C#

IN A NUTSHELL

D1493909

Other Microsoft .NET resources from O'Reilly

Related titles	
Learning C#	ADO.NET in a Nutshell
Programming C#	.NET Windows Forms in a Nutshell
Programming Visual Basic .NET	.NET Framework Essentials
Programming ASP.NET	Mastering Visual Studio .NET
ASP.NET in a Nutshell	

.NET Books Resource Center

dotnet.oreilly.com is a complete catalog of O'Reilly's books on .NET and related technologies, including sample chapters and code examples.

ONDotnet.com provides independent coverage of fundamental, interoperable, and emerging Microsoft .NET programming and web services technologies.

Conferences

O'Reilly & Associates bring diverse innovators together to nurture the ideas that spark revolutionary industries. We specialize in documenting the latest tools and systems, translating the innovator's knowledge into useful skills for those in the trenches. Visit *conferences.oreilly.com* for our upcoming events.

Safari Bookshelf (*safari.oreilly.com*) is the premier online reference library for programmers and IT professionals. Conduct searches across more than 1,000 books. Subscribers can zero in on answers to time-critical questions in a matter of seconds. Read the books on your Bookshelf from cover to cover or simply flip to the page you need. Try it today with a free trial.

C#

IN A NUTSHELL

Second Edition

Peter Drayton,
Ben Albahari, and Ted Neward

O'REILLY®

Beijing • Cambridge • Farnham • Köln • Paris • Sebastopol • Taipei • Tokyo

C# in a Nutshell, Second Edition

by Peter Drayton, Ben Albahari, and Ted Neward

Copyright © 2003, 2002 O'Reilly & Associates, Inc. All rights reserved.
Printed in the United States of America.

Published by O'Reilly & Associates, Inc., 1005 Gravenstein Highway North, Sebastopol, CA 95472.

O'Reilly & Associates books may be purchased for educational, business, or sales promotional use. Online editions are also available for most titles (*safari.oreilly.com*). For more information, contact our corporate/institutional sales department: 800-998-9938 or *corporate@oreilly.com*.

Editor:	Brian Jepson
Production Editor:	Philip Dangler
Cover Designer:	Emma Colby
Interior Designer:	David Futato

Printing History:

March 2002:	First Edition.
August 2003:	Second Edition.

ISBN: 0-596-00526-1

[M]

Table of Contents

Part I. Programming with C#

Part II. Programming with the .NET Framework

Part III. Language and Tools Reference

Part IV. API Quick Reference

Part V. Appendixes

Preface

This book is a desktop reference for Microsoft's C# programming language, designed to sit comfortably next to you while you program and to accompany you faithfully in your travels. The first version of C# shipped in January 2002 as part of Visual Studio .NET and the .NET Framework, after an extensive public beta release.

C# in a Nutshell is divided into four parts (along with five appendixes and a Type, Method, Property, Event, and Field Index). Part I introduces the C# language and the .NET Common Language Runtime (CLR). It is a fast-paced, no-fluff introduction to the C# programming language, from its data types through all of the statements and features that make it the modern component-oriented language it was designed to be.

Part II shows how to use the C# language in conjunction with core classes of the .NET Framework Class Library (FCL) to accomplish a variety of common programming tasks, from manipulating strings to interacting with legacy COM components. Part III contains a number of useful references, including a summary of C# syntax, presented in the unique notation developed for both this title and *C# Essentials*, as well as a reference to useful command-line tools that ship with Visual Studio .NET and the .NET Framework.

Part IV is a quick reference to 21 of the most important namespaces of the FCL and their more than 700 types, complete with namespace maps, type descriptions, member signatures, and useful cross references and annotations. Also included is a class and method index that can be used to locate the type in which a given member is found or the namespace that contains a given type.

Audience

If you're a working C# programmer, we think you'll want *C# in a Nutshell* to be part of your reference library regardless of your present level of ability. With its thorough coverage of language elements, its compact language and tools reference, and its unique, jam-packed guide to the core FCL APIs, you should easily be able to find answers to most questions of syntax and functionality that you will encounter on the job.

If you are an experienced Java, C++, or Visual Basic programmer encountering the C# language and the CLR for the first time, this book will enable you to master the essentials of the language. Less experienced programmers may wish to first work through an introductory text, such as *Programming C#*, by Jesse Liberty (O'Reilly & Associates).

Contents of This Book

Parts I, II, and III of this book document the C# language, the .NET CLR, and relevant tools that ship with the .NET Framework downloadable SDK. Part I, *Programming with C#*, introduces the C# language and the .NET Framework:

Introducing C# and the .NET Framework
> Chapter 1 provides an overview of the C# language and the .NET Framework, with special attention to their key features and benefits.

C# Language Basics
> This chapter introduces the elements of the C# language, including data types and basic constructs such as expressions and statements. Special notation is used throughout the chapter to summarize C# syntax rules for later reference.

Creating Types in C#
> Chapter 3 explains how to define and instantiate new types in C#. In C#, all classes are components that embody both executable code and metadata used by the CLR at runtime.

Advanced C# Features
> This chapter explains features of the C# language used to handle events and exceptions, callbacks, custom attributes and more.

Part II, *Programming with the .NET Framework*, contains:

Framework Class Library Overview
> Chapter 5 is an overview of the core .NET Framework APIs covered in this book. The APIs themselves are covered in Part IV. Here you will find a summary of the support you can expect in each functional area of the FCL, along with lists of the namespaces in which the relevant types are found.

String Handling
> This chapter describes key FCL types available for string manipulation and shows how to program them using C#. The FCL offers a wide range of advanced string handling features. FCL types for regular expression matching and replacement capabilities based on Perl5 regular expressions are also covered.

Collections
> Chapter 7 presents the most important FCL types for working with common data structures such as arrays, hashtables, dictionaries, stacks, and more. Also covered are key collection interfaces such as IEnumerable, ICollection, and IComparable.

XML I/O

This chapter introduces built-in FCL support for XML, explains the relationships between XML and the I/O system in general, demonstrates the consumption and production of XML documents in both node-based and Infoset-based forms, highlights the use of XPath, and explores XSLT.

Networking

The FCL includes a number of types that make accessing networked resources easy. Chapter 9 describes the core networking support in the FCL and provides numerous examples leveraging the predefined classes.

Streams and I/O

This chapter introduces built-in FCL support for handling streams and I/O, explains relationships between the abstract and concrete classes in the streams architecture, demonstrates their usage, and explores the filesystem-specific support.

Serialization

Chapter 11 introduces the built-in support for object serialization and deserialization, and demonstrates how clients and objects can participate in the serialization and deserialization process.

Assemblies

This chapter explains the configuration and use of assemblies, the fundamental unit of deployment in .NET. The FCL provides attributes and types for managing assemblies, which are also covered.

Reflection

Chapter 13 describes the key FCL types available for examining the metadata of existing types using reflection. Creating new types (and associated metadata) is termed Reflection.Emit, and is done via the types in the System.Reflection.Emit namespace, which is also explored in this chapter.

Custom Attributes

Types, members, modules, and assemblies all have associated metadata that is used by all the major CLR services, which is considered an indivisible part of an application, and can be accessed via reflection, as explained in Chapter 13. This chapter explains how to add custom metadata to application elements by writing custom attributes.

Memory Management

The .NET Framework provides automatic garbage collection of types no longer in use, and allows programmers to provide their own finalizers via C# destructors. This chapter also shows how to provide Dispose( ) or Close( ) methods to clean up after an object whose work is finished.

Threading

Chapter 16 explains the use of FCL types to manage application threads. C# provides a lock statement to synchronize access to shared resources, and the FCL includes a Monitor class to implement pulse and wait, atomic, and other thread operations.

Integrating with Native DLLs

This chapter explains the PInvoke services through which C# programs can interact with legacy DLLs.

Integrating with COM Components
> Chapter 18 discusses FCL types and attributes used to expose COM objects to C# programs and to expose C# objects to COM.

Diagnostics
> Because providing integrated error handling and reporting is such a common need among applications, the .NET Framework provides a diverse set of facilities to monitor application behavior, detect runtime errors, inspect the application environment, report application status, and integrate with debugging tools if available. This chapter introduces the debugging and diagnostics support provided by the FCL.

C# Language Reference
> Chapter 20 contains a concise alphabetical listing of all C# language constructs and their syntax.

Part III, *Language and Tools Reference*, contains:

XML Documentation Tag Reference
> C# provides XML documentation tags that facilitate the development of application documentation within the source code itself. This chapter presents the tags available to programmers and illustrates their use.

C# Naming and Coding Conventions
> Chapter 22 proposes guidelines for naming and casing elements of C# programs. The guidelines are drawn from official Microsoft documents and the experiences of the authors.

C# Development Tools
> This chapter is a reference to useful command-line tools that ship with Visual Studio .NET and the .NET Framework, including the compiler and debugger.

The 23 chapters in Parts I–III of *C# in a Nutshell* teach you the C# language and get you up and running with many of the most important APIs of the .NET Framework. The other half of the book is Part IV, *API Quick Reference*, which is a succinct but detailed API reference of 21 important namespaces and more than 700 core types and their members. Please be sure to read Chapter 24, *How to Use This Quick Reference*, which appears at the beginning of Part IV and explains how to get the most from its content.

Part V, *Appendixes*, includes additional reference tables for regular expression syntax (*Regular Expressions*); format specifiers (*Format Specifiers*); C#-to-COM default data mapping (*Data Marshaling*); a glossary of C# keywords (*C# Keywords*); an alphabetical list of .NET namespaces and the DLLs that expose them (*Namespaces and Assemblies*); and a *Type, Method, Property, Event, and Field Index* in which you can look up a method or field and find what type it is defined in.

Assumptions This Book Makes

To program in C#, you must have installed one of the many editions of Visual Studio .NET on your system (Standard, Professional, Enterprise, or Architect), or have downloaded and installed the .NET Framework SDK. Visual Studio provides a complete interactive developer environment that simplifies many of the tasks of

C# programming, especially the development of Windows clients, server-side web applications and web services. In addition, Visual Studio provides excellent support for the debugging and project management of applications.

However, with the .NET Framework SDK installed on your system you can write C# programs using an editor such as emacs, SharpDevelop, or Microsoft Notepad, and compile, debug, and execute them using the command-line utilities described in Chapter 23.

To download the .NET Framework SDK (currently a 106 MB file), see *http://msdn.microsoft.com/net/*.

What's on the CD

The CD that accompanies this book contains a copy of *C# in a Nutshell for Microsoft Visual Studio .NET*. This software plugs directly into Microsoft Visual Studio .NET and makes the contents of the C# in a Nutshell API Quick Reference (Part IV) available to you as a fully integrated member of Visual Studio .NET Dynamic Help.

By making *C# in a Nutshell* a part of your Visual Studio .NET development environment, you gain the following benefits:

- Continuous access to the contents of the C# API Quick Reference as you work in the online Visual Studio .NET development environment.
- The ability to browse the contents of the API Quick Reference in the Visual Studio .NET Help Contents window.
- Constantly updated Dynamic Help links to relevant API Quick Reference entries as you write C# code (these links appear in a separate Dynamic Help window link group named "O'Reilly Help").
- Links to both API Quick Reference topics and Microsoft documentation topics when you use either the Help Search facility or interactive index.
- Access to the O'Reilly web site, *www.oreilly.com*, for additional books and articles on C# and the .NET Framework.
- Cross-links from API Quick Reference topics to related topics in MSDN documentation.

For more information on *C# in a Nutshell for Microsoft Visual Studio .NET*, please read the release notes on the CD.

To use C# in a Nutshell for Microsoft Visual Studio .NET you must be running a version of Visual C# .NET or Visual Studio .NET on your computer. To install C# in a Nutshell for Microsoft Visual Studio .NET:

1. Place the CD in the CD player.
2. If you are running Visual C# 2003 or Visual Studio .NET 2003, double-click on the file named *CSharpInANutshell-vs2003.msi*. If you are still running Visual C# 2002 or Visual Studio .NET 2002, double-click on the file named *CSharpInANutshell-vs2002.msi*
3. Follow the instructions contained in the install program windows. Be sure to read and to accept the terms of the software license before proceeding.

To uninstall *C# in a Nutshell for Microsoft Visual Studio .NET*, repeat the above procedure, but click on the Remove button when the program prompts you to select an install option.

Making the *C# in a Nutshell Quick Reference* available as a Visual Studio .NET plug-in is a new venture for O'Reilly & Associates and Microsoft. We welcome your comments and ideas.

Please send your comments to:

> *bookquestions@oreilly.com*

If you discover errors in content or encounter any problems in using this product, please report them to:

> *bookquestions@oreilly.com*

Conventions Used in This Book

The following typographical conventions are used in this book.

Italic is used for:

- Directory pathnames and filenames
- Domain names and URLs
- New terms where they are first defined

`Constant width` is used for:

- Code examples and output
- Names and keywords in C# programs, including method or field names, variable names, and class names
- XML and HTML element tags
- Registry keys

`Constant width italic` is used for:

- Replaceable parameter names or user-provided elements in syntax

In several parts of this book, we have included simple grammar specifications for many, but not all, of the language constructs introduced in this book, to provide you with a fast way to understand the grammar of a particular construct and its valid combinations. In this grammar syntax, the XML occurrence operators (?, *, and +) are used to specify more precisely the number of times an element may occur in a particular construct:

x

> Indicates *x* is to be used verbatim (`constant width`)

x

> Indicates *x* is supplied by the programmer (`constant width italic`)

x?

> Indicates *x* may occur zero or one times.

x*

Indicates *x* may occur zero or more times, separated by commas.

x+

Indicates *x* may occur one or more times, separated by commas.

[...]

Indicates a logical grouping of code elements, when not implicitly grouped using the verbatim terms { }, ( ), and [ ].

[x|y]

Indicates only one of a choice of code elements may occur.

 This icon designates a note, which is an important aside to the nearby text.

Related Books

O'Reilly & Associates, Inc., publishes an entire series of books on C# programming and .NET, including several companion books to this one. Some recommended books in the O'Reilly .NET series include:

- *Programming C#*, by Jesse Liberty
- *.NET Framework Essentials*, by Thuan Thai and Hoang Q. Lam
- *VB.NET Language in a Nutshell*, by Steven Roman, Ron Petrusha, and Paul Lomax
- *Programming Visual Basic .NET*, by Dave Grundgeiger
- *Programming ASP.NET*, by Jesse Liberty and Dan Hurwitz
- *C# and VB.NET Conversion Pocket Reference*, by Jose Mojica

You can find a complete list of O'Reilly .NET books and other programming titles at *http://dotnet.oreilly.com*.

We also recommend *C# Primer: A Practical Approach*, by Stanley B. Lippman (Addison-Wesley Professional) and *Effective Java*, by Joshua Bloch (Addison-Wesley Professional) (an excellent programming book for C# programmers as well).

C# Resources Online

Even this book cannot answer every question you might have about the language. There are many online resources that can help you get the most out of C#. We recommend the following sites:

http://msdn.microsoft.com/net/

The Microsoft .NET Developer Center is the official site for all things .NET, including the latest version of the .NET Framework SDK, as well as documentation, technical articles, sample code, pointers to discussion groups, and third-party resources.

http://www.gotdotnet.com
> Community support site run by the .NET Framework team. Includes articles, specifications, and numerous samples from .NET Framework team members and the community at large.

http://discuss.develop.com
> The DevelopMentor DOTNET discussion lists are the best site for free-wheeling, independent discussion of the .NET Framework; participants often include key Microsoft engineers and program managers.

http://www.ecma.ch/ecma1/stand/ECMA-334.htm
http://www.ecma.ch/ecma1/stand/ECMA-335.htm
> The official ECMA C# (ECMA-334) and CLI (ECMA-335) specifications.

http://www.ondotnet.com
> The .NET DevCenter on the O'Reilly Network, featuring original articles, news, and weblogs of interest to .NET programmers.

http://dotnet.oreilly.com
> The O'Reilly .NET Center. Visit this page frequently for information on current and upcoming books from O'Reilly. You'll find sample chapters, articles, and other resources.

http://msdn.microsoft.com/community/net.asp
> A list of third-party resources for C# and .NET Framework developers.

You can also find Usenet discussions about .NET in the *microsoft.public.dotnet.** family of newsgroups. In addition, the newsgroup *microsoft.public.dotnet. languages.csharp* specifically addresses C#. If your news server does not carry these groups, you can find them at *news://msnews.microsoft.com*.

Lastly, two articles of interest are:

http://windows.oreilly.com/news/hejlsberg_0800.html
> An interview with chief C# architect Anders Hejlsberg, by O'Reilly editor John Osborn.

http://www.genamics.com/developer/csharp_comparative.htm
> A comparison of C# to C++ and Java by coauthor Ben Albahari.

How to Contact Us

We have tested and verified the information in this book to the best of our ability, but you may find that features have changed (or even that we have made mistakes!). Please let us know about any errors you find, as well as your suggestions for future editions, by writing to:

O'Reilly & Associates, Inc.
1005 Gravenstein Highway North
Sebastopol, CA 95472
(800) 998-9938 (in the U.S. or Canada)
(707) 829-0515 (international/local)
(707) 829-0104 (fax)

You can also send us messages electronically. To be put on the mailing list or request a catalog, send email to:

info@oreilly.com

To ask technical questions or comment on the book, send email to:

bookquestions@oreilly.com

We have a web site for the book, where we'll list examples, errata, and any plans for future editions. You can access this page at:

http://www.oreilly.com/catalog/csharpnut2/

For more information about this book and others, see the following O'Reilly web sites:

http://www.oreilly.com
http://dotnet.oreilly.com

How the Quick Reference Is Generated

Part IV, *API Quick Reference*, was generated using .NET's reflection API (described in Chapter 13). Using reflection, we drilled down into selected classes, structs, enums, delegates, and interfaces from the Framework Class Library, and extracted detailed information on each type and its members. Next, we structured this information as DocBook XML, which we used to generate the printed pages.

Each detailed type listing is accompanied by one or more paragraphs describing the type and its significant members. These descriptions offer an overview of how you can use the type in your own applications and describe related types, pitfalls, and useful features.

Acknowledgments

This book would not be possible without the contribution and support of many individuals, including family, friends, and the hard-working folks at O'Reilly & Associates, Inc.

Brian Jepson and Lenny Muellner developed the programs responsible for generating Part IV and the *Type, Method, Property, Event, and Field Index*. Brian also developed the namespace maps that are found in the overviews that begin each chapter of the Reference with input from Ted and Peter. Peter Drayton developed the program that generated material for Appendix E. Ted Neward, Matthew MacDonald, Martin Smith, Steve Spainhour, and Brian Jepson wrote the more than 700 insightful namespace and type descriptions that make the API reference so valuable.

Brad Merrill of Microsoft wrote the sections on regular expressions and provided content for Appendix A.

Brad Abrams and members of his .NET Framework team contributed to the design of the API reference and provided technical review that immeasurably improved its quality. Additional technical review of the manuscript was provided by Joe Nalewabau and Kerry Loynd of Microsoft.

The C# in a Nutshell for Visual Studio .NET CD that accompanies this book is the work of many individuals. Mike Sierra of O'Reilly converted the API Quick Reference entries to Microsoft Help 2.0 format and added the XML tags needed to integrate their content with the Visual Studio .NET Dynamic Help system. His work was made easier by former O'Reilly tools group members Lenny Muellner and Erik Ray who wrote the scripts for converting Frame pages to HTML. The O'Reilly Tech Support group tested each pre-release build of the software.

Our thanks also to Kipper York and Shane McRoberts, former members of the Microsoft Help team, who provided invaluable technical assistance at critical moments during our initial encounters with Visual Studio .NET Dynamic Help. Erik Promislow of Active State built the install packages that make our Help files an integral part of the Visual Studio .NET developer environment. Frank Gocinski of the Visual Studio .NET third-party integration program was instrumental in making O'Reilly a full Microsoft VSIP partner. A special tip of the hat as well to Rob Howard of Microsoft who understood our original vision and helped us make the right connections to get this project off the ground

Peter Drayton

Above all, I'd like to thank my wife Julie DuBois, who never fails to make days spent without .NET even more wonderful than days spent *with* .NET. I'd also like to thank Ben Albahari, for charging the C# and .NET hill with me for the second time in less than 18 months; Ted Neward, who played the role of the cavalry, arriving at an opportune time and making the back half of the book all that it could be; and Brian Jepson, Nancy Kotary, and John Osborn for their tireless support and efforts (editorial and otherwise).

Casting a slightly wider net, the stories in this book were immeasurably improved by comments and insights from Simon Fell, Don Box, Brock Allen, and all the other incredibly smart, talented DevelopMentor instructors I am fortunate to count as colleagues.

Lastly, I'd like to dedicate this book to my father, Peter Drayton, Sr., and my late mother, Irene Mary Rochford Drayton, for giving me a strong rudder to navigate life.

Ben Albahari

I'd like to thank Peter, for asking me to participate in this book and who has yet to fail at making me enthusiastic about what I do; the O'Reilly editors (Brian, Nancy, and John) for their commitment and courteous patience required to finish this project; Ted, for joining us to tackle the most formidable part of the book; and my girlfriend, Karen, who motivated me with a mixture of love and logic.

Ted Neward

First and foremost, my thanks to Peter for inviting (dragging?) me into this project. I've had nothing but fun working with him and Ben on what I hope is a useful resource for the thousands of expatriate C++, Java, and VB programmers flocking to this new language. Second, my thanks to the team at O'Reilly, for making my first O'Reilly book a wonderful experience. Third, my thanks to my students, past and present, who challenged, questioned, argued, and laughed (hysterically, maybe) at my C# teaching efforts. Fourth, my thanks to Don Box and Mike Abercrombie, for DevelopMentor and the wonderful culture they created there, and for allowing me to be a part of it. Last, but of course not least, I want to thank my wonderful family: my wife Charlotte, and my sons Michael and Matthew, for putting up with Dad while he once again disappeared into the study for a while.

I would also like to thank you, the reader, for taking the time to include us as part of your C# experience. It is my hope that our efforts will yield fruit in the form of less time to learn C#, leaving you more time to spend with your family and friends. It may seem trite to say it, but in this "new age" in which we find ourselves, such things are as valuable as gold; as for me and my newfound time, I'm going off for pizza with my family.

Programming with C#

Part I, *Programming with C#*, introduces the C# language and the .NET Framework:

Introducing C# and the .NET Framework

C# is a programming language from Microsoft designed specifically to target the .NET Framework. Microsoft's .NET Framework is a runtime environment and class library that dramatically simplifies the development and deployment of modern, component-based applications.

When the .NET Framework and C# language compiler were shipped in final form in January 2002, both the platform and programming language had already garnered much industry attention and widespread use among Microsoft-centric early adopters. Why this level of success? Certainly, the C# language and the .NET Framework address many of the technical challenges facing modern developers as they strive to develop increasingly complex distributed systems with ever-shrinking schedules and team sizes.

However, in addition to its technical merits, one of the main reasons for the success that the language and platform has enjoyed thus far is the unprecedented degree of openness that Microsoft has shown. From July 2000 to January 2002, the .NET Framework underwent an extensive public beta that allowed tens of thousands of developers to "kick the tires" of the programming environment. This allowed Microsoft to both solicit and react to developer community feedback before finalizing the new platform.

Additionally, the key specifications for both the language and the platform have been published, reviewed, and ratified by an international standards organization called the European Computer Manufacturers Association (ECMA). These standardization efforts have led to multiple third-party initiatives that bring the C# language and the .NET platform to non-Microsoft environments. They have also prompted renewed interest among academics in the use of Microsoft technologies as teaching and research vehicles.

Lastly, although the language and platform are shiny and new, the foundations for the C# language and the .NET Framework have been years in the making, reaching back more than half a decade. Understanding where the language and platform have come from gives us a better understanding of where they are headed.

The C# Language

Reports of a new language from Microsoft first started surfacing in 1998. At that time the language was called COOL, and was said to be very similar to Java. Although Microsoft consistently denied the reports of the new language, rumors persisted.

In June 2000, Microsoft ended the speculation by releasing the specifications for a new language called C# (pronounced "see-sharp"). This was rapidly followed by the release of a preview version of the .NET Framework SDK (which included a C# compiler) at the July 2000 Professional Developer's Conference (PDC) in Orlando, Florida.

The new language was designed by Anders Hejlsberg (creator of Turbo Pascal and architect of Delphi), Scott Wiltamuth, and Peter Golde. Described in the C# Language Specification as a "...simple, modern, object-oriented, and type-safe programming language derived from C and C++," C# bears many syntactic similarities to C++ and Java.

However, focusing on the syntactic similarities between C# and Java does the C# language a disservice. Semantically, C# pushes the language-design envelope substantially beyond where the Java language was circa 2001, and could rightfully be viewed as the next step in the evolution of component-oriented programming languages. While it is outside the scope of this book to perform a detailed comparison between C# and Java, we urge interested readers to read the widely cited article "A Comparative Overview of C# and Java," by co-author Ben Albahari, available at *http://genamics.com/developer/csharp_comparative.htm*.

Enabling Component-Based Development

Over the last 10 years, programming techniques such as object-oriented design, interface-based programming, and component-based software have become ubiquitous. However, programming language support for these constructs has always lagged behind the current state-of-the-art best practices. As a result, developers tend to either depend on programming conventions and custom code rather than direct compiler and runtime support, or to not take advantage of the techniques at all.

As an example, consider that C++ supported object orientation, but had no formal concept of interfaces. C++ developers resorted to abstract base classes and mix-in interfaces to simulate interface-based programming, and relied on external component programming models such as COM or CORBA to provide the benefits of component-based software.

While Java extended C++ to add language-level support for interfaces and packages (among other things), it too had very little language-level support for building long-lived component-based systems (in which one needs to develop, interconnect, deploy, and version components from various sources over an

---

extended period of time). This is not to say that the Java community hasn't built many such systems, but rather that these needs were addressed by programming conventions and custom code: relying on naming conventions to identify common design patterns such as properties and events, requiring external metadata for deployment information, and developing custom class loaders to provide stronger component versioning semantics.

By comparison, the C# language was designed from the ground up around the assumption that modern systems are built using components. Consequently, C# provides direct language support for common component constructs such as properties, methods, and events (used by RAD tools to build applications out of components, setting properties, responding to events, and wiring components together via method calls). C# also allows developers to directly annotate and extend a component's type information to provide deployment, design, or runtime support, integrate component versioning directly into the programming model, and integrate XML-based documentation directly into C# source files. C# also discards the C++ and COM approach of spreading source artifacts across header files, implementation files, and type libraries in favor of a much simpler source organization and component reuse model.

While this is by no means an exhaustive list, the enhancements in C# over Java and C++ qualify it as the next major step in the evolution of component-based development languages.

A Modern Object-Oriented Language

In addition to deeply integrated support for building component-based systems, C# is also a fully capable object-oriented language, supporting all the common concepts and abstractions that exist in languages such as C++ and Java.

As is expected of any modern object-oriented language, C# supports concepts such as inheritance, encapsulation, polymorphism, and interface-based programming. C# supports common C, C++, and Java language constructs such as classes, structs, interfaces, and enums, as well as more novel constructs such as delegates, which provide a type-safe equivalent to C/C++ function pointers, and custom attributes, which allow annotation of code elements with additional information.

In addition, C# incorporates features from C++ such as operator overloading, user-defined conversions, true rectangular arrays, and pass-by-reference semantics that are currently missing from Java.

Unlike most programming languages, C# has no runtime library of its own. Instead, C# relies on the vast class library in the .NET Framework for all its needs, including console I/O, network and file handling, collection data structures, and many other facilities. Implemented primarily in C# and spanning more than a million lines of code, this class library served as an excellent torture-test during the development cycle for both the C# language and the C# compiler.

The C# language strives to balance the need for consistency and efficiency. Some object-oriented languages (such as Smalltalk) take the viewpoint that "everything is an object." This approach has the advantage that instances of primitive types (such as integers) are first-class objects. However, it has the disadvantage of being very inefficient. To avoid this overhead, other languages (such as Java) choose to bifurcate the type system into primitives and everything else, leading to less overhead, but also to a schism between primitive and user-defined types.

C# balances these two conflicting viewpoints by presenting a unified type system in which all types (including primitive types) are derived from a common base type, while simultaneously allowing for performance optimizations that allow primitive types and simple user-defined types to be treated as raw memory, with minimal overhead and increased efficiency.

Building Robust and Durable Software

In a world of always-on connectivity and distributed systems, software robustness takes on new significance. Servers need to stay up and running 24×7 to service clients, and clients need to be able to download code off the network and run it locally with some guarantee that it will not misbehave. The C# language (in concert with the .NET Framework) promotes software robustness in a number of different ways.

First and foremost, C# is a type-safe language, meaning that programs are prevented from accessing objects in inappropriate ways. All code and data is associated with a type, all objects have an associated type, and only operations defined by the associated type can be performed on an object. Type-safety eliminates an entire category of errors in C and C++ programs stemming from invalid casts, bad pointer arithmetic, and even malicious code.

C# also provides automatic memory management in the form of a high-performance tracing generational garbage collector. This frees programmers from performing manual memory management or reference counting, and eliminates an entire category of errors, such as dangling pointers, memory leaks, and circular references.

Even good programs can have bad things happen to them, and it is important to have a consistent mechanism for detecting errors. Over the years, Windows developers have had to contend with numerous error reporting mechanisms, such as simple failure return codes, Win32 structured exceptions, C++ exceptions, COM error HResults, and OLE automation IErrorInfo objects. This proliferation of approaches breeds complexity and makes it difficult for designers to create standardized error-handling strategies. The .NET Framework eliminates this complexity by standardizing on a single exception-handling mechanism that is used throughout the framework, and exposed in all .NET languages including C#.

The C# language design also includes numerous other features that promote robustness, such as language-level support for independently versioning base classes (without changing derived class semantics or mandating recompilation of derived classes), detection of attempts to use uninitialized variables, array bounds checking, and support for checked arithmetic.

A Pragmatic World View

Many of the design decisions in the C# language represent a pragmatic world view on the part of the designers. For example, the syntax was selected to be familiar to C, C++, and Java developers, making it easier to learn C# and aiding source code porting.

While C# provides many useful, high-level object-oriented features, it recognizes that in certain limited cases these features can work against raw performance. Rather than dismiss these concerns as unimportant, C# includes explicit support for features such as direct pointer manipulation, unsafe type casts, declarative pinning of garbage-collected objects, and direct memory allocation on the stack. Naturally, these features come at a cost, both in terms of the complexity they add and the elevated security privileges required to use them. However, the existence of these features gives C# programmers much more headroom than other, more restrictive languages do.

Lastly, the interop facilities in the .NET Framework make it easy to leverage existing DLLs and COM components from C# code, and to use C# components in classic COM applications. Although not strictly a function of the C# language, this capability reflects a similarly pragmatic world view, in which new functionality coexists peacefully with legacy code for as long as needed.

The .NET Framework

The Microsoft .NET Framework consists of two elements: a runtime environment called the Common Language Runtime (CLR), and a class library called the Framework Class Library (FCL). The FCL is built on top of the CLR and provides services needed by modern applications.

While applications targeting the .NET Framework interact directly with the FCL, the CLR serves as the underlying engine. In order to understand the .NET Framework, one first must understand the role of the CLR.

The Common Language Runtime

The CLR is a modern runtime environment that manages the execution of user code, providing services such as JIT compilation, memory management, exception management, debugging and profiling support, and integrated security and permission management.

Essentially, the CLR represents the foundation of Microsoft's computing platform for the next decade. However, it has been a long time in the making. Its origins can be traced back to early 1997, when products such as Microsoft Transaction Server (MTS) were starting to deliver on the promise of a more declarative, service-oriented programming model. This new model allowed developers to declaratively annotate their components at development time, and then rely on the services of a runtime (such as MTS) to hijack component activation and intercept method calls, transparently layering in additional services such as transactions, security, just-in-time (JIT) activation, and more. This need to augment COM type information pushed the limits of what was possible and useful with IDL and type libraries. The COM+ team set out to find a generalized solution to this problem.

The first public discussion of a candidate solution occurred at the 1997 PDC in San Diego, when Mary Kirtland and other members of the COM+ team discussed a future version of COM centered on something called the COM+ Runtime, and providing many of the services such as extensible type information, cross-language integration, implementation inheritance, and automatic memory management that ultimately resurfaced in the CLR.*

Soon after the 1997 PDC, Microsoft stopped talking publicly about the technology, and the product known as COM+ that was released with Windows 2000 bore little resemblance to the COM+ Runtime originally described. Behind the scenes, however, work was continuing and the scope of the project was expanding significantly as it took on a much larger role within Microsoft.

Initially codenamed Lightning, the project underwent many internal (and some external) renamings, and was known at various times as COM3, COM+ 2.0, the COM+ Runtime, the NGWS Runtime, the Universal Runtime (URT), and the Common Language Runtime. This effort ultimately surfaced as the .NET Framework, announced at the July 2000 PDC in Orlando, Florida. During the following 18 months, the .NET Framework underwent an extensive public beta, culminating in the release of Version 1.0 of the Microsoft .NET Framework on January 15, 2002.

Compilation and Execution Model

To better understand the CLR, consider how compilers that target the .NET Framework differ from traditional compilers.

Traditional compilers target a specific processor, consuming source files in a specific language, and producing binary files containing streams of instructions in the native language of the target processor. These binary files may then be executed directly on the target processor.

.NET compilers function a little differently, as they do not target a specific native processor. Instead, they consume source files and produce binary files containing an intermediate representation of the source constructs, expressed as a combination of metadata and Common Intermediate Language (CIL). In order for these binaries to be executed, the CLR must be present on the target machine.

When these binaries are executed, they cause the CLR to load. The CLR then takes over and manages execution, providing a range of services such as JIT compilation (converting the CIL as needed into the correct stream of instructions for the underlying processor), memory management (in the form of a garbage collector), exception management, debugger and profiler integration, and security services (stack walking and permission checks).

---

* Two sites, *http://www.microsoft.com/msj/defaulttop.asp?page=/msj/1197/inthisissuefeatures1197.htm* and *http://www.microsoft.com/msj/defaulttop.asp?page=/msj/1297/inthisissuefeatures1297.htm*, contain articles by Mary Kirtland on the COM+ Runtime.

This compilation and execution model explains why C# is referred to as a *managed language*, why code running in the CLR is referred to as *managed code*, and why the CLR is said to provide *managed execution*.

Although this dependency on a runtime environment might initially appear to be a drawback, substantial benefits arise from this architecture. Since the metadata and CIL representations are processor architecture–neutral, binaries may be used on any machine in which the Common Language Runtime is present, regardless of underlying processor architecture. Additionally, since processor-specific code generation is deferred until runtime, the CLR has the opportunity to perform processor-specific optimizations based on the target architecture the code is running on. As processor technology advances, all applications need to take advantage of these advances is an updated version of the CLR.

Unlike traditional binary representations, which are primarily streams of native processor instructions, the combination of metadata and CIL retains almost all of the original source language constructs. In addition, this representation is source language-neutral, which allows developers to build applications using multiple source languages. They can select the best language for a particular task, rather than being forced to standardize on a particular source language for each application or needing to rely on component technologies, such as COM or CORBA, to mask the differences between the source languages used to build the separate components of an application.

The Common Type System

Ultimately, the CLR exists to safely execute managed code, regardless of source language. In order to provide for cross-language integration, to ensure type safety, and to provide managed execution services such as JIT compilation, garbage collection, exception management, etc., the CLR needs intimate knowledge of the managed code that it is executing.

To meet this requirement, the CLR defines a shared type system called the Common Type System (CTS). The CTS defines the rules by which all types are declared, defined and managed, regardless of source language. The CTS is designed to be rich and flexible enough to support a wide variety of source languages, and is the basis for cross-language integration, type safety, and managed execution services.

Compilers for managed languages that wish to be first-class citizens in the world of the CLR are responsible for mapping source language constructs onto the CTS analogs. In cases in which there is no direct analog, the language designers may decide to either adapt the source language to better match the CTS (ensuring more seamless cross-language integration), or to provide additional plumbing that preserves the original semantics of the source language (possibly at the expense of cross-language integration capabilities).

Since all types are ultimately represented as CTS types, it now becomes possible to combine types authored in different languages in new and interesting ways. For example, since managed languages ultimately declare CTS types, and the CTS supports inheritance, it follows that the CLR supports cross-language inheritance.

The Common Language Specification

Not all languages support the exact same set of constructs, and this can be a barrier to cross-language integration. Consider this example: Language A allows unsigned types (which are supported by the CTS), while Language B does not. How should code written in Language B call a method written in Language A, which takes an unsigned integer as a parameter?

The solution is the Common Language Specification (CLS). The CLS defines the reasonable subset of the CTS that should be sufficient to support cross-language integration, and specifically excludes problem areas such as unsigned integers, operator overloading, and more.

Each managed language decides how much of the CTS to support. Languages that can consume any CLS-compliant type are known as CLS Consumers. Languages which can extend any existing CLS-compliant type are known as CLS Extenders. Naturally, managed languages are free to support CTS features over and above the CLS, and most do. As an example, the C# language is both a CLS Consumer and a CLS Extender, and supports all of the important CTS features.

The combination of the rich and flexible CTS and the widely supported CLS has led to many languages being adapted to target the .NET platform. At the time of this writing, Microsoft was offering compilers for six managed languages (C#, VB.NET, JScript, Managed Extensions for C++, Microsoft IL, and J#), and a host of other commercial vendors and academics were offering managed versions of languages, such as COBOL, Eiffel, Haskell, Mercury, Mondrian, Oberon, Forth, Scheme, Smalltalk, APL, several flavors of Pascal, and more.

Given the level of interest from industry and academia, one might say that .NET has spawned something of a renaissance in programming-language innovation.

The Framework Class Library

Developer needs (and Windows capabilities) have evolved much since Windows 1.0 was introduced in November 1985. As Windows has grown to meet new customer needs, the accompanying APIs have grown by orders of magnitude over time, becoming ever more complex, increasingly inconsistent, and almost impossible to comprehend in their totality.

Additionally, while modern paradigms such as object orientation, component software, and Internet standards had emerged and, in many cases, joined the mainstream, these advances had not yet been incorporated into the Windows programming model in a comprehensive and consistent manner.

Given the issues, and the degree of change already inherent in the move to a managed execution environment, the time was ripe for a clean start. As a result, the .NET Framework replaces most (though not all) of the traditional Windows API sets with a well-factored, object-oriented class library called the Framework Class Library (FCL).

The FCL provides a diverse array of higher-level software services, addressing the needs of modern applications. Conceptually, these can be grouped into several categories such as:

- Support for core functionality, such as interacting with basic data types and collections; console, network and file I/O; and interacting with other runtime-related facilities
- Support for interacting with databases, consuming and producing XML, and manipulating tabular and tree-structured data
- Support for building web-based (thin client) applications with a rich server-side event model
- Support for building desktop-based (thick client) applications with broad support for the Windows GUI
- Support for building SOAP-based XML web services

The FCL is vast, including more than 3,500 classes. For a more detailed overview of the facilities in the FCL, see Chapter 5.

ECMA Standardization

One of the most encouraging aspects about the .NET Framework is the degree of openness that Microsoft has shown during its development. From the earliest public previews, core specifications detailing the C# language, the classes in the FCL, and the inner workings of the CLR have been freely available.

However, this openness was taken to a new level in November 2000 when Microsoft, along with co-sponsors Intel and HP, officially submitted the specifications for the C# language, a subset of the FCL, and the runtime environment to ECMA for standardization.

This action began an intense standardization process. Organizations participating in the effort included Microsoft, HP, Intel, IBM, Fujitsu Software, ISE, Plum Hall, Monash University, and others. The work was performed under the auspices of ECMA technical committee TC39, the same committee that had previously standardized the JavaScript language as ECMAScript.

TC39 chartered two new task groups to perform the actual standardization work: one to focus on the C# language, the other to focus on what became known as the Common Language Infrastructure (CLI).

The CLI consisted of the runtime engine and the subset of the FCL being standardized. Conceptually, Microsoft's CLR is intended to be a conforming commercial implementation of the runtime engine specified in the CLI, and Microsoft's FCL is intended to be a conforming commercial implementation of the class library specified in the CLI (although obviously, it is a massive superset of the 294 classes ultimately specified in the CLI).

After more than a year of intense effort, the task groups completed their standardization work and presented the specifications to the ECMA General Assembly. In December 2001 the General Assembly ratified the C# and CLI specifications, assigning them the ECMA standards numbers of ECMA-334 (C#) and ECMA-335 (the CLI). In late December, 2001, ECMA submitted the standards to the International Organization for Standardization (ISO) via the Fast-Track process, and in April 2003, ISO ratified the standards as ISO/IEC 23270 (C#) and ISO/IEC 23271 (CLI), giving C# and the CLI bona-fide international standard status.

Critics have claimed that the standardization process was merely a ploy by Microsoft to deflect Java's cross-platform advantages. However, the qualifications and seniority of the people working on the standardization effort, and their level of involvement during the lengthy standardization cycle, tell a different story. Microsoft, along with its co-sponsors and the other members of the standardization task groups, committed some of its best and brightest minds to this effort, spending a huge amount of time and attention on the standardization process. Given that this effort occurred concurrently with the development and release of the .NET Framework itself, this level of investment by Microsoft and others flies in the face of the conspiracy theories.

Of course, for standards to have an impact there must be implementations. In addition to the commercial .NET Framework, Microsoft itself has two other CLI implementations: the Shared Source CLI (SSCLI) and the .NET Compact Framework.

In November 2002 Microsoft released the Shared Source CLI (SSCLI) (*http://msdn.microsoft.com/net/sscli*). Formerly known by its code-name, Rotor, the SSCLI is source code for a working implementation of the CLI and C# standards that builds and runs on Windows XP, FreeBSD, and Mac OS X. Licensed for non-commercial use, the SSCLI provides academics, researchers, and technology enthusiasts a vehicle for teaching and research on the inner workings of a CLI implementation, and it also serves as a valuable resource for CLI implementers. Community response has been very positive: a substantial number of research projects and teaching efforts have been based on the SSCLI, and in April 2003 Cornell University launched a community site (*http://www.sscli.net*) that includes a CVS repository, discussion lists, and a bug tracker to coordinate these efforts.

The .NET Compact Framework, now available with Visual Studio .NET 2003, is an implementation of the CLI designed to target resource-constrained devices, and is initially available for Pocket PC 2000+ and Windows CE 4.1+ operating systems.

However, Microsoft's implementations are not the only game in town. Other CLI implementations include the Mono project and dotGNU.

The Mono project (*http://www.go-mono.com*), started by Ximian Corporation, is aiming to provide an implementation of not only the CLI platform and the C# compiler, but also a larger set of classes selected from Microsoft's .NET Framework FCL. In addition to the internal resources that Ximian has committed to the project, the Mono project has also attracted attention from the broader open source community, and appears to be gathering steam.

Another community effort to create an implementation of the C# and CLI standards is the dotGNU project (*http://www.dotgnu.org*). While not as high-profile as Mono, dotGNU has also been making headway, and includes some interesting and unique concepts. The core of dotGNU is Portable.NET, which was originally developed by a lone developer (Rhys Weatherley) before merging his project with dotGNU in August 2000. There are unique aspects to the dotGNU project, including the fact that it was originally designed around a CIL interpreter rather than a JIT compiler, and the developers' plan to support directly executing Java binaries.

It is very likely that more implementations of the CLI will arise over time. While it is too early to say whether the .NET Framework (in the form of the CLI) will ever be available on as many platforms as Java is, the degree of openness and the level of community interest is very encouraging.

Changes in Visual C# 2003

There have been a few minor additions and changes to the C# language in Visual Studio .NET 2003. Most of these changes were made to tighten the language, to conform more precisely to the ECMA specification of C#, and to address bugs in control flow optimizations made by the compiler. These changes have been included in the language reference. (For example, documentation comments may now use standard /* ... */ notation. See Chapter 4.)

The 1.1 version of the Framework Class Libraries has some minor changes from 1.0, which are reflected in the updated API reference section of this book. With the exception of signature changes on two methods on the XslTransform class, there are no breaking changes that would prevent a 1.0 application from working on the 1.1 Framework.

2

C# Language Basics

In this chapter, we explain a simple C# program and introduce the basics of the C# language.

A First C# Program

Here is a simple C# program:

```
namespace FirstProgram {
  using System;
  class Example {
    static void Main () {
      Console.WriteLine ("Hello world!");
    }
  }
}
```

A C# program is composed of types (typically classes) that we organize into namespaces. Each type contains function members (typically methods and properties), as well as data members (typically fields). Methods contain a series of statements that are executed sequentially. In our program, we define a class named Example that contains a method named Main, which has a single statement that writes Hello world! to the console window. C# recognizes this method as the default entry point of execution, so that's where the program begins.

The Console class encapsulates standard input/output functionality, providing methods such as WriteLine. To use types from another namespace, use the using directive. Since the Console class resides in the System namespace, we write using System; similarly, types from other namespaces could use our Example class by using FirstProgram.

In C#, there are no standalone functions; they are always associated with a type, or, as we will see, instances of that type. Our program is simple, and makes use of only static members, which means the member is associated with its type, rather than instances of its type. In addition, we make use of only void methods, which means these methods do not return a value.

Throughout this book, most of the examples contain this stub code:

```
using System;
class Test {
  static void Main () {
    ...
  }
}
```

Identifiers and Keywords

Identifiers are names programmers choose for their types, methods, variables, etc. An identifier must be a whole word, essentially made up of Unicode characters starting with a letter or underscore, and may not clash with a keyword. As a special case, the @ prefix may be used to avoid a clash with a keyword, but is not considered part of the identifier. For instance, the following two identifiers are equivalent:

```
KoЯn
@KoЯn
```

C# identifiers are case-sensitive, though for compatibility with other languages, you should not differentiate public or protected identifiers by case alone.

Here is a list of C# keywords:

abstract	as	base	bool	break
byte	case	catch	char	checked
class	const	continue	decimal	default
delegate	do	double	else	enum
event	explicit	extern	false	finally
fixed	float	for	foreach	goto
if	implicit	in	int	interface
internal	is	lock	long	namespace
new	null	object	operator	out
override	params	private	protected	public
readonly	ref	return	sbyte	sealed
short	sizeof	stackalloc	static	string
struct	switch	this	throw	true
try	typeof	uint	ulong	unchecked
unsafe	ushort	using	virtual	void
while				

Type Basics

A C# program is best understood in terms of three basic elements: functions, data, and types. This book assumes you have some programming experience, so let's start with a brief overview of functions and data (which you should have some familiarity with) and then move on to explain types in more detail.

Functions

A function performs an action by executing a series of statements. For example, you may have a function that returns the distance between two points, or a function that calculates the average of an array of values. A function is a way of manipulating data.

Data

Data is values that functions operate on. For example, you may have data holding the coordinates of a point, or data holding an array of values. Data always has a particular type.

Types

A type has a set of data members and function members. The function members are used to manipulate the data members. The most common types are classes and structs, which provide a template for creating data; data is always an instance of a type.

Types are quite an abstract concept, so let's look at two concrete examples.

The String Class

The string class specifies a sequence of characters. This means you can store values such as ".NET" or "http://oreilly.com". You can also perform functions such as returning the character at a particular position on the string or getting its lowercase representation.

In this example, we output the lower case representation of ".NET" (which will be ".net"), and return the length of the string (which will be 4). To do this, we first create an instance of a string, then use the ToLower method and Length property, which are function members of that string.

```
using System;
class Test {
  static void Main () {
    string s = ".NET";
    Console.WriteLine (s.ToLower()); // outputs ".net"
    Console.WriteLine (s.Length); // outputs 4
  }
}
```

The int Struct

The int struct specifies a signed integer (a positive or negative whole number) that is 32 bits long. This means you can store values ranging from −2,147,483,648 to 2,147,483,647 (or -2^{n-1} to $2^{n-1}-1$, in which $n=32$). With an int, you can perform functions such as adding, multiplying, etc.

In this example, we output the result of multiplying 3 by 4. To do this, we create two instances of the int, and then use the * operator. The int type is actually a built-in type that supports primitive arithmetic functionality (such as *), but it is helpful to think of the * operator as a function member of the int type.

```
using System;
class Example {
  static void Main () {
```

```
    int a = 3;
    int b = 4;
    Console.WriteLine (a * b);
  }
}
```

A Custom Type

You can also define custom types in C#. In fact, a program is built by defining new types, each with a set of data members and function members. In this example, we build our own type, called Counter:

```
// Imports types from System namespace, such as Console
using System;
class Counter { // New types are typically classes or structs
  // --- Data members ---
  int value; // field of type int
  int scaleFactor; // field of type int

  // Constructor, used to initialize a type instance
  public Counter(int scaleFactor) {
    this.scaleFactor = scaleFactor;
  }
  // Method
  public void Inc() {
    value+=scaleFactor;
  }
  // Property
  public int Count {
    get {return value; }
  }
}
class Test {
  // Execution begins here
  static void Main( ) {

    // Create an instance of counter type
    Counter c = new Counter(5);
    c.Inc();
    c.Inc();
    Console.WriteLine(c.Count); // prints "10";

    // create another instance of counter type
    Counter d = new Counter(7);
    d.Inc();
    Console.WriteLine(d.Count); // prints "7";
  }
}
```

Type Instances

Generally, you must create instances of a type to use that type. Data members and function members that require a type to be instantiated in order to be used are called instance members (by default, members are instance members). Data members and function members that can be used on the type itself are called static members.

In this example, the instance method PrintName prints the name of a particular panda, while the static method PrintSpeciesName prints the name shared by all pandas in the application (AppDomain):

```
using System;
class Panda {
  string name;
  static string speciesName = "Ailuropoda melanoleuca";
  // Initializes Panda(See Instance Constructors)
  public Panda(string n) {
    name = n;
  }
  public void PrintName() {
    Console.WriteLine(name);
  }
  public static void PrintSpeciesName() {
    Console.WriteLine(speciesName);
  }
}
class Test {
  static void Main() {
    Panda.PrintSpeciesName(); // invoke static method
    Panda p1 = new Panda("Petey");
    Panda p2 = new Panda("Jimmy");
    p1.PrintName(); // invoke instance method
    p2.PrintName(); // invoke instance method
  }
}
```

Note that the invocation of static members from outside of their enclosing type requires specifying the type name. You may have deduced that Console's WriteLine method is a static member. It is associated with the Console class, rather than an instance of the Console class. A function member should be static when it doesn't rely on any instance data members. Similarly, the Main method of all programs is a static member, which means that this method can be called without instantiating the enclosing class.

Conversions

Each type has its own set of rules defining how it can be converted to and from other types. Conversions between types may be implicit or explicit. Implicit conversions can be performed automatically, while explicit conversions require a cast:

```
int x = 123456; // int is a 4-byte integer
long y = x; // implicit conversion to 8-byte integer
short z =(short)x // explicit conversion to 2-byte integer
```

The rationale behind implicit conversions is they are guaranteed to succeed and do not lose information. Conversely, an explicit conversion is required either when runtime circumstances determine whether the conversion will succeed or whether information may be lost during the conversion.

Most conversion rules are supplied by the language, such as the previously shown numeric conversions. Occasionally it is useful for developers to define their own implicit and explicit conversions, explained later in this chapter.

Value Types and Reference Types

All C# types fall into the following categories:

- Value types (struct, enum)
- Reference types (class, array, delegate, interface)
- Pointer types

The fundamental difference between the three main categories (value types, reference types, and pointer types) is how they are handled in memory. The following sections explain the essential differences between value types and reference types. Pointer types fall outside mainstream C# usage, and are covered later in Chapter 4.

Value Types

Value types are the easiest types to understand. They directly contain data, such as the int type (holds an integer), or the bool type (holds a true or false value). A value type's key characteristic is when you assign one value to another, you make a copy of that value. For example:

```
using System;
class Test {
  static void Main () {
    int x = 3;
    int y = x; // assign x to y, y is now a copy of x
    x++; // increment x to 4
    Console.WriteLine (y); // prints 3
  }
}
```

Reference Types

Reference types are a little more complex. A reference type really defines two separate entities: an object, and a reference to that object. This example follows exactly the same pattern as our previous example, but notice how the variable y is updated, while in our previous example, y remained unchanged:

```
using System;
using System.Text;
class Test {
  static void Main () {
    StringBuilder x = new StringBuilder ("hello");
    StringBuilder y = x;
    x.Append (" there");
    Console.WriteLine (y); // prints "hello there"
  }
}
```

This is because the StringBuilder type is a reference type, while the int type is a value type. When we declared the StringBuilder variable, we were actually doing two separate things, which can be separated into these two lines:

```
StringBuilder x;
x = new StringBuilder ("hello");
```

The first line creates a new reference to a StringBuilder. The second line assigns a new StringBuilder object to the reference. Let's look at the next line:

```
StringBuilder y = x;
```

When we assign x to y, we are saying, "make y point to the same thing that x points to." A reference stores the address of an object (an address is a memory location, stored as a four-byte number). We're actually still making a copy of x, but we're copying this four-byte number as opposed to the StringBuilder object itself.

Let's look at this line:

```
x.Append (" there");
```

This line actually does two things. It first finds the memory location represented by x, and then it tells the StringBuilder object that lies at that memory location to append " there" to it. We could have achieved exactly the same effect by appending " there" to y, because x and y refer to the same object:

```
y.Append (" there");
```

A reference may point at no object, by assigning the reference to null. In this code sample, we assign null to x, but can still access the same StringBuilder object we created via y:

```
using System;
using System.Text;
class Test {
  static void Main () {
    StringBuilder x;
    x = new StringBuilder ("hello");
    StringBuilder y = x;
    x = null;
    y.Append (" there");
    Console.WriteLine (y); // prints "hello there"
  }
}
```

The Heap and the Stack

The stack is a block of memory that grows each time a function is entered (basically to store local variables) and shrinks each time a function exits (because the local variables are no longer needed). In our previous example, when the main function finishes executing, the references x and y go out of scope, as do any value types declared in the function. This is because these values are stored on the stack.

The heap is a block of memory in which reference type objects are stored. Whenever a new object is created, it is allocated on the heap, and returns a reference to that object. During a program's execution, the heap starts filling up as new objects are created. The runtime has a garbage collector that deallocates objects from the heap so your computer does not run out of memory. An object is deallocated when it is determined that it has zero references to it.

You can't explicitly delete objects in C#. An object is either automatically popped off the stack or automatically collected by the garbage collector.

Value types and reference types side-by-side

A good way to understand the difference between value types and reference types is to see them side-by-side. In C#, you can define your own reference types or your own value types. If you want to define a simple type such as a number, it makes sense to define a value type, in which efficiency and copy-by-value semantics are desirable. Otherwise you should define a reference type. You can define a new value type by declaring a struct, and define a new reference type by defining a class.

To create a value-type or reference-type instance, the constructor for the type may be called, with the new keyword. A value-type constructor simply initializes an object. A reference-type constructor creates a new object on the heap, and then initializes the object:

```
// Reference-type declaration
class PointR {
  public int x, y;
}
// Value-type declaration
struct PointV {
  public int x, y;
}
class Test {
  static void Main( ) {
    PointR a; // Local reference-type variable, uses 4 bytes of
              // memory on the stack to hold address
    PointV b; // Local value-type variable, uses 8 bytes of
              // memory on the stack for x and y
    a = new PointR( ); // Assigns the reference to address of new
                       // instance of PointR allocated on the
                       // heap. The object on the heap uses 8
                       // bytes of memory for x and y, and an
                       // additional 8 bytes for core object
                       // requirements, such as storing the
                       // object's type  synchronization state
    b = new PointV( ); // Calls the value-type's default
                       // constructor.  The default constructor
                       // for both PointR and PointV will set
                       // each field to its default value, which
                       // will be 0 for both x and y.
    a.x = 7;
    b.x = 7;
  }
}
// At the end of the method the local variables a and b go out of
// scope, but the new instance of a PointR remains in memory until
// the garbage collector determines it is no longer referenced
```

Assignment to a reference type copies an object reference, while assignment to a value type copies an object value:

```
    ...
    PointR c = a;
    PointV d = b;
    c.x = 9;
    d.x = 9;
    Console.WriteLine(a.x); // Prints 9
    Console.WriteLine(b.x); // Prints 7
  }
}
```

As with this example, an object on the heap can be pointed at by multiple variables, whereas an object on the stack or inline can only be accessed via the variable it was declared with. "Inline" means that the variable is part of a larger object; i.e., it exists as a data member or an array member.

Type System Unification

C# provides a unified type system, whereby the object class is the ultimate base type for both reference types and value types. This means all types, apart from the occasionally used pointer types, share the same basic set of characteristics.

Simple types are value types

Simple types are so called because most have a direct representation in machine code. For example, the floating-point numbers in C# are matched by the floating-point numbers in most processors, such as Pentium processors. For this reason, most languages treat them specially, but in doing so create two separate sets of rules for simple types and user-defined types. In C#, all types follow the same set of rules, resulting in greater programming simplicity.

To do this, the simple types in C# alias structs found in the System namespace. For instance, the int type aliases the System.Int32 struct, the long type aliases the System.Int64 struct, etc. Simple types therefore have the same features one would expect any user-defined type to have. For instance, the int type has function members:

```
int i = 3;
string s = i.ToString();
```

This is equivalent to:

```
// This is an explanatory version of System.Int32
namespace System {
  struct Int32 {
    ...
    public string ToString() {
      return ...;
    }
  }
}
// This is valid code, but we recommend you use the int alias
System.Int32 i = 5;
string s = i.ToString();
```

Value types expand the set of simple types

Simple types have two useful features: they are efficient, and their copy-by-value semantics are intuitive. Consider again how natural it is assigning one number to another and getting a copy of the value of that number, as opposed to getting a copy of a reference to that number. In C#, value types are defined to expand the set of simple types. In this example, we revisit our PointV and PointR example, but this time look at efficiency.

Creating an array of 1,000 ints is very efficient. This allocates 1,000 ints in one contiguous block of memory:

```
int[ ] a = new int[1000];
```

Similarly, creating an array of a value type PointV is very efficient too:

```
struct PointV {
  public int x, y
}
PointV[ ] a = new PointV[1000];
```

If we used a reference type PointR, we would need to instantiate 1,000 individual points after instantiating the array:

```
class PointR {
    public int x, y;
}
PointR[ ] a = new PointR[1000]; // creates an array of 1000 null references
for (int i=0; i<a.Length; i++)
    a[i] = new PointR( );
```

In Java, only the simple types (int, float, etc.) can be treated with this efficiency, while in C# one can expand the set of simple types by declaring a struct.

Furthermore, C#'s operators may be overloaded, so that operations that are typically applicable only to simple types are applicable to any class or struct, such as +, −, etc. (see "Operator Overloading", in Chapter 4).

Boxing and unboxing value types

So that common operations can be performed on both reference types and value types, each value type has a corresponding hidden reference type. This is created when it is cast to a reference type. This process is called boxing. A value type may be cast to the "object" class, which is the ultimate base class for all value types and reference types, or an interface it implements.

In this example, we box and unbox an int to and from its corresponding reference type:

```
class Test {
  static void Main () {
    int x = 9;
    object o = x; // box the int
    int y = (int)o; // unbox the int
  }
}
```

When a value type is boxed, a new reference type is created to hold a copy of the value type. Unboxing copies the value from the reference type back into a value type. Unboxing requires an explicit cast, and a check is made to ensure the value type to convert to matches the type contained in the reference type. An InvalidCastException is thrown if the check fails. You never need to worry about what happens to boxed objects once you've finished with them; the garbage collector take cares of them for you.

Using collection classes is a good example of boxing and unboxing. In this example, we use the Queue class with value types:

```
using System;
using System.Collections;
class Test {
  static void Main () {
    Queue q = new Queue ();
    q.Enqueue (1); // box an int
    q.Enqueue (2); // box an int
    Console.WriteLine ((int)q.Dequeue()); // unbox an int
    Console.WriteLine ((int)q.Dequeue()); // unbox an int
  }
}
```

Predefined Types

This section explains each of C#'s predefined types:

- Value types
    —Integer, signed (sbyte, short, int, long)
    —Integer, unsigned (byte, ushort, uint, ulong)
    —Floating-point (float, decimal, double)
- Reference types
    —Object
    —String

All of these types alias types found in the System namespace. For example, there is only a syntactic difference between these two statements:

```
int i = 5;
System.Int32 i = 5;
```

Integral Types

C# type	System type	Size	Signed
sbyte	System.SByte	1 byte	yes
short	System.Int16	2 bytes	yes
int	System.Int32	4 bytes	yes
long	System.Int64	8 bytes	yes
byte	System.Byte	1 byte	no
ushort	System.UInt16	2 bytes	no

C# type	System type	Size	Signed
uint	System.UInt32	4 bytes	no
ulong	System.UInt64	8 bytes	no

For unsigned integers that are n bits wide, possible values range from 0 to 2^{n-1}. For signed integers that are n bits wide, their possible values range from -2^{n-1} to $2^{n-1}-1$. Integer literals can use either decimal or hexadecimal notation:

```
int x = 5;
ulong y = 0x1234AF; // prefix with 0x for hexadecimal
```

When an integral literal is valid for several possible integral types, the default type chosen goes in this order: int, uint, long, and ulong. The following suffixes may be used to explicitly specify the chosen type:

U   uint or ulong

L   long or ulong

U   ulong

Integral conversions

An implicit conversion between integral types is permitted when the type to convert to contains every possible value of the type to convert from. Otherwise an explicit conversion is required. For instance, you can implicitly convert an int to a long, but must explicitly convert an int to a short:

```
int x = 123456;
long y = x; // implicit, no information lost
short z = (short)x; // explicit, truncates x
```

Floating-Point Types

C# type	System type	Size
float	System.Single	4 Bytes
double	System.Double	8 Bytes

A float can hold values from approximately $\pm 1.5 \times 10^{-45}$ to approximately $\pm 3.4 \times 10^{38}$ with 7 significant figures.

A double can hold values from approximately $\pm 5.0 \times 10^{-324}$ to approximately $\pm 1.7 \times 10^{308}$ with 15–16 significant figures.

Floating-point types can hold the special values +0, −0, +∞, −∞, and NaN (not a number), which represent the outcome of mathematical operations such as division by zero. float and double implement the specification of the IEEE 754 format types, supported by almost all processors, and defined by the IEEE at *http://www.ieee.org*.

Floating-point literals can use decimal or exponential notation. A float literal requires the suffix f or F. A double literal may choose to add the suffix d or D.

```
float x = 9.81f;
double y = 7E-02; // 0.07
```

Floating-point conversions

An implicit conversion from a `float` to a `double` loses no information and is permitted, but not vice versa. An implicit conversion from an `int`, `uint`, and `long` to a `float`, and from a `long` to a `double` is allowed, for readability:

```
int strength = 2;
int offset = 3;
float x = 9.53f * strength - offset;
```

If this example uses larger values, precision may be lost. However, the possible range of values is not truncated, since both a `float` and a `double`'s lowest and highest possible values exceed an `int`, `uint`, or `long`'s lowest or highest value. All other conversions between integral and floating-point types must be explicit:

```
float x = 3.53f;
int offset = (int)x;
```

Decimal Type

The decimal type can hold values from $\pm 1.0 \times 10^{-28}$ to approximately $\pm 7.9 \times 10^{28}$ with 28–29 significant figures.

The `decimal` type holds 28 digits and the position of the decimal point on those digits. Unlike a floating-point value, it has more precision, but a smaller range. It is typically useful in financial calculations, in which the combination of its high precision and the ability to store a base10 number without rounding errors is very valuable. The number 0.1, for instance, is represented exactly with a decimal, but as a recurring binary number with a floating-point type. There is no concept of +0, −0, +∞, −∞, and NaN for a decimal.

A decimal literal requires the suffix m or M.

```
decimal x = 80603.454327m; // holds exact value
```

Decimal conversions

An implicit conversion from all integral types to a decimal type is permitted because a decimal type can represent every possible integer value. A conversion from a decimal to floating type or vice versa requires an explicit conversion, since floating-point types have a bigger range than a decimal, and a decimal has more precision than a floating-point type.

Char Type

C# type	System type	Size
char	System.Char	2 Bytes

The char type represents a Unicode character. A char literal consists of either a character, Unicode format, or escape character enclosed in single quote marks:

```
`A' // simple character
`\u0041' // Unicode
```

```
`\x0041' // unsigned short hexadecimal
`\n' // escape sequence character
```

Table 2-1 lists the escape sequence characters.

Table 2-1. Escape sequence characters

Char	Meaning	Value
\'	Single quote	0x0027
\"	Double quote	0x0022
\\	Backslash	0x005C
\0	Null	0x0000
\a	Alert	0x0007
\b	Backspace	0x0008
\f	Form feed	0x000C
\n	New line	0x000A
\r	Carriage return	0x000D
\t	Horizontal tab	0x0009
\v	Vertical tab	0x000B

Char conversions

An implicit conversion from a char to most numeric types works—it's dependent upon whether the numeric type can accommodate an unsigned short. If it cannot, an explicit conversion is required.

Bool Type

C# type	System type	Size
bool	System.Boolean	1 Byte / 2Byte

The bool type is a logical value that can be assigned the literal true or false.

Although a boolean value requires only one bit (0 or 1), it occupies one byte of storage, since this is the minimum chunk that addressing on most processor architectures can work with. Each element in a boolean array uses two bytes of memory.

Bool conversions

No conversions can be made from booleans to numeric types or vice versa.

Object Type

C# type	System type	Size
object	System.Object	0 byte/8 byte overhead

The object class is the ultimate base type for both value types and reference types. Value types have no storage overhead from an object. Reference types, which are stored on the heap, intrinsically require an overhead. In the .NET runtime, a reference-type instance has an eight-byte overhead, which stores the object's type, as well as temporary information such as its synchronization lock state or whether it has been fixed from movement by the garbage collector. Note that each reference to a reference-type instance uses four bytes of storage.

For more information about the System.Object type, see Chapter 26.

String Type

C# type	System type	Size
string	System.String	20 bytes minimum

The C# string represents an immutable sequence of Unicode characters, and aliases the System.String class (see Chapter 26).

Although string is a class, its use is so ubiquitous in programming that it is given special privileges by both the C# compiler and .NET runtime.

Unlike other classes, a new instance can be created using a string literal:

```
string a = "Heat";
```

Strings can also be created with verbatim string literals. Verbatim string literals start with @, and indicate that the string should be used verbatim, even if it spans multiple lines or includes escape characters, i.e. "\". In this example, the pairs a1 and a2 represent the same string, and the pairs b1 and b2 represent the same string:

```
string a1 = "\\\\server\\fileshare\\helloworld.cs";
string a2 = @"\\server\fileshare\helloworld.cs";
Console.WriteLine(a1==a2); // Prints "True"

string b1 = "First Line\r\nSecond Line";
string b2 = @"First Line
Second Line";
Console.WriteLine(b1==b2); // Prints "True"
```

Arrays

```
type [*]
+ array-name =
[
  new type [ dimension+ ][*]*; |
  { value1, value2, ... };
]
```

Note that [*] is the set: [ ] [,] [,,] ...

Arrays allow a group of elements of a particular type to be stored in a contiguous block of memory. An array is specified by placing square brackets after the element type. For example:

```
char[ ] vowels = new char[ ] {'a','e','i','o','u'};
Console.WriteLine(vowels [1]); // Prints "e"
```

This prints "e" because array indexes start at 0. To support other languages, .NET can create arrays based on arbitrary start indexes, but all the libraries use zero-based indexing. Once an array has been created, its length cannot be changed. However, the System.Collection classes provide dynamically sized arrays, as well as other data structures, such as associative (key/value) arrays.

Multidimensional Arrays

Multidimensional arrays come in two varieties: rectangular and jagged. Rectangular arrays represent an *n*-dimensional block, while jagged arrays are arrays of arrays. In this example we make use of the for loop, which is explained in the statements section. The for loops here simply iterate through each item in the arrays.

```
// rectangular
int [,,] matrixR = new int [3, 4, 5]; // creates 1 big cube
// jagged
int [ ][ ][ ] matrixJ = new int [3][ ][ ];
for (int i = 0; i < 3; i++) {
    matrixJ[i] = new int [4][ ];
    for (int j = 0; j < 4; j++)
        matrixJ[i][j] = new int [5];
}
// assign an element
matrixR [1,1,1] = matrixJ [1][1][1] = 7;
```

Local Field Array Declarations

For convenience, local and field declarations may omit the array type when assigning a known value, since the type is specified in the declaration anyway:

```
int[,] array = {{1,2},{3,4}};
```

Array Length and Rank ·

Arrays know their own length. For multidimensional array methods, the array's GetLength method returns the number of elements for a given dimension, which is from 0 (the outermost) to the array's rank-1 (the innermost).

```
// single dimensional
for(int i = 0; i < vowels.Length; i++);
// multi-dimensional
for(int i = 0; i < matrixR.GetLength(2); i++);
```

Bounds Checking

All array indexing is bounds-checked by the runtime, with IndexOutOfRangeException thrown for invalid indices. Like Java, this prevents program faults and debugging difficulties while enabling code to execute with security restrictions.

Generally, the performance hit from bounds-checking is minor, and the JIT (Just-in-Time compiler) can perform optimizations, such as determining each array index is safe before entering a loop, thus avoiding a check made for each iteration. In addition, C# provides "unsafe" code that can explicitly bypass bounds-checking (see "Unsafe Code and Pointers" in Chapter 4).

Array Conversions

Arrays of reference types may be converted to other arrays, using the same logic you would apply to its element type (this is called *array covariance*). All arrays implement System.Array, which provides methods to generically get and set elements regardless of the array type.

Variables and Parameters

A variable represents a typed storage location. A variable can be a local variable, parameter, array element, an instance field, or a static field.

All variables have an associated type, which essentially defines the possible values the variable can have and the operations that can be performed on that variable. C# is strongly typed, which means the set of operations that can be performed on a type are enforced at compile time, rather than at runtime. In addition, C# is type-safe, which ensures that a variable can be operated on only via the correct type with the help of runtime checking (except in unsafe blocks; see "Unsafe Code and Pointers" in Chapter 4).

Definite Assignment

All variables in C# (except in unsafe contexts) must be assigned a value before they are used. A variable is either explicitly assigned a value or automatically assigned a default value. Automatic assignment occurs for static fields, class instance fields, and array elements not explicitly assigned a value. For example:

```
using System;
class Test {
  int v;
  // Constructors that initalize an instance of a Test
  public Test() {} // v will be automatically assigned to 0
  public Test(int a) { // explicitly assign v a value
    v = a;
  }
  static void Main() {
    Test[] tests = new Test [2]; // declare array
    Console.WriteLine(tests[1]); // ok, elements assigned to null
    Test t;
    Console.WriteLine(t); // error, t not assigned before use
  }
}
```

Default Values

Essentially the default value for all primitive (or atomic) types is zero:

Type	Default value
Numeric types	0
Bool type	false
Char type	'\0'
Enum types	0
Reference type	null

The default value for each field in a complex (or composite) type is one of these aforementioned values.

Parameters

A method has a sequence of parameters. Parameters define the set of arguments that must be provided for that method. In this example the method Foo has a single parameter named p, of type int:

```
static void Foo(int p) {++p;}
static void Main( ) {
  Foo(8);
}
```

Passing arguments by value

By default, arguments in C# are passed by value, which is by far the most common case. This means a copy of the value is created when passed to the method:

```
static void Foo(int p) {++p;}
static void Main( ) {
  int x = 8;
  Foo(x); // make a copy of the value-type x
  Console.WriteLine(x); // x will still be 8
}
```

Assigning p a new value does not change the contents of x, since p and x reside in different memory locations.

Ref modifier

To pass by reference, C# provides athe parameter modifier ref, which allows p and x to refer to the same memory locations:

```
class Test {
  static void Foo(ref int p) {++p;}
  static void Main () {
    int x = 8;
    Foo(ref x); // send reference of x to Foo
    Console.WriteLine(x); // x is now 9
  }
}
```

Now assigning p a new value changes the contents of x. This is usually the reason we want to pass by reference, though occasionally it is more efficient when passing large structs. Notice how the ref modifier and the method definition are required in the method call. This makes it very clear what's going on, and clears ambiguity since parameter modifiers change the signature of a method.

The ref modifier is essential when implementing a swap method:

```
class Test {
  static void Swap (ref string a, ref string b) {
    string temp = a;
    a = b;
    b = temp;
  }
  static void Main () {
    string x = "Bush";
    string y = "Gore";
    Swap(ref x, ref y);
    System.Console.WriteLine("x is {0}, y is {1}", x, y);
  }
}
// outputs: x is Gore, y is Bush
```

The out modifier

C# is a language that enforces that variables are assigned before use, so it also provides the out modifier, which is the natural complement of the ref modifier. While a ref modifier requires that a variable is assigned a value before being passed to a method, the out modifier requires that a variable is assigned a value before returning from a method:

```
using System;
class Test {
  static void Split(string name, out string firstNames,
                    out string lastName) {
    int i = name.LastIndexOf(' ');
    firstNames = name.Substring(0, i);
    lastName = name.Substring(i+1);
  }
  static void Main() {
    string a, b;
    Split("Nuno Bettencourt", out a, out b);
    Console.WriteLine("FirstName:{0}, LastName:{1}", a, b);
  }
}
```

The params modifier

The params parameter modifier may be specified on the last parameter of a method so that the method accepts any number of parameters of a particular type. For example:

```
using System;
class Test {
  static int Add(params int[ ] iarr) {
```

```
      int sum = 0;
      foreach(int i in iarr)
        sum += i;
      return sum;
    }
    static void Main( ) {
      int i = Add(1, 2, 3, 4);
      Console.WriteLine(i); // 10
    }
  }
```

Expressions and Operators

An expression is a sequence of operators and operands that specifies a computation. C# has unary operators, binary operators, and one ternary operator. Complex expressions can be built because an operand may itself be an expression, such as the operand (1 + 2) shown in the following example:

```
((1 + 2) / 3)
```

Operator Precedence

When an expression contains multiple operators, the precedence of the operators controls the order in which the individual operators are evaluated. When the operators are of the same precedence, their associativity determines the order. Binary operators (except for assignment operators) are left-associative; i.e., they are evaluated from left to right. The assignment operators, unary operators, and the conditional operator are right-associative; i.e., they are evaluated from right to left.

For example:

```
1 + 2 + 3 * 4
```

is evaluated as:

```
((1 + 2) + (3 * 4))
```

because * has a higher precedence than +, and + is a binary operator that is left-associative. You can insert parentheses to change the default order of evaluation. C# overloads operators, which means the same operator may have different meanings for different types.

Table 2-2 lists C#'s operators in order of precedence. Operators in the same box have the same precedence, and operators in italic may be overloaded for custom types.

Table 2-2. Operator precedence

Category	Operators
Primary	Grouping: (x) Member access: x.y Struct pointer member access: -> Method call: f(x) Indexing: a[x] *Post increment*: x++ *Post decrement*: x-- Constructor call: new Array stack allocation: `stackalloc` Type retrieval: `typeof` Struct size retrieval: `sizeof` Arithmetic check on: `checked` Arithmetic check off: `unchecked`
Unary	*Positive value of (passive)*: + *Negative value of*: − *Not*: ! *Bitwise complement*: ~ *Pre increment*: ++x *Pre decrement*: --x Type cast: (T)x Value at address: * Address of value: &
Multiplicative	*Multiply*: * *Divide*: / *Division remainder*: %
Additive	*Add*: + *Subtract*: −
Shift	*Shift bits left*: << *Shift bits right*: >>
Relational	*Less than*: < *Greater than*: > *Less than or equal to*: <= *Greater than or equal to*: >= Type equality/compatibility: `is` Conditional type conversion: `as`
Equality	*Equals*: == *Not equals*: !=
Logical bitwise	*And*: & *Exclusive or*: ^ *Or*:	

Table 2-2. Operator precedence (continued)

Category	Operators
Logical Boolean	And: &&
	Or: ||
	Ternary conditional: ? :
	e.g., `int x = a > b ? 2 : 7;`
	is equivalent to:
	`int x;`
	`if (a > b) x = 2;`
	`else x = 7;`
Assignment	Assign/modify:
	`= *= /= %= += -= <<= >>= &= ^= |=`

Arithmetic Overflow Check Operators

The syntax for the checked and unchecked operators is:

```
checked (expression)
unchecked (expression)
```

The syntax for the checked and unchecked statements is:

```
checked statement-or-statement-block
unchecked statement-or-statement-block
```

The checked operator tells the runtime to generate an `OverflowException` if an integral expression exceeds the arithmetic limits of that type. The checked operator affects expressions with the ++, --, (unary)-, +, -, *, /, and explicit conversion operators between integral types. For example:

```
int a = 1000000;
int b = 1000000;

// Check an expression
int c = checked(a*b);

// Check every expression in a statement-block
checked {
    ...
    c = a * b;
    ...
}
```

The checked operator only applies to runtime expressions, since constant expressions are checked during compilation (though this can be turned off with the /checked [+|-] command-line switch). The unchecked operator disables arithmetic checking at compile time, and is seldom useful, but does make expressions such as the following compile:

```
const int signedBit = unchecked((int)0x80000000);
```

Statements

Execution in a C# program is specified by a series of statements that execute sequentially in the textual order in which they appear. All statements in a procedural-based language such as C# are executed for their effect. For instance, a statement may assign an expression to a variable, repeatedly execute a list of statements, or jump to another statement.

So that multiple statements can be grouped together, zero or more statements may be enclosed in braces to form a statement block.

Expression Statements

```
[variable =]? expr;
```

An expression statement evaluates an expression, either assigning its result to a variable or generating side effects (i.e., invocation, new, ++, --). An expression statement ends in a semicolon. For example:

```
x = 5 + 6; // assign result
x++; // side effect
y = Math.Min(x, 20); // side effect and assign result
Math.Min(x, y); // discards result, but ok, there is a side effect
x == y; // error, has no side effect, and does not assign result
```

Declaration Statements

The variable declaration syntax is:

```
type [variable [ = expr ]?]+ ;
```

The constant declaration syntax is:

```
const type [variable = constant-expr]+;
```

A declaration statement declares a new variable, optionally assigning the result of an expression to that variable. A declaration statement ends in a semicolon.

The scope of a local or constant variable extends to the end of the current block. You cannot declare another local variable with the same name in the current block or in any nested blocks. For example:

```
bool a = true;
while(a) {
  int x = 5;
  if (x==5) {
    int y = 7;
    int x = 2; // error, x already defined
  }
  Console.WriteLine(y); // error, y is out of scope
}
```

A constant declaration is like a variable declaration, except that the variable cannot be changed after it has been declared:

```
const double speedOfLight = 2.99792458E08;
speedOfLight+=10; // error
```

Selection Statements

C# has many ways to conditionally control the flow of program execution. This section covers the simplest two constructs: the if-else statement and the switch statement. In addition, C# also provides the conditional operator and loop statements that conditionally execute based on a boolean expression. Finally, C# provides object-oriented ways of conditionally controlling the flow of execution, namely virtual method invocations and delegate invocations.

The if-else statement

```
if (Boolean-expr)
  [statement | statement-block]
[ else
  [statement | statement-block] ]?
```

An if-else statement executes code depending on whether a boolean expression is true. Unlike in C, only a boolean expression is permitted. In this example, the Compare method will return 1 if a is greater than b, -1 if a is less than b, and 0 if a is equal to b.

```
int Compare(int a, int b) {
   if (a>b)
      return 1;
   else if (a<b)
      return -1;
   return 0;
}
```

It is very common to use the && and || and ! operators to test for AND, OR, and NOT conditions. In this example, our GetUmbrellaNeeded method returns an umbrella if it's rainy or sunny (to protect us from the rain or the sun), as long as it's not also windy (since umbrellas are useless in the wind):

```
Umbrella GetUmbrella (bool rainy, bool sunny, bool windy) {
   if ((rainy || sunny) && ! windy)
      return umbrella;
   return null;
}
```

The switch statement

```
switch (expr) {
[ case constant-expr : statement* ]*
[ default : statement* ]?
}
```

switch statements let you branch program execution based on a selection of possible values a variable may have. switch statements may result in cleaner code than multiple if statements, since switch statements require an expression to be evaluated only once. For instance:

```
void Award(int x) {
  switch(x) {
    case 1:
      Console.WriteLine("Winner!");
```

```
      break;
    case 2:
      Console.WriteLine("Runner-up");
      break;
    case 3:
    case 4:
      Console.WriteLine("Highly commended");
      break;
    default:
      Console.WriteLine("Don't quit your day job!");
      break;
  }
}
```

The switch statement can only evaluate a predefined type (including the string type) or enum, though user-defined types may provide an implicit conversion to these types.

The end of each case statement must be unreachable. This typically means each case statement ends with a jump statement. The options are:

- Use the break statement to jump to the end of the switch statement (this is by far the most common option).

- Use the goto case <*constant expression*> or goto default statements to jump to either another case statement or to the default case statement.

- Use any other jump statement—namely, return, throw, continue, or goto *label*.

Unlike in Java and C++, the end of a case statement must explicitly state where to go to next. There is no error-prone "default fall through" behavior; not specifying a break results in the next case statement being executed:

```
void Greet(string title) {
  switch (title) {
    case null:
      Console.WriteLine("And you are?");
      goto default;
    case "King":
      Console.WriteLine("Greetings your highness");
      // error, should specify break, otherwise...
    default :
      Console.WriteLine("How's it hanging?");
      break;
  }
}
```

Loop Statements

C# enables a sequence of statements to execute repeatedly with the while, do while, for, and foreach statements.

while loops

```
while (Boolean-expr)
[statement | statement-block]
```

---

while loops repeatedly execute a statement block when a boolean expression is true. The expression is tested before the statement block is executed. For example:

```
int i = 0;
while (i<5) {
   Console.WriteLine (i);
   i++;
}

output:
0
1
2
3
4
```

do-while loops

```
do
  [statement |statement-block]
while (Boolean-expr);
```

do-while loops differ only in functionality from while loops in that they allow the expression to be tested after the statement block has executed. In this example, a do-while loop prints 8, while a while loop would have not printed anything. For example:

```
int i = 8;
do {
   Console.WriteLine (i);
   i++;
}
while (i<5);

output:
8
```

for loops

```
for (statement?;
     Boolean-expr?;
     statement?)
  [statement | statement-block]
```

for loops can be more convenient than while loops when you need to maintain an iterator value. As in Java and C, for loops contain three parts. The first part is a statement executed before the loop begins, and by convention is used to initialize an iterator variable; the second part is a boolean expression that, while true, will execute the statement block, and the third part is a statement executed after each iteration of the statement block, which convention is used to iterate the iterator variable. For example:

```
for (int i=0; i<10; i++)
   Console.WriteLine(i);
```

Any of the three parts of the for statement may be omitted. One can implement an infinite loop such as the following (though while (true) may be used instead):

```
for (;;)
    Console.WriteLine("Hell ain't so bad");
```

foreach loops

```
foreach ( type-value in IEnumerable )
    [statement | statement-block ]
```

It is very common for for loops to iterate over a collection, so C#, like Visual Basic, has a foreach statement.

For instance, instead of doing the following:

```
for (int i=0; i<dynamite.Length; i++)
    Console.WriteLine(dynamite [i]);
```

You can perform this action:

```
foreach (Stick stick in dynamite)
    Console.WriteLine(stick);
```

The foreach statement works on any collection (including arrays). Although not strictly necessary, all collections leverage this functionality by supporting IEnumerable and IEnumerator, which are explained in Chapter 7. Here is an equivalent way to iterate over our collection:

```
IEnumerator ie = dynamite.GetEnumerator( );
while (ie.MoveNext( )) {
    Stick stick = (Stick)ie.Current;
    Console.WriteLine(stick);
}
```

Under the hood, the foreach statement also acts as a using statement (covered later in this chapter) on the enumerator object (ie in the example above). In Visual C# 2003, Dispose( ) will be called on the enumerator, even if the enumerator does not implement IEnumerable.

Jump Statements

The C# jump statements are break, continue, goto, return, and throw. All jump statements obey sensible restrictions imposed by try statements (see "Try Statements and Exceptions" in Chapter 4). First, a jump out of a try block always executes the try's finally block before reaching the target of the jump. Second, a jump cannot be made from the inside to the outside of a finally block.

The break statement

```
break;
```

The break statement transfers execution from the enclosing while loop, for loop, or switch statement block to the next statement block.

```
int x = 0;
while (true) {
```

```
    x++;
    if (x>5)
        break; // break from the loop
}
```

The continue statement

```
continue;
```

The continue statement forgoes the remaining statements in the loop and makes an early start on the next iteration.

```
int x = 0;
int y = 0;
while (y<100) {
    x++;
    if ((x%7)==0)
        continue; // continue with next iteration
    y++;
}
```

The goto statement

```
goto statement-label;
goto case-constant;
```

The goto statement transfers execution to another label within the statement block. A label statement is just a placeholder in a method:

```
int x = 4;
start:
x++;
if (x==5)
    goto start;
```

The goto case statement transfers execution to another case label in a switch block (as explained earlier in the "Switch" section).

The return statement

```
return expr?;
```

The return statement exits the method, and must return an expression of the method's return type if the method is nonvoid.

```
int CalcX(int a) {
    int x = a * 100;
    return x; // return to the calling method with value
}
```

The throw statement

```
throw exception-expr?;
```

The throw statement throws an exception to indicate an abnormal condition has occurred (see "Try Statements and Exceptions" in Chapter 4).

```
if (w==null)
    throw new ArgumentException("w can't be null");
```

The lock statement

```
lock (expr)
  [statement | statement-block]
```

The lock statement is actually a syntactic shortcut for calling the Enter and Exit methods of the Monitor class (see Chapter 16).

The using statement

```
using (declaration-expr)
  [statement | statement-block]
```

Many classes encapsulate nonmemory resources, such as file handles, graphics handles, or database connections. These classes implement System.IDisposable, which defines a single parameterless method named Dispose called to clean up these resources. The using statement provides an elegant syntax for declaring and then calling the Dispose method of variables that implement IDisposable. For example:

```
using (FileStream fs = new FileStream (fileName, FileMode.Open)) {
  ...
}
```

This is precisely equivalent to:

```
FileStream fs = new FileStream (fileName, FileMode.Open);
try {
  ...
}
finally {
  if (fs != null)
    ((IDispoable)fs).Dispose( );
}
```

For more on IDisposable, see Chapter 15.

Namespaces

These are defined in files, organized by namespaces, compiled into a module, then grouped into an assembly.

These organizational units are crosscutting. For example, typically a group of namespaces belong to one assembly, but a single namespace may in fact be spread over multiple assemblies (see Chapter 12).

Files

File organization is almost of no significance to the C# compiler—a whole project could be merged into one .cs file and it would still compile (preprocessor statements are the only exception to this). However, it's generally tidy to have one type in one file, with the filename matching the name of the class and the directory the file is in matching the name of the class's namespace.

Namespaces

```
namespace name+          // Dot-delimited
{
 using-statement*
 [namespace-declaration |
  type-declaration]*      // No delimiters
}
```

A namespace lets you group related types into a hierarchical categorization. Generally the first name is the name of your organization, and it gets more specific from there:

```
namespace MyCompany.MyProduct.Drawing {
   class Point {int x, y, z;}
   delegate void PointInvoker(Point p);
}
```

Nesting namespaces

You may also nest namespaces instead of using dots. This example is semantically identical to the previous example:

```
namespace MyCompany {
  namespace MyProduct {
    namespace Drawing {
       class Point {int x, y, z;}
       delegate void PointInvoker(Point p);
    }
  }
}
```

Using a type with its fully qualified name

To use the Point from another namespace, you may refer to it with its fully qualified name. The namespace a type is within actually becomes part of the type name:

```
namespace TestProject {
  class Test {
    static void Main( ) {
      MyCompany.MyProduct.Drawing.Point x;
    }
  }
}
```

The using keyword

The using keyword is a convenient way to avoid using the fully qualified name of types in other namespaces. This example is semantically identical to our previous example:

```
namespace TestProject {
  using MyCompany.MyProduct.Drawing;
  class Test {
    static void Main( ) {
      Point x;
```

```
      }
    }
  }
```

Aliasing types and namespaces

Type names must be unique within a namespace. To avoid naming conflicts without having to use fully qualified names, C# allows you to specify an alias for a type or namespace. Here is an example:

```
using sys = System;        // Namespace alias
using txt = System.String; // Type alias
class Test {
  static void Main() {
    txt s = "Hello, World!";
    sys.Console.WriteLine(s); // Hello, World!
    sys.Console.WriteLine(s.GetType()); // System.String
  }
}
```

Global namespace

The global namespace is the outermost level that all namespaces and types are implicitly declared in. When a type is not explicitly declared within a namespace, it may be used without qualification from any other namespace, since it a member of the global namespace. However, apart from the smallest programs, it is always good practice to organize types within logical namespaces.

In this example, the class Test is declared in the global namespace, so it can be used without qualification from the Noo namespace.

```
class Test {
  public static void Foo () {
    System.Console.WriteLine ("hello!");
  }
}
namespace Noo {
  class Test2 {
    static void Main() {
      Test.Foo();
    }
  }
}
```

3

Creating Types in C#

In this chapter, we cover creation of types in C#, including classes, inheritance, access modifiers, structs, interfaces, and enums.

Classes

```
attributes? unsafe? access-modifier?
new?
[ abstract | sealed ]?
class class-name
[: base-class |
 : interface+ |
 : base-class, interface+ ]?
{ class-members }
```

In C#, a program is built by defining new types, each with a set of data members and function members. Custom types should form higher-level building blocks that are easy to use, and closely model your problem space.

In this example, we simulate an astronaut jumping on different planets, using three classes, Planet, Astronaut, and Test, to test our simulation.

First, let's define the Planet class. By convention, we define the data members of the class at the top of the class declaration. There are two data members here: the name and gravity fields, which store the name and gravity of a planet. We then define a constructor for the planet. Constructors are function members that allow you to initialize an instance of your class. We initialize the data members with values fed to the parameters of the constructor. Finally, we define two more function members, which are properties that allow us to get the "Name" and "Gravity" of a planet. The Planet class looks like this:

```
using System;

class Planet {
```

```
    string name; // field
    double gravity; // field
    // constructor
    public Planet (string n, double g) {
      name = n;
      gravity = g;
    }
    // property
    public string Name {
      get {return name;}
    }
    // property
    public double Gravity {
      get {return gravity;}
    }
}
```

Next, we define the Astronaut class. As with the Planet class, we first define our data members. Here an astronaut has two fields: the astronaut's fitness, and the current planet the astronaut is on. We then provide a constructor, which initializes the fitness of an astronaut. Next we define a CurrentPlanet property that allows us to get or set the planet an astronaut is on. Finally we define a jump method that outputs how far the astronaut jumps, based on the fitness of the astronaut and the planet he is on.

```
using System;

class Astronaut {
  double fitness; // field
  Planet currentPlanet; // field

  // constructor
  public Astronaut (double f) {
    fitness = f;
  }
  // property
  public Planet CurrentPlanet {
    get {
      return currentPlanet;
    }
    set {
      currentPlanet = value;
    }
  }
  // method
  public void Jump () {
    if (currentPlanet == null)
      Console.WriteLine ("Bye Bye!");
    else {
      double distance = fitness/currentPlanet.Gravity;
      Console.WriteLine ("Jumped {0} metres on {1}", distance,
                         currentPlanet.Name);
    }
  }
}
```

Last, we define the Test class, which uses the Planet and Astronaut classes. Here we create two planets, earth and moon, and one astronaut, forestGump. Then we see how far forestGump jumps on each of these planets:

```
class Test {
  static void Main () {
    // create a new instance of a planet
    Planet earth = new Planet ("earth", 9.8);
    // create another new instance of a planet
    Planet moon = new Planet ("moon", 1.6);
    // create a new instance of an astronaut
    Astronaut forestGump = new Astronaut (20);
    forestGump.CurrentPlanet = earth;
    forestGump.Jump();
    forestGump.CurrentPlanet = moon;
    forestGump.Jump();
  }
}
// output
Jumped 2.04 metres on earth
Jumped 12.50 metres on moon
```

If a class is designed well, it becomes a new higher-level building block that is easy for someone else to use. The user of a class seldom cares about the data members or implementation details of another class, merely its specification. To use a planet or an astronaut, all you need to know is how to use their public function members.

In the following section, we look at each kind of type members a class can have, namely fields, constants, properties, indexers, methods, operators, constructors, destructors, and nested types. (Operators and events are explained in Chapter 4.)

The this Keyword

The this keyword denotes a variable that is a reference to a class or struct instance and is only accessible from within nonstatic function members of the class or struct. The this keyword is also used by a constructor to call an overloaded constructor (explained later in this chapter) or declare or access indexers (also explained later in this chapter). A common use of the this variable is to distinguish a field name from a parameter name.

```
class Dude {
  string name;
  public Dude (string name) {
    this.name = name;
  }
  public void Introduce(Dude a) {
    if (a!=this)
      Console.WriteLine("Hello, I'm "+name);
  }
}
```

Fields

```
attributes? unsafe? access-modifier?
new?
static?
[readonly | volatile]?
type [ field-name [ = expr]? ]+ ;
```

Fields hold data for a class or struct:

```
class MyClass {
  int x;
  float y = 1, z = 2;
  static readonly int MaxSize = 10;
  ...
}
```

Nonstatic fields

Nonstatic fields are also referred to as instance variables or instance data members. Static variables are also referred to as static variables or static data members.

The readonly modifier

As the name suggests, the readonly modifier prevents a field from being modified after it has been assigned. Such a field is termed a *read-only field*. A read-only field is always evaluated at runtime, not at compile time. A read-only field must be assigned in its declaration or within the type's constructor in order to compile (see more on constructors, later in this chapter), while non-read-only fields merely generate a warning when left unassigned.

Constants

```
attributes? access-modifier?
new?
const type [constant-name = constant-expr]+;
```

A constant is a field that is evaluated at compile time and is implicitly static. The logical consequence of this is that a constant may not defer evaluation to a method or constructor, and may only be one of a few built-in types. These types are sbyte, byte, short, ushort, int, uint, long, ulong, float, double, decimal, bool, char, string, and enum. For example:

```
public const double PI = 3.14159265358979323846;
```

The benefit of a constant is that it is evaluated at compile time, permitting additional optimization by the compiler. For instance:

```
public static double Circumference(double radius) {
  return 2 * Math.PI * radius;
}
```

evaluates to:

```
public static double Circumference(double radius) {
  return 6.2831853071795862 * radius;
}
```

A read-only field would not make this optimization, but is more versionable. For instance, suppose there was a mistake in calculation of *pi*, and Microsoft releases a patch to their library that contains the Math class, which is deployed to each client computer. If your software that uses the Circumference method is already deployed on a client machine, then the mistake is not fixed until you recompile your application with the latest version of the Math class. With a read-only field, however, this mistake is automatically fixed. Generally, this scenario occurs when a field value changes not as a result of a mistake, but simply because of an upgrade (such as MaxThreads changing from 500 to 1,000).

Properties

```
attributes? unsafe? access-modifier?
[
  [[sealed | abstract]? override] |
  new? [virtual | abstract | static]?
]?
type property-name { [
 attributes? get      // read-only
  statement-block |
 attributes? set      // write-only
  statement-block |
 attributes? get      // read-write
  statement-block
 attributes? set
  statement-block
] }
```

Properties can be characterized as object-oriented fields. Properties promote encapsulation by allowing a class or struct to control access to its data, and by hiding the internal representation of the data. For instance:

```
public class Well {
    decimal dollars; // private field
    public int Cents {
      get { return(int)(dollars * 100); }
      set {
        // value is an implicit variable in a set
        if (value>=0) // typical validation code
            dollars = (decimal)value/100;
      }
    }
}
class Test {
    static void Main( ) {
        Well w = new Well( );
        w.Cents = 25; // set
        int x = w.Cents; // get
        w.Cents += 10; // get and set(throw a dime in the well)
    }
}
```

The get accessor returns a value of the property's type. The set accessor has an implicit parameter named value that is of the property's type. A property can be

Creating Types

read-only if it specifies only a get method, and write-only if it specifies only a write method (though rarely desirable).

Many languages loosely implement properties with a get/set method convention, and C# properties are in fact compiled to get_*XXX*/set_*XXX* methods. This is the representation in MSIL:

```
public int get_Cents {...}
public void set_Cents (int value) {...}
```

 Simple property accessors are inlined by the JIT (Just-In-Time compiler), which means there is no performance difference between a property access and a field access. Inlining is an optimization in which a method call is replaced with the body of that method.

Indexers

```
attributes? unsafe? access-modifier?
[
  [[sealed | abstract]? override] |
  new? [virtual | abstract | static]?
]?
type this [ attributes? [type arg]+ ] {
  attributes? get        // read-only
  statement-block |
  attributes? set        // write-only
  statement-block |
  attributes? get        // read-write
  statement-block
  attributes? set
  statement-block
}
```

Indexers provide a natural way of indexing elements in a class or struct that encapsulate a collection, via an array's [ ] syntax. Indexers are similar to properties, but are accessed via an index, as opposed to a property name. The index can be any number of parameters. In the following example, the ScoreList class can be used to maintain the list of scores given by five judges. The indexer uses a single int index to get or set a particular judge's score.

```
public class ScoreList {
  int[ ] scores = new int [5];
  // indexer
  public int this[int index] {
    get {
      return scores[index]; }
    set {
      if(value >= 0 && value <= 10)
        scores[index] = value;
    }
  }
  // property (read-only)
  public int Average {
    get {
```

```
            int sum = 0;
            foreach(int score in scores)
                sum += score;
            return sum / scores.Length;
        }
    }
}
class Test {
    static void Main( ) {
        ScoreList sl = new ScoreList( );
        sl[0] = 9;
        sl[1] = 8;
        sl[2] = 7;
        sl[3] = sl[4] = sl[1];
        System.Console.WriteLine(sl.Average);
    }
}
```

A type may declare multiple indexers that take different parameters. Our example
could be extended to return the score by a judge's name, as opposed to a numeric
index.

Indexers are compiled to get_Item (...)/set_Item (...) methods, which is the
representation in MSIL.

```
public Story get_Item (int index) {...}
public void set_Item (int index, Story value) {...}
```

Methods

```
attributes? unsafe? access-modifier?
[
    [[sealed | abstract]? override] |
    new? [virtual | abstract |
      static extern?]?
]?
[ void | type ]
  method-name (parameter-list)
    statement-blockParameter list syntax:
[ attributes? [ref | out]? type arg ]*
[ params attributes? type[ ] arg ]?
```

All C# code executes in a method or in a special form of a method. Constructors,
destructors, and operators are special types of methods, and properties and
indexers are internally implemented with get/set methods.

Signatures

A method's signature is characterized by the type and modifier of each parameter
in its parameter list. The parameter modifiers ref and out allow arguments to be
passed by reference, rather than by value. These characteristics are referred to as a
method signature, because they uniquely distinguish one method from another.

Overloading methods

A type may overload methods (have multiple methods with the same name), as long as the signatures are different.* For example, the following methods can all coexist in the same type:

```
void Foo(int x);
void Foo(double x);
void Foo(int x, float y);
void Foo(float x, int y);
void Foo(ref int x);
```

However, the following pairs of methods cannot coexist in the same type, since the return type and params modifier do not qualify as part of a method's signature.

```
void Foo(int x);
float Foo(int x); // compile error
void Goo (int[ ] x);
void Goo (params int[ ] x); // compile error
```

Instance Constructors

```
attributes? unsafe? access-modifier?
class-name (parameter-list)
[ :[ base | this ] (argument-list) ]?
statement-block
```

Constructors allow initialization code to execute for a class or struct. A class constructor first creates a new instance of that class on the heap and then performs initialization, while a struct constructor merely performs initialization.

Unlike ordinary methods, a constructor has the same name as the class or struct and has no return type:

```
class MyClass {
  public MyClass( ) {
    // initialization code
  }
}
```

A class or struct may overload constructors, and may call one of its overloaded constructors before executing its method body using the this keyword:

```
class MyClass {
  public int x;
  public MyClass( ) : this(5) { }
  public MyClass(int v) {
    x = v;
  }
}
MyClass m1 = new MyClass( );
MyClass m2 = new MyClass(10);
Console.WriteLine(m1.x) // 5
Console.WriteLine(m2.x) // 10;
```

---

* An exception to this rule is that two otherwise identical signatures cannot coexist if one parameter has the ref modifier and the other parameter has the out modifier.

If a class does not define any constructors, an implicit parameter-free constructor is created. A struct cannot define a parameter-free constructor, since a constructor that initializes each field with a default value (effectively zero) is always implicitly defined.

Field initialization order

Another useful way to perform initialization is to assign fields an initial value in their declaration:

```
class MyClass {
    int x = 5;
}
```

Field assignments are performed before the constructor is executed, and are initialized in the textual order in which they appear.

Constructor access modifiers

A class or struct may choose any access modifier for a constructor. It is occasionally useful to specify a private constructor to prevent a class from being constructed. This is appropriate for utility classes made up entirely of static members, such as the System.Math class.

Static Constructors

```
attributes? unsafe? extern?
static class-name ( )
statement-block
```

A static constructor allows initialization code to execute before the first instance of a class or struct is created, or before any static member of the class or struct is · accessed. A class or struct can define only one static constructor, and it must be parameter-free and have the same name as the class or struct:

```
class Test {
    static Test( ) {
        Console.WriteLine("Test Initialized");
    }
}
```

Static field initialization order

Each static field assignment is made before any of the static constructors are called, and are initialized in the textual order in which they appear, which is consistent with instance fields.

```
class Test {
    public static int x = 5;
    public static void Foo( ) { }
    static Test( ) {
        Console.WriteLine("Test Initialized");
    }
}
```

Accessing either Test.x or Test.Foo assigns 5 to x, and then prints Test Initialized.

Nondeterminism of static constructors

Static constructors cannot be called explicitly, and the runtime may invoke them well before they are first used. Programs should not make any assumptions about the timing of a static constructor's invocation. In this example, Test Initialized may be printed after Test2 Initialized:

```
class Test2 {
  public static void Foo() { }
  static Test2 () {
    Console.WriteLine("Test2 Initialized");
  }
}
Test.Foo();
Test2.Foo();
```

Destructors and Finalizers

```
attributes? unsafe?
~class-name ( )
statement-block
```

Destructors are class-only methods that are used to clean up nonmemory resources just before the garbage collector reclaims the memory for an object. Just as a constructor is called when an object is created, a destructor is called when an object is destroyed. C# destructors are very different from C++ destructors, primarily because of the presence of the garbage collector. First, memory is automatically reclaimed with a garbage collector, so a destructor in C# is used solely for nonmemory resources. Second, destructor calls are nondeterministic. The garbage collector calls an object's destructor when it determines it is no longer referenced; however, it may determine this after an undefined period of time has passed after the last reference to the object disappeared.

A destructor is actually a syntactic shortcut for declaring a Finalize method (known as a finalizer), and is expanded by the compiler into the following method declaration:

```
protected override void Finalize() {
  ...
  base.Finalize();
}
```

For more details on the garbage collector and finalizers, see Chapter 18.

Nested Types

A nested type is declared within the scope of another type. Nesting a type has three benefits:

- A nested type can access all the members of its enclosing type, regardless of a member's access modifier.

- A nested type can be hidden from other types with type-member access modifiers.
- Accessing a nested type from outside of its enclosing type requires specifying the type name. This is the same principle used for static members.

For example:

```
using System;
class A {
    int x = 3; // private member
    protected internal class Nested {// choose any access-level
        public void Foo () {
            A a = new A ();
            Console.WriteLine (a.x); //can access A's private members
        }
    }
}
class B {
    static void Main () {
        A.Nested n = new A.Nested (); // Nested is scoped to A
        n.Foo ();
    }
}
// an example of using "new" on a type declaration
class C : A {
    new public class Nested { } // hide inherited type member
}
```

Nested classes in C# are roughly equivalent to static inner classes in Java. There is no C# equivalent to Java's nonstatic inner classes; there is no "outer this" in C#.

Inheritance

A class can inherit from another class to extend or customize the original class. Inheriting from a class allows you to reuse the functionality in that class instead of building it from scratch. A class can inherit from only a single class, but can itself be inherited by many classes, thus forming a class hierarchy. A well-designed class hierarchy is one that reasonably generalizes the nouns in a problem space. For example, there is a class called Image in the System.Drawing namespace, which the Bitmap, Icon, and Metafile classes inherit from. All classes are ultimately part of a single giant class hierarchy, of which the root is the Object class. All classes implicitly inherit from it.

In this example, we start by defining a class called Location. This class is very basic, and provides a location with a name property and a way to display itself to the console window:

```
class Location { // Implicitly inherits from object
    string name;

    // The constructor that initializes Location
```

```
public Location(string n) {
   name = n;
}
public string Name {get {return name;}}
public void Display() {
   System.Console.WriteLine(Name);
}
}
```

Next, we define a class called URL, which will inherit from Location. The URL class has all the same members as Location, as well as a new member, Navigate. Inheriting from a class requires specifying the class to inherit from the class declaration, using the C++ colon notation:

```
class URL : Location { // Inherit from Location
   public void Navigate() {
      System.Console.WriteLine("Navigating to "+Name);
   }
   // The constructor for URL, which calls Location's constructor
   public URL(string name) : base(name) { }
}
```

Now, we instantiate a URL, then invoke both the Display method (which is defined in Location) and the navigate method (which is defined in URL):

```
class Test {
   static void Main() {
      URL u = new URL("http://microsoft.com");
      u.Display();
      u.Navigate();
   }
}
```

The specialized class/general class is referred to as the derived class/base class or the subclass/superclass.

Class Conversions

A class *D* may be implicitly upcast to the class *B* that it derives from, and a class *B* may be explicitly downcast to the class *D* that derives from it. For instance:

```
URL u = new URL();
Location l = u; // upcast
u = (URL)l; // downcast
```

If the downcast fails, an InvalidCastException is thrown.

The as operator

The as operator makes a downcast that evaluates to null if the downcast fails:

```
u = l as URL;
```

The is operator

The is operator tests whether an object is or derives from a specified class (or implements an interface). It is often used to perform a test before a downcast:

```
if (l is URL)
    ((URL)l).Navigate( );
```

Polymorphism

Polymorphism is the ability to perform the same operations on many types, as long as each type shares a common subset of characteristics. C# custom types exhibit polymorphism by inheriting classes and implementing interfaces (see "Interfaces" later in this chapter).

To continue with our inheritance example, the Show method can perform the operation Display on both a URL and a LocalFile, because both types inherit a Location's set of characteristics:

```
class LocalFile : Location {
  public void Execute( ) {
    System.Console.WriteLine("Executing "+Name);
  }
  // The constructor for LocalFile, which calls URL's constructor
  public LocalFile(string name) : base(name) { }
}
class Test {
  static void Main( ) {
    URL u = new URL("http://microsoft.com");
    LocalFile l = new LocalFile("c:\\readme.txt");
    Show(u);
    Show(l);
  }
  public static void Show(Location loc) {
    System.Console.Write("Location is: ");
    loc.Display( );
  }
}
```

Virtual Function Members

A key aspect of polymorphism is the ability for each type to exhibit a shared characteristic in its own way. A base class may have virtual function members, which enable a derived class to provide its own implementation for that function member (also see "Interfaces" later in this chapter):

```
class Location {
  public virtual void Display( ) {
    Console.WriteLine(Name);
  }
    ...
}
class URL : Location {
  // chop off the http:// at the start
```

```
  public override void Display( ) {
    Console.WriteLine(Name.Substring(6));
  }
  ...
}
```

URL now has a custom way of displaying itself. The Show method in the Test class in the previous section now calls the new implementation of Display. The signatures of the overridden method and the virtual method must be identical, but unlike Java and C++, the override keyword is also required.

Abstract Classes and Abstract Members

A class may be declared abstract. An abstract class may have abstract members. These are function members without implementation that are implicitly virtual. In our earlier examples, we had a Navigate method for the URL and an Execute method for the LocalFile. Instead, Location could be an abstract class with an abstract method called Launch:

```
abstract class Location {
  public abstract void Launch( );
}
class URL : Location {
  public override void Launch( ) {
    Console.WriteLine("Run Internet Explorer...");
  }
}
class LocalFile : Location {
  public override void Launch( ) {
    Console.WriteLine("Run Win32 Program...");
  }
}
```

A derived class must override all its inherited abstract members, or must itself be declared abstract. An abstract class cannot be instantiated. For instance, if LocalFile does not override Launch, then LocalFile itself must be declared abstract, perhaps so that Shortcut and PhysicalFile can derive from it.

Sealed Classes

A class may prevent other classes from inheriting from it by specifying the sealed modifier in the class declaration:

```
sealed class Math {
  ...
}
```

The most common scenario for sealing a class is when a class is composed of only static members, which is the case with the Math class. Another effect of sealing a class is that it enables the compiler to turn all virtual method invocations made on that class into faster nonvirtual method invocations.

Hiding Inherited Members

Aside from calling a constructor, the new keyword can also be used to hide the base class data members, function members, and type members of a class. Overriding a virtual method with the new keyword hides, rather than overrides, the base class implementation of the method:

```
class B {
  public virtual void Foo() { }
}
class D : B {
  public override void Foo() { }
}
class N : D {
  public new void Foo() { } // hides D's Foo
}
N n = new N();
n.Foo(); // calls N's Foo
((D)n).Foo(); // calls D's Foo
((B)n).Foo(); // calls D's Foo
```

A method declaration with the same signature as its base class must explicitly state whether it overrides or hides the inherited member.

Advanced Features of Virtual Function Members

This section deals with the subtleties of the virtual function member calling mechanism.

Versionioning virtual function members

In C#, a method is compiled with a flag that is true if it overrides a virtual method. This flag is important for versioning. Suppose you write a class that derives from a base class in the .NET Framework, and deploy your application to a client computer. Later, the client upgrades the .NET Framework, and that base class now has a virtual method that matches the signature of one of your methods in the derived class:

```
class B { // written by the library people
  virtual void Foo() {...} // added in latest update
}
class D : B { // written by you
  void Foo() {...}
}
```

In most object-oriented languages such as Java, methods are not compiled with this flag, so a derived class's method with the same signature is assumed to override the base class's virtual method. This means a virtual call is made to D's Foo, even though D's Foo was unlikely to have been made according to the specification intended by the author of B. This could easily break your application. In C#, the flag for D's Foo is false, so the runtime knows to treat D's Foo as new, which ensures that your application functions as it was originally intended. When you get the chance to recompile with the latest framework, you can add the new modifier to Foo, or perhaps rename Foo to something else.

Creating Types

Sealed virtual function members

An overridden function member may seal its implementation, so that it cannot be overridden. In our earlier virtual function member example, we could have sealed the URL's implementation of Display. This prevents a class that derives from URL from overriding Display, which provides a guarantee on the behavior of a URL.

```
class Location {
  public virtual void Display() {
    Console.WriteLine(Name);
    }
    ...
}
class URL : Location {
  public sealed override void Display() {
    Console.WriteLine(Name.Substring(6));
  }
  ...
}
```

Overriding a virtual function member

Very occasionally, it is useful to override a virtual function member with an abstract one. In this example, the abstract Editor class overrides the Text property to ensure that concrete classes deriving from Editor provide an implementation for Text.

```
class Control {
  public virtual string Text {
    get {
      return null;
    }
  }
}
abstract class Editor : Control {
  abstract override string Text {get;}
}
```

The base Keyword

The base keyword is similar to the this keyword, except that it accesses an overridden or hidden base class function member. The base keyword is also used to call a base class constructor (see the next section) or access a base class indexer (by using base instead of this). Calling base accesses the next most derived class that defines that member. The following builds upon our example from the section on the this keyword:

```
class Hermit : Dude {
  public void new Introduce(Dude a) {
    base.Introduce(a);
    Console.WriteLine("Nice Talking To You");
  }
}
```

There is no way to access an instance member of a specific base class, as with the C++ scope resolution :: operator.

Constructor and Field Initialization in the Inheritance Chain

Initialization code can execute for each class in an inheritance chain, in constructors as well as field initializers. There are two rules. The first is field initialization occurs before *any* constructor in the inheritance chain is called. The second is the base class executes its initialization code before the derived class does.

A constructor must call its base class constructors first. In a case in which the base class has a parameterless constructor, the constructor is implicitly called. In a case in which the base class provides only constructors that require parameters, the derived class constructor must explicitly call one of the base class constructors with the base keyword. A constructor may also call an overloaded constructor (which calls base for it):

```
class B {
  public int x ;
  public B(int a) {
    x = a;
  }
  public B(int a, int b) {
    x = a * b;
  }
  // Notice how all of B's constructors need parameters
}
class D : B {
  public D( ) : this(7) { } // call an overloaded constructor
  public D(int a) : base(a) { } // call a base class constructor
}
```

Consistent with instance constructors, static constructors respect the inheritance chain, so each static constructor from the least derived to the most derived is called.

Access Modifiers

To promote encapsulation, a type or type member may hide itself from other types or other assemblies by adding one of the following five access modifiers to the declaration:

public
> The type or type member is fully accessible. This is the implicit accessibility for enum members (see "Enums" later in this chapter) and interface members (see "Interfaces" later in this chapter).

internal
> The type or type member in assembly *A* is accessible only from within *A*. This is the default accessibility for nonnested types, and so may be omitted.

private

    The type member in type *T* is accessible only from within *T*. This is the default accessibility for class and struct members, and so may be omitted.

protected

    The type member in class *C* is accessible only from within *C*, or from within a class that derives from *C*.

protected internal

    The type member in class *C* and assembly *A* is accessible only from within *C*, from within a class that derives from *C*, or from within *A*. Note that C# has no concept of protected and internal, whereby "a type member in class *C* and assembly *A* is accessible only from within *C*, or from within a class that both derives from *C* and is within *A*."

Note that a type member may be a nested type. Here is an example of using access modifiers:

```
// Assembly1.dll
using System;
public class A {
  private int x=5;
  public void Foo() {Console.WriteLine (x);}
  protected static void Goo() { }
  protected internal class NestedType { }
}
internal class B {
  private void Hoo () {
    A a1 = new A (); // ok
    Console.WriteLine(a1.x); // error, A.x is private
    A.NestedType n; // ok, A.NestedType is internal
    A.Goo(); // error, A's Goo is protected
  }
}

// Assembly2.exe (references Assembly1.dll)
using System;
class C : A { // C defaults to internal
  static void Main() { // Main defaults to private
    A a1 = new A(); // ok
    a1.Foo(); // ok
    C.Goo(); // ok, inherits A's protected static member
    new A.NestedType(); // ok, A.NestedType is protected
    new B(); // error, Assembly 1's B is internal
    Console.WriteLine(x); // error, A's x is private
  }
}
```

Restrictions on Access Modifiers

A type or type member cannot declare itself to be more accessible than any of the types it uses in the declaration. For instance, a class cannot be public if it derives from an internal class, or a method cannot be protected if the type of one of its parameters is internal to the assembly. The rationale behind this restriction is whatever is accessible to another type is actually usable by that type.

In addition, access modifiers cannot be used when they conflict with the purpose of inheritance modifiers. For example, a virtual (or abstract) member cannot be declared private, since it would be impossible to override. Similarly, a sealed class cannot define new protected members, since there is no class that could benefit from this accessibility.

Finally, to maintain the contract of a base class, a function member with the override modifier must have the same accessibility as the virtual member it overrides.

Structs

```
attributes? unsafe? access-modifier?
new?
struct struct-name [: interface+]?
{ struct-members }
```

A struct is similar to a class, with the following major differences:

- A class is a reference type, while a struct is a value type. Consequently, structs are typically used to express simple types, in which value-type semantics are desirable (e.g., assignment copies a value rather than a reference).

- A class fully supports inheritance (see Chapter 5), whereas a struct can inherit only from an object and is implicitly sealed (in the runtime structs actually inherit from System.ValueType). Both classes and structs can implement interfaces.

- A class can have a destructor, and a struct cannot.

- A class can define a custom parameterless constructor and initialize instance fields, while a struct cannot. The default parameterless constructor for a struct initializes each field with a default value (effectively zero). If a struct declares a constructor(s), then all of its fields must be assigned in that constructor call.

Interfaces

```
attributes? unsafe? access-modifier?
new?
interface interface-name
[ : base-interface+ ]?
{ interface-members }
```

An interface is similar to a class, but with the following major differences:

- An interface provides a specification rather than an implementation for its members. This is similar to a pure abstract class, which is an abstract class consisting of only abstract members.

- A class and struct can implement multiple interfaces, while a class can inherit only from a single class.

- A struct can implement an interface, but a struct cannot inherit from a class.

Earlier in this chapter, we defined polymorphism as the ability to perform the same operations on many types, as long as each type shares a common subset of characteristics. The purpose of an interface is precisely for defining such a set of characteristics.

An interface is comprised of a set of the following members:

- Method
- Property
- Indexer
- Event

These members are always implicitly public and implicitly abstract (and therefore virtual and nonstatic).

Defining an Interface

An interface declaration is like a class declaration, but it provides no implementation for its members, since all its members are implicitly abstract. These members are intended to be implemented by a class or struct that implements the interface. Here is a very simple interface that defines a single method:

```
public interface IDelete {
    void Delete();
}
```

Implementing an Interface

Classes or structs that implement an interface may be said to "fulfill the contract of the interface." In this example, our IDelete interface can be implemented by GUI controls that support the concept of deleting, such as a TextBox, TreeView, or your own custom GUI control.

```
public class TextBox : IDelete {
    public void Delete() {...}
}
public class TreeView : IDelete {
    public void Delete() {...}
}
```

If a class inherits from a base class, then each interface implemented must appear after the base class:

```
public class TextBox : Control, IDelete {...}
public class TreeView : Control, IDelete {...}
```

Using an Interface

An interface is useful when you need multiple classes to share characteristics not present in a common base class. In addition, an interface is a good way to ensure that these classes provide their own implementation for the interface member, since interface members are implicitly abstract.

The following example assumes a form containing many GUI controls (including some TextBox and TreeView controls) in which the currently focused control is accessed with the ActiveControl property. When a user clicks Delete on a menu item or toolbar button, the example tests to see whether ActiveControl implements IDelete, and if so, casts it to IDelete to call its Delete method:

```
class MyForm {
  ...
  void DeleteClick( ) {
    if (ActiveControl is IDelete)
      PerformDelete ((IDelete)ActiveControl);
  }
}
```

Extending an Interface

Interfaces may extend other interfaces. For instance:

```
ISuperDelete : IDelete {
  bool CanDelete {get;}
  event EventHandler CanDeleteChanged;
}
```

A control implements the CanDelete property to indicate that it has something to delete and is not read-only, and implements the CanDeleteChanged event to fire an event whenever its CanDelete property changes. This framework allows our application to ghost its Delete menu item and toolbar button when the ActiveControl is unable to delete.

Explicit Interface Implementation

If there is a name collision between an interface member and an existing member in the class or struct, C# allows you to explicitly implement an interface member to resolve the conflict. In this example, we resolve a conflict when implementing two interfaces that both define a Delete method:

```
public interface IDesignTimeControl {
  ...
  object Delete( );
}
public class TextBox : IDelete, IDesignTimeControl {
  ...
  void IDelete.Delete( ) { }
  object IDesignTimeControl.Delete( ) {...}
  // Note that explicitly implementing just one of them would
  // be enough to resolve the conflict
}
```

Unlike implicit interface implementations, explicit interface implementations can't be declared with abstract, virtual, override, or new modifiers. In addition, while an implicit implementation requires the use of the public modifier, an explicit implementation has no access modifier. However, to access the method, the class or struct must be cast to the appropriate interface first:

```
TextBox tb = new TextBox( );
IDesignTimeControl idtc = (IDesignTimeControl)tb;
IDelete id = (IDelete)tb;
idtc.Delete( );
id.Delete( );
```

Reimplementing an Interface

If a base class implements an interface member with the virtual (or abstract) modifier, then a derived class can override it. If not, the derived class must reimplement the interface to override that member:

```
public class RichTextBox : TextBox, IDelete {
    // TextBox's IDelete.Delete is not virtual (since explicit
    // interface implementations cannot be virtual)
    public void Delete( ) { }
}
```

This lets us use a RichTextBox as an IDelete, and calls RichTextBox's version of Delete.

Interface Conversions

A class or struct T may be implicitly cast to an interface I that T implements. Similarly, an interface X may be implicitly cast to an interface Y that X inherits from. An interface may be explicitly cast to any other interface or nonsealed class. However, an explicit cast from an interface I to a sealed class or struct T is permitted only if it is possible that T could implement I. For example:

```
interface IDelete {...}
interface IDesignTimeControl {...}
class TextBox : IDelete, IDesignTimeControl {...}
sealed class Timer : IDesignTimeControl {...}

TextBox tb1 = new TextBox ( );
IDelete d = tb1; // implicit cast
IDesignTimeControl dtc = (IDesignTimeControl)d;
TextBox tb2 = (TextBox)dtc;
Timer t = (Timer)d; // illegal, a Timer can never implement IDelete
```

Standard boxing conversions happen when converting between structs and interfaces.

Enums

```
attributes? access-modifier?
new?
enum enum-name [ : integer-type ]?
{ [attributes? enum-member-name
[ = value ]? ]* }
```

Enums specify a group of named numeric constants:

```
public enum Direction {North, East, West, South}
```

Unlike in C, enum members must be used with the enum type name. This resolves naming conflicts and makes code clearer:

```
Direction walls = Direction.East;
```

By default, enums are assigned integer constants 0, 1, 2, etc. You may optionally specify an alternative numeric type to base your enum on, and explicitly specify values for each enum member:

```
[Flags]
public enum Direction : byte {
   North=1, East=2, West=4, South=8
}
Direction walls = Direction.North | Direction.West;
if((walls & Direction.North) != 0)
    System.Console.WriteLine("Can't go north!");
```

The [Flags] attribute is optional, and informs the runtime that the values in the enum can be bit-combined, and should be decoded accordingly in the debugger or when outputting text to the console. For example:

```
Console.WriteLine(walls.Format()); // Displays "North|West"
Console.WriteLine(walls); // Calls walls.ToString, displays "5"
```

The System.Enum type also provides many useful static methods for enums that allow one to determine the underlying type of an enum, to check if a specific value is supported, to initialize an enum from a string constant, to retrieve a list of the valid values, and other common operations such as conversions. Here is an example of the usage:

```
using System;
public enum Toggle : byte { Off=0, On=1 }
class Test {
   static void Main() {
     Type t = Enum.GetUnderlyingType(typeof(Toggle));
     Console.WriteLine(t); // Prints "Byte"

     bool bDimmed = Enum.IsDefined(typeof(Toggle), "Dimmed");
     Console.WriteLine(bDimmed); // Prints "False"

     Toggle tog =(Toggle)Enum.Parse(typeof(Toggle), "On");
     Console.WriteLine(Enum.Format(typeof(Toggle), tog, "D")); // Prints "1"
     Console.WriteLine(tog); // Prints "On"

     object[ ] oa = Enum.GetValues(typeof(Toggle));
     foreach(Toggle toggle in oa) // Prints "On=1, Off=0"
       Console.WriteLine("{0}={1}", toggle,Enum.Format(typeof(Toggle),
                                  toggle, "D"));
   }
}
```

Enum Operators

The operators relevant to enums are:

```
== != < > <= >= + - ^ & | ~
=  += -= ++ -- sizeof
```

Enum Conversions

Enums may be explicitly converted to other enums. Enums and numeric types may be explicitly converted to one another. A special case is the numeric literal 0, which may be implicitly converted to an enum.

4

Advanced C# Features

In this chapter, we cover advanced C# topics, including events, operator overloading, try statements and exceptions, attributes, unsafe code and pointers, preprocessor directives, and XML documentation.

Delegates

attributes? unsafe? *access-modifier*?
new?
delegate
[void | *type*]
delegate-name (*parameter-list*);

A *delegate* is a type defining a method signature, so that delegate instances can hold and invoke a method or list of methods that match its signature. A delegate declaration consists of a name and a method signature. For example:

```
using System;
delegate bool Filter (string s);

class Test {
  static void Main( ) {
    Filter f = new Filter(FirstHalfOfAlphabet);
    Display(new String [ ] {"Ant","Lion","Yak"}, f);
  }
  static bool FirstHalfOfAlphabet(string s) {
    return "N".CompareTo(s) > 0;
  }
  static void Display(string[ ] names, Filter f) {
    int count = 0;
    foreach(string s in names)
      if(f(s)) // invoke delegate
        Console.WriteLine("Item {0} is {1}", count++, s);
  }
```

}

Note that the signature of a delegate method includes its return type. It also allows the use of a params modifier in its parameter list, which expands the list of elements that characterize an ordinary method signature. The actual name of the target method is irrelevant to the delegate.

Multicast Delegates

Delegates can hold and invoke multiple methods. In this example, we declare a very simple delegate called MethodInvoker, which we use to hold and then invoke the Foo and Goo methods sequentially. The += method creates a new delegate by adding the right delegate operand to the left delegate operand:

```
using System;
delegate void MethodInvoker();
class Test {
    static void Main() {
        new Test(); // prints "Foo","Goo"
    }
    Test () {
        MethodInvoker m = null;
        m += new MethodInvoker(Foo);
        m += new MethodInvoker(Goo);
        m();
    }
    void Foo() {
        Console.WriteLine("Foo");
    }
    void Goo() {
        Console.WriteLine("Goo");
    }
}
```

A delegate can also be removed from another delegate using the -= operator:

```
Test {
    MethodInvoker m = null;
    m += new MethodInvoker(Foo);
    m -= new MethodInvoker(Foo);
    // m is now null
}
```

Delegates are invoked in the order they are added. If a delegate has a nonvoid return type, then the value of the last delegate invoked is returned. Note that the += and -= operations on a delegate are not thread-safe. (For more information on thread safety, see Chapter 16.)

> To work with the .NET runtime, C# compiles += and -= operations made on a delegate to the static Combine and Remove methods of the System.Delegate class.

Delegates Versus Function Pointers

A delegate is behaviorally similar to a C function pointer (or Delphi closure), but delegates can hold multiple methods, as well as hold the instance associated with each nonstatic method. In addition, delegates, like all other C# constructs used outside unsafe blocks, are type-safe and secure. This means that you're protected from pointing to the wrong type of method or to a method you don't have permission to access.

Delegates Versus Interfaces

A problem that can be solved with a delegate can also be solved with an interface. For instance, the following explains how to solve our filter problem using an IFilter interface:

```
using System;
interface IFilter {
    bool Filter(string s);
}
class Test {
  class FirstHalfOfAlphabetFilter : IFilter {
    public bool Filter(string s) {
      return ("N".CompareTo(s) > 0);
    }
  }
  static void Main() {
    FirstHalfOfAlphabetFilter f = new FirstHalfOfAlphabetFilter();
    Display(new string [] {"Ant", "Lion", "Yak"}, f);
  }
  static void Display(string[] names, IFilter f) {
    int count = 0;
    foreach (string s in names)
      if (f.Filter(s))
        Console.WriteLine("Item {0} is {1}", count++, s);
  }
}
```

In this case, the problem is slightly more elegantly handled with a delegate, but generally delegates are best used for event handling.

Events

Event handling is essentially a process in which one object can notify other objects that an event has occurred. This process is largely encapsulated by multicast delegates, which have this ability built in.

Defining a Delegate for an Event

The .NET Framework provides many event-handling delegates, but you can write your own. For example:

```
delegate void MoveEventHandler(object source, MoveEventArgs e);
```

By convention, the delegate's first parameter denotes the source of the event, and the delegate's second parameter derives from System.EventArgs and contains data about the event.

Storing Data for an Event with EventArgs

The EventArgs class may be derived from to include information relevant to a particular event:

```
public class MoveEventArgs : EventArgs {
  public int newPosition;
  public bool cancel;
  public MoveEventArgs(int newPosition) {
    this.newPosition = newPosition;
  }
}
```

Declaring and Firing an Event

A class or struct can declare an event by applying the event modifier to a delegate field. In this example, the slider class has a Position property that fires a Move event whenever its Position changes:

```
class Slider {
  int position;
  public event MoveEventHandler Move;
  public int Position {
    get { return position; }
    set {
      if (position != value) { // if position changed
        if (Move != null) { // if invocation list not empty
          MoveEventArgs args = new MoveEventArgs(value);
          Move(this, args); // fire event
          if (args.cancel)
            return;
        }
        position = value;
      }
    }
  }
}
```

The event keyword promotes encapsulation by ensuring that only the += and -= operations can be performed on the delegate. Other classes may act on the event, but only the Slider can invoke the delegate (fire the event) or clear the delegate's invocation list.

Acting on an Event with an Event Handler

We are able to act on an event by adding an event handler to it. An event handler is a delegate that wraps the method we want invoked when the event is fired.

In this example, we want our Form to act on changes made to a Slider's Position. This is done by creating a MoveEventHandler delegate that wraps our event-handling method (the slider_Move method). This delegate is added to the Move event's existing list of MoveEventHandlers (which is initially empty). Changing the position on the slider fires the Move event, which invokes our slider_Move method:

```
using System;
class Form {
  static void Main( ) {
    Slider slider = new Slider( );
    // register with the Move event
    slider.Move += new MoveEventHandler(slider_Move);
    slider.Position = 20;
    slider.Position = 60;
  }
  static void slider_Move(object source, MoveEventArgs e) {
    if(e.newPosition < 50)
      Console.WriteLine("OK");
    else {
      e.cancel = true;
      Console.WriteLine("Can't go that high!");
    }
  }
}
```

Typically, the Slider class is extended so that it fires the Move event whenever its Position is changed by a mouse movement, keypress, etc.

Event Accessors

```
attributes? unsafe? access-modifier?
[
  [[sealed | abstract]? override] |
  new? [virtual | static]?
]?
event delegate type event-property accessor-name
{
  attributes? add statement-block
  attributes? remove statement-block
}
```

 Abstract accessors don't specify an implementation, so they replace an add/remove block with a semicolon.

Similar to the way properties provide controlled access to fields, event accessors provide controlled access to an event. Consider the following field declaration:

```
public event MoveEventHandler Move;
```

Except for the underscore prefix added to the field (to avoid a name collision), this is semantically identical to:

```
private MoveEventHandler _Move;
public event MoveEventHandler Move {
  add {
```

```
   _Move += value;
  }
  remove {
   _Move -= value;
  }
}
```

The ability to specify a custom implementation of add and remove handlers for an event allows a class to proxy an event generated by another class, thus acting as a relay for an event rather than the generator of that event. Another advantage of this technique is to eliminate the need to store a delegate as a field, which can be costly in terms of storage space. For instance, a class with 100 event fields would store 100 delegate fields, even though maybe only 4 of those events are actually assigned. Instead, you can store these delegates in a dictionary, and add and remove the delegates from that dictionary (assuming the dictionary holding 4 elements uses less storage space than 100 delegate references).

 The add and remove parts of an event are compiled to add_XXX and remove_XXX methods.

Operator Overloading

C# lets you overload operators to work with operands that are custom classes or structs using operators. An operator is a static method with the keyword operator preceding the operator to overload (instead of a method name), parameters representing the operands, and return types representing the result of an expression. Table 4-1 lists the available overloadable operators.

Table 4-1. Overloadable operators

+	-	!	~	++
--	+	-	* (binary only)	/
%	& (binary only)	|	^	<<
>>	==	!=	>	<
>=	<=			

Literals that also act as overloadable operators are true and false.

Implementing Value Equality

A pair of references exhibit referential equality when both references point to the same object. By default, the == and != operators will compare two reference-type variables by reference. However, it is occasionally more natural for the == and != operators to exhibit value equality, whereby the comparison is based on the value of the objects that the references point to.

Whenever overloading the == and != operators, you should always override the virtual Equals method to route its functionality to the == operator. This allows a class to be used polymorphically (which is essential if you want to take advantage of functionality such as the collection classes). It also provides compatibility with other .NET languages that don't overload operators.

A good guideline for knowing whether to implement the == and != operators is if it is natural for the class to overload other operators too, such as <, >, +, or -; otherwise, don't bother—just implement the Equals method. For structs, overloading the == and != operators provides a more efficient implementation than the default one.

```
class Note {
  int value;
  public Note(int semitonesFromA) {
    value = semitonesFromA;
  }
  public static bool operator ==(Note x, Note y) {
    return x.value == y.value;
  }
  public static bool operator !=(Note x, Note y) {
    return x.value != y.value;
  }
  public override bool Equals(object o) {
    if(!(o is Note))
      return false;
    return this ==(Note)o;
  }
}
Note a = new Note(4);
Note b = new Note(4);
Object c = a;
Object d = b;

// To compare a and b by reference
Console.WriteLine((object)a ==(object)b; // false

//To compare a and b by value:
Console.WriteLine(a == b); // true

//To compare c and d by reference:
Console.WriteLine(c == d); // false

//To compare c and d by value:
Console.WriteLine(c.Equals(d)); // true
```

Logically Paired Operators

The C# compiler enforces operators that are logical pairs to both be defined. These operators are == !=, < >, and <= >=.

Custom Implicit and Explicit Conversions

As explained in the discussion on types, the rationale behind implicit conversions is they are guaranteed to succeed and do not lose information during the conversion. Conversely, an explicit conversion is required either when runtime circumstances will determine whether the conversion will succeed or if information may be lost during the conversion. In this example, we define conversions between our musical Note type and a double (which represents the frequency in hertz of that note):

```
...
// Convert to hertz
public static implicit operator double(Note x) {
  return 440*Math.Pow(2,(double)x.value/12);
}

// Convert from hertz(only accurate to nearest semitone)
public static explicit operator Note(double x) {
  return new Note((int)(0.5+12*(Math.Log(x/440)/Math.Log(2))));
}
...

Note n =(Note)554.37; // explicit conversion
double x = n; // implicit conversion
```

Three-State Logic Operators

The true and false keywords are used as operators when defining types with three-state logic to enable these types to work seamlessly with constructs that take boolean expressions—namely, the if, do, while, for, and conditional (?:) statements. The System.Data.SQLTypes.SQLBoolean struct provides this functionality:

```
public struct SQLBoolean ... {
  ...
  public static bool operator true(SQLBoolean x) {
    return x.value == 1;
  }
  public static bool operator false(SQLBoolean x) {
    return x.value == -1;
  }
  public static SQLBoolean operator !(SQLBoolean x) {
    return new SQLBoolean(- x.value);
  }
  public bool IsNull {
    get { return value == 0;}
  }
  ...
}
class Test {
  void Foo(SQLBoolean a) {
    if (a)
      Console.WriteLine("True");
    else if (! a)
      Console.WriteLine("False");
    else
```

```
        Console.WriteLine("Null");
    }
}
```

Indirectly Overloadable Operators

The && and || operators are automatically evaluated from & and |, so they do not
need to be overloaded. The [ ] operators can be customized with indexers (see
"Indexers in Chapter 3). The assignment operator = cannot be overloaded, but all
other assignment operators are automatically evaluated from their corresponding
binary operators (e.g., += is evaluated from +).

Try Statements and Exceptions

```
try statement-block
[catch (exception type value?)?
 statement-block]+ |
finally statement-block |
[catch (exception type value?)?
 statement-block]+
finally statement-block
```

The purpose of a try statement is to simplify program execution in exceptional
circumstances—typically, an error. A try statement does two things. First, it lets
the catch block catch exceptions thrown during the try block's execution.
Second, it ensures that execution cannot leave the try block without first
executing the finally block. A try block must be followed by a catch block(s), a
finally block, or both. The form of a try block looks like this:

```
try {
    ... // exception may be thrown during execution of this function
}
catch (ExceptionA ex) {
    ... // react to exception of type ExceptionA
}
catch (ExceptionB ex) {
    ... // react to exception of type ExceptionB
}
finally {
    ... // code to always run after try block executes, even if
    ... // an exception is not thrown
}
```

Exceptions

C# exceptions are objects that contain information representing the occurrence of
an exceptional program state. When an exceptional state has occurred (e.g., a
method receives an illegal value), an exception object may be thrown, and the
call-stack is unwound until the exception is caught by an exception-handling
block. For example:

```
using System;
```

```
namespace TryStatementsAndExceptions {
  public class WeightCalculator {
    public static float CalcBMI (float weightKilos, float metersTall) {
      if (metersTall < 0 || metersTall > 3)
        throw new ArgumentException ("Impossible Height", "metersTall");
      if (weightKilos < 0 || weightKilos > 1000)
        throw new ArgumentException ("Impossible Weight", "weightKilos");
      return weightKilos / (metersTall*metersTall);
    }
  }
  class Test {
    static void Main () {
      TestIt ();
    }
    static void TestIt () {
      try {
        float bmi = WeightCalculator.CalcBMI (100, 5);
        Console.WriteLine(bmi);
      }
      catch(ArgumentException ex) {
        Console.WriteLine(ex);
      }
      finally {
        Console.WriteLine ("Thanks for running the program");
      }
      Console.Read( );
    }
  }
}
```

In this example, calling CalcBMI throws an ArgumentException indicating that it's impossible for someone to be five meters tall. Execution leaves CalcBMI and returns to the calling method, TestIt, which handles the ArgumentException, and displays the exception to the Console. Next, the finally method is executed, which prints "Thanks for running the program" to the Console. Without our try statement, the call stack would have been unwound right back to the Main method, and the program would terminate.

The catch Clause

A catch clause specifies the exception type (including derived types) to catch. An exception must be of type System.Exception, or a type that derives from System. Exception. Catching System.Exception provides the widest possible net for catching errors, which is useful if your handling of the error is totally generic, such as an error-logging mechanism. Otherwise, you should catch a more specific exception type, to prevent your catch block from having to deal with a circumstance it wasn't designed to handle (e.g., an out-of-memory exception).

Omitting the exception variable

Specifying only an exception type without a variable name allows an exception to be caught when we don't need to use the exception instance and merely knowing its type is enough. The previous example could be written like this:

```
catch(ArgumentException) { // don't specify variable
  Console.WriteLine("Couldn't calculate ideal weight!");
}
```

Omitting the catch expression

You may also entirely omit the catch expression. This catches an exception of any type, even types thrown by other non-CLS-compliant languages that are not derived from System.Exception. The previous example could be written like this:

```
catch {
  Console.WriteLine("Couldn't calculate ideal weight!");
}
```

Specifying multiple catch clauses

When declaring multiple catch clauses, only the first catch clause with an exception type that matches the thrown exception executes its catch block. It is illegal for an exception type *B* to precede an exception type *D* if *B* is a base class of *D*, since it would be unreachable.

```
try {...}
catch (NullReferenceException) {...}
catch (ArgumentException) {...}
catch {...}
```

The finally Block

A finally block is always executed when control leaves the try block. A finally block is executed at any of the following periods:

- Immediately after the try block completes
- Immediately after the try block prematurely exits with a jump statement (e.g., return, goto), and immediately before the target of the jump statement
- Immediately after a catch block executes

finally blocks can add determinism to a program's execution by ensuring that the specified code always gets executed.

In our main example, if the height passed to the calculator is invalid, an ArgumentException is thrown that executes the catch block, followed by the finally block. However, if anything else goes wrong, the finally block is still executed. This ensures that we say goodbye to our user before exiting the program.

Key Properties of System.Exception

Notable properties of `System.Exception` include:

`StackTrace`
    A string representing all the methods that are called from the origin of the exception to the `catch` block.

`Message`
    A string with a description of the error.

`InnerException`
    This cascading exception structure can be particularly useful when debugging. Sometimes it is useful to catch an exception, then throw a new, more specific exception. For instance, we may catch an `IOException`, and then throw a `ProblemFooingException` that contains more specific information on what went wrong. In this scenario, the `ProblemFooingException` should include the `IOException` as the `InnerException` argument in its constructor, which is assigned to the `InnerException` property.

Note that in C# all exceptions are runtime exceptions—there is no equivalent to Java's compile-time checked exceptions.

Attributes

```
[[target:]? attribute-name (
positional-param+ |
[named-param = expr]+ |
positional-param+, [named-param = expr]+)?]
```

Attributes are language constructs that can decorate a code element (assemblies, modules, types, members, return values, and parameters) with additional information.

In every language, you specify information associated with the types, methods, parameters, and other elements of your program. For example, a type can specify a list of interfaces it derives from, or a parameter can specify modifiers, such as the `ref` modifier in C#. The limitation of this approach is you can associate information with code elements using only the predefined constructs that the language provides.

Attributes allow programmers to extend the types of information associated with these code elements. For example, serialization in the .NET Framework uses various serialization attributes applied to types and fields to define how these code elements are serialized. This approach is more flexible than requiring the language to have special syntax for serialization.

Attribute Classes

An attribute is defined by a class that inherits (directly or indirectly) from the abstract class `System.Attribute`. When specifying an attribute to an element, the attribute name is the name of the type. By convention, the derived type name ends in Attribute, although specifying the suffix is not required when specifying the attribute.

In this example, the Foo class is specified as serializable using the Serializable attribute:

```
[Serializable]
public class Foo {...}
```

The Serializable attribute is actually a type declared in the System namespace, as follows:

```
class SerializableAttribute : Attribute {...}
```

We could also specify the Serializable attribute using its fully qualified type name, as follows:

```
[System.SerializableAttribute]
public class Foo {...}
```

The preceding two examples of using the Serializable attribute are semantically identical.

The C# language and the FCL include a number of predefined attributes. For more information about the other attributes included in the FCL and creating your own attributes, see Chapter 14.

Named and Positional Parameters

Attributes can take parameters, which can specify additional information on the code element beyond the mere presence of the attribute.

In this example, the class Foo is specified as obsolete using the Obsolete attribute. This attribute allows parameters to be included to specify both a message and whether the compiler should treat the use of this class as an error:

```
[Obsolete("Use Bar class instead", IsError=true)]
public class Foo {...}
```

Attribute parameters fall into one of two categories: positional and named. In the preceding example, Use Bar class instead is a positional parameter and IsError=true is a named parameter.

The positional parameters for an attribute correspond to the parameters passed to the attribute type's public constructors. The named parameters for an attribute correspond to the set of public read-write or write-only instance properties and fields of the attribute type.

When specifying an attribute of an element, positional parameters are mandatory and named parameters are optional. Since the parameters used to specify an attribute are evaluated at compile time, they are generally limited to constant expressions.

Attribute Targets

Implicitly, the target of an attribute is the code element it immediately precedes, such as with the attributes we have covered so far. Sometimes it is necessary to explicitly specify that the attribute applies to particular target.

Here is an example of using the `CLSCompliant` attribute to specify the level of CLS compliance for an entire assembly:

```
[assembly:CLSCompliant(true)]
```

Specifying Multiple Attributes

Multiple attributes can be specified for a single code element. Each attribute can be listed within the same pair of square brackets (separated by a comma), in separate pairs of square brackets, or in any combination of the two.

Consequently, the following three examples are semantically identical:

```
[Serializable, Obsolete, CLSCompliant(false)]
public class Bar {...}
```

```
[Serializable]
[Obsolete]
[CLSCompliant(false)]
public class Bar {...}
```

```
[Serializable, Obsolete]
[CLSCompliant(false)]
public class Bar {...}
```

Unsafe Code and Pointers

C# supports direct memory manipulation via pointers within blocks of code marked unsafe and compiled with the /unsafe compiler option. Pointer types are primarily useful for interoperability with C APIs, but may also be used for accessing memory outside the managed heap or for performance-critical hotspots.

Pointer Basics

For every value type or pointer type *V*, there is a corresponding pointer type *V**. A pointer instance holds the address of a value. This is considered to be of type *V*, but pointer types can be (unsafely) cast to any other pointer type. Table 4-2 lists the main pointer operators.

Table 4-2. Principal pointer operators

Operator	Meaning
&	The address-of operator returns a pointer to the address of a value.
*	The dereference operator returns the value at the address of a pointer.
->	The pointer-to-member operator is a syntactic shortcut, in which x->y is equivalent to (*x).y.

Unsafe Code

By marking a type, type member, or statement block with the unsafe keyword, you're permitted to use pointer types and perform C++ style pointer operations on memory within that scope. Here is an example of using pointers with a managed object:

```
unsafe void RedFilter(int[,] bitmap) {
  const int length = bitmap.Length;
  fixed (int* b = bitmap) {
    int* p = b;
    for(int i = 0; i < length; i++)
      *p++ &= 0xFF;
  }
}
```

Unsafe code typically runs faster than a corresponding safe implementation, which in this case would have required a nested loop with array indexing and bounds checking. An unsafe C# method may also be faster than calling an external C function, since there is no overhead associated with leaving the managed execution environment.

The fixed Statement

```
fixed ([value-type | void ]* name = [&]? expr )
  statement-block
```

The fixed statement is required to pin a managed object, such as the bitmap in the previous example. During the execution of a program, many objects are allocated and deallocated from the heap. In order to avoid unnecessary waste or fragmentation of memory, the garbage collector moves objects around. Pointing to an object is futile if its address could change while referencing it, so the fixed statement tells the garbage collector to "pin" the object and not move it around. This may have an impact on the efficiency of the runtime, so fixed blocks should be used only briefly, and heap allocation should be avoided within the fixed block.

C# returns a pointer only from a value type, never directly from a reference type. Syntactically, arrays and strings are an exception to this, since they actually return a pointer to their first element (which must be a value type), rather than the objects themselves.

Value types declared inline within reference types require the reference type to be pinned, as follows:

```
class Test {
  int x;
  static void Main( ) {
    Test test = new Test ( );
    unsafe {
      fixed(int* p = &test.x) { // pins test
        *p = 9;
      }
      System.Console.WriteLine(test.x);
    }
  }
}
```

The Pointer-to-Member Operator

In addition to the & and * operators, C# also provides the C++-style -> operator, which can be used on structs:

```
struct Test {
    int x;
    unsafe static void Main() {
        Test test = new Test();
        Test* p = &test;
        p->x = 9;
        System.Console.WriteLine(test.x);
    }
}
```

The stackalloc Keyword

Memory can be allocated in a block on the stack explicitly using the stackalloc keyword. Since it is allocated on the stack, its lifetime is limited to the execution of the method, just as with any other local variable. The block may use [ ] indexing, but is purely a value type with no additional self-describing information or bounds-checking that an array provides.

```
int* a = stackalloc int [10];
for (int i = 0; i < 10; ++i)
    Console.WriteLine(a[i]); // print raw memory
```

Void*

Rather than pointing to a specific value type, a pointer may make no assumptions about the type of the underlying data. This approach is useful for functions that deal with raw memory. An implicit conversion exists from any pointer type to a void*. A void* cannot be dereferenced and arithmetic operations cannot be performed on void pointers. For example:

```
class Test {
    unsafe static void Main () {
        short[ ] a = {1,1,2,3,5,8,13,21,34,55};
        fixed (short* p = a) {
            // sizeof returns size of value-type in bytes
            Zap (p, a.Length * sizeof (short));
        }
        foreach (short x in a)
            System.Console.WriteLine (x); // prints all zeros
    }
    unsafe static void Zap (void* memory, int byteCount) {
        byte* b = (byte*)memory;
        for (int i = 0; i < byteCount; i++)
            *b++ = 0;
    }
}
```

Pointers to Unmanaged Code

Pointers are also useful for accessing data outside the managed heap (such as when interacting with C DLLs or COM), or when dealing with data not in the main memory (such as graphics memory or a storage medium on an embedded device).

Preprocessor Directives

Preprocessor directives supply the compiler with additional information about regions of code. The most common preprocessor directives are the conditional directives, which provide a way to include or exclude regions of code from compilation. For example:

```
#define DEBUG
class MyClass {
   int x;
   void Foo() {
   # if DEBUG
      Console.WriteLine("Testing: x = {0}", x);
   # endif
   ...
}
```

In this class, the statement in Foo is compiled as conditionally dependent upon the presence of the DEBUG symbol. If we remove the DEBUG symbol, the statement is not compiled. Preprocessor symbols can be defined within a source file (as we have done), and they can be passed to the compiler with the /define: symbol command-line option. All preprocessor symbols are implicitly true, so the #define statement in the previous example is effectively same as the following:

```
#define DEBUG = true
```

The #error and #warning symbols prevent accidental misuse of conditional directives by making the compiler generate a warning or error given an undesirable set of compilation symbols. See Table 4-3 for a list of preprocessor directives and their actions.

Table 4-3. Preprocessor directives

Preprocessor directive	Action
#define *symbol*	Defines *symbol*.
#undef *symbol*	Undefines *symbol*.
#if *symbol* [*operator symbol2*] ...	*symbol* to test. *operators* are ==, !=, &&, || followed by #else, #elif, and #endif.
#else	Executes code to subsequent #endif.
#elif *symbol* [*operator symbol2*]	Combines #else branch and #if test.
#endif	Ends conditional directives.
#warning *text*	*text* of the warning to appear in compiler output.
#error *text*	*text* of the error to appear in compiler output.

Table 4-3. Preprocessor directives (continued)

Preprocessor directive	Action
#line [*number* ["*file*"] | hidden]	*number* specifies the line in source code; *file* is the filename to appear in computer output; hidden specifies that the compiler should generate debugger information (this feature was added in Visual C# 2003).
#region *name*	Marks the beginning of outline.
#end *region*	Ends an outline region.

XML Documentation

C# offers three different styles of source-code documentation: single-line comments, multiline comments, and documentation comments.

C/C++–Style Comments

Single- and multiline comments use the C++ syntax, // and /*...*/:

```
int x = 3; // this is a comment
MyMethod( ); /* this is a
comment that spans two lines */
```

The disadvantage of this style of commenting is that there is no predetermined standard for documenting types. Consequently, it cannot be easily parsed to automate the production of documentation. C# improves on this by allowing you to embed documentation comments in the source, and by providing an automated mechanism for extracting and validating documentation at compile time.

Documentation Comments

Documentation comments are composed of embedded XML tags. These tags allow one to mark up the descriptive text to better define the semantics of the type or member, and also to incorporate cross-references. Documentation comments must either start with /// (that's *three* slashes), or (as of Visual C# 2003) be contained in multiline comments (that's /* ... */). They can be applied to any user-defined type or member.

These comments can then be extracted at compile time into a separate output file containing the documentation. The compiler validates the comments for internal consistency, expands cross-references into fully qualified type IDs, and outputs a well-formed XML file. Further processing is left up to you, although a common next step is to run the XML through XSLT, generating HTML documentation.

Here is an example of documentation comments for a very simple type:

```
// Filename: DocTest.cs
using System;
class MyClass {
  /// <summary>
  /// The Foo method is called from
  ///    <see cref="Main">Main</see>
  /// </summary>
```

```
/// <mytag>Secret stuff</mytag>
/// <param name="s">Description for s</param>
static void Foo(string s) { Console.WriteLine(s); }
static void Main() { Foo("42"); }
}
```

XML Documentation Files

When run through the compiler using the /doc:*<filename>* command-line option, the following XML file is generated:

```
<?xml version="1.0"?>
<doc>
  <assembly>
    <name>DocTest</name>
  </assembly>
  <members>
    <member name="M:MyClass.Foo(System.String)">
      <summary>
      The Foo method is called from
        <see cref="M:MyClass.Main">Main</see>
      </summary>
      <mytag>Secret stuff</mytag>
      <param name="s">Description for s</param>
    </member>
  </members>
</doc>
```

The <?xml...>, <doc>, and <members> tags are generated automatically and form the skeleton for the XML file. The <assembly> and <name> tags indicate the assembly this type lives in. Every member that was preceded by a documentation comment is included in the XML file via a <member> tag with a name attribute that identifies the member. Note that the cref attribute in the <see> tag has also been expanded to refer to a fully qualified type and member. The predefined XML documentation tags that were embedded in the documentation comments are also included in the XML file, and have been validated to ensure that all parameters are documented, that the names are accurate, and that any cross-references to other types or members can be resolved. Finally, any additional user-defined tags are transferred verbatim.

Predefined XML Tags

The predefined set of XML tags that can be used to mark up the descriptive text are listed here:

<summary>

> <summary>*description*</summary>

This tag describes a type or member. Typically, <summary> contains the description of a member at a fairly high level.

<remarks>

> <remarks>*description*</remarks>

This tag provides additional information regarding a particular member. Information about side effects within the method, or particular behavior that may not otherwise be intuitive (such as the idea that this method may throw an ArrayOutOfBoundsException if a parameter is greater than 5) is listed here.

`<param>`

> `<param name="`*name*`">description</param>`

This tag describes a parameter on a method. The name attribute is mandatory, and must refer to a parameter on the method. If this tag is applied to any parameter on a method, all of the parameters on that method must be documented. Enclose *name* in double quotation marks ("").

`<returns>`

> `<returns>`*description*`</returns>`

This tag describes the return values for a method.

`<exception>`

> `<exception [cref="`*type*`"]>`*description*`</exception>`

This tag documents the exceptions a method may throw. If present, the optional cref attribute should refer to the type of the exception. The type name must be enclosed in double quotation marks ("").

`<permission>`

> `<permission [cref="`*type*`"]>`*description*`</permission>`

This tag documents the permissions requirement for a type or member. If present, the optional cref attribute should refer to the type that represents the permission set required by the member, although the compiler does not validate this. The type name must be enclosed in double quotation marks ("").

`<example>`

> `<example>`*description*`</example>`

This tag provides a description and sample source code explaining the use of a type or member. Typically, the `<example>` tag provides the description and contains the `<c>` and `<code>` tags, although they can also be used independently.

`<c>`

> `<c>`*code*`</c>`

This tag indicates an inline code snippet. Typically, this tag is used inside an `<example>` block (described previously).

`<code>`

> `<code>`*code*`</code>`

This tag is used to indicate multiline code snippets. Again, this is typically used inside of an `<example>` block (described previously).

`<see>`

> `<see cref="`*member*`">`*text*`</see>`

This tag identifies cross-references in the documentation to other types or members. Typically, the `<see>` tag is used inline within a description (as opposed to the <seealso> tag, which is broken out into a separate "See Also" section). This tag is useful because it allows tools to generate cross-references, indexes, and hyperlinked views of the documentation. Member names must be enclosed by double quotation marks ("").

<seealso>

```
<seealso cref="member">text</seealso>
```

This tag identifies cross-references in the documentation to other types or members. Typically, <seealso> tags are broken out into a separate "See Also" section. This tag is useful because it allows tools to generate cross-references, indexes, and hyperlinked views of the documentation. Member names must be enclosed by double quotation marks ("").

<value>

```
<value>description</value>
```

This tag describes a property on a class.

<paramref>

```
<paramref name="name"/>
```

This tag identifies the use of a parameter name within descriptive text, such as <remarks>. The name must be enclosed by double quotation marks ("").

<list>

```
<list type=[ bullet | number | table ]>
  <listheader>
    <term>name</term>
    <description>description</description>
  </listheader>
  <item>
    <term>name</term>
    <description>description</description>
  </item>
</list>
```

This tag provides hints to documentation generators about how to format the documentation—in this case, as a list of items.

<para>

```
<para>text</para>
```

This tag sets off the text as a paragraph to documentation generators.

<include>

```
<include file='filename' path='path-to-element'>
```

This tag specifies an external file that contains documentation and an XPath path to a specific element in that file. For example, a path of docs[@id="001"]/* retrieves whatever is inside of <docs id="001"/>. The filename and path must be enclosed by single quotation marks (''), but you must use double quotation marks ("") for the id attribute within the path-to-element expression.

User-Defined Tags

There is little that is special about the predefined XML tags recognized by the C# compiler, and you are free to define your own. The only special processing done by the compiler is on the <param> tag (in which it verifies the parameter name and that all the parameters on the method are documented) and the cref attribute (in which it verifies that the attribute refers to a real type or member, and expands it to a fully qualified type or member ID). The cref attribute can also be used in your own tags, and is verified and expanded just as it is in the predefined <exception>, <permission>, <see>, and <seealso> tags.

Generated Documentation

Once an XML file is generated from documentation comments, it typically requires another step before becoming generally useful to programmers, since most of us aren't quite able to parse and use an XML file "in the raw."

The most common approach is to run the XML output through an XSLT stylesheet to generate some more human-friendly format, such as HTML. (Variations on this idea include generating PDF, RTF, or even Microsoft Word documents.) While Microsoft may publish a standardized XSLT file for this, companies may want to create their own to establish their own "look" for documentation of components they sell. Alternatively, several open source projects have already begun to explore this area, and produce neatly formatted documentation files; one example is *http://ndoc.sourceforge.net*.

The ability to put user-defined tags into the XML documentation sections represents a powerful extensibility point—for example, a company may put implementation details about the method or class inside of <implementation> tags and define two XSLT files: one excluding the implementation tags, and the other including it. The non-<implementation>-aware files can be distributed publicly, while the <implementation>-aware files are used internally by developers. An automated test tool might run tests against those methods or classes described by a <test name=test-to-run> tag. Types meant to be stored in the database might use XML documentation tags to indicate the SQL required to create the tables, and a custom tool could be written to extract the necessary SQL from the XML documentation files in order to run it. Non-public information about the code can be embedded within the code itself or in the documentation comments and processed by an external tool via this mechanism, which makes it quite powerful.

Type or Member Cross-References

Type names and type or member cross-references are translated into IDs that uniquely define the type or member. These names are composed of a prefix that defines what the ID represents and a signature of the type or member.

Table 4-4 lists the set of type or member prefixes.

Table 4-4. XML type ID prefixes

XML type prefix	ID prefixes applied to
N	Namespace
T	Type (class, struct, enum, interface, delegate)
F	Field
P	Property (includes indexers)
M	Method (includes special methods)
E	Event
!	Error

The rules describing how the signatures are generated are well documented, although fairly complex.

Here is an example of a type and the IDs that are generated:

```
// Namespaces do not have independent signatures
namespace NS {
  /// T:NS.MyClass
  class MyClass {
    /// F:NS.MyClass.aField
    string aField;
    /// P:NS.MyClass.aProperty
    short aProperty {get {...} set {...}}
    /// T:NS.MyClass.NestedType
    class NestedType {...};
    /// M:NS.MyClass.X()
    void X() {...}
    /// M:NS.MyClass.Y(System.Int32,System.Double@,System.Decimal@)
    void Y(int p1, ref double p2, out decimal p3) {...}
    /// M:NS.MyClass.Z(System.Char[],System.Single[0:,0:])
    void Z(char[] p1, float[,] p2) {...}
    /// M:NS.MyClass.op_Addition(NS.MyClass,NS.MyClass)
    public static MyClass operator+(MyClass c1, MyClass c2) {...}
    /// M:NS.MyClass.op_Implicit(NS.MyClass)~System.Int32
    public static implicit operator int(MyClass c) {...}
    /// M:NS.MyClass.#ctor
    MyClass() {...}
    /// M:NS.MyClass.Finalize
    ~MyClass() {...}
    /// M:NS.MyClass.#cctor
    static MyClass() {...}
  }
}
```

Programming with the .NET Framework

Part II, *Programming with the .NET Framework*, contains:

Framework Class Library Overview

Almost all the capabilities of the .NET Framework are exposed via a set of managed types known as the Framework Class Library (FCL). Because these types are CLS-compliant, they are accessible from almost any .NET language. FCL types are grouped logically by namespace and are packaged in a set of assemblies that are part of the .NET platform. Using these types in a C# application requires you to reference the appropriate assembly when compiling (most essential assemblies are referenced by default; see Appendix E). In order to work effectively in C# on the .NET platform, it is important to understand the general capabilities in the predefined class library. However, the library is far too large to cover completely in this book, as it encompasses 3,744 types grouped into 124 namespaces and packaged in 34 different assemblies.

Instead, in this chapter, we give an overview of the entire FCL (broken down by logical area) and provide references to relevant types and namespaces so that you can explore their details in the .NET Framework SDK on your own.

The specific types and namespaces mentioned in this overview are based on the 1.1 version of the .NET Framework.

Useful tools for exploring the FCL include the .NET Framework SDK documentation, the Visual Studio .NET documentation, the *WinCV.exe* class browser, and the *ILDasm.exe* disassembler (see Chapter 23).

Core Types

The core types are contained in the System namespace. This namespace is the heart of the FCL and contains classes, interfaces, and attributes that all other types depend on. The root of the FCL is the type Object, from which all other .NET types derive. Other fundamental types are ValueType (the base type for structs), Enum (the base type for enums), Convert (used to convert between base types), Exception (the base type for all exceptions), and the boxed versions of the predefined value types. Interfaces that are used throughout the FCL, such as ICloneable, IComparable, IFormattable, and IConvertible, are also defined here. Extended types such as DateTime, TimeSpan, and DBNull are available as well. Other classes include support for delegates (see "Delegates" in Chapter 4), basic math operations, custom attributes (see "Attributes" in Chapter 4 and Chapter 14), and exception handling (see "Try Statements and Exceptions" in Chapter 4).

For more information, see the System namespace.

Text

The FCL provides rich support for text. Important types include the System.String class for handling immutable strings, a StringBuilder class that provides string-handling operations with support for locale-aware comparison operations and multiple string encoding formats (ASCII, Unicode, UTF-7, and UTF-8), as well as a set of classes that provide regular expression support (see Chapter 6).

For more information, see the following namespaces:

```
System.Text
System.Text.RegularExpressions
```

An important related type in another namespace is System.String.

Collections

The FCL provides a set of general-purpose data structures such as System.Array, ArrayList, Hashtable, Queue, Stack, BitArray, and more. Standardized design patterns using common base types and public interfaces allow consistent handling of collections throughout the FCL for both predefined and user-defined collection types (see Chapter 7).

For more information, see the following namespaces:

```
System.Collections
System.Collections.Specialized
```

An important related type in another namespace is System.Array.

Streams and I/O

The FCL provides good support for accessing the standard input, output, and error streams. Classes are also provided for performing binary and text file I/O, registering for notification of filesystem events, and for accessing a secure user-specific storage area known as Isolated Storage (see Chapter 10).

For more information, see the following namespaces:

```
System.IO
System.IO.IsolatedStorage
```

An important related type in another namespace is System.Console.

Networking

The FCL provides a layered set of classes for communicating over the network using different levels of abstraction, including raw socket access; TCP, UDP, and HTTP protocol support; a high-level request/response mechanism based on URIs and streams; and pluggable protocol handlers (see Chapter 9).

For more information, see the following namespaces:

```
System.Net
System.Net.Sockets
```

An important related type in another namespace is `System.IO.Stream`.

Threading

The FCL provides rich support for building multithreaded applications, including thread and thread-pool management, thread-synchronization mechanisms, such as monitors, mutexes, events, reader/writer locks, etc., and access to such underlying platform features as I/O completion ports and system timers (see Chapter 16).

For more information, see the following namespaces:

```
System.Threading
System.Timers
```

Important related types in other namespaces include `System.Thread` and `System.ThreadStaticAttribute`.

Security

The FCL provides classes for manipulating all elements of the .NET Framework's Code Access Security model, including security policies, security principals, permission sets, and evidence. These classes also support cryptographic algorithms such as DES, 3DES, RC2, RSA, DSig, MD5, SHA1, and Base64 encoding for stream transformations.

For more information, see the following namespaces:

```
System.Security
System.Security.Cryptography
System.Security.Cryptography.X509Certificates
System.Security.Cryptography.Xml
System.Security.Permissions
System.Security.Policy
System.Security.Principal
```

Reflection and Metadata

The .NET runtime depends heavily on the existence of metadata and the ability to inspect and manipulate it dynamically. The FCL exposes this via a set of abstract classes that mirror the significant elements of an application (assemblies, modules, types, and members) and provide support for creating instances of FCL types and new types on the fly (see Chapter 13).

For more information, see the following namespaces:

```
System.Reflection
System.Reflection.Emit
```

Important related types in other namespaces include System.Type, System. Activator, and System.AppDomain.

Assemblies

The FCL provides attributes that tag the metadata on an assembly with information such as target OS and processor, assembly version, and other information. The FCL also provides classes to manipulate assemblies, modules, and assembly strong names (see Chapter 12).

For more information, see the following namespace:

```
System.Reflection
```

Serialization

The FCL includes support for serializing arbitrary object graphs to and from a stream. This serialization can store and transmit complex data structures via files or the network. The default serializers provide binary and XML-based formatting but can be extended with user-defined formatters.

For more information, see the following namespaces:

```
System.Runtime.Serialization
System.Runtime.Serialization.Formatters
System.Runtime.Serialization.Formatters.Binary
System.Runtime.Serialization.Formatters.Soap
```

Important related types in other namespaces include System. NonSerializedAttribute and System.SerializableAttribute.

Remoting

Remoting is the cornerstone of a distributed application, and the FCL provides excellent support for making and receiving remote method calls. Calls may be synchronous or asynchronous, support request/response or one-way modes, delivered over multiple transports (TCP, HTTP, and SMTP), and serialized in multiple formats (SOAP and binary). The remoting infrastructure supports multiple activation models, lease-based object lifetimes, distributed object identity, object marshaling by reference and by value, and message interception. These types can be extended with user-defined channels, serializers, proxies, and call context.

For more information, see the following namespaces:

```
System.Runtime.Remoting
System.Runtime.Remoting.Activation
```

```
System.Runtime.Remoting.Channels
System.Runtime.Remoting.Channels.Http
System.Runtime.Remoting.Channels.Tcp
System.Runtime.Remoting.Contexts
System.Runtime.Remoting.Lifetime
System.Runtime.Remoting.Messaging
System.Runtime.Remoting.Metadata
System.Runtime.Remoting.MetadataServices
System.Runtime.Remoting.Proxies
System.Runtime.Remoting.Services
```

Important related types in other namespaces include:

```
System.AppDomain
System.ContextBoundObject
System.ContextStaticAttribute
System.MarshalByRefObject
```

Web Services

Logically, web services are simply another form of remoting. In reality, the FCL support for web services is considered part of ASP.NET and is entirely separate from the CLR remoting infrastructure. Classes and attributes exist for describing and publishing web services, discovering what web services are exposed at a particular endpoint (URI), and invoking a web service method.

For more information, see the following namespaces:

```
System.Web.Services
System.Web.Services.Configuration
System.Web.Services.Description
System.Web.Services.Discovery
System.Web.Services.Protocols
```

Data Access

The FCL includes a set of classes that access data sources and manage complex data sets. Known as ADO.NET, these classes are the managed replacement for ADO under Win32. ADO.NET supports both connected and disconnected operations, multiple data providers (including nonrelational data sources), and serialization to and from XML.

For more information, see the following namespaces:

```
System.Data
System.Data.Common
System.Data.Odbc (.NET 1.1)
System.Data.OleDb
System.Data.OracleClient (.NET 1.1)
System.Data.SqlClient
System.Data.SqlTypes
```

XML

The FCL provides broad support for XML 1.0, XML schemas, XML namespaces with two separate XML parsing models (a DOM2-based model and a pull-mode variant of SAX2), and implementations of XSLT, XPath, and SOAP 1.1.

For more information, see the following namespaces:

```
System.Xml
System.Xml.Schema
System.Xml.Serialization
System.Xml.XPath
System.Xml.Xsl
```

Graphics

The FCL includes classes to support working with graphic images. Known as GDI+, these classes are the managed equivalent of GDI under Win32, and include support for brushes, fonts, bitmaps, text rendering, drawing primitives, image conversions, and print-preview capabilities.

For more information, see the following namespaces:

```
System.Drawing
System.Drawing.Design
System.Drawing.Drawing2D
System.Drawing.Imaging
System.Drawing.Printing
System.Drawing.Text
```

Rich Client Applications

The FCL includes support for creating classic GUI applications. This support is known as Windows Forms, and consists of a forms package, a predefined set of GUI components, and a component model suited to RAD designer tools. These classes provide varying degrees of abstraction from low-level message-loop handler classes to high-level layout managers and visual inheritance.

For more information, see the following namespaces:

```
System.Windows.Forms
System.Windows.Forms.Design
```

Web-Based Applications

The FCL includes support for creating web-based applications. This support is known as Web Forms, and consists of a server-side forms package that generates browser-specific UI (e.g. HTML, DHTML, WAP for Mobile devices, etc.), a predefined set of HTML-based GUI widgets, and a component model suited to RAD designer tools. The FCL also includes a set of classes that manage session state, security, caching, debugging, tracing, localization, configuration, and deployment for web-based applications. Finally, the FCL includes the classes and attributes that produce and consume web services, which are described previously in this chapter in the "Web Services" section. Collectively, these capabilities are known as ASP.NET and are a complete replacement for ASP under Win32.

For more information, see the following namespaces:

```
System.Web
System.Web.Caching
System.Web.Configuration
System.Web.Hosting
System.Web.Mail
System.Web.Mobile (.NET 1.1)
System.Web.Security
System.Web.SessionState
System.Web.UI
System.Web.UI.Design
System.Web.UI.Design.WebControls
System.Web.UI.HtmlControls
System.Web.UI.MobileControls (.NET 1.1)
System.Web.UI.MobileControls.Adapters (.NET 1.1)
System.Web.UI.WebControls
```

Globalization

The FCL provides classes that aid globalization by supporting code-page conversions, locale-aware string operations, date/time conversions, and the use of resource files to centralize localization work.

For more information, see the following namespaces:

```
System.Globalization
System.Resources
```

Configuration

The FCL provides access to the .NET configuration system, which includes a per-user and per-application configuration model with inheritance of configuration settings, and a transacted installer framework. Classes exist both to use the configuration framework and to extend it.

For more information, see the following namespaces:

```
System.Configuration
System.Configuration.Assemblies
System.Configuration.Install
```

Advanced Component Services

The FCL provides support for building on the COM+ services such as distributed transactions, JIT activation, object pooling, queuing, and events. The FCL also includes types that provide access to reliable, asynchronous, one-way messaging via an existing Message Queue infrastructure (MSMQ), in addition to classes that provide access to existing directory services (Active Directory).

For more information, see the following namespaces:

```
System.EnterpriseServices
System.EnterpriseServices.CompensatingResourceManager
System.DirectoryServices
System.Messaging
```

Diagnostics and Debugging

The FCL includes classes that provide debug tracing with multilistener support, access to the event log, access to process, thread, and stack frame information, and the ability to create and consume performance counters (see Chapter 19).

For more information, see the following namespaces:

```
System.Diagnostics
System.Diagnostics.SymbolStore
```

Interoperating with Unmanaged Code

The .NET runtime supports bidirectional interop with unmanaged code via COM, COM+, and native Win32 API calls. The FCL provides a set of classes and attributes that support this, including precise control of managed object lifetime, and the option of creating user-defined custom marshallers to handle specific interop situations (see Chapter 17 and Chapter 18).

For more information, see the following namespaces:

```
System.Runtime.InteropServices
System.Runtime.InteropServices.CustomMarshalers
System.Runtime.InteropServices.Expando
```

An important related type in another namespace is System.Buffer.

Compiler and Tool Support

In the .NET runtime, components are distinguished from classes by the presence of additional metadata and other apparatus that facilitates the use of the component forms packages such as Windows Forms and Web Forms. The FCL provides classes and attributes that support both the creation of components and the creation of tools that consume components. These classes also include the ability to generate and compile C#, JScript, and VB.NET source code.

For more information, see the following namespaces:

```
Microsoft.CSharp
Microsoft.JScript
Microsoft.VisualBasic
Microsoft.Vsa
System.CodeDom
System.CodeDom.Compiler
System.ComponentModel
System.ComponentModel.Design
System.ComponentModel.Design.Serialization
System.Runtime.CompilerServices
```

Runtime Facilities

The FCL provides classes that can control runtime behavior. The canonical examples are the classes that control the garbage collector and those that provide strong and weak reference support.

For more information, see the following namespace:

```
System
```

An important related type in another namespace is `System.Runtime.InteropServices.GCHandle`.

Native OS Facilities

The FCL provides support for controlling existing NT services and creating new ones. It also provides access to certain native Win32 facilities such as the Windows registry and the Windows Management Instrumentation (WMI).

For more information, see the following namespaces:

```
Microsoft.Win32
System.Management
System.Management.Instrumentation
System.ServiceProcess
```

Undocumented Types

The assemblies that make up the .NET Framework also export many types and namespaces that are not documented. These types and namespaces generally represent either implementation details that are subject to change, vestigial code from earlier betas, or tool-specific code that happens to be managed and is therefore subject to examination via reflection. Regardless of the reason, one cannot count on undocumented types, nor expect any support from Microsoft.

That said, there is useful information to be gained from investigating these private implementation details. Examples of this include programmatic access to the GAC, predefined Win32 structures and COM interfaces (internals of *SoapSuds.exe*, *RegAsm.exe*, *TlbImp.exe*, and *TlbExp.exe*), and browser, tool, and OS integration helpers.

Many of the documented namespaces include additional undocumented types. Additionally, the following namespaces are completely undocumented:

```
Accessibility
IEHost.Execute
Microsoft.CLRAdmin
Microsoft.IE
Microsoft.JScript.Vsa
Microsoft.VisualBasic.CompilerServices
Microsoft.VisualBasic.Helpers
Microsoft.VisualBasic.Vsa
Microsoft.VisualC
Microsoft.Vsa.Vb.CodeDOM
```

```
Microsoft_VsaVb
RegCode
SoapSudsCode
System.Diagnostics.Design
System.EnterpriseServices.Internal
System.Messaging.Design
System.ServiceProcess.Design
System.Web.Handlers
System.Web.RegularExpressions
System.Web.Util
System.Windows.Forms.ComponentModel.Com2Interop
System.Windows.Forms.PropertyGridInternal
TlbExpCode
TlbImpCode
```

To investigate these types and namespaces, use *ILDasm.exe* to examine the metadata and MSIL (see Appendix E to match DLLs with their namespaces).

6

String Handling

C# offers a wide range of string-handling features. Support is provided for both mutable and immutable strings, extensible string formatting, locale-aware string comparisons, and multiple string encoding systems. The string handling support also includes regular expression matching and replacement capabilities based on Perl 5 regular expressions, including lazy quantifiers (??, *?, +?, {n,m}?), positive and negative look-ahead, and conditional evaluation.

This chapter introduces and demonstrates the most common types you'll use in working with strings. The types mentioned in this section all exist in the System, System.Text, or System.Text.RegularExpressions namespaces (unless otherwise stated).

String Class

A C# string represents an immutable sequence of characters, and aliases the System.String class. Strings have comparison, appending, inserting, conversion, copying, formatting, indexing, joining, splitting, padding, trimming, removing, replacing, and searching methods. The compiler converts addition (+) operations on operands, in which the left operand is a string to Concat( ) methods (assuming it can't fold the concatenation together directly at compile time), and also preevaluates and interns string constants where possible (see Chapter 6 later in this chapter).

Comparing Strings

Although System.String is a reference type, the == operator is overloaded, so you can easily compare two strings by value, as follows:

```
string a = "abracadabra";
string b = "abracadabra";
Console.WriteLine(a==b); // Prints "True"
```

Immutability of Strings

Strings are *immutable*, which means they can't be modified after creation. Consequently, many of the methods that initially appear to modify a string actually create a new string:

```
string a = "Heat";
string b = a.Insert(3, "r")
Console.WriteLine(b); // Prints Heart
```

If you need a mutable string, see the `StringBuilder` class, discussed later in this chapter.

String Interning

In addition, the immutability of strings enables all strings in an application to be *interned*. Interning is the process in which all the constant strings in an application are stored in a common place and any duplicate strings are eliminated. This saves space at runtime but creates the possibility that multiple string references will point to the same location in memory. This can be the source of unexpected results when comparing two constant strings, as follows:

```
string a = "hello";
string b = "hello";
Console.WriteLine(a == b); // True for String only
Console.WriteLine(a.Equals(b)); // True for all objects
Console.WriteLine((object)a == (object)b); // True!!
```

Formatting Strings

The `Format()` method provides a convenient way to build strings that make use of embedded parameters. Parameters in such strings can be of any type, including both predefined and user-defined types.

The `String.Format()` method takes *a format-specification string*, followed by a variable number of parameters. The format-specification string defines the template for the string; the position and format of each parameter within the string is specified by a *format specifier* for each of its parameters.

The syntax of a format specifier looks like this:

```
{ParamIndex[,MinWidth][:FormatString]}
```

It has the following parameters:

ParamIndex
> This is the zero-based index of the parameter to be formatted. This number specifies a position in the parameter list that follows the format-specification string.

MinWidth
> This is the minimum number of characters required for the string representation of the parameter, to be padded by spaces if necessary (a negative number is left-justified, a positive number is right-justified). If not specified, the string representation consumes the minimum number of characters possible.

FormatString

This is passed to the ToString( ) method on IFormattable to construct the string if the parameter represents an object that implements IFormattable. If not, the ToString( ) method on System.Object is used to construct the string.

 All of the common types (int, string, DateTime, etc.) implement IFormattable. A table of the numeric and picture format specifiers supported by the common predefined types is provided in Appendix B.

In the following example, we embed string specifiers for the integer account variable i (parameter 0 in the parameter list), and the decimal cash variable m (parameter 1 in the parameter list, with C = currency) in the format-specification string:

```
Account {0} has {1:C}
```

The parameters themselves are listed immediately following the string template:

```
using System;
class TestFormatting {
  static void Main( ) {
    int i = 2;
    decimal m = 42.73m;
    string s = String.Format("Account {0} has {1:C}.", i, m);
    Console.WriteLine(s); // Prints "Account 2 has $42.73"
  }
}
```

Indexing Strings

Consistent with all other indexing in the CLR, the characters in a string are accessed with a zero-based index:

```
using System;
class TestIndexing {
  static void Main( ) {
    string s = "Going down?";
    for (int i=0; i<s.Length; i++)
      Console.WriteLine(s[i]); // Prints s vertically
  }
}
```

Encoding Strings

Strings can be converted between different character encodings using the Encoding type. The Encoding type can't be created directly, but the ASCII, Unicode, UTF7, UTF8, and BigEndianUnicode static properties on the Encoding type return correctly constructed instances.

Here is an example that converts an array of bytes into a string using the ASCII encoding:

```
using System;
using System.Text;
```

```
class TestEncoding {
  static void Main( ) {
    byte[ ] ba = new byte[ ] { 67, 35, 32, 105, 115,
                               32, 67, 79, 79, 76, 33 };
    string s = Encoding.ASCII.GetString(ba);
    Console.WriteLine(s);
  }
}
```

StringBuilder Class

The StringBuilder class represents mutable strings. It starts at a predefined size (16 characters, by default) and grows dynamically as more characters are added. It can grow either unbounded or up to a configurable maximum. For example:

```
using System;
using System.Text;
class TestStringBuilder {
  static void Main( ) {
    StringBuilder sb = new StringBuilder("Hello, ");
    sb.Append("World");
    sb[11] = '!';
    Console.WriteLine(sb); // Hello, World!
  }
}
```

Regular Expression Support

Regular expressions have been used in various programming languages and tools for many years. The FCL includes a set of classes for utilizing the power of regular expressions that are designed to be compatible with Perl 5 regular expressions. In addition, the regular expression classes implement some additional functionality, such as named capture groups, right-to-left pattern matching, and expression compilation.

Regular expression knowledge seems to be one of those topics that most programmers have learned and then forgotten more than once. For the purposes of this chapter, we presume some previous use and experience with regular expressions within Perl 5. The .NET regexp classes are a superset of Perl 5 functionality, so this will serve as a good conceptual starting point.

For readers new to regular expressions, we suggest starting with some basic Perl 5 introductions. The *perl.com* site has some great resource materials and introductory tutorials. In addition, the definitive work on regular expressions is *Mastering Regular Expressions*, by Jeffrey E. F. Friedl (O'Reilly & Associates). For those who want to get the most out of working with regular expressions, this book is highly recommended.

The Regex Class

The Regex class is the heart of the BCL regular expression support. Used both as an object instance and as a static type, the Regex class represents an immutable, compiled instance of a regular expression that can be applied to a string via a matching process.

Internally, the regular expression is stored as either a sequence of internal regular expression bytecodes that are interpreted at match time or as compiled MSIL opcodes that are JIT-compiled by the CLR at runtime. This allows you to make a trade-off between a worsened regular expression startup time and memory utilization versus higher raw match performance at runtime.

The Regex class contains several static methods:

Method	Purpose
Escape()	Ignores regex metacharacters within a string
IsMatch()	Methods that return a bool result if the supplied regular expression matches within the string
Match()	Methods that return a Match instance
Matches()	Methods that return a list of Match instances as a collection
Replace()	Methods that replace the matched regular expressions with replacement strings
Split()	Methods that return an array of strings determined by the expression
Unescape()	Unescapes any escaped characters within a string

For more information on the regular-expression options, supported character escapes, substitution patterns, character sets, positioning assertions, quantifiers, grouping constructs, backreferences, and alternation, see Appendix A.

The Match and MatchCollection Classes

The Match class represents the result of applying a regular expression to a string, looking for the first successful match. The MatchCollection class contains a collection of Match instances that represent the result of applying a regular expression to a string recursively until the first unsuccessful match occurs.

The Group Class

The Group class represents the results from a single grouping expression. From this class, it is possible to drill down to the individual subexpression matches with the Captures property.

The Capture and Capture Collection Classes

The CaptureCollection class contains a collection of Capture instances, each representing the results of a single subexpression match.

Regular Expression Basics

Let's start with simple expressions using the Regex and the Match classes.

```
Match m = Regex.Match("abracadabra", "(a|b|r)+");
```

This results in an instance of the Match class that can be tested for success without examining the contents of the matched string, as follows:

```
if (m.Success) {
    ...
}
```

To use the matched substring, simply convert it to a string:

```
Console.WriteLine("Match="+m.ToString());
```

The output of this example is the portion of the string that has been successfully matched, as follows:

```
Match=abra
```

Simple string replacements are also very straightforward. For example, consider the following statement:

```
string s = Regex.Replace("abracadabra", "abra", "zzzz");
```

This returns the string zzzzcadzzzz, in which all occurrences of the matching pattern are replaced by the replacement string zzzzz.

Now let's look at a more complex expression:

```
string s = Regex.Replace("  abra  ", @"^\s*(.*?)\s*$", "$1");
```

This returns the string abra, with preceding and trailing spaces removed. This pattern is generally useful for removing leading and trailing spaces from any string. We could also have used the literal string quote construct in C#. Within a literal string, the compiler does not process the backslash character (\) as an escape character. Consequently, the @"..." is very useful when working with regular expressions, and when you are specifying escaped metacharacters with a \. Also of note is the use of $1 as the replacement string. The replacement string can contain only substitutions, which are references to capture groups in the regular expression.

Now let's try a slightly more complex sample by doing a walk-through of a grouping structure. For example:

```
string text = "abracadabra1abracadabra2abracadabra3";
string pat = @"
    (       # start the first group
      abra# match the literal 'abra'
      (# start the second (inner) group
      cad# match the literal 'cad'
      )?# end the second (optional) group
    )# end the first group
    +# match one or more occurences
    ";
// create a new regex that ignores comments
Regex r = new Regex(pat, RegexOptions.IgnorePatternWhitespace);
// get the list of group numbers
int[] gnums = r.GetGroupNumbers();
// get first match
Match m = r.Match(text);
while (m.Success) {
```

```
// start at group 1
  for (int i = 1; i < gnums.Length; i++) {
    Group g = m.Group(gnums[i]);
// get the group for this match
    Console.WriteLine("Group"+gnums[i]+"=["+g.ToString()+"]");
// get caps for this group
    CaptureCollection cc = g.Captures;
    for (int j = 0; j < cc.Count; j++) {
      Capture c = cc[j];
      Console.WriteLine("Capture" + j + "=["+c.ToString()
        + "] Index=" + c.Index + " Length=" + c.Length);
    }
  }
// get next match
  m = m.NextMatch();
}
```

The output of this example is:

```
Group1=[abra]
        Capture0=[abracad] Index=0 Length=7
        Capture1=[abra] Index=7 Length=4
Group2=[cad]
        Capture0=[cad] Index=4 Length=3
Group1=[abra]
        Capture0=[abracad] Index=12 Length=7
        Capture1=[abra] Index=19 Length=4
Group2=[cad]
        Capture0=[cad] Index=16 Length=3
Group1=[abra]
        Capture0=[abracad] Index=24 Length=7
        Capture1=[abra] Index=31 Length=4
Group2=[cad]
        Capture0=[cad] Index=28 Length=3
```

We'll first examine the string pat, which contains the regular expression. The first capture group is marked by the first parenthesis, and then the expression matches an abra, if the regex engine matches the expression to that found in the text. Then the second capture group begins, marked by the second parenthesis, but the definition of the first capture group is still ongoing. What this means is that the first group must match abracad and the second group matches the cad. So, if we decided to make the cad match an optional occurrence with the ? metacharacter, then abra or abracad is matched. Next, we end the first group, and ask the expression to match one or more occurrences by specifying the + metacharacter.

During the matching process we create an instance of the expression by calling the Regex constructor, which is also where you specify your options. In this case, we used the RegexOptions.IgnorePatternWhitespace option, as the regular expression itself includes comments and whitespace for formatting purposes. The RegexOptions.IgnorePatternWhitespace option instructs the regex engine to ignore both the comments and all the whitespace that is not explicitly escaped.

Next, we retrieve the list of group numbers (gnums) defined in this regular expression. Although this could have been done explicitly, this sample demonstrates a programmatic approach. This approach is also useful if we have specified named groups as a way of quickly indexing through the set of groups.

Then we perform the first match and enter a loop to test for success of the current match. The next step is to iterate through the list of groups starting at group 1. The reason we do not use group 0 in this sample is that group 0 is the fully captured match string, and what we usually (but not always) want to pick out of a string is a subgroup. You might use group 0 if you want to collect the fully matched string as a single string.

Within each group, we iterate through the CaptureCollection. There is usually only one capture per match, per group—in this case two captures show for Group1: Capture0 and Capture1. And if we ask only for the ToString of Group1, we receive abra, although it does also match the abracad sub string. The group ToString value is the value of the last Capture in its CaptureCollection. This is the expected behavior, and if we want the match to stop after just the abra, we can remove the + from the expression, telling the regular expression engine to match on just the expression.

Procedural- and Expression-Based Patterns

Generally, users of regular expressions fall into one of two groups. The first group tends to use minimal regular expressions that provide matching or grouping behaviors, and then write procedural code to perform some iterative behavior. The second group tries to utilize the maximum power and functionality of the expression-processing engine itself, with as little procedural logic as possible. For most of us, the best answer is somewhere in between. We'll now explore the trade-offs in complexity and performance of these two approaches.

Procedural-Based Patterns

A common processing need is to match certain parts of a string and perform some processing. So, here's an example that matches words within a string and capital-izes them:

```
using System;
using System.Text.RegularExpressions;

class ProceduralFun {
  static void Main( ) {
    string txt = "the quick red fox jumped over the lazy brown dog.";
    Console.WriteLine("text=["+txt+"]");
    string res = "";
    string pat = @"\w+|\W+";

    // Loop through all the matches
    foreach (Match m in Regex.Matches(txt, pat)) {
      string s = m.ToString( );

      // If the first char is lower case, capitalize it
      if (char.IsLower(s[0]))
        s = char.ToUpper(s[0])+s.Substring(1, s.Length-1);
```

```
        res += s; // Collect the text
    }
    Console.WriteLine("result=["+res+"]");
  }
}
```

As you can see, you use the C# foreach statement to process the set of matches found, and perform some processing (in this case, creating a new result string).

The output of the sample is:

```
text=[the quick red fox jumped over the lazy brown dog.]
result=[The Quick Red Fox Jumped Over The Lazy Brown Dog.]
```

Expression-Based Patterns

Another way to implement the previous example is by providing a MatchEvaluator, which processes it as a single result set.

So the new sample looks like:

```
using System;
using System.Text.RegularExpressions;

class ExpressionFun {
  static string CapText(Match m) {
    // Get the matched string
    string s = m.ToString();

    // If the first char is lower case, capitalize it
    if (char.IsLower(s[0]))
      return char.ToUpper(s[0]) + s.Substring(1, s.Length-1);
    return s;
  }
  static void Main() {
    string txt = "the quick red fox jumped over the lazy brown dog.";
    Console.WriteLine("text=[" + txt + "]");
    string pat = @"\w+";
    MatchEvaluator me = new MatchEvaluator(CapText);
    string res = Regex.Replace(txt, pat, me);
    Console.WriteLine("result=[" + res + "]");
  }
}
```

Also of note is that the pattern is simplified, since we need only to modify the words, not the nonwords.

Cookbook Regular Expressions

To wrap up this overview of how regular expressions are used in C# applications, the following is a set of useful expressions that have been used in other environments.[*]

---

[*] These expressions were taken from the *Perl Cookbook* by Tom Christiansen and Nathan Torkington (O'Reilly), and updated for the C# environment by Brad Merrill of Microsoft.

- Matching roman numerals:

```
string p1 = "^m*(d?c{0,3}|c[dm])"
   + "(l?x{0,3}|x[lc])(v?i{0,3}|i[vx])$";
string t1 = "vii";
Match m1 = Regex.Match(t1, p1);
```

- Swapping first two words:

```
string t2 = "the quick brown fox";
string p2 = @"(\S+)(\s+)(\S+)";
Regex x2 = new Regex(p2);
string r2 = x2.Replace(t2, "$3$2$1", 1);
```

- Matching "keyword = value" patterns:

```
string t3 = "myval = 3";
string p3 = @"(\w+)\s*=\s*(.*)\s*$";
Match m3 = Regex.Match(t3, p3);
```

- Matching lines of at least 80 characters:

```
string t4 = "*********************"
   + "****************************"
   + "*****************************";
string p4 = ".{80,}";
Match m4 = Regex.Match(t4, p4);
```

- Extracting date/time values (MM/DD/YY HH:MM:SS):

```
string t5 = "01/01/01 16:10:01";
string p5 =
   @"(\d+)/(\d+)/(\d+) (\d+):(\d+):(\d+)";
Match m5 = Regex.Match(t5, p5);
```

- Changing directories (for Windows):

```
string t6 =
   @"C:\Documents and Settings\user1\Desktop\";
string r6 = Regex.Replace(t6,
   @"\\user1\\",
   @"\user2\");
```

- Expanding (%nn) hex escapes:

```
string t7 = "%41"; // capital A
string p7 = "%([0-9A-Fa-f][0-9A-Fa-f])";
// uses a MatchEvaluator delegate
string r7 = Regex.Replace(t7, p7,
   HexConvert);
```

- Deleting C comments (imperfectly):

```
string t8 = @"
/*
 * this is an old cstyle comment block
 */
";
string p8 = @"
 /\*  # match the opening delimiter
 .*? # match a minimal numer of characters
 \*/ # match the closing delimiter
";
```

```
string r8 = Regex.Replace(t8, p8, "", RegexOptions.Singleline
                | RegexOptions.IgnorePatternWhitespace);
```

- Removing leading and trailing whitespace:

```
string t9a = "   leading";
string p9a = @"^\s+";
string r9a = Regex.Replace(t9a, p9a, "");

string t9b = "trailing   ";
string p9b = @"\s+$";
string r9b = Regex.Replace(t9b, p9b, "");
```

- Turning "\" followed by "n" into a real newline:

```
string t10 = @"\ntest\n";
string r10 = Regex.Replace(t10, @"\\n", "\n");
```

- Detecting IP addresses:

```
string t11 = "55.54.53.52";
string p11 = "^" +
  @"([01]?\d\d|2[0-4]\d|25[0-5])\." +
  @"([01]?\d\d|2[0-4]\d|25[0-5])\." +
  @"([01]?\d\d|2[0-4]\d|25[0-5])\." +
  @"([01]?\d\d|2[0-4]\d|25[0-5])" +
  "$";
Match m11 = Regex.Match(t11, p11);
```

- Removing leading path from filename:

```
string t12 = @"c:\file.txt";
string p12 = @"^.*\\";
string r12 = Regex.Replace(t12, p12, "");
```

- Joining lines in multiline strings:

```
string t13 = @"this is
a split line";
string p13 = @"\s*\r?\n\s*";
string r13 = Regex.Replace(t13, p13, " ");
```

- Extracting all numbers from a string:

```
string t14 = @"
test 1
test 2.3
test 47
";
string p14 = @"(\d+\.?\d*|\.\d+)";
MatchCollection mc14 = Regex.Matches(t14, p14);
```

- Finding all caps words:

```
string t15 = "This IS a Test OF ALL Caps";
string p15 = @"(\b[^\Wa-z0-9_]+\b)";
MatchCollection mc15 = Regex.Matches(t15, p15);
```

- Finding all lowercase words:

```
string t16 = "This is A Test of lowercase";
string p16 = @"(\b[^\WA-Z0-9_]+\b)";
MatchCollection mc16 = Regex.Matches(t16, p16);
```

- Finding all initial caps words:

```
string t17 = "This is A Test of Initial Caps";
string p17 = @"(\b[^\Wa-z0-9_][^\WA-Z0-9_]*\b)";
MatchCollection mc17 = Regex.Matches(t17, p17);
```

- Finding links in simple HTML:

```
string t18 = @"
<html>
<a href=""http://windows.oreilly.com/news/first.htm"">first tag text</a>
<a href=""http://windows.oreilly.com/news/next.htm"">next tag text</a>
</html>
";
string p18 = @"<A[^>]*?HREF\s*=\s*[""']?"
    + @"([^'"" >]+?)[ '""]?>";
MatchCollection mc18 = Regex.Matches(t18, p18, RegexOptions.IgnoreCase
            | RegexOptions.Singleline);
```

- Finding middle initials:

```
string t19 = "Hanley A. Strappman";
string p19 = @"^\S+\s+(\S)\S*\s+\S";
Match m19 = Regex.Match(t19, p19);
```

- Changing inch marks to quotation marks:

```
string t20 = @"2' 2"" ";
string p20 = "\"([^\"]*)";
string r20 = Regex.Replace(t20, p20, "``$1''");
```

Collections

Collections are standard data structures that supplement arrays, which are the only built-in data structures in C#. In this, C# differs from languages such as Perl and Python, which incorporate key/value data structures and dynamically sized arrays into the language itself.

The FCL includes a set of types that provide commonly required data structures and support for creating your own. These types are typically broken down into two categories: interfaces that define a standardized set of design patterns for collection classes in general, and concrete classes that implement these interfaces and provide a usable range of data structures.

This chapter introduces all the concrete collection classes and abstract collection interfaces and provides examples of their use. Unless otherwise stated, the types mentioned in this section all exist in the System.Collections or System.Collections.Specialized namespaces, which are both documented in the reference section of this book, Part V.

Iterating Over Collections

In computing, there are many different kinds of collections ranging from simple data structures, such as arrays or linked lists, to more complex ones, such as red/black trees and priority queues. While the internal implementation and external characteristics of these data structures vary widely, the ability to traverse the contents of the collection is an almost universal need. In the FCL, this is supported via a pair of interfaces (IEnumerable and IEnumerator) that allow different data structures to expose a common traversal API.

IEnumerable and IEnumerator Interfaces

To expose an enumerator, a collection implements IEnumerable. This interface allows clients to retrieve an enumerator, typed as an IEnumerator interface reference. The enumerator is a logical cursor that can be used to iterate over the elements of the collection in a forward-only manner. The interfaces look like this:

```
public interface IEnumerable {
  IEnumerator GetEnumerator( );
}
public interface IEnumerator {
  bool MoveNext( );
  object Current {get;}
  void Reset( );
}
```

The IEnumerable interface has a single GetEnumerator( ) method that returns an IEnumerator interface reference, with the enumerator positioned before the first element in the collection. The IEnumerator interface provides standard mechanisms (the MoveNext( ) and Reset( ) methods) to iterate over the collection and to retrieve the current element (the Current property) as a generic object reference.

The collection can then be enumerated as follows, or as in the next code example:

```
MyCollection mcoll = new MyCollection( );
...
// Using IEnumerator: substitute your typename for XXX
IEnumerator ie = myc.GetEnumerator( );
while (myc.MoveNext( )) {
  XXX item = (XXX)myc.Current;
  Console.WriteLine(item);
  ...
}
```

C# also provides the foreach statement, which works on any collection that either implements the IEnumerable interface, or provides an accessible GetEnumerator( ) method that returns a type with accessible MoveNext( ) and Reset( ) methods. Using foreach can simplify iteration code, as follows:

```
MyCollection mcoll = new MyCollection
...
// Using foreach: substitute your typename for XXX
foreach (XXX item in mcoll) {
  Console.WriteLine(item);
  ...
}
```

Implementing IEnumerable and IEnumerator

To allow your data types to be enumerated via the standard mechanisms, implement IEnumerable and IEnumerator, taking care to follow the interface's semantic contract. IEnumerator is often implemented as a nested helper type, which is initialized by passing the collection to the constructor of the IEnumerator:

```
using System.Collections;
public class MyCollection : IEnumerable {
  // ...
  int[ ] data;
  public virtual IEnumerator GetEnumerator ( ) {
    return new MyCollection.Enumerator(this);
```

```
      }
    private class Enumerator : IEnumerator {
      MyCollection outer;
      int currentIndex = -1;
      internal Enumerator(MyCollection outer) {
        this.outer = outer;
      }
      public object Current {
        get {
          if (currentIndex == outer.data.Length)
            throw new InvalidOperationException( );
          return outer.data[currentIndex]; // boxed!
        }
      }
      public bool MoveNext( ) {
        if (currentIndex > outer.data.Length)
          throw new InvalidOperationException( );
        return ++currentIndex < outer.data.Length;
      }
      public void Reset( ) {
        currentIndex = -1;
      }
    }
  }
```

Optimizing foreach

One of the downsides of implementing IEnumerable and IEnumerator, as shown in the previous example, is the return type of IEnumerator.Current is object. This approach has two main disadvantages:

1. Clients need to cast the object reference to a more specific type, which is both inefficient compared to a more strongly typed interface for homogenous collections, and may also cause TypeCastExceptions to be thrown if the casts fail.

2. When a collection contains value types, returning them as object references results in their being boxed and unboxed, which is inefficient, creates excess garbage on the heap, and makes it impossible to edit the contents of the collection directly.

Fortunately, there are some ways to resolve these issues. Although the foreach statement is designed to work with types that implement IEnumerable and IEnumerator, the C# compiler actually allows foreach iteration over types that merely provide a type-compatible subset of the methods and semantics in IEnumerable and IEnumerator. It does this by looking first at the type used for the collection in the foreach statement to see if it has an accessible method called GetEnumerator( ) that takes no parameters, and then returns a publicly accessible type. If it does, it then looks at the return type to see if it has loosely equivalent functionality to the IEnumerator interface. To do this, the compiler checks whether the type has an accessible MoveNext method (taking no parameters and returning a bool result) and an accessible Current property (matching the type of the individual element in the foreach statement). If all of these requirements are met, the C# compiler emits IL code to use these types and methods directly, without going through the interfaces. This means that client code does not need to downcast from object, and in the case of collections returning value types, no boxing occurs. Modifying the previous example to work this way looks like the following:

```
using System.Collections;
public class MyCollection {
  // ...
  int[] data;
  public Enumerator GetEnumerator () {
    return new MyCollection.Enumerator(this);
  }
  public class Enumerator  {
    MyCollection outer;
    int currentIndex = -1;
    internal Enumerator(MyCollection outer) {
      this.outer = outer;
    }
    public int Current {
      get {
        if (currentIndex == outer.data.Length)
          throw new InvalidOperationException();
        return outer.data[currentIndex]; // no boxing!
      }
    }
    public bool MoveNext() {
      if (currentIndex > outer.data.Length)
        throw new InvalidOperationException();
      return ++currentIndex < outer.data.Length;
    }
  }
}
```

The problem with this approach is that when used in languages other than C#, this type does not appear to be a collection since it does not implement the standard interfaces. Fortunately, explicit interface implementation can be used to support both approaches concurrently, as follows:

```
using System.Collections;
public class MyCollection : IEnumerable  {
  // ...
  int[] data;
  public Enumerator GetEnumerator() {
    return new MyCollection.Enumerator(this);
  }
  IEnumerator IEnumerable.GetEnumerator() {
    return this.GetEnumerator;
  }
  public class Enumerator : IEnumerator {
    MyCollection outer;
    int currentIndex = -1;
    internal Enumerator(MyCollection outer) {
      this.outer = outer;
```

```
          }
          public int Current {
            get {
              if (currentIndex == outer.data.Length)
                throw new InvalidOperationException( );
              return outer.data[currentIndex];
            }
          }
          public bool MoveNext( ) {
            if (currentIndex > outer.data.Length)
              throw new InvalidOperationException( );
            return ++currentIndex < outer.data.Length;
          }
          object IEnumerator.Current {
              get { return this.Current; }
          }
          bool IEnumerator.MoveNext( ) {
            return this.MoveNext( );
          }
          void IEnumerator.Reset( ) {
            currentIndex = -1;
          }
        }
      }
```

This approach allows C# clients to bind to the more efficient, type-safe version of
the methods, while other languages such as VB.NET bind to the more generic
interface-based implementations.

IDictionaryEnumerator Interface

Later in this chapter we discuss the use of dictionary data structures. The
IDictionaryEnumerator interface is a standardized interface used to enumerate
over the contents of a dictionary, in which each element has both a key and a
value. The Entry property is a more type-safe version of the Current property, and
the Key and Value properties provide access to the element keys and values
directly. The interface looks like this:

```
public interface IDictionaryEnumerator : IEnumerator {
    DictionaryEntry Entry {get;}
    object Key {get;}
    object Value {get;}
}
```

Standard Collection Interfaces

While IEnumerable and IEnumerator provide standard ways to access the contents
of a collection, they don't provide any way to modify it, nor any way to easily
perform other common tasks, such as determine the size, search the collection,
etc. The .NET Framework also defines a set of three standardized interfaces
(ICollection, IList, and IDictionary), which collections should implement to
provide support for these types of operations.

ICollection Interface

The ICollection interface is the standard interface for countable collections of objects. It provides the ability to determine the size of a collection, to determine if it can be modified or synchronized, and to copy the collection into an array for sequential processing. Since ICollection extends IEnumerable, types that implement ICollection can also be traversed via IEnumerable and IEnumerator. The interface looks like this:

```
public interface ICollection : IEnumerable {
    void CopyTo(Array array, int index);
    int Count {get;}
    bool IsReadOnly {get;}
    bool IsSynchronized {get;}
    object SyncRoot {get;}
}
```

IList Interface

The IList interface is the standard interface for array-indexable collections. In addition to the functionality inherent in ICollection and IEnumerable, it also provides the ability to index directly into the collection by position (using the overloaded indexer), to add, remove, and change elements in the collection by position, and to search for elements in the collection. The interface looks like this:

```
public interface IList : ICollection, IEnumerable {
    object this[int index] {get; set}
    int Add(object o);
    void Clear();
    bool Contains(object value);
    int IndexOf(object value);
    void Insert(int index, object value);
    void Remove(object value);
    void RemoveAt(int index);
}
```

IDictionary Interface

The IDictionary interface is the standard interface for key/value–based collections such as hashtables, maps, and property bags. Similar to the IList interface, it provides the functionality inherent in ICollection and IEnumerable, as well as the ability to access elements in the collection based on key, remove them, search the collection for an element, and access lists of the keys and values already in the collection. The interface looks like this:

```
public interface IDictionary : ICollection, IEnumerable {
    object this[object key] {get; set};
    ICollection Keys {get;}
    ICollection Values {get;}
    void Clear();
    bool Contains(object value);
    IDictionaryEnumerator GetEnumerator();
    void Remove(object key);
}
```

Predefined Collection Classes

The FCL provides a reasonably comprehensive set of prebuilt data structures providing concrete implementations of all the interfaces described in this chapter. However, since C# does not yet support generics, the implementations work in terms of the generic object type, which has the same disadvantages (excessive casting, boxing) as the generic IEnumerator interface described earlier. If you prefer more type-safe collection classes, you may use one of these predefined types as a starting point for your own type-safe variant.

The Array Class

The Array class is the canonical aggregate data structure in the FCL, representing a fixed-size array of object references of uniform type. Since the Array data structure is fundamental, the C# language provides explicit array declaration and initialization syntax (for more details, see Chapters 2 and 3). The storage for the array is allocated on the GC heap at the time a class is instantiated, and cannot change (see the ArrayList class for a growable array-like data structure). The Array class implements ICollection, IList, and IEnumerable, so arrays can be treated as lists, generic cloneable collections, or sets of elements that can be enumerated. In addition, the Array class supports sorting and searching of the array. Sorting of the array is often accomplished by delegating to IComparable implementations on the contained elements, which requires that you implement IComparable on types that are intended for use in arrays that need to be sorted. The following is an example of using the Array class:

```
string[ ] strs1 = { "time", "the", "now", "is" };
Array.Reverse(strs1);
Array strs2 = Array.CreateInstance(typeof(string), 4);
strs2.SetValue("for", 0);
strs2.SetValue("all", 1);
strs2.SetValue("good", 2);
strs2.SetValue("men", 3);
Array strings = Array.CreateInstance(typeof(string), 8);
Array.Copy(strs1, strings, 4);
strs2.CopyTo(strings, 4);
foreach (string s in strings)
    Console.WriteLine(s);
```

The ArrayList Class

The ArrayList class provides a dynamically sized array of objects that implements the IList interface. An ArrayList works by maintaining an internal array of objects that is replaced with a larger array when it reaches its capacity of elements. It is very efficient at adding elements (since there is usually a free slot at the end), but is inefficient at inserting elements (since all elements have to be shifted to make a free slot). Searching can be efficient if the BinarySearch( ) method is used on an ArrayList that has been sorted, but is otherwise inefficient as it requires that each item is checked individually. The following is an example of using the ArrayList class:

```
ArrayList a = new ArrayList();
a.Add("Vernon");
a.Add("Corey");
a.Add("William");
a.Add("Muzz");
a.Sort();
for (int i = 0; i < a.Count; i++)
    Console.WriteLine(a[i]);
```

The Hashtable Class

A Hashtable is a standard dictionary (key/value) data structure that uses a hashing algorithm to store and index values efficiently. This hashing algorithm is performed using the hashcode returned by the GetHashCode() method on System. Object. Types stored in a Hashtable should therefore override GetHashCode() to return a good hash of the object's internal value. Hashtable also implements the IDictionary interface, and therefore can also be manipulated as a normal dictionary data structure. The following is an example of using the Hashtable class:

```
Hashtable ht = new Hashtable();
ht["One"] = 1;
ht["Two"] = 2;
ht["Three"] = 3;
Console.WriteLine(ht["Two"]); // Prints "2"
```

The Queue Class

A Queue is a standard first-in first-out (FIFO) data structure, providing simple operations to enqueue, dequeue, peek at the element at the top of the queue, etc. The following is an example of using the Queue class:

```
Queue q = new Queue();
q.Enqueue(1);
q.Enqueue(2);
Console.WriteLine(q.Dequeue()); // Prints "1"
Console.WriteLine(q.Dequeue()); // Prints "2"
```

The Stack Class

A Stack is a standard last-in first-out (LIFO) data structure, providing simple operations to Push and Pop elements on and off the stack. The following is an example of using the Stack class:

```
Stack s = new Stack();
s.Push(1); // Stack = 1
s.Push(2); // Stack = 1,2
s.Push(3); // Stack = 1,2,3
Console.WriteLine(s.Pop()); // Prints 3, Stack=1,2
Console.WriteLine(s.Pop()); // Prints 2, Stack=1
Console.WriteLine(s.Pop()); // Prints 1, Stack=
```

The BitArray Class

A BitArray is a dynamically sized array of bool values. It is more memory-efficient than a simple array of bools, because it uses only one bit for each value, whereas a bool array uses one byte for each value. The following is an example of using the BitArray class:

```
BitArray bits = new BitArray( );
bits.Length = 2;
bits[1] = true;
bits.Xor(bits); // Xor the array with itself
```

The SortedList Class

A SortedList is a standard dictionary data structure that uses a binary-chop search to index efficiently. SortedList implements the IDictionary interface and is manipulated like any other dictionary data structure. SortedList also implements the ICollection and IEnumerable interfaces. The following is an example of using a SortedList:

```
SortedList s = new SortedList( );
s["Zebra"] = 1;
s["Antelope"] = 2;
s["Eland"] = 3;
s["Giraffe"] = 4;
s["Meerkat"] = 5;
s["Dassie"] = 6;
s["Tokoloshe"] = 7;
Console.WriteLine(s["Meerkat"]); // Prints "5" in 3 lookups
```

The StringCollection Class

The StringCollection class is a standard collection data structure for storing strings. StringCollection implements the ICollection interface and can be manipulated like any other collection data structure. The following is an example of using a StringCollection:

```
StringCollection sc = new StringCollection( );
sc.Add("s1");
string[ ] sarr = {"s2", "s3", "s4"};
sc.AddRange(sarr);
foreach (string s in sc)
  Console.Write("{0} ", s); // s1 s2 s3 s4
```

The StringDictionary Class

The StringDictionary class is a dictionary data structure for storing key/value pairs in which the type of the key is a string. This class offers very similar methods to the Hashtable class, although the only standard interface it implements is IEnumerable. The following is an example of using a StringDictionary:

```
StringDictionary sd = new StringDictionary( );
sd["One"] = 1;
sd["Two"] = 2;
```

```
sd["Three"] = 3;
Console.WriteLine(sd["Two"]); // Prints "2"
```

Ordering Instances

The implementations of the collection classes' sorting and searching capabilities
depend on certain facilities in the contained objects themselves. The most
common of these are the ability to order the contained objects (used for sorting
and efficient searching) and the ability to hash an object (to speed storage and
retrieval in dictionary-based structures such as Hashtable). As with most other
parts of the FCL's collections framework, this is accomplished via standardized
interfaces and overridden virtual methods on System.Object.

The IComparable Interface

The IComparable interface allows one object to indicate its ordering relative to
another instance of the same type. To allow sorting and searching of your types in
an array, implement the IComparable interface, which looks like this:

```
public interface IComparable {
    int CompareTo(object rhs);
}
```

Implementation of this interface should follow the following semantic rules:

1. If a comes before b → a.CompareTo(b) < 0
2. If a is equal b → a.CompareTo(b) == 0
3. If a comes after b → a.CompareTo(b) > 0
4. null comes first: a.CompareTo(null) > 0
5. a.CompareTo(b) → a.GetType() == b.GetType()

An example implementation of this interface might look like this:

```
public sealed class Person : IComparable {
   public string Name;
   public int Age;
   public int CompareTo(object o) {
// Check for null
      if (o==null) return 1;
// Check for concrete type match
      if (o.GetType() != this.GetType())
         throw new ArgumentException();
// Sort instances by ascending Age
      Person rhs = (Person)o;
      if (Age < rhs.Age) return -1;
      if (Age > rhs.Age) return 1;
      return 0;
   }
}
```

Note that in this example Person is marked as sealed. This is intended to simplify
implementation, which can be complex in the face of future, unexpected inheritance. Remember to always ensure that the rules in the semantic contract are

followed, including the one that states you can only compare identical types. One way of enforcing this is by explicitly comparing the types using GetType( ), as the previous sample does. Additionally, ensure that comparing to a null reference doesn't throw an exception, but returns 0, which sorts the null entries to the front of the list.

Implementing IComparable allows you to provide a default ordering for a type. However, sometimes more than one ordering for a type is needed. This can be accomplished using implementations of the IComparer interface.

The IComparer Interface

The collection classes actually perform their sorting using an implementation of the IComparer interface, which compares two independent object instances for their relative ordering. The IComparer interface looks likes this:

```
public interface IComparer {
  int Compare(object x, object y);
}
```

You generally don't need to implement this interface, since a default implementation that delegates to the IComparable interface is already provided by the Comparer type (which is used by the Array class by default). However, if you wish to provide additional ordering options for a type, you can provide additional concrete implementations of the IComparer interface that performed type-specific comparisons (these are often implemented as nested helper types).

Generating Hash Code

All object instances can provide a signed 32-bit integer hash of their contents via the GetHashCode( ) method on System.Object. Good hashes can have a dramatic effect on Hashtable speed (they are used to determine which bucket to add entries to in the hashtable), and can also provide a low-fidelity (but possibly more efficient) equivalence test. Using GetHashCode in this way is demonstrated in the following examples:

```
void Enroll(Student s, CourseList cl) {
  hashtable.Add(s, cl); // GHC called on key (s)
}
bool FastCompare(Student s1, Student s2) {
  // Use GHC to test for possible equivalence
  if (s1.GetHashCode( ) != s2.GetHashCode( )) return false;

  // Use Equals to test for definite equivalence
  return s1.Equals(s2);
}
```

The default implementation of GetHashCode( ) on System.Object returns a semi-unique member #, while the implementation of GetHashCode( ) on System.ValueType merely returns the hash of the first field in the value type. Although these defaults work in a lot of cases, there are sometimes performance benefits gained from implementing GetHashCode( ) on your own type. Additionally, if a type overrides the Equals( ) method, it is required to override the GetHashCode( ) method, which means that many framework types override GetHashCode( ), as shown here:

```
void DumpHashes(object o, int i, Version v) {
    Console.WriteLine(o.GetHashCode()); // object index
    Console.WriteLine(i.GetHashCode()); // integer value
    Console.WriteLine(v.GetHashCode()); // hash of fields
}
```

The Object.GetHashCode Method

The System.GetHashCode method is declared as follows:

```
public virtual int GetHashCode();
```

It is important to understand the general contract for GetHashCode( ), which looks like this:

1. A.GetHashCode( ) → even distribution across all a's
2. a.Equals(b) → a.GetHashCode( ) == b.GetHashCode( )
3. A overrides GetHashCode → A overrides Equals
4. Safe: no exceptions thrown; no circular references

The idea is that good implementations use all 32 bits to provide a good even distribution and ideally preserve the significance of field ordering (to ensure that Point(10,20) hashes differently to Point(20,10)). Preserving field ordering is traditionally done by multiplying the hash for each field by some odd prime constant (37 is a popular choice in the Java world, in which a similar construct exists). Additionally, if you have not derived directly from System.Object, consider combining the hash of your base type with the hash of your contained members. Lastly, remember that contained aggregate data structures (such as Arrays) may not hash their contents correctly, and therefore may need to be hashed by hand. The following is an example implementing some of these rules, in order to provide a good hash distribution that includes all the type's data in the hash calculation.

```
public sealed class Data {
    public readonly short x, y;
    public readonly Color c;
    ArrayList al = new ArrayList();

    public override int GetHashCode() {
        int hc = 1; // base.GetHashCode if base!=object
        hc = 37*hc + x<<16|(ushort)x;
        hc = 37*hc + y.GetHashCode();
        hc = 37*hc + (c==null ? 0 : c.GetHashCode());
        foreach (object o in al)
            hc = 37*hc + o.GetHashCode();
        return hc;
    }
}
```

8

XML I/O

XML has, for better or worse, taken the programming industry by storm. It has become, in a matter of a few short years, the *de facto* standard for exchanging data between heterogeneous systems as well as the format of choice for storing just about any kind of data. The .NET runtime uses XML as part of its configuration, and the .NET Framework contains a redesigned set of classes for accessing, consuming, producing, and transforming XML documents.

This chapter introduces the built-in support for XML, explains the relationships between XML and the I/O system in general, demonstrates the consumption and production of XML documents in both node-based and Infoset-based forms, highlights the use of XPath, and finally explores XSLT. All types within this namespace come from the System.Xml and System.Xml.XPath namespaces and are contained in the System.Xml.dll assembly. (When using these types, remember to reference the assembly either at the command line or from Visual Studio's project dialogs.)

Accessing XML Documents

Like the I/O mechanism described in Chapter 10, the XML libraries in the .NET FCL follow a pattern of an "abstract base class with concrete backing store implementation classes." The two abstract base classes themselves are XmlReader and XmlWriter, used respectively for consuming and producing XML.

XmlReader

The XmlReader class, as its name implies, provides the ability to consume XML documents. It is an abstract base class, intended to be subclassed for working against a particular source of XML. There are three concrete implementations of XmlReader in the FCL: XmlTextReader (used for parsing XML from any arbitrary stream of text), XmlNodeReader (used for parsing XML from an XmlNode), and

XmlValidatingReader, which is an XmlReader that performs DTD and/or Schema validation against the parsed document.

Most often, an XmlTextReader is all that's necessary to begin working with XML input, as shown in the following example:

```
using System.Xml;
class XmlFun {
  static void Main( ) {
    XmlTextReader tr = new XmlTextReader("xmlfun.xml");
    // use tr as described later
  }
}
```

This code expects to find a file named *xmlfun.xml* within the current directory. This constructor is a shortcut notation for the more powerful Stream-based constructor that XmlTextReader also supports:

```
using System.IO;
using System.Xml;
class XmlFun {
  static void Main( ) {
    XmlTextReader tr =
      new XmlTextReader(
        new TextReader(
          new FileStream("xmlfun.xml", FileMode.Open)));
    // use tr as described later
  }
}
```

This highlights an important point: XmlTextReader can pull XML from any Stream-based input source, including HTTP URLs and database text columns. For example, it becomes possible to parse XML out of an in-memory String-based representation:

```
using System.IO;
using System.Xml;
class XmlFun {
  static void Main( ) {
    string xmlContent =
      "<book>" +
      "  <title>C# in a Nutshell</title>" +
      "  <author>Drayton</author>" +
      "  <author>Neward</author>" +
      "  <author>Albahari</author>" +
      "</book>";

    XmlTextReader tr =
      new XmlTextReader(new StringReader(xmlContent));
  }
}
```

The ability to parse in-memory strings permits the parsing of XML-generated in-process without having to write the XML first to a file. This can be particularly powerful as a means of decoupling between components.

Once the XmlReader instance is created, it can be used to extract the XML elements in a pull-driven mode. XmlReader itself serves as a cursor to the various XML constructs contained within the stream, such as elements, attributes, and so forth. The current construct can be accessed using a variety of properties: Name (to return the qualified name of the element or attribute), Value (to return the value of the raw text), and so on. The Read method is commonly used to iterate to the next element in the stream; otherwise, one of the various MoveXXX methods, such as MoveToNextElement, can be used to perform higher-level navigation within the stream. (Note that all navigation must be forward-only; once bypassed, a node cannot be retrieved.) The following code demonstrates how to pull all the XML elements from an XML stream and echo them back to the console:

```
using System;
using System.IO;
using System.Xml;
class XmlFun {
  static void Main( ) {
    try
    {
      string xmlContent =
        "<book>" +
        "  <title>C# in a Nutshell</title>" +
        "  <authors>" +
        "    <author>Drayton</author>" +
        "    <author>Neward</author>" +
        "    <author>Albahari</author>" +
        "  </authors>" +
        "</book>";

      XmlTextReader reader =
        new XmlTextReader(new StringReader(xmlContent));

      //Parse the file and display each of the nodes.
      while (reader.Read( ))
      {
        switch (reader.NodeType)
        {
          case XmlNodeType.Element:
            Console.Write("<{0}>", reader.Name);
            break;
          case XmlNodeType.Text:
            Console.Write(reader.Value);
            break;
          case XmlNodeType.CDATA:
            Console.Write("<![CDATA[{0}]]>", reader.Value);
            break;
          case XmlNodeType.ProcessingInstruction:
            Console.Write("<?{0} {1}?>", reader.Name, reader.Value);
            break;
          case XmlNodeType.Comment:
            Console.Write("<!--{0}-->", reader.Value);
            break;
          case XmlNodeType.XmlDeclaration:
```

```
            Console.Write("<?xml version='1.0'?>");
            break;
         case XmlNodeType.Document:
            break;
         case XmlNodeType.DocumentType:
            Console.Write("<!DOCTYPE {0} [{1}]", reader.Name,
               reader.Value);
            break;
         case XmlNodeType.EntityReference:
            Console.Write(reader.Name);
            break;
         case XmlNodeType.EndElement:
            Console.Write("</{0}>", reader.Name);
            break;
      }
    }
   }
  }
}
```

In the preceding example, the actual data of interest is found in either the Name or Value property of the XmlTextReader, depending on the actual type of the Read node.

XmlWriter

Just as XmlReader serves as the abstract type for consuming XML, XmlWriter serves as an abstract type for producing XML-compliant data. It is always possible to emit XML "in the raw" by creating a String and appending XML tags to it, as in the following:

```
string xml = "<greeting>" +
messageOfTheDay +
"< /greeting>";
```

However, there are numerous problems with this technique, most notably the possibility that typos and accidental programmer errors will render the XML ill-formed and therefore unparseable. XmlWriter provides a less error-prone way of generating well-formed XML. The following code generates the XML data string of the preceding example (without the XML error), complete with document declaration:

```
XmlTextWriter xw = new XmlTextWriter("greetings.xml", null);
xw.Formatting = Formatting.Indented;
xw.Indentation = 2;
xw.WriteStartDocument();
xw.WriteStartElement("greeting");
xw.WriteString(messageOfTheDay);
xw.WriteEndElement();
xw.WriteEndDocument();
xw.Close();
```

This writes the XML to a file named *greetings.xml*, indenting the code two spaces on each level. To write the data to an in-memory string, pass either a System.IO.

TextWriter instance into the constructor of XmlTextWriter, or else pass a System. IO.Stream object and a System.Text.Encoding enumeration instance (to tell the Writer how to treat character data; by default, it uses UTF-8).

Parsing an XML Stream

Of course, simply reading and writing XML in this form, while of some use, is somewhat limiting. Much of XML's attraction is in its ability to provide structure over data; using XmlReader "in the raw," however, hides the very hierarchical structure XML imposes. In many cases, XML data is best viewed as an arranged tree of data, complete with the XML structuring elements (the tags and attributes surrounding the data) found within it.

Fortunately, the .NET XML architecture supports such a view, using the XmlDocument class to model the entire XML document itself. To see the hierarchical structure in an XML document, you must first pass the XML into the XmlDocument instance for parsing:

```
XmlDocument doc = new XmlDocument( );
doc.Load(new XmlReader(...));
```

Alternatively, you can use LoadXml to parse an arbitrary string instance.

Once the XmlDocument is populated with data, the document's document element can be obtained from the XmlDocument instance via the DocumentElement property. From there, it is a simple matter to walk the various child nodes, all the way to the elements of interest:

```
XmlNode docNode = doc.DocumentElement;
//print out all the first-level children
foreach (XmlNode n in docNode.ChildNodes)
    System.Console.WriteLine(n.Name);
```

At this point, navigation becomes an exercise in using the various properties and methods on XmlNode. The Attributes property returns an XmlAttributeCollection containing the attributes (if any) on this node, the ChildNodes property (shown in the previous code snippet) returns an XmlNodeList instance containing the child nodes of this node, and the Name and Value properties return various information depending on the current node's type.

Selecting Nodes Using XPath

Walking the resulting tree of XmlNode instances that is created by XML readers can be tedious and error-prone in its own right, particularly when a specific set of nodes scattered throughout the tree is desired. To address this requirement, the W3C defined a query API called XPath for selecting nodes within an Infoset (the tree-like hierarchy a DOM-compliant parser transforms XML input into, according to the W3C Specifications) representation. In the .NET XML libraries, this is implemented by specifying the IXPathNavigable interface, with any type that supports the interface in turn supporting XPath queries against it.

Without the availability of XPath, programmers must write code like that in the following example in order to list the author names found in a given book element:

```csharp
using System;
using System.IO;
using System.Xml;

class App
{
  public static void Main(string[] args)
  {
    string xmlContent =
      "<book>" +
      " <title>C# in a Nutshell</title>" +
      " <authors>" +
      "   <author>Drayton</author>" +
      "   <author>Neward</author>" +
      "   <author>Albahari</author>" +
      " </authors>" +
      "</book>";
    XmlTextReader xtr =
      new XmlTextReader(new StringReader(xmlContent));

    XmlDocument doc = new XmlDocument();
    doc.Load(xtr);
    XmlNode docElement = doc.DocumentElement;

    // This gets us title and authors
    foreach (XmlNode n2 in docElement.ChildNodes)
    {
      if (n2.Name == "authors")
      {
        // This gets us author tags
        foreach (XmlNode n3 in n2.ChildNodes)
        {
          // This gets us the text inside the author tag;
          // could also get the child element, a text node,
          // and examine its Value property
          Console.WriteLine(n3.InnerText);
        }
      }
    }
  }
}
```

Because, however, XMLNode implements the IXPathNavigable interface, we can instead write an XPath query that does the selection for us, as well as returns an XmlNodeList that we can walk in the usual fashion:

```csharp
using System;
using System.IO;
using System.Xml;

class App
{
```

```
public static void Main(string[ ] args)
{
  string xmlContent =
    "<book>" +
    "  <title>C# in a Nutshell</title>" +
    "  <authors>" +
    "    <author>Drayton</author>" +
    "    <author>Neward</author>" +
    "    <author>Albahari</author>" +
    "  </authors>" +
    "</book>";
  XmlTextReader xtr =
    new XmlTextReader(new StringReader(xmlContent));

  XmlDocument doc = new XmlDocument( );
  doc.Load(xtr);
  XmlNode docElement = doc.DocumentElement;

  XmlNodeList result =
    docElement.SelectNodes("/book/authors/author/text( )");
  foreach (XmlNode n in result)
  {
    Console.WriteLine(n.Value);
  }
}
}
```

While the preceding code may not seem like much of an improvement over the earlier XPath-free approach, the real power of XPath becomes apparent when doing far more complex queries. For example, consider the following code, which returns the list of books authored by either Drayton or Neward:

```
using System;
using System.IO;
using System.Xml;

class App
{
  public static void Main(string[ ] args)
  {
    string xmlContent =
      "<book>" +
      "  <title>C# in a Nutshell</title>" +
      "  <authors>" +
      "    <author>Drayton</author>" +
      "    <author>Neward</author>" +
      "    <author>Albahari</author>" +
      "  </authors>" +
      "</book>";
    XmlTextReader xtr =
      new XmlTextReader(new StringReader(xmlContent));

    XmlDocument doc = new XmlDocument( );
    doc.Load(xtr);
```

```
XmlNode docElement = doc.DocumentElement;

XmlNodeList result =
  docElement.SelectNodes("/book" +
                        "[authors/author/text( )='Drayton' or " +
                        "authors/author/text( )='Neward']" +
                        "/title/text( )");
foreach (XmlNode n in result)
{
  Console.WriteLine(n.Value);
}
}
}
```

Notice that in the XPath-related code, the conditional logic is contained within the XPath statement itself—the subquery contained inside the square brackets acts as a predicate constraining the rest of the statement. Writing the code to produce similar results in C# would be at least a page long. You can find more information on XPath in *XML in a Nutshell*, by Elliotte Rusty Harold and W. Scott Means, or *Learning XML*, by Erik T. Ray (both published by O'Reilly).

Transforming a Document Using XSLT

A frequent usage of XPath is to find nodes for extraction and possible transformation into other XML documents, or into non-XML data, such as HTML or flat-file format for legacy consumption. While XPath provides a powerful API for selecting nodes from within an Infoset, writing the procedural code to execute query after query, along with the code to execute against each query result, is tedious and error-prone. Again, the W3C has anticipated this need and provided another XML-based standard, the XSL: Transformations specification (in which XSL originally stood for "eXtensible Stylesheet Language:"), for doing precisely this.

In the following example, we continue to use this XML book as our source data:

```
<book>
  <title>C# in a Nutshell</title>
  <authors>
    <author>Drayton</author>
    <author>Neward</author>
    <author>Albahari</author>
  </authors>
</book>
```

Suppose you wish to transform this source XML into a format more suitable for end-user consumption, such as HTML. For purely pedagogical reasons, we wish the title to display in bold font in an H1-style heading, with the authors' names displayed in order in italic text.

Certainly, you could write the necessary C# code to execute two XPath queries, one to retrieve the title of the book (/book/title/text( )) and another to retrieve the list of authors for the book (/book/authors/author/text( )). You could then take each resulting XmlNodeList, walk through the results, and echo the HTML back to the caller. However, it is much simpler to write a single file that describes

---

these transformation rules without having to worry about how the work gets done:

```
<xsl:transform xmlns:xsl="">
  <xsl:template match="title">
    <h1><xsl:value-of select="text( )" /></h1>
  </xsl:template>
  <xsl:template match="author">
    <i><xsl:value-of select="text( )" /></i>
  </xsl:template>
</xsl:transform>
```

When this transform is run through an XSLT engine, the engine starts at the root node of the source XML (our book element, in this case), and begins to evaluate each <xsl:template> rule specified. Here, the <xsl:template> tags specify a criteria (i.e., an XPath set of nodes) that indicate when this template should be invoked. If a match occurs (such as the case when the current node is the book/title node against the first template in the XSLT), the body of the <xsl:template> tag is fired. Literal text, such as the <h1> and </h1> text, is copied directly to the XSLT engine's output stream; other XSLT tags are in turn evaluated. The <xsl:value-of> tag also specifies an XPath query, but takes the resulting nodes and echoes their "values" (the text in the case of a text( ) node) to the XSLT engine's output stream. Thus, running an XSLT engine using the books that XML input and the XSLT transformation described earlier produces the following:

```
<h1>C# In A Nutshell</h1><i>Drayton</i><i>Neward</i><i>Albahari</i>
```

This is, of course, browseable HTML.

The .NET Framework Class Library support for XML includes the programmatic execution of XSLT, using the System.Xml.Xsl.XslTransform class:

```
using System;
using System.IO;
using System.Xml;
using System.Xml.Xsl;

class App
{
  public static void Main(string[ ] args)
  {
    // Load the transform int the XSLT Engine
    XslTransform transform = new XslTransform( );
    transform.Load("book2html.xsl");

    /* book2html.xsl contains this code:
      <xsl:transform xmlns:xsl="http://www.w3.org/1999/XSL/Transform">
        <xsl:template match="title">
          <h1><xsl:value-of select="text( )" /></h1>
        </xsl:template>
        <xsl:template match="author">
          <i><xsl:value-of select="text( )" /></i>
        </xsl:template>
      </xsl:transform>
```

```
    */
    // Obtain the data to transform
    string xmlContent =
      "<book>" +
      "  <title>C# in a Nutshell</title>" +
      "  <authors>" +
      "    <author>Drayton</author>" +
      "    <author>Neward</author>" +
      "    <author>Albahari</author>" +
      "  </authors>" +
      "</book>";
    XmlTextReader xtr =
      new XmlTextReader(new StringReader(xmlContent));
    XmlDocument doc = new XmlDocument( );
    doc.Load(xtr);

    // Define where the results should go
    StringWriter output = new StringWriter( );

    // Transform
    transform.Transform(doc, null, output);

    Console.WriteLine(output);
  }
}
```

This XSLT Engine is quite powerful; the middle argument to the XslTransform object allows the .NET programmer to pass in an argument list, which is a collection of parameters from outside the engine to inside the engine, including callback methods that the XSLT Engine can invoke (using Microsoft-specific extensions) when a particular rule is evaluated. See the System.Xsl.Xsl namespace for more details on .NET's support for XSLT. See *XSLT*, by Doug Tidwell (O'Reilly) for more general information on XSLT.

9

Networking

The FCL includes a number of types that make accessing networked resources easy. Offering different levels of abstraction, these types allow an application to ignore much of the detail normally required to access networked resources while retaining a high degree of control.

This chapter describes the core networking support in the FCL, and provides numerous examples leveraging the predefined classes. The types mentioned in this section all exist in the System.Net and System.Net.Sockets namespaces.

Network Programming Models

High-level access is performed using a set of types that implement a generic request/response architecture, which is extensible, to support new protocols. The implementation of this architecture in the FCL also includes HTTP-specific extensions to make interacting with web servers easy.

Should the application require lower-level access to the network, types exist to support the Transmission Control Protocol (TCP) and User Datagram Protocol (UDP). Finally, in situations in which direct transport-level access is required, there are types that provide raw socket access.

Generic Request/Response Architecture

The request/response architecture is based on Uniform Resource Indicator (URI) and stream I/O, follows the factory design pattern, and makes good use of abstract types and interfaces. A factory method, WebRequest.Create( ), parses the URI and creates the appropriate protocol handler to fulfill the request.

Protocol handlers share a common abstract base type (WebRequest), which exposes properties that configure the request and methods used to retrieve the response.

Responses are also represented as types and share a common abstract base type (WebResponse), which exposes a NetworkStream, providing a simple streams-based I/O and easy integration into the rest of the FCL.

This example is a simple implementation of the popular Unix snarf utility. It demonstrates the use of the WebRequest and WebResponse classes to retrieve the contents of a URI and print them to the console:

```
// Snarf.cs
// Run Snarf.exe <http-uri> to retrieve a web page
// e.g. snarf.exe http://www.oreilly.com/catalog/csharpnut/
using System;
using System.IO;
using System.Net;
using System.Text;
class Snarf {
  static void Main(string[ ] args) {

    // Retrieve the data at the URL with a WebRequest instance
    WebRequest req = WebRequest.Create(args[0]);
    WebResponse resp = req.GetResponse( );

    // Read in the data, performing ASCII->Unicode encoding
    Stream s = resp.GetResponseStream( );
    StreamReader sr = new StreamReader(s, Encoding.ASCII);
    string doc = sr.ReadToEnd( );

    Console.WriteLine(doc); // Print result to console
  }
}
```

HTTP-Specific Support

The request/response architecture inherently supports protocol-specific extensions via the use of subtyping. Since WebRequest.Create( ) creates and returns the appropriate handler type based on the URI, accessing protocol-specific features is as easy as downcasting the returned WebRequest object to the appropriate protocol-specific handler and accessing the extended functionality.

The FCL includes specific support for the HTTP protocol, including the ability to easily access and control elements of an interactive web session, such as the HTTP headers, user-agent strings, proxy support, user credentials, authentication, keep-alives, pipelining, and more.

This example demonstrates the use of the HTTP-specific request/response classes to control the user-agent string for the request and retrieve the server type:

```
// ProbeSvr.cs
// Run ProbeSvr.exe <servername> to retrieve the server type
using System;
using System.Net;
class ProbeSvr {
  static void Main(string[ ] args) {
```

```csharp
// Get instance of WebRequest ABC, convert to HttpWebRequest
WebRequest req = WebRequest.Create(args[0]);
req.Method = "HEAD"; // we're just looking at headers
HttpWebRequest httpReq = (HttpWebRequest)req;

// Access HTTP-specific features such as User-Agent
httpReq.UserAgent = "CSPRProbe/1.0";

// Retrieve response and print to console
WebResponse resp = req.GetResponse();
HttpWebResponse httpResp = (HttpWebResponse)resp;
Console.WriteLine(httpResp.Server);
    }
}
```

WebClient

WebClient provides a higher-level interface to network resources than WebRequest. DownloadData() and DownloadFile() retrieve resources from a URI into a byte array or a file. UploadData() and UploadFile() sends the contents of a byte array or a file to a resource identified by a URI. Use WebClient to rewrite Snarf.cs as:

```csharp
// Snarf2.cs
// Run Snarf.exe <http-uri> to retrieve a web page
using System;
using System.Net;
using System.Text;
class Snarf {
  static void Main(string[] args) {
    WebClient wc = new WebClient();
    byte[] buffer = wc.DownloadData(args[0]);
    string doc = Encoding.ASCII.GetString(buffer);
    Console.WriteLine(doc);
  }
}
```

Adding New Protocol Handlers

Adding handlers to support new protocols is trivial; simply implement a new set of derived types based on WebRequest and WebResponse, implement the IWebRequestCreate interface on your WebRequest-derived type, and register it as a new protocol handler with the WebRequest.RegisterPrefix() at runtime. Once this is done, any code that uses the request/response architecture can access networked resources using the new URI format (and underlying protocol).

Using TCP, UDP, and Sockets

The System.Net.Sockets namespace includes types that provide protocol-level support for TCP and UDP. These types are built on the underlying Socket type, which is itself directly accessible for transport-level access to the network.

Two classes provide the TCP support: TcpListener and TcpClient. TcpListener listens for incoming connections, creating Socket instances that respond to the connection request. TcpClient connects to a remote host, hiding the details of the underlying socket in a Stream-derived type that allows stream I/O over the network.

A class called UdpClient provides the UDP support. UdpClient serves as both a client and a listener, and includes multicast support, allowing individual datagrams to be sent and received as byte arrays.

Both the TCP and the UDP classes help to access the underlying network socket (represented by the Socket class). The Socket class is a thin wrapper over the native Windows sockets functionality and is the lowest level of networking accessible to managed code.

The following example is a simple implementation of the Quote of the Day (qotd) protocol, as defined by the IETF in RFC 865. It demonstrates the use of a TCP listener to accept incoming requests and the use of the lower-level Socket type to fulfill the request:

```
// QOTDListener.cs
// Run QOTDListener.exe to service incoming QOTD requests
using System;
using System.Net;
using System.Net.Sockets;
using System.Text;
class QOTDListener {
  static string[ ] quotes =
{@"Sufficiently advanced magic is indistinguishable from technology --
Terry Pratchett",
 @"Sufficiently advanced technology is indistinguishable from magic --
 Arthur C Clarke" };
  static void Main( ) {

    // Start a TCP listener on port 17
    TcpListener l = new TcpListener(17);
    l.Start( );
    Console.WriteLine("Waiting for clients to connect");
    Console.WriteLine("Press Ctrl+C to quit...");
    int numServed = 1;
    while (true) {

      // Block waiting for an incoming socket connect request
      Socket s = l.AcceptSocket( );

      // Encode alternating quotes as bytes for sending
      Char[ ] carr = quotes[numServed%2].ToCharArray( );
      Byte[ ] barr = Encoding.ASCII.GetBytes(carr);

      // Return data to client, then clean up socket & repeat
      s.Send(barr, barr.Length, 0);
      s.Shutdown(SocketShutdown.Both);
      s.Close( );
```

```
        Console.WriteLine("{0} quotes served...", numServed++);
      }
    }
  }
```

To test this example, run the listener and try connecting to port 17 on localhost using a telnet client. Under Windows 2000, this can be done from the command line by entering:

```
telnet localhost 17
```

Notice the use of Socket.Shutdown and Socket.Close at the end of the while loop; this is required to flush and close the socket immediately, rather than wait for the garbage collector to finalize and collect unreachable Socket objects later.

Using DNS

The networking types in the base class library also support normal and reverse Domain Name System (DNS) resolution. Here's an example using these types:

```
// DNSLookup.cs
// Run DNSLookup.exe <servername> to determine IP addresses
using System;
using System.Net;
class DNSLookup {
  static void Main(string[ ] args) {
    IPHostEntry he = Dns.GetHostByName(args[0]);
    IPAddress[ ] addrs = he.AddressList;
    foreach (IPAddress addr in addrs)
      Console.WriteLine(addr);
  }
}
```

10

Streams and I/O

Almost all nontrivial programs need to store and retrieve persistent data, whether in a database, on a local or remote file system, or over the network. Since this is a common need, many programming environments define an abstraction called a stream that is used to model reading and writing to/from files on disk. The .NET Framework supports this abstraction fully, and also extends it into other areas such as network I/O, buffering and in-memory operations, and cryptographic services.

This chapter introduces the built-in support for streams and I/O, explains the relationships between the abstract and concrete classes in the streams architecture, demonstrates their usage, and finally explores the filesystem-specific support. Unless otherwise stated, the types mentioned in this chapter all exist in the System, System.IO, or System.IO.IsolatedStorage namespaces.

Streams and Backing Stores

The stream is a fundamental abstraction used throughout the .NET Framework to model access to persistent data. A stream represents the flow of data coming in and out of a backing store. A backing store represents the endpoint of a stream. Although a backing store is often a file or network connection, in reality it can represent any medium capable of reading or writing raw data.

A simple example is to use a stream to read and write to a file on disk. However, streams and backing stores are not limited to disk and network I/O. A more sophisticated example is to use the cryptography support in the .NET Framework to encrypt or decrypt a stream of bytes as they move around in memory.

The Abstract Stream Class

Stream is an abstract class that defines operations for reading and writing a stream of raw typeless data as bytes. Once a stream is opened, it stays open and can be read from or written to until the stream is flushed and closed. Flushing a stream updates the writes made to the stream; closing a stream first flushes the stream, then closes the stream.

Stream has the methods CanRead, CanWrite, and CanSeek, for streams that support only sequential access. If a stream supports random access, the SetPosition method can move to a linear position on that stream.

The Stream class provides synchronous and asynchronous read and write operations. By default, an asynchronous method calls the stream's corresponding synchronous method by wrapping the synchronous method in a delegate type and starting a new thread. Similarly, by default, a synchronous method calls the stream's corresponding asynchronous method and waits until the thread has completed its operation. Classes that derive from Stream must override either the synchronous or asynchronous methods but may override both sets of methods if the need arises.

Concrete Stream-Derived Classes

The framework includes a number of different concrete implementations of the abstract base class Stream. Each implementation represents a different storage medium and allows a raw stream of bytes to be read from and written to the backing store.

Examples of this include the FileStream class (which reads and writes bytes to and from a file), the NetworkStream class (which sends and receives bytes over the network), and the stream returned from the static Stream.Null property (which serves as /dev/null for this platform).

The following example creates a text file on disk and uses the abstract File type to write data to it:

```
using System.IO;
class StreamFun {
  static void Main( ) {
    Stream s = new FileStream("foo.txt", FileMode.Create);
    s.WriteByte(67);
    s.WriteByte(35);
    s.Close( );
  }
}
```

In addition, one stream may act as the frontend to another stream, performing additional processing on the underlying stream as needed. Examples of this include stream encryption/decryption and stream buffering.

The following is an example that converts the file output from the previous sample into its Base64 representation using the CryptoStream class:

```
using System;
using System.IO;
using System.Security.Cryptography;
class EncoderFun {
  static void Main( ) {
    Stream stm = new FileStream("foo.txt", FileMode.Open, FileAccess.Read);
```

```
        ICryptoTransform ict = new ToBase64Transform( );
        CryptoStream cs = new CryptoStream(stm, ict, CryptoStreamMode.Read);
        TextReader tr = new StreamReader(cs);
        string s = tr.ReadToEnd( );
        Console.WriteLine(s);
    }
}
```

Encapsulating Raw Streams

While the Stream class reads and writes raw bytes, most programs prefer to
produce and consume data either in the form of native data types or lines of text.
To make this easy, the framework includes related pairs of XXXReader/XXXWriter
classes that provide this higher-level, encapsulated access to the raw underlying
data stream.

The BinaryReader and BinaryWriter Classes

BinaryReader and BinaryWriter are concrete classes that define operations for
reading and writing a stream of native data types. The most fundamental operations of the BinaryReader and BinaryWriter classes are the methods that read and
write instances of the primitive data types: bool, byte, char, decimal, float,
double, short, int, long, sbyte, ushort, uint, and ulong. Additionally, methods are
provided to read and write strings and arrays of the primitive data types.

Imagine we have a simple class, defined as follows, that we want to read and write
from a stream:

```
public class Student {
    public string Name;
    public int     Age;
    public double GPA;
}
```

Methods that read and write instances of the Student class from a stream in a
binary format might look like this:

```
void SaveToStream(Stream stm, Student s) {
    BinaryWriter bw = new BinaryWriter(stm);
    bw.Write(s.Name);
    bw.Write(s.Age);
    bw.Write(s.GPA);
    bw.Flush( ); // Ensure the BinaryWriter buffer is empty
}
void ReadFromStream(Stream stm, Student s) {
    BinaryReader br = new BinaryReader(stm);
    s.Name = br.ReadString( );
    s.Age = br.ReadInt32( );
    s.GPA = br.ReadDouble( );
}
```

The Abstract TextReader and TextWriter Classes

TextReader and TextWriter are abstract base classes that define operations for reading and writing a stream of characters. The most fundamental operations of the TextReader and TextWriter classes are the methods that read and write a single character to or from a stream.

The TextReader class provides default implementations for methods that read in an array of characters or a string representing a line of characters. The TextWriter class provides default implementations for methods that write an array of characters, as well as methods that convert common types (optionally with formatting options) to a sequence of characters.

The framework includes a number of different concrete implementations of the abstract base classes TextReader and TextWriter. Some of the most prominent include StreamReader and StreamWriter, and StringReader and StringWriter.

The StreamReader and StreamWriter Classes

StreamReader and StreamWriter are concrete classes that derive from TextReader and TextWriter, respectively, and operate on a Stream that may be passed as a constructor parameter.

These classes allow you to combine a Stream (which can have a backing store but knows only about raw data) with a TextReader or TextWriter (which knows about character data, but doesn't have a backing store).

In addition, StreamReader and StreamWriter can perform special translations between characters and raw bytes. Such translations include translating Unicode characters to ANSI characters to either big-endian or little-endian format.

Assuming the existence of a Student class as defined in the previous example, methods to read and write instances of the Student class to/from a stream in a binary format might look like this:

```
void SaveToStream(Stream stm, Student s) {
  TextWriter tw = new StreamWriter(stm);
  tw.WriteLine(s.Name);
  tw.WriteLine(s.Age);
  tw.WriteLine(s.GPA);
  tw.Flush( ); // Ensure the TextWriter buffer is empty
}
void ReadFromStream(Stream stm, Student s) {
  TextReader tr = new StreamReader(stm);
  s.Name = tr.ReadLine( );
  s.Age = Int32.Parse(tr.ReadLine( ));
  s.GPA = Double.Parse(tr.ReadLine( ));
}
```

The StringReader and StringWriter Classes

StringReader and StringWriter are concrete classes that derive from TextReader and TextWriter, respectively, and operate on a string or StringBuilder, which may be passed in as a constructor parameter.

The StringReader class can be thought of as the simplest possible read-only backing store, because it simply performs read operations on the underlying string. Also, the StringWriter class can be thought of as the simplest possible write-only backing store, because it simply performs write operations on that StringBuilder.

The following example uses a StringWriter wrapped around an underlying StringBuilder backing store to write to a string:

```
using System;
using System.IO;
using System.Text;
class Test {
  static void Main( ) {
    StringBuilder sb = new StringBuilder( );
    StringWriter sw = new StringWriter(sb);
    WriteHello(sw);
    Console.WriteLine(sb);
  }
  static void WriteHello(TextWriter tw) {
    tw.Write("Hello, String I/O!");
  }
}
```

Directories and Files

The File and Directory classes contain static methods and properties that encapsulate the operations typically associated with file I/O, such as copying, moving, deleting, renaming, and enumerating files and directories.

The actual manipulation of the contents of a file is done with a FileStream. The File class has methods that return a FileStream, though you may directly instantiate a FileStream.

Reading and Writing Files

This example reads in and prints out the first line of a text file specified on the command line:

```
using System;
using System.IO;
class FileDumper {
  static void Main(string[ ] args) {
    Stream s = File.OpenRead(args[0]);
    StreamReader sr = new StreamReader(s);
    Console.WriteLine(sr.ReadLine( ));
    sr.Close( );
  }
}
```

Examining Directories

To examine the contents of the filesystem, use the DirectoryInfo and FileInfo
classes, both of which are derived from a common FileSystemInfo base class.
These provide access to most of the filesystem information, which the following
example demonstrates by replicating the results of the dir command:

```csharp
using System;
using System.IO;
using System.Text;
class DirCommand {
  static void Main( ) {
    long numFiles=0, numDirs=0, totalBytes=0;
    string currentDir = Directory.GetCurrentDirectory( );
    DirectoryInfo currentDirInfo = new DirectoryInfo(currentDir);
    StringBuilder sb = new StringBuilder( );
    sb.AppendFormat(" Directory of {0}\n\n", currentDirInfo.FullName);
    DirectoryInfo rootDirInfo = currentDirInfo.Root;
    if (rootDirInfo != null) {
      sb.AppendFormat("{0:dd/MM/yyyy  hh:mm tt}    <DIR>          .\n",
                    rootDirInfo.LastWriteTime);
      numDirs++;
    }
    DirectoryInfo parentDirInfo = currentDirInfo.Parent;
    if (parentDirInfo != null) {
      sb.AppendFormat("{0:dd/MM/yyyy  hh:mm tt}    <DIR>          ..\n",
                    parentDirInfo.LastWriteTime);
      numDirs++;
    }
    FileSystemInfo[ ] fsis = currentDirInfo.GetFileSystemInfos( );
    foreach (FileSystemInfo fsi in fsis) {
      FileInfo fi = fsi as FileInfo;
      if (fi != null) {
        sb.AppendFormat("{0:dd/MM/yyyy  hh:mm tt}    {1,14:N0} {2}\n",
                      fi.LastWriteTime, fi.Length, fi.Name);
        numFiles++;
        totalBytes += fi.Length;
      }
      DirectoryInfo di = fsi as DirectoryInfo;
      if (di != null) {
        sb.AppendFormat("{0:dd/MM/yyyy  hh:mm tt}    <DIR>          {1}\n",
                      di.LastWriteTime, di.Name);
        numDirs++;
      }
    }
    sb.AppendFormat("{0,16:G} File(s) {1,14:N0} bytes\n", numFiles,
                  totalBytes);
    sb.AppendFormat("{0,16:G} Dir(s)\n", numDirs);
    Console.WriteLine(sb.ToString( ));
  }
}
```

Catching Filesystem Events

To monitor a filesystem for changes (creation, modification, or deletion of a file, for example), use a FileSystemWatcher with the FileSystemEventHandler, RenamedEventHandler, and ErrorEventHandler delegates. ErrorEventHandler does not inform you of filesystem errors. Instead, it indicates that the FileSystemWatcher's event buffer overflowed because it was overwhelmed by Changed, Created, Deleted, or Renamed events.

The following example monitors whatever directory you specify on the command line. Run it using the name of an existing directory, and then rename, delete, create, and modify some files in that directory:

```
// WatchFS.cs - use WatchFS.exe <path> to monitor file system
using System;
using System.IO;
using System.Threading;
class WatchFS {
  static void FSErrorCallback(object o, ErrorEventArgs eea) {
    Console.WriteLine("Error: {0}", eea.GetException().Message);
  }
  static void FSRenamedCallback(object o, RenamedEventArgs rea) {
    Console.WriteLine("Renamed: {0}->{1}", rea.OldFullPath, rea.FullPath);
  }
  static void FSEventCallback(object o, FileSystemEventArgs fsea) {
    Console.WriteLine("Event: {0}->{1}", fsea.ChangeType,  fsea.FullPath);
  }
  static void Main(string[] args) {
    // Register handlers for file system events
    FileSystemWatcher fsw = new FileSystemWatcher(args[0]);
    fsw.Changed += new FileSystemEventHandler(FSEventCallback);
    fsw.Created += new FileSystemEventHandler(FSEventCallback);
    fsw.Deleted += new FileSystemEventHandler(FSEventCallback);
    fsw.Renamed += new RenamedEventHandler(FSRenamedCallback);
    fsw.Error   += new ErrorEventHandler(FSErrorCallback);
    fsw.EnableRaisingEvents = true;

    Console.WriteLine("Listening for events - press <enter> to end");
    Console.ReadLine(); // Wait for keypress to end
  }
}
```

Asynchronous I/O

I/O doesn't always happen on your terms—all too often, it takes a lot more time than you would like. Since I/O tasks are not necessarily CPU-bound, your code might be free to do some other things while a large file transfer runs in the background. For example, your CPU could be busy handling user input, rather than hanging while your user saves a 10 MB file across a VPN connection that's riding on top of a 56K dialup session.

The .NET Framework provides an asynchronous I/O for these cases. The first thing to do is create a class to maintain state between asynchronous calls. The following example uses the ReadState class to maintain state. It contains a buffer, an input stream, an AsyncCallback, and a StringBuilder. The first three are needed only during the asynchronous calls. The last, which accumulates the contents of the stream during each call, is also used after all the calls have completed.

The AsyncCallback delegate is defined in IOReadCallback. It's responsible for pausing the asynchronous operation using Stream.EndRead( ), appending the contents of the buffer to the StringBuilder, and restarting the operation with Stream.BeginRead( ).

Inside the delegate, the arguments to BeginRead( ) are identical to those used in the first call to BeginRead( ), which kicks off the asynchronous operation in the Main( ) method. Each call to BeginRead( ) returns an IAsyncResult object, which is a token that represents the asynchronous operation. While the asynchronous read is proceeding, the Main( ) method uses System.Net.WebClient to download a file. When it's done, it waits on the IAsyncResult's WaitHandle until the entire file has been read. Then, it prints out the contents of the file.

```
// AsyncRead.cs - use AsyncRead.exe <filename> to test
using System;
using System.IO;
using System.Text;
class AsyncReadFun {
  class AsyncReadState {
    public Stream stm; // Underlying stream
    public byte[ ] buf = new byte[256]; // Read buffer
    public StringBuilder sb = new StringBuilder( ); // Result buffer
    public AsyncCallback acb = new AsyncCallback(AsyncReadCallback);
  }
  static void AsyncReadCallback(IAsyncResult iar) {
    AsyncReadState ars = (AsyncReadState)iar.AsyncState;
    int bytes = ars.stm.EndRead(iar); // Get count of bytes read
    if (bytes > 0) { // Copy read bytes and restart read
      ars.sb.Append(Encoding.ASCII.GetString(ars.buf, 0, bytes));
      Console.WriteLine("Read chunk of {0} bytes", bytes);
      ars.stm.BeginRead(ars.buf, 0, ars.buf.Length, ars.acb, ars);
    }
  }
  static void Main(string[ ] args) {
    // Open the stream & start reading
    Stream s = File.OpenRead(args[0]);
    AsyncReadState ars = new AsyncReadState( );
    ars.stm = s; // Save the stream reference
    IAsyncResult iar = s.BeginRead(ars.buf, 0, ars.buf.Length,
                                   ars.acb, ars);
    // Download a file while we're reading the stream
    System.Net.WebClient wc = new System.Net.WebClient( );
    wc.DownloadFile("http://www.oreilly.com", "index.html");
    Console.WriteLine("Finished downloading index.html.");
    iar.AsyncWaitHandle.WaitOne( ); // Wait until the async read is done
    Console.WriteLine(ars.sb);
  }
}
```

Isolated Storage

The .NET Framework's isolated storage classes create and manipulate data compartments that are unique to a user and an assembly. For example, suppose that the user *joe* runs the .NET application *someapp.exe*. If *someapp.exe* uses isolated storage to create directories and files, the .NET runtime guarantees that another program (such as *anotherapp.exe*) cannot access those files, even if *joe* runs *anotherapp.exe*. Further, if another user, *bob*, runs *someapp.exe*, he won't be able to access the files that *someapp.exe* created when *joe* ran it.

Isolated storage is limited by a quota, so even if it's manipulated by untrusted mobile code, you don't need to worry about that code performing a denial-of-service attack by filling your disk with useless data.

Where does isolated storage live? This depends on your operating system, but in Windows 2000 and XP, it is either found in *\Documents and Settings\<username>\ Local Settings\Application Data\Microsoft\IsolatedStorage* (the nonroaming profile) or in *\Documents and Settings\<username>\Application Data\Microsoft\IsolatedStorage* (the roaming profile). For other operating systems, such as Windows NT 4.0 or Windows 98, see *Introduction to Isolated Storage* in the .NET Framework SDK documentation.

Reading and Writing Isolated Storage

To create or access a file in isolated storage, create an instance of `IsolatedStorageFileStream` (pass in the desired filename and combination of `FileMode` constants). If your assembly doesn't currently have an area of isolated storage set up, .NET creates it at this time. The following example creates a new file in isolated storage, writes some data to it, and then displays the contents of that file:

```
using System;
using System.IO;
using System.IO.IsolatedStorage;
class Isolated {
  static void WriteToIS() {
    // Create a file in isolated storage
    IsolatedStorageFileStream stm =
      new IsolatedStorageFileStream("test.txt", FileMode.Create);
    // Write some text to the stream
    StreamWriter sw = new StreamWriter(stm);
    sw.WriteLine("Hello, World");
    sw.Close();
    stm.Close();
  }
  static void ReadFromIS() {
    // Open an existing file in isolated storage
    IsolatedStorageFileStream stm =
      new IsolatedStorageFileStream("test.txt", FileMode.Open);
    // Read the file
    StreamReader sr = new StreamReader(stm);
    string s = sr.ReadToEnd();
    sr.Close();
```

```
      stm.Close( );
      Console.WriteLine(s);
    }
    static void Main( ) {
      WriteToIS( );
      ReadFromIS( );
    }
  }
```

After running this sample you will find the resulting file in the appropriate *IsolatedStorage* folder for your operating system, as described in the previous section.

Enumerating the Contents of Isolated Storage

The .NET Framework includes the *storadm.exe* utility for listing (/LIST) the current user's isolated storage or for removing (/REMOVE) all of the user's isolated storage.

You can also access the current user's stores using IsolatedStorageFile. Use the static IsolatedStorageFile.GetEnumerator( ) method with an argument of IsolatedStorageScope.User to enumerate all the isolated storage for the current user. Once you have a store, you can inspect it or modify it, or open one of the files it contains by passing the store to the IsolatedStorageFileStream constructor.

```
using System;
using System.Collections;
using System.IO;
using System.IO.IsolatedStorage;
using System.Security.Policy;
class EnumIsolated {
  static void Main( ) {
    // Get all the current user's isolated stores
    IEnumerator ie =
      IsolatedStorageFile.GetEnumerator(IsolatedStorageScope.User);
    while (ie.MoveNext( )) {
      IsolatedStorageFile isf = (IsolatedStorageFile) e.Current;
      // Find the location of the associated assembly
      Url url = (Url)isf.AssemblyIdentity;
      Console.WriteLine("Assembly: {0}", url.Value);
      Console.WriteLine("Size: {0}", isf.CurrentSize);
      // List all the files in the store
      Console.WriteLine("Files:");
      string[ ] files = isf.GetFileNames("*");
      foreach (string file in files) {
        IsolatedStorageFileStream isfs =
          new IsolatedStorageFileStream(file, FileMode.Open, isf);
        Console.WriteLine(" {0}\t{1} bytes", file, isfs.Length);
      }
    }
  }
}
```

11

Serialization

The .NET Framework includes extensive support for serialization and deserialization, allowing clients to explicitly and implicitly serialize object instances and arbitrarily complex object graphs, and allowing types a wide degree of control over how and where they are serialized and deserialized.

This chapter introduces the support for object serialization and deserialization that is built into the .NET Framework, and shows how clients and objects can participate in the serialization and deserialization process. Unless otherwise stated, the types mentioned in this chapter all exist in the System or System. Runtime.Serialization namespaces.

What Is Serialization?

Some types are like mosquitoes: once instantiated, they live a short life near to where they were born, and then die quietly. Types such as these don't store important nontransient data and are used by clients in the same context they were created in. These types are trivial, and generally don't need serialization. However, many important types are not like this, storing data that needs to be persisted to some backing store (e.g. a database, file, or network), or being passed back and forth between different contexts as parameters in method calls. These types need to support serialization.

Serialization is the act of taking an in-memory object or object graph and flattening it into a stream of bytes that may be stored or transmitted. Deserialization works in reverse, taking a stream of bytes and reconstituting it into an in-memory object instance or object graph. Serialization and deserialization can happen either explicitly or implicitly, but the basic mechanism remains the same.

Serialization Support in the Framework

The .NET Framework includes extensive support for both serialization and deserialization, both from the perspective of clients wanting to serialize and deserialize objects, and from the perspective of types wanting some control over how and where they are serialized. This support is found in two sets of namespaces: System.Runtime.Serialization.* and System.Xml.Serialization.*.

Each of these namespaces includes a suite of types that, together with your types, form a serialization "engine," which has the ability to serialize one or more objects into a stream of some kind. Additionally, each of these namespaces supports XML as a serialization format (the System.Runtime.Serialization.* namespaces also support a binary serialization format).

The primary differences between the two serialization engines are that the one contained in the System.Runtime.Serialization.* namespaces supports arbitrary object graphs and can serialize any .NET type using SOAP Section 5 encoding. However, this engine produces XML that is very CLR-centric, describing primitive types using XML namespaces and schemas that assume the reader understands the CLR type system. On the other hand, the serialization engine contained in the System.Xml.Serialization.* namespaces produces very clean XSD schemas and matching XML instances, describing primitive types in terms of XSD data types wherever possible. However, it cannot handle arbitrary object graphs, and in some cases doesn't support all of the CLR paradigms naturally.

While both serialization engines fulfill valid (and different) needs, the rest of this chapter concentrates on the System.Runtime.Serialization.* serialization support because of its natural advantages for serializing the widest possible range of types in a CLR-centric manner.

Explicit Serialization

Consider a case in which a client wants to serialize a complex graph of objects to a file on disk. Furthermore, let's assume that the objects already support serialization (if not, the client's job is much harder). Fundamentally, there are two things the client needs to initiate an explicit serialization: an object reference identifying the root of the object graph, and a Stream reference identifying the place to serialize the object graph to.

Given these two references, the client needs some way to initiate the serialization and deserialization process. Since this is a common need, the Framework defines a standard interface called IFormatter that provides Serialize and Deserialize methods that work in terms of object and Stream references.

The Framework also provides two concrete implementations of this interface: the BinaryFormatter class (which lives in the System.Runtime.Serialization.Formatters.Binary namespace, and serializes object graphs using a binary format), and the SoapFormatter class (which lives in the System.Runtime.Serialization.Formatters.Soap namespace, and serializes object graphs as XML using SOAP Section 5 encoding rules).

Using these classes, clients can serialize graphs of objects with almost no code:

```
public void SerializeGraph(string file, object root) {
   Stream stm = new FileStream(file, FileMode.Create);
   IFormatter fmt = new BinaryFormatter( );
   fmt.Serialize(stm, root);
   stm.Flush( );
   stm.Close( );
}
```

When passed a target filename and the root of an object graph supporting serialization, SerializeGraph creates a new file and serializes the object graph into it in a binary format. Changing the serialization format to an XML representation of the object graph (using SOAP Section 5 encoding rules) is as simple as replacing the call to instantiate the BinaryFormatter with one to instantiate a SoapFormatter.

Deserialization is just as simple—the following code assumes an XML serialization format, and deserializes the contents of a file into an in-memory object graph. To use the object reference returned by the function in client code, downcast to the appropriate type:

```
public object DeserializeGraph(string file) {
   Stream stm = new FileStream(file, FileMode.Open);
   IFormatter fmt = new SoapFormatter( );
   object o = fmt.Deserialize(stm);
   stm.Close( );
   return o;
}
```

Implicit Serialization

Not all serialization and deserialization is explicit. Consider the following set of serializable classes:

```
[Serializable]
public sealed class Person {
   public string Name;
   public int Age;
}

[Serializable]
public sealed class Team {
   public string Name;
   public Person[ ] Players;
}
```

Serializing an instance of Team causes the embedded array of Person instances to implicitly be serialized.

Additionally, types can be serialized as part of method invocations. For example, imagine a function that merges two Teams using some complex algorithm, declared as follows:

```
public Team MergeTeams(Team teamOne, Team teamTwo) {...}
```

If instances of the type containing this method were always created and then used from within the same AppDomain, the calling code and the method itself could share the Team references. However, if we want to invoke this method from outside the AppDomain it was created in (or even from off the machine it was created on), the method invocation needs to be remoted across the AppDomain machine boundary.

While the remoting process and the supporting infrastructure in the Framework is rich, powerful, and complex, this chapter doesn't delve into remoting. However, it is helpful to understand that one of the steps in remoting involves turning a method call into a pair of request and response messages that can be transmitted across AppDomain or machine boundaries. If the MergeTeams method is remoted, the teamOne and teamTwo parameters are implicitly serialized into the request message by the same serialization infrastructure we used explicitly earlier in the chapter, and the resulting merged Team instance is implicitly serialized into the response message on method completion.

[Serializable]

In the preceding examples we assumed for simplicity's sake that the object graph was serializable, and we focused on how serialization and deserialization occurred. Now let's spend some time defining what it means for an object or object graph to be serializable, and how to mark your classes and structs as such.

Types that should support being serialized and deserialized by the runtime must be marked with the [Serializable] attribute, as follows:

```
[Serializable]
public sealed class Person {
  public string Name;
  public int Age;
}
```

This sets a special serializable bit in the metadata for the type that instructs the runtime to provide serialization and deserialization support. The [Serializable] attribute is not inherited, thus derived types are not automatically serializable. To provide for the serialization of derived types, mark each type as [Serializable].

As we saw earlier in the section "Implicit Serialization," serializing a type implicitly serializes all members of the type, recursively. This implies that all members of a type must themselves be serializable for the type to successfully serialize. This is true regardless of the accessibility of the members. For example, if you modify the Person class as follows, it will no longer be serializable:

```
[Serializable]
public sealed class Person {
  public string Name;
  public int Age;
  private Company Employer; // Person no longer Serializable!
}

public class Company {...}
```

Attempting to serialize an instance of Person now results in a SerializationException being thrown.

Although the combination of the [Serializable] attribute and the runtime's built-in support for serializing arbitrary object graphs is powerful, it doesn't give you much control over the serialization and deserialization process. However, there are several other ways for a type to participate in serialization, as we shall see.

[NonSerialized]

Even types with large amounts of important nontransient data sometimes contain members that are not appropriate for serialization. Common examples of transient members are fields that hold resources, such as file or window handles, that would not make sense on another machine or at a later time. Other examples of transient members that do not deserve to be serialized are fields that were calculated and cached in the type, but can be recreated from other, nontransient members. Lastly, a type may sometimes need to contain a member that is not serializable, yet still support serialization of the rest of the type.

To instruct the runtime's serialization engine to ignore a member when serializing a type, mark it with the [NonSerialized] attribute, as follows:

```
[Serializable]
public sealed class Person {
  public string Name;
  public DateTime DateOfBirth;
  [NonSerialized] public int Age; // Can be calculated
  // Rest of class...
}
```

When serializing an instance of Person, the runtime ignores the Age member and does not write it to the output stream. Similarly, when deserializing an instance of Person, the input stream does not contain data for the Age member, which is set to the bit pattern representing 0 (i.e., null for references, 0 for integrals, etc.). Consequently, when using an object instance of a type such as Person that has been deserialized, remember to watch out for null and zeroed members.

IDeserializationCallback

It is helpful to think of deserialization as a special form of constructor call, since the end result is a valid object reference. While the [NonSerialized] attribute is useful for controlling which data is stored in the serialized form of the object or sent over the wire on a remoting call, the problem is that the fields marked with [NonSerialized] are not assigned meaningful values when the constructor (i.e., the deserialization process) finishes executing. This can result in class invariants being violated, such as the implicit in the preceding sample, in which Age is intended to store the Person's age based on the DateOfBirth.

One possible solution to this problem is the IDeserializationCallback interface. Implementing this interface on your type indicates to the runtime that you wish to participate in the deserialization process. This interface contains a single method,

OnDeserialization, which the runtime invokes after it has finished constructing your object, but before it returns the fully constructed instance to the client. This method gives you a chance to perform whatever fixups you need to inside the object, and is a way to ensure that class invariants are preserved before clients can access the instance.

Using our sample Person class, the IDeserializationCallback interface implementation might look like this:

```
[Serializable]
public sealed class Person : IDeserializationCallback {
  public string Name;
  public DateTime DateOfBirth;
  [NonSerialized] public int Age; // Can be calculated
  public void OnDeserialization(object o) {
    TimeSpan ts = DateTime.Now - DateOfBirth;
    Age = ts.Days/365; // Rough age in years
  }

  // Rest of class...
}
```

By combining the [Serializable] attribute with the [NonSerialized] attribute and the IDeserializationCallback interface, it is possible to add serialization support to complex object graphs with relatively little code.

ISerializable

As flexible as the preceding approaches are, they still constrain the type implementer somewhat. Type implementers who need the serialized format to use different names than the in-memory members, or who need the mapping of members to serialized data to be something other than 1:1, or who would like to serialize as one type and deserialize as another (proxy) type, may want to take control of their own serialization via ISerializable and the other interfaces and attributes that make up the serialization architecture.

To indicate to the runtime that it wants to fully control serialization and deserialization, a type implements the ISerializable interface, which looks like this:

```
namespace System.Runtime.Serialization {
  public interface ISerializable {
    void GetObjectData(SerializationInfo si, StreamingContext sc);
  }
}
```

The SerializationInfo parameter is a reference to a property bag* that you should store the type member values in. Additionally, SerializationInfo also contains properties that you can use to control the type and assembly the instance should deserialize as. The StreamingContext parameter is a structure that contains, among

---

* A common data structure storing a collection of key/value pairs; also known as a hashtable or dictionary.

other things, an enumeration value indicating where the serialized instance is headed (to disk, into the remoting plumbing, etc.).

In addition to implementing ISerializable, a type that is controlling its own serialization needs to provide a deserialization constructor that takes two parameters: a SerializationInfo object reference and a StreamingContext structure. The accessibility of this constructor is not important, and can even be private to prevent other clients from using it to create unofficial instances.

Putting this together with the Teams class from the previous example, an implementation of ISerializable with a deserialization constructor might look like the following:

```
[Serializable]
public sealed class Team : ISerializable {
    public string Name;
    public Person[ ] Players;
    public void GetObjectData(SerializationInfo si, StreamingContext sc) {
        si.AddValue("IChangedTheFieldName", Name);
        si.AddValue("Players", Players);
    }
    private Team(SerializationInfo si, StreamingContext sc)  {
        Name = si.GetString("IChangedTheFieldName");
        Players = (Person[ ])si.GetValue("Players", typeof(Person[ ]));
    }
    // Rest of class...
}
```

This implementation of the deserialization constructor is illustrative, but not robust—real implementations should consider comparing the version of the deserializing type with the version in the SerializationInfo's AssemblyName property to detect version mismatches and code accordingly.

[Serializable] and ISerializable

Eagle-eyed readers will have noticed that in all the preceding examples the classes are sealed. This is no accident. Marking a class as [Serializable] and deciding whether to implement ISerializable has some specific implications for both base and derived types, and deserves separate discussion.

Consider the following serializable class hierarchy:

```
[Serializable]
public class Person {
  public string Name;
  public int Age;
  // Rest of class...
}

[Serializable]
public sealed class Student: Person {
  public string Course;
  // Rest of class...
}
```

In this example both `Person` and `Student` are serializable, and both classes use the default runtime serialization behavior since neither class implements `ISerializable`.

Now imagine that the developer of `Person` decides for some reason to implement `ISerializable` and provide a deserialization constructor to control `Person` serialization. The new version of `Person` might look like this:

```
[Serializable]
public class Person : ISerialization {
  public string Name;
  public int Age;
  public void GetObjectData(SerializationInfo si, StreamingContext sc) {
    si.AddValue("IChangedTheNameFieldName", Name);
    si.AddValue("IChangedTheAgeFieldName", Age);
  }
  protected Person(SerializationInfo si, StreamingContext sc)  {
    Name = si.GetString("IChangedTheNameFieldName");
    Age = sc.GetInt32("IChangedTheAgeFieldName");
  }
  // Rest of class...
}
```

Although this works for instances of `Person`, this change breaks serialization of `Student` instances. Serializing a `Student` instance would appear to succeed, but the `Course` field in the `Student` type isn't saved to the stream because the implementation of `ISerializable.GetObjectData` on `Person` has no knowledge of the members of the `Student` derived type. Additionally, deserialization of `Student` instances throws an exception since the runtime is looking (unsuccessfully) for a deserialization constructor on `Student`.

Fundamentally, if a base class implements `ISerializable` and the other serialization-related interfaces and base classes, derived classes need to follow suit. There are a several ways of accomplishing this. One option is for the base class to declare `GetObjectData` as `virtual`, allowing derived classes to simply override it as needed and call up the base type's `GetObjectData` as needed. Another option is for the derived class to reimplement `ISerializable` using explicit interface implementation, calling up to the base implementation as needed. In all cases, derived types need to provide deserialization constructors, and chain up to the base deserialization constructor as needed. An implementation of `Student` that takes the latter approach looks like this:

```
[Serializable]
public sealed class Student : Person, ISerialization {
  public string Course;
  void ISerialization.GetObjectData(SerializationInfo si,
                                    StreamingContext sc) {
    si.AddValue("IChangedTheCourseFieldName", Course);
    base.GetObjectData(si, sc);
  }
  private Student(SerializationInfo si, StreamingContext sc)
    : base(si, sc) {
    Course = si.GetString("IChangedTheCourseFieldName");
  }
```

```
  // Rest of class...
}
```

Now imagine a case in which the developer of Person elects not to implement
ISerializable, relying instead on the default runtime serialization behavior. A
derived type such as Student wishing to control its serialization by implementing
ISerializable needs to ensure that the Person members are correctly serialized as
part of the GetObjectData call, and correctly initialized by the Student deserialization constructor. While this could be performed manually in the derived type for
public and protected members of the base type, the problem remains for private
members of the base type that need serialization and deserialization.

The problem is that Person does not have an ISerializable.GetObjectData
method or a deserialization constructor that the Student type can delegate to. The
solution to this problem is the FormatterServices class, which provides a standard way to retrieve the list of all members in a type that need to be serialized
(GetSerializableMembers), as well as a standard way to retrieve a serialized representation of these members (GetObjectData), and a standard way to deserialize this
representation back into a new instance (PopulateObjectMembers). An implementation of Student that uses FormatterServices looks like this:

```
[Serializable]
public sealed class Student : Person, ISerializable {
  public string Course;
  public void GetObjectData(SerializationInfo si, StreamingContext sc) {
    Type t = typeof(Person);
    MemberInfo[ ] mbrs = FormatterServices.GetSerializableMembers(t);
    object[ ] data = FormatterServices.GetObjectData(this, mbrs);
    si.AddValue("BaseData", data);
    si.AddValue("IChangedTheCourseFieldName", Course);
  }
  private Student(SerializationInfo si, StreamingContext sc) {
    Type t = typeof(Person);
    MemberInfo[ ] mbrs = FormatterServices.GetSerializableMembers( );
    object[ ] data = (object[ ])si.GetValue("BaseData", typeof(object[ ]));
    FormatterServices.PopulateObjectMembers(this, mbrs, data);
    Course = si.GetString("IChangedTheCourseFieldName");
  }
  // Rest of class...
}
```

12

Assemblies

An assembly is a logical package (similar to a DLL in Win32) that consists of a manifest, a set of one or more modules, and an optional set of resources. This package forms the basic unit of deployment and versioning, and creates a boundary for type resolution and security permissioning.

Elements of an Assembly

Every .NET application consists of at least one assembly, which is in turn built from a number of three basic elements: a manifest, modules, and resources.

The manifest contains a set of metadata that describes everything the runtime needs to know about the assembly. This information includes:

- The simple name of the assembly
- The version number of the assembly
- An optional originator public key and assembly hash
- The list of files in the assembly, with file hashes
- The list of referenced assemblies, including versioning information and an optional public key
- The list of types included in the assembly, with a mapping to the module containing the type
- The set of minimum and optional security permissions requested by the assembly
- The set of security permissions explicitly refused by the assembly
- Culture, processor, and OS information
- A set of custom attributes to capture details such as product name, owner information, etc.

Modules are Portable Executable (PE) files that contain types described using metadata and implemented using MSIL. Additionally, modules have module manifests that define the external assemblies they are dependent on.

Resources contain nonexecutable data that is logically included with the assembly. Examples of this include bitmaps, localizable text, persisted objects, and so on.

Assemblies and Modules

The simplest assembly contains an assembly manifest and a single module containing the application's types, packaged as an EXE with a Main entry point. More complex assemblies may be composed of multiple modules (PE files), separate resource files, manifest, etc.

The element that defines the presence of an assembly is termed the assembly manifest. The assembly manifest is not a physical construct, but rather a set of metadata that can either be included in one of the existing PE files in the assembly, or can live in a standalone PE file.

An assembly may also contain multiple modules. This technique can increase the performance of applications that use assemblies that are loaded over the network, since the CLR only loads modules as the types contained within them are needed. In addition, each module can be written in a different language, allowing a mixture of C#, VB.NET, and raw MSIL. Although not common, a single module could also be included in several different assemblies. When using multimodule assemblies, the convention is for the module PE files to have a .netmodule extension.

Finally, an assembly may contain a set of resources, which can either be kept in standalone files or included in one of the PE files in the assembly.

Scoping Types and Type References

The assembly boundary also forms a type accessibility boundary: the C# internal accessibility modifier allows types to restrict method accessibility to a single assembly.

Additionally, references to types are always scoped by the assembly in which the type resides—the unique reference for a type (known as a TypeRef) is the combination of a reference to the assembly it was defined in and the fully qualified type name including any namespaces. For example, this local variable declaration:

```
System.Net.WebRequest wr;
```

is represented in MSIL as follows:

```
.assembly extern System.Net { .ver 1:0:2914:16 ... }
.locals(class [System.Net]System.Net.WebRequest wr)
```

As you can see from this example, in order to reference a type unambiguously, we need to be able to identify the assembly that contains it unambiguously. The .NET Framework's mechanism for naming assemblies is very powerful, and is a giant step beyond the use of ProgIDs and GUIDs in classic COM development.

Naming and Signing Assemblies

Assemblies are identified with a four-part name, consisting of:

- The simple name of the assembly
- The version number of the assembly
- An optional originator public key (and associated digital signature)
- An optional set of culture information

The assembly's simple name is defined in the assembly manifest, and is generally the same as the name of the module that contains the manifest, minus the extension (i.e., the simple name for the assembly MyAssembly.dll is MyAssembly).

The assembly's version number is divided into four parts and looks like this:

```
<major>.<minor>.<build>.<revision>
```

The System.Reflection.AssemblyVersionAttribute assembly-level custom attribute allows you to specify either a full or partial version number for the assembly, as well as allowing you to have the <build> and <revision> portions of the version number automatically change for each build. For example, apply the following custom attribute to an assembly:

```
using System.Reflection;
[assembly:AssemblyVersion("1.0.0.*")]
```

This results in an assembly in which the revision number is different every time the assembly is compiled. This represents the number of seconds since midnight, divided by two, since the day the assembly was built.

Assemblies can also be digitally signed using public-key technology to identify the developer (known as the "originator") and to detect tampering with the assembly after it has been signed. When an assembly is signed, an eight-byte originator ID (known as a public-key token) forms part of the assembly's name.

In order to sign an assembly, the originator needs to first generate an RSA public/private key pair, which can be done using the *sn.exe* utility, as follows:

```
sn.exe -k PublicPrivate.snk
```

This generates a file (*PublicPrivate.snk*) containing both a 128-byte RSA public key and a matching private key.

Once this is done, the System.Reflection.AssemblyKeyFileAttribute assembly-level custom attribute is used to tell the compiler where to find the key pair. This attribute also tells the compiler that after generating the assembly it should sign it with the private key, insert the signature into the PE file, and add the public key to the assembly manifest.

```
using System.Reflection;
[assembly:AssemblyKeyFile("PublicPrivate.snk")]
```

The presence of this additional information in the PE file and assembly manifest allows the CLR to, before loading the assembly at runtime, verify that it hasn't been tampered with. The *sn.exe* utility can also be used to manually verify that a signed assembly has not been tampered with, by using the -v option:

```
sn.exe -v MyAssembly.dll
```

Additionally, clients that use types from a signed assembly include a simplified 8-byte MD5 hash of the public key (again, this is known as a public key token) directly in the assembly reference.

This further protects clients, since re-signing an assembly that has been tampered with either requires the originator's private key (something most originators guard closely), or the use of a different public/private key pair. In the latter case, the public key token for the new key pair doesn't match the original public key token embedded in the client's assembly reference, and the modified assembly is not loaded.

To determine what the public key token is for a given originator's public/private key pair, use the *sn.exe* utility with the -T (for assemblies) or with -t (for public-key-only keyfiles), as follows:

```
sn.exe -T MyAssembly.dll
sn.exe -t Public.snk
```

Since the originator's private key is so critical, some organizations prefer to centralize signing authority, and not to distribute the key widely even within the organization. It is also possible to delay-sign an assembly, in which the compiler embeds the public key in the manifest and preserves space in the PE file for the signature, but doesn't actually sign the assembly.

The first step in this procedure is to generate a file that only contains the public key:

```
sn.exe -p PublicPrivate.snk Public.snk
```

The resulting *Public.snk* file can then be used in place of the *PublicPrivate.snk* file. Additionally, the System.Reflection.AssemblyDelaySign attribute is used to tell the compiler we wish to delay-sign the assembly:

```
using System.Reflection;
[assembly:AssemblyKeyFile("Public.snk")]
[assembly:AssemblyDelaySign(true)]
```

The resulting assembly can be used almost identically to normally signed assemblies for development purposes, except it cannot be placed in the Global Assembly Cache and it cannot be verified with *sn.exe*.

Delay-signing the assembly means that the compiler (and consequently, the developers) only needs access to the public key. At some later point a trusted member of the organization can use the *sn.exe* tool and the closely guarded private key to re-sign the assembly, which inserts the appropriate digital signature in the PE file. This is done using the *sn.exe* utility, as follows:

```
sn.exe -R MyAssembly.dll PublicPrivate.snk
```

Once the assembly has been re-signed, it can be verified using *sn.exe* and placed in the GAC using *gactutil.exe*.

The final part of the assembly name is the culture information. This is used when the assembly contains only culture-specific resources such as localized strings, dialogs, and other interface elements. The culture is controlled by the presence of the `System.Reflection.AssemblyCulture` custom attribute on the assembly, as follows:

```
using System.Reflection;
[assembly:AssemblyCulture("en-US")]
```

If no culture is specified, the assembly is considered to be culture-neutral.

When combined, the four elements name, version, culture and originator make up a unique identifier (known as an `AssemblyRef`) for an assembly, which is part of a `TypeRef` to unambiguously identify a type.

To allow user code to refer to a unique assembly in this way (e.g., for programmatic loading of assemblies via reflection), these four elements can be combined in a stringified, human-readable format known as the assembly display name. The display name is built up from the four elements like this:

```
<name>, Version=<version>, Culture=<culture>, PublicKeyToken=<originator>
```

The display name may be used as input to the `System.Reflection.Assembly.Load` method, as follows:

```
Assembly a = Assembly.Load(@"MyAssembly, Version="1.0.0.0",
            Culture=neutral, PublicKeyToken=70e2f3b624e8bfa5");
```

Resolving and Loading Assemblies

At the point that the CLR first needs to access the metadata for a type (e.g., when JIT-ing methods that use the type), it must first locate and load the assembly containing the type. The process of determining exactly which assembly to load is called "resolving," and is performed by the assembly resolver. Once the assembly resolver has determined which physical file to load, the assembly loader is responsible for loading it into memory.

The assembly resolver performs a relatively complex set of operations, controlled by application and machine-level configuration files. These configuration files can tell the resolver to bind to a different version of the assembly than specified in the assembly reference, and can give the resolver hints about where to look for the physical file the loader should load (either at a URI endpoint, or in subdirectories under the application directory).

Once the resolver has identified which file to load and has verified that the name, version, culture, and originator information in the assembly manifest in the located file matches what the resolver is expecting, it hands off to the loader, which physically loads and verifies the file.

Deployment

An assembly is the smallest .NET unit of deployment. Due to the self-describing nature of a manifest, deployment can be as simple as copying the assembly (and in the case of a multifile assembly, all the associated files) into the application directory.

This is a vast improvement over traditional COM development, in which components, their supporting DLLs, and their configuration information are spread out over multiple directories and the Windows registry.

In many cases, we want to share assemblies between applications. The foremost way to do this is to sign the assemblies, then place them in the machine-wide global assembly cache (GAC), which all applications have access to. The assembly resolver always consults the GAC before looking elsewhere for the assembly, so this is the fastest option.

Next, assemblies may be deployed at *http*: and *file*: URI endpoints. To do this, deploy them in the correct location and use the application and machine configuration files to tell the assembly resolver where to look using the `<codeBase>` element. (See the .NET Framework SDK documentation for the specific format of the configuration files.)

Lastly, if we do not wish to share assemblies between applications, we can place them in or beneath the application directory. When deployed in this way, the assembly resolver finds them by probing for a file with the name matching the simple name of the assembly and either a *.dll* or *.exe* extension. The directories that the resolver probes in follow a well-defined set of rules (see the .NET Framework SDK documentation for more details) and can be controlled by the configuration files with the `<probing>` element.

Security Permissions

The assembly forms a boundary for security permissioning. The assembly manifest contains hashes for any referenced assemblies (determined at compile time), a list of the minimum set of security permissions the assembly requires in order to function, a list of the optional permissions that it requests, and a list of the permissions that it explicitly refuses (i.e., never wants to receive).

To illustrate how these permissions might be used, imagine an email client similar to Microsoft Outlook, developed using the .NET Framework. It probably requires the ability to communicate over the network on ports 110 (POP3), 25 (SMTP), and 143 (IMAP4). It might request the ability to run JavaScript functions in a sandbox to allow full interactivity when presenting HTML emails. Finally, it probably refuses ever being granted the ability to write to disk or read the local address book, thus avoiding scripting attacks such as the ILoveYou virus.

Essentially, the assembly declares its security needs and assumptions, but leaves the final decision on permissioning up to the CLR, which enforces local security policy.

At runtime the CLR uses the hashes to determine whether a dependent assembly has been tampered with, and combines the assembly permission information with local security policy to determine whether to load the assembly and which permissions to grant it.

This mechanism provides fine-grained control over security and is a major advantage of the .NET Framework over traditional Windows applications.

13

Reflection

Many of the services available in .NET and exposed via C# (such as late binding, serialization, remoting, attributes, etc.) depend on the presence of metadata. Your own programs can also take advantage of this metadata, and even extend it with new information. Examining existing types via their metadata is called *reflection*, and is done using a rich set of types in the System.Reflection namespace. It is also possible to dynamically create new types at runtime via the classes in the System. Reflection.Emit namespace. You can extend the metadata for existing types with custom attributes. For more information, see Chapter 14.

Type Hierarchy

Reflection involves traversing and manipulating an object model that represents an application, including all its compile-time and runtime elements. Consequently, it is important to understand the various logical units of a .NET application and their roles and relationships.

The fundamental units of an application are its types, which contain members and nested types. Types are contained in modules, which are composed into assemblies. All these elements are described with metadata. Metadata is generally produced by the compiler at compile time, although it may also be created on the fly via Reflection.Emit (which is described in the later section "Creating New Types at Runtime").

At runtime, these elements are all contained within an AppDomain. An AppDomain isn't described with metadata, yet it plays an important role in reflection because it forms a logical process that a .NET application runs in.

Each of these elements is exposed via a matching type from the System or System. Reflection namespaces. Figure 13-1 shows the inheritance hierarchy for key reflection types.

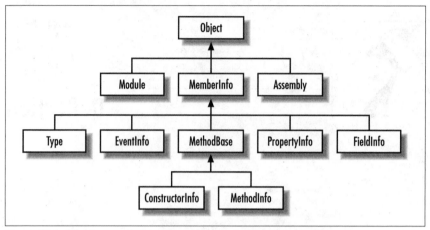

Figure 13-1. Inheritance relationships among the .NET reflection types

Given a reference to any of these elements, you can navigate the relationships between it and the related elements, as shown in Figure 13-2.

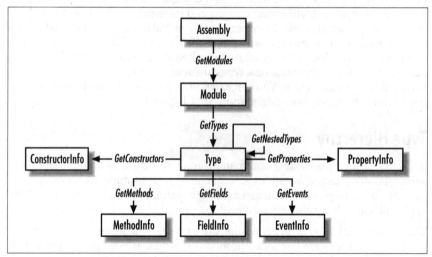

Figure 13-2. Traversing the .NET reflection hierarchy

Types, Members, and Nested Types

The most basic element that reflection deals with is the Type class. This class represents the metadata for each type declaration in an application (both predefined and user-defined types).

Types contain members, which include constructors, fields, properties, events, and methods. In addition, types may contain nested types, which exist within the scope of an outer type and are typically used as helper classes. Types are grouped into modules, which are, in turn, contained within assemblies.

Assemblies and Modules

Assemblies are the logical equivalent of DLLs in Win32 and the basic unit of deployment, versioning, and reuse for types. In addition, assemblies create a security, visibility, and scope resolution boundary for types (for more information, see Chapter 12).

A module is a physical file such as a DLL, an EXE, or a resource (such as GIFs or JPGs). While it isn't common practice, an assembly can be composed of multiple modules, allowing you to control application working set size, use multiple languages within one assembly, and share a module across multiple assemblies.

AppDomains

From the perspective of reflection, an AppDomain is the root of the type hierarchy and serves as the container for assemblies and types when they are loaded into memory at runtime. A helpful way to think about an AppDomain is to view it as the logical equivalent of a process in a Win32 application.

AppDomains provide isolation, creating a hard boundary for managed code just like the process boundary under Win32. Similar to processes, AppDomains can be started and stopped independently, and application faults take down only the AppDomain the fault occurs in, not the process hosting the AppDomain.

Retrieving the Type for an Instance

At the heart of reflection is System.Type, which is an abstract base class that provides access to the metadata of a type.

You can access the Type class for any instance using GetType( ), which is a method implemented on System.Object. When you call GetType( ), the method returns a concrete subtype of System.Type, which can reflect over and manipulate the type.

Retrieving a Type Directly

You can also retrieve a Type class by name (without needing an instance) using the static method GetType on the Type class. When specifying which type to retrieve, you can provide either the namespace-qualified name of the type, or the assembly-qualified name, as follows:

```
Type t = Type.GetType("System.Int32");
Type t2 = Type.GetType("MyNamespace.MyType, MyAssembly");
```

In the case in which you provide only the namespace-qualified name, GetType looks first in the calling assembly, and then in *mscorlib.dll*.

Finally, C# provides the typeof operator, which returns the Type class for any type known at compile time:

```
Type t = typeof(System.Int32);
```

The main difference between these two approaches is that Type.GetType is evaluated at runtime and thus is more dynamic, binding to a type in an assembly by name, while the typeof operator is evaluated at compile time and thus is slightly faster, binding to a type in a specific assembly version via a type token.

Reflecting Over a Type Hierarchy

Once you have retrieved a Type instance, you can navigate the application hierarchy described earlier, accessing the metadata via types that represent members, modules, assemblies, namespaces, AppDomains, and nested types. You can also inspect the metadata and any custom attributes, create new instances of the types, and invoke members.

Here is an example that uses reflection to display the members in three different types:

```
using System;
using System.Reflection;
class Test {
  static void Main( ) {
    object o = new Object( );
    DumpTypeInfo(o.GetType( ));
    DumpTypeInfo(typeof(int));
    DumpTypeInfo(Type.GetType("System.String"));
  }
  static void DumpTypeInfo(Type t) {
    Console.WriteLine("Type: {0}", t);

    // Retrieve the list of members in the type
    MemberInfo[ ] miarr = t.GetMembers( );

    // Print out details on each of them
    foreach (MemberInfo mi in miarr)
      Console.WriteLine("  {0}={1}", mi.MemberType, mi);
  }
}
```

Late Binding

Reflection can also perform late binding, in which the application dynamically loads, instantiates, and uses a type at runtime. This provides greater flexibility at the expense of invocation overhead.

In this section, we create an example that uses very late binding, dynamically discovers new types at runtime, and uses them as well.

In the next example, one or more assemblies are loaded by name (as specified on the command line). The example then iterates through the types in the assembly looking for subtypes of the Greeting abstract base class. When one is found, the type is instantiated and its SayHello( ) method invoked, which displays an appropriate greeting.

To perform the runtime discovery of types, we use an abstract base class that's compiled into an assembly as follows (see the source comment for filename and compilation information):

```
// Greeting.cs - compile with /t:library
public abstract class Greeting {
  public abstract void SayHello( );
}
```

Compiling this code produces a file named *Greeting.dll*, which the other parts of the sample can use.

We now create a new assembly containing two concrete subtypes of the abstract type Greeting, as follows (see the source comment for filename and compilation information):

```
// English.cs - compile with /t:library /r:Greeting.dll
using System;
public class AmericanGreeting : Greeting {
  private string msg = "Hey, dude. Wassup!";
  public override void SayHello( ) {
    Console.WriteLine(msg);
  }
}
public class BritishGreeting : Greeting {
  private string msg = "Good morning, old chap!";
  public override void SayHello( ) {
    Console.WriteLine(msg);
  }
}
```

Compiling the source file *English.cs* produces a file named *English.dll*, which the main program can now dynamically reflect over and use.

Now we create the main sample, as follows (see the source comment for filename and compilation information):

```
// SayHello.cs - compile with /r:Greeting.dll
// Run with SayHello.exe <dllname1> <dllname2> ... <dllnameN>
using System;
using System.Reflection;
class Test {
  static void Main (string[ ] args) {

    // Iterate over the cmd-line options,
    // trying to load each assembly
    foreach (string s in args) {
      Assembly a = Assembly.LoadFrom(s);

      // Pick through all the public types, looking for
      // subtypes of the abstract base class Greeting
      foreach (Type t in a.GetTypes( ))
        if (t.IsSubclassOf(typeof(Greeting))) {

          // Having found an appropriate subtype, create it
          object o = Activator.CreateInstance(t);
```

```
                // Retrieve the SayHello MethodInfo & invoke it
                MethodInfo mi = t.GetMethod("SayHello");
                mi.Invoke(o, null);
            }
        }
    }
}
```

Running the sample now with SayHello English.dll produces the following output:

```
Hey, dude. Wassup!
Good morning, old chap!
```

The interesting aspect of the preceding sample is that it's completely late-bound; i.e., long after the *SayHello* program is shipped you can create a new type and have *SayHello* automatically take advantage of it by simply specifying it on the command line. This is one of the key benefits of late binding via reflection. You could use this pattern to develop an application that supports third-party plug-ins. Each plug-in would have to implement the same interface and be stored in its own assembly. Your application could then use Assembly.LoadFrom( ) and Activator. CreateInstance( ) to activate the plug-in.

Activation

In the previous examples, you loaded an assembly by hand and used the System. Activator class to create a new instance based on a type. There are many overrides of the CreateInstance( ) method that provide a wide range of creation options, including the ability to short-circuit the process and create a type directly:

```
    object o = Activator.CreateInstance("Assem1.dll",
                                        "Friendly.Greeting");
```

Other capabilities of the Activator type include creating types on remote machines, creating types in specific AppDomains (sandboxes), and creating types by invoking a specific constructor (rather than using the default constructor as these examples show).

Advanced Uses of Reflection

The preceding example demonstrates the use of reflection, but doesn't perform any tasks you can't accomplish using normal C# language constructs. However, reflection can also manipulate types in ways not supported directly in C#, as demonstrated in this section.

While the CLR enforces access controls on type members (specified using access modifiers such as private and protected), these restrictions don't apply to reflection. Assuming you have the correct set of permissions, you can use reflection to access and manipulate private data and function members, as this example using the Greeting subtypes from the previous section shows (see the source comment for filename and compilation information):

```
    // InControl.cs - compile with /r:Greeting.dll,English.dll
    using System;
```

```
using System.Reflection;
class TestReflection {
  // Note: This method requires the ReflectionPermission perm.
  static void ModifyPrivateData(object o, string msg) {

    // Get a FieldInfo type for the private data member
    Type t = o.GetType();
    FieldInfo fi = t.GetField("msg", BindingFlags.NonPublic|
                                    BindingFlags.Instance);

    // Use the FieldInfo to adjust the data member value
    fi.SetValue(o, msg);
  }
  static void Main() {
    // Create instances of both types
    BritishGreeting bg = new BritishGreeting();
    AmericanGreeting ag = new AmericanGreeting();

    // Adjust the private data via reflection
    ModifyPrivateData(ag, "Things are not the way they seem");
    ModifyPrivateData(bg, "The runtime is in total control!");

    // Display the modified greeting strings
    ag.SayHello(); // "Things are not the way they seem"
    bg.SayHello(); // "The runtime is in total control!"
  }
}
```

When run, this sample generates the following output:

```
Things are not the way they seem
The runtime is in total control!
```

This demonstrates that the private msg data members in both types are modified via reflection, although there are no public members defined on the types that allow that operation. Note that while this technique can bypass access controls, it still doesn't violate type safety.

Although this is a somewhat contrived example, the capability can be useful when building utilities such as class browsers and test suite automation tools that need to inspect and interact with a type at a deeper level than its public interface.

Creating New Types at Runtime

The System.Reflection.Emit namespace contains classes that can create entirely new types at runtime. These classes can define a dynamic assembly in memory, define a dynamic module in the assembly, define a new type in the module, including all its members, and emit the MSIL opcodes needed to implement the application logic in the members.

Here is an example that creates and uses a new type called HelloWorld with a member called SayHello:

```
using System;
using System.Reflection;
```

```csharp
using System.Reflection.Emit;
public class Test
{
  static void Main( )
  {
    // Create a dynamic assembly in the current AppDomain
    AppDomain ad = AppDomain.CurrentDomain;
    AssemblyName an = new AssemblyName( );
    an.Name = "DynAssembly";
    AssemblyBuilder ab =
      ad.DefineDynamicAssembly(an, AssemblyBuilderAccess.Run);

    // Create a module in the assembly & a type in the module
    ModuleBuilder modb = ab.DefineDynamicModule("DynModule");
    TypeBuilder tb = modb.DefineType("AgentSmith",
                                     TypeAttributes.Public);

    // Add a SayHello member to the type
    MethodBuilder mb = tb.DefineMethod("SayHello",
                                       MethodAttributes.Public,
                                       null, null);

    // Generate the MSIL for the SayHello Member
    ILGenerator ilg = mb.GetILGenerator( );
    ilg.EmitWriteLine("Never send a human to do a machine's job.");
    ilg.Emit(OpCodes.Ret);

    // Finalize the type so we can create it
    tb.CreateType( );

    // Create an instance of the new type
    Type t = ab.GetType("AgentSmith");
    object o = Activator.CreateInstance(t);

    // Prints "Never send a human to do a machine's job."
    t.GetMethod("SayHello").Invoke(o, null);
  }
}
```

A common example using Reflection.Emit is the regular expression support in the FCL, which can emit new types that are tuned to search for specific regular expressions, eliminating the overhead of interpreting the regular expression at runtime.

Other uses of Reflection.Emit in the FCL include dynamically generating transparent proxies for remoting and generating types that perform specific XSLT transforms with the minimum runtime overhead.

14

Custom Attributes

Types, members, modules, and assemblies all have associated metadata that is used by all the major CLR services, is considered an indivisible part of an application, and can be accessed via reflection (see Chapter 13).

A key characteristic of metadata is it can be extended. Extend the metadata with custom attributes, which allow you to "decorate" a code element with additional information stored in the metadata associated with the element.

This additional information can then be retrieved at runtime and used to build services that work declaratively, which is the way that the CLR implements core features such as serialization and interception.

Language Support

Decorating an element with a custom attribute is known as specifying the custom attribute. This is done by writing the name of the attribute enclosed in brackets ([ ]) immediately before the element declaration as follows:

```
[Serializable] public class Foo {...}
```

In this example, the Foo class is specified as serializable. This information is saved in the metadata for Foo, and affects the way the CLR treats an instance of this class.

A useful way to think about custom attributes is they expand the built-in set of declarative constructs in the C# language, such as public, private, and sealed.

Compiler Support

In reality, custom attributes are simply types derived from System.Attribute with language constructs for specifying them on an element (see "Attributes" in Chapter 4).

These language constructs are recognized by the compiler, which emits a small chunk of data into the metadata. This custom data includes a serialized call to the constructor of the custom attribute type (containing the values for the positional parameters), and a collection of property set operations (containing the values for the named parameters).

The compiler also recognizes a small number of pseudocustom attributes. These are special attributes that have direct representation in metadata and are stored natively (i.e., not as chunks of custom data). This is primarily a runtime performance optimization, although it has some implications for retrieving attributes via reflection, as discussed later.

To understand this, consider the following class with two specified attributes:

```
[Serializable, Obsolete]
class Foo {...}
```

When compiled in MSIL, the metadata for the class Foo looks like this:

```
.class private auto ansi serializable beforefieldinit Foo
        extends [mscorlib]System.Object
{
    .custom instance void
        [mscorlib]System.ObsoleteAttribute::.ctor() = ( 01 00 00 00 )
        ...
    }
}
```

Compare the different treatment by the compiler of the Obsolete attribute, which is a custom attribute and is stored as a serialized constructor call to the System. ObsoleteAttribute type, to the treatment of the Serializable attribute, which is a pseudocustom attribute represented directly in the metadata with the serializable token.

Runtime Support

At runtime the core CLR services, such as serialization and remoting, inspect the custom and pseudocustom attributes to determine how to handle an instance of a type.

In the case of custom attributes, this is done by creating an instance of the attribute (invoking the relevant constructor call and property-set operations), then performing whatever steps are needed to determine how to handle an instance of the type.

In the case of pseudocustom attributes, this is done by inspecting the metadata directly and determining how to handle an instance of the type. Consequently, handling pseudocustom attributes is more efficient than handling custom attributes.

Note that none of these steps is initiated until a service or user program actually tries to access the attributes, so there is little runtime overhead unless required.

Predefined Attributes

The .NET Framework makes extensive use of attributes for purposes ranging from simple documentation to advanced support for threading, remoting, serialization, and COM interop. These attributes are all defined in the FCL, and can be used, extended, and retrieved by your own code.

However, certain attributes are treated specially by the compiler and the runtime. Three attributes considered general enough to be defined in the C# specification are AttributeUsage, Conditional, and Obsolete. Other attributes, such as CLSCompliant, Serializable, and NonSerialized, are also treated specially.

The AttributeUsage Attribute

```
[AttributeUsage(target-enum
    [, AllowMultiple=[true|false]]?
    [, Inherited=[true|false]]?
    ] (for classes)
```

The AttributeUsage attribute is applied to a new attribute class declaration. It controls how the new attribute should be treated by the compiler—specifically, which set of targets (classes, interfaces, properties, methods, parameters, etc.) the new attribute can be specified on. This is true whether multiple instances of this attribute may be applied to the same target, and whether this attribute propagates to subtypes of the target.

target-enum is a bitwise mask of values from the System.AttributeTargets enum, which looks like this:

```
namespace System {
  [Flags]
  public enum AttributeTargets {
    Assembly    = 0x0001,
    Module      = 0x0002,
    Class       = 0x0004,
    Struct      = 0x0008,
    Enum        = 0x0010,
    Constructor = 0x0020,
    Method      = 0x0040,
    Property    = 0x0080,
    Field       = 0x0100,
    Event       = 0x0200,
    Interface   = 0x0400,
    Parameter   = 0x0800,
    Delegate    = 0x1000,
    ReturnValue = 0x2000,
    All         = 0x3fff,
  }
}
```

The Conditional Attribute

```
[Conditional(symbol)] (for methods)
```

The Conditional attribute can be applied to any method with a void return type. The presence of this attribute tells the compiler to conditionally omit calls to the method unless *symbol* is defined in the calling code. This is similar to wrapping every call to the method with #if and #endif preprocessor directives, but Conditional has the advantage of needing to be specified only in one place.

The Obsolete Attribute

```
[Obsolete([Message=]? message
   IsError= [true|false]]
 ] (for all attribute targets)
```

Applied to any valid attribute target, the Obsolete attribute indicates that the target is obsolete. Obsolete can include a message that explains which alternative types or members to use and a flag that tells the compiler to treat the use of this type or member as an error instead of a warning.

For example, referencing type Bar in the following example causes the compiler to display an error message and halts compilation:

```
[Obsolete("Don't try this at home", IsError=true)]
class Bar { ... }
```

The CLSCompliant Attribute

```
[CLSCompliant(true|false)]
(for all attribute targets)
```

Applied to an assembly, the CLSCompliant attribute tells the compiler whether to validate CLS compliance for all the exported types in the assembly. Applied to any other attribute target, this attribute allows the target to declare if it should be considered CLS-compliant. In order to mark a target as CLS-compliant, the entire assembly needs to be considered as such.

In the following example, the CLSCompliant attribute is used to specify an assembly as CLS-compliant and a class within it as *not* CLS-compliant:

```
[assembly:CLSCompliant(true)]

[CLSCompliant(false)]
public class Bar {
  public ushort Answer { get {return 42;} }
}
```

The Serializable Attribute

```
[Serializable]
(for classes, structs, enums, delegates)
```

Applied to a class, struct, enum, or delegate, the Serializable attribute marks it as being serializable. This attribute is a pseudocustom attribute and is represented specially in the metadata.

The NonSerialized attribute

```
[NonSerialized] (for fields)
```

Applied to a field, the NonSerialized attribute prevents it from being serialized along with its containing class or struct. This attribute is a pseudocustom attribute and is represented specially in the metadata.

Defining a New Custom Attribute

In addition to using the predefined attributes supplied by the .NET Framework, you can also create your own.

To create a custom attribute, use the following steps:

1. Derive a class from System.Attribute or from a descendent of System. Attribute. By convention the class name should end with the word Attribute, although this isn't required.

2. Provide the class with a public constructor. The parameters to the constructor define the positional parameters of the attribute and are mandatory when specifying the attribute on an element.

3. Declare public-instance fields, public-instance read/write properties, or public-instance write-only properties to specify the named parameters of the attribute. Unlike positional parameters, these are optional when specifying the attribute on an element.

   The types that can be used for attribute constructor parameters and properties are bool, byte, char, double, float, int, long, short, string, object, the Type type, enum, or a one-dimensional array of all of these.

4. Finally, as described in the preceding section, define what the attribute may be specified on using the AttributeUsage attribute.

Consider the following example of a custom attribute, CrossRefAttribute, which removes the limitation that the CLR metadata contains only information about statically linked types, but not dynamically linked ones.

```
// Xref.cs - cross-reference custom attribute
// compile with:
//    csc /t:library XRef.cs
using System;
[AttributeUsage(AttributeTargets.All, AllowMultiple=true)]
public class CrossRefAttribute : Attribute {
    Type   xref;
    string desc = "";
    public string Description { set { desc=value; } }
    public CrossRefAttribute(Type xref) { this.xref=xref; }
    public override string ToString( ) {
        string tmp = (desc.Length>0) ? " ("+desc+")" : "";
        return "CrossRef to "+xref.ToString( )+tmp;
    }
}
```

From the attribute user's perspective, this attribute can be applied to any target multiple times (note the use of the AttributeUsage attribute to control this).

CrossRefAttribute takes one mandatory positional parameter (namely the type to cross reference) and one optional named parameter (the description), and is used as follows:

```
[CrossRef(typeof(Bar), Description="Foos often hang around Bars")]
class Foo {...}
```

Essentially, this attribute embeds cross references to dynamically linked types (with optional descriptions) in the metadata. This information can then be retrieved at runtime by a class browser to present a more complete view of a type's dependencies.

Retrieving a Custom Attribute at Runtime

Retrieving attributes at runtime is done using reflection via one of System. Attribute's GetCustomAttribute or GetCustomAttributes overloads. Here is an example that uses and inspects the CrossRefAttribute using GetCustomAttribute:

```
// XRefTest.cs - apply and inspect a CrossRefAttribute
// Compile with: csc /r:XRef.dll XRefTest.cs
using System;
class Bar { }
[CrossRef(typeof(Bar), Description="Foos often hang around Bars")]
class Foo {
  static void Main( ) {
    // Retrieve the custom attribute from type Foo
    Attribute attr =
      Attribute.GetCustomAttribute(typeof(Foo),
                              typeof(CrossRefAttribute));
    // Display the attribute.
    if (attr != null) {
      CrossRefAttribute cr = (CrossRefAttribute)attr;
      Console.WriteLine(cr);
    }
  }
}
```

This is one of the few circumstances where the difference between custom attributes and pseudocustom attributes becomes apparent, since pseudocustom attributes can't be retrieved with GetCustomAttribute. Here is another example that uses reflection to determine which attributes are on a specific type:

```
using System;
[Serializable, Obsolete]
class Test {
  static void Main( ) {
    Type t = typeof(Test);
    object[ ] caarr = Attribute.GetCustomAttributes(t);
    Console.WriteLine("{0} has {1} custom attribute(s)",
                      t, caarr.Length);
    foreach (object ca in caarr)
      Console.WriteLine(ca);
  }
}
```

Although the Test class of the preceding example has two attributes specified, the sample produces the following output:

```
Test has 1 custom attribute(s)
System.ObsoleteAttribute
```

This demonstrates how the Serializable attribute (a pseudocustom attribute) isn't accessible via reflection, while the Obsolete attribute (a custom attribute) is.

15

Memory Management

Almost all modern programming languages allocate memory in two places: on the stack and on the heap. Memory allocated on the stack stores local variables, parameters, and return values, and is generally managed automatically by the operating system. Memory allocated on the heap, however, is treated differently by different languages. In C and C++, memory allocated on the heap is managed manually. In C# and Java, however, memory allocated on the heap is managed automatically.

While manual memory management has the advantage of being simple for runtimes to implement, it has drawbacks that tend not to exist in systems that offer automatic memory management. For example, a large percentage of bugs in C and C++ programs stem from using an object after it has been deleted (dangling pointers) or forgetting to delete an object when it is no longer needed (memory leaks).

The process of automatically managing memory is known as garbage collection. While generally more complex for runtimes to implement than traditional manual memory management, garbage collection greatly simplifies development and eliminates many common errors related to manual memory management.

For example, it is almost impossible to generate a traditional memory leak in C#, and common bugs such as circular references in traditional COM development simply go away.

The Garbage Collector

C# depends on the CLR for many of its runtime services, and garbage collection is no exception.

The CLR includes a high-performing generational mark-and-compact garbage collector (GC) that performs automatic memory management for type instances stored on the managed heap.

The GC is considered to be a *tracing* garbage collector in that it doesn't interfere with every access to an object, but rather wakes up intermittently and traces the graph of objects stored on the managed heap to determine which objects can be considered garbage and therefore collected.

The GC generally initiates a garbage collection when a memory allocation occurs and memory is too low to fulfill the request. This process can also be initiated manually using the System.GC type. Initiating a garbage collection freezes all threads in the process to allow the GC time to examine the managed heap.

The GC begins with the set of object references considered roots, and walks the object graph, marking all the objects it touches as reachable. Once this process is complete, all objects that have not been marked are considered to be garbage.

Objects that are considered garbage and don't have finalizers are immediately discarded, and the memory is reclaimed. Objects that are considered garbage and do have finalizers are flagged for additional asynchronous processing on a separate thread to invoke their Finalize methods before they can be considered garbage and reclaimed at the next collection.

Objects considered still live are then shifted down to the bottom of the heap (compacted), hopefully freeing space to allow the memory allocation to succeed.

At this point the memory allocation is attempted again, the threads in the process are unfrozen, and either normal processing continues or an OutOfMemoryException is thrown.

Optimization Techniques

Although this may sound like an inefficient process compared to simply managing memory manually, the GC incorporates various optimization techniques to reduce the time an application is frozen while waiting for the GC to complete (known as pause time).

The most important of these optimizations is one that makes the GC generational. This technique takes advantage of the fact that while many objects tend to be allocated and discarded rapidly, certain objects are long-lived and thus don't need to be traced during every collection.

Basically, the GC divides the managed heap into three generations. Objects that have just been allocated are considered to be in Gen0, objects that have survived one collection cycle are considered to be in Gen1, and all other objects are considered to be in Gen2.

When it performs a collection, the GC initially collects only Gen0 objects. If not enough memory is reclaimed to fulfill the request, both Gen0 and Gen1 objects are collected; if that fails as well, a full collection of the Gen0, Gen1, and Gen2 objects is attempted.

Many other optimizations are also used to enhance the performance of automatic memory management, and in general a GC-based application can be expected to approach the performance of an application that uses manual memory management.

Finalizers

When implementing your own types, you can choose to give them finalizers (by providing C# destructors). Finalizers are methods called asynchronously by the GC once an object is determined to be garbage.

Although this is required in certain cases, in general there are many good technical reasons to avoid the use of finalizers.

As described in the previous section, objects with finalizers incur significant overhead when they are collected, requiring asynchronous invocation of their Finalize methods and taking two full GC cycles for their memory to be reclaimed.

Other reasons not to use finalizers include:

- Objects with finalizers take longer to allocate on the managed heap than objects without finalizers.
- Objects with finalizers that refer to other objects (even those without finalizers) can prolong the life of the referred objects unnecessarily.
- It's impossible to predict in what order the finalizers for a set of objects will be called.
- You have limited control over when (or even if!) the finalizer for an object will be called.

In summary, finalizers are somewhat like lawyers—while there are cases in which you really need them, in general you don't want to use them unless absolutely necessary. If you do use them, you need to be 100 percent sure you understand what they are doing for you.

If you have to implement a finalizer, follow these guidelines or have a very good reason for not doing so:

- Ensure that your finalizer executes quickly.
- Never block in your finalizer.
- Free any unmanaged resources you own.
- Don't reference any other objects.
- Don't throw any unhandled exceptions.

Dispose and Close Methods

Implementing a finalizer gives your type an opportunity to release any external unmanaged resources (such as database connections or file handles) that it may be holding onto. From the perspective of the users of your type, this makes the resource management implicit: they interact with your type, and your type interacts with the resource as needed. However, since GC happens asynchronously and there are no guarantees as to exactly when the finalizers will be called, this level of control may not be sufficient. In these cases, it is good practice to also offer clients explicit resource management controls.

To provide explicit resource management to clients of your type, implement the IDisposable interface. This offers clients a Dispose( ) method they can call to explicitly instruct you to release resources. For types in which Dispose( ) doesn't make sense, provide an explicit Close( ) method that optionally forwards to a private implementation of IDisposable.Dispose. If your type also has a finalizer (via a C# destructor), your Dispose( ) or Close( ) implementation should include a special call to the static SuppressFinalize( ) method on the System.GC type to indicate that the destructor no longer needs to be called. Typically, the real finalizer is written to call the Dispose/Close method, as follows:

```
using System;
public class Worker : IDisposable {
  int id;
  public Worker(int id) {
    this.id = id;
  }
  // ...
  protected virtual void Dispose(bool disposing) {
    if (disposing) {
      // Not in finalizer, can reference other managed objects here
      Console.WriteLine("Disposing {0}: Releasing managed resources", id);
      // Call Dispose on other managed resources you're holding refs to
    }
    Console.WriteLine("Disposing {0}: Releasing unmanaged resources", id);
    // Release any unmanaged resources you're holding
  }
  public void Dispose( ) {
    Dispose(true);
    GC.SuppressFinalize(this); // Mark this object finalized
  }
  ~Worker( ) {
    Console.WriteLine("Finalizing {0}: Calling Dispose( )", id);
    Dispose(false);
  }
  public static void Main( ) {
    // create a worker and call Dispose when we're done.
    using(Worker w1 = new Worker(1)) {
      // ...
    }
    // create a worker that will get cleaned up when the CLR
    // gets around to it.
    Worker w2 = new Worker(2);
  }
}
```

If you run this code, you will see that the finalizer for Worker(1) is never called, since its Dispose( ) method is called once execution leaves the using block, and the Dispose( ) method calls GC.SuppressFinalize( ).

```
Disposing 1: Releasing managed resources
Disposing 1: Releasing unmanaged resources
Finalizing 2: Calling Dispose( )
Disposing 2: Releasing unmanaged resources
```

Worker 2 is finalized and disposed when the CLR gets around to it, but it's never given a chance to clean up other objects. The disposable pattern gives you a way to close or dispose of any external objects you might be using, such as an I/O stream, in a safe and consistent manner.

16

Threading

A C# application runs in one or more threads that effectively execute in parallel within the same application. Here is a simple multithreaded application:

```
using System;
using System.Threading;
class ThreadTest {
  static void Main( ) {
  Thread t = new Thread(new ThreadStart(Go));
    t.Start( );
    Go( );
  }
  static void Go( ) {
    for (char c='a'; c<='z'; c++ )
      Console.Write(c);
  }
}
```

In this example, a new thread object is constructed by passing it a ThreadStart delegate that wraps the method that specifies where to start execution for that thread. Then start the thread and call Go, so two separate threads are running Go in parallel. However, there's one problem. Both threads share a common resource: the console. If you run ThreadTest, you receive output something like this:

```
abcdabcdefghijklmnopqrsefghijklmnopqrstuvwxyztuvwxyz
```

Thread Synchronization

Thread synchronization comprises techniques for ensuring that multiple threads coordinate their access to shared resources.

The lock Statement

C# provides the lock statement to ensure that only one thread at a time can access a block of code. Consider the following example:

```
using System;
using System.Threading;
class LockTest {
  static void Main( ) {
    LockTest lt = new LockTest ( );
    Thread t = new Thread(new ThreadStart(lt.Go));
    t.Start( );
    lt.Go( );
  }
  void Go( ) {
    lock(this)
      for ( char c='a'; c<='z'; c++)
        Console.Write(c);
  }
}
```

Running LockTest produces the following output:

```
abcdefghijklmnopqrstuvwxyzabcdefghijklmnopqrstuvwxyz
```

The lock statement acquires a lock on any reference type instance. If another thread has already acquired the lock, the thread doesn't continue until the other thread relinquishes its lock on that instance.

The lock statement is actually a syntactic shortcut for calling the Enter( ) and Exit( ) methods of the FCL Monitor class (see "The Monitor Class"):

```
System.Threading.Monitor.Enter(expression);
try {
  ...
}
finally {
  System.Threading.Monitor.Exit(expression);
}
```

Pulse and Wait Operations

The next most common threading operations are Pulse and Wait in combination with locks. These operations let threads communicate with each other via a monitor that maintains a list of threads waiting to grab an object's lock:

```
using System;
using System.Threading;
class MonitorTest {
  static void Main( ) {
    MonitorTest mt = new MonitorTest( );
    Thread t = new Thread(new ThreadStart(mt.Go));
    t.Start( );
    mt.Go( );
  }
  void Go( ) {
```

```
        for ( char c='a'; c<='z'; c++)
          lock(this) {
             Console.Write(c);
             Monitor.Pulse(this);
             Monitor.Wait(this);
          }
    }
}
```

Running MonitorTest produces the following result:

aabbccddeeffgghhiijjkkllmmnnooppqqrrssttuuvvwwxxyyzz

The Pulse method tells the monitor to wake up the next thread that is waiting to get a lock on that object as soon as the current thread has released it. The current thread typically releases the monitor in one of two ways. First, execution may leave the lock statement blocked. Alternatively, calling the Wait method temporarily releases the lock on an object and makes the thread fall asleep until another thread wakes it up by pulsing the object.

Deadlocks

The MonitorTest example actually contains a type of bug called a deadlock. When you run the program, it prints the correct output, but then the console window locks up. This is because there are two sleeping threads, and neither will wake the other. The deadlock occurs because when printing z, each thread goes to sleep but never gets pulsed. Solve the problem by replacing the Go method with this new implementation:

```
    void Go( ) {
      for ( char c='a'; c<='z'; c++)
         lock(this) {
            Console.Write(c);
            Monitor.Pulse(this);
            if (c<'z')
               Monitor.Wait(this);
         }
    }
```

In general, the danger of using locks is that two threads may both end up being blocked waiting for a resource held by the other thread. Most common deadlock situations can be avoided by ensuring that you always acquire resources in the same order.

Atomic Operations

Atomic operations are operations the system promises will not be interrupted. In the previous examples, the Go method isn't atomic, because it can be interrupted while it is running so another thread can run. However, updating a variable is atomic, because the operation is guaranteed to complete without control being passed to another thread. The Interlocked class provides additional atomic operations, which allow basic operations to perform without requiring a lock. This can be useful, since acquiring a lock is many times slower than a simple atomic operation.

Common Thread Types

Much of the functionality of threads is provided through the classes in the System. Threading namespace. The most basic thread class to understand is the Monitor class, which is explained next.

The Monitor Class

The System.Threading.Monitor class provides an implementation of Hoare's Monitor that allows you to use any reference-type instance as a monitor.

The Enter and Exit Methods

The Enter( ) and Exit( ) methods respectively obtain and release a lock on an object. If the object is already held by another thread, Enter( ) waits until the lock is released, or the thread is interrupted by a ThreadInterruptedException. Every call to Enter( ) for a given object on a thread should be matched with a call to Exit( ) for the same object on the same thread.

The TryEnter Methods

The TryEnter( ) methods are similar to the Enter( ) method, but they don't require a lock on the object to proceed. These methods return true if the lock is obtained, and false if it isn't, optionally passing in a timeout parameter that specifies the maximum time to wait for the other threads to relinquish the lock.

The Wait Methods

The thread holding a lock on an object may call one of the Wait( ) methods to temporarily release the lock and block itself, while it waits for another thread to notify it by executing a pulse on the monitor. This approach can tell a worker thread there is work to perform on that object. The overloaded versions of Wait( ) allow you to specify a timeout that reactivates the thread if a pulse hasn't arrived within the specified duration. When the thread wakes up, it reacquires the monitor for the object (potentially blocking until the monitor becomes available). Wait( ) returns true if the thread is reactivated by another thread pulsing the monitor and returns false if the Wait( ) call times out without receiving a pulse.

The Pulse and PulseAll Methods

A thread holding a lock on an object may call Pulse( ) on that object to wake up a blocked thread as soon as the thread calling Pulse( ) has released its lock on the monitor. If multiple threads are waiting on the same monitor, Pulse( ) activates only the first in the queue (successive calls to Pulse( ) wake up other waiting threads, one per call). The PulseAll( ) method successively wakes up all the threads.

Asynchronous Delegates

Sometimes it is desirable to call a method asynchronously, so the call returns immediately while the method executes on a separate thread. The runtime provides a standard way that any method can be called asynchronously, taking into account retrieving return values and ref/in parameters supplied to the method. When the C# compiler encounters a delegate, the delegate derived class it generates contains three key methods:

```
return-type Invoke (parameter-list);
IAsyncResult BeginInvoke (parameter-list, AsyncCallback ac, object state);
return-type EndInvoke (ref/out-only parameter-list, IAsyncCallback ac);
```

Calling Invoke() calls the method synchronously, and the caller has to wait until the delegate finishes executing (a standard delegate invocation in C# calls Invoke()).

Calling BeginInvoke() invokes the delegate with the supplied parameter list, then immediately returns. This asynchronous call is performed as soon as a thread is available in the ThreadPool. Two additional parameters are added to BeginInvoke(): an AsyncCallback object, to optionally specify a delegate to execute by the ThreadPool thread just before it returns, and an arbitrary object to hold state. The AsyncCallback delegate signature is a void method with a single IAsyncResult parameter, which lets you access information about the call.

Calling EndInvoke() retrieves the return value of the called method, along with any ref/out parameters that may have been modified.

In the following example, we call TimeConsumingFunction() twice asynchronously, whereby the Main method can continue executing while work is being done by each TimeConsumingFunction. To keep the example simple, these functions happen to execute very fast, but this methodology could be applied to much slower functions such as file I/O functions.

```
using System;
using System.Threading;
using System.Runtime.Remoting.Messaging;

delegate int Compute (string s);

public class Test {
  static int TimeConsumingFunction (string s) {
    return s.Length;
  }

  static void DisplayFunctionResult (IAsyncResult ar) {
    Compute c = (Compute)((AsyncResult)ar).AsyncDelegate;
    int result = c.EndInvoke(ar);
    string s = (string)ar.AsyncState;
    Console.WriteLine ("{0} is {1} characters long", s, result);
  }

  static void Main () {
    Compute c = new Compute (TimeConsumingFunction);
```

```
        AsyncCallback ac = new AsyncCallback (DisplayFunctionResult);
        string s1 = "Christopher";
        string s2 = "Nolan";
        IAsyncResult ar1 = c.BeginInvoke (s1, ac, s1);
        IAsyncResult ar2 = c.BeginInvoke (s2, ac, s2);
        Console.WriteLine ("Ready");
        Console.Read( );
    }
}
```

The output is:

```
Ready
Christopher is 11 characters long
Nolan is 5 characters long
```

17

Integrating with Native DLLs

While it would be convenient if all applications could be written entirely in managed code, and you never had to depend on the services of "legacy" code, this situation is not likely to occur in the immediate future. For the purposes of this discussion, legacy code is defined as any code written in a traditional Microsoft language, such as Visual C++ or VB, for an already released operating system, such as Windows 2000 or Windows XP, or a virtual machine such as the VB runtime. Practically speaking, it is essential that managed code be able to draw on the services of unmanaged code in an efficient and well-integrated manner. Thankfully, the .NET Framework is an over-achiever in this area, providing excellent support for integrating with traditional DLLs as well as COM components and COM+ applications.

This section introduces and demonstrates the facilities for integrating with existing unmanaged code packaged in traditional DLLs. Unless otherwise stated, the types mentioned in this section all exist in either the System or System. Runtime.InteropServices namespaces.

Calling Into DLLs

PInvoke, short for Platform Invocation Services, lets C# access functions, structs, and callbacks in unmanaged DLLs. For example, perhaps you wish to call the MessageBox function in the Windows DLL *user32.dll*:

```
int MessageBox(HWND hWnd, LPCTSTR lpText,
               LPCTSTR lpCation, UINT uType);
```

To call this function, you can write a static extern method decorated with the DllImport attribute:

```
using System.Runtime.InteropServices;
class MsgBoxTest {
  [DllImport("user32.dll")]
```

```
static extern int MessageBox(int hWnd, string text,
                             string caption, int type);
public static void Main( ) {
    MessageBox(0, "Please do not press this button again.",
             "Attention", 0);
}
}
```

PInvoke then finds and loads the required Win32 DLLs and resolves the entry point of the requested function. The CLR includes a marshaler that knows how to convert parameters and return values between .NET types and unmanaged types. In this example the int parameters translate directly to four-byte integers that the function expects, and the string parameters are converted into null-terminated arrays of characters using one-byte ANSI characters under Win9x, or into two-byte Unicode characters under WinNT/Win2K.

Marshaling Common Types

The CLR marshaler is a .NET facility that knows about the core types used by COM and the Windows API, and provides default translations to CLR types for you. The bool type, for instance, can be translated into a two-byte Windows BOOL type or a four-byte Boolean type. Using the MarshalAs attribute, you can override a default translation:

```
using System.Runtime.InteropServices;
static extern int Foo([MarshalAs(UnmanagedType.LPStr)]
                      string s);
```

In this case, the marshaler was told to use LPStr, so it will always use ANSI characters. Array classes and the StringBuilder class copy the marshaled value from an external function back to the managed value, as follows:

```
using System;
using System.Text;
using System.Runtime.InteropServices;
class Test {
    [DllImport("kernel32.dll")]
    static extern int GetWindowsDirectory(StringBuilder sb,
                                          int maxChars);

    static void Main( ) {
        StringBuilder s = new StringBuilder(256);
        GetWindowsDirectory(s, 256);
        Console.WriteLine(s);
    }
}
```

Marshaling Classes and Structs

Passing a class or struct to a C function requires marking the struct or class with the StructLayout attribute:

```
// InteropFun.cs - compile with /nowarn:649 or add "=0;" default
//    initializers to the fields in SystemTime to avoid warnings
```

```csharp
using System;
using System.Runtime.InteropServices;
[StructLayout(LayoutKind.Sequential)]
class SystemTime {
    public ushort wYear;
    public ushort wMonth;
    public ushort wDayOfWeek;
    public ushort wDay;
    public ushort wHour;
    public ushort wMinute;
    public ushort wSecond;
    public ushort wMilliseconds;
}
class InteropFun {
    [DllImport("kernel32.dll")]
    static extern void GetSystemTime(SystemTime t);
    static void Main() {
        SystemTime t = new SystemTime();
        GetSystemTime(t);
        Console.WriteLine(t.wYear);
    }
}
```

In both C and C#, fields in an object are located at *n* number of bytes from the address of that object. The difference is that in a C# program, the CLR finds this offset by looking it up using the field name; C field names are compiled directly into offsets. For instance, in C, wDay is just a token to represent whatever is at the address of a SystemTime instance plus 24 bytes.

For access speed and future widening of a data type, these offsets are usually in multiples of a minimum width, called the *pack size*. For .NET types, the pack size is usually set at the discretion of the runtime, but by using the StructLayout attribute, field offsets can be controlled. When using this attribute, the default pack size is 8 bytes, but it can be set to 1, 2, 4, 8, or 16 bytes (pass Pack=*packsize* to the StructLayout constructor). There are also explicit options to control individual field offsets (see "Simulating a C Union" later in this chapter). This lets a .NET type pass to a C function.

In and Out Marshaling

The previous Test example works if SystemTime is a struct and t is a ref parameter, but is actually less efficient:

```csharp
struct SystemTime {...}
static extern void GetSystemTime(ref SystemTime t);
```

This is because the marshaler must always create fresh values for external parameters, so the previous method copies t when going in to the function. It then copies the marshaled t when coming out of the function. By default, pass-by-value parameters are copied in, C# ref parameters are copied in/out, and C# out parameters are copied out, but there are exceptions for the types that have custom conversions. For instance, array classes and the StringBuilder class require copying when coming out of a function, so they are in/out. It is occasionally useful to override this behavior, with the In and Out attributes. For example, if an array should be read-only, the in modifier indicates to only copy the array going into the function, and not come out of it:

```
static extern void Foo([In] int[ ] array);
```

Callbacks from Unmanaged Code

The P/Invoke layer does its best to present a natural programming model on both sides of the boundary, mapping between the relevant constructs where possible. Since C# not only can call out to C functions but can also be called back from the C functions (via function pointers), the P/Invoke layer needs to map unmanaged function pointers onto something natural for the managed world. The managed equivalent of a function pointer is a delegate, so the P/Invoke layer automatically maps between delegates (in C#) and function pointers (in C). To call a function in a DLL that takes a callback function pointer as a parameter, declare a delegate with the correct signature for the callback function and pass an instance of the delegate when calling the function that performs the callback, as follows:

```
using System;
using System.Runtime.InteropServices;

class CallbackFun {
    delegate bool CallBack(int hWnd, int lParam);
    [DllImport("user32.dll")]
    static extern int EnumWindows(CallBack hWnd, int lParam);
    static bool PrintWindow(int hWnd, int lParam) {
        Console.WriteLine(hWnd);
        return true;
    }
    static void Main( ) {
        CallBack e = new CallBack(PrintWindow);
        EnumWindows(e, 0);
    }
}
```

Simulating a C Union

Each field in a struct is given enough room to store its data. Consider a struct containing one int and one char. The int is likely to start at an offset of 0, and is guaranteed at least four bytes. So, the char could start at an offset of 4. If, for some reason, the char started at an offset of 2, then you'd change the value of the int if you assigned a value to the char. Sounds like mayhem, doesn't it? Strangely enough, the C language supports a variation on a struct called a *union* that does exactly this. You can simulate this in C# using LayoutKind.Explicit and the FieldOffset attribute.

It might be hard to think of a case in which this would be useful. However, consider a situation in which you want to create a vast quantity of different primitive types, but store them in one array. You have to store them all in an object array, and the primitive values are boxed every time they go into the array. This means you're going to start using a lot of heap memory, and you'll pay the cost of boxing and unboxing as you go from primitive to object and back again. This example shows how this works with three objects, but if it were thousands or millions of objects, the impact on performance would be noticeable:

```
using System;
public class BoxMe {
  public static void Main() {
    // Stuff some primitive values into an array.
    object[ ] a = new object[3];
    a[0] = 1073741824;
    a[1] = 'A';
    a[2] = true;
    // Display each value
    foreach (object o in a) {
      Console.WriteLine("Value: {0}", o);
    }
  }
}
```

To avoid the boxing and unboxing operations, you can use a union to create a *variant type*, which is a type that can take on one value at a time, but can represent a variety of types. Your variant type has a flag field that tells you the type that the variant represents. It also includes one value field for each of the possible types it can take on. Since each value field starts at the same offset, a variant instance never takes up more memory than the largest type plus the size of the flag field (it may also take a couple of bytes to optimally align the fields in memory).

The next example shows the use of a variant struct called MyVariant. It can be an int, char, or bool. The value fields intVal, charVal, and boolVal are stored at an offset (sizeof(byte)) that sets aside enough memory for the flag field vType. This means that the value fields are overlapped. Since the variant can only represent one value at any given time, initializing charVal as "A" will produce that same value even if you inspect intVal. However, the value is treated as an int giving 65, the ASCII value of "A", as shown in this example:

```
using System;
using System.Runtime.InteropServices;

// Enumerate the possible types for MyVariant
public enum MyVariantType : byte { Int, Char, Bool };

// Define a structure for MyVariant
[StructLayout(LayoutKind.Explicit)]
public struct MyVariant {
  // Type flag
  [FieldOffset (0)] public MyVariantType vType;
  // Start the fields, leaving enough room for vType
  [FieldOffset (sizeof(byte))] public int  intVal;
  [FieldOffset (sizeof(byte))] public char charVal;
  [FieldOffset (sizeof(byte))] public bool boolVal;

  // Return a string representation of this Variant
  public override string ToString() {
```

```
      switch (vType) {
        case MyVariantType.Int:
          return intVal.ToString( );
        case MyVariantType.Char:
          return charVal.ToString( );
        case MyVariantType.Bool:
          return boolVal.ToString( );
      }
      throw new Exception("Unknown Variant type: " + vType);
    }
}

// Create an array of variants and display their values
public class VariantTest {
  public static void Main( ) {
    MyVariant[ ] a = new MyVariant[3];
    a[0].vType = MyVariantType.Int;
    a[0].intVal = 1073741824;
    a[1].vType = MyVariantType.Char;
    a[1].charVal = 'A';
    a[2].vType = MyVariantType.Bool;
    a[2].boolVal = true;

    // Display each variant's value
    foreach (MyVariant mv in a) {
      Console.WriteLine("Value: {0}", mv);
    }
    // Reinterpret the char as an int
    Console.WriteLine("{0} is: {1}", a[1], a[1].intVal);
  }
}
```

Mapping a Struct to a Binary Format

You can use the LayoutKind.Sequential argument with the StructLayout attribute
to tell .NET to ensure that struct fields are laid out in the order in which they are
defined. You can use this to create a struct that maps to a binary format, such as a
GIF image. If you use this in conjunction with Win32 APIs for mapping a file into
memory, you can define such a struct, load a file into memory, and superimpose
the struct over that region of memory.

The next example features a struct, Gif89a, whose fields map directly to the
layout of a GIF image. Because you can't define a fixed-length array in a C#
struct, use a sequence of three bytes to hold the GIF signature ("GIF") and the
version ("89a"). The Signature and Version properties each have an accessor
method that turns these bytes into a string. The Dump( ) method displays the
version and the dimensions of the GIF.

The Main( ) method uses three functions defined in *kernel32.dll* to map a GIF file
into memory. Then, it casts that memory region (starting at baseAddress) to a
Gif89a. This maps the struct onto the binary file format, eliminating the need to
write code that parses each individual field of the GIF header.

```
// GIFInspects.cs - compile with /unsafe
using System;
using System.IO;
using System.Runtime.InteropServices;

[StructLayout(LayoutKind.Sequential)]
public struct Gif89a {
  byte sig0, sig1, sig2; // Signature
  byte ver0, ver1, ver2; // Version
  public ushort ScreenWidth;
  public ushort ScreenHeight;
  // other members of GIF89a header removed for brevity
  public string Signature { // concatenate the bytes to get a string
    get {
      char[ ] c = {(char) sig0, (char) sig1, (char) sig2};
      return new String(c);
    }
  }
  public string Version {
    get {
      char[ ] c = {(char) ver0, (char) ver1, (char) ver2};
      return new String(c);
    }
  }
  public void Dump( ) {
    Console.WriteLine("Image size: {0}x{1}", ScreenWidth, ScreenHeight);
    Console.WriteLine("GIF Type: {0}{1}", Signature, Version);
  }
}

public class GIFInspect {
  const uint PAGE_READONLY = 0x02; // from winnt.h
  const uint FILE_MAP_READ = 0x04; // from WinBASE.h
  [DllImport("kernel32.dll")]
  private static extern int CreateFileMapping(IntPtr hFile,
                                              int lpAttributes,
                                              uint flProtect,
                                              uint dwMaximumSizeHigh,
                                              uint dwMaximumSizeLow,
                                              string lpName);
  [DllImport("kernel32.dll")]
  private static extern uint MapViewOfFile(int hFileMappingObject,
                                           uint dwDesiredAccess,
                                           uint dwFileOffsetHigh,
                                           uint dwFileOffsetLow,
                                           uint dwNumberOfBytesToMap);
  [DllImport("kernel32.dll")]
  private static extern int CloseHandle(int hObject);

  public static void Main(string[ ] args) {
    // Open the file
    FileStream fs = new FileStream(args[0],
                                   FileMode.Open,
                                   FileAccess.Read,
```

```
                            FileShare.Read);
    // Map the file into memory
    int hSection = CreateFileMapping(fs.Handle, 0, PAGE_READONLY,
                                     0, 0, null);
    uint baseAddress = MapViewOfFile(hSection, FILE_MAP_READ,
                                     0, 0, 0);
    // Cast the memory at baseAddress to a Gif89a
    unsafe {
      Gif89a* ptr = (Gif89a*) baseAddress;
      ptr->Dump( ); // display information about the GIF
    }
    fs.Close( );
    CloseHandle(hSection);
  }
}
```

Predefined Interop Support Attributes

The FCL provides a set of attributes you can use to mark up your objects with information that is used by the CLR marshaling services to alter their default marshaling behavior.

This section describes the most common attributes you need when interoperating with native Win32 DLLs. These attributes all exist in the System.Runtime. InteropServices namespace.

The DllImport Attribute

```
[DllImport (dll-name
  [, EntryPoint=function-name]?
  [, CharSet=charset-enum]?
  [, SetLastError=true|false]?
  [, ExactSpelling=true|false]?
  [, PreserveSig=true|false]?
  [, CallingConvention=callconv-enum?)]
  (for methods)
```

The DllImport attribute annotates an external function that defines a DLL entry point. The parameters for this attribute are as follows:

dll-name
    A string specifying the name of the DLL.

function-name
    A string specifying the function name in the DLL. This is useful if you want the name of your C# function to be different from the name of the DLL function.

charset-enum
    A CharSet enum, specifying how to marshal strings. The default value is CharSet.Auto, which converts strings to ANSI characters on Win98, and to Unicode characters on WinNT.

SetLastError

    If true, preserves the Win32 error info. The default is false.

ExactSpelling

    If true, the EntryPoint must exactly match the function. If false, name-matching heuristics are used. The default is false.

PreserveSig

    If true, the method signature is preserved exactly as it was defined. If false, an HRESULT transformation is performed (see the documentation for "PreserveSigAttribute" in Chapter 36).

callconv-enum

    A CallingConvention enum, specifying the mode to use with the EntryPoint. The default is StdCall.

The StructLayout Attribute

```
[StructLayout(layout-enum
    [, Pack=packing-size]?
    [, CharSet=charset-enum]?
    [, Size=absolute-size?)]
    (for classes, structs)
```

The StructLayout attribute specifies how the data members of a class or struct should be laid out in memory. Although this attribute is commonly used when declaring structures that are passed to or returned from native DLLs, it can also define data structures suited to file and network I/O. The parameters for this attribute are as follows:

layout-enum

    A LayoutKind enum, which can be *sequential* (which lays out fields one after the next with a minimum pack size), *union* (which makes all fields have an offset of 0, so long as they are value types) or *explicit* (which lets each field have a custom offset).

packing-size

    An int specifying whether the packing size is 1, 2, 4, 8, or 16 bytes. The default value is 8.

charset-enum

    A CharSet enum, specifying how to marshal strings. The default value is CharSet.Auto, which converts strings to ANSI characters on Win98, and Unicode characters on WinNT.

absolute-size

    Specifies the size of the struct or class. This has to be at least as large as the sum of all the members.

The FieldOffset Attribute

```
[FieldOffset (byte-offset)]
(for fields)
```

The FieldOffset attribute is used within a class or struct that has explicit field layout. This attribute can be applied to a field and specifies the field offset in bytes from the start of the class or struct. Note that these offsets don't have to be strictly increasing and can overlap, thus creating a union data structure.

The MarshalAs Attribute

```
[MarshalAs(unmanaged-type)
    [, named-parameters]?]
(for fields, parameters, return values)
```

The MarshalAs attribute overrides the default marshaling behavior the marshaler applies to a parameter or field. The *unmanaged-type* value is taken from the UnmanagedType enum; see the following list for the permissible values:

Bool	LPStr	VBByRefStr
I1	LPWStr	AnsiBStr
U1	LPTStr	TBStr
I2	ByValTStr	VariantBool
U2	IUnknown	FunctionPtr
I4	IDispatch	LPVoid
U4	Struct	AsAny
I8	Interface	RPrecise
U8	SafeArray	LPArray
R4	ByValArray	LPStruct
R8	SysInt	CustomMarshaler
BStr	SysUInt	NativeTypeMax
Error		

For a detailed description of how and when to use each of these enum values, as well as other legal *named parameters*, see the .NET Framework SDK documentation.

The In Attribute

```
[In]
(for parameters)
```

The In attribute specifies that data should be marshaled into the caller and can be combined with the Out attribute.

The Out Attribute

```
[Out]
(for parameters)
```

The Out attribute specifies that data should be marshaled out from the called method to the caller and can be combined with the In attribute.

DLLs

18

Integrating with COM Components

The CLR provides support both for exposing C# objects as COM objects and for using COM objects from C#. Additionally, CLR components can make use of COM+ services and can be used as configured components by CLR and classic COM applications.

Binding COM and C# Objects

Interoperating between COM and C# works through either early or late binding. Early binding allows you to program with types known at compile time, while late binding forces you to program with types via dynamic discovery, using reflection on the C# side and IDispatch on the COM side.

When calling COM programs from C#, early binding works by providing metadata in the form of an assembly for the COM object and its interfaces. *TlbImp.exe* takes a COM type library and generates the equivalent metadata in an assembly. With the generated assembly, it's possible to instantiate and call methods on a COM object just as you would on any other C# object.

When calling C# programs from COM, early binding works via a type library. Both *TlbExp.exe* and *RegAsm.exe* allow you to generate a COM type library from your assembly. You can then use this type library with tools that support early binding via type libraries such as Visual Basic 6.

Exposing COM Objects to C#

When you instantiate a COM object, you are actually working with a proxy known as the Runtime Callable Wrapper (RCW). The RCW is responsible for managing the lifetime requirements of the COM object and translating the methods called on it into the appropriate calls on the COM object. When the garbage collector finalizes the RCW, it releases all references to the object it was holding. For situations in which you need to release the COM object without waiting for the garbage collector to finalize the RCW, you can use the static ReleaseComObject method of the System.Runtime.InteropServices.Marshal type.

The following example demonstrates how to change your MSN Instant Messenger friendly name using C# via COM Interop:

```
// RenameMe.cs - compile with:
//    csc RenameMe.cs /r:Messenger.dll
// Run RenameMe.exe "new name" to change your name
//    as it is displayed to other users.
// Run TlbImp.exe "C:\Program Files\Messenger\msmsgs.exe"
//    to create Messenger.dll
using System;
using Messenger;
class MSNFun {
    static void Main(string[ ] args) {
        MsgrObject mo = new MsgrObject( );
        IMsgrService ims = mo.Services.PrimaryService;
        ims.FriendlyName = args[0];
    }
}
```

You can also work with COM objects using the reflection API. This is more cumbersome than using *TlbImp.exe*, but is handy in cases in which it's impossible or inconvenient to run *TlbImp.exe*. To use COM through reflection, you have to get a Type from Type.GetTypeFromProgID( ) for each COM type you want to work with. Then, use Activator.CreateInstance( ) to create an instance of the type. To invoke methods or set or get properties, use the reflection API, which is covered in Chapter 13:

```
using System;
using System.Reflection;
public class ComReflect {
  public static void Main( ) {
    object obj_msword;   // Microsoft Word Application
    Type wa = Type.GetTypeFromProgID("Word.Application", true);
    // Create an instance of Microsoft Word
    obj_msword = Activator.CreateInstance(wa);

    // Use the reflection API from here on in...
  }
}
```

Exposing C# Objects to COM

Just as an RCW proxy wraps a COM object when you access it from C#, code that accesses a C# object as a COM object must do so through a proxy as well. When your C# object is marshaled out to COM, the runtime creates a COM Callable Wrapper (CCW). The CCW follows the same lifetime rules as other COM objects, and as long as it is alive, a CCW maintains a traceable reference to the object it wraps. This keeps the object alive when the garbage collector is run.

The following example shows how you can export both a class and an interface from C# and control the Global Unique Identifiers (GUIDs) and Dispatch IDs (DISPIDs) assigned. After compiling IRunInfo and StackSnapshot, you can register both using *RegAsm.exe*.

```
// IRunInfo.cs
// Compile with:
//    csc /t:library IRunInfo.cs
using System;
using System.Runtime.InteropServices;
[GuidAttribute("aa6b10a2-dc4f-4a24-ae5e-90362c2142c1")]
public interface IRunInfo {
  [DispId(1)]
  string GetRunInfo( );
}

// StackSnapshot.cs
//    compile with csc /t:library /r:IRunInfo.dll StackSnapShot.cs
using System;
using System.Runtime.InteropServices;
using System.Diagnostics;
[GuidAttribute("b72ccf55-88cc-4657-8577-72bd0ff767bc")]
public class StackSnapshot : IRunInfo {
  public StackSnapshot( ) {
    st = new StackTrace( );
  }
  [DispId(1)]
  public string GetRunInfo( ) {
    return st.ToString( );
  }
  private StackTrace st;
}
```

COM Mapping in C#

When you use a COM object from C#, the RCW makes a COM method look like a normal C# instance method. In COM, methods normally return an HRESULT to indicate success or failure and use an out parameter to return a value. In C#, however, methods normally return their result values and use exceptions to report errors. The RCW handles this by checking the HRESULT returned from the call to a COM method and throwing a C# exception when it finds a failure result. With a success result, the RCW returns the parameter marked as the return value in the COM method signature.

 For more information on the argument modifiers and default mappings from COM type library types to C# types, see Appendix C.

Common COM Interop Support Attributes

The FCL provides a set of attributes you can use to mark up your objects with information needed by the CLR interop services to expose managed types to the unmanaged world as COM objects. See Chapter 37, *System.Runtime.InteropServices*, for documentation about these attributes.

COM+ Support

The CLR also includes special plumbing and interop services that allow CLR classes to be deployed as COM+ configured components. This allows both CLR clients and classic COM clients to make use of COM+ services for building scalable applications.

What Is COM+?

COM+ provides a set of services that are designed to help build scalable distributed systems, such as distributed transaction support, object pooling, Just-In-Time activation, synchronization, role-based security, loosely coupled events, and others.

These services are provided by a runtime environment called the COM+ runtime, and are based on the idea of intercepting new COM object creation and (possibly) method calls to layer in the additional services as needed.

COM classes that use COM+ services are called Configured Components because the exact set of services each COM class requires is controlled and configured using declarative attributes that are stored in a metadata repository called the COM+ Catalog.

The COM+ Catalog groups a set of configured components together into something called an Application, which also has metadata settings that control which process the COM components end up in when they are created at runtime (the options here are Library and Server, where Library components end up in the creator's process, while Server components are hosted in a separate process), the security principal the new process runs as, and other settings.

Using COM+ Services with CLR Classes

Naturally, CLR classes can also take advantage of COM+ services. Although the underlying implementation of this is currently the classic COM+ runtime, the mechanics of it are largely hidden from the .NET programmer, who may choose to work almost entirely in terms of normal CLR base classes, interfaces, and custom attributes.

The bulk of the functionality in .NET for using COM+ services is exposed via the System.EnterpriseServices namespace. The most important type in this namespace is the ServicedComponent class, which is the base class that all CLR classes must derive from if they wish to use COM+ services (i.e., if they want to be configured components).

There is a suite of custom attributes in this namespace that can control almost all of the configuration settings that would otherwise be stored in the COM+ Catalog. Examples of these attributes include both assembly-level attributes which control the settings for the entire COM+ application, the ApplicationActivationAttributes, which controls whether the CLR class is deployed in a COM+ Library or Server application, and component-level attributes, which declare and configure the COM+ services the CLR class wishes to be provided at runtime. Examples of component-level custom attributes include the TransactionAttribute (which specifies the COM+ transaction semantics for the class), the JustInTimeActivationAttribute (which specifies that the CLR class should have JITA semantics), the SynchronizationAttribute (which controls the synchronization behavior of methods), the ObjectPoolingAttribute (which controls whether the CLR class is pooled), and many, many others.

Although ServicedComponent serves as a special base class which signals the .NET Framework that a class needs COM+ services, it also provides other capabilities. In classic COM+ work, COM classes implement interfaces such as IObjectConstruct and IObjectControl to customize aspects of their behavior. When using COM+ services in .NET, your classes can override virtual methods provided by ServicedComponent that mirror the functionality in IObjectConstruct and IObjectControl, allowing a very natural, .NET-centric way of accomplishing the same thing.

Other important classes in the System.EnterpriseServices namespace include ContextUtil and SecurityCallContext. These classes provide static methods that allow a CLR-configured component to access COM+ context. This is used to control things like transaction status and to access information such as the security role a caller is in.

Lastly, let's discuss deployment. Deploying traditional COM+ applications requires one to configure the component's COM+ Catalog settings. This is typically done using either the COM+ Explorer (by hand, really only suitable for toy applications) or using custom registration code. When configuring CLR classes, there are two different approaches.

The first approach is using the *RegSvcs.exe* command-line tool. This tool performs all the relevant COM Interop and COM+ Catalog configuration, using both command-line options and the custom attributes applied to your assembly and classes to control the COM+ metadata. While this requires an extra step, arguably this approach is the most powerful and flexible, resulting in CLR-configured classes that can be used from both COM and .NET clients.

Alternatively, the .NET COM+ integration is able to automatically register classes that derive from ServicedComponent in the COM+ catalog when they are first instantiated. This has the advantage of not requiring any additional setup, but also has several disadvantages, most notably that the client code that indirectly causes the registration to occur needs elevated privileges, and until the class is configured, it is invisible to COM clients.

A simple C# configured class might look like this:

```
using System;
using System.EnterpriseServices;
```

```
[assembly:ApplicationName("MyCOMPlusApplication")]
[assembly:ApplicationActivation(ActivationOption.Server)]

[ObjectPooling(true), Transaction(TransactionOption.Required)]
public class MyConfiguredComponent : ServicedComponent {
  public void DoDBWork() {
    ContextUtil.SetAbort();
    // ... do database work...
    ContextUtil.SetComplete();
  }
  public override bool CanBePooled() {
    return true;
  }
}
```

19

Diagnostics

Even good applications sometimes have bad things happen to them. When things go wrong, it is important to detect this as soon as possible, and to gather information to aid in diagnosing the source of the problem. On the developer's desktop, the tools for doing this include debuggers and profilers. However, once the application leaves the desktop, these tools are generally no longer available. Consequently, it becomes the application's responsibility to perform this detection and information-gathering role.

Because providing integrated error handling and reporting is such a common need among applications, the .NET Framework provides a diverse set of facilities to monitor application behavior, detect runtime errors, inspect the application environment, report application status, and integrate with debugging tools if available.

This chapter introduces the debugging and diagnostics support in the .NET Framework, which is primarily contained in the System.Diagnostics namespace. Unless otherwise stated, the types mentioned in this chapter all exist in either the System or System.Diagnostics namespaces.

Logging and Assertion Facilities

The Debug and Trace classes provide error logging and assertion capabilities. These two classes are almost identical; the main differentiator is how they are used. The Debug class is used primarily in debug builds, while the Trace class is used in both debug and release builds.

For error logging and assertion, make use of the Debug and Trace classes where appropriate, then compile with the DEBUG symbol to enable the Debug class and the TRACE symbol to enable the Trace class. This is done using the /define:*symbol* compiler switch, or by using the #define preprocessor directive:

```
#define DEBUG // Equivalent to /d:DEBUG, activates Debug class
#define TRACE // Equivalent to /d:TRACE, activates Trace class
```

Note that using the compiler switch defines the symbols for all the source files in the compilation, while using the preprocessor directive defines only the symbol for the source file the directive appears in.

If these symbols are defined, the Debug and Trace methods function normally. If these symbols are not defined, many of the calls into the Debug and Trace classes are optimized away by the compiler.

Since the Debug and Trace classes are almost identical, we will concentrate on the Debug class in the rest of this section, identifying anything that is specific to either the Debug or Trace classes separately.

The Debug class maintains a collection of TraceListener instances that are responsible for handling (storing, reporting, etc.) application messages. Applications log status messages using the static Debug.WriteXXX methods, which forward the messages to each of the listeners in the Debug.Listeners collection. By default the Listeners collection includes a single listener (DefaultTraceListener), which outputs the message to the system debug console. However, the application is free to add and remove listeners to direct the messages elsewhere.

Adding and removing listeners can be done using a custom listener or one of the predefined listeners, such as the EventLogTraceListener, which logs messages to the Win32 event log, or the TextWriterTraceListener, which logs messages to a file or forwards them to another concrete type via an abstract TextWriter or Stream class, as the following code fragment demonstrates:

```
// Log messages to a file
Debug.Listeners.Add(new TextWriteTraceListener("Debug.out"));

TextWriter tw = Console.Out; // Get TextWriter for stdout
Debug.Listeners.Add(new TextWriterTraceListener(tw));

Stream stm = GetNetworkStream(); // Connects to remote listener
Debug.Listeners.Add(new TextWriterTraceListener(stm));
```

Messages are written using the Write, WriteLine, WriteIf, and WriteLineIf overloads. Messages may optionally be assigned to a category, allowing listeners to group related messages. Messages may also be indented. Examples of using these methods are as follows:

```
Debug.Write("Send this to all listeners, uncategorized");
Debug.WriteLine("Error", "Group this message with other errors");

Debug.Indent();
Debug.WriteLineIf(bLogging, "Hug a tree (indented)"); // conditional
Debug.Unindent();
```

When using listeners that may require cleanup, such as the TextWriterTraceListener, remember to call the Flush and Close methods on application shutdown, as follows:

```
Debug.Flush(); // Flush underlying FileStream
Debug.Close(); // Close Debug.out file
```

A useful technique for detecting error conditions early is using asserts to verify class or method invariants. The Debug and Trace classes both provide Assert and

Fail methods that test expressions and can optionally invoke the debugger or log messages when an assertion fails, as follows:

```
Debug.Assert(expression); // Use to check class or method invariants
Debug.Assert(false, "Alert the listeners!"); // Log invalid assertions
...
Trace.Fail("Unknown error - about to die horribly");
Trace.Assert(veryImportantInvariant); // Asserts in release builds too...
```

Conditional Compilation

The presence or absence of the DEBUG and TRACE symbols tell the compiler how to handle calls to methods in the Debug and Trace classes. If the DEBUG or TRACE symbols are not defined, many of the method calls into the Debug and Trace classes are optimized away completely. This can be a desirable feature for your own types, and there are a number of ways to accomplish this with the .NET Framework and the C# language.

One option is to bracket the calls with #if/#endif preprocessor directives, as follows:

```
void DoWork() {
#if METHODCALL
    Debug.WriteLine("MethodCall", "Entering MyClass::DoWork");
#endif
    Console.WriteLine("Working...");
}
```

Compiling this function with /d:METHODCALL,DEBUG results in a call to Debug. WriteLine and a log of the method entry. The downside to this approach is using preprocessor directives such as this is arduous and error-prone, and the code quickly becomes unreadable.

An alternative is to use the ConditionalAttribute custom attribute. When placed on a method, this attribute instructs the C# compiler to conditionally omit calls to the method.

Using this approach we can define a reflection-driven logger, as follows:

```
public class Logger {
  [Conditional("METHODCALL")]
  public static void LogMethodCall() {
    StackFrame sf = new StackFrame(1); // Get preceding stack frame
    MethodBase mb = sf.GetMethod(); // Get refl. info for method
    Type t = mb.DeclaringType; // Get refl. info for type
    string s = String.Format("Entering {0}::{1}", t.Name, mb.Name);
    Debug.WriteLine("MethodCall", s); // Dump methodcall
  }
}
```

Client code can simply call this method on method entry, as follows:

```
void DoWork() {
  Logger.LogMethodCall();
  Console.WriteLine("Working...");
}
```

When client code is compiled with METHODCALL defined, the C# compiler emits calls to the LogMethodCall function. If METHODCALL is not defined, the compiler omits the calls entirely.

Debugger Integration

Sometimes it is useful for an application to interact with a debugger if one is present. This is done using the System.Diagnostics.Debugger class. Properties and methods on this class allow one to detect if a debugger is attached (IsAttached) and logging messages (IsLogged); launch, attach, and signal a debugger (Launch); signal an attached debugger, launching one if necessary (Break); and log messages to a debugger if one is attached (Log).

Additionally, there are two custom attributes (DebuggerStepThroughAttribute and DebuggerHiddenAttribute) that can be placed on methods to control how the debugger handles the method.

DebuggerStepThroughAttribute indicates to the debugger that the method should be automatically stepped through without any user interaction. This attribute is suited for use in proxies and functions where the proxy method or thunk* performs some trivial and/or predictable setup, calls the real method, and then performs some similarly trivial and/or predictable teardown. When single-stepping through code that calls the proxy method or thunk, the debugger automatically steps down into the real method.

When stepping through the "real" method, the call stack in the debugger still lists the proxy method or thunk. To hide it completely, use the related DebuggerHiddenAttribute attribute. These two attributes can be combined on proxies and thunks to help the user focus on debugging the application logic, not the plumbing.

```
void DoWork( ) {...} // Real method...
...
[DebuggerStepThrough, DebuggerHidden]
void DoWorkProxy( ) {
  // setup...
  DoWork( );
  // teardown...
}
...
o.DoWorkProxy( ); // "Step into" passes control into DoWork( )
```

Processes, Threads, and Stacks

The .NET Framework provides managed execution of code. However, managed applications live alongside unmanaged applications, and need to coexist. It can be useful for a managed application to have access to information about the atoms of unmanaged execution, namely operating system processes and threads.

* A "thunk" is a small piece of code that forwards a call to another function.

Additionally, since "managed execution" implies the existence of some over-arching facility monitoring the execution process itself, it is not unreasonable to wish for access to detailed information about the execution process. Both of these needs are met by the classes in the System.Diagnostics namespace, providing access to unmanaged processes and threads, as well as access to managed stack frames. Access to managed threads and AppDomains, which are the managed equivalent of processes, is accomplished using the System and System.Threading namespaces.

Launching a New Process

The Process class can be used to launch new operating system processes, enumerate and kill existing ones, and monitor the vital statistics of a running process. The Process.Start method has overloads that range from taking the file-name of an EXE to launch to taking a populated ProcessStartInfo instance, which fully specifies the parameters for process launching. The latter approach can also be used to capture and redirect the launched process's stdin, stdout and stderr, as the following sample demonstrates:

```
public void LaunchDirCommand( ) {
    ProcessStartInfo psi = new ProcessStartInfo( );
    psi.FileName = "cmd.exe";
    psi.Arguments = "/c dir";
    psi.RedirectStandardOutput = true;
    psi.UseShellExecute = false;
    Process p = Process.Start(psi);
    StreamReader stm = p.StandardOutput;
    string s = stm.ReadToEnd( );
    Console.WriteLine(s);
}
```

Examining Running Processes

The Process.GetProcessXXX methods allow an application to retrieve a specific process by name or process ID, and to enumerate all running processes. Given a valid process instance, a wealth of properties provide access to the process's vital statistics such as name, ID, priority, memory and processor utilization, window handles, etc. The following sample enumerates some basic information for all the running processes in the system:

```
public void EnumerateRunningProcesses( ) {
    Process[ ] procs = Process.GetProcesses( );
    foreach (Process p in procs) {
        Console.WriteLine("{0} ({1})", p.ProcessName, p.Id);
        Console.WriteLine("  Started: {0}", p.StartTime);
        Console.WriteLine("  Working set: {0}", p.WorkingSet);
        Console.WriteLine("  Processor time: {0}", p.TotalProcessorTime);
        Console.WriteLine("  Threads: {0}", p.Threads.Count);
    }
}
```

Examining Threads in a Process

Building on the previous example, it is also possible to retrieve information on the operating system threads in a process using the Process.Threads property. This returns a collection of ProcessThread instances, each representing an underlying operating system thread (which may or may not have a managed System.Threading.Thread counterpart). Given a reference to a ProcessThread instance we can discover a host of information about the underlying thread and even control aspects such as thread priority and processor affinity.

```
public void EnumerateThreads(Process p) {
  ProcessThreadCollection ptc = p.Threads;
  foreach (ProcessThread pt in ptc) {
    Console.WriteLine("Thread {0} ({1})", pt.Id, pt.ThreadState);
    Console.WriteLine("  Priority Level: {0}", pt.PriorityLevel);
    Console.WriteLine("  Started: {0}", pt.StartTime);
    Console.WriteLine("  Processor time: {0}", pt.TotalProcessorTime);
  }
}
...
Process p = Process.GetCurrentProcess();
EnumerateThreads(p);
```

Examining Stack Frames for a Thread

One of the benefits of managed execution is that the Execution Engine has visibility into the execution process for managed applications. The StackTrace and StackFrame classes provide read-only access to some of this information, namely the application call stack and the individual stack frames. This information can be used in exception handling code to determine what led up to the failure, and to improve the quality of error reporting.

```
// Compile with /debug+ to disable JIT inlining, provide src debug info
using System;
using System.Diagnostics;

class DumpStackFrames {
  static void WalkStack() {
    StackTrace st = new StackTrace(true); // true==use .PDB if available
    Console.Write("Current stack has {0} frames", st.FrameCount);
    for (int i=0; i<st.FrameCount; i++) {
      StackFrame sf = st.GetFrame(i);
      Console.Write("\nFrame {0}: {1}, ", i, sf.GetMethod().Name);
      Console.Write("{0}@{1}", sf.GetFileName(), sf.GetFileLineNumber());
    }
  }
  static void A() { B(); }
  static void B() { C(); }
  static void C() { WalkStack(); }
  static void Main() { A(); }
}
```

A run of the preceding example produces the following output:

```
Current stack has 5 frames
Frame 0: WalkStack, c:\CSiaN\Diagnostics\DumpStack.cs@7
Frame 1: C, c:\CSiaN\Diagnostics\DumpStack.cs@17
Frame 2: B, c:\CSiaN\Diagnostics\DumpStack.cs@16
Frame 3: A, c:\CSiaN\Diagnostics\DumpStack.cs@15
Frame 4: Main, c:\CSiaN\Diagnostics\DumpStack.cs@18
```

Event Logs

Useful as the Debug and Trace classes are, the Win32 platform already provides a logging mechanism in the form of the event log. Classes are provided in the System.Diagnostics namespace that allow applications to enumerate the existing event sources and logs, read from and write to an event log manually, use an event log as a backing store for Trace or Debug output, create and install new event sources, and monitor an event log for changes.

Reading the Event Log

To read an event log, create an instance of the EventLog class with the name of the log you wish to access, and optionally the name of the machine on which the log resides and the event source with which to filter the log entries. Once you have a valid EventLog instance, it provides a wealth of properties and methods that let you examine and manipulate the log as a whole. To read the individual entries in the log, use the EventLog.Entries property to retrieve a collection of EventLogEntry instances. The following sample displays information on any log on your system:

```
// DumpLog.cs - use DumpLog <logname>
using System;
using System.Diagnostics;

class DumpLog {
  static void Main(string[] args) {
    // Present the alternatives
    if (args.Length <= 0) {
      EventLog[] ela = EventLog.GetEventLogs();
      Console.WriteLine("Usage:  DumpLog <logname>");
      Console.WriteLine("\n\tWhere <logname> is one of:\n");
      foreach (EventLog el in ela) {
        Console.WriteLine("\t{0}", el.LogDisplayName);
      }
      return;
    }
    // Extract the parameters
    string logName = args[0];
    // Check the log actually exists
    if (!EventLog.Exists(logName)) {
      Console.WriteLine("Unknown log name {0}", logName);
      return;
    }
```

```
// Iterate over the entire log, dumping the events
EventLog el = new EventLog(logName);
Console.WriteLine("{0} on {1}", el.LogDisplayName, el.MachineName);
EventLogEntryCollection elec = el.Entries;
foreach (EventLogEntry ele in elec) {
  Console.WriteLine("Event ID {0} ({1}):{2}",
      ele.EventID, ele.EntryType, ele.Message);
  Console.WriteLine("  generated by {0} on {1} for {2}@{3}",
      ele.Source, ele.TimeGenerated, ele.UserName, ele.MachineName);
    }
  }
}
```

Writing to the Event Log

Similarly, one can write to the event log using the same EventLog class used in the previous example. The only complexity arises because log entries need a source—if the event source doesn't already exist, you need to create it. As the following sample demonstrates, creating a command-line utility to add events to an event log on the local machine is trivial:

```
// WriteLog.cs - use WriteLog <logname> <message>
using System;
using System.Diagnostics;
class WriteLog {
  const string SOURCE = "CSiaN";
  static void Main(string[] args) {
    // Extract the parameters
    string logName = args[0], message = args[1];
    // Verify the log actually exists
    if (!EventLog.Exists(logName)) {
      Console.WriteLine("Unknown log name '{0}'", logName);
      return;
    }
    // Create the CSiaN event source if necessary
    if (!EventLog.SourceExists(SOURCE) ) {
      EventLog.CreateEventSource(SOURCE, logName);
    }
    // Write the event to the log on the local machine
    EventLog el = new EventLog(logName, ".", SOURCE);
    el.WriteEntry(message)
  }
}
```

Monitoring the Event Log

In some cases it can be useful to monitor the event log, examining new entries as they are written and taking appropriate action. To do this, register a listener for the EventLog.EntryWritten event on a log we are interested in monitoring. As new event log entries are added to the log, you receive callbacks, and can access the details of the new event log entry and take appropriate action. The following sample demonstrates registering a listener to display new events in a log as they are written. (To generate new events in the log, use the preceding WriteLog sample.)

```
// WatchLog.cs - use WatchLog <logname>
using System;
using System.Diagnostics;
class WatchLog {
  static void NewEntryCallback(object o, EntryWrittenEventArgs ewea) {
    // The new entry is included in the event arguments
    EventLogEntry ele = ewea.Entry;
    Console.WriteLine("New event in log: {0}", ele.Message);
  }
  static void Main(string[] args) {
    // Check the arguments and provide help
    if (args.Length != 1) {
      Console.WriteLine("Usage: WatchLog <logname>");
      return;
    }
    // Verify the log actually exists
    string logName = args[0];
    if (!EventLog.Exists(logName)) {
      Console.WriteLine("Unknown log name '{0}'", logName);
      return;
    }
    // Register handler and wait for keypress
    EventLog el = new EventLog(logName);
    el.EntryWritten += new EntryWrittenEventHandler(NewEntryCallback);
    el.EnableRaisingEvents = true;
    Console.WriteLine("Listening for events - press <enter> to end");
    Console.ReadLine();
  }
}
```

Performance Counters

Event logs are useful for capturing application status that is not of a time-sensitive nature, yet needs to be recorded for future analysis. However, to gain insight into the current state of an application (or the system as a whole), a more real-time approach is needed.

The Win32 solution to this need is the performance-monitoring infrastructure, which consists of a set of performance counters that the system and applications expose, and the Microsoft Management Console (MMC) snap-ins used to monitor these counters in real time.

Performance counters are grouped into categories such as "System," "Processor," ".NET CLR Memory," and so on. These categories are sometimes also referred to as "performance objects" by the GUI tools. Each category groups a related set of performance counters that monitor one aspect of the system or application. Examples of performance counters in the ".NET CLR Memory" category include "% Time in GC," "# Bytes in All Heaps," and "Allocated bytes/sec."

Each category may optionally have one or more instances that can be monitored independently. For example, this is useful in the "% Processor Time" performance counter in the "Processor" category, which allows one to monitor CPU utilization. On a multiprocessor machine, this counter supports an instance for each CPU, allowing one to monitor the utilization of each CPU independently.

The following sections illustrate how to perform commonly needed tasks, such as determining which counters are exposed, monitoring a counter, and creating your own counters to expose application status information.

Enumerating the Available Counters

In the following example, enumerate all of the available performance counters on the system. To do this, first retrieve a list of the categories, then iterate through the list displaying the counters and instances for each category, as follows:

```
// DumpCounters.cs
using System;
using System.Diagnostics;
class DumpCounters {
  static void Main( ) {
    PerformanceCounterCategory[ ] cats;
    cats = PerformanceCounterCategory.GetCategories( );
    foreach (PerformanceCounterCategory cat in cats) {
      try {
        Console.WriteLine("Category: {0}", cat.CategoryName);
        string[ ] instances = cat.GetInstanceNames( );
        if (instances.Length == 0) {
          // Dump counters without instances
          foreach (PerformanceCounter ctr in cat.GetCounters( ))
            Console.WriteLine("  Counter: {0}", ctr.CounterName);
        } else {
          // Dump counters with instances
          foreach (string instance in instances) {
            Console.WriteLine("  Instance: {0}", instance);
            foreach (PerformanceCounter ctr in cat.GetCounters(instance))
              Console.WriteLine("    Counter: {0}", ctr.CounterName);
          }
        }
      } catch (Exception e) { // Some perf counters don't provide details
        Console.WriteLine("Exception: {0}", e.Message);
      }
    }
  }
}
```

Reading Performance Counter Data

The following sample demonstrates how to retrieve the current value for an arbitrary performance counter. It incorporates error-handling code to illustrate how to verify category, counter, and instance name before attempting to read a performance counter value. Use the preceding DumpCounters sample to enumerate the available categories, counters, and instances on your machine, and pass them to the sample on the command line:

```
// WatchCounter.cs - use WatchCounter <category> <counter> [<instance>]
using System;
```

```
using System.Threading;
using System.Diagnostics;
class WatchCounter {
  static void Main(string[] args) {
    // Extract the parameters
    string cat = args[0], ctr = args[1];
    string inst = (args.Length==3) ? args[2] : "";
    // Check the category is OK
    if (!PerformanceCounterCategory.Exists(cat)) {
      Console.WriteLine("Unknown category {0}", cat);
      return;
    }
    // Check the counter is OK
    if (!PerformanceCounterCategory.CounterExists(ctr, cat)) {
      Console.WriteLine("Unknown counter {0}", ctr);
      return;
    }
    // Check the instance is OK
    if (inst.Length>0 &&
        !PerformanceCounterCategory.InstanceExists(inst, cat)) {
      Console.WriteLine("Unknown instance {0}", inst);
      return;
    }
    // Spin in a loop, dumping the counter
    Console.WriteLine("Press <ctrl+c> to end");
    PerformanceCounter pc = new PerformanceCounter(cat, ctr, inst);
    while (true) {
      Console.WriteLine("Counter value is {0}", pc.NextValue());
      Thread.Sleep(1000); // No! Bad programmer!
    }
  }
}
```

Adding a New Performance Counter

To expose real-time status information about your applications, instantiate a
read/write PerformanceCounter object with the name of an existing category, the
name of the new counter, and the name of the new instance, then update the
value of the counter as the application status changes. The following sample
demonstrates how to create your own counter and expose application status
values through it. (To watch the changing counter values, use the preceding
WatchCounter sample.)

```
// WriteCounter.cs - use WriteCounter <category> <counter> [<instance>]
using System;
using System.Threading;
using System.Diagnostics;
class WriteCounter {
  static void Main(string[] args) {
    // Extract the parameters
    string cat = args[0], ctr = args[1];
    string inst = (args.Length==3) ? args[2] : "";
    // Create the category if it doesn't already exist
```

```csharp
      if (!PerformanceCounterCategory.Exists(cat)) {
        PerformanceCounterCategory.Create(cat, "", ctr, "");
      }
      // Check the counter is OK
      if (!PerformanceCounterCategory.CounterExists(ctr, cat)) {
        Console.WriteLine("Unknown counter {0}", ctr);
        return;
      }
      // Create a new read/write counter & instance for an existing category
      PerformanceCounter pc = new PerformanceCounter(cat, ctr, inst, false);
      // Create counter and spin in a loop, incrementing it
      Console.WriteLine("Press <ctrl+c> to end");
      while (true) {
        Console.WriteLine("Incrementing counter...");
        pc.Increment();
        Thread.Sleep(1000); // No! Bad programmer!
      }
    }
  }
}
```

20

C# Language Reference

The following table describes the syntax of various C# language elements. The left column shows the syntax for each element, and the right column includes one or more examples.

Arrays

```
type [*]
+ array-name =
[
  new type [ dimension+ ][*]*; |
  { value1, value2, ... };
]
```

```
byte[ ] arr1 = new byte[10];
int[ ] arr2 = {0, 1, 2};

([*] is the set: [ ] [,] [,,] etc.)
```

Attributes

```
[[target:]? attribute-name (
positional-param+ |
[named-param = expr]+ |
positional-param+, [named-param =
                    expr]+)?]
```

```
[assembly:CLSCompliant(false)]
[WebMethod(true,
  Description="My web method")]
```

Break statement

```
break;
```

```
break;
```

Checked/unchecked

```
checked (expr)



unchecked (expr)
```

```
// throws exception
short x = 32767;
int i = checked( (short) ++x );
// silently overflows to -32768
short y = 32767;
int j = unchecked( (short) ++y );
```

```
checked [statement | statement-block]        // throws exception
                                             public short foo( ) {
                                               short y = 32767;
                                               checked {
                                                 return ++y;
                                               }
                                             }
unchecked [statement | statement-block]      // silently overflows
                                             public short bar( ) {
                                               short y = 32767;
                                               unchecked {
                                                 return ++y;
                                               }
                                             }
```

Class declaration

```
attributes? unsafe? access-modifier?         public class MyClass : Base, IFoo {
new?                                           // ...
[ abstract | sealed ]?                       }
class class-name
[: base-class |
 : interface+ |
 : base-class, interface+ ]?
{ class-members }
```

Constant declaration

```
const type [variable = constant-expr]+;      const int xyzzy = 42;
```

Constant fields

```
attributes? access-modifier?                 internal const byte fnord = 23;
new?
const type [constant-name =
                       constant-expr]+;
```

Continue statement

```
continue;                                    continue;
```

Delegates

```
attributes? unsafe? access-modifier?         public delegate void
new?                                           MyHandler(object s, EventArgs e);
delegate
[ void | type ]
delegate-name (parameter-list);
```

Destructors

```
attributes? unsafe?                          ~SomeClass( ) {
~class-name ( )                                // destructor code
statement-block                              }
```

Do-While loops

```
do                                           int i = 0;
 [statement |statement-block]                do { // print 0 through 9
while (Boolean-expr);                          Console.WriteLine(i++);
                                             } while(i < 10);
```

Empty statements

```
;
```

```
i = 0;
while(i++ < 10)
  ; // take no action
Console.WriteLine(i); // prints 11
```

Enums

```
attributes? access-modifier?
new?
enum enum-name [ : integer-type ]?
{ [attributes? enum-member-name
[ = value ]? ]* }
```

```
[Flags] public enum Color : long {
  Red = 0xff0000,
  Green = 0x00ff00,
  Blue = 0x0000ff
};
//...
// prints "Green, Red"
Color yellow = (Color) 0xffff00;
Console.WriteLine(yellow);
```

Events

```
attributes? unsafe? access-modifier?
[
  [[sealed | abstract]? override] |
  new? [virtual | static]?
]?
event delegate-type event-name
```

```
event MyDelegate OnClickedSomething;
// ...
OnClickedSomething(arg1, arg2);
```

Event accessors

```
attributes? unsafe? access-modifier?
[
  [[sealed | abstract]? override] |
  new? [virtual | static]?
]?
event delegate-type event-accessor-name
{
  attributes? add statement-block
  attributes? remove statement-block
}
```

```
event MyDelegate OnAction {
  add {
    // ...
  }
  remove {
    // ...
  }
}
```

Expression statements

```
[variable =]? expr;
```

```
a = 10 * 10;
a++;
b = ++a;
```

Fields

```
attributes? unsafe? access-modifier?
new?
static?
[readonly | volatile]?
type [ field-name [ = expr]? ]+ ;
```

```
protected int agent = 0x007;
```

Fixed statements

```
fixed ([value-type | void ]* name =
                   [&]? expr )
  statement-block
```

```
byte[ ] b = {0, 1, 2};
fixed (byte* p = b) {
  *p = 100; // b[0] = 100
}
```

For loops

```
for (statement?;
     Boolean-expr?;
     statement?)
[statement | statement-block]
```

```
// print 0 through 9
for(int j=0; j<10; j++)
  Console.WriteLine(j);
```

Foreach loops

```
foreach ( type-value in IEnumerable )
statement or statement-block
```

```
StringCollection sc =
  new StringCollection( );
sc.Add("Hello");
sc.Add("World");
foreach(String s in sc)
  Console.WriteLine(s);
```

Goto statement

```
goto statement-label;
goto case-constant;
```

```
i = 0;
MyLabel:
if(++i < 100)
  goto MyLabel;
Console.WriteLine(i);
```

If-Else statement

```
if (Boolean-expr)
[statement | statement-block]
[ else
[statement | statement-block] ]?
```

```
if(choice == "A") {
  // ...
} else if (choice == "B") {
  // ...
} else {
  // ...
}
```

Indexers

```
attributes? unsafe? access-modifier?
[
  [[sealed | abstract]? override] |
  new? [virtual | abstract | static]?
]?
type this [ attributes? [type arg]+ ] {
  attributes? get    // read-only
  statement-block |
  attributes? set    // write-only
  statement-block |
  attributes? get    // read-write
  statement-block
  attributes? set
  statement-block
}
```

```
string this[int index] {
  get {
    return somevalue;
  }
  set {
    // do something with
    // implicit "value" arg
  }
}
```

Instance constructors

```
attributes? unsafe? access-modifier?
class-name (parameter-list)
[ :[ base | this ] (argument-list) ]?
statement-block
```

```
MyClass(int i) {
  // perform initialization
}
// Initialize with default
MyClass( ) : this(42) { }
```

Interfaces

```
attributes? unsafe? access-modifier?
new?
interface interface-name
[ : base-interface+ ]?
{ interface-members }
```

```
interface IFoo :
  IDisposable, IComparable
{
  // member declarations
}
```

Lock statement

```
lock (expr)
 [statement | statement-block]
```

```
lock(this) {
  int tmp = a;
  a = b;
  b = tmp;
}
```

Method declaration syntax

```
attributes? unsafe? access-modifier?
[
  [[sealed | abstract]? override] |
  new? [virtual | abstract |
   static extern?]?
]?
[ void | type ]
  method-name (parameter-list)
    statement-block
```

```
public abstract int MethA(object o);
public virtual void MethB(int i,
                          object o)
{
  // statements...
}
```

Namespace

```
namespace name+
{
 using-statement*
 [namespace-declaration |
  type-declaration]*
}
```

```
namespace OReilly.CSharp {
  using System;
  interface IFoo : IComparable { }
  public class MyClass { }
}
```

```
(namespace is dot-delimited)
(namespace-declaration has no delim-
iters)
```

Parameter list

```
[ attributes? [ref | out]? type arg ]*
[ params attributes? type[ ] arg ]?
```

```
void MethA(ref int a, out int b) {
  b = ++a;
}
void MethB(params string[ ] args)
{
  foreach (string s in args)
    Console.WriteLine(s);
}
// ...
int a = 20, b;
MethA(ref a, out b);
Console.WriteLine("a={0}, b={1}",
                  a, b);
MethB("hello", "world");
```

Properties

```
attributes? unsafe? access-modifier?
[
  [[sealed | abstract]? override] |
  new? [virtual | abstract | static]?
]?
type property-name { [
 attributes? get    // read-only
  statement-block |
 attributes? set    // write-only
  statement-block |
 attributes? get    // read-write
  statement-block
 attributes? set
  statement-block
] }
```

```
private string name;
public string Name {
  get {
    return name;
  }
  set {
    name = value;
  }
}
```

Return statement

```
return expr?;
```

```
return;
return x;
```

Statements and statement blocks

```
statement
```

```
int x = 100;
```

```
statement-block
```

```
{
  int x = 100;
  Console.WriteLine(x);
  return x;
}
```

Static constructors

```
attributes? unsafe? extern?
static class-name ( )
statement-block
```

```
static MyClass( ) {
  // initialize static members
}
```

Struct declaration

```
attributes? unsafe? access-modifier?
new?
struct struct-name [: interface+]?
{ struct-members }
```

```
public struct TwoFer {
  public int part1, part2;
}
```

Switch statement

```
switch (expr) {
[ case constant-expr : statement* ]*
[ default : statement* ]?
}
```

```
switch(choice) {
  case "A":
    // ... do something
    break;
  case "B":
    // ... do something
    // then branch to A
    goto case "A";
  case "C":
  case "D":
    // ... do something
    break;
  default:
    Console.WriteLine("bad choice");
    break;
}
```

Throw statement

```
throw exception-expr?;
```

```
throw new
  Exception("something's wrong");
```

Try statements and exceptions

```
try statement-block
[catch (exception type value?)?
 statement-block]+ |
finally statement-block |
[catch (exception type value?)?
 statement-block]+
finally statement-block
```

```
try {
  // do something
} catch (Exception) {
  // recover
} finally {
  // this will always
  // be called
}
```

Using statement

```
using (declaration-expr)
 [statement | statement-block]
```

```
using(StreamReader s =
  new StreamReader("README.TXT"))
{
  // ...
}
// s is disposed here
```

Variable declaration

```
type [variable [ = expr ]?]+ ;
```

```
long a, b, c;
int x = 100;
```

While loops

```
while (Boolean-expr)
 [statement | statement-block]
```

```
int i = 0;
while(i < 10) {
 // print 0 through 9
 Console.WriteLine(i++);
}
```

Language and Tools Reference

Part III, *Language and Tools Reference*, contains:

21

XML Documentation Tag Reference

Table 21-1 lists the predefined set of XML tags that can be used to mark up the descriptive text. Table 21-2 lists possible prefixes for type and member cross-references.

Table 21-1. Predefined XML tags

Tag	Description
`<summary>`	`<summary>`*description*`</summary>`
	Describes a type or member. Typically, this contains the description of a member at a fairly high level.
`<remarks>`	`<remarks>`*description*`</remarks>`
	Provides additional information regarding a particular member. Information about side effects within the method, or particular behavior that may not otherwise be intuitive (such as the idea that this method may throw an `ArrayOutOfBoundsException` if a parameter is greater than 5) should be listed here.
`<param>`	`<param name="name">`*description*`</param>`
	Describes a parameter on a method. The name attribute is mandatory and must refer to a parameter on the method. If this tag is applied to any parameter on a method, all parameters on that method must be documented. You must enclose name in double quotation marks ("").
`<returns>`	`<returns>`*description*`</returns>`
	This tag describes the return values for a method.
`<exception>`	`<exception [cref="`*type*`"]>`*description*`</exception>`
	Describes the exceptions a method may throw. If present, the optional `cref` attribute should refer to the type of exception. You must enclose `type` in double quotation marks ("").
`<permission>`	`<permission [cref="`*type*`"]>`*description*`</permission>`
	Describes the permission requirements for a type or member. If present, the optional `cref` attribute should refer to the type that represents the permission set required by the member, although the compiler doesn't validate this. You must enclose `type` in double quotation marks ("").
`<example>`	`<example>`*description*`</example>`
	Provide a description and sample source code explaining the use of a type or member. Typically, the `<example>` tag provides the description and contains the `<c>` and `<code>` tags (described next), although these can also be used independently.

Table 21-1. Predefined XML tags (continued)

Tag	Description
`<c>`	`<c>code</c>`
	Indicates an inline code snippet. Typically, this is used inside of an `<example>` block (just described).
`<code>`	`<code>code</code>`
	Used to indicate multiline code snippets. Again, typically used inside of an `<example>` block.
`<see>`	`<see cref="member">text</see>`
	Identifies cross-references in the documentation to other types or members. Typically, the `<see>` tag is used inline within a description (as opposed to the `<seealso>` tag, below, which is broken out into a separate "See Also" section). These tags are useful because they allow tools to generate cross-references, indexes, and hyperlinked views of the documentation. Member names must be enclosed by double quotation marks ("").
`<seealso>`	`<seealso cref="member">text</seealso>`
	Identifies cross-references in the documentation to other types or members. Typically, `<seealso>` tags are broken out into a separate "See Also" section. These tags are useful because they allow tools to generate cross-references, indexes, and hyperlinked views of the documentation. Member names must be enclosed by double quotation marks ("").
`<value>`	`<value>description</value>`
	Describes a property on a class.
`<paramref>`	`<paramref name="name"/>`
	Identifies the use of a parameter name within descriptive text, such as `<remarks>` or `<summary>`. The name must be enclosed by double quotation marks ("").

`<list>`	`<list type=[bullet|number|table]>`
	 `<listheader>`
	 `<term>name</term>`
	 `<description>description</description>`
	 `</listheader>`
	 `<item>`
	 `<term>name</term>`
	 `<description>description</description>`
	 `</item>`
	 `</list>`

	Provide hints to documentation generators on how to format the documentation—in this case as a list of items.
`<para>`	`<para>text</para>`
	Sets off the text as a paragraph to documentation generators.
`<include>`	`<include file='filename' path='path-to-element'>`
	Specifies an external file that contains documentation and an XPath path to a specific element in that file. For example, a path of `docs[@id="001"]/*` retrieves whatever is inside of `<docs id="001"/>`. The filename and path must be enclosed by single quotation marks (' ').

Table 21-2. XML type ID prefixes

Prefix	Applied to
N	Namespace
T	Type (class, struct, enum, interface, delegate)
F	Field

Table 21-2. XML type ID prefixes (continued)

Prefix	Applied to
P	Property (includes indexers)
M	Method (includes special methods)
E	Event
!	Error

22

C# Naming and Coding Conventions

Naming conventions have long been understood to be a beneficial practice in software development, for a variety of reasons elucidated more clearly and persuasively elsewhere. The benefits of a naming convention, however, take special meaning in the cross-language environment that .NET offers—for the first time, a class library written in C# can be accessed verbatim from VB, C++, Eiffel, and any other ".NET-consumer" language, compiler, or environment. While "industry practices" are hard to discuss in an industry that has yet to even ship its first release, Microsoft has released some guidelines to its own naming conventions, used predominantly in the Framework Class Library; even if you and your development shop choose to use alternative conventions, understanding the naming conventions of the FCL is key to using it effectively.

There are three elements of naming guidelines:

- Case (capitalization)
- Mechanics (class names, method names, and so on)
- Word choice (consistent terminology and phraseology)

Much of this information can also be found in the Microsoft documentation set.

Case

Throughout the years, computer scientists have never been able to agree on one common way in which to express human-readable concepts (including word breaks for compound names such as "XML reader" or "input stream") in arenas in which normal rules of English, such as spaces, cannot apply. As a result, various languages have used different rules and formats to indicate where a logical word break should occur.

A variety of styles have emerged over the years, summarized here:

Pascal

The Pascal language was the first to use this style of capitalization, hence its name. In a compound name (such as "input stream" or "base type"), capitalize the first letter of each word, then eliminate the space. Thus, "input stream" becomes "InputStream" and "base type" becomes "BaseType". Proponents of this style like the fact that each word is distinctly separated (the uppercase letter always signifies a new word), while detractors point out that acronyms become difficult to work with. "xml parser" becomes "XMLParser", and "HTTP IO Factory" becomes "HTTPIOFactory".

Camel

"Camel-casing," as its called, is the style used frequently in Java. Again, in a compound name, the first letter of each word is capitalized, except for the first word, which is left lowercase. This produces, for example, "baseType" and "inputStream". Acronyms become particularly difficult if they come as the first word and styles diverge. The general agreement seems to be to have the entire acronym lowercased, as in "xmlParser".

All-caps

This style is distinctive, if a bit difficult to read. All letters of the word are uppercased (as if typing with the caps-lock key down), and spaces are again eliminated. While it becomes visually distinctive, all-caps identifiers tend to become hard to read—for example "BASETYPE" or "INPUTSTREAM". As a result, aside from die-hard COBOL programmers, all-caps casing tends to be used only sporadically within a modern language.

Underscore-separation

Also known as "C-casing," this style has recently fallen out of favor, particularly in C++ and Java programming circles. C-casing keeps all words in lowercase, using the underscore (_) to replace spaces. Proponents like this style because it makes the compound name look nearly identical to the English equivalent ("input_stream" or "base_type"); detractors claim the underscore is overused and abused in names ("prepare_to_accept_the_users_input"). Underscore-separation case doesn't show up in the .NET Framework directly, but will probably appear as legacy C and C++ applications are ported (or simply recompiled) for the .NET environment.

As with many things, no one style fits all, and the Microsoft naming conventions use the first three (particularly Pascal casing) throughout.

Capitalization rules can be mostly summarized as the following:

- Any name which is visible to consumers of the assembly (that is, anything declared with an access specifier of "public" or "protected") should be Pascal-cased. This means class names, properties, methods, and events.

- Names internal to the assembly can be pretty much anything the component developer wishes (subject to corporate standards, of course); however, the Microsoft convention appears to continue the use of Pascal-casing for methods, events and properties. Fields are camel-cased.

- Symbolic constants (the value of pi, the HTTP response code for a "File Not Found" error, and so forth) should be written using all-caps.

Remember that other languages in .NET are not case-sensitive; never differentiate between two C# methods using only case. (On top of being not CLS-compliant, this is just bad form and confusing.)

Mechanics

Mechanics, in this case, refers to the process of selecting a name for a given metadata token in the language such as class, interface, field, parameter, and so on.

Microsoft, in its "Naming Guidelines" topic (under the ".NET Framework Design Guidelines" in the .NET SDK Documentation), contains a list of "Do's" and "Don'ts" regarding naming guidelines. Rather than reprint that list here in either parroted or paraphrased form, we just make the following general suggestions.

Names should be descriptive and concise. More importantly, they should be meaningful to the principal consumers of the name—use syntax, phraseology, and terms that are familiar to the developers who will use the code you are writing.

As suggested, since classes and interfaces and value types are often marked "public," use Pascal-case for their names.

Interfaces should always be prefixed with I, following in COM tradition. Following the Pascal-casing rules, make sure the next letter of the interface is also capitalized, as in IComparable (indicating an interface that provides comparable behavior). Frequently, interfaces are also descriptive names (Comparable, Disposable, and so on), rather than nouns.

Other than the I for interfaces, do not use any sort of prefixes on names. This is what namespaces are for.

Attributes should always end in the Attribute suffix. The C# compiler can use shorthand naming rules (allowing you to leave off the Attribute portion of the name when using the attribute) if you follow this convention.

Enums should use Pascal-casing, both for the typename and the values within the enumerated type.

Fields should be named relative to what they store. Microsoft specifically recommends against using Hungarian notation, even the MFC m_ style; however, this style shows up in a few places inside the FCL. Use what feels right to you and your peers, but be consistent.

Events should be suffixed with EventHandler; event argument types should be suffixed with EventArgs. Frequently, events are prefixed with an On, indicating the event is fired "on button clicks" or "on window closing"; this is not entirely consistent, however.

Exceptions should always be suffixed with Exception.

Word Choice

It's wise to avoid using class names duplicated in heavily used namespaces. For instance, do not use the following for a class name:

    System   Collections   Forms   UI

Also avoid using identifiers that conflict with common keywords; remember that all keywords must be escapable (and therefore usable) within any .NET language, but that doesn't mean it's easy to do. Avoid the identifier names listed in Table 22-1.

Table 22-1. Common keywords best avoided in class names

AddHandler	AddressOf	Alias	And	Ansi
As	Assembly	Auto	BitAnd	BitNot
BitOr	BitXor	Boolean	ByRef	Byte
ByVal	Call	Case	Catch	CBool
CByte	CChar	CDate	CDec	CDbl
Char	CInt	Class	CLng	CObj
Const	CShort	CSng	CStr	CType
Date	Decimal	Declare	Default	Delegate
Dim	Do	Double	Each	Else
ElseIf	End	Enum	Erase	Error
Eval	Event	Exit	Extends	ExternalSource
False	Finally	For	Friend	Function
Get	GetType	Goto	Handles	If
Implements	Imports	In	Inherits	Integer
Interface	Is	InstanceOf	Let	Lib
Like	Long	Loop	Me	Mod
Module	MustInherit	MustOverride	MyBase	MyClass
Namespace	New	Next	Not	Nothing
NotInheritable	NotOverridable	Object	On	Option
Optional	Or	Overloads	Overridable	Overrides
Package	ParamArray	Preserve	Private	Property
Protected	Public	RaiseEvent	ReadOnly	ReDim
Region	REM	RemoveHandler	Resume	Return
Select	Set	Shadows	Shared	Short
Single	Static	Step	Stop	String
Structure	Sub	SyncLock	Then	Throw
To	True	Try	TypeOf	Unicode
Until	Var	Variant	When	While
With	WithEvents	WriteOnly	Xor	

Try to avoid using abbreviations in identifiers (including parameter names), but if doing so renders the name more unintelligible, use camel-casing rules for any abbreviation over two characters, even if this is not the standard abbreviation. (Thus, the compound name "XML reader" should be called "XmlReader").

Namespaces

The general pattern to follow when naming namespaces is:

```
CompanyName.TechnologyName
```

Some examples of well-formed namespaces are:

```
Microsoft.Office
Corel.OfficePerfect
OReilly.CSharpInANutshell
```

One problem that may arise, particularly as more companies begin to write code for the .NET platform, is that the "company-level" namespaces may clash. Java sought to avoid this problem by strongly suggesting companies use their reverse-DNS name ("oreilly.com" produces "com.oreilly" top-level namespace names), since DNS names are guaranteed to be unique. Over time, however, this proved to be less of an issue than originally thought, and many companies began to use the "center" name in the DNS name (for instance "oreilly" in "oreilly.com"). There is no reason to believe this convention won't continue to work in .NET.

For legibility, use Pascal case, and separate logical components with periods (for example, `Microsoft.Office.PowerPoint`). However, if your product involves nontraditional capitalization, it's okay to use that system, even if it deviates from normal namespace casing (for example `NeXT.WebObjects`, `OReilly.Network` and ee. cummings).

Plural namespace names are recommended where appropriate—for example, use `System.Collections`, not `System.Collection`. Exceptions to this rule are brand names and abbreviations—for example, use `System.IO`, not `System.IOs`.

Never reuse names across namespace and class names—for example, the `System.Debug` namespace should never have a class named `Debug` within it. (Naturally, this is scoped to the namespace itself; it is perfectly acceptable to have a class called `Debug` in the `System.IO` namespace.)

23

C# Development Tools

The .NET Framework SDK contains many useful programming tools. Here is an alphabetical list of those we have found most useful or necessary for developing C# applications. Unless otherwise noted, the tools in this list can be found either in the \bin directory of your .NET Framework SDK installation or in the %SystemRoot%\Microsoft.NET\Framework\VERSION directory (replace VERSION with the framework version). Once the .NET Framework is installed, you can access these tools from any directory. To use any of these tools, invoke a Command Prompt window and enter the name of the desired tool.

This chapter uses the following conventions:

Italic
> Used as a placeholder to indicate an item that should be replaced with an actual value.

[item]
> The brackets indicate an optional item. In some cases, [item] is used to indicate that part of a word is optional. For example, /v[erbose] indicates that the options /v and /verbose are equivalent.

(item1 | item2)
> The pipe (|) symbol indicates alternation, and the parentheses group the choices together; you must choose one of the specified options.

[item1 | item2]
> The pipe (|) symbol indicates alternation, and the brackets indicate that the choice is optional; you *may* choose one of the specified options. This is often used with the + and - symbols. For example, /verbose[+|-] indicates that you may choose /verbose, /verbose+, or /verbose-. The first two (/verbose and /verbose+) are equivalent.

item1, item2
> Comma-separated items indicate equivalent items. For example, the -C and -console options of the *ADepends.exe* tool are equivalent.

Synopsis

```
adepends [options] | [file] ...
```

Description

Displays all assemblies that a given assembly is dependent on to load. This is a useful C# program found among the samples in the *Tool Developers Guide* directory beneath the .NET Framework or Visual Studio .NET directory tree. You need to install these samples before you can use them, because they are not installed by default.

Options

--appbase *path*, -A *path*

Specify a directory path to use for the application base path (see the BaseDirectory property of the System.AppDomain type).

--config *configfile*, -O *configfile*

Generate an application configuration file. Requires the -console option.

--console, -C

Send output to the console (standard output).

--gui, -G

Display output in a window (default).

--help

Displays usage information and exits.

--relative *path*, -R *path*

Specify a directory path to use for the relative search path (see the RelativeSearchPath property of the System.AppDomain type).

--

Suspends interpretation of command-line arguments as options. Use this if *file* has the same name as an option.

See Also

ILDasm.exe, *WinCV.exe*

Al.exe

Assembly Linker

Synopsis

```
al /out:manifestfile [options] source
```

Description

Creates an assembly manifest from the modules and resources files you name. You can also include Win32 resources files. See *GacUtil.exe* for an example of creating an assembly.

Example

```
al /out:c.dll a.netmodule b.netmodule
```

Source

You may specify one or more of these sources:

file

> The name of a .NET module, which is produced by using the /t:module argument with the C# compiler. These modules typically have the extension *.netmodule*. The resulting *manifestfile* contains a reference to the *.netmodule* file.

file,target

> The name of a .NET module, along with a target filename (a .NET assembly, typically a DLL). The target is created and the .NET module is copied into it. The resulting *manifestfile* contains a reference to the target rather than the .NET module.

/embed[resource]:*file*[,*name*[,Private]]

> Embeds (copy) a resource file into the file that contains the manifest. Use *name* to associate an internal identifier with the resource. Resources are public by default; use Private to hide the resource from other assemblies.

/link[resource]:*file*[,*name*[,*target*[,Private]]]

> Makes a resource file part of the assembly described by the manifest. This links the resource file to the manifest but does not make a copy (see /embed). Use *name* to associate an internal identifier with the resource. Use *target* to specify a .NET assembly to copy the resource into (as with *file,target*). Resources are public by default; use Private to hide the resource from other assemblies.

Options

/?, /help

> Displays usage information and exits.

@*file*

> Specifies a response file containing arguments to *al*.

/algid:*id*

> The algorithm for hashing files. Specify the hexadecimal ID of the algorithm (use *WinCV.exe* to inspect the AssemblyHashAlgorithm enumeration in the System.Configuration.Assemblies namespace). Valid algorithm IDs for the first release of .NET include 0x0000 (None), 0x8003 (MD5), or 0x8004 (SHA1, the default).

/base[address]:*addr*

> Specifies the base address at which to load DLLs.

/bugreport:*file*

> Generates a text file that contains a bug report. Use this to report a bug in *al.exe*.

/comp[any]:*text*

> Specifies the text of the assembly's Company field. This has the same effect as the System.Reflection.AssemblyCompanyAttribute custom attribute. This is also used as the Win32 Company resource (unless you specify /win32res).

/config[uration]:*text*

> Specifies the text of the assembly's Configuration field. This has the same effect as the System.Reflection.AssemblyConfigurationAttribute custom attribute.

/copy[right]:*text*

> Specifies the text of the assembly's Copyright field. This has the same effect as the System.Reflection.AssemblyCopyrightAttribute custom attribute. This is also used as the Win32 Copyright resource (unless you specify /win32res).

`/c[ulture]:`*text*

> Specifies the assembly's culture string. This has the same effect as the `System.Reflection.AssemblyCultureAttribute` custom attribute.

`/delay[sign][+|-]`

> Use `/delaysign+` or `/delaysign` to partially sign the assembly, and `/delaysign-` (the default) to fully sign it. This option requires the `/keyfile` or `/keyname` option. See the `System.Reflection.AssemblyDelaySignAttribute` custom attribute for more details.

`/descr[iption]:`*text*

> Specifies the assembly's Description field. This has the same effect as the `System.Reflection.AssemblyDescriptionAttribute` custom attribute. This is also used as the Win32 Comments resource (unless you specify `/win32res`).

`/e[vidence]:`*file*

> The name of the security evidence file to embed.

`/fileversion:`*version*

> Specifies the assembly's File Version field in *major.minor.build.revision* format (such as 6.0.2600.0). This has the same effect as the `System.Reflection.AssemblyFileVersionAttribute` custom attribute. This is also used as the Win32 File Version resource (unless you specify `/win32res`). This version corresponds to the Win32 File Version, and is *not* used to determine compatibility for side-by-side execution.

`/flags:`*flags*

> Specify flags for side-by-side operation. Possible values are `0x0000` (side-by-side compatible), `0x0010` (side-by-side operation is prohibited within the same application domain), `0x0020` (side-by-side operation prohibited within same process), or `0x0030` (side-by-side operation prohibited within the same machine boundary). This has the same effect as the `System.Reflection.AssemblyFlagsAttribute` custom attribute.

`/fullpaths`

> Use fully qualified filenames in error messages.

`/keyf[ile]:`*file*

> Specifies the name of the file that contains the key or key-pair with which to sign the assembly. This has the same effect as the `System.Reflection.AssemblyKeyFileAttribute` custom attribute. You can generate a key file with the *Sn* utility.

`/keyn[ame]:`*name*

> Specifies a key container that contains the key-pair with which to sign the assembly. This has the same effect as the `System.Reflection.AssemblyKeyNameAttribute` custom attribute. You can add keys to a container using `sn -i`.

`/main:`*method*

> Specifies the fully qualified method name (`type.method` or `namespace.type.method`) to use as the entry point. Must be used in conjunction with `/target:exe`.

`/nologo`

> Suppresses display of the banner and copyright messages.

`/out:`*file*

> Specifies the output filename.

/prod[uct]:text

Specifies the assembly's Product field. This has the same effect as the System.Reflection.AssemblyProductAttribute custom attribute. This is also used as the Win32 Product resource (unless you specify /win32res).

/productv[ersion]:text

Specifies the assembly's Product Version field. This has the same effect as the System.Reflection.AssemblyInformationalVersionAttribute custom attribute. This is also used as the Win32 Product Version resource (unless you specify /win32res).

/t[arget]:format

Specifies the format of the file identified by */out:file*. The valid formats are lib[rary] (DLL library), exe (console application), or win[exe] (Windows application).

/template:file

Specifies another assembly from which to import all metadata (except culture). The assembly must have a strong name.

/title:text

Specifies the assembly's Title field. This has the same effect as the System.Reflection.AssemblyTitleAttribute custom attribute. This is also used as the Win32 Description resource (unless you specify /win32res).

/trade[mark]:text

Specifies the assembly's Trademark field. This has the same effect as the System.Reflection.AssemblyTrademarkAttribute custom attribute. This is also used as the Win32 Trademark resource (unless you specify /win32res).

/v[ersion]:version

Specifies the assembly version in *major.minor.build.revision* format. This has the same effect as the System.Reflection.AssemblyVersionAttribute custom attribute. This is also used as the Win32 Assembly Version resource (unless you specify /win32res). This version is used to determine side-by-side compatibility.

/win32icon:file

Specifies an icon (*.ico*) file to be used as the application's icon.

/win32res:file

Specifies a Win32 resource (*.res*) file to insert in the output file.

See Also

Csc.exe, Sn.exe

Cordbg.exe

Command-line debugger

Synopsis

```
cordbg [program [program-arguments]] [!command ...]
```

Description

This is a general source-level, command-line debug utility for MSIL programs. It's a very useful tool for C# source debugging (make sure you compiled your program with /debug). Source for *cordbg* is available in the *\Tool Developers Guide* directory. You can start *cordbg* with the name of a program and the arguments to pass to that program. You can also supply one or more commands (prefixed with !) on the command line.

After you launch *cordbg*, you are greeted by the (cordbg) prompt, where you can type commands until you exit *cordbg* with the quit command.

Sample Sessions

Set a breakpoint, start the program, and step through a few lines of code:

```
c:\home>cordbg Tester.exe
Microsoft (R) Common Language Runtime Test Debugger Shell
Version 1.1.4322.573
Copyright (C) Microsoft Corporation 1998-2002. All rights reserved.

(cordbg) run Tester.exe
Process 2024/0x7e8 created.
Warning: couldn't load symbols for
c:\windows\microsoft.net\framework\v1.0.3617\mscorlib.dll
[thread 0xee8] Thread created.

004:     for (int i = 0; i < 3; i++) {
(cordbg) show
001: using System;
002: class Tester {
003:    public static void Main( ) {
004:*      for (int i = 0; i < 3; i++) {
005:           object o = i;
006:           Console.Write(i + " ");
007:      }
008:      Console.Write("\n");
009:   }
(cordbg) b 6
Breakpoint #1 has bound to c:\home\Tester.exe.
#1      c:\home\Tester.cs:6  Main+0xb(il) [active]
(cordbg) go
break at #1     c:\home\Tester.cs:6  Main+0xb(il) [active]

006:           Console.Write(i + " ");
(cordbg) next
0
004:     for (int i = 0; i < 3; i++) {
(cordbg) step

005:           object o = i;
(cordbg) step
break at #1     c:\home\Tester.cs:6  Main+0xb(il) [active]
```

Swap two string variables by changing the addresses they refer to:

```
017:     string a = "A";
(cordbg) step

018:     string b = "B";
(cordbg) step

019:     Console.WriteLine(a + ", " + b);
```

```
(cordbg) print a
a=(0x00c51abc) "A"
(cordbg) print b
b=(0x00c51ad0) "B"
(cordbg) set a 0x00c51ad0
a=(0x00c51ad0) "B"
(cordbg) set b 0x00c51abc
b=(0x00c51abc) "A"
(cordbg) next
B, A
```

Invoke a static and instance method using funceval:

```
014:        TestClass my_instance = new TestClass( );
(cordbg) next

015:        return;
(cordbg) funceval TestClass::MyStaticMethod
In MyStaticMethod( )
Function evaluation complete.
$result=0x0000002a
015:        return;
(cordbg) funceval TestClass::MyInstanceMethod my_instance
In MyInstanceMethod( )
Function evaluation complete.
$result=0x00000017
015:        return;
(cordbg) print $result
$result=0x00000017
```

Commands

? [*command*], h[elp] [*command*]
> Displays general help. If *command* is specified, displays help for that command.

> [*file*]
> Writes all subsequent commands to a file. If *file* is not specified, this command stops writing commands to that file.

< *file*
> Read and execute commands from a file.

ap[pdomainenum] [*option*]
> Lists all the AppDomains inside the current process. Valid choices for *option* are attach (list all AppDomains and prompt for which appdomain to attach to), detach (list all AppDomains and prompt for which AppDomain to detach from), 0 (list the AppDomains), or 1 (AppDomains and assemblies; the default list).

as[sociatesource] (s | b *breakpoint*) *filename*
> Associate the specified source file with the current stackframe (s) or an existing breakpoint (b *breakpoint*).

a[ttach] *pid*
> Attach to a managed process (use pro[cessenum] to get a list of *pid*s).

b[reak] ([*file*:]*line* | [*class*::]*function*[:*offset*])
> Set a breakpoint at a given line number or function. With no arguments, lists all breakpoints.

ca[tch] [*event*]
> Specify an event type to suspend execution when that event occurs. Valid types are e[xceptions] [*exception-type*] (an exception is thrown), u[nhandled] (an exception is thrown that is not handled by the program), c[lass] (a class is loaded), m[odule] (a module is loaded), or t[hread] (a thread is started). With no arguments, catch displays a list of event types with the current catch/ignore settings.

cont [*count*], g[o]
> Continues until the next breakpoint or until the program terminates, whichever comes first. Use *count* to continue over breakpoints multiple times.

del[ete] [*breakpoint* ...], rem[ove] [*breakpoint* ...]
> Delete the specified breakpoint(s). Use the breakpoint IDs as listed by the break command. If you don't specify a breakpoint, all breakpoints are deleted.

de[tach]
> Detach from the current process and let it run to completion.

dis[assemble] [0x*address*] [{+|-}*delta*] [*lines*]
> Displays native code disassembly for the current instruction pointer (IP) or address. By default, five lines of surrounding context before and after the IP are shown (use the *lines* argument to change this).

d[own] [*count*]
> Move the stack pointer down one stack frame or the specified number of stack frames. This does not affect the instruction pointer, but it does affect the output of subsequent show commands.

du[mp] *address* [*count*]
> Dump memory at the specified address. The optional *count* argument specifies how many bytes to dump.

f[unceval] [*class*::]*function* [*args*]
> Execute a function. For instance, with methods, you must supply an instance of the class as the first argument (see Sample Sessions for an example). The return value is stored in the variable $result, which you can inspect with the p[rint] command.

ig[nore]
> Specify an event type to ignore when that event occurs (use catch to suspend execution whenever that event occurs). See catch for a list and description of valid events. With no arguments, ignore displays a list of event types with the current catch/ignore settings.

k[ill]
> Stops the current process, but does not exit the debugger.

l[ist] *option*
> Lists the loaded modules (*option*=mod), classes (*option*=cl), or global functions (*option*=fu).

m[ode] *option* (0 | 1)
> Sets debugger modes. Type help mode for a list of valid modes and their descriptions. With no arguments, mode displays current mode settings.

newo[bj] *type*
> Creates a new object, stored in the variable $result.

newobjnc *type*
> Creates a new object without calling the constructor. The new object is stored in the variable $result.

news[tr] "*string*"
> Creates a new string, stored in the variable $result.

ns[ingle] [*count*]
> Step to the next native instruction, stepping over function calls. If *count* is specified, steps the next *count* instructions.

o[ut] [*count*]
> Steps out of the current function. If *count* is specified, steps out of *count* functions.

pa[th] [*path*]
> Sets or (with no argument) displays the path used to search for source code files.

p[rint] [*variable*]
> Prints a list of all local variables and their values, or if *variable* is specified, prints the value of that variable.

pro[cessenum]
> Displays a list of each managed process along with its process id (*pid*).

q[uit], ex[it]
> Terminates the current process and exits the debugger.

ref[reshsource] *file*
> Reloads the source code for the specified file.

reg[isters]
> Displays the CPU registers and their contents for the current thread.

re[sume] [~] tid
> With tid, resumes the specified thread ID. With ~, resumes all threads except the specified thread ID. See the t[hreads] command.

r[un] [*program* [*program-arguments*]]
> With no arguments, kills and restarts the current process. With arguments, starts a new program with the specified program arguments.

set *variable* *value*
> Set a variable to a given value. You can set the address of a reference type to a valid address for that type (see Sample Sessions). The C# or JIT compiler may perform optimizations that make certain variables unavailable, in which case you see the message "Variable *variable* is in scope but unavailable."

setip *line*
> Set the instruction pointer to the specified line number.

sh[ow] [*number-of-lines*]
> Displays source code. The current line is shown with an asterisk (*).

si [*count*], s[tep] [*count*], i[n] [*count*]
> Steps to the next line of code, stepping into functions. If *count* is specified, steps the next *count* lines of code.

so [*count*], n[ext]
> Steps to the next line of source code, stepping over functions. If *count* is specified, steps the next *count* lines of code.

ss[ingle] [*count*]

Step to the next native instruction, stepping into function calls. If *count* is specified, steps the next *count* instructions.

stop

See break.

su[spend] [~] tid

With tid, suspends the specified thread ID. With ~, suspends all threads except the specified thread ID. See the t[hreads] command.

t[hreads] [*tid*]

With no arguments, lists all threads and their IDs. With the *tid* argument, sets the current thread.

uc[lear] tid

Clears the current unmanaged exception for the thread ID specified by *tid*.

u[p] [*count*]

Move the stack pointer up one stack frame or the specified number of stack frames. This does not affect the instruction pointer, but it does affect the output of subsequent show commands.

ut[hreads] [*tid*]

With no arguments, lists all unmanaged threads and their IDs. With the *tid* argument, sets the current unmanaged thread.

uw[here]

Displays an unmanaged stack trace.

w[here] [*count*]

Displays a stack trace for the currently executing thread. This displays up to 10 (or *count*) stack frames.

wr[itememory] *addresscountbyte1* [*byte2* ...]

Writes *count* bytes to the specified memory address.

wt

Steps through the program, one native instruction at a time, and prints a call tree containing a count of instructions in each function.

x *pattern*

Displays symbols matching *pattern*. Use * as a wild card character (trailing characters are ignored). The symbol format is module!symbol.

IL Debugging

If you'd like to step through the MSIL instead of the C# source code, you can use *ILDasm* to disassemble your program and then use *ILasm* to assemble it into an executable (don't forget the /debug switch). Then, run that executable under *cordbg*:

```
C:\home>csc Tester.cs
Microsoft (R) Visual C# .NET Compiler version 7.10.3052.4
for Microsoft (R) .NET Framework version 1.1.4322
Copyright (C) Microsoft Corporation 2001-2002. All rights reserved.

C:\home>ILDasm /text Tester.exe > TesterIL.il

C:\home>ILasm /debug TesterIL.il

Microsoft (R) .NET Framework IL Assembler.  Version 1.1.4322.573
```

Copyright (C) Microsoft Corporation 1998-2002. All rights reserved.
Assembling 'TesterIL.il' , no listing file, to EXE --> 'TesterIL.EXE'
Source file is ANSI

Assembled method Tester::Main
Assembled method Tester::.ctor
Creating PE file

Emitting members:
Global
Class 1 Methods: 2;
Writing PE file
Operation completed successfully

C:\home>**cordbg TesterIL.exe**
Microsoft (R) Common Language Runtime Test Debugger Shell
Version 1.1.4322.573
Copyright (C) Microsoft Corporation 1998-2002. All rights reserved.

(cordbg) run TesterIL.exe
Process 1004/0x3ec created.
Warning: couldn't load symbols for
c:\windows\microsoft.net\framework\v1.0.3617\mscorlib.dll
[thread 0x61c] Thread created.

```
057:      IL_0000:  ldc.i4.0
(cordbg) show
052:      .entrypoint
053:      // Code size       51 (0x33)
054:      .maxstack  2
055:      .locals init (int32 V_0,
056:              object V_1)
057:*     IL_0000:  ldc.i4.0
058:      IL_0001:  stloc.0
059:      IL_0002:  br.s       IL_0024
060:
061:      IL_0004:  ldloc.0
062:      IL_0005:  box        [mscorlib]System.Int32
(cordbg)
```

See Also
Csc.exe, ILAsm.exe, ILDasm.exe

Csc.exe

C# compiler

Synopsis
csc [*options*] *files*

Description
Compiles C# sources and incorporates resource files and separately compiled modules. Also allows you to specify conditional compilation options, XML documentation, and path information.

Examples

```
csc foo.cs /r:bar.dll /win32res:foo.res
csc foo.cs /debug /define:TEMP
```

Options

/?, /help

Displays usage information and exits.

@file

Specifies a response file containing arguments to *csc*.

/addmodule:*file1*[;*file2* ...]

Imports metadata from one or more named modules (files with the extension
.netmodule). To create a module, use /target:module.

/baseaddress:*addr*

Specifies the base address at which to load DLLs.

/bugreport:*file*

Generates a text file that contains a bug report. Use this to report a bug in *csc.exe*.

/checked[+|-]

If you specify /checked+, the runtime throws an exception when an integer operation results in a value outside the range of the associated data type. This only
affects code that has not been wrapped in a checked or unchecked block of code.
If you specify /checked-, an exception is not thrown.

/codepage:*id*

Specifies the code page to use for all source files.

/d[efine]:*symbol1*[;*symbol2* ...]

Specify one or more symbols to define. This has the same effect as the #define
preprocessor directive.

/debug[+|-]

Enables or disables debugging information. You may specify /debug instead of
/debug+. The default is /debug-.

/debug:(full|pdbonly)

Specifies the debug modes that are supported by the generated assembly. The
full option is the default and allows you to perform source code debugging when
attaching a debugger to the program before or after it is started. The pdbonly
option only permits source code debugging if you start the program under control
of the debugger. If you attach the debugger to the program after it is started, it
displays only native assembly in the debugger.

/doc:*file*

Specify the XML documentation file to generate.

/filealign:*size*

Specifies the size, in bytes, of sections in the output file. Valid sizes are 512, 1024,
2048, 4096, 8192, and 16384.

/fullpaths

Use fully qualified filenames in error messages.

/incr[emental][+|-]

Enables or disables incremental compilation. By default, incremental compilation
is off.

/lib:*dir1*[;*dir2* ...]
  Specifies directories to search for assemblies imported with the /reference option.

/linkres[ource]:*file*[,*id*]
  Specifies a .NET resource (and optional identifier) to link to the generated assembly. Not valid with /target:module.

/m[ain]:*type*
  Specifies the name of the type that contains the entry point. This is only valid for executables. The entry point method must be named Main, and must be declared static.

/noconfig
  Do not use the global or local configuration file (*csc.rsp*). You can find the global *csc.rsp* file in *%SystemRoot%\Microsoft.NET\Framework\VERSION*, in which *VERSION* is a version of the .NET Framework. This file contains default arguments for the C# compiler, including the list of assemblies that are imported by default. If you create a file named *csc.rsp* in the same directory as your source code, it is processed after the global configuration file.

/nologo
  Suppresses display of the banner and copyright messages.

/nostdlib[+|-]
  With /nostdlib+ or /nostdlib, the C# compiler will not import *mscorlib.dll*, which defines the fundamental types used in .NET and most of the System namespace.

/nowarn:*number1*[;*number2* ...]
  Specifies a list of warning numbers to ignore. Do not include the alphabetic part of the warning. For example, to suppress warning *CS0169*, use /nowarn:169.

/o[ptimize][+|-]
  Enables or disables compiler optimizations. By default, optimizations are enabled.

/out:*file*
  Specifies the output filename.

/recurse:*wildcard*
  Recursively searches directories for source code files matching *wildcard* (which may include directory names).

/r[eference]:*file1*[;*file2* ...]
  Imports metadata from one or more named assemblies. Generally used with DLLs, but you may also specify executables.

/res[ource]:*file*[,*id*]
  Specifies a .NET resource (and optional identifier) to embed in the generated assembly.

/t[arget]:*format*
  Specifies the format of the output file. The valid formats are library (DLL library), module (a library without an assembly manifest), exe (console application), or winexe (Windows application).

/unsafe[+|-]
  Enables or disables (the default) unsafe code. Unsafe code is enclosed in a block marked by the unsafe keyword.

/utf8output
  Displays compiler console output using UTF-8 encoding.

/w[arn]:*level*

Sets the compiler warning level from 0 (no warnings) to 4 (the default, all warnings).

/warnaserror[+|-]

Enables or disables (the default) treating warnings as errors (warnings halt compilation).

/win32icon:*file*

Specifies an icon (*.ico*) file to use as the application's icon.

/win32res:*file*

Specifies a Win32 resource (*.res*) file to insert in the output file.

DbgCLR.exe

Microsoft CLR Debugger

Synopsis

```
DbgCLR [options]
```

Description

Windows-based, source-level debugger. Available in the *GuiDebug* directory of the .NET Framework SDK installation.

Options

/mdi

Uses multiple document interface.

/sdi

Uses single document interface.

/fn *name*

Specifies font name.

/fn *size*

Specifies font size.

GacUtil.exe

Global Assembly Cache Utility

Synopsis

```
gacutil command [options]
```

Description

Allows you to install, uninstall, and list the contents of the Global Assembly Cache (GAC).

Examples

Create a module, generate a key-pair, build a signed manifest assembly containing the module, and install the assembly in the GAC:

```
C:\home>csc /t:module Example.cs
Microsoft (R) Visual C# .NET Compiler version 7.10.3052.4
for Microsoft (R) .NET Framework version 1.1.4322
Copyright (C) Microsoft Corporation 2001-2002. All rights reserved.
```

```
C:\home>sn -k example.key

Microsoft (R) .NET Framework Strong Name Utility  Version 1.1.4322.573
Copyright (C) Microsoft Corporation 1998-2002. All rights reserved.

Key pair written to example.key

C:\home>al /keyfile:example.key /out:Example.dll Example.netmodule
Microsoft (R) Assembly Linker version 7.10.3077
for Microsoft (R) .NET Framework version 1.1.4322
Copyright (C) Microsoft Corporation 2001-2002. All rights reserved.

C:\home>gacutil /i Example.dll

Microsoft (R) .NET Global Assembly Cache Utility.  Version 1.1.4322.573
Copyright (C) Microsoft Corporation 1998-2002. All rights reserved.

Assembly successfully added to the cache
```

Delete all assemblies named Example from the GAC:

```
C:\home>gacutil /u Example

Microsoft (R) .NET Global Assembly Cache Utility.  Version 1.1.4322.573
Copyright (C) Microsoft Corporation 1998-2002. All rights reserved.

Assembly: Example, Version=2.0.0.0, Culture=neutral,
PublicKeyToken=9a587aa1499c251f, Custom=null
Uninstalled: Example, Version=2.0.0.0, Culture=neutral,
PublicKeyToken=9a587aa1499c251f, Custom=null

Number of items uninstalled = 1
Number of failures = 0
```

Find a list of all assemblies named Example and delete a specific version:

```
C:\home>gacutil /l Example

Microsoft (R) .NET Global Assembly Cache Utility.  Version 1.1.4322.573
Copyright (C) Microsoft Corporation 1998-2002. All rights reserved.

The Global Assembly Cache contains the following assemblies:
  Example, Version=1.0.0.0, Culture=neutral,
    PublicKeyToken=093bfe6ba64f6b38, Custom=null
  Example, Version=1.2.0.0, Culture=neutral,
    PublicKeyToken=4644a63cb9786bcc, Custom=null

The cache of ngen files contains the following entries:

Number of items = 2

C:\home>gacutil /u Example,Version=1.2.0.0

Microsoft (R) .NET Global Assembly Cache Utility.  Version 1.1.4322.573
Copyright (C) Microsoft Corporation 1998-2002. All rights reserved.
```

```
Assembly: Example, Version=1.2.0.0, Culture=neutral,
PublicKeyToken=4644a63cb9786bcc, Custom=null
Uninstalled: Example, Version=1.2.0.0, Culture=neutral,
PublicKeyToken=4644a63cb9786bcc, Custom=null

Number of items uninstalled = 1
Number of failures = 0
```

Commands

/?

Displays usage information and exits.

/cdl

Removes all assemblies that were downloaded from the network.

/i [/f] [/r] *assemblypath*

Installs the specified assembly into the GAC. The assembly must have a strong name (see *Sn.exe*).

/il [/f /r] *assemblylistfile*

Installs one or more assemblies into the GAC. *assemblylistfile* is a file that contains a cr/lf-delimited list of assembly file names.

/l [/r] [*name*]

Lists all assemblies in the GAC. If you supply a name, it lists all versions of the named assembly.

/ldl

Lists all assemblies that were downloaded from the network.

/nologo

Suppresses display of the banner and copyright messages.

/silent

Suppresses display of all console output.

/u [/f] [/r] *assembly*

Remove an assembly from the GAC.

/ul [/r] *assemblylistfile*

Removes one or more assemblies from the GAC. *assemblylistfile* is a file that contains a cr/lf-delimited list of assembly file names.

/ungen *assembly*

Removes an assembly from the cache of *ngen*'d files (see *Ngen.exe*).

Options

/f

Use with the /i or /il commands to force installation, even if the assembly already exists. With /u, /f forces removal by uninstalling all traced references (this fails if the assembly is referenced by the Windows Installer).

/r *scheme id description*

Specifies a traced reference (use this with /i, /il, /u, or /ul). Valid options for *scheme* are FILEPATH (*id* must be a path to a file), UNINSTALL_KEY (*id* must be a registry key), or OPAQUE (*id* must be an identifier). *id* is the referencing application's identifier (for a scheme of FILEPATH, it would be the application's full path), and *description* is a friendly name for the referencing application.

See Also

Sn.exe, Al.exe, Csc.exe

ILasm.exe

Synopsis

```
ilasm [options] file1 [[options] file2 ...]
```

Description

Creates MSIL modules and assemblies directly from an MSIL textual representation.
See *IL Debugging* elsewhere in this chapter for an example that uses *ILasm.exe*.

Options

/?

    Displays usage information and exits.

/ali[gnment]=*int*

    Specifies a value for File Alignment in the NT Optional Header. Overrides the MSIL .alignment directive.

/bas[e]=*int*

    Specifies a value for ImageBase in the NT Optional Header. Overrides the MSIL .imagebase directive.

/clo[ck]

    Reports on how long the assembly takes.

/deb[ug]

    Includes debugging information in the output file.

/dll

    Assembles source file to a DLL.

/exe

    Assembles source file to an executable file (the default).

/fla[gs]=*int*

    Sets ImageFlags in the CLR header. Overrides the MSIL .corflags directive.

/key:*file*

    Specifies the name of the file that contains the key or key-pair with which to sign the assembly. You can generate a key file with the *sn* utility.

/key:@*text*

    Specifies a key container that contains the key-pair with which to sign the assembly. You can add keys to a container using sn -i.

/lis[ting]

    Emits a listing to the console as the file is assembled.

/nol[ogo]

    Suppresses display of the banner and copyright messages.

/out[put]:*file*

    Specifies the output filename.

/qui[et]

    Suppresses display of assembly progress to console.

/res[ource]:*file*

Specifies a Win32 resource (*.res*) file to include in the generated assembly.

/sub[system]=*int*

Specifies a value for the subsystem in the NT Optional Header. Overrides the MSIL .subsystem directive.

See Also

Csc.exe, ILDasm.exe

ILDasm.exe

MSIL Disassembler

Synopsis

```
ildasm [options] file [options]
```

Description

Disassembles modules and assemblies. The default is to display a GUI with a tree-style representation, but you can also specify an output file. See *IL Debugging* elsewhere in this chapter for an extended example that uses *ILDasm.exe*.

Examples

```
ildasm b.dll
ildasm b.dll /out=b.asm
```

Options

/?

Displays usage information and exits.

/all

Combines /header, /bytes, and /tokens. Requires the /text or /out option.

/byt[es]

Displays actual bytes (in hexadecimal) as comments amongst the MSIL.

/hea[der]

Includes file header information. Requires the /text or /out option.

/ite[m]=class[::method[(sig)]]

Disassembles only the specified class or member. Requires /text or /out option.

/lin[enum]

Displays references to line numbers from the original source code. To use this option, *file* must be compiled with /debug.

/nob[ar]

By default, *ILDasm* displays a progress bar while disassembling, even with /text. Use /nobar to suppress that progress bar.

/out:*file*

Displays output to a file instead of creating GUI.

/noi[l]

Suppresses display of MSIL. Requires the /text or /out option.

/pub[only]

Disassembles only public types (equivalent to /vis=pub).

/quo[teallnames]
>   Encloses all names in single quotes.

/raw[eh]
>   Displays exception handling clauses in raw form.

/sou[rce]
>   Displays original source code lines as comments.

/tex[t]
>   Displays output to console instead of creating GUI.

/tok[ens]
>   Displays class and member metadata tokens.

/uni[code]
>   Displays output in UNICODE. Requires the /text or /out option.

/utf[8]
>   Displays output in UTF-8. Requires the /text or /out option.

/vis[ibility]=vis[+vis...]
>   Restricts disassembly to types and members matching specified visibility. Available visibilities are PUB (public), PRI (private), FAM (family), ASM (assembly), FAA (family and assembly), FOA (family or assembly), and PSC (private scope).

See Also

Csc.exe, ILasm.exe

InstallUtil.exe

Synopsis

>   InstallUtil [/u[ninstall]] [*options*] *assembly1* [[*options*] *assembly2*] ...

Description

Executes installers and uninstallers contained within the assembly. A log file can be written, and state information can be persisted. For complete details, see the *Installer Tool (Installutil.exe)* topic in the .NET Framework SDK Documentation.

Options

/? [*assemblypath*], /h[elp] [*assemblypath*]
>   Prints a usage message and exits. If *assemblypath* is supplied, it displays help for any additional options supported by installers in the assembly.

/logFile=*file*
>   Logs installation progress to a file (defaults to *assemblyname.InstallLog*).

/logToConsole=(true|false)
>   If true, logs output to the console. The default is false.

/showCallStack
>   Prints the call stack to the log file if an exception is thrown during installation.

/u[ninstall]
>   Uninstalls assemblies. This option applies to all assemblies specified on the command line.

Ngen.exe

Synopsis

```
ngen [options] [assembly-path-or-display-name ...]
```

Description

Compiles an assembly to native code and installs a native image in the local computer's native image cache. That native image is used each time you access the original assembly, even though the original assembly contains MSIL. If the runtime can't locate the native image, it falls back on JIT compilation.

Examples

```
ngen foo.exe
ngen foo.dll
```

Options

/debug

Generates a native image that can be used with a debugger.

/debugopt

Generates a native image that can be used with a debugger in optimized debugging mode.

/delete

Deletes native images matching *assembly-path-or-display-name*. Use * for *assembly-path-or-display-name* to delete *all* native images.

/nologo

Suppresses display of the banner and copyright messages.

/prof

Generates a native image that can be used with a profiler.

/show

Lists native images matching *assembly-path-or-display-name*. If *assembly-path-or-display-name* is not supplied, lists all native images.

/showversion

Displays the version of the .NET runtime that would be used to generate the native image. Does not actually generate the image. (Added in .NET 1.1.)

/silent

Suppresses display of success messages.

Nmake.exe

Synopsis

```
nmake [options] [macro=value ...] [targets]
```

Description

Common utility that scripts building of multiple components and source files and tracks rebuild dependency information. If a target is not specified, *Nmake* looks for a target called *all*.

Options

/@file
> Specifies a response file containing arguments to *nmake*.

/?, /help
> Displays usage information and exits.

/a
> Build all targets, even if they are up-to-date.

/b
> Builds if timestamps are equal.

/c
> Suppresses output messages.

/d
> Displays build information.

/e
> Overrides environment variable macros.

/f makefile
> Specifies a makefile. The default is *Makefile* in the current directory.

/i
> Ignores command exit codes. Continues building even if an error occurs in an external program, such as a compiler.

/k
> If an error occurs while building a target, /k causes *nmake* to continue building other targets.

/n
> Displays commands, but does not actually execute them.

/nologo
> Suppresses display of the banner and copyright messages.

/p
> Displays *nmake* settings and information about the current makefile.

/q
> Checks time stamps, but does not perform the build.

/r
> Ignores predefined rules. (Compare the output of nmake /pq to the output of nmake /p).

/s
> Suppresses display of commands as they are executed.

/t
> Changes timestamps, but does not perform the build

/u
> Dumps inline files.

/y
> Disables batch mode.

/x file
> Sends all standard error messages to *file*.

See Also

Managing Projects with make, by Andrew Oram and Steve Talbott (O'Reilly & Associates).

PEVerify.exe

Synopsis

```
PEverify file [options]
```

Description

Verifies that your compiler has generated type-safe MSIL. C# always generates type-safe MSIL. Useful for ILASM-generated programs.

Options

/?

Displays usage information and exits.

/break=*count*

Aborts execution after *count* errors. The default is one error.

/clock

Reports on how long verification took.

/hresult

Displays error codes in hexadecimal.

/ignore=*code1*[,*code2* ...]

Ignores specified error codes. You must specify the error codes in hexadecimal format (such as 0x0000001F).

/ignore=@*file*

Specifies a file containing error codes to ignore. The error codes must be in hexadecimal format.

/il

Verifies only the PE structure and MSIL.

/md

Verifies only the PE structure and metadata.

/quiet

Suppresses display of errors.

/unique

Ignores duplicate error codes.

See Also

ILasm.exe

RegAsm.exe

Synopsis

```
RegAsm assembly [options]
```

Description

Registers an assembly in the system registry. This allows COM clients to call managed methods. You can also use it to generate the registry file for future registration. If the assembly is only accessed from one COM client, and that client lives in the same directory as the assembly, you do not need to add the assembly to the GAC. If you want the assembly to be accessible to all COM clients, you should add it to the GAC (see *GacUtil.exe*).

Example

```
regasm /regfile:c.reg c.dll
```

Options

`/?, /help`
> Displays usage information and exits.

`/codebase`
> Specifies a file path for the assembly. Do not use this if the assembly is in the GAC, or if you later plan to add it to the GAC. The assembly must be signed with a strong name (see *Sn.exe*).

`/nologo`
> Suppresses display of the banner and copyright messages.

`/regfile[:file]`
> Generates a *.reg* file that you can use to add the assembly to the registry. This option does not change the registry; you need to double-click on the generated *.reg* file to add the assembly to the registry. You cannot use this option with `/unregister` or `/tlb`.

`/registered`
> Refers only to type libraries that are already registered.

`/silent`
> Suppresses display of success messages.

`/tlb[:file]`
> Generates a type library (*.tlb*).

`/unregister`
> Unregisters the assembly.

`/verbose`
> Displays verbose output.

See Also

GacUtil.exe, Sn.exe

RegSvcs.exe
Service Installation Utility

Synopsis

```
regsvcs [options] assembly
```

Description

Registers an assembly to COM+, and installs its typelib into a new or existing application. Can also generate a typelib. The assembly must be signed with a strong name (see *Sn.exe*).

Example

```
regsvcs foo.dll /appname:comapp /tlb:newfoo.tlb
```

Options

/?, /help
Displays usage information and exits.

/appdir:path
Specifies application root directory. (Added in .NET 1.1.)

/appname:name
Specifies the name of the COM+ application.

/c
Creates the application.

/componly
Configures only components, ignoring methods and interfaces.

/exapp
Expects that the application already exists. *RegSvcs.exe* fails if the application does not exist.

/extlb
Uses an existing type library. Requires the /tlb option.

/fc
Finds and uses an existing application or creates a new one if it does not exist. This is the default mode.

/nologo
Suppresses display of the banner and copyright messages.

/noreconfig
Does not reconfigure an existing application.

/parname:name
Specifies the name or ID of the COM+ application to find or create.

/quiet
Suppresses display of success, banner, and copyright messages.

/reconfig
Reconfigures an existing application. This is the default behavior.

/tlb:file
Specifies the type library.

/u
Uninstall the assembly from the application.

Synopsis

```
sn options
```

Description

Verifies assemblies and their key information. Also generates key files and manages Cryptographic Service Provider (CSP) containers, which provide a layer of abstraction over key storage and management. CSPs are enumerated in the *HKLM\SOFTWARE\ Microsoft\Cryptography\Defaults\Provider* registry key. See *GacUtil.exe* for an example of signing an assembly.

Examples

Create a new key-pair:

```
C:\home>sn -k mykey.snk

Microsoft (R) .NET Framework Strong Name Utility  Version 1.1.4322.573
Copyright (C) Microsoft Corporation 1998-2002. All rights reserved.

Key pair written to mykey.snk
```

Add that key-pair to a container:

```
C:\home>sn -i mykey.snk MyContainer

Microsoft (R) .NET Framework Strong Name Utility  Version 1.1.4322.573
Copyright (C) Microsoft Corporation 1998-2002. All rights reserved.

Key pair installed into 'MyContainer'
```

Extract the public key from the key in the container:

```
C:\home>sn -pc MyContainer pubkey.out

Microsoft (R) .NET Framework Strong Name Utility  Version 1.1.4322.573
Copyright (C) Microsoft Corporation 1998-2002. All rights reserved.

Public key written to pubkey.out
```

Options

-?, help

Displays usage information and exits.

-c [csp]

Sets the default CSP for your machine. With no arguments, resets the CSP to the default.

-d container

Deletes the specified key container.

-D assembly1assembly2

Compares two assemblies and verifies that they differ only by signature.

-e assemblyfile

Extracts an assembly's public key into *file*.

`-i` *filecontainer*

> Installs a key-pair from *file* in the container.

`-k` *file*

> Generates a new key-pair and stores it in *file*.

`-m` [y|n]

> With y, specifies that key containers are machine-specific. With n, specifies that they are user-specific. With no arguments, displays the current settings.

`-o` *keyfile* [*csvfile*]

> Converts a public key to comma-separated value (CSV) format and stores it in the *csvfile*. If *csvfile* is not specified, stores the data in the clipboard.

`-p` *infileoutfile*

> Extracts the public key from *infile* and stores it in *outfile*. Use the extracted public key for delay signing (see *Al.exe*).

`-pc` *containerfile*

> Extracts the public key from the key-pair that is stored in the container. The public key is stored in *file*.

`-q`

> Suppresses display of success messages.

`-R` *assembly* file

> Re-signs a previously signed (or delay-signed) assembly.

`-Rc` *assemblycontainer*

> Re-signs a previously signed (or delay-signed) assembly using the key-pair in the specified container.

`-t`[p] *file*

> Displays a public key's token (-t) or the token and public key (-tp). The file must be generated with -p.

`-T`[p] *assembly*

> Displays an assembly's public key token (-T) or the token and public key (-Tp).

`-v`[f] *assembly*

> Verifies an assembly's strong name. Use f to force verification even if you have disabled it with -Vr.

`-Vl`

> Lists the machine's current settings for strong name verification.

`-Vr` *assembly* [*userlist*]

> Registers the assembly for verification skipping. You can optionally supply a list of users that this applies to.

`-Vu` *assembly*

> Unregisters the assembly for verification skipping.

`-Vx`

> Unregisters all verification skipping entries.

See Also

Al.exe, GacUtil.exe

SoapSuds.exe

Synopsis

soapsuds (-url:*args* | -types:*args* | -is:*args* | -ia:*args*) [*options*]

Description

Creates XML schemas for services in an assembly and creates assemblies from a schema. You can also reference the schema via its URL. Use *SoapSuds* to create client applications that communicate with .NET remoting servers. Use *Wsdl.exe* to create clients that communicate with .NET Web Services.

Example

```
soapsuds
  -url:http://localhost/myapp/app.soap?wsdl
  -os:app.xml
```

Options and Arguments

-d[omain]:*domain*
  Specifies a domain name, if one is required for authentication.

-GenerateCode, -gc
  Generates code (equivalent to -od:.).

-httpProxyName:*name*, -hpn:*name*
  Specifies an HTTP proxy name (use this when connecting through an HTTP proxy).

-httpProxyPort:*port*, -hpp:*port*
  Specifies an HTTP proxy port (use this when connecting through an HTTP proxy).

-inputAssemblyFile:*file*, -ia:*file*
  Specifies an input assembly file from which to import types. Do not include the *.exe* or *.dll* extension.

-inputDirectory:*directory*, -id:*directory*
  Specifies the directory that contains *.dll* files.

-inputSchemaFile:*file*, -is:*file*
  Specifies the input schema file.

-NoWrappedProxy, -nowp
  Creates a proxy that is not wrapped (the default is a wrapped proxy).

-outputAssemblyFile:*file*, -oa:*file*
  Writes output to an assembly file. *SoapSuds* also generates source code.

-outputDirectory:*directory*, -od:*directory*
  Specifies the output directory.

-outputSchemaFile:*file*, -os:*file*
  Writes output to an XML schema file.

-p[assword]:*password*
  Specifies a password, if one is required for authentication.

-proxyNamespace:*namespace*, -pn:*namespace*
> Specifies the namespace for generated proxy code. This should only be used for interop namespaces.

-se[rviceEndpoint]:*url*
> Specifies the URL for the WSDL's service endpoint.

-StrongNameFile:*file*, -sn:*file*
> Signs the generated assembly using the specified key file. See *Sn.exe*.

-types:*type1,assembly*[,*endpoint*][;*type2,assembly*[,*endpoint*] ...]
> Specifies one or more input types, with optional assembly name and service endpoint.

-url[ToSchema]:*url*
> Specifies the location of the XML schema.

-u[sername]:*username*
> Specifies a username, if one is required for authentication.

-WrappedProxy, -wp
> Creates a proxy that is wrapped (this is the default).

TlbExp.exe
Type Library Exporter

Synopsis
    tlbexp *assembly* [*options*]

Description
Exports a COM typelib derived from the public types within the supplied assembly. Differs from *RegAsm.exe* in that it doesn't perform any registration.

Example
    tlbexp /out:c.tlb c.dll

Options
/?, /help
> Displays usage information and exits.

/names:*file*
> Supplies a filename that controls the capitalization of names in the type library. Each line in *file* should contain one name.

/nologo
> Suppresses display of the banner and copyright messages.

/out:*file*
> Specifies the filename of type library.

/silent
> Suppresses display of success messages.

/verbose
> Displays verbose output.

See Also
TlbImp.exe, *RegAsm.exe*

Synopsis

```
tlbimp file[\resourceid] [options]
```

Description

Creates a managed assembly from the supplied COM typelib, mapping the type definitions to .NET types. You need to import this new assembly into your C# program for use.

Example

```
tlbimp /out:MyOldCom.dll MyCom.tlb
```

Options

`/?, /help`

Displays usage information and exits.

`/asmversion:version`

Specifies the generated assembly's version in *major.minor.build.revision* format (such as 6.0.2600.0).

`/delaysign`

Partially signs the generated assembly. Requires /keycontainer, /keyfile, or /publickey.

`/keycontainer:name`

Specifies a key container that contains the key-pair with which to sign the assembly.

`/keyfile:file`

Specifies the name of the file that contains the key or key-pair with which to sign the assembly.

`/namespace:namespace`

Specifies the namespace of the generated assembly.

`/nologo`

Suppresses display of the banner and copyright messages.

`/out:file`

Specifies the filename of the generated assembly.

`/primary`

Generates a primary interop assembly.

`/publickey:file`

Specifies a file that contains a public key with which to sign the assembly. To create such a file, use the -p option of the *Sn.exe* utility.

`/reference:file`

Specifies an assembly that contains external type definitions.

`/silent`

Suppresses display of success messages.

`/strictref`

Causes *TlbImp.exe* to fail if it cannot resolve all references within the imported file or an assembly listed with the /reference option.

`/sysarray`
Imports COM SAFEARRAYs as the .NET managed System.Array type.

`/transform:name`
Performs the specified transformation. Currently, only DispRet is available (performs [out,retval] transformation on methods of disp-only interfaces). (Added in .NET 1.1.)

`/unsafe`
Disables security checks in the generated assembly. Use with caution, since this poses a security risk.

`/verbose`
Displays verbose output.

See Also

TlbExp.exe

Wsdl.exe
Web Services Description Language Utility

Synopsis

```
wsdl.exe options url-or-path [url-or-path ...]
```

Description

Creates service descriptions and generates proxy clients for ASP.NET web-service methods. See the ASP.NET documentation in the .NET Framework SDK for more detail on web services.

Example

Create the proxy client *Service1.cs* from the .NET web service at the specified URL:

```
wsdl http://localhost/MyService/Service1.asmx?WSDL
```

Options

`/?`
Displays usage information and exits.

`/appsettingbaseurl:url, /baseurl:url`
Specifies the base URL for calculating the URL fragment. Requires /appsettingurlkey.

`/appsettingurlkey:key, /urlkey:key`
Specifies application settings configuration key to read the default value for the proxy client's Url property.

`/d[omain]:domain`
Specifies a domain name, if one is required for authentication.

`/l[anguage]:language`
Specifies the language for the generated proxy client. Valid options are CS (C#), VB (Visual Basic .NET), JS (JScript.NET), and VJS (J#).

`/namespace:namespace`
Specifies a namespace for the generated proxy client class.

`/nologo`
Suppresses display of the banner and copyright messages.

/o[ut]:*file*

Specifies the filename of the generated proxy client class. If not specified, *Wsdl* bases the filename on the name of the web service.

/parsableerrors

Displays error messages using a format similar to that used by the compilers. (Added in .NET 1.1.)

/p[assword]:*password*

Specifies a password, if one is required for authentication.

/protocol:*protocol*

Specifies the protocol to implement. Valid protocols are *SOAP* (the default), *SOAP12*, *HttpGet*, or *HttpPost*.

/proxy:*url*

Specifies the URL of an HTTP proxy server.

/proxydomain:*domain*, /pd:*domain*

Specifies a domain name, if one is required for HTTP proxy server authentication.

/proxypassword:*password*, /pp:*password*

Specifies a password, if one is required for HTTP proxy server authentication.

/proxyusername:*username*, /pu:*username*

Specifies a user name, if one is required for HTTP proxy server authentication.

/server

Generates an abstract class instead of a concrete proxy client class.

/u[sername]:*username*

Specifies a user name, if one is required for authentication.

WinCV.exe

Windows Class Viewer

Synopsis

```
wincv [options]
```

Description

Searches for matching names within a supplied assembly and displays types and member signatures as C# code. If no assemblies are supplied, it uses the default libraries. The namespaces and classes are displayed in a listbox, and the selected type information is displayed in another window.

Options

/?, /h

Displays usage information and exits.

@*file*

Specifies a response file containing *WinCV.exe* options.

/hide:*option*

Hides types matching the specified option. Valid options are protected, private, internal, and inherited. You may supply this option multiple times.

/nostdlib[+|-]

Use /nostdlib+ or /nostdlib to suppress loading default assemblies.

/r:file

Specifies an assembly. You may supply this option multiple times to specify multiple assemblies. Use */nostdlib* to hide everything else but the types in the specified assemblies.

/show:option

Shows types matching the specified option. Valid options are protected, private, internal, and inherited. You may supply this option multiple times.

See Also

ILDasm.exe

Xsd.exe

XML Schema Definition Tool

Synopsis

```
xsd.exe assembly.[dll|exe] [/outputdir:dir] [/type:type1 [/type:type2 ...]]
xsd.exe instance.xml [/outputdir:dir]
xsd.exe schema.xdr [/outputdir:dir]
xsd.exe schema.xsd (/classes|/dataset) [/e] [/l] [/n] [/o] [/uri]
```

Description

Generates XML schemas from XDR, XML files, or class information. Can also generate DataSet or class information from a schema.

Examples

```
xsd foo.xdr
xsd bar.dll
```

Arguments

assembly.[dll|exe]

The name of a .NET assembly. *Xsd.exe* infers a schema from the assembly's types and generates an *.xsd* file.

*instance.*xml

The name of an XML document. *Xsd.exe* infers a schema from it and generates an *.xsd* file.

*schema.*xdr

The name of an XML Data Reduced schema document. *Xsd.exe* converts it to an *.xsd* file.

*schema.*xsd

The name of an XML Schema Description Language schema document. *Xsd.exe* generates either a dataset (/dataset) or source code (/classes) for types that correspond to the schema.

Options

/c[lasses]

Generates types that correspond to an XML schema.

/d[ataset]

Generates a subclass of DataSet that corresponds to an XML schema.

/e[lement]:*element*

　　Specifies a particular element in the XML schema. To specify multiple elements, use this option more than once. By default, *Xsd.exe* processes all elements.

/l[anguage]:*language*

　　Specifies the language for the generated code. Valid options are CS (C#), VB (Visual Basic .NET), JS (JScript.NET), and VJS (J#).

/n[amespace]:*namespace*

　　Specifies the namespace for the generated types.

/nologo

　　Suppresses display of the banner and copyright messages.

/o[ut]:*directory*

　　Specifies the directory to store generated files.

/t[ype]:*type*

　　Specifies a particular type in the assembly. To specify multiple types, use this option more than once. By default, *Xsd.exe* processes all types.

/u[ri]:*uri*

　　Specifies the URI of the elements in the schema file to process.

IV

API Quick Reference

Part IV, *API Quick Reference*, is a succinct but detailed API reference of 21 important namespaces and more than 700 core types and their members. Chapter 24, *How to Use This Quick Reference*, appears at the beginning of Part IV and explains how to get the most from its content.

24

How to Use This Quick Reference

The quick-reference section that follows packs a lot of information into a small space. This introduction explains how to get the most out of that information. It describes how the quick reference is organized and how to read the individual quick-ref entries.

Finding a Quick-Reference Entry

The quick reference is organized into chapters, one per namespace. Each chapter begins with an overview of the namespace and includes a hierarchy diagram for the types (classes, interfaces, enumerations, delegates, and structs) in the namespace. Following the overview are quick-reference entries for all of the types in the namespace.

Figure 24-1 is a sample diagram showing the notation used in this book. This notation is similar to that used in *Java in a Nutshell*, but borrows some features from UML. Abstract classes are shown as a slanted rectangle, and sealed classes as an octagonal rectangle. Inheritance is shown as a solid line from the subtype, ending with a hollow triangle that points to the supertype. There are two notations that indicate interface implementation. The lollipop notation is used most of the time, since it is easier to read. In some cases, especially where many types implement a given interface, the shaded box notation with the dashed line is used.

Important relationships between types (associations) are shown with a dashed line ending with an arrow. The figures don't show every possible association. Some types have strong containing relationships with one another. For example, a System.Net.WebException includes a System.Net.WebResponse that represents the HTTP response containing the error details (HTTP status code and error message). To show this relationship, a filled diamond is attached to the containing type with a solid line that points to the contained type.

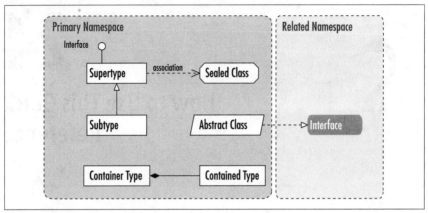

Figure 24-1. Class hierarchy notation

Entries are organized alphabetically by type *and* namespace, so that related types are grouped near each other. Thus, in order to look up a quick reference entry for a particular type, you must also know the name of the namespace that contains that type. Usually, the namespace is obvious from the context, and you should have no trouble looking up the quick-reference entry you want. Use the tabs on the outside edge of the book and the dictionary-style headers on the upper outside corner of each page to help you find the namespace and type you are looking for.

Occasionally, you may need to look up a type for which you do not already know the namespace. In this case, refer to the *Type, Method, Property, Event, and Field Index*. This index allows you to look up a type by its name and find out what namespace it is part of.

Reading a Quick-Reference Entry

Each quick-reference entry contains quite a bit of information. The sections that follow describe the structure of a quick-reference entry, explaining what information is available, where it is found, and what it means. While reading the descriptions that follow, you will find it helpful to flip through the reference section itself to find examples of the features being described.

Type Name, Namespace, Assembly, Type Category, and Flags

Each quick-reference entry begins with a four-part title that specifies the name, namespace (followed by the assembly in parentheses), and type category of the type, and may also specify various additional flags that describe the type. The type name appears in bold at the upper left of the title. The namespace and assembly appear, in smaller print, in the lower left, below the type name.

The upper-right portion of the title indicates the type category of the type (class, delegate, enum, interface, or struct). The class category may include modifiers such as sealed or abstract.

In the lower-right corner of the title you may find a list of flags that describe the type. The possible flags and their meanings are as follows:

ECMA
> The type is part of the ECMA CLI specification.

serializable
> The type, or a supertype, implements `System.Runtime.Serialization.ISerializable` or has been flagged with the `System.Serializable` attribute.

marshal by reference
> This class, or a superclass, derives from `System.MarshalByRefObject`.

context bound
> This class, or a superclass, derives from `System.ContextBoundObject`.

disposable
> The type implements the `System.IDisposable` interface.

flag
> The enumeration is marked with the `System.FlagsAttribute`.

Description

The title of each quick-reference entry is followed by a short description of the most important features of the type. This description may be anywhere from a couple of sentences to several paragraphs long.

Synopsis

The most important part of every quick-reference entry is the synopsis, which follows the title and description. The synopsis for a type looks a lot like its source code, except that the member bodies are omitted and some additional annotations are added. If you know C# syntax, you know how to read the type synopsis.

The first line of the synopsis contains information about the type itself. It begins with a list of type modifiers, such as abstract and sealed. These modifiers are followed by the class, delegate, enum, interface, or struct keyword and then by the name of the type. The type name may be followed by a colon (:) and a supertype or interfaces that the type implements.

The type definition line is followed by a list of the members that the type defines. This list includes only those members that are explicitly declared in the type, are overridden from a base class, or are implementations of an interface member. Members that are simply inherited from a base class are not shown; you will need to look up the base class definition to find those members. Once again, if you understand basic C# syntax, you should have no trouble making sense of these lines. The listing for each member includes the modifiers, type, and name of the member. For methods, the synopsis also includes the type and name of each method parameter. The member names are in boldface, so it is easy to scan the list of members looking for the one you want. The names of method parameters are in italics to indicate that they are not to be used literally. The member listings are printed on alternating gray and white backgrounds to keep them visually separate.

Member availability and flags

Each member listing is a single line that defines the API for that member. These listings use C# syntax, so their meaning is immediately clear to any C# programmer. There is some auxiliary information associated with each member synopsis, however, that requires explanation.

The area to the right of the member synopsis is used to display a variety of flags that provide additional information about the member. Some of these flags indicate additional specification details that do not appear in the member API itself.

The following flags may be displayed to the right of a member synopsis:

Overrides
> Indicates that a method overrides a method in one of its supertypes. The flag is followed by the name of the supertype that the method overrides.

Implements
> Indicates that a method implements a method in an interface. The flag is followed by the name of the interface that is implemented.

=
> For enumeration fields and constant fields, this flag is followed by the constant value of the field. Only constants of primitive and String types and constants with the value null are displayed. Some constant values are specification details, while others are implementation details. Some constants are platform-dependent, such as System.BitConverter.IsLittleEndian. Platform-dependent values shown in this book conform to the System.PlatformID. Win32NT platform (32-bit Windows NT, 2000, or XP). The reason that symbolic constants are defined, however, is so you can write code that does not rely directly upon the constant value. Use this flag to help you understand the type, but do not rely upon the constant values in your own programs.

Functional grouping of members

Within a type synopsis, the members are not listed in strict alphabetical order. Instead, they are broken down into functional groups and listed alphabetically within each group. Constructors, events, fields, methods, and properties are all listed separately. Instance methods are kept separate from static (class) methods. Public members are listed separately from protected members. Grouping members by category breaks a type down into smaller, more comprehensible segments, making the type easier to understand. This grouping also makes it easier for you to find a desired member.

Functional groups are separated from each other in a type synopsis with C# comments, such as // Public Constructors, // Protected Instance Properties, and // Events. The various functional categories are as follows (in the order in which they appear in a type synopsis):

Constructors
> Displays the constructors for the type. Public constructors and protected constructors are displayed separately in subgroupings. If a type defines no constructor at all, the C# compiler adds a default no-argument constructor

that is displayed here. If a type defines only private constructors, it cannot be instantiated, so no constructor appears. Constructors are listed first because the first thing you do with most types is instantiate them by calling a constructor.

Fields
Displays all of the fields defined by the type, including constants. Public and protected fields are displayed in separate subgroups. Fields are listed here, near the top of the synopsis, because constant values are often used throughout the type as legal values for method parameters and return values.

Properties
Lists all the properties of the type, breaking them down into subgroups for public and protected static properties and public and protected instance properties. After the property name, its accessors (get or set) are shown.

Static Methods
Lists the static methods (class methods) of the type, broken down into subgroups for public static methods and protected static methods.

Public Instance Methods
Contains all of the public instance methods.

Protected Instance Methods
Contains all of the protected instance methods.

Class Hierarchy

For any type that has a non-trivial inheritance hierarchy, the synopsis is followed by a "Hierarchy" section. This section lists all of the supertype of the type, as well as any interfaces implemented by those supertypes. It will also list any interfaces implemented by an interface. In the hierarchy listing, arrows indicate supertype to subtype relationships, while the interfaces implemented by a type follow the type name in parentheses. For example, the following hierarchy indicates that System.IO.Stream implements IDisposable and extends MarshalByRefObject, which itself extends Object:

```
System.Object → System.MarshalByRefObject →
System.IO.Stream(System.IDisposable)
```

If a type has subtypes, the "Hierarchy" section is followed by a "Subtypes" section that lists those subtypes. If an interface has implementations, the "Hierarchy" section is followed by an "Implementations" section that lists those implementations. While the "Hierarchy" section shows ancestors of the type, the "Subtypes" or "Implementations" section shows descendants.

Cross References

The hierarchy section of a quick-reference entry is followed by a number of optional cross reference sections that indicate other, related types and methods that may be of interest. These sections are the following:

Passed To

This section lists all of the members (from other types) that are passed an object of this type as an argument, including properties whose values can be set to this type. This is useful when you have an object of a given type and want to know where it can be used.

Returned By

This section lists all of the members that return an object of this type, including properties whose values can take on this type. This is useful when you know that you want to work with an object of this type, but don't know how to obtain one.

Valid On

For attributes, this lists the attribute targets that the attribute can be applied to.

Associated Events

For delegates, lists the events it can handle.

A Note About Type Names

Throughout the quick reference, you'll notice that types are sometimes referred to by type name alone and at other times referred to by type name and namespace. If namespaces were always used, the type synopses would become long and hard to read. On the other hand, if namespaces were never used, it would sometimes be difficult to know what type was being referred to. The rules for including or omitting the namespace name are complex. They can be summarized approximately as follows, however:

• If the type name alone is ambiguous, the namespace name is always used.

• If the type is part of the System namespace or is a very commonly used type like System.Collection.ICollection, the namespace is omitted.

• If the type being referred to is part of the current namespace (and has a quick-reference entry in the current chapter), the namespace is omitted. The namespace is also omitted if the type being referred to is part of a namespace that contains the current namespace.

The Microsoft.Win32 Namespace

The Microsoft.Win32 namespace includes types you can use to interact with the Microsoft Windows platform. These types concentrate on two aspects of Windows-specific programming: receiving operating system events and manipulating the registry. Essentially, the classes, delegates, and enumerations in this namespace provide a type-safe object wrapper around a few select functions in the Windows API.

Use the Registry class to access the root-level registry keys, which are provided as RegistryKey objects. These have built-in methods for retrieving and modifying key values. The SystemEvents class allows you to respond to system events such as timers, preference changes, and shutdown operations. All other types in this namespace are used to support the SystemEvents class, by providing delegates for each event and custom System.EventArgs objects that provide additional information to the corresponding event handlers.

PowerModeChangedEventArgs

Microsoft.Win32 (system.dll)   class

This class creates a custom System.EventArgs object for the PowerModeChangedEventHandler delegate. It provides additional information to your event handler, identifying the new power mode that the system has entered.

```
public class PowerModeChangedEventArgs : EventArgs {
// Public Constructors
   public PowerModeChangedEventArgs(PowerModes mode);
// Public Instance Properties
   public PowerModes Mode{get; }
}
```

Hierarchy   System.Object → System.EventArgs → PowerModeChangedEventArgs

Passed To   PowerModeChangedEventHandler.{BeginInvoke( ), Invoke( )}

Figure 25-1 shows the inheritance diagram for this namespace.

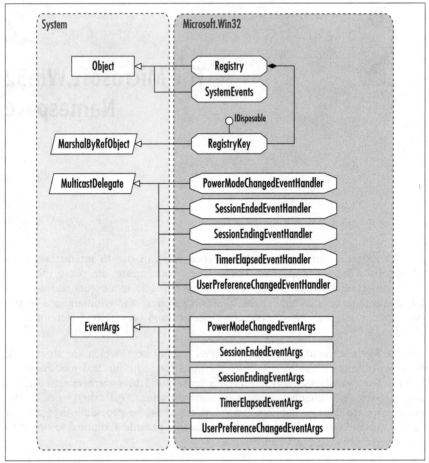

Figure 25-1. The Microsoft.Win32 namespace

PowerModeChangedEventHandler

serializable

Microsoft.Win32 (system.dll)

delegate

This delegate defines the signature that an event handler must use to receive the SystemEvents.PowerModeChanged event. This event is raised when the computer enters or exits suspend mode, and when the power consumption level changes. A computer requires Advanced Power Management (APM) or Advanced Configuration and Power Interface (ACPI) support in order to use these operating system features. APM/ACPI is usually supported on (but not restricted to) portable computers and devices.

```
public delegate void PowerModeChangedEventHandler(object sender, PowerModeChangedEventArgs e);
```

Associated Events SystemEvents.PowerModeChanged( )

PowerModes

Microsoft.Win32 (system.dll)

serializable

enum

This enumeration is used for the PowerModeChangedEventArgs class. It provides information about the current power modes, such as Suspend, which indicates that the computer is preparing to enter suspend mode, and Resume, which indicates that the computer is about to leave it. StatusChange simply indicates that the power mode status has changed, possibly due to automatic power-down settings, a weak or charging battery, or a transition between AC power and battery power.

```
public enum PowerModes {
   Resume = 1,
   StatusChange = 2,
   Suspend = 3
}
```

Hierarchy   System.Object → System.ValueType → System.Enum(System.IComparable, System.IFormattable, System.IConvertible) → PowerModes

Returned By   PowerModeChangedEventArgs.Mode

Passed To   PowerModeChangedEventArgs.PowerModeChangedEventArgs( )

Registry

Microsoft.Win32 (mscorlib.dll)

sealed class

This class is the starting point when using the Windows registry, which is the central repository used by most Windows applications for storing user-specific settings and preferences. Each static field of this class represents a root RegistryKey object, which has values and multiple levels of subkeys. These keys are read-only, but can be manipulated using the methods of the RegistryKey class.

Most applications store their settings in CurrentUser (HKEY_CURRENT_USER). The recommended standard is to use the Software subkey, create a subkey for your organization, and then create a subkey for each specific application (for example, Internet Explorer preferences are stored in HKEY_CURRENT_USER\Software\Microsoft\Internet Explorer). Analogous global settings that should affect all users on the current computer can be placed in a similar subkey in LocalMachine (HKEY_LOCAL_MACHINE). For example, setup programs often use this key to store information about installed applications. The full collection of user settings for all the users of the current computer can be retrieved from the Users key, as can the default settings for new users, which are contained in the .DEFAULT subkey of users. CurrentUser is actually a mapped subkey of Users, much as CurrentConfig is a subkey of LocalMachine.

The ClassesRoot key contains information used for Windows 3.1–compatible DDE and OLE support. Information for file viewers, Windows Explorer extensions, and file associations is also stored in this key. You can use the PerformanceData key to retrieve performance-related information. This data is not actually stored in the registry. Instead, it is automatically collected from the appropriate system object managers when this key is accessed. Lastly, the DynData key is used to support Virtual Device Drivers (VxDs) and allow them to provide real-time data to remote Win32 applications. It is used only in Windows 95, 98, and ME systems.

Much more information about the system registry is available from Microsoft's Windows platform documentation.

```
public sealed class Registry {
// Public Static Fields
  public static readonly RegistryKey ClassesRoot;              // =HKEY_CLASSES_ROOT [0x80000000]
  public static readonly RegistryKey CurrentConfig;           // =HKEY_CURRENT_CONFIG [0x80000005]
  public static readonly RegistryKey CurrentUser;             // =HKEY_CURRENT_USER [0x80000001]
  public static readonly RegistryKey DynData;                 // =HKEY_DYN_DATA [0x80000006]
  public static readonly RegistryKey LocalMachine;            // =HKEY_LOCAL_MACHINE [0x80000002]
  public static readonly RegistryKey PerformanceData;         // =HKEY_PERFORMANCE_DATA [0x80000004]
  public static readonly RegistryKey Users;                   // =HKEY_USERS [0x80000003]
}
```

RegistryHive
serializable

Microsoft.Win32 (mscorlib.dll) enum

This enumeration provides values for the RegistryKey.OpenRemoteBaseKey( ) method. These values identify a registry key, just like the fields in the Registry class.

```
public enum RegistryHive {
  ClassesRoot = 0x80000000,
  CurrentUser = 0x80000001,
  LocalMachine = 0x80000002,
  Users = 0x80000003,
  PerformanceData = 0x80000004,
  CurrentConfig = 0x80000005,
  DynData = 0x80000006
}
```

Hierarchy   System.Object → System.ValueType → System.Enum(System.IComparable, System.IFormattable, System.IConvertible) → RegistryHive

Passed To   RegistryKey.OpenRemoteBaseKey( )

RegistryKey
marshal by reference, disposable

Microsoft.Win32 (mscorlib.dll) sealed class

The RegistryKey class contains the core functionality for reading and writing to the Windows registry. Each RegistryKey object represents an individual key in the registry. You can use the properties of this class to find out how many values this key contains (ValueCount), how many subkeys (SubKeyCount) there are, and the fully qualified key name (Name).

To open a subkey for modification, use the overloaded version of the OpenSubKey( ) method—which allows you to specify the writable parameter—and set it to true. You can open subkeys that are several levels deep by separating keys with a backslash (\). In C#, the backslash must be escaped, as in mykey.OpenKey("Software\\Microsoft"). You can also use methods such as CreateSubKey( ) and DeleteSubKey( ). In the registry, keys are logical groupings, and values are the entries used to store the actual data. You can use the GetValue( ), SetValue( ), and DeleteValue( ) methods to manipulate a named value in the current key.

Changes to the registry are propagated across the system automatically and are flushed to disk automatically by the system. You should never need to use methods such as

Flush(), unless you require absolute certainty that a registry change has been written to disk. The OpenRemoteBaseKey() method opens the registry on a remote computer, provided both machines are running the remote registry service and have remote administration enabled.

```
public sealed class RegistryKey : MarshalByRefObject, IDisposable {
// Public Instance Properties
  public string Name{get; }
  public int SubKeyCount{get; }
  public int ValueCount{get; }
// Public Static Methods
  public static RegistryKey OpenRemoteBaseKey(RegistryHive hKey, string machineName);
// Public Instance Methods
  public void Close( );
  public RegistryKey CreateSubKey(string subkey);
  public void DeleteSubKey(string subkey);
  public void DeleteSubKey(string subkey, bool throwOnMissingSubKey);
  public void DeleteSubKeyTree(string subkey);
  public void DeleteValue(string name);
  public void DeleteValue(string name, bool throwOnMissingValue);
  public void Flush( );
  public string[ ] GetSubKeyNames( );
  public object GetValue(string name);
  public object GetValue(string name, object defaultValue);
  public string[ ] GetValueNames( );
  public RegistryKey OpenSubKey(string name);
  public RegistryKey OpenSubKey(string name, bool writable);
  public void SetValue(string name, object value);
  public override string ToString( );                                   // overrides object
// Protected Instance Methods
  protected override void Finalize( );                                  // overrides object
}
```

Hierarchy   System.Object → System.MarshalByRefObject → RegistryKey(System.IDisposable)

SessionEndedEventArgs

Microsoft.Win32 (system.dll)   class

This class is a custom System.EventArgs object for the SystemEvents.SessionEnded delegate. It provides additional information to your event handler about why the current session has ended.

```
public class SessionEndedEventArgs : EventArgs {
// Public Constructors
  public SessionEndedEventArgs(SessionEndReasons reason);
// Public Instance Properties
  public SessionEndReasons Reason{get; }
}
```

Hierarchy   System.Object → System.EventArgs → SessionEndedEventArgs

Passed To   SessionEndedEventHandler.{BeginInvoke( ), Invoke( )}

Microsoft.
Win32

SessionEndedEventHandler

serializable

Microsoft.Win32 (system.dll)   delegate

This delegate defines the signature that an event handler must use to receive the System-Events.SessionEnded event. This event is raised just before the system finishes its logoff or shutdown procedure.

```
public delegate void SessionEndedEventHandler(object sender, SessionEndedEventArgs e);
```

Associated Events SystemEvents.SessionEnded( )

SessionEndingEventArgs

class

Microsoft.Win32 (system.dll)   class

This class is a custom System.EventArgs object for the SystemEvents.SessionEnding delegate. It provides additional information to your event handler about why the session is ending, and allows you to request that the session continue, by setting the Cancel property to true. Note that this is only a request, and you may not always be able to successfully cancel a shutdown operation.

```
public class SessionEndingEventArgs : EventArgs {
// Public Constructors
  public SessionEndingEventArgs(SessionEndReasons reason);
// Public Instance Properties
  public bool Cancel{set; get; }
  public SessionEndReasons Reason{get; }
}
```

Hierarchy   System.Object → System.EventArgs → SessionEndingEventArgs

Passed To   SessionEndingEventHandler.{BeginInvoke( ), Invoke( )}

SessionEndingEventHandler

serializable

Microsoft.Win32 (system.dll)   delegate

This delegate defines the signature that an event handler must use to receive the System-Events.SessionEnding event. This event is raised when the user has chosen to log off or shutdown the system. It occurs before the SystemEvents.SessionEnded event. SessionEndingEventArgs provides a Cancel property, which you can set in the event handler to cancel the pending shutdown.

```
public delegate void SessionEndingEventHandler(object sender, SessionEndingEventArgs e);
```

Associated Events SystemEvents.SessionEnding( )

SessionEndReasons

serializable

Microsoft.Win32 (system.dll)   enum

This enumeration specifies information for the Reason property of the SessionEndingEventArgs and SessionEndedEventArgs event arguments. It specifies whether the user who started the current application is logging off (Logoff) (in which case the system may continue to run) or whether the operating system is shutting down (SystemShutdown).

```
public enum SessionEndReasons {
  Logoff = 1,
  SystemShutdown = 2
}
```

Hierarchy   System.Object → System.ValueType → System.Enum(System.IComparable, System.
                  IFormattable, System.IConvertible) → SessionEndReasons

Returned By   SessionEndedEventArgs.Reason, SessionEndingEventArgs.Reason

Passed To   SessionEndedEventArgs.SessionEndedEventArgs( ), SessionEndingEventArgs.
                  SessionEndingEventArgs( )

SystemEvents

Microsoft.Win32 (system.dll)   sealed class

This class provides global events for select Windows operating system events. You can
write event handlers to receive these. Some of the events include notifications that
occur when user settings are changed (DisplaySettingsChanged, TimeChanged, and UserPrefer-
enceChanged) or when the system state changes (LowMemory, PowerModeChangedSessionEnded,
and SessionEnding). You can also receive notifications about new fonts (Installed-
FontsChanged) and palette switching in 256-color mode (PaletteChanged).

System event handlers are executed on a different thread than the rest of your
program. For this reason, code in the event handler must be thread-safe. If your event
handler needs access to other objects from your program, you can use the static
method InvokeOnEventsThread( ) to instantiate these objects on the system event listener
thread. This way, they are easily accessible to the event handler code.

Do not perform time-consuming tasks in a system event handler, as it may cause problems with other applications that are also trying to handle the event.

```
public sealed class SystemEvents {
// Public Static Methods
  public static IntPtr CreateTimer(int interval);
  public static void InvokeOnEventsThread(Delegate method);
  public static void KillTimer(IntPtr timerId);
// Events
  public event EventHandler DisplaySettingsChanged;
  public event EventHandler EventsThreadShutdown;
  public event EventHandler InstalledFontsChanged;
  public event EventHandler LowMemory;
  public event EventHandler PaletteChanged;
  public event PowerModeChangedEventHandler PowerModeChanged;
  public event SessionEndedEventHandler SessionEnded;
  public event SessionEndingEventHandler SessionEnding;
  public event EventHandler TimeChanged;
  public event TimerElapsedEventHandler TimerElapsed;
  public event UserPreferenceChangedEventHandler UserPreferenceChanged;
  public event UserPreferenceChangingEventHandler UserPreferenceChanging;
}
```

TimerElapsedEventArgs

Microsoft.Win32 (system.dll)   class

This class is a custom System.EventArgs object used for the SystemEvents.TimerElapsed delegate. It provides additional information to your event handler, identifying the ID of the timer that has changed.

```
public class TimerElapsedEventArgs : EventArgs {
// Public Constructors
  public TimerElapsedEventArgs(IntPtr timerId);
// Public Instance Properties
  public IntPtr TimerId{get; }
}
```

Hierarchy   System.Object → System.EventArgs → TimerElapsedEventArgs

Passed To   TimerElapsedEventHandler.{BeginInvoke( ), Invoke( )}

TimerElapsedEventHandler   serializable

Microsoft.Win32 (system.dll)   delegate

This delegate defines the signature an event handler must use to receive the SystemEvents.TimerElapsed event. This event is raised whenever a windows timer interval expires.

```
public delegate void TimerElapsedEventHandler(object sender, TimerElapsedEventArgs e);
```

Associated Events SystemEvents.TimerElapsed( )

UserPreferenceCategory   serializable

Microsoft.Win32 (system.dll)   enum

This enumeration is used for the UserPreferenceChangedEventArgs class. It provides information identifying the type of preference that was changed.

```
public enum UserPreferenceCategory {
  Accessibility = 1,
  Color = 2,
  Desktop = 3,
  General = 4,
  Icon = 5,
  Keyboard = 6,
  Menu = 7,
  Mouse = 8,
  Policy = 9,
  Power = 10,
  Screensaver = 11,
  Window = 12,
  Locale = 13
}
```

Hierarchy	System.Object → System.ValueType → System.Enum(System.IComparable, System.IFormattable, System.IConvertible) → UserPreferenceCategory
Returned By	UserPreferenceChangedEventArgs.Category, UserPreferenceChangingEventArgs.Category
Passed To	UserPreferenceChangedEventArgs.UserPreferenceChangedEventArgs( ), UserPreferenceChangingEventArgs.UserPreferenceChangingEventArgs( )

UserPreferenceChangedEventArgs

Microsoft.Win32 (system.dll)   class

This class is a custom System.EventArgs object used for the UserPreferenceChangedEventHandler delegate. It provides additional information to your event handler, identifying the type of preference that was changed.

```
public class UserPreferenceChangedEventArgs : EventArgs {
// Public Constructors
  public UserPreferenceChangedEventArgs(UserPreferenceCategory category);
// Public Instance Properties
  public UserPreferenceCategory Category{get; }
}
```

Hierarchy	System.Object → System.EventArgs → UserPreferenceChangedEventArgs
Passed To	UserPreferenceChangedEventHandler.{BeginInvoke( ), Invoke( )}

UserPreferenceChangedEventHandler   serializable

Microsoft.Win32 (system.dll)   delegate

This delegate defines the signature an event handler must use to receive the SystemEvents.UserPreferenceChanged event. This event is raised when a user applies configuration changes, usually through one of the setting modules in the Control Panel. Note that not all changes raise this event, so it is best to first test it to make sure it accomplishes everything you need before you rely on it.

```
public delegate void UserPreferenceChangedEventHandler(object sender, UserPreferenceChangedEventArgs e);
```

Associated Events SystemEvents.UserPreferenceChanged( )

UserPreferenceChangingEventArgs

Microsoft.Win32 (system.dll)   class

This class represents the event arguments sent to a UserPreferenceChangingEventHandler. Category specifies the UserPreferenceCategory of user preferences that is changing.

```
public class UserPreferenceChangingEventArgs : EventArgs {
// Public Constructors
  public UserPreferenceChangingEventArgs(UserPreferenceCategory category);
// Public Instance Properties
  public UserPreferenceCategory Category{get; }
}
```

Hierarchy	System.Object → System.EventArgs → UserPreferenceChangingEventArgs
Passed To	UserPreferenceChangingEventHandler.{BeginInvoke( ), Invoke( )}

UserPreferenceChangingEventHandler   serializable

Microsoft.Win32 (system.dll)   delegate

This delegate receives the SystemEvents.UserPreferenceChanging event, which is similar to SystemEvents.UserPreferenceChanged, except it is raised as the event is changing, not after it has changed.

```
public delegate void UserPreferenceChangingEventHandler(object sender, UserPreferenceChangingEventArgs e);
```

Associated Events SystemEvents.UserPreferenceChanging( )

26

System

In many respects, the System namespace serves as the core namespace for the .NET libraries, in much the same way java.lang does for Java programmers or stdlib.h does for C/C++ programmers. For example, the ECMA-compliant primitive-type value types are defined in the System namespace, along with complementary composite types and base types. These are used in the synthesis of type generation, which is done by the compiler on the .NET programmer's behalf (for an example of this on-the-fly type synthesis, see Array). Figure 26-1 shows many of the types in this namespace.

System serves as the home for key base-type definitions, including Object, the root of every type in the .NET hierarchy. Every type in the system ultimately extends this class, making it the "root of all evil" in .NET. In addition, this namespace contains ValueType, the base type for all value types in .NET (such as the primitive types listed later in this chapter, shown in Figure 26-5), and Type, which in turn represents compile-time type information about other types defined within the .NET environment (the type metadata). More on Type can be found in Chapter 35.

ECMA-compliant primitive-type value types include the fundamental types used for all .NET applications, which are basic value types such as Int32, Single, Double, Decimal, Char, Byte, and Boolean. All of the primitive types are aliased in C# with keywords such as int, double, and bool. See the description of each type for more details. See also "Predefined Types" in Chapter 2. In addition to these fundamental types, there are composite types such as DateTime and TimeSpan, used to handle date- and time-based calculations without having to drop down to integer math, and Uri, used to represent references to a Universal Resource Identifier, which is the more generic form of the ubiquitous HTTP URL identifier used on the Web.

In addition to these primitive and composite types, several interfaces defined here are intended as support interfaces. For example, the interfaces IConvertible, IComparable,

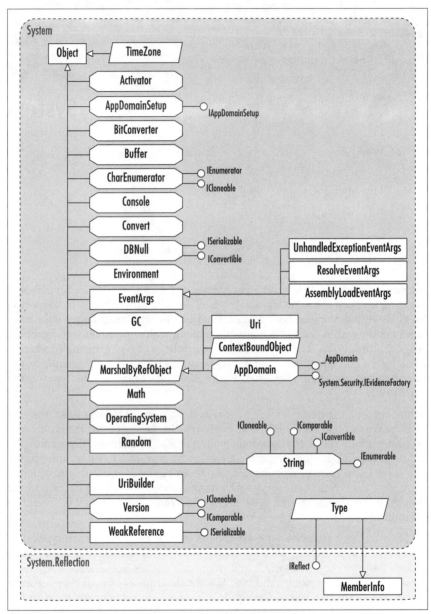

Figure 26-1. The System namespace

and ICloneable let types support the same basic operations (conversion, comparison, and cloning, respectively) that the primitive types offer.

Along with the base types described earlier, System contains base types that programmers do not directly reference, such as the following:

System.Array

The base type for any array-type declaration, allowing .NET developers to refer to any type (or rank) array without having to specify exact type.

System.Delegate *and* **System.MulticastDelegate**

Base types for delegate types (see Figure 26-2) created using the delegate keyword in C#.

System.Attribute

The base type required for any type that wishes to be used as an attribute on other types, or methods, fields, etc. (see Figure 26-2).

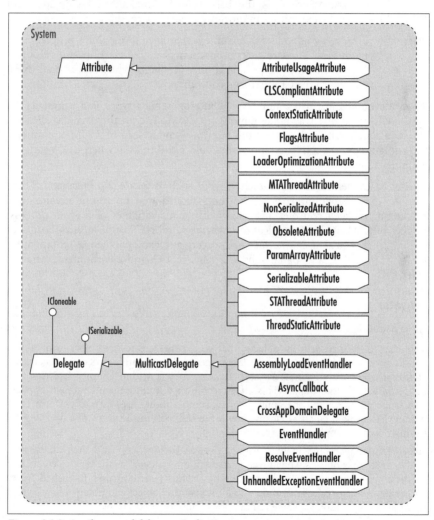

Figure 26-2. Attributes and delegates in the System namespace

Because delegates are often used in conjunction with events and event handlers, System also contains the definitions for EventHandler, the universal delegate type, and EventArgs, the base type representing data sent as part of an event-handler call.

System also serves as the heart of the exception-handling hierarchy in .NET, defining the base type Exception, which is the base type for all exceptions. The exception hierarchy is then bifurcated into two realms: *system exceptions*, which are exceptions generated by or relating to the runtime itself, and *application exceptions*, which are exceptions relating to the target business domain and typically are used on a per-application basis. SystemException serves as the base type for the former, and ApplicationException is the base type for the latter. Figure 26-3 and Figure 26-4 show the exceptions in the System namespace.

System also contains two definitions of some importance to the .NET programmer: the IDisposable interface, used to help programmers define cleanup and resource-release semantics for their types, and the GC class, which gives the .NET programmer access to the CLR garbage collector.

The System namespace also contains a few interoperability types. Guid represents the OSF UUID type that was made famous by COM. The attributes STAThreadAttribute and MTAThreadAttribute indicate to the runtime which sort of COM apartment-threading model the .NET component should use (but only when COM interoperability comes into play).

Finally, System defines the fundamental types such as Console and Environment. These give the .NET programmer access to the standard-in/standard-out streams (i.e., the command-shell console) and the environment variables of a given process, respectively. Most .NET applications will use ASP.NET or Windows Forms to present a graphical user interface. However, applications such as compilation tools, XML filters, and batch jobs use console I/O and environment variables extensively.

Activator   CF 1.0

System (mscorlib.dll)   sealed class

This class is used to *activate* objects; that is, it either creates an object or obtains a handle to an existing object. This class is generally used in a variety of specialized conditions. For example, Activator can create an object within another AppDomain and hold a handle to that object. This effectively gives a multidomain container application (such as ASP.NET) the ability to reach into another AppDomain to perform tasks within that domain (such as closing down the AppDomain in the event of a user request to shut down the application server).

Activator's methods come in two distinct flavors: CreateInstance() and CreateInstanceFrom(). These create new objects when given particular criteria (such as the type to create and the assembly from which to create it). The GetObject() method uses published System.Runtime.Remoting.RemotingConfiguration data to locate another object and obtain a handle to it (usually in preparation for some remote-object method invocations).

All of the methods in Activator return a System.Runtime.Remoting.ObjectHandle, not the actual object itself; this object is actually a proxy to the created/remote object. As such, programmers must call Unwrap() on the returned ObjectHandle to use the object. (Note that an explicit downcast is required, since the return value is declared to be a generic object.)

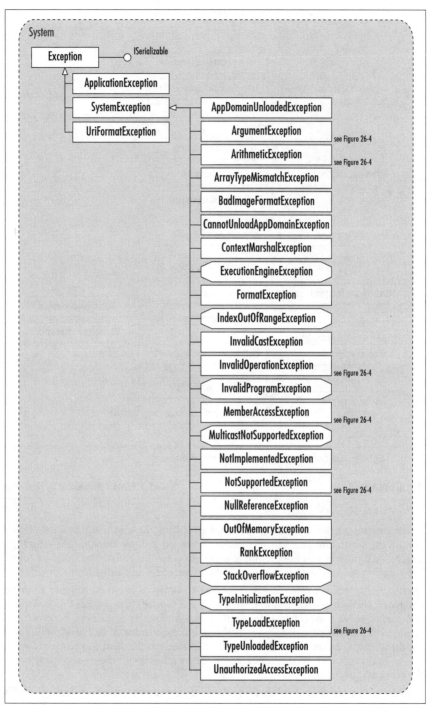

Figure 26-3. Exceptions in the System namespace

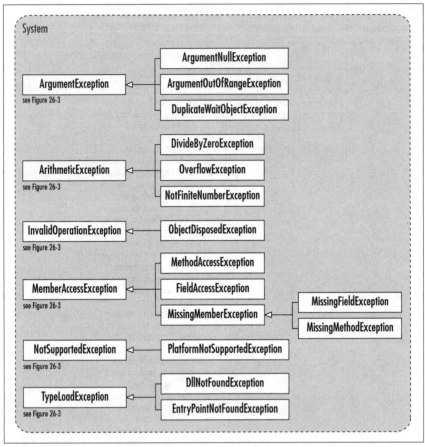

Figure 26-4. Specialized exceptions in the System namespace

AppDomain

CF 1.0, ECMA 1.0, marshal by reference

System (mscorlib.dll)   sealed class

This class represents an abstract separation within the executing process, which mimics the separation between processes running on a single machine. As a result, a single .NET process can host multiple other processes that offer the isolation found between processes, while keeping the low overhead of a single process.

Every .NET process created has at least one AppDomain, even when running a simple command shell–driven application, such as *Hello, world*, created by the shim code at the start of a .NET executable file. Applications that act as containers, however, can create multiple AppDomains, loading assemblies into each AppDomain independently of one another. This is, in fact, precisely how ASP.NET keeps multiple web applications separate from one another, so that an exception thrown from within one won't tear down the entire IIS process.

Creating a new AppDomain involves using the static CreateDomain() method. This method is overloaded four ways, but the most common use is simply to pass in a friendly name for the AppDomain. When finished with a given AppDomain, use the Unload() method to close

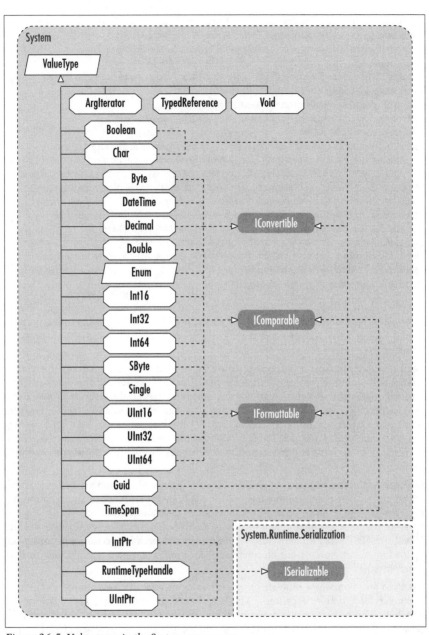

Figure 26-5. Value types in the System namespace

```
public sealed class Activator {
// Public Static Methods
   public static ObjectHandle CreateComInstanceFrom(string assemblyName, string typeName);
   public static ObjectHandle CreateComInstanceFrom(string assemblyName, string typeName, byte[] hashValue,
      System.Configuration.Assemblies.AssemblyHashAlgorithm hashAlgorithm);
```

```
public static object CreateInstance(Type type);
public static object CreateInstance(Type type, System.Reflection.BindingFlags bindingAttr,
    System.Reflection.Binder binder, object[ ] args, System.Globalization.CultureInfo culture);
public static object CreateInstance(Type type, System.Reflection.BindingFlags bindingAttr,
    System.Reflection.Binder binder, object[ ] args, System.Globalization.CultureInfo culture, object[ ] activationAttributes);
public static object CreateInstance(Type type, bool nonPublic);
public static object CreateInstance(Type type, object[ ] args);
public static object CreateInstance(Type type, object[ ] args, object[ ] activationAttributes);
public static ObjectHandle CreateInstance(string assemblyName, string typeName);
public static ObjectHandle CreateInstance(string assemblyName, string typeName, bool ignoreCase,
    System.Reflection.BindingFlags bindingAttr, System.Reflection.Binder binder, object[ ] args,
    System.Globalization.CultureInfo culture, object[ ] activationAttributes, System.Security.Policy.Evidence securityInfo);
public static ObjectHandle CreateInstance(string assemblyName, string typeName, object[ ] activationAttributes);
public static ObjectHandle CreateInstanceFrom(string assemblyFile, string typeName);
public static ObjectHandle CreateInstanceFrom(string assemblyFile, string typeName, bool ignoreCase,
    System.Reflection.BindingFlags bindingAttr, System.Reflection.Binder binder, object[ ] args,
    System.Globalization.CultureInfo culture, object[ ] activationAttributes, System.Security.Policy.Evidence securityInfo);
public static ObjectHandle CreateInstanceFrom(string assemblyFile, string typeName, object[ ] activationAttributes);
public static object GetObject(Type type, string url);
public static object GetObject(Type type, string url, object state);
}
```

down the AppDomain and all objects stored within it. Should a .NET programmer wish to obtain a reference to the AppDomain she is currently executing within, the static property CurrentDomain returns the current AppDomain.

Each AppDomain contains an entirely separate list of loaded assemblies accessible via the GetAssemblies() method, which returns the list of assemblies loaded for this particular AppDomain. AppDomains can also create instances of types within the given AppDomain, using the CreateInstance() family of methods. An AppDomain can also load and execute the entry point of an assembly using the ExecuteAssembly() method, or it can load an assembly directly using one of the Load() methods. AppDomains even support the ability to create dynamic (that is, transient or temporary) assemblies through the DefineDynamicAssembly() method.

AppDomains also offer a number of .NET events for interested consumers, notifying .NET programmers when an assembly has been loaded (AssemblyLoad), when an exception has been thrown out of a thread within that assembly (UnhandledException), or when the AppDomain—or the process containing it—is being unloaded and torn down (DomainUnload and ProcessExit). .NET programmers can use these events to perform necessary actions, such as loading an assembly from an alternative location when an assembly fails to load (AssemblyResolve).

AppDomain also contains a number of properties, which act in a role similar to environment variables within a process. These AppDomain properties are, like environment variables, simple name-value mapping pairs, retrievable in one of two ways: via the GetData() method or via a set of predefined properties on the AppDomain class (such as BaseDirectory).

```
public sealed class AppDomain : MarshalByRefObject, _AppDomain, System.Security.IEvidenceFactory {
// Public Static Properties
    public static AppDomain CurrentDomain{get; }
// Public Instance Properties
    public string BaseDirectory{get; }                                      // implements _AppDomain
```

```
public string DynamicDirectory{get; }                                              // implements _AppDomain
public Evidence Evidence{get; }                                  // implements System.Security.IEvidenceFactory
public string FriendlyName{get; }                                                  // implements _AppDomain
public string RelativeSearchPath{get; }                                            // implements _AppDomain
public AppDomainSetup SetupInformation{get; }
public bool ShadowCopyFiles{get; }                                                 // implements _AppDomain
// Public Static Methods
public static AppDomain CreateDomain(string friendlyName);
public static AppDomain CreateDomain(string friendlyName, System.Security.Policy.Evidence securityInfo);
public static AppDomain CreateDomain(string friendlyName, System.Security.Policy.Evidence securityInfo,
    AppDomainSetup info);
public static AppDomain CreateDomain(string friendlyName, System.Security.Policy.Evidence securityInfo,
    string appBasePath, string appRelativeSearchPath, bool shadowCopyFiles);
public static int GetCurrentThreadId( );
public static void Unload(AppDomain domain);
// Public Instance Methods
public void AppendPrivatePath(string path);                                        // implements _AppDomain
public void ClearPrivatePath( );                                                   // implements _AppDomain
public void ClearShadowCopyPath( );                                                // implements _AppDomain
public ObjectHandle CreateComInstanceFrom(string assemblyName, string typeName);
public ObjectHandle CreateComInstanceFrom(string assemblyFile, string typeName, byte[ ] hashValue,
    System.Configuration.Assemblies.AssemblyHashAlgorithm hashAlgorithm);
public ObjectHandle CreateInstance(string assemblyName, string typeName);          // implements _AppDomain
public ObjectHandle CreateInstance(string assemblyName, string typeName, bool ignoreCase,
    System.Reflection.BindingFlags bindingAttr, System.Reflection.Binder binder, object[ ] args,
    System.Globalization.CultureInfo culture, object[ ] activationAttributes,
    System.Security.Policy.Evidence securityAttributes);                           // implements _AppDomain
public ObjectHandle CreateInstance(string assemblyName, string typeName,
    object[ ] activationAttributes);                                               // implements _AppDomain
public object CreateInstanceAndUnwrap(string assemblyName, string typeName);
public object CreateInstanceAndUnwrap(string assemblyName, string typeName, bool ignoreCase,
    System.Reflection.BindingFlags bindingAttr, System.Reflection.Binder binder, object[ ] args,
    System.Globalization.CultureInfo culture, object[ ] activationAttributes,
    System.Security.Policy.Evidence securityAttributes);
public object CreateInstanceAndUnwrap(string assemblyName, string typeName, object[ ] activationAttributes);
public ObjectHandle CreateInstanceFrom(string assemblyFile, string typeName);      // implements _AppDomain
public ObjectHandle CreateInstanceFrom(string assemblyFile, string typeName, bool ignoreCase,
    System.Reflection.BindingFlags bindingAttr, System.Reflection.Binder binder, object[ ] args,
    System.Globalization.CultureInfo culture, object[ ] activationAttributes,
    System.Security.Policy.Evidence securityAttributes);                           // implements _AppDomain
public ObjectHandle CreateInstanceFrom(string assemblyFile, string typeName,
    object[ ] activationAttributes);                                               // implements _AppDomain
public object CreateInstanceFromAndUnwrap(string assemblyName, string typeName);
public object CreateInstanceFromAndUnwrap(string assemblyName, string typeName, bool ignoreCase,
    System.Reflection.BindingFlags bindingAttr, System.Reflection.Binder binder, object[ ] args,
    System.Globalization.CultureInfo culture, object[ ] activationAttributes,
    System.Security.Policy.Evidence securityAttributes);
public object CreateInstanceFromAndUnwrap(string assemblyName, string typeName, object[ ] activationAttributes);
public AssemblyBuilder DefineDynamicAssembly(System.Reflection.AssemblyName name,
    System.Reflection.Emit.AssemblyBuilderAccess access);                          // implements _AppDomain
public AssemblyBuilder DefineDynamicAssembly(System.Reflection.AssemblyName name,
    System.Reflection.Emit.AssemblyBuilderAccess access, System.Security.Policy.Evidence evidence);
                                                                                   // implements _AppDomain
```

```
public AssemblyBuilder DefineDynamicAssembly(System.Reflection.AssemblyName name,
    System.Reflection.Emit.AssemblyBuilderAccess access, System.Security.Policy.Evidence evidence,
    System.Security.PermissionSet requiredPermissions, System.Security.PermissionSet optionalPermissions,
    System.Security.PermissionSet refusedPermissions);                          // implements _AppDomain
public AssemblyBuilder DefineDynamicAssembly(System.Reflection.AssemblyName name,
    System.Reflection.Emit.AssemblyBuilderAccess access, System.Security.PermissionSet requiredPermissions,
    System.Security.PermissionSet optionalPermissions, System.Security.PermissionSet refusedPermissions);
                                                                                // implements _AppDomain
public AssemblyBuilder DefineDynamicAssembly(System.Reflection.AssemblyName name,
    System.Reflection.Emit.AssemblyBuilderAccess access, string dir);           // implements _AppDomain
public AssemblyBuilder DefineDynamicAssembly(System.Reflection.AssemblyName name,
    System.Reflection.Emit.AssemblyBuilderAccess access, string dir, System.Security.Policy.Evidence evidence);
                                                                                // implements _AppDomain
public AssemblyBuilder DefineDynamicAssembly(System.Reflection.AssemblyName name,
    System.Reflection.Emit.AssemblyBuilderAccess access, string dir, System.Security.Policy.Evidence evidence,
    System.Security.PermissionSet requiredPermissions, System.Security.PermissionSet optionalPermissions,
    System.Security.PermissionSet refusedPermissions);                          // implements _AppDomain
public AssemblyBuilder DefineDynamicAssembly(System.Reflection.AssemblyName name,
    System.Reflection.Emit.AssemblyBuilderAccess access, string dir, System.Security.Policy.Evidence evidence,
    System.Security.PermissionSet requiredPermissions, System.Security.PermissionSet optionalPermissions,
    System.Security.PermissionSet refusedPermissions, bool isSynchronized);     // implements _AppDomain
public AssemblyBuilder DefineDynamicAssembly(System.Reflection.AssemblyName name,
    System.Reflection.Emit.AssemblyBuilderAccess access, string dir,
    System.Security.PermissionSet requiredPermissions, System.Security.PermissionSet optionalPermissions,
    System.Security.PermissionSet refusedPermissions);                          // implements _AppDomain
public void DoCallBack(CrossAppDomainDelegate callBackDelegate);                // implements _AppDomain
public int ExecuteAssembly(string assemblyFile);                                // implements _AppDomain
public int ExecuteAssembly(string assemblyFile,
    System.Security.Policy.Evidence assemblySecurity);                          // implements _AppDomain
public int ExecuteAssembly(string assemblyFile, System.Security.Policy.Evidence assemblySecurity,
    string[] args);                                                             // implements _AppDomain
public int ExecuteAssembly(string assemblyFile, System.Security.Policy.Evidence assemblySecurity,
    string[] args, byte[] hashValue, System.Configuration.Assemblies.AssemblyHashAlgorithm hashAlgorithm);
public Assembly[] GetAssemblies();                                              // implements _AppDomain
public object GetData(string name);                                            // implements _AppDomain
public Type GetType();                                                                 // overrides object
public override object InitializeLifetimeService();                      // overrides MarshalByRefObject
public bool IsFinalizingForUnload();
public Assembly Load(System.Reflection.AssemblyName assemblyRef);               // implements _AppDomain
public Assembly Load(System.Reflection.AssemblyName assemblyRef,
    System.Security.Policy.Evidence assemblySecurity);                          // implements _AppDomain
public Assembly Load(byte[] rawAssembly);                                       // implements _AppDomain
public Assembly Load(byte[] rawAssembly, byte[] rawSymbolStore);                // implements _AppDomain
public Assembly Load(byte[] rawAssembly, byte[] rawSymbolStore, System.Security.Policy.Evidence securityEvidence);
                                                                                // implements _AppDomain
public Assembly Load(string assemblyString);                                    // implements _AppDomain
public Assembly Load(string assemblyString, System.Security.Policy.Evidence assemblySecurity);
                                                                                // implements _AppDomain
public void SetAppDomainPolicy(System.Security.Policy.PolicyLevel domainPolicy);  // implements _AppDomain
public void SetCachePath(string path);                                          // implements _AppDomain
public void SetData(string name, object data);                                  // implements _AppDomain
public void SetDynamicBase(string path);
public void SetPrincipalPolicy(System.Security.Principal.PrincipalPolicy policy);  // implements _AppDomain
```

```
    public void SetShadowCopyFiles( );
    public void SetShadowCopyPath(string path);                                      // implements _AppDomain
    public void SetThreadPrincipal(System.Security.Principal.IPrincipal principal);  // implements _AppDomain
    public override string ToString( );                                              // overrides object
// Events
    public event AssemblyLoadEventHandler AssemblyLoad;                              // implements _AppDomain
    public event ResolveEventHandler AssemblyResolve;                               // implements _AppDomain
    public event EventHandler DomainUnload;                                         // implements _AppDomain
    public event EventHandler ProcessExit;                                          // implements _AppDomain
    public event ResolveEventHandler ResourceResolve;                              // implements _AppDomain
    public event ResolveEventHandler TypeResolve;                                  // implements _AppDomain
    public event UnhandledExceptionEventHandler UnhandledException;                 // implements _AppDomain
}
```

Hierarchy   Object → MarshalByRefObject → AppDomain(_AppDomain, System.Security.
                     IEvidenceFactory)

Returned By   System.Threading.Thread.GetDomain( )

AppDomainSetup   serializable

System (mscorlib.dll)   sealed class

This class allows you to configure some settings for an application domain before
creating an AppDomain object. Create an instance of this class, set its properties, and pass
it to the appropriate AppDomain factory method.

```
public sealed class AppDomainSetup : IAppDomainSetup {
// Public Constructors
    public AppDomainSetup( );
// Public Instance Properties
    public string ApplicationBase{set; get; }                                      // implements IAppDomainSetup
    public string ApplicationName{set; get; }                                      // implements IAppDomainSetup
    public string CachePath{set; get; }                                            // implements IAppDomainSetup
    public string ConfigurationFile{set; get; }                                    // implements IAppDomainSetup
    public bool DisallowBindingRedirects{set; get; }
    public bool DisallowCodeDownload{set; get; }
    public bool DisallowPublisherPolicy{set; get; }
    public string DynamicBase{set; get; }                                          // implements IAppDomainSetup
    public string LicenseFile{set; get; }                                          // implements IAppDomainSetup
    public LoaderOptimization LoaderOptimization{set; get; }
    public string PrivateBinPath{set; get; }                                       // implements IAppDomainSetup
    public string PrivateBinPathProbe{set; get; }                                  // implements IAppDomainSetup
    public string ShadowCopyDirectories{set; get; }                                // implements IAppDomainSetup
    public string ShadowCopyFiles{set; get; }                                      // implements IAppDomainSetup
}
```

Returned By   AppDomain.SetupInformation

Passed To   AppDomain.CreateDomain( )

AppDomainUnloadedException

serializable

System (mscorlib.dll)   class

This exception signals an attempt to access an **AppDomain** that has been unloaded by AppDomain.Unload( ).

```
public class AppDomainUnloadedException : SystemException {
// Public Constructors
  public AppDomainUnloadedException( );
  public AppDomainUnloadedException(string message);
  public AppDomainUnloadedException(string message, Exception innerException);
// Protected Constructors
  protected AppDomainUnloadedException(System.Runtime.Serialization.SerializationInfo info,
    System.Runtime.Serialization.StreamingContext context);
}
```

Hierarchy   Object → Exception(System.Runtime.Serialization.ISerializable) → SystemException →
                     AppDomainUnloadedException

ApplicationException

CF 1.0, ECMA 1.0, serializable

System (mscorlib.dll)   class

Derive from this class to create your own application-specific exceptions when a system-supplied exception is inappropriate. For example, if an application's methods receive an invalid argument, it makes sense to throw an **ArgumentException**. However, if an internal calculation results in a value that violates your business rules, you might choose to throw an application exception. Application exceptions should be treated as nonfatal.

```
public class ApplicationException : Exception {
// Public Constructors
  public ApplicationException( );
  public ApplicationException(string message);
  public ApplicationException(string message, Exception innerException);
// Protected Constructors
  protected ApplicationException(System.Runtime.Serialization.SerializationInfo info,
    System.Runtime.Serialization.StreamingContext context);
}
```

Hierarchy   Object → Exception(System.Runtime.Serialization.ISerializable) → ApplicationException

Subclasses   System.Reflection.{InvalidFilterCriteriaException, TargetException,
                     TargetInvocationException, TargetParameterCountException}

ArgIterator

System (mscorlib.dll)   struct

The .NET runtime uses this class to handle methods that take a variable number of parameters (C# uses the **params** keyword; C++ uses ...; VB.NET uses **ParamArray**). The use of this class is completely hidden by language features. Unless you are writing a language compiler that needs to implement this feature, you do not need to use this class.

```
public struct ArgIterator {
// Public Constructors
  public ArgIterator(RuntimeArgumentHandle arglist);
  public ArgIterator(RuntimeArgumentHandle arglist, void *ptr);
// Public Instance Methods
  public void End( );
  public override bool Equals(object o);                              // overrides ValueType
  public override int GetHashCode( );                                // overrides ValueType
  public TypedReference GetNextArg( );
  public TypedReference GetNextArg(RuntimeTypeHandle rth);
  public RuntimeTypeHandle GetNextArgType( );
  public int GetRemainingCount( );
}
```

Hierarchy   Object → ValueType → ArgIterator

ArgumentException   CF 1.0, ECMA 1.0, serializable

System (mscorlib.dll)   class

This exception indicates that illegal data was passed to a method or constructor call. Note that *illegal* data is entirely contextual—the data may be a legitimate .NET value, but inappropriate for the use in question. Although .NET languages are type-safe in that you can't pass a string as a parameter when an integer is expected, there is nothing to keep you from passing a null or invalid value, such as sending (2001, 13, 32) to DateTime's constructor. However, there is no 32nd day of the 13th month of the year 2001, and if you try to initialize such a date, you'll get an exception.

The ArgumentException class (or one of its subclasses, ArgumentNullException or ArgumentOutOfRangeException) indicates that a method argument violated such a constraint. If you need to implement this exception in your own code, consider using one of its subclasses instead, since they represent common argument exceptions.

```
public class ArgumentException : SystemException {
// Public Constructors
  public ArgumentException( );
  public ArgumentException(string message);
  public ArgumentException(string message, Exception innerException);
  public ArgumentException(string message, string paramName);
  public ArgumentException(string message, string paramName, Exception innerException);
// Protected Constructors
  protected ArgumentException(System.Runtime.Serialization.SerializationInfo info,
      System.Runtime.Serialization.StreamingContext context);
// Public Instance Properties
  public override string Message{get; }                              // overrides Exception
  public virtual string ParamName{get; }
// Public Instance Methods
  public override void GetObjectData(System.Runtime.Serialization.SerializationInfo info,
      System.Runtime.Serialization.StreamingContext context);        // overrides Exception
}
```

System

Hierarchy   Object → Exception(System.Runtime.Serialization.ISerializable) → SystemException → ArgumentException

Subclasses   ArgumentNullException, ArgumentOutOfRangeException, DuplicateWaitObjectException

ArgumentNullException   CF 1.0, ECMA 1.0, serializable

System (mscorlib.dll)   class

This exception is a subclass of ArgumentException and indicates that a null parameter value was received by a method that does not accept nulls.

```
public class ArgumentNullException : ArgumentException {
// Public Constructors
  public ArgumentNullException( );
  public ArgumentNullException(string paramName);
  public ArgumentNullException(string paramName, string message);
// Protected Constructors
  protected ArgumentNullException(System.Runtime.Serialization.SerializationInfo info,
    System.Runtime.Serialization.StreamingContext context);
}
```

Hierarchy   Object → Exception(System.Runtime.Serialization.ISerializable) → SystemException → ArgumentException → ArgumentNullException

ArgumentOutOfRangeException   CF 1.0, ECMA 1.0, serializable

System (mscorlib.dll)   class

This exception is a subclass of ArgumentException and indicates that a method received an out-of-range parameter value.

```
public class ArgumentOutOfRangeException : ArgumentException {
// Public Constructors
  public ArgumentOutOfRangeException( );
  public ArgumentOutOfRangeException(string paramName);
  public ArgumentOutOfRangeException(string paramName, object actualValue, string message);
  public ArgumentOutOfRangeException(string paramName, string message);
// Protected Constructors
  protected ArgumentOutOfRangeException(System.Runtime.Serialization.SerializationInfo info,
    System.Runtime.Serialization.StreamingContext context);
// Public Instance Properties
  public virtual object ActualValue{get; }
  public override string Message{get; }                                    // overrides ArgumentException
// Public Instance Methods
  public override void GetObjectData(System.Runtime.Serialization.SerializationInfo info,
    System.Runtime.Serialization.StreamingContext context);                // overrides ArgumentException
}
```

Hierarchy   Object → Exception(System.Runtime.Serialization.ISerializable) → SystemException → ArgumentException → ArgumentOutOfRangeException

ArithmeticException

System (mscorlib.dll) class

This is the base class for all math-related exceptions. You can throw this class from your own code, but use a subclass (if one exists) that specifically addresses the type of error you have encountered.

```
public class ArithmeticException : SystemException {
// Public Constructors
   public ArithmeticException( );
   public ArithmeticException(string message);
   public ArithmeticException(string message, Exception innerException);
// Protected Constructors
   protected ArithmeticException(System.Runtime.Serialization.SerializationInfo info,
      System.Runtime.Serialization.StreamingContext context);
}
```

Hierarchy   Object → Exception(System.Runtime.Serialization.ISerializable) → SystemException → ArithmeticException

Subclasses   DivideByZeroException, NotFiniteNumberException, OverflowException

Array

CF 1.0, ECMA 1.0, serializable

System (mscorlib.dll) abstract class

Unlike other environments (such as C++), .NET has arrays of first-class type, in that all array types are derivatives of the base type Array. All methods are available on any array type, regardless of its declaration. In fact, the CLR is required to synthesize a *pseudotype* that matches the declaration. Thus, when you declare a variable of type string[], the CLR creates an anonymous type, deriving from Array specifically for storing Strings in a one-dimensional array.

The Array class has a number of useful array-related methods, such as checking for bounds violations (attempting to access an element of the array that isn't in the array's declared size) and retrieval of array length. In addition, because Array also implements the ICloneable, System.Collections.IList, System.Collections.ICollection, and System.Collections.IEnumerable interfaces, arrays can be used anywhere these interface types are expected.

Starting with .NET 1.1, Array now has support for 64-bit indexer values, meaning that an array can stretch to include 2^{64} possible elements. As a result, several methods, including Copy( ), GetValue( ), and SetValue( ), among others, take Int64 parameters as well as Int32.

Arrays are reference types. This means that the statement ArrayB = ArrayA results in two objects that reference the same array. Use ArrayB = ArrayA.Clone( ) to create a duplicate copy of an array. This will be a shallow copy with identical references to subobjects. To create a deep copy in which each array has its own copy of subobjects, you must loop through the array and assign values manually.

The Array class also contains useful static methods. These include IndexOf( ), which returns the offset of the first matching occurrence of an object in an array. For one-dimensional arrays, you can also use Reverse( ) to reverse a subset of rows, and Sort( ) to sort a subset of rows (provided the objects in the array implement the IComparable interface). If the objects in the array do not implement that interface, you can implement System.Collections.IComparer in a custom class and pass an instance of it to Sort( ).

The static Copy( ) method works like the C function memmove: it copies a portion of an array to a different position in the current array (or to a different array). When copying between multidimensional arrays, the array is treated like a long one-dimensional array in which each element occupies a separate row. (For example, if an array has three columns, copying five elements from the beginning of the array copies all three elements in the first row and the first two elements from the second row.) The source and destination ranges can overlap without causing a problem.

Note that you can create both multidimensional arrays and ragged arrays (arrays of arrays). Arrays are fixed in size and zero-based by default, although you can use the CreateInstance( ) method to create an array with a different lower bound. This is not recommended, as the array won't be CLS (Common Language Specification)–compliant. Lastly, if you need a dynamically resizable array, consider the collection System.Collections.ArrayList, which provides Add( ) and Remove( ) methods.

```
public abstract class Array : ICloneable, IList, ICollection, IEnumerable {
// Public Instance Properties
   public virtual bool IsFixedSize{get; }                                                    // implements IList
   public virtual bool IsReadOnly{get; }                                                     // implements IList
   public virtual bool IsSynchronized{get; }                                                 // implements ICollection
   public int Length{get; }
   public long LongLength{get; }
   public int Rank{get; }
   public virtual object SyncRoot{get; }                                                     // implements ICollection
// Public Static Methods
   public static int BinarySearch(Array array, int index, int length, object value);
   public static int BinarySearch(Array array, int index, int length, object value, System.Collections.IComparer comparer);
   public static int BinarySearch(Array array, object value);
   public static int BinarySearch(Array array, object value, System.Collections.IComparer comparer);
   public static void Clear(Array array, int index, int length);
   public static void Copy(Array sourceArray, Array destinationArray, int length);
   public static void Copy(Array sourceArray, Array destinationArray, long length);
   public static void Copy(Array sourceArray, int sourceIndex, Array destinationArray, int destinationIndex, int length);
   public static void Copy(Array sourceArray, long sourceIndex, Array destinationArray, long destinationIndex, long length);
   public static Array CreateInstance(Type elementType, int length);
   public static Array CreateInstance(Type elementType, params int[ ] lengths);
   public static Array CreateInstance(Type elementType, int[ ] lengths, int[ ] lowerBounds);
   public static Array CreateInstance(Type elementType, int length1, int length2);
   public static Array CreateInstance(Type elementType, int length1, int length2, int length3);
   public static Array CreateInstance(Type elementType, params long[ ] lengths);
   public static int IndexOf(Array array, object value);
   public static int IndexOf(Array array, object value, int startIndex);
   public static int IndexOf(Array array, object value, int startIndex, int count);
   public static int LastIndexOf(Array array, object value);
   public static int LastIndexOf(Array array, object value, int startIndex);
   public static int LastIndexOf(Array array, object value, int startIndex, int count);
   public static void Reverse(Array array);
   public static void Reverse(Array array, int index, int length);
   public static void Sort(Array array);
   public static void Sort(Array keys, Array items);
   public static void Sort(Array keys, Array items, System.Collections.IComparer comparer);
   public static void Sort(Array keys, Array items, int index, int length);
```

```
public static void Sort(Array keys, Array items, int index, int length, System.Collections.IComparer comparer);
public static void Sort(Array array, System.Collections.IComparer comparer);
public static void Sort(Array array, int index, int length);
public static void Sort(Array array, int index, int length, System.Collections.IComparer comparer);
// Public Instance Methods
public virtual object Clone( );                                                      // implements ICloneable
public virtual void CopyTo(Array array, int index);                                  // implements ICollection
public virtual void CopyTo(Array array, long index);
public virtual IEnumerator GetEnumerator( );                                         // implements IEnumerable
public int GetLength(int dimension);
public long GetLongLength(int dimension);
public int GetLowerBound(int dimension);
public int GetUpperBound(int dimension);
public object GetValue(int index);
public object GetValue(params int[ ] indices);
public object GetValue(int index1, int index2);
public object GetValue(int index1, int index2, int index3);
public object GetValue(long index);
public object GetValue(params long[ ] indices);
public object GetValue(long index1, long index2);
public object GetValue(long index1, long index2, long index3);
public void Initialize( );
public void SetValue(object value, int index);
public void SetValue(object value, params int[ ] indices);
public void SetValue(object value, int index1, int index2);
public void SetValue(object value, int index1, int index2, int index3);
public void SetValue(object value, long index);
public void SetValue(object value, params long[ ] indices);
public void SetValue(object value, long index1, long index2);
public void SetValue(object value, long index1, long index2, long index3);
}
```

Returned By   System.Collections.ArrayList.ToArray( ), Enum.GetValues( )

Passed To   Multiple types

ArrayTypeMismatchException   CF 1.0, ECMA 1.0, serializable

System (mscorlib.dll)   class

This exception is thrown when you store an element in an array that has a different type than the array's declared type. For example, trying to store a String object into an array declared to hold Int32 instances causes this exception to be thrown.

```
public class ArrayTypeMismatchException : SystemException {
// Public Constructors
public ArrayTypeMismatchException( );
public ArrayTypeMismatchException(string message);
public ArrayTypeMismatchException(string message, Exception innerException);
// Protected Constructors
protected ArrayTypeMismatchException(System.Runtime.Serialization.SerializationInfo info,
    System.Runtime.Serialization.StreamingContext context);
}
```

Hierarchy   Object → Exception(System.Runtime.Serialization.ISerializable) → SystemException → ArrayTypeMismatchException

AssemblyLoadEventArgs

ECMA 1.0

System (mscorlib.dll)   class

This class is used by the .NET Framework to pass information to the AppDomain.Assembly-Load event. This information consists of a System.Reflection.Assembly object that represents the newly loaded assembly.

```
public class AssemblyLoadEventArgs : EventArgs {
// Public Constructors
  public AssemblyLoadEventArgs(System.Reflection.Assembly loadedAssembly);
// Public Instance Properties
  public Assembly LoadedAssembly{get; }
}
```

Hierarchy   Object → EventArgs → AssemblyLoadEventArgs

Passed To   AssemblyLoadEventHandler.{BeginInvoke( ), Invoke( )}

AssemblyLoadEventHandler

ECMA 1.0, serializable

System (mscorlib.dll)   delegate

This delegate represents the event-handler method for the AppDomain.AssemblyLoad event.

```
public delegate void AssemblyLoadEventHandler(object sender, AssemblyLoadEventArgs args);
```

Associated Events   AppDomain.AssemblyLoad( )

AsyncCallback

CF 1.0, ECMA 1.0, serializable

System (mscorlib.dll)   delegate

This delegate type is used as part of asynchronous operations on delegates in general. As described in Chapter 16, delegates can be executed in an asynchronous fashion, using a random thread out of the system-managed thread pool. Frequently, however, programmers desire notification of the asynchronously executing delegate's completion, and the AsyncCallback is used to achieve that.

Using an AsyncCallback is fairly straightforward. At the asynchronous delegate's invocation, pass in an instance of this delegate (referring to a void-returning IAsyncResult-accepting method) as part of the BeginInvoke( ) call. When the asynchronously executing delegate has finished execution, the method on the other end of the AsyncCallback is invoked, with an IAsyncResult object as the sole parameter. (This IAsyncResult object contains the output parameters from the delegate's call: the return value, along with any out or ref parameters declared as part of the method's signature.)

```
public delegate void AsyncCallback(IAsyncResult ar);
```

Passed To   Multiple types

This is the base class for all custom attributes. Attributes are the .NET programmer's means of inserting additional metadata into a type's definition. For example, the .NET Serialization mechanism uses an attribute to indicate which fields in a type should not be serialized (see the System.Reflection.FieldAttributes.NotSerialized enumeration value). .NET programmers are free to create their own attributes (called *custom attributes*, although from a certain perspective all attributes are inherently custom) by creating a new type that claims Attribute as its base class type.

By themselves, attributes offer no modification to a type's behavioral semantics; that is, attributes don't modify the type's methods or execution in any way. In fact, attribute instances aren't even created until they are retrieved out of the type's metadata via the Reflection APIs. The entire purpose of an attribute is to act as a marker inside the type's metadata for consumption by some other API, library, or facility. For example, the Serialization APIs in the .NET Framework Class Library use the Serializable attribute to indicate which types are serializable. However, by themselves, the attributes carry no code to perform the actual act of serialization. This must be done by passing the instance of the type into instances of the Serialization classes, in which the attribute is retrieved and examined, and "appropriate" action is taken.

Attributes can be attached to any metadata component in the .NET system. This means fields, methods, properties, events, types (classes and value types), assemblies, modules, and more can all be the target of attribute declarations. (An attribute indicates which types it is restricted to by using the AttributeTargets enumeration.)

The base Attribute class provides helper functions for testing custom attributes, including the IsDefined() method, which examines a code element and indicates whether its metadata is decorated with a specified type of attribute. To use this method, you must provide the element using the appropriate reflection type (e.g., System.Reflection. Assembly or System.Reflection.ParameterInfo). You can also use the GetCustomAttribute() method to get a reference to an attribute of a specified type, or the GetCustomAttributes() method to get an array that contains all matching attributes. When applied to a class or class member, these methods consider all ancestors. To disable this default behavior, use one of the overloaded methods that allows you to supply the inherit parameter, and set it to false.

Custom attributes should override the TypeId property so that it supplies a user-defined identifier that uniquely describes the instance of this attribute on the type. This is entirely because more than one instance of an attribute can be associated with any particular metadata-token (field, type, parameter, and so on) instance.

```
public abstract class Attribute {
// Protected Constructors
  protected Attribute( );
// Public Instance Properties
  public virtual object TypeId{get; }
// Public Static Methods
  public static Attribute GetCustomAttribute(System.Reflection.Assembly element, Type attributeType);
  public static Attribute GetCustomAttribute(System.Reflection.Assembly element, Type attributeType, bool inherit);
  public static Attribute GetCustomAttribute(System.Reflection.MemberInfo element, Type attributeType);
  public static Attribute GetCustomAttribute(System.Reflection.MemberInfo element, Type attributeType, bool inherit);
  public static Attribute GetCustomAttribute(System.Reflection.Module element, Type attributeType);
```

```
public static Attribute GetCustomAttribute(System.Reflection.Module element, Type attributeType, bool inherit);
public static Attribute GetCustomAttribute(System.Reflection.ParameterInfo element, Type attributeType);
public static Attribute GetCustomAttribute(System.Reflection.ParameterInfo element, Type attributeType, bool inherit);
public static Attribute[ ] GetCustomAttributes(System.Reflection.Assembly element);
public static Attribute[ ] GetCustomAttributes(System.Reflection.Assembly element, bool inherit);
public static Attribute[ ] GetCustomAttributes(System.Reflection.Assembly element, Type attributeType);
public static Attribute[ ] GetCustomAttributes(System.Reflection.Assembly element, Type attributeType, bool inherit);
public static Attribute[ ] GetCustomAttributes(System.Reflection.MemberInfo element);
public static Attribute[ ] GetCustomAttributes(System.Reflection.MemberInfo element, bool inherit);
public static Attribute[ ] GetCustomAttributes(System.Reflection.MemberInfo element, Type type);
public static Attribute[ ] GetCustomAttributes(System.Reflection.MemberInfo element, Type type, bool inherit);
public static Attribute[ ] GetCustomAttributes(System.Reflection.Module element);
public static Attribute[ ] GetCustomAttributes(System.Reflection.Module element, bool inherit);
public static Attribute[ ] GetCustomAttributes(System.Reflection.Module element, Type attributeType);
public static Attribute[ ] GetCustomAttributes(System.Reflection.Module element, Type attributeType, bool inherit);
public static Attribute[ ] GetCustomAttributes(System.Reflection.ParameterInfo element);
public static Attribute[ ] GetCustomAttributes(System.Reflection.ParameterInfo element, bool inherit);
public static Attribute[ ] GetCustomAttributes(System.Reflection.ParameterInfo element, Type attributeType);
public static Attribute[ ] GetCustomAttributes(System.Reflection.ParameterInfo element, Type attributeType,
    bool inherit);
public static bool IsDefined(System.Reflection.Assembly element, Type attributeType);
public static bool IsDefined(System.Reflection.Assembly element, Type attributeType, bool inherit);
public static bool IsDefined(System.Reflection.MemberInfo element, Type attributeType);
public static bool IsDefined(System.Reflection.MemberInfo element, Type attributeType, bool inherit);
public static bool IsDefined(System.Reflection.Module element, Type attributeType);
public static bool IsDefined(System.Reflection.Module element, Type attributeType, bool inherit);
public static bool IsDefined(System.Reflection.ParameterInfo element, Type attributeType);
public static bool IsDefined(System.Reflection.ParameterInfo element, Type attributeType, bool inherit);
// Public Instance Methods
public override bool Equals(object obj);                                      // overrides object
public override int GetHashCode( );                                          // overrides object
public virtual bool IsDefaultAttribute( );
public virtual bool Match(object obj);
}
```

Subclasses	Multiple types
Valid On	All

AttributeTargets

CF 1.0, ECMA 1.0, serializable, flag

System (mscorlib.dll)   enum

This enumeration is used to set the AttributeUsageAttribute.ValidOn property when creating a custom attribute. It allows you to specify the code elements for which a custom attribute can be used. You can use a bitwise combination of these values to specify multiple elements.

Using this attribute is the only means by which a custom attribute can declare a restriction of its usage against various metadata types. For example, when using the System.Reflection.AssemblyKeyFileAttribute attribute, which simply tells the compiler which public/private keyfile to use to sign the assembly, it makes no sense to apply to any other metadata type besides the assembly. Therefore, the AssemblyKeyFileAttribute attribute has an AttributeUsageAttribute (see the AttributeUsageAttribute entry) declared on it with the value Assembly. As a result, any attempt to use the AssemblyKeyFileAttribute attribute on anything other than an assembly results in a compilation error.

```
public enum AttributeTargets {
  Assembly = 0x00000001,
  Module = 0x00000002,
  Class = 0x00000004,
  Struct = 0x00000008,
  Enum = 0x00000010,
  Constructor = 0x00000020,
  Method = 0x00000040,
  Property = 0x00000080,
  Field = 0x00000100,
  Event = 0x00000200,
  Interface = 0x00000400,
  Parameter = 0x00000800,
  Delegate = 0x00001000,
  ReturnValue = 0x00002000,
  All = 0x00003FFF
}
```

Hierarchy   Object → ValueType → Enum(IComparable, IFormattable, IConvertible) → AttributeTargets

Returned By   AttributeUsageAttribute.ValidOn

Passed To   AttributeUsageAttribute.AttributeUsageAttribute( )

AttributeUsageAttribute   CF 1.0, ECMA 1.0, serializable

System (mscorlib.dll)   sealed class

This attribute is used when developing a custom attribute class. It allows you to specify how your custom attribute must be used. The ValidOn property uses a bitwise combination of values from AttributeTargets to specify the code elements that can use your custom attribute. It's read-only and must be initialized using the constructor, as in [AttributeUsage(AttributeTargets.Field | AttributeTargets.Property)].

The AllowMultiple property specifies whether the attribute can be used more than once for the same element. The Inherited attribute specifies whether your custom attribute will be applied to derived classes and overridden members. These are indicated using the usual *named parameter* syntax supported by attributes, as in [AttributeUsage(Inherited = true, AllowMultiple = true)].

```
public sealed class AttributeUsageAttribute : Attribute {
// Public Constructors
  public AttributeUsageAttribute(AttributeTargets validOn);
// Public Instance Properties
  public bool AllowMultiple{set; get; }
  public bool Inherited{set; get; }
  public AttributeTargets ValidOn{get; }
}
```

System

Valid On   Class

BadImageFormatException   ECMA 1.0, serializable

System (mscorlib.dll)   class

This exception occurs when .NET tries to load a DLL or executable that is either corrupt or invalid for the platform on which you are running.

```
public class BadImageFormatException : SystemException {
// Public Constructors
  public BadImageFormatException( );
  public BadImageFormatException(string message);
  public BadImageFormatException(string message, Exception inner);
  public BadImageFormatException(string message, string fileName);
  public BadImageFormatException(string message, string fileName, Exception inner);
// Protected Constructors
  protected BadImageFormatException(System.Runtime.Serialization.SerializationInfo info,
     System.Runtime.Serialization.StreamingContext context);
// Public Instance Properties
  public string FileName{get; }
  public string FusionLog{get; }
  public override string Message{get; }                          // overrides Exception
// Public Instance Methods
  public override void GetObjectData(System.Runtime.Serialization.SerializationInfo info,
     System.Runtime.Serialization.StreamingContext context);     // overrides Exception
  public override string ToString( );                            // overrides Exception
}
```

Hierarchy   Object → Exception(System.Runtime.Serialization.ISerializable) → SystemException →
BadImageFormatException

BitConverter   CF 1.0

System (mscorlib.dll)   sealed class

This class provides static methods that can be used to convert portions of a byte array to simple value types. It also contains the overloaded **GetBytes( )** method, which converts simple data types to byte arrays. These functions can be useful for creating custom reader and writer classes. For example, a typical writer class might take specific data, convert it to a byte array, then pass the byte array to some type of stream object.

```
public sealed class BitConverter {
// Public Static Fields
  public static readonly bool IsLittleEndian;                    // =True
// Public Static Methods
  public static long DoubleToInt64Bits(double value);
  public static byte[ ] GetBytes(bool value);
  public static byte[ ] GetBytes(char value);
  public static byte[ ] GetBytes(double value);
  public static byte[ ] GetBytes(short value);
```

```
public static byte[ ] GetBytes(int value);
public static byte[ ] GetBytes(long value);
public static byte[ ] GetBytes(float value);
public static byte[ ] GetBytes(ushort value);
public static byte[ ] GetBytes(uint value);
public static byte[ ] GetBytes(ulong value);
public static double Int64BitsToDouble(long value);
public static bool ToBoolean(byte[ ] value, int startIndex);
public static char ToChar(byte[ ] value, int startIndex);
public static double ToDouble(byte[ ] value, int startIndex);
public static short ToInt16(byte[ ] value, int startIndex);
public static int ToInt32(byte[ ] value, int startIndex);
public static long ToInt64(byte[ ] value, int startIndex);
public static float ToSingle(byte[ ] value, int startIndex);
public static string ToString(byte[ ] value);
public static string ToString(byte[ ] value, int startIndex);
public static string ToString(byte[ ] value, int startIndex, int length);
public static ushort ToUInt16(byte[ ] value, int startIndex);
public static uint ToUInt32(byte[ ] value, int startIndex);
public static ulong ToUInt64(byte[ ] value, int startIndex);
}
```

Boolean

CF 1.0, ECMA 1.0, serializable

System (mscorlib.dll)   struct

This is a simple value type that contains either true or false. When converting to or from a string or comparing with a string, the TrueString and FalseString fields are used (these return True and False). This type is available in C# through the bool alias.

```
public struct Boolean : IComparable, IConvertible {
// Public Static Fields
  public static readonly string FalseString;                                    // =False
  public static readonly string TrueString;                                     // =True
// Public Static Methods
  public static bool Parse(string value);
// Public Instance Methods
  public int CompareTo(object obj);                                  // implements IComparable
  public override bool Equals(object obj);                            // overrides ValueType
  public override int GetHashCode( );                                // overrides ValueType
  public TypeCode GetTypeCode( );                                    // implements IConvertible
  public override string ToString( );                                // overrides ValueType
  public string ToString(IFormatProvider provider);                  // implements IConvertible
}
```

Hierarchy   Object → ValueType → Boolean(IComparable, IConvertible)

Returned By   Multiple types

Passed To   Multiple types

System (mscorlib.dll)   sealed class

The Buffer class provides static methods used to manipulate a region of unmanaged memory as though it were an array of Bytes. Byte arrays are traditionally used in unmanaged code to represent blocks of contiguous memory. This class includes the ByteLength() method, which indicates the total number of bytes in an array, and the GetByte() and SetByte() methods, which allow you to retrieve or set a specific Byte object in an array by specifying a zero-based index. Additionally, the BlockCopy() method can be used to move contiguous groups of bytes from one position in a buffer to another.

Note that BlockCopy() ignores types when conducting its byte-shuffling operations. If you use BlockCopy() to insert an otherwise incompatible type into the buffer, the copy goes through, but unpredictable results will arise later when you try to work with the buffer as its original type. For example, if you use the BlockCopy() method to insert an Int32 into an array of String objects, the copy goes through, but the next time the array is accessed, there is no longer a String reference. It is an Int32, and what the CLR will do at that point is undocumented.

```
public sealed class Buffer {
// Public Static Methods
   public static void BlockCopy(Array src, int srcOffset, Array dst, int dstOffset, int count);
   public static int ByteLength(Array array);
   public static byte GetByte(Array array, int index);
   public static void SetByte(Array array, int index, byte value);
}
```

Byte

CF 1.0, ECMA 1.0, serializable

System (mscorlib.dll)   struct

This simple value type represents an unsigned 8-bit integer that can vary in value from 0 to 255. The Parse() method converts a number in a string (such as 122) into a Byte object. This type is available in C# through the byte alias.

```
public struct Byte : IComparable, IFormattable, IConvertible {
// Public Static Fields
   public const byte MaxValue;                                                                        // =255
   public const byte MinValue;                                                                        // =0
// Public Static Methods
   public static byte Parse(string s);
   public static byte Parse(string s, IFormatProvider provider);
   public static byte Parse(string s, System.Globalization.NumberStyles style);
   public static byte Parse(string s, System.Globalization.NumberStyles style, IFormatProvider provider);
// Public Instance Methods
   public int CompareTo(object value);                                                  // implements IComparable
   public override bool Equals(object obj);                                                // overrides ValueType
   public override int GetHashCode();                                                      // overrides ValueType
   public TypeCode GetTypeCode();                                                       // implements IConvertible
   public override string ToString();                                                      // overrides ValueType
   public string ToString(IFormatProvider provider);                                    // implements IConvertible
   public string ToString(string format);
   public string ToString(string format, IFormatProvider provider);                    // implements IFormattable
}
```

Hierarchy	Object → ValueType → Byte(IComparable, IFormattable, IConvertible)
Returned By	Multiple types
Passed To	Multiple types

CannotUnloadAppDomainException

ECMA 1.0, serializable

System (mscorlib.dll)   class

This exception signals that an attempt to invoke **AppDomain.Unload( )** failed. This indicates that you either tried to unload the default application domain (**AppDomain.CurrentDomain**), the domain has a thread that cannot be stopped, or the domain has already been unloaded.

```
public class CannotUnloadAppDomainException : SystemException {
// Public Constructors
  public CannotUnloadAppDomainException( );
  public CannotUnloadAppDomainException(string message);
  public CannotUnloadAppDomainException(string message, Exception innerException);
// Protected Constructors
  protected CannotUnloadAppDomainException(System.Runtime.Serialization.SerializationInfo info,
    System.Runtime.Serialization.StreamingContext context);
}
```

Hierarchy	Object → Exception(System.Runtime.Serialization.ISerializable) → SystemException → CannotUnloadAppDomainException

Char

CF 1.0, ECMA 1.0, serializable

System (mscorlib.dll)   struct

This simple value type represents a 16-bit Unicode character (from hexadecimal 0x0000 to 0xFFFF). You can convert a character to upper- or lowercase and get its numeric representation using the methods of a **Char** object. You can also test if it is a number, letter, or symbol by using the methods prefixed with **Is**. For exact information, use the **GetUnicodeCategory( )** method to get an enumerated value from **System. Globalization.UnicodeCategory**. This classifies the character into one of about thirty categories.

This type is aliased as **char** in C#. If you need an array of chars, use the **String** class.

```
public struct Char : IComparable, IConvertible {
// Public Static Fields
  public const char MaxValue;                                                              // =0x0000FFFF
  public const char MinValue;                                                              // =0x00000000
// Public Static Methods
  public static double GetNumericValue(char c);
  public static double GetNumericValue(string s, int index);
  public static UnicodeCategory GetUnicodeCategory(char c);
  public static UnicodeCategory GetUnicodeCategory(string s, int index);
  public static bool IsControl(char c);
  public static bool IsControl(string s, int index);
  public static bool IsDigit(char c);
  public static bool IsDigit(string s, int index);
```

System

```
public static bool IsLetter(char c);
public static bool IsLetter(string s, int index);
public static bool IsLetterOrDigit(char c);
public static bool IsLetterOrDigit(string s, int index);
public static bool IsLower(char c);
public static bool IsLower(string s, int index);
public static bool IsNumber(char c);
public static bool IsNumber(string s, int index);
public static bool IsPunctuation(char c);
public static bool IsPunctuation(string s, int index);
public static bool IsSeparator(char c);
public static bool IsSeparator(string s, int index);
public static bool IsSurrogate(char c);
public static bool IsSurrogate(string s, int index);
public static bool IsSymbol(char c);
public static bool IsSymbol(string s, int index);
public static bool IsUpper(char c);
public static bool IsUpper(string s, int index);
public static bool IsWhiteSpace(char c);
public static bool IsWhiteSpace(string s, int index);
public static char Parse(string s);
public static char ToLower(char c);
public static char ToLower(char c, System.Globalization.CultureInfo culture);
public static string ToString(char c);
public static char ToUpper(char c);
public static char ToUpper(char c, System.Globalization.CultureInfo culture);
// Public Instance Methods
public int CompareTo(object value);                                    // implements IComparable
public override bool Equals(object obj);                               // overrides ValueType
public override int GetHashCode( );                                    // overrides ValueType
public TypeCode GetTypeCode( );                                        // implements IConvertible
public override string ToString( );                                   // overrides ValueType
public string ToString(IFormatProvider provider);                     // implements IConvertible
}
```

Hierarchy	Object → ValueType → Char(IComparable, IConvertible)
Returned By	Multiple types
Passed To	Multiple types

CharEnumerator

CF 1.0, ECMA 1.0, serializable

System (mscorlib.dll)

sealed class

This class allows you to access and iterate through individual chars in an array. You can manually retrieve a CharEnumerator from a String object using the String.GetEnumerator() method and then using the MoveNext() method to step through the string. However, C# provides built-in support with the convenient foreach statement, which uses a CharEnumerator transparently.

By convention, a CharEnumerator starts just before the first character. When using a CharEnumerator manually, you need to call the MoveNext( ) method before you can access the first character.

```
public sealed class CharEnumerator : IEnumerator, ICloneable {
// Public Instance Properties
  public char Current{get; }
// Public Instance Methods
  public object Clone( );                                              // implements ICloneable
  public bool MoveNext( );                                            // implements IEnumerator
  public void Reset( );                                              // implements IEnumerator
}
```

Returned By   String.GetEnumerator( )

CLSCompliantAttribute   CF 1.0, ECMA 1.0, serializable

System (mscorlib.dll)   sealed class

This attribute indicates that a program element is compliant with the CLS. If you use non-CLS-compliant classes (such as UInt32) in a class marked as compliant, the compiler generates a compliance warning.

By default, types without this attribute are not CLS-compliant unless they are contained in a CLS-compliant type or assembly. You can specifically mark non-CLS-compliant members inside a CLS-compliant type using [CLSCompliant(false)].

```
public sealed class CLSCompliantAttribute : Attribute {
// Public Constructors
  public CLSCompliantAttribute(bool isCompliant);
// Public Instance Properties
  public bool IsCompliant{get; }
}
```

Hierarchy   Object → Attribute → CLSCompliantAttribute

Valid On   All

Console   CF 1.0, ECMA 1.0

System (mscorlib.dll)   sealed class

The Console class provides static methods that allow you to create console, or command-line, applications. If you attempt to use these methods in a Windows Forms application, they are ignored. For a console application, data is transmitted through three streams. Input is received from the *standard input stream*, output is written through the *standard output stream*, and error data is written to the *standard error output stream*. These streams are provided through the In property, which is a System.IO. TextReader object, and through the Out and Error properties, which are System.IO.TextWriter objects. You can use the methods of these objects directly, or you can use the methods provided by the Console class. For example, you can use the Write( ) method to write any basic data type to the console window (or use WriteLine( ) to write data with a trailing hard return). You can also use the ReadLine( ) method to cause the console window to wait for input. When the user presses the Enter key, this method returns with a string containing the input characters (except the final hard return).

You can use the SetIn(), SetOut(), and SetError() methods to bind the console to different stream objects, such as System.IO.FileStream. To reset the streams to their default objects, use the methods prefixed with OpenStandard.

```
public sealed class Console {
// Public Static Properties
  public static TextWriter Error{get; }
  public static TextReader In{get; }
  public static TextWriter Out{get; }
// Public Static Methods
  public static Stream OpenStandardError( );
  public static Stream OpenStandardError(int bufferSize);
  public static Stream OpenStandardInput( );
  public static Stream OpenStandardInput(int bufferSize);
  public static Stream OpenStandardOutput( );
  public static Stream OpenStandardOutput(int bufferSize);
  public static int Read( );
  public static string ReadLine( );
  public static void SetError(System.IO.TextWriter newError);
  public static void SetIn(System.IO.TextReader newIn);
  public static void SetOut(System.IO.TextWriter newOut);
  public static void Write(bool value);
  public static void Write(char value);
  public static void Write(char[ ] buffer);
  public static void Write(char[ ] buffer, int index, int count);
  public static void Write(decimal value);
  public static void Write(double value);
  public static void Write(int value);
  public static void Write(long value);
  public static void Write(object value);
  public static void Write(float value);
  public static void Write(string value);
  public static void Write(string format, object arg0);
  public static void Write(string format, params object[ ] arg);
  public static void Write(string format, object arg0, object arg1);
  public static void Write(string format, object arg0, object arg1, object arg2);
  public static void Write(string format, object arg0, object arg1, object arg2, object arg3);
  public static void Write(uint value);
  public static void Write(ulong value);
  public static void WriteLine( );
  public static void WriteLine(bool value);
  public static void WriteLine(char value);
  public static void WriteLine(char[ ] buffer);
  public static void WriteLine(char[ ] buffer, int index, int count);
  public static void WriteLine(decimal value);
  public static void WriteLine(double value);
  public static void WriteLine(int value);
  public static void WriteLine(long value);
  public static void WriteLine(object value);
  public static void WriteLine(float value);
  public static void WriteLine(string value);
```

```
public static void WriteLine(string format, object arg0);
public static void WriteLine(string format, params object[ ] arg);
public static void WriteLine(string format, object arg0, object arg1);
public static void WriteLine(string format, object arg0, object arg1, object arg2);
public static void WriteLine(string format, object arg0, object arg1, object arg2, object arg3);
public static void WriteLine(uint value);
public static void WriteLine(ulong value);
}
```

ContextBoundObject   serializable, marshal by reference, context bound

System (mscorlib.dll)   abstract class

An object inheriting from ContextBoundObject shares characteristics with an object inheriting from MarshalByRefObject. The difference is that a context further subdivides a
domain. While instances of MarshalByRefObject are passed to other domains by reference
and must interact through proxy objects, instances of ContextBoundObject are passed by
reference to other contexts, even in the same domain. Unlike domains, contexts can
provide a rich environment with other services such as synchronization, transactions,
just-in-time activation, and security.

For more information, consult the System.Runtime.Remoting.Contexts namespace.

```
public abstract class ContextBoundObject : MarshalByRefObject {
// Protected Constructors
  protected ContextBoundObject( );
}
```

Hierarchy   Object → MarshalByRefObject → ContextBoundObject

ContextMarshalException   serializable

System (mscorlib.dll)   class

This exception is thrown when a marshaler fails to move an object across a context
boundary. This is usually the case if a nonserializable object is passed as a parameter to
a cross-context call, such as an instance of the CrossAppDomainDelegate.

```
public class ContextMarshalException : SystemException {
// Public Constructors
  public ContextMarshalException( );
  public ContextMarshalException(string message);
  public ContextMarshalException(string message,
    Exception inner);
// Protected Constructors
  protected ContextMarshalException(System.Runtime.Serialization.SerializationInfo info,
    System.Runtime.Serialization.StreamingContext context);
}
```

Hierarchy   Object → Exception(System.Runtime.Serialization.ISerializable) → SystemException →
                     ContextMarshalException

ContextStaticAttribute

serializable

System (mscorlib.dll)

class

This attribute designates that a static field should not be shared between contexts. Each context accesses a separate copy of this field and is able to set and retrieve values without accidentally overwriting data set by another context. Just as thread-local storage is used to store data in a per-thread fashion, this is used to store static data in a per-context fashion.

```
public class ContextStaticAttribute : Attribute {
// Public Constructors
  public ContextStaticAttribute( );
}
```

Hierarchy   Object → Attribute → ContextStaticAttribute

Valid On   Field

Convert

CF 1.0, ECMA 1.0

System (mscorlib.dll)

sealed class

This class provides static helper methods that convert base data types to other base data types. You can also convert objects to base data types, provided they implement the IConvertible interface and cast objects to different types with the ChangeType( ) method.

CLR languages typically allow widening conversions (e.g., Int16 to Int32) through direct assignment. Narrowing conversions require the Convert class or explicit casting. The Convert class does not generate an exception when you lose numeric precision, but it does throw an overflow exception if the source value is too large for the destination data type.

Note that implicit and explicit conversions can return different results than the Convert class. Namely, they truncate significant digits in a narrowing conversion (for example, changing 32.6 to the integer 32), while the Convert class rounds the number automatically (converting 32.6 to 33). The Convert class uses banker's rounding, meaning that the fraction 1/2 is rounded down for even numbers (so 4.5 becomes 4) and rounded up for odd numbers (so 5.5 becomes 6). This helps combat rounding bias.

The ToString( ) methods are functionally equivalent to the Object.ToString( ) method of the corresponding base data types. The conversions from strings to numeric or date data are functionally equivalent to the Parse( ) method of the appropriate data type (e.g., Int32. Parse( )). For string conversions, you can also supply an IFormatProvider object to specify culture-specific formatting information used to interpret or encode a string.

For Boolean conversions, any nonzero number becomes true, except for strings, which are compared against the Boolean.TrueString and Boolean.FalseString fields. When converted to a number, a Boolean false becomes a 0, and a Boolean true becomes a 1.

Some conversion methods are provided only for symmetry and always throw an Invalid-CastException. These include any conversion between date and any data type other than string.

```
public sealed class Convert {
// Public Static Fields
  public static readonly object DBNull;
```

// Public Static Methods
```
public static object ChangeType(object value,  Type conversionType);
public static object ChangeType(object value, TypeCode typeCode);
public static object ChangeType(object value, TypeCode typeCode, IFormatProvider provider);
public static object ChangeType(object value, Type conversionType, IFormatProvider provider);
public static byte[ ] FromBase64CharArray(char[ ] inArray,  int offset, int length);
public static byte[ ] FromBase64String(string s);
public static TypeCode GetTypeCode(object value);
public static bool IsDBNull(object value);
public static int ToBase64CharArray(byte[ ] inArray,  int offsetIn, int length, char[ ] outArray, int offsetOut);
public static string ToBase64String(byte[ ] inArray);
public static string ToBase64String(byte[ ] inArray,  int offset, int length);
public static bool ToBoolean(bool value);
public static bool ToBoolean(byte value);
public static bool ToBoolean(char value);
public static bool ToBoolean(DateTime value);
public static bool ToBoolean(decimal value);
public static bool ToBoolean(double value);
public static bool ToBoolean(short value);
public static bool ToBoolean(int value);
public static bool ToBoolean(long value);
public static bool ToBoolean(object value);
public static bool ToBoolean(object value,  IFormatProvider provider);
public static bool ToBoolean(sbyte value);
public static bool ToBoolean(float value);
public static bool ToBoolean(string value);
public static bool ToBoolean(string value,  IFormatProvider provider);
public static bool ToBoolean(ushort value);
public static bool ToBoolean(uint value);
public static bool ToBoolean(ulong value);
public static byte ToByte(bool value);
public static byte ToByte(byte value);
public static byte ToByte(char value);
public static byte ToByte(DateTime value);
public static byte ToByte(decimal value);
public static byte ToByte(double value);
public static byte ToByte(short value);
public static byte ToByte(int value);
public static byte ToByte(long value);
public static byte ToByte(object value);
public static byte ToByte(object value, IFormatProvider provider);
public static byte ToByte(sbyte value);
public static byte ToByte(float value);
public static byte ToByte(string value);
public static byte ToByte(string value,  IFormatProvider provider);
public static byte ToByte(string value, int fromBase);
public static byte ToByte(ushort value);
public static byte ToByte(uint value);
public static byte ToByte(ulong value);
public static char ToChar(bool value);
public static char ToChar(byte value);
```

System

```
public static char ToChar(char value);
public static char ToChar(DateTime value);
public static char ToChar(decimal value);
public static char ToChar(double value);
public static char ToChar(short value);
public static char ToChar(int value);
public static char ToChar(long value);
public static char ToChar(object value);
public static char ToChar(object value, IFormatProvider provider);
public static char ToChar(sbyte value);
public static char ToChar(float value);
public static char ToChar(string value);
public static char ToChar(string value, IFormatProvider provider);
public static char ToChar(ushort value);
public static char ToChar(uint value);
public static char ToChar(ulong value);
public static DateTime ToDateTime(bool value);
public static DateTime ToDateTime(byte value);
public static DateTime ToDateTime(char value);
public static DateTime ToDateTime(DateTime value);
public static DateTime ToDateTime(decimal value);
public static DateTime ToDateTime(double value);
public static DateTime ToDateTime(short value);
public static DateTime ToDateTime(int value);
public static DateTime ToDateTime(long value);
public static DateTime ToDateTime(object value);
public static DateTime ToDateTime(object value, IFormatProvider provider);
public static DateTime ToDateTime(sbyte value);
public static DateTime ToDateTime(float value);
public static DateTime ToDateTime(string value);
public static DateTime ToDateTime(string value, IFormatProvider provider);
public static DateTime ToDateTime(ushort value);
public static DateTime ToDateTime(uint value);
public static DateTime ToDateTime(ulong value);
public static decimal ToDecimal(bool value);
public static decimal ToDecimal(byte value);
public static decimal ToDecimal(char value);
public static decimal ToDecimal(DateTime value);
public static decimal ToDecimal(decimal value);
public static decimal ToDecimal(double value);
public static decimal ToDecimal(short value);
public static decimal ToDecimal(int value);
public static decimal ToDecimal(long value);
public static decimal ToDecimal(object value);
public static decimal ToDecimal(object value, IFormatProvider provider);
public static decimal ToDecimal(sbyte value);
public static decimal ToDecimal(float value);
public static decimal ToDecimal(string value);
public static decimal ToDecimal(string value, IFormatProvider provider);
public static decimal ToDecimal(ushort value);
public static decimal ToDecimal(uint value);
```

```
public static decimal ToDecimal(ulong value);
public static double ToDouble(bool value);
public static double ToDouble(byte value);
public static double ToDouble(char value);
public static double ToDouble(DateTime value);
public static double ToDouble(decimal value);
public static double ToDouble(double value);
public static double ToDouble(short value);
public static double ToDouble(int value);
public static double ToDouble(long value);
public static double ToDouble(object value);
public static double ToDouble(object value, IFormatProvider provider);
public static double ToDouble(sbyte value);
public static double ToDouble(float value);
public static double ToDouble(string value);
public static double ToDouble(string value, IFormatProvider provider);
public static double ToDouble(ushort value);
public static double ToDouble(uint value);
public static double ToDouble(ulong value);
public static short ToInt16(bool value);
public static short ToInt16(byte value);
public static short ToInt16(char value);
public static short ToInt16(DateTime value);
public static short ToInt16(decimal value);
public static short ToInt16(double value);
public static short ToInt16(short value);
public static short ToInt16(int value);
public static short ToInt16(long value);
public static short ToInt16(object value);
public static short ToInt16(object value, IFormatProvider provider);
public static short ToInt16(sbyte value);
public static short ToInt16(float value);
public static short ToInt16(string value);
public static short ToInt16(string value, IFormatProvider provider);
public static short ToInt16(string value, int fromBase);
public static short ToInt16(ushort value);
public static short ToInt16(uint value);
public static short ToInt16(ulong value);
public static int ToInt32(bool value);
public static int ToInt32(byte value);
public static int ToInt32(char value);
public static int ToInt32(DateTime value);
public static int ToInt32(decimal value);
public static int ToInt32(double value);
public static int ToInt32(short value);
public static int ToInt32(int value);
public static int ToInt32(long value);
public static int ToInt32(object value);
public static int ToInt32(object value, IFormatProvider provider);
public static int ToInt32(sbyte value);
public static int ToInt32(float value);
```

```
public static int ToInt32(string value);
public static int ToInt32(string value, IFormatProvider provider);
public static int ToInt32(string value, int fromBase);
public static int ToInt32(ushort value);
public static int ToInt32(uint value);
public static int ToInt32(ulong value);
public static long ToInt64(bool value);
public static long ToInt64(byte value);
public static long ToInt64(char value);
public static long ToInt64(DateTime value);
public static long ToInt64(decimal value);
public static long ToInt64(double value);
public static long ToInt64(short value);
public static long ToInt64(int value);
public static long ToInt64(long value);
public static long ToInt64(object value);
public static long ToInt64(object value, IFormatProvider provider);
public static long ToInt64(sbyte value);
public static long ToInt64(float value);
public static long ToInt64(string value);
public static long ToInt64(string value, IFormatProvider provider);
public static long ToInt64(string value, int fromBase);
public static long ToInt64(ushort value);
public static long ToInt64(uint value);
public static long ToInt64(ulong value);
public static sbyte ToSByte(bool value);
public static sbyte ToSByte(byte value);
public static sbyte ToSByte(char value);
public static sbyte ToSByte(DateTime value);
public static sbyte ToSByte(decimal value);
public static sbyte ToSByte(double value);
public static sbyte ToSByte(short value);
public static sbyte ToSByte(int value);
public static sbyte ToSByte(long value);
public static sbyte ToSByte(object value);
public static sbyte ToSByte(object value, IFormatProvider provider);
public static sbyte ToSByte(sbyte value);
public static sbyte ToSByte(float value);
public static sbyte ToSByte(string value);
public static sbyte ToSByte(string value, IFormatProvider provider);
public static sbyte ToSByte(string value, int fromBase);
public static sbyte ToSByte(ushort value);
public static sbyte ToSByte(uint value);
public static sbyte ToSByte(ulong value);
public static float ToSingle(bool value);
public static float ToSingle(byte value);
public static float ToSingle(char value);
public static float ToSingle(DateTime value);
public static float ToSingle(decimal value);
public static float ToSingle(double value);
public static float ToSingle(short value);
```

```
public static float ToSingle(int value);
public static float ToSingle(long value);
public static float ToSingle(object value);
public static float ToSingle(object value, IFormatProvider provider);
public static float ToSingle(sbyte value);
public static float ToSingle(float value);
public static float ToSingle(string value);
public static float ToSingle(string value, IFormatProvider provider);
public static float ToSingle(ushort value);
public static float ToSingle(uint value);
public static float ToSingle(ulong value);
public static string ToString(bool value);
public static string ToString(bool value, IFormatProvider provider);
public static string ToString(byte value);
public static string ToString(byte value, IFormatProvider provider);
public static string ToString(byte value, int toBase);
public static string ToString(char value);
public static string ToString(char value, IFormatProvider provider);
public static string ToString(DateTime value);
public static string ToString(DateTime value, IFormatProvider provider);
public static string ToString(decimal value);
public static string ToString(decimal value, IFormatProvider provider);
public static string ToString(double value);
public static string ToString(double value, IFormatProvider provider);
public static string ToString(short value);
public static string ToString(short value, IFormatProvider provider);
public static string ToString(short value, int toBase);
public static string ToString(int value);
public static string ToString(int value, IFormatProvider provider);
public static string ToString(int value, int toBase);
public static string ToString(long value);
public static string ToString(long value, IFormatProvider provider);
public static string ToString(long value, int toBase);
public static string ToString(object value);
public static string ToString(object value, IFormatProvider provider);
public static string ToString(sbyte value);
public static string ToString(sbyte value, IFormatProvider provider);
public static string ToString(float value);
public static string ToString(float value, IFormatProvider provider);
public static string ToString(string value);
public static string ToString(string value, IFormatProvider provider);
public static string ToString(ushort value);
public static string ToString(ushort value, IFormatProvider provider);
public static string ToString(uint value);
public static string ToString(uint value, IFormatProvider provider);
public static string ToString(ulong value);
public static string ToString(ulong value, IFormatProvider provider);
public static ushort ToUInt16(bool value);
public static ushort ToUInt16(byte value);
public static ushort ToUInt16(char value);
public static ushort ToUInt16(DateTime value);
```

```
public static ushort ToUInt16(decimal value);
public static ushort ToUInt16(double value);
public static ushort ToUInt16(short value);
public static ushort ToUInt16(int value);
public static ushort ToUInt16(long value);
public static ushort ToUInt16(object value);
public static ushort ToUInt16(object value, IFormatProvider provider);
public static ushort ToUInt16(sbyte value);
public static ushort ToUInt16(float value);
public static ushort ToUInt16(string value);
public static ushort ToUInt16(string value, IFormatProvider provider);
public static ushort ToUInt16(string value, int fromBase);
public static ushort ToUInt16(ushort value);
public static ushort ToUInt16(uint value);
public static ushort ToUInt16(ulong value);
public static uint ToUInt32(bool value);
public static uint ToUInt32(byte value);
public static uint ToUInt32(char value);
public static uint ToUInt32(DateTime value);
public static uint ToUInt32(decimal value);
public static uint ToUInt32(double value);
public static uint ToUInt32(short value);
public static uint ToUInt32(int value);
public static uint ToUInt32(long value);
public static uint ToUInt32(object value);
public static uint ToUInt32(object value, IFormatProvider provider);
public static uint ToUInt32(sbyte value);
public static uint ToUInt32(float value);
public static uint ToUInt32(string value);
public static uint ToUInt32(string value, IFormatProvider provider);
public static uint ToUInt32(string value, int fromBase);
public static uint ToUInt32(ushort value);
public static uint ToUInt32(uint value);
public static uint ToUInt32(ulong value);
public static ulong ToUInt64(bool value);
public static ulong ToUInt64(byte value);
public static ulong ToUInt64(char value);
public static ulong ToUInt64(DateTime value);
public static ulong ToUInt64(decimal value);
public static ulong ToUInt64(double value);
public static ulong ToUInt64(short value);
public static ulong ToUInt64(int value);
public static ulong ToUInt64(long value);
public static ulong ToUInt64(object value);
public static ulong ToUInt64(object value, IFormatProvider provider);
public static ulong ToUInt64(sbyte value);
public static ulong ToUInt64(float value);
public static ulong ToUInt64(string value);
public static ulong ToUInt64(string value, IFormatProvider provider);
public static ulong ToUInt64(string value, int fromBase);
```

```
public static ulong ToUInt64(ushort value);
public static ulong ToUInt64(uint value);
public static ulong ToUInt64(ulong value);
}
```

CrossAppDomainDelegate   serializable

System (mscorlib.dll)   delegate

This delegate invokes a method in a different application domain using the AppDomain.
DoCallBack( ) method. You can then invoke a delegate instance within another AppDomain,
which provides you with the ability to check on an AppDomain's status or information.

```
public delegate void CrossAppDomainDelegate( );
```

Passed To   AppDomain.DoCallBack( )

DateTime   CF 1.0, ECMA 1.0, serializable

System (mscorlib.dll)   struct

This simple value type represents a moment in time from 12:00:00 A.M., 1/1/0001
C.E. (Common Era), to 11:59:59 P.M., 12/31/9999 C.E., which is measured to the
nearest *tick*, or 100-nanosecond interval. You can use this type in greater-than/less-
than comparisons, sorting, and in calculations using other DateTime or TimeSpan
instances. You can also use convenient Add... methods, such as AddSeconds( ), with a
positive or negative value.

To extract part of a date, use properties such as Day and Minute. All properties except
Ticks represent a single component of a compound date, not the whole date. You can
convert a string into a DateTime using the static Parse( ) or ParseExact( ) methods, which
require that the date match the pattern specified by a supplied format string.

The DateTime class also provides valuable static functions that can determine the
number of days in a month (DaysInMonth( )), evaluate whether a year is a leap year
(IsLeapYear( )), and retrieve the date stamp from a file (FromFileTime( )). You can also get the
current date from the static property Today (or UtcNow for the coordinated universal
time).

```
public struct DateTime : IComparable, IFormattable, IConvertible {
// Public Constructors
  public DateTime(int year, int month, int day);
  public DateTime(int year, int month, int day, System.Globalization.Calendar calendar);
  public DateTime(int year, int month, int day, int hour, int minute, int second);
  public DateTime(int year, int month, int day, int hour, int minute, int second, System.Globalization.Calendar calendar);
  public DateTime(int year, int month, int day, int hour, int minute, int second, int millisecond);
  public DateTime(int year, int month, int day, int hour, int minute, int second, int millisecond,
     System.Globalization.Calendar calendar);
  public DateTime(long ticks);
// Public Static Fields
  public static readonly DateTime MaxValue;                    // =12/31/9999 11:59:59 PM
  public static readonly DateTime MinValue;                    // =1/1/0001 12:00:00 AM
// Public Static Properties
  public static DateTime Now{get; }
  public static DateTime Today{get; }
```

```
public static DateTime UtcNow{get; }
```
// Public Instance Properties
```
public DateTime Date{get; }
public int Day{get; }
public DayOfWeek DayOfWeek{get; }
public int DayOfYear{get; }
public int Hour{get; }
public int Millisecond{get; }
public int Minute{get; }
public int Month{get; }
public int Second{get; }
public long Ticks{get; }
public TimeSpan TimeOfDay{get; }
public int Year{get; }
```
// Public Static Methods
```
public static int Compare(DateTime t1, DateTime t2);
public static int DaysInMonth(int year, int month);
public static bool Equals(DateTime t1, DateTime t2);
public static DateTime FromFileTime(long fileTime);
public static DateTime FromFileTimeUtc(long fileTime);
public static DateTime FromOADate(double d);
public static bool IsLeapYear(int year);
public static DateTime Parse(string s);
public static DateTime Parse(string s, IFormatProvider provider);
public static DateTime Parse(string s, IFormatProvider provider, System.Globalization.DateTimeStyles styles);
public static DateTime ParseExact(string s, string[ ] formats, IFormatProvider provider,
    System.Globalization.DateTimeStyles style);
public static DateTime ParseExact(string s, string format, IFormatProvider provider);
public static DateTime ParseExact(string s, string format, IFormatProvider provider,
    System.Globalization.DateTimeStyles style);
public static DateTime operator −(DateTime d, TimeSpan t);
public static TimeSpan operator −(DateTime d1, DateTime d2);
public static DateTime operator +(DateTime d, TimeSpan t);
public static bool operator !=(DateTime d1, DateTime d2);
public static bool operator <(DateTime t1, DateTime t2);
public static bool operator <=(DateTime t1, DateTime t2);
public static bool operator = =(DateTime d1, DateTime d2);
public static bool operator >(DateTime t1, DateTime t2);
public static bool operator >=(DateTime t1, DateTime t2);
```
// Public Instance Methods
```
public DateTime Add(TimeSpan value);
public DateTime AddDays(double value);
public DateTime AddHours(double value);
public DateTime AddMilliseconds(double value);
public DateTime AddMinutes(double value);
public DateTime AddMonths(int months);
public DateTime AddSeconds(double value);
public DateTime AddTicks(long value);
public DateTime AddYears(int value);
public int CompareTo(object value);                                    // implements IComparable
public override bool Equals(object value);                             // overrides ValueType
```

```
public string[ ] GetDateTimeFormats( );
public string[ ] GetDateTimeFormats(char format);
public string[ ] GetDateTimeFormats(char format, IFormatProvider provider);
public string[ ] GetDateTimeFormats(IFormatProvider provider);
public override int GetHashCode( );                                          // overrides ValueType
public TypeCode GetTypeCode( );                                              // implements IConvertible
public DateTime Subtract(TimeSpan value);
public TimeSpan Subtract(DateTime value);
public long ToFileTime( );
public long ToFileTimeUtc( );
public DateTime ToLocalTime( );
public string ToLongDateString( );
public string ToLongTimeString( );
public double ToOADate( );
public string ToShortDateString( );
public string ToShortTimeString( );
public override string ToString( );                                          // overrides ValueType
public string ToString(IFormatProvider provider);                            // implements IConvertible
public string ToString(string format);
public string ToString(string format, IFormatProvider provider);            // implements IFormattable
public DateTime ToUniversalTime( );
}
```

Hierarchy   Object → ValueType → DateTime(IComparable, IFormattable, IConvertible)

Returned By   Multiple types

Passed To   Multiple types

DayOfWeek

CF 1.0, serializable

System (mscorlib.dll)   enum

This enumeration is used by the DateTime.DayOfWeek property.

```
public enum DayOfWeek {
  Sunday = 0,
  Monday = 1,
  Tuesday = 2,
  Wednesday = 3,
  Thursday = 4,
  Friday = 5,
  Saturday = 6
}
```

Hierarchy   Object → ValueType → Enum(IComparable, IFormattable, IConvertible) → DayOfWeek

Returned By   DateTime.DayOfWeek, System.Globalization.Calendar.GetDayOfWeek( ), System.
                   Globalization.DateTimeFormatInfo.FirstDayOfWeek

Passed To   System.Globalization.Calendar.GetWeekOfYear( ), System.Globalization.DateTimeFormatInfo.
                   {FirstDayOfWeek, GetAbbreviatedDayName( ), GetDayName( )}

System

DBNull

System (mscorlib.dll)   sealed class

DBNull indicates the absence of information, typically in a database application in which a field does not contain any data. The types in the System.Data.SqlTypes namespace have built-in support for DBNull.

Note that Value is not the same as the null keyword in C#. The null keyword can be used to release an object by clearing the reference. System.DBNull.Value, on the other hand, is a reference to a special value (a member of the singleton class DBNull) that is used to indicate missing information.

This class has some other uses, namely in COM Interop, in which it represents a VT_ EMPTY variant (as opposed to a VT_NULL variant, which is a null reference).

```
public sealed class DBNull : System.Runtime.Serialization.ISerializable, IConvertible {
// Public Static Fields
  public static readonly DBNull Value;
// Public Instance Methods
  public void GetObjectData(System.Runtime.Serialization.SerializationInfo info,
    System.Runtime.Serialization.StreamingContext context);              // implements ISerializable
  public TypeCode GetTypeCode( );                                        // implements IConvertible
  public override string ToString( );                                          // overrides object
  public string ToString(IFormatProvider provider);                       // implements IConvertible
}
```

Decimal

System (mscorlib.dll)   struct

This simple value type is commonly used for financial calculations, which can preserve a significant number of fractional digits with no round-off error. Decimals are stored as 12-byte signed integers scaled by a variable power of 10. This means that a decimal data type can effectively hold 28 significant digits without losing any information. With a scale of 0 (no decimal places), the largest possible value is approximately $7.92*10^{28}$. This type is available in C# through the decimal alias.

```
public struct Decimal : IFormattable, IComparable, IConvertible {
// Public Constructors
  public Decimal(double value);
  public Decimal(int value);
  public Decimal(int[ ] bits);
  public Decimal(int lo, int mid, int hi, bool isNegative, byte scale);
  public Decimal(long value);
  public Decimal(float value);
  public Decimal(uint value);
  public Decimal(ulong value);
// Public Static Fields
  public static readonly decimal MaxValue;           // =79228162514264337593543950335
  public static readonly decimal MinusOne;                                      // =-1
  public static readonly decimal MinValue;          // =-79228162514264337593543950335
  public static readonly decimal One;                                          // =1
  public static readonly decimal Zero;                                         // =0
// Public Static Methods
```

```
public static decimal Add(decimal d1, decimal d2);
public static int Compare(decimal d1, decimal d2);
public static decimal Divide(decimal d1, decimal d2);
public static bool Equals(decimal d1, decimal d2);
public static decimal Floor(decimal d);
public static decimal FromOACurrency(long cy);
public static int[ ] GetBits(decimal d);
public static decimal Multiply(decimal d1, decimal d2);
public static decimal Negate(decimal d);
public static decimal Parse(string s);
public static decimal Parse(string s, IFormatProvider provider);
public static decimal Parse(string s, System.Globalization.NumberStyles style);
public static decimal Parse(string s, System.Globalization.NumberStyles style, IFormatProvider provider);
public static decimal Remainder(decimal d1, decimal d2);
public static decimal Round(decimal d, int decimals);
public static decimal Subtract(decimal d1, decimal d2);
public static byte ToByte(decimal value);
public static double ToDouble(decimal d);
public static short ToInt16(decimal value);
public static int ToInt32(decimal d);
public static long ToInt64(decimal d);
public static long ToOACurrency(decimal value);
public static sbyte ToSByte(decimal value);
public static float ToSingle(decimal d);
public static ushort ToUInt16(decimal value);
public static uint ToUInt32(decimal d);
public static ulong ToUInt64(decimal d);
public static decimal Truncate(decimal d);
public static decimal operator %(decimal d1, decimal d2);
public static decimal operator *(decimal d1, decimal d2);
public static decimal operator /(decimal d1, decimal d2);
public static decimal operator--(decimal d);
public static decimal operator -(decimal d);
public static decimal operator -(decimal d1, decimal d2);
public static decimal operator +(decimal d);
public static decimal operator +(decimal d1, decimal d2);
public static decimal operator ++(decimal d);
public static bool operator !=(decimal d1, decimal d2);
public static bool operator <(decimal d1, decimal d2);
public static bool operator <=(decimal d1, decimal d2);
public static bool operator = =(decimal d1, decimal d2);
public static bool operator >(decimal d1, decimal d2);
public static bool operator >=(decimal d1, decimal d2);
public static explicit operator byte(decimal value);
public static explicit operator char(decimal value);
public static explicit operator decimal(double value);
public static explicit operator decimal(float value);
public static explicit operator double(decimal value);
public static explicit operator short(decimal value);
public static explicit operator int(decimal value);
public static explicit operator long(decimal value);
```

```
public static explicit operator sbyte(decimal value);
public static explicit operator float(decimal value);
public static explicit operator ushort(decimal value);
public static explicit operator uint(decimal value);
public static explicit operator ulong(decimal value);
public static implicit operator decimal(byte value);
public static implicit operator decimal(char value);
public static implicit operator decimal(short value);
public static implicit operator decimal(int value);
public static implicit operator decimal(long value);
public static implicit operator decimal(sbyte value);
public static implicit operator decimal(ushort value);
public static implicit operator decimal(uint value);
public static implicit operator decimal(ulong value);
// Public Instance Methods
public int CompareTo(object value);                                     // implements IComparable
public override bool Equals(object value);                              // overrides ValueType
public override int GetHashCode();                                      // overrides ValueType
public TypeCode GetTypeCode();                                          // implements IConvertible
public override string ToString();                                     // overrides ValueType
public string ToString(IFormatProvider provider);                      // implements IConvertible
public string ToString(string format);
public string ToString(string format, IFormatProvider provider);       // implements IFormattable
}
```

Hierarchy   Object → ValueType → Decimal(IFormattable, IComparable, IConvertible)

Returned By   Convert.ToDecimal( ), IConvertible.ToDecimal( ), System.IO.BinaryReader.ReadDecimal( ),
                   System.Runtime.InteropServices.CurrencyWrapper.WrappedObject, System.Runtime.
                   Serialization.FormatterConverter.ToDecimal( ), System.Runtime.Serialization.
                   IFormatterConverter.ToDecimal( ), System.Runtime.Serialization.SerializationInfo.
                   GetDecimal( ), System.Xml.XmlConvert.ToDecimal( )

Passed To   Multiple types

Delegate   CF 1.0, ECMA 1.0, serializable

System (mscorlib.dll)   abstract class

A delegate is used to provide a decoupling of caller from callee; that is, a delegate
points to a given method (instance or static) in a class, and callers can call through the
delegate without having to know the target of the call. In many respects, the delegate is
conceptually similar to the C/C++ *function pointer*, with a number of important
advantages. A delegate is strongly typed, meaning that only methods that match the
delegate's declared signature are acceptable when constructing the delegate instance,
and the compiler enforces the delegate's declared signature when called. A delegate
can distinguish between a static and an instance method. This avoids the C++ application associated with pointers to member functions, which require a literal pointer to the
object upon which to invoke the method.

Delegates are usually constructed by the language compiler, varying in syntax from
language to language. In C#, the construct public delegate void CallbackDelegate(int param1, string
param2); declares a new type that derives from the Delegate type (its immediate superclass

is actually MulticastDelegate). This new CallbackDelegate type is also declared with a constructor (to take the method to call when the delegate is invoked) and an Invoke method (to do the actual call), along with asynchronous versions of Invoke (the BeginInvoke and EndInvoke methods).

In many cases, you will want to use delegates as an *invocation chain*, where a single call to the delegate should result in a series of calls against a collection of delegate targets. (This is most easily seen in .NET's publish-subscribe event-handling idiom—C#'s event keyword.) To achieve this, Delegate contains static methods allowing delegates to combine into a single delegate instance that calls into multiple delegate targets. The Combine( ) method takes two existing delegate instances (with identical signatures) and returns a single delegate instance that calls both targets when invoked. (There is another form of Combine( ) that takes an array of delegates instead of just a pair.) Remove( ) does the opposite of Combine( ), removing a delegate from the multicast call chain. (See the MulticastDelegate entry for more information on multicast delegates.)

Delegates can also be invoked using the DynamicInvoke( ) method, without knowing the actual concretely generated Delegate subtype. This method expects an array of object references, whose type should match those of the expected parameters to the delegate. If any of the parameters to DynamicInvoke( ) do not match those expected by the target method, an exception is thrown. Delegates can also be constructed in the same generic fashion using one of the overloaded forms of CreateDelegate( ).

Delegates can be invoked either synchronously or asynchronously. To invoke a delegate synchronously (that is, block until the call(s) return), simply use the delegate as if it is a method, as shown in "Delegates" in Chapter 4. The call to a delegate is executed completely before execution resumes in the calling method. Should you wish the call to the delegate to occur in parallel with the calling method, use the BeginInvoke method to start execution and the EndInvoke method to wait for the asynchronous delegate call's completion (if it hasn't finished by the time the EndInvoke call is made). If any of the delegate's parameters are declared as ref or out parameters, these parameters will be available on the parameter list to EndInvoke.

```
public abstract class Delegate : ICloneable, System.Runtime.Serialization.ISerializable {
// Protected Constructors
   protected Delegate(object target, string method);
   protected Delegate(Type target, string method);
// Public Instance Properties
   public MethodInfo Method{get; }
   public object Target{get; }
// Public Static Methods
   public static Delegate Combine(Delegate[ ] delegates);
   public static Delegate Combine(Delegate a, Delegate b);
   public static Delegate CreateDelegate(Type type, System.Reflection.MethodInfo method);
   public static Delegate CreateDelegate(Type type, object target, string method);
   public static Delegate CreateDelegate(Type type, object target, string method, bool ignoreCase);
   public static Delegate CreateDelegate(Type type, Type target, string method);
   public static Delegate Remove(Delegate source, Delegate value);
   public static Delegate RemoveAll(Delegate source, Delegate value);
   public static bool operator !=(Delegate d1, Delegate d2);
   public static bool operator = =(Delegate d1, Delegate d2);
// Public Instance Methods
   public virtual object Clone( );                                    // implements ICloneable
```

```
public object DynamicInvoke(object[ ] args);
public override bool Equals(object obj);                                              // overrides object
public override int GetHashCode( );                                                  // overrides object
public virtual Delegate[ ] GetInvocationList( );
public virtual void GetObjectData(System.Runtime.Serialization.SerializationInfo info,
    System.Runtime.Serialization.StreamingContext context);                          // implements ISerializable
// Protected Instance Methods
protected virtual Delegate CombineImpl(Delegate d);
protected virtual object DynamicInvokeImpl(object[ ] args);
protected virtual MethodInfo GetMethodImpl( );
protected virtual Delegate RemoveImpl(Delegate d);
}
```

Subclasses	MulticastDelegate
Returned By	MulticastDelegate.{CombineImpl( ), GetInvocationList( ), RemoveImpl( )}
Passed To	Microsoft.Win32.SystemEvents.InvokeOnEventsThread( ), MulticastDelegate.{CombineImpl ( ), RemoveImpl( )}, System.Reflection.EventInfo.{AddEventHandler( ), RemoveEventHandler( )}, System.Runtime.InteropServices.Expando.IExpando.AddMethod( )

DivideByZeroException

CF 1.0, ECMA 1.0, serializable

System (mscorlib.dll)   class

This exception is thrown when a math operation attempts to divide by zero.

```
public class DivideByZeroException : ArithmeticException {
// Public Constructors
  public DivideByZeroException( );
  public DivideByZeroException(string message);
  public DivideByZeroException(string message, Exception innerException);
// Protected Constructors
  protected DivideByZeroException(System.Runtime.Serialization.SerializationInfo info,
    System.Runtime.Serialization.StreamingContext context);
}
```

Hierarchy	Object → Exception(System.Runtime.Serialization.ISerializable) → SystemException → ArithmeticException → DivideByZeroException

DllNotFoundException

CF 1.0, serializable

System (mscorlib.dll)   class

This exception indicates that the file specified in a DLL import could not be found (see System.Runtime.InteropServices.DllImportAttribute). This exception is thrown only when you attempt to link against a method declared using the P/Invoke features of .NET. Any managed DLL (such as those produced by C# or Visual Basic .NET) that cannot be found instead generates TypeLoadExceptions when you attempt to resolve types out of an assembly that cannot be found.

```
public class DllNotFoundException : TypeLoadException {
// Public Constructors
  public DllNotFoundException( );
```

```
    public DllNotFoundException(string message);
    public DllNotFoundException(string message, Exception inner);
// Protected Constructors
    protected DllNotFoundException(System.Runtime.Serialization.SerializationInfo info,
        System.Runtime.Serialization.StreamingContext context);
}
```

Hierarchy   Object → Exception(System.Runtime.Serialization.ISerializable) → SystemException →
             TypeLoadException → DllNotFoundException

Double   CF 1.0, ECMA 1.0, serializable

System (mscorlib.dll)   struct

This represents a 64-bit double-precision floating number as a value type. The value of
a double can range, approximately from -1.8×10^{308} to 1.8×10^{308} and can be set to one
of the following fields: PositiveInfinity, NegativeInfinity, and NaN (not a number). This type is
aliased as double in C#.

```
public struct Double : IComparable, IFormattable, IConvertible {
// Public Static Fields
    public const double Epsilon;                              // =4.94065645841247E-324
    public const double MaxValue;                             // =1.79769313486232E+308
    public const double MinValue;                             // =-1.79769313486232E+308
    public const double NaN;                                  // =NaN
    public const double NegativeInfinity;                     // =-Infinity
    public const double PositiveInfinity;                     // =Infinity
// Public Static Methods
    public static bool IsInfinity(double d);
    public static bool IsNaN(double d);
    public static bool IsNegativeInfinity(double d);
    public static bool IsPositiveInfinity(double d);
    public static double Parse(string s);
    public static double Parse(string s, IFormatProvider provider);
    public static double Parse(string s, System.Globalization.NumberStyles style);
    public static double Parse(string s, System.Globalization.NumberStyles style, IFormatProvider provider);
    public static bool TryParse(string s, System.Globalization.NumberStyles style, IFormatProvider provider, out double result);
// Public Instance Methods
    public int CompareTo(object value);                              // implements IComparable
    public override bool Equals(object obj);                         // overrides ValueType
    public override int GetHashCode( );                              // overrides ValueType
    public TypeCode GetTypeCode( );                                  // implements IConvertible
    public override string ToString( );                             // overrides ValueType
    public string ToString(IFormatProvider provider);               // implements IConvertible
    public string ToString(string format);
    public string ToString(string format, IFormatProvider provider); // implements IFormattable
}
```

Hierarchy   Object → ValueType → Double(IComparable, IFormattable, IConvertible)

Returned By   Multiple types

Passed To   Multiple types

DuplicateWaitObjectException

ECMA 1.0, serializable

System (mscorlib.dll)

class

This exception is thrown when an object shows up more than once in the array passed to System.Threading.WaitHandle.WaitAll( ) or System.Threading.WaitHandle.WaitAny( ).

```
public class DuplicateWaitObjectException : ArgumentException {
// Public Constructors
  public DuplicateWaitObjectException( );
  public DuplicateWaitObjectException(string parameterName);
  public DuplicateWaitObjectException(string parameterName, string message);
// Protected Constructors
  protected DuplicateWaitObjectException(System.Runtime.Serialization.SerializationInfo info,
    System.Runtime.Serialization.StreamingContext context);
}
```

Hierarchy   Object → Exception(System.Runtime.Serialization.ISerializable) → SystemException → ArgumentException → DuplicateWaitObjectException

EntryPointNotFoundException

CF 1.0, ECMA 1.0, serializable

System (mscorlib.dll)

class

This exception indicates that an entry point could not be found when .NET loaded an assembly flagged for execution; that is, an AppDomain was instructed to execute an assembly, but no method in that assembly was marked with the .entrypoint metadata flag.

```
public class EntryPointNotFoundException : TypeLoadException {
// Public Constructors
  public EntryPointNotFoundException( );
  public EntryPointNotFoundException(string message);
  public EntryPointNotFoundException(string message, Exception inner);
// Protected Constructors
  protected EntryPointNotFoundException(System.Runtime.Serialization.SerializationInfo info,
    System.Runtime.Serialization.StreamingContext context);
}
```

Hierarchy   Object → Exception(System.Runtime.Serialization.ISerializable) → SystemException → TypeLoadException → EntryPointNotFoundException

Enum

CF 1.0, ECMA 1.0, serializable

System (mscorlib.dll)

abstract class

This is the base class for all enumerations. In C#, you can use the enum keyword to create an enumeration type consisting of named constants and their values. By default, the underlying type used for enumeration elements is Int32, but you can use any integer data type.

```
public abstract class Enum : ValueType : IComparable, IFormattable, IConvertible {
// Protected Constructors
  protected Enum( );
```

```
// Public Static Methods
    public static string Format(Type enumType, object value, string format);
    public static string GetName(Type enumType, object value);
    public static string[ ] GetNames(Type enumType);
    public static Type GetUnderlyingType(Type enumType);
    public static Array GetValues(Type enumType);
    public static bool IsDefined(Type enumType, object value);
    public static object Parse(Type enumType, string value);
    public static object Parse(Type enumType, string value, bool ignoreCase);
    public static object ToObject(Type enumType, byte value);
    public static object ToObject(Type enumType, short value);
    public static object ToObject(Type enumType, int value);
    public static object ToObject(Type enumType, long value);
    public static object ToObject(Type enumType, object value);
    public static object ToObject(Type enumType, sbyte value);
    public static object ToObject(Type enumType, ushort value);
    public static object ToObject(Type enumType, uint value);
    public static object ToObject(Type enumType, ulong value);
// Public Instance Methods
    public int CompareTo(object target);                                    // implements IComparable
    public override bool Equals(object obj);                                // overrides ValueType
    public override int GetHashCode( );                                     // overrides ValueType
    public TypeCode GetTypeCode( );                                         // implements IConvertible
    public override string ToString( );                                     // overrides ValueType
    public string ToString(IFormatProvider provider);                       // implements IConvertible
    public string ToString(string format);
    public string ToString(string format, IFormatProvider provider);        // implements IFormattable
}
```

Hierarchy   Object → ValueType → Enum(IComparable, IFormattable, IConvertible)

Subclasses   Multiple types

Environment

CF 1.0, ECMA 1.0

System (mscorlib.dll)   sealed class

This class represents an application's operating environment, which includes details about the operating system, the current user, and other environment variables. This information is provided through static properties and some helper methods.

You can retrieve command-line arguments as a string from CommandLine or as an array of strings using GetCommandLineArgs( ). Use the GetLogicalDrives( ) method to get an array of strings containing drive names (for example, C:\), and use the GetFolderPath( ) method to get the physical location of a special system folder. You can also retrieve environment variables by key name using the GetEnvironmentVariable( ) method and automatically replace environment variables in a string with the ExpandEnvironmentVariables( ) method, as long as they are delimited with the percent sign (%). For example, on a system with the environment variable MAC_ADDR set to 123456789012, the string MAC_ADDR=%MAC_ADDR% would be converted to MAC_ADDR=123456789012.

```
public sealed class Environment {
// Public Static Properties
   public static string CommandLine{get; }
   public static string CurrentDirectory{set; get; }
   public static int ExitCode{set; get; }
   public static bool HasShutdownStarted{get; }
   public static string MachineName{get; }
   public static string NewLine{get; }
   public static OperatingSystem OSVersion{get; }
   public static string StackTrace{get; }
   public static string SystemDirectory{get; }
   public static int TickCount{get; }
   public static string UserDomainName{get; }
   public static bool UserInteractive{get; }
   public static string UserName{get; }
   public static Version Version{get; }
   public static long WorkingSet{get; }
// Public Static Methods
   public static void Exit(int exitCode);
   public static string ExpandEnvironmentVariables(string name);
   public static string[ ] GetCommandLineArgs( );
   public static string GetEnvironmentVariable(string variable);
   public static IDictionary GetEnvironmentVariables( );
   public static string GetFolderPath(SpecialFolder folder);
   public static string[ ] GetLogicalDrives( );
}
```

Environment.SpecialFolder   serializable

System (mscorlib.dll)   enum

This enumeration is used by the Environment.GetFolderPath( ) method to allow you to
retrieve the physical path of commonly used system (or "special") folders, including
everything from the Internet cache to the Start menu.

```
public enum Environment.SpecialFolder {
   Desktop = 0,
   Programs = 2,
   Personal = 5,
   Favorites = 6,
   Startup = 7,
   Recent = 8,
   SendTo = 9,
   StartMenu = 11,
   MyMusic = 13,
   DesktopDirectory = 16,
   MyComputer = 17,
   Templates = 21,
   ApplicationData = 26,
   LocalApplicationData = 28,
   InternetCache = 32,
   Cookies = 33,
```

```
History = 34,
CommonApplicationData = 35,
System = 37,
ProgramFiles = 38,
MyPictures = 39,
CommonProgramFiles = 43
}
```

Hierarchy   Object → ValueType → Enum(IComparable, IFormattable, IConvertible) → SpecialFolder

EventArgs   CF 1.0, ECMA 1.0, serializable

System (mscorlib.dll)   class

See the EventHandler entry for details regarding the EventArgs/EventHandler idiom for delegates in .NET. If .NET developers wish to follow this idiom, they should create new subtypes of EventArgs for each new collection of data to be sent to interested parties; otherwise, they should pass Empty, indicating that no event data is to be passed as part of this event notification.

```
public class EventArgs {
// Public Constructors
  public EventArgs( );
// Public Static Fields
  public static readonly EventArgs Empty;                           // =System.EventArgs
}
```

Subclasses   Multiple types

Passed To   EventHandler.{BeginInvoke( ), Invoke( )}

EventHandler   CF 1.0, ECMA 1.0, serializable

System (mscorlib.dll)   delegate

Shortly after Beta 1 of .NET was released, Microsoft .NET developers realized that prolific use of delegates could easily lead to type-bloat; since each declared delegate created a new type in the system, a large number of delegates would lead to a huge number of types to load, verify, and initialize. In Beta 2, Microsoft introduced an idiom that, it's hoped, will keep type-bloat down to reasonable levels in .NET.

Microsoft defines two types, EventHandler (a delegate type) and EventArgs, a glorified C construct. EventHandler is declared to expect two parameters: an object reference indicating the sender of the event, and an event data parameter (the EventArgs or some derived-type instance).

This delegate represents the base type for .NET event handlers. (In Beta 2 and later, all .NET Framework Class Library types with declared events use this same idiom, so as to remain consistent.) Its arguments include a sender parameter, which refers to the object that issued the event, and an e parameter, which contains additional event data. Events that do not require additional information use the EventHandler delegate directly.

Events that need to send additional information derive their own custom delegate from this type. Custom event delegates look similar, except that they replace the EventArgs parameter with a custom object derived from EventArgs. This object contains additional properties or methods that are specific to the event.

```
public delegate void EventHandler(object sender,
    EventArgs e);
```

Associated Events Multiple types

Exception

CF 1.0, ECMA 1.0, serializable

System (mscorlib.dll)   class

This is the base class for all .NET exceptions. .NET Framework exceptions are generally derived from SystemException, and user-defined exceptions are generally derived from
ApplicationException.

In some cases, one exception may throw another; this is often the case when using
layered architectures. For example, a persistence layer may throw a persistence-related
exception (DatabaseNotFoundException), whose semantics are undefined at a higher level
(such as the UI layer). In this case, a middle layer may throw a new exception-derived
type (such as PersistenceException), but doesn't wish to lose the original source of the
exception—instead, it wraps the original exception by setting it to be the InnerException.
In this way, a layer can communicate a lower-level exception to higher layers without
losing information or violating encapsulation.

The StackTrace property is a string containing the stacktrace. This permits determination
of the call sequence leading up to the line that threw the exception. HelpLink contains a
link to a help file with information about the exception. Message contains a text message
that describes the exception.

```
public class Exception : System.Runtime.Serialization.ISerializable {
// Public Constructors
  public Exception( );
  public Exception(string message);
  public Exception(string message, Exception innerException);
// Protected Constructors
  protected Exception(System.Runtime.Serialization.SerializationInfo info,
    System.Runtime.Serialization.StreamingContext context);
// Public Instance Properties
  public virtual string HelpLink{set; get; }
  public Exception InnerException{get; }
  public virtual string Message{get; }
  public virtual string Source{set; get; }
  public virtual string StackTrace{get; }
  public MethodBase TargetSite{get; }
// Protected Instance Properties
  protected int HResult{set; get; }
// Public Instance Methods
  public virtual Exception GetBaseException( );
  public virtual void GetObjectData(System.Runtime.Serialization.SerializationInfo info,
    System.Runtime.Serialization.StreamingContext context);              // implements ISerializable
  public override string ToString( );                                        // overrides object
}
```

Subclasses   ApplicationException, SystemException, System.IO.IsolatedStorage.IsolatedStorageException

System.IO.ErrorEventArgs.GetException( ), System.Reflection.ReflectionTypeLoadException. LoaderExceptions, System.Threading.ThreadExceptionEventArgs.Exception

Passed To   Multiple types

ExecutionEngineException   ECMA 1.0, serializable

System (mscorlib.dll)   sealed class

This exception indicates that an error has occurred deep within the innards of the .NET CLR.

```
public sealed class ExecutionEngineException : SystemException {
// Public Constructors
  public ExecutionEngineException( );
  public ExecutionEngineException(string message);
  public ExecutionEngineException(string message, Exception innerException);
}
```

Hierarchy   Object → Exception(System.Runtime.Serialization.ISerializable) → SystemException → ExecutionEngineException

FieldAccessException   ECMA 1.0, serializable

System (mscorlib.dll)   class

This exception is thrown when you try to access a protected or private field that you would not normally have access to. Most compilers will not let you compile code that does this directly. However, late-bound code can sneak by the compiler and throw this exception at runtime. For example, if you lack sufficient privileges to modify a field using System.Reflection.FieldInfo.SetValue( ), this exception is thrown.

```
public class FieldAccessException : MemberAccessException {
// Public Constructors
  public FieldAccessException( );
  public FieldAccessException(string message);
  public FieldAccessException(string message, Exception inner);
// Protected Constructors
  protected FieldAccessException(System.Runtime.Serialization.SerializationInfo info,
    System.Runtime.Serialization.StreamingContext context);
}
```

Hierarchy   Object → Exception(System.Runtime.Serialization.ISerializable) → SystemException → MemberAccessException → FieldAccessException

FlagsAttribute   CF 1.0, ECMA 1.0, serializable

System (mscorlib.dll)   class

This attribute indicates that an enumeration should be treated as a set of on/off flags (i.e., a bit field). Unlike enumerated constants, bit fields can be combined with a bitwise OR operation.

```
public class FlagsAttribute : Attribute {
// Public Constructors
  public FlagsAttribute( );
}
```

Hierarchy   Object → Attribute → FlagsAttribute

Valid On   Enum

FormatException   CF 1.0, ECMA 1.0, serializable

System (mscorlib.dll)   class

This exception signals that an error occurred during the handling of a format string. Format strings are used by methods such as Console.WriteLine( ) to replace a format specification with one or more parameters. This exception may be triggered by supplying too few arguments to replace all the format strings (for example, supplying only two arguments to Console.WriteLine( ) when your format string is "{0} {1} {2}"). See Appendix B for more information on format strings.

```
public class FormatException : SystemException {
// Public Constructors
  public FormatException( );
  public FormatException(string message);
  public FormatException(string message, Exception innerException);
// Protected Constructors
  protected FormatException(System.Runtime.Serialization.SerializationInfo info,
    System.Runtime.Serialization.StreamingContext context);
}
```

Hierarchy   Object → Exception(System.Runtime.Serialization.ISerializable) → SystemException →
                     FormatException

Subclasses   UriFormatException, System.Net.CookieException, System.Reflection.
                     CustomAttributeFormatException

GC   CF 1.0, ECMA 1.0

System (mscorlib.dll)   sealed class

This class allows you to control garbage collection programmatically. Garbage collection is the .NET service that periodically scans for unreferenced objects and reclaims the memory they occupy.

The garbage-collection service distinguishes between older and more recently allocated memory using *generations*. The most recently allocated memory is considered generation zero, and the oldest memory is in generation MaxGeneration. Because new allocations are likely to be freed before long-standing memory allocations, the garbage collector improves its performance by concentrating on lower generations of memory. You can find out the generation of an object using the GetGeneration( ) method. You can also get the number of memory bytes that are currently allocated using the GetTotalMemory( ) method. A forceFullCollection parameter indicates whether this method should wait a short interval before returning to collect and finalize some objects.

To force a *full sweep* garbage collection, use the Collect() method. You can improve performance by specifying the maximum generation that will be examined. Generally, it is best to let .NET perform garbage collection automatically when the system is idle.

Some developers have lamented a noticeable lack of *deterministic finalization* within a garbage-collected system; that is, because the object's lifetime is under the control of the garbage collector, there is no guarantee that an object is destroyed as soon as it becomes unreferenced. One approach used to try to compensate for this phenomenon is to call GC repeatedly in an effort to force the object's cleanup. This is both time-consuming and wasteful of the garbage collector's efforts, since a collection may involve not only recollection, but readjustment of object locations in memory. If a programmer requires more explicit control over when an object is cleaned up, the class can be declared as implementing the IDisposable interface (which consists of a single method, Dispose()). This interface allows the object to participate in a using declaration, which guarantees that the object's Dispose() method is invoked when control leaves the declared scope block (see "Using Statement" in Chapter 2). Use of IDisposable is recommended over the use of Finalize() methods. This is due to a variety of reasons too numerous to explore here.

The KeepAlive() method is used to preserve the life of an object that is not strongly referenced. This is sometimes required when interacting with methods in unmanaged code (such as Win32 APIs or COM). The KeepAlive() method works in an unusual manner: it makes an object ineligible for garbage collection from the start of the current routine to the point where the KeepAlive() method is called. This unusual system prevents problems that could otherwise be created by compiler optimizations.

```
public sealed class GC {
// Public Static Properties
  public static int MaxGeneration{get; }
// Public Static Methods
  public static void Collect( );
  public static void Collect(int generation);
  public static int GetGeneration(object obj);
  public static int GetGeneration(WeakReference wo);
  public static long GetTotalMemory(bool forceFullCollection);
  public static void KeepAlive(object obj);
  public static void ReRegisterForFinalize(object obj);
  public static void SuppressFinalize(object obj);
  public static void WaitForPendingFinalizers( );
}
```

Guid
CF 1.0, serializable

System (mscorlib.dll)   struct

This value type represents a Globally Unique Identifier (GUID). A GUID is a 128-bit integer (16 bytes) that can be used across all computers and networks and will be statistically unique (for all practical purposes, the number cannot be duplicated coincidentally). GUIDs are used to identify COM (but not .NET) objects uniquely for registration purposes.

```
public struct Guid : IFormattable, IComparable {
// Public Constructors
  public Guid(byte[ ] b);
```

```
public Guid(int a, short b, short c, byte[ ] d);
public Guid(int a, short b, short c, byte d, byte e, byte f, byte g, byte h, byte i, byte j, byte k);
public Guid(string g);
public Guid(uint a, ushort b, ushort c, byte d, byte e, byte f, byte g, byte h, byte i, byte j, byte k);
// Public Static Fields
public static readonly Guid Empty;                          // =00000000-0000-0000-0000-000000000000
// Public Static Methods
public static Guid NewGuid( );
public static bool operator !=(Guid a,  Guid b);
public static bool operator = =(Guid a, Guid b);
// Public Instance Methods
public int CompareTo(object value);                                          // implements IComparable
public override bool Equals(object o);                                        // overrides ValueType
public override int GetHashCode( );                                           // overrides ValueType
public byte[ ] ToByteArray( );
public override string ToString( );                                          // overrides ValueType
public string ToString(string format);
public string ToString(string format, IFormatProvider provider);            // implements IFormattable
}
```

Hierarchy	Object → ValueType → Guid(IFormattable, IComparable)
Returned By	System.Reflection.Emit.UnmanagedMarshal.IIDGuid, System.Runtime.InteropServices. IRegistrationServices.GetManagedCategoryGuid( ), System.Runtime.InteropServices.Marshal. {GenerateGuidForType( ), GetTypeLibGuid( ), GetTypeLibGuidForAssembly( )}, System. Runtime.InteropServices.RegistrationServices.GetManagedCategoryGuid( ), Type.GUID, System.Xml.XmlConvert.ToGuid( )
Passed To	System.Reflection.Emit.ModuleBuilder.DefineDocument( ), System.Runtime.InteropServices.IRegistrationServices.RegisterTypeForComClients( ), System. Runtime.InteropServices.Marshal.QueryInterface( ), System.Runtime.InteropServices.Regis-trationServices.RegisterTypeForComClients( ), Type.GetTypeFromCLSID( ), System.Xml. XmlConvert.ToString( )

IAsyncResult   CF 1.0, ECMA 1.0

System (mscorlib.dll)   interface

This interface is used in asynchronous programming to act as a placeholder for the result of the async call. It is most commonly used when an instance of a delegate type is fired using the BeginInvoke method. (This idiom is used extensively throughout the .NET Framework Class Library.)

Asynchronous method calls can be harvested in a number of ways. A programmer can poll the call by checking the IsCompleted property of the IAsyncResult object to see if the call has completed yet. This, while perhaps the simplest approach, is also likely the most wasteful, as the caller needs to be in some sort of spin loop, repeatedly checking the property until a true is received.

A variant of the polling spin loop is to use the AsyncWaitHandle property of IAsyncResult. This is a standard Win32 handle that can be used in some of the synchronization primitives provided in the System.Threading namespace. Specifically, this property is a System. Threading.WaitHandle instance, meaning that the programmer can call any of the Wait methods: WaitOne( ), WaitAny( ), or WaitAll( ). The net effect is the same—put the calling thread to sleep until the async call completes.

Although not formally part of the IAsyncResult interface, a corresponding EndInvoke method is supported by delegates. The EndInvoke method blocks the calling thread until the async call completes. Alternatively, at the point of the async delegate call, a programmer can specify a callback delegate to call when the async call completes. This callback, a delegate instance of type AsyncCallback, is passed this IAsyncResult instance as part of the call. An optional generic argument can also be passed in as part of the async call, and this generic argument is available on the IAsyncResult through the AsyncState property. For an example of using IAsyncResult, see "Asynchronous Delegates" in Chapter 16.

```
public interface IAsyncResult {
// Public Instance Properties
  public object AsyncState{get; }
  public WaitHandle AsyncWaitHandle{get; }
  public bool CompletedSynchronously{get; }
  public bool IsCompleted{get; }
}
```

Returned By   Multiple types

Passed To   Multiple types

ICloneable   CF 1.0, ECMA 1.0

System (mscorlib.dll)   interface

ICloneable is a marker interface, indicating that an object can be cloned (that is, have a completely identical copy created). It consists of a single method, Clone( ), which is called by clients wishing to create a complete copy of the ICloneable-implementing class.

When speaking of cloning, the terms *deep copy cloning* and *shallow copy cloning* indicate how deeply into the object graph a clone operation will carry itself. A deep copy not only clones the object called, but in turn seeks to clone any objects to which it holds reference. This sort of operation must be handled by the programmer, usually by calling Clone( ) in turn on each object this object references. A shallow copy is a complete bitwise copy of this object; any objects referenced by this object are also referenced by the cloned object.

The simplest way to implement a shallow clone is to use the Object.MemberwiseClone( ) method to copy this object's fields directly and then return. A deep clone also calls MemberwiseClone( ), but then also asks each object reference held within this object to Clone( ) itself.

```
public interface ICloneable {
// Public Instance Methods
  public object Clone( );
}
```

Implemented By Multiple types

IComparable

System (mscorlib.dll)   interface

This interface is implemented by classes that can be ordered in a list. Classes such as String and Int32 implement this interface. You can also implement it in your own classes to create a type-specific method that allows your objects to be sorted in arrays. This interface does not allow classes to be compared with the greater-than and less-than operators; that requires operator overloading. This interface simply provides a well-known protocol for doing comparisons of objects. (Of course, nothing prevents a C# programmer from defining overloaded comparison operations and calling CompareTo() as the implementation.)

To implement IComparable, override the CompareTo() method. This method accepts another instance of your IComparable object and returns an integer that indicates the result of the comparison. (Zero means equal, less than zero indicates that the supplied object is less than the current instance, and greater than zero indicates that the object is greater than the current instance.) Note that the actual value of the integer is irrelevant other than its positive, negative, or zero status (similar to the way strcmp works in C). Also note that because CompareTo() accepts an argument of IComparable type, care must be taken to ensure that it is a legitimate comparison—for example, myInt.CompareTo(myString) throws an ArgumentException.

```
public interface IComparable {
// Public Instance Methods
  public int CompareTo(object obj);
}
```

Implemented By Multiple types

IConvertible

System (mscorlib.dll)   interface

The IConvertible interface allows conversion of an object to basic data types and allows the conversion methods in the Convert class to use that object. When implementing the IConvertible interface, create your own type-specific methods for each of the supplied conversion methods.

Note that IConvertible allows one-way conversion from a custom type to other data types, but does not allow a conversion from a basic data type to a custom type.

```
public interface IConvertible {
// Public Instance Methods
  public TypeCode GetTypeCode( );
  public bool ToBoolean(IFormatProvider provider);
  public byte ToByte(IFormatProvider provider);
  public char ToChar(IFormatProvider provider);
  public DateTime ToDateTime(IFormatProvider provider);
  public decimal ToDecimal(IFormatProvider provider);
  public double ToDouble(IFormatProvider provider);
  public short ToInt16(IFormatProvider provider);
  public int ToInt32(IFormatProvider provider);
  public long ToInt64(IFormatProvider provider);
  public sbyte ToSByte(IFormatProvider provider);
```

```
public float ToSingle(IFormatProvider provider);
public string ToString(IFormatProvider provider);
public object ToType(Type conversionType, IFormatProvider provider);
public ushort ToUInt16(IFormatProvider provider);
public uint ToUInt32(IFormatProvider provider);
public ulong ToUInt64(IFormatProvider provider);
}
```

Implemented By   Multiple types

ICustomFormatter   CF 1.0

System (mscorlib.dll)   interface

This interface provides a custom formatter, which returns string information for supplied objects based on custom criteria. The ICustomFormatter interface contains a single Format() method. This method accepts a format string and an IFormatProvider object and uses this criteria to determine which string to return for the specified object.

```
public interface ICustomFormatter {
// Public Instance Methods
  public string Format(string format, object arg, IFormatProvider formatProvider);
}
```

IDisposable   CF 1.0, ECMA 1.0

System (mscorlib.dll)   interface

This interface provides a last-ditch cleanup hook with well-known timing semantics (similar in concept to a C++ destructor). This is called *deterministic finalization*.

As part of normal garbage-collection operation, the CLR looks for (and calls if available) the object's Finalize method right before it removes an object from heap memory. Unfortunately, because the CLR may not garbage-collect the object as soon as it becomes available for collection, objects may hold onto resources for longer than necessary. The IDisposable interface is intended to work with language constructs to let you ensure that key resources are released in a time-efficient manner.

Any object whose type implements the IDisposable interface must have a corresponding Dispose() method defined for it. This in turn makes the object eligible for use in the C# using block declaration. For more details, see "Using Statement" in Chapter 2.

If a type provides a Finalize method, then it should also inherit this interface and provide a corresponding Dispose() method. In addition, once the Dispose() method is called, part of its implementation should be to call the GC.SuppressFinalize() method to prevent the garbage collector from finalizing this object again when garbage collection occurs.

```
public interface IDisposable {
// Public Instance Methods
  public void Dispose( );
}
```

Implemented By   Multiple types

IFormatProvider

CF 1.0, ECMA 1.0

System (mscorlib.dll)   interface

This interface provides a way to retrieve an object that controls formatting through the GetFormat( ) method. For example, the System.Globalization.CultureInfo class can return a System. Globalization.NumberFormatInfo object, a System.Globalization.DateTimeFormatInfo object, or a null reference, depending on the supplied formatType parameter.

```
public interface IFormatProvider {
// Public Instance Methods
  public object GetFormat(Type formatType);
}
```

Implemented By   System.Globalization.{CultureInfo, DateTimeFormatInfo, NumberFormatInfo}

Returned By   System.IO.TextWriter.FormatProvider

Passed To   Multiple types

IFormattable

CF 1.0, ECMA 1.0

System (mscorlib.dll)   interface

This interface is implemented in your objects to provide a custom ToString( ) method that accepts a format string and an IFormatProvider instance. You can then use this information to determine how the return string should be rendered. All numeric value types in the System namespace implement this interface.

```
public interface IFormattable {
// Public Instance Methods
  public string ToString(string format, IFormatProvider formatProvider);
}
```

Implemented By   Multiple types

IndexOutOfRangeException

CF 1.0, ECMA 1.0, serializable

System (mscorlib.dll)   sealed class

This exception signals an attempt to access an index beyond the bounds of a collection or array.

```
public sealed class IndexOutOfRangeException : SystemException {
// Public Constructors
  public IndexOutOfRangeException( );
  public IndexOutOfRangeException(string message);
  public IndexOutOfRangeException(string message, Exception innerException);
}
```

Hierarchy   Object → Exception(System.Runtime.Serialization.ISerializable) → SystemException → IndexOutOfRangeException

System (mscorlib.dll)   struct

This is the value type for 16-bit integers (which can range from –32768 to 32767). This is also available in C# through the short alias.

```
public struct Int16 : IComparable, IFormattable, IConvertible {
// Public Static Fields
  public const short MaxValue;                                                            // =32767
  public const short MinValue;                                                            // =-32768
// Public Static Methods
  public static short Parse(string s);
  public static short Parse(string s, IFormatProvider provider);
  public static short Parse(string s, System.Globalization.NumberStyles style);
  public static short Parse(string s, System.Globalization.NumberStyles style, IFormatProvider provider);
// Public Instance Methods
  public int CompareTo(object value);                                                     // implements IComparable
  public override bool Equals(object obj);                                                // overrides ValueType
  public override int GetHashCode( );                                                     // overrides ValueType
  public TypeCode GetTypeCode( );                                                         // implements IConvertible
  public override string ToString( );                                                     // overrides ValueType
  public string ToString(IFormatProvider provider);                                       // implements IConvertible
  public string ToString(string format);
  public string ToString(string format, IFormatProvider provider);                        // implements IFormattable
}
```

Hierarchy   Object → ValueType → Int16(IComparable, IFormattable, IConvertible)

Returned By   Multiple types

Passed To   Multiple types

Int32

System (mscorlib.dll)   struct

This is the value type for 32-bit integers (which can range from –2,147,483,648 to 2,147,483,647). This is also available in C# through the int alias.

```
public struct Int32 : IComparable, IFormattable, IConvertible {
// Public Static Fields
  public const int MaxValue;                                                              // =2147483647
  public const int MinValue;                                                              // =-2147483648
// Public Static Methods
  public static int Parse(string s);
  public static int Parse(string s, IFormatProvider provider);
  public static int Parse(string s, System.Globalization.NumberStyles style);
  public static int Parse(string s, System.Globalization.NumberStyles style, IFormatProvider provider);
// Public Instance Methods
  public int CompareTo(object value);                                                     // implements IComparable
  public override bool Equals(object obj);                                                // overrides ValueType
  public override int GetHashCode( );                                                     // overrides ValueType
```

System

```
public TypeCode GetTypeCode( );                                              // implements IConvertible
public override string ToString( );                                            // overrides ValueType
public string ToString(IFormatProvider provider);                          // implements IConvertible
public string ToString(string format);
public string ToString(string format, IFormatProvider provider);            // implements IFormattable
}
```

Hierarchy   Object → ValueType → Int32(IComparable, IFormattable, IConvertible)

Returned By   Multiple types

Passed To   Multiple types

Int64   CF 1.0, ECMA 1.0, serializable

System (mscorlib.dll)   struct

This is the value type for 64-bit integers (which can range, approximately, from -9.22×10^{18} to 9.22×10^{18}). This is also available in C# through the long alias.

```
public struct Int64 : IComparable, IFormattable, IConvertible {
// Public Static Fields
  public const long MaxValue;                                        // =9223372036854775807
  public const long MinValue;                                        // =-9223372036854775808
// Public Static Methods
  public static long Parse(string s);
  public static long Parse(string s, IFormatProvider provider);
  public static long Parse(string s, System.Globalization.NumberStyles style);
  public static long Parse(string s, System.Globalization.NumberStyles style, IFormatProvider provider);
// Public Instance Methods
  public int CompareTo(object value);                                     // implements IComparable
  public override bool Equals(object obj);                                 // overrides ValueType
  public override int GetHashCode( );                                      // overrides ValueType
  public TypeCode GetTypeCode( );                                          // implements IConvertible
  public override string ToString( );                                        // overrides ValueType
  public string ToString(IFormatProvider provider);                      // implements IConvertible
  public string ToString(string format);
  public string ToString(string format, IFormatProvider provider);        // implements IFormattable
}
```

Hierarchy   Object → ValueType → Int64(IComparable, IFormattable, IConvertible)

Returned By   Multiple types

Passed To   Multiple types

IntPtr   CF 1.0, ECMA 1.0, serializable

System (mscorlib.dll)   struct

This is the value type used to store unmanaged pointers or handles (e.g., IntPtr objects are used in the System.IO.FileStream class to hold file handles).

Using this type allows your pointers to be platform-independent, as IntPtr is automatically mapped to a 32-bit integer on 32-bit operating systems and to a 64-bit integer on 64-bit operating systems. The IntPtr type is CLS-compliant and should be used in preference of the UIntPtr.

```
public struct IntPtr : System.Runtime.Serialization.ISerializable {
// Public Constructors
  public IntPtr(int value);
  public IntPtr(long value);
  public IntPtr(void *value);
// Public Static Fields
  public static readonly IntPtr Zero;                                          // =0
// Public Static Properties
  public static int Size{get; }
// Public Static Methods
  public static bool operator !=(IntPtr value1, IntPtr value2);
  public static bool operator = =(IntPtr value1,  IntPtr value2);
  public static explicit operator int(IntPtr value);
  public static explicit operator long(IntPtr value);
  public static explicit operator IntPtr(int value);
  public static explicit operator IntPtr(long value);
  public static explicit operator IntPtr(void *value);
  public static explicit operator Void(IntPtr value);
// Public Instance Methods
  public override bool Equals(object obj);                              // overrides ValueType
  public override int GetHashCode( );                                   // overrides ValueType
  public int ToInt32( );
  public long ToInt64( );
  public void* ToPointer( );
  public override string ToString( );                                  // overrides ValueType
}
```

Hierarchy   Object → ValueType → IntPtr(System.Runtime.Serialization.ISerializable)

Returned By   Multiple types

Passed To   Multiple types

InvalidCastException   CF 1.0, ECMA 1.0, serializable

System (mscorlib.dll)   class

This exception signals a failure during a cast or explicit conversion.

```
public class InvalidCastException : SystemException {
// Public Constructors
  public InvalidCastException( );
  public InvalidCastException(string message);
  public InvalidCastException(string message, Exception innerException);
// Protected Constructors
  protected InvalidCastException(System.Runtime.Serialization.SerializationInfo info,
    System.Runtime.Serialization.StreamingContext context);
}
```

System

Hierarchy   Object → Exception(System.Runtime.Serialization.ISerializable) → SystemException → InvalidCastException

InvalidOperationException   CF 1.0, ECMA 1.0, serializable

System (mscorlib.dll)   class

This exception indicates that a user attempted to use a method when the object was not in an appropriate state. For example, this exception is thrown if you attempt to write data with a System.Xml.XmlTextWriter that is already closed.

```
public class InvalidOperationException : SystemException {
// Public Constructors
  public InvalidOperationException( );
  public InvalidOperationException(string message);
  public InvalidOperationException(string message, Exception innerException);
// Protected Constructors
  protected InvalidOperationException(System.Runtime.Serialization.SerializationInfo info,
    System.Runtime.Serialization. StreamingContext context);
}
```

Hierarchy   Object → Exception(System.Runtime.Serialization.ISerializable) → SystemException → InvalidOperationException

Subclasses   ObjectDisposedException, System.Net.{ProtocolViolationException, WebException}

InvalidProgramException   CF 1.0, ECMA 1.0, serializable

System (mscorlib.dll)   sealed class

This exception indicates that the .NET execution engine found some invalid code or metadata in a program. This can be caused by a compiler bug that generates malformed MSIL (Microsoft Intermediate Language) instructions.

```
public sealed class InvalidProgramException : SystemException {
// Public Constructors
  public InvalidProgramException( );
  public InvalidProgramException(string message);
  public InvalidProgramException(string message, Exception inner);
}
```

Hierarchy   Object → Exception(System.Runtime.Serialization.ISerializable) → SystemException → InvalidProgramException

IServiceProvider   CF 1.0

System (mscorlib.dll)   interface

This interface defines a mechanism for retrieving a service object. A class implementing this interface provides a service object to other objects through its GetService( ) method.

```
public interface IServiceProvider {
// Public Instance Methods
  public object GetService(Type serviceType);
}
```

LoaderOptimization

serializable

System (mscorlib.dll)

enum

This enumeration is used for the LoaderOptimizationAttribute constructor. It specifies whether your application will use more than one AppDomain. Use the MultiDomain value if your application contains many domains that use the same code, and use MultiDomain-Host if your application hosts multiple domains with unique code—in which case resources are shared for globally available assemblies only. NotSpecified reverts to SingleDomain, unless the default domain or host specifies otherwise.

```
public enum LoaderOptimization {
  NotSpecified = 0,
  SingleDomain = 1,
  MultiDomain = 2,
  MultiDomainHost = 3,
  DomainMask = 3,
  DisallowBindings = 4
}
```

Hierarchy   Object → ValueType → Enum(IComparable, IFormattable, IConvertible) → LoaderOptimization

Returned By   AppDomainSetup.LoaderOptimization, LoaderOptimizationAttribute.Value

Passed To   AppDomainSetup.LoaderOptimization, LoaderOptimizationAttribute. LoaderOptimizationAttribute( )

LoaderOptimizationAttribute

System (mscorlib.dll)

sealed class

This attribute can be used only on your application's Main method. It sets the type of default optimization used to share internal resources across application domains. It is most relevant when you use the AppDomain class to create more than one domain from your application. By default, if you do not use this attribute, the .NET Framework makes optimizations with the assumption that your application has only a single domain.

```
public sealed class LoaderOptimizationAttribute : Attribute {
// Public Constructors
  public LoaderOptimizationAttribute(byte value);
  public LoaderOptimizationAttribute(LoaderOptimization value);
// Public Instance Properties
  public LoaderOptimization Value{get; }
}
```

Hierarchy	Object → Attribute → LoaderOptimizationAttribute
Valid On	Method

LocalDataStoreSlot

CF 1.0

System (mscorlib.dll)   sealed class

The CLR allocates a multislot local data store to each process when it starts. These slots are used for thread-specific and context-specific data, and are not shared between threads or contexts. The LocalDataStoreSlot class encapsulates one of these slots. It's used by the GetData( ) and SetData( ) methods in the System.Threading.Thread and System.Runtime.Remoting.Contexts.Context classes.

```
public sealed class LocalDataStoreSlot {
// Protected Instance Methods
  protected override void Finalize( );                                            // overrides object
}
```

Returned By	System.Threading.Thread.{AllocateDataSlot( ), AllocateNamedDataSlot( ), GetNamedDataSlot( )}
Passed To	System.Threading.Thread.{GetData( ), SetData( )}

MarshalByRefObject   CF 1.0, ECMA 1.0, serializable, marshal by reference

System (mscorlib.dll)   abstract class

MarshalByRefObject is the base class for objects that are marshaled by reference across AppDomain boundaries. If you attempt to transmit an object that derives from this class to another domain (e.g., as a parameter in a method call to a remote machine), an object reference is sent. (In actuality, this is an object proxy, which provides the same interface—methods, properties, and so forth.) If the other domain uses this reference (e.g., sets an object property or calls one of its methods), the call is automatically marshaled back to the original domain in which the object was created, and it is invoked there, using the proxy object the .NET Framework creates automatically.

You can inherit from this class to create a remotable object. Values that should be marshaled by reference include unmanaged pointers and file handles, which do not have any meaning in another domain. Objects that are marshaled by reference live until their lifetime lease expires. The MarshalByRefObject class includes methods for getting and setting the ILease object from the System.Runtime.Remoting.Lifetime namespace. More information about remoting can be found in the System.Runtime.Remoting namespace.

```
public abstract class MarshalByRefObject {
// Protected Constructors
  protected MarshalByRefObject( );
// Public Instance Methods
  public virtual ObjRef CreateObjRef(Type requestedType);
  public object GetLifetimeService( );
  public virtual object InitializeLifetimeService( );
}
```

Subclasses	Multiple types

System (mscorlib.dll)   sealed class

This class provides static helper functions for many trigonometric, logarithmic, and other mathematical operations, including methods for rounding numbers, getting absolute values, retrieving the largest whole divisor (Floor()), and determining the remainder (IEEERemainder()). The constants *pi* and *e* are provided as fields.

```
public sealed class Math {
// Public Static Fields
  public const double E;                                          // =2.71828182845905
  public const double PI;                                         // =3.14159265358979
// Public Static Methods
  public static decimal Abs(decimal value);
  public static double Abs(double value);
  public static short Abs(short value);
  public static int Abs(int value);
  public static long Abs(long value);
  public static sbyte Abs(sbyte value);
  public static float Abs(float value);
  public static double Acos(double d);
  public static double Asin(double d);
  public static double Atan(double d);
  public static double Atan2(double y, double x);
  public static long BigMul(int a, int b);
  public static double Ceiling(double a);
  public static double Cos(double d);
  public static double Cosh(double value);
  public static int DivRem(int a, int b, out int result);
  public static long DivRem(long a, long b, out long result);
  public static double Exp(double d);
  public static double Floor(double d);
  public static double IEEERemainder(double x, double y);
  public static double Log(double d);
  public static double Log(double a, double newBase);
  public static double Log10(double d);
  public static byte Max(byte val1, byte val2);
  public static decimal Max(decimal val1, decimal val2);
  public static double Max(double val1, double val2);
  public static short Max(short val1, short val2);
  public static int Max(int val1, int val2);
  public static long Max(long val1, long val2);
  public static sbyte Max(sbyte val1, sbyte val2);
  public static float Max(float val1, float val2);
  public static ushort Max(ushort val1, ushort val2);
  public static uint Max(uint val1, uint val2);
  public static ulong Max(ulong val1, ulong val2);
  public static byte Min(byte val1, byte val2);
  public static decimal Min(decimal val1, decimal val2);
  public static double Min(double val1, double val2);
  public static short Min(short val1, short val2);
```

System

```
public static int Min(int val1, int val2);
public static long Min(long val1, long val2);
public static sbyte Min(sbyte val1, sbyte val2);
public static float Min(float val1, float val2);
public static ushort Min(ushort val1, ushort val2);
public static uint Min(uint val1, uint val2);
public static ulong Min(ulong val1, ulong val2);
public static double Pow(double x, double y);
public static decimal Round(decimal d);
public static decimal Round(decimal d, int decimals);
public static double Round(double a);
public static double Round(double value, int digits);
public static int Sign(decimal value);
public static int Sign(double value);
public static int Sign(short value);
public static int Sign(int value);
public static int Sign(long value);
public static int Sign(sbyte value);
public static int Sign(float value);
public static double Sin(double a);
public static double Sinh(double value);
public static double Sqrt(double d);
public static double Tan(double a);
public static double Tanh(double value);
}
```

MemberAccessException

CF 1.0, ECMA 1.0, serializable

System (mscorlib.dll)   class

This is the superclass of several exceptions that indicate a failed attempt to access a class member.

```
public class MemberAccessException : SystemException {
// Public Constructors
  public MemberAccessException( );
  public MemberAccessException(string message);
  public MemberAccessException(string message, Exception inner);
// Protected Constructors
  protected MemberAccessException(System.Runtime.Serialization.SerializationInfo info,
    System.Runtime.Serialization.StreamingContext context);
}
```

Hierarchy   Object → Exception(System.Runtime.Serialization.ISerializable) → SystemException → MemberAccessException

Subclasses   FieldAccessException, MethodAccessException, MissingMemberException

MethodAccessException

ECMA 1.0, serializable

System (mscorlib.dll)   class

This exception indicates a failed attempt to access a method.

```
public class MethodAccessException : MemberAccessException {
// Public Constructors
  public MethodAccessException( );
  public MethodAccessException(string message);
  public MethodAccessException(string message, Exception inner);
// Protected Constructors
  protected MethodAccessException(System.Runtime.Serialization.SerializationInfo info,
    System.Runtime.Serialization.StreamingContext context);
}
```

Hierarchy   Object → Exception(System.Runtime.Serialization.ISerializable) → SystemException →
MemberAccessException → MethodAccessException

MissingFieldException   CF 1.0, ECMA 1.0, serializable

System (mscorlib.dll)   class

MissingMemberException indicates an attempt to access a nonexistent field.

```
public class MissingFieldException : MissingMemberException {
// Public Constructors
  public MissingFieldException( );
  public MissingFieldException(string message);
  public MissingFieldException(string message, Exception inner);
  public MissingFieldException(string className, string fieldName);
// Protected Constructors
  protected MissingFieldException(System.Runtime.Serialization.SerializationInfo info,
    System.Runtime.Serialization.StreamingContext context);
// Public Instance Properties
  public override string Message{get; }                         // overrides MissingMemberException
}
```

Hierarchy   Object → Exception(System.Runtime.Serialization.ISerializable) → SystemException →
MemberAccessException → MissingMemberException → MissingFieldException

MissingMemberException   CF 1.0, ECMA 1.0, serializable

System (mscorlib.dll)   class

This is the superclass of several exceptions that indicate an attempt to access a nonexistent member. Although the compiler detects explicit attempts of this sort, it does not protect against attempts to access nonexistent members using reflection.

```
public class MissingMemberException : MemberAccessException {
// Public Constructors
  public MissingMemberException( );
  public MissingMemberException(string message);
  public MissingMemberException(string message, Exception inner);
  public MissingMemberException(string className, string memberName);
// Protected Constructors
  protected MissingMemberException(System.Runtime.Serialization.SerializationInfo info,
    System.Runtime.Serialization.StreamingContext context);
// Protected Instance Fields
```

```
protected string ClassName;
protected string MemberName;
protected byte[ ] Signature;
// Public Instance Properties
public override string Message{get; }                                                        // overrides Exception
// Public Instance Methods
public override void GetObjectData(System.Runtime.Serialization.SerializationInfo info,
    System.Runtime.Serialization.StreamingContext context);                                  // overrides Exception
}
```

Hierarchy   Object → Exception(System.Runtime.Serialization.ISerializable) → SystemException →
                     MemberAccessException → MissingMemberException

Subclasses   MissingFieldException, MissingMethodException

MissingMethodException   CF 1.0, ECMA 1.0, serializable

System (mscorlib.dll)   class

This exception indicates an attempt to access a nonexistent method.

```
public class MissingMethodException : MissingMemberException {
// Public Constructors
  public MissingMethodException( );
  public MissingMethodException(string message);
  public MissingMethodException(string message, Exception inner);
  public MissingMethodException(string className, string methodName);
// Protected Constructors
  protected MissingMethodException(System.Runtime.Serialization.SerializationInfo info,
    System.Runtime.Serialization.StreamingContext context);
// Public Instance Properties
  public override string Message{get; }                                     // overrides MissingMemberException
}
```

Hierarchy   Object → Exception(System.Runtime.Serialization.ISerializable) → SystemException →
                     MemberAccessException → MissingMemberException → MissingMethodException

MTAThreadAttribute

System (mscorlib.dll)   sealed class

This attribute is used entirely for COM interoperability in .NET; it has no effect on a
pure .NET application or system.

This attribute can be used only on the Main method of the application. It sets the
default threading model to MTA (multithreaded apartment). Alternatively, you can
use the STAThreadAttribute attribute for a single-threaded apartment model.

```
public sealed class MTAThreadAttribute : Attribute {
// Public Constructors
  public MTAThreadAttribute( );
}
```

Valid On   Method

MulticastDelegate   CF 1.0, ECMA 1.0, serializable

System (mscorlib.dll)   abstract class

This is the base class for multicast delegates. Multicast delegates are identical to normal delegates, except that their invocation list can hold more than one method at a time. You can use Delegate.Combine( ) to add a method to the list and Delegate.Remove( ) to remove one. In C#, you can also use the + operator (or +=) to add methods. When you invoke a multicast delegate, the methods are invoked synchronously one after the other. An error in one method can prevent the delegate from calling the other methods in its list.

Multicast delegates can also be invoked asynchronously, meaning that the entire call chain is invoked serially by a single thread out of the system thread pool. If it is desirable to invoke each delegate in the chain on its own asynchronous thread instead, then use GetInvocationList( ) to obtain the list of delegates and asynchronously invoke each one.

```
public abstract class MulticastDelegate : Delegate {
// Protected Constructors
  protected MulticastDelegate(object target, string method);
  protected MulticastDelegate(Type target, string method);
// Public Static Methods
  public static bool operator !=(MulticastDelegate d1, MulticastDelegate d2);
  public static bool operator = =(MulticastDelegate d1, MulticastDelegate d2);
// Public Instance Methods
  public sealed override bool Equals(object obj);                           // overrides Delegate
  public sealed override int GetHashCode( );                                // overrides Delegate
  public sealed override Delegate[ ] GetInvocationList( );                   // overrides Delegate
  public override void GetObjectData( System.Runtime.Serialization.SerializationInfo info,
    System.Runtime.Serialization.StreamingContext context);                 // overrides Delegate
// Protected Instance Methods
  protected sealed override Delegate CombineImpl( Delegate follow);          // overrides Delegate
  protected sealed override object DynamicInvokeImpl(object[ ] args);        // overrides Delegate
  protected sealed override Delegate RemoveImpl(Delegate value);            // overrides Delegate
}
```

Hierarchy   Object → Delegate(ICloneable, System.Runtime.Serialization.ISerializable) →
                     MulticastDelegate

Subclasses   Multiple types

MulticastNotSupportedException   CF 1.0, serializable

System (mscorlib.dll)   sealed class

This exception is thrown when two uncombinable delegates are combined; see Delegate and MulticastDelegate for details regarding what constitutes *combinable* delegates.

```
public sealed class MulticastNotSupportedException : SystemException {
// Public Constructors
  public MulticastNotSupportedException( );
  public MulticastNotSupportedException(string message);
  public MulticastNotSupportedException(string message, Exception inner);
}
```

Hierarchy   Object → Exception(System.Runtime.Serialization.ISerializable) → SystemException → MulticastNotSupportedException

NonSerializedAttribute   CF 1.0

System (mscorlib.dll)   sealed class

This attribute lets you mark properties of fields in a class as nonserializable, so that they are ignored during a serialization operation. Typical examples of nonserializable data include pointers, handles, and other data structures that can't be re-created during deserialization.

By default, a class is not eligible for serialization unless it implements System.Runtime.Serialization.ISerializable or is marked with a SerializableAttribute. Once a class is marked as serializable, you must mark all fields or properties that are not to be serialized with a NonSerializedAttribute.

```
public sealed class NonSerializedAttribute : Attribute {
// Public Constructors
  public NonSerializedAttribute( );
}
```

Hierarchy   Object → Attribute → NonSerializedAttribute

Valid On   Field

NotFiniteNumberException   CF 1.0, ECMA 1.0, serializable

System (mscorlib.dll)   class

This exception is thrown when certain languages encounter floating-point infinity or NaN (not a number) values. These values can be represented in C# with Double.NegativeInfinity, Double.PositiveInfinity, and Double.NaN. (Similar fields are available in Single.)

```
public class NotFiniteNumberException : ArithmeticException {
// Public Constructors
  public NotFiniteNumberException( );
  public NotFiniteNumberException(double offendingNumber);
  public NotFiniteNumberException(string message);
  public NotFiniteNumberException(string message, double offendingNumber);
  public NotFiniteNumberException(string message, double offendingNumber, Exception innerException);
// Protected Constructors
  protected NotFiniteNumberException(System.Runtime.Serialization.SerializationInfo info,
     System.Runtime.Serialization.StreamingContext context);
// Public Instance Properties
  public double OffendingNumber{get; }
```

```
  public override void GetObjectData(System.Runtime.Serialization.SerializationInfo info,
    System.Runtime.Serialization.StreamingContext context);            // overrides Exception
}
```

Hierarchy   Object → Exception(System.Runtime.Serialization.ISerializable) → SystemException →
ArithmeticException → NotFiniteNumberException

NotImplementedException   ECMA 1.0, serializable

System (mscorlib.dll)   class

This exception signals an attempt to access an unimplemented method or operation.

Suppose you have a base class with a number of unimplemented methods. You may have reason not to mark them as abstract (perhaps you want to let programmers develop subclasses that only implement some of the base class methods). You can throw this exception in those methods, letting users of the subclass know that they are not implemented.

```
public class NotImplementedException : SystemException {
// Public Constructors
  public NotImplementedException( );
  public NotImplementedException(string message);
  public NotImplementedException(string message, Exception inner);
// Protected Constructors
  protected NotImplementedException(System.Runtime.Serialization.SerializationInfo info,
    System.Runtime.Serialization.StreamingContext context);
}
```

Hierarchy   Object → Exception(System.Runtime.Serialization.ISerializable) → SystemException →
NotImplementedException

NotSupportedException   CF 1.0, ECMA 1.0, serializable

System (mscorlib.dll)   class

This exception indicates an attempt to use an unsupported method. For example, if you try to seek on a stream that is based on unidirectional input—for example, a standard input stream from a console utility such as *sort.exe*—this exception could be thrown.

```
public class NotSupportedException : SystemException {
// Public Constructors
  public NotSupportedException( );
  public NotSupportedException(string message);
  public NotSupportedException(string message, Exception innerException);
// Protected Constructors
  protected NotSupportedException(System.Runtime.Serialization.SerializationInfo info,
    System.Runtime.Serialization.StreamingContext context);
}
```

System

Hierarchy   Object → Exception(System.Runtime.Serialization.ISerializable) → SystemException → NotSupportedException

Subclasses   PlatformNotSupportedException

NullReferenceException   CF 1.0, ECMA 1.0, serializable

System (mscorlib.dll)   class

This exception is thrown when you try to dereference a null pointer (for example, accessing an instance field on an object reference that currently points to no instance).

```
public class NullReferenceException : SystemException {
// Public Constructors
  public NullReferenceException( );
  public NullReferenceException(string message);
  public NullReferenceException(string message, Exception innerException);
// Protected Constructors
  protected NullReferenceException(System.Runtime.Serialization.SerializationInfo info,
      System.Runtime.Serialization.StreamingContext context);
}
```

Hierarchy   Object → Exception(System.Runtime.Serialization.ISerializable) → SystemException → NullReferenceException

Object   CF 1.0, ECMA 1.0, serializable

System (mscorlib.dll)   class

This class is the root of all .NET types, including value types and reference types. Some CLR languages such as C# and VB.NET do not require a type to inherit from Object explicitly. If no base type is listed in a class declaration, it is assumed that the type is to inherit from Object. Therefore, all types derive from it implicitly and can use any of its methods.

Use the GetType( ) method to obtain a description of your object's internal metadata as a Type object. Use the ToString( ) method to get a String that represents your object. By default, this is the fully qualified type name of your object, but most classes override this method to provide something more useful, such as a string representation of the object's content. For example, System.Drawing.Point.ToString( ) might return (10, 5).

The MemberwiseClone( ) method returns a new object of the same type that is a member-by-member duplicate. This object is called a shallow copy because any subobjects are not copied. Instead, the references are duplicated, meaning that both the original and cloned type refer to the same subobjects. MemberwiseClone( ) is protected, so it can be called only from methods of your derived object. Usually, you will implement the ICloneable interface for your objects and call MemberwiseClone( ) from a customized ICloneable. Clone( ) method.

Use the Equals( ) method to test for reference equality. Derived value-type classes override this method to provide value equality (which returns true for identical content, even if it is stored in different objects at different memory addresses). Note that the equality operator (== in C#, = in VB.NET) does not call Equals( ) unless the equality operator is overloaded for the appropriate type (as it is with String, for example).

The ReferenceEquals( ) method, while perhaps seeming somewhat similar, compares object identity rather than object equality. That is, while Equals( ) might return true for two independent objects that contain the same state, ReferenceEquals( ) checks to see if the two references passed to it point to the same object. These two objects are identical, which is only the case when both references point to the same location in memory. Because the == operator compares references by default, but could be changed later to compare state (or anything else), ReferenceEquals( ) is the only safe way to test references for identity.

The GetHashCode( ) method returns a hash code so the object can be used as a key in a System.Collections.Hashtable collection. By default, GetHashCode( ) returns a unique hash code for each object, which is sufficient for reference types but must be overridden by all value types so that equivalent types return identical hash codes.

```
public class Object {
// Public Constructors
  public Object( );
// Public Static Methods
  public static bool Equals(object objA, object objB);
  public static bool ReferenceEquals(object objA, object objB);
// Public Instance Methods
  public virtual bool Equals(object obj);
  public virtual int GetHashCode( );
  public Type GetType( );
  public virtual string ToString( );
// Protected Instance Methods
  protected override void Finalize( );
  protected object MemberwiseClone( );
}
```

Subclasses   Multiple types

Returned By   Multiple types

Passed To   Multiple types

ObjectDisposedException

CF 1.0, ECMA 1.0, serializable

System (mscorlib.dll)   class

This exception is thrown when certain operations are performed on an object that has been disposed. For example, trying to read from an I/O stream that has been closed by the System.IO.Stream.Close( ) method should raise this exception.

```
public class ObjectDisposedException : InvalidOperationException {
// Public Constructors
  public ObjectDisposedException(string objectName);
  public ObjectDisposedException(string objectName, string message);
// Protected Constructors
  protected ObjectDisposedException(System.Runtime.Serialization.SerializationInfo info,
    System.Runtime.Serialization.StreamingContext context);
// Public Instance Properties
  public override string Message{get; }                              // overrides Exception
  public string ObjectName{get; }
```

public override void **GetObjectData**(System.Runtime.Serialization.SerializationInfo *info*,
   System.Runtime.Serialization.StreamingContext *context*);   // overrides Exception
}

Hierarchy   Object → Exception(System.Runtime.Serialization.ISerializable) → SystemException →
                    InvalidOperationException → ObjectDisposedException

ObsoleteAttribute   **CF 1.0, ECMA 1.0, serializable**

System (mscorlib.dll)   **sealed class**

This attribute is used to mark program elements that will be removed in future versions or are no longer fully supported. The use of an element with this attribute (e. g., calling a method or setting a property marked with ObsoleteAttribute) causes a compile-time warning. You can set the Message property to supply a string to display to the user, typically specifying a workaround or the program element that should be used as a replacement. You can also use the IsError property to specify that the compiler treats the use of this element as an error. The default is **false**. These properties are set through the constructor, as in [Obsolete ("OldMethod has been replaced by NewMethod", **true**)].

```
public sealed class ObsoleteAttribute : Attribute {
// Public Constructors
  public ObsoleteAttribute( );
  public ObsoleteAttribute(string message);
  public ObsoleteAttribute(string message, bool error);
// Public Instance Properties
  public bool IsError{get; }
  public string Message{get; }
}
```

Hierarchy   Object → Attribute → ObsoleteAttribute

Valid On   Class, Struct, Enum, Constructor, Method, Property, Field, Event, Interface, Delegate

OperatingSystem   **CF 1.0, serializable**

System (mscorlib.dll)   **sealed class**

This class represents the current operating system by combining an instance of the PlatformID and Version classes. It is returned by the Environment.OSVersion property.

```
public sealed class OperatingSystem : ICloneable {
// Public Constructors
  public OperatingSystem(PlatformID platform, Version version);
// Public Instance Properties
  public PlatformID Platform{get; }
  public Version Version{get; }
// Public Instance Methods
  public object Clone( );                                    // implements ICloneable
  public override string ToString( );                        // overrides object
}
```

Returned By   Environment.OSVersion

OutOfMemoryException

System (mscorlib.dll)   class

This exception indicates that the .NET runtime has exhausted all available memory and usually means the CLR is in deep danger of dying altogether.

```
public class OutOfMemoryException : SystemException {
// Public Constructors
  public OutOfMemoryException( );
  public OutOfMemoryException(string message);
  public OutOfMemoryException(string message, Exception innerException);
// Protected Constructors
  protected OutOfMemoryException(System.Runtime.Serialization.SerializationInfo info,
    System.Runtime.Serialization.StreamingContext context);
}
```

Hierarchy   Object → Exception(System.Runtime.Serialization.ISerializable) → SystemException →
                   OutOfMemoryException

OverflowException

System (mscorlib.dll)   class

This exception indicates an attempt to store a value that exceeds the limit of the target type. This could be caused by an arithmetic operation, cast, or conversion.

```
public class OverflowException : ArithmeticException {
// Public Constructors
  public OverflowException( );
  public OverflowException(string message);
  public OverflowException(string message, Exception innerException);
// Protected Constructors
  protected OverflowException(System.Runtime.Serialization.SerializationInfo info,
    System.Runtime.Serialization.StreamingContext context);
}
```

Hierarchy   Object → Exception(System.Runtime.Serialization.ISerializable) → SystemException →
                   ArithmeticException → OverflowException

ParamArrayAttribute

System (mscorlib.dll)   sealed class

This attribute is used on a method to indicate that it can accept a variable number of parameters. The method has an array as its last parameter, and the list of values passed to the method are stored in the array. In C#, use the **params** keyword to create methods with a variable number of arguments, rather than using this attribute directly.

```
public sealed class ParamArrayAttribute : Attribute {
// Public Constructors
  public ParamArrayAttribute( );
}
```

Hierarchy	Object → Attribute → ParamArrayAttribute
Valid On	Parameter

PlatformID

System (mscorlib.dll) CF 1.0, serializable

enum

This enumerated value indicates the type of operating platform that .NET is currently running on and is returned by the OperatingSystem.Platform property. Win32Windows indicates a Windows 9x–based operating system, while Win32NT indicates an operating system based on Windows NT, including Windows 2000, XP, and .NET Server. Win32S is a layer that can run on 16-bit versions of Windows (Windows 3.x) to provide access to some 32-bit applications, and WinCE represents the Pocket PC flavor of the Win32 operating system.

```
public enum PlatformID {
    Win32S = 0,
    Win32Windows = 1,
    Win32NT = 2,
    WinCE = 3
}
```

Hierarchy	Object → ValueType → Enum(IComparable, IFormattable, IConvertible) → PlatformID
Returned By	OperatingSystem.Platform
Passed To	OperatingSystem.OperatingSystem( )

PlatformNotSupportedException

CF 1.0, serializable

System (mscorlib.dll)

class

This exception signals an attempt to access a class or member that is not available on the current platform. For example, many properties from System.Diagnostics.Process are not available on Windows 95, 98, or ME.

```
public class PlatformNotSupportedException : NotSupportedException {
// Public Constructors
    public PlatformNotSupportedException( );
    public PlatformNotSupportedException(string message);
    public PlatformNotSupportedException(string message, Exception inner);
// Protected Constructors
    protected PlatformNotSupportedException(System.Runtime.Serialization.SerializationInfo info,
        System.Runtime.Serialization.StreamingContext context);
}
```

Hierarchy	Object → Exception(System.Runtime.Serialization.ISerializable) → SystemException → NotSupportedException → PlatformNotSupportedException

Random

System (mscorlib.dll) class

This class encapsulates a *pseudorandom number* (one chosen from a list of pregenerated numbers, but that is statistically random). After creating an instance of this class, use the Next(), NextDouble(), or NextBytes() methods to return random information. NextDouble() returns a fraction value between 0.0 and 1.0, while Next() returns an integer between 0 and the maximum bound that you specify. NextBytes() fills a supplied array of bytes with random numbers.

When creating a Random object, you supply a seed value to the constructor, which determines the place on the list from where the random number is drawn. If you supply the same seed value to multiple Random instances, you will receive the same random number. Computers are incapable of generating truly random numbers, and Random should not be used for cryptographic algorithms. For a cryptographically strong random number generator, see the System.Security.Cryptography.RandomNumberGenerator in the .NET Framework SDK Documentation.

```
public class Random {
// Public Constructors
  public Random();
  public Random(int Seed);
// Public Instance Methods
  public virtual int Next();
  public virtual int Next(int maxValue);
  public virtual int Next(int minValue, int maxValue);
  public virtual void NextBytes(byte[ ] buffer);
  public virtual double NextDouble();
// Protected Instance Methods
  protected virtual double Sample();
}
```

RankException

System (mscorlib.dll) class

This exception signals an attempt to send an array of the wrong rank to a method. For example, this exception is thrown when you pass a multidimensional array to Array.Sort() or Array.Reverse().

```
public class RankException : SystemException {
// Public Constructors
  public RankException();
  public RankException(string message);
  public RankException(string message, Exception innerException);
// Protected Constructors
  protected RankException(System.Runtime.Serialization.SerializationInfo info,
    System.Runtime.Serialization. StreamingContext context);
}
```

Hierarchy   Object → Exception(System.Runtime.Serialization.ISerializable) → SystemException → RankException

ResolveEventArgs

System (mscorlib.dll)   class

This object is provided to methods with the **ResolveEventHandler** signature, indicating additional information about the reference that could not be resolved in the **Name** property.

```
public class ResolveEventArgs : EventArgs {
// Public Constructors
  public ResolveEventArgs(string name);
// Public Instance Properties
  public string Name{get; }
}
```

Hierarchy   Object → EventArgs → ResolveEventArgs

Passed To   System.Reflection.ModuleResolveEventHandler.{BeginInvoke( ), Invoke( )},
                       ResolveEventHandler.{BeginInvoke( ), Invoke( )}

ResolveEventHandler   serializable

System (mscorlib.dll)   delegate

This delegate defines the event handler that can be created to respond to **AppDomain. TypeResolve**, **AppDomain.ResourceResolve**, and **AppDomain.AssemblyResolve** events. These events are raised when the runtime cannot find a type, assembly, or resource. Use this delegate to catch that event, then find and return the assembly that contains the missing type, resource, or assembly.

```
public delegate Assembly ResolveEventHandler(object sender, ResolveEventArgs args);
```

Associated Events AppDomain.{AssemblyResolve( ), ResourceResolve( ), TypeResolve( )}

RuntimeTypeHandle   CF 1.0, ECMA 1.0, serializable

System (mscorlib.dll)   struct

This structure is a handle to the internal metadata representation of a type. The **Value** property provides an **IntPtr** reference. You can use this class with the **Type. GetTypeFromHandle( )** static method.

```
public struct RuntimeTypeHandle : System.Runtime.Serialization.ISerializable {
// Public Instance Properties
  public IntPtr Value{get; }
// Public Instance Methods
  public void GetObjectData(System.Runtime.Serialization.SerializationInfo info,
    System.Runtime.Serialization.StreamingContext context);             // implements ISerializable
}
```

Hierarchy   Object → ValueType → RuntimeTypeHandle(System.Runtime.Serialization.ISerializable)

Returned By   ArgIterator.GetNextArgType( ), Type.{GetTypeHandle( ), TypeHandle}

Passed To   ArgIterator.GetNextArg( ), Type.GetTypeFromHandle( )

System (mscorlib.dll)   struct

This structure represents an 8-bit signed integer (from −128 to 127). It is not CLS-compliant. Use Int16 instead. In C#, this type is aliased as **sbyte**.

```
public struct SByte : IComparable, IFormattable, IConvertible {
// Public Static Fields
  public const sbyte MaxValue;                                           // =127
  public const sbyte MinValue;                                           // =-128
// Public Static Methods
  public static sbyte Parse(string s);
  public static sbyte Parse(string s, IFormatProvider provider);
  public static sbyte Parse(string s, System.Globalization.NumberStyles style);
  public static sbyte Parse(string s, System.Globalization.NumberStyles style, IFormatProvider provider);
// Public Instance Methods
  public int CompareTo(object obj);                                // implements IComparable
  public override bool Equals(object obj);                         // overrides ValueType
  public override int GetHashCode( );                              // overrides ValueType
  public TypeCode GetTypeCode( );                                  // implements IConvertible
  public override string ToString( );                             // overrides ValueType
  public string ToString(IFormatProvider provider);               // implements IConvertible
  public string ToString(string format);
  public string ToString(string format, IFormatProvider provider); // implements IFormattable
}
```

Hierarchy   Object → ValueType → SByte(IComparable, IFormattable, IConvertible)

Returned By   Convert.ToSByte( ), Decimal.ToSByte( ), IConvertible.ToSByte( ), System.IO.BinaryReader.
                     ReadSByte( ), Math.{Abs( ), Max( ), Min( )}, System.Runtime.Serialization.
                     FormatterConverter.ToSByte( ), System.Runtime.Serialization.IFormatterConverter.
                     ToSByte( ), System.Runtime.Serialization.SerializationInfo.GetSByte( ), System.Xml.
                     XmlConvert.ToSByte( )

Passed To   Multiple types

SerializableAttribute

System (mscorlib.dll)   sealed class

This attribute is used in the class definition to indicate that a class can be serialized. By default, all fields in the class are serialized except for the fields that are marked with a NonSerializedAttribute.

It is not necessary to use this attribute if a given type implements the System.Runtime.Serialization.ISerializable interface, which indicates that a class provides its own methods for serialization.

```
public sealed class SerializableAttribute : Attribute {
// Public Constructors
  public SerializableAttribute( );
}
```

System

Hierarchy   Object → Attribute → SerializableAttribute

Valid On   Class, Struct, Enum, Delegate

Single   CF 1.0, ECMA 1.0, serializable

System (mscorlib.dll)   struct

This represents a 32-bit single-precision floating number as a value type. The value of a single can range approximately from -3.4×10^{38} to 3.4×10^{38}, and can also be set to one of the following fields: PositiveInfinity, NegativeInfinity, and NaN (not a number). In C#, this type is aliased as float.

public struct **Single** : IComparable, IFormattable, IConvertible {	
// Public Static Fields	
public const float **Epsilon**;	// =1.401298E-45
public const float **MaxValue**;	// =3.402823E+38
public const float **MinValue**;	// =-3.402823E+38
public const float **NaN**;	// =NaN
public const float **NegativeInfinity**;	// =-Infinity
public const float **PositiveInfinity**;	// =Infinity
// Public Static Methods	
public static bool **IsInfinity**(float *f*);	
public static bool **IsNaN**(float *f*);	
public static bool **IsNegativeInfinity**(float *f*);	
public static bool **IsPositiveInfinity**(float *f*);	
public static float **Parse**(string *s*);	
public static float **Parse**(string *s*, IFormatProvider *provider*);	
public static float **Parse**(string *s*, System.Globalization.NumberStyles *style*);	
public static float **Parse**(string *s*, System.Globalization.NumberStyles *style*, IFormatProvider *provider*);	
// Public Instance Methods	
public int **CompareTo**(object *value*);	// implements IComparable
public override bool **Equals**(object *obj*);	// overrides ValueType
public override int **GetHashCode**( );	// overrides ValueType
public TypeCode **GetTypeCode**( );	// implements IConvertible
public override string **ToString**( );	// overrides ValueType
public string **ToString**(IFormatProvider *provider*);	// implements IConvertible
public string **ToString**(string *format*);	
public string **ToString**(string *format*, IFormatProvider *provider*);	// implements IFormattable
}	

Hierarchy   Object → ValueType → Single(IComparable, IFormattable, IConvertible)

Returned By   BitConverter.ToSingle( ), Convert.ToSingle( ), Decimal.ToSingle( ), System.Diagnostics. CounterSample.Calculate( ), System.Diagnostics.CounterSampleCalculator. ComputeCounterValue( ), System.Diagnostics.PerformanceCounter.NextValue( ), IConvertible.ToSingle( ), System.IO.BinaryReader.ReadSingle( ), System.Runtime. Serialization.FormatterConverter.ToSingle( ), System.Runtime.Serialization. IFormatterConverter.ToSingle( ), System.Runtime.Serialization.SerializationInfo.GetSingle( ), System.Xml.XmlConvert.ToSingle( )

Passed To   Multiple types

StackOverflowException

System (mscorlib.dll)   sealed class

This exception indicates that the .NET runtime environment experienced a stack overflow. This can be caused by pathologically deep recursion.

```
public sealed class StackOverflowException : SystemException {
// Public Constructors
  public StackOverflowException( );
  public StackOverflowException(string message);
  public StackOverflowException(string message, Exception innerException);
}
```

Hierarchy   Object → Exception(System.Runtime.Serialization.ISerializable) → SystemException →
                     StackOverflowException

STAThreadAttribute

System (mscorlib.dll)   sealed class

This attribute can be used only on the Main method of an application. It sets the default threading model to STA (single-threaded apartment). Alternatively, you can use the MTAThreadAttribute attribute to use a multithreaded apartment model. See Chapter 17.

Like its counterpart, MTAThreadAttribute, this attribute has no meaning outside of COM interoperability.

```
public sealed class STAThreadAttribute : Attribute {
// Public Constructors
  public STAThreadAttribute( );
}
```

Hierarchy   Object → Attribute → STAThreadAttribute

Valid On   Method

String

System (mscorlib.dll)   sealed class

This class consists of an immutable array of Char characters and built-in helper functions. Methods that appear to modify a string, such as Concat( ), actually create and return a new String object. To modify a string directly, use the System.Text.StringBuilder class. This can enhance performance in some routines that make intensive use of string-manipulation operations. In C#, String is aliased as string.

A string is slightly unusual because it is a reference type that behaves like a value type for comparison and assignment operations. Two String objects with the same content but different locations in memory return true when tested for equality. Also, assigning one String to another clones the string itself, rather than just duplicating the reference.

On the other hand, a String is a fully featured object with a Length property and a wide variety of methods for the following: padding or trimming specified characters on either side, converting case, performing inline substitutions (with Replace( )), and dividing a string into an array of strings (with Split( )). There's also a default indexer that lets you retrieve a single character. Note that strings are zero-based, and the first character is string[0].

You can create a string made up of a single repeated character by using an alternate constructor and supplying a char and the number of repetitions.

```
public sealed class String : IComparable, ICloneable, IConvertible, IEnumerable {
// Public Constructors
  public String(char *value);
  public String(char *value, int startIndex, int length);
  public String(char[ ] value);
  public String(char[ ] value, int startIndex, int length);
  public String(char c, int count);
  public String(sbyte *value);
  public String(sbyte *value, int startIndex, int length);
  public String(sbyte *value, int startIndex, int length, System.Text.Encoding enc);
// Public Static Fields
  public static readonly string Empty;
// Public Instance Properties
  public int Length{get; }
  public char this[int index]{get; }
// Public Static Methods
  public static int Compare(string strA, int indexA, string strB, int indexB, int length);
  public static int Compare(string strA, int indexA, string strB, int indexB, int length, bool ignoreCase);
  public static int Compare(string strA, int indexA, string strB, int indexB, int length, bool ignoreCase,
    System.Globalization.CultureInfo culture);
  public static int Compare(string strA, string strB);
  public static int Compare(string strA, string strB, bool ignoreCase);
  public static int Compare(string strA, string strB, bool ignoreCase, System.Globalization.CultureInfo culture);
  public static int CompareOrdinal(string strA, int indexA, string strB, int indexB, int length);
  public static int CompareOrdinal(string strA, string strB);
  public static string Concat(object arg0);
  public static string Concat(params object[ ] args);
  public static string Concat(object arg0, object arg1);
  public static string Concat(object arg0, object arg1, object arg2);
  public static string Concat(object arg0, object arg1, object arg2, object arg3);
  public static string Concat(params string[ ] values);
  public static string Concat(string str0, string str1);
  public static string Concat(string str0, string str1, string str2);
  public static string Concat(string str0, string str1, string str2, string str3);
  public static string Copy(string str);
  public static bool Equals(string a, string b);
  public static string Format(IFormatProvider provider, string format, params object[ ] args);
  public static string Format(string format, object arg0);
  public static string Format(string format, params object[ ] args);
  public static string Format(string format, object arg0, object arg1);
  public static string Format(string format, object arg0, object arg1, object arg2);
  public static string Intern(string str);
  public static string IsInterned(string str);
  public static string Join(string separator, string[ ] value);
  public static string Join(string separator, string[ ] value, int startIndex, int count);
  public static bool operator !=(string a, string b);
```

```csharp
public static bool operator = =(string a, string b);
// Public Instance Methods
    public object Clone( );                                                              // implements ICloneable
    public int CompareTo(object value);                                                  // implements IComparable
    public int CompareTo(string strB);
    public void CopyTo(int sourceIndex, char[ ] destination, int destinationIndex, int count);
    public bool EndsWith(string value);
    public override bool Equals(object obj);                                             // overrides object
    public bool Equals(string value);
    public CharEnumerator GetEnumerator( );
    public override int GetHashCode( );                                                  // overrides object
    public TypeCode GetTypeCode( );                                                      // implements IConvertible
    public int IndexOf(char value);
    public int IndexOf(char value, int startIndex);
    public int IndexOf(char value, int startIndex, int count);
    public int IndexOf(string value);
    public int IndexOf(string value, int startIndex);
    public int IndexOf(string value, int startIndex, int count);
    public int IndexOfAny(char[ ] anyOf);
    public int IndexOfAny(char[ ] anyOf, int startIndex);
    public int IndexOfAny(char[ ] anyOf, int startIndex, int count);
    public string Insert(int startIndex, string value);
    public int LastIndexOf(char value);
    public int LastIndexOf(char value, int startIndex);
    public int LastIndexOf(char value, int startIndex, int count);
    public int LastIndexOf(string value);
    public int LastIndexOf(string value, int startIndex);
    public int LastIndexOf(string value, int startIndex, int count);
    public int LastIndexOfAny(char[ ] anyOf);
    public int LastIndexOfAny(char[ ] anyOf, int startIndex);
    public int LastIndexOfAny(char[ ] anyOf, int startIndex, int count);
    public string PadLeft(int totalWidth);
    public string PadLeft(int totalWidth, char paddingChar);
    public string PadRight(int totalWidth);
    public string PadRight(int totalWidth, char paddingChar);
    public string Remove(int startIndex, int count);
    public string Replace(char oldChar, char newChar);
    public string Replace(string oldValue, string newValue);
    public string[ ] Split(params char[ ] separator);
    public string[ ] Split(char[ ] separator, int count);
    public bool StartsWith(string value);
    public string Substring(int startIndex);
    public string Substring(int startIndex, int length);
    public char[ ] ToCharArray( );
    public char[ ] ToCharArray(int startIndex, int length);
    public string ToLower( );
    public string ToLower(System.Globalization.CultureInfo culture);
    public override string ToString( );                                                 // overrides object
    public string ToString(IFormatProvider provider);                                   // implements IConvertible
    public string ToUpper( );
    public string ToUpper(System.Globalization.CultureInfo culture);
```

```
  public string Trim( );
  public string Trim(params char[ ] trimChars);
  public string TrimEnd(params char[ ] trimChars);
  public string TrimStart(params char[ ] trimChars);
}
```

Returned By   Multiple types

Passed To   Multiple types

SystemException   CF 1.0, ECMA 1.0, serializable

System (mscorlib.dll)   class

This class is the base class of exceptions that represent .NET runtime errors. In contrast, ApplicationException is the base class for user-defined exceptions.

```
public class SystemException : Exception {
// Public Constructors
  public SystemException( );
  public SystemException(string message);
  public SystemException(string message, Exception innerException);
// Protected Constructors
  protected SystemException(System.Runtime.Serialization.SerializationInfo info,
    System.Runtime.Serialization.StreamingContext context);
}
```

Hierarchy   Object → Exception(System.Runtime.Serialization.ISerializable) → SystemException

Subclasses   Multiple types

ThreadStaticAttribute   serializable

System (mscorlib.dll)   class

This attribute designates that a static field should not be shared between threads. Each thread receives a separate instance of this field and can set and retrieve values for it without causing potential synchronization problems. This also means that each thread has a copy of the static field that may contain different values.

```
public class ThreadStaticAttribute : Attribute {
// Public Constructors
  public ThreadStaticAttribute( );
}
```

Hierarchy   Object → Attribute → ThreadStaticAttribute

Valid On   Field

System (mscorlib.dll) **struct**

This class encapsulates a positive or negative interval of time that can be used for arithmetic operations and greater-than or less-than comparisons. Internally, the TimeSpan is stored as a number of *ticks*, each of which is equal to 100 nanoseconds. You can convert a string into a TimeSpan using the static Parse( ) method.

You can evaluate a time span in terms of days, hours, seconds, and so on, by using the appropriate Total property. The corresponding properties that are not preceded with the word Total return only one component of the time span. (For example, the TotalHours property returns 1.5 for a time span of an hour and a half, while Hours returns 1 for a time span of one hour.)

The TimeSpan static methods prefixed with From are useful for quickly creating a time span for use as an argument for a method call, as in myApp.SetTimeSpan(TimeSpan.FromMinutes(10)).

```
public struct TimeSpan : IComparable {
// Public Constructors
   public TimeSpan(int hours, int minutes, int seconds);
   public TimeSpan(int days, int hours, int minutes, int seconds);
   public TimeSpan(int days, int hours, int minutes, int seconds, int milliseconds);
   public TimeSpan(long ticks);
// Public Static Fields
   public static readonly TimeSpan MaxValue;              // =10675199.02:48:05.4775807
   public static readonly TimeSpan MinValue;              // =-10675199.02:48:05.4775808
   public const long TicksPerDay;                         // =864000000000
   public const long TicksPerHour;                        // =36000000000
   public const long TicksPerMillisecond;                 // =10000
   public const long TicksPerMinute;                      // =600000000
   public const long TicksPerSecond;                      // =10000000
   public static readonly TimeSpan Zero;                  // =00:00:00
// Public Instance Properties
   public int Days{get; }
   public int Hours{get; }
   public int Milliseconds{get; }
   public int Minutes{get; }
   public int Seconds{get; }
   public long Ticks{get; }
   public double TotalDays{get; }
   public double TotalHours{get; }
   public double TotalMilliseconds{get; }
   public double TotalMinutes{get; }
   public double TotalSeconds{get; }
// Public Static Methods
   public static int Compare(TimeSpan t1, TimeSpan t2);
   public static bool Equals(TimeSpan t1, TimeSpan t2);
   public static TimeSpan FromDays(double value);
   public static TimeSpan FromHours(double value);
   public static TimeSpan FromMilliseconds(double value);
   public static TimeSpan FromMinutes(double value);
   public static TimeSpan FromSeconds(double value);
```

```
public static TimeSpan FromTicks(long value);
public static TimeSpan Parse(string s);
public static TimeSpan operator –(TimeSpan t);
public static TimeSpan operator –(TimeSpan t1, TimeSpan t2);
public static TimeSpan operator +(TimeSpan t);
public static TimeSpan operator +(TimeSpan t1, TimeSpan t2);
public static bool operator !=(TimeSpan t1, TimeSpan t2);
public static bool operator <(TimeSpan t1, TimeSpan t2);
public static bool operator <=(TimeSpan t1, TimeSpan t2);
public static bool operator = =(TimeSpan t1, TimeSpan t2);
public static bool operator >(TimeSpan t1, TimeSpan t2);
public static bool operator >=(TimeSpan t1, TimeSpan t2);
// Public Instance Methods
public TimeSpan Add(TimeSpan ts);
public int CompareTo(object value);                                          // implements IComparable
public TimeSpan Duration( );
public override bool Equals(object value);                                     // overrides ValueType
public override int GetHashCode( );                                           // overrides ValueType
public TimeSpan Negate( );
public TimeSpan Subtract(TimeSpan ts);
public override string ToString( );                                           // overrides ValueType
}
```

Hierarchy   Object → ValueType → TimeSpan(IComparable)

Returned By   DateTime.{Subtract( ), TimeOfDay}, System.Diagnostics.Process.{PrivilegedProcessorTime,
                   TotalProcessorTime, UserProcessorTime}, System.Diagnostics.ProcessThread.
                   {PrivilegedProcessorTime, TotalProcessorTime, UserProcessorTime}, System.Globalization.
                   DaylightTime.Delta, TimeZone.GetUtcOffset( ), System.Xml.XmlConvert.ToTimeSpan( )

Passed To   Multiple types

TimeZone   CF 1.0, serializable

System (mscorlib.dll)   abstract class

This abstract class encapsulates a time zone. You cannot create a TimeZone instance
directly because different time zones require different implementations of methods
that involve time offsets due to daylight savings time. The most useful member of the
TimeZone class is the static CurrentTimeZone property, which provides a TimeZone object based
on the localization settings of the current system.

```
public abstract class TimeZone {
// Protected Constructors
  protected TimeZone( );
// Public Static Properties
  public static TimeZone CurrentTimeZone{get; }
// Public Instance Properties
  public abstract string DaylightName{get; }
  public abstract string StandardName{get; }
// Public Static Methods
  public static bool IsDaylightSavingTime(DateTime time, System.Globalization.DaylightTime daylightTimes);
```

```
// Public Instance Methods
  public abstract DaylightTime GetDaylightChanges(int year);
  public abstract TimeSpan GetUtcOffset(DateTime time);
  public virtual bool IsDaylightSavingTime(DateTime time);
  public virtual DateTime ToLocalTime(DateTime time);
  public virtual DateTime ToUniversalTime(DateTime time);
}
```

Type

System (mscorlib.dll)   abstract class

Type is an abstract base class that encapsulates the metadata for any .NET type. You can get a Type object by using the System.Object.GetType( ) method, which is inherited by all .NET types, or by the typeof operator in C#.

The Type is used most often for reflection. You can get a complete description of an object's metadata, including information about the constructors, methods, fields, properties, and events of a class, as well as the module and the assembly in which the class is deployed by using it. Do this by using the supplied Get methods, such as GetEvents( ) and GetConstructors( ), which return arrays of the appropriate System.Reflection class. You can also use the singular methods, such as GetEvent( ), to retrieve a single type object that matches specific criteria. Note that all members can be retrieved, including inherited, private, and protected members.

```
public abstract class Type : System.Reflection.MemberInfo, System.Reflection.IReflect {
// Protected Constructors
  protected Type( );
// Public Static Fields
  public static readonly char Delimiter;                              // =0x0000002E
  public static readonly Type[ ] EmptyTypes;                          // =System.Type[ ]
  public static readonly MemberFilter FilterAttribute;               // =System.Reflection.MemberFilter
  public static readonly MemberFilter FilterName;                    // =System.Reflection.MemberFilter
  public static readonly MemberFilter FilterNameIgnoreCase;         // =System.Reflection.MemberFilter
  public static readonly object Missing;                            // =System.Reflection.Missing
// Public Static Properties
  public static Binder DefaultBinder{get; }
// Public Instance Properties
  public abstract Assembly Assembly{get; }
  public abstract string AssemblyQualifiedName{get; }
  public TypeAttributes Attributes{get; }
  public abstract Type BaseType{get; }
  public override Type DeclaringType{get; }                         // overrides System.Reflection.MemberInfo
  public abstract string FullName{get; }
  public abstract Guid GUID{get; }
  public bool HasElementType{get; }
  public bool IsAbstract{get; }
  public bool IsAnsiClass{get; }
  public bool IsArray{get; }
  public bool IsAutoClass{get; }
  public bool IsAutoLayout{get; }
  public bool IsByRef{get; }
  public bool IsClass{get; }
```

```
public bool IsCOMObject{get; }
public bool IsContextful{get; }
public bool IsEnum{get; }
public bool IsExplicitLayout{get; }
public bool IsImport{get; }
public bool IsInterface{get; }
public bool IsLayoutSequential{get; }
public bool IsMarshalByRef{get; }
public bool IsNestedAssembly{get; }
public bool IsNestedFamANDAssem{get; }
public bool IsNestedFamily{get; }
public bool IsNestedFamORAssem{get; }
public bool IsNestedPrivate{get; }
public bool IsNestedPublic{get; }
public bool IsNotPublic{get; }
public bool IsPointer{get; }
public bool IsPrimitive{get; }
public bool IsPublic{get; }
public bool IsSealed{get; }
public bool IsSerializable{get; }
public bool IsSpecialName{get; }
public bool IsUnicodeClass{get; }
public bool IsValueType{get; }
public override MemberTypes MemberType{get; }                    // overrides System.Reflection.MemberInfo
public abstract Module Module{get; }
public abstract string Namespace{get; }
public override Type ReflectedType{get; }                        // overrides System.Reflection.MemberInfo
public abstract RuntimeTypeHandle TypeHandle{get; }
public ConstructorInfo TypeInitializer{get; }
public abstract Type UnderlyingSystemType{get; }                 // implements System.Reflection.IReflect
// Public Static Methods
public static Type GetType(string typeName);
public static Type GetType(string typeName, bool throwOnError);
public static Type GetType(string typeName, bool throwOnError, bool ignoreCase);
public static Type[ ] GetTypeArray(object[ ] args);
public static TypeCode GetTypeCode(Type type);
public static Type GetTypeFromCLSID(Guid clsid);
public static Type GetTypeFromCLSID(Guid clsid,  bool throwOnError);
public static Type GetTypeFromCLSID(Guid clsid,  string server);
public static Type GetTypeFromCLSID(Guid clsid, string server, bool throwOnError);
public static Type GetTypeFromHandle(RuntimeTypeHandle handle);
public static Type GetTypeFromProgID(string progID);
public static Type GetTypeFromProgID(string progID, bool throwOnError);
public static Type GetTypeFromProgID(string progID, string server);
public static Type GetTypeFromProgID(string progID, string server, bool throwOnError);
public static RuntimeTypeHandle GetTypeHandle(object o);
// Public Instance Methods
public override bool Equals(object o);                            // overrides object
public bool Equals(Type o);
public virtual Type[ ] FindInterfaces(System.Reflection.TypeFilter filter, object filterCriteria);
```

public virtual MemberInfo[ ] **FindMembers**(System.Reflection.MemberTypes *memberType*,
   System.ReflectionSystemobject *filterCriteria*);.Reflection.MemberFilter *filter*,.BindingFlags *bindingAttr*,
public virtual int **GetArrayRank**( );
public ConstructorInfo **GetConstructor**(System.Reflection.BindingFlags *bindingAttr*, System.Reflection.Binder *binder*,
   Type[System.Reflection.ParameterModifier[ ] *modifiers*);] *types*, System.Reflection.CallingConventions *callConvention*,
public ConstructorInfo **GetConstructor**(System.Reflection.BindingFlags *bindingAttr*,
   System.Reflection.ParameterModifier[ ] *modifiers*); System.Reflection.Binder *binder*, Type[ ] *types*,
public ConstructorInfo **GetConstructor**(Type[ ] *types*);
public ConstructorInfo[ ] **GetConstructors**( );
public abstract ConstructorInfo[ ] **GetConstructors**(System.Reflection.BindingFlags *bindingAttr*);
public virtual MemberInfo[ ] **GetDefaultMembers**( );
public abstract Type **GetElementType**( );
public EventInfo **GetEvent**(string *name*);
public abstract EventInfo **GetEvent**(string *name*, System.Reflection.BindingFlags *bindingAttr*);
public virtual EventInfo[ ] **GetEvents**( );
public abstract EventInfo[ ] **GetEvents**(System.Reflection.BindingFlags *bindingAttr*);
public FieldInfo **GetField**(string *name*);
public abstract FieldInfo **GetField**(string *name*, System.Reflection.BindingFlags *bindingAttr*);
                                             // implements System.Reflection.IReflect
public FieldInfo[ ] **GetFields**( );
public abstract FieldInfo[ ] **GetFields**(System.Reflection.BindingFlags *bindingAttr*); *// implements System.Reflection.IReflect*
public override int **GetHashCode**( );   *// overrides object*
public Type **GetInterface**(string *name*);
public abstract Type **GetInterface**(string *name*, bool *ignoreCase*);
public virtual InterfaceMapping **GetInterfaceMap**(Type *interfaceType*);
public abstract Type[ ] **GetInterfaces**( );
public MemberInfo[ ] **GetMember**(string *name*);
public virtual MemberInfo[ ] **GetMember**(string *name*, System.Reflection.BindingFlags *bindingAttr*);
                                             // implements System.Reflection.IReflect
public virtual MemberInfo[ ] **GetMember**(string *name*, System.Reflection.MemberTypes *type*,
   System.Reflection.BindingFlags *bindingAttr*);
public MemberInfo[ ] **GetMembers**( );
public abstract MemberInfo[ ] **GetMembers**(System.Reflection.BindingFlags *bindingAttr*);
                                             // implements System.Reflection.IReflect
public MethodInfo **GetMethod**(string *name*);
public MethodInfo **GetMethod**(string *name*, System.Reflection.BindingFlags *bindingAttr*);
                                             // implements System.Reflection.IReflect

public MethodInfo **GetMethod**(string *name*, System.Reflection.BindingFlags *bindingAttr*,
   System.Reflection.BinderSystem. Reflection.ParameterModifier[ ] *modifiers*); *binder*,Type[ ] *types*,
   System.Reflection.CallingConventions *callConvention*,
public MethodInfo **GetMethod**(string *name*, System.Reflection.BindingFlags *bindingAttr*,
System.Reflection.Binder *binder*, Type[ ] *types*, System.Reflection.ParameterModifier[ ] *modifiers*);
                                             // implements System.Reflection.IReflect
public MethodInfo **GetMethod**(string *name*, Type[ ] *types*);
public MethodInfo **GetMethod**(string *name*, Type[ ] *types*, System.Reflection.ParameterModifier[ ] *modifiers*);
public MethodInfo[ ] **GetMethods**( );
public abstract MethodInfo[ ] **GetMethods**(System.Reflection.BindingFlags *bindingAttr*);
                                             // implements System.Reflection.IReflect
public Type **GetNestedType**(string *name*);
public abstract Type **GetNestedType**(string *name*, System.Reflection.BindingFlags *bindingAttr*);
public Type[ ] **GetNestedTypes**( );

public abstract Type[ ] **GetNestedTypes**(System.Reflection.BindingFlags *bindingAttr*);
public PropertyInfo[ ] **GetProperties**( );
public abstract PropertyInfo[ ]**GetProperties**(System.Reflection.BindingFlags *bindingAttr*);
// implements System.Reflection.IReflect

public PropertyInfo **GetProperty**(string *name*);
public PropertyInfo **GetProperty**(string *name*, System.Reflection.BindingFlags *bindingAttr*);
// implements System.Reflection.IReflect

public PropertyInfo **GetProperty**(string *name*, System.Reflection.BindingFlags *bindingAttr*,
  System.Reflection.Binder *binder*, Type *returnType*, Type[ ] *types*,
  System.Reflection.ParameterModifier[ ] *modifiers*);   *// implements System.Reflection.IReflect*
public PropertyInfo **GetProperty**(string *name*, Type *returnType*);
public PropertyInfo **GetProperty**(string *name*, Type[ ] *types*);
public PropertyInfo **GetProperty**(string *name*, Type *returnType*, Type[ ] *types*);
public PropertyInfo **GetProperty**(string *name*, Type *returnType*, Type[ ] *types*,
  System.Reflection.ParameterModifier[ ] *modifiers*);
public object **InvokeMember**(string *name*, System.Reflection.BindingFlags *invokeAttr*,
  System.Reflection.Binder *binder*, object *target*, object[ ] *args*);
public object **InvokeMember**(string *name*, System.Reflection.BindingFlags *invokeAttr*,
  System.Reflection.Binder *binder*, object *target*, object[ ] *args*, System.Globalization.CultureInfo *culture*);
public abstract object **InvokeMember**(string *name*, System.Reflection.BindingFlags *invokeAttr*,
  System.Reflection.Binder *binder*, object *target*, object[ ] *args*, System.Reflection.ParameterModifier[ ] *modifiers*
  System.Globalization.CultureInfo *culture*, string[ ] *namedParameters*);   *// implements System.Reflection.IReflect*
public virtual bool **IsAssignableFrom**(Type *c*);
public virtual bool **IsInstanceOfType**(object *o*);
public virtual bool **IsSubclassOf**(Type *c*);
public override string **ToString**( );   *// overrides object*
// Protected Instance Methods
protected abstract TypeAttributes **GetAttributeFlagsImpl**( );
protected abstract ConstructorInfo **GetConstructorImpl**(System.Reflection.BindingFlags *bindingAttr*,
  System.Reflection.Binder *binder*, System.Reflection.CallingConventions *callConvention*, Type[ ] *types*,
  System.Reflection.ParameterModifier[ ] *modifiers*);
protected abstract MethodInfo **GetMethodImpl**(string *name*,
  System.Reflection.BindingFlags *bindingAttr*, System.Reflection.Binder *binder*,
  System.Reflection.CallingConventions *callConvention*, Type[ ] *types*, System.Reflection.ParameterModifier[ ] *modifiers*);
protected abstract PropertyInfo **GetPropertyImpl**(string *name*, System.Reflection.BindingFlags *bindingAttr*,
  System.Reflection.Binder *binder*, Type *returnType*, Type[ ] *types*, System.Reflection.ParameterModifier[ ] *modifiers*);
protected abstract bool **HasElementTypeImpl**( );
protected abstract bool **IsArrayImpl**( );
protected abstract bool **IsByRefImpl**( );
protected abstract bool **IsCOMObjectImpl**( );
protected virtual bool **IsContextfulImpl**( );
protected virtual bool **IsMarshalByRefImpl**( );
protected abstract bool **IsPointerImpl**( );
protected abstract bool **IsPrimitiveImpl**( );
protected virtual bool **IsValueTypeImpl**( );
}

Hierarchy   Object → System.Reflection.MemberInfo(System.Reflection.ICustomAttributeProvider) →
                Type(System.Reflection.IReflect)

Subclasses   System.Reflection.TypeDelegator, System.Reflection.Emit.{EnumBuilder, TypeBuilder}

TypeCode

System (mscorlib.dll)   enum

This enumeration specifies the type of an object. It is available for all objects that implement the IConvertible interface. If the object does not implement this interface, use its GetType( ) method (derived from System.Object) to return an instance of the Type class, which provides a Type.GetTypeCode( ) method.

The TypeCode enumeration includes members for most simple value types. If you use this method on an object that is not explicitly represented in this enumeration, the catch-all value Object is returned.

```
public enum TypeCode {
  Empty = 0,
  Object = 1,
  DBNull = 2,
  Boolean = 3,
  Char = 4,
  SByte = 5,
  Byte = 6,
  Int16 = 7,
  UInt16 = 8,
  Int32 = 9,
  UInt32 = 10,
  Int64 = 11,
  UInt64 = 12,
  Single = 13,
  Double = 14,
  Decimal = 15,
  DateTime = 16,
  String = 18
}
```

Hierarchy   Object → ValueType → Enum(IComparable, IFormattable, IConvertible) → TypeCode

Returned By   Multiple types

Passed To   Convert.ChangeType( ), System.Runtime.Serialization.FormatterConverter.Convert( ), System.Runtime.Serialization.IFormatterConverter.Convert( )

TypeInitializationException

System (mscorlib.dll)   sealed class

This class provides a wrapper around an exception thrown by the .NET class initializer. The underlying exception is accessible through InnerException.

System

```
public sealed class TypeInitializationException : SystemException {
// Public Constructors
  public TypeInitializationException(string fullTypeName, Exception innerException);
// Public Instance Properties
  public string TypeName{get; }
// Public Instance Methods
  public override void GetObjectData(System.Runtime.Serialization.SerializationInfo info,
    System.Runtime.Serialization.StreamingContext context);                          // overrides Exception
}
```

Hierarchy   Object → Exception(System.Runtime.Serialization.ISerializable) → SystemException →
                 TypeInitializationException

TypeLoadException   CF 1.0, ECMA 1.0, serializable

System (mscorlib.dll)   class

This exception signals that a class (or its assembly) cannot be found or loaded by the
.NET runtime.

```
public class TypeLoadException : SystemException {
// Public Constructors
  public TypeLoadException( );
  public TypeLoadException(string message);
  public TypeLoadException(string message, Exception inner);
// Protected Constructors
  protected TypeLoadException(System.Runtime.Serialization.SerializationInfo info,
    System.Runtime.Serialization.StreamingContext context);
// Public Instance Properties
  public override string Message{get; }                                              // overrides Exception
  public string TypeName{get; }
// Public Instance Methods
  public override void GetObjectData( System.Runtime.Serialization.SerializationInfo info,
    System.Runtime.Serialization.StreamingContext context);                          // overrides Exception
}
```

Hierarchy   Object → Exception(System.Runtime.Serialization.ISerializable) → SystemException →
                 TypeLoadException

Subclasses   DllNotFoundException, EntryPointNotFoundException

TypeUnloadedException   ECMA 1.0, serializable

System (mscorlib.dll)   class

This exception signals an attempt to access a Type that has been unloaded.

```
public class TypeUnloadedException : SystemException {
// Public Constructors
  public TypeUnloadedException( );
  public TypeUnloadedException(string message);
  public TypeUnloadedException(string message, Exception innerException);
```

```
    protected TypeUnloadedException(System.Runtime.Serialization.SerializationInfo info,
       System.Runtime.Serialization.StreamingContext context);
}
```

Hierarchy   Object → Exception(System.Runtime.Serialization.ISerializable) → SystemException →
                     TypeUnloadedException

UInt16   CF 1.0, ECMA 1.0, serializable

System (mscorlib.dll)   struct

This structure is the value type for 16-bit unsigned integers (which range from 0 to
65,535). It is not CLS-compliant (although Int16 is). This is also available in C#
through the ushort alias.

```
public struct UInt16 : IComparable, IFormattable, IConvertible {
// Public Static Fields
  public const ushort MaxValue;                                                    // =65535
  public const ushort MinValue;                                                    // =0
// Public Static Methods
  public static ushort Parse(string s);
  public static ushort Parse(string s, IFormatProvider provider);
  public static ushort Parse(string s, System.Globalization.NumberStyles style);
  public static ushort Parse(string s, System.Globalization.NumberStyles style, IFormatProvider provider);
// Public Instance Methods
  public int CompareTo(object value);                                        // implements IComparable
  public override bool Equals(object obj);                                   // overrides ValueType
  public override int GetHashCode( );                                        // overrides ValueType
  public TypeCode GetTypeCode( );                                            // implements IConvertible
  public override string ToString( );                                        // overrides ValueType
  public string ToString(IFormatProvider provider);                          // implements IConvertible
  public string ToString(string format);
  public string ToString(string format, IFormatProvider provider);           // implements IFormattable
}
```

Hierarchy   Object → ValueType → UInt16(IComparable, IFormattable, IConvertible)

Returned By   BitConverter.ToUInt16( ), Convert.ToUInt16( ), Decimal.ToUInt16( ), IConvertible.ToUInt16( ),
                     System.IO.BinaryReader.ReadUInt16( ), System.Runtime.Serialization.FormatterConverter.
                     ToUInt16( ), System.Runtime.Serialization.IFormatterConverter.ToUInt16( ), System.Runtime.
                     Serialization.SerializationInfo.GetUInt16( ), System.Xml.XmlConvert.ToUInt16( )

Passed To   Multiple types

UInt32   CF 1.0, ECMA 1.0, serializable

System (mscorlib.dll)   struct

This structure is the value type for 32-bit unsigned integers (which range from 0 to
4,294,967,295). It is not CLS-compliant (although Int32 is). This structure is also available in C# through the uint alias.

```
public struct UInt32 : IComparable, IFormattable, IConvertible {
// Public Static Fields
  public const uint MaxValue;                                                      // =4294967295
  public const uint MinValue;                                                      // =0
// Public Static Methods
  public static uint Parse(string s);
  public static uint Parse(string s, IFormatProvider provider);
  public static uint Parse(string s, System.Globalization.NumberStyles style);
  public static uint Parse(string s, System.Globalization.NumberStyles style, IFormatProvider provider);
// Public Instance Methods
  public int CompareTo(object value);                                              // implements IComparable
  public override bool Equals(object obj);                                         // overrides ValueType
  public override int GetHashCode();                                               // overrides ValueType
  public TypeCode GetTypeCode();                                                   // implements IConvertible
  public override string ToString();                                              // overrides ValueType
  public string ToString(IFormatProvider provider);                               // implements IConvertible
  public string ToString(string format);
  public string ToString(string format, IFormatProvider provider);                // implements IFormattable
}
```

Hierarchy   Object → ValueType → UInt32(IComparable, IFormattable, IConvertible)

Returned By   BitConverter.ToUInt32( ), Convert.ToUInt32( ), Decimal.ToUInt32( ), IConvertible.ToUInt32( ),
System.IO.BinaryReader.ReadUInt32( ), System.Reflection.AssemblyAlgorithmIdAttribute.
AlgorithmId, System.Reflection.AssemblyFlagsAttribute.Flags, System.Runtime.Serialization.
FormatterConverter.ToUInt32( ), System.Runtime.Serialization.IFormatterConverter.
ToUInt32( ), System.Runtime.Serialization.SerializationInfo.GetUInt32( ), UIntPtr.ToUInt32( ),
System.Xml.XmlConvert.ToUInt32( )

Passed To   Multiple types

UInt64
CF 1.0, ECMA 1.0, serializable

System (mscorlib.dll)   struct

This structure is the value type for 64-bit unsigned integers (which range from 0 to 1.
84×10^{20}). It is not CLS-compliant (although Int64 is). This structure is also available in
C# through the ulong alias.

```
public struct UInt64 : IComparable, IFormattable, IConvertible {
// Public Static Fields
  public const ulong MaxValue;                                                     // =18446744073709551615
  public const ulong MinValue;                                                     // =0
// Public Static Methods
  public static ulong Parse(string s);
  public static ulong Parse(string s,
      IFormatProvider provider);
  public static ulong Parse(string s, System.Globalization.NumberStyles style);
  public static ulong Parse(string s, System.Globalization.NumberStyles style, IFormatProvider provider);
// Public Instance Methods
  public int CompareTo(object value);                                              // implements IComparable
  public override bool Equals(object obj);                                         // overrides ValueType
  public override int GetHashCode();                                               // overrides ValueType
```

```
public TypeCode GetTypeCode( );                                            // implements IConvertible
public override string ToString( );                                         // overrides ValueType
public string ToString(IFormatProvider provider);                          // implements IConvertible
public string ToString(string format);
public string ToString(string format, IFormatProvider provider);           // implements IFormattable
}
```

Hierarchy   Object → ValueType → UInt64(IComparable, IFormattable, IConvertible)

Returned By   BitConverter.ToUInt64( ), Convert.ToUInt64( ), Decimal.ToUInt64( ), IConvertible.ToUInt64( ),
                    System.IO.BinaryReader.ReadUInt64( ), System.IO.IsolatedStorage.IsolatedStorage.
                    {CurrentSize, MaximumSize}, System.Runtime.Serialization.FormatterConverter.ToUInt64( ),
                    System.Runtime.Serialization.IFormatterConverter.ToUInt64( ), System.Runtime.
                    Serialization.SerializationInfo.GetUInt64( ), UIntPtr.ToUInt64( ), System.Xml.XmlConvert.
                    ToUInt64( )

Passed To   Multiple types

UIntPtr   CF 1.0, ECMA 1.0, serializable

System (mscorlib.dll)   struct

This structure is provided mainly for symmetry with IntPtr. Use IntPtr, which is CLS-compliant, instead.

```
public struct UIntPtr : System.Runtime.Serialization.ISerializable {
// Public Constructors
  public UIntPtr(uint value);
  public UIntPtr(ulong value);
  public UIntPtr(void *value);
// Public Static Fields
  public static readonly UIntPtr Zero;                                              // =0
// Public Static Properties
  public static int Size{get; }
// Public Static Methods
  public static bool operator !=(UIntPtr value1, UIntPtr value2);
  public static bool operator = =(UIntPtr value1, UIntPtr value2);
  public static explicit operator uint(UIntPtr value);
  public static explicit operator ulong(UIntPtr value);
  public static explicit operator UIntPtr(uint value);
  public static explicit operator UIntPtr(ulong value);
  public static explicit operator UIntPtr(void *value);
  public static explicit operator Void(UIntPtr value);
// Public Instance Methods
  public override bool Equals(object obj);                                  // overrides ValueType
  public override int GetHashCode( );                                       // overrides ValueType
  public void* ToPointer( );
  public override string ToString( );                                       // overrides ValueType
  public uint ToUInt32( );
  public ulong ToUInt64( );
}
```

Hierarchy • Object → ValueType → UIntPtr(System.Runtime.Serialization.ISerializable)

Passed To System.Threading.Thread.{VolatileRead( ), VolatileWrite( )}

UnauthorizedAccessException

CF 1.0, ECMA 1.0, serializable

System (mscorlib.dll)   class

This exception signals a failed attempt to access a resource (for example, trying to delete a read-only file).

```
public class UnauthorizedAccessException : SystemException {
// Public Constructors
   public UnauthorizedAccessException( );
   public UnauthorizedAccessException(string message);
   public UnauthorizedAccessException(string message,
      Exception inner);
// Protected Constructors
   protected UnauthorizedAccessException(System.Runtime.Serialization.SerializationInfo info,
      System.Runtime.Serialization.StreamingContext context);
}
```

Hierarchy Object → Exception(System.Runtime.Serialization.ISerializable) → SystemException → UnauthorizedAccessException

UnhandledExceptionEventArgs

ECMA 1.0, serializable

System (mscorlib.dll)   class

This class is passed as an argument to an UnhandledExceptionEventHandler event handler. Its IsTerminating property specifies whether the CLR is in the process of shutting down.

```
public class UnhandledExceptionEventArgs : EventArgs {
// Public Constructors
   public UnhandledExceptionEventArgs(object exception, bool isTerminating);
// Public Instance Properties
   public object ExceptionObject{get; }
   public bool IsTerminating{get; }
}
```

Hierarchy Object → EventArgs → UnhandledExceptionEventArgs

Passed To UnhandledExceptionEventHandler.{BeginInvoke( ), Invoke( )}

UnhandledExceptionEventHandler

ECMA 1.0, serializable

System (mscorlib.dll)   delegate

This delegate specifies the signature for an event handler that responds to the AppDomain. UnhandledException event. This event is triggered by an exception that is not handled by the application domain.

```
public delegate void UnhandledExceptionEventHandler(object sender, UnhandledExceptionEventArgs e);
```

Uri

CF 1.0, ECMA 1.0, serializable, marshal by reference

System (system.dll)   class

This class encapsulates a complete URI (Uniform Resource Identifier) and provides various parts of it through properties. For example, you can get the Scheme (e.g., http, https, mailto) and the Port number. For http, the default port is 80, if not specified in the Uri (ftp uses port 21, https uses 443, and mailto uses 25). You can also retrieve the query-string arguments—including the initial question mark—from the Query property, or the fragment portion—including the fragment marker (#)—from the Fragment property. Some Boolean properties include IsLoopback, which indicates true if the Uri references the local host, and IsUnc, which indicates true if the Uri is a UNC path (such as \\server\folder).

The Uri constructors perform some basic cleanup of your parameters before creating a Uri, including converting the scheme and hostname to lowercase, removing default and blank port numbers, and removing the trailing slash (/). Instances of Uri have read-only properties. To modify a Uri, use a UriBuilder object.

The Uri class also provides static helper methods such as EscapeString( ), which converts a string to a valid URL by converting all characters with an ASCII value greater than 127 to hexadecimal representation. The CheckHostName( ) and CheckSchemeName( ) methods accept a string and check if it is syntactically valid for the given property (although they do not attempt to determine if a host or URI exists).

The Uri class is used by many .NET types, including some in ASP.NET, although you may find many other uses for it as a type-safe way to store and exchange URL information.

```
public class Uri : MarshalByRefObject , System.Runtime.Serialization.ISerializable {
// Public Constructors
  public Uri(string uriString);
  public Uri(string uriString, bool dontEscape);
  public Uri(Uri baseUri, string relativeUri);
  public Uri(Uri baseUri, string relativeUri, bool dontEscape);
// Protected Constructors
  protected Uri(System.Runtime.Serialization.SerializationInfo serializationInfo,
    System.Runtime.Serialization.StreamingContext streamingContext);
// Public Static Fields
  public static readonly string SchemeDelimiter;                                            // =://
  public static readonly string UriSchemeFile;                                              // =file
  public static readonly string UriSchemeFtp;                                               // =ftp
  public static readonly string UriSchemeGopher;                                            // =gopher
  public static readonly string UriSchemeHttp;                                              // =http
  public static readonly string UriSchemeHttps;                                             // =https
  public static readonly string UriSchemeMailto;                                            // =mailto
  public static readonly string UriSchemeNews;                                              // =news
  public static readonly string UriSchemeNntp;                                              // =nntp
// Public Instance Properties
  public string AbsolutePath{get; }
  public string AbsoluteUri{get; }
  public string Authority{get; }
  public string Fragment{get; }
```

```
public string Host{get; }
public UriHostNameType HostNameType{get; }
public bool IsDefaultPort{get; }
public bool IsFile{get; }
public bool IsLoopback{get; }
public bool IsUnc{get; }
public string LocalPath{get; }
public string PathAndQuery{get; }
public int Port{get; }
public string Query{get; }
public string Scheme{get; }
public string[ ] Segments{get; }
public bool UserEscaped{get; }
public string UserInfo{get; }
// Public Static Methods
public static UriHostNameType CheckHostName(string name);
public static bool CheckSchemeName(string schemeName);
public static int FromHex(char digit);
public static string HexEscape(char character);
public static char HexUnescape(string pattern, ref int index);
public static bool IsHexDigit(char character);
public static bool IsHexEncoding(string pattern, int index);
// Protected Static Methods
protected static string EscapeString(string str);
protected static bool IsExcludedCharacter(char character);
// Public Instance Methods
public override bool Equals(object comparand);                                // overrides object
public override int GetHashCode( );                                          // overrides object
public string GetLeftPart(UriPartial part);
public string MakeRelative(Uri toUri);
public override string ToString( );                                          // overrides object
// Protected Instance Methods
protected virtual void Canonicalize( );
protected virtual void CheckSecurity( );
protected virtual void Escape( );
protected virtual bool IsBadFileSystemCharacter(char character);
protected virtual bool IsReservedCharacter(char character);
protected virtual void Parse( );
protected virtual string Unescape(string path);
}
```

Hierarchy   Object → MarshalByRefObject → Uri(System.Runtime.Serialization.ISerializable)

Returned By   System.Net.Cookie.CommentUri, System.Net.HttpWebRequest.Address, System.Net.IWeb-
                    Proxy.GetProxy( ), System.Net.ServicePoint.Address, System.Net.WebProxy.{Address,
                    GetProxy( )}, System.Net.WebRequest.RequestUri, System.Net.WebResponse.ResponseUri,
                    UriBuilder.Uri, System.Xml.XmlResolver.ResolveUri( )

Passed To   Multiple types

System (system.dll)   class

Every instance of Uri is immutable. This class wraps a Uri object and allows you to modify some of its properties without needing to create a new Uri. It is analogous to the System.Text.StringBuilder class for strings.

```
public class UriBuilder {
// Public Constructors
  public UriBuilder( );
  public UriBuilder(string uri);
  public UriBuilder(string schemeName, string hostName);
  public UriBuilder(string scheme, string host, int portNumber);
  public UriBuilder(string scheme, string host, int port, string pathValue);
  public UriBuilder(string scheme, string host, int port, string path, string extraValue);
  public UriBuilder(Uri uri);
// Public Instance Properties
  public string Fragment{set; get; }
  public string Host{set; get; }
  public string Password{set; get; }
  public string Path{set; get; }
  public int Port{set; get; }
  public string Query{set; get; }
  public string Scheme{set; get; }
  public Uri Uri{get; }
  public string UserName{set; get; }
// Public Instance Methods
  public override bool Equals(object rparam);                              // overrides object
  public override int GetHashCode( );                                     // overrides object
  public override string ToString( );                                    // overrides object
}
```

UriFormatException   CF 1.0, ECMA 1.0, serializable

System (system.dll)   class

This exception indicates that you attempted to use an invalid URI, usually in the Uri constructor. For a description of the URI format, see *http://www.ietf.org/rfc/rfc2396.txt*.

```
public class UriFormatException : FormatException {
// Public Constructors
  public UriFormatException( );
  public UriFormatException(string textString);
// Protected Constructors
  protected UriFormatException(System.Runtime.Serialization.SerializationInfo serializationInfo,
    System.Runtime.Serialization.StreamingContext streamingContext);
}
```

Hierarchy   Object → Exception(System.Runtime.Serialization.ISerializable) → SystemException → FormatException → UriFormatException

System

UriHostNameType

System (system.dll)   enum

This enumeration is used for the Uri.CheckHostName( ) method. Basic indicates that the host is set, but cannot be determined.

```
public enum UriHostNameType {
  Unknown = 0,
  Basic = 1,
  Dns = 2,
  IPv4 = 3,
  IPv6 = 4
}
```

Hierarchy   Object → ValueType → Enum(IComparable, IFormattable, IConvertible) → UriHostNameType

Returned By   Uri.{CheckHostName( ), HostNameType}

UriPartial

CF 1.0, ECMA 1.0, serializable

System (system.dll)   enum

This enumeration is used for the Uri.GetLeftPart( ) method. For example, the URL *http:// www.oreilly.com/index.html#toc* has a Scheme of *http://*, an Authority of *http://www.oreilly. com*, and a Path of *http://www.oreilly.com/index.html* (everything up to, but not including, the query delimiter ? or the fragment delimiter #).

```
public enum UriPartial {
  Scheme = 0,
  Authority = 1,
  Path = 2
}
```

Hierarchy   Object → ValueType → Enum(IComparable, IFormattable, IConvertible) → UriPartial

Passed To   Uri.GetLeftPart( )

ValueType

CF 1.0, ECMA 1.0, serializable

System (mscorlib.dll)   abstract class

This is the base class for all value types. A value type is a simple data structure, such as UInt32, or an enumeration. It is differentiated from a reference type (or object). Value types are stored on the stack rather than the .NET managed heap and are accessed directly rather than through a reference. Value types also behave differently from reference types, most notably in assignment operations (which create a copy of the data, not a duplicate reference to the same data) and comparison operations (which return true as long as the content of the two value types is the same). To define your own simple value types, use the struct keyword (use the enum keyword to define an enumeration). Value types are implicitly sealed.

```
public abstract class ValueType {
// Protected Constructors
```

```
    protected ValueType( );
// Public Instance Methods
    public override bool Equals(object obj);                                              // overrides object
    public override int GetHashCode( );                                                  // overrides object
    public override string ToString( );                                                  // overrides object
}
```

Subclasses   Multiple types

Version   CF 1.0, ECMA 1.0, serializable

System (mscorlib.dll)   sealed class

This class represents a version number. The .NET framework uses it as the version of
assemblies, operating systems, and network protocols. A version number consists of as
many as four parts: a major, minor, build, and revision number. For some applications, such as the HTTP protocol, only the first two numbers (major and minor) are
used.

```
public sealed class Version : ICloneable, IComparable {
// Public Constructors
    public Version( );
    public Version(int major, int minor);
    public Version(int major, int minor, int build);
    public Version(int major, int minor, int build, int revision);
    public Version(string version);
// Public Instance Properties
    public int Build{get; }
    public int Major{get; }
    public int Minor{get; }
    public int Revision{get; }
// Public Static Methods
    public static bool operator !=(Version v1, Version v2);
    public static bool operator <(Version v1, Version v2);
    public static bool operator <=(Version v1, Version v2);
    public static bool operator = =(Version v1, Version v2);
    public static bool operator >(Version v1, Version v2);
    public static bool operator >=(Version v1, Version v2);
// Public Instance Methods
    public object Clone( );                                                       // implements ICloneable
    public int CompareTo(object version);                                        // implements IComparable
    public override bool Equals(object obj);                                      // overrides object
    public override int GetHashCode( );                                          // overrides object
    public override string ToString( );                                          // overrides object
    public string ToString(int fieldCount);
}
```

Returned By   Environment.Version, System.Net.HttpWebRequest.ProtocolVersion, System.Net.
                     HttpWebResponse.ProtocolVersion, System.Net.ServicePoint.ProtocolVersion,
                     OperatingSystem.Version, System.Reflection.AssemblyName.Version

System

Passed To   System.Net.HttpWebRequest.ProtocolVersion, OperatingSystem.OperatingSystem( ), System.
Reflection.Assembly.GetSatelliteAssembly( ), System.Reflection.AssemblyName.Version

Void   CF 1.0, ECMA 1.0, serializable

System (mscorlib.dll)   struct

This structure indicates that a method does not return any information, as in public void
Main( ). This type is available in C# through the void alias.

```
public struct Void {
// No public or protected members
}
```

Hierarchy   Object → ValueType → Void

Returned By   Multiple types

Passed To   ArgIterator.ArgIterator( ), IntPtr.IntPtr( ), System.Reflection.Pointer.Box( ), UIntPtr.UIntPtr( )

WeakReference   CF 1.0, serializable

System (mscorlib.dll)   class

This class encapsulates a *weak reference* to an object. By default, when you instantiate
a .NET class, you create a strong reference, which prevents the garbage collector from
removing the object and reclaiming memory. A weak reference, however, does not
prevent an object from being released.

Objects that are weakly referenced can still be kept alive as long as there is at least one
strong reference to them. That means a weak reference allows you to access an object
as long as it is in use by another part of your application. For example, objects can be
stored in a collection using a weak reference, but not kept alive just because they are in
the collection.

To create a weakly referenced object, pass the name of the object to the WeakReference
constructor. You can use the IsAlive property to check if the reference is valid, and the
Target property to get a reference to the actual object. Assigning the Target property to
another variable creates a strong reference.

You can set the TrackResurrection property to true in the constructor to maintain a *long*
weak reference, which tracks an object during (or after) finalization.

```
public class WeakReference : System.Runtime.Serialization.ISerializable {
// Public Constructors
  public WeakReference(object target);
  public WeakReference(object target, bool trackResurrection);
// Protected Constructors
  protected WeakReference(System.Runtime.Serialization.SerializationInfo info,
    System.Runtime.Serialization.StreamingContext context);
// Public Instance Properties
  public virtual bool IsAlive{get; }
  public virtual object Target{set; get; }
  public virtual bool TrackResurrection{get; }
```

```
// Public Instance Methods
   public virtual void GetObjectData(System.Runtime.Serialization.SerializationInfo info,
      System.Runtime.Serialization.StreamingContext context);                // implements ISerializable
// Protected Instance Methods
   protected override void Finalize( );                                                      // overrides object
}
```

Passed To   GC.GetGeneration( )

27

System.Collections

The System.Collections namespace provides basic functionality for collections of objects. It defines interfaces, base classes, and implementations for collections such as dictionaries, sorted lists, queues, and stacks. The base classes can also be extended to create specialized collection types. However, the System.Collections. Specialized namespace contains a set of extended collection types based on this namespace, so check there before creating your own types. Figures 27-1 and 27-2 show the types in this namespace.

On first observation, the design of these collections seems somewhat awkward—for example, why does a "list" seem to be broken into two pieces: the IList interface and the ArrayList implementation? On top of this, the namespace defines a number of other interfaces, such as IEnumerable and IEnumerator, that seem unnecessary.

In fact, the design of the collection types in this namespace is quite similar to the designs of other container libraries such as the STL (Standard Template Library) in C++ and the Java Collections library in JDK 1.2. By separating the interface of a collection type (the concept of "list-ness" or "dictionary-ness") from the actual implementation, you are free to assume only the absolute minimum about the actual implementation used, and instead focus only on what is needed in order to carry out the work. For example, C#'s foreach construct works by silently using the IEnumerable interface to obtain an object that inherits the IEnumerator interface. Thus, a programmer could, if desired, create a custom type (perhaps modeling a hand of cards) that acts just as any other collection class does. Alternatively, the iterator (the type that inherits from IEnumerator) could be a "smart" iterator, knowing how to walk through (or skip past) types in the container itself. All this is possible solely because the interface is separated from the implementation; it is *decoupled*.

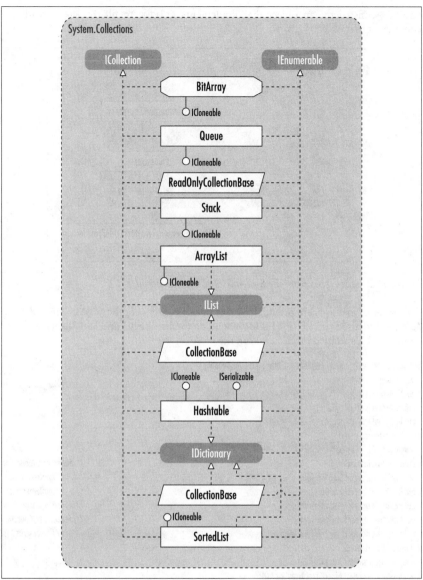

Figure 27-1. Collection types implementing ICollection and IEnumerable

ArrayList

CF 1.0, ECMA 1.0, serializable

System.Collections (mscorlib.dll)   class

This class is similar to an array, but it can grow or shrink as needed. The Capacity property returns the maximum number of elements the ArrayList can hold. You can reduce the size by setting Capacity explicitly or using the TrimToSize( ) method. An ArrayList can be constructed empty or with an integer argument that sets its initial size. You can also

System.
Collections

pass the constructor an object that implements ICollection to fill the ArrayList with the contents of that object.

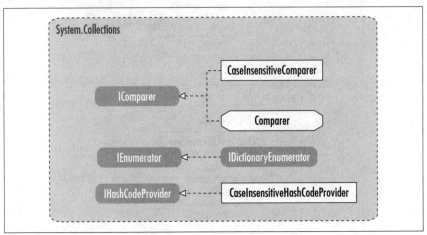

Figure 27-2. More types from the System.Collections namespace

A number of methods are provided to modify the contents of the ArrayList. The Add() and AddRange() methods add elements to the end of the list. Insert() and InsertRange() add new elements at a specified location within the list.

```
public class ArrayList : IList, ICollection, IEnumerable, ICloneable {
// Public Constructors
   public ArrayList( );
   public ArrayList(ICollection c);
   public ArrayList(int capacity);
// Public Instance Properties
   public virtual int Capacity{set; get; }
   public virtual int Count{get; }                                          // implements ICollection
   public virtual bool IsFixedSize{get; }                                        // implements IList
   public virtual bool IsReadOnly{get; }                                         // implements IList
   public virtual bool IsSynchronized{get; }                              // implements ICollection
   public virtual object SyncRoot{get; }                                  // implements ICollection
   public virtual object this[object key]{set; get; }                            // implements IList
// Public Static Methods
   public static ArrayList Adapter(IList list);
   public static ArrayList FixedSize(ArrayList list);
   public static IList FixedSize(IList list);
   public static ArrayList ReadOnly(ArrayList list);
   public static IList ReadOnly(IList list);
   public static ArrayList Repeat(object value, int count);
   public static ArrayList Synchronized(ArrayList list);
   public static IList Synchronized(IList list);
// Public Instance Methods
   public virtual int Add(object value);                                         // implements IList
   public virtual void AddRange(ICollection c);
   public virtual int BinarySearch(int index, int count, object value, IComparer comparer);
   public virtual int BinarySearch(object value);
```

```
public virtual int BinarySearch(object value, IComparer comparer);
public virtual void Clear( );                                                    // implements IList
public virtual object Clone( );                                                  // implements ICloneable
public virtual bool Contains(object item);                                       // implements IList
public virtual void CopyTo(Array array);
public virtual void CopyTo(Array array, int arrayIndex);                          // implements ICollection
public virtual void CopyTo(int index, Array array, int arrayIndex, int count);
public virtual IEnumerator GetEnumerator( );                                      // implements IEnumerable
public virtual IEnumerator GetEnumerator(int index, int count);
public virtual ArrayList GetRange(int index, int count);
public virtual int IndexOf(object value);                                        // implements IList
public virtual int IndexOf(object value, int startIndex);
public virtual int IndexOf(object value, int startIndex, int count);
public virtual void Insert(int index, object value);                             // implements IList
public virtual void InsertRange(int index, ICollection c);
public virtual int LastIndexOf(object value);
public virtual int LastIndexOf(object value, int startIndex);
public virtual int LastIndexOf(object value, int startIndex, int count);
public virtual void Remove(object obj);                                          // implements IList
public virtual void RemoveAt(int index);                                         // implements IList
public virtual void RemoveRange(int index, int count);
public virtual void Reverse( );
public virtual void Reverse(int index, int count);
public virtual void SetRange(int index, ICollection c);
public virtual void Sort( );
public virtual void Sort(IComparer comparer);
public virtual void Sort(int index, int count, IComparer comparer);
public virtual Array ToArray(Type type);
public virtual object[ ] ToArray( );
public virtual void TrimToSize( );
}
```

Returned By   CollectionBase.InnerList, ReadOnlyCollectionBase.InnerList, System.Net.WebProxy.
BypassArrayList

BitArray   CF 1.0, serializable

System.Collections (mscorlib.dll)   sealed class

This class stores a collection of bit values as Boolean types. The constructor takes many different forms of input to build the initial array, including arguments that specify the initial values and the size of the array. You can construct the BitArray with an existing array of bools, or with a byte or integer array. With an integer array, each int value becomes 32 bits of the BitArray, with the least significant bit mapped to the lowest index value (MyBitArray[0]) of the 32-bit range. A byte array uses 8 bits for each value in a similar fashion. A "bare" array can be constructed by simply providing an integer value for the number of bits in the BitArray, which are all set to false by default. Provide an additional Boolean value as a second argument to set the default values to either true or false.

The main functions of the BitArray class allow you to perform bitwise operations with two BitArrays of the same length. There are methods for And( ), Or( ), and Xor( ) that correspond to their respective bitwise operations. The Not( ) method inverts each bit value in the BitArray.

```
public sealed class BitArray : ICollection, IEnumerable, ICloneable {
// Public Constructors
  public BitArray(BitArray bits);
  public BitArray(bool[ ] values);
  public BitArray(byte[ ] bytes);
  public BitArray(int length);
  public BitArray(int[ ] values);
  public BitArray(int length, bool defaultValue);
// Public Instance Properties
  public int Count{get; }                                            // implements ICollection
  public bool IsReadOnly{get; }
  public bool IsSynchronized{get; }                                  // implements ICollection
  public int Length{set; get; }
  public object SyncRoot{get; }                                      // implements ICollection
  public bool this[int index]{set; get; }
// Public Instance Methods
  public BitArray And(BitArray value);
  public object Clone( );                                            // implements ICloneable
  public void CopyTo(Array array, int index);                        // implements ICollection
  public bool Get(int index);
  public IEnumerator GetEnumerator( );                               // implements IEnumerable
  public BitArray Not( );
  public BitArray Or(BitArray value);
  public void Set(int index, bool value);
  public void SetAll(bool value);
  public BitArray Xor(BitArray value);
}
```

CaseInsensitiveComparer

CF 1.0, serializable

System.Collections (mscorlib.dll)

class

This type provides a means for case-insensitive comparison of string objects. This class implements the IComparer.Compare( ) method. You can obtain a standard comparer that uses the System.Globalization.InvariantCulture rules for string comparisons by using the CaseInsensitiveComparer instance returned from the static DefaultInvariant property.

```
public class CaseInsensitiveComparer : IComparer {
// Public Constructors
  public CaseInsensitiveComparer( );
  public CaseInsensitiveComparer(System.Globalization.CultureInfo culture);
// Public Static Properties
  public static CaseInsensitiveComparer Default{get; }
  public static CaseInsensitiveComparer DefaultInvariant{get; }
// Public Instance Methods
  public int Compare(object a, object b);                            // implements IComparer
}
```

CaseInsensitiveHashCodeProvider

System.Collections (mscorlib.dll) class

When this object is passed to a Hashtable constructor, it overrides the GetHashCode( ) method to allow string comparison without regard to case. If you pass an instance of this type into the Hashtable constructor, you should also pass in an instance of CaseInsensitiveComparer to ensure that any comparison operations (such as sorting) are also performed in a case-insensitive fashion. You can obtain a standard provider that uses the System.Globalization.InvariantCulture rules for generating hashcodes by using the CaseInsensitiveComparer instance returned from the static DefaultInvariant property.

```
public class CaseInsensitiveHashCodeProvider : IHashCodeProvider {
// Public Constructors
  public CaseInsensitiveHashCodeProvider( );
  public CaseInsensitiveHashCodeProvider(System.Globalization.CultureInfo culture);
// Public Static Properties
  public static CaseInsensitiveHashCodeProvider Default{get; }
  public static CaseInsensitiveHashCodeProvider DefaultInvariant{get; }
// Public Instance Methods
  public int GetHashCode(object obj);                          // implements IHashCodeProvider
}
```

CollectionBase

System.Collections (mscorlib.dll) abstract class

This base collection type must be extended to create strongly typed collection objects. CollectionBase provides a modifiable collection. For a read-only collection of objects, use ReadOnlyCollectionBase. Many special collection types throughout the .NET framework derive from this class.

```
public abstract class CollectionBase : IList, ICollection, IEnumerable {
// Protected Constructors
  protected CollectionBase( );
// Public Instance Properties
  public int Count{get; }                                      // implements ICollection
// Protected Instance Properties
  protected ArrayList InnerList{get; }
  protected IList List{get; }
// Public Instance Methods
  public void Clear( );                                        // implements IList
  public IEnumerator GetEnumerator( );                         // implements IEnumerable
  public void RemoveAt(int index);                             // implements IList
// Protected Instance Methods
  protected virtual void OnClear( );
  protected virtual void OnClearComplete( );
  protected virtual void OnInsert(int index, object value);
  protected virtual void OnInsertComplete(int index, object value);
  protected virtual void OnRemove(int index, object value);
  protected virtual void OnRemoveComplete(int index, object value);
  protected virtual void OnSet(int index, object oldValue, object newValue);
```

```
protected virtual void OnSetComplete(int index, object oldValue, object newValue);
protected virtual void OnValidate(object value);
}
```

Subclasses   System.Diagnostics.{CounterCreationDataCollection, EventLogPermissionEntryCollection, PerformanceCounterPermissionEntryCollection}

Comparer   CF 1.0, ECMA 1.0, serializable

System.Collections (mscorlib.dll)   sealed class

The Comparer class is used to compare two objects of the same type. The Compare() method takes two objects. If the first object is less than the second, a negative value is returned. If the first object is greater than the second, a positive value is returned. If the objects are equal, zero is returned. The comparisons of strings are case-sensitive. For case-insensitive string comparisons, use CaseInsensitiveComparer. You can obtain a standard comparer that uses the System.Globalization.InvariantCulture rules for string comparisons by using the CaseInsensitiveComparer instance returned from the static DefaultInvariant property.

```
public sealed class Comparer : IComparer {
// Public Constructors
  public Comparer(System.Globalization.CultureInfo culture);
// Public Static Fields
  public static readonly Comparer Default;                          // =System.Collections.Comparer
  public static readonly Comparer DefaultInvariant;                 // =System.Collections.Comparer
// Public Instance Methods
  public int Compare(object a, object b);                           // implements IComparer
}
```

DictionaryBase   serializable

System.Collections (mscorlib.dll)   abstract class

This abstract base class is used to implement specialized dictionary style collections. Classes derived from DictionaryBase allow for strongly typed key and value pairs. A set of protected instance methods is defined to be overridden by derived classes. These methods allow a class to specify customized processes when functions are performed on the derived object. For example, OnSet() lets you perform a function before you set a new element in the dictionary, while OnSetComplete() lets you perform a function after a value is set.

```
public abstract class DictionaryBase : IDictionary, ICollection, IEnumerable {
// Protected Constructors
  protected DictionaryBase();
// Public Instance Properties
  public int Count{get; }                                          // implements ICollection
// Protected Instance Properties
  protected IDictionary Dictionary{get; }
  protected Hashtable InnerHashtable{get; }
// Public Instance Methods
  public void Clear();                                             // implements IDictionary
  public void CopyTo(Array array, int index);                      // implements ICollection
  public IDictionaryEnumerator GetEnumerator();                    // implements IDictionary
```

```
// Protected Instance Methods
  protected virtual void OnClear( );
  protected virtual void OnClearComplete( );
  protected virtual object OnGet(object key, object currentValue);
  protected virtual void OnInsert(object key, object value);
  protected virtual void OnInsertComplete(object key, object value);
  protected virtual void OnRemove(object key, object value);
  protected virtual void OnRemoveComplete(object key, object value);
  protected virtual void OnSet(object key, object oldValue, object newValue);
  protected virtual void OnSetComplete(object key, object oldValue, object newValue);
  protected virtual void OnValidate(object key, object value);
}
```

Subclasses   System.Diagnostics.{InstanceDataCollection, InstanceDataCollectionCollection}

DictionaryEntry   CF 1.0, ECMA 1.0, serializable

System.Collections (mscorlib.dll)   struct

This structure defines the special value type used for the elements of a dictionary collection. This type consists of a key and a value. A DictionaryEntry is retrieved by the IDictionaryEnumerator.Entry property.

```
public struct DictionaryEntry {
// Public Constructors
  public DictionaryEntry(object key, object value);
// Public Instance Properties
  public object Key{set; get; }
  public object Value{set; get; }
}
```

Hierarchy   System.Object → System.ValueType → DictionaryEntry

Returned By   IDictionaryEnumerator.Entry

Hashtable   CF 1.0, ECMA 1.0, serializable

System.Collections (mscorlib.dll)   class

A *hashtable* is an associative array (dictionary) that contains key-value pairs. Each value is identified and retrieved by a specific key that is transformed into an integer value called a *hashcode*.

A hashtable is an efficient way to store and retrieve values in memory. It uses a fast algorithm to convert a hashcode into a hash key. This hash key is used internally to determine which "bucket" a hashtable entry belongs to. Although the algorithm selects a bucket quickly, each bucket may contain more than one value. In this case, a linear search locates the desired value based on its hashcode. However, the fast bucket search offers such an advantage that a subsequent linear search has a negligible impact on the overall performance of the hashtable.

Initially, a 1-to-1 ratio of buckets to values applies (called the *load factor*). However, as more items are added to the hashtable, the load factor is changed, and each bucket ends up holding more elements. Greater load factors reduce the amount of memory required to store the hashtable, but increase lookup time.

The first argument to the Hashtable constructor gives a value for its initial size or provides an existing IDictionary whose values will fill the Hashtable. A Hashtable automatically increases its size when all buckets are full. The loadFactor argument is optionally used to specify the load factor; the default is 1.0. You can also provide references to IHashCodeProvider and IComparer instances in the constructor to provide custom hashcode and key-sorting functionality.

Keys of varying types can be used as in a regular dictionary collection. A hashing algorithm is used to convert the key into the hashcode. This is accomplished by the GetHashCode() method of each key object, which is a virtual method provided by Object. GetHashCode() can be overridden to use a custom algorithm instead of the default hashing algorithm provided by the CLR. (See CaseInsensitiveHashCodeProvider.)

The Keys and Values properties retrieve ICollection objects containing the keys and values, respectively, of the Hashtable.

The Hashtable indexer allows you to get or retrieve a value by specific key. If a key already exists, its value is overwritten. The Add() method can also add a new key and value to a Hashtable, but throws an exception if the key already exists.

```
public class Hashtable : IDictionary, ICollection, IEnumerable, System.Runtime.Serialization.ISerializable,
    System.Runtime.Serialization.IDeserializationCallback, ICloneable {
// Public Constructors
  public Hashtable( );
  public Hashtable(IDictionary d);
  public Hashtable(IDictionary d, IHashCodeProvider hcp, IComparer comparer);
  public Hashtable(IDictionary d, float loadFactor);
  public Hashtable(IDictionary d, float loadFactor, IHashCodeProvider hcp, IComparer comparer);
  public Hashtable(IHashCodeProvider hcp, IComparer comparer);
  public Hashtable(int capacity);
  public Hashtable(int capacity, IHashCodeProvider hcp, IComparer comparer);
  public Hashtable(int capacity, float loadFactor);
  public Hashtable(int capacity, float loadFactor, IHashCodeProvider hcp, IComparer comparer);
// Protected Constructors
  protected Hashtable(System.Runtime.Serialization.SerializationInfo info,
      System.Runtime.Serialization.StreamingContext context);
// Public Instance Properties
  public virtual int Count{get; }                                     // implements ICollection
  public virtual bool IsFixedSize{get; }                              // implements IDictionary
  public virtual bool IsReadOnly{get; }                              // implements IDictionary
  public virtual bool IsSynchronized{get; }                          // implements ICollection
  public virtual ICollection Keys{get; }                             // implements IDictionary
  public virtual object SyncRoot{get; }                              // implements ICollection
  public virtual object this[object key]{set; get; }                 // implements IDictionary
  public virtual ICollection Values{get; }                           // implements IDictionary
// Protected Instance Properties
  protected IComparer comparer{set; get; }
  protected IHashCodeProvider hcp{set; get; }
// Public Static Methods
  public static Hashtable Synchronized(Hashtable table);
// Public Instance Methods
  public virtual void Add(object key, object value);                 // implements IDictionary
  public virtual void Clear( );                                       // implements IDictionary
  public virtual object Clone( );                                     // implements ICloneable
```

```
public virtual bool Contains(object key);                                      // implements IDictionary
public virtual bool ContainsKey(object key);
public virtual bool ContainsValue(object value);
public virtual void CopyTo(Array array, int arrayIndex);                        // implements ICollection
public virtual IDictionaryEnumerator GetEnumerator( );                          // implements IDictionary
public virtual void GetObjectData(System.Runtime.Serialization.SerializationInfo info,
    System.Runtime.Serialization.StreamingContext context);                    // implements ISerializable
public virtual void OnDeserialization(object sender);    // implements System.Runtime.Serialization.IDeserializationCallback
public virtual void Remove(object key);                                        // implements IDictionary
// Protected Instance Methods
protected virtual int GetHash(object key);
protected virtual bool KeyEquals(object item, object key);
}
```

Returned By DictionaryBase.InnerHashtable, System.Collections.Specialized.CollectionsUtil.
CreateCaseInsensitiveHashtable( )

ICollection   CF 1.0, ECMA 1.0

System.Collections (mscorlib.dll)   interface

This interface defines the basic characteristics of collection objects and implements
three properties. Count gets the number of elements contained in a collection; IsSynchronized indicates whether the collection is thread-safe, and SyncRoot returns an object that
synchronizes access to the collection (this is the object itself if the implementing class
does not provide a Synchronized( ) method). ICollection also implements the CopyTo( ) method
for copying elements to an Array object at a specified index.

```
public interface ICollection : IEnumerable {
// Public Instance Properties
  public int Count{get; }
  public bool IsSynchronized{get; }
  public object SyncRoot{get; }
// Public Instance Methods
  public void CopyTo(Array array, int index);
}
```

Implemented By Multiple types

Returned By Multiple types

Passed To ArrayList.{AddRange( ), ArrayList( ), InsertRange( ), SetRange( )}, Queue.Queue( ), Stack.
Stack( )

IComparer   CF 1.0, ECMA 1.0

System.Collections (mscorlib.dll)   interface

This interface implements a method for comparing objects. Compare( ) determines
whether an object is greater than (positive return value), less than (negative return
value), or equal (zero) to another object. This interface is required for classes that need
to sort elements or search collections.

```
public interface IComparer {
// Public Instance Methods
  public int Compare(object x, object y);
}
```

Implemented By CaseInsensitiveComparer, Comparer

Returned By Hashtable.comparer

Passed To System.Array.{BinarySearch( ), Sort( )}, ArrayList.{BinarySearch( ), Sort( )}, Hashtable.
{comparer, Hashtable( )}, SortedList.SortedList( ), System.Collections.Specialized.
ListDictionary.ListDictionary( ), System.Collections.Specialized.NameObjectCollectionBase.
NameObjectCollectionBase( ), System.Collections.Specialized.NameValueCollection.
NameValueCollection( ), System.Xml.XPath.XPathExpression.AddSort( )

IDictionary

CF 1.0, ECMA 1.0

System.Collections (mscorlib.dll)

interface

This base interface for a collection of key/value elements defines the indexer (in C#,
the this property; in VB.NET, the property marked as Default), as well as the Keys and
Values properties that return collections containing the dictionary's keys or values,
respectively. This interface also defines the methods by which the entries may be
modified, such as Add( ), Clear( ), and Remove( ).

```
public interface IDictionary : ICollection, IEnumerable {
// Public Instance Properties
  public bool IsFixedSize{get; }
  public bool IsReadOnly{get; }
  public ICollection Keys{get; }
  public object this[object key]{set; get; }
  public ICollection Values{get; }
// Public Instance Methods
  public void Add(object key, object value);
  public void Clear( );
  public bool Contains(object key);
  public IDictionaryEnumerator GetEnumerator( );
  public void Remove(object key);
}
```

Implemented By DictionaryBase, Hashtable, SortedList, System.Collections.Specialized.{HybridDictionary,
ListDictionary}

Returned By DictionaryBase.Dictionary, System.Environment.GetEnvironmentVariables( )

Passed To Hashtable.Hashtable( ), SortedList.SortedList( ), System.Collections.Specialized.Collection-
sUtil.CreateCaseInsensitiveHashtable( ), System.Diagnostics.EventLogInstaller.{Install( ),
Rollback( ), Uninstall( )}

IDictionaryEnumerator

System.Collections (mscorlib.dll)   interface

This interface is an enumerator for Dictionary collections. It defines three read-only properties that can be obtained from the currently selected element of the collection. The Entry property gets an entry (key and value) in the form of a DictionaryEntry object. Key and Value return the key and value of the current element.

```
public interface IDictionaryEnumerator : IEnumerator {
// Public Instance Properties
  public DictionaryEntry Entry{get; }
  public object Key{get; }
  public object Value{get; }
}
```

Returned By   DictionaryBase.GetEnumerator( ), Hashtable.GetEnumerator( ), IDictionary.GetEnumerator( ),
SortedList.GetEnumerator( ), System.Collections.Specialized.HybridDictionary.
GetEnumerator( ), System.Collections.Specialized.ListDictionary.GetEnumerator( )

IEnumerable

System.Collections (mscorlib.dll)   interface

This interface exposes an enumerator to iterate over a collection. The GetEnumerator( ) method returns an IEnumerator for the object.

```
public interface IEnumerable {
// Public Instance Methods
  public IEnumerator GetEnumerator( );
}
```

Implemented By   Multiple types

IEnumerator

System.Collections (mscorlib.dll)   interface

This interface provides an enumerator to iterate over the elements of a collection. The Current property gets the current element in the iteration. MoveNext( ) advances to the next collection element. Reset( ) returns the position of the iteration to the start of the collection, just before the first element; an initial call to MoveNext( ) is necessary to retrieve the first element of the collection.

```
public interface IEnumerator {
// Public Instance Properties
  public object Current{get; }
// Public Instance Methods
  public bool MoveNext( );
  public void Reset( );
}
```

Implemented By   IDictionaryEnumerator, System.CharEnumerator, System.Globalization.
TextElementEnumerator, System.Runtime.Serialization.SerializationInfoEnumerator

IHashCodeProvider

CF 1.0, ECMA 1.0

System.Collections (mscorlib.dll)

interface

This interface implements a custom hash function to supply a hashcode to an object. Normally hashtables use System.Object.GetHashCode( ) for hash keys. However, if a Hashtable is constructed using an object that implements this interface, GetHashCode( ) can be used to provide a customized hash function. CaseInsensitiveHashCodeProvider is an example of a custom hash function.

```
public interface IHashCodeProvider {
// Public Instance Methods
  public int GetHashCode(object obj);
}
```

Implemented By   CaseInsensitiveHashCodeProvider

Returned By   Hashtable.hcp

Passed To   Hashtable.{Hashtable( ), hcp}, System.Collections.Specialized.NameObjectCollectionBase. NameObjectCollectionBase( ), System.Collections.Specialized.NameValueCollection. NameValueCollection( )

IList

CF 1.0, ECMA 1.0

System.Collections (mscorlib.dll)

interface

This interface defines the basic characteristics of an indexable collection of objects. All array and collection classes implement this interface. IList defines methods by adding an element to the end of a list (Add( )), inserting or removing an element at a specific index (Insert( ) and RemoveAt( )), or removing all elements. Remove( ) removes the first occurrence of a specific object from a list. Changing the elements of a list requires that the class be resizable and modifiable (see the IsFixedSize property). The Contains( ) method checks to see if a given value is contained in the list, while IndexOf( ) returns the index of an existing list value.

```
public interface IList : ICollection, IEnumerable {
// Public Instance Properties
  public bool IsFixedSize{get; }
  public bool IsReadOnly{get; }
  public object this[int index]{set; get; }
// Public Instance Methods
  public int Add(object value);
  public void Clear( );
  public bool Contains(object value);
  public int IndexOf(object value);
  public void Insert(int index, object value);
  public void Remove(object value);
  public void RemoveAt(int index);
}
```

Implemented By	ArrayList, CollectionBase, System.Array, System.Collections.Specialized.StringCollection, System.Diagnostics.TraceListenerCollection
Returned By	ArrayList.{FixedSize( ), ReadOnly( ), Synchronized( )}, CollectionBase.List, SortedList. {GetKeyList( ), GetValueList( )}
Passed To	ArrayList.{Adapter( ), FixedSize( ), ReadOnly( ), Synchronized( )}, System.Net.Sockets.Socket. Select( )

Queue

CF 1.0, serializable

System.Collections (mscorlib.dll) class

This class describes a collection manipulated on a first-in, first-out basis. The newest elements are added to one end with the Enqueue( ) method, and the oldest are taken off the other end with Dequeue( ). A Queue can be constructed as an empty collection or with the elements of an existing collection. The initial capacity can also be specified, although the default for an empty queue is 32. Normally, a Queue automatically increases its capacity when new elements exceed the current capacity, using a default growth factor of 2.0. (The growth factor is multiplied by the current capacity to determine the new capacity.) You may specify your own growth factor when you specify an initial capacity for the Queue.

The Dequeue( ) method returns the element at the beginning of the Queue, and simultaneously removes it. You can get the first element without removal by using Peek( ). The contents of a Queue can be copied to an existing Array object using the CopyTo( ) method. ToArray( ) creates a new Array object with the contents of the Queue.

The Queue is not threadsafe. The Synchronize( ) method provides a wrapper for thread safety.

```
public class Queue : ICollection, IEnumerable, ICloneable {
// Public Constructors
  public Queue( );
  public Queue(ICollection col);
  public Queue(int capacity);
  public Queue(int capacity, float growFactor);
// Public Instance Properties
  public virtual int Count{get; }                                    // implements ICollection
  public virtual bool IsSynchronized{get; }                          // implements ICollection
  public virtual object SyncRoot{get; }                              // implements ICollection
// Public Static Methods
  public static Queue Synchronized(Queue queue);
// Public Instance Methods
  public virtual void Clear( );
  public virtual object Clone( );                                    // implements ICloneable
  public virtual bool Contains(object obj);
  public virtual void CopyTo(Array array, int index);               // implements ICollection
  public virtual object Dequeue( );
  public virtual void Enqueue(object obj);
  public virtual IEnumerator GetEnumerator( );                      // implements IEnumerable
```

```
public virtual object Peek( );
public virtual object[ ] ToArray( );
public virtual void TrimToSize( );
}
```

ReadOnlyCollectionBase   serializable

System.Collections (mscorlib.dll)   abstract class

This abstract base class is for read-only collections, similar to CollectionBase.

```
public abstract class ReadOnlyCollectionBase : ICollection, IEnumerable {
// Protected Constructors
  protected ReadOnlyCollectionBase( );
// Public Instance Properties
  public int Count{get; }                                               // implements ICollection
// Protected Instance Properties
  protected ArrayList InnerList{get; }
// Public Instance Methods
  public IEnumerator GetEnumerator( );                                  // implements IEnumerable
}
```

Subclasses   System.Diagnostics.{ProcessModuleCollection, ProcessThreadCollection}

SortedList   serializable

System.Collections (mscorlib.dll)   class

This class is a dictionary collection in which values can be retrieved either by associated key or by index (meaning that the elements are specifically ordered). Keys are sorted based on their object type (e.g., strings are alphabetically sorted). You can override the default key comparison methods by providing your own IComparer-implementing object to the SortedList constructor.

Many methods are defined to allow you to retrieve values by either key name or index value. The IndexOfKey( ) and IndexOfValue( ) methods return the zero-based index value of the specified key or value. GetByIndex( ) and SetByIndex( ) use the index values for their functionality.

```
public class SortedList : IDictionary, ICollection, IEnumerable, ICloneable {
// Public Constructors
  public SortedList( );
  public SortedList(IComparer comparer);
  public SortedList(IComparer comparer, int capacity);
  public SortedList(IDictionary d);
  public SortedList(IDictionary d, IComparer comparer);
  public SortedList(int initialCapacity);
// Public Instance Properties
  public virtual int Capacity{set; get; }
  public virtual int Count{get; }                                       // implements ICollection
  public virtual bool IsFixedSize{get; }                                // implements IDictionary
  public virtual bool IsReadOnly{get; }                                 // implements IDictionary
  public virtual bool IsSynchronized{get; }                             // implements ICollection
  public virtual ICollection Keys{get; }                                // implements IDictionary
```

```
public virtual object SyncRoot{get; }                                         // implements ICollection
public virtual object this[object key]{set; get; }                            // implements IDictionary
public virtual ICollection Values{get; }                                      // implements IDictionary
// Public Static Methods
public static SortedList Synchronized(SortedList list);
// Public Instance Methods
public virtual void Add(object key, object value);                            // implements IDictionary
public virtual void Clear( );                                                 // implements IDictionary
public virtual object Clone( );                                               // implements ICloneable
public virtual bool Contains(object key);                                     // implements IDictionary
public virtual bool ContainsKey(object key);
public virtual bool ContainsValue(object value);
public virtual void CopyTo(Array array, int arrayIndex);                      // implements ICollection
public virtual object GetByIndex(int index);
public virtual IDictionaryEnumerator GetEnumerator( );                        // implements IDictionary
public virtual object GetKey(int index);
public virtual IList GetKeyList( );
public virtual IList GetValueList( );
public virtual int IndexOfKey(object key);
public virtual int IndexOfValue(object value);
public virtual void Remove(object key);                                       // implements IDictionary
public virtual void RemoveAt(int index);
public virtual void SetByIndex(int index, object value);
public virtual void TrimToSize( );
}
```

Returned By   System.Collections.Specialized.CollectionsUtil.CreateCaseInsensitiveSortedList( )

Stack   CF 1.0, serializable

System.Collections (mscorlib.dll)   class

This class implements a collection of objects manipulated in a last-in, first-out manner. The primary methods of a Stack are Push( ) and Pop( ). Push( ) adds an element to the top of a stack and Pop( ) removes the top element from the stack. Peek( ) returns the top element without removing it from the stack.

```
public class Stack : ICollection, IEnumerable, ICloneable {
// Public Constructors
public Stack( );
public Stack(ICollection col);
public Stack(int initialCapacity);
// Public Instance Properties
public virtual int Count{get; }                                              // implements ICollection
public virtual bool IsSynchronized{get; }                                    // implements ICollection
public virtual object SyncRoot{get; }                                        // implements ICollection
// Public Static Methods
public static Stack Synchronized(Stack stack);
// Public Instance Methods
public virtual void Clear( );
public virtual object Clone( );                                              // implements ICloneable
```

```
public virtual bool Contains(object obj);
public virtual void CopyTo(Array array, int index);                          // implements ICollection
public virtual IEnumerator GetEnumerator( );                                 // implements IEnumerable
public virtual object Peek( );
public virtual object Pop( );
public virtual void Push(object obj);
public virtual object[ ] ToArray( );
}
```

System.Collections.
Specialized

The types defined in the System.Collections namespace are fine as general-purpose collection types, but frequently programmers require specialized semantics around a collection class; for example, a collection of booleans could be more efficiently stored as a single System.Int64, whereas simply placing System.Boolean instances into a general-purpose collection is far more wasteful, in both memory and processing time.

Additionally, programmers often grow frustrated with the lack of type-safety in the general-purpose containers; not only does a programmer have to typecast any object obtained out of the container, but the container itself holds no intrinsic logic to "screen out" unwanted types being inserted into the container. (This is in marked contrast to C++ template-based collections such as the STL, in which the attempt to put a string into a container of integers causes a compile-time error.)

Container specialization isn't limited to storage type; at times, a programmer desires different processing behavior than the general-purpose container provides. As an example, consider the System.Collections.IDictionary interface. Note that it clearly defines a mapping of keys to values; however, it is only implicitly understood that the exact same key must be produced to obtain the value desired. In most cases, this is exactly what's needed; however, there are times when a less stringent retrieval mechanism is preferred. For example, perhaps a case-insensitive match is wanted instead of doing an exact match for a string key. The System.Collections.Specialized namespace includes collections designed to address these cases. Figure 28-1 shows the types in this namespace.

BitVector32   CF 1.0

System.Collections.Specialized (system.dll)   struct

This structure defines a lightweight bit vector that can store booleans and 16-bit integers in a 32-bit structure. Sections hold single 16-bit integer values and are the building blocks of a BitVector32. Sections are created with CreateSection(). Each section is

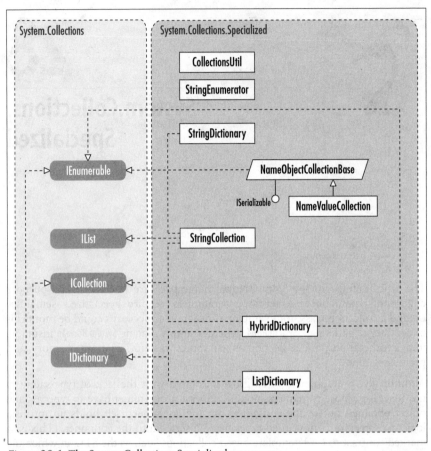

Figure 28-1. The System.Collections.Specialized namespace

constructed with a maximum value for the integer it can hold. Except for the initial section, each subsequent section must provide a reference to the previous section in addition to the maximum value.

The indexer takes two forms. When indexed by a section name, that section's value can be set or retrieved. When indexed by an integer that specifies a bit in the vector, you can determine whether that bit is set or not (**true** or **false**).

```
public struct BitVector32 {
// Public Constructors
  public BitVector32(BitVector32 value);
  public BitVector32(int data);
// Public Instance Properties
  public int Data{get; }
  public int this(Section section)){set; get; }
  public bool this[int bit]{set; get; }
// Public Static Methods
  public static int CreateMask( );
  public static int CreateMask(int previous);
```

```
public static Section CreateSection(short maxValue);
public static Section CreateSection(short maxValue, Section previous);
public static string ToString(BitVector32 value);
// Public Instance Methods
public override bool Equals(object o);                                    // overrides ValueType
public override int GetHashCode( );                                       // overrides ValueType
public override string ToString( );                                      // overrides ValueType
}
```

Hierarchy   System.Object → System.ValueType → BitVector32

BitVector32.Section   CF 1.0

System.Collections.Specialized (system.dll)   struct

This structure represents a section of a bit vector that holds a single integer value. A
BitVector32.Section instance is created by the BitVector32.CreateSection( ) method, which specifies the maximum value the Section can hold, and references the preceding Section, unless
it is the first Section in the vector.

```
public struct BitVector32.Section {
// Public Instance Properties
public short Mask{get; }
public short Offset{get; }
// Public Static Methods
public static string ToString(Section value);
// Public Instance Methods
public override bool Equals(object o);                                    // overrides ValueType
public override int GetHashCode( );                                       // overrides ValueType
public override string ToString( );                                      // overrides ValueType
}
```

Hierarchy   System.Object → System.ValueType → Section

CollectionsUtil

System.Collections.Specialized (system.dll)   class

This class defines static methods to create special collections in which keys are sorted
without respect to case. CreateCaseInsensitiveHashtable( ) creates a Hashtable, and
CreateCaseInsensitiveSortedList( ) creates a System.Collections.SortedList.

```
public class CollectionsUtil {
// Public Constructors
public CollectionsUtil( );
// Public Static Methods
public static Hashtable CreateCaseInsensitiveHashtable( );
public static Hashtable CreateCaseInsensitiveHashtable(System.Collections.IDictionary d);
public static Hashtable CreateCaseInsensitiveHashtable(int capacity);
public static SortedList CreateCaseInsensitiveSortedList( );
}
```

HybridDictionary

System.Collections.Specialized (system.dll)   class

This class implements a standard dictionary collection with built-in capability for case-insensitive key comparison. Case-insensitivity can be specified during construction with a Boolean argument.

```
public class HybridDictionary : IDictionary, ICollection, IEnumerable {
// Public Constructors
  public HybridDictionary( );
  public HybridDictionary(bool caseInsensitive);
  public HybridDictionary(int initialSize);
  public HybridDictionary(int initialSize, bool caseInsensitive);
// Public Instance Properties
  public int Count{get; }                                   // implements ICollection
  public bool IsFixedSize{get; }                  // implements System.Collections.IDictionary
  public bool IsReadOnly{get; }                   // implements System.Collections.IDictionary
  public bool IsSynchronized{get; }                         // implements ICollection
  public ICollection Keys{get; }                  // implements System.Collections.IDictionary
  public object SyncRoot{get; }                             // implements ICollection
  public object this[object key]{set; get; }      // implements System.Collections.IDictionary
  public ICollection Values{get; }                // implements System.Collections.IDictionary
// Public Instance Methods
  public void Add(object key, object value);      // implements System.Collections.IDictionary
  public void Clear( );                           // implements System.Collections.IDictionary
  public bool Contains(object key);               // implements System.Collections.IDictionary
  public void CopyTo(Array array, int index);               // implements ICollection
  public IDictionaryEnumerator GetEnumerator( );  // implements System.Collections.IDictionary
  public void Remove(object key);                 // implements System.Collections.IDictionary
}
```

ListDictionary

System.Collections.Specialized (system.dll)   class

This class is a simple implementation of a dictionary collection (System.Collections.IDictionary) for small lists. It implements the IDictionary methods and properties, and it is suggested for use with a small number of elements (less than 10). The overloaded constructor can optionally pass an System.Collections.IComparer reference, which may be used for case-insensitive key comparison or other special key type conversions.

```
public class ListDictionary : IDictionary, ICollection, IEnumerable {
// Public Constructors
  public ListDictionary( );
  public ListDictionary(System.Collections.IComparer comparer);
// Public Instance Properties
  public int Count{get; }                                   // implements ICollection
  public bool IsFixedSize{get; }                  // implements System.Collections.IDictionary
  public bool IsReadOnly{get; }                   // implements System.Collections.IDictionary
  public bool IsSynchronized{get; }                         // implements ICollection
  public ICollection Keys{get; }                  // implements System.Collections.IDictionary
  public object SyncRoot{get; }                             // implements ICollection
```

public object **this**[object *key*]{set; get; }	// implements System.Collections.IDictionary
public ICollection **Values**{get; }	// implements System.Collections.IDictionary
// Public Instance Methods	
public void **Add**(object *key*, object *value*);	// implements System.Collections.IDictionary
public void **Clear**( );	// implements System.Collections.IDictionary
public bool **Contains**(object *key*);	// implements System.Collections.IDictionary
public void **CopyTo**(Array *array*, int *index*);	// implements ICollection
public IDictionaryEnumerator **GetEnumerator**( );	// implements System.Collections.IDictionary
public void **Remove**(object *key*);	// implements System.Collections.IDictionary

}

NameObjectCollectionBase
CF 1.0, serializable

System.Collections.Specialized (system.dll)   abstract class

This abstract base class is for a hashtable-based collection of key/value pairs, in which
the key is specifically typed as a string. This class defines methods to be overridden by
derived classes that allow for special comparing and sorting of key strings.

public abstract class **NameObjectCollectionBase** : ICollection, IEnumerable, System.Runtime.Serialization.ISerializable,
System.Runtime.Serialization.IDeserializationCallback {
// Protected Constructors
  protected **NameObjectCollectionBase**( );
  protected **NameObjectCollectionBase**(System.Collections.IHashCodeProvider *hashProvider*,
    System.Collections.IComparer *comparer*);
  protected **NameObjectCollectionBase**(int *capacity*);
  protected **NameObjectCollectionBase**(int *capacity*, System.Collections.IHashCodeProvider *hashProvider*,
    System.Collections.IComparer *comparer*);
  protected **NameObjectCollectionBase**(System.Runtime.Serialization.SerializationInfo *info*,
    System.Runtime.Serialization.StreamingContext *context*);
// Public Instance Properties
  public virtual int **Count**{get; }   // implements ICollection
  public virtual KeysCollection **Keys**{get; }
// Protected Instance Properties
  protected bool **IsReadOnly**{set; get; }
// Public Instance Methods
  public IEnumerator **GetEnumerator**( );   // implements IEnumerable
  public virtual void **GetObjectData**(System.Runtime.Serialization.SerializationInfo *info*,
    System.Runtime.Serialization.StreamingContext *context*);   // implements ISerializable
  public virtual void **OnDeserialization**(object *sender*);   // implements System.Runtime.Serialization.IDeserializationCallback
// Protected Instance Methods
  protected void **BaseAdd**(string *name*, object *value*);
  protected void **BaseClear**( );
  protected object **BaseGet**(int *index*);
  protected object **BaseGet**(string *name*);
  protected string[ ] **BaseGetAllKeys**( );
  protected object[ ] **BaseGetAllValues**( );
  protected object[ ] **BaseGetAllValues**(Type *type*);
  protected string **BaseGetKey**(int *index*);
  protected bool **BaseHasKeys**( );
  protected void **BaseRemove**(string *name*);
  protected void **BaseRemoveAt**(int *index*);

```
protected void BaseSet(int index, object value);
protected void BaseSet(string name, object value);
}
```

Subclasses   NameValueCollection

NameObjectCollectionBase.KeysCollection

CF 1.0, serializable

System.Collections.Specialized (system.dll)   class

This class is a collection of key strings retrieved by the NameObjectCollectionBase.Keys property.

```
public class NameObjectCollectionBase.KeysCollection : ICollection, IEnumerable {
// Public Instance Properties
    public int Count{get; }                                      // implements ICollection
    public string this[int index]{get; }
// Public Instance Methods
    public virtual string Get(int index);
    public IEnumerator GetEnumerator( );                          // implements IEnumerable
}
```

NameValueCollection

CF 1.0, ECMA 1.0, serializable

System.Collections.Specialized (system.dll)   class

This class is a collection of keys and associated values composed of strings in which a single key may have multiple values associated with it. A multivalued entry is stored as a comma-separated list of the string values. Use the Add() method to append new values to existing values of a key. Using Set() or setting the value by key name overwrites the existing value. You can use a string containing a comma-separated list to assign multiple values to a key.

The GetValues() method returns a string array containing all the values of the specified key (or index). An example of how this class is used is System.Net.WebHeaderCollection, which derives from it. A WebHeaderCollection contains the collection of various HTTP header names as key strings and their values. HTTP headers such as Accept: often have multiple values (for example, MIME types for Accept).

```
public class NameValueCollection : NameObjectCollectionBase {
// Public Constructors
    public NameValueCollection( );
    public NameValueCollection(System.Collections.IHashCodeProvider hashProvider,
        System.Collections.IComparer comparer);
    public NameValueCollection(int capacity);
    public NameValueCollection(int capacity, System.Collections.IHashCodeProvider hashProvider,
        System.Collections.IComparer comparer);
    public NameValueCollection(int capacity, NameValueCollection col);
    public NameValueCollection(NameValueCollection col);
// Protected Constructors
    protected NameValueCollection(System.Runtime.Serialization.SerializationInfo info,
        System.Runtime.Serialization.StreamingContext context);
// Public Instance Properties
    public virtual string[ ] AllKeys{get; }
```

```
   public string this[int index]{get; }
   public string this[string name]{set; get; }
// Public Instance Methods
   public void Add(NameValueCollection c);
   public virtual void Add(string name, string value);
   public void Clear( );
   public void CopyTo(Array dest, int index);                              // implements ICollection
   public virtual string Get(int index);
   public virtual string Get(string name);
   public virtual string GetKey(int index);
   public virtual string[ ] GetValues(int index);
   public virtual string[ ] GetValues(string name);
   public bool HasKeys( );
   public virtual void Remove(string name);
   public virtual void Set(string name, string value);
// Protected Instance Methods
   protected void InvalidateCachedArrays( );
}
```

Hierarchy	System.Object → NameObjectCollectionBase(System.Collections.ICollection, System. Collections.IEnumerable, System.Runtime.Serialization.ISerializable, System.Runtime. Serialization.IDeserializationCallback) → NameValueCollection
Subclasses	System.Net.WebHeaderCollection
Returned By	System.Net.WebClient.QueryString
Passed To	System.Net.WebClient.{QueryString, UploadValues( )}

StringCollection   serializable

System.Collections.Specialized (system.dll)   class

This class is a special collection in which the elements are strings.

```
public class StringCollection : IList, ICollection, IEnumerable {
// Public Constructors
   public StringCollection( );
// Public Instance Properties
   public int Count{get; }                                                // implements ICollection
   public bool IsReadOnly{get; }                                          // implements IList
   public bool IsSynchronized{get; }                                      // implements ICollection
   public object SyncRoot{get; }                                          // implements ICollection
   public string this[int index]{set; get; }
// Public Instance Methods
   public int Add(string value);
   public void AddRange(string[ ] value);
   public void Clear( );                                                  // implements IList
   public bool Contains(string value);
   public void CopyTo(string[ ] array, int index);
   public StringEnumerator GetEnumerator( );
   public int IndexOf(string value);
```

```
public void Insert(int index, string value);
public void Remove(string value);
public void RemoveAt(int index);                                        // implements IList
}
```

StringDictionary

System.Collections.Specialized (system.dll)   class

This class is a dictionary collection in which keys and values are all strings.

```
public class StringDictionary : IEnumerable {
// Public Constructors
  public StringDictionary( );
// Public Instance Properties
  public virtual int Count{get; }
  public virtual bool IsSynchronized{get; }
  public virtual ICollection Keys{get; }
  public virtual object SyncRoot{get; }
  public virtual string this[string key]{set; get; }
  public virtual ICollection Values{get; }
// Public Instance Methods
  public virtual void Add(string key, string value);
  public virtual void Clear( );
  public virtual bool ContainsKey(string key);
  public virtual bool ContainsValue(string value);
  public virtual void CopyTo(Array array, int index);
  public virtual IEnumerator GetEnumerator( );                          // implements IEnumerable
  public virtual void Remove(string key);
}
```

Returned By   System.Diagnostics.ProcessStartInfo.EnvironmentVariables

StringEnumerator

System.Collections.Specialized (system.dll)   class

This type implements an enumerator for a StringCollection. This is returned by StringCollection.GetEnumerator( ).

```
public class StringEnumerator {
// Public Instance Properties
  public string Current{get; }
// Public Instance Methods
  public bool MoveNext( );
  public void Reset( );
}
```

Returned By   StringCollection.GetEnumerator( )

29

System.Diagnostics

Diagnostics are an important part of any software system. In addition to the obvious necessity of debugging the code, diagnostics can keep track of application performance and liveness, thus indicating a problem proactively, rather than waiting for the phone call from the system administrators.

Diagnostics means more than just compiling with debug symbols turned on. Certain code paths might want to execute only when diagnostics are turned on to full power, indicated by a compile-time switch. At other times, particularly in long-running systems (such as WebService-based systems), developers want to keep a log of the system's actions; frequently, debug reports from users are sketchy ("Um, when I clicked the button, it all just crashed"), and having a complete log of the system's actions can be invaluable in tracking the problem down. Not only can the log consist of custom-written messages (usually to a file), but the Windows Event Log is also available for use from within this namespace.

Diagnostics also includes the ability to track the health and performance of the application; under Windows 2000 and XP, this means interaction with the Performance utility. This is a powerful tool that can be launched from the Administrative Tools program group (under Windows NT, it is called Performance Monitor). By creating appropriate performance counters within the application, .NET programmers can give the system support staff (system administrators and production monitoring personnel, among others) the ability to monitor and track the application, even remotely. In addition to its diagnostic facilities, this namespace exposes operating system processes using the Process type. Use this type to launch new processes or take control of processes currently running on the system. The ProcessThread type lets you drill down into each thread that's running within a process for fine-grained control over running applications.

Most of the functionality in this namespace is disabled at runtime unless you've enabled debugging. If you are using command-line compilers, you can pass the /d:DEBUG switch to enable debugging (to enable tracing, use /d:TRACE). Alternatively, you can use the preprocessor directives #define TRACE or #define DEBUG. The advantage here is that you can leave all your debugging code in, and it does not affect your release builds. The related **/debug** switch adds debug symbols to your program. You need the debug symbols to obtain source file and line number information in stack traces or to run your program under the control of a debugger. In Visual Studio .NET, you can enable debugging and debug symbols by creating a debug build of your application.

Some diagnostic settings can be controlled using the application configuration file (appname.exe.config). This lets you control trace and debugging behavior without having to recompile. The root element in an application configuration file is the <configuration> element. Create a <system.diagnostics> element within that root element. All the settings mentioned in this chapter must be contained in that <system.diagnostics> element. Figure 29-1, Figure 29-2, Figure 29-3, and Figure 29-4 show the types in this namespace.

BooleanSwitch

System.Diagnostics (system.dll)   class

This class provides a simple on/off switch for debugging and tracing. Consult **Enabled** to check if the switch has been set. You can configure a Boolean switch using the application configuration file (see **Switch**). To use a **BooleanSwitch**, you must enable tracing or debugging at compilation time.

```
public class BooleanSwitch : Switch {
// Public Constructors
  public BooleanSwitch(string displayName, string description);
// Public Instance Properties
  public bool Enabled{set; get; }
}
```

Hierarchy   System.Object → Switch → BooleanSwitch

ConditionalAttribute   CF 1.0, ECMA 1.0, serializable

System.Diagnostics (mscorlib.dll)   sealed class

This attribute marks a method as callable only if a compilation variable, given by conditionString, is set. Compilation variables can be set by supplying /define:VARIABLE as a command-line argument to the compiler or by supplying #define VARIABLE directives in the source code itself. If the compilation variable is not set, calls to the marked method are ignored.

```
public sealed class ConditionalAttribute : Attribute {
// Public Constructors
  public ConditionalAttribute(string conditionString);
// Public Instance Properties
  public string ConditionString{get; }
}
```

Hierarchy   System.Object → System.Attribute → ConditionalAttribute

Valid On   Method

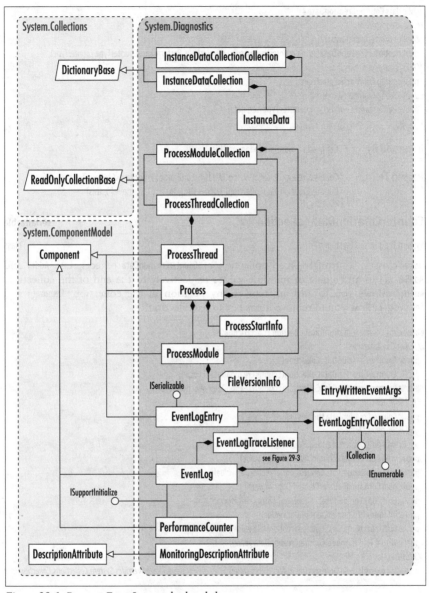

Figure 29-1. Process, EventLog, and related classes

CounterCreationData

serializable

System.Diagnostics (system.dll)

class

This class is used to specify a type, name, and help string for a custom counter.

```
public class CounterCreationData {
// Public Constructors
  public CounterCreationData( );
  public CounterCreationData(string counterName, string counterHelp, PerformanceCounterType counterType);
// Public Instance Properties
  public string CounterHelp{set; get; }
  public string CounterName{set; get; }
  public PerformanceCounterType CounterType{set; get; }
}
```

Returned By   CounterCreationDataCollection.this

Passed To   CounterCreationDataCollection.{Add( ), AddRange( ), Contains( ), CopyTo( ),
                     CounterCreationDataCollection( ), IndexOf( ), Insert( ), Remove( ), this}

CounterCreationDataCollection   serializable

System.Diagnostics (system.dll)   class

This class is a strongly-typed collection of CounterCreationData objects. Use Add( ) and
AddRange( ) to add single or multiple values respectively to the end of the collection.
Insert( ) allows you to add an item at any position in the collection. Remove( ) and
RemoveAt( ) allow you to remove items from the collection.

```
public class CounterCreationDataCollection : CollectionBase {
// Public Constructors
  public CounterCreationDataCollection( );
  public CounterCreationDataCollection(CounterCreationData[ ] value);
  public CounterCreationDataCollection(CounterCreationDataCollection value);
// Public Instance Properties
  public CounterCreationData this[int index]{set; get; }
// Public Instance Methods
  public int Add(CounterCreationData value);
  public void AddRange(CounterCreationData[ ] value);
  public void AddRange(CounterCreationDataCollection value);
  public bool Contains(CounterCreationData value);
  public void CopyTo(CounterCreationData[ ] array,  int index);
  public int IndexOf(CounterCreationData value);
  public void Insert(int index, CounterCreationData value);
  public virtual void Remove(CounterCreationData value);
// Protected Instance Methods
  protected override void OnInsert(int index, object value);        // overrides System.Collections.CollectionBase
}
```

Hierarchy   System.Object → System.Collections.CollectionBase(System.Collections.IList, System.
                     Collections.ICollection, System.Collections.IEnumerable) → CounterCreationDataCollection

Returned By   PerformanceCounterInstaller.Counters

Passed To   PerformanceCounterCategory.Create( )

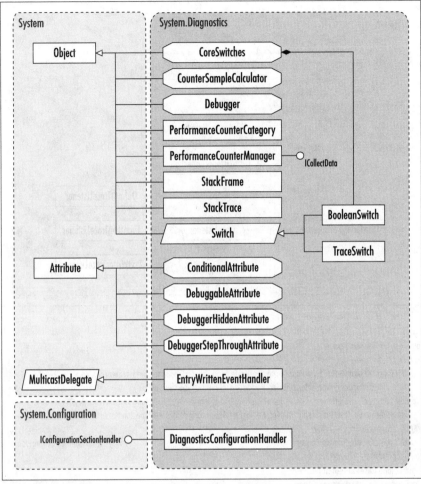

Figure 29-2. More classes from the System.Diagnostics namespace

CounterSample

System.Diagnostics (system.dll)   **struct**

This structure contains a performance counter's raw data. It represents a sample taken at a particular point in time (the `CounterTimeStamp` property). `Calculate()` returns a counter's performance data as a **float** value. The two-argument form returns values for calculated performance counters, such as averages.

`TimeStamp` and `TimeStamp100nSec` return the system timestamp, with varying degrees of accuracy. (`TimeStamp100nSec` is the most precise, reporting a timestamp within .1 milliseconds.) `BaseValue` specifies a base raw value for samples based on multiple counters. `RawValue` contains the sample's numeric value. `SystemFrequency` represents how often the system reads the counter, and `CounterFrequency` represents how often samples are taken by the counter. Both frequencies are represented in milliseconds..

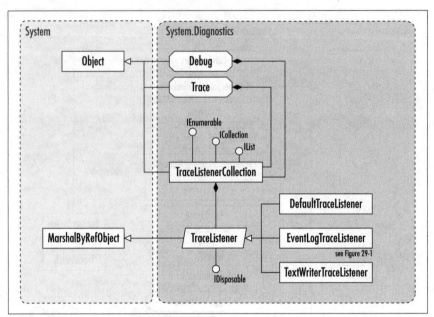

Figure 29-3. TraceListener and related classes

```
public struct CounterSample {
// Public Constructors
    public CounterSample(long rawValue, long baseValue, long counterFrequency, long systemFrequency,
        long timeStamp, long timeStamp100nSec, PerformanceCounterType counterType);
    public CounterSample(long rawValue, long baseValue, long counterFrequency, long systemFrequency,
        long timeStamp, long timeStamp100nSec, PerformanceCounterType counterType, long counterTimeStamp);
// Public Static Fields
    public static CounterSample Empty;                                    // =System.Diagnostics.CounterSample
// Public Instance Properties
    public long BaseValue{get; }
    public long CounterFrequency{get; }
    public long CounterTimeStamp{get; }
    public PerformanceCounterType CounterType{get; }
    public long RawValue{get; }
    public long SystemFrequency{get; }
    public long TimeStamp{get; }
    public long TimeStamp100nSec{get; }
// Public Static Methods
    public static float Calculate(CounterSample counterSample);
    public static float Calculate(CounterSample counterSample, CounterSample nextCounterSample);
}
```

Hierarchy	System.Object → System.ValueType → CounterSample
Returned By	InstanceData.Sample, PerformanceCounter.NextSample( )
Passed To	CounterSampleCalculator.ComputeCounterValue( ), InstanceData.InstanceData( )

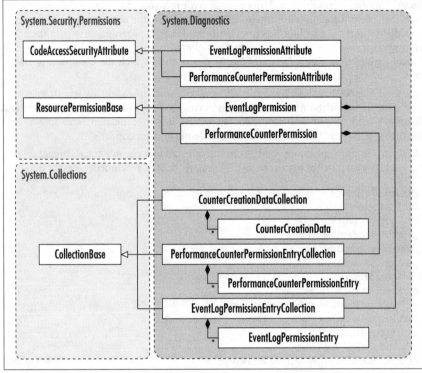

Figure 29-4. CodeAccessSecurityAttributes, collections, and related classes

CounterSampleCalculator

System.Diagnostics (system.dll)   sealed class

This class provides ComputeCounterValue( ), which interprets CounterSample structures. It
returns a floating-point value that represents the data contained in one or two samples.

```
public sealed class CounterSampleCalculator {
// Public Static Methods
  public static float ComputeCounterValue(CounterSample newSample);
  public static float ComputeCounterValue(CounterSample oldSample, CounterSample newSample);
}
```

Debug   CF 1.0

System.Diagnostics (system.dll)   sealed class

This class provides methods that allow you to print debugging information and use
assertions. The Listeners collection contains a set of listeners that are responsible for
reporting debugging operations through the user interface or trace log. That collection
initially includes an instance of DefaultTraceListener. Add a TraceListener using the Add( )
method of the Listeners property. Use Close( ) or Flush( ) to close or flush all listeners that
write output to a file, such as the TextWriterTraceListener. Set AutoFlush to true to automatically flush each listener after a write operation.

Assert( ) specifies a condition and an optional error message to display if the condition is false. If the DefaultTraceListener's AssertUiEnabled property is true, the error message is displayed as a dialog, and the user has the opportunity to abort the program, retry (test the assertion again), or ignore the failed assertion. Otherwise, the error message is written to DefaultTraceListener.LogFileName. Fail( ) acts like an assertion in which the condition is always false.

Indent( ) and Unindent( ) allow you to set the level of indentation when you call WriteLine( ). Use IndentSize to set the number of spaces corresponding to indented text. Write( ) and WriteLine( ) send output to each TraceListener in the Listeners collection, and WriteIf( ) and WriteLineIf( ) allow you to conditionally output debug information.

You can use the application configuration file to add or remove trace listeners. Look up System.Diagnostics.TraceListener in the .NET Framework SDK Documentation for details.

```
public sealed class Debug {
// Public Static Properties
  public static bool AutoFlush{set; get; }
  public static int IndentLevel{set; get; }
  public static int IndentSize{set; get; }
  public static TraceListenerCollection Listeners{get; }
// Public Static Methods
  public static void Assert(bool condition);
  public static void Assert(bool condition, string message);
  public static void Assert(bool condition, string message, string detailMessage);
  public static void Close( );
  public static void Fail(string message);
  public static void Fail(string message, string detailMessage);
  public static void Flush( );
  public static void Indent( );
  public static void Unindent( );
  public static void Write(object value);
  public static void Write(object value, string category);
  public static void Write(string message);
  public static void Write(string message, string category);
  public static void WriteIf(bool condition, object value);
  public static void WriteIf(bool condition, object value, string category);
  public static void WriteIf(bool condition, string message);
  public static void WriteIf(bool condition, string message, string category);
  public static void WriteLine(object value);
  public static void WriteLine(object value, string category);
  public static void WriteLine(string message);
  public static void WriteLine(string message, string category);
  public static void WriteLineIf(bool condition, object value);
  public static void WriteLineIf(bool condition, object value, string category);
  public static void WriteLineIf(bool condition, string message);
  public static void WriteLineIf(bool condition, string message, string category);
}
```

DebuggableAttribute

System.Diagnostics (mscorlib.dll)   sealed class

This attribute contains two properties that indicate if code can be debugged. IsJITOptimizerDisabled indicates whether optimization has been turned off, and IsJITTrackingEnabled indicates whether debug symbols have been placed in the code. This attribute is automatically applied by the compiler, with isJITTrackingEnabled set to false and isJITOptimizerDisabled set to true. Use the /debug command-line compiler switch to include debug symbols (isJIT-TrackingEnabled=true), and use /optimize to enable compile-time optimizations (isJITOptimizerDisabled=false).

```
public sealed class DebuggableAttribute : Attribute {
// Public Constructors
   public DebuggableAttribute(bool isJITTrackingEnabled, bool isJITOptimizerDisabled);
// Public Instance Properties
   public bool IsJITOptimizerDisabled{get; }
   public bool IsJITTrackingEnabled{get; }
}
```

Hierarchy   System.Object → System.Attribute → DebuggableAttribute

Valid On   Assembly, Module

Debugger

System.Diagnostics (mscorlib.dll)   sealed class

This class enables you to control the debugger from the debugged code. If a debugger is executing your code, IsAttached returns true. Break() sets a breakpoint and causes the debugger to pause. Log() logs output to the debugger window. The Launch() method launches the debugger and attaches it to your process, returning true if successful or if the debugger is already attached. Launch() returns false if the debugger could not be attached.

```
public sealed class Debugger {
// Public Constructors
   public Debugger( );
// Public Static Fields
   public static readonly string DefaultCategory;
// Public Static Properties
   public static bool IsAttached{get; }
// Public Static Methods
   public static void Break( );
   public static bool IsLogging( );
   public static bool Launch( );
   public static void Log(int level, string category, string message);
}
```

DebuggerHiddenAttribute

serializable

System.Diagnostics (mscorlib.dll)

sealed class

This attribute is used by the Visual Studio debugger. Visual Studio does not allow you to set a breakpoint in a method marked with this attribute, nor does it stop inside such a method.

```
public sealed class DebuggerHiddenAttribute : Attribute {
// Public Constructors
  public DebuggerHiddenAttribute( );
}
```

Hierarchy   System.Object → System.Attribute → DebuggerHiddenAttribute

Valid On   Constructor, Method, Property

DebuggerStepThroughAttribute

CF 1.0, serializable

System.Diagnostics (mscorlib.dll)

sealed class

This attribute is used by the Visual Studio debugger. Visual Studio does not stop in a method marked with this attribute, but it does allow you to set a breakpoint in such a method.

```
public sealed class DebuggerStepThroughAttribute : Attribute {
// Public Constructors
  public DebuggerStepThroughAttribute( );
}
```

Hierarchy   System.Object → System.Attribute → DebuggerStepThroughAttribute

Valid On   Class, Struct, Constructor, Method

DefaultTraceListener

CF 1.0, marshal by reference, disposable

System.Diagnostics (system.dll)

class

This class provides the default TraceListener. By default, an instance of this class is available in the Listeners collection of the Debug and Trace classes. The Write( ) and WriteLine( ) methods output to the log and to the active debugger (if any) via the Win32 API function OutputDebugString. The log file is initially unset, so output goes only to the debugger. To specify a log file, set LogFileName. You may also set a logfile in the <assert> element of the application configuration file's <system.diagnostics> section, as in <assert logfilename="logfile.log"/>.

AssertUiEnabled determines whether to use the user interface for failed assertions. If true, .NET uses a dialog box with the options Abort, Retry, or Fail. Whether this property is set to true or false, .NET always writes messages to the LogFileName, if one is specified. The AssertUiEnabled property can be set using the <assert> element, as in <assert assertuienabled="false"/> (the default is true).

```
public class DefaultTraceListener : TraceListener {
// Public Constructors
  public DefaultTraceListener( );
```

```
// Public Instance Properties
  public bool AssertUiEnabled{set; get; }
  public string LogFileName{set; get; }
// Public Instance Methods
  public override void Fail(string message);                              // overrides TraceListener
  public override void Fail(string message, string detailMessage);       // overrides TraceListener
  public override void Write(string message);                            // overrides TraceListener
  public override void WriteLine(string message);                        // overrides TraceListener
}
```

Hierarchy   System.Object → System.MarshalByRefObject → TraceListener(System.IDisposable) →
                     DefaultTraceListener

EntryWrittenEventArgs

System.Diagnostics (system.dll)   class

These event arguments are passed by an EventLog.EntryWritten event.

```
public class EntryWrittenEventArgs : EventArgs {
// Public Constructors
  public EntryWrittenEventArgs( );
  public EntryWrittenEventArgs(EventLogEntry entry);
// Public Instance Properties
  public EventLogEntry Entry{get; }
}
```

Hierarchy   System.Object → System.EventArgs → EntryWrittenEventArgs

Passed To   EntryWrittenEventHandler.{BeginInvoke( ), Invoke( )}

EntryWrittenEventHandler   serializable

System.Diagnostics (system.dll)   delegate

This delegate supports the EventLog.EntryWritten event.

```
public delegate void EntryWrittenEventHandler(object sender, EntryWrittenEventArgs e);
```

Associated Events   EventLog.EntryWritten( )

EventLog   marshal by reference, disposable

System.Diagnostics (system.dll)   class

This class accesses Windows event logs that are accessible through the *Event Viewer*
administrative tool. Windows contains three logs by default: the Application Log,
System Log, and Security Log. The Security Log is read-only, so you can't write events
to it. Whenever you need to raise an event, you must select a system-wide unique
event source. This source can be any keyword, as long as it is unique. To write an
event to the Application log, use the static two-argument version of WriteEntry( ),
supplying the source name and message as string arguments. If the source does not
exist, it is automatically registered.

You can manually register a new event source several ways. First, call CreateEventSource( ). If you do not specify a log name, then your events are registered with the generic Application Log. Otherwise, a new *.evt* file is created (in the *%SystemRoot%\system32\ config* directory). Alternatively, create a new EventLog object, and set Source, Log, and MachineName to the appropriate values. To delete a source, call DeleteEventSource( ). Delete( ) lets you delete an entire log, but be careful not to delete one of the Windows event logs! GetEventLogs( ) allows you to find the logs on the system, and LogNameFromSourceName( ) allows you to determine the log file for a given source.

You can interact with a log in many ways. Add to it using WriteEntry( ) and remove all log entries by calling Clear( ). Examine the Entries property to view the individual log entries. An EventLog can raise the EntryWritten event if you set EnableRaisingEvents to true.

```
public class EventLog : System.ComponentModel.Component, System.ComponentModel.ISupportInitialize {
// Public Constructors
  public EventLog( );
  public EventLog(string logName);
  public EventLog(string logName, string machineName);
  public EventLog(string logName, string machineName, string source);
// Public Instance Properties
  public bool EnableRaisingEvents{set; get; }
  public EventLogEntryCollection Entries{get; }
  public string Log{set; get; }
  public string LogDisplayName{get; }
  public string MachineName{set; get; }
  public string Source{set; get; }
  public ISynchronizeInvoke SynchronizingObject{set; get; }
// Public Static Methods
  public static void CreateEventSource(string source, string logName);
  public static void CreateEventSource(string source, string logName, string machineName);
  public static void Delete(string logName);
  public static void Delete(string logName, string machineName);
  public static void DeleteEventSource(string source);
  public static void DeleteEventSource(string source, string machineName);
  public static bool Exists(string logName);
  public static bool Exists(string logName, string machineName);
  public static EventLog[ ] GetEventLogs( );
  public static EventLog[ ] GetEventLogs(string machineName);
  public static string LogNameFromSourceName(string source, string machineName);
  public static bool SourceExists(string source);
  public static bool SourceExists(string source, string machineName);
  public static void WriteEntry(string source, string message);
  public static void WriteEntry(string source, string message, EventLogEntryType type);
  public static void WriteEntry(string source, string message, EventLogEntryType type, int eventID);
  public static void WriteEntry(string source, string message, EventLogEntryType type, int eventID, short category);
  public static void WriteEntry(string source, string message, EventLogEntryType type, int eventID, short category,
    byte[ ] rawData);
// Public Instance Methods
  public void BeginInit( );                                    // implements System.ComponentModel.ISupportInitialize
  public void Clear( );
  public void Close( );
  public void EndInit( );                                      // implements System.ComponentModel.ISupportInitialize
  public void WriteEntry(string message);
```

```
public void WriteEntry(string message, EventLogEntryType type);
public void WriteEntry(string message, EventLogEntryType type, int eventID);
public void WriteEntry(string message, EventLogEntryType type, int eventID, short category);
public void WriteEntry(string message, EventLogEntryType type, int eventID, short category, byte[ ] rawData);
// Protected Instance Methods
    protected override void Dispose(bool disposing);                    // overrides System.ComponentModel.Component
// Events
    public event EntryWrittenEventHandler EntryWritten;
}
```

Hierarchy   System.Object → System.MarshalByRefObject → System.ComponentModel.
                   Component(System.ComponentModel.IComponent, System.IDisposable) →
                   EventLog(System.ComponentModel.ISupportInitialize)

Returned By   EventLogTraceListener.EventLog

Passed To   EventLogTraceListener.{EventLog, EventLogTraceListener( )}

EventLogEntry   serializable, marshal by reference, disposable

System.Diagnostics (system.dll)   sealed class

This class represents an individual entry from an EventLog. A collection of these objects
is available through EventLog.Entries. This class exposes all the properties of an event log
entry.

```
public sealed class EventLogEntry : System.ComponentModel.Component, System.Runtime.Serialization.ISerializable {
// Public Instance Properties
    public string Category{get; }
    public short CategoryNumber{get; }
    public byte[ ] Data{get; }
    public EventLogEntryType EntryType{get; }
    public int EventID{get; }
    public int Index{get; }
    public string MachineName{get; }
    public string Message{get; }
    public string[ ] ReplacementStrings{get; }
    public string Source{get; }
    public DateTime TimeGenerated{get; }
    public DateTime TimeWritten{get; }
    public string UserName{get; }
// Public Instance Methods
    public bool Equals(EventLogEntry otherEntry);
}
```

Hierarchy   System.Object → System.MarshalByRefObject → System.ComponentModel.
                   Component(System.ComponentModel.IComponent, System.IDisposable) →
                   EventLogEntry(System.Runtime.Serialization.ISerializable)

Returned By   EntryWrittenEventArgs.Entry, EventLogEntryCollection.this

Passed To   EntryWrittenEventArgs.EntryWrittenEventArgs( ), EventLogEntryCollection.CopyTo( )

EventLogEntryCollection

System.Diagnostics (system.dll)   class

This class is an ICollection implementation for EventLogEntry objects.

```
public class EventLogEntryCollection : ICollection, IEnumerable {
// Public Instance Properties
  public int Count{get; }                                                          // implements ICollection
  public virtual EventLogEntry this[int index]){get; }
// Public Instance Methods
  public void CopyTo(EventLogEntry[ ] entries, int index);
  public IEnumerator GetEnumerator( );                                             // implements IEnumerable
}
```

Returned By   EventLog.Entries

EventLogEntryType   serializable

System.Diagnostics (system.dll)   enum

This enumeration represents an event log entry's severity level. Error indicates that the
message contains an error. SuccessAudit and FailureAudit indicate that an audited access
attempt, such as a user logon, has succeeded or failed. Information represents that a
significant operation, such as starting or stopping a service, has taken place. Warning
indicates that a problem has occurred. Warnings are not as serious as Errors, but they
should be investigated and resolved whenever possible, so your log does not fill up
with warning messages.

```
public enum EventLogEntryType {
  Error = 1,
  Warning = 2,
  Information = 4,
  SuccessAudit = 8,
  FailureAudit = 16
}
```

Hierarchy   System.Object → System.ValueType → System.Enum(System.IComparable, System.
                     IFormattable, System.IConvertible) → EventLogEntryType

Returned By   EventLogEntry.EntryType

Passed To   EventLog.WriteEntry( )

EventLogInstaller   marshal by reference, disposable

System.Diagnostics (system.configuration.install.dll)   class

This class is a System.Configuration.Install.Installer to install EventLogs. To install a new source,
set the appropriate Source and Log properties.

```
public class EventLogInstaller : System.Configuration.Install.ComponentInstaller {
// Public Constructors
  public EventLogInstaller( );
```

```
// Public Instance Properties
    public string Log{set; get; }
    public string Source{set; get; }
    public UninstallAction UninstallAction{set; get; }
// Public Instance Methods
    public override void CopyFromComponent(System.ComponentModel.IComponent component);
                                    // overrides System.Configuration.Install.ComponentInstaller
    public override void Install(System.Collections.IDictionary stateSaver);     // overrides System.Configuration.Install.Installer
    public override bool IsEquivalentInstaller(System.Configuration.Install.ComponentInstaller otherInstaller);
                                    // overrides System.Configuration.Install.ComponentInstaller
    public override void Rollback(System.Collections.IDictionary savedState);   // overrides System.Configuration.Install.Installer
    public override void Uninstall(System.Collections.IDictionary savedState);  // overrides System.Configuration.Install.Installer
}
```

Hierarchy   System.Object → System.MarshalByRefObject → System.ComponentModel.Compo-
nent(System.ComponentModel.IComponent, System.IDisposable) → System.Configuration.
Install.Installer → System.Configuration.Install.ComponentInstaller → EventLogInstaller

EventLogPermission   serializable

System.Diagnostics (system.dll)   sealed class

This class is a System.Security.Permissions.ResourcePermissionBase object, which indicates whether
or not the executing code has permission to access the Windows event logs.

```
public sealed class EventLogPermission : System.Security.Permissions.ResourcePermissionBase {
// Public Constructors
    public EventLogPermission( );
    public EventLogPermission(EventLogPermissionAccess permissionAccess, string machineName);
    public EventLogPermission(EventLogPermissionEntry[ ] permissionAccessEntries);
    public EventLogPermission(System.Security.Permissions.PermissionState state);
// Public Instance Properties
    public EventLogPermissionEntryCollection PermissionEntries{get; }
}
```

Hierarchy   System.Object → System.Security.CodeAccessPermission(System.Security.IPermission,
System.Security.ISecurityEncodable, System.Security.IStackWalk) →
System.Security.Permissions.ResourcePermissionBase(System.Security.Permissions.IUnre-
strictedPermission) → EventLogPermission

EventLogPermissionAccess   serializable, flag

System.Diagnostics (system.dll)   enum

This enumeration is used by EventLogPermissionAttribute. None indicates no access, and Browse
allows you to read logs. Instrument allows reading and writing. Audit represents the
highest level of access. It lets you read logs, clear a log, monitor events, respond to
entries, delete logs and event sources, and enumerate a collection of all logs.

```
public enum EventLogPermissionAccess {
    None = 0x00000000,
    Browse = 0x00000002,
```

```
Instrument = 0x00000006,
Audit = 0x0000000A
}
```

Hierarchy	System.Object → System.ValueType → System.Enum(System.IComparable, System. IFormattable, System.IConvertible) → EventLogPermissionAccess
Returned By	EventLogPermissionAttribute.PermissionAccess, EventLogPermissionEntry.PermissionAccess
Passed To	EventLogPermission.EventLogPermission( ), EventLogPermissionAttribute.PermissionAccess, EventLogPermissionEntry.EventLogPermissionEntry( )

EventLogPermissionAttribute   serializable

System.Diagnostics (system.dll)   class

This security attribute specifies the EventLogPermissionAccess required by your code.

```
public class EventLogPermissionAttribute : System.Security.Permissions.CodeAccessSecurityAttribute {
// Public Constructors
  public EventLogPermissionAttribute(System.Security.Permissions.SecurityAction action);
// Public Instance Properties
  public string MachineName{set; get; }
  public EventLogPermissionAccess PermissionAccess{set; get; }
// Public Instance Methods
  public override IPermission CreatePermission( );        // overrides System.Security.Permissions.SecurityAttribute
}
```

Hierarchy	System.Object → System.Attribute → System.Security.Permissions.SecurityAttribute → System.Security.Permissions.CodeAccessSecurityAttribute → EventLogPermissionAttribute
Valid On	Assembly, Class, Struct, Constructor, Method, Event

EventLogPermissionEntry   serializable

System.Diagnostics (system.dll)   class

This class represents a single permission from an EventLogPermission's PermissionEntries collection. MachineName checks the machine name the entry is for, and PermissionAccess gets an EventLogPermissionAccess that represents the granted permissions.

```
public class EventLogPermissionEntry {
// Public Constructors
  public EventLogPermissionEntry(EventLogPermissionAccess permissionAccess, string machineName);
// Public Instance Properties
  public string MachineName{get; }
  public EventLogPermissionAccess PermissionAccess{get; }
}
```

Returned By	EventLogPermissionEntryCollection.this
Passed To	EventLogPermission.EventLogPermission( ), EventLogPermissionEntryCollection.{Add( ), AddRange( ), Contains( ), CopyTo( ), IndexOf( ), Insert( ), Remove( ), this}

EventLogPermissionEntryCollection

serializable

System.Diagnostics (system.dll)

class

A strongly typed collection that contains EventLogPermissionEntry objects.

```
public class EventLogPermissionEntryCollection : CollectionBase {
// Public Instance Properties
  public EventLogPermissionEntry this(int index){set; get; }
// Public Instance Methods
  public int Add(EventLogPermissionEntry value);
  public void AddRange(EventLogPermissionEntry[ ] value);
  public void AddRange(EventLogPermissionEntryCollection value);
  public bool Contains(EventLogPermissionEntry value);
  public void CopyTo(EventLogPermissionEntry[ ] array, int index);
  public int IndexOf(EventLogPermissionEntry value);
  public void Insert(int index, EventLogPermissionEntry value);
  public void Remove(EventLogPermissionEntry value);
// Protected Instance Methods
  protected override void OnClear( );                                  // overrides System.Collections.CollectionBase
  protected override void OnInsert(int index, object value);            // overrides System.Collections.CollectionBase
  protected override void OnRemove(int index, object value);            // overrides System.Collections.CollectionBase
  protected override void OnSet(int index, object oldValue, object newValue);  // overrides System.Collections.CollectionBase
}
```

Hierarchy　　　System.Object → System.Collections.CollectionBase(System.Collections.IList, System.Collections.ICollection, System.Collections.IEnumerable) → EventLogPermissionEntryCollection

Returned By　　　EventLogPermission.PermissionEntries

EventLogTraceListener

marshal by reference, disposable

System.Diagnostics (system.dll)

sealed class

To capture trace and debug output to an EventLog, add an instance of this class to Debug.
Listeners, or Trace.Listeners. You can specify an EventLog instance in the constructor or the
name of an event source as a string.

```
public sealed class EventLogTraceListener : TraceListener {
// Public Constructors
  public EventLogTraceListener( );
  public EventLogTraceListener(EventLog eventLog);
  public EventLogTraceListener(string source);
// Public Instance Properties
  public EventLog EventLog{set; get; }
  public override string Name{set; get; }                               // overrides TraceListener
// Public Instance Methods
  public override void Close( );                                        // overrides TraceListener
  public override void Write(string message);                          // overrides TraceListener
  public override void WriteLine(string message);                      // overrides TraceListener
// Protected Instance Methods
  protected override void Dispose(bool disposing);                     // overrides TraceListener
}
```

System.
Diagnostics

FileVersionInfo

System.Diagnostics (system.dll)   **sealed class**

This class provides access to the attributes specific to binary files. Use GetVersionInfo( ) to obtain a reference to a file, and then inspect the object's properties to determine information about the file.

```
public sealed class FileVersionInfo {
// Public Instance Properties
  public string Comments{get; }
  public string CompanyName{get; }
  public int FileBuildPart{get; }
  public string FileDescription{get; }
  public int FileMajorPart{get; }
  public int FileMinorPart{get; }
  public string FileName{get; }
  public int FilePrivatePart{get; }
  public string FileVersion{get; }
  public string InternalName{get; }
  public bool IsDebug{get; }
  public bool IsPatched{get; }
  public bool IsPreRelease{get; }
  public bool IsPrivateBuild{get; }
  public bool IsSpecialBuild{get; }
  public string Language{get; }
  public string LegalCopyright{get; }
  public string LegalTrademarks{get; }
  public string OriginalFilename{get; }
  public string PrivateBuild{get; }
  public int ProductBuildPart{get; }
  public int ProductMajorPart{get; }
  public int ProductMinorPart{get; }
  public string ProductName{get; }
  public int ProductPrivatePart{get; }
  public string ProductVersion{get; }
  public string SpecialBuild{get; }
// Public Static Methods
  public static FileVersionInfo GetVersionInfo(string fileName);
// Public Instance Methods
  public override string ToString( );                                                      // overrides object
}
```

Returned By   ProcessModule.FileVersionInfo

InstanceData

System.Diagnostics (system.dll)   class

This type represents the instance data for a performance counter sample. InstanceName returns the InstanceData's name. RawValue returns the sample's raw data. Sample returns the CounterSample responsible for the data.

```
public class InstanceData {
// Public Constructors
  public InstanceData(string instanceName, CounterSample sample);
// Public Instance Properties
  public string InstanceName{get; }
  public long RawValue{get; }
  public CounterSample Sample{get; }
}
```

Returned By   InstanceDataCollection.this

Passed To   InstanceDataCollection.CopyTo( )

InstanceDataCollection

System.Diagnostics (system.dll)   class

This type is a strongly typed collection of InstanceData objects.

```
public class InstanceDataCollection : DictionaryBase {
// Public Constructors
  public InstanceDataCollection(string counterName);
// Public Instance Properties
  public string CounterName{get; }
  public ICollection Keys{get; }                               // implements System.Collections.IDictionary
  public InstanceData this[string instanceName]{get; }
  public ICollection Values{get; }                             // implements System.Collections.IDictionary
// Public Instance Methods
  public bool Contains(string instanceName);
  public void CopyTo(InstanceData[ ] instances, int index);
}
```

Hierarchy   System.Object → System.Collections.DictionaryBase(System.Collections.IDictionary,
                     System.Collections.ICollection, System.Collections.IEnumerable) → InstanceDataCollection

Returned By   InstanceDataCollectionCollection.this

Passed To   InstanceDataCollectionCollection.CopyTo( )

InstanceDataCollectionCollection

System.Diagnostics (system.dll)   class

This type is a strongly typed collection of InstanceDataCollection objects (e.g., a collection of collections).

```
public class InstanceDataCollectionCollection : DictionaryBase {
// Public Constructors
   public InstanceDataCollectionCollection( );
// Public Instance Properties
   public ICollection Keys{get; }                                        // implements System.Collections.IDictionary
   public InstanceDataCollection this[string counterName]){get; }
   public ICollection Values{get; }                                      // implements System.Collections.IDictionary
// Public Instance Methods
   public bool Contains(string counterName);
   public void CopyTo(InstanceDataCollection[ ] counters, int index);
}
```

Hierarchy System.Object → System.Collections.DictionaryBase(System.Collections.IDictionary, System.
Collections.ICollection, System.Collections.IEnumerable) → InstanceDataCollectionCollection

Returned By PerformanceCounterCategory.ReadCategory( )

MonitoringDescriptionAttribute

System.Diagnostics (system.dll)   class

This type is a System.ComponentModel.DescriptionAttribute that holds an informative description
of one of the System.Diagnostics monitoring members.

```
public class MonitoringDescriptionAttribute : System.ComponentModel.DescriptionAttribute {
// Public Constructors
   public MonitoringDescriptionAttribute(string description);
// Public Instance Properties
   public override string Description{get; }                          // overrides System.ComponentModel.DescriptionAttribute
}
```

Hierarchy System.Object → System.Attribute → System.ComponentModel.DescriptionAttribute →
MonitoringDescriptionAttribute

Valid On All

PerformanceCounter   marshal by reference, disposable

System.Diagnostics (system.dll)   sealed class

This class represents a Windows NT, 2000, or XP performance counter that can be
accessed using the Performance Administrative Tool. PerformanceCounters already exist for
system devices, such as processor, disk, or memory usage, as well as for system
resources, such as processes or threads. Using the PerformanceCounter class, you can both
read from and write performance data to existing custom counters.

To create your own custom performance counters, use PerformanceCounterCategory.Create( ).
You can write to a performance counter by using one of the PerformanceCounter constructors that takes the boolean readonly argument. Set that argument to false to create a
performance counter that you can write to. To set the value of a performance counter,
call IncrementBy( ), Increment( ), or Decrement( ), or set the RawValue to the desired value.

To access an existing performance counter, create an instance of PerformanceCounter with
the CategoryName and CounterName set to that of an available category and an existing

performance counter. The category and counter names are case-insensitive, so you could sample the available memory by calling the constructor as Performance-Counter("memory", "available mbytes"). Consult the Performance Administrative Tool for the available performance counters. You can explicitly set the CategoryName and CounterName (and the optional InstanceName and MachineName) properties, if you choose not to set these using the constructor.

To obtain a new data sample for a counter, call either NextValue( ) or NextSample( ). NextSample( ) returns a CounterSample structure that represents the raw captured performance data. NextValue( ) fetches the next sample and calculates its value based on the raw data it contains. To permanently remove a counter, call RemoveInstance( ). If you attempt to modify or remove a counter in which the ReadOnly property is set to true, an InvalidOperationException is returned.

```
public sealed class PerformanceCounter : System.ComponentModel.Component,
    System.ComponentModel.ISupportInitialize {
// Public Constructors
  public PerformanceCounter( );
  public PerformanceCounter(string categoryName, string counterName);
  public PerformanceCounter(string categoryName, string counterName, bool readOnly);
  public PerformanceCounter(string categoryName, string counterName, string instanceName);
  public PerformanceCounter(string categoryName, string counterName, string instanceName, bool readOnly);
  public PerformanceCounter(string categoryName, string counterName, string instanceName, string machineName);
// Public Static Fields
  public static int DefaultFileMappingSize;                                    // =524288
// Public Instance Properties
  public string CategoryName{set; get; }
  public string CounterHelp{get; }
  public string CounterName{set; get; }
  public PerformanceCounterType CounterType{get; }
  public string InstanceName{set; get; }
  public string MachineName{set; get; }
  public long RawValue{set; get; }
  public bool ReadOnly{set; get; }
// Public Static Methods
  public static void CloseSharedResources( );
// Public Instance Methods
  public void BeginInit( );                        // implements System.ComponentModel.ISupportInitialize
  public void Close( );
  public long Decrement( );
  public void EndInit( );                          // implements System.ComponentModel.ISupportInitialize
  public long Increment( );
  public long IncrementBy(long value);
  public CounterSample NextSample( );
  public float NextValue( );
  public void RemoveInstance( );
// Protected Instance Methods
  protected override void Dispose(bool disposing);        // overrides System.ComponentModel.Component
}
```

Hierarchy	System.Object → System.MarshalByRefObject → System.ComponentModel.Compo-nent(System.ComponentModel.IComponent, System.IDisposable) → PerformanceCounter(System.ComponentModel.ISupportInitialize)
Returned By	PerformanceCounterCategory.GetCounters( )

PerformanceCounterCategory

System.Diagnostics (system.dll)   sealed class

This class allows you to create and manage categories of performance counters. You can see the categories recognized by your system when you use the Performance Administrative Tool. When you attempt to add a counter, you'll see the categories listed in the Performance object drop-list, such as Processor, Memory, Thread, and Network Interface.

Use Create( ) to add a new category. The three-argument form lets you supply a category name, a description of the category, and a collection of CounterCreationData objects. Each CounterCreationData object describes a counter to create in the new category. Use the four-argument form of Create( ) to create a new category with only a single counter.

Delete( ) removes a counter category, and Exists( ) checks whether a given category exists. If you want to check if a specific counter exists in a category, call CounterExists( ). To check for an instance in a category, use InstanceExists( ). GetCategories( ) returns all the categories recognized by the system.

The CategoryHelp, CategoryName, and MachineName properties provide access to the name, help text, and machine name for a given category. You can use the nonstatic versions of CounterExists( ) and InstanceExists( ) to check if a specified counter or instance exists in the inspected category. GetCounters( ) and GetInstanceNames( ) retrieve a list of the counters and instances in a category.

```
public sealed class PerformanceCounterCategory {
// Public Constructors
  public PerformanceCounterCategory( );
  public PerformanceCounterCategory(string categoryName);
  public PerformanceCounterCategory(string categoryName, string machineName);
// Public Instance Properties
  public string CategoryHelp{get; }
  public string CategoryName{set; get; }
  public string MachineName{set; get; }
// Public Static Methods
  public static bool CounterExists(string counterName, string categoryName);
  public static bool CounterExists(string counterName, string categoryName, string machineName);
  public static PerformanceCounterCategory Create(string categoryName, string categoryHelp,
      CounterCreationDataCollection counterData);
  public static PerformanceCounterCategory Create(string categoryName, string categoryHelp,
      string counterName, string counterHelp);
  public static void Delete(string categoryName);
  public static bool Exists(string categoryName);
  public static bool Exists(string categoryName, string machineName);
  public static PerformanceCounterCategory[ ] GetCategories( );
  public static PerformanceCounterCategory[ ] GetCategories(string machineName);
  public static bool InstanceExists(string instanceName, string categoryName);
```

```
public static bool InstanceExists(string instanceName, string categoryName, string machineName);
// Public Instance Methods
  public bool CounterExists(string counterName);
  public PerformanceCounter[ ] GetCounters( );
  public PerformanceCounter[ ] GetCounters(string instanceName);
  public string[ ] GetInstanceNames( );
  public bool InstanceExists(string instanceName);
  public InstanceDataCollectionCollection ReadCategory( );
}
```

PerformanceCounterInstaller   marshal by reference, disposable

System.Diagnostics (system.configuration.install.dll)   class

This is an installer for a PerformanceCounter component. CategoryName and CategoryHelp contain the name and help text pertinent to the category to install the counters into, and Counters contains the counters that will be installed.

```
public class PerformanceCounterInstaller : System.Configuration.Install.ComponentInstaller {
// Public Constructors
  public PerformanceCounterInstaller( );
// Public Instance Properties
  public string CategoryHelp{set; get; }
  public string CategoryName{set; get; }
  public CounterCreationDataCollection Counters{get; }
  public UninstallAction UninstallAction{set; get; }
// Public Instance Methods
  public override void CopyFromComponent(System.ComponentModel.IComponent component);
                              // overrides System.Configuration.Install.ComponentInstaller
  public override void Install(System.Collections.IDictionary stateSaver);    // overrides System.Configuration.Install.Installer
  public override void Rollback(System.Collections.IDictionary savedState);   // overrides System.Configuration.Install.Installer
  public override void Uninstall(System.Collections.IDictionary savedState);  // overrides System.Configuration.Install.Installer
}
```

Hierarchy   System.Object → System.MarshalByRefObject → System.ComponentModel.Compo-
               nent(System.ComponentModel.IComponent, System.IDisposable) → System.Configuration.
               Install.Installer → System.Configuration.Install.ComponentInstaller →
               PerformanceCounterInstaller

PerformanceCounterPermission   serializable

System.Diagnostics (system.dll)   sealed class

This class is a System.Security.CodeAccessPermission object that specifies code access to PerformanceCounter instances. The PermissionEntries property returns a collection of
PerformanceCounterPermissionEntry objects representing the specific permissions granted.

```
public sealed class PerformanceCounterPermission : System.Security.Permissions.ResourcePermissionBase {
// Public Constructors
  public PerformanceCounterPermission( );
  public PerformanceCounterPermission(PerformanceCounterPermissionAccess permissionAccess,
    string machineName, string categoryName);
  public PerformanceCounterPermission(PerformanceCounterPermissionEntry[ ] permissionAccessEntries);
```

```
public PerformanceCounterPermission(System.Security.Permissions.PermissionState state);
// Public Instance Properties
public PerformanceCounterPermissionEntryCollection PermissionEntries{get; }
}
```

Hierarchy   System.Object → System.Security.CodeAccessPermission(System.Security.IPermission,
System.Security.ISecurityEncodable, System.Security.IStackWalk) →
System.Security.Permissions.ResourcePermissionBase(System.Security.Permissions.
IUnrestrictedPermission) → PerformanceCounterPermission

PerformanceCounterPermissionAccess   serializable, flag

System.Diagnostics (system.dll)   enum

This enumeration represents the different types of access that can be granted to
executing code. Administer allows full control over a PerformanceCounter, while Browse allows
you to view, but not modify, PerformanceCounter data. Instrument allows the code to act as a
performance counter (you may read and write, but not create, categories). None explicitly denies access to a PerformanceCounterCategory.

```
public enum PerformanceCounterPermissionAccess {
  None = 0x00000000,
  Browse = 0x00000002,
  Instrument = 0x00000006,
  Administer = 0x0000000E
}
```

Hierarchy   System.Object → System.ValueType → System.Enum(System.IComparable, System.IFor-
mattable, System.IConvertible) → PerformanceCounterPermissionAccess

Returned By   PerformanceCounterPermissionAttribute.PermissionAccess, PerformanceCounterPermission-
Entry.PermissionAccess

Passed To   PerformanceCounterPermission.PerformanceCounterPermission( ), PerformanceCounterPer-
missionAttribute.PermissionAccess, PerformanceCounterPermissionEntry.
PerformanceCounterPermissionEntry( )

PerformanceCounterPermissionAttribute   serializable

System.Diagnostics (system.dll)   class

This class is a System.Security.Permissions.SecurityAttribute that explicitly allows you to set
required or denied performance counter permissions. You can use the CategoryName,
MachineName, and PermissionAccess properties to indicate the required permissions for a
specific PerformanceCounter.

```
public class PerformanceCounterPermissionAttribute : System.Security.Permissions.CodeAccessSecurityAttribute {
// Public Constructors
  public PerformanceCounterPermissionAttribute(System.Security.Permissions.SecurityAction action);
// Public Instance Properties
  public string CategoryName{set; get; }
  public string MachineName{set; get; }
  public PerformanceCounterPermissionAccess PermissionAccess{set; get; }
```

```
// Public Instance Methods
    public override IPermission CreatePermission( );                // overrides System.Security.Permissions.SecurityAttribute
}
```

Hierarchy	System.Object → System.Attribute → System.Security.Permissions.SecurityAttribute → System.Security.Permissions.CodeAccessSecurityAttribute → PerformanceCounterPermissionAttribute
Valid On	Assembly, Class, Struct, Constructor, Method, Event

PerformanceCounterPermissionEntry   serializable

System.Diagnostics (system.dll)   class

This class holds the necessary information for a given permission. The PermissionAccess property sets the PerformanceCounterPermissionAccess level for a specific CategoryName and MachineName.

```
public class PerformanceCounterPermissionEntry {
// Public Constructors
    public PerformanceCounterPermissionEntry(PerformanceCounterPermissionAccess permissionAccess,
        string machineName, string categoryName);
// Public Instance Properties
    public string CategoryName{get; }
    public string MachineName{get; }
    public PerformanceCounterPermissionAccess PermissionAccess{get; }
}
```

Returned By	PerformanceCounterPermissionEntryCollection.this
Passed To	PerformanceCounterPermission.PerformanceCounterPermission( ), PerformanceCounterPermissionEntryCollection.{Add( ), AddRange( ), Contains( ), CopyTo( ), IndexOf( ), Insert( ), Remove( ), this}

PerformanceCounterPermissionEntryCollection   serializable

System.Diagnostics (system.dll)   class

This strongly typed collection contains PerformanceCounterPermissionEntry objects.

```
public class PerformanceCounterPermissionEntryCollection : CollectionBase {
// Public Instance Properties
    public PerformanceCounterPermissionEntry this[int index]{set; get; }
// Public Instance Methods
    public int Add(PerformanceCounterPermissionEntry value);
    public void AddRange(PerformanceCounterPermissionEntry[ ] value);
    public void AddRange(PerformanceCounterPermissionEntryCollection value);
    public bool Contains(PerformanceCounterPermissionEntry value);
    public void CopyTo(PerformanceCounterPermissionEntry[ ] array, int index);
    public int IndexOf(PerformanceCounterPermissionEntry value);
    public void Insert(int index, PerformanceCounterPermissionEntry value);
    public void Remove(PerformanceCounterPermissionEntry value);
```

```
// Protected Instance Methods
  protected override void OnClear( );                                    // overrides System.Collections.CollectionBase
  protected override void OnInsert(int index, object value);             // overrides System.Collections.CollectionBase
  protected override void OnRemove(int index, object value);             // overrides System.Collections.CollectionBase
  protected override void OnSet(int index, object oldValue, object newValue);  // overrides System.Collections.CollectionBase
}
```

Hierarchy   System.Object → System.Collections.CollectionBase(System.Collections.IList, System.Collec-
tions.ICollection, System.Collections.IEnumerable) →
PerformanceCounterPermissionEntryCollection

Returned By   PerformanceCounterPermission.PermissionEntries

PerformanceCounterType   serializable

System.Diagnostics (system.dll)   enum

This enumeration represents the different types of performance counters available.
Look up System.Diagnostics.PerformanceCounterType in the .NET Framework SDK Documentation for complete details.

```
public enum PerformanceCounterType {
  NumberOfItemsHEX32 = 0,
  NumberOfItemsHEX64 = 256,
  NumberOfItems32 = 65536,
  NumberOfItems64 = 65792,
  CounterDelta32 = 4195328,
  CounterDelta64 = 4195584,
  SampleCounter = 4260864,
  CountPerTimeInterval32 = 4523008,
  CountPerTimeInterval64 = 4523264,
  RateOfCountsPerSecond32 = 272696320,
  RateOfCountsPerSecond64 = 272696576,
  RawFraction = 537003008,
  CounterTimer = 541132032,
  Timer100Ns = 542180608,
  SampleFraction = 549585920,
  CounterTimerInverse = 557909248,
  Timer100NsInverse = 558957824,
  CounterMultiTimer = 574686464,
  CounterMultiTimer100Ns = 575735040,
  CounterMultiTimerInverse = 591463680,
  CounterMultiTimer100NsInverse = 592512256,
  AverageTimer32 = 805438464,
  ElapsedTime = 807666944,
  AverageCount64 = 1073874176,
  SampleBase = 1073939457,
  AverageBase = 1073939458,
  RawBase = 1073939459,
  CounterMultiBase = 1107494144
}
```

Hierarchy	System.Object → System.ValueType → System.Enum(System.IComparable, System. IFormattable, System.IConvertible) → PerformanceCounterType
Returned By	CounterCreationData.CounterType, CounterSample.CounterType, PerformanceCounter. CounterType
Passed To	CounterCreationData.{CounterCreationData( ), CounterType}, CounterSample. CounterSample( )

Process

marshal by reference, disposable

System.Diagnostics (system.dll)   class

This class represents a system process. Use it to start, stop, and interact with a process. To launch a new process, create an instance of ProcessStartInfo, set its properties, and pass it to the single-argument form of the static Start( ) method. This offers a great deal of control over process creation. To launch a process without customizing its StartInfo, simply call the one-string or two-string argument form of the static Start( ) method. The first string argument is the name of the program, batch file, or document to start, and the optional second argument contains any command-line arguments. You can also explicitly create a new instance of Process, set its StartInfo property, and call the Start( ) method to start the process.

GetCurrentProcess( ) creates a Process instance that represents the current process. Enumerate all running processes on the system by using GetProcesses( ). Use GetProcessesByName( ) to get all processes for a given program. GetProcessById( ) retrieves a Process given its process ID.

Use CloseMainWindow( ) to shut down a process that has a user interface. You can terminate a process with Kill( ), but this forces an abnormal termination, which may result in data corruption. If you would like to raise an event when the process finishes executing, use Exited (EnableRaisingEvents must be set to true).

Most of the properties allow you to access general information about the running process. However, this information is populated at the time you associate a Process object with a running process. You can call Refresh( ) each time you need to update this information. Modules allows you to inspect the code modules the process has loaded into memory, and MainModule returns the module that started the process. StandardInput, StandardOutput, and StandardError allow access to the default I/O streams (see the ProcessStartInfo.Redirect* methods). Threads returns the threads in use by the process, and WorkingSet returns the physical memory usage of the process.

```
public class Process : System.ComponentModel.Component {
// Public Constructors
  public Process( );
// Public Instance Properties
  public int BasePriority{get; }
  public bool EnableRaisingEvents{set; get; }
  public int ExitCode{get; }
  public DateTime ExitTime{get; }
  public IntPtr Handle{get; }
  public int HandleCount{get; }
  public bool HasExited{get; }
  public int Id{get; }
  public string MachineName{get; }
```

System. Diagnostics

Process | 443

```
public ProcessModule MainModule{get; }
public IntPtr MainWindowHandle{get; }
public string MainWindowTitle{get; }
public IntPtr MaxWorkingSet{set; get; }
public IntPtr MinWorkingSet{set; get; }
public ProcessModuleCollection Modules{get; }
public int NonpagedSystemMemorySize{get; }
public int PagedMemorySize{get; }
public int PagedSystemMemorySize{get; }
public int PeakPagedMemorySize{get; }
public int PeakVirtualMemorySize{get; }
public int PeakWorkingSet{get; }
public bool PriorityBoostEnabled{set; get; }
public ProcessPriorityClass PriorityClass{set; get; }
public int PrivateMemorySize{get; }
public TimeSpan PrivilegedProcessorTime{get; }
public string ProcessName{get; }
public IntPtr ProcessorAffinity{set; get; }
public bool Responding{get; }
public StreamReader StandardError{get; }
public StreamWriter StandardInput{get; }
public StreamReader StandardOutput{get; }
public ProcessStartInfo StartInfo{set; get; }
public DateTime StartTime{get; }
public ISynchronizeInvoke SynchronizingObject{set; get; }
public ProcessThreadCollection Threads{get; }
public TimeSpan TotalProcessorTime{get; }
public TimeSpan UserProcessorTime{get; }
public int VirtualMemorySize{get; }
public int WorkingSet{get; }
// Public Static Methods
public static void EnterDebugMode( );
public static Process GetCurrentProcess( );
public static Process GetProcessById(int processId);
public static Process GetProcessById(int processId, string machineName);
public static Process[ ] GetProcesses( );
public static Process[ ] GetProcesses(string machineName);
public static Process[ ] GetProcessesByName(string processName);
public static Process[ ] GetProcessesByName(string processName, string machineName);
public static void LeaveDebugMode( );
public static Process Start(ProcessStartInfo startInfo);
public static Process Start(string fileName);
public static Process Start(string fileName, string arguments);
// Public Instance Methods
public void Close( );
public bool CloseMainWindow( );
public void Kill( );
public void Refresh( );
public bool Start( );
public override string ToString( );                    // overrides System.ComponentModel.Component
public bool WaitForExit(int milliseconds);
```

```
  public void WaitForExit( );
  public bool WaitForInputIdle( );
  public bool WaitForInputIdle(int milliseconds);
// Protected Instance Methods
  protected override void Dispose(bool disposing);              // overrides System.ComponentModel.Component
  protected void OnExited( );
// Events
  public event EventHandler Exited;
}
```

Hierarchy　　System.Object → System.MarshalByRefObject → System.ComponentModel.
　　　　　　　　Component(System.ComponentModel.IComponent, System.IDisposable) → Process

ProcessModule   marshal by reference, disposable

System.Diagnostics (system.dll)   class

This class represents a DLL or EXE file loaded by a process. BaseAddress returns the starting
memory address of the loaded module and EntryPointAddress returns the memory address
of the module's entry point (such as Main( ), WinMain( ), or DllMain( )). You can also check
the size of the loaded module by checking ModuleMemorySize. FileName returns the full path
to the file of a loaded module, and FileVersionInfo allows you to access the version information of a file. Lastly, you can view the name of the module with ModuleName.

```
public class ProcessModule : System.ComponentModel.Component {
// Public Instance Properties
  public IntPtr BaseAddress{get; }
  public IntPtr EntryPointAddress{get; }
  public string FileName{get; }
  public FileVersionInfo FileVersionInfo{get; }
  public int ModuleMemorySize{get; }
  public string ModuleName{get; }
// Public Instance Methods
  public override string ToString( );                           // overrides System.ComponentModel.Component
}
```

Hierarchy　　System.Object → System.MarshalByRefObject → System.ComponentModel.Compo-
　　　　　　　　nent(System.ComponentModel.IComponent, System.IDisposable) → ProcessModule

Returned By　　Process.MainModule, ProcessModuleCollection.this

Passed To　　ProcessModuleCollection.{Contains( ), CopyTo( ), IndexOf( ), ProcessModuleCollection( )}

ProcessModuleCollection

System.Diagnostics (system.dll)   class

This class is a strongly typed collection that contains ProcessModule objects.

```
public class ProcessModuleCollection : ReadOnlyCollectionBase {
// Public Constructors
  public ProcessModuleCollection(ProcessModule[ ] processModules);
// Protected Constructors
```

```
  protected ProcessModuleCollection( );
// Public Instance Properties
  public ProcessModule this[int index]{get; }
// Public Instance Methods
  public bool Contains(ProcessModule module);
  public void CopyTo(ProcessModule[ ] array, int index);
  public int IndexOf(ProcessModule module);
}
```

Hierarchy System.Object → System.Collections.ReadOnlyCollectionBase(System.Collections.ICollection, System.Collections.IEnumerable) → ProcessModuleCollection

Returned By Process.Modules

ProcessPriorityClass   serializable

System.Diagnostics (system.dll)   enum

This enumeration represents the different priorities given to a process. Process priorities, along with thread priorities, determine how processor time is allocated. Most processes run with Normal priority. Use Idle to specify that processor time should be allocated to a process only when the processor is idle. AboveNormal and BelowNormal allow you to set priorities slightly above or below Normal, but are not supported by Windows 95, 98, or Me. An exception is thrown if you attempt to use them.

High should be used only for time-critical tasks, but use care in choosing this priority because little time will be available to other applications. RealTime is the maximum allowable priority. When this priority is used, the process runs with higher priority than even the operating system. Assigning High and RealTime to a process will almost certainly make your system's user interface unresponsive. For this reason, be careful when using these.

```
public enum ProcessPriorityClass {
  Normal = 32,
  Idle = 64,
  High = 128,
  RealTime = 256,
  BelowNormal = 16384,
  AboveNormal = 32768
}
```

Hierarchy System.Object → System.ValueType → System.Enum(System.IComparable, System.IFormattable, System.IConvertible) → ProcessPriorityClass

Returned By Process.PriorityClass

Passed To Process.PriorityClass

ProcessStartInfo

System.Diagnostics (system.dll)   sealed class

This class is used to configure how a process is started or to view the settings a process was started with. To start a process, set FileName to the full path of the application or file, then pass the ProcessStartInfo instance to Process.Start( ). FileName is the only property you must set. Use the other properties for more control. (Use Arguments to specify the command-line arguments.)

In Windows, each document type has a verb that you can use to do different things with (for example, a Microsoft Word document has an open and a print verb). To consult the possible verbs for a specific file, enumerate the Verbs property after you set FileName. To start a process with a specific verb, set Verb.

To change the standard error, input, or output source or targets (usually the system console), set one or more of RedirectStandardError, RedirectStandardInput, or RedirectStandardOutput to true. This enables the Process.StandardError, Process.StandardInput, and Process.StandardOutput properties, which you can then set as needed. Set the EnvironmentVariables and WorkingDirectory to change the default process start behavior. If the process cannot be started, you can display an error dialog window by setting ErrorDialog (set the handle of the dialog's parent window with ErrorDialogParentHandle). If you set CreateNoWindow, a new window is not created to start the new process. However, if you want a window, set its style by setting WindowStyle. You can also specify that the file should be executed from a Windows command prompt with UseShellExecute.

```
public sealed class ProcessStartInfo {
// Public Constructors
  public ProcessStartInfo( );
  public ProcessStartInfo(string fileName);
  public ProcessStartInfo(string fileName, string arguments);
// Public Instance Properties
  public string Arguments{set; get; }
  public bool CreateNoWindow{set; get; }
  public StringDictionary EnvironmentVariables{get; }
  public bool ErrorDialog{set; get; }
  public IntPtr ErrorDialogParentHandle{set; get; }
  public string FileName{set; get; }
  public bool RedirectStandardError{set; get; }
  public bool RedirectStandardInput{set; get; }
  public bool RedirectStandardOutput{set; get; }
  public bool UseShellExecute{set; get; }
  public string Verb{set; get; }
  public string[ ] Verbs{get; }
  public ProcessWindowStyle WindowStyle{set; get; }
  public string WorkingDirectory{set; get; }
}
```

Returned By   Process.StartInfo

Passed To   Process.{Start( ), StartInfo}

ProcessThread   marshal by reference, disposable

System.Diagnostics (system.dll)   class

This class represents a thread, the smallest unit of execution under Win32. Use Process. Threads to get an array of all the threads contained within a given process. As with processes, a thread runs with a given priority. BasePriority represents the base priority for a thread. From time to time, the operating system changes a thread's priority; a thread's current priority is available from CurrentPriority. Threads in background applications run with a lower priority, as do threads that are sleeping. BasePriorityPriorityLevel specifies a range of appropriate priorities for a thread.

If a process is ProcessPriorityClass.Normal, ProcessPriorityClass.High, or ProcessPriorityClass.RealTime, you can set a thread's PriorityBoostEnabled to true. This gives the thread an extra boost whenever the user is interacting with the program's user interface. You can make a thread prefer one processor over another by setting the value of IdealProcessor. ProcessorAffinity allows you to set up a bitfield that represents one or more preferred processors. Bit 0 represents the first processor, bit 1 the second, and so on. For example, a ProcessorAffinity of 0x0005 (bits 0 and 2 on) indicates that the first and third processor are preferred. Use ResetIdealProcessor( ) to tell the thread that it can run on any processor, leaving the processor choice up to the operating system.

The current state of a thread is returned by ThreadState. If a thread is waiting, you can retrieve the reason the thread is waiting via WaitReason. PrivilegedProcessorTime and UserProcessorTime return the privileged and user processor time, and TotalProcessorTime returns the sum of those two.

The ProcessThread class differs from the System.Threading.Thread type. ProcessThread represents the view of a thread from an administrative viewpoint, while System.Threading.Thread represents a thread from its creator's viewpoint. When you want to enumerate and interact with the threads of an external process, use ProcessThread. When you need to create a new thread in your own program, use System.Threading.Thread.

```
public class ProcessThread : System.ComponentModel.Component {
// Public Instance Properties
  public int BasePriority{get; }
  public int CurrentPriority{get; }
  public int Id{get; }
  public int IdealProcessor{set; }
  public bool PriorityBoostEnabled{set; get; }
  public ThreadPriorityLevel PriorityLevel{set; get; }
  public TimeSpan PrivilegedProcessorTime{get; }
  public IntPtr ProcessorAffinity{set; }
  public IntPtr StartAddress{get; }
  public DateTime StartTime{get; }
  public ThreadState ThreadState{get; }
  public TimeSpan TotalProcessorTime{get; }
  public TimeSpan UserProcessorTime{get; }
  public ThreadWaitReason WaitReason{get; }
// Public Instance Methods
  public void ResetIdealProcessor( );
}
```

Hierarchy   System.Object → System.MarshalByRefObject → System.ComponentModel.Component(System.ComponentModel.IComponent, System.IDisposable) → ProcessThread

Returned By   ProcessThreadCollection.this

Passed To   ProcessThreadCollection.{Add( ), Contains( ), CopyTo( ), IndexOf( ), Insert( ), ProcessThreadCollection( ), Remove( )}

ProcessThreadCollection

System.Diagnostics (system.dll)   class

This strongly typed collection contains ProcessThread objects.

```
public class ProcessThreadCollection : ReadOnlyCollectionBase {
// Public Constructors
  public ProcessThreadCollection(ProcessThread[ ] processThreads);
// Protected Constructors
  protected ProcessThreadCollection( );
// Public Instance Properties
  public ProcessThread this[int index]{get; }
// Public Instance Methods
  public int Add(ProcessThread thread);
  public bool Contains(ProcessThread thread);
  public void CopyTo(ProcessThread[ ] array, int index);
  public int IndexOf(ProcessThread thread);
  public void Insert(int index, ProcessThread thread);
  public void Remove(ProcessThread thread);
}
```

Hierarchy   System.Object → System.Collections.ReadOnlyCollectionBase(System.Collections.ICollection,
                       System.Collections.IEnumerable) → ProcessThreadCollection

Returned By   Process.Threads

ProcessWindowStyle   serializable

System.Diagnostics (system.dll)   enum

This enumeration contains the window states you can choose from when starting a
Process.

```
public enum ProcessWindowStyle {
  Normal = 0,
  Hidden = 1,
  Minimized = 2,
  Maximized = 3
}
```

Hierarchy   System.Object → System.ValueType → System.Enum(System.IComparable, System.
                       IFormattable, System.IConvertible) → ProcessWindowStyle

Returned By   ProcessStartInfo.WindowStyle

Passed To   ProcessStartInfo.WindowStyle

StackFrame   serializable

System.Diagnostics (mscorlib.dll)   class

A stack frame is an abstraction of the current state of an executing method. Use Stack-
Trace to enumerate all the stack frames that led up to the current process. Use GetMethod( )

to obtain information about the method represented by a stack frame. Use GetFileName( ) to retrieve the name of the module that contains the method. The column and line numbers of the method, which are determined from debugging symbols, can be accessed with GetFileColumnNumber( ) and GetFileLineNumber( ). To obtain the location in memory of the StackFrame, use GetNativeOffset( ), or, alternatively, for the offset of IL code, call GetILOffset( ). If the JIT compiler is not generating debugging symbols, this number is approximated by the runtime.

```
public class StackFrame {
// Public Constructors
  public StackFrame( );
  public StackFrame(bool fNeedFileInfo);
  public StackFrame(int skipFrames);
  public StackFrame(int skipFrames, bool fNeedFileInfo);
  public StackFrame(string fileName, int lineNumber);
  public StackFrame(string fileName, int lineNumber, int colNumber);
// Public Static Fields
  public const int OFFSET_UNKNOWN;                                       // = -1
// Public Instance Methods
  public virtual int GetFileColumnNumber( );
  public virtual int GetFileLineNumber( );
  public virtual string GetFileName( );
  public virtual int GetILOffset( );
  public virtual MethodBase GetMethod( );
  public virtual int GetNativeOffset( );
  public override string ToString( );                               // overrides object
}
```

Returned By   StackTrace.GetFrame( )

Passed To   StackTrace.StackTrace( )

StackTrace   serializable

System.Diagnostics (mscorlib.dll)   class

A stack trace is an ordered list of StackFrame objects. Call the constructor to create a stack trace that starts with a StackFrame corresponding to the current method. The optional boolean argument fNeedFileInfo indicates that the stack trace should include the filename as well as the line and column number. (The program must have been compiled with /debug to get this information.)

When one method calls another, a new stack frame is created and FrameCount is incremented. To get a specific StackFrame, use GetFrame( ). The static constant METHODS_TO_SKIP returns the number of methods skipped at the beginning of the StackTrace.

```
public class StackTrace {
// Public Constructors
  public StackTrace( );
  public StackTrace(bool fNeedFileInfo);
  public StackTrace(Exception e);
  public StackTrace(Exception e, bool fNeedFileInfo);
  public StackTrace(Exception e, int skipFrames);
```

```
public StackTrace(Exception e, int skipFrames, bool fNeedFileInfo);
public StackTrace(int skipFrames);
public StackTrace(int skipFrames, bool fNeedFileInfo);
public StackTrace(StackFrame frame);
public StackTrace(System.Threading.Thread targetThread, bool needFileInfo);
// Public Static Fields
public const int METHODS_TO_SKIP;                                              // =0
// Public Instance Properties
public virtual int FrameCount{get; }
// Public Instance Methods
public virtual StackFrame GetFrame(int index);
public override string ToString( );                                    // overrides object
}
```

Switch

System.Diagnostics (system.dll)   abstract class

Consult this class in a conditional statement to execute special tracing or debugging code. To use a switch you must have debugging enabled. Each Switch has a DisplayName and Description. SwitchSetting contains the current setting.

Specify the value of a switch in the application configuration file. Under the <system.diagnostics> element, add an element <switches> to hold all the switches. Within the <switches> element, define each switch you want with <add name="switchname" value="value"/>. For a BooleanSwitch, any nonzero value sets BooleanSwitch.Enabled to true. For a TraceSwitch, use a value from the TraceLevel enumeration.

```
public abstract class Switch {
// Protected Constructors
   protected Switch(string displayName, string description);
// Public Instance Properties
   public string Description{get; }
   public string DisplayName{get; }
// Protected Instance Properties
   protected int SwitchSetting{set; get; }
// Protected Instance Methods
   protected virtual void OnSwitchSettingChanged( );
}
```

Subclasses   BooleanSwitch, TraceSwitch

TextWriterTraceListener   marshal by reference, disposable

System.Diagnostics (system.dll)   class

This class writes to a System.IO.TextWriter. Use Writer to set or change the TextWriter.

```
public class TextWriterTraceListener : TraceListener {
// Public Constructors
   public TextWriterTraceListener( );
   public TextWriterTraceListener(System.IO.Stream stream);
   public TextWriterTraceListener(System.IO.Stream stream, string name);
   public TextWriterTraceListener(string fileName);
```

```
public TextWriterTraceListener(string fileName, string name);
public TextWriterTraceListener(System.IO.TextWriter writer);
public TextWriterTraceListener(System.IO.TextWriter writer, string name);
// Public Instance Properties
public TextWriter Writer{set; get; }
// Public Instance Methods
public override void Close( );                                          // overrides TraceListener
public override void Flush( );                                         // overrides TraceListener
public override void Write(string message);                           // overrides TraceListener
public override void WriteLine(string message);                      // overrides TraceListener
// Protected Instance Methods
protected override void Dispose(bool disposing);                     // overrides TraceListener
}
```

Hierarchy   System.Object → System.MarshalByRefObject → TraceListener(System.IDisposable) →
TextWriterTraceListener

ThreadPriorityLevel   serializable

System.Diagnostics (system.dll)   enum

This enumeration represents the different thread priority levels. A thread's priority
level is computed relative to the process priority level using ProcessThread.PriorityLevel.

```
public enum ThreadPriorityLevel {
  Normal = 0,
  AboveNormal = 1,
  Highest = 2,
  TimeCritical = 15,
  Idle = -15,
  Lowest = -2,
  BelowNormal = -1
}
```

Hierarchy   System.Object → System.ValueType → System.Enum(System.IComparable,
System.IFormattable, System.IConvertible) → ThreadPriorityLevel

Returned By ProcessThread.PriorityLevel

Passed To   ProcessThread.PriorityLevel

ThreadState   serializable

System.Diagnostics (system.dll)   enum

This enumeration represents the different thread states as recognized by the operating
system. They mostly correspond to the states defined by System.Threading.ThreadState, but
also include Transition for when a thread is waiting on something other than the CPU (it
might be waiting on disk I/O, for example).

```
public enum ThreadState {
  Initialized = 0,
  Ready = 1,
```

```
  Running = 2,
  Standby = 3,
  Terminated = 4,
  Wait = 5,
  Transition = 6,
  Unknown = 7
}
```

Hierarchy   System.Object → System.ValueType → System.Enum(System.IComparable,
                 System.IFormattable, System.IConvertible) → ThreadState

Returned By ProcessThread.ThreadState

ThreadWaitReason   serializable

System.Diagnostics (system.dll)   enum

This enumeration specifies the reason a thread is waiting. VirtualMemory indicates that a
thread is waiting for virtual memory to be allocated, and PageIn and PageOut indicate that
a thread is waiting for virtual memory to page in or out, respectively. FreePage is for
threads waiting for a free virtual memory page. EventPairHigh and EventPairLow signal that
the thread is waiting on events. LpcReceive indicates that a thread is waiting for a local
procedure call, and LpcReply means that it is waiting for a reply to a local procedure call.
If thread execution has been suspended or delayed, you will see either Suspended or Execu-
tionDelay. SystemAllocation means that the thread is waiting for a system allocation, and
Executive indicates that it is waiting for the scheduler. Unknown is for when the operating
system cannot report why a thread is waiting.

```
public enum ThreadWaitReason {
  Executive = 0,
  FreePage = 1,
  PageIn = 2,
  SystemAllocation = 3,
  ExecutionDelay = 4,
  Suspended = 5,
  UserRequest = 6,
  EventPairHigh = 7,
  EventPairLow = 8,
  LpcReceive = 9,
  LpcReply = 10,
  VirtualMemory = 11,
  PageOut = 12,
  Unknown = 13
}
```

Hierarchy   System.Object → System.ValueType → System.Enum(System.IComparable,
                 System.IFormattable, System.IConvertible) → ThreadWaitReason

Returned By ProcessThread.WaitReason

This class supplies static methods and properties to provide tracing ability. The calls to the Trace methods and properties are executed only if tracing is enabled. (See the introduction to this chapter for instructions on enabling tracing.)

The static properties allow you to adjust the settings that are used when you call the methods. You can specify that output be indented a certain amount with IndentLevel or increase or decrease the IndentLevel by one using Indent( ) and Unindent( ). You can also adjust the number of spaces each indent level adds using IndentSize. AutoFlush makes sure that after each use of a Trace method, the Listeners are flushed.

Write( ) and WriteLine( ) simply write to each TraceListener in the Listeners collection (by default, this collection includes an instance of DefaultTraceListener). WriteIf( ) and WriteLineIf( ) do the same, but only if the specified condition evaluates to true. Assert( ) emits an error message if a condition evaluates to false, and Fail( ) always emits an error message.

One possible point of confusion is that Listeners is read-only. This means that you may not point Listeners to a different collection. You can, however, add new TraceListener objects to the TraceListenerCollection with the TraceListenerCollection.Add( ) method.

You can use the application configuration file to configure this class. Under the <system. diagnostics> element, add a <trace> element. You can set attributes for this element that correspond to Trace properties, as in <trace autoflush="true" indentsize="4"/>.

```
public sealed class Trace {
// Public Static Properties
  public static bool AutoFlush{set; get; }
  public static int IndentLevel{set; get; }
  public static int IndentSize{set; get; }
  public static TraceListenerCollection Listeners{get; }
// Public Static Methods
  public static void Assert(bool condition);
  public static void Assert(bool condition, string message);
  public static void Assert(bool condition, string message, string detailMessage);
  public static void Close( );
  public static void Fail(string message);
  public static void Fail(string message, string detailMessage);
  public static void Flush( );
  public static void Indent( );
  public static void Unindent( );
  public static void Write(object value);
  public static void Write(object value, string category);
  public static void Write(string message);
  public static void Write(string message, string category);
  public static void WriteIf(bool condition, object value);
  public static void WriteIf(bool condition, object value, string category);
  public static void WriteIf(bool condition, string message);
  public static void WriteIf(bool condition, string message, string category);
  public static void WriteLine(object value);
  public static void WriteLine(object value, string category);
  public static void WriteLine(string message);
  public static void WriteLine(string message, string category);
```

```
  public static void WriteLineIf(bool condition, object value);
  public static void WriteLineIf(bool condition, object value, string category);
  public static void WriteLineIf(bool condition, string message);
  public static void WriteLineIf(bool condition, string message, string category);
}
```

TraceLevel   serializable

System.Diagnostics (system.dll)   enum

This enumeration represents the possible levels for a trace. Use a TraceSwitch to inspect a
switch's current level. Error indicates that tracing code should emit messages for error
conditions, while Warning indicates that tracing code should emit both warnings and
error messages. Info adds to Warning by including informational messages along with
warnings and errors. Verbose indicates that *all* trace messages should be emitted. Turn
tracing messages off with Off.

```
public enum TraceLevel {
  Off = 0,
  Error = 1,
  Warning = 2,
  Info = 3,
  Verbose = 4
}
```

Hierarchy	System.Object → System.ValueType → System.Enum(System.IComparable, System. IFormattable, System.IConvertible) → TraceLevel
Returned By	TraceSwitch.Level
Passed To	TraceSwitch.Level

TraceListener   CF 1.0, marshal by reference, disposable

System.Diagnostics (system.dll)   abstract class

This abstract class TraceListener is associated with a trace through inclusion in the Trace.
Listeners collection. Each TraceListener is responsible for sending trace output somewhere.
For example, when you call Trace.WriteLine( ), each TraceListener sends the same output to its
respective output destination. Use Name to give a name to your TraceListener instances.

Use IndentLevel to control the level of indentation in the output. IndentSize specifies the
number of spaces in each level of indent. NeedIndent toggles whether to indent the
output at all. Use Write( ) and WriteLine( ) to send output to the TraceListener's destination.
WriteIndent( ) emits whitespace according to the current IndentLevel and IndentSize. It has the
side effect of setting NeedIndent to false, so the next time you call one of the Write*
methods, it will not emit extra indentation.

You can use the application configuration file to add or remove TraceListeners. Look up
System.Diagnostics.TraceListener in the .NET Framework SDK Documentation for details.

```
public abstract class TraceListener : MarshalByRefObject, IDisposable {
// Protected Constructors
  protected TraceListener( );
  protected TraceListener(string name);
```

```
// Public Instance Properties
  public int IndentLevel{set; get; }
  public int IndentSize{set; get; }
  public virtual string Name{set; get; }
// Protected Instance Properties
  protected bool NeedIndent{set; get; }
// Public Instance Methods
  public virtual void Close( );
  public void Dispose( );                                                      // implements IDisposable
  public virtual void Fail(string message);
  public virtual void Fail(string message, string detailMessage);
  public virtual void Flush( );
  public virtual void Write(object o);
  public virtual void Write(object o, string category);
  public abstract void Write(string message);
  public virtual void Write(string message, string category);
  public virtual void WriteLine(object o);
  public virtual void WriteLine(object o, string category);
  public abstract void WriteLine(string message);
  public virtual void WriteLine(string message, string category);
// Protected Instance Methods
  protected virtual void Dispose(bool disposing);
  protected virtual void WriteIndent( );
}
```

Hierarchy	System.Object → System.MarshalByRefObject → TraceListener(System.IDisposable)
Subclasses	DefaultTraceListener, EventLogTraceListener, TextWriterTraceListener
Returned By	TraceListenerCollection.this
Passed To	TraceListenerCollection.{Add( ), AddRange( ), Contains( ), CopyTo( ), IndexOf( ), Insert( ), Remove( ), this}

TraceListenerCollection   CF 1.0

System.Diagnostics (system.dll)   class

This class is a strongly typed, thread-safe collection that contains **TraceListener** objects.

```
public class TraceListenerCollection : IList, ICollection, IEnumerable {
// Public Instance Properties
  public int Count{get; }                                                      // implements ICollection
  public TraceListener this[string name]{get; }
  public TraceListener this[int i]{set; get; }
// Public Instance Methods
  public int Add(TraceListener listener);
  public void AddRange(TraceListener[ ] value);
  public void AddRange(TraceListenerCollection value);
  public void Clear( );                                                        // implements IList
  public bool Contains(TraceListener listener);
  public void CopyTo(TraceListener[ ] listeners, int index);
```

```
public IEnumerator GetEnumerator( );                                    // implements IEnumerable
public int IndexOf(TraceListener listener);
public void Insert(int index, TraceListener listener);
public void Remove(string name);
public void Remove(TraceListener listener);
public void RemoveAt(int index);                                        // implements IList
}
```

Returned By   Debug.Listeners, Trace.Listeners

TraceSwitch

System.Diagnostics (system.dll)   class

This class provides a switch that can be set to one of the values in the TraceLevel enumeration. These values are inclusive and cumulative (for example, if Level is set to TraceLevel. Info, then TraceInfo, TraceWarning, and TraceError are true). See TraceLevel for more details. You can configure a trace switch using the application configuration file (see Switch).

```
public class TraceSwitch : Switch {
// Public Constructors
    public TraceSwitch(string displayName, string description);
// Public Instance Properties
    public TraceLevel Level{set; get; }
    public bool TraceError{get; }
    public bool TraceInfo{get; }
    public bool TraceVerbose{get; }
    public bool TraceWarning{get; }
// Protected Instance Methods
    protected override void OnSwitchSettingChanged( );                  // overrides Switch
}
```

Hierarchy   System.Object → Switch → TraceSwitch

30

System.Globalization

The System.Globalization namespace provides classes that assist in localization of applications based on language and culture. The CultureInfo class is the primary container for a set of resources that is used for a specified language and culture implementation. It describes how strings are sorted, the specifics of calendars and date and time formats, as well as language and dialect code pages. An application obtains its culture information based on either the CultureInfo specified by the current thread or from the user or local machine's preferences. Specific cultural information is contained in resource files deployed in satellite assemblies. System.Resources.ResourceManager marshals these resource files into System.Resources.ResourceSets that provide the objects and methods specific to a localization.

The System.Globalization namespace provides a base Calendar class, as well as specific calendar implementations for major cultures. CompareInfo defines how string comparison and sorting are handled. DateTimeFormatInfo defines how DateTime values are formatted, and NumberFormatInfo defines various formatting styles, such as currency symbols and decimal and grouping separators. Figure 30-1 shows the types in this namespace.

Calendar   CF 1.0, serializable

System.Globalization (mscorlib.dll)   abstract class

This abstract class determines the division and measurement of time in units, such as day, months, years, and eras. It is an abstract base class for culture-specific calendar implementations included in this namespace. Derived classes store the specific information about a calendar's eras, lengths of years and months, and the sometimes esoteric rules for calculating leap years. These properties get used by DateTimeFormatInfo to properly display a date and time string from a specific DateTime value.

```
public abstract class Calendar {
// Protected Constructors
  protected Calendar( );
```

```
// Public Static Fields
  public const int CurrentEra;                                                          // =0
// Public Instance Properties
  public abstract int[ ] Eras{get; }
  public virtual int TwoDigitYearMax{set; get; }
// Public Instance Methods
  public virtual DateTime AddDays(DateTime time, int days);
  public virtual DateTime AddHours(DateTime time, int hours);
  public virtual DateTime AddMilliseconds(DateTime time, double milliseconds);
  public virtual DateTime AddMinutes(DateTime time, int minutes);
  public abstract DateTime AddMonths(DateTime time, int months);
  public virtual DateTime AddSeconds(DateTime time, int seconds);
  public virtual DateTime AddWeeks(DateTime time, int weeks);
  public abstract DateTime AddYears(DateTime time, int years);
  public abstract int GetDayOfMonth(DateTime time);
  public abstract DayOfWeek GetDayOfWeek(DateTime time);
  public abstract int GetDayOfYear(DateTime time);
  public virtual int GetDaysInMonth(int year, int month);
  public abstract int GetDaysInMonth(int year, int month, int era);
  public virtual int GetDaysInYear(int year);
  public abstract int GetDaysInYear(int year, int era);
  public abstract int GetEra(DateTime time);
  public virtual int GetHour(DateTime time);
  public virtual double GetMilliseconds(DateTime time);
  public virtual int GetMinute(DateTime time);
  public abstract int GetMonth(DateTime time);
  public virtual int GetMonthsInYear(int year);
  public abstract int GetMonthsInYear(int year, int era);
  public virtual int GetSecond(DateTime time);
  public virtual int GetWeekOfYear(DateTime time, CalendarWeekRule rule, DayOfWeek firstDayOfWeek);
  public abstract int GetYear(DateTime time);
  public virtual bool IsLeapDay(int year, int month, int day);
  public abstract bool IsLeapDay(int year, int month, int day, int era);
  public virtual bool IsLeapMonth(int year, int month);
  public abstract bool IsLeapMonth(int year, int month, int era);
  public virtual bool IsLeapYear(int year);
  public abstract bool IsLeapYear(int year, int era);
  public virtual DateTime ToDateTime(int year, int month, int day, int hour, int minute, int second, int millisecond);
  public abstract DateTime ToDateTime(int year, int month, int day, int hour, int minute, int second, int millisecond, int era);
  public virtual int ToFourDigitYear(int year);
}
```

Subclasses	GregorianCalendar, HebrewCalendar, HijriCalendar, JapaneseCalendar, JulianCalendar, KoreanCalendar, TaiwanCalendar, ThaiBuddhistCalendar
Returned By	CultureInfo.{Calendar, OptionalCalendars}, DateTimeFormatInfo.Calendar
Passed To	System.DateTime.DateTime( ), DateTimeFormatInfo.Calendar

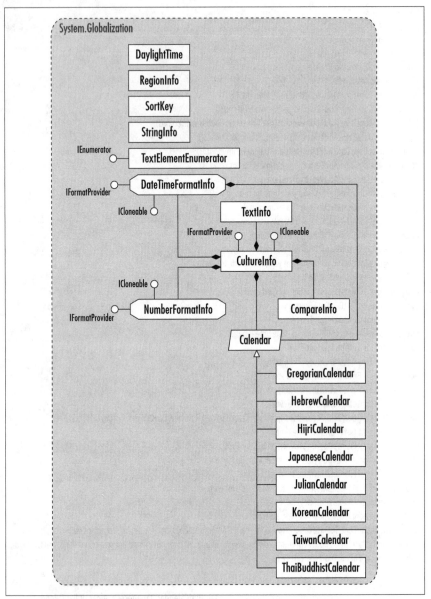

Figure 30-1. The System.Globalization namespace

CalendarWeekRule

CF 1.0, serializable

System.Globalization (mscorlib.dll)   enum

This enumeration contains values that specify how the first week of a calendar year is determined. Each calendar requires that the starting day of a week is designated (i.e., Sunday in the Gregorian calendar). The value FirstDay designates that the first calendar week begins on the first day of the year regardless of the number of days left in the week. The FirstFourDayWeek specifies the first week that has at least four days in it. FirstFull-Week uses the first complete week as the first in the calendar.

```
public enum CalendarWeekRule {
  FirstDay = 0,
  FirstFullWeek = 1,
  FirstFourDayWeek = 2
}
```

Hierarchy	System.Object → System.ValueType → System.Enum(System.IComparable, System. IFormattable, System.IConvertible) → CalendarWeekRule
Returned By	DateTimeFormatInfo.CalendarWeekRule
Passed To	Calendar.GetWeekOfYear( ), DateTimeFormatInfo.CalendarWeekRule

CompareInfo
CF 1.0, serializable

System.Globalization (mscorlib.dll)
class

This class defines methods of string comparison that follow culture-specific rules. The CultureInfo.CompareInfo property contains an instance of this class. The Compare() method and other string searching methods, such as IndexOf() and IsPrefix(), can be passed a set of CompareOptions, which provide culture-specific flags related to strings. The GetCompareInfo() method is used instead of a public constructor to retrieve an instance of this class.

```
public class CompareInfo : System.Runtime.Serialization.IDeserializationCallback {
// Public Instance Properties
  public int LCID{get; }
// Public Static Methods
  public static CompareInfo GetCompareInfo(int culture);
  public static CompareInfo GetCompareInfo(int culture, System.Reflection.Assembly assembly);
  public static CompareInfo GetCompareInfo(string name);
  public static CompareInfo GetCompareInfo(string name, System.Reflection.Assembly assembly);
// Public Instance Methods
  public virtual int Compare(string string1, int offset1, int length1, string string2, int offset2, int length2);
  public virtual int Compare(string string1, int offset1, int length1, string string2, int offset2, int length2,
    CompareOptions options);
  public virtual int Compare(string string1, int offset1, string string2, int offset2);
  public virtual int Compare(string string1, int offset1, string string2, int offset2, CompareOptions options);
  public virtual int Compare(string string1, string string2);
  public virtual int Compare(string string1, string string2, CompareOptions options);
  public override bool Equals(object value);                                    // overrides object
  public override int GetHashCode( );                                          // overrides object
  public virtual SortKey GetSortKey(string source);
  public virtual SortKey GetSortKey(string source, CompareOptions options);
  public virtual int IndexOf(string source, char value);
  public virtual int IndexOf(string source, char value, CompareOptions options);
  public virtual int IndexOf(string source, char value, int startIndex);
  public virtual int IndexOf(string source, char value, int startIndex, CompareOptions options);
  public virtual int IndexOf(string source, char value, int startIndex, int count);
  public virtual int IndexOf(string source, char value, int startIndex, int count, CompareOptions options);
```

```
public virtual int IndexOf(string source, string value);
public virtual int IndexOf(string source, string value, CompareOptions options);
public virtual int IndexOf(string source, string value, int startIndex);
public virtual int IndexOf(string source, string value, int startIndex, CompareOptions options);
public virtual int IndexOf(string source, string value, int startIndex, int count);
public virtual int IndexOf(string source, string value, int startIndex, int count, CompareOptions options);
public virtual bool IsPrefix(string source, string prefix);
public virtual bool IsPrefix(string source, string prefix, CompareOptions options);
public virtual bool IsSuffix(string source, string suffix);
public virtual bool IsSuffix(string source, string suffix, CompareOptions options);
public virtual int LastIndexOf(string source, char value);
public virtual int LastIndexOf(string source, char value, CompareOptions options);
public virtual int LastIndexOf(string source, char value, int startIndex);
public virtual int LastIndexOf(string source, char value, int startIndex, CompareOptions options);
public virtual int LastIndexOf(string source, char value, int startIndex, int count);
public virtual int LastIndexOf(string source, char value, int startIndex, int count, CompareOptions options);
public virtual int LastIndexOf(string source, string value);
public virtual int LastIndexOf(string source, string value, CompareOptions options);
public virtual int LastIndexOf(string source, string value, int startIndex);
public virtual int LastIndexOf(string source, string value, int startIndex, CompareOptions options);
public virtual int LastIndexOf(string source, string value, int startIndex, int count);
public virtual int LastIndexOf(string source, string value, int startIndex, int count, CompareOptions options);
public override string ToString( );                                        // overrides object
}
```

Returned By   CultureInfo.CompareInfo

CompareOptions   CF 1.0, serializable, flag

System.Globalization (mscorlib.dll)   enum

This enumeration defines a set of constants that set culture-specific behavior on string comparisons in the CompareInfo class. IgnoreKanaType treats phonetic Japanese symbols the same whether they are in hiragana or katagana characters. IgnoreNonSpace disregards nonspacing characters such as diacritics. Ordinal specifies that comparison is done with Unicode values.

```
public enum CompareOptions {
  None = 0x00000000,
  IgnoreCase = 0x00000001,
  IgnoreNonSpace = 0x00000002,
  IgnoreSymbols = 0x00000004,
  IgnoreKanaType = 0x00000008,
  IgnoreWidth = 0x00000010,
  StringSort = 0x20000000,
  Ordinal = 0x40000000
}
```

Hierarchy   System.Object → System.ValueType → System.Enum(System.IComparable, System. IFormattable, System.IConvertible) → CompareOptions

Passed To   CompareInfo.{Compare( ), GetSortKey( ), IndexOf( ), IsPrefix( ), IsSuffix( ), LastIndexOf( )}

System.Globalization (mscorlib.dll)   class

The CultureInfo class encapsulates information about handling information according to the special requirements of a particular culture and language. Culture information is identified by language and country/region codes as specified in RFC 1766. For example, U.S. English is identified as en-US. The two-letter, lowercase language codes are defined in ISO 639-1. The two-letter, uppercase region codes are defined in ISO 3166.

The specific CultureInfo to use at runtime can be found in a number of ways. The class provides four public properties that return the current CultureInfo instance. CurrentCulture returns the value of Thread.CurrentCulture, which is the CultureInfo used by the current thread. CurrentUICulture returns the CultureInfo used by the System.Resources.ResourceManager. This can be a user, machine, or application-based locale setting. It is set in Thread.CurrentUICulture. InstalledUICulture gets the default CultureInfo used by the ResourceManager and represents the locale of the Operating system. InvariantCulture returns the CultureInfo for the invariant locale, which is non-culture-specific, as well as in the default OS language. This is used with non-culture-specific functions such as system-level calls.

The instance properties of the class provide a number of ways to retrieve the culture name. For example, NativeName gets the culture name in the language of that culture. LCID gets the NLS-specified number for a culture name. Other properties get or set the various class instances used for localization. Calendar, CompareInfo, DateTimeFormat, Number-Format, and TextInfo return instances of the analogous classes that set their functionality.

```
public class CultureInfo : ICloneable, IFormatProvider {
// Public Constructors
  public CultureInfo(int culture);
  public CultureInfo(int culture, bool useUserOverride);
  public CultureInfo(string name);
  public CultureInfo(string name, bool useUserOverride);
// Public Static Properties
  public static CultureInfo CurrentCulture{get; }
  public static CultureInfo CurrentUICulture{get; }
  public static CultureInfo InstalledUICulture{get; }
  public static CultureInfo InvariantCulture{get; }
// Public Instance Properties
  public virtual Calendar Calendar{get; }
  public virtual CompareInfo CompareInfo{get; }
  public virtual DateTimeFormatInfo DateTimeFormat{set; get; }
  public virtual string DisplayName{get; }
  public virtual string EnglishName{get; }
  public virtual bool IsNeutralCulture{get; }
  public bool IsReadOnly{get; }
  public virtual int LCID{get; }
  public virtual string Name{get; }
  public virtual string NativeName{get; }
  public virtual NumberFormatInfo NumberFormat{set; get; }
  public virtual Calendar[ ] OptionalCalendars{get; }
  public virtual CultureInfo Parent{get; }
  public virtual TextInfo TextInfo{get; }
  public virtual string ThreeLetterISOLanguageName{get; }
```

```
  public virtual string ThreeLetterWindowsLanguageName{get; }
  public virtual string TwoLetterISOLanguageName{get; }
  public bool UseUserOverride{get; }
// Public Static Methods
  public static CultureInfo CreateSpecificCulture(string name);
  public static CultureInfo[ ] GetCultures(CultureTypes types);
  public static CultureInfo ReadOnly(CultureInfo ci);
// Public Instance Methods
  public void ClearCachedData( );
  public virtual object Clone( );                                               // implements ICloneable
  public override bool Equals(object value);                                    // overrides object
  public virtual object GetFormat(Type formatType);                             // implements IFormatProvider
  public override int GetHashCode( );                                           // overrides object
  public override string ToString( );                                          // overrides object
}
```

Returned By   System.Reflection.AssemblyName.CultureInfo, System.Threading.Thread.{CurrentCulture, CurrentUICulture}

Passed To   Multiple types

CultureTypes   CF 1.0, serializable, flag

System.Globalization (mscorlib.dll)   enum

The values of this enumeration determine which cultures are returned by CultureInfo. GetCultures( ). NeutralCultures specifies language-specific cultures without any regional or country association. SpecificCultures specifies cultures that are identified by both language and region.

```
public enum CultureTypes {
  NeutralCultures = 0x00000001,
  SpecificCultures = 0x00000002,
  InstalledWin32Cultures = 0x00000004,
  AllCultures = 0x00000007
}
```

Hierarchy   System.Object → System.ValueType → System.Enum(System.IComparable, System. IFormattable, System.IConvertible) → CultureTypes

Passed To   CultureInfo.GetCultures( )

DateTimeFormatInfo   CF 1.0, ECMA 1.0, serializable

System.Globalization (mscorlib.dll)   sealed class

This class defines how DateTime values are formatted for a culture. Several standard patterns are defined with the default property values. These standard patterns are designated by a format character. The format character provides a shortcut to specify the format of a DateTime with the ToString( ) method. You can create custom formats using a set of format pattern characters. These characters represent different styles of day and time representations and allow you to build customized pattern strings. To create custom patterns, first you need to construct a writable instance of DateTimeFormatInfo by using its constructor. Use InvariantInfo to fetch a culture-independent, read-only instance of this class.

```
public sealed class DateTimeFormatInfo : ICloneable, IFormatProvider {
// Public Constructors
  public DateTimeFormatInfo( );
// Public Static Properties
  public static DateTimeFormatInfo CurrentInfo{get; }
  public static DateTimeFormatInfo InvariantInfo{get; }
// Public Instance Properties
  public string[ ] AbbreviatedDayNames{set; get; }
  public string[ ] AbbreviatedMonthNames{set; get; }
  public string AMDesignator{set; get; }
  public Calendar Calendar{set; get; }
  public CalendarWeekRule CalendarWeekRule{set; get; }
  public string DateSeparator{set; get; }
  public string[ ] DayNames{set; get; }
  public DayOfWeek FirstDayOfWeek{set; get; }
  public string FullDateTimePattern{set; get; }
  public bool IsReadOnly{get; }
  public string LongDatePattern{set; get; }
  public string LongTimePattern{set; get; }
  public string MonthDayPattern{set; get; }
  public string[ ] MonthNames{set; get; }
  public string PMDesignator{set; get; }
  public string RFC1123Pattern{get; }
  public string ShortDatePattern{set; get; }
  public string ShortTimePattern{set; get; }
  public string SortableDateTimePattern{get; }
  public string TimeSeparator{set; get; }
  public string UniversalSortableDateTimePattern{get; }
  public string YearMonthPattern{set; get; }
// Public Static Methods
  public static DateTimeFormatInfo GetInstance(IFormatProvider provider);
  public static DateTimeFormatInfo ReadOnly(DateTimeFormatInfo dtfi);
// Public Instance Methods
  public object Clone( );                                          // implements ICloneable
  public string GetAbbreviatedDayName(DayOfWeek dayofweek);
  public string GetAbbreviatedEraName(int era);
  public string GetAbbreviatedMonthName(int month);
  public string[ ] GetAllDateTimePatterns( );
  public string[ ] GetAllDateTimePatterns(char format);
  public string GetDayName(DayOfWeek dayofweek);
  public int GetEra(string eraName);
  public string GetEraName(int era);
  public object GetFormat(Type formatType);                       // implements IFormatProvider
  public string GetMonthName(int month);
}
```

Returned By   CultureInfo.DateTimeFormat

Passed To   CultureInfo.DateTimeFormat

DateTimeStyles

CF 1.0, ECMA 1.0, serializable, flag

System.Globalization (mscorlib.dll)   enum

This enumeration provides several formatting options for the DateTime.Parse() and DateTime.ParseExact() methods to use. The values supplied mostly determine how whitespace is dealt with when a string is parsed into a DateTime value by ParseExact(). When the string is compared to a format pattern, some whitespace can be disregarded if it is not exactly aligned with the pattern. Parse() ignores whitespace by default, so AdjustToUniversal and NoCurrentDateDefault are the only relevant values for that method. If the string to parse does not include a date with NoCurrentDateDefault, its result is created with day, month, and year values all set to 1. The date and time are converted to coordinated universal time (UTC) with AdjustToUniversal.

```
public enum DateTimeStyles {
  None = 0x00000000,
  AllowLeadingWhite = 0x00000001,
  AllowTrailingWhite = 0x00000002,
  AllowInnerWhite = 0x00000004,
  AllowWhiteSpaces = 0x00000007,
  NoCurrentDateDefault = 0x00000008,
  AdjustToUniversal = 0x00000010
}
```

Hierarchy   System.Object → System.ValueType → System.Enum(System.IComparable, System. IFormattable, System.IConvertible) → DateTimeStyles

Passed To   System.DateTime.{Parse( ), ParseExact( )}

DaylightTime

CF 1.0, serializable

System.Globalization (mscorlib.dll)   class

This setting defines when daylight saving time begins and ends. It uses three properties: Start is the time when daylight saving time begins; End is when standard time resumes; and Delta is the length of time (measured in ticks) that the clock is adjusted from standard time during this period. Delta is a System.TimeSpan value measured in "ticks," or 100-nanosecond periods.

```
public class DaylightTime {
// Public Constructors
  public DaylightTime(DateTime start, DateTime end, TimeSpan delta);
// Public Instance Properties
  public TimeSpan Delta{get; }
  public DateTime End{get; }
  public DateTime Start{get; }
}
```

Returned By   System.TimeZone.GetDaylightChanges( )

Passed To   System.TimeZone.IsDaylightSavingTime( )

466 | Chapter 30: System.Globalization

GregorianCalendar

System.Globalization (mscorlib.dll)   class

This class implements the standard Western calendar, and also the default culture-invariant calendar. It defines two eras (B.C./B.C.E. and A.D./C.E.), 12 months per year. A leap year occurs every 4 years except for years divisible by 100. However, years divisible by 400 are leap years. Only the current era (A.D./C.E.) is recognized by .NET's implementation of the Gregorian calendar.

```
public class GregorianCalendar : Calendar {
// Public Constructors
  public GregorianCalendar( );
  public GregorianCalendar(GregorianCalendarTypes type);
// Public Static Fields
  public const int ADEra;                                                              // =1
// Public Instance Properties
  public virtual GregorianCalendarTypes CalendarType{set; get; }
  public override int[ ] Eras{get; }                                       // overrides Calendar
  public override int TwoDigitYearMax{set; get; }                          // overrides Calendar
// Public Instance Methods
  public override DateTime AddMonths(DateTime time, int months);            // overrides Calendar
  public override DateTime AddWeeks(DateTime time, int weeks);              // overrides Calendar
  public override DateTime AddYears(DateTime time, int years);              // overrides Calendar
  public override int GetDayOfMonth(DateTime time);                        // overrides Calendar
  public override DayOfWeek GetDayOfWeek(DateTime time);                    // overrides Calendar
  public override int GetDayOfYear(DateTime time);                         // overrides Calendar
  public override int GetDaysInMonth(int year, int month, int era);        // overrides Calendar
  public override int GetDaysInYear(int year, int era);                    // overrides Calendar
  public override int GetEra(DateTime time);                               // overrides Calendar
  public override int GetMonth(DateTime time);                             // overrides Calendar
  public override int GetMonthsInYear(int year, int era);                  // overrides Calendar
  public override int GetYear(DateTime time);                              // overrides Calendar
  public override bool IsLeapDay(int year, int month, int day, int era);   // overrides Calendar
  public override bool IsLeapMonth(int year, int month, int era);          // overrides Calendar
  public override bool IsLeapYear(int year, int era);                      // overrides Calendar
  public override DateTime ToDateTime(int year, int month, int day,
      int hour, int minute, int second, int millisecond, int era);         // overrides Calendar
  public override int ToFourDigitYear(int year);                           // overrides Calendar
}
```

Hierarchy   System.Object → Calendar → GregorianCalendar

GregorianCalendarTypes

System.Globalization (mscorlib.dll)   enum

This enumeration specifies some language-specific variations of the Gregorian calendar that can be set with the GregorianCalendar.CalendarType property.

```
public enum GregorianCalendarTypes {
  Localized = 1,
  USEnglish = 2,
```

GregorianCalendarTypes | 467

```
MiddleEastFrench = 9,
Arabic = 10,
TransliteratedEnglish = 11,
TransliteratedFrench = 12
}
```

Hierarchy	System.Object → System.ValueType → System.Enum(System.IComparable, System. IFormattable, System.IConvertible) → GregorianCalendarTypes

Returned By	GregorianCalendar.CalendarType

Passed To	GregorianCalendar.{CalendarType, GregorianCalendar( )}

HebrewCalendar

serializable

System.Globalization (mscorlib.dll)   class

This calendar class implements the Hebrew calendar. This complicated calendar determines leap years within a 19-year cycle. The 3rd, 6th, 8th, 11th, 14th, 17th, and 19th years are leap years. Regular years have 12 months and between 353 and 355 days, and leap years have 13 months and between 383 and 385 days; the variance is determined by the placement of Jewish holidays. This implementation recognizes the years 5343 to 6000 (A.M.), which is equivalent to the Gregorian years 1582 to 2240.

```
public class HebrewCalendar : Calendar {
// Public Constructors
  public HebrewCalendar( );
// Public Static Fields
  public static readonly int HebrewEra;                                                    // =1
// Public Instance Properties
  public override int[ ] Eras{get; }                                               // overrides Calendar
  public override int TwoDigitYearMax{set; get; }                                  // overrides Calendar
// Public Instance Methods
  public override DateTime AddMonths(DateTime time, int months);                   // overrides Calendar
  public override DateTime AddYears(DateTime time, int years);                     // overrides Calendar
  public override int GetDayOfMonth(DateTime time);                               // overrides Calendar
  public override DayOfWeek GetDayOfWeek(DateTime time);                          // overrides Calendar
  public override int GetDayOfYear(DateTime time);                               // overrides Calendar
  public override int GetDaysInMonth(int year, int month, int era);              // overrides Calendar
  public override int GetDaysInYear(int year, int era);                          // overrides Calendar
  public override int GetEra(DateTime time);                                     // overrides Calendar
  public override int GetMonth(DateTime time);                                   // overrides Calendar
  public override int GetMonthsInYear(int year, int era);                        // overrides Calendar
  public override int GetYear(DateTime time);                                    // overrides Calendar
  public override bool IsLeapDay(int year, int month, int day, int era);         // overrides Calendar
  public override bool IsLeapMonth(int year, int month, int era);                // overrides Calendar
  public override bool IsLeapYear(int year, int era);                            // overrides Calendar
  public override DateTime ToDateTime(int year, int month, int day, int hour,
    int minute, int second, int millisecond, int era);                          // overrides Calendar
  public override int ToFourDigitYear(int year);                                 // overrides Calendar
}
```

Hierarchy	System.Object → Calendar → HebrewCalendar

HijriCalendar

System.Globalization (mscorlib.dll)   class

This calendar class implements the Islamic Hijri calendar. This calendar is based from the time of Mohammed's migration from Mecca (denoted as A.H.). Regular years have 12 months and 354 days. Leap years have 355 days. Leap years are calculated in 30-year cycles, occurring in the 2nd, 5th, 7th, 10th, 13th, 16th, 18th, 21st, 24th, 26th, and 29th years.

```
public class HijriCalendar : Calendar {
// Public Constructors
  public HijriCalendar( );
// Public Static Fields
  public static readonly int HijriEra;                                               // =1
// Public Instance Properties
  public override int[ ] Eras{get; }                                          // overrides Calendar
  public int HijriAdjustment{set; get; }
  public override int TwoDigitYearMax{set; get; }                             // overrides Calendar
// Public Instance Methods
  public override DateTime AddMonths(DateTime time, int months);              // overrides Calendar
  public override DateTime AddYears(DateTime time, int years);                // overrides Calendar
  public override int GetDayOfMonth(DateTime time);                           // overrides Calendar
  public override DayOfWeek GetDayOfWeek(DateTime time);                      // overrides Calendar
  public override int GetDayOfYear(DateTime time);                           // overrides Calendar
  public override int GetDaysInMonth(int year, int month, int era);          // overrides Calendar
  public override int GetDaysInYear(int year, int era);                      // overrides Calendar
  public override int GetEra(DateTime time);                                 // overrides Calendar
  public override int GetMonth(DateTime time);                               // overrides Calendar
  public override int GetMonthsInYear(int year, int era);                    // overrides Calendar
  public override int GetYear(DateTime time);                                // overrides Calendar
  public override bool IsLeapDay(int year, int month, int day, int era);     // overrides Calendar
  public override bool IsLeapMonth(int year, int month, int era);            // overrides Calendar
  public override bool IsLeapYear(int year, int era);                        // overrides Calendar
  public override DateTime ToDateTime(int year, int month, int day,
       int hour, int minute, int second, int millisecond, int era);          // overrides Calendar
  public override int ToFourDigitYear(int year);                             // overrides Calendar
}
```

Hierarchy   System.Object → Calendar → HijriCalendar

JapaneseCalendar

System.Globalization (mscorlib.dll)   class

This calendar class implements the Japanese or Wareki calendar. This calendar follows the same rules and settings as the Gregorian calendar, except that it is divided into eras based on the reign of each Japanese Emperor.

```
public class JapaneseCalendar : Calendar {
// Public Constructors
  public JapaneseCalendar( );
// Public Instance Properties
```

public override int[ ] **Eras**{get; }	// overrides Calendar
public override int **TwoDigitYearMax**{set; get; }	// overrides Calendar
// Public Instance Methods	
public override DateTime **AddMonths**(DateTime *time*, int *months*);	// overrides Calendar
public override DateTime **AddYears**(DateTime *time*, int *years*);	// overrides Calendar
public override int **GetDayOfMonth**(DateTime *time*);	// overrides Calendar
public override DayOfWeek **GetDayOfWeek**(DateTime *time*);	// overrides Calendar
public override int **GetDayOfYear**(DateTime *time*);	// overrides Calendar
public override int **GetDaysInMonth**(int *year*, int *month*, int *era*);	// overrides Calendar
public override int **GetDaysInYear**(int *year*, int *era*);	// overrides Calendar
public override int **GetEra**(DateTime *time*);	// overrides Calendar
public override int **GetMonth**(DateTime *time*);	// overrides Calendar
public override int **GetMonthsInYear**(int *year*, int *era*);	// overrides Calendar
public override int **GetYear**(DateTime *time*);	// overrides Calendar
public override bool **IsLeapDay**(int *year*, int *month*, int *day*, int *era*);	// overrides Calendar
public override bool **IsLeapMonth**(int *year*, int *month*, int *era*);	// overrides Calendar
public override bool **IsLeapYear**(int *year*, int *era*);	// overrides Calendar
public override DateTime **ToDateTime**(int *year*, int *month*, int *day*, int *hour*,int *minute*, int *second*, int *millisecond*, int *era*);	// overrides Calendar
public override int **ToFourDigitYear**(int *year*);	// overrides Calendar
}	

Hierarchy   System.Object → Calendar → JapaneseCalendar

JulianCalendar   serializable

System.Globalization (mscorlib.dll)   class

This calendar class implements the calendar created by a decree from Julius Caesar in 45 B.C.E. The calendar recognizes a leap year every four years without exception, but in all other respects is the same as the Gregorian calendar, which replaced it in 1582 C.E. Due to the difference in leap-year calculation, the Julian calendar is currently 12 days behind the Gregorian calendar.

public class **JulianCalendar** : Calendar {	
// Public Constructors	
public **JulianCalendar**( );	
// Public Static Fields	
public static readonly int **JulianEra**;	// =1
// Public Instance Properties	
public override int[ ] **Eras**{get; }	// overrides Calendar
public override int **TwoDigitYearMax**{set; get; }	// overrides Calendar
// Public Instance Methods	
public override DateTime **AddMonths**(DateTime *time*, int *months*);	// overrides Calendar
public override DateTime **AddYears**(DateTime *time*, int *years*);	// overrides Calendar
public override int **GetDayOfMonth**(DateTime *time*);	// overrides Calendar
public override DayOfWeek **GetDayOfWeek**(DateTime *time*);	// overrides Calendar
public override int **GetDayOfYear**(DateTime *time*);	// overrides Calendar
public override int **GetDaysInMonth**(int *year*, int *month*, int *era*);	// overrides Calendar
public override int **GetDaysInYear**(int *year*, int *era*);	// overrides Calendar
public override int **GetEra**(DateTime *time*);	// overrides Calendar
public override int **GetMonth**(DateTime *time*);	// overrides Calendar
public override int **GetMonthsInYear**(int *year*, int *era*);	// overrides Calendar

```
public override int GetYear(DateTime time);                              // overrides Calendar
public override bool IsLeapDay(int year, int month, int day, int era);   // overrides Calendar
public override bool IsLeapMonth(int year, int month, int era);          // overrides Calendar
public override bool IsLeapYear(int year, int era);                      // overrides Calendar
public override DateTime ToDateTime(int year, int month, int day, int hour,
    int minute, int second, int millisecond, int era);                  // overrides Calendar
public override int ToFourDigitYear(int year);                           // overrides Calendar
}
```

Hierarchy System.Object → Calendar → JulianCalendar

KoreanCalendar   CF 1.0, serializable

System.Globalization (mscorlib.dll)   class

This calendar class implements the Korean calendar. The Korean calendar is the same as the Gregorian calendar except that the eras are defined differently. 01 January, 2001 on the Gregorian calendar is 01 January, 4334 on the Korean calendar.

```
public class KoreanCalendar : Calendar {
// Public Constructors
  public KoreanCalendar( );
// Public Static Fields
  public const int KoreanEra;                                           // =1
// Public Instance Properties
  public override int[ ] Eras{get; }                                    // overrides Calendar
  public override int TwoDigitYearMax{set; get; }                       // overrides Calendar
// Public Instance Methods
  public override DateTime AddMonths(DateTime time,                     // overrides Calendar
    int months);
  public override DateTime AddYears(DateTime time,                      // overrides Calendar
    int years);
  public override int GetDayOfMonth(DateTime time);                     // overrides Calendar
  public override DayOfWeek GetDayOfWeek(DateTime time);                // overrides Calendar
  public override int GetDayOfYear(DateTime time);                      // overrides Calendar
  public override int GetDaysInMonth(int year, int month,              // overrides Calendar
    int era);
  public override int GetDaysInYear(int year, int era);                // overrides Calendar
  public override int GetEra(DateTime time);                           // overrides Calendar
  public override int GetMonth(DateTime time);                         // overrides Calendar
  public override int GetMonthsInYear(int year, int era);              // overrides Calendar
  public override int GetYear(DateTime time);                          // overrides Calendar
  public override bool IsLeapDay(int year, int month,                  // overrides Calendar
    int day, int era);
  public override bool IsLeapMonth(int year, int month,                // overrides Calendar
    int era);
  public override bool IsLeapYear(int year, int era);                  // overrides Calendar
  public override DateTime ToDateTime(int year, int month,             // overrides Calendar
    int day, int hour, int minute, int second,  int millisecond, int era);
  public override int ToFourDigitYear(int year);                       // overrides Calendar
}
```

Hierarchy System.Object → Calendar → KoreanCalendar

NumberFormatInfo

CF 1.0, ECMA 1.0, serializable

System.Globalization (mscorlib.dll)   sealed class

This class defines how numbers are displayed according to culture and language. Formats for currency and its symbols and types of numeric formats, such as scientific and hexadecimal notations and their separators, are described by the properties of this class. As with DateTimeFormatInfo, a set of standard numeric formats is predefined and specified by format characters.

The default property values apply to the invariant culture settings. The culture-specific NumberFormatInfo instance is retrieved by CurrentInfo, which is determined by the CultureInfo of the current thread or environment.

```
public sealed class NumberFormatInfo : ICloneable, IFormatProvider {
// Public Constructors
  public NumberFormatInfo( );
// Public Static Properties
  public static NumberFormatInfo CurrentInfo{get; }
  public static NumberFormatInfo InvariantInfo{get; }
// Public Instance Properties
  public int CurrencyDecimalDigits{set; get; }
  public string CurrencyDecimalSeparator{set; get; }
  public string CurrencyGroupSeparator{set; get; }
  public int[ ] CurrencyGroupSizes{set; get; }
  public int CurrencyNegativePattern{set; get; }
  public int CurrencyPositivePattern{set; get; }
  public string CurrencySymbol{set; get; }
  public bool IsReadOnly{get; }
  public string NaNSymbol{set; get; }
  public string NegativeInfinitySymbol{set; get; }
  public string NegativeSign{set; get; }
  public int NumberDecimalDigits{set; get; }
  public string NumberDecimalSeparator{set; get; }
  public string NumberGroupSeparator{set; get; }
  public int[ ] NumberGroupSizes{set; get; }
  public int NumberNegativePattern{set; get; }
  public int PercentDecimalDigits{set; get; }
  public string PercentDecimalSeparator{set; get; }
  public string PercentGroupSeparator{set; get; }
  public int[ ] PercentGroupSizes{set; get; }
  public int PercentNegativePattern{set; get; }
  public int PercentPositivePattern{set; get; }
  public string PercentSymbol{set; get; }
  public string PerMilleSymbol{set; get; }
  public string PositiveInfinitySymbol{set; get; }
  public string PositiveSign{set; get; }
// Public Static Methods
  public static NumberFormatInfo GetInstance(IFormatProvider formatProvider);
  public static NumberFormatInfo ReadOnly(NumberFormatInfo nfi);
// Public Instance Methods
  public object Clone( );                                    // implements ICloneable
```

```
public object GetFormat(Type formatType);                              // implements IFormatProvider
}
```

Returned By   CultureInfo.NumberFormat

Passed To   CultureInfo.NumberFormat

NumberStyles

CF 1.0, ECMA 1.0, serializable, flag

System.Globalization (mscorlib.dll)   enum

This enumeration specifies a number of style rules that may be used when a numeric
type uses the Parse( ) method to convert a string into a number.

```
public enum NumberStyles {
  None = 0x00000000,
  AllowLeadingWhite = 0x00000001,
  AllowTrailingWhite = 0x00000002,
  AllowLeadingSign = 0x00000004,
  Integer = 0x00000007,
  AllowTrailingSign = 0x00000008,
  AllowParentheses = 0x00000010,
  AllowDecimalPoint = 0x00000020,
  AllowThousands = 0x00000040,
  Number = 0x0000006F,
  AllowExponent = 0x00000080,
  Float = 0x000000A7,
  AllowCurrencySymbol = 0x00000100,
  Currency = 0x0000017F,
  Any = 0x000001FF,
  AllowHexSpecifier = 0x00000200,
  HexNumber = 0x00000203
}
```

Hierarchy   System.Object → System.ValueType → System.Enum(System.IComparable, System.
IFormattable, System.IConvertible) → NumberStyles

Passed To   System.Byte.Parse( ), System.Decimal.Parse( ), System.Double.{Parse( ), TryParse( )}, System.
Int16.Parse( ), System.Int32.Parse( ), System.Int64.Parse( ), System.SByte.Parse( ), System.
Single.Parse( ), System.UInt16.Parse( ), System.UInt32.Parse( ), System.UInt64.Parse( )

RegionInfo

CF 1.0, serializable

System.Globalization (mscorlib.dll)   class

This class contains properties for the selected region or country settings. It stores information on the name and standard letter codes for the region, the currency symbol, and
whether the metric system is used or not. The region names are the two- and three-
letter codes defined in ISO 3166. Currency strings are defined by ISO 4217.

```
public class RegionInfo {
// Public Constructors
  public RegionInfo(int culture);
```

```
    public RegionInfo(string name);
// Public Static Properties
    public static RegionInfo CurrentRegion{get; }
// Public Instance Properties
    public virtual string CurrencySymbol{get; }
    public virtual string DisplayName{get; }
    public virtual string EnglishName{get; }
    public virtual bool IsMetric{get; }
    public virtual string ISOCurrencySymbol{get; }
    public virtual string Name{get; }
    public virtual string ThreeLetterISORegionName{get; }
    public virtual string ThreeLetterWindowsRegionName{get; }
    public virtual string TwoLetterISORegionName{get; }
// Public Instance Methods
    public override bool Equals(object value);                        // overrides object
    public override int GetHashCode( );                              // overrides object
    public override string ToString( );                             // overrides object
}
```

SortKey   serializable

System.Globalization (mscorlib.dll)   class

This class represents a set of weighted classifications used to sort individual elements
of a string.

```
public class SortKey {
// Public Instance Properties
    public virtual byte[ ] KeyData{get; }
    public virtual string OriginalString{get; }
// Public Static Methods
    public static int Compare(SortKey sortkey1, SortKey sortkey2);
// Public Instance Methods
    public override bool Equals(object value);                        // overrides object
    public override int GetHashCode( );                              // overrides object
    public override string ToString( );                             // overrides object
}
```

Returned By   CompareInfo.GetSortKey( )

StringInfo   CF 1.0, serializable

System.Globalization (mscorlib.dll)   class

This class allows you to manipulate a string by its individual elements. Each separately displayed character is considered a text element. This includes base characters
and the Unicode-defined surrogate pairs and combining character sequences. The class
provides enumeration of the elements in the string, as well as a means of further identifying combining characters. ParseCombiningCharacters( ) returns only the indexes of the base
characters, high surrogates, and combined characters within a string.

```
public class StringInfo {
// Public Constructors
   public StringInfo( );
// Public Static Methods
   public static string GetNextTextElement(string str);
   public static string GetNextTextElement(string str, int index);
   public static TextElementEnumerator GetTextElementEnumerator(string str);
   public static TextElementEnumerator GetTextElementEnumerator(string str, int index);
   public static int[ ] ParseCombiningCharacters(string str);
}
```

TaiwanCalendar
CF 1.0, serializable

System.Globalization (mscorlib.dll)   class

This class implements the Taiwanese calendar. This calendar works like the Gregorian calendar, except for difference in the year and era. 2001 in the Gregorian calendar is the year 90 in the Taiwanese calendar.

```
public class TaiwanCalendar : Calendar {
// Public Constructors
   public TaiwanCalendar( );
// Public Instance Properties
   public override int[ ] Eras{get; }                                    // overrides Calendar
   public override int TwoDigitYearMax{set; get; }                       // overrides Calendar
// Public Instance Methods
   public override DateTime AddMonths(DateTime time, int months);        // overrides Calendar
   public override DateTime AddYears(DateTime time, int years);          // overrides Calendar
   public override int GetDayOfMonth(DateTime time);                     // overrides Calendar
   public override DayOfWeek GetDayOfWeek(DateTime time);                // overrides Calendar
   public override int GetDayOfYear(DateTime time);                      // overrides Calendar
   public override int GetDaysInMonth(int year, int month, int era);     // overrides Calendar
   public override int GetDaysInYear(int year, int era);                 // overrides Calendar
   public override int GetEra(DateTime time);                            // overrides Calendar
   public override int GetMonth(DateTime time);                          // overrides Calendar
   public override int GetMonthsInYear(int year, int era);               // overrides Calendar
   public override int GetYear(DateTime time);                           // overrides Calendar
   public override bool IsLeapDay(int year, int month, int day, int era); // overrides Calendar
   public override bool IsLeapMonth(int year, int month, int era);       // overrides Calendar
   public override bool IsLeapYear(int year, int era);                   // overrides Calendar
   public override DateTime ToDateTime(int year, int month, int day, int hour,
      int minute, int second, int millisecond, int era);                // overrides Calendar
   public override int ToFourDigitYear(int year);                        // overrides Calendar
}
```

Hierarchy   System.Object → Calendar → TaiwanCalendar

TextElementEnumerator
CF 1.0, serializable

System.Globalization (mscorlib.dll)   class

This class provides enumeration for individual text elements in a string composed of complex characters. This enumerator is retrieved by StringInfo.GetTextElementEnumerator( ).

```
public class TextElementEnumerator : IEnumerator {
// Public Instance Properties
  public object Current{get; }                                              // implements IEnumerator
  public int ElementIndex{get; }
// Public Instance Methods
  public string GetTextElement( );
  public bool MoveNext( );                                                  // implements IEnumerator
  public void Reset( );                                                     // implements IEnumerator
}
```

Returned By   StringInfo.GetTextElementEnumerator( )

TextInfo   CF 1.0, serializable

System.Globalization (mscorlib.dll)   class

This class is used to describe certain properties of the writing system in use by a
culture. The properties of this class specify system-specific and standardized code
pages for text, as well as the ListSeparator string (a "," for the invariant culture). TextInfo
defines methods that determine casing semantics per culture. For example, ToLower( )
returns the lowercase version of the specified character or string. The ToTitleCase( )
method capitalizes the first letter of each word in a string.

```
public class TextInfo : System.Runtime.Serialization.IDeserializationCallback {
// Public Instance Properties
  public virtual int ANSICodePage{get; }
  public virtual int EBCDICCodePage{get; }
  public virtual string ListSeparator{get; }
  public virtual int MacCodePage{get; }
  public virtual int OEMCodePage{get; }
// Public Instance Methods
  public override bool Equals(object obj);                                  // overrides object
  public override int GetHashCode( );                                      // overrides object
  public virtual char ToLower(char c);
  public virtual string ToLower(string str);
  public override string ToString( );                                     // overrides object
  public string ToTitleCase(string str);
  public virtual char ToUpper(char c);
  public virtual string ToUpper(string str);
}
```

Returned By   CultureInfo.TextInfo

ThaiBuddhistCalendar   CF 1.0, serializable

System.Globalization (mscorlib.dll)   class

This class implements the Thai Buddhist calendar. This calendar works like the Gregorian calendar except for the year and era. 2001 in the Gregorian calendar is the year
2544 in the Thai Buddhist calendar.

```
public class ThaiBuddhistCalendar : Calendar {
// Public Constructors
  public ThaiBuddhistCalendar( );
// Public Static Fields
  public const int ThaiBuddhistEra;                                              // =1
// Public Instance Properties
  public override int[ ] Eras{get; }                                  // overrides Calendar
  public override int TwoDigitYearMax{set; get; }                     // overrides Calendar
// Public Instance Methods
  public override DateTime AddMonth4s(DateTime time, int months);     // overrides Calendar
  public override DateTime AddYears(DateTime time, int years);        // overrides Calendar
  public override int GetDayOfMonth(DateTime time);                   // overrides Calendar
  public override DayOfWeek GetDayOfWeek(DateTime time);              // overrides Calendar
  public override int GetDayOfYear(DateTime time);                    // overrides Calendar
  public override int GetDaysInMonth(int year, int month, int era);   // overrides Calendar
  public override int GetDaysInYear(int year, int era);               // overrides Calendar
  public override int GetEra(DateTime time);                          // overrides Calendar
  public override int GetMonth(DateTime time);                        // overrides Calendar
  public override int GetMonthsInYear(int year, int era);             // overrides Calendar
  public override int GetYear(DateTime time);                         // overrides Calendar
  public override bool IsLeapDay(int year, int month, int day, int era); // overrides Calendar
  public override bool IsLeapMonth(int year, int month, int era);     // overrides Calendar
  public override bool IsLeapYear(int year, int era);                 // overrides Calendar
  public override DateTime ToDateTime(int year, int month, int day, int hour,
    int minute, int second, int millisecond, int era);               // overrides Calendar
  public override int ToFourDigitYear(int year);                      // overrides Calendar
}
```

Hierarchy System.Object → Calendar → ThaiBuddhistCalendar

UnicodeCategory

CF 1.0, ECMA 1.0, serializable

System.Globalization (mscorlib.dll)   enum

The values of this enumeration specify the specific category of a character defined by the Unicode standard. This enumeration supports the **System.Char** class in determining properties of Unicode characters such as case with regard to the **CultureInfo** setting.

```
public enum UnicodeCategory {
  UppercaseLetter = 0,
  LowercaseLetter = 1,
  TitlecaseLetter = 2,
  ModifierLetter = 3,
  OtherLetter = 4,
  NonSpacingMark = 5,
  SpacingCombiningMark = 6,
  EnclosingMark = 7,
  DecimalDigitNumber = 8,
  LetterNumber = 9,
  OtherNumber = 10,
  SpaceSeparator = 11,
  LineSeparator = 12,
```

System.
Globalization

```
ParagraphSeparator = 13,
Control = 14,
Format = 15,
Surrogate = 16,
PrivateUse = 17,
ConnectorPunctuation = 18,
DashPunctuation = 19,
OpenPunctuation = 20,
ClosePunctuation = 21,
InitialQuotePunctuation = 22,
FinalQuotePunctuation = 23,
OtherPunctuation = 24,
MathSymbol = 25,
CurrencySymbol = 26,
ModifierSymbol = 27,
OtherSymbol = 28,
OtherNotAssigned = 29
}
```

Hierarchy System.Object → System.ValueType → System.Enum(System.IComparable, System. IFormattable, System.IConvertible) → UnicodeCategory

Returned By System.Char.GetUnicodeCategory( )

31

System.IO

The System.IO types serve as the primary means for stream-oriented I/O—files, principally, although the abstract types defined here serve as base classes for other forms of I/O, such as the XML stack in System.Xml. The System.IO namespace is shown in Figures 31-1 and 31-2.

The System.IO namespace can be seen as two distinct partitions: a set of utility types for using and working with the local machine's filesystem, and a protocol stack for working with bytestream-oriented input and output. The former partition is the collection of classes such as Directory and FileSystemWatcher, whereas the latter partition is the set of Stream and Reader/Writer types.

The Stream types in System.IO follow a basic object model, similar to the I/O model used by the C/C++ runtime library: all serial byte access is a stream, and there are different sources and sinks for this serialized byte data. In the System.IO package, this is represented directly by the abstract base type Stream; its concrete subtypes represent the actual I/O access: FileStream represents I/O to a file, and MemoryStream represents I/O to a literal array of bytes (whose size is dynamically managed) in memory. Other packages within the .NET Framework Class Library offer up their own Stream-derived types. For example, in the System.Net namespace, socket connections and HTTP responses are offered up as Stream-derived types, giving .NET programmers the ability to treat any sort of input or output data as "just a stream."

Simply reading and writing to these streams is not enough of an abstraction, however. In particular, programmers often need to perform one of two sorts of I/O: binary I/O, which is writing actual binary representations of objects or data to disk, or text I/O, which is writing the textual representations of that data. These operations are fundamentally different—writing the text representation of the integer value 5 produces the literal text "5" within the stream, whereas writing the binary value generates the hex value 0x00000005 (represented as four bytes, 05 00 00 00, in the file). In the .NET libraries, because these types of I/O operations are different from one another, these operations are abstracted out into two sets of abstract base types. BinaryReader and BinaryWriter are for reading and writing binary values to streams, and TextReader and TextWriter are for reading and writing character-based data.

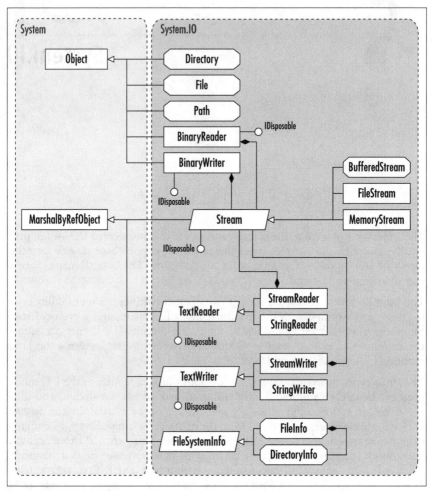

Figure 31-1. The System.IO namespace

Note that the System.IO namespace also offers some interesting stream-on-stream options. Like the Java java.io package, Stream types can layer on top of other Stream types to offer additional functionality—this is the Decorator pattern (from the *Design Patterns* book). The sole example of this in the System.IO namespace is the BufferedStream, which maintains a buffer on top of the Stream object passed to it in its constructor.

All of these types work together to provide some powerful abstraction and composite behaviors. For example, when working with random-access data, create a BinaryReader around a BufferedStream, which in turn wraps around a FileStream. If you decide later to store the random-access data in memory for optimization's

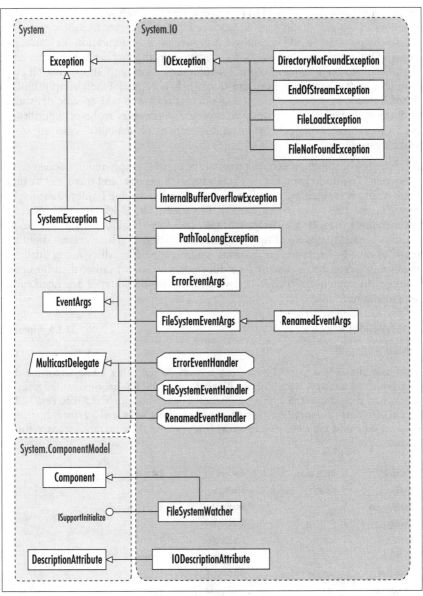

Figure 31-2. Exceptions, delegates, event arguments, and components in the System.IO namespace

sake, change the BufferedStream/FileStream pair to a MemoryStream. When reading a configuration file, choose to declare the ReadConfiguration method you have written to take an arbitrary TextReader, rather than ask for a string containing the filename. This allows for flexibility later—perhaps the configuration wants to be stored into a CLOB field in an RDBMS. Simply change the actual Stream instance passed into the TextReader, and start reading the configuration out of the RDBMS, off of a socket request, or out of the HTTP response sent to a web server. Similarly, when planning to extend the System.IO namespace's capabilities, try to follow this same model. If you want to add compression to save on a configuration file's size, just build a CompressingStream that wraps another Stream in the manner BufferedStream does. If you want to have some interprocess communication with an existing "legacy" Win32 app (perhaps communicate over an NT Named Pipe), simply build a NamedPipeStream. In general, there is no particular reason to take specific derivatives of Stream as parameters—by limiting expected parameters to be of type Stream, .NET programmers can gain an incredible amount of flexibility regarding where and how data lives.

All this notwithstanding, certain programmatic tasks simply require access to the filesystem. The underlying filesystem is a hierarchical one, and there will be times there is simply no escaping that fact. For these tasks, the .NET System.IO namespace provides the filesystem types: Directory, DirectoryInfo, File, FileInfo and its associated enumerations, FileSystemInfo, FileSystemWatcher, and Path (finally, a class that understands directory paths in all their various incarnations!). These classes should be used for mostly "meta-file" operations (enumerating files, discovering attributes about a file, creating or destroying a directory, and so on) rather than for operations on the contents of the file (for which the Stream-based types described earlier are more appropriate).

BinaryReader   CF 1.0, disposable

System.IO (mscorlib.dll)   class

This class allows you to read data from a Stream. When using a BinaryReader, the data represented by a Stream is regarded as a binary format, and bits are merely read from the stream and copied into the appropriate types. The methods prefixed with Read() allow you to grab data of a specific type from the front of the Stream and advance the current position. The next table shows how many bytes each of these methods reads in from a stream.

Method	Bytes read	Method	Bytes read
Read	variable	ReadInt32	4
ReadBoolean	1	ReadInt64	8
ReadByte	1	ReadSByte	1
ReadBytes	variable	ReadSingle	4
ReadChar	2	ReadString	variable
ReadChars	variable	ReadUInt16	2
ReadDecimal	16	ReadUInt32	4
ReadDouble	8	ReadUInt64	8

ReadString() uses the current encoding of the BinaryReader, which can be set when you call the constructor. Strings are prefixed with their length. PeekChar() allows you to look at the first character of a stream (a System.Char, which is two bytes) without advancing the position of the Stream. Because a binary reader may hold on to resources that should be freed when not needed, the BinaryReader must be closed using Close() or by wrapping it in a using block (which calls the protected Dispose() method to do the cleanup at the end of the using block).

```
public class BinaryReader : IDisposable {
// Public Constructors
  public BinaryReader(Stream input);
  public BinaryReader(Stream input,
    System.Text.Encoding encoding);
// Public Instance Properties
  public virtual Stream BaseStream{get; }
// Public Instance Methods
  public virtual void Close( );
  public virtual int PeekChar( );
  public virtual int Read( );
  public virtual int Read(byte[ ] buffer, int index, int count);
  public virtual int Read(char[ ] buffer, int index, int count);
  public virtual bool ReadBoolean( );
  public virtual byte ReadByte( );
  public virtual byte[ ] ReadBytes(int count);
  public virtual char ReadChar( );
  public virtual char[ ] ReadChars(int count);
  public virtual decimal ReadDecimal( );
  public virtual double ReadDouble( );
  public virtual short ReadInt16( );
  public virtual int ReadInt32( );
  public virtual long ReadInt64( );
  public virtual sbyte ReadSByte( );
  public virtual float ReadSingle( );
  public virtual string ReadString( );
  public virtual ushort ReadUInt16( );
  public virtual uint ReadUInt32( );
  public virtual ulong ReadUInt64( );
// Protected Instance Methods
  protected virtual void Dispose(bool disposing);
  protected virtual void FillBuffer(int numBytes);
  protected int Read7BitEncodedInt( );
}
```

BinaryWriter

CF 1.0, serializable, disposable

System.IO (mscorlib.dll)   class

This class complements BinaryReader. To write binary data, simply call Write( ) and pass data of the desired type; the method is overloaded for all "primitive types" (but not the generic System.Object type—that is the subject of the System.Runtime.Serialization namespaces). Be aware, however, that because BinaryWriter is not the actual destination of the data (the wrapped Stream object is) the data may be cached in a buffer somewhere between the BinaryWriter and the sink. To ensure data is completely written, call the Flush( ) method. When working with a BinaryWriter in a sensitive code area, consider placing it in a using block to ensure cleanup (in this case, release of the Stream it wraps after flushing the data).

```
public class BinaryWriter : IDisposable {
// Public Constructors
  public BinaryWriter(Stream output);
```

```
   public BinaryWriter(Stream output,
      System.Text.Encoding encoding);
// Protected Constructors
   protected BinaryWriter( );
// Public Static Fields
   public static readonly BinaryWriter Null;                                    // =System.IO.BinaryWriter
// Protected Instance Fields
   protected Stream OutStream;
// Public Instance Properties
   public virtual Stream BaseStream{get; }
// Public Instance Methods
   public virtual void Close( );
   public virtual void Flush( );
   public virtual long Seek(int offset, SeekOrigin origin);
   public virtual void Write(bool value);
   public virtual void Write(byte value);
   public virtual void Write(byte[ ] buffer);
   public virtual void Write(byte[ ] buffer, int index, int count);
   public virtual void Write(char ch);
   public virtual void Write(char[ ] chars);
   public virtual void Write(char[ ] chars, int index, int count);
   public virtual void Write(decimal value);
   public virtual void Write(double value);
   public virtual void Write(short value);
   public virtual void Write(int value);
   public virtual void Write(long value);
   public virtual void Write(sbyte value);
   public virtual void Write(float value);
   public virtual void Write(string value);
   public virtual void Write(ushort value);
   public virtual void Write(uint value);
   public virtual void Write(ulong value);
// Protected Instance Methods
   protected virtual void Dispose(bool disposing);
   protected void Write7BitEncodedInt(int value);
}
```

BufferedStream

marshal by reference, disposable

System.IO (mscorlib.dll)   sealed class

This type buffers read and write operations to a stream. Because the I/O devices are usually the slowest part of the machine, it usually makes sense to write larger amounts of data at a time, so buffering can improve I/O performance dramatically.

Note that many of the Stream-based types automatically buffer data or represent resources that also buffer data, not only in the System.IO namespace, but also in other namespaces. For example, the filesystem usually has several buffers in place at various levels. This type, however, offers some optimization capabilities, since data won't be sent to the underlying Stream until this object's buffer is full. This can help with accidental flushing in the middle of sensitive operations, such as a tightly executing loop.

```
public sealed class BufferedStream : Stream {
// Public Constructors
  public BufferedStream(Stream stream);
  public BufferedStream(Stream stream, int bufferSize);
// Public Instance Properties
  public override bool CanRead{get; }                                          // overrides Stream
  public override bool CanSeek{get; }                                          // overrides Stream
  public override bool CanWrite{get; }                                         // overrides Stream
  public override long Length{get; }                                          // overrides Stream
  public override long Position{set; get; }                                   // overrides Stream
// Public Instance Methods
  public override void Close( );                                              // overrides Stream
  public override void Flush( );                                              // overrides Stream
  public override int Read(in byte[ ] array, int offset, int count);          // overrides Stream
  public override int ReadByte( );                                           // overrides Stream
  public override long Seek(long offset, SeekOrigin origin);                  // overrides Stream
  public override void SetLength(long value);                                 // overrides Stream
  public override void Write(byte[ ] array, int offset, int count);           // overrides Stream
  public override void WriteByte(byte value);                                // overrides Stream
}
```

Hierarchy   System.Object → System.MarshalByRefObject → Stream(System.IDisposable) →
              BufferedStream

Directory   CF 1.0, ECMA 1.0

System.IO (mscorlib.dll)   sealed class

This class provides many static methods for working with filesystem directories. Most
of the methods behave as expected. GetLogicalDrives( ) returns an array of all of the drives
of a system in the format "k:", in which "k" is the drive letter. GetParent( ) returns the
parent path of the specified path, and GetDirectoryRoot( ) returns the root directory of the
specified path.

```
public sealed class Directory {
// Public Static Methods
  public static DirectoryInfo CreateDirectory(string path);
  public static void Delete(string path);
  public static void Delete(string path, bool recursive);
  public static bool Exists(string path);
  public static DateTime GetCreationTime(string path);
  public static DateTime GetCreationTimeUtc(string path);
  public static string GetCurrentDirectory( );
  public static string[ ] GetDirectories(string path);
  public static string[ ] GetDirectories(string path, string searchPattern);
  public static string GetDirectoryRoot(string path);
  public static string[ ] GetFiles(string path);
  public static string[ ] GetFiles(string path, string searchPattern);
  public static string[ ] GetFileSystemEntries(string path);
  public static string[ ] GetFileSystemEntries(string path, string searchPattern);
  public static DateTime GetLastAccessTime(string path);
  public static DateTime GetLastAccessTimeUtc(string path);
  public static DateTime GetLastWriteTime(string path);
```

```
public static DateTime GetLastWriteTimeUtc(string path);
public static string[ ] GetLogicalDrives( );
public static DirectoryInfo GetParent(string path);
public static void Move(string sourceDirName, string destDirName);
public static void SetCreationTime(string path, DateTime creationTime);
public static void SetCreationTimeUtc(string path, DateTime creationTimeUtc);
public static void SetCurrentDirectory(string path);
public static void SetLastAccessTime(string path, DateTime lastAccessTime);
public static void SetLastAccessTimeUtc(string path, DateTime lastAccessTimeUtc);
public static void SetLastWriteTime(string path, DateTime lastWriteTime);
public static void SetLastWriteTimeUtc(string path, DateTime lastWriteTimeUtc);
}
```

DirectoryInfo

CF 1.0, serializable, marshal by reference

System.IO (mscorlib.dll)   sealed class

This class provides the same functionality as Directory, but in a strongly typed, object-oriented manner. An instance of this type represents a single directory. This class extends FileSystemInfo and implements all its methods. In addition, it adds Parent and Root properties to return the parent and root directories, respectively. Similarly, it also supplies GetDirectories( ) and GetFiles( ), to retrieve its subdirectories and files, as well as GetFileSystemInfos( ), which returns both the files and subdirectories contained by the current directory. MoveTo( ) allows you to move a directory from one place to another.

Given the similarity between this type and the Directory type, it may not be clear when one should be used in place of the other. The key difference is the Directory class is a collection of static utility functions, whereas a DirectoryInfo object is an actual object, maintaining state and identity in the classic style of all objects. (In fact, the DirectoryInfo methods often map over to use the corresponding Directory methods.)

```
public sealed class DirectoryInfo : FileSystemInfo {
// Public Constructors
  public DirectoryInfo(string path);
// Public Instance Properties
  public override bool Exists{get; }                              // overrides FileSystemInfo
  public override string Name{get; }                             // overrides FileSystemInfo
  public DirectoryInfo Parent{get; }
  public DirectoryInfo Root{get; }
// Public Instance Methods
  public void Create( );
  public DirectoryInfo CreateSubdirectory(string path);
  public override void Delete( );                                // overrides FileSystemInfo
  public void Delete(bool recursive);
  public DirectoryInfo[ ] GetDirectories( );
  public DirectoryInfo[ ] GetDirectories(string searchPattern);
  public FileInfo[ ] GetFiles( );
  public FileInfo[ ] GetFiles(string searchPattern);
  public FileSystemInfo[ ] GetFileSystemInfos( );
  public FileSystemInfo[ ] GetFileSystemInfos(string searchPattern);
  public void MoveTo(string destDirName);
  public override string ToString( );                            // overrides object
}
```

Hierarchy	System.Object → System.MarshalByRefObject →
	FileSystemInfo(System.Runtime.Serialization.ISerializable) → DirectoryInfo

Returned By	Directory.{CreateDirectory( ), GetParent( )}, FileInfo.Directory

DirectoryNotFoundException
CF 1.0, ECMA 1.0, serializable

System.IO (mscorlib.dll) class

This exception is thrown if you attempt to access a directory that does not exist.

```
public class DirectoryNotFoundException : IOException {
// Public Constructors
  public DirectoryNotFoundException( );
  public DirectoryNotFoundException(string message);
  public DirectoryNotFoundException(string message, Exception innerException);
// Protected Constructors
  protected DirectoryNotFoundException(System.Runtime.Serialization.SerializationInfo info,
    System.Runtime.Serialization.StreamingContext context);
}
```

Hierarchy	System.Object → System.Exception(System.Runtime.Serialization.ISerializable) →
	System.SystemException → IOException → DirectoryNotFoundException

EndOfStreamException
CF 1.0, ECMA 1.0, serializable

System.IO (mscorlib.dll) class

This exception is thrown if you attempt to read data from a stream at its end position.

```
public class EndOfStreamException : IOException {
// Public Constructors
  public EndOfStreamException( );
  public EndOfStreamException(string message);
  public EndOfStreamException(string message,
    Exception innerException);
// Protected Constructors
  protected EndOfStreamException(System.Runtime.Serialization.SerializationInfo info,
    System.Runtime.Serialization.StreamingContext context);
}
```

Hierarchy	System.Object → System.Exception(System.Runtime.Serialization.ISerializable) →
	System.SystemException → IOException → EndOfStreamException

ErrorEventArgs

System.IO (system.dll) class

This type defines the event arguments that are passed when a FileSystemWatcher.Error event occurs. It contains the exception that was raised by the error, which you can access by calling GetException( ).

```
public class ErrorEventArgs : EventArgs {
// Public Constructors
  public ErrorEventArgs(Exception exception);
// Public Instance Methods
  public virtual Exception GetException( );
}
```

Hierarchy   System.Object → System.EventArgs → ErrorEventArgs

Passed To   ErrorEventHandler.{BeginInvoke( ), Invoke( )}, FileSystemWatcher.OnError( )

ErrorEventHandler   serializable

System.IO (system.dll)   delegate

This is a delegate for the FileSystemWatcher.Error event.

```
public delegate void ErrorEventHandler(object sender,
    ErrorEventArgs e);
```

Associated Events FileSystemWatcher.Error( )

File   CF 1.0, ECMA 1.0

System.IO (mscorlib.dll)   sealed class

Like the Directory type, this type offers a collection of static utility methods for working with files on the filesystem. In most cases, these methods are simply shortcuts for working with the System.IO types directly; for example, the AppendText( ) method returns a StreamWriter that can append text to the file specified in the path argument. This could be accomplished just as easily by creating a StreamWriter around a FileStream opened to the same file, with the FileMode.Append flag passed into the constructor.

That stated, there are methods on this type that aren't available through the Stream-based API. For example, the file's creation time, last-accessed time, last-modified times, and attributes are all available via this type, whereas no such corresponding call exists on the Stream type.

```
public sealed class File {
// Public Static Methods
  public static StreamWriter AppendText(string path);
  public static void Copy(string sourceFileName, string destFileName);
  public static void Copy(string sourceFileName, string destFileName, bool overwrite);
  public static FileStream Create(string path);
  public static FileStream Create(string path, int bufferSize);
  public static StreamWriter CreateText(string path);
  public static void Delete(string path);
  public static bool Exists(string path);
  public static FileAttributes GetAttributes(string path);
  public static DateTime GetCreationTime(string path);
  public static DateTime GetCreationTimeUtc(string path);
  public static DateTime GetLastAccessTime(string path);
  public static DateTime GetLastAccessTimeUtc(string path);
  public static DateTime GetLastWriteTime(string path);
  public static DateTime GetLastWriteTimeUtc(string path);
```

```
public static void Move(string sourceFileName, string destFileName);
public static FileStream Open(string path, FileMode mode);
public static FileStream Open(string path, FileMode mode, FileAccess access);
public static FileStream Open(string path, FileMode mode, FileAccess access, FileShare share);
public static FileStream OpenRead(string path);
public static StreamReader OpenText(string path);
public static FileStream OpenWrite(string path);
public static void SetAttributes(string path, FileAttributes fileAttributes);
public static void SetCreationTime(string path, DateTime creationTime);
public static void SetCreationTimeUtc(string path, DateTime creationTimeUtc);
public static void SetLastAccessTime(string path, DateTime lastAccessTime);
public static void SetLastAccessTimeUtc(string path, DateTime lastAccessTimeUtc);
public static void SetLastWriteTime(string path, DateTime lastWriteTime);
public static void SetLastWriteTimeUtc(string path, DateTime lastWriteTimeUtc);
}
```

FileAccess

CF 1.0, ECMA 1.0, serializable, flag

System.IO (mscorlib.dll)

enum

System.IO

This enumeration represents the various access levels a program can exercise on a file. Programs can either read, write, or do both.

```
public enum FileAccess {
  Read = 0x00000001,
  Write = 0x00000002,
  ReadWrite = 0x00000003
}
```

Hierarchy   System.Object → System.ValueType → System.Enum(System.IComparable, System. IFormattable, System.IConvertible) → FileAccess

Passed To   File.Open( ), FileInfo.Open( ), FileStream.FileStream( ), System.IO.IsolatedStorage. IsolatedStorageFileStream.IsolatedStorageFileStream( ), System.Net.Sockets.NetworkStream. NetworkStream( )

FileAttributes

CF 1.0, serializable, flag

System.IO (mscorlib.dll)

enum

This enumeration represents the various attributes a file can have in the .NET environment; many, if not most, of these attributes parallel the standard Win32 filesystem attributes of the same name.

```
public enum FileAttributes {
  ReadOnly = 0x00000001,
  Hidden = 0x00000002,
  System = 0x00000004,
  Directory = 0x00000010,
  Archive = 0x00000020,
  Device = 0x00000040,
  Normal = 0x00000080,
  Temporary = 0x00000100,
  SparseFile = 0x00000200,
```

```
ReparsePoint = 0x00000400,
Compressed = 0x00000800,
Offline = 0x00001000,
NotContentIndexed = 0x00002000,
Encrypted = 0x00004000
}
```

Hierarchy	System.Object → System.ValueType → System.Enum(System.IComparable, System.IFormattable, System.IConvertible) → FileAttributes
Returned By	File.GetAttributes( ), FileSystemInfo.Attributes
Passed To	File.SetAttributes( ), FileSystemInfo.Attributes

FileInfo   CF 1.0, serializable, marshal by reference

System.IO (mscorlib.dll)   sealed class

Like the parallels between Directory and DirectoryInfo, this class offers an object-centric spin on the static functions offered in the File type.

```
public sealed class FileInfo : FileSystemInfo {
// Public Constructors
  public FileInfo(string fileName);
// Public Instance Properties
  public DirectoryInfo Directory{get; }
  public string DirectoryName{get; }
  public override bool Exists{get; }                              // overrides FileSystemInfo
  public long Length{get; }
  public override string Name{get; }                             // overrides FileSystemInfo
// Public Instance Methods
  public StreamWriter AppendText( );
  public FileInfo CopyTo(string destFileName);
  public FileInfo CopyTo(string destFileName, bool overwrite);
  public FileStream Create( );
  public StreamWriter CreateText( );
  public override void Delete( );                                // overrides FileSystemInfo
  public void MoveTo(string destFileName);
  public FileStream Open(FileMode mode);
  public FileStream Open(FileMode mode, FileAccess access);
  public FileStream Open(FileMode mode, FileAccess access, FileShare share);
  public FileStream OpenRead( );
  public StreamReader OpenText( );
  public FileStream OpenWrite( );
  public override string ToString( );                            // overrides object
}
```

Hierarchy	System.Object → System.MarshalByRefObject → FileSystemInfo(System.Runtime. Serialization.ISerializable) → FileInfo
Returned By	DirectoryInfo.GetFiles( )

FileLoadException

System.IO (mscorlib.dll)   class

This exception is thrown when a file cannot be loaded.

```
public class FileLoadException : IOException {
// Public Constructors
  public FileLoadException( );
  public FileLoadException(string message);
  public FileLoadException(string message, Exception inner);
  public FileLoadException(string message, string fileName);
  public FileLoadException(string message, string fileName, Exception inner);
// Protected Constructors
  protected FileLoadException(System.Runtime.Serialization.SerializationInfo info,
    System.Runtime.Serialization.StreamingContext context);
// Public Instance Properties
  public string FileName{get; }
  public string FusionLog{get; }
  public override string Message{get; }                                                          // overrides Exception
// Public Instance Methods
  public override void GetObjectData(System.Runtime.Serialization.SerializationInfo info,
    System.Runtime.Serialization.StreamingContext context);                                      // overrides Exception
  public override string ToString( );                                                            // overrides Exception
}
```

Hierarchy   System.Object → System.Exception(System.Runtime.Serialization.ISerializable) →
              System.SystemException → IOException → FileLoadException

FileMode

System.IO (mscorlib.dll)   enum

This enumeration allows you to specify how you want to open a file. If you use Create, and the file already exists, an IOException is thrown. If you use CreateNew, any file that currently exists is overwritten. OpenOrCreate indicates that if a file already exists, it must be opened; otherwise, a new file must be created. Similarly, Truncate indicates that the file must be opened and all its data erased (writing then begins at the first byte in the file). Append indicates that the file must be opened and the "file position" set to the end of the file (the opposite of Truncate).

```
public enum FileMode {
  CreateNew = 1,
  Create = 2,
  Open = 3,
  OpenOrCreate = 4,
  Truncate = 5,
  Append = 6
}
```

Hierarchy   System.Object → System.ValueType → System.Enum(System.IComparable,
              System.IFormattable, System.IConvertible) → FileMode

File.Open( ), FileInfo.Open( ), FileStream.FileStream( ), System.IO.IsolatedStorage.
IsolatedStorageFileStream.IsolatedStorageFileStream( )

FileNotFoundException

CF 1.0, ECMA 1.0, serializable

System.IO (mscorlib.dll)

class

This exception is thrown when you attempt to access a file that does not exist.

```
public class FileNotFoundException : IOException {
// Public Constructors
  public FileNotFoundException( );
  public FileNotFoundException(string message);
  public FileNotFoundException(string message, Exception innerException);
  public FileNotFoundException(string message, string fileName);
  public FileNotFoundException(string message, string fileName, Exception innerException);
// Protected Constructors
  protected FileNotFoundException(System.Runtime.Serialization.SerializationInfo info,
    System.Runtime.Serialization.StreamingContext context);
// Public Instance Properties
  public string FileName{get; }
  public string FusionLog{get; }
  public override string Message{get; }                            // overrides Exception
// Public Instance Methods
  public override void GetObjectData(System.Runtime.Serialization.SerializationInfo info,
    System.Runtime.Serialization.StreamingContext context);        // overrides Exception
  public override string ToString( );                              // overrides Exception
}
```

Hierarchy System.Object → System.Exception(System.Runtime.Serialization.ISerializable) →
System.SystemException → IOException → FileNotFoundException

FileShare

CF 1.0, ECMA 1.0, serializable, flag

System.IO (mscorlib.dll)

enum

This enumeration defines how two different processes can access the same file. If one
process is using ReadWrite or Write, no other process can use the file. Similarly, if another
process is using Read, then other processes can read from the file, but not write to it.

```
public enum FileShare {
  None = 0x00000000,
  Read = 0x00000001,
  Write = 0x00000002,
  ReadWrite = 0x00000003,
  Inheritable = 0x00000010
}
```

Hierarchy System.Object → System.ValueType → System.Enum(System.IComparable,
System.IFormattable, System.IConvertible) → FileShare

Passed To File.Open( ), FileInfo.Open( ), FileStream.FileStream( ), System.IO.IsolatedStorage.
IsolatedStorageFileStream.IsolatedStorageFileStream( )

System.IO (mscorlib.dll)   class

This class is the basic implementation of Stream for files. It implements Stream, and adds a few methods specifically for working with files. Handle allows you to grab the underlying system handle to the file resource. IsAsync tells you if the file was opened asynchronously or synchronously. If you want to prevent other processes from accessing parts (or all) of the file, call Lock( ). Subsequently, to free the lock, call Unlock( ).

Note that using the Lock( ) or Unlock( ) methods is not the same as using the lock keyword in C#. The lock action locks only for this process, whereas the file-range locks used in the Lock/Unlock methods are implemented at the filesystem level and are therefore a cross-process mechanism.

```
public class FileStream : Stream {
// Public Constructors
   public FileStream(IntPtr handle, FileAccess access);
   public FileStream(IntPtr handle, FileAccess access, bool ownsHandle);
   public FileStream(IntPtr handle, FileAccess access, bool ownsHandle, int bufferSize);
   public FileStream(IntPtr handle, FileAccess access, bool ownsHandle, int bufferSize, bool isAsync);
   public FileStream(string path, FileMode mode);
   public FileStream(string path, FileMode mode, FileAccess access);
   public FileStream(string path, FileMode mode, FileAccess access, FileShare share);
   public FileStream(string path, FileMode mode, FileAccess access, FileShare share, int bufferSize);
   public FileStream(string path, FileMode mode, FileAccess access, FileShare share, int bufferSize, bool useAsync);
// Public Instance Properties
   public override bool CanRead{get; }                                              // overrides Stream
   public override bool CanSeek{get; }                                              // overrides Stream
   public override bool CanWrite{get; }                                             // overrides Stream
   public virtual IntPtr Handle{get; }
   public virtual bool IsAsync{get; }
   public override long Length{get; }                                              // overrides Stream
   public string Name{get; }
   public override long Position{set; get; }                                       // overrides Stream
// Public Instance Methods
   public override IAsyncResult BeginRead(byte[ ] array, int offset, int numBytes,
      AsyncCallback userCallback, object stateObject);                             // overrides Stream
   public override IAsyncResult BeginWrite(byte[ ] array, int offset, int numBytes,
      AsyncCallback userCallback, object stateObject);                             // overrides Stream
   public override void Close( );                                                  // overrides Stream
   public override int EndRead(IAsyncResult asyncResult);                          // overrides Stream
   public override void EndWrite(IAsyncResult asyncResult);                        // overrides Stream
   public override void Flush( );                                                  // overrides Stream
   public virtual void Lock(long position, long length);
   public override int Read(in byte[ ] array, int offset, int count);              // overrides Stream
   public override int ReadByte( );                                               // overrides Stream
   public override long Seek(long offset, SeekOrigin origin);                      // overrides Stream
   public override void SetLength(long value);                                     // overrides Stream
   public virtual void Unlock(long position, long length);
   public override void Write(byte[ ] array, int offset, int count);               // overrides Stream
   public override void WriteByte(byte value);                                     // overrides Stream
```

System.IO

```
// Protected Instance Methods
  protected virtual void Dispose(bool disposing);
  protected override void Finalize( );                                        // overrides object
}
```

Hierarchy   System.Object → System.MarshalByRefObject → Stream(System.IDisposable) → FileStream

Subclasses   System.IO.IsolatedStorage.IsolatedStorageFileStream

Returned By   File.{Create( ), Open( ), OpenRead( ), OpenWrite( )}, FileInfo.{Create( ), Open( ), OpenRead( ),
                   OpenWrite( )}, System.Reflection.Assembly.{GetFile( ), GetFiles( )}

Passed To   System.Reflection.StrongNameKeyPair.StrongNameKeyPair( )

FileSystemEventArgs

System.IO (system.dll)   class

This class offers the arguments for a FileSystemEventHandler.

```
public class FileSystemEventArgs : EventArgs {
// Public Constructors
  public FileSystemEventArgs(WatcherChangeTypes changeType, string directory, string name);
// Public Instance Properties
  public WatcherChangeTypes ChangeType{get; }
  public string FullPath{get; }
  public string Name{get; }
}
```

Hierarchy   System.Object → System.EventArgs → FileSystemEventArgs

Subclasses   RenamedEventArgs

Passed To   FileSystemEventHandler.{BeginInvoke( ), Invoke( )}, FileSystemWatcher.{OnChanged( ),
                   OnCreated( ), OnDeleted( )}

FileSystemEventHandler   serializable

System.IO (system.dll)   delegate

This delegate is for the FileSystemWatcher.Changed, FileSystemWatcher.Created, and FileSystemWatcher.
Deleted events.

```
public delegate void FileSystemEventHandler(object sender, FileSystemEventArgs e);
```

Associated Events FileSystemWatcher.{Changed( ), Created( ), Deleted( )}

FileSystemInfo   CF 1.0, serializable, marshal by reference

System.IO (mscorlib.dll)   abstract class

This serves as the base class for both FileInfo and DirectoryInfo, and allows access to the
basic filesystem information relating to both.

```
public abstract class FileSystemInfo : MarshalByRefObject, System.Runtime.Serialization.ISerializable {
// Protected Constructors
  protected FileSystemInfo( );
  protected FileSystemInfo(System.Runtime.Serialization.SerializationInfo info,
    System.Runtime.Serialization.StreamingContext context);
// Protected Instance Fields
  protected string FullPath;
  protected string OriginalPath;
// Public Instance Properties
  public FileAttributes Attributes{set; get; }
  public DateTime CreationTime{set; get; }
  public DateTime CreationTimeUtc{set; get; }
  public abstract bool Exists{get; }
  public string Extension{get; }
  public virtual string FullName{get; }
  public DateTime LastAccessTime{set; get; }
  public DateTime LastAccessTimeUtc{set; get; }
  public DateTime LastWriteTime{set; get; }
  public DateTime LastWriteTimeUtc{set; get; }
  public abstract string Name{get; }
// Public Instance Methods
  public abstract void Delete( );
  public virtual void GetObjectData(                                          // implements ISerializable
    System.Runtime.Serialization.SerializationInfo info, System.Runtime.Serialization.StreamingContext context);
  public void Refresh( );
}
```

Hierarchy   System.Object → System.MarshalByRefObject → FileSystemInfo(System.Runtime.
                   Serialization.ISerializable)

Subclasses   DirectoryInfo, FileInfo

Returned By   DirectoryInfo.GetFileSystemInfos( )

FileSystemWatcher   marshal by reference, disposable

System.IO (system.dll)   class

This class allows you to listen to the filesystem and respond to different operations on
it. To register a watch on files or directories, first set Path to the path you wish to
watch. Next, set the Filter property. If you want to respond to all file changes, set it to
an empty ("") string. To watch an individual file, set Filter to the filename. You can also
use wildcards (such as *) in the filename. You must then also set NotifyFilter to register
the types of events you wish to be notified of. If you want to monitor the subdirectories as well, set IncludeSubdirectories. EnableRaisingEvents allows you to enable or disable the
FileSystemWatcher. The watcher then exposes the following events: Changed, Created, Deleted,
Disposed, Error, and Renamed. An Error is raised if too many events occur on a filesystem for
the watcher to correctly monitor it.

```
public class FileSystemWatcher : System.ComponentModel.Component, System.ComponentModel.ISupportInitialize {
// Public Constructors
  public FileSystemWatcher( );
  public FileSystemWatcher(string path);
```

```
  public FileSystemWatcher(string path, string filter);
// Public Instance Properties
  public bool EnableRaisingEvents{set; get; }
  public string Filter{set; get; }
  public bool IncludeSubdirectories{set; get; }
  public int InternalBufferSize{set; get; }
  public NotifyFilters NotifyFilter{set; get; }
  public string Path{set; get; }
  public override ISite Site{set; get; }                              // overrides System.ComponentModel.Component
  public ISynchronizeInvoke SynchronizingObject{set; get; }
// Public Instance Methods
  public void BeginInit( );                                           // implements System.ComponentModel.ISupportInitialize
  public void EndInit( );                                             // implements System.ComponentModel.ISupportInitialize
  public WaitForChangedResult WaitForChanged(WatcherChangeTypes changeType);
  public WaitForChangedResult WaitForChanged(WatcherChangeTypes changeType, int timeout);
// Protected Instance Methods
  protected override void Dispose(bool disposing);                    // overrides System.ComponentModel.Component
  protected void OnChanged(FileSystemEventArgs e);
  protected void OnCreated(FileSystemEventArgs e);
  protected void OnDeleted(FileSystemEventArgs e);
  protected void OnError(ErrorEventArgs e);
  protected void OnRenamed(RenamedEventArgs e);
// Events
  public event FileSystemEventHandler Changed;
  public event FileSystemEventHandler Created;
  public event FileSystemEventHandler Deleted;
  public event ErrorEventHandler Error;
  public event RenamedEventHandler Renamed;
}
```

Hierarchy   System.Object → System.MarshalByRefObject → System.ComponentModel.
                 Component(System.ComponentModel.IComponent, System.IDisposable) →
                 FileSystemWatcher(System.ComponentModel.ISupportInitialize)

InternalBufferOverflowException   serializable

System.IO (system.dll)   class

This exception is passed by a FileSystemWatcher.Error event. This occurs when the internal
buffer of a FileSystemWatcher overflows because too many events have occurred.

```
public class InternalBufferOverflowException : SystemException {
// Public Constructors
  public InternalBufferOverflowException( );
  public InternalBufferOverflowException(string message);
  public InternalBufferOverflowException(string message, Exception inner);
// Protected Constructors
  protected InternalBufferOverflowException(System.Runtime.Serialization.SerializationInfo info,
    System.Runtime.Serialization.StreamingContext context);
}
```

Hierarchy   System.Object → System.Exception(System.Runtime.Serialization.ISerializable) →
                 System.SystemException → InternalBufferOverflowException

---

IODescriptionAttribute

System.IO (system.dll)   class

This custom attribute describes an I/O property or event.

```
public class IODescriptionAttribute : System.ComponentModel.DescriptionAttribute {
// Public Constructors
  public IODescriptionAttribute(string description);
// Public Instance Properties
  public override string Description{get; }                    // overrides System.ComponentModel.DescriptionAttribute
}
```

Hierarchy   System.Object → System.Attribute → System.ComponentModel.DescriptionAttribute →
                    IODescriptionAttribute

Valid On   All

IOException   CF 1.0, ECMA 1.0, serializable

System.IO (mscorlib.dll)   class

This is the base class of all the I/O related exceptions.

```
public class IOException : SystemException {
// Public Constructors
  public IOException( );
  public IOException(string message);
  public IOException(string message, Exception innerException);
  public IOException(string message, int hresult);
// Protected Constructors
  protected IOException(System.Runtime.Serialization.SerializationInfo info,
    System.Runtime.Serialization.StreamingContext context);
}
```

Hierarchy   System.Object → System.Exception(System.Runtime.Serialization.ISerializable) →
                    System.SystemException → IOException

Subclasses   DirectoryNotFoundException, EndOfStreamException, FileLoadException,
                    FileNotFoundException, PathTooLongException

MemoryStream   CF 1.0, ECMA 1.0, serializable, marshal by reference, disposable

System.IO (mscorlib.dll)   class

This class is a stream that keeps its data in memory as opposed to on the disk (as a
FileStream does). In addition to the Stream methods, ToArray( ) writes the entire stream to a
byte array, and WriteTo( ) dumps the contents of this stream to a different one.

```
public class MemoryStream : Stream {
// Public Constructors
  public MemoryStream( );
  public MemoryStream(byte[ ] buffer);
  public MemoryStream(byte[ ] buffer, bool writable);
```

System.IO

```
public MemoryStream(byte[ ] buffer, int index, int count);
public MemoryStream(byte[ ] buffer, int index, int count, bool writable);
public MemoryStream(byte[ ] buffer, int index, int count, bool writable, bool publiclyVisible);
public MemoryStream(int capacity);
// Public Instance Properties
public override bool CanRead{get; }                                        // overrides Stream
public override bool CanSeek{get; }                                        // overrides Stream
public override bool CanWrite{get; }                                       // overrides Stream
public virtual int Capacity{set; get; }
public override long Length{get; }                                         // overrides Stream
public override long Position{set; get; }                                  // overrides Stream
// Public Instance Methods
public override void Close( );                                             // overrides Stream
public override void Flush( );                                             // overrides Stream
public virtual byte[ ] GetBuffer( );
public override int Read(in byte[ ] buffer, int offset, int count);        // overrides Stream
public override int ReadByte( );                                          // overrides Stream
public override long Seek(long offset, SeekOrigin loc);                    // overrides Stream
public override void SetLength(long value);                                // overrides Stream
public virtual byte[ ] ToArray( );
public override void Write(byte[ ] buffer, int offset, int count);         // overrides Stream
public override void WriteByte(byte value);                                // overrides Stream
public virtual void WriteTo(Stream stream);
}
```

Hierarchy System.Object → System.MarshalByRefObject → Stream(System.IDisposable) → MemoryStream

NotifyFilters   serializable, flag

System.IO (system.dll)   enum

This type represents the different types of filesystem events you can use a FileSystem-Watcher to look for. NotifyFilters allows you to indicate what kind of changes a FileSystemWatcher should respond to.

```
public enum NotifyFilters {
  FileName = 0x00000001,
  DirectoryName = 0x00000002,
  Attributes = 0x00000004,
  Size = 0x00000008,
  LastWrite = 0x00000010,
  LastAccess = 0x00000020,
  CreationTime = 0x00000040,
  Security = 0x00000100
}
```

Hierarchy System.Object → System.ValueType → System.Enum(System.IComparable, System.IFormattable, System.IConvertible) → NotifyFilters

Returned By FileSystemWatcher.NotifyFilter

Passed To FileSystemWatcher.NotifyFilter

System.IO (mscorlib.dll)   sealed class

This class provides many static methods for processing strings representing file paths in a platform-independent manner. The static properties allow you to inspect the file conventions of the system on which the software is running. The static methods supply an implementation of the frequently performed path manipulations. ChangeExtension() allows you to change the extension of a file, and GetExtension() allows you to retrieve it. Combine() combines two file paths (the second argument cannot contain a UNC or a drive letter). GetTempPath() returns the current system temporary storage folder, and the infinitely cooler GetTempFileName() creates a unique temporary filename, then creates a zero-byte file there. IsPathRooted() checks to see if a path contains a root, which can also be retrieved by calling GetPathRoot().

```
public sealed class Path {
// Public Static Fields
    public static readonly char AltDirectorySeparatorChar;              // =0x0000002F
    public static readonly char DirectorySeparatorChar;                 // =0x0000005C
    public static readonly char[ ] InvalidPathChars;                    // =System.Char[ ]
    public static readonly char PathSeparator;                          // =0x0000003B
    public static readonly char VolumeSeparatorChar;                    // =0x0000003A
// Public Static Methods
    public static string ChangeExtension(string path, string extension);
    public static string Combine(string path1, string path2);
    public static string GetDirectoryName(string path);
    public static string GetExtension(string path);
    public static string GetFileName(string path);
    public static string GetFileNameWithoutExtension(string path);
    public static string GetFullPath(string path);
    public static string GetPathRoot(string path);
    public static string GetTempFileName( );
    public static string GetTempPath( );
    public static bool HasExtension(string path);
    public static bool IsPathRooted(string path);
}
```

PathTooLongException   CF 1.0, ECMA 1.0, serializable

System.IO (mscorlib.dll)   class

This exception is thrown when you attempt to access or create a file with a name that is too long for the filesystem.

```
public class PathTooLongException : IOException {
// Public Constructors
    public PathTooLongException( );
    public PathTooLongException(string message);
    public PathTooLongException(string message, Exception innerException);
// Protected Constructors
    protected PathTooLongException(System.Runtime.Serialization.SerializationInfo info,
        System.Runtime.Serialization.StreamingContext context);
}
```

System.IO

Hierarchy   System.Object → System.Exception(System.Runtime.Serialization.ISerializable) →
System.SystemException → IOException → PathTooLongException

RenamedEventArgs

System.IO (system.dll)   class

This type represents the arguments passed by a FileSystemWatcher.Renamed event.

```
public class RenamedEventArgs : FileSystemEventArgs {
// Public Constructors
  public RenamedEventArgs(WatcherChangeTypes changeType, string directory, string name, string oldName);
// Public Instance Properties
  public string OldFullPath{get; }
  public string OldName{get; }
}
```

Hierarchy   System.Object → System.EventArgs → FileSystemEventArgs → RenamedEventArgs

Passed To   FileSystemWatcher.OnRenamed( ), RenamedEventHandler.{BeginInvoke( ), Invoke( )}

RenamedEventHandler   serializable

System.IO (system.dll)   delegate

This delegate is for the FileSystemWatcher.Renamed event.

```
public delegate void RenamedEventHandler(object sender, RenamedEventArgs e);
```

Associated Events

FileSystemWatcher.Renamed( )

SeekOrigin   CF 1.0, ECMA 1.0, serializable

System.IO (mscorlib.dll)   enum

This enumeration is used by the Stream.Seek( ) method. You can specify that you want to
seek either from the beginning with Begin, from the current position with Current, or end
with End.

```
public enum SeekOrigin {
  Begin = 0,
  Current = 1,
  End = 2
}
```

Hierarchy   System.Object → System.ValueType → System.Enum(System.IComparable,
System.IFormattable, System.IConvertible) → SeekOrigin

Passed To   BinaryWriter.Seek( ), Stream.Seek( )

This class is the basic building block of I/O in the .NET Framework. Many types of application use a Stream in one way or another. When calling System.Console.WriteLine( ), you use a TextWriter, which contains a StreamWriter. When you design an ASP.NET application, the System.Web.UI.Page uses a System.Net.Sockets.NetworkStream. In fact, whenever you access a remote database server you are using a NetworkStream.

To determine whether a given Stream can read, write, or seek, check CanRead, CanWrite, or CanSeek, respectively. If your stream can seek, you may seek forward or backward using Seek( ). Length reveals the length of the stream, which can also be set by calling SetLength( ), and Position allows you to check your current position in the stream.

To perform asynchronous I/O, call BeginRead( ) or BeginWrite( ). Notification of an asynchronous operation comes in two ways: either via an System.AsyncCallback delegate callback passed in as part of the BeginRead( )/BeginWrite( ) call, or else by calling the EndRead( ) or EndWrite( ) method explicitly, which blocks the calling thread until the async operation completes.

Streams usually hold on to a precious resource (a network connection or a file handle), which should be freed as soon as it is not needed any more. Because destruction is completely nondeterministic with garbage collection, be sure to call Close( ) at the end of the Stream's useful lifetime. (Alternatively, wrap the use of the Stream in a using block to have the compiler generate the call to Dispose( )—which in turn calls Close( )—when the block finishes.)

```
public abstract class Stream : MarshalByRefObject, IDisposable {
// Protected Constructors
  protected Stream( );
// Public Static Fields
  public static readonly Stream Null;                                            // =System.IO.Stream+NullStream
// Public Instance Properties
  public abstract bool CanRead{get; }
  public abstract bool CanSeek{get; }
  public abstract bool CanWrite{get; }
  public abstract long Length{get; }
  public abstract long Position{set; get; }
// Public Instance Methods
  public virtual IAsyncResult BeginRead(byte[ ] buffer, int offset, int count, AsyncCallback callback, object state);
  public virtual IAsyncResult BeginWrite(byte[ ] buffer, int offset, int count, AsyncCallback callback, object state);
  public virtual void Close( );
  public virtual int EndRead(IAsyncResult asyncResult);
  public virtual void EndWrite(IAsyncResult asyncResult);
  public abstract void Flush( );
  public abstract int Read(in byte[ ] buffer, int offset, int count);
  public virtual int ReadByte( );
  public abstract long Seek(long offset, SeekOrigin origin);
  public abstract void SetLength(long value);
  public abstract void Write(byte[ ] buffer, int offset, int count);
  public virtual void WriteByte(byte value);
// Protected Instance Methods
  protected virtual WaitHandle CreateWaitHandle( );
}
```

Hierarchy	System.Object → System.MarshalByRefObject → Stream(System.IDisposable)
Subclasses	BufferedStream, FileStream, MemoryStream, System.Net.Sockets.NetworkStream
Returned By	Multiple types
Passed To	Multiple types

StreamReader   CF 1.0, ECMA 1.0, serializable, marshal by reference, disposable

System.IO (mscorlib.dll)   class

This class is an extension of a TextReader and provides implementations for all its methods. CurrentEncoding returns the current encoding the StreamReader is using. If you would like to discard the buffered data (so it isn't written to a disk or other resource), call DiscardBufferedData( ).

This class is a quick way to open a file for reading. Simply call the constructor with a string containing the filename, and you can immediately begin reading from the file with methods such as Read( ), ReadLine( ), or ReadToEnd( ).

```
public class StreamReader : TextReader {
// Public Constructors
  public StreamReader(Stream stream);
  public StreamReader(Stream stream, bool detectEncodingFromByteOrderMarks);
  public StreamReader(Stream stream, System.Text.Encoding encoding);
  public StreamReader(Stream stream, System.Text.Encoding encoding, bool detectEncodingFromByteOrderMarks);
  public StreamReader(Stream stream, System.Text.Encoding encoding,
     bool detectEncodingFromByteOrderMarks, int bufferSize);
  public StreamReader(string path);
  public StreamReader(string path, bool detectEncodingFromByteOrderMarks);
  public StreamReader(string path, System.Text.Encoding encoding);
  public StreamReader(string path, System.Text.Encoding encoding, bool detectEncodingFromByteOrderMarks);
  public StreamReader(string path, System.Text.Encoding encoding,
     bool detectEncodingFromByteOrderMarks, int bufferSize);
// Public Static Fields
  public static readonly StreamReader Null;                  // =System.IO.StreamReader+NullStreamReader
// Public Instance Properties
  public virtual Stream BaseStream{get; }
  public virtual Encoding CurrentEncoding{get; }
// Public Instance Methods
  public override void Close( );                              // overrides TextReader
  public void DiscardBufferedData( );
  public override int Peek( );                               // overrides TextReader
  public override int Read( );                               // overrides TextReader
  public override int Read(in char[ ] buffer, int index, int count);    // overrides TextReader
  public override string ReadLine( );                        // overrides TextReader
  public override string ReadToEnd( );                       // overrides TextReader
// Protected Instance Methods
  protected override void Dispose(bool disposing);           // overrides TextReader
}
```

Hierarchy   System.Object → System.MarshalByRefObject → TextReader(System.IDisposable) →
StreamReader

Returned By   System.Diagnostics.Process.{StandardError, StandardOutput}, File.OpenText( ),
FileInfo.OpenText( )

StreamWriter   CF 1.0, ECMA 1.0, serializable, marshal by reference, disposable

System.IO (mscorlib.dll)   class

This class implements TextWriter and provides all its methods. If you set the AutoFlush
property, every call to Write( ) or WriteLine( ) flushes the buffer.

This class is a quick way to open a file for writing. Call the constructor with a string
containing the filename, and you can immediately begin writing to the file with Write( )
or WriteLine( ).

```
public class StreamWriter : TextWriter {
// Public Constructors
  public StreamWriter(Stream stream);
  public StreamWriter(Stream stream, System.Text.Encoding encoding);
  public StreamWriter(Stream stream, System.Text.Encoding encoding, int bufferSize);
  public StreamWriter(string path);
  public StreamWriter(string path, bool append);
  public StreamWriter(string path, bool append, System.Text.Encoding encoding);
  public StreamWriter(string path, bool append, System.Text.Encoding encoding, int bufferSize);
// Public Static Fields
  public static readonly StreamWriter Null;                         // =System.IO.StreamWriter
// Public Instance Properties
  public virtual bool AutoFlush{set; get; }
  public virtual Stream BaseStream{get; }
  public override Encoding Encoding{get; }                          // overrides TextWriter
// Public Instance Methods
  public override void Close( );                                    // overrides TextWriter
  public override void Flush( );                                    // overrides TextWriter
  public override void Write(char value);                          // overrides TextWriter
  public override void Write(char[ ] buffer);                      // overrides TextWriter
  public override void Write(char[ ] buffer, int index, int count); // overrides TextWriter
  public override void Write(string value);                        // overrides TextWriter
// Protected Instance Methods
  protected override void Dispose(bool disposing);                 // overrides TextWriter
  protected override void Finalize( );                             // overrides object
}
```

Hierarchy   System.Object → System.MarshalByRefObject → TextWriter(System.IDisposable) →
StreamWriter

Returned By   System.Diagnostics.Process.StandardInput, File.{AppendText( ), CreateText( )},
FileInfo.{AppendText( ), CreateText( )}

StringReader

CF 1.0, ECMA 1.0, serializable, marshal by reference, disposable

System.IO (mscorlib.dll)   class

This class implements TextReader and provides all its methods. It is useful when you would like to deal with a System.String in the same way you would work with a TextReader.

```
public class StringReader : TextReader {
// Public Constructors
  public StringReader(string s);
// Public Instance Methods
  public override void Close( );                                      // overrides TextReader
  public override int Peek( );                                       // overrides TextReader
  public override int Read( );                                       // overrides TextReader
  public override int Read(in char[ ] buffer, int index, int count);  // overrides TextReader
  public override string ReadLine( );                                // overrides TextReader
  public override string ReadToEnd( );                               // overrides TextReader
// Protected Instance Methods
  protected override void Dispose(bool disposing);                    // overrides TextReader
}
```

Hierarchy   System.Object → System.MarshalByRefObject → TextReader(System.IDisposable) →
                       StringReader

StringWriter

CF 1.0, ECMA 1.0, serializable, marshal by reference, disposable

System.IO (mscorlib.dll)   class

This class provides an alternative to using a System.Text.StringBuilder to create a string. This allows you to create a string in the exact same manner you would create a text file, which can be very useful. It implements all of the TextWriter methods.

```
public class StringWriter : TextWriter {
// Public Constructors
  public StringWriter( );
  public StringWriter(IFormatProvider formatProvider);
  public StringWriter(System.Text.StringBuilder sb);
  public StringWriter(System.Text.StringBuilder sb, IFormatProvider formatProvider);
// Public Instance Properties
  public override Encoding Encoding{get; }                            // overrides TextWriter
// Public Instance Methods
  public override void Close( );                                      // overrides TextWriter
  public virtual StringBuilder GetStringBuilder( );
  public override string ToString( );                                 // overrides object
  public override void Write(char value);                             // overrides TextWriter
  public override void Write(char[ ] buffer, int index, int count);   // overrides TextWriter
  public override void Write(string value);                           // overrides TextWriter
// Protected Instance Methods
  protected override void Dispose(bool disposing);                    // overrides TextWriter
}
```

Hierarchy   System.Object → System.MarshalByRefObject → TextWriter(System.IDisposable) →
                       StringWriter

CF 1.0, ECMA 1.0, serializable, marshal by reference, disposable

System.IO (mscorlib.dll)   abstract class

This class is optimized to read a stream of sequential characters. The Read() methods read data from the front of a stream, and Peek() looks at the first character without advancing the position of an associated stream. If you need a thread-safe TextReader, use Synchronized() to create a thread-safe copy of a TextReader.

```
public abstract class TextReader : MarshalByRefObject, IDisposable {
// Protected Constructors
  protected TextReader();
// Public Static Fields
  public static readonly TextReader Null;                        // =System.IO.TextReader+NullTextReader
// Public Static Methods
  public static TextReader Synchronized(TextReader reader);
// Public Instance Methods
  public virtual void Close();
  public virtual int Peek();
  public virtual int Read();
  public virtual int Read(in char[] buffer, int index, int count);
  public virtual int ReadBlock(in char[] buffer, int index, int count);
  public virtual string ReadLine();
  public virtual string ReadToEnd();
// Protected Instance Methods
  protected virtual void Dispose(bool disposing);
}
```

Hierarchy	System.Object → System.MarshalByRefObject → TextReader(System.IDisposable)
Subclasses	StreamReader, StringReader
Returned By	System.Console.In, System.Xml.XmlTextReader.GetRemainder()
Passed To	System.Console.SetIn(), System.Xml.XmlDocument.Load(), System.Xml.XmlTextReader. XmlTextReader(), System.Xml.XPath.XPathDocument.XPathDocument()

CF 1.0, ECMA 1.0, serializable, marshal by reference, disposable

System.IO (mscorlib.dll)   abstract class

This class writes strings of characters to a stream. Encoding sets the encoding of the produced text; change the object that provides formatting by setting FormatProvider. To change the newline character produced in your text, set the NewLine property. To write to a stream, call either Write() or WriteLine(). To clear the current buffer of characters, use Flush(). As always, Close() allows you to free the resources in use by the TextWriter.

```
public abstract class TextWriter : MarshalByRefObject, IDisposable {
// Protected Constructors
  protected TextWriter();
  protected TextWriter(IFormatProvider formatProvider);
// Public Static Fields
  public static readonly TextWriter Null;                       // =System.IO.TextWriter+NullTextWriter
```

```
// Protected Instance Fields
  protected char[ ] CoreNewLine;
// Public Instance Properties
  public abstract Encoding Encoding{get; }
  public virtual IFormatProvider FormatProvider{get; }
  public virtual string NewLine{set; get; }
// Public Static Methods
  public static TextWriter Synchronized(TextWriter writer);
// Public Instance Methods
  public virtual void Close( );
  public virtual void Flush( );
  public virtual void Write(bool value);
  public virtual void Write(char value);
  public virtual void Write(char[ ] buffer);
  public virtual void Write(char[ ] buffer, int index, int count);
  public virtual void Write(decimal value);
  public virtual void Write(double value);
  public virtual void Write(int value);
  public virtual void Write(long value);
  public virtual void Write(object value);
  public virtual void Write(float value);
  public virtual void Write(string value);
  public virtual void Write(string format, object arg0);
  public virtual void Write(string format, params object[ ] arg);
  public virtual void Write(string format, object arg0, object arg1);
  public virtual void Write(string format, object arg0, object arg1, object arg2);
  public virtual void Write(uint value);
  public virtual void Write(ulong value);
  public virtual void WriteLine( );
  public virtual void WriteLine(bool value);
  public virtual void WriteLine(char value);
  public virtual void WriteLine(char[ ] buffer);
  public virtual void WriteLine(char[ ] buffer, int index, int count);
  public virtual void WriteLine(decimal value);
  public virtual void WriteLine(double value);
  public virtual void WriteLine(int value);
  public virtual void WriteLine(long value);
  public virtual void WriteLine(object value);
  public virtual void WriteLine(float value);
  public virtual void WriteLine(string value);
  public virtual void WriteLine(string format, object arg0);
  public virtual void WriteLine(string format, params object[ ] arg);
  public virtual void WriteLine(string format, object arg0, object arg1);
  public virtual void WriteLine(string format, object arg0, object arg1, object arg2);
  public virtual void WriteLine(uint value);
  public virtual void WriteLine(ulong value);
// Protected Instance Methods
  protected virtual void Dispose(bool disposing);
}
```

Hierarchy	System.Object → System.MarshalByRefObject → TextWriter(System.IDisposable)
Subclasses	StreamWriter, StringWriter
Returned By	System.Console.{Error, Out}, System.Diagnostics.TextWriterTraceListener.Writer
Passed To	System.Console.{SetError( ), SetOut( )}, System.Diagnostics.TextWriterTraceListener. {TextWriterTraceListener( ), Writer}, System.Xml.XmlDocument.Save( ), System.Xml. XmlTextWriter.XmlTextWriter( ), System.Xml.Xsl.XslTransform.Transform( )

WaitForChangedResult

System.IO (system.dll)   struct

This structure contains the changes on a file. This is used to construct FileSystemEventArgs and RenamedEventArgs.

```
public struct WaitForChangedResult {
// Public Instance Properties
  public WatcherChangeTypes ChangeType{set; get; }
  public string Name{set; get; }
  public string OldName{set; get; }
  public bool TimedOut{set; get; }
}
```

Hierarchy	System.Object → System.ValueType → WaitForChangedResult
Returned By	FileSystemWatcher.WaitForChanged( )

WatcherChangeTypes

serializable, flag

System.IO (system.dll)   enum

This enumeration represents the different types of changes that can occur on a file. It is used by FileSystemEventArgs.

```
public enum WatcherChangeTypes {
  Created = 0x00000001,
  Deleted = 0x00000002,
  Changed = 0x00000004,
  Renamed = 0x00000008,
  All = 0x0000000F
}
```

Hierarchy	System.Object → System.ValueType → System.Enum(System.IComparable, System.IFormattable, System.IConvertible) → WatcherChangeTypes
Returned By	FileSystemEventArgs.ChangeType, WaitForChangedResult.ChangeType
Passed To	FileSystemEventArgs.FileSystemEventArgs( ), FileSystemWatcher.WaitForChanged( ), RenamedEventArgs.RenamedEventArgs( ), WaitForChangedResult.ChangeType

32

System.IO.IsolatedStorage

System.IO.IsolatedStorage allows you to access an isolated area of a filesystem for your application. This is useful when access to the System.IO classes is not possible. The security settings of the .NET Framework prohibit web applications and downloaded controls from accessing the local filesystem directly, but those settings allow them to use System.IO.IsolatedStorage. Applications' storage areas are isolated from one another, so anything in isolated storage is protected from untrusted applications. The size of isolated storage is limited, so an untrusted application cannot create a denial-of-service condition by filling your hard disk with data.

When you use isolated storage, the runtime sets aside disk space for a given level of isolation (specified using IsolatedStorageScope). If you use Windows 2000 or XP, *<SYSTEMDRIVE>\Documents and Settings\<user>\Application Data* contains the isolated storage area if roaming is turned on, and *<SYSTEMDRIVE>\Documents and Settings\<user>\Local Settings\Application Data* contains the storage area if roaming is not on. Applications can use this area as a data store for their particular persistence needs. Figure 32-1 shows the inheritance diagram for this namespace. For more information, see "Isolated Storage" in Chapter 10.

INormalizeForIsolatedStorage

System.IO.IsolatedStorage (mscorlib.dll)   interface

This interface exposes Normalize(), which returns a normalized copy of the object on which it is called. You usually use this method if you are inheriting from IsolatedStorage and you want to see if a store already exists.

```
public interface INormalizeForIsolatedStorage {
// Public Instance Methods
  public object Normalize( );
}
```

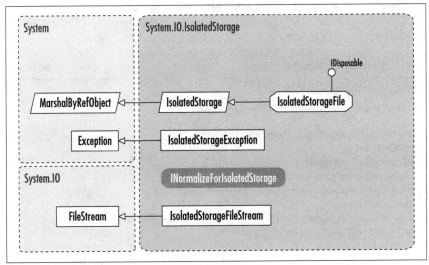

Figure 32-1. The System.IO.IsolatedStorage namespace

IsolatedStorage

marshal by reference

System.IO.IsolatedStorage (mscorlib.dll)

abstract class

This is the abstract base class from which all isolated storage classes must inherit. AssemblyIdentity returns the assembly identity associated with the isolated store, and DomainIdentity returns the domain associated with the store. Use CurrentSize to detect how much space the store takes up on the disk, and use MaximumSize to detect the maximum storage allowed. Scope returns an IsolatedStorageScope enumeration for the store. If you wish to delete the isolated store and all its contents completely, call Remove( ).

```
public abstract class IsolatedStorage : MarshalByRefObject {
// Protected Constructors
  protected IsolatedStorage( );
// Public Instance Properties
  public object AssemblyIdentity{get; }
  public virtual ulong CurrentSize{get; }
  public object DomainIdentity{get; }
  public virtual ulong MaximumSize{get; }
  public IsolatedStorageScope Scope{get; }
// Protected Instance Properties
  protected virtual char SeparatorExternal{get; }
  protected virtual char SeparatorInternal{get; }
// Public Instance Methods
  public abstract void Remove( );
// Protected Instance Methods
  protected abstract IsolatedStoragePermission GetPermission(System.Security.PermissionSet ps);
  protected void InitStore(IsolatedStorageScope scope, Type domainEvidenceType,Type assemblyEvidenceType);
}
```

Hierarchy	System.Object → System.MarshalByRefObject → IsolatedStorage
Subclasses	IsolatedStorageFile

IsolatedStorageException   serializable

System.IO.IsolatedStorage (mscorlib.dll)   class

This exception represents isolated storage errors.

```
public class IsolatedStorageException : Exception {
// Public Constructors
  public IsolatedStorageException( );
  public IsolatedStorageException(string message);
  public IsolatedStorageException(string message, Exception inner);
// Protected Constructors
  protected IsolatedStorageException(System.Runtime.Serialization.SerializationInfo info,
    System.Runtime.Serialization.StreamingContext context);
}
```

Hierarchy	System.Object → System.Exception(System.Runtime.Serialization.ISerializable) → IsolatedStorageException

IsolatedStorageFile   marshal by reference, disposable

System.IO.IsolatedStorage (mscorlib.dll)   sealed class

This class represents an isolated-storage filesystem area that can contain files and directories. The static GetStore( ) returns a reference to the current store. Call GetStore( ) only with the proper IsolatedStorageScope enumerations set. There are two shortcuts for this method: GetUserStoreForAssembly( ) returns the same store as GetStore( ) with IsolatedStorage-Scope.User | IsolatedStorageScope.Assembly as its first argument, and GetUserStoreForDomain( ) returns as though GetStore( ) was called with IsolatedStorageScope.User | IsolatedStorageScope.Assembly | IsolatedStorageScope.Domain. GetEnumerator( ) returns all valid types of storage isolation for the specified assembly and domain.

The rest of the methods for this class allow you to work with files and directories. CreateDirectory( ) and DeleteDirectory( ) allow you to create and delete directories, just as DeleteFile( ) allows you to delete files (use an IsolatedStorageFileStream to create them). Close( ) allows you to close a store opened with GetStore( ). GetFileNames( ) returns an array of filenames matching a given filter.

```
public sealed class IsolatedStorageFile : IsolatedStorage, IDisposable {
// Public Instance Properties
  public override ulong CurrentSize{get; }                             // overrides IsolatedStorage
  public override ulong MaximumSize{get; }                             // overrides IsolatedStorage
// Public Static Methods
  public static IEnumerator GetEnumerator(IsolatedStorageScope scope);
  public static IsolatedStorageFile GetStore(IsolatedStorageScope scope, System.Security.Policy.Evidence domainEvidence,
    Type domainEvidenceType, System.Security.Policy.Evidence assemblyEvidence,Type assemblyEvidenceType);
  public static IsolatedStorageFile GetStore(IsolatedStorageScope scope, object domainIdentity, object assemblyIdentity);
  public static IsolatedStorageFile GetStore(IsolatedStorageScope scope,Type domainEvidenceType,
    Type assemblyEvidenceType);
  public static IsolatedStorageFile GetUserStoreForAssembly( );
```

```
public static IsolatedStorageFile GetUserStoreForDomain( );
public static void Remove(IsolatedStorageScope scope);
// Public Instance Methods
public void Close( );
public void CreateDirectory(string dir);
public void DeleteDirectory(string dir);
public void DeleteFile(string file);
public void Dispose( );                                              // implements IDisposable
public string[ ] GetDirectoryNames(string searchPattern);
public string[ ] GetFileNames(string searchPattern);
public override void Remove( );                                      // overrides IsolatedStorage
// Protected Instance Methods
protected override void Finalize( );                                 // overrides object
protected override IsolatedStoragePermission
  GetPermission(System.Security.PermissionSet ps);                   // overrides IsolatedStorage
}
```

Hierarchy	System.Object → System.MarshalByRefObject → IsolatedStorage → IsolatedStorageFile(System.IDisposable)
Passed To	IsolatedStorageFileStream.IsolatedStorageFileStream( )

IsolatedStorageFileStream
marshal by reference, disposable

System.IO.IsolatedStorage (mscorlib.dll)
class

System.IO.
IsolatedStor

This class is simply a System.IO.FileStream implementation for isolated storage. Use it to create and modify isolated storage files.

```
public class IsolatedStorageFileStream : System.IO.FileStream {
// Public Constructors
public IsolatedStorageFileStream(string path, System.IO.FileMode mode);
public IsolatedStorageFileStream(string path, System.IO.FileMode mode, System.IO.FileAccess access);
public IsolatedStorageFileStream(string path, System.IO.FileMode mode,
  System.IO.FileAccess access, System.IO.FileShare share);
public IsolatedStorageFileStream(string path, System.IO.FileMode mode,
  System.IO.FileAccess access, System.IO.FileShare share, int bufferSize);
public IsolatedStorageFileStream(string path, System.IO.FileMode mode,
  System.IO.FileAccess access, System.IO.FileShare share, int bufferSize, IsolatedStorageFile isf);
public IsolatedStorageFileStream(string path, System.IO.FileMode mode,
  System.IO.FileAccess access, System.IO.FileShare share, IsolatedStorageFile isf);
public IsolatedStorageFileStream(string path, System.IO.FileMode mode,
  System.IO.FileAccess access, IsolatedStorageFile isf);
public IsolatedStorageFileStream(string path, System.IO.FileMode mode, IsolatedStorageFile isf);
// Public Instance Properties
public override bool CanRead{get; }                                  // overrides System.IO.FileStream
public override bool CanSeek{get; }                                  // overrides System.IO.FileStream
public override bool CanWrite{get; }                                 // overrides System.IO.FileStream
public override IntPtr Handle{get; }                                 // overrides System.IO.FileStream
public override bool IsAsync{get; }                                  // overrides System.IO.FileStream
public override long Length{get; }                                   // overrides System.IO.FileStream
public override long Position{set; get; }                            // overrides System.IO.FileStream
```

```
// Public Instance Methods
    public override IAsyncResult BeginRead(byte[ ] buffer, int offset,
        int numBytes, AsyncCallback userCallback, object stateObject);          // overrides System.IO.FileStream
    public override IAsyncResult BeginWrite(byte[ ] buffer, int offset, int numBytes,
        AsyncCallback userCallback, object stateObject);                        // overrides System.IO.FileStream
    public override void Close( );                                             // overrides System.IO.FileStream
    public override int EndRead(IAsyncResult asyncResult);                     // overrides System.IO.FileStream
    public override void EndWrite(IAsyncResult asyncResult);                   // overrides System.IO.FileStream
    public override void Flush( );                                            // overrides System.IO.FileStream
    public override int Read(byte[ ] buffer, int offset, int count);          // overrides System.IO.FileStream
    public override int ReadByte( );                                          // overrides System.IO.FileStream
    public override long Seek(long offset, System.IO.SeekOrigin origin);      // overrides System.IO.FileStream
    public override void SetLength(long value);                               // overrides System.IO.FileStream
    public override void Write(byte[ ] buffer, int offset, int count);        // overrides System.IO.FileStream
    public override void WriteByte(byte value);                              // overrides System.IO.FileStream
// Protected Instance Methods
    protected override void Dispose(bool disposing);                          // overrides System.IO.FileStream
}
```

Hierarchy   System.Object → System.MarshalByRefObject → System.IO.Stream(System.IDisposable) → System.IO.FileStream → IsolatedStorageFileStream

IsolatedStorageScope   serializable, flag

System.IO.IsolatedStorage (mscorlib.dll)   enum

This enumeration allows you to specify the levels of isolation an **IsolatedStorageFile** store should have. For example, if you call **IsolatedStorageFile.GetStore( )** with **Assembly**, the isolated storage cannot be accessed by code from another assembly. **Roaming** allows the isolated store to be placed in a roaming profile; without it, the store does not roam with the user.

```
public enum IsolatedStorageScope {
    None = 0x00000000,
    User = 0x00000001,
    Domain = 0x00000002,
    Assembly = 0x00000004,
    Roaming = 0x00000008
}
```

Hierarchy   System.Object → System.ValueType → System.Enum(System.IComparable,
                 System.IFormattable, System.IConvertible) → IsolatedStorageScope

Returned By   IsolatedStorage.Scope

Passed To   IsolatedStorage.InitStore( ), IsolatedStorageFile.{GetEnumerator( ), GetStore( ), Remove( )}

33

System.Net

System.Net supports a high-level API for working with common Internet protocols (HTTP being the principal example) without having to deal with low-level details (such as the actual protocol format). In addition, this namespace provides some high-level constructs for working with networks—TCP/IP in particular.

Most .NET programmers will work with either the WebClient type, which provides the most high-level view of doing HTTP-style request/response communications over a TCP/IP network (such as the Internet), or else the slightly lower-level WebRequest and WebResponse types. The choice between the two is really not all that difficult: for most high-level, protocol-agnostic work, WebClient will likely be the preferred choice. If protocol-specific actions need to be taken (such as specifying additional headers as part of an HTTP request, for example), then likely the .NET programmer will want to work with WebRequest and WebResponse. To be specific, the .NET programmer will work with the concrete derived types HttpWebRequest and HttpWebResponse.

As shipped, the .NET Framework Class Library provides implementations for three URI protocol schemes: HTTP, HTTPS, and files (http:, https:, and file:, respectively). For support of other URI types (such as FTP, NNTP, or POP3), a new derivative of WebRequest and WebResponse must be written, an Abstract Factory type implementing the IWebRequestCreate interface must be created, and an instance of it (along with the protocol scheme prefix) must be registered with WebRequest. RegisterPrefix(). Figure 33-1 shows the collaborations between the concrete classes HttpWebRequest, HttpWebResponse, FileWebRequest, and FileWebResponse.

Figure 33-2 shows the composition of the ServicePoint class, and Figure 33-3 shows the remaining types in this namespace.

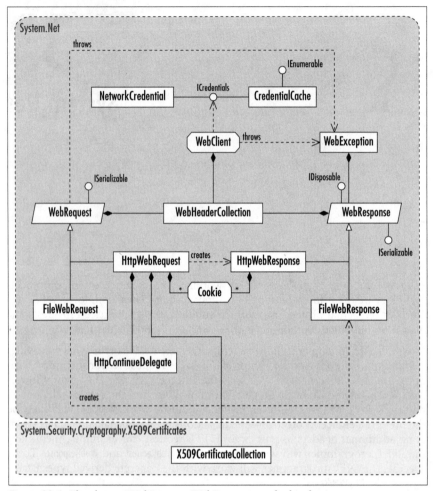

Figure 33-1. The abstract WebRequest, WebResponse, and related concrete types

AuthenticationManager

CF 1.0, ECMA 1.0

System.Net (system.dll)

class

This class is responsible for finding an authentication module to authorize access to network resources. You do not need to use this class unless you have defined your own authentication scheme. By default, Basic, Digest, NTLM, and Kerberos authentication schemes are supported. This, for the most part, covers the needs of 99.9% of all .NET programmers in the world. Kerberos is not supported on Windows 95/98 or on Windows Me..

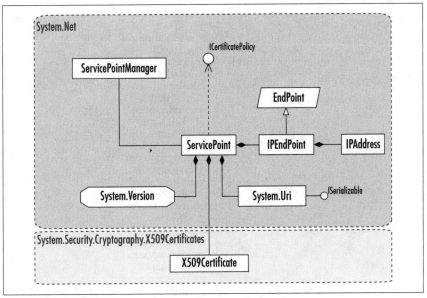

Figure 33-2. Endpoints, service points, and associated types

```
public class AuthenticationManager {
// Public Static Properties
   public static IEnumerator RegisteredModules{get; }
// Public Static Methods
   public static Authorization Authenticate(string challenge, WebRequest request, ICredentials credentials);
   public static Authorization PreAuthenticate(WebRequest request, ICredentials credentials);
   public static void Register(IAuthenticationModule authenticationModule);
   public static void Unregister(IAuthenticationModule authenticationModule);
   public static void Unregister(string authenticationScheme);
}
```

Authorization

CF 1.0, ECMA 1.0

System.Net (system.dll)   class

This class encapsulates an authentication message that AuthenticationManager sends to a remote server. The Message property contains the string that is sent to the server in response to its authentication challenge.

The Authorization class is used by implementations of IAuthenticationModule and by AuthenticationManager. You should not need to use it directly unless you have implemented your own authentication scheme.

Returned By

AuthenticationManager.{Authenticate(),   PreAuthenticate()},   IAuthenticationModule.{Authenticate(),
PreAuthenticate()}

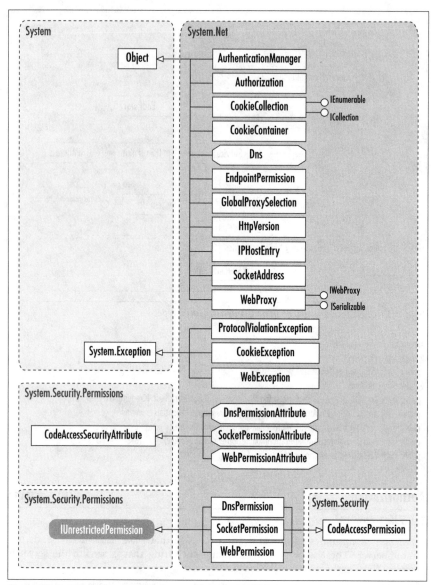

Figure 33-3. Other classes in the System.Net namespace

```
public class Authorization {
// Public Constructors
  public Authorization(string token);
  public Authorization(string token, bool finished);
  public Authorization(string token, bool finished, string connectionGroupId);
// Public Instance Properties
  public bool Complete{get; }
  public string ConnectionGroupId{get; }
```

```
public string Message{get; }
public string[ ] ProtectionRealm{set; get; }
}
```

Cookie   serializable

System.Net (system.dll)   sealed class

This class represents an HTTP cookie, as standardized by RFC 2965 (*ftp://ftp.isi.edu/in-notes/rfc2965.txt*). A cookie represents a simple name-value pair that is sent back by the HTTP User-Agent on each subsequent request to the URL host that set the cookie. The rules governing the visibility, scope, and lifetime of cookies is well documented in the RFC; see that document for details. The Cookie has properties defined on it corresponding to the settable values in the RFC: principally, the Value property sets the value of the cookie, and the Name property sets the name by which the cookie's value can be retrieved.

As a User-Agent, adding a Cookie to an HttpWebRequest is as simple as adding the Cookie instance to the HttpWebRequest.CookieContainer property. When you receive a response from an HTTP server, it may contain one or more cookies. Use the HttpWebResponse.Cookies collection to obtain the cookies that the HTTP server sent you.

Note that, as a User-Agent (the client), it is the .NET programmer's responsibility for maintaining all the semantics of the RFC—that is, the cookie must only be sent back to the host that set it, the cookie can only be sent back if it obeys the "path" prefix set on the cookie, and so forth. Failure to do so could result in different hosts viewing cookies that they didn't set, which is a potential security hole (albeit only if a host puts sensitive material into the cookie in the first place). None of this is implemented in the HttpWebRequest or Cookie types.

```
public sealed class Cookie {
// Public Constructors
  public Cookie( );
  public Cookie(string name, string value);
  public Cookie(string name, string value, string path);
  public Cookie(string name, string value, string path, string domain);
// Public Instance Properties
  public string Comment{set; get; }
  public Uri CommentUri{set; get; }
  public bool Discard{set; get; }
  public string Domain{set; get; }
  public bool Expired{set; get; }
  public DateTime Expires{set; get; }
  public string Name{set; get; }
  public string Path{set; get; }
  public string Port{set; get; }
  public bool Secure{set; get; }
  public DateTime TimeStamp{get; }
  public string Value{set; get; }
  public int Version{set; get; }
// Public Instance Methods
  public override bool Equals(object comparand);                  // overrides object
  public override int GetHashCode( );                             // overrides object
```

```
public override string ToString( );                                              // overrides object
}
```

Returned By   CookieCollection.this

Passed To   CookieCollection.Add( ), CookieContainer.Add( )

CookieCollection   serializable

System.Net (system.dll)   class

This class is a specialized collection for holding cookies. It's used by **HttpWebResponse** to represent a set of cookies returned by a server. By default, the **IsReadOnly** property is set to **true**.

```
public class CookieCollection : ICollection, IEnumerable {
// Public Constructors
  public CookieCollection( );
// Public Instance Properties
  public int Count{get; }                                                        // implements ICollection
  public bool IsReadOnly{get; }
  public bool IsSynchronized{get; }                                              // implements ICollection
  public object SyncRoot{get; }                                                  // implements ICollection
  public Cookie this[int index]{get; }
  public Cookie this[string name]{get; }
// Public Instance Methods
  public void Add(Cookie cookie);
  public void Add(CookieCollection cookies);
  public void CopyTo(Array array, int index);                                    // implements ICollection
  public IEnumerator GetEnumerator( );                                           // implements IEnumerable
}
```

Returned By   CookieContainer.GetCookies( ), HttpWebResponse.Cookies

Passed To   CookieContainer.Add( ), HttpWebResponse.Cookies

CookieContainer   serializable

System.Net (system.dll)   class

This class is a container that holds cookies and organizes them by URI. You can add a **Cookie** or **CookieCollection** to a container using the simplest forms of the **Add( )** method, or you can use the forms of the **Add( )** method that take a **System.Uri** argument. You can retrieve all the cookies for a given URI using the **GetCookies( )** method.

```
public class CookieContainer {
// Public Constructors
  public CookieContainer( );
  public CookieContainer(int capacity);
  public CookieContainer(int capacity, int perDomainCapacity, int maxCookieSize);
// Public Static Fields
  public const int DefaultCookieLengthLimit;                                     // =4096
  public const int DefaultCookieLimit;                                           // =300
```

```
  public const int DefaultPerDomainCookieLimit;                                   // =20
// Public Instance Properties
  public int Capacity{set; get; }
  public int Count{get; }
  public int MaxCookieSize{set; get; }
  public int PerDomainCapacity{set; get; }
// Public Instance Methods
  public void Add(Cookie cookie);
  public void Add(CookieCollection cookies);
  public void Add(Uri uri, Cookie cookie);
  public void Add(Uri uri, CookieCollection cookies);
  public string GetCookieHeader(Uri uri);
  public CookieCollection GetCookies(Uri uri);
  public void SetCookies(Uri uri, string cookieHeader);
}
```

Returned By   HttpWebRequest.CookieContainer

Passed To   HttpWebRequest.CookieContainer

CookieException   serializable

System.Net (system.dll)   class

This exception signals an error encountered during a cookie-related operation.

```
public class CookieException : FormatException {
// Public Constructors
  public CookieException( );
// Protected Constructors
  protected CookieException(System.Runtime.Serialization.SerializationInfo serializationInfo,
    System.Runtime.Serialization.StreamingContext streamingContext);
}
```

Hierarchy   System.Object → System.Exception(System.Runtime.Serialization.ISerializable) →
                System.SystemException → System.FormatException → CookieException

CredentialCache   ECMA 1.0

System.Net (system.dll)   class

This class maintains credentials for multiple network resources. If you are developing a
client application that needs to authenticate itself to more than one server, you can
store an instance of this class in the WebRequest.Credentials property.

After you create an instance of this class, use the Add( ) method to associate NetworkCredential objects with a URI and authentication type (using a string such as "Basic" or "Digest").
Then you can assign the CredentialCache instance to the WebRequest.Credentials property to use
the credentials for future web requests.

```
public class CredentialCache : ICredentials, IEnumerable {
// Public Constructors
  public CredentialCache( );
```

```
// Public Static Properties
  public static ICredentials DefaultCredentials{get; }
// Public Instance Methods
  public void Add(Uri uriPrefix, string authType, NetworkCredential cred);
  public NetworkCredential GetCredential(Uri uriPrefix, string authType);          // implements ICredentials
  public IEnumerator GetEnumerator( );                                            // implements IEnumerable
  public void Remove(Uri uriPrefix, string authType);
}
```

Dns

CF 1.0, ECMA 1.0

System.Net (system.dll)

sealed class

This type offers up a collection of static methods for resolving DNS (Domain Name Service) operations. Because raw IP addresses (such as 192.168.0.1) can be difficult for humans to remember, DNS servers take human-friendly names (such as "www.oreilly. com") and in turn translate them into IP addresses and/or back again. This ability can be useful in a variety of scenarios, including the simple logging of clients who have visited a web site recently. (Note that this is not a secure way of tracking usage—even a simple attacker can spoof the return address of an IP packet, so don't rely on this mechanism for any kind of security validation or audit trail.)

The GetHostByName( ) method takes a hostname (such as "www.oreilly.com") and returns the corresponding IPHostEntry instance; this IPHostEntry instance is used later in several of the System.Net and System.Net.Sockets types. This method (along with the paired method Resolve( )) can be invoked asynchronously using the BeginGetHostByName( ) or BeginResolve( ) methods. Like all async methods in the .NET Framework, they take two additional parameters: an AsyncCallback object, and a generic object parameter that is passed to the AsyncCallback when the call completes.

At the surface, there would appear to be no difference between calling Resolve( ) or GetHostByName( ); in fact, the Resolve( ) method calls into GetHostByName( ) after doing a small amount of preprocessing to check if the string passed is either a standard host name ("www.oreilly.com") or a dotted-quad IP address ("192.168.0.1"); GetHostByName( ) requires a hostname. (For those familiar with the Berkeley sockets API, the GetHostByName( ) method is a wrapper around the native BSD gethostbyname function.)

```
public sealed class Dns {
// Public Static Methods
  public static IAsyncResult BeginGetHostByName(string hostName, AsyncCallback requestCallback, object stateObject);
  public static IAsyncResult BeginResolve(string hostName, AsyncCallback requestCallback, object stateObject);
  public static IPHostEntry EndGetHostByName(IAsyncResult asyncResult);
  public static IPHostEntry EndResolve(IAsyncResult asyncResult);
  public static IPHostEntry GetHostByAddress(IPAddress address);
  public static IPHostEntry GetHostByAddress(string address);
  public static IPHostEntry GetHostByName(string hostName);
  public static string GetHostName( );
  public static IPHostEntry Resolve(string hostName);
}
```

DnsPermission

ECMA 1.0, serializable

System.Net (system.dll)   sealed class

This class controls access to DNS services. The constructor accepts one argument, either System.Security.Permissions.PermissionState.None (no access to DNS services) or System.Security.Permissions.PermissionState.Unrestricted (all access).

This permission is Demand( )ed by all of the methods on the Dns class.

```
public sealed class DnsPermission : System.Security.CodeAccessPermission,
    System.Security.Permissions.IUnrestrictedPermission {
// Public Constructors
    public DnsPermission(System.Security.Permissions.PermissionState state);
// Public Instance Methods
    public override IPermission Copy( );                                  // overrides CodeAccessPermission
    public override void FromXml(System.Security.SecurityElement securityElement);   // overrides CodeAccessPermission
    public override IPermission Intersect(System.Security.IPermission target);   // overrides CodeAccessPermission
    public override bool IsSubsetOf(System.Security.IPermission target);   // overrides CodeAccessPermission
    public bool IsUnrestricted( );                                        // implements IUnrestrictedPermission
    public override SecurityElement ToXml( );                            // overrides CodeAccessPermission
    public override IPermission Union(System.Security.IPermission target);   // overrides CodeAccessPermission
}
```

Hierarchy   System.Object → System.Security.CodeAccessPermission(System.Security.IPermission,
                 System.Security.ISecurityEncodable, System.Security.IStackWalk) →
                 DnsPermission(System.Security.Permissions.IUnrestrictedPermission)

DnsPermissionAttribute

ECMA 1.0, serializable

System.Net (system.dll)   sealed class

This attribute is used to declare in metadata that the attributed method or class requires DnsPermission of the declared form.

```
public sealed class DnsPermissionAttribute : System.Security.Permissions.CodeAccessSecurityAttribute {
// Public Constructors
    public DnsPermissionAttribute(System.Security.Permissions.SecurityAction action);
// Public Instance Methods
    public override IPermission CreatePermission( );       // overrides System.Security.Permissions.SecurityAttribute
}
```

Hierarchy   System.Object → System.Attribute → System.Security.Permissions.SecurityAttribute →
                 System.Security.Permissions.CodeAccessSecurityAttribute → DnsPermissionAttribute

Valid On   Assembly, Class, Struct, Constructor, Method

EndPoint

CF 1.0, ECMA 1.0, serializable

System.Net (system.dll)   abstract class

This abstract class represents a network address. It is extended by IPEndPoint, which represents an IP network address. It could later be extended to represent other kinds of networking endpoints for other protocol stacks beyond TCP/IP.

```
public abstract class EndPoint {
// Protected Constructors
  protected EndPoint( );
// Public Instance Properties
  public virtual AddressFamily AddressFamily{get; }
// Public Instance Methods
  public virtual EndPoint Create(SocketAddress socketAddress);
  public virtual SocketAddress Serialize( );
}
```

Subclasses   IPEndPoint

Returned By   IPEndPoint.Create( ), System.Net.Sockets.Socket.{LocalEndPoint, RemoteEndPoint}, System.
                    Net.Sockets.TcpListener.LocalEndpoint

Passed To   System.Net.Sockets.Socket.{BeginConnect( ), BeginReceiveFrom( ), BeginSendTo( ), Bind( ),
                    Connect( ), EndReceiveFrom( ), ReceiveFrom( ), SendTo( )}

EndpointPermission   serializable

System.Net (system.dll)   class

This permission is Demand( )ed by all of the methods on the EndPoint class.

```
public class EndpointPermission {
// Public Instance Properties
  public string Hostname{get; }
  public int Port{get; }
  public TransportType Transport{get; }
// Public Instance Methods
  public override bool Equals(object obj);                                 // overrides object
  public override int GetHashCode( );                                      // overrides object
  public override string ToString( );                                     // overrides object
}
```

FileWebRequest   serializable, marshal by reference

System.Net (system.dll)   class

This subclass of WebRequest provides access to resources that use the file URL scheme
(such as a file on your local filesystem). Use WebRequest.Create( ) with a *file://* URL to
create an instance of this class. The WebRequest.Create( ) method returns an instance of this
class as a reference of type WebRequest.

You may feel a small sense of confusion regarding this type and the "file:" protocol
scheme; if a program needs access to a file on the filesystem, why not simply open a
System.IO.FileStream instead of using WebRequest.Create("file:/...")? In terms of straight functionality, the System.IO.FileStream call more closely represents the fact that this resource is
coming from disk; however, due to the ubiquity of HTTP servers growing within the
enterprise, there are often times when a system wishes to equally represent HTTP
URLs and filesystem paths within an arbitrary context. For example, a configuration
file might be used to indicate where to retrieve user preferences; by specifying the location as a URL rather than an absolute file location, storage of user preferences is
permitted on a centralized server without any additional code. (This allows a kind of

"roaming preferences" capability within the system.) Many of the .NET tools also use this approach to identify "files" to act upon via command-line parameters.

```
public class FileWebRequest : WebRequest {
// Protected Constructors
  protected FileWebRequest(System.Runtime.Serialization.SerializationInfo serializationInfo,
    System.Runtime.Serialization.StreamingContext streamingContext);
// Public Instance Properties
  public override string ConnectionGroupName{set; get; }                                          // overrides WebRequest
  public override long ContentLength{set; get; }                                                  // overrides WebRequest
  public override string ContentType{set; get; }                                                  // overrides WebRequest
  public override ICredentials Credentials{set; get; }                                             // overrides WebRequest
  public override WebHeaderCollection Headers{get; }                                               // overrides WebRequest
  public override string Method{set; get; }                                                        // overrides WebRequest
  public override bool PreAuthenticate{set; get; }                                                 // overrides WebRequest
  public override IWebProxy Proxy{set; get; }                                                      // overrides WebRequest
  public override Uri RequestUri{get; }                                                            // overrides WebRequest
  public override int Timeout{set; get; }                                                          // overrides WebRequest
// Public Instance Methods
  public override IAsyncResult BeginGetRequestStream(AsyncCallback callback, object state);        // overrides WebRequest
  public override IAsyncResult BeginGetResponse(AsyncCallback callback, object state);             // overrides WebRequest
  public override Stream EndGetRequestStream(IAsyncResult asyncResult);                            // overrides WebRequest
  public override WebResponse EndGetResponse(IAsyncResult asyncResult);                            // overrides WebRequest
  public override Stream GetRequestStream( );                                                      // overrides WebRequest
  public override WebResponse GetResponse( );                                                      // overrides WebRequest
}
```

Hierarchy   System.Object → System.MarshalByRefObject → WebRequest(System.Runtime.Serializa-
                       tion.ISerializable) → FileWebRequest

FileWebResponse   serializable, marshal by reference, disposable

System.Net (system.dll)   class

This subclass of WebResponse is returned by WebRequest.GetResponse() when you request access to a file URI. Since this subclass does not add any new methods, there's no need to cast the return value to a FileWebResponse; the GetResponseStream() method returns a System. IO.Stream from which the file's contents can be retrieved.

```
public class FileWebResponse : WebResponse {
// Protected Constructors
  protected FileWebResponse(System.Runtime.Serialization.SerializationInfo serializationInfo,
    System.Runtime.Serialization.StreamingContext streamingContext);
// Public Instance Properties
  public override long ContentLength{get; }                                                        // overrides WebResponse
  public override string ContentType{get; }                                                        // overrides WebResponse
  public override WebHeaderCollection Headers{get; }                                               // overrides WebResponse
  public override Uri ResponseUri{get; }                                                           // overrides WebResponse
// Public Instance Methods
  public override void Close( );                                                                   // overrides WebResponse
  public override Stream GetResponseStream( );                                                     // overrides WebResponse
```

```
// Protected Instance Methods
  protected virtual void Dispose(bool disposing);
}
```

Hierarchy   System.Object → System.MarshalByRefObject → WebResponse(System.Runtime.
                    Serialization.ISerializable, System.IDisposable) → FileWebResponse

GlobalProxySelection

CF 1.0, ECMA 1.0

System.Net (system.dll)   class

This class holds the default IWebProxy object used by all HTTP requests. To change it, set the Select property to an instance of WebProxy.

```
public class GlobalProxySelection {
// Public Constructors
  public GlobalProxySelection( );
// Public Static Properties
  public static IWebProxy Select{set; get; }
// Public Static Methods
  public static IWebProxy GetEmptyWebProxy( );
}
```

HttpContinueDelegate

CF 1.0, ECMA 1.0, serializable

System.Net (system.dll)   delegate

The HttpWebRequest.ContinueDelegate property uses this class to handle HttpStatusCode.Continue responses. These responses are sent when the server receives the HTTP request, is able to process it, and wishes to notify the client that the request was successfully received. (Most HTTP servers will send this only if the request processing would take longer than expected.)

```
public delegate void HttpContinueDelegate(int StatusCode, WebHeaderCollection httpHeaders);
```

Returned By   HttpWebRequest.ContinueDelegate

Passed To   HttpWebRequest.ContinueDelegate

HttpStatusCode

CF 1.0, ECMA 1.0, serializable

System.Net (system.dll)   enum

This enumeration contains HTTP 1.1 status codes as defined in RFC 2616 (*ftp://ftp.isi. edu/in-notes/rfc2616.txt*).

```
public enum HttpStatusCode {
  Continue = 100,
  SwitchingProtocols = 101,
  OK = 200,
  Created = 201,
  Accepted = 202,
  NonAuthoritativeInformation = 203,
  NoContent = 204,
```

```
ResetContent = 205,
PartialContent = 206,
MultipleChoices = 300,
Ambiguous = 300,
MovedPermanently = 301,
Moved = 301,
Found = 302,
Redirect = 302,
SeeOther = 303,
RedirectMethod = 303,
NotModified = 304,
UseProxy = 305,
Unused = 306,
TemporaryRedirect = 307,
RedirectKeepVerb = 307,
BadRequest = 400,
Unauthorized = 401,
PaymentRequired = 402,
Forbidden = 403,
NotFound = 404,
MethodNotAllowed = 405,
NotAcceptable = 406,
ProxyAuthenticationRequired = 407,
RequestTimeout = 408,
Conflict = 409,
Gone = 410,
LengthRequired = 411,
PreconditionFailed = 412,
RequestEntityTooLarge = 413,
RequestUriTooLong = 414,
UnsupportedMediaType = 415,
RequestedRangeNotSatisfiable = 416,
ExpectationFailed = 417,
InternalServerError = 500,
NotImplemented = 501,
BadGateway = 502,
ServiceUnavailable = 503,
GatewayTimeout = 504,
HttpVersionNotSupported = 505
}
```

Hierarchy System.Object → System.ValueType → System.Enum(System.IComparable, System.IFormattable, System.IConvertible) → HttpStatusCode

Returned By HttpWebResponse.StatusCode

HttpVersion

CF 1.0, ECMA 1.0

System.Net (system.dll)   class

This class contains System.Version values that represent versions for HTTP 1.0 and 1.1.

```
public class HttpVersion {
// Public Constructors
  public HttpVersion( );
// Public Static Fields
  public static readonly Version Version10;                                           // =1.0
  public static readonly Version Version11;                                           // =1.1
}
```

HttpWebRequest   CF 1.0, ECMA 1.0, serializable, marshal by reference

System.Net (system.dll)   class

This is a subclass of WebRequest. .NET uses this subclass to request documents from the
http and https URI schemes (RFCs 2616 and 2818, respectively). An instance of this type
is returned by WebRequest.Create( ) when a URI starting with the *http://* or *https://* prefix is
passed in. Since that method's return value is WebRequest, cast it to HttpWebRequest if you
need access to any of the methods or properties that are unique to this class (and the
HTTP or HTTPS protocol).

The properties on this type correspond directly to the headers documented in the RFC
standard documentation; see that document for details regarding their contents. Note
that because these headers are sent as part of the HTTP request, any modification of
the headers must be done before the request is sent to the remote host. (Calling either
GetResponse( ) or BeginGetResponse( ), the asynchronous version of GetResponse( ), sends the
request.)

When a WebRequest encounters an error, a WebException is thrown.

```
public class HttpWebRequest : WebRequest {
// Protected Constructors
  protected HttpWebRequest(System.Runtime.Serialization.SerializationInfo serializationInfo,
     System.Runtime.Serialization.StreamingContext streamingContext);
// Public Static Properties
  public static int DefaultMaximumResponseHeadersLength{set; get; }
// Public Instance Properties
  public string Accept{set; get; }
  public Uri Address{get; }
  public bool AllowAutoRedirect{set; get; }
  public bool AllowWriteStreamBuffering{set; get; }
  public X509CertificateCollection ClientCertificates{get; }
  public string Connection{set; get; }
  public override string ConnectionGroupName{set; get; }                       // overrides WebRequest
  public override long ContentLength{set; get; }                               // overrides WebRequest
  public override string ContentType{set; get; }                              // overrides WebRequest
  public HttpContinueDelegate ContinueDelegate{set; get; }
  public CookieContainer CookieContainer{set; get; }
  public override ICredentials Credentials{set; get; }                         // overrides WebRequest
  public string Expect{set; get; }
  public bool HaveResponse{get; }
  public override WebHeaderCollection Headers{set; get; }                       // overrides WebRequest
  public DateTime IfModifiedSince{set; get; }
  public bool KeepAlive{set; get; }
  public int MaximumAutomaticRedirections{set; get; }
```

public int **MaximumResponseHeadersLength**{set; get; }	
public string **MediaType**{set; get; }	
public override string **Method**{set; get; }	// overrides WebRequest
public bool **Pipelined**{set; get; }	
public override bool **PreAuthenticate**{set; get; }	// overrides WebRequest
public Version **ProtocolVersion**{set; get; }	
public override IWebProxy **Proxy**{set; get; }	// overrides WebRequest
public int **ReadWriteTimeout**{set; get; }	
public string **Referer**{set; get; }	
public override Uri **RequestUri**{get; }	// overrides WebRequest
public bool **SendChunked**{set; get; }	
public ServicePoint **ServicePoint**{get; }	
public override int **Timeout**{set; get; }	// overrides WebRequest
public string **TransferEncoding**{set; get; }	
public bool **UnsafeAuthenticatedConnectionSharing**{set; get; }	
public string **UserAgent**{set; get; }	
// Public Instance Methods	
public override void **Abort**( );	// overrides WebRequest
public void **AddRange**(int *range*);	
public void **AddRange**(int *from*, int *to*);	
public void **AddRange**(string *rangeSpecifier*, int *range*);	
public void **AddRange**(string *rangeSpecifier*, int *from*, int *to*);	
public override IAsyncResult **BeginGetRequestStream**(AsyncCallback *callback*, object *state*);	// overrides WebRequest
public override IAsyncResult **BeginGetResponse**(AsyncCallback *callback*, object *state*);	// overrides WebRequest
public override Stream **EndGetRequestStream**(IAsyncResult *asyncResult*);	// overrides WebRequest
public override WebResponse **EndGetResponse**(IAsyncResult *asyncResult*);	// overrides WebRequest
public override int **GetHashCode**( );	// overrides object
public override Stream **GetRequestStream**( );	// overrides WebRequest
public override WebResponse **GetResponse**( );	// overrides WebRequest
}	

Hierarchy   System.Object → System.MarshalByRefObject → WebRequest(System.Runtime.
Serialization.ISerializable) → HttpWebRequest

HttpWebResponse   CF 1.0, ECMA 1.0, serializable, marshal by reference, disposable

System.Net (system.dll)   class

This class represents a response from an HTTP server. This is usually returned from
WebRequest.GetResponse( ) or WebRequest.EndGetResponse( ). Use GetResponseStream( ) to obtain a
System.IO.Stream object containing the response body. Use GetResponseHeader( ) to fetch a
specific HTTP header.

```
public class HttpWebResponse : WebResponse {
// Protected Constructors
   protected HttpWebResponse(System.Runtime.Serialization.SerializationInfo serializationInfo,
      System.Runtime.Serialization.StreamingContext streamingContext);
// Public Instance Properties
   public string CharacterSet{get; }
   public string ContentEncoding{get; }
   public override long ContentLength{get; }                          // overrides WebResponse
   public override string ContentType{get; }                          // overrides WebResponse
```

```
public CookieCollection Cookies{set; get; }
public override WebHeaderCollection Headers{get; }                          // overrides WebResponse
public DateTime LastModified{get; }
public string Method{get; }
public Version ProtocolVersion{get; }
public override Uri ResponseUri{get; }                                      // overrides WebResponse
public string Server{get; }
public HttpStatusCode StatusCode{get; }
public string StatusDescription{get; }
// Public Instance Methods
public override void Close( );                                              // overrides WebResponse
public override int GetHashCode( );                                        // overrides object
public string GetResponseHeader(string headerName);
public override Stream GetResponseStream( );                                // overrides WebResponse
// Protected Instance Methods
protected virtual void Dispose(bool disposing);
}
```

Hierarchy   System.Object → System.MarshalByRefObject → WebResponse(System.Runtime.
Serialization.ISerializable, System.IDisposable) → HttpWebResponse

IAuthenticationModule   CF 1.0, ECMA 1.0

System.Net (system.dll)   interface

This interface is implemented by all authentication modules. If you develop a custom
authentication module, you must implement this interface and register an instance of
your module with AuthenticationManager.Register( ).

```
public interface IAuthenticationModule {
// Public Instance Properties
 public string AuthenticationType{get; }
 public bool CanPreAuthenticate{get; }
// Public Instance Methods
 public Authorization Authenticate(string challenge,WebRequest request, ICredentials credentials);
 public Authorization PreAuthenticate(WebRequest request, ICredentials credentials);
}
```

Passed To   AuthenticationManager.{Register( ), Unregister( )}

ICertificatePolicy   CF 1.0

System.Net (system.dll)   interface

This interface validates the certificates that web servers present to your applications. If
you create a web request that uses the https protocol, the .NET Framework uses the
default certificate policy to validate the server's certificate.

You can implement this interface to create your own custom certificate policy. Unlike
authentication modules, only one certificate policy may be active at a time. To set this,
create an instance of your implementation and assign it to ServicePointManager.
CertificatePolicy.

```
public interface ICertificatePolicy {
// Public Instance Methods
    public bool CheckValidationResult(ServicePoint srvPoint,
        System.Security.Cryptography.X509Certificates.X509Certificate certificate, WebRequest request, int certificateProblem);
}
```

Returned By   ServicePointManager.CertificatePolicy

Passed To   ServicePointManager.CertificatePolicy

ICredentials

CF 1.0, ECMA 1.0

System.Net (system.dll)   interface

This interface is implemented by all web-client credentials. The class NetworkCredential works with authentication schemes such as Basic and Digest authentication, NTLM, and Kerberos. If you need to implement a client authentication scheme not supported by .NET (such as SSL client certificates), you need to implement ICredentials and add a new instance of your implementation to your application's credential cache. For more information on using a credential cache, see CredentialCache.

```
public interface ICredentials {
// Public Instance Methods
    public NetworkCredential GetCredential(Uri uri, string authType);
}
```

Implemented By CredentialCache, NetworkCredential

Returned By   CredentialCache.DefaultCredentials, IWebProxy.Credentials, WebClient.Credentials, WebProxy.Credentials, WebRequest.Credentials

Passed To   AuthenticationManager.{Authenticate( ), PreAuthenticate( )}, IAuthenticationModule. {Authenticate( ), PreAuthenticate( )}, IWebProxy.Credentials, WebClient.Credentials, WebProxy.{Credentials, WebProxy( )}, WebRequest.Credentials, System.Xml.XmlResolver. Credentials

IPAddress

CF 1.0, ECMA 1.0, serializable

System.Net (system.dll)   class

This class represents an IP address. Use the Parse( ) method to turn a dotted-quad string (such as "192.168.0.1") into an IPAddress. Use the ToString( ) method to convert an IPAddress into a string.

```
public class IPAddress {
// Public Constructors
    public IPAddress(byte[ ] address);
    public IPAddress(byte[ ] address, long scopeid);
    public IPAddress(long newAddress);
// Public Static Fields
    public static readonly IPAddress Any;                    // =0.0.0.0
    public static readonly IPAddress Broadcast;              // =255.255.255.255
    public static readonly IPAddress IPv6Any;
    public static readonly IPAddress IPv6Loopback;
```

```
public static readonly IPAddress IPv6None;
public static readonly IPAddress Loopback;                                    // =127.0.0.1
public static readonly IPAddress None;                                        // =255.255.255.255
// Public Instance Properties
public long Address{set; get; }                                              // obsolete
public AddressFamily AddressFamily{get; }
public long ScopeId{set; get; }
// Public Static Methods
public static short HostToNetworkOrder(short host);
public static int HostToNetworkOrder(int host);
public static long HostToNetworkOrder(long host);
public static bool IsLoopback(IPAddress address);
public static short NetworkToHostOrder(short network);
public static int NetworkToHostOrder(int network);
public static long NetworkToHostOrder(long network);
public static IPAddress Parse(string ipString);
// Public Instance Methods
public override bool Equals(object comparand);                               // overrides object
public byte[ ] GetAddressBytes( );
public override int GetHashCode( );                                         // overrides object
public override string ToString( );                                        // overrides object
}
```

Returned By   IPEndPoint.Address, IPHostEntry.AddressList, System.Net.Sockets.IPv6MulticastOption.
                   Group, System.Net.Sockets.MulticastOption.{Group, LocalAddress}

Passed To   Multiple types

IPEndPoint   CF 1.0, ECMA 1.0, serializable

System.Net (system.dll)   class

This class represents a network endpoint as a combination of IPAddress and an integer
port number. The static fields MinPort and MaxPort represent the minimum and maximum
acceptable values for Port. These values are operating system–dependent.

This class does not represent an open socket connection, which contains two
endpoints (local and remote). To create a socket, use System.Net.Sockets.Socket.

```
public class IPEndPoint : EndPoint {
// Public Constructors
public IPEndPoint(long address, int port);
public IPEndPoint(IPAddress address, int port);
// Public Static Fields
public const int MaxPort;                                                    // =65535
public const int MinPort;                                                    // =0
// Public Instance Properties
public IPAddress Address{set; get; }
public override AddressFamily AddressFamily{get; }                          // overrides EndPoint
public int Port{set; get; }
// Public Instance Methods
public override EndPoint Create(SocketAddress socketAddress);              // overrides EndPoint
public override bool Equals(object comparand);                             // overrides object
```

```
public override int GetHashCode( );                                          // overrides object
public override SocketAddress Serialize( );                                  // overrides EndPoint
public override string ToString( );                                          // overrides object
}
```

Hierarchy   System.Object → EndPoint → IPEndPoint

Passed To   System.Net.Sockets.TcpClient.{Connect( ), TcpClient( )}, System.Net.Sockets.TcpListener.
                     TcpListener( ), System.Net.Sockets.UdpClient.{Connect( ), Receive( ), Send( ), UdpClient( )}

IPHostEntry   CF 1.0, ECMA 1.0

System.Net (system.dll)   class

The Dns class uses this class to represent hosts. A host is named by its HostName property, and its aliases are stored in the Aliases property. The AddressList property contains all the IP addresses for that host.

```
public class IPHostEntry {
// Public Constructors
  public IPHostEntry( );
// Public Instance Properties
  public IPAddress[ ] AddressList{set; get; }
  public string[ ] Aliases{set; get; }
  public string HostName{set; get; }
}
```

Returned By   Dns.{EndGetHostByName( ), EndResolve( ), GetHostByAddress( ), GetHostByName( ),
                     Resolve( )}

IWebProxy   CF 1.0, ECMA 1.0

System.Net (system.dll)   interface

IWebProxy defines the interface used by the WebProxy class. Parties interested in creating customized proxy handlers would implement this interface to do so, but the WebProxy implementation is sufficient for most HTTP access purposes.

To use an implementation of IWebProxy, see the GlobalProxySelection class or the WebRequest. Proxy property.

```
public interface IWebProxy {
// Public Instance Properties
  public ICredentials Credentials{set; get; }
// Public Instance Methods
  public Uri GetProxy(Uri destination);
  public bool IsBypassed(Uri host);
}
```

Implemented By   WebProxy

Returned By   GlobalProxySelection.{GetEmptyWebProxy( ), Select}, WebRequest.Proxy

Passed To   GlobalProxySelection.Select, ServicePointManager.FindServicePoint( ), WebRequest.Proxy

IWebRequestCreate

CF 1.0, ECMA 1.0

System.Net (system.dll)   interface

This interface is for objects that create protocol-specific instances of WebRequest. For example, the private class HttpRequestCreator is the underlying class that implements this interface. WebRequest uses that class under the hood to create instances of HttpWebRequest when an application connects to an http or https URI.

If you create your own protocol-specific implementation of this interface, you can register it with the WebRequest.RegisterPrefix( ) static method.

```
public interface IWebRequestCreate {
// Public Instance Methods
  public WebRequest Create(Uri uri);
}
```

Passed To   WebRequest.RegisterPrefix( )

NetworkAccess

ECMA 1.0, serializable

System.Net (system.dll)   enum

This enumeration specifies network access permissions. Accept indicates that an application has permission to accept network connections. Connect indicates that the application can connect to network hosts.

Both WebPermission and SocketPermission use this enumeration.

```
public enum NetworkAccess {
  Connect = 64,
  Accept = 128
}
```

Hierarchy   System.Object → System.ValueType → System.Enum(System.IComparable,
                       System.IFormattable, System.IConvertible) → NetworkAccess

Passed To   SocketPermission.{AddPermission( ), SocketPermission( )}, WebPermission
                       {AddPermission( ), WebPermission( )}

NetworkCredential

CF 1.0, ECMA 1.0

System.Net (system.dll)   class

This class is an implementation of ICredentials for authentication schemes that use passwords, such as basic and digest authentication, NTLM, and Kerberos. See CredentialCache for more details.

```
public class NetworkCredential : ICredentials {
// Public Constructors
  public NetworkCredential( );
  public NetworkCredential(string userName, string password);
  public NetworkCredential(string userName, string password, string domain);
// Public Instance Properties
  public string Domain{set; get; }
  public string Password{set; get; }
```

```
    public string UserName{set; get; }
// Public Instance Methods
    public NetworkCredential GetCredential(Uri uri, string authType);                        // implements ICredentials
}
```

Returned By   CredentialCache.GetCredential( ), ICredentials.GetCredential( )

Passed To   CredentialCache.Add( )

ProtocolViolationException
CF 1.0, ECMA 1.0, serializable

System.Net (system.dll)   class

This exception is thrown when a network protocol error occurs.

```
public class ProtocolViolationException : InvalidOperationException {
// Public Constructors
    public ProtocolViolationException( );
    public ProtocolViolationException(string message);
// Protected Constructors
    protected ProtocolViolationException(System.Runtime.Serialization.SerializationInfo serializationInfo,
        System.Runtime.Serialization.StreamingContext streamingContext);
}
```

Hierarchy   System.Object → System.Exception(System.Runtime.Serialization.ISerializable) →
                     System.SystemException → System.InvalidOperationException →
                     ProtocolViolationException

SecurityProtocolType
.NET 1.1, serializable, flag

System.Net (system.dll)   enum

This enumeration specifies the available security protocol types.

```
public enum SecurityProtocolType {
    Ssl3 = 0x00000030,
    Tls = 0x000000C0
}
```

Hierarchy   System.Object → System.ValueType → System.Enum(System.IComparable,
                     System.IFormattable, System.IConvertible) → SecurityProtocolType

Returned By   ServicePointManager.SecurityProtocol

Passed To   ServicePointManager.SecurityProtocol

ServicePoint
CF 1.0, ECMA 1.0

System.Net (system.dll)   class

This class is used by ServicePointManager to manage connections to remote hosts. The .NET
Framework reuses service points for all requests to a given URI. The lifetime of a given
ServicePoint is governed by its MaxIdleTime property.

The ServicePoint class is a high-level abstraction of the underlying implementation. Details of the implementation, such as the sockets used for HTTP transport, are not publicly exposed.

```
public class ServicePoint {
// Public Instance Properties
  public Uri Address{get; }
  public X509Certificate Certificate{get; }
  public X509Certificate ClientCertificate{get; }
  public int ConnectionLimit{set; get; }
  public string ConnectionName{get; }
  public int CurrentConnections{get; }
  public bool Expect100Continue{set; get; }
  public DateTime IdleSince{get; }
  public int MaxIdleTime{set; get; }
  public virtual Version ProtocolVersion{get; }
  public bool SupportsPipelining{get; }
  public bool UseNagleAlgorithm{set; get; }
// Public Instance Methods
  public override int GetHashCode( );                                          // overrides object
}
```

Returned By   HttpWebRequest.ServicePoint, ServicePointManager.FindServicePoint( )

Passed To   ICertificatePolicy.CheckValidationResult( )

ServicePointManager   CF 1.0, ECMA 1.0

System.Net (system.dll)   class

This class is responsible for managing ServicePoint instances. As your applications make HTTP connections to network resources, this class is working behind the scenes to maintain the connections. When your application makes many connections to the same server, this class eliminates the overhead of making a new connection each time you connect.

The ServicePointManager also sets the default certificate policy for new connections. In most cases, the default certificate policy should suit your needs. If you need to change it, see ICertificatePolicy for more details.

```
public class ServicePointManager {
// Public Static Fields
  public const int DefaultNonPersistentConnectionLimit;                          // =4
  public const int DefaultPersistentConnectionLimit;                             // =2
// Public Static Properties
  public static ICertificatePolicy CertificatePolicy{set; get; }
  public static bool CheckCertificateRevocationList{set; get; }
  public static int DefaultConnectionLimit{set; get; }
  public static bool Expect100Continue{set; get; }
  public static int MaxServicePointIdleTime{set; get; }
  public static int MaxServicePoints{set; get; }
  public static SecurityProtocolType SecurityProtocol{set; get; }
  public static bool UseNagleAlgorithm{set; get; }
```

```
// Public Static Methods
  public static ServicePoint FindServicePoint(string uriString, IWebProxy proxy);
  public static ServicePoint FindServicePoint(Uri address);
  public static ServicePoint FindServicePoint(Uri address, IWebProxy proxy);
}
```

SocketAddress

System.Net (system.dll)   class

This type defines an address of a particular socket; in particular, it defines the family of networking protocols to which the address belongs (for example, IP or IPv6), as well as the size of the address itself. This type can be safely ignored for most high-level (and, arguably, most low-level) networking operations.

```
public class SocketAddress {
// Public Constructors
  public SocketAddress(System.Net.Sockets.AddressFamily family);
  public SocketAddress(System.Net.Sockets.AddressFamily family, int size);
// Public Instance Properties
  public AddressFamily Family{get; }
  public int Size{get; }
  public byte this[int offset]{set; get; }
// Public Instance Methods
  public override bool Equals(object comparand);                    // overrides object
  public override int GetHashCode( );                               // overrides object
  public override string ToString( );                               // overrides object
}
```

Returned By   EndPoint.Serialize( )

Passed To   EndPoint.Create( )

SocketPermission

ECMA 1.0, serializable

System.Net (system.dll)   sealed class

This permission controls whether code can make or accept socket connections for a given NetworkAccess, TransportType, hostname, and port number (see the four-argument form of the constructor). The static field AllPorts is a constant that represents permission to all ports and can be used as the port argument to the constructor.

```
public sealed class SocketPermission : System.Security.CodeAccessPermission,
  System.Security.Permissions.IUnrestrictedPermission {
// Public Constructors
  public SocketPermission(NetworkAccess access, TransportType transport, string hostName, int portNumber);
  public SocketPermission(System.Security.Permissions.PermissionState state);
// Public Static Fields
  public const int AllPorts;                                                    // =-1
// Public Instance Properties
  public IEnumerator AcceptList{get; }
  public IEnumerator ConnectList{get; }
// Public Instance Methods
```

```
public void AddPermission(NetworkAccess access, TransportType transport,string hostName, int portNumber);
public override IPermission Copy( );                                                        // overrides CodeAccessPermission
public override void FromXml(System.Security.SecurityElement securityElement);              // overrides CodeAccessPermission
public override IPermission Intersect(System.Security.IPermission target);                  // overrides CodeAccessPermission
public override bool IsSubsetOf(System.Security.IPermission target);                        // overrides CodeAccessPermission
public bool IsUnrestricted( );                                                              // implements IUnrestrictedPermission
public override SecurityElement ToXml( );                                                   // overrides CodeAccessPermission
public override IPermission Union(System.Security.IPermission target);                      // overrides CodeAccessPermission
}
```

Hierarchy   System.Object → System.Security.CodeAccessPermission(System.Security.IPermission,
                  System.Security.ISecurityEncodable, System.Security.IStackWalk) →
                  SocketPermission(System.Security.Permissions.IUnrestrictedPermission)

SocketPermissionAttribute   ECMA 1.0, serializable

System.Net (system.dll)   sealed class

This attribute is used to declare in metadata that the attributed method or class
requires SocketPermission of the declared form.

```
public sealed class SocketPermissionAttribute : System.Security.Permissions.CodeAccessSecurityAttribute {
// Public Constructors
  public SocketPermissionAttribute(System.Security.Permissions.SecurityAction action);
// Public Instance Properties
  public string Access{set; get; }
  public string Host{set; get; }
  public string Port{set; get; }
  public string Transport{set; get; }
// Public Instance Methods
  public override IPermission CreatePermission( );                     // overrides System.Security.Permissions.SecurityAttribute
}
```

Hierarchy   System.Object → System.Attribute → System.Security.Permissions.SecurityAttribute →
                  System.Security.Permissions.CodeAccessSecurityAttribute → SocketPermissionAttribute

Valid On   Assembly, Class, Struct, Constructor, Method

TransportType   ECMA 1.0, serializable

System.Net (system.dll)   enum

This enumeration defines the transport protocols that can be used to communicate
over a socket.

```
public enum TransportType {
  Udp = 1,
  Connectionless = 1,
  Tcp = 2,
  ConnectionOriented = 2,
  All = 3
}
```

Hierarchy	System.Object → System.ValueType → System.Enum(System.IComparable, System.IFormattable, System.IConvertible) → TransportType
Returned By	EndpointPermission.Transport
Passed To	SocketPermission.{AddPermission( ), SocketPermission( )}

WebClient

ECMA 1.0, marshal by reference, disposable

System.Net (system.dll)   sealed class

This class is a simple HTTP User-Agent. Use DownloadData( ) to fetch a document as an array of bytes. The DownloadFile( ) method fetches a document and stores it in a file. You can upload data to a URI using UploadFile( ) or UploadData( ) (which uploads the contents of a byte array).

Before connecting to a URI, invoke the Add( ) method of the QueryString or Headers properties to add a key/value pair to the HTTP query string or HTTP request headers. Set the credentials property to authenticate the WebClient to the remote server, if necessary.

```
public sealed class WebClient : System.ComponentModel.Component {
// Public Constructors
  public WebClient( );
// Public Instance Properties
  public string BaseAddress{set; get; }
  public ICredentials Credentials{set; get; }
  public WebHeaderCollection Headers{set; get; }
  public NameValueCollection QueryString{set; get; }
  public WebHeaderCollection ResponseHeaders{get; }
// Public Instance Methods
  public byte[ ] DownloadData(string address);
  public void DownloadFile(string address, string fileName);
  public Stream OpenRead(string address);
  public Stream OpenWrite(string address);
  public Stream OpenWrite(string address, string method);
  public byte[ ] UploadData(string address, byte[ ] data);
  public byte[ ] UploadData(string address, string method, byte[ ] data);
  public byte[ ] UploadFile(string address, string fileName);
  public byte[ ] UploadFile(string address, string method, string fileName);
  public byte[ ] UploadValues(string address, System.Collections.Specialized.NameValueCollection data);
  public byte[ ] UploadValues(string address, string method, System.Collections.Specialized.NameValueCollection data);
}
```

Hierarchy	System.Object → System.MarshalByRefObject → System.ComponentModel. Component(System.ComponentModel.IComponent, System.IDisposable) → WebClient

WebException

CF 1.0, ECMA 1.0, serializable

System.Net (system.dll)   class

This exception represents an error that occurred while using a protocol-specific implementation of WebRequest. In the case of some protocols, such as HTTP, the exception's Response property contains information about the error that occurred.

```
public class WebException : InvalidOperationException {
// Public Constructors
  public WebException( );
  public WebException(string message);
  public WebException(string message, Exception innerException);
  public WebException(string message, Exception innerException, WebExceptionStatus status, WebResponse response);
  public WebException(string message, WebExceptionStatus status);
// Protected Constructors
  protected WebException(System.Runtime.Serialization.SerializationInfo serializationInfo,
    System.Runtime.Serialization.StreamingContext streamingContext);
// Public Instance Properties
  public WebResponse Response{get; }
  public WebExceptionStatus Status{get; }
}
```

Hierarchy   System.Object → System.Exception(System.Runtime.Serialization.ISerializable) →
                System.SystemException → System.InvalidOperationException → WebException

WebExceptionStatus   CF 1.0, ECMA 1.0, serializable

System.Net (system.dll)   enum

This enumeration defines constants for the status codes used in WebException.Status.

```
public enum WebExceptionStatus {
  Success = 0,
  NameResolutionFailure = 1,
  ConnectFailure = 2,
  ReceiveFailure = 3,
  SendFailure = 4,
  PipelineFailure = 5,
  RequestCanceled = 6,
  ProtocolError = 7,
  ConnectionClosed = 8,
  TrustFailure = 9,
  SecureChannelFailure = 10,
  ServerProtocolViolation = 11,
  KeepAliveFailure = 12,
  Pending = 13,
  Timeout = 14,
  ProxyNameResolutionFailure = 15,
  UnknownError = 16,
  MessageLengthLimitExceeded = 17
}
```

Hierarchy   System.Object → System.ValueType → System.Enum(System.IComparable,
                System.IFormattable, System.IConvertible) → WebExceptionStatus

Returned By   WebException.Status

Passed To   WebException.WebException( )

WebHeaderCollection

System.Net (system.dll)   class

This class contains the headers that are part of a WebRequest or WebResponse. Some headers should not be accessed through this collection. Instead, use the corresponding properties of the WebRequest or WebResponse (or the HTTP-specific subclasses). These headers are Accept, Connection, Content-Length, Content-Type, Date, Expect, Host, Range, Referer, Transfer-Encoding, and User-Agent.

```
public class WebHeaderCollection : System.Collections.Specialized.NameValueCollection {
// Public Constructors
  public WebHeaderCollection( );
// Protected Constructors
  protected WebHeaderCollection(System.Runtime.Serialization.SerializationInfo serializationInfo,
    System.Runtime.Serialization.StreamingContext streamingContext);
// Public Static Methods
  public static bool IsRestricted(string headerName);
// Public Instance Methods
  public void Add(string header);
  public override void Add(string name, string value);                      // overrides NameValueCollection
  public override string[ ] GetValues(string header);                       // overrides NameValueCollection
  public override void OnDeserialization(object sender);
                                // overrides System.Collections.Specialized.NameObjectCollectionBase
  public override void Remove(string name);                                 // overrides NameValueCollection
  public override void Set(string name, string value);                      // overrides NameValueCollection
  public byte[ ] ToByteArray( );
  public override string ToString( );                                                    // overrides object
// Protected Instance Methods
  protected void AddWithoutValidate(string headerName, string headerValue);
}
```

Hierarchy	System.Object → System.Collections.Specialized.NameObjectCollectionBase(System. Collections.ICollection, System.Collections.IEnumerable, System.Runtime.Serialization. ISerializable, System.Runtime.Serialization.IDeserializationCallback) → System.Collections. Specialized.NameValueCollection → WebHeaderCollection
Returned By	WebClient.{Headers, ResponseHeaders}, WebRequest.Headers, WebResponse.Headers
Passed To	HttpContinueDelegate.{BeginInvoke( ), Invoke( )}, WebClient.Headers, WebRequest.Headers

WebPermission

System.Net (system.dll)   sealed class

This permission controls which connections an application can make or accept.

```
public sealed class WebPermission : System.Security.CodeAccessPermission,
  System.Security.Permissions.IUnrestrictedPermission {
// Public Constructors
  public WebPermission( );
  public WebPermission(NetworkAccess access, System.Text.RegularExpressions.Regex uriRegex);
  public WebPermission(NetworkAccess access, string uriString);
```

```
public WebPermission(System.Security.Permissions.PermissionState state);
// Public Instance Properties
public IEnumerator AcceptList{get; }
public IEnumerator ConnectList{get; }
// Public Instance Methods
public void AddPermission(NetworkAccess access, System.Text.RegularExpressions.Regex uriRegex);
public void AddPermission(NetworkAccess access, string uriString);
public override IPermission Copy( );                                          // overrides CodeAccessPermission
public override void FromXml(System.Security.SecurityElement securityElement);  // overrides CodeAccessPermission
public override IPermission Intersect(System.Security.IPermission target);    // overrides CodeAccessPermission
public override bool IsSubsetOf(System.Security.IPermission target);          // overrides CodeAccessPermission
public bool IsUnrestricted( );                                                // implements IUnrestrictedPermission
public override SecurityElement ToXml( );                                     // overrides CodeAccessPermission
public override IPermission Union(System.Security.IPermission target);        // overrides CodeAccessPermission
}
```

Hierarchy   System.Object → System.Security.CodeAccessPermission(System.Security.IPermission,
System.Security.ISecurityEncodable, System.Security.IStackWalk) →
WebPermission(System.Security.Permissions.IUnrestrictedPermission)

WebPermissionAttribute   ECMA 1.0, serializable

System.Net (system.dll)   sealed class

This attribute is used to declare in metadata that the attributed method or class
requires WebPermission of the declared form.

```
public sealed class WebPermissionAttribute : System.Security.Permissions.CodeAccessSecurityAttribute {
// Public Constructors
public WebPermissionAttribute(System.Security.Permissions.SecurityAction action);
// Public Instance Properties
public string Accept{set; get; }
public string AcceptPattern{set; get; }
public string Connect{set; get; }
public string ConnectPattern{set; get; }
// Public Instance Methods
public override IPermission CreatePermission( );           // overrides System.Security.Permissions.SecurityAttribute
}
```

Hierarchy   System.Object → System.Attribute → System.Security.Permissions.SecurityAttribute →
System.Security.Permissions.CodeAccessSecurityAttribute → WebPermissionAttribute

Valid On   Assembly, Class, Struct, Constructor, Method

WebProxy   CF 1.0, ECMA 1.0, serializable

System.Net (system.dll)   class

This implementation of IWebProxy supports HTTP proxies. Use the one-argument
form of the constructor to specify the URI of the proxy server. The second argument, BypassOnLocal, if set to true, bypasses the proxy server for local (intranet)
addresses. Other forms of the constructor allow you to specify an array that lists
servers for which you should bypass the proxy (this list can contain regular

expression strings containing URI patterns to match). You can also supply network credentials to authenticate your application to the proxy server.

See GlobalProxySelection or the WebRequest.Proxy property for details on configuring a proxy.

```
public class WebProxy : IWebProxy, System.Runtime.Serialization.ISerializable {
// Public Constructors
  public WebProxy( );
  public WebProxy(string Address);
  public WebProxy(string Address, bool BypassOnLocal);
  public WebProxy(string Address, bool BypassOnLocal, string[ ] BypassList);
  public WebProxy(string Address, bool BypassOnLocal, string[ ] BypassList, ICredentials Credentials);
  public WebProxy(string Host, int Port);
  public WebProxy(Uri Address);
  public WebProxy(Uri Address, bool BypassOnLocal);
  public WebProxy(Uri Address, bool BypassOnLocal, string[ ] BypassList);
  public WebProxy(Uri Address, bool BypassOnLocal, string[ ] BypassList, ICredentials Credentials);
// Protected Constructors
  protected WebProxy(System.Runtime.Serialization.SerializationInfo serializationInfo,
    System.Runtime.Serialization.StreamingContext streamingContext);
// Public Instance Properties
  public Uri Address{set; get; }
  public ArrayList BypassArrayList{get; }
  public string[ ] BypassList{set; get; }
  public bool BypassProxyOnLocal{set; get; }
  public ICredentials Credentials{set; get; }                          // implements IWebProxy
// Public Static Methods
  public static WebProxy GetDefaultProxy( );
// Public Instance Methods
  public Uri GetProxy(Uri destination);                                // implements IWebProxy
  public bool IsBypassed(Uri host);                                    // implements IWebProxy
}
```

WebRequest   CF 1.0, ECMA 1.0, serializable, marshal by reference

System.Net (system.dll)   abstract class

Because many Internet protocols are request-response synchronous protocols, this class serves as a base type for any and all request-response style of network communication. As such, a .NET programmer will never create a WebRequest type directly—instead, a static method on this class, Create( ), is used as a "virtual constructor" to create a subtype of WebRequest that matches the protocol scheme requested. For example, if the string *http://www.oreilly.com* is passed to Create( ), an instance of HttpWebRequest is handed back. Out of the box, only "http", "https", and "file" are supported.

Once obtained, a .NET programmer can manipulate the common properties of the WebRequest type to control various aspects of the request. Alternatively, downcast the generic WebRequest reference to the concrete type returned to access protocol-specific aspects of that protocol—for example, the returned object from WebRequest.Create("http://www.oreilly.com") will be a HttpWebRequest, so it is safe to cast it as such. This allows access to the Accept and SendChunked properties/headers in the request. Be sure to manipulate these properties before the request is sent, or the modifications will have no effect.

Use the GetResponse( ) method to obtain a WebResponse object corresponding to the response that the remote server sent. This means that the request is sent, and the response harvested. The methods BeginGetResponse( ) and EndGetResponse( ) are asynchronous versions of GetResponse( ).

By default, WebRequest uses the proxy server specified in GlobalProxySelection.Select. Override that setting by assigning an IWebProxy implementation to the Proxy property.

```
public abstract class WebRequest : MarshalByRefObject, System.Runtime.Serialization.ISerializable {
// Protected Constructors
  protected WebRequest( );
  protected WebRequest(System.Runtime.Serialization.SerializationInfo serializationInfo,
    System.Runtime.Serialization. StreamingContext streamingContext);
// Public Instance Properties
  public virtual string ConnectionGroupName{set; get; }
  public virtual long ContentLength{set; get; }
  public virtual string ContentType{set; get; }
  public virtual ICredentials Credentials{set; get; }
  public virtual WebHeaderCollection Headers{set; get; }
  public virtual string Method{set; get; }
  public virtual bool PreAuthenticate{set; get; }
  public virtual IWebProxy Proxy{set; get; }
  public virtual Uri RequestUri{get; }
  public virtual int Timeout{set; get; }
// Public Static Methods
  public static WebRequest Create(string requestUriString);
  public static WebRequest Create(Uri requestUri);
  public static WebRequest CreateDefault(Uri requestUri);
  public static bool RegisterPrefix(string prefix, IWebRequestCreate creator);
// Public Instance Methods
  public virtual void Abort( );
  public virtual IAsyncResult BeginGetRequestStream(AsyncCallback callback, object state);
  public virtual IAsyncResult BeginGetResponse(AsyncCallback callback, object state);
  public virtual Stream EndGetRequestStream(IAsyncResult asyncResult);
  public virtual WebResponse EndGetResponse(IAsyncResult asyncResult);
  public virtual Stream GetRequestStream( );
  public virtual WebResponse GetResponse( );
}
```

Hierarchy	System.Object → System.MarshalByRefObject → WebRequest(System.Runtime. Serialization.ISerializable)
Subclasses	FileWebRequest, HttpWebRequest
Returned By	IWebRequestCreate.Create( )
Passed To	AuthenticationManager.{Authenticate( ), PreAuthenticate( )}, IAuthenticationModule. {Authenticate( ), PreAuthenticate( )}, ICertificatePolicy.CheckValidationResult( )

System.Net (system.dll)   abstract class

This class represents a response received from a WebRequest. A response consists of
headers (stored as key/value pairs in the Headers property) and a response body. You
can obtain the response body as a System.IO.Stream using the GetResponseStream( ) method.

When you are finished with the response, call its Close( ) method; this releases any open
resources still held by the WebResponse without having to wait for garbage collection to
do so (which could take longer than desired).

```
public abstract class WebResponse : MarshalByRefObject, System.Runtime.Serialization.ISerializable, IDisposable {
// Protected Constructors
  protected WebResponse( );
  protected WebResponse(System.Runtime.Serialization.SerializationInfo serializationInfo,
    System.Runtime.Serialization.StreamingContext streamingContext);
// Public Instance Properties
  public virtual long ContentLength{set; get; }
  public virtual string ContentType{set; get; }
  public virtual WebHeaderCollection Headers{get; }
  public virtual Uri ResponseUri{get; }
// Public Instance Methods
  public virtual void Close( );
  public virtual Stream GetResponseStream( );
}
```

Hierarchy	System.Object → System.MarshalByRefObject → WebResponse(System.Runtime. Serialization.ISerializable, System.IDisposable)
Subclasses	FileWebResponse, HttpWebResponse
Returned By	WebException.Response, WebRequest.{EndGetResponse( ), GetResponse( )}
Passed To	WebException.WebException( )

34

System.Net.Sockets

The System.Net.Sockets namespace classes implement standard Berkeley sockets APIs for cross-process/cross-host communication. Sockets are low-level objects (abstractions, really) that provide the foundation for most Internet networking. A socket binds to a local address and port, and either waits for a connection from a remote address or connects to a remote address and exchanges data across the network. Two socket implementations are made available in this namespace, TCP/IP and UDP/IP. Most Internet applications, such as FTP clients and web browsers, are built upon socket connections.

Although many system-level programmers feel a close kinship with these types, .NET programmers are greatly encouraged to consider using higher-level constructs, such as HTTP (see the System.Net namespace) or the System.Runtime. Remoting types, to facilitate remote communications. If you need to work at the socket level, consider using TcpClient or TcpListener. These are high-level abstractions of the socket API that support client and server functionality.

For more details regarding many of the options mentioned in this namespace, consult a low-level sockets reference, such as W. Richard Stevens' *Network Programming in the Unix Environment* (Volumes 1 and 2) or *TCP/IP Illustrated* (Volumes 1, 2, and 3). Although the books were written for a Unix environment, . NET faithfully mirrors much, if not all, of the Berkeley sockets API (which originally came from Unix). Figure 34-1 shows the types in this namespace.

AddressFamily   CF 1.0, ECMA 1.0, serializable

System.Net.Sockets (system.dll)   enum

This enumeration contains values to specify the address family used by a socket. This indicates to which family of addressing schemes the address of the socket belongs. Note that the standard four-digit IP scheme falls under the enumeration InterNetwork, and its successor, IPv6, under the enumeration InterNetworkV6.

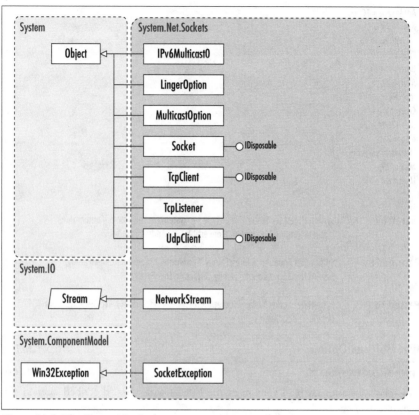

Figure 34-1. The System.Net.Sockets namespace

```
public enum AddressFamily {
  Unspecified = 0,
  Unix = 1,
  InterNetwork = 2,
  ImpLink = 3,
  Pup = 4,
  Chaos = 5,
  Ipx = 6,
  NS = 6,
  Iso = 7,
  Osi = 7,
  Ecma = 8,
  DataKit = 9,
  Ccitt = 10,
  Sna = 11,
  DecNet = 12,
  DataLink = 13,
  Lat = 14,
  HyperChannel = 15,
```

```
   AppleTalk = 16,
   NetBios = 17,
   VoiceView = 18,
   FireFox = 19,
   Banyan = 21,
   Atm = 22,
   InterNetworkV6 = 23,
   Cluster = 24,
   Ieee12844 = 25,
   Irda = 26,
   NetworkDesigners = 28,
   Max = 29,
   Unknown = -1
}
```

Hierarchy   System.Object → System.ValueType → System.Enum(System.IComparable, System.IFormattable, System.IConvertible) → AddressFamily

Returned By   System.Net.EndPoint.AddressFamily, System.Net.IPAddress.AddressFamily, System.Net.SocketAddress.Family, Socket.AddressFamily

Passed To   System.Net.SocketAddress.SocketAddress( ), Socket.Socket( ), TcpClient.TcpClient( ), UdpClient.UdpClient( )

IPv6MulticastOption   .NET 1.1

System.Net.Sockets (system.dll)   class

This class specifies an IPv6 version of the MulticastOption class, described later in this chapter.

```
public class IPv6MulticastOption {
// Public Constructors
   public IPv6MulticastOption(System.Net.IPAddress group);
   public IPv6MulticastOption(System.Net.IPAddress group, long ifindex);
// Public Instance Properties
   public IPAddress Group{set; get; }
   public long InterfaceIndex{set; get; }
}
```

LingerOption   CF 1.0, ECMA 1.0

System.Net.Sockets (system.dll)   class

This class is a socket option object that enables a socket to continue to send queued data after a call to Socket.Close( ). If the Enabled property is True, the connection lingers for the number of seconds given by LingerTime. The LingerOption object is set on a socket with the Socket.SetSocketOption( ) method and a SocketOptionName of SocketOptionName.Linger.

```
public class LingerOption {
// Public Constructors
   public LingerOption(bool enable, int seconds);
```

```
// Public Instance Properties
  public bool Enabled{set; get; }
  public int LingerTime{set; get; }
}
```

Returned By   TcpClient.LingerState

Passed To   TcpClient.LingerState

MulticastOption

System.Net.Sockets (system.dll)   class

This class specifies an IP address for IP-multicast packets. IP-multicast addresses must be in the range of 224.0.0.0 to 239.255.255.255. The MulticastOption is set on a socket using the SocketOptionName.AddMembership value with Socket.SetSocketOption( ). You can drop multicast with SocketOptionName.DropMembership.

```
public class MulticastOption {
// Public Constructors
  public MulticastOption(System.Net.IPAddress group);
  public MulticastOption(System.Net.IPAddress group, System.Net.IPAddress mcint);
// Public Instance Properties
  public IPAddress Group{set; get; }
  public IPAddress LocalAddress{set; get; }
}
```

NetworkStream   CF 1.0, ECMA 1.0, marshal by reference, disposable

System.Net.Sockets (system.dll)   class

This class creates a basic network stream from an underlying socket. It allows for simple data access to the stream and supports permissions settings.

```
public class NetworkStream : System.IO.Stream {
// Public Constructors
  public NetworkStream(Socket socket);
  public NetworkStream(Socket socket, bool ownsSocket);
  public NetworkStream(Socket socket, System.IO.FileAccess access);
  public NetworkStream(Socket socket, System.IO.FileAccess access, bool ownsSocket);
// Public Instance Properties
  public override bool CanRead{get; }                        // overrides System.IO.Stream
  public override bool CanSeek{get; }                        // overrides System.IO.Stream
  public override bool CanWrite{get; }                       // overrides System.IO.Stream
  public virtual bool DataAvailable{get; }
  public override long Length{get; }                         // overrides System.IO.Stream
  public override long Position{set; get; }                  // overrides System.IO.Stream
// Protected Instance Properties
  protected bool Readable{set; get; }
  protected Socket Socket{get; }
  protected bool Writeable{set; get; }
// Public Instance Methods
  public override IAsyncResult BeginRead(byte[ ] buffer, int offset, int size,
    AsyncCallback callback, object state);                   // overrides System.IO.Stream
```

```
public override IAsyncResult BeginWrite(byte[ ] buffer, int offset, int size,
    AsyncCallback callback, object state);                          // overrides System.IO.Stream
public override void Close( );                                       // overrides System.IO.Stream
public override int EndRead(IAsyncResult asyncResult);              // overrides System.IO.Stream
public override void EndWrite(IAsyncResult asyncResult);           // overrides System.IO.Stream
public override void Flush( );                                       // overrides System.IO.Stream
public override int Read(in byte[ ] buffer, int offset, int size);  // overrides System.IO.Stream
public override long Seek(long offset, System.IO.SeekOrigin origin); // overrides System.IO.Stream
public override void SetLength(long value);                         // overrides System.IO.Stream
public override void Write(byte[ ] buffer, int offset, int size);   // overrides System.IO.Stream
// Protected Instance Methods
protected virtual void Dispose(bool disposing);
protected override void Finalize( );                                // overrides object
}
```

Hierarchy System.Object → System.MarshalByRefObject → System.IO.Stream(System.IDisposable) →
NetworkStream

Returned By TcpClient.GetStream( )

ProtocolFamily   CF 1.0, serializable

System.Net.Sockets (system.dll)   enum

This enumeration contains settings for the protocol family of a socket.

```
public enum ProtocolFamily {
    Unspecified = 0,
    Unix = 1,
    InterNetwork = 2,
    ImpLink = 3,
    Pup = 4,
    Chaos = 5,
    Ipx = 6,
    NS = 6,
    Iso = 7,
    Osi = 7,
    Ecma = 8,
    DataKit = 9,
    Ccitt = 10,
    Sna = 11,
    DecNet = 12,
    DataLink = 13,
    Lat = 14,
    HyperChannel = 15,
    AppleTalk = 16,
    NetBios = 17,
    VoiceView = 18,
    FireFox = 19,
    Banyan = 21,
    Atm = 22,
    InterNetworkV6 = 23,
```

```
Cluster = 24,
Ieee12844 = 25,
Irda = 26,
NetworkDesigners = 28,
Max = 29,
Unknown = -1
}
```

Hierarchy   System.Object → System.ValueType → System.Enum(System.IComparable,
System.IFormattable, System.IConvertible) → ProtocolFamily

ProtocolType   CF 1.0, ECMA 1.0, serializable

System.Net.Sockets (system.dll)   enum

This enumeration contains settings for the protocol type of a socket. A protocol type
must be specified for every Socket instance.

```
public enum ProtocolType {
  Unspecified = 0,
  IP = 0,
  Icmp = 1,
  Igmp = 2,
  Ggp = 3,
  Tcp = 6,
  Pup = 12,
  Udp = 17,
  Idp = 22,
  IPv6 = 41,
  ND = 77,
  Raw = 255,
  Ipx = 1000,
  Spx = 1256,
  SpxII = 1257,
  Unknown = -1
}
```

Hierarchy   System.Object → System.ValueType → System.Enum(System.IComparable,
System.IFormattable, System.IConvertible) → ProtocolType

Returned By   Socket.ProtocolType

Passed To   Socket.Socket( )

SelectMode   CF 1.0, ECMA 1.0, serializable

System.Net.Sockets (system.dll)   enum

This enumeration contains the settings for polling modes used by Socket.Poll( ).

```
public enum SelectMode {
  SelectRead = 0,
  SelectWrite = 1,
```

```
SelectError = 2
}
```

Hierarchy System.Object → System.ValueType → System.Enum(System.IComparable,
System.IFormattable, System.IConvertible) → SelectMod3e

Passed To Socket.Poll( )

Socket

CF 1.0, ECMA 1.0, disposable

System.Net.Sockets (system.dll)   class

This class implements a standard Berkeley socket. Each socket is constructed with
the address family to use, the socket type (datagram or stream), and the protocol
that the socket will use. Every socket must be bound to a local endpoint before you
can use it. The Bind( ) method takes a System.Net.IPEndPoint object that contains the local
IP address and port number to bind the socket to. Bind( ) must be called before any
connection can be made through the socket. To establish a connection to a remote
address, use Connect( ).

To listen for connections from remote clients, use Listen( ) to set the socket in listening
mode where it waits for incoming connections. The integer argument to Listen( ) specifies how many remote connection requests can be queued at one time, waiting for a
socket connection. A call to Accept( ) returns a new socket that connects to the first
pending connection request in the listening queue. This new socket exists only for this
connection and is destroyed once the connection is closed.

You can interrogate the socket to determine if it supports IPv4 (standard TCP/IP quad-
style addresses) by examining the SupportsIPV4 property; similarly, you can determine if
the socket supports IPv6 by examining SupportsIPv6.

Data is written to a socket using Send( ). Data from a specified buffer is sent through the
socket to its remote endpoint. Data is read from a socket using Receive( ). Receive( ) gets
data from the socket connection and stores it in a specified receive buffer.

You can set several socket options to control the behavior of a socket with
SetSocketOption( ). This method requires a SocketOptionLevel value, which determines the type
of socket option to set. For example, SocketOptionLevel.IP is used for options related to an
IP socket. The SocketOptionName value gives the specific option, which must be applicable
to the SocketOptionLevel. The last argument to SetSocketOption( ) provides the value of the
option. SetSocketOption( ) enables features such as SocketOptionName.KeepAlive, in which a
connection is maintained even when no data transfer is occurring, or SocketOptionName.
MaxConnections, which sets the maximum permitted size of a listen queue.

When a session is finished, the connection can be gracefully closed with Shutdown( ).
When send or receive options are called with a SocketShutdown value, they are no longer
allowed on the socket. A call to Close( ) terminates the socket connection.

```
public class Socket : IDisposable {
// Public Constructors
  public Socket(AddressFamily addressFamily, SocketType socketType, ProtocolType protocolType);
// Public Static Properties
  public static bool SupportsIPv4{get; }
  public static bool SupportsIPv6{get; }
// Public Instance Properties
  public AddressFamily AddressFamily{get; }
```

```
public int Available{get; }
public bool Blocking{set; get; }
public bool Connected{get; }
public IntPtr Handle{get; }
public EndPoint LocalEndPoint{get; }
public ProtocolType ProtocolType{get; }
public EndPoint RemoteEndPoint{get; }
public SocketType SocketType{get; }
// Public Static Methods
public static void Select(System.Collections.IList checkRead, System.Collections.IList checkWrite,
    System.Collections.IList checkError, int microSeconds);
// Public Instance Methods
public Socket Accept( );
public IAsyncResult BeginAccept(AsyncCallback callback, object state);
public IAsyncResult BeginConnect(System.Net.EndPoint remoteEP, AsyncCallback callback, object state);
public IAsyncResult BeginReceive(byte[ ] buffer, int offset, int size, SocketFlags socketFlags,
    AsyncCallback callback, object state);
public IAsyncResult BeginReceiveFrom(byte[ ] buffer, int offset, int size, SocketFlags socketFlags,
    ref System.Net.EndPoint remoteEP, AsyncCallback callback, object state);
public IAsyncResult BeginSend(byte[ ] buffer, int offset, int size, SocketFlags socketFlags,
    AsyncCallback callback, object state);
public IAsyncResult BeginSendTo(byte[ ] buffer, int offset, int size, SocketFlags socketFlags,
    System.Net.EndPoint remoteEP, AsyncCallback callback, object state);
public void Bind(System.Net.EndPoint localEP);
public void Close( );
public void Connect(System.Net.EndPoint remoteEP);
public Socket EndAccept(IAsyncResult asyncResult);
public void EndConnect(IAsyncResult asyncResult);
public int EndReceive(IAsyncResult asyncResult);
public int EndReceiveFrom(IAsyncResult asyncResult, ref System.Net.EndPoint endPoint);
public int EndSend(IAsyncResult asyncResult);
public int EndSendTo(IAsyncResult asyncResult);
public override int GetHashCode( );                                          // overrides object
public byte[ ] GetSocketOption(SocketOptionLevel optionLevel, SocketOptionName optionName, int optionLength);
public object GetSocketOption(SocketOptionLevel optionLevel, SocketOptionName optionName);
public void GetSocketOption(SocketOptionLevel optionLevel, SocketOptionName optionName, byte[ ] optionValue);
public int IOControl(int ioControlCode, byte[ ] optionInValue, byte[ ] optionOutValue);
public void Listen(int backlog);
public bool Poll(int microSeconds, SelectMode mode);
public int Receive(byte[ ] buffer);
public int Receive(byte[ ] buffer, int offset, int size, SocketFlags socketFlags);
public int Receive(byte[ ] buffer, int size, SocketFlags socketFlags);
public int Receive(byte[ ] buffer, SocketFlags socketFlags);
public int ReceiveFrom(byte[ ] buffer, ref System.Net.EndPoint remoteEP);
public int ReceiveFrom(byte[ ] buffer, int offset, int size, SocketFlags socketFlags, ref System.Net.EndPoint remoteEP);
public int ReceiveFrom(byte[ ] buffer, int size, SocketFlags socketFlags, ref System.Net.EndPoint remoteEP);
public int ReceiveFrom(byte[ ] buffer, SocketFlags socketFlags, ref System.Net.EndPoint remoteEP);
public int Send(byte[ ] buffer);
public int Send(byte[ ] buffer, int offset, int size, SocketFlags socketFlags);
public int Send(byte[ ] buffer, int size, SocketFlags socketFlags);
public int Send(byte[ ] buffer, SocketFlags socketFlags);
```

```
public int SendTo(byte[ ] buffer, System.Net.EndPoint remoteEP);
public int SendTo(byte[ ] buffer, int offset, int size, SocketFlags socketFlags, System.Net.EndPoint remoteEP);
public int SendTo(byte[ ] buffer, int size, SocketFlags socketFlags, System.Net.EndPoint remoteEP);
public int SendTo(byte[ ] buffer, SocketFlags socketFlags, System.Net.EndPoint remoteEP);
public void SetSocketOption(SocketOptionLevel optionLevel, SocketOptionName optionName, byte[ ] optionValue);
public void SetSocketOption(SocketOptionLevel optionLevel, SocketOptionName optionName, int optionValue);
public void SetSocketOption(SocketOptionLevel optionLevel, SocketOptionName optionName, object optionValue);
public void Shutdown(SocketShutdown how);
// Protected Instance Methods
protected virtual void Dispose(bool disposing);
protected override void Finalize( );                                                          // overrides object
}
```

Returned By	NetworkStream.Socket, TcpClient.Client, TcpListener.{AcceptSocket( ), Server}, UdpClient.Client
Passed To	NetworkStream.NetworkStream( ), TcpClient.Client, UdpClient.Client

SocketException   CF 1.0, ECMA 1.0, serializable

System.Net.Sockets (system.dll)   class

This exception represents a socket-related error.

```
public class SocketException : System.ComponentModel.Win32Exception {
// Public Constructors
  public SocketException( );
  public SocketException(int errorCode);
// Protected Constructors
  protected SocketException(System.Runtime.Serialization.SerializationInfo serializationInfo,
    System.Runtime.Serialization.StreamingContext streamingContext);
// Public Instance Properties
  public override int ErrorCode{get; }              // overrides System.Runtime.InteropServices.ExternalException
}
```

Hierarchy	System.Object → System.Exception(System.Runtime.Serialization.ISerializable) → System.SystemException → System.Runtime.InteropServices.ExternalException → System.ComponentModel.Win32Exception → SocketException

SocketFlags   CF 1.0, ECMA 1.0, serializable, flag

System.Net.Sockets (system.dll)   enum

This enumeration contains values for setting flags for socket messages. SocketFlags are provided to Socket.Send( ) and Socket.Receive( ) to specify parameters for how data is transferred. The OutOfBand flag tells the socket to process out-of-band data in the stream. DontRoute tells the socket to send data to the remote endpoint without using routing tables.

```
public enum SocketFlags {
  None = 0x00000000,
  OutOfBand = 0x00000001,
  Peek = 0x00000002,
```

```
DontRoute = 0x00000004,
MaxIOVectorLength = 0x00000010,
Partial = 0x00008000
}
```

Hierarchy	System.Object → System.ValueType → System.Enum(System.IComparable, System.IFormattable, System.IConvertible) → SocketFlags
Passed To	Socket.{BeginReceive( ), BeginReceiveFrom( ), BeginSend( ), BeginSendTo( ), Receive( ), ReceiveFrom( ), Send( ), SendTo( )}

SocketOptionLevel

CF 1.0, ECMA 1.0, serializable

System.Net.Sockets (system.dll)   enum

This enumeration contains values for the type of socket option specified in Socket. SetSocketOption( ).

```
public enum SocketOptionLevel {
  IP = 0,
  Tcp = 6,
  Udp = 17,
  IPv6 = 41,
  Socket = 65535
}
```

Hierarchy	System.Object → System.ValueType → System.Enum(System.IComparable, System.IFormattable, System.IConvertible) → SocketOptionLevel
Passed To	Socket.{GetSocketOption( ), SetSocketOption( )}

SocketOptionName

CF 1.0, ECMA 1.0, serializable

System.Net.Sockets (system.dll)   enum

This enumeration contains the names of socket options set by Socket.SetSocketOption( ). The socket option named must be applicable to the option level from SocketOptionLevel.

```
public enum SocketOptionName {
  IPOptions = 1,
  Debug = 1,
  NoDelay = 1,
  NoChecksum = 1,
  HeaderIncluded = 2,
  AcceptConnection = 2,
  Expedited = 2,
  BsdUrgent = 2,
  TypeOfService = 3,
  ReuseAddress = 4,
  IpTimeToLive = 4,
  KeepAlive = 8,
  MulticastInterface = 9,
  MulticastTimeToLive = 10,
```

```
MulticastLoopback = 11,
AddMembership = 12,
DropMembership = 13,
DontFragment = 14,
AddSourceMembership = 15,
DropSourceMembership = 16,
DontRoute = 16,
BlockSource = 17,
UnblockSource = 18,
PacketInformation = 19,
ChecksumCoverage = 20,
Broadcast = 32,
UseLoopback = 64,
Linger = 128,
OutOfBandInline = 256,
SendBuffer = 4097,
ReceiveBuffer = 4098,
SendLowWater = 4099,
ReceiveLowWater = 4100,
SendTimeout = 4101,
ReceiveTimeout = 4102,
Error = 4103,
Type = 4104,
MaxConnections = 2147483647,
DontLinger = -129,
ExclusiveAddressUse = -5
}
```

Hierarchy	System.Object → System.ValueType → System.Enum(System.IComparable, System.IFormattable, System.IConvertible) → SocketOptionName
Passed To	Socket.{GetSocketOption( ), SetSocketOption( )}

SocketShutdown   CF 1.0, ECMA 1.0, serializable

System.Net.Sockets (system.dll)   enum

This enumeration provides values used by Socket.Shutdown( ). Receive specifies that receiving will be disabled on a socket. Send specifies that sending will be disabled. Both disables sending and receiving.

```
public enum SocketShutdown {
  Receive = 0,
  Send = 1,
  Both = 2
}
```

Hierarchy	System.Object → System.ValueType → System.Enum(System.IComparable, System.IFormattable, System.IConvertible) → SocketShutdown
Passed To	Socket.Shutdown( )

CF 1.0, ECMA 1.0, serializable

System.Net.Sockets (system.dll)   enum

This enumeration contains the names for the type of socket that is created.

```
public enum SocketType {
  Stream = 1,
  Dgram = 2,
  Raw = 3,
  Rdm = 4,
  Seqpacket = 5,
  Unknown = -1
}
```

Hierarchy   System.Object → System.ValueType → System.Enum(System.IComparable,
                   System.IFormattable, System.IConvertible) → SocketType

Returned By   Socket.SocketType

Passed To   Socket.Socket( )

TcpClient
CF 1.0, disposable

System.Net.Sockets (system.dll)   class

This class provides a client-side abstraction of the sockets API. The zero-argument
form of the constructor creates the client. Connect to a remote server with the Connect( )
method (you must specify an existing System.Net.IPEndPoint or a remote IP address and
port number). Alternatively, use an overloaded form of the constructor to simultaneously create the client and make the connection.

This class completely obscures the underlying socket. However, the GetStream( ) method
returns a NetworkStream that you can use to send and receive data across the network.

```
public class TcpClient : IDisposable {
// Public Constructors
  public TcpClient( );
  public TcpClient(AddressFamily family);
  public TcpClient(System.Net.IPEndPoint localEP);
  public TcpClient(string hostname, int port);
// Public Instance Properties
  public LingerOption LingerState{set; get; }
  public bool NoDelay{set; get; }
  public int ReceiveBufferSize{set; get; }
  public int ReceiveTimeout{set; get; }
  public int SendBufferSize{set; get; }
  public int SendTimeout{set; get; }
// Protected Instance Properties
  protected bool Active{set; get; }
  protected Socket Client{set; get; }
// Public Instance Methods
  public void Close( );
  public void Connect(System.Net.IPAddress address, int port);
```

```
    public void Connect(System.Net.IPEndPoint remoteEP);
    public void Connect(string hostname, int port);
    public NetworkStream GetStream( );
// Protected Instance Methods
    protected virtual void Dispose(bool disposing);
    protected override void Finalize( );                                        // overrides object
}
```

Returned By   TcpListener.AcceptTcpClient( )

TcpListener   CF 1.0

System.Net.Sockets (system.dll)   class

This class provides a server-side abstraction of the sockets API. The TcpListener is
constructed with a local address and port to which it is automatically bound. A call to
Start( ) initiates listening for connection requests. When a request is received, either
AcceptSocket( ) or AcceptTcpClient( ) accepts the connection and returns a Socket or a TcpClient
you can use to exchange data with the remote client.

```
public class TcpListener {
// Public Constructors
    public TcpListener(int port);                                               // obsolete
    public TcpListener(System.Net.IPAddress localaddr, int port);
    public TcpListener(System.Net.IPEndPoint localEP);
// Public Instance Properties
    public EndPoint LocalEndpoint{get; }
// Protected Instance Properties
    protected bool Active{get; }
    protected Socket Server{get; }
// Public Instance Methods
    public Socket AcceptSocket( );
    public TcpClient AcceptTcpClient( );
    public bool Pending( );
    public void Start( );
    public void Stop( );
// Protected Instance Methods
    protected override void Finalize( );                                        // overrides object
}
```

UdpClient   CF 1.0, disposable

System.Net.Sockets (system.dll)   class

This class is used to create UDP client sockets. UDP-based clients transmit messages
called datagrams across a connection. Unlike TCP, control data is not sent to ensure
the integrity and order of the data (so UDP is faster than TCP, but not as reliable).
UDP is often used to broadcast media streams, such as video, and to support multi-
casting. The UdpClient can be constructed with a binding to a local address and port, or
it can be constructed given the IP address and port number of the remote server to
which it connects.

The JoinMulitcastGroup() method sets the addres of an IP-multicast group to join. DropMulti-
castGroup() drops the client from the group.

```
public class UdpClient : IDisposable {
// Public Constructors
  public UdpClient( );
  public UdpClient(AddressFamily family);
  public UdpClient(int port);
  public UdpClient(int port, AddressFamily family);
  public UdpClient(System.Net.IPEndPoint localEP);
  public UdpClient(string hostname, int port);
// Protected Instance Properties
  protected bool Active{set; get; }
  protected Socket Client{set; get; }
// Public Instance Methods
  public void Close( );
  public void Connect(System.Net.IPAddress addr, int port);
  public void Connect(System.Net.IPEndPoint endPoint);
  public void Connect(string hostname, int port);
  public void DropMulticastGroup(System.Net.IPAddress multicastAddr);
}
```

35

System.Reflection

System.Reflection is the API that exposes the full-fidelity metadata of the .NET environment to the .NET programmer. In short, it permits complete access to compile-time data at runtime. Everything is available, including fields, methods, constructors, properties, delegate types, and events. The reflection API (as exposed by the System.Reflection namespace) offers some truly unique capabilities unavailable in other compile-time bound languages such as C++. The closest the average COM programmer has come to using reflection is the IDispatch interface and/or type libraries. Reflection, fortunately, is at once both easier to use and far more powerful.

Reflection offers up a number of possible approaches to use. Introspection is the act of using the reflection APIs to discover information about a component assembly (and its constituent types) at runtime without any prior (compile-time) knowledge of it. This approach was first popularized by tools such as Visual Basic and numerous Java IDEs that offered GUI-based construction of visual interfaces. The third-party component was dropped into some well-known location, and the IDE "discovered" it and offered it on a toolbar the next time the IDE was started.

Along similar lines, reflection is often used as part of development tools; for example, the .NET utility *xsd.exe* uses metadata to generate XML Schema documents that correspond to .NET declared types. A .NET programmer could use reflection to generate SQL (Structured Query Language) statements for storing object instances into a relational database, or even into the SQL DDL (Data Definition Language) itself. Other tools could produce remoting proxies, transparently adding the necessary code to marshal and unmarshal parameters and return values across a network connection, even for types that weren't designed to be remoted in the first place.

Lastly, reflection isn't just a read-only view of a type's construction; the reflective APIs in .NET also allow for manipulation of methods and state (although not the rewriting of code—once loaded, a type's methods remain exactly as they were defined). The most prevalent example of this sort of usage of reflection is in the .NET Object Serialization code (in the System.Runtime.Serialization namespace). Serialization takes an existing object instance, uses reflection to suck out the object's state, transforms it into a binary representation, and stores that representation (a stream of bytes) to some source, such as a file on disk, a socket, a binary column in a database, and so on. Later, serialization can also take that same stream of bytes and rehydrate the serialized object back into existence.

Careful readers will note that last sentence and wonder, if only for a moment, how it could be possible for code to reach into an object and directly manipulate its state; after all, any object-oriented developer worthy of the name knows to mark all fields as "private," which should make said fields completely inaccessible. The fact is, reflection can violate even these most sacrosanct of boundaries—it can reach in and manipulate any private member it finds—thus it is highly sensitive to any changes in the definition of fields inside of a type.

Figure 35-1 shows the inheritance diagram for this namespace. Figure 35-2 shows the exceptions, delegates, and attributes from this namespace.

AmbiguousMatchException
CF 1.0, ECMA 1.0, serializable

System.Reflection (mscorlib.dll) sealed class

This exception is thrown when you attempt to bind to a method with the Binder and the given criteria matches more than one method; this is the case, for example, when binding against an overloaded method solely by its name.

```
public sealed class AmbiguousMatchException : SystemException {
// Public Constructors
  public AmbiguousMatchException( );
  public AmbiguousMatchException(string message);
  public AmbiguousMatchException(string message, Exception inner);
}
```

Hierarchy   System.Object → System.Exception(System.Runtime.Serialization.ISerializable) → System.SystemException → AmbiguousMatchException

Assembly
CF 1.0, ECMA 1.0, serializable

System.Reflection (mscorlib.dll) class

In the .NET environment, assemblies are the fundamental units of development and deployment; although the various languages allow the .NET programmer to work with elements as fine-grained as classes or functions, these types must belong as part of an assembly in order to be loaded and used. Consequently, the assembly is the core of the component model in .NET.

The Assembly type is the Reflection API object representing the assembly. An assembly (either a .DLL or .EXE—to the CLR, there is no difference) consists of one or more modules; most assemblies are in fact single-module assemblies. (Multimodule assemblies are certainly possible, but usually not necessary for most developers' needs. As such, they are not discussed here.) .NET programmers can use the object model in the Assembly class to discover information about a particular assembly—for example, an assembly knows the modules contained within it, and each module knows the types defined and bound to that module. Thus, for any random assembly, a .NET program

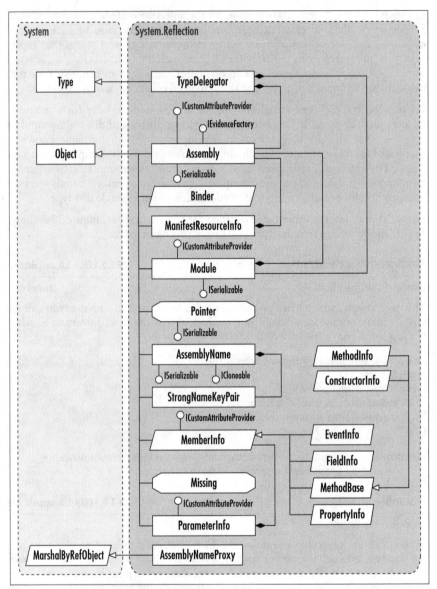

Figure 35-1. The System.Reflection namespace

can enumerate each type defined inside that assembly. This is, in fact, what the *WinCV.exe* sample program (see the .NET SDK, in the *\bin* subdirectory) does. (The *ILDasm.exe* application provides similar results, but uses unmanaged APIs to view into an assembly, rather than Reflection.)

The Assembly API can be broken into two collections: those representing operations against a particular assembly (indicated by a particular Assembly instance), and those that work independently of a particular instance—loading an assembly into the CLR, for example.

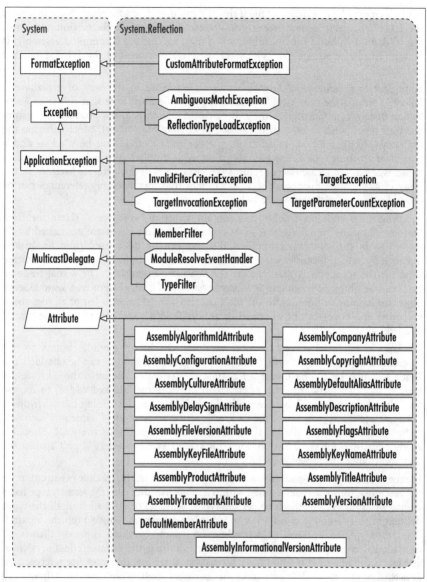

Figure 35-2. Exceptions, delegates, and attributes from System.Reflection

The instance-specific methods of Assembly are, for the most part, self-describing. The properties of Assembly, in particular, are straightforward. CodeBase describes the URL from which this assembly was loaded, EntryPoint describes the entry point (the Main()) of the assembly, if it has one, Evidence is the security information regarding this particular assembly, and FullName is the fully qualified (name, culture, version info, and public key token) for this assembly. The remaining two properties are a bit more obscure: GlobalAssemblyCache is a simple boolean value indicating whether this assembly was loaded out of the global assembly cache or not, and Location describes the location of the manifest file (which may be in a different file if this is a multimodule assembly). Note that as of the 1.1 .NET release, a new property, ImageRuntimeVersion, returns the version number of the CLR used to build the assembly; when used against a 1.0-compiled assembly, it may return illegal strings like "v1.x86ret" or "retail" instead of the 1.1-documented "v1.1.4322".

Some instance methods of Assembly require a bit more in the way of explanation. GetName( ) returns the fully qualified name for this assembly; note that this is an AssemblyName instance, rather than a string. Because an Assembly is also a producer of custom attribute types (such as AssemblyVersionAttribute or AssemblyKeyFileAttribute), Assembly also has the GetCustomAttributes( ) method. In addition, the IsDefined( ) method can be used to find a particular attribute type defined in this assembly; it simply returns a boolean true/false value, whereas GetCustomAttributes( ) returns the instance(s) of the attribute itself. A list (an array of AssemblyName instances) of all assemblies that this assembly references can be found by calling GetReferencedAssemblies( ).

In addition to code, assemblies can contain arbitrary "resources." (Here the term "resource" means "anything that's not code.") These resources are contained as .file references in the assembly's manifest file and can be discovered from an Assembly instance by calling GetManifestResourceNames( ). Information about the persistence scheme used for the resources is available via the GetManifestResourceInfo( ). The actual resource itself can be obtained by calling GetManifestResourceStream( ), which returns a System.IO.Stream object containing or pointing to the file's contents. In addition, a list of all files (both resources and code) can be obtained by calling GetFiles( ), and a particular file can be opened by calling GetFile( ).

An assembly consists of one or more modules; the list of modules bound to this assembly are available via the GetModules( ) call. A particular module can be obtained as a Module instance by calling GetModule( ) against the assembly. Because the CLR delays loading modules until required, Assembly also provides the GetLoadedModules( ) to list the modules of this assembly that have been loaded into the CLR. Going the other direction, the LoadModule( ) call forces the CLR to load the given module name into memory, rather than waiting for the usual on-demand loading policy of the CLR. Should a module-load fail for some reason, the CLR signals event handlers bound against the Assembly instance's ModuleResolve event.

Frequently, a .NET programmer will not be interested in the modules that comprise the assembly, only the types defined within it. Towards that end, the Assembly type has a couple of "shortcut" methods to get the types. GetTypes( ) returns a list of all the types defined in this assembly as an array of System.Type references. GetType( ) returns a particular System.Type, or optionally (depending on which overload is used) throws an exception if the type cannot be found. Take note that the parameterless version of GetType( ) is the inherited method from System.Object; it returns the System.Type reference for Assembly, not any types defined within the assembly itself. Note that the GetTypes( ) call returns a list of all types defined in the assembly, even those declared as private to the assembly (which normally should not be seen by assembly consumers); to see a list of only the "public" types, call GetExportedTypes( ) instead.

Once a particular type within the assembly has been located, an instance of that type can be created by calling CreateInstance( ). This uses the system activator (see System.Activator) to create an instance of that type and hand it back as a generic object reference. For example, calling object o = typeof(Object).Assembly.CreateInstance("DateTime"); is a roundabout way to create an instance of a System.DateTime; the typeof(Object) returns the System.Type for System.Object. That type lives in the mscorlib.dll assembly, and calling CreateInstance("DateTime") succeeds because DateTime is defined within that assembly. .NET programmers typically only use this method when building a container application (such as ASP.NET) that will be creating instances of objects not known at compile-time.

The Assembly type also contains a number of static methods for use in referencing assemblies as a collective whole; for example, the GetAssembly() call returns the Assembly in which a particular Type is defined. (Knowing this, we could change the example in the last paragraph to read object o = Assembly.GetAssembly(typeof(object)).CreateInstance("DateTime");, which is a bit clearer if a bit longer.) Likewise, the GetExecutingAssembly() returns the assembly in which the current code is executing, and GetCallingAssembly() returns the assembly whose code called the methods in this assembly. (These methods by themselves may seem less than useful, until the idea of walking the call-stack, as Code Access Security does, is considered.)

However, the two most important static methods on the Assembly class by far are Load() and LoadFrom(). Both load an assembly into the CLR, but in drastically different ways. LoadFrom() is the simpler of the two, taking a filename and loading it as an assembly into the CLR—no questions asked. Load() goes through the assembly-load algorithm and checks the private probe path and the Global Assembly Cache before giving up on finding the assembly. (Note that if an assembly-load request fails, the appropriate events on the containing AppDomain instance are signaled.) In addition, starting with the 1.1 release, these two are joined by a new method, LoadFile(), which will load an assembly specified by a file location passed as a string.

```
public class Assembly : System.Security.IEvidenceFactory, ICustomAttributeProvider,
    System.Runtime.Serialization.ISerializable {
// Public Instance Properties
    public virtual string CodeBase{get; }
    public virtual MethodInfo EntryPoint{get; }
    public virtual string EscapedCodeBase{get; }
    public virtual Evidence Evidence{get; }                          // implements System.Security.IEvidenceFactory
    public virtual string FullName{get; }
    public bool GlobalAssemblyCache{get; }
    public virtual string ImageRuntimeVersion{get; }
    public virtual string Location{get; }
// Public Static Methods
    public static string CreateQualifiedName(string assemblyName, string typeName);
    public static Assembly GetAssembly(Type type);
    public static Assembly GetCallingAssembly( );
    public static Assembly GetEntryAssembly( );
    public static Assembly GetExecutingAssembly( );
    public static Assembly Load(AssemblyName assemblyRef);
    public static Assembly Load(AssemblyName assemblyRef, System.Security.Policy.Evidence assemblySecurity);
    public static Assembly Load(byte[ ] rawAssembly);
    public static Assembly Load(byte[ ] rawAssembly, byte[ ] rawSymbolStore);
    public static Assembly Load(byte[ ] rawAssembly, byte[ ] rawSymbolStore,
        System.Security.Policy.Evidence securityEvidence);
    public static Assembly Load(string assemblyString);
    public static Assembly Load(string assemblyString, System.Security.Policy.Evidence assemblySecurity);
    public static Assembly LoadFile(string path);
    public static Assembly LoadFile(string path, System.Security.Policy.Evidence securityEvidence);
    public static Assembly LoadFrom(string assemblyFile);
    public static Assembly LoadFrom(string assemblyFile, System.Security.Policy.Evidence securityEvidence);
```

public static Assembly **LoadFrom**(string *assemblyFile*, System.Security.Policy.Evidence *securityEvidence*, byte[ ] *hashValue*,
   System.Configuration.Assemblies.AssemblyHashAlgorithm *hashAlgorithm*);
public static Assembly **LoadWithPartialName**(string *partialName*);
public static Assembly **LoadWithPartialName**(string *partialName*, System.Security.Policy.Evidence *securityEvidence*);
// Public Instance Methods
public object **CreateInstance**(string *typeName*);
public object **CreateInstance**(string *typeName*, bool *ignoreCase*);
public object **CreateInstance**(string *typeName*, bool *ignoreCase*, BindingFlags *bindingAttr*,
   Binder *binder*, object[ ] *args*, System.Globalization.CultureInfo *culture*, object[ ] *activationAttributes*);
public virtual object[ ] **GetCustomAttributes**(bool *inherit*);   // implements ICustomAttributeProvider
public virtual object[ ] **GetCustomAttributes**(Type *attributeType*, bool *inherit*);   // implements ICustomAttributeProvider
public virtual Type[ ] **GetExportedTypes**( );
public virtual FileStream **GetFile**(string *name*);
public virtual FileStream[ ] **GetFiles**( );
public virtual FileStream[ ] **GetFiles**(bool *getResourceModules*);
public Module[ ] **GetLoadedModules**( );
public Module[ ] **GetLoadedModules**(bool *getResourceModules*);
public virtual ManifestResourceInfo **GetManifestResourceInfo**(string *resourceName*);
public virtual string[ ] **GetManifestResourceNames**( );
public virtual Stream **GetManifestResourceStream**(string *name*);
public virtual Stream **GetManifestResourceStream**(Type *type*, string *name*);
public Module **GetModule**(string *name*);
public Module[ ] **GetModules**( );
public Module[ ] **GetModules**(bool *getResourceModules*);
public virtual AssemblyName **GetName**( );
public virtual AssemblyName **GetName**(bool *copiedName*);
public virtual void **GetObjectData**(System.Runtime.Serialization.SerializationInfo *info*,
   System.Runtime.Serialization.StreamingContext *context*);   // implements ISerializable
public AssemblyName[ ] **GetReferencedAssemblies**( );
public Assembly **GetSatelliteAssembly**(System.Globalization.CultureInfo *culture*);
public Assembly **GetSatelliteAssembly**(System.Globalization.CultureInfo *culture*, Version *version*);
public virtual Type **GetType**(string *name*);
public virtual Type **GetType**(string *name*, bool *throwOnError*);
public Type **GetType**(string *name*, bool *throwOnError*, bool *ignoreCase*);
public virtual Type[ ] **GetTypes**( );
public virtual bool **IsDefined**(Type *attributeType*, bool *inherit*);   // implements ICustomAttributeProvider
public Module **LoadModule**(string *moduleName*, byte[ ] *rawModule*);
public Module **LoadModule**(string *moduleName*, byte[ ] *rawModule*, byte[ ] *rawSymbolStore*);
public override string **ToString**( );   // overrides object
// Events
public event ModuleResolveEventHandler **ModuleResolve**;
}

Subclasses   System.Reflection.Emit.AssemblyBuilder

Returned By   System.AppDomain.{GetAssemblies( ), Load( )}, System.AssemblyLoadEventArgs.
               LoadedAssembly, ManifestResourceInfo.ReferencedAssembly, Module.Assembly,
               System.ResolveEventHandler.{EndInvoke( ), Invoke( )}, System.Type.Assembly

Passed To   Multiple types

AssemblyAlgorithmIdAttribute

System.Reflection (mscorlib.dll)   sealed class

The assembly manifest contains a hash of all of the files in the assembly. This attribute allows you to specify and change which hashing algorithm is used to hash these files.

```
public sealed class AssemblyAlgorithmIdAttribute : Attribute {
// Public Constructors
   public AssemblyAlgorithmIdAttribute(System.Configuration.Assemblies.AssemblyHashAlgorithm algorithmId);
   public AssemblyAlgorithmIdAttribute(uint algorithmId);
// Public Instance Properties
   public uint AlgorithmId{get; }
}
```

Hierarchy   System.Object → System.Attribute → AssemblyAlgorithmIdAttribute

Valid On   Assembly

AssemblyCompanyAttribute

System.Reflection (mscorlib.dll)   sealed class

This custom attribute is applied on an assembly that allows you to specify the company that created the assembly.

```
public sealed class AssemblyCompanyAttribute : Attribute {
// Public Constructors
   public AssemblyCompanyAttribute(string company);
// Public Instance Properties
   public string Company{get; }
}
```

Hierarchy   System.Object → System.Attribute → AssemblyCompanyAttribute

Valid On   Assembly

AssemblyConfigurationAttribute

System.Reflection (mscorlib.dll)   sealed class

This custom attribute allows you to specify a configuration for the assembly (such as debug, release, beta, etc.).

```
public sealed class AssemblyConfigurationAttribute : Attribute {
// Public Constructors
   public AssemblyConfigurationAttribute(string configuration);
// Public Instance Properties
   public string Configuration{get; }
}
```

Hierarchy   System.Object → System.Attribute → AssemblyConfigurationAttribute

Valid On   Assembly

AssemblyCopyrightAttribute

CF 1.0

System.Reflection (mscorlib.dll)   sealed class

This custom attribute string contains copyright information.

```
public sealed class AssemblyCopyrightAttribute : Attribute {
// Public Constructors
  public AssemblyCopyrightAttribute(string copyright);
// Public Instance Properties
  public string Copyright{get; }
}
```

Hierarchy   System.Object → System.Attribute → AssemblyCopyrightAttribute

Valid On   Assembly

AssemblyCultureAttribute

CF 1.0

System.Reflection (mscorlib.dll)   sealed class

This custom attribute specifies the supported culture of an assembly.

```
public sealed class AssemblyCultureAttribute : Attribute {
// Public Constructors
  public AssemblyCultureAttribute(string culture);
// Public Instance Properties
  public string Culture{get; }
}
```

Hierarchy   System.Object → System.Attribute → AssemblyCultureAttribute

Valid On   Assembly

AssemblyDefaultAliasAttribute

CF 1.0

System.Reflection (mscorlib.dll)   sealed class

This custom attribute specifies a friendly name for an assembly. This is useful when
assemblies have cryptic names such as GUIDs, as COM components do.

```
public sealed class AssemblyDefaultAliasAttribute : Attribute {
// Public Constructors
  public AssemblyDefaultAliasAttribute(string defaultAlias);
// Public Instance Properties
  public string DefaultAlias{get; }
}
```

Hierarchy   System.Object → System.Attribute → AssemblyDefaultAliasAttribute

Valid On   Assembly

AssemblyDelaySignAttribute

System.Reflection (mscorlib.dll)   sealed class

When an assembly designer does not have access to a key-pair to sign a component, this attribute reserves space in the manifest to be filled by a signing utility. The framework's sn.exe utility has a command-line switch (-R or -Rc) just for this purpose.

```
public sealed class AssemblyDelaySignAttribute : Attribute {
// Public Constructors
  public AssemblyDelaySignAttribute(bool delaySign);
// Public Instance Properties
  public bool DelaySign{get; }
}
```

Hierarchy   System.Object → System.Attribute → AssemblyDelaySignAttribute

Valid On   Assembly

AssemblyDescriptionAttribute

System.Reflection (mscorlib.dll)   sealed class

This custom attribute allows a description to be stored with an assembly.

```
public sealed class AssemblyDescriptionAttribute : Attribute {
// Public Constructors
  public AssemblyDescriptionAttribute(string description);
// Public Instance Properties
  public string Description{get; }
}
```

Hierarchy   System.Object → System.Attribute → AssemblyDescriptionAttribute

Valid On   Assembly

AssemblyFileVersionAttribute

System.Reflection (mscorlib.dll)   sealed class

This custom attribute stores a given version number in the assembly's Win32 VERSIONINFO resource. This is not the same as the assembly's version (given by the AssemblyVersionAttribute).

```
public sealed class AssemblyFileVersionAttribute : Attribute {
// Public Constructors
  public AssemblyFileVersionAttribute(string version);
// Public Instance Properties
  public string Version{get; }
}
```

Hierarchy   System.Object → System.Attribute → AssemblyFileVersionAttribute

Valid On   Assembly

AssemblyFlagsAttribute

CF 1.0

System.Reflection (mscorlib.dll)

sealed class

Use this attribute to specify the side-by-side execution behavior of this assembly. The flags parameter may take one of the following values: 0x0000 (side-by-side compatible), 0x0010 (side-by-side operation is prohibited within the same application domain), 0x0020 (side-by-side operation prohibited within same process), or 0x0030 (side-by-side operation prohibited within the same machine boundary).

```
public sealed class AssemblyFlagsAttribute : Attribute {
// Public Constructors
  public AssemblyFlagsAttribute(int assemblyFlags);
  public AssemblyFlagsAttribute(uint flags);
// Public Instance Properties
  public int AssemblyFlags{get; }
  public uint Flags{get; }
}
```

Hierarchy   System.Object → System.Attribute → AssemblyFlagsAttribute

Valid On   Assembly

AssemblyInformationalVersionAttribute

CF 1.0

System.Reflection (mscorlib.dll)

sealed class

This custom attribute allows a version number to be stored. This stored version is purely for documentation and is not used by the runtime.

```
public sealed class AssemblyInformationalVersionAttribute : Attribute {
// Public Constructors
  public AssemblyInformationalVersionAttribute(string informationalVersion);
// Public Instance Properties
  public string InformationalVersion{get; }
}
```

Hierarchy   System.Object → System.Attribute → AssemblyInformationalVersionAttribute

Valid On   Assembly

AssemblyKeyFileAttribute

CF 1.0

System.Reflection (mscorlib.dll)

sealed class

To create a strong-named assembly, use this attribute, specifying a file containing a key-pair. Alternatively, you could use an AssemblyDelaySignAttribute or an AssemblyKeyNameAttribute.

```
public sealed class AssemblyKeyFileAttribute : Attribute {
// Public Constructors
  public AssemblyKeyFileAttribute(string keyFile);
// Public Instance Properties
  public string KeyFile{get; }
}
```

Hierarchy   System.Object → System.Attribute → AssemblyKeyFileAttribute

Valid On   Assembly

AssemblyKeyNameAttribute

CF 1.0

System.Reflection (mscorlib.dll)   sealed class

This attribute serves the same purpose as an AssemblyKeyFileAttribute, but allows you to specify a key container instead of a file.

```
public sealed class AssemblyKeyNameAttribute : Attribute {
// Public Constructors
  public AssemblyKeyNameAttribute(string keyName);
// Public Instance Properties
  public string KeyName{get; }
}
```

Hierarchy   System.Object → System.Attribute → AssemblyKeyNameAttribute

Valid On   Assembly

AssemblyName

CF 1.0, serializable

System.Reflection (mscorlib.dll)   sealed class

This class represents an assembly's fully qualified name, which makes it unique. An assembly's identity consists of a simple name (the Name property), supported culture (CultureInfo), version number, and key pair. The version number itself has four parts: major version, minor version, build number, and revision number. The Flags property allows you to set the flags for an assembly (see the AssemblyNameFlags enumeration). Use HashAlgorithm to access the hash algorithm used with the manifest to verify that the files of an assembly are correct. VersionCompatibility is a System.Configuration.Assemblies.AssemblyVersion-Compatibility enumeration, which allows specification of the compatibility between versions.

Both FullName and ToString( ) return a comma-delimited string formatted, such as Name, Culture = CultureInfo, Version = Version Number, SN = StrongName, PK = Public Key Token. Any of the parameters except Name are optional. SetPublicKey( ) and SetPublicKeyToken( ) allow you to specify a public key for an originator or the strong name, respectively, and the complementary Get methods allow you to retrieve the same information.

```
public sealed class AssemblyName : ICloneable, System.Runtime.Serialization.ISerializable,
    System.Runtime.Serialization.IDeserializationCallback {
// Public Constructors
  public AssemblyName( );
// Public Instance Properties
  public string CodeBase{set; get; }
  public CultureInfo CultureInfo{set; get; }
  public string EscapedCodeBase{get; }
  public AssemblyNameFlags Flags{set; get; }
  public string FullName{get; }
  public AssemblyHashAlgorithm HashAlgorithm{set; get; }
  public StrongNameKeyPair KeyPair{set; get; }
```

System. Reflection

```
    public string Name{set; get; }
    public Version Version{set; get; }
    public AssemblyVersionCompatibility VersionCompatibility{set; get; }
// Public Static Methods
    public static AssemblyName GetAssemblyName(string assemblyFile);
// Public Instance Methods
    public object Clone( );                                                          // implements ICloneable
    public void GetObjectData(System.Runtime.Serialization.SerializationInfo info,
        System.Runtime.Serialization.StreamingContext context);                     // implements ISerializable
    public byte[ ] GetPublicKey( );
    public byte[ ] GetPublicKeyToken( );
    public void OnDeserialization(object sender);       // implements System.Runtime.Serialization.IDeserializationCallback
    public void SetPublicKey(byte[ ] publicKey);
    public void SetPublicKeyToken(byte[ ] publicKeyToken);
    public override string ToString( );                                             // overrides object
}
```

Returned By   Assembly.{GetName( ), GetReferencedAssemblies( )},
                    AssemblyNameProxy.GetAssemblyName( )

Passed To   System.AppDomain.{DefineDynamicAssembly( ), Load( )}, Assembly.Load( ),
                    System.Text.RegularExpressions.Regex.CompileToAssembly( )

AssemblyNameFlags   CF 1.0, serializable, flag

System.Reflection (mscorlib.dll)   enum

This enumeration represents the possible flags for an AssemblyName. AssemblyName.Flags can
either be set to None or PublicKey. PublicKey specifies that the originator is fully given by the
public key, rather than by a token. Retargetable indicates that the assembly can be retar-
geted at runtime to an assembly from a different publisher, meaning we can "alias" the
assembly to a third-party assembly (that, implicitly, would have a different public key
token than this one).

```
public enum AssemblyNameFlags {
    None = 0x00000000,
    PublicKey = 0x00000001,
    Retargetable = 0x00000100
}
```

Hierarchy   System.Object → System.ValueType → System.Enum(System.IComparable,
                   System.IFormattable, System.IConvertible) → AssemblyNameFlags

Returned By   AssemblyName.Flags

Passed To   AssemblyName.Flags

AssemblyNameProxy   marshal by reference

System.Reflection (mscorlib.dll)   class

This class is a remotable wrapper around AssemblyName. To access the underlying AssemblyName, call AssemblyName.GetAssemblyName( ).

```
public class AssemblyNameProxy : MarshalByRefObject {
// Public Constructors
  public AssemblyNameProxy( );
// Public Instance Methods
  public AssemblyName GetAssemblyName(string assemblyFile);
}
```

Hierarchy   System.Object → System.MarshalByRefObject → AssemblyNameProxy

AssemblyProductAttribute   CF 1.0

System.Reflection (mscorlib.dll)   sealed class

This class is a custom attribute for the product name.

```
public sealed class AssemblyProductAttribute : Attribute {
// Public Constructors
  public AssemblyProductAttribute(string product);
// Public Instance Properties
  public string Product{get; }
}
```

Hierarchy   System.Object → System.Attribute → AssemblyProductAttribute

Valid On   Assembly

AssemblyTitleAttribute   CF 1.0

System.Reflection (mscorlib.dll)   sealed class

This class is a custom attribute for an assembly title.

```
public sealed class AssemblyTitleAttribute : Attribute {
// Public Constructors
  public AssemblyTitleAttribute(string title);
// Public Instance Properties
  public string Title{get; }
}
```

Hierarchy   System.Object → System.Attribute → AssemblyTitleAttribute

Valid On   Assembly

AssemblyTrademarkAttribute   CF 1.0

System.Reflection (mscorlib.dll)   sealed class

This custom attribute is used to add a trademark.

```
public sealed class AssemblyTrademarkAttribute : Attribute {
// Public Constructors
  public AssemblyTrademarkAttribute(string trademark);
// Public Instance Properties
```

```
public string Trademark{get;}
}
```

Hierarchy   System.Object → System.Attribute → AssemblyTrademarkAttribute

Valid On   Assembly

AssemblyVersionAttribute   CF 1.0

System.Reflection (mscorlib.dll)   sealed class

This attribute is the version of the assembly. This version is used by the framework to check compatibility and determine if side-by-side execution is needed.

```
public sealed class AssemblyVersionAttribute : Attribute {
// Public Constructors
  public AssemblyVersionAttribute(string version);
// Public Instance Properties
  public string Version{get;}
}
```

Hierarchy   System.Object → System.Attribute → AssemblyVersionAttribute

Valid On   Assembly

Binder   CF 1.0, ECMA 1.0, serializable

System.Reflection (mscorlib.dll)   abstract class

This type is used by the .NET runtime for method argument conversion. It is responsible for such things as determining whether it is permissible to pass a short to a method that takes a long parameter. If you need to override .NET's default conversion rules, you could subclass this type (however, most programmers will never need to do this). For more details, see the .NET Framework SDK documentation on this type.

```
public abstract class Binder {
// Protected Constructors
  protected Binder( );
// Public Instance Methods
  public abstract FieldInfo BindToField(BindingFlags bindingAttr, FieldInfo[ ] match, object value,
    System.Globalization.CultureInfo culture);
  public abstract MethodBase BindToMethod(BindingFlags bindingAttr, MethodBase[ ] match, ref object[ ] args,
    ParameterModifier[ ] modifiers, System.Globalization.CultureInfo culture, string[ ] names, out object state);
  public abstract object ChangeType(object value, Type type, System.Globalization.CultureInfo culture);
  public abstract void ReorderArgumentArray(ref object[ ] args, object state);
  public abstract MethodBase SelectMethod(BindingFlags bindingAttr, MethodBase[ ] match,
    Type[ ] types, ParameterModifier[ ] modifiers);
  public abstract PropertyInfo SelectProperty(BindingFlags bindingAttr, PropertyInfo[ ] match,
    Type returnType, Type[ ] indexes, ParameterModifier[ ] modifiers);
}
```

Returned By   System.Type.DefaultBinder

BindingFlags

System.Reflection (mscorlib.dll)   enum

This enumeration specifies how reflection searches for members. It is used by many types in the System and System.Reflection namespaces. The following list describes each enumeration member:

CreateInstance
> Tells reflection to call a constructor that matches the specified arguments. If a member name is supplied, it is ignored.

DeclaredOnly
> Specifies to search only from the declared methods, and not from the inherited ones.

Default
> Specifies that all the default search parameters should be used.

ExactBinding
> Ensures that arguments must match exactly (no downcasting is performed).

Static
> Allows static members to match.

FlattenHierarchy
> Allows matching of static methods from inherited classes.

GetField

GetProperty
> Specify that the value of a specified field or property should be returned.

SetField

SetProperty
> Allow you to set fields and properties.

IgnoreCase
> Causes the search to be case-insensitive.

IgnoreReturn
> Tells the search to ignore the return value. This is used primarily for COM Interop.

Public
> Allows public members to be searched.

Instance
> Specifies that instance members must be searched.

NonPublic
> Allows nonpublic members to be searched.

InvokeMethod
> Says that a method that is not a constructor should be invoked.

OptionalParamBinding
> Allows matching based on the number of parameters for methods with optional arguments.

System.
Reflection

SuppressChangeType

Specifies that the CLR should not perform type coercions to invoke a method (as of this writing, SuppressChangeType is unimplemented).

PutDispProperty
PutRefDispProperty

Allow you to call the COM accessors. If the put method expects a COM intrinsic type, use PutDispProperty; if the put method expects a COM object, use PutRefDispProperty.

```
public enum BindingFlags {
    Default = 0x00000000,
    IgnoreCase = 0x00000001,
    DeclaredOnly = 0x00000002,
    Instance = 0x00000004,
    Static = 0x00000008,
    Public = 0x00000010,
    NonPublic = 0x00000020,
    FlattenHierarchy = 0x00000040,
    InvokeMethod = 0x00000100,
    CreateInstance = 0x00000200,
    GetField = 0x00000400,
    SetField = 0x00000800,
    GetProperty = 0x00001000,
    SetProperty = 0x00002000,
    PutDispProperty = 0x00004000,
    PutRefDispProperty = 0x00008000,
    ExactBinding = 0x00010000,
    SuppressChangeType = 0x00020000,
    OptionalParamBinding = 0x00040000,
    IgnoreReturn = 0x01000000
}
```

Hierarchy   System.Object → System.ValueType → System.Enum(System.IComparable, System.IFormattable, System.IConvertible) → BindingFlags

Passed To   Multiple types

CallingConventions   CF 1.0, serializable, flag

System.Reflection (mscorlib.dll)   enum

Calling conventions are the rules that govern the semantics of how method arguments and return values are passed. They also specify which registers to use, and designate what this method does with the stack. The following list describes each enumeration member:

Standard

Designates the default CLR conventions.

VarArgs

Allows variable arguments.

Any

Allows either convention.

HasThis

Passes the target method the this (or Me) reference as the first argument and cannot be used for static methods.

ExplicitThis

Represents a call to a nonstatic method and is a function pointer (for delegates). If ExplicitThis is set, HasThis must also be set.

```
public enum CallingConventions {
    Standard = 0x00000001,
    VarArgs = 0x00000002,
    Any = 0x00000003,
    HasThis = 0x00000020,
    ExplicitThis = 0x00000040
}
```

Hierarchy	System.Object → System.ValueType → System.Enum(System.IComparable, System.IFormattable, System.IConvertible) → CallingConventions
Returned By	MethodBase.CallingConvention
Passed To	Multiple types

ConstructorInfo

CF 1.0, ECMA 1.0, serializable

System.Reflection (mscorlib.dll)   abstract class

This class is an implementation of MethodBase explicitly for constructors. It adds the two static read-only properties ConstructorName and TypeConstructorName, which are defined in metadata as methods of the name .ctor and .cctor, respectively. (Recall that a "type constructor" is executed as soon as the type is loaded into the CLR; hence the name "class constructor"—"cctor" for short.)

```
public abstract class ConstructorInfo : MethodBase {
// Protected Constructors
    protected ConstructorInfo( );
// Public Static Fields
    public static readonly string ConstructorName;                              // =.ctor
    public static readonly string TypeConstructorName;                          // =.cctor
// Public Instance Properties
    public override MemberTypes MemberType{get; }                        // overrides MemberInfo
// Public Instance Methods
    public abstract object Invoke(BindingFlags invokeAttr, Binder binder, object[ ] parameters,
        System.Globalization.CultureInfo culture);
    public object Invoke(object[ ] parameters);
}
```

Hierarchy	System.Object → MemberInfo(ICustomAttributeProvider) → MethodBase → ConstructorInfo
Subclasses	System.Reflection.Emit.ConstructorBuilder

Returned By   System.Type.{GetConstructor( ), GetConstructorImpl( ), GetConstructors( ), TypeInitializer}

Passed To   Multiple types

CustomAttributeFormatException CF 1.0, serializable

System.Reflection (mscorlib.dll) class

This exception is thrown when the binary format of an attribute of a type cannot be read. This can occur when custom attributes and types are created at runtime.

```
public class CustomAttributeFormatException : FormatException {
// Public Constructors
  public CustomAttributeFormatException( );
  public CustomAttributeFormatException(string message);
  public CustomAttributeFormatException(string message, Exception inner);
// Protected Constructors
  protected CustomAttributeFormatException(System.Runtime.Serialization.SerializationInfo info,
    System.Runtime.Serialization.StreamingContext context);
}
```

Hierarchy   System.Object → System.Exception(System.Runtime.Serialization.ISerializable) →
           System.SystemException → System.FormatException → CustomAttributeFormatException

DefaultMemberAttribute CF 1.0, ECMA 1.0, serializable

System.Reflection (mscorlib.dll) sealed class

This attribute allows you to specify the default member of a class. It corresponds to the VB.NET Default keyword. C# does not permit the use of default members as part of the language, although other .NET languages (most notably VB.NET) do.

```
public sealed class DefaultMemberAttribute : Attribute {
// Public Constructors
  public DefaultMemberAttribute(string memberName);
// Public Instance Properties
  public string MemberName{get; }
}
```

Hierarchy   System.Object → System.Attribute → DefaultMemberAttribute

Valid On   Class, Struct, Interface

EventAttributes CF 1.0, ECMA 1.0, serializable, flag

System.Reflection (mscorlib.dll) enum

This is an enumeration of the attributes that can be placed on events. None specifies no attributes. ReservedMask is a reserved flag for use only by the runtime. SpecialName indicates that the event is described by the name. RTSpecialName is similar, but states that the runtime should check the encoding of the name.

```
public enum EventAttributes {
  None = 0x00000000,
  SpecialName = 0x00000200,
  ReservedMask = 0x00000400,
  RTSpecialName = 0x00000400
}
```

Hierarchy   System.Object → System.ValueType → System.Enum(System.IComparable,
                     System.IFormattable, System.IConvertible) → EventAttributes

Returned By   EventInfo.Attributes

Passed To   System.Reflection.Emit.TypeBuilder.DefineEvent( )

EventInfo   CF 1.0, ECMA 1.0

System.Reflection (mscorlib.dll)   abstract class

This class allows you to access events through reflection and is, itself, an implementation of MemberInfo. Attributes gets the EventAttributes object, and EventHandlerType gets the System. Type of the event-handler delegate for the event. IsMulticast returns true if the event is multicast, and IsSpecialName indicates whether this has special meaning. AddEventHandler( ) adds the passed delegate to the event handler, and GetAddMethod( ), GetRaiseMethod( ), and GetRemoveMethod( ) return a MethodInfo for the method used to add an event handler, raise an event, or remove an event handler, respectively.

```
public abstract class EventInfo : MemberInfo {
// Protected Constructors
  protected EventInfo( );
// Public Instance Properties
  public abstract EventAttributes Attributes{get; }
  public Type EventHandlerType{get; }
  public bool IsMulticast{get; }
  public bool IsSpecialName{get; }
  public override MemberTypes MemberType{get; }                    // overrides MemberInfo
// Public Instance Methods
  public void AddEventHandler(object target, Delegate handler);
  public MethodInfo GetAddMethod( );
  public abstract MethodInfo GetAddMethod(bool nonPublic);
  public MethodInfo GetRaiseMethod( );
  public abstract MethodInfo GetRaiseMethod(bool nonPublic);
  public MethodInfo GetRemoveMethod( );
  public abstract MethodInfo GetRemoveMethod(bool nonPublic);
  public void RemoveEventHandler(object target, Delegate handler);
}
```

Hierarchy   System.Object → MemberInfo(ICustomAttributeProvider) → EventInfo

Returned By   System.Type.{GetEvent( ), GetEvents( )}

FieldAttributes

System.Reflection (mscorlib.dll) enum

This is an enumeration of the attributes that can be specified on a field. Assembly means that the field is internal (that is, private to the assembly); Family indicates that the field is protected. Private, Public, and Static are self-explanatory. If the field has a default value, HasDefault is marked; if a field is constant, Literal is marked. InitOnly indicates that the field can only be set on object initialization. To exclude a field from being serialized, NotSerialized should be asserted. HasFieldMarshal specifies that the field has special marshaling information.

```
public enum FieldAttributes {
  PrivateScope = 0x00000000,
  Private = 0x00000001,
  FamANDAssem = 0x00000002,
  Assembly = 0x00000003,
  Family = 0x00000004,
  FamORAssem = 0x00000005,
  Public = 0x00000006,
  FieldAccessMask = 0x00000007,
  Static = 0x00000010,
  InitOnly = 0x00000020,
  Literal = 0x00000040,
  NotSerialized = 0x00000080,
  HasFieldRVA = 0x00000100,
  SpecialName = 0x00000200,
  RTSpecialName = 0x00000400,
  HasFieldMarshal = 0x00001000,
  PinvokeImpl = 0x00002000,
  HasDefault = 0x00008000,
  ReservedMask = 0x00009500
}
```

Hierarchy   System.Object → System.ValueType → System.Enum(System.IComparable,
                  System.IFormattable, System.IConvertible) → FieldAttributes

Returned By   FieldInfo.Attributes

Passed To   System.Reflection.Emit.ModuleBuilder.{DefineInitializedData( ), DefineUninitializedData( )},
                  System.Reflection.Emit.TypeBuilder.{DefineField( ), DefineInitializedData( ),
                  DefineUninitializedData( )}

FieldInfo

System.Reflection (mscorlib.dll) abstract class

This class is an implementation of MemberInfo and allows access to an instance field. Note that, like all reflective objects, the FieldInfo instance refers to the metadata concept of the field within the type, not a particular field within a particular instance of that type. (This is important when working with or manipulating the value stored in object instance fields.)

IsAssembly, IsFamily, IsFamilyAndAssembly, IsFamilyOrAssembly, IsPublic, and IsPrivate allow you to check the visibility of the field. FieldType returns the declared type of this field. FieldHandle is a System.RuntimeFieldHandle. Use Attributes to retrieve the attributes. To see if the FieldInfo has the NotSerialized or PinvokeImplFieldAttributes set, inspect the IsNotSerialized and IsPinvokeImpl properties. If the field is static, IsStatic is true. The Set and Get methods allow you set the values, and the ones with Direct in their name take a typed reference as opposed to an object.

```
public abstract class FieldInfo : MemberInfo {
// Protected Constructors
  protected FieldInfo( );
// Public Instance Properties
  public abstract FieldAttributes Attributes{get; }
  public abstract RuntimeFieldHandle FieldHandle{get; }
  public abstract Type FieldType{get; }
  public bool IsAssembly{get; }
  public bool IsFamily{get; }
  public bool IsFamilyAndAssembly{get; }
  public bool IsFamilyOrAssembly{get; }
  public bool IsInitOnly{get; }
  public bool IsLiteral{get; }
  public bool IsNotSerialized{get; }
  public bool IsPinvokeImpl{get; }
  public bool IsPrivate{get; }
  public bool IsPublic{get; }
  public bool IsSpecialName{get; }
  public bool IsStatic{get; }
  public override MemberTypes MemberType{get; }                          // overrides MemberInfo
// Public Static Methods
  public static FieldInfo GetFieldFromHandle(RuntimeFieldHandle handle);
// Public Instance Methods
  public abstract object GetValue(object obj);
  public virtual object GetValueDirect(TypedReference obj);
  public void SetValue(object obj, object value);
  public abstract void SetValue(object obj, object value, BindingFlags invokeAttr, Binder binder,
    System.Globalization.CultureInfo culture);
  public virtual void SetValueDirect(TypedReference obj, object value);
}
```

Hierarchy   System.Object → MemberInfo(ICustomAttributeProvider) → FieldInfo

Subclasses   System.Reflection.Emit.FieldBuilder

Returned By   Binder.BindToField( ), IReflect.{GetField( ), GetFields( )}, Module.{GetField( ), GetFields( )},
                    System.Runtime.InteropServices.Expando.IExpando.AddField( ), System.Type.{GetField( ),
                    GetFields( )}

Passed To   Binder.BindToField( ), System.Reflection.Emit.CustomAttributeBuilder.
                    CustomAttributeBuilder( ), System.Reflection.Emit.ILGenerator.{Emit( ), EmitWriteLine( )},
                    System.Reflection.Emit.ModuleBuilder.GetFieldToken( )

ICustomAttributeProvider

System.Reflection (mscorlib.dll)   interface

This interface is implemented if an object supports custom attributes. GetCustomAttributes() returns the custom attributes, and IsDefined() returns true if an attribute of a passed System.Type is defined on this member.

```
public interface ICustomAttributeProvider {
// Public Instance Methods
   public object[ ] GetCustomAttributes(bool inherit);
   public object[ ] GetCustomAttributes(Type attributeType, bool inherit);
   public bool IsDefined(Type attributeType, bool inherit);
}
```

Implemented By   Assembly, MemberInfo, Module, ParameterInfo

Returned By   MethodInfo.ReturnTypeCustomAttributes

InterfaceMapping

System.Reflection (mscorlib.dll)   struct

This value type allows you to retrieve information about interfaces. To access the Type for an interface, use InterfaceType. TargetType contains the Type of the implementing class. Similarly, InterfaceMethods and TargetMethods return the methods of the interface and the implementing class, respectively.

```
public struct InterfaceMapping {
// Public Instance Fields
   public MethodInfo[ ] InterfaceMethods;
   public Type InterfaceType;
   public MethodInfo[ ] TargetMethods;
   public Type TargetType;
}
```

Hierarchy   System.Object → System.ValueType → InterfaceMapping

Returned By   System.Type.GetInterfaceMap( )

InvalidFilterCriteriaException   serializable

System.Reflection (mscorlib.dll)   class

This exception is thrown when the filter criteria passed to System.Type.FindMembers( ) is invalid.

```
public class InvalidFilterCriteriaException : ApplicationException {
// Public Constructors
   public InvalidFilterCriteriaException( );
   public InvalidFilterCriteriaException(string message);
   public InvalidFilterCriteriaException(string message, Exception inner);
```

```
// Protected Constructors
  protected InvalidFilterCriteriaException(System.Runtime.Serialization.SerializationInfo info,
    System.Runtime.Serialization.StreamingContext context);
}
```

Hierarchy   System.Object → System.Exception(System.Runtime.Serialization.ISerializable) →
                  System.ApplicationException → InvalidFilterCriteriaException

IReflect

System.Reflection (mscorlib.dll)   interface

This interface defines how types are reflected and provides all the relevant information about the members of a class (methods, fields, and properties). The Get methods allow access to these members. The methods GetField(), GetMethod(), GetProperty(), and GetMember() return single members of the specified type by name. The methods GetFields(), GetMethods(), GetProperties(), and GetMembers() return all of the specified type of members contained by the class.

```
public interface IReflect {
// Public Instance Properties
  public Type UnderlyingSystemType{get; }
// Public Instance Methods
  public FieldInfo GetField(string name, BindingFlags bindingAttr);
  public FieldInfo[ ] GetFields(BindingFlags bindingAttr);
  public MemberInfo[ ] GetMember(string name, BindingFlags bindingAttr);
  public MemberInfo[ ] GetMembers(BindingFlags bindingAttr);
  public MethodInfo GetMethod(string name, BindingFlags bindingAttr);
  public MethodInfo GetMethod(string name, BindingFlags bindingAttr, Binder binder, Type[ ] types,
    ParameterModifier[ ] modifiers);
  public MethodInfo[ ] GetMethods(BindingFlags bindingAttr);
  public PropertyInfo[ ] GetProperties(BindingFlags bindingAttr);
  public PropertyInfo GetProperty(string name, BindingFlags bindingAttr);
  public PropertyInfo GetProperty(string name, BindingFlags bindingAttr, Binder binder, Type returnType,
    Type[ ] types, ParameterModifier[ ] modifiers);
  public object InvokeMember(string name, BindingFlags invokeAttr, Binder binder, object target, object[ ] args,
    ParameterModifier[ ] modifiers, System.Globalization.CultureInfo culture, string[ ] namedParameters);
}
```

Implemented By   System.Type, System.Runtime.InteropServices.Expando.IExpando

ManifestResourceInfo

System.Reflection (mscorlib.dll)   class

This class represents a resource from an assembly manifest. As assemblies can span multiple files, this resource represents one file from an assembly. The FileName returns the name of the file containing the resource if it is not the same as the file containing the manifest. ResourceLocation allows you to inspect the ResourceLocation enumeration for this resource, telling you whether the resource is contained in the same file as the manifest. ReferencedAssembly returns the Assembly object representing the specified assembly.

```
public class ManifestResourceInfo {
// Public Instance Properties
  public virtual string FileName{get; }
  public virtual Assembly ReferencedAssembly{get; }
  public virtual ResourceLocation ResourceLocation{get; }
}
```

Returned By   Assembly.GetManifestResourceInfo( )

MemberFilter   serializable

System.Reflection (mscorlib.dll)   delegate

This delegate defines a function that is used to filter an array of MemberInfo objects. This
method is run for each MemberInfo and should return true to include the MemberInfo. The
second parameter, filterCriteria, is an arbitrary argument that you may specify to be
passed to the filter.

This delegate is used from the System.Type.FindMembers( ) method and is designed to allow
for high-level "searches" of a type's members (fields, methods, properties, and so on)
without having to code the actual looping logic itself.

```
public delegate bool MemberFilter(MemberInfo m, object filterCriteria);
```

Passed To   System.Type.FindMembers( )

MemberInfo   CF 1.0, ECMA 1.0, serializable

System.Reflection (mscorlib.dll)   abstract class

This class is the base type for all reflective types defined in the .NET environment; it
defines the basic data associated with any member (field, method, property, event,
nested type) of a given type. Note that even System.Type itself inherits from this class.

By itself, MemberInfo is a fairly simple type. It consists of four properties: DeclaringType (a
reference to the System.Type in which this member was declared, which might be a base
type to the class being reflected over), MemberType (an enumeration describing the type
of the member), Name, and ReflectedType (the System.Type instance from which this Member-
Info object was received in the first place). MemberInfo also consists of two methods,
GetCustomAttributes( ) and IsDefined( ), both of which deal with any custom attributes defined
on this member.

```
public abstract class MemberInfo : ICustomAttributeProvider {
// Protected Constructors
  protected MemberInfo( );
// Public Instance Properties
  public abstract Type DeclaringType{get; }
  public abstract MemberTypes MemberType{get; }
  public abstract string Name{get; }
  public abstract Type ReflectedType{get; }
// Public Instance Methods
  public abstract object[ ] GetCustomAttributes( bool inherit);                  // implements ICustomAttributeProvider
  public abstract object[ ] GetCustomAttributes(Type attributeType, bool inherit);   // implements ICustomAttributeProvider
  public abstract bool IsDefined(Type attributeType, bool inherit);              // implements ICustomAttributeProvider
}
```

Subclasses	EventInfo, FieldInfo, MethodBase, PropertyInfo, System.Type
Returned By	IReflect.{GetMember( ), GetMembers( )}, ParameterInfo.Member, System.Runtime. InteropServices.Marshal.GetMethodInfoForComSlot( ), System.Runtime.Serialization. FormatterServices.GetSerializableMembers( ), System.Type.{FindMembers( ), GetDefaultMembers( ), GetMember( ), GetMembers( )}
Passed To	System.Attribute.{GetCustomAttribute( ), GetCustomAttributes( ), IsDefined( )}, MemberFilter.{BeginInvoke( ), Invoke( )}, System.Runtime.InteropServices.Expando. IExpando.RemoveMember( ), System.Runtime.InteropServices.Marshal. GetComSlotForMethodInfo( ), System.Runtime.Serialization.FormatterServices. {GetObjectData( ), PopulateObjectMembers( )}, System.Runtime.Serialization. ObjectManager.{RecordFixup( ), RegisterObject( )}

MemberTypes
CF 1.0, serializable, flag

System.Reflection (mscorlib.dll)   enum

This enumeration represents the different types of MemberInfo objects. All specifies all member types, and Custom specifies a custom member type. All of the other enumerated values specify the type of the MemberInfo object. For example, Field designates that the MemberInfo object is actually a FieldInfo object.

```
public enum MemberTypes {
   Constructor = 0x00000001,
   Event = 0x00000002,
   Field = 0x00000004,
   Method = 0x00000008,
   Property = 0x00000010,
   TypeInfo = 0x00000020,
   Custom = 0x00000040,
   NestedType = 0x00000080,
   All = 0x000000BF
}
```

Hierarchy	System.Object → System.ValueType → System.Enum(System.IComparable, System.IFormattable, System.IConvertible) → MemberTypes
Returned By	MemberInfo.MemberType
Passed To	System.Type.{FindMembers( ), GetMember( )}

MethodAttributes
CF 1.0, ECMA 1.0, serializable, flag

System.Reflection (mscorlib.dll)   enum

These attributes can be placed on methods. The behavior of most of these is obvious and the same as for FieldAttributes. The others are used for specifying the structure of the object vTable.

```
public enum MethodAttributes {
   ReuseSlot = 0x00000000,
   PrivateScope = 0x00000000,
```

```
    Private = 0x00000001,
    FamANDAssem = 0x00000002,
    Assembly = 0x00000003,
    Family = 0x00000004,
    FamORAssem = 0x00000005,
    Public = 0x00000006,
    MemberAccessMask = 0x00000007,
    UnmanagedExport = 0x00000008,
    Static = 0x00000010,
    Final = 0x00000020,
    Virtual = 0x00000040,
    HideBySig = 0x00000080,
    NewSlot = 0x00000100,
    VtableLayoutMask = 0x00000100,
    CheckAccessOnOverride = 0x00000200,
    Abstract = 0x00000400,
    SpecialName = 0x00000800,
    RTSpecialName = 0x00001000,
    PinvokeImpl = 0x00002000,
    HasSecurity = 0x00004000,
    RequireSecObject = 0x00008000,
    ReservedMask = 0x0000D000
}
```

Hierarchy	System.Object → System.ValueType → System.Enum(System.IComparable, System.IFormattable, System.IConvertible) → MethodAttributes
Returned By	MethodBase.Attributes
Passed To	System.Reflection.Emit.ModuleBuilder.{DefineGlobalMethod( ), DefinePInvokeMethod( )}, System.Reflection.Emit.TypeBuilder.{DefineConstructor( ), DefineDefaultConstructor( ), DefineMethod( ), DefinePInvokeMethod( )}

MethodBase

CF 1.0, ECMA 1.0, serializable

System.Reflection (mscorlib.dll)

abstract class

This is an abstract base class representing executable method calls, which fall into two categories: regular methods and constructors. GetCurrentMethod( ) and GetMethodFromHandle( ) are static methods that return the currently executing method and a method represented by a System.RuntimeMethodHandle object, respectively. The MethodHandle returns the handle for a specific method instance.

The properties prefixed by Is return boolean values, allowing inspection of the modifiers of the reflected method. Only some require explanation: IsAssembly returns true if the method is internal, and IsFamily returns true for protected methods. If a member of exactly the same name and signature is hidden by a derived class, IsHideBySig is true. IsSpecialName indicates whether this method has a special name, such as a property accessor, get_PropertyName or set_PropertyName.

Similarly, the attributes on a given method can be inspected from the Attributes property. GetParameters( ) returns the parameters of a method or constructor, and GetMethodImplementationFlags( ) returns the MethodImplAttributes flags set on the method.

In addition to introspecting on a method, the MethodBase also allows for reflective invocation of a method, using the Invoke() method. Note that Invoke() requires both the object instance against which to invoke the method (or null if the method is declared static), as well as an array of object references containing the arguments to the method, in their proper order. Should the argument array mismatch in any way (wrong number of arguments, wrong type of arguments, wrong order of arguments, and so on), an exception is thrown and the method call is not even attempted. Method invocation in this manner is much slower than direct compile-time-bound method execution.

```
public abstract class MethodBase : MemberInfo {
// Protected Constructors
  protected MethodBase( );
// Public Instance Properties
  public abstract MethodAttributes Attributes{get; }
  public virtual CallingConventions CallingConvention{get; }
  public bool IsAbstract{get; }
  public bool IsAssembly{get; }
  public bool IsConstructor{get; }
  public bool IsFamily{get; }
  public bool IsFamilyAndAssembly{get; }
  public bool IsFamilyOrAssembly{get; }
  public bool IsFinal{get; }
  public bool IsHideBySig{get; }
  public bool IsPrivate{get; }
  public bool IsPublic{get; }
  public bool IsSpecialName{get; }
  public bool IsStatic{get; }
  public bool IsVirtual{get; }
  public abstract RuntimeMethodHandle MethodHandle{get; }
// Public Static Methods
  public static MethodBase GetCurrentMethod( );
  public static MethodBase GetMethodFromHandle(RuntimeMethodHandle handle);
// Public Instance Methods
  public abstract MethodImplAttributes GetMethodImplementationFlags( );
  public abstract ParameterInfo[ ] GetParameters( );
  public abstract object Invoke(object obj, BindingFlags invokeAttr, Binder binder, object[ ] parameters,
    System.Globalization.CultureInfo culture);
  public object Invoke(object obj, object[ ] parameters);
}
```

Hierarchy	System.Object → MemberInfo(ICustomAttributeProvider) → MethodBase
Subclasses	ConstructorInfo, MethodInfo
Returned By	System.Diagnostics.StackFrame.GetMethod( ), System.Exception.TargetSite, Binder.{BindToMethod( ), SelectMethod( )}
Passed To	Binder.{BindToMethod( ), SelectMethod( )}

MethodImplAttributes

System.Reflection (mscorlib.dll)   enum

These flags specify how a method has been implemented. Managed, Unmanaged, and ManagedMask indicate whether the method is managed or unmanaged code. If a method allows only one thread to execute it at a time, then its Synchronized flag is set. ForwardRef specifies that the method has not been defined, and InternalCall indicates that the method is an internal call. IL and OPTIL specify that the code is IL or optimized IL. If the method is provided by the runtime, Runtime should be set, and if the method implementation is native, Native is marked. When a method should not be inlined during optimization, NoInlining is set. When the method signature should be exported exactly as specified, PreserveSig is set.

```
public enum MethodImplAttributes {
  Managed = 0x00000000,
  IL = 0x00000000,
  Native = 0x00000001,
  OPTIL = 0x00000002,
  Runtime = 0x00000003,
  CodeTypeMask = 0x00000003,
  Unmanaged = 0x00000004,
  ManagedMask = 0x00000004,
  NoInlining = 0x00000008,
  ForwardRef = 0x00000010,
  Synchronized = 0x00000020,
  PreserveSig = 0x00000080,
  InternalCall = 0x00001000,
  MaxMethodImplVal = 0x0000FFFF
}
```

Hierarchy   System.Object → System.ValueType → System.Enum(System.IComparable, System.IFormattable, System.IConvertible) → MethodImplAttributes

Returned By   MethodBase.GetMethodImplementationFlags( )

Passed To   System.Reflection.Emit.ConstructorBuilder.SetImplementationFlags( ), System.Reflection.Emit.MethodBuilder.SetImplementationFlags( )

MethodInfo

System.Reflection (mscorlib.dll)   abstract class

This class is an implementation of MethodBase for methods (ConstructorInfo is the other implementation for constructors). It adds two properties: ReturnType and ReturnTypeCustomAttributes, which allow access to the System.Type object of the value returned and to the custom attributes set on that value. If the method is overridden from a base class, then GetBaseDefinition( ) returns the MethodInfo for the overridden method.

```
public abstract class MethodInfo : MethodBase {
// Protected Constructors
  protected MethodInfo( );
// Public Instance Properties
```

```
public override MemberTypes MemberType{get; }                          // overrides MemberInfo
public abstract Type ReturnType{get; }
public abstract ICustomAttributeProvider ReturnTypeCustomAttributes{get; }
// Public Instance Methods
public abstract MethodInfo GetBaseDefinition( );
}
```

Hierarchy	System.Object → MemberInfo(ICustomAttributeProvider) → MethodBase → MethodInfo
Subclasses	System.Reflection.Emit.MethodBuilder
Returned By	Multiple types
Passed To	System.Delegate.CreateDelegate( ), System.Reflection.Emit.AssemblyBuilder. SetEntryPoint( ), System.Reflection.Emit.ILGenerator.{Emit( ), EmitCall( )}, System.Reflection. Emit.ModuleBuilder.{GetMethodToken( ), SetUserEntryPoint( )}, System.Reflection.Emit. TypeBuilder.DefineMethodOverride( ), System.Runtime.InteropServices.Marshal. {NumParamBytes( ), Prelink( )}

Missing   CF 1.0

System.Reflection (mscorlib.dll)   sealed class

Because C# (as well as some other languages) does not allow optional parameters, Missing allows those languages to pass this value to indicate that a value will not be specified for those optional parameters. The only way to access an instance of this class—there can only be one—is by the return value of the static field, called Value.

```
public sealed class Missing {
// Public Static Fields
  public static readonly Missing Value;                          // =System.Reflection.Missing
}
```

Module   CF 1.0, ECMA 1.0, serializable

System.Reflection (mscorlib.dll)   class

Modules are .NET executable files (either .EXE or .DLL files) consisting of classes or interfaces. One or more modules and other resources (such as graphics) make up an assembly. The Module class allows reflection of these executables. FilterTypeName and Filter-TypeNameIgnoreCase are static properties that return a TypeFilter delegate that filters types by name. The first is case-sensitive, and the second is case-insensitive. Assembly returns the appropriate Assembly object that this is part of. Name returns the filename of this module and FullyQualifiedName returns that filename as well as the full path. Use FindTypes( ) to return a list of types from a module accepted by a TypeFilter delegate. The methods prefixed with Get return the specific methods, types, or fields contained in this module, and IsDefined( ) checks whether a specific attribute is defined on the module.

```
public class Module : System.Runtime.Serialization.ISerializable, ICustomAttributeProvider {
// Public Static Fields
  public static readonly TypeFilter FilterTypeName;              // =System.Reflection.TypeFilter
  public static readonly TypeFilter FilterTypeNameIgnoreCase;    // =System.Reflection.TypeFilter
// Public Instance Properties
```

```
public Assembly Assembly{get; }
public virtual string FullyQualifiedName{get; }
public string Name{get; }
public string ScopeName{get; }
// Public Instance Methods
public virtual Type[ ] FindTypes(TypeFilter filter, object filterCriteria);
public virtual object[ ] GetCustomAttributes(bool inherit);                                      // implements ICustomAttributeProvider
public virtual object[ ] GetCustomAttributes(Type attributeType, bool inherit);                  // implements ICustomAttributeProvider
public FieldInfo GetField(string name);
public FieldInfo GetField(string name, BindingFlags bindingAttr);
public FieldInfo[ ] GetFields( );
public MethodInfo GetMethod(string name);
public MethodInfo GetMethod(string name, BindingFlags bindingAttr, Binder binder,
    CallingConventions callConvention, Type[ ] types, ParameterModifier[ ] modifiers);
public MethodInfo GetMethod(string name, Type[ ] types);
public MethodInfo[ ] GetMethods( );
public virtual void GetObjectData(System.Runtime.Serialization.SerializationInfo info,
    System.Runtime.Serialization.StreamingContext context);                                       // implements ISerializable
public X509Certificate GetSignerCertificate( );
public virtual Type GetType(string className);
public virtual Type GetType(string className, bool ignoreCase);
public virtual Type GetType(string className, bool throwOnError, bool ignoreCase);
public virtual Type[ ] GetTypes( );
public virtual bool IsDefined(Type attributeType, bool inherit);                                  // implements ICustomAttributeProvider
public bool IsResource( );
public override string ToString( );                                                               // overrides object
// Protected Instance Methods
protected virtual MethodInfo GetMethodImpl(string name, BindingFlags bindingAttr, Binder binder,
    CallingConventions callConvention, Type[ ] types, ParameterModifier[ ] modifiers);
}
```

Subclasses   System.Reflection.Emit.ModuleBuilder

Returned By   Assembly.{GetLoadedModules( ), GetModule( ), GetModules( ), LoadModule( )}, System.
                     Reflection.Emit.ConstructorBuilder.GetModule( ), System.Reflection.Emit.MethodBuilder.
                     GetModule( ), ModuleResolveEventHandler.{EndInvoke( ), Invoke( )}, System.Type.Module

Passed To   System.Attribute.{GetCustomAttribute( ), GetCustomAttributes( ), IsDefined( )}, System.
                     Reflection.Emit.SignatureHelper.{GetFieldSigHelper( ), GetLocalVarSigHelper( ),
                     GetMethodSigHelper( ), GetPropertySigHelper( )}, System.Runtime.InteropServices.Marshal.
                     GetHINSTANCE( )

ModuleResolveEventHandler   serializable

System.Reflection (mscorlib.dll)   delegate

This delegate is used as an event handler by Assembly when it cannot resolve a reference
to a module that is part of an assembly. One instance in which this might occur is if
one resource is not present.

```
public delegate Module ModuleResolveEventHandler(object sender, ResolveEventArgs e);
```

Associated Events Assembly.ModuleResolve( ), System.Reflection.Emit.AssemblyBuilder.ModuleResolve( )

ParameterAttributes

System.Reflection (mscorlib.dll)   enum

These attributes are specified on a parameter. When the parameter has a default value, HasDefault is asserted. Optional, Out, In, and Retval all behave as you would expect them to. If a parameter has no attribute, None must be marked alone. If the parameter contains locale identifying information, Lcid should be set. Lastly, if the parameter is for marshaling information, HasFieldMarshal is asserted.

```
public enum ParameterAttributes {
  None = 0x00000000,
  In = 0x00000001,
  Out = 0x00000002,
  Lcid = 0x00000004,
  Retval = 0x00000008,
  Optional = 0x00000010,
  HasDefault = 0x00001000,
  HasFieldMarshal = 0x00002000,
  Reserved3 = 0x00004000,
  Reserved4 = 0x00008000,
  ReservedMask = 0x0000F000
}
```

Hierarchy   System.Object → System.ValueType → System.Enum(System.IComparable, System.IFormattable, System.IConvertible) → ParameterAttributes

Returned By   ParameterInfo.Attributes

Passed To   System.Reflection.Emit.ConstructorBuilder.DefineParameter( ), System.Reflection.Emit.MethodBuilder.DefineParameter( )

ParameterInfo

System.Reflection (mscorlib.dll)   class

This class allows the inspection of the type and behavior of a method parameter. Because parameters can have custom attributes on them, the class implements ICustomAttributeProvider. Attributes returns the attributes defined on this parameter. If the parameter has a default, it is stored in DefaultValue. Retrieve the name, type, and member the parameter is from by inspecting Name, ParameterType, and Member. Position returns the ordinal position of this parameter. IsOptional returns true if the parameter is optional, and IsLcid indicates when the parameter is a locale identifier.

A parameter is passed by reference if the IsByRef property of its ParameterType property is true and the IsOut property is false (*out* parameters have IsByRef and IsOut set to true). A parameter that has been marked as [In] has IsOut set to false and IsIn set to true.

```
public class ParameterInfo : ICustomAttributeProvider {
// Protected Constructors
  protected ParameterInfo( );
// Protected Instance Fields
  protected ParameterAttributes AttrsImpl;
  protected Type ClassImpl;
```

System.
Reflection

```
  protected object DefaultValueImpl;
  protected MemberInfo MemberImpl;
  protected string NameImpl;
  protected int PositionImpl;
// Public Instance Properties
  public virtual ParameterAttributes Attributes{get; }
  public virtual object DefaultValue{get; }
  public bool IsIn{get; }
  public bool IsLcid{get; }
  public bool IsOptional{get; }
  public bool IsOut{get; }
  public bool IsRetval{get; }
  public virtual MemberInfo Member{get; }
  public virtual string Name{get; }
  public virtual Type ParameterType{get; }
  public virtual int Position{get; }
// Public Instance Methods
  public virtual object[ ] GetCustomAttributes(bool inherit);                        // implements ICustomAttributeProvider
  public virtual object[ ] GetCustomAttributes(Type attributeType, bool inherit);    // implements ICustomAttributeProvider
  public virtual bool IsDefined(Type attributeType, bool inherit);                   // implements ICustomAttributeProvider
}
```

Returned By   MethodBase.GetParameters( ), PropertyInfo.GetIndexParameters( )

Passed To   System.Attribute.{GetCustomAttribute( ), GetCustomAttributes( ), IsDefined( )}

ParameterModifier   CF 1.0, ECMA 1.0, serializable

System.Reflection (mscorlib.dll)   struct

This value type acts much like an array of boolean values. It can be constructed to a
certain size, and then each index can be set or retrieved.

```
public struct ParameterModifier {
// Public Constructors
  public ParameterModifier(int parameterCount);
// Public Instance Properties
  public bool this[int index]{set; get; }
}
```

Hierarchy   System.Object → System.ValueType → ParameterModifier

Passed To   Multiple types

Pointer

System.Reflection (mscorlib.dll)   sealed class

This class allows access to direct pointers to .NET objects through two static
methods. Unbox( ) returns a void* pointer to the passed object and pins it, not allowing
the garbage collector to move its place in memory, and Box( ) returns control over the
object to the .NET runtime.

```
public sealed class Pointer : System.Runtime.Serialization.ISerializable {
// Public Static Methods
  public static object Box(void *ptr, Type type);
  public static void* Unbox(object ptr);
}
```

PropertyAttributes

CF 1.0, ECMA 1.0, serializable, flag

System.Reflection (mscorlib.dll)   enum

Specifies the attributes that can be placed on properties. The important ones that you
will encounter are None and HasDefault, which specify either the absence of attributes or
that there is a default.

```
public enum PropertyAttributes {
  None = 0x00000000,
  SpecialName = 0x00000200,
  RTSpecialName = 0x00000400,
  HasDefault = 0x00001000,
  Reserved2 = 0x00002000,
  Reserved3 = 0x00004000,
  Reserved4 = 0x00008000,
  ReservedMask = 0x0000F400,
}
```

Hierarchy   System.Object → System.ValueType → System.Enum(System.IComparable,
                   System.IFormattable, System.IConvertible) → PropertyAttributes

Returned By   PropertyInfo.Attributes

Passed To   System.Reflection.Emit.TypeBuilder.DefineProperty( )

PropertyInfo

CF 1.0, ECMA 1.0, serializable

System.Reflection (mscorlib.dll)   abstract class

This class implements MemberInfo and represents a declared property on a type. CanRead
and CanWrite check whether this property has get or set behaviors defined. These
methods can be inspected directly (as MethodInfo instances) by calling GetGetMethod() and
GetSetMethod(), or together by calling GetAccessors(), which returns an array of all defined
accessors. If the property is an indexer, GetIndexParameters() returns parameters to access
the indexer. GetValue() and SetValue() allow the instance of this property to be set or
retrieved; these act as a shortcut to calling Invoke on the methods returned from
GetGetMethod() or GetSetMethod().

```
public abstract class PropertyInfo : MemberInfo {
// Protected Constructors
  protected PropertyInfo( );
// Public Instance Properties
  public abstract PropertyAttributes Attributes{get; }
  public abstract bool CanRead{get; }
  public abstract bool CanWrite{get; }
  public bool IsSpecialName{get; }
```

```
public override MemberTypes MemberType{get; }                              // overrides MemberInfo
public abstract Type PropertyType{get; }
// Public Instance Methods
public MethodInfo[ ] GetAccessors( );
public abstract MethodInfo[ ] GetAccessors(bool nonPublic);
public MethodInfo GetGetMethod( );
public abstract MethodInfo GetGetMethod(bool nonPublic);
public abstract ParameterInfo[ ] GetIndexParameters( );
public MethodInfo GetSetMethod( );
public abstract MethodInfo GetSetMethod(bool nonPublic);
public abstract object GetValue(object obj, BindingFlags invokeAttr, Binder binder, object[ ] index,
   System.Globalization.CultureInfo culture);
public virtual object GetValue(object obj, object[ ] index);
public abstract void SetValue(object obj, object value, BindingFlags invokeAttr, Binder binder,
   object[ ] index, System.Globalization.CultureInfo culture);
public virtual void SetValue(object obj, object value, object[ ] index);
}
```

Hierarchy	System.Object → MemberInfo(ICustomAttributeProvider) → PropertyInfo
Subclasses	System.Reflection.Emit.PropertyBuilder
Returned By	Binder.SelectProperty( ), IReflect.{GetProperties( ), GetProperty( )}, System.Runtime.InteropServices.Expando.IExpando.AddProperty( ), System.Type.{GetProperties( ), GetProperty( ), GetPropertyImpl( )}
Passed To	Binder.SelectProperty( ), System.Reflection.Emit.CustomAttributeBuilder.CustomAttributeBuilder( )

ReflectionTypeLoadException   serializable

System.Reflection (mscorlib.dll)   sealed class

This exception is thrown if any of the types from a module cannot be loaded when Module.GetTypes( ) is called. This exception provides access to the correctly loaded classes via Types.

```
public sealed class ReflectionTypeLoadException : SystemException {
// Public Constructors
public ReflectionTypeLoadException(Type[ ] classes, Exception[ ] exceptions);
public ReflectionTypeLoadException(Type[ ] classes, Exception[ ] exceptions, string message);
// Public Instance Properties
public Exception[ ] LoaderExceptions{get; }
public Type[ ] Types{get; }
// Public Instance Methods
public override void GetObjectData(System.Runtime.Serialization.SerializationInfo info,
   System.Runtime.Serialization.StreamingContext context);               // overrides Exception
}
```

Hierarchy	System.Object → System.Exception(System.Runtime.Serialization.ISerializable) → System.SystemException → ReflectionTypeLoadException

ResourceAttributes

System.Reflection (mscorlib.dll)   enum

This enumeration includes the only two flags that can be placed on resources: Public
and Private.

```
public enum ResourceAttributes {
  Public = 0x00000001,
  Private = 0x00000002
}
```

Hierarchy   System.Object → System.ValueType → System.Enum(System.IComparable,
                       System.IFormattable, System.IConvertible) → ResourceAttributes

Passed To   System.Reflection.Emit.AssemblyBuilder.{AddResourceFile( ), DefineResource( )},
                       System.Reflection.Emit.ModuleBuilder.DefineResource( )

ResourceLocation

serializable, flag

System.Reflection (mscorlib.dll)   enum

This enumeration returns the location of a resource relative to the assembly.

```
public enum ResourceLocation {
  Embedded = 0x00000001,
  ContainedInAnotherAssembly = 0x00000002,
  ContainedInManifestFile = 0x00000004
}
```

Hierarchy   System.Object → System.ValueType → System.Enum(System.IComparable,
                       System.IFormattable, System.IConvertible) → ResourceLocation

Returned By   ManifestResourceInfo.ResourceLocation

StrongNameKeyPair

serializable

System.Reflection (mscorlib.dll)   class

This property allows reflection of an assembly's strong name. Use PublicKey to decrypt
the encrypted name to verify the authenticity of the assembly.

```
public class StrongNameKeyPair {
// Public Constructors
  public StrongNameKeyPair(byte[ ] keyPairArray);
  public StrongNameKeyPair(System.IO.FileStream keyPairFile);
  public StrongNameKeyPair(string keyPairContainer);
// Public Instance Properties
  public byte[ ] PublicKey{get; }
}
```

Returned By   AssemblyName.KeyPair

Passed To   AssemblyName.KeyPair

System.
Reflection

TargetException

System.Reflection (mscorlib.dll)   class

This exception is thrown when you attempt to invoke a nonstatic method on a null object reference. (Note that in Beta1 of the .NET SDK, it was permissible to call a nonvirtual method against a null reference, so long as that method didn't access any of the fields in the type. In Beta2 and beyond, this "feature" has been closed and removed.)

```
public class TargetException : ApplicationException {
// Public Constructors
  public TargetException( );
  public TargetException(string message);
  public TargetException(string message, Exception inner);
// Protected Constructors
  protected TargetException(System.Runtime.Serialization.SerializationInfo info,
    System.Runtime.Serialization.StreamingContext context);
}
```

Hierarchy   System.Object → System.Exception(System.Runtime.Serialization.ISerializable) → System.ApplicationException → TargetException

TargetInvocationException

System.Reflection (mscorlib.dll)   sealed class

This exception is thrown by methods invoked via Reflection when they raise exceptions. Check InnerException to view the actual exception raised.

```
public sealed class TargetInvocationException : ApplicationException {
// Public Constructors
  public TargetInvocationException(Exception inner);
  public TargetInvocationException(string message, Exception inner);
}
```

Hierarchy   System.Object → System.Exception(System.Runtime.Serialization.ISerializable) → System.ApplicationException → TargetInvocationException

TargetParameterCountException

System.Reflection (mscorlib.dll)   sealed class

This exception is thrown when a method is invoked with an incorrect number of parameters. Note that this can only come when invoking methods via reflection, since the compiler detects any normal parameter count errors.

```
public sealed class TargetParameterCountException : ApplicationException {
// Public Constructors
  public TargetParameterCountException( );
  public TargetParameterCountException(string message);
  public TargetParameterCountException(string message, Exception inner);
}
```

Hierarchy   System.Object → System.Exception(System.Runtime.Serialization.ISerializable) → System.ApplicationException → TargetParameterCountException

System.Reflection (mscorlib.dll)   enum

These attributes can be applied to a type. A type is either a class or interface, so either Class or Interface must be set. Most of the modifiers share the same keywords with C# and VB.NET, so they are easy to understand. The values prefixed with Nested indicate a class that is nested as well as its visibility.

```
public enum TypeAttributes {
  Class = 0x00000000,
  AutoLayout = 0x00000000,
  AnsiClass = 0x00000000,
  NotPublic = 0x00000000,
  Public = 0x00000001,
  NestedPublic = 0x00000002,
  NestedPrivate = 0x00000003,
  NestedFamily = 0x00000004,
  NestedAssembly = 0x00000005,
  NestedFamANDAssem = 0x00000006,
  VisibilityMask = 0x00000007,
  NestedFamORAssem = 0x00000007,
  SequentialLayout = 0x00000008,
  ExplicitLayout = 0x00000010,
  LayoutMask = 0x00000018,
  Interface = 0x00000020,
  ClassSemanticsMask = 0x00000020,
  Abstract = 0x00000080,
  Sealed = 0x00000100,
  SpecialName = 0x00000400,
  RTSpecialName = 0x00000800,
  Import = 0x00001000,
  Serializable = 0x00002000,
  UnicodeClass = 0x00010000,
  AutoClass = 0x00020000,
  StringFormatMask = 0x00030000,
  HasSecurity = 0x00040000,
  ReservedMask = 0x00040800,
  BeforeFieldInit = 0x00100000
}
```

Hierarchy   System.Object → System.ValueType → System.Enum(System.IComparable,
                   System.IFormattable, System.IConvertible) → TypeAttributes

Returned By   System.Type.{Attributes, GetAttributeFlagsImpl( )}

Passed To   System.Reflection.Emit.ModuleBuilder.{DefineEnum( ), DefineType( )},
                   System.Reflection.Emit.TypeBuilder.DefineNestedType( )

System.
Reflection

Because System.Type is an abstract class, TypeDelegator simply wraps System.Type methods and provides the necessary implementations.

```
public class TypeDelegator : Type {
// Public Constructors
   public TypeDelegator(Type delegatingType);
// Protected Constructors
   protected TypeDelegator( );
// Protected Instance Fields
   protected Type typeImpl;
// Public Instance Properties
   public override Assembly Assembly{get; }                                    // overrides Type
   public override string AssemblyQualifiedName{get; }                         // overrides Type
   public override Type BaseType{get; }                                        // overrides Type
   public override string FullName{get; }                                      // overrides Type
   public override Guid GUID{get; }                                            // overrides Type
   public override Module Module{get; }                                        // overrides Type
   public override string Name{get; }                                          // overrides MemberInfo
   public override string Namespace{get; }                                     // overrides Type
   public override RuntimeTypeHandle TypeHandle{get; }                         // overrides Type
   public override Type UnderlyingSystemType{get; }                            // overrides Type
// Public Instance Methods
   public override ConstructorInfo[ ] GetConstructors(BindingFlags bindingAttr);      // overrides Type
   public override object[ ] GetCustomAttributes(bool inherit);                // overrides MemberInfo
   public override object[ ] GetCustomAttributes(Type attributeType, bool inherit);   // overrides MemberInfo
   public override Type GetElementType( );                                     // overrides Type
   public override EventInfo GetEvent(string name, BindingFlags bindingAttr);   // overrides Type
   public override EventInfo[ ] GetEvents( );                                  // overrides Type
   public override EventInfo[ ] GetEvents(BindingFlags bindingAttr);           // overrides Type
   public override FieldInfo GetField(string name, BindingFlags bindingAttr);   // overrides Type
   public override FieldInfo[ ] GetFields(BindingFlags bindingAttr);           // overrides Type
   public override Type GetInterface(string name, bool ignoreCase);            // overrides Type
   public override InterfaceMapping GetInterfaceMap(Type interfaceType);       // overrides Type
   public override Type[ ] GetInterfaces( );                                   // overrides Type
   public override MemberInfo[ ] GetMember(string name, MemberTypes type, BindingFlags bindingAttr);   // overrides Type
   public override MemberInfo[ ] GetMembers(BindingFlags bindingAttr);         // overrides Type
   public override MethodInfo[ ] GetMethods(BindingFlags bindingAttr);         // overrides Type
   public override Type GetNestedType(string name, BindingFlags bindingAttr);   // overrides Type
   public override Type[ ] GetNestedTypes(BindingFlags bindingAttr);           // overrides Type
   public override PropertyInfo[ ] GetProperties(BindingFlags bindingAttr);    // overrides Type
   public override object InvokeMember(string name, BindingFlags invokeAttr,
      Binder binder, object target, object[ ] args, ParameterModifier[ ] modifiers,
      System.Globalization.CultureInfo culture, string[ ] namedParameters);    // overrides Type
   public override bool IsDefined(Type attributeType, bool inherit);           // overrides MemberInfo
// Protected Instance Methods
   protected override TypeAttributes GetAttributeFlagsImpl( );                 // overrides Type
   protected override ConstructorInfo GetConstructorImpl(BindingFlags bindingAttr, Binder binder,
      CallingConventions callConvention, Type[ ] types, ParameterModifier[ ] modifiers);   // overrides Type
```

```
    protected override MethodInfo GetMethodImpl(string name, BindingFlags bindingAttr,
        Binder binder, CallingConventions callConvention, Type[ ] types, ParameterModifier[ ] modifiers);    // overrides Type
    protected override PropertyInfo GetPropertyImpl(string name, BindingFlags bindingAttr,
        Binder binder, Type returnType, Type[ ] types, ParameterModifier[ ] modifiers);                       // overrides Type
    protected override bool HasElementTypeImpl( );                                                             // overrides Type
    protected override bool IsArrayImpl( );                                                                    // overrides Type
    protected override bool IsByRefImpl( );                                                                    // overrides Type
    protected override bool IsCOMObjectImpl( );                                                                // overrides Type
    protected override bool IsPointerImpl( );                                                                  // overrides Type
    protected override bool IsPrimitiveImpl( );                                                                // overrides Type
    protected override bool IsValueTypeImpl( );                                                                // overrides Type
}
```

Hierarchy   System.Object → MemberInfo(ICustomAttributeProvider) → System.Type(IReflect) →
                 TypeDelegator

TypeFilter   serializable

System.Reflection (mscorlib.dll)   delegate

This delegate maps to a function that will be applied individually to a list of System.Type
objects. A filter runs through the list, and if this delegate returns true, the filtered list
includes this object; otherwise it is excluded.

public delegate bool **TypeFilter**(Type m, object filterCriteria);

Passed To   Module.FindTypes( ), System.Type.FindInterfaces( )

36

System.Reflection.Emit

There are several ways to use reflection in .NET. Reflection can be used for runtime-type inspection and late-bound object creation using the types in the System.Reflection namespace. Reflection can also be used for dynamic code creation, which is supported by the types in this namespace, System.Reflection.Emit. Dynamic code creation means a programmer can programmatically create code constructs such as methods and events from within code, using the appropriate corresponding type (for example, MethodBuilder and EventBuilder). These code elements are all ingredients that can be added to a dynamic assembly, represented by an AssemblyBuilder object. Dynamic assemblies can be saved to disk as PE (Portable Executable) files, typically in DLL form. Or, alternatively, emit it directly to memory for immediate use, at the expense of persistence (memory-only types disappear when the containing AppDomain terminates).

The ILGenerator class allows you to emit the MSIL (Microsoft Intermediate Language) for your code, using the corresponding GetILGenerator() method from a *builder* class. This process (sometimes known as "baking") allows you to convert the information in the builder object into a legitimate .NET type. You can then instantiate this newly created type on the spot.

The primary use of the System.Reflection.Emit namespace is to create compilers and script hosts, although many other uses are possible, including programs that dynamically create code that is fine-tuned to process a specific regular expression (see System.Text.RegularExpressions.Regex.CompileToAssembly()). When creating dynamic types, you generally begin by creating an AssemblyBuilder, which contains one or more ModuleBuilder objects. This in turn contains TypeBuilder instances. TypeBuilder objects contain most of the other ingredients in this namespace, including classes for building events, properties, methods, and enumerations.

Many of the builder classes in this namespace use similar methods and properties for retrieving information about the containing module (for example, ConstructorBuilder.GetModule()), getting an internal handle to the metadata (for example, EnumBuilder.TypeHandle()), and retrieving attributes (MethodBuilder.Attributes). Also note that though the builder classes derive from the corresponding "-Info" class (for example, MethodBuilder derives from System.Reflection.MethodInfo), not all of the inherited properties are currently supported. This includes methods such as Invoke( ). To use these methods, you may need to reflect on the object with System.Type.GetType( ). Figure 36-1 shows the types in this namespace.

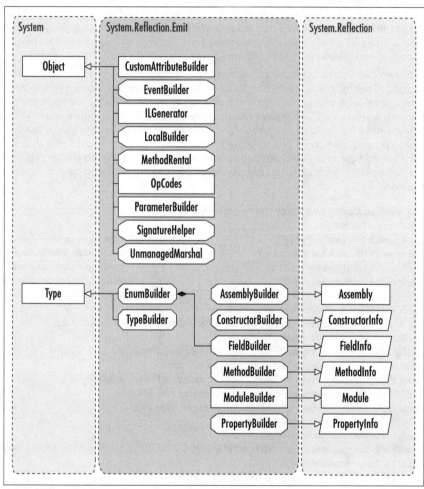

Figure 36-1. The System.Reflection.Emit namespace

AssemblyBuilder

System.Reflection.Emit (mscorlib.dll)   sealed class

This class represents a dynamic assembly. A dynamic assembly is the root container for all the builder objects in the System.Reflection.Emit namespace. You can create an AssemblyBuilder object by using the DefineDynamicAssembly( ) method of the System.AppDomain class. When you create a dynamic assembly, specify a name and the access mode, using the AssemblyBuilderAccess enumeration. If you plan to save the assembly to disk using the the Save() method, be sure to specify AssemblyBuilderAccess.Save or AssemblyBuilderAccess. RunAndSave.

A dynamic assembly can contain one or more modules, which are defined by Module-Builder objects. Use the DefineDynamicModule() method to define, create, and return a ModuleBuilder object, as in ModuleBuilder myModB = myAssemblyB.DefineDynamicModule("ModuleName");. By default, this is a transient module that cannot be saved, regardless of the Assembly-BuilderAccess specified. To create a module that can be saved to disk, use a version of the overloaded DefineDynamicModule() that requires a fileName argument. You can also use other methods to add an attribute to the assembly, add or create managed and unmanaged resources, and retrieve a System.IO.FileStream object for any of the files in the assembly.

When you are finished creating an assembly and all its members, you can use the Save() method. This method takes a simple filename as a parameter, which can't include directory or drive information. To use a different directory or drive, you must specify the path when you create the dynamic assembly by using the appropriate constructor. When you save a dynamic assembly, all nontransient modules are saved using the file-name specified when you created them. By default, the assembly is saved as a DLL file (as if you had used the /target:library command-line compiler switch). To change this, use the SetEntryPoint() method to specify the assembly's startup method and to specify PEFileKinds.

```
public sealed class AssemblyBuilder : System.Reflection.Assembly {
// Public Instance Properties
   public override string CodeBase{get; }                          // overrides System.Reflection.Assembly
   public override MethodInfo EntryPoint{get; }                    // overrides System.Reflection.Assembly
   public override string ImageRuntimeVersion{get; }              // overrides System.Reflection.Assembly
   public override string Location{get; }                          // overrides System.Reflection.Assembly
// Public Instance Methods
   public void AddResourceFile(string name, string fileName);
   public void AddResourceFile(string name, string fileName, System.Reflection.ResourceAttributes attribute);
   public ModuleBuilder DefineDynamicModule(string name);
   public ModuleBuilder DefineDynamicModule(string name, bool emitSymbolInfo);
   public ModuleBuilder DefineDynamicModule(string name, string fileName);
   public ModuleBuilder DefineDynamicModule(string name, string fileName, bool emitSymbolInfo);
   public IResourceWriter DefineResource(string name, string description, string fileName);
   public IResourceWriter DefineResource(string name, string description, string fileName,
      System.Reflection.ResourceAttributes attribute);
   public void DefineUnmanagedResource(byte[ ] resource);
   public void DefineUnmanagedResource(string resourceFileName);
   public void DefineVersionInfoResource( );
   public void DefineVersionInfoResource(string product, string productVersion, string company,
      string copyright, string trademark);
   public ModuleBuilder GetDynamicModule(string name);
   public override Type[ ] GetExportedTypes( );                    // overrides System.Reflection.Assembly
   public override FileStream GetFile(string name);               // overrides System.Reflection.Assembly
   public override FileStream[ ] GetFiles(bool getResourceModules); // overrides System.Reflection.Assembly
   public override ManifestResourceInfo GetManifestResourceInfo(string resourceName);
                                                                    // overrides System.Reflection.Assembly
   public override string[ ] GetManifestResourceNames( );          // overrides System.Reflection.Assembly
   public override Stream GetManifestResourceStream(string name);  // overrides System.Reflection.Assembly
   public override Stream GetManifestResourceStream(Type type, string name); // overrides System.Reflection.Assembly
   public void Save(string assemblyFileName);
```

```
    public void SetCustomAttribute(System.Reflection.ConstructorInfo con, byte[ ] binaryAttribute);
    public void SetCustomAttribute(CustomAttributeBuilder customBuilder);
    public void SetEntryPoint(System.Reflection.MethodInfo entryMethod);
    public void SetEntryPoint(System.Reflection.MethodInfo entryMethod, PEFileKinds fileKind);
}
```

Hierarchy   System.Object → System.Reflection.Assembly(System.Security.IEvidenceFactory,
                 System.Reflection.ICustomAttributeProvider, System.Runtime.Serialization.ISerializable) →
                 AssemblyBuilder

Returned By System.AppDomain.DefineDynamicAssembly( )

AssemblyBuilderAccess   serializable, flag

System.Reflection.Emit (mscorlib.dll)   enum

This enumeration is used by the System.AppDomain.DefineDynamicAssembly( ) method. It specifies whether a dynamic assembly will support dynamic execution only (Run), save to
disk only (Save), or both (RunAndSave).

```
public enum AssemblyBuilderAccess {
    Run = 0x00000001,
    Save = 0x00000002,
    RunAndSave = 0x00000003
}
```

Hierarchy   System.Object → System.ValueType → System.Enum(System.IComparable,
                 System.IFormattable, System.IConvertible) → AssemblyBuilderAccess

Passed To   System.AppDomain.DefineDynamicAssembly( )

ConstructorBuilder

System.Reflection.Emit (mscorlib.dll)   sealed class

This class represents a dynamically created constructor method. Create a constructor
and add it to a type using either the TypeBuilder.DefineConstructor( ) method or the TypeBuilder.
DefineDefaultConstructor( ) method. The default constructor accepts no parameters, and just
calls the constructor of the parent class. You cannot use the ILGenerator class with a
default constructor, because its code is provided by the runtime. Generally, a default
constructor does not need to be created, as the CLR provides it for you.

If you create a custom constructor with TypeBuilder.DefineConstructor( ), you can specify the
constructor's parameters as an array of System.Type objects. Alternatively, you can use
the DefineParameter( ) method to create a ParameterBuilder. You can also add MSIL code to
the constructor using the GetILGenerator( ) method.

```
public sealed class ConstructorBuilder : System.Reflection.ConstructorInfo {
// Public Instance Properties
    public override MethodAttributes Attributes{get; }              // overrides System.Reflection.MethodBase
    public override Type DeclaringType{get; }                       // overrides System.Reflection.MemberInfo
    public bool InitLocals{set; get; }
    public override RuntimeMethodHandle MethodHandle{get; }         // overrides System.Reflection.MethodBase
    public override string Name{get; }                              // overrides System.Reflection.MemberInfo
    public override Type ReflectedType{get; }                       // overrides System.Reflection.MemberInfo
```

```
public Type ReturnType{get; }
public string Signature{get; }
// Public Instance Methods
public void AddDeclarativeSecurity(System.Security.Permissions.SecurityAction action,
    System.Security.PermissionSet pset);
public ParameterBuilder DefineParameter(int iSequence,
    System.Reflection.ParameterAttributes attributes, string strParamName);
public override object[ ] GetCustomAttributes(bool inherit);                          // overrides System.Reflection.MemberInfo
public override object[ ] GetCustomAttributes(Type attributeType, bool inherit);      // overrides System.Reflection.MemberInfo
public ILGenerator GetILGenerator( );
public override MethodImplAttributes GetMethodImplementationFlags( );                 // overrides System.Reflection.MethodBase
public Module GetModule( );
public override ParameterInfo[ ] GetParameters( );                                   // overrides System.Reflection.MethodBase
public MethodToken GetToken( );
public override object Invoke(System.Reflection.BindingFlags invokeAttr, System.Reflection.Binder binder,
    object[ ] parameters, System.Globalization.CultureInfo culture);                 // overrides System.Reflection.ConstructorInfo
public override object Invoke(object obj, System.Reflection.BindingFlags invokeAttr, System.Reflection.Binder binder,
    object[ ] parameters, System.Globalization.CultureInfo culture);                 // overrides System.Reflection.MethodBase
public override bool IsDefined(Type attributeType, bool inherit);                     // overrides System.Reflection.MemberInfo
public void SetCustomAttribute(System.Reflection.ConstructorInfo con, byte[ ] binaryAttribute);
public void SetCustomAttribute(CustomAttributeBuilder customBuilder);
public void SetImplementationFlags(System.Reflection.MethodImplAttributes attributes);
public void SetSymCustomAttribute(string name, byte[ ] data);
public override string ToString( );                                                  // overrides object
}
```

Hierarchy	System.Object → System.Reflection.MemberInfo(System.Reflection.ICustomAttributeProvider) → System.Reflection.MethodBase → System.Reflection.ConstructorInfo → ConstructorBuilder
Returned By	TypeBuilder.{DefineConstructor( ), DefineDefaultConstructor( ), DefineTypeInitializer( )}

CustomAttributeBuilder

System.Reflection.Emit (mscorlib.dll)   class

This class represents a dynamically created custom attribute. To apply a custom attribute, pass an instance of this type to the SetCustomAttribute( ) method for the appropriate builder (PropertyBuilder.SetCustomAttribute( ) or MethodBuilder.SetCustomAttribute( ),for example). The constructor allows you to specify the custom attribute's named properties and fields, their values, and a constructor.

```
public class CustomAttributeBuilder {
// Public Constructors
  public CustomAttributeBuilder(System.Reflection.ConstructorInfo con, object[ ] constructorArgs);
  public CustomAttributeBuilder(System.Reflection.ConstructorInfo con, object[ ] constructorArgs,
    System.Reflection.FieldInfo[ ] namedFields, object[ ] fieldValues);
  public CustomAttributeBuilder(System.Reflection.ConstructorInfo con, object[ ] constructorArgs,
    System.Reflection.PropertyInfo[ ] namedProperties, object[ ] propertyValues);
  public CustomAttributeBuilder(System.Reflection.ConstructorInfo con, object[ ] constructorArgs,
    System.Reflection.PropertyInfo[ ] namedProperties, object[ ] propertyValues,
    System.Reflection.FieldInfo[ ] namedFields, object[ ] fieldValues);
}
```

AssemblyBuilder.SetCustomAttribute( ), ConstructorBuilder.
SetCustomAttribute( ), EnumBuilder.SetCustomAttribute( ), EventBuilder.
SetCustomAttribute( ), FieldBuilder.SetCustomAttribute( ), MethodBuilder.
SetCustomAttribute( ), ModuleBuilder.SetCustomAttribute( ), ParameterBuilder.
SetCustomAttribute( ), PropertyBuilder.SetCustomAttribute( ), TypeBuilder.
SetCustomAttribute( ), System.Text.RegularExpressions.Regex.CompileToAssembly( )

EnumBuilder

System.Reflection.Emit (mscorlib.dll)   sealed class

This class represents a dynamically created enumeration. Enumerations are created at module scope using the ModuleBuilder.DefineEnum( ) method. Before using a dynamically created enumeration, you must use the CreateType( ) method to complete it.

```
public sealed class EnumBuilder : Type {
// Public Instance Properties
  public override Assembly Assembly{get; }                                       // overrides Type
  public override string AssemblyQualifiedName{get; }                           // overrides Type
  public override Type BaseType{get; }                                          // overrides Type
  public override Type DeclaringType{get; }                                     // overrides Type
  public override string FullName{get; }                                        // overrides Type
  public override Guid GUID{get; }                                              // overrides Type
  public override Module Module{get; }                                          // overrides Type
  public override string Name{get; }                          // overrides System.Reflection.MemberInfo
  public override string Namespace{get; }                                       // overrides Type
  public override Type ReflectedType{get; }                                     // overrides Type
  public override RuntimeTypeHandle TypeHandle{get; }                           // overrides Type
  public TypeToken TypeToken{get; }
  public FieldBuilder UnderlyingField{get; }
  public override Type UnderlyingSystemType{get; }                              // overrides Type
// Public Instance Methods
  public Type CreateType( );
  public FieldBuilder DefineLiteral(string literalName, object literalValue);
  public override ConstructorInfo[ ] GetConstructors(System.Reflection.BindingFlags bindingAttr);    // overrides Type
  public override object[ ] GetCustomAttributes(bool inherit);              // overrides System.Reflection.MemberInfo
  public override object[ ] GetCustomAttributes(Type attributeType, bool inherit);  // overrides System.Reflection.MemberInfo
  public override Type GetElementType( );                                       // overrides Type
  public override EventInfo GetEvent(string name, System.Reflection.BindingFlags bindingAttr);    // overrides Type
  public override EventInfo[ ] GetEvents( );                                    // overrides Type
  public override EventInfo[ ] GetEvents(System.Reflection.BindingFlags bindingAttr);    // overrides Type
  public override FieldInfo GetField(string name, System.Reflection.BindingFlags bindingAttr);    // overrides Type
  public override FieldInfo[ ] GetFields(System.Reflection.BindingFlags bindingAttr);    // overrides Type
  public override Type GetInterface(string name, bool ignoreCase);              // overrides Type
  public override InterfaceMapping GetInterfaceMap(Type interfaceType);         // overrides Type
  public override Type[ ] GetInterfaces( );                                     // overrides Type
  public override MemberInfo[ ] GetMember(string name, System.Reflection.MemberTypes type,
    System.Reflection.BindingFlags bindingAttr);                               // overrides Type
  public override MemberInfo[ ] GetMembers(System.Reflection.BindingFlags bindingAttr);    // overrides Type
  public override MethodInfo[ ] GetMethods(System.Reflection.BindingFlags bindingAttr);    // overrides Type
  public override Type GetNestedType(string name, System.Reflection.BindingFlags bindingAttr);    // overrides Type
```

```
public override Type[ ] GetNestedTypes(System.Reflection.BindingFlags bindingAttr);                    // overrides Type
public override PropertyInfo[ ] GetProperties(System.Reflection.BindingFlags bindingAttr);             // overrides Type
public override object InvokeMember(string name, System.Reflection.BindingFlags invokeAttr,
    System.Reflection.Binder binder, object target, object[ ] args, System.Reflection.ParameterModifier[ ] modifiers,
    System.Globalization.CultureInfo culture, string[ ] namedParameters);                              // overrides Type
public override bool IsDefined(Type attributeType, bool inherit);            // overrides System.Reflection.MemberInfo
public void SetCustomAttribute(System.Reflection.ConstructorInfo con, byte[ ] binaryAttribute);
public void SetCustomAttribute(CustomAttributeBuilder customBuilder);
// Protected Instance Methods
protected override TypeAttributes GetAttributeFlagsImpl( );                                            // overrides Type
protected override ConstructorInfo GetConstructorImpl(System.Reflection.BindingFlags bindingAttr,
    System.Reflection.Binder binder, System.Reflection.CallingConventions callConvention,
    Type[ ] types, System.Reflection.ParameterModifier[ ] modifiers);                                  // overrides Type
protected override MethodInfo GetMethodImpl(string name, System.Reflection.BindingFlags bindingAttr,
    System.Reflection.Binder binder, System.Reflection.CallingConventions callConvention, Type[ ] types,
    System.Reflection.ParameterModifier[ ] modifiers);                                                 // overrides Type
protected override PropertyInfo GetPropertyImpl(string name,
    System.Reflection.BindingFlags bindingAttr,
    System.Reflection.Binder binder, Type returnType, Type[ ] types,
    System.Reflection.ParameterModifier[ ] modifiers);                                                 // overrides Type
protected override bool HasElementTypeImpl( );                                                         // overrides Type
protected override bool IsArrayImpl( );                                                                // overrides Type
protected override bool IsByRefImpl( );                                                                // overrides Type
protected override bool IsCOMObjectImpl( );                                                            // overrides Type
protected override bool IsPointerImpl( );                                                              // overrides Type
protected override bool IsPrimitiveImpl( );                                                            // overrides Type
protected override bool IsValueTypeImpl( );                                                            // overrides Type
}
```

Hierarchy System.Object → System.Reflection.MemberInfo(System.Reflection.
ICustomAttributeProvider) → System.Type(System.Reflection.IReflect) → EnumBuilder

Returned By ModuleBuilder.DefineEnum( )

EventBuilder

System.Reflection.Emit (mscorlib.dll)   sealed class

This class represents a dynamically created event. Events are created with the TypeBuilder.
DefineEvent( ) method. You can then attach a MethodBuilder object to represent one of three
methods: the method used to raise the event (SetRaiseMethod( )), the method used to
subscribe to the event (SetAddOnMethod( )), and the method used to unsubscribe
(SetRemoveOnMethod( )).

```
public sealed class EventBuilder {
// Public Instance Methods
public void AddOtherMethod(MethodBuilder mdBuilder);
public EventToken GetEventToken( );
public void SetAddOnMethod(MethodBuilder mdBuilder);
public void SetCustomAttribute(System.Reflection.ConstructorInfo con, byte[ ] binaryAttribute);
```

```
public void SetCustomAttribute(CustomAttributeBuilder customBuilder);
public void SetRaiseMethod(MethodBuilder mdBuilder);
public void SetRemoveOnMethod(MethodBuilder mdBuilder);
}
```

Returned By   TypeBuilder.DefineEvent( )

EventToken   serializable

System.Reflection.Emit (mscorlib.dll)   struct

This class represents the token for an event. A token is a 4-byte number that points to
the metadata description of a program element in MSIL. The first byte in the token
identifies the metadata table, which depends on the type of program element. The
remaining 3 bytes specify the row in the metadata table. For example, the token
0x06000004 specifies that the corresponding metadata is stored in the fourth row of
table 0x06 (the MethodDef table).

```
public struct EventToken {
// Public Static Fields
  public static readonly EventToken Empty;                        // =System.Reflection.Emit.EventToken
// Public Instance Properties
  public int Token{get; }
// Public Instance Methods
  public override bool Equals(object obj);                                  // overrides ValueType
  public override int GetHashCode( );                                      // overrides ValueType
}
```

Hierarchy   System.Object → System.ValueType → EventToken

Returned By   EventBuilder.GetEventToken( )

FieldBuilder

System.Reflection.Emit (mscorlib.dll)   sealed class

This class represents a dynamically created field. Fields are created with the TypeBuilder.
DefineField( ) method, which allows you to specify the field's characteristics using the
System.Reflection.FieldAttributes enumeration. The TypeBuilder.DefineField( ) method also determines the name and type of the field. Fields must be a simple data type such as a string
or integer. Use SetConstant( ) to set the default value of the field.

```
public sealed class FieldBuilder : System.Reflection.FieldInfo {
// Public Instance Properties
  public override FieldAttributes Attributes{get; }              // overrides System.Reflection.FieldInfo
  public override Type DeclaringType{get; }                      // overrides System.Reflection.MemberInfo
  public override RuntimeFieldHandle FieldHandle{get; }          // overrides System.Reflection.FieldInfo
  public override Type FieldType{get; }                          // overrides System.Reflection.FieldInfo
  public override string Name{get; }                             // overrides System.Reflection.MemberInfo
  public override Type ReflectedType{get; }                      // overrides System.Reflection.MemberInfo
// Public Instance Methods
  public override object[ ] GetCustomAttributes(bool inherit);   // overrides System.Reflection.MemberInfo
  public override object[ ] GetCustomAttributes(Type attributeType, bool inherit); // overrides System.Reflection.MemberInfo
```

```
public FieldToken GetToken( );
public override object GetValue(object obj);                              // overrides System.Reflection.FieldInfo
public override bool IsDefined(Type attributeType, bool inherit);         // overrides System.Reflection.MemberInfo
public void SetConstant(object defaultValue);
public void SetCustomAttribute(System.Reflection.ConstructorInfo con, byte[ ] binaryAttribute);
public void SetCustomAttribute(CustomAttributeBuilder customBuilder);
public void SetMarshal(UnmanagedMarshal unmanagedMarshal);
public void SetOffset(int iOffset);
public override void SetValue(object obj, object val, System.Reflection.BindingFlags invokeAttr,
    System.Reflection.Binder binder, System.Globalization.CultureInfo culture);    // overrides System.Reflection.FieldInfo
}
```

Hierarchy	System.Object → System.Reflection.MemberInfo(System.Reflection. ICustomAttributeProvider) → System.Reflection.FieldInfo → FieldBuilder

Returned By	EnumBuilder.{DefineLiteral( ), UnderlyingField}, ModuleBuilder.{DefineInitializedData( ), DefineUninitializedData( )}, TypeBuilder.{DefineField( ), DefineInitializedData( ), DefineUninitializedData( )}

FieldToken   serializable

System.Reflection.Emit (mscorlib.dll)   struct

This class represents the token for a field. See EventToken for more details on tokens.

```
public struct FieldToken {
// Public Static Fields
  public static readonly FieldToken Empty;                    // =System.Reflection.Emit.FieldToken
// Public Instance Properties
  public int Token{get; }
// Public Instance Methods
  public override bool Equals(object obj);                     // overrides ValueType
  public override int GetHashCode( );                         // overrides ValueType
}
```

Hierarchy	System.Object → System.ValueType → FieldToken

Returned By	FieldBuilder.GetToken( ), ModuleBuilder.GetFieldToken( )

FlowControl   serializable

System.Reflection.Emit (mscorlib.dll)   enum

This enumeration is used by the OpCode.FlowControl property. It describes how the instruction alters the flow of control. Next indicates a normal flow of control, while Cond_Branch indicates a conditional branch instruction. The Meta value provides information about a subsequent instruction.

```
public enum FlowControl {
  Branch = 0,
  Break = 1,
  Call = 2,
  Cond_Branch = 3,
```

```
  Meta = 4,
  Next = 5,
  Phi = 6,
  Return = 7,
  Throw = 8
}
```

Hierarchy   System.Object → System.ValueType → System.Enum(System.IComparable,
                   System.IFormattable, System.IConvertible) → FlowControl

Returned By   OpCode.FlowControl

ILGenerator

System.Reflection.Emit (mscorlib.dll)   class

This class generates MSIL (Microsoft Intermediate Language) instructions. You receive
an ILGenerator object from a GetILGenerator method in a builder class. For example, you can
use the ConstructorBuilder.GetILGenerator() to create MSIL instructions for a constructor, or
MethodBuilder.GetILGenerator() to create MSIL instructions for a method. Use BeginScope() and
EndScope() to start and stop a lexical scope.

To emit instructions, use the Emit() method. The Emit() method requires an OpCode
object. The easiest way to supply this is by using one of the constant fields from
OpCodes, as in myGenerator.Emit(OpCodes.Ret);. EmitWriteLine() creates the MSIL code required to
call System.Console.WriteLine() with the supplied variable. You can also define and mark
labels in the instruction stream (DefineLabel() and MarkLabel()), emit an instruction for
throwing an exception (ThrowException()), and define local variables (DeclareLocal()).

Emit error handling blocks with BeginExceptionBlock() and EndExceptionBlock() (which emits
the equivalent of a C# try statement), BeginCatchBlock() (which emits the equivalent of the
catch statement), and BeginFinallyBlock() (which emits the equivalent of the finally statement). You must end the exception block using EndExceptionBlock().

```
public class ILGenerator {
// Public Instance Methods
  public virtual void BeginCatchBlock(Type exceptionType);
  public virtual void BeginExceptFilterBlock( );
  public virtual Label BeginExceptionBlock( );
  public virtual void BeginFaultBlock( );
  public virtual void BeginFinallyBlock( );
  public virtual void BeginScope( );
  public LocalBuilder DeclareLocal(Type localType);
  public virtual Label DefineLabel( );
  public virtual void Emit(OpCode opcode);
  public virtual void Emit(OpCode opcode, byte arg);
  public virtual void Emit(OpCode opcode, System.Reflection.ConstructorInfo con);
  public virtual void Emit(OpCode opcode, double arg);
  public virtual void Emit(OpCode opcode, System.Reflection.FieldInfo field);
  public virtual void Emit(OpCode opcode, short arg);
  public virtual void Emit(OpCode opcode, int arg);
  public virtual void Emit(OpCode opcode, long arg);
  public virtual void Emit(OpCode opcode, Label label);
```

```
public virtual void Emit(OpCode opcode, Label[ ] labels);
public virtual void Emit(OpCode opcode, LocalBuilder local);
public virtual void Emit(OpCode opcode, System.Reflection.MethodInfo meth);
public void Emit(OpCode opcode, sbyte arg);
public virtual void Emit(OpCode opcode, SignatureHelper signature);
public virtual void Emit(OpCode opcode, float arg);
public virtual void Emit(OpCode opcode, string str);
public virtual void Emit(OpCode opcode, Type cls);
public void EmitCall(OpCode opcode, System.Reflection.MethodInfo methodInfo, Type[ ] optionalParameterTypes);
public void EmitCalli(OpCode opcode, System.Reflection.CallingConventions callingConvention, Type returnType,
    Type[ ] parameterTypes, Type[ ] optionalParameterTypes);
public void EmitCalli(OpCode opcode, System.Runtime.InteropServices.CallingConvention unmanagedCallConv,
    Type returnType, Type[ ] parameterTypes);
public virtual void EmitWriteLine(System.Reflection.FieldInfo fld);
public virtual void EmitWriteLine(LocalBuilder localBuilder);
public virtual void EmitWriteLine(string value);
public virtual void EndExceptionBlock( );
public virtual void EndScope( );
public virtual void MarkLabel(Label loc);
public virtual void MarkSequencePoint(System.Diagnostics.SymbolStore.ISymbolDocumentWriter document,
    int startLine, int startColumn, int endLine, int endColumn);
public virtual void ThrowException(Type excType);
public void UsingNamespace(string usingNamespace);
}
```

Returned By   ConstructorBuilder.GetILGenerator( ), MethodBuilder.GetILGenerator( )

Label   serializable

System.Reflection.Emit (mscorlib.dll)   struct

This class represents a label in the MSIL instruction stream. You can create a label
with ILGenerator.DefineLabel( ) and place it in the stream with ILGenerator.MarkLabel( ).

```
public struct Label {
// Public Instance Methods
  public override bool Equals(object obj);                      // overrides ValueType
  public override int GetHashCode( );                          // overrides ValueType
}
```

Hierarchy   System.Object → System.ValueType → Label

Returned By   ILGenerator.{BeginExceptionBlock( ), DefineLabel( )}

Passed To   ILGenerator.{Emit( ), MarkLabel( )}

LocalBuilder

System.Reflection.Emit (mscorlib.dll)   sealed class

This class represents a dynamically created local variable. Local variables are created
for methods and constructors through the ILGenerator object, using the ILGenerator.
DeclareLocal( ).

```
public sealed class LocalBuilder {
// Public Instance Properties
  public Type LocalType{get; }
// Public Instance Methods
  public void SetLocalSymInfo(string name);
  public void SetLocalSymInfo(string name, int startOffset, int endOffset);
}
```

Returned By   ILGenerator.DeclareLocal( )

Passed To   ILGenerator.{Emit( ), EmitWriteLine( )}

MethodBuilder

System.Reflection.Emit (mscorlib.dll)   sealed class

This class represents a dynamically created method. Methods are created with **Type-Builder.DefineMethod( )**. When creating a method, specify the name, parameters, and return type. You can also specify other characteristics of the method, such as whether it is static, abstract, or virtual, by using the **System.Reflection.MethodAttributes** enumeration. After creating a method, you can specify how the return value will be marshaled to unmanaged code using **SetMarshal( )**, and add declarative security using **AddDeclarativeSecurity( )**. You must specify the security action (such as Demand, Assert, Deny) using the **System.Security.Permissions.SecurityAction** enumeration and the permissions required using the **System.Security.PermissionSet** collection class. You can call **AddDeclarativeSecurity( )** several times to specify different security actions.

To create a global method builder, use **ModuleBuilder.DefineGlobalMethod( )**. You must also use **ModuleBuilder.CreateGlobalFunctions( )** to finish creating global methods before you persist or use the dynamic module. Global methods must be static. You can also create a global native method using **ModuleBuilder.DefinePInvokeMethod( )**. PInvoke methods cannot be abstract or virtual.

```
public sealed class MethodBuilder : System.Reflection.MethodInfo {
// Public Instance Properties
  public override MethodAttributes Attributes{get; }                                    // overrides System.Reflection.MethodBase
  public override CallingConventions CallingConvention{get; }                           // overrides System.Reflection.MethodBase
  public override Type DeclaringType{get; }                                             // overrides System.Reflection.MemberInfo
  public bool InitLocals{set; get; }
  public override RuntimeMethodHandle MethodHandle{get; }                               // overrides System.Reflection.MethodBase
  public override string Name{get; }                                                    // overrides System.Reflection.MemberInfo
  public override Type ReflectedType{get; }                                             // overrides System.Reflection.MemberInfo
  public override Type ReturnType{get; }                                                // overrides System.Reflection.MethodInfo
  public override ICustomAttributeProvider ReturnTypeCustomAttributes{get; }   // overrides System.Reflection.MethodInfo
  public string Signature{get; }
// Public Instance Methods
  public void AddDeclarativeSecurity(System.Security.Permissions.SecurityAction action,
      System.Security.PermissionSet pset);
  public void CreateMethodBody(byte[ ] il, int count);
  public ParameterBuilder DefineParameter(int position, System.Reflection.ParameterAttributes attributes,
      string strParamName);
  public override bool Equals(object obj);                                              // overrides object
  public override MethodInfo GetBaseDefinition( );                                      // overrides System.Reflection.MethodInfo
```

```
public override object[ ] GetCustomAttributes(bool inherit);              // overrides System.Reflection.MemberInfo
public override object[ ] GetCustomAttributes(Type attributeType,bool inherit);  // overrides System.Reflection.MemberInfo
public override int GetHashCode( );                                        // overrides object
public ILGenerator GetILGenerator( );
public ILGenerator GetILGenerator(int size);
public override MethodImplAttributes GetMethodImplementationFlags( );      // overrides System.Reflection.MethodBase
public Module GetModule( );
public override ParameterInfo[ ] GetParameters( );                         // overrides System.Reflection.MethodBase
public MethodToken GetToken( );
public override object Invoke(object obj, System.Reflection.BindingFlags invokeAttr, System.Reflection.Binder binder,
     object[ ] parameters, System.Globalization.CultureInfo culture);
                                                                           // overrides System.Reflection.MethodBase
public override bool IsDefined(Type attributeType, bool inherit);          // overrides System.Reflection.MemberInfo
public void SetCustomAttribute(System.Reflection.ConstructorInfo con, byte[ ] binaryAttribute);
public void SetCustomAttribute(CustomAttributeBuilder customBuilder);
public void SetImplementationFlags(System.Reflection.MethodImplAttributes attributes);
public void SetMarshal(UnmanagedMarshal unmanagedMarshal);
public void SetSymCustomAttribute(string name, byte[ ] data);
public override string ToString( );                                        // overrides object
}
```

Hierarchy	System.Object → System.Reflection.MemberInfo(System.Reflection. ICustomAttributeProvider) → System.Reflection.MethodBase → System.Reflection. MethodInfo → MethodBuilder
Returned By	ModuleBuilder.{DefineGlobalMethod( ), DefinePInvokeMethod( )}, TypeBuilder.{DefineMethod( ), DefinePInvokeMethod( )}
Passed To	EventBuilder.{AddOtherMethod( ), SetAddOnMethod( ), SetRaiseMethod( ), SetRemoveOnMethod( )}, PropertyBuilder.{AddOtherMethod( ), SetGetMethod( ), SetSetMethod( )}

MethodRental

System.Reflection.Emit (mscorlib.dll)   sealed class

This class can be used to swap a method "body" (the MSIL code inside the method).
To do this, use the static SwapMethodBody( ) method and specify the target Type, the token
of the method that should receive the new body, a pointer to the new method, the size
of the new method, and a flag specifying the type of compilation using the appropriate
field constant (either JitImmediate or JitOnDemand). The IntPtr to the new method body
should point to an array of bytes that contain the IL for the method's header and body.

```
public sealed class MethodRental {
// Public Static Fields
  public const int JitImmediate;                                           // =1
  public const int JitOnDemand;                                            // =0
// Public Static Methods
  public static void SwapMethodBody(Type cls, int methodtoken, IntPtr rgIL, int methodSize, int flags);
}
```

MethodToken

System.Reflection.Emit (mscorlib.dll)   struct

This class represents the token for a method. See EventToken for more details on tokens.

```
public struct MethodToken {
// Public Static Fields
  public static readonly MethodToken Empty;                        // =System.Reflection.Emit.MethodToken
// Public Instance Properties
  public int Token{get; }
// Public Instance Methods
  public override bool Equals(object obj);                                     // overrides ValueType
  public override int GetHashCode( );                                         // overrides ValueType
}
```

Hierarchy   System.Object → System.ValueType → MethodToken

Returned By   ConstructorBuilder.GetToken( ), MethodBuilder.GetToken( ), ModuleBuilder.
                    {GetArrayMethodToken( ), GetConstructorToken( ), GetMethodToken( )}

ModuleBuilder

System.Reflection.Emit (mscorlib.dll)   class

This class represents a dynamically created module inside a dynamic assembly.
Dynamic modules are created with the AssemblyBuilder.DefineDynamicModule( ) method. A
dynamic module can be either transient or persistable, which means you can save it to
disk as part of a PE file. To create a persistable module, use a version of the Assembly-
Builder.DefineDynamicModule( ) method that allows you to specify a filename.

You can use the methods that begin with Define to create types, managed and unmanaged resources, global methods, and PInvoke (global native) methods.

```
public class ModuleBuilder : System.Reflection.Module {
// Public Instance Properties
  public override string FullyQualifiedName{get; }                      // overrides System.Reflection.Module
// Public Instance Methods
  public void CreateGlobalFunctions( );
  public ISymbolDocumentWriter DefineDocument(string url, Guid language, Guid languageVendor,
    Guid documentType);
  public EnumBuilder DefineEnum(string name, System.Reflection.TypeAttributes visibility, Type underlyingType);
  public MethodBuilder DefineGlobalMethod(string name, System.Reflection.MethodAttributes attributes,
    System.Reflection.CallingConventions callingConvention,Type returnType, Type[ ] parameterTypes);
  public MethodBuilder DefineGlobalMethod(string name, System.Reflection.MethodAttributes attributes,
    Type returnType, Type[ ] parameterTypes);
  public FieldBuilder DefineInitializedData(string name, byte[ ] data, System.Reflection.FieldAttributes attributes);
  public MethodBuilder DefinePInvokeMethod(string name, string dllName,
    System.Reflection.MethodAttributes attributes, System.Reflection.CallingConventions callingConvention,Type returnType,
    Type[ ] parameterTypes, System.Runtime.InteropServices.CallingConvention nativeCallConv,
    System.Runtime.InteropServices.CharSet nativeCharSet);
  public MethodBuilder DefinePInvokeMethod(string name, string dllName, string entryName,
    System.Reflection.MethodAttributes attributes, System.Reflection.CallingConventions callingConvention,
    Type returnType, Type[ ] parameterTypes, System.Runtime.InteropServices.CallingConvention nativeCallConv,
    System.Runtime.InteropServices.CharSet nativeCharSet);
```

```
public IResourceWriter DefineResource(string name, string description);
public IResourceWriter DefineResource(string name, string description, System.Reflection.ResourceAttributes attribute);
public TypeBuilder DefineType(string name);
public TypeBuilder DefineType(string name, System.Reflection.TypeAttributes attr);
public TypeBuilder DefineType(string name, System.Reflection.TypeAttributes attr, Type parent);
public TypeBuilder DefineType(string name, System.Reflection.TypeAttributes attr, Type parent, int typesize);
public TypeBuilder DefineType(string name, System.Reflection.TypeAttributes attr, Type parent, PackingSize packsize);
public TypeBuilder DefineType(string name, System.Reflection.TypeAttributes attr, Type parent,
    PackingSize packingSize, int typesize);
public TypeBuilder DefineType(string name, System.Reflection.TypeAttributes attr, Type parent, Type[ ] interfaces);
public FieldBuilder DefineUninitializedData(string name, int size, System.Reflection.FieldAttributes attributes);
public void DefineUnmanagedResource(byte[ ] resource);
public void DefineUnmanagedResource(string resourceFileName);
public MethodInfo GetArrayMethod(Type arrayClass, string methodName,
    System.Reflection.CallingConventions callingConvention, Type returnType, Type[ ] parameterTypes);
public MethodToken GetArrayMethodToken(Type arrayClass, string methodName,
    System.Reflection.CallingConventions callingConvention,Type returnType, Type[ ] parameterTypes);
public MethodToken GetConstructorToken(System.Reflection.ConstructorInfo con);
public FieldToken GetFieldToken(System.Reflection.FieldInfo field);
public MethodToken GetMethodToken(System.Reflection.MethodInfo method);
public SignatureToken GetSignatureToken(byte[ ] sigBytes, int sigLength);
public SignatureToken GetSignatureToken(SignatureHelper sigHelper);
public StringToken GetStringConstant(string str);
public ISymbolWriter GetSymWriter( );
public override Type GetType(string className);                              // overrides System.Reflection.Module
public override Type GetType(string className, bool ignoreCase);             // overrides System.Reflection.Module
public override Type GetType(string className, bool throwOnError, bool ignoreCase); // overrides System.Reflection.Module
public override Type[ ] GetTypes( );                                         // overrides System.Reflection.Module
public TypeToken GetTypeToken(string name);
public TypeToken GetTypeToken(Type type);
public bool IsTransient( );
public void SetCustomAttribute(System.Reflection.ConstructorInfo con, byte[ ] binaryAttribute);
public void SetCustomAttribute(CustomAttributeBuilder customBuilder);
public void SetSymCustomAttribute(string name, byte[ ] data);
public void SetUserEntryPoint(System.Reflection.MethodInfo entryPoint);
}
```

Hierarchy   System.Object → System.Reflection.Module(System.Runtime.Serialization.ISerializable,
                 System.Reflection.ICustomAttributeProvider) → ModuleBuilder

Returned By AssemblyBuilder.{DefineDynamicModule( ), GetDynamicModule( )}

OpCode

System.Reflection.Emit (mscorlib.dll)   struct

This structure describes a single MSIL instruction. It is used by the ILGenerator.Emit( )
method. Alternatively, use a field from the OpCodes class to supply a specific instruction
without needing to create an OpCode object. Instructions are characterized by several
pieces of information, represented as properties, such as OpCode, Operand, and flow
control.

```
public struct OpCode {
// Public Instance Properties
  public FlowControl FlowControl{get; }
  public string Name{get; }
  public OpCodeType OpCodeType{get; }
  public OperandType OperandType{get; }
  public int Size{get; }
  public StackBehaviour StackBehaviourPop{get; }
  public StackBehaviour StackBehaviourPush{get; }
  public short Value{get; }
// Public Instance Methods
  public override bool Equals(object obj);                              // overrides ValueType
  public override int GetHashCode( );                                  // overrides ValueType
  public override string ToString( );                                  // overrides ValueType
}
```

Hierarchy   System.Object → System.ValueType → OpCode

Passed To   ILGenerator.{Emit( ), EmitCall( ), EmitCalli( )}, OpCodes.TakesSingleByteArgument( )

OpCodes

System.Reflection.Emit (mscorlib.dll)   class

This class provides the set of MSIL instructions through static fields. Each field returns the OpCode object that represents the corresponding instruction, and can be used in the ILGenerator.Emit( ) method. For a detailed description of these opcodes, see *Partition III, CIL* of the ECMA CLI specification (*http://msdn.microsoft.com/net/ecma/*).

```
public class OpCodes {
// Public Static Fields
  public static readonly OpCode Add;                                         // =add
  public static readonly OpCode Add_Ovf;                                     // =add.ovf
  public static readonly OpCode Add_Ovf_Un;                                  // =add.ovf.un
  public static readonly OpCode And;                                         // =and
  public static readonly OpCode Arglist;                                     // =arglist
  public static readonly OpCode Beq;                                         // =beq
  public static readonly OpCode Beq_S;                                       // =beq.s
  public static readonly OpCode Bge;                                         // =bge
  public static readonly OpCode Bge_S;                                       // =bge.s
  public static readonly OpCode Bge_Un;                                      // =bge.un
  public static readonly OpCode Bge_Un_S;                                    // =bge.un.s
  public static readonly OpCode Bgt;                                         // =bgt
  public static readonly OpCode Bgt_S;                                       // =bgt.s
  public static readonly OpCode Bgt_Un;                                      // =bgt.un
  public static readonly OpCode Bgt_Un_S;                                    // =bgt.un.s
  public static readonly OpCode Ble;                                         // =ble
  public static readonly OpCode Ble_S;                                       // =ble.s
  public static readonly OpCode Ble_Un;                                      // =ble.un
  public static readonly OpCode Ble_Un_S;                                    // =ble.un.s
  public static readonly OpCode Blt;                                         // =blt
  public static readonly OpCode Blt_S;                                       // =blt.s
```

System.Re-
flection.Emit

```csharp
public static readonly OpCode Blt_Un;                  // =blt.un
public static readonly OpCode Blt_Un_S;                // =blt.un.s
public static readonly OpCode Bne_Un;                  // =bne.un
public static readonly OpCode Bne_Un_S;                // =bne.un.s
public static readonly OpCode Box;                     // =box
public static readonly OpCode Br;                      // =br
public static readonly OpCode Br_S;                    // =br.s
public static readonly OpCode Break;                   // =break
public static readonly OpCode Brfalse;                 // =brfalse
public static readonly OpCode Brfalse_S;               // =brfalse.s
public static readonly OpCode Brtrue;                  // =brtrue
public static readonly OpCode Brtrue_S;                // =brtrue.s
public static readonly OpCode Call;                    // =call
public static readonly OpCode Calli;                   // =calli
public static readonly OpCode Callvirt;                // =callvirt
public static readonly OpCode Castclass;               // =castclass
public static readonly OpCode Ceq;                     // =ceq
public static readonly OpCode Cgt;                     // =cgt
public static readonly OpCode Cgt_Un;                  // =cgt.un
public static readonly OpCode Ckfinite;                // =ckfinite
public static readonly OpCode Clt;                     // =clt
public static readonly OpCode Clt_Un;                  // =clt.un
public static readonly OpCode Conv_I;                  // =conv.i
public static readonly OpCode Conv_I1;                 // =conv.i1
public static readonly OpCode Conv_I2;                 // =conv.i2
public static readonly OpCode Conv_I4;                 // =conv.i4
public static readonly OpCode Conv_I8;                 // =conv.i8
public static readonly OpCode Conv_Ovf_I;              // =conv.ovf.i
public static readonly OpCode Conv_Ovf_I_Un;           // =conv.ovf.i.un
public static readonly OpCode Conv_Ovf_I1;             // =conv.ovf.i1
public static readonly OpCode Conv_Ovf_I1_Un;          // =conv.ovf.i1.un
public static readonly OpCode Conv_Ovf_I2;             // =conv.ovf.i2
public static readonly OpCode Conv_Ovf_I2_Un;          // =conv.ovf.i2.un
public static readonly OpCode Conv_Ovf_I4;             // =conv.ovf.i4
public static readonly OpCode Conv_Ovf_I4_Un;          // =conv.ovf.i4.un
public static readonly OpCode Conv_Ovf_I8;             // =conv.ovf.i8
public static readonly OpCode Conv_Ovf_I8_Un;          // =conv.ovf.i8.un
public static readonly OpCode Conv_Ovf_U;              // =conv.ovf.u
public static readonly OpCode Conv_Ovf_U_Un;           // =conv.ovf.u.un
public static readonly OpCode Conv_Ovf_U1;             // =conv.ovf.u1
public static readonly OpCode Conv_Ovf_U1_Un;          // =conv.ovf.u1.un
public static readonly OpCode Conv_Ovf_U2;             // =conv.ovf.u2
public static readonly OpCode Conv_Ovf_U2_Un;          // =conv.ovf.u2.un
public static readonly OpCode Conv_Ovf_U4;             // =conv.ovf.u4
public static readonly OpCode Conv_Ovf_U4_Un;          // =conv.ovf.u4.un
public static readonly OpCode Conv_Ovf_U8;             // =conv.ovf.u8
public static readonly OpCode Conv_Ovf_U8_Un;          // =conv.ovf.u8.un
public static readonly OpCode Conv_R_Un;               // =conv.r.un
public static readonly OpCode Conv_R4;                 // =conv.r4
public static readonly OpCode Conv_R8;                 // =conv.r8
public static readonly OpCode Conv_U;                  // =conv.u
```

public static readonly OpCode **Conv_U1**;	// =conv.u1
public static readonly OpCode **Conv_U2**;	// =conv.u2
public static readonly OpCode **Conv_U4**;	// =conv.u4
public static readonly OpCode **Conv_U8**;	// =conv.u8
public static readonly OpCode **Cpblk**;	// =cpblk
public static readonly OpCode **Cpobj**;	// =cpobj
public static readonly OpCode **Div**;	// =div
public static readonly OpCode **Div_Un**;	// =div.un
public static readonly OpCode **Dup**;	// =dup
public static readonly OpCode **Endfilter**;	// =endfilter
public static readonly OpCode **Endfinally**;	// =endfinally
public static readonly OpCode **Initblk**;	// =initblk
public static readonly OpCode **Initobj**;	// =initobj
public static readonly OpCode **Isinst**;	// =isinst
public static readonly OpCode **Jmp**;	// =jmp
public static readonly OpCode **Ldarg**;	// =ldarg
public static readonly OpCode **Ldarg_0**;	// =ldarg.0
public static readonly OpCode **Ldarg_1**;	// =ldarg.1
public static readonly OpCode **Ldarg_2**;	// =ldarg.2
public static readonly OpCode **Ldarg_3**;	// =ldarg.3
public static readonly OpCode **Ldarg_S**;	// =ldarg.s
public static readonly OpCode **Ldarga**;	// =ldarga
public static readonly OpCode **Ldarga_S**;	// =ldarga.s
public static readonly OpCode **Ldc_I4**;	// =ldc.i4
public static readonly OpCode **Ldc_I4_0**;	// =ldc.i4.0
public static readonly OpCode **Ldc_I4_1**;	// =ldc.i4.1
public static readonly OpCode **Ldc_I4_2**;	// =ldc.i4.2
public static readonly OpCode **Ldc_I4_3**;	// =ldc.i4.3
public static readonly OpCode **Ldc_I4_4**;	// =ldc.i4.4
public static readonly OpCode **Ldc_I4_5**;	// =ldc.i4.5
public static readonly OpCode **Ldc_I4_6**;	// =ldc.i4.6
public static readonly OpCode **Ldc_I4_7**;	// =ldc.i4.7
public static readonly OpCode **Ldc_I4_8**;	// =ldc.i4.8
public static readonly OpCode **Ldc_I4_M1**;	// =ldc.i4.m1
public static readonly OpCode **Ldc_I4_S**;	// =ldc.i4.s
public static readonly OpCode **Ldc_I8**;	// =ldc.i8
public static readonly OpCode **Ldc_R4**;	// =ldc.r4
public static readonly OpCode **Ldc_R8**;	// =ldc.r8
public static readonly OpCode **Ldelem_I**;	// =ldelem.i
public static readonly OpCode **Ldelem_I1**;	// =ldelem.i1
public static readonly OpCode **Ldelem_I2**;	// =ldelem.i2
public static readonly OpCode **Ldelem_I4**;	// =ldelem.i4
public static readonly OpCode **Ldelem_I8**;	// =ldelem.i8
public static readonly OpCode **Ldelem_R4**;	// =ldelem.r4
public static readonly OpCode **Ldelem_R8**;	// =ldelem.r8
public static readonly OpCode **Ldelem_Ref**;	// =ldelem.ref
public static readonly OpCode **Ldelem_U1**;	// =ldelem.u1
public static readonly OpCode **Ldelem_U2**;	// =ldelem.u2
public static readonly OpCode **Ldelem_U4**;	// =ldelem.u4
public static readonly OpCode **Ldelema**;	// =ldelema
public static readonly OpCode **Ldfld**;	// =ldfld

```
public static readonly OpCode Ldflda;                  // =ldflda
public static readonly OpCode Ldftn;                   // =ldftn
public static readonly OpCode Ldind_I;                 // =ldind.i
public static readonly OpCode Ldind_I1;                // =ldind.i1
public static readonly OpCode Ldind_I2;                // =ldind.i2
public static readonly OpCode Ldind_I4;                // =ldind.i4
public static readonly OpCode Ldind_I8;                // =ldind.i8
public static readonly OpCode Ldind_R4;                // =ldind.r4
public static readonly OpCode Ldind_R8;                // =ldind.r8
public static readonly OpCode Ldind_Ref;               // =ldind.ref
public static readonly OpCode Ldind_U1;                // =ldind.u1
public static readonly OpCode Ldind_U2;                // =ldind.u2
public static readonly OpCode Ldind_U4;                // =ldind.u4
public static readonly OpCode Ldlen;                   // =ldlen
public static readonly OpCode Ldloc;                   // =ldloc
public static readonly OpCode Ldloc_0;                 // =ldloc.0
public static readonly OpCode Ldloc_1;                 // =ldloc.1
public static readonly OpCode Ldloc_2;                 // =ldloc.2
public static readonly OpCode Ldloc_3;                 // =ldloc.3
public static readonly OpCode Ldloc_S;                 // =ldloc.s
public static readonly OpCode Ldloca;                  // =ldloca
public static readonly OpCode Ldloca_S;                // =ldloca.s
public static readonly OpCode Ldnull;                  // =ldnull
public static readonly OpCode Ldobj;                   // =ldobj
public static readonly OpCode Ldsfld;                  // =ldsfld
public static readonly OpCode Ldsflda;                 // =ldsflda
public static readonly OpCode Ldstr;                   // =ldstr
public static readonly OpCode Ldtoken;                 // =ldtoken
public static readonly OpCode Ldvirtftn;               // =ldvirtftn
public static readonly OpCode Leave;                   // =leave
public static readonly OpCode Leave_S;                 // =leave.s
public static readonly OpCode Localloc;                // =localloc
public static readonly OpCode Mkrefany;                // =mkrefany
public static readonly OpCode Mul;                     // =mul
public static readonly OpCode Mul_Ovf;                 // =mul.ovf
public static readonly OpCode Mul_Ovf_Un;              // =mul.ovf.un
public static readonly OpCode Neg;                     // =neg
public static readonly OpCode Newarr;                  // =newarr
public static readonly OpCode Newobj;                  // =newobj
public static readonly OpCode Nop;                     // =nop
public static readonly OpCode Not;                     // =not
public static readonly OpCode Or;                      // =or
public static readonly OpCode Pop;                     // =pop
public static readonly OpCode Prefix1;                 // =prefix1
public static readonly OpCode Prefix2;                 // =prefix2
public static readonly OpCode Prefix3;                 // =prefix3
public static readonly OpCode Prefix4;                 // =prefix4
public static readonly OpCode Prefix5;                 // =prefix5
public static readonly OpCode Prefix6;                 // =prefix6
public static readonly OpCode Prefix7;                 // =prefix7
public static readonly OpCode Prefixref;               // =prefixref
```

public static readonly OpCode **Refanytype**;	// =refanytype
public static readonly OpCode **Refanyval**;	// =refanyval
public static readonly OpCode **Rem**;	// =rem
public static readonly OpCode **Rem_Un**;	// =rem.un
public static readonly OpCode **Ret**;	// =ret
public static readonly OpCode **Rethrow**;	// =rethrow
public static readonly OpCode **Shl**;	// =shl
public static readonly OpCode **Shr**;	// =shr
public static readonly OpCode **Shr_Un**;	// =shr.un
public static readonly OpCode **Sizeof**;	// =sizeof
public static readonly OpCode **Starg**;	// =starg
public static readonly OpCode **Starg_S**;	// =starg.s
public static readonly OpCode **Stelem_I**;	// =stelem.i
public static readonly OpCode **Stelem_I1**;	// =stelem.i1
public static readonly OpCode **Stelem_I2**;	// =stelem.i2
public static readonly OpCode **Stelem_I4**;	// =stelem.i4
public static readonly OpCode **Stelem_I8**;	// =stelem.i8
public static readonly OpCode **Stelem_R4**;	// =stelem.r4
public static readonly OpCode **Stelem_R8**;	// =stelem.r8
public static readonly OpCode **Stelem_Ref**;	// =stelem.ref
public static readonly OpCode **Stfld**;	// =stfld
public static readonly OpCode **Stind_I**;	// =stind.i
public static readonly OpCode **Stind_I1**;	// =stind.i1
public static readonly OpCode **Stind_I2**;	// =stind.i2
public static readonly OpCode **Stind_I4**;	// =stind.i4
public static readonly OpCode **Stind_I8**;	// =stind.i8
public static readonly OpCode **Stind_R4**;	// =stind.r4
public static readonly OpCode **Stind_R8**;	// =stind.r8
public static readonly OpCode **Stind_Ref**;	// =stind.ref
public static readonly OpCode **Stloc**;	// =stloc
public static readonly OpCode **Stloc_0**;	// =stloc.0
public static readonly OpCode **Stloc_1**;	// =stloc.1
public static readonly OpCode **Stloc_2**;	// =stloc.2
public static readonly OpCode **Stloc_3**;	// =stloc.3
public static readonly OpCode **Stloc_S**;	// =stloc.s
public static readonly OpCode **Stobj**;	// =stobj
public static readonly OpCode **Stsfld**;	// =stsfld
public static readonly OpCode **Sub**;	// =sub
public static readonly OpCode **Sub_Ovf**;	// =sub.ovf
public static readonly OpCode **Sub_Ovf_Un**;	// =sub.ovf.un
public static readonly OpCode **Switch**;	// =switch
public static readonly OpCode **Tailcall**;	// =tail.
public static readonly OpCode **Throw**;	// =throw
public static readonly OpCode **Unaligned**;	// =unaligned.
public static readonly OpCode **Unbox**;	// =unbox
public static readonly OpCode **Volatile**;	// =volatile.
public static readonly OpCode **Xor**;	// =xor

```
// Public Static Methods
   public static bool TakesSingleByteArgument(OpCode inst);
}
```

OpCodeType

System.Reflection.Emit (mscorlib.dll)   enum

This enumeration specifies the type of an MSIL OpCode, which is provided through the OpCode.OpCodeType property. These types include Annotation (an instruction that carries extra information for specific MSIL processors, but can usually be ignored), Macro (a synonym for another MSIL instruction), Nternal (a reserved instruction), Objmodel (an instruction that applies to objects), Prefix (an instruction that specifies an action that must be taken before the next instruction is executed), and Primitive (a built-in instruction).

```
public enum OpCodeType {
  Annotation = 0,
  Macro = 1,
  Nternal = 2,
  Objmodel = 3,
  Prefix = 4,
  Primitive = 5
}
```

Hierarchy   System.Object → System.ValueType → System.Enum(System.IComparable,
                    System.IFormattable, System.IConvertible) → OpCodeType

Returned By   OpCode.OpCodeType

OperandType

System.Reflection.Emit (mscorlib.dll)   enum

This enumeration specifies the operand type of an MSIL OpCode, which is provided through the OpCode.OperandType property. Operands include tokens (InlineField, InlineMethod, InlineType, and InlineTok) and integers (InlineI8, InlineI8, ShortInlineI, and ShortInlineR).

```
public enum OperandType {
  InlineBrTarget = 0,
  InlineField = 1,
  InlineI = 2,
  InlineI8 = 3,
  InlineMethod = 4,
  InlineNone = 5,
  InlinePhi = 6,
  InlineR = 7,
  InlineSig = 9,
  InlineString = 10,
  InlineSwitch = 11,
  InlineTok = 12,
  InlineType = 13,
  InlineVar = 14,
  ShortInlineBrTarget = 15,
  ShortInlineI = 16,
  ShortInlineR = 17,
  ShortInlineVar = 18
}
```

Hierarchy	System.Object → System.ValueType → System.Enum(System.IComparable, System.IFormattable, System.IConvertible) → OperandType
Returned By	OpCode.OperandType

PackingSize
serializable, flag

System.Reflection.Emit (mscorlib.dll)   enum

This enumeration defines the packing size for a type and is set in the ModuleBuilder. DefineType( ) and TypeBuilder.DefineNestedType( ) methods. The digit at the end of each value name in this enumeration specifies a number of bytes.

```
public enum PackingSize {
  Unspecified = 0x00000000,
  Size1 = 0x00000001,
  Size2 = 0x00000002,
  Size4 = 0x00000004,
  Size8 = 0x00000008,
  Size16 = 0x00000010
}
```

Hierarchy	System.Object → System.ValueType → System.Enum(System.IComparable, System.IFormattable, System.IConvertible) → PackingSize
Returned By	TypeBuilder.PackingSize
Passed To	ModuleBuilder.DefineType( ), TypeBuilder.DefineNestedType( )

ParameterBuilder

System.Reflection.Emit (mscorlib.dll)   class

This class represents a dynamically created parameter, which is created through the MethodBuilder.DefineParameter( ) or ConstructorBuilder.DefineParameter( ) method. When creating a ParameterBuilder with these methods, specify the name of the parameter and its position in the list of arguments. This list is 1-based, so the first parameter is given an index of 1. Use the SetMarshal( ) method to specify how the parameter is marshaled from unmanaged code. The SetConstant( ) method specifies the default value for a parameter.

```
public class ParameterBuilder {
// Public Instance Properties
  public virtual int Attributes{get; }
  public bool IsIn{get; }
  public bool IsOptional{get; }
  public bool IsOut{get; }
  public virtual string Name{get; }
  public virtual int Position{get; }
// Public Instance Methods
  public virtual ParameterToken GetToken( );
  public virtual void SetConstant(object defaultValue);
  public void SetCustomAttribute(System.Reflection.ConstructorInfo con, byte[ ] binaryAttribute);
```

```
public void SetCustomAttribute(CustomAttributeBuilder customBuilder);
public virtual void SetMarshal(UnmanagedMarshal unmanagedMarshal);
}
```

Returned By   ConstructorBuilder.DefineParameter( ), MethodBuilder.DefineParameter( )

ParameterToken   serializable

System.Reflection.Emit (mscorlib.dll)   struct

This class represents the token for a parameter. See EventToken for more details on tokens.

```
public struct ParameterToken {
// Public Static Fields
  public static readonly ParameterToken Empty;                    // =System.Reflection.Emit.ParameterToken
// Public Instance Properties
  public int Token{get; }
// Public Instance Methods
  public override bool Equals(object obj);                                      // overrides ValueType
  public override int GetHashCode( );                                          // overrides ValueType
}
```

Hierarchy   System.Object → System.ValueType → ParameterToken

Returned By   ParameterBuilder.GetToken( )

PEFileKinds   serializable

System.Reflection.Emit (mscorlib.dll)   enum

This enumeration is used by the AssemblyBuilder.SetEntryPoint( ) method. It specifies the type of PE file that will be created by the AssemblyBuilder.

```
public enum PEFileKinds {
  Dll = 1,
  ConsoleApplication = 2,
  WindowApplication = 3
}
```

Hierarchy   System.Object → System.ValueType → System.Enum(System.IComparable,
                      System.IFormattable, System.IConvertible) → PEFileKinds

Passed To   AssemblyBuilder.SetEntryPoint( )

PropertyBuilder

System.Reflection.Emit (mscorlib.dll)   sealed class

This class represents a dynamically created property. To create a PropertyBuilder object, use the TypeBuilder.DefineProperty( ) method and specify the parameter types, return value type, and any additional special settings through the System.Reflection.PropertyAttributes enumeration. You can specify MethodBuilder objects for the property get and property set methods using SetGetMethod( ) and SetSetMethod( ). You can also set the property's default value using the SetConstant( ) method.

```
public sealed class PropertyBuilder : System.Reflection.PropertyInfo {
// Public Instance Properties
  public override PropertyAttributes Attributes{get; }                                    // overrides System.Reflection.PropertyInfo
  public override bool CanRead{get; }                                                     // overrides System.Reflection.PropertyInfo
  public override bool CanWrite{get; }                                                    // overrides System.Reflection.PropertyInfo
  public override Type DeclaringType{get; }                                               // overrides System.Reflection.MemberInfo
  public override string Name{get; }                                                      // overrides System.Reflection.MemberInfo
  public PropertyToken PropertyToken{get; }
  public override Type PropertyType{get; }                                                // overrides System.Reflection.PropertyInfo
  public override Type ReflectedType{get; }                                               // overrides System.Reflection.MemberInfo
// Public Instance Methods
  public void AddOtherMethod(MethodBuilder mdBuilder);
  public override MethodInfo[ ] GetAccessors(bool nonPublic);                             // overrides System.Reflection.PropertyInfo
  public override object[ ] GetCustomAttributes(bool inherit);                            // overrides System.Reflection.MemberInfo
  public override object[ ] GetCustomAttributes(Type attributeType, bool inherit);        // overrides System.Reflection.MemberInfo
  public override MethodInfo GetGetMethod(bool nonPublic);                                // overrides System.Reflection.PropertyInfo
  public override ParameterInfo[ ] GetIndexParameters( );                                 // overrides System.Reflection.PropertyInfo
  public override MethodInfo GetSetMethod(bool nonPublic);                                // overrides System.Reflection.PropertyInfo
  public override object GetValue(object obj, System.Reflection.BindingFlags invokeAttr, System.Reflection.Binder binder,
      object[ ] index, System.Globalization.CultureInfo culture);                         // overrides System.Reflection.PropertyInfo
  public override object GetValue(object obj, object[ ] index);                           // overrides System.Reflection.PropertyInfo
  public override bool IsDefined(Type attributeType,bool inherit);                        // overrides System.Reflection.MemberInfo
  public void SetConstant(object defaultValue);
  public void SetCustomAttribute(System.Reflection.ConstructorInfo con, byte[ ] binaryAttribute);
  public void SetCustomAttribute(CustomAttributeBuilder customBuilder);
  public void SetGetMethod(MethodBuilder mdBuilder);
  public void SetSetMethod(MethodBuilder mdBuilder);
  public override void SetValue(object obj, object value, System.Reflection.BindingFlags invokeAttr,
      System.Reflection.Binder binder, object[ ] index, System.Globalization.CultureInfo culture);
                                                                                          // overrides System.Reflection.PropertyInfo
  public override void SetValue(object obj, object value, object[ ] index);               // overrides System.Reflection.PropertyInfo
}
```

Hierarchy   System.Object → System.Reflection.MemberInfo(System.Reflection.
                   ICustomAttributeProvider) → System.Reflection.PropertyInfo → PropertyBuilder

Returned By   TypeBuilder.DefineProperty( )

PropertyToken   serializable

System.Reflection.Emit (mscorlib.dll)   struct

This class represents the token for a property. See EventToken for more details on tokens.

```
public struct PropertyToken {
// Public Static Fields
  public static readonly PropertyToken Empty;                                             // =System.Reflection.Emit.PropertyToken
// Public Instance Properties
  public int Token{get; }
// Public Instance Methods
  public override bool Equals(object obj);                                                // overrides ValueType
  public override int GetHashCode( );                                                     // overrides ValueType
}
```

Hierarchy   System.Object → System.ValueType → PropertyToken

Returned By   PropertyBuilder.PropertyToken

SignatureHelper

System.Reflection.Emit (mscorlib.dll)   sealed class

This class contains helper functions that allow you to build a signature for a method, such as AddArgument( ). Use one of the static methods to get a SignatureHelper, which you can pass to ILGenerator.Emit( ).

```
public sealed class SignatureHelper {
// Public Static Methods
  public static SignatureHelper GetFieldSigHelper(System.Reflection.Module mod);
  public static SignatureHelper GetLocalVarSigHelper(System.Reflection.Module mod);
  public static SignatureHelper GetMethodSigHelper(System.Reflection.Module mod,
    System.Reflection.CallingConventions callingConvention,Type returnType);
  public static SignatureHelper GetMethodSigHelper(System.Reflection.Module mod,
    System.Runtime.InteropServices.CallingConvention unmanagedCallConv, Type returnType);
  public static SignatureHelper GetMethodSigHelper(System.Reflection.Module mod,
    Type returnType,Type[ ] parameterTypes);
  public static SignatureHelper GetPropertySigHelper(System.Reflection.Module mod,
    Type returnType, Type[ ] parameterTypes);
// Public Instance Methods
  public void AddArgument(Type clsArgument);
  public void AddSentinel( );
  public override bool Equals(object obj);                                    // overrides object
  public override int GetHashCode( );                                        // overrides object
  public byte[ ] GetSignature( );
  public override string ToString( );                                        // overrides object
}
```

Passed To   ILGenerator.Emit( ), ModuleBuilder.GetSignatureToken( )

SignatureToken   serializable

System.Reflection.Emit (mscorlib.dll)   struct

This class represents the token for a method signature. See EventToken for more details on tokens.

```
public struct SignatureToken {
// Public Static Fields
  public static readonly SignatureToken Empty;            // =System.Reflection.Emit.SignatureToken
// Public Instance Properties
  public int Token{get; }
// Public Instance Methods
  public override bool Equals(object obj);                                  // overrides ValueType
  public override int GetHashCode( );                                      // overrides ValueType
}
```

Hierarchy	System.Object → System.ValueType → SignatureToken
Returned By	ModuleBuilder.GetSignatureToken( )

StackBehaviour

System.Reflection.Emit (mscorlib.dll)

serializable

enum

This enumeration is used to set the OpCode.StackBehaviourPush( ) and OpCode.StackBehaviourPop( ) methods, which determine how an MSIL instruction pushes an operand onto the stack and pops it off.

```
public enum StackBehaviour {
  Pop0 = 0,
  Pop1 = 1,
  Pop1_pop1 = 2,
  Popi = 3,
  Popi_pop1 = 4,
  Popi_popi = 5,
  Popi_popi8 = 6,
  Popi_popi_popi = 7,
  Popi_popr4 = 8,
  Popi_popr8 = 9,
  Popref = 10,
  Popref_pop1 = 11,
  Popref_popi = 12,
  Popref_popi_popi = 13,
  Popref_popi_popi8 = 14,
  Popref_popi_popr4 = 15,
  Popref_popi_popr8 = 16,
  Popref_popi_popref = 17,
  Push0 = 18,
  Push1 = 19,
  Push1_push1 = 20,
  Pushi = 21,
  Pushi8 = 22,
  Pushr4 = 23,
  Pushr8 = 24,
  Pushref = 25,
  Varpop = 26,
  Varpush = 27
}
```

Hierarchy	System.Object → System.ValueType → System.Enum(System.IComparable, System.IFormattable, System.IConvertible) → StackBehaviour
Returned By	OpCode.{StackBehaviourPop, StackBehaviourPush}

StringToken

System.Reflection.Emit (mscorlib.dll)   struct

This class represents the token for a string constant in a module's constant pool. See
EventToken for more details on tokens.

```
public struct StringToken {
// Public Instance Properties
  public int Token{get; }
// Public Instance Methods
  public override bool Equals(object obj);                                                   // overrides ValueType
  public override int GetHashCode( );                                                        // overrides ValueType
}
```

Hierarchy   System.Object → System.ValueType → StringToken

Returned By   ModuleBuilder.GetStringConstant( )

TypeBuilder

System.Reflection.Emit (mscorlib.dll)   sealed class

This class represents a dynamically created type in a dynamic module (ModuleBuilder
object). Generally, a type is either a class or an interface. To create a TypeBuilder, use the
overloaded ModuleBuilder.DefineType( ) method. Depending on which overload you use, you
can specify different information including the type name, superclass, and implemented interfaces. You can also use the System.Reflection.TypeAttributes enumeration to
specify other options, such as making a class sealed, abstract, or public, or defining it
as an interface. Once the type is created, you can add members such as constructors,
events, fields, properties, methods, and other nested types, using the corresponding
Define method.

Before using a type you created, you must use the CreateType( ) method to get a Type
object. After that, you can instantiate the Type with the System.Activator.CreateInstance( )
method, and invoke members of the type with the System.Type.InvokeMember( ) method.
After creating a type, you can no longer use TypeBuilder methods that would change the
type, such as a Define method.

```
public sealed class TypeBuilder : Type {
// Public Static Fields
  public const int UnspecifiedTypeSize;                                                              // =0
// Public Instance Properties
  public override Assembly Assembly{get; }                                                           // overrides Type
  public override string AssemblyQualifiedName{get; }                                                // overrides Type
  public override Type BaseType{get; }                                                               // overrides Type
  public override Type DeclaringType{get; }                                                          // overrides Type
  public override string FullName{get; }                                                             // overrides Type
  public override Guid GUID{get; }                                                                   // overrides Type
  public override Module Module{get; }                                                               // overrides Type
  public override string Name{get; }                               // overrides System.Reflection.MemberInfo
  public override string Namespace{get; }                                                            // overrides Type
  public PackingSize PackingSize{get; }
  public override Type ReflectedType{get; }                                                          // overrides Type
```

public int **Size**{get; }

public override RuntimeTypeHandle **TypeHandle**{get; } // overrides Type

public TypeToken **TypeToken**{get; }

public override Type **UnderlyingSystemType**{get; } // overrides Type

// Public Instance Methods

public void **AddDeclarativeSecurity**(System.Security.Permissions.SecurityAction *action*,
    System.Security.PermissionSet *pset*);

public void **AddInterfaceImplementation**(Type *interfaceType*);

public Type **CreateType**( );

public ConstructorBuilder **DefineConstructor**(System.Reflection.MethodAttributes *attributes*,
    System.Reflection.CallingConventions *callingConvention*,Type[ ] *parameterTypes*);

public ConstructorBuilder **DefineDefaultConstructor**(System.Reflection.MethodAttributes *attributes*);

public EventBuilder **DefineEvent**(string *name*, System.Reflection.EventAttributes *attributes*, Type *eventtype*);

public FieldBuilder **DefineField**(string *fieldName*, Type *type*, System.Reflection.FieldAttributes *attributes*);

public FieldBuilder **DefineInitializedData**(string *name*, byte[ ] *data*, System.Reflection.FieldAttributes *attributes*);

public MethodBuilder **DefineMethod**(string *name*, System.Reflection.MethodAttributes *attributes*,
    System.Reflection.CallingConventions *callingConvention*,Type *returnType*, Type[ ] *parameterTypes*);

public MethodBuilder **DefineMethod**(string *name*, System.Reflection.MethodAttributes *attributes*,
    Type *returnType*, Type[ ] *parameterTypes*);

public void **DefineMethodOverride**(System.Reflection.MethodInfo *methodInfoBody*,
    System.Reflection.MethodInfo *methodInfoDeclaration*);

public TypeBuilder **DefineNestedType**(string *name*);

public TypeBuilder **DefineNestedType**(string *name*, System.Reflection.TypeAttributes *attr*);

public TypeBuilder **DefineNestedType**(string *name*, System.Reflection.TypeAttributes *attr*, Type *parent*);

public TypeBuilder **DefineNestedType**(string *name*, System.Reflection.TypeAttributes *attr*, Type *parent*, int *typeSize*);

public TypeBuilder **DefineNestedType**(string *name*, System.Reflection.TypeAttributes *attr*,
    Type *parent*,PackingSize *packSize*);

public TypeBuilder **DefineNestedType**(string *name*, System.Reflection.TypeAttributes *attr*, Type *parent*, Type[ ] *interfaces*);

public MethodBuilder **DefinePInvokeMethod**(string *name*, string *dllName*,
    System.Reflection.MethodAttributes *attributes*, System.Reflection.CallingConventions *callingConvention*,
    Type *returnType*, Type[ ] *parameterTypes*, System.Runtime.InteropServices.CallingConvention *nativeCallConv*,
    System.Runtime.InteropServices.CharSet *nativeCharSet*);

public MethodBuilder **DefinePInvokeMethod**(string *name*, string *dllName*, string *entryName*,
System.Reflection.MethodAttributes *attributes*, System.Reflection.CallingConventions *callingConvention*,
    Type *returnType*, Type[ ] *parameterTypes*, System.Runtime.InteropServices.CallingConvention *nativeCallConv*,
    System.Runtime.InteropServices.CharSet *nativeCharSet*);

public PropertyBuilder **DefineProperty**(string *name*, System.Reflection.PropertyAttributes *attributes*,
    Type *returnType*, Type[ ] *parameterTypes*);

public ConstructorBuilder **DefineTypeInitializer**( );

public FieldBuilder **DefineUninitializedData**(string *name*, int *size*, System.Reflection.FieldAttributes *attributes*);

public override ConstructorInfo[ ] **GetConstructors**(System.Reflection.BindingFlags *bindingAttr*); // overrides Type

public override object[ ] **GetCustomAttributes**(bool *inherit*); // overrides System.Reflection.MemberInfo

public override object[ ] **GetCustomAttributes**(Type *attributeType*,bool *inherit*); // overrides System.Reflection.MemberInfo

public override Type **GetElementType**( ); // overrides Type

public override EventInfo **GetEvent**(string *name*, System.Reflection.BindingFlags *bindingAttr*); // overrides Type

public override EventInfo[ ] **GetEvents**( ); // overrides Type

public override EventInfo[ ] **GetEvents**(System.Reflection.BindingFlags *bindingAttr*); // overrides Type

public override FieldInfo **GetField**(string *name*, System.Reflection.BindingFlags *bindingAttr*); // overrides Type

public override FieldInfo[ ] **GetFields**(System.Reflection.BindingFlags *bindingAttr*); // overrides Type

public override Type **GetInterface**(string *name*, bool *ignoreCase*); // overrides Type

public override InterfaceMapping **GetInterfaceMap**(Type *interfaceType*); // overrides Type

public override Type[ ] **GetInterfaces**( ); // overrides Type

```
public override MemberInfo[ ] GetMember(string name, System.Reflection.MemberTypes type,
    System.Reflection.BindingFlags bindingAttr);                                          // overrides Type
public override MemberInfo[ ] GetMembers(System.Reflection.BindingFlags bindingAttr);     // overrides Type
public override MethodInfo[ ] GetMethods(System.Reflection.BindingFlags bindingAttr);     // overrides Type
public override Type GetNestedType(string name, System.Reflection.BindingFlags bindingAttr); // overrides Type
public override Type[ ] GetNestedTypes(System.Reflection.BindingFlags bindingAttr);       // overrides Type
public override PropertyInfo[ ] GetProperties(System.Reflection.BindingFlags bindingAttr); // overrides Type
public override object InvokeMember(string name, System.Reflection.BindingFlags invokeAttr,
    System.Reflection.Binder binder, object target, object[ ] args, System.Reflection.ParameterModifier[ ] modifiers,
    System.Globalization.CultureInfo culture, string[ ] namedParameters);                 // overrides Type
public override bool IsAssignableFrom(Type c);                                            // overrides Type
public override bool IsDefined(Type attributeType, bool inherit);         // overrides System.Reflection.MemberInfo
public override bool IsSubclassOf(Type c);                                                // overrides Type
public void SetCustomAttribute(System.Reflection.ConstructorInfo con, byte[ ] binaryAttribute);
public void SetCustomAttribute(CustomAttributeBuilder customBuilder);
public void SetParent(Type parent);
public override string ToString( );                                                       // overrides Type
// Protected Instance Methods
protected override TypeAttributes GetAttributeFlagsImpl( );                               // overrides Type
protected override ConstructorInfo GetConstructorImpl(System.Reflection.BindingFlags bindingAttr,
    System.Reflection.Binder binder, System.Reflection.CallingConventions callConvention,Type[ ] types,
    System.Reflection.ParameterModifier[ ] modifiers);                                    // overrides Type
protected override MethodInfo GetMethodImpl(string name, System.Reflection.BindingFlags bindingAttr,
    System.Reflection.Binder binder, System.Reflection.CallingConventions callConvention, Type[ ] types,
    System.Reflection.ParameterModifier[ ] modifiers);                                    // overrides Type
protected override PropertyInfo GetPropertyImpl(string name,
    System.Reflection.BindingFlags bindingAttr, System.Reflection.Binder binder, Type returnType, Type[ ] types,
    System.Reflection.ParameterModifier[ ] modifiers);                                    // overrides Type
protected override bool HasElementTypeImpl( );                                            // overrides Type
protected override bool IsArrayImpl( );                                                   // overrides Type
protected override bool IsByRefImpl( );                                                   // overrides Type
protected override bool IsCOMObjectImpl( );                                               // overrides Type
protected override bool IsPointerImpl( );                                                 // overrides Type
protected override bool IsPrimitiveImpl( );                                               // overrides Type
}
```

Hierarchy	System.Object → System.Reflection.MemberInfo(System.Reflection. ICustomAttributeProvider) → System.Type(System.Reflection.IReflect) → TypeBuilder

Returned By	ModuleBuilder.DefineType( )

TypeToken   serializable

System.Reflection.Emit (mscorlib.dll)   struct

This class represents the token for a type. See EventToken for more details on tokens.

```
public struct TypeToken {
// Public Static Fields
    public static readonly TypeToken Empty;                             // =System.Reflection.Emit.TypeToken
// Public Instance Properties
    public int Token{get; }
```

```
// Public Instance Methods
  public override bool Equals(object obj);                                          // overrides ValueType
  public override int GetHashCode( );                                              // overrides ValueType
}
```

Hierarchy   System.Object → System.ValueType → TypeToken

Returned By   EnumBuilder.TypeToken, ModuleBuilder.GetTypeToken( ), TypeBuilder.TypeToken

UnmanagedMarshal   serializable

System.Reflection.Emit (mscorlib.dll)   sealed class

This class defines how parameters or fields should be marshaled in function calls to
unmanaged code. By default, the CLR applies certain format conversions automatically during this marshaling (for example, it might change a System.String object to an
unmanaged BSTR). Use this class to override this default behavior.

To create an instance of this class, use one of the static methods to define the unmanaged type you want. Typically, you will use DefineUnmanagedMarshal( ) for this purpose and
specify the unmanaged type using the System.Runtime.InteropServices.UnmanagedType enumeration. Alternatively, use DefineByValTStr( ) to specify marshaling to a string in a fixed array
buffer, and specify the other methods for various types of unmanaged arrays. These
static methods all return an UnmanagedMarshal object, with its read-only properties set
accordingly. Lastly, associate the UnmanagedMarshal with the appropriate type using the
SetMarshal( ) method for the ParameterBuilder, MethodBuilder, or FieldBuilder class.

```
public sealed class UnmanagedMarshal {
// Public Instance Properties
  public UnmanagedType BaseType{get; }
  public int ElementCount{get; }
  public UnmanagedType GetUnmanagedType{get; }
  public Guid IIDGuid{get; }
// Public Static Methods
  public static UnmanagedMarshal DefineByValArray(int elemCount);
  public static UnmanagedMarshal DefineByValTStr(int elemCount);
  public static UnmanagedMarshal DefineLPArray(System.Runtime.InteropServices.UnmanagedType elemType);
  public static UnmanagedMarshal DefineSafeArray(System.Runtime.InteropServices.UnmanagedType elemType);
  public static UnmanagedMarshal DefineUnmanagedMarshal
    System.Runtime.InteropServices.UnmanagedType unmanagedType);
}
```

Passed To   FieldBuilder.SetMarshal( ), MethodBuilder.SetMarshal( ), ParameterBuilder.SetMarshal( )

37

System.Runtime.
InteropServices

The types in this namespace work with unmanaged code using either PInvoke or COM. PInvoke (short for Platform Invoke) lets you access functions that reside in underlying operating system–specific shared libraries (on Win32, these are DLLs). COM (Component Object Model) is a Win32 legacy component architecture that is used throughout Windows and Windows applications. Many programmers experience COM through the object models of applications such as Microsoft Office, Exchange, and SQL Server. The COM support in .NET lets you access COM components as though they were native .NET classes. For an overview of PInvoke, see Chapter 17 and Chapter 18. Many of the types in this namespace are custom attributes. For information on how the flags and properties of a custom attribute map to its actual usage, see Chapter 14.

We have omitted some of the more esoteric parts of this namespace, so there are some classes that aren't discussed here. For the most part, you will not need those classes unless you are developing specialized code that handles marshaling data types between managed and unmanaged code. If so, you should consult the MSDN .NET reference materials. Figures 37-1 and 37-2 show the types in this namespace.

ArrayWithOffset

System.Runtime.InteropServices (mscorlib.dll)   struct

This class converts an array of value type instances to an unmanaged array. Your unmanaged code accesses this array as a pointer that initially points to the first array element. Each time the pointer increments, it points to the next element in the array. The constructor takes a mandatory **offset** argument that specifies which element should be the first element in the unmanaged array. If you want to pass the whole array, specify an offset of zero.

Hierarchy   System.Object → System.ValueType → ArrayWithOffset

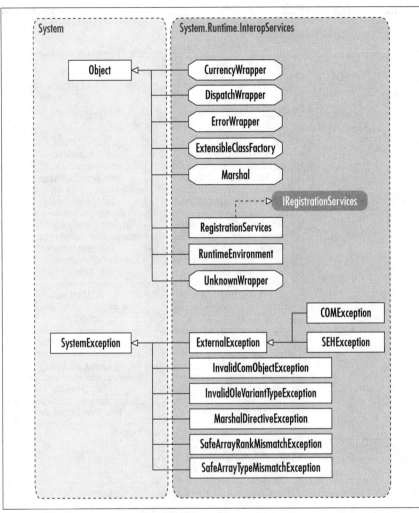

Figure 37-1. The System.Runtime.InteropServices namespace

```
public struct ArrayWithOffset {
// Public Constructors
    public ArrayWithOffset(object array, int offset);
// Public Instance Methods
    public override bool Equals(object obj);                                    // overrides ValueType
    public object GetArray( );
    public override int GetHashCode( );                                         // overrides ValueType
    public int GetOffset( );
}
```

System.Runtime.InteropServices (mscorlib.dll)   enum

This enumeration specifies the flags you can use with IRegistrationServices.RegisterAssembly( ).

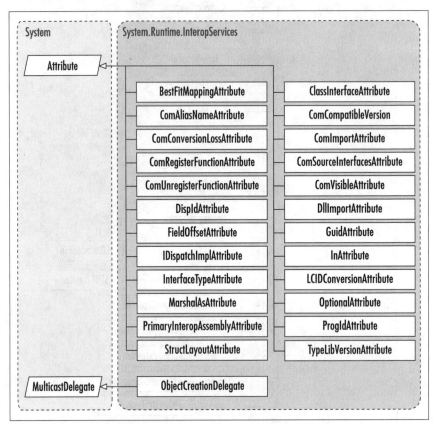

Figure 37-2. Attributes and delegates from System.Runtime.InteropServices

```
public enum AssemblyRegistrationFlags {
  None = 0x00000000,
  SetCodeBase = 0x00000001
}
```

Hierarchy   System.Object → System.ValueType → System.Enum(System.IComparable,
                    System.IFormattable, System.IConvertible) → AssemblyRegistrationFlags

Passed To   IRegistrationServices.RegisterAssembly( ), RegistrationServices.RegisterAssembly( )

BestFitMappingAttribute   .NET 1.1

System.Runtime.InteropServices (mscorlib.dll)   sealed class

This class determines whether Unicode characters are converted to ANSI characters by
selecting the closest matching character.

```
public sealed class BestFitMappingAttribute : Attribute {
// Public Constructors
  public BestFitMappingAttribute(bool BestFitMapping);
// Public Instance Fields
  public bool ThrowOnUnmappableChar;
// Public Instance Properties
  public bool BestFitMapping{get; }
}
```

Hierarchy   System.Object → System.Attribute → BestFitMappingAttribute

Valid On   Assembly, Class, Struct, Interface

CallingConvention   CF 1.0, ECMA 1.0, serializable

System.Runtime.InteropServices (mscorlib.dll)   enum

This enumeration specifies the calling convention to use when you invoke a function. DllImportAttribute uses this in its CallingConvention parameter.

Cdecl specifies the standard calling convention used by C++ and C programs. This is required for functions that take a variable number of arguments, such as printf( ). FastCall attempts to put function arguments into registers. StdCall is the convention used for calling Win32 API functions. ThisCall is the calling convention used by C++ member functions taking fixed arguments. Use the Winapi calling convention for function calls that use PASCAL or __far __pascal.

```
public enum CallingConvention {
  Winapi = 1,
  Cdecl = 2,
  StdCall = 3,
  ThisCall = 4,
  FastCall = 5
}
```

Hierarchy   System.Object → System.ValueType → System.Enum(System.IComparable,
                     System.IFormattable, System.IConvertible) → CallingConvention

Passed To   System.Reflection.Emit.ILGenerator.EmitCalli( ), System.Reflection.Emit.ModuleBuilder.
                     DefinePInvokeMethod( ), System.Reflection.Emit.SignatureHelper.GetMethodSigHelper( ),
                     System.Reflection.Emit.TypeBuilder.DefinePInvokeMethod( )

CharSet   CF 1.0, ECMA 1.0, serializable

System.Runtime.InteropServices (mscorlib.dll)   enum

This enumeration specifies the character set that is used for marshaled strings. It is used by DllImportAttribute and StructLayoutAttribute.

Ansi marshals strings using one-byte ANSI characters, while Unicode uses two bytes to represent a single Unicode character. The Auto value is used only for PInvoke and specifies that PInvoke should decide how to marshal the strings based on your operating system (Unicode for Windows NT/2000/XP and ANSI for Windows 9x/Me).

```
public enum CharSet {
  None = 1,
  Ansi = 2,
  Unicode = 3,
  Auto = 4
}
```

Hierarchy   System.Object → System.ValueType → System.Enum(System.IComparable,
                  System.IFormattable, System.IConvertible) → CharSet

Passed To   System.Reflection.Emit.ModuleBuilder.DefinePInvokeMethod( ), System.Reflection.Emit.
                  TypeBuilder.DefinePInvokeMethod( )

ClassInterfaceAttribute

System.Runtime.InteropServices (mscorlib.dll)   sealed class

This attribute specifies the interface that should be exposed to COM when you
generate a type library. See ClassInterfaceType for the possible arguments to this attribute.

```
public sealed class ClassInterfaceAttribute : Attribute {
// Public Constructors
  public ClassInterfaceAttribute(ClassInterfaceType classInterfaceType);
  public ClassInterfaceAttribute(short classInterfaceType);
// Public Instance Properties
  public ClassInterfaceType Value{get; }
}
```

Hierarchy   System.Object → System.Attribute → ClassInterfaceAttribute

Valid On   Assembly, Class

ClassInterfaceType   serializable

System.Runtime.InteropServices (mscorlib.dll)   enum

This enumeration contains values to use as arguments for ClassInterfaceAttribute. AutoDispatch
specifies that a dispatch-only interface should be generated. AutoDual specifies that a
dual interface should be generated, and None specifies that no interface should be
generated.

```
public enum ClassInterfaceType {
  None = 0,
  AutoDispatch = 1,
  AutoDual = 2
}
```

Hierarchy   System.Object → System.ValueType → System.Enum(System.IComparable, System.IFor-
                  mattable, System.IConvertible) → ClassInterfaceType

Returned By   ClassInterfaceAttribute.Value

Passed To   ClassInterfaceAttribute.ClassInterfaceAttribute( )

CoClassAttribute

System.Runtime.InteropServices (mscorlib.dll)   sealed class

This attribute describes the class ID of a coclass that was imported from a type library.

```
public sealed class CoClassAttribute : Attribute {
// Public Constructors
  public CoClassAttribute(Type coClass);
// Public Instance Properties
  public Type CoClass{get; }
}
```

Hierarchy   System.Object → System.Attribute → CoClassAttribute

Valid On   Interface

ComAliasNameAttribute

System.Runtime.InteropServices (mscorlib.dll)   sealed class

This attribute is automatically added when COM type libraries are imported into the .NET runtime. COM uses alias names for various data types (such as typedef [public] int SHOE_SIZE). When you import a COM object that uses such an alias, .NET automatically decorates each parameter, property, field, and return value with this attribute. If you need to know the name of the COM alias, use the System.Reflection API to see if this custom attribute has been attached to the parameter, property, field, or return value you are interested in.

Since .NET automatically converts COM aliases to the underlying .NET types when it imports a type library, you do not need to use this attribute for typical applications (tool developers will find this attribute useful, though).

```
public sealed class ComAliasNameAttribute : Attribute {
// Public Constructors
  public ComAliasNameAttribute(string alias);
// Public Instance Properties
  public string Value{get; }
}
```

Hierarchy   System.Object → System.Attribute → ComAliasNameAttribute

Valid On   Property, Field, Parameter, ReturnValue

ComCompatibleVersionAttribute   .NET 1.1

System.Runtime.InteropServices (mscorlib.dll)   sealed class

This attribute tells COM clients that the types in the assembly are backward-compatible with those from an earlier version.

```
public sealed class ComCompatibleVersionAttribute : Attribute {
// Public Constructors
  public ComCompatibleVersionAttribute(int major, int minor, int build, int revision);
```

```
// Public Instance Properties
  public int BuildNumber{get; }
  public int MajorVersion{get; }
  public int MinorVersion{get; }
  public int RevisionNumber{get; }
}
```

Hierarchy System.Object → System.Attribute → ComCompatibleVersionAttribute

Valid On Assembly

ComConversionLossAttribute

System.Runtime.InteropServices (mscorlib.dll)   sealed class

The presence of this attribute indicates that information about a type was lost as it was imported from a type library.

```
public sealed class ComConversionLossAttribute : Attribute {
// Public Constructors
  public ComConversionLossAttribute( );
}
```

Hierarchy System.Object → System.Attribute → ComConversionLossAttribute

Valid On All

COMException   serializable

System.Runtime.InteropServices (mscorlib.dll)   class

When a COM error occurs, .NET tries to map it to an exception in the .NET Framework and throws that exception. If the COM error does not map to any exception in the .NET Framework, this exception is thrown instead. It's the "couldn't find an exception" exception.

```
public class COMException : ExternalException {
// Public Constructors
  public COMException( );
  public COMException(string message);
  public COMException(string message, Exception inner);
  public COMException(string message, int errorCode);
// Protected Constructors
  protected COMException(System.Runtime.Serialization.SerializationInfo info,
    System.Runtime.Serialization.StreamingContext context);
// Public Instance Methods
  public override string ToString( );                                          // overrides Exception
}
```

Hierarchy System.Object → System.Exception(System.Runtime.Serialization.ISerializable) → System.SystemException → ExternalException → COMException

ComImportAttribute

System.Runtime.InteropServices (mscorlib.dll)   sealed class

This attribute indicates that the type decorated by this attribute is in fact an unmanaged type defined in a previously published type library and should be treated differently internally to support that.

This attribute is necessary only if the .NET type definition—the class definition in C#—This interface indicates a type whose members can be removed or added. The members are represented as System.Reflection.MemberInfo objects.

is merely a "shim" for interacting with the unmanaged version. In most cases, .NET programmers only use this type when interacting with existing COM APIs, such as when building Explorer Shell Extensions.

```
public sealed class ComImportAttribute : Attribute {
// Public Constructors
  public ComImportAttribute( );
}
```

Hierarchy   System.Object → System.Attribute → ComImportAttribute

Valid On   Class, Interface

ComInterfaceType   serializable

System.Runtime.InteropServices (mscorlib.dll)   enum

This enumeration specifies the COM interface type. Use this attribute with InterfaceType-Attribute to specify how your .NET interfaces are exposed to COM.

```
public enum ComInterfaceType {
  InterfaceIsDual = 0,
  InterfaceIsIUnknown = 1,
  InterfaceIsIDispatch = 2
}
```

Hierarchy   System.Object|aut System.ValueType → System.Enum(System.IComparable,
                   System.IFormattable, System.IConvertible) → ComInterfaceType

Returned By   InterfaceTypeAttribute.Value

Passed To   InterfaceTypeAttribute.InterfaceTypeAttribute( )

ComMemberType   serializable

System.Runtime.InteropServices (mscorlib.dll)   enum

This enumeration describes a COM member. Method indicates that the member is an ordinary method. PropGet and PropSet identify methods that get and set the values of properties (getters and setters).

```
public enum ComMemberType {
  Method = 0,
```

```
  PropGet = 1,
  PropSet = 2
}
```
/

Hierarchy   System.Object → System.ValueType → System.Enum(System.IComparable,
                  System.IFormattable, System.IConvertible) → ComMemberType

Passed To   Marshal.GetMethodInfoForComSlot( )

ComRegisterFunctionAttribute

System.Runtime.InteropServices (mscorlib.dll)   sealed class

This attribute is attached to a static method to indicate that it should be invoked when
the enclosing assembly is registered with COM. The method should take two string
arguments. The first is the name of the registry key being updated, and the second is
the namespace-qualified name of the type being registered (such as System.String). There
can only be one registration function in each assembly.

Microsoft suggests that you do not use this feature and includes it only for backward
compatibility. If you use this feature to specify a registration method, you must also
specify an unregistration method (see ComUnregisterFunctionAttribute) that reverses all
changes you made in the registration function.

```
public sealed class ComRegisterFunctionAttribute : Attribute {
// Public Constructors
  public ComRegisterFunctionAttribute( );
}
```

Hierarchy   System.Object → System.Attribute → ComRegisterFunctionAttribute

Valid On   Method

ComSourceInterfacesAttribute

System.Runtime.InteropServices (mscorlib.dll)   sealed class

This attribute indicates the unmanaged event (using the COM IConnectionPoint
architecture) interfaces that are available on the decorated type. For each method
defined in the COM interface, the type must provide a corresponding "event" instance
that the COM architecture will plug into.

This attribute is only necessary when building .NET objects for plugging into COM
event-aware systems, such as ActiveX control containers.

```
public sealed class ComSourceInterfacesAttribute : Attribute {
// Public Constructors
  public ComSourceInterfacesAttribute(string sourceInterfaces);
  public ComSourceInterfacesAttribute(Type sourceInterface);
  public ComSourceInterfacesAttribute(Type sourceInterface1, Type sourceInterface2);
  public ComSourceInterfacesAttribute(Type sourceInterface1, Type sourceInterface2, Type sourceInterface3);
  public ComSourceInterfacesAttribute(Type sourceInterface1, Type sourceInterface2,
    Type sourceInterface3, Type sourceInterface4);
```

```
// Public Instance Properties
  public string Value{get; }
}
```

Hierarchy   System.Object → System.Attribute → ComSourceInterfacesAttribute

Valid On   Class

ComUnregisterFunctionAttribute

System.Runtime.InteropServices (mscorlib.dll)   sealed class

This attribute is attached to a static method to indicate that it should be invoked when the enclosing assembly is unregistered from COM. There can only be one unregistration function in each assembly.

For more details, see ComRegisterFunctionAttribute.

```
public sealed class ComUnregisterFunctionAttribute : Attribute {
// Public Constructors
  public ComUnregisterFunctionAttribute( );
}
```

Hierarchy   System.Object → System.Attribute → ComUnregisterFunctionAttribute

Valid On   Method

ComVisibleAttribute   CF 1.0

System.Runtime.InteropServices (mscorlib.dll)   sealed class

By default, all public assemblies, types, and members that are registered with COM are visible to COM. This attribute is used with a false argument to hide an assembly, type, or member from COM. This attribute has a cascading effect: if you hide an assembly, all the public types in that assembly are hidden as well.

You can override this attribute on individual types. If, for example, you want to make only one public type visible from an assembly, add the attribute [ComVisible(false)] to the assembly, but also add [ComVisible(true)] to the one type that you want to expose.

```
public sealed class ComVisibleAttribute : Attribute {
// Public Constructors
  public ComVisibleAttribute(bool visibility);
// Public Instance Properties
  public bool Value{get; }
}
```

Hierarchy   System.Object → System.Attribute → ComVisibleAttribute

Valid On   Assembly, Class, Struct, Enum, Method, Property, Field, Interface, Delegate

CurrencyWrapper

System.Runtime.InteropServices (mscorlib.dll) sealed class

This class is used to create a wrapper around a decimal value. Then, when you pass the newly created CurrencyWrapper to an unmanaged method, the object is marshaled as the VT_CURRENCY type.

```
public sealed class CurrencyWrapper {
// Public Constructors
  public CurrencyWrapper(decimal obj);
  public CurrencyWrapper(object obj);
// Public Instance Properties
  public decimal WrappedObject{get; }
}
```

DispatchWrapper

System.Runtime.InteropServices (mscorlib.dll) sealed class

By default, objects are passed to unmanaged methods as the VT_UNKNOWN type. This wrapper is used to send an object as type VT_DISPATCH.

```
public sealed class DispatchWrapper {
// Public Constructors
  public DispatchWrapper(object obj);
// Public Instance Properties
  public object WrappedObject{get; }
}
```

DispIdAttribute   CF 1.0

System.Runtime.InteropServices (mscorlib.dll) sealed class

Specifies a member's DispId when it is exposed to COM.

```
public sealed class DispIdAttribute : Attribute {
// Public Constructors
  public DispIdAttribute(int dispId);
// Public Instance Properties
  public int Value{get; }
}
```

Hierarchy   System.Object → System.Attribute → DispIdAttribute

Valid On   Method, Property, Field, Event

DllImportAttribute   CF 1.0, ECMA 1.0

System.Runtime.InteropServices (mscorlib.dll) sealed class

This attribute (and, in C#, the keyword "extern") specifies that a method definition is implemented externally (usually in a DLL). Apply this attribute to a method that has been declared (but not defined) to specify the DLL name and entry point in which the method can be found.

The attribute can be customized in a number of different ways to help control the binding against the external method. The CallingConvention value dictates how the parameters to the call (and return value coming back) should be sent to the function. CallingConvention.StdCall (used for calling into _stdcall-declared functions, which is most of the Win32 API set) and CallingConvention.Cdecl (used for calling functions declared directly from C or C++) are the two most common values. The CharSet value indicates which character set parameters to the call are expected to be, either two-byte Unicode or one-byte ANSI. EntryPoint indicates the name of the exported function from the DLL to bind to (normally this is guessed from the name of the .NET-declared method), and ExactSpelling indicates whether the .NET compiler should attempt to "best match" a declared DllImport method against a possible set of exported functions. The PreserveSig value indicates how .NET should treat [out]-declared and [retval]-declared parameters. By default, the .NET compilers ignore the HRESULT return value on IDL-declared methods and use the [retval]-declared parameter as the return value; setting PreserveSig to true turns this off. BestFitMapping is used to define whether the CLR should try to "best fit" Unicode characters to ANSI equivalents, and is turned on by default. ThrowOnUnmappableChar indicates whether an exception should be thrown when the interop marshaler attempts to convert an unmappable character, and is turned off by default. Finally, because many Win32 APIs use the GetLastError API call to note the exact reason a call fails, the SetLastError value indicates whether the caller should use that API to discover the reason for failures.

```
public sealed class DllImportAttribute : Attribute {
// Public Constructors
   public DllImportAttribute(string dllName);
// Public Instance Fields
   public bool BestFitMapping;
   public CallingConvention CallingConvention;
   public CharSet CharSet;
   public string EntryPoint;
   public bool ExactSpelling;
   public bool PreserveSig;
   public bool SetLastError;
   public bool ThrowOnUnmappableChar;
// Public Instance Properties
   public string Value{get; }
}
```

Hierarchy   System.Object → System.Attribute → DllImportAttribute

Valid On   Method

ErrorWrapper

System.Runtime.InteropServices (mscorlib.dll)   **sealed class**

This wrapper is used to force an integer, Exception, or other object to be marshaled as type VT_ERROR.

```
public sealed class ErrorWrapper {
// Public Constructors
   public ErrorWrapper(Exception e);
   public ErrorWrapper(int errorCode);
```

```
  public ErrorWrapper(object errorCode);
// Public Instance Properties
  public int ErrorCode{get; }
}
```

ExtensibleClassFactory

System.Runtime.InteropServices (mscorlib.dll)   sealed class

This class exposes the method RegisterObjectCreationCallback( ), which specifies a delegate
that manufactures instances of a managed type. Use this to build managed types that
extend unmanaged types. Since a managed type cannot directly inherit from an
unmanaged type, the managed type needs to aggregate an instance of the unmanaged
type. The delegate that you register with RegisterObjectCreationCallback( ) takes care of
creating the unmanaged type.

```
public sealed class ExtensibleClassFactory {
// Public Static Methods
  public static void RegisterObjectCreationCallback(ObjectCreationDelegate callback);
}
```

ExternalException   CF 1.0, serializable

System.Runtime.InteropServices (mscorlib.dll)   class

This is the base class for COM interop and SEH (Structured Exception Handler)
exceptions.

```
public class ExternalException : SystemException {
// Public Constructors
  public ExternalException( );
  public ExternalException(string message);
  public ExternalException(string message, Exception inner);
  public ExternalException(string message, int errorCode);
// Protected Constructors
  protected ExternalException(System.Runtime.Serialization.SerializationInfo info,
    System.Runtime.Serialization.StreamingContext context);
// Public Instance Properties
  public virtual int ErrorCode{get; }
}
```

Hierarchy   System.Object → System.Exception(System.Runtime.Serialization.ISerializable) →
                     System.SystemException → ExternalException

Subclasses   COMException, SEHException

FieldOffsetAttribute   ECMA 1.0

System.Runtime.InteropServices (mscorlib.dll)   sealed class

This attribute controls the offset, in bytes, of a field. Use it to match your .NET types
to the layout of C and C++ structures exactly. This attribute can be used only within
classes that have the StructLayoutAttribute attribute where LayoutKind.Explicit was used.

```
public sealed class FieldOffsetAttribute : Attribute {
// Public Constructors
  public FieldOffsetAttribute(int offset);
// Public Instance Properties
  public int Value{get; }
}
```

Hierarchy   System.Object → System.Attribute → FieldOffsetAttribute

Valid On   Field

GCHandle   CF 1.0, ECMA 1.0

System.Runtime.InteropServices (mscorlib.dll)   struct

This class is used when you need to pass a managed object to unmanaged code. To use this class, pass an instance of a .NET-managed type to the Alloc() method. The single-argument form of Alloc() creates the GCHandle with GCHandleType.Normal, which ensures that the object will not be freed by the garbage collector. (This means that some kind of user code must also call the Free() method in order to release the object.) Managed code can use the Target property to access the underlying object.

```
public struct GCHandle {
// Public Instance Properties
  public bool IsAllocated{get; }
  public object Target{set; get; }
// Public Static Methods
  public static GCHandle Alloc(object value);
  public static GCHandle Alloc(object value, GCHandleType type);
  public static explicit operator GCHandle(IntPtr value);
  public static explicit operator IntPtr(GCHandle value);
// Public Instance Methods
  public IntPtr AddrOfPinnedObject( );
  public void Free( );
}
```

Hierarchy   System.Object → System.ValueType → GCHandle

GCHandleType   CF 1.0, ECMA 1.0, serializable

System.Runtime.InteropServices (mscorlib.dll)   enum

This enumeration contains values for the two-argument form of GCHandle.Alloc(). Normal protects the object from being garbage collected, and Pinned does the same (but it also enables the GCHandle.AddrOfPinnedObject() method). Weak and WeakTrackResurrection both allow the object to be garbage-collected. However, Weak causes the object to be zeroed out before the finalizer runs, but WeakTrackResurrection does not zero the object, so the object's finalizer can safely resurrect it.

```
public enum GCHandleType {
  Weak = 0,
  WeakTrackResurrection = 1,
  Normal = 2,
```

```
Pinned = 3
}
```

Hierarchy   System.Object → System.ValueType → System.Enum(System.IComparable,
                     System.IFormattable, System.IConvertible) → GCHandleType

Passed To   GCHandle.Alloc( )

GuidAttribute   CF 1.0

System.Runtime.InteropServices (mscorlib.dll)   sealed class

This attribute is used to specify the GUID of assemblies, modules, or types you
expose to COM. If you don't use this attribute to specify a GUID, one is automatically generated. When you apply this attribute, use its full name ([GuidAttribute( )] rather
than [Guid( )]) to avoid clashes with the System.Guid type.

```
public sealed class GuidAttribute : Attribute {
// Public Constructors
  public GuidAttribute(string guid);
// Public Instance Properties
  public string Value{get; }
}
```

Hierarchy   System.Object → System.Attribute → GuidAttribute

Valid On   Assembly, Class, Struct, Enum, Interface, Delegate

HandleRef

System.Runtime.InteropServices (mscorlib.dll)   struct

When you pass a managed object into unmanaged code using PInvoke, there is a
chance that the garbage collector will finalize the object before the unmanaged code is
finished with it. This can only happen when your managed code does not reference the
object after the PInvoke call. Because the garbage collector's reach does not extend
into unmanaged code, this fools the garbage collector into thinking that you are
finished with it.

This class is used to wrap your managed object before passing it into unmanaged code,
and you are guaranteed that the garbage collector will not touch it until the PInvoke
call returns.

```
public struct HandleRef {
// Public Constructors
  public HandleRef(object wrapper, IntPtr handle);
// Public Instance Properties
  public IntPtr Handle{get; }
  public object Wrapper{get; }
// Public Static Methods
  public static explicit operator IntPtr(HandleRef value);
}
```

Hierarchy   System.Object → System.ValueType → HandleRef

IDispatchImplAttribute

System.Runtime.InteropServices (mscorlib.dll)   sealed class

There are multiple implementations of IDispatch available for you to expose dual inter-faces and dispinterfaces to COM. Attach this attribute to a class or an assembly to specify which IDispatch implementation to use. If you apply this attribute to an assembly, it applies to all classes within that assembly. For a list of available IDispatch implementa-tions, see IDispatchImplType.

```
public sealed class IDispatchImplAttribute : Attribute {
// Public Constructors
  public IDispatchImplAttribute(IDispatchImplType implType);
  public IDispatchImplAttribute(short implType);
// Public Instance Properties
  public IDispatchImplType Value{get; }
}
```

Hierarchy   System.Object → System.Attribute → IDispatchImplAttribute

Valid On   Assembly, Class

IDispatchImplType   serializable

System.Runtime.InteropServices (mscorlib.dll)   enum

This enumeration contains the values used by IDispatchImplAttribute. SystemDefinedImpl tells the runtime to decide which IDispatch implementation to use. InternalImpl tells .NET to use its own IDispatch implementation, and CompatibleImpl uses an IDispatch implementation that is compatible with OLE automation. If you use this last implementation, it requires static type information. Because this information is automatically generated at runtime, CompatibleImpl may have an adverse impact on performance.

```
public enum IDispatchImplType {
  SystemDefinedImpl = 0,
  InternalImpl = 1,
  CompatibleImpl = 2
}
```

Hierarchy   System.Object → System.ValueType → System.Enum(System.IComparable,
                      System.IFormattable, System.IConvertible) → IDispatchImplType

Returned By   IDispatchImplAttribute.Value

Passed To   IDispatchImplAttribute.IDispatchImplAttribute( )

InAttribute   CF 1.0, ECMA 1.0

System.Runtime.InteropServices (mscorlib.dll)   sealed class

This attribute is attached to a parameter to marshal it as an in parameter. By default, parameters are marshaled based on their modifiers, so this attribute is only necessary if you want to override the defaults. Parameters with no modifiers are marshaled as [In].

Parameters with the ref modifier are marshaled as [In, Out]. Parameters with the out modifier are marshaled as [Out].

```
public sealed class InAttribute : Attribute {
// Public Constructors
  public InAttribute( );
}
```

Hierarchy   System.Object → System.Attribute → InAttribute

Valid On   Parameter

InterfaceTypeAttribute

System.Runtime.InteropServices (mscorlib.dll)   sealed class

This attribute is used to create a .NET interface that maps a COM interface into your managed application. See ComInterfaceType for the available values.

```
public sealed class InterfaceTypeAttribute : Attribute {
// Public Constructors
  public InterfaceTypeAttribute(ComInterfaceType interfaceType);
  public InterfaceTypeAttribute(short interfaceType);
// Public Instance Properties
  public ComInterfaceType Value{get; }
}
```

Hierarchy   System.Object → System.Attribute → InterfaceTypeAttribute

Valid On   Interface

InvalidComObjectException   serializable

System.Runtime.InteropServices (mscorlib.dll)   class

This exception signals that an invalid COM object has been used.

```
public class InvalidComObjectException : SystemException {
// Public Constructors
  public InvalidComObjectException( );
  public InvalidComObjectException(string message);
  public InvalidComObjectException(string message, Exception inner);
// Protected Constructors
  protected InvalidComObjectException(System.Runtime.Serialization.SerializationInfo info,
    System.Runtime.Serialization.StreamingContext context);
}
```

Hierarchy   System.Object → System.Exception(System.Runtime.Serialization.ISerializable) →
                       System.SystemException → InvalidComObjectException

InvalidOleVariantTypeException

serializable

System.Runtime.InteropServices (mscorlib.dll)

class

This exception signals that the marshaler failed in an attempt to marshal a variant to managed code.

```
public class InvalidOleVariantTypeException : SystemException {
// Public Constructors
  public InvalidOleVariantTypeException( );
  public InvalidOleVariantTypeException(string message);
  public InvalidOleVariantTypeException(string message, Exception inner);
// Protected Constructors
  protected InvalidOleVariantTypeException(System.Runtime.Serialization.SerializationInfo info,
    System.Runtime.Serialization.StreamingContext context);
}
```

Hierarchy System.Object → System.Exception(System.Runtime.Serialization.ISerializable) → System.SystemException → InvalidOleVariantTypeException

IRegistrationServices

System.Runtime.InteropServices (mscorlib.dll)

interface

This interface defines the interface used by classes that register and unregister assemblies with COM.

```
public interface IRegistrationServices {
// Public Instance Methods
  public Guid GetManagedCategoryGuid( );
  public string GetProgIdForType(Type type);
  public Type[ ] GetRegistrableTypesInAssembly(System.Reflection.Assembly assembly);
  public bool RegisterAssembly(System.Reflection.Assembly assembly, AssemblyRegistrationFlags flags);
  public void RegisterTypeForComClients(Type type, ref Guid g);
  public bool TypeRepresentsComType(Type type);
  public bool TypeRequiresRegistration(Type type);
  public bool UnregisterAssembly(System.Reflection.Assembly assembly);
}
```

Implemented By RegistrationServices

LayoutKind

CF 1.0, ECMA 1.0, serializable

System.Runtime.InteropServices (mscorlib.dll)

enum

This enumeration is used to specify how objects are laid out when they are passed to unmanaged code. Auto specifies that .NET should choose the best method to lay out the objects. Explicit gives you complete control over how the object's data members are laid out. You must use FieldOffsetAttribute with each member if you specify Explicit. Sequential lays out the object's members one after the other, in the same order that they are defined in the class definition.

```
public enum LayoutKind {
  Sequential = 0,
```

```
    Explicit = 2,
    Auto = 3
}
```

Hierarchy	System.Object → System.ValueType → System.Enum(System.IComparable, System.IFormattable, System.IConvertible) → LayoutKind

Returned By	StructLayoutAttribute.Value

Passed To	StructLayoutAttribute.StructLayoutAttribute( )

LCIDConversionAttribute

System.Runtime.InteropServices (mscorlib.dll)   sealed class

This attribute indicates that a parameter within the method's unmanaged signature expects an [lcid] argument. Pass an integer value to the constructor to specify which parameter, starting with 0 for the first parameter.

```
public sealed class LCIDConversionAttribute : Attribute {
// Public Constructors
  public LCIDConversionAttribute(int lcid);
// Public Instance Properties
  public int Value{get; }
}
```

Hierarchy	System.Object → System.Attribute → LCIDConversionAttribute

Valid On	Method

Marshal   CF 1.0

System.Runtime.InteropServices (mscorlib.dll)   sealed class

This class offers a collection of static methods for working with unmanaged memory and converting managed types to unmanaged types. Unless you are developing specialized code for marshaling types between managed and unmanaged code, you probably do not need to use any of these methods.

GetHRForException( ) converts a .NET exception to a COM HResult. If you are curious about the platform you are running on, you can find out the size of a character with the SystemDefaultCharSize field, which is 1 on an ANSI platform (Windows 9x/Me) and 2 on a Unicode platform (Windows NT, 2000, and XP).

Use the IsComObject( ) method to determine whether an object is actually an unmanaged COM object. The AddRef( ) method increments a COM object's reference count.

```
public sealed class Marshal {
// Public Static Fields
  public static readonly int SystemDefaultCharSize;                                            // =2
  public static readonly int SystemMaxDBCSCharSize;                                            // =1
// Public Static Methods
  public static int AddRef(IntPtr pUnk);
  public static IntPtr AllocCoTaskMem(int cb);
  public static IntPtr AllocHGlobal(int cb);
```

```
public static IntPtr AllocHGlobal(IntPtr cb);
public static object BindToMoniker(string monikerName);
public static void ChangeWrapperHandleStrength(object otp, bool flsWeak);
public static void Copy(byte[ ] source, int startIndex, IntPtr destination, int length);
public static void Copy(char[ ] source, int startIndex, IntPtr destination, int length);
public static void Copy(double[ ] source, int startIndex, IntPtr destination, int length);
public static void Copy(short[ ] source, int startIndex, IntPtr destination, int length);
public static void Copy(int[ ] source, int startIndex, IntPtr destination, int length);
public static void Copy(long[ ] source, int startIndex, IntPtr destination, int length);
public static void Copy(IntPtr source, byte[ ] destination, int startIndex, int length);
public static void Copy(IntPtr source, char[ ] destination, int startIndex, int length);
public static void Copy(IntPtr source, double[ ] destination, int startIndex, int length);
public static void Copy(IntPtr source, short[ ] destination, int startIndex, int length);
public static void Copy(IntPtr source, int[ ] destination, int startIndex, int length);
public static void Copy(IntPtr source, long[ ] destination, int startIndex, int length);
public static void Copy(IntPtr source, float[ ] destination, int startIndex, int length);
public static void Copy(float[ ] source, int startIndex, IntPtr destination, int length);
public static object CreateWrapperOfType(object o, Type t);
public static void DestroyStructure(IntPtr ptr, Type structuretype);
public static void FreeBSTR(IntPtr ptr);
public static void FreeCoTaskMem(IntPtr ptr);
public static void FreeHGlobal(IntPtr hglobal);
public static Guid GenerateGuidForType(Type type);
public static string GenerateProgIdForType(Type type);
public static object GetActiveObject(string progID);
public static IntPtr GetComInterfaceForObject(object o, Type T);
public static object GetComObjectData(object obj, object key);
public static int GetComSlotForMethodInfo(System.Reflection.MemberInfo m);
public static int GetEndComSlot(Type t);
public static int GetExceptionCode( );
public static IntPtr GetExceptionPointers( );
public static IntPtr GetHINSTANCE(System.Reflection.Module m);
public static int GetHRForException(Exception e);
public static int GetHRForLastWin32Error( );
public static IntPtr GetIDispatchForObject(object o);
public static IntPtr GetITypeInfoForType(Type t);
public static IntPtr GetIUnknownForObject(object o);
public static int GetLastWin32Error( );
public static IntPtr GetManagedThunkForUnmanagedMethodPtr(IntPtr pfnMethodToWrap, IntPtr pbSignature,
    int cbSignature);
public static MemberInfo GetMethodInfoForComSlot(Type t, int slot, ref ComMemberType memberType);
public static void GetNativeVariantForObject(object obj, IntPtr pDstNativeVariant);
public static object GetObjectForIUnknown(IntPtr pUnk);
public static object GetObjectForNativeVariant(IntPtr pSrcNativeVariant);
public static object[ ] GetObjectsForNativeVariants(IntPtr aSrcNativeVariant, int cVars);
public static int GetStartComSlot(Type t);
public static Thread GetThreadFromFiberCookie(int cookie);
public static object GetTypedObjectForIUnknown(IntPtr pUnk, Type t);
public static Type GetTypeForITypeInfo(IntPtr piTypeInfo);
public static string GetTypeInfoName(UCOMITypeInfo pTI);
public static Guid GetTypeLibGuid(UCOMITypeLib pTLB);
public static Guid GetTypeLibGuidForAssembly(System.Reflection.Assembly asm);
```

```
public static int GetTypeLibLcid(UCOMITypeLib pTLB);
public static string GetTypeLibName(UCOMITypeLib pTLB);
public static IntPtr GetUnmanagedThunkForManagedMethodPtr(IntPtr pfnMethodToWrap, IntPtr pbSignature,
    int cbSignature);
public static bool IsComObject(object o);
public static bool IsTypeVisibleFromCom(Type t);
public static int NumParamBytes(System.Reflection.MethodInfo m);
public static IntPtr OffsetOf(Type t, string fieldName);
public static void Prelink(System.Reflection.MethodInfo m);
public static void PrelinkAll(Type c);
public static string PtrToStringAnsi(IntPtr ptr);
public static string PtrToStringAnsi(IntPtr ptr, int len);
public static string PtrToStringAuto(IntPtr ptr);
public static string PtrToStringAuto(IntPtr ptr, int len);
public static string PtrToStringBSTR(IntPtr ptr);
public static string PtrToStringUni(IntPtr ptr);
public static string PtrToStringUni(IntPtr ptr, int len);
public static object PtrToStructure(IntPtr ptr, Type structureType);
public static void PtrToStructure(IntPtr ptr, object structure);
public static int QueryInterface(IntPtr pUnk, ref Guid iid, out IntPtr ppv);
public static byte ReadByte(IntPtr ptr);
public static byte ReadByte(IntPtr ptr, int ofs);
public static byte ReadByte(in object ptr, int ofs);
public static short ReadInt16(IntPtr ptr);
public static short ReadInt16(IntPtr ptr, int ofs);
public static short ReadInt16(in object ptr, int ofs);
public static int ReadInt32(IntPtr ptr);
public static int ReadInt32(IntPtr ptr, int ofs);
public static int ReadInt32(in object ptr, int ofs);
public static long ReadInt64(IntPtr ptr);
public static long ReadInt64(IntPtr ptr, int ofs);
public static long ReadInt64(in object ptr, int ofs);
public static IntPtr ReadIntPtr(IntPtr ptr);
public static IntPtr ReadIntPtr(IntPtr ptr, int ofs);
public static IntPtr ReadIntPtr(in object ptr, int ofs);
public static IntPtr ReAllocCoTaskMem(IntPtr pv, int cb);
public static IntPtr ReAllocHGlobal(IntPtr pv, IntPtr cb);
public static int Release(IntPtr pUnk);
public static int ReleaseComObject(object o);
public static void ReleaseThreadCache( );
public static bool SetComObjectData(object obj, object key, object data);
public static int SizeOf(object structure);
public static int SizeOf(Type t);
public static IntPtr StringToBSTR(string s);
public static IntPtr StringToCoTaskMemAnsi(string s);
public static IntPtr StringToCoTaskMemAuto(string s);
public static IntPtr StringToCoTaskMemUni(string s);
public static IntPtr StringToHGlobalAnsi(string s);
public static IntPtr StringToHGlobalAuto(string s);
public static IntPtr StringToHGlobalUni(string s);
public static void StructureToPtr(object structure, IntPtr ptr, bool fDeleteOld);
```

```
public static void ThrowExceptionForHR(int errorCode);
public static void ThrowExceptionForHR(int errorCode, IntPtr errorInfo);
public static IntPtr UnsafeAddrOfPinnedArrayElement(Array arr, int index);
public static void WriteByte(IntPtr ptr, byte val);
public static void WriteByte(IntPtr ptr, int ofs, byte val);
public static void WriteByte(in object ptr, int ofs, byte val);
public static void WriteInt16(IntPtr ptr, char val);
public static void WriteInt16(IntPtr ptr, short val);
public static void WriteInt16(IntPtr ptr, int ofs, char val);
public static void WriteInt16(IntPtr ptr, int ofs, short val);
public static void WriteInt16(in object ptr, int ofs, char val);
public static void WriteInt16(in object ptr, int ofs, short val);
public static void WriteInt32(IntPtr ptr, int val);
public static void WriteInt32(IntPtr ptr, int ofs, int val);
public static void WriteInt32(in object ptr, int ofs, int val);
public static void WriteInt64(IntPtr ptr, int ofs, long val);
public static void WriteInt64(IntPtr ptr, long val);
public static void WriteInt64(in object ptr, int ofs, long val);
public static void WriteIntPtr(IntPtr ptr, int ofs, IntPtr val);
public static void WriteIntPtr(IntPtr ptr, IntPtr val);
public static void WriteIntPtr(in object ptr, int ofs, IntPtr val);
}
```

MarshalAsAttribute

System.Runtime.InteropServices (mscorlib.dll)   sealed class

This optional attribute is used to explicitly specify the unmanaged type a parameter, field, or return value should be marshaled to. If you do not specify this attribute, .NET uses the type's default marshaler. The UnmanagedType enumeration contains the unmanaged types you can marshal to with this attribute.

```
public sealed class MarshalAsAttribute : Attribute {
// Public Constructors
  public MarshalAsAttribute(short unmanagedType);
  public MarshalAsAttribute(UnmanagedType unmanagedType);
// Public Instance Fields
  public UnmanagedType ArraySubType;
  public string MarshalCookie;
  public string MarshalType;
  public Type MarshalTypeRef;
  public VarEnum SafeArraySubType;
  public Type SafeArrayUserDefinedSubType;
  public int SizeConst;
  public short SizeParamIndex;
// Public Instance Properties
  public UnmanagedType Value{get; }
}
```

Hierarchy   System.Object → System.Attribute → MarshalAsAttribute

Valid On   Field, Parameter, ReturnValue

MarshalDirectiveException

serializable

System.Runtime.InteropServices (mscorlib.dll)

class

This exception is thrown when the marshaler encounters an unsupported MarshalAsAttribute.

```
public class MarshalDirectiveException : SystemException {
// Public Constructors
  public MarshalDirectiveException( );
  public MarshalDirectiveException(string message);
  public MarshalDirectiveException(string message, Exception inner);
// Protected Constructors
  protected MarshalDirectiveException(System.Runtime.Serialization.SerializationInfo info,
    System.Runtime.Serialization.StreamingContext context);
}
```

Hierarchy System.Object → System.Exception(System.Runtime.Serialization.ISerializable) →
System.SystemException → MarshalDirectiveException

ObjectCreationDelegate

serializable

System.Runtime.InteropServices (mscorlib.dll)

delegate

Use this delegate with the ExtensibleClassFactory.RegisterObjectCreationCallback( ) method to create a COM object.

```
public delegate IntPtr ObjectCreationDelegate(IntPtr aggregator);
```

Passed To ExtensibleClassFactory.RegisterObjectCreationCallback( )

OptionalAttribute

System.Runtime.InteropServices (mscorlib.dll)

sealed class

This attribute is attached to a parameter to indicate that it is optional.

```
public sealed class OptionalAttribute : Attribute {
// Public Constructors
  public OptionalAttribute( );
}
```

Hierarchy System.Object → System.Attribute → OptionalAttribute

Valid On Parameter

OutAttribute

CF 1.0, ECMA 1.0

System.Runtime.InteropServices (mscorlib.dll)

sealed class

This attribute is attached to a parameter to cause it to be marshaled as an out parameter. See InAttribute for more details, including information on the default behavior.

```
public sealed class OutAttribute : Attribute {
// Public Constructors
   public OutAttribute( );
}
```

Hierarchy   System.Object → System.Attribute → OutAttribute

Valid On   Parameter

PreserveSigAttribute

System.Runtime.InteropServices (mscorlib.dll)   sealed class

When .NET converts a managed method signature to an unmanaged signature, it changes the return value to a parameter that has the out and retval COM attributes. Instead of the original return value, the unmanaged method returns a COM HRESULT. If you want to override this behavior, attach the PreserveSigAttribute to the method.

Something similar happens when you call unmanaged methods from managed code. In that case, the [out, retval] parameter on the COM side becomes the return value, and an HRESULT that indicates an error condition is translated into a .NET exception. If you want to be able to access the HRESULT as a long return value, use the PreserveSigAttribute on the methods in your COM interface declaration (see InterfaceTypeAttribute).

```
public sealed class PreserveSigAttribute : Attribute {
// Public Constructors
   public PreserveSigAttribute( );
}
```

Hierarchy   System.Object → System.Attribute → PreserveSigAttribute

Valid On   Method

ProgIdAttribute

System.Runtime.InteropServices (mscorlib.dll)   sealed class

This attribute is attached to a class to specify its COM ProgID.

```
public sealed class ProgIdAttribute : Attribute {
// Public Constructors
   public ProgIdAttribute(string progId);
// Public Instance Properties
   public string Value{get; }
}
```

Hierarchy   System.Object → System.Attribute → ProgIdAttribute

Valid On   Class

RegistrationServices

System.Runtime.InteropServices (mscorlib.dll)   class

This class is responsible for registering and unregistering assemblies with COM.

```
public class RegistrationServices : IRegistrationServices {
// Public Constructors
  public RegistrationServices( );
// Public Instance Methods
  public virtual Guid GetManagedCategoryGuid( );                        // implements IRegistrationServices
  public virtual string GetProgIdForType(Type type);                    // implements IRegistrationServices
  public virtual Type[ ] GetRegistrableTypesInAssembly(System.Reflection.Assembly assembly);
                                                                        // implements IRegistrationServices
  public virtual bool RegisterAssembly(System.Reflection.Assembly assembly, AssemblyRegistrationFlags flags);
                                                                        // implements IRegistrationServices
  public virtual void RegisterTypeForComClients(Type type, ref Guid g); // implements IRegistrationServices
  public virtual bool TypeRepresentsComType(Type type);                 // implements IRegistrationServices
  public virtual bool TypeRequiresRegistration(Type type);              // implements IRegistrationServices
  public virtual bool UnregisterAssembly(System.Reflection.Assembly assembly);  // implements IRegistrationServices
}
```

RuntimeEnvironment

System.Runtime.InteropServices (mscorlib.dll)   class

This type exposes static methods you can use to get information about the CLR's environment.

```
public class RuntimeEnvironment {
// Public Constructors
  public RuntimeEnvironment( );
// Public Static Properties
  public static string SystemConfigurationFile{get; }
// Public Static Methods
  public static bool FromGlobalAccessCache(System.Reflection.Assembly a);
  public static string GetRuntimeDirectory( );
  public static string GetSystemVersion( );
}
```

SafeArrayRankMismatchException   serializable

System.Runtime.InteropServices (mscorlib.dll)   class

This exception signals that a SAFEARRAY's rank does not match the rank in the method signature; it might be thrown when invoking a managed method.

```
public class SafeArrayRankMismatchException : SystemException {
// Public Constructors
  public SafeArrayRankMismatchException( );
  public SafeArrayRankMismatchException(string message);
  public SafeArrayRankMismatchException(string message, Exception inner);
```

```
// Protected Constructors
  protected SafeArrayRankMismatchException(System.Runtime.Serialization.SerializationInfo info,
    System.Runtime.Serialization.StreamingContext context);
}
```

Hierarchy   System.Object → System.Exception(System.Runtime.Serialization.ISerializable) →
                     System.SystemException → SafeArrayRankMismatchException

SafeArrayTypeMismatchException   serializable

System.Runtime.InteropServices (mscorlib.dll)   class

This exception signals that a SAFEARRAY's type does not match the type in the method
signature; it might be thrown when invoking a managed method.

```
public class SafeArrayTypeMismatchException : SystemException {
// Public Constructors
  public SafeArrayTypeMismatchException( );
  public SafeArrayTypeMismatchException(string message);
  public SafeArrayTypeMismatchException(string message, Exception inner);
// Protected Constructors
  protected SafeArrayTypeMismatchException(System.Runtime.Serialization.SerializationInfo info,
    System.Runtime.Serialization.StreamingContext context);
}
```

Hierarchy   System.Object → System.Exception(System.Runtime.Serialization.ISerializable) →
                     System.SystemException → SafeArrayTypeMismatchException

SEHException   serializable

System.Runtime.InteropServices (mscorlib.dll)   class

This class is used as a wrapper for an unmanaged C++ exception that was thrown.

```
public class SEHException : ExternalException {
// Public Constructors
  public SEHException( );
  public SEHException(string message);
  public SEHException(string message, Exception inner);
// Protected Constructors
  protected SEHException(System.Runtime.Serialization.SerializationInfo info,
    System.Runtime.Serialization.StreamingContext context);
// Public Instance Methods
  public virtual bool CanResume( );
}
```

Hierarchy   System.Object → System.Exception(System.Runtime.Serialization.ISerializable) →
                     System.SystemException → ExternalException → SEHException

StructLayoutAttribute

System.Runtime.InteropServices (mscorlib.dll)   sealed class

Use this attribute to control how the members of a class are laid out in memory. See LayoutKind for the possible values you can use with this attribute.

```
public sealed class StructLayoutAttribute : Attribute {
// Public Constructors
  public StructLayoutAttribute(short layoutKind);
  public StructLayoutAttribute(LayoutKind layoutKind);
// Public Instance Fields
  public CharSet CharSet;
  public int Pack;
  public int Size;
// Public Instance Properties
  public LayoutKind Value{get; }
}
```

Hierarchy   System.Object → System.Attribute → StructLayoutAttribute

Valid On   Class, Struct

TypeLibVersionAttribute

System.Runtime.InteropServices (mscorlib.dll)   sealed class

This attribute specifies the exported type library's version.

```
public sealed class TypeLibVersionAttribute : Attribute {
// Public Constructors
  public TypeLibVersionAttribute(int major, int minor);
// Public Instance Properties
  public int MajorVersion{get; }
  public int MinorVersion{get; }
}
```

Hierarchy   System.Object → System.Attribute → TypeLibVersionAttribute

Valid On   Assembly

UnknownWrapper

System.Runtime.InteropServices (mscorlib.dll)   sealed class

Use this wrapper to pass a managed object into unmanaged code as type VT_UNKNOWN.

```
public sealed class UnknownWrapper {
// Public Constructors
  public UnknownWrapper(object obj);
// Public Instance Properties
  public object WrappedObject{get; }
}
```

UnmanagedType

CF 1.0, ECMA 1.0, serializable

System.Runtime.InteropServices (mscorlib.dll)   enum

This enumeration contains constant values that represent various unmanaged types.

```
public enum UnmanagedType {
  Bool = 2,
  I1 = 3,
  U1 = 4,
  I2 = 5,
  U2 = 6,
  I4 = 7,
  U4 = 8,
  I8 = 9,
  U8 = 10,
  R4 = 11,
  R8 = 12,
  Currency = 15,
  BStr = 19,
  LPStr = 20,
  LPWStr = 21,
  LPTStr = 22,
  ByValTStr = 23,
  IUnknown = 25,
  IDispatch = 26,
  Struct = 27,
  Interface = 28,
  SafeArray = 29,
  ByValArray = 30,
  SysInt = 31,
  SysUInt = 32,
  VBByRefStr = 34,
  AnsiBStr = 35,
  TBStr = 36,
  VariantBool = 37,
  FunctionPtr = 38,
  AsAny = 40,
  LPArray = 42,
  LPStruct = 43,
  CustomMarshaler = 44,
  Error = 45
}
```

Hierarchy   System.Object → System.ValueType → System.Enum(System.IComparable,
System.IFormattable, System.IConvertible) → UnmanagedType

Returned By   System.Reflection.Emit.UnmanagedMarshal.{BaseType, GetUnmanagedType},
MarshalAsAttribute.Value

Passed To   System.Reflection.Emit.UnmanagedMarshal.{DefineLPArray( ), DefineSafeArray( ),
DefineUnmanagedMarshal( )}, MarshalAsAttribute.MarshalAsAttribute( )

System.Runtime.InteropServices (mscorlib.dll)   enum

This enumeration contains constants that can be used with MarshalAsAttribute.SafeArraySub-Type to specify how to marshal arrays that are passed from managed to unmanaged code.

```
public enum VarEnum {
  VT_EMPTY = 0,
  VT_NULL = 1,
  VT_I2 = 2,
  VT_I4 = 3,
  VT_R4 = 4,
  VT_R8 = 5,
  VT_CY = 6,
  VT_DATE = 7,
  VT_BSTR = 8,
  VT_DISPATCH = 9,
  VT_ERROR = 10,
  VT_BOOL = 11,
  VT_VARIANT = 12,
  VT_UNKNOWN = 13,
  VT_DECIMAL = 14,
  VT_I1 = 16,
  VT_UI1 = 17,
  VT_UI2 = 18,
  VT_UI4 = 19,
  VT_I8 = 20,
  VT_UI8 = 21,
  VT_INT = 22,
  VT_UINT = 23,
  VT_VOID = 24,
  VT_HRESULT = 25,
  VT_PTR = 26,
  VT_SAFEARRAY = 27,
  VT_CARRAY = 28,
  VT_USERDEFINED = 29,
  VT_LPSTR = 30,
  VT_LPWSTR = 31,
  VT_RECORD = 36,
  VT_FILETIME = 64,
  VT_BLOB = 65,
  VT_STREAM = 66,
  VT_STORAGE = 67,
  VT_STREAMED_OBJECT = 68,
  VT_STORED_OBJECT = 69,
  VT_BLOB_OBJECT = 70,
  VT_CF = 71,
  VT_CLSID = 72,
  VT_VECTOR = 4096,
```

```
    VT_ARRAY = 8192,
    VT_BYREF = 16384
}
```

Hierarchy System.Object → System.ValueType → System.Enum(System.IComparable,
System.IFormattable, System.IConvertible) → VarEnum

IExpando

System.Runtime.InteropServices.Expando (mscorlib.dll)   interface

This interface indicates a type whose members can be removed or added. The
members are represented as **System.Reflection.MemberInfo** objects.

```
public interface IExpando : System.Reflection.IReflect {
// Public Instance Methods
   public FieldInfo AddField(string name);
   public MethodInfo AddMethod(string name, Delegate method);
   public PropertyInfo AddProperty(string name);
   public void RemoveMember(System.Reflection.MemberInfo m);
}
```

38

System.Runtime.Serialization

The act of serialization transforms an object (and all of its associated objects and/ or data elements) into a stream of bytes, suitable for storage or transmission across a network. The reverse of this act, called deserialization, is to take the same stream of bytes and reconstitute the objects exactly as they were at the time of serialization.

This act, which sounds simple in theory, encompasses a number of points that must be addressed. For starters, the serialization libraries must provide complete reference semantics—that is, if an object holds two references to other objects, both of which happen to point to the same object, then the serialization mechanism needs to keep that in place. Therefore, when the stream is deserialized, both references point to the same object again.

In addition, the actual format of the stream of bytes may be different from application to application. For example, for storage into a binary column in a database, the serialized representation must be as compact and succinct as possible—no "wasted" bytes. But if we want to send the serialized data over an HTTP link to a non-.NET process, then a binary format is entirely inappropriate, and an XML-based one is more useful.

The System.Runtime.Serialization namespace and its child namespace, System.Runtime.Serialization.Formatters (with its own two child namespaces, System.Runtime.Serialization.Formatters. Binary and System.Runtime.Serialization.Formatters.Soap), directly addresses these needs. System.Runtime.Serialization contains the types necessary to perform the serialization of an object into a stream of bytes, using an alternative object (which implements the IFormatter interface) to actually format the bytes into either binary or XML form. While it is certainly feasible to write your own custom formatters, most .NET programmers have no real practical need to do so, since a binary format and an XML format cover most needs.

Serialization does not necessarily come for free, however—there are a few things a .NET programmer must do in order to take advantage of the Serialization mechanism. For starters, a type must be marked as serializable in order to be eligible for serialization; this requires adding the System.SerializableAttribute to the type's declaration. By default, when a type becomes serializable, all nonstatic fields within that type are transformed into bytes when serialized. If a field is itself nonserializable, an exception is thrown; fields that wish to remain unserialized (that is, remain empty during the serialization process) must be marked with the System.NonSerializedAttribute in the type declaration.

It is possible to take greater control over the serialization process by implementing the ISerializable interface and providing definitions for the methods declared there; however, most .NET programmers are generally satisfied with the default serialization behavior.

Figure 38-1 shows the types in this namespace.

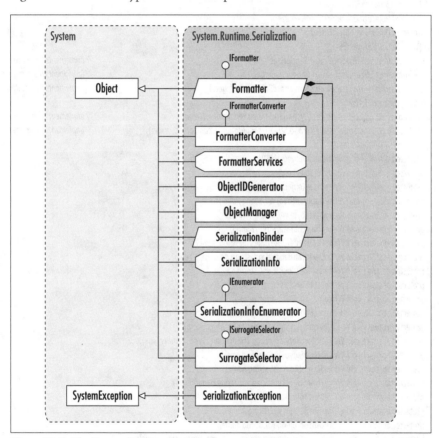

Figure 38-1. The System.Runtime.Serialization namespace

Formatter

System.Runtime.Serialization (mscorlib.dll)   abstract class

This is the abstract base class for all runtime serialization formatters. It implements the IFormatter interface, which provides the properties that select the binder, surrogates, and streaming context of the formatter. This interface also implements the Serialize() and Deserialize() methods.

Additionally, the Formatter manages the queue of objects to serialize and provides a set of Write* methods for writing types to the stream.

```
public abstract class Formatter : IFormatter {
// Protected Constructors
  protected Formatter( );
// Protected Instance Fields
  protected ObjectIDGenerator m_idGenerator;
  protected Queue m_objectQueue;
// Public Instance Properties
  public abstract SerializationBinder Binder{set; get; }                    // implements IFormatter
  public abstract StreamingContext Context{set; get; }                      // implements IFormatter
  public abstract ISurrogateSelector SurrogateSelector{set; get; }          // implements IFormatter
// Public Instance Methods
  public abstract object Deserialize(System.IO.Stream serializationStream);  // implements IFormatter
  public abstract void Serialize(System.IO.Stream serializationStream, object graph);  // implements IFormatter
// Protected Instance Methods
  protected virtual object GetNext(out long objID);
  protected virtual long Schedule(object obj);
  protected abstract void WriteArray(object obj, string name, Type memberType);
  protected abstract void WriteBoolean(bool val, string name);
  protected abstract void WriteByte(byte val, string name);
  protected abstract void WriteChar(char val, string name);
  protected abstract void WriteDateTime(DateTime val, string name);
  protected abstract void WriteDecimal(decimal val, string name);
  protected abstract void WriteDouble(double val, string name);
  protected abstract void WriteInt16(short val, string name);
  protected abstract void WriteInt32(int val, string name);
  protected abstract void WriteInt64(long val, string name);
  protected virtual void WriteMember(string memberName, object data);
  protected abstract void WriteObjectRef(object obj, string name, Type memberType);
  protected abstract void WriteSByte(sbyte val, string name);
  protected abstract void WriteSingle(float val, string name);
  protected abstract void WriteTimeSpan(TimeSpan val, string name);
  protected abstract void WriteUInt16(ushort val, string name);
  protected abstract void WriteUInt32(uint val, string name);
  protected abstract void WriteUInt64(ulong val, string name);
  protected abstract void WriteValueType(object obj, string name, Type memberType);
}
```

FormatterConverter

System.Runtime.Serialization (mscorlib.dll) class

This class is a basic implementation of the IFormatterConverter interface. It provides a formatter with a means to convert values to different base types. The generic Convert() method converts a value into a specified type. The various To* methods convert values into specific types.

```
public class FormatterConverter : IFormatterConverter {
// Public Constructors
  public FormatterConverter();
// Public Instance Methods
  public object Convert(object value, Type type);                    // implements IFormatterConverter
  public object Convert(object value, TypeCode typeCode);            // implements IFormatterConverter
  public bool ToBoolean(object value);                              // implements IFormatterConverter
  public byte ToByte(object value);                                // implements IFormatterConverter
  public char ToChar(object value);                                // implements IFormatterConverter
  public DateTime ToDateTime(object value);                        // implements IFormatterConverter
  public decimal ToDecimal(object value);                          // implements IFormatterConverter
  public double ToDouble(object value);                            // implements IFormatterConverter
  public short ToInt16(object value);                              // implements IFormatterConverter
  public int ToInt32(object value);                                // implements IFormatterConverter
  public long ToInt64(object value);                               // implements IFormatterConverter
  public sbyte ToSByte(object value);                              // implements IFormatterConverter
  public float ToSingle(object value);                             // implements IFormatterConverter
  public string ToString(object value);                            // implements IFormatterConverter
  public ushort ToUInt16(object value);                            // implements IFormatterConverter
  public uint ToUInt32(object value);                              // implements IFormatterConverter
  public ulong ToUInt64(object value);                             // implements IFormatterConverter
}
```

FormatterServices

System.Runtime.Serialization (mscorlib.dll) sealed class

The methods of this sealed class provide some background functionality to a formatter when serializing and deserializing objects. For example, GetObjectData() creates an array of System.Reflection.MemberInfo object data. GetSerializableMembers() retrieves all the serializable members of a given class. PopulateObjectMembers() is the basic deserialization method, using a MemberInfo array of member names and an array of corresponding data values to repopulate a specified object.

```
public sealed class FormatterServices {
// Public Static Methods
  public static void CheckTypeSecurity(Type t, System.Runtime.Serialization.Formatters.TypeFilterLevel securityLevel);
  public static object[] GetObjectData(object obj, System.Reflection.MemberInfo[] members);
  public static object GetSafeUninitializedObject(Type type);
  public static MemberInfo[] GetSerializableMembers(Type type);
  public static MemberInfo[] GetSerializableMembers(Type type, StreamingContext context);
  public static Type GetTypeFromAssembly(System.Reflection.Assembly assem, string name);
  public static object GetUninitializedObject(Type type);
  public static object PopulateObjectMembers(object obj, System.Reflection.MemberInfo[] members, object[] data);
}
```

IDeserializationCallback

System.Runtime.Serialization (mscorlib.dll)   interface

This interface implements a notification triggered when deserialization of an object is completed. Specify callback functionality with the OnDeserialization( ) method. This class is useful for restoring members that can be computed after deserialization, instead of serializing them and using more storage resources.

```
public interface IDeserializationCallback {
// Public Instance Methods
  public void OnDeserialization(object sender);
}
```

Implemented By   System.Collections.Hashtable, System.Collections.Specialized.NameObjectCollectionBase,
                     System.Globalization.{CompareInfo, TextInfo}, System.Reflection.AssemblyName

IFormatter

System.Runtime.Serialization (mscorlib.dll)   interface

This interface defines the basic serialization and deserialization functionality for a formatter. Its three properties determine the SerializationBinder, StreamingContext, and Surrogate-Selector of the formatter. It also defines the two basic methods of Serialize( ) and Deserialize( ).

```
public interface IFormatter {
// Public Instance Properties
  public SerializationBinder Binder{set; get; }
  public StreamingContext Context{set; get; }
  public ISurrogateSelector SurrogateSelector{set; get; }
// Public Instance Methods
  public object Deserialize(System.IO.Stream serializationStream);
  public void Serialize(System.IO.Stream serializationStream, object graph);
}
```

Implemented By   Formatter, System.Runtime.Serialization.Formatters.Binary.BinaryFormatter,
                     System.Runtime.Serialization.Formatters.Soap.SoapFormatter

IFormatterConverter

System.Runtime.Serialization (mscorlib.dll)   interface

This interface defines the basic methods that convert serializable data into base class types. These conversion methods are used to parse the data contained in SerializationInfo instances.

```
public interface IFormatterConverter {
// Public Instance Methods
  public object Convert(object value, Type type);
  public object Convert(object value, TypeCode typeCode);
  public bool ToBoolean(object value);
  public byte ToByte(object value);
  public char ToChar(object value);
  public DateTime ToDateTime(object value);
```

```
    public decimal ToDecimal(object value);
    public double ToDouble(object value);
    public short ToInt16(object value);
    public int ToInt32(object value);
    public long ToInt64(object value);
    public sbyte ToSByte(object value);
    public float ToSingle(object value);
    public string ToString(object value);
    public ushort ToUInt16(object value);
    public uint ToUInt32(object value);
    public ulong ToUInt64(object value);
}
```

Implemented By   FormatterConverter

Passed To   SerializationInfo.SerializationInfo( )

IObjectReference

System.Runtime.Serialization (mscorlib.dll)   interface

This interface indicates that an object references another object. Use of this interface means that during deserialization, the object must be dereferenced during fixup so the "real" object is placed in the object graph.

```
public interface IObjectReference {
// Public Instance Methods
    public object GetRealObject(StreamingContext context);
}
```

ISerializable

System.Runtime.Serialization (mscorlib.dll)   interface

Indicates that an object is serializable and provides serialization information to the formatter. This interface defines GetObjectData( ), which specifies the member information that will be provided to a SerializationInfo instance in a specific StreamingContext. Classes that implement ISerializable must also provide a constructor that takes the same arguments as GetObjectData( ). The constructor must use those arguments to deserialize an instance of the class.

```
public interface ISerializable {
// Public Instance Methods
    public void GetObjectData(SerializationInfo info, StreamingContext context);
}
```

Implemented By   Multiple types

ISerializationSurrogate

System.Runtime.Serialization (mscorlib.dll)   interface

Objects that implement this interface can be delegated to perform the serialization and deserialization of another object by providing customized methods for GetObjectData( )

and SetObjectData( ). GetObjectData( ) gets the member information to create a SerializationInfo instance, while SetObjectData( ) uses information from a SerializationInfo instance to recreate an object.

```
public interface ISerializationSurrogate {
// Public Instance Methods
  public void GetObjectData(object obj, SerializationInfo info, StreamingContext context);
  public object SetObjectData(object obj, SerializationInfo info, StreamingContext context, ISurrogateSelector selector);
}
```

Returned By   ISurrogateSelector.GetSurrogate( ), SurrogateSelector.GetSurrogate( )

Passed To   SurrogateSelector.AddSurrogate( )

ISurrogateSelector

System.Runtime.Serialization (mscorlib.dll)   interface

This interface is implemented by classes that help the formatter decide the appropriate surrogate to serialize or deserialize a particular type.

```
public interface ISurrogateSelector {
// Public Instance Methods
  public void ChainSelector(ISurrogateSelector selector);
  public ISurrogateSelector GetNextSelector( );
  public ISerializationSurrogate GetSurrogate(Type type, StreamingContext context, out ISurrogateSelector selector);
}
```

Implemented By   SurrogateSelector

Returned By   Formatter.SurrogateSelector, System.Runtime.Serialization.Formatters.Binary.BinaryFormatter.SurrogateSelector, System.Runtime.Serialization.Formatters.Soap.SoapFormatter.SurrogateSelector, IFormatter.SurrogateSelector, SurrogateSelector.GetNextSelector( )

Passed To   Formatter.SurrogateSelector, System.Runtime.Serialization.Formatters.Binary.BinaryFormatter.{BinaryFormatter( ), SurrogateSelector}, System.Runtime.Serialization.Formatters.Soap.SoapFormatter.{SoapFormatter( ), SurrogateSelector}, IFormatter.SurrogateSelector, ISerializationSurrogate.SetObjectData( ), ObjectManager.ObjectManager( ), SurrogateSelector.{ChainSelector( ), GetSurrogate( )}

ObjectIDGenerator   serializable

System.Runtime.Serialization (mscorlib.dll)   class

This class is used by formatters to identify objects within a serialized stream in order to track object references. The IDs are 64-bit numbers that are generated when an object is referenced or is referencing another. (An ID with a zero value is a null reference.) The GetId( ) method creates and returns an ID for an object if it does not already have one.

```
public class ObjectIDGenerator {
// Public Constructors
  public ObjectIDGenerator( );
```

```
// Public Instance Methods
  public virtual long GetId(object obj, out bool firstTime);
  public virtual long HasId(object obj, out bool firstTime);
}
```

ObjectManager

System.Runtime.Serialization (mscorlib.dll)   class

This class is used by a formatter to manage object references during deserialization.
Objects in the stream can refer to already deserialized objects. This causes the
formatter to ask the ObjectManager to complete the reference after the deserialization is
completed (i.e., on "fixup").

```
public class ObjectManager {
// Public Constructors
  public ObjectManager(ISurrogateSelector selector, StreamingContext context);
// Public Instance Methods
  public virtual void DoFixups( );
  public virtual object GetObject(long objectID);
  public virtual void RaiseDeserializationEvent( );
  public virtual void RecordArrayElementFixup(long arrayToBeFixed, int[ ] indices, long objectRequired);
  public virtual void RecordArrayElementFixup(long arrayToBeFixed, int index, long objectRequired);
  public virtual void RecordDelayedFixup(long objectToBeFixed, string memberName, long objectRequired);
  public virtual void RecordFixup(long objectToBeFixed, System.Reflection.MemberInfo member, long objectRequired);
  public virtual void RegisterObject(object obj, long objectID);
  public void RegisterObject(object obj, long objectID, SerializationInfo info);
  public void RegisterObject(object obj, long objectID, SerializationInfo info, long idOfContainingObj,
    System.Reflection.MemberInfo member);
  public void RegisterObject(object obj, long objectID, SerializationInfo info, long idOfContainingObj,
    System.Reflection.MemberInfo member, int[ ] arrayIndex);
}
```

SerializationBinder   serializable

System.Runtime.Serialization (mscorlib.dll)   abstract class

This abstract base class provides a binder to a formatter that controls which classes are
loaded during deserialization according to assembly information.

```
public abstract class SerializationBinder {
// Protected Constructors
  protected SerializationBinder( );
// Public Instance Methods
  public abstract Type BindToType(string assemblyName, string typeName);
}
```

Returned By   Formatter.Binder, System.Runtime.Serialization.Formatters.Binary.BinaryFormatter.Binder,
                     System.Runtime.Serialization.Formatters.Soap.SoapFormatter.Binder, IFormatter.Binder

Passed To   Formatter.Binder, System.Runtime.Serialization.Formatters.Binary.BinaryFormatter.Binder,
                     System.Runtime.Serialization.Formatters.Soap.SoapFormatter.Binder, IFormatter.Binder

SerializationEntry

System.Runtime.Serialization (mscorlib.dll)   struct

This class encapsulates the information used for a single member stored within Serialization-Info. This object stores the Name of the object, its Value, and the ObjectType. SerializationEntry instances are the elements returned via the SerializationInfoEnumerator.

```
public struct SerializationEntry {
// Public Instance Properties
  public string Name{get; }
  public Type ObjectType{get; }
  public object Value{get; }
}
```

Hierarchy   System.Object → System.ValueType → SerializationEntry

Returned By   SerializationInfoEnumerator.Current

SerializationException   **serializable**

System.Runtime.Serialization (mscorlib.dll)   class

This class contains the exceptions thrown on serialization and deserialization errors.

```
public class SerializationException : SystemException {
// Public Constructors
  public SerializationException( );
  public SerializationException(string message);
  public SerializationException(string message, Exception innerException);
// Protected Constructors
  protected SerializationException(SerializationInfo info, StreamingContext context);
}
```

Hierarchy   System.Object → System.Exception(ISerializable) → System.SystemException →
                       SerializationException

SerializationInfo

System.Runtime.Serialization (mscorlib.dll)   .   sealed class

SerializationInfo objects are used by classes that customize serialization behavior. The data required for each member is the name of the member, its type, and its value. Within a class's ISerializable.GetObjectData( ) block, the AddValue( ) method is used to add member data. Deserialization is defined within a deserialization constructor (see ISerializable). It is specified by retrieving member data with GetValue( ), or one of the many other Get* methods, and assigning the data to the appropriate members.

```
public sealed class SerializationInfo {
// Public Constructors
  public SerializationInfo(Type type, IFormatterConverter converter);
// Public Instance Properties
  public string AssemblyName{set; get; }
  public string FullTypeName{set; get; }
```

```
    public int MemberCount{get; }
    // Public Instance Methods
    public void AddValue(string name, bool value);
    public void AddValue(string name, byte value);
    public void AddValue(string name, char value);
    public void AddValue(string name, DateTime value);
    public void AddValue(string name, decimal value);
    public void AddValue(string name, double value);
    public void AddValue(string name, short value);
    public void AddValue(string name, int value);
    public void AddValue(string name, long value);
    public void AddValue(string name, object value);
    public void AddValue(string name, object value, Type type);
    public void AddValue(string name, sbyte value);
    public void AddValue(string name, float value);
    public void AddValue(string name, ushort value);
    public void AddValue(string name, uint value);
    public void AddValue(string name, ulong value);
    public bool GetBoolean(string name);
    public byte GetByte(string name);
    public char GetChar(string name);
    public DateTime GetDateTime(string name);
    public decimal GetDecimal(string name);
    public double GetDouble(string name);
    public SerializationInfoEnumerator GetEnumerator( );
    public short GetInt16(string name);
    public int GetInt32(string name);
    public long GetInt64(string name);
    public sbyte GetSByte(string name);
    public float GetSingle(string name);
    public string GetString(string name);
    public ushort GetUInt16(string name);
    public uint GetUInt32(string name);
    public ulong GetUInt64(string name);
    public object GetValue(string name, Type type);
    public void SetType(Type type);
}
```

Passed To   Multiple types

SerializationInfoEnumerator

System.Runtime.Serialization (mscorlib.dll)   sealed class

This class provides an enumerator to iterate over the elements contained in the SerializationInfo. Each element is of type SerializationEntry.

```
public sealed class SerializationInfoEnumerator : IEnumerator {
    // Public Instance Properties
    public SerializationEntry Current{get; }
    public string Name{get; }
    public Type ObjectType{get; }
```

```
  public object Value{get; }
// Public Instance Methods
  public bool MoveNext( );                                                        // implements IEnumerator
  public void Reset( );                                                           // implements IEnumerator
}
```

Returned By   SerializationInfo.GetEnumerator( )

StreamingContext   serializable

System.Runtime.Serialization (mscorlib.dll)   struct

This class describes the source or destination of a serialized stream. The context can
determine how classes are serialized and require special parsing during deserialization.
The State property holds a value from StreamingContextStates that indicates the destination
of object data during serialization and the source of data during deserialization. This
could indicate that you are serializing data to a file, for example, or deserializing data
that came from another process.

```
public struct StreamingContext {
// Public Constructors
  public StreamingContext(StreamingContextStates state);
  public StreamingContext(StreamingContextStates state, object additional);
// Public Instance Properties
  public object Context{get; }
  public StreamingContextStates State{get; }
// Public Instance Methods
  public override bool Equals(object obj);                                          // overrides ValueType
  public override int GetHashCode( );                                              // overrides ValueType
}
```

Hierarchy   System.Object → System.ValueType → StreamingContext

Returned By   Formatter.Context, System.Runtime.Serialization.Formatters.Binary.BinaryFormatter.
                   Context, System.Runtime.Serialization.Formatters.Soap.SoapFormatter.Context,
                   IFormatter.Context

Passed To   Multiple types

StreamingContextStates   serializable, flag

System.Runtime.Serialization (mscorlib.dll)   enum

This enumeration contains values that describe types of streams that serialized data
derives from or targets.

```
public enum StreamingContextStates {
  CrossProcess = 0x00000001,
  CrossMachine = 0x00000002,
  File = 0x00000004,
  Persistence = 0x00000008,
  Remoting = 0x00000010,
  Other = 0x00000020,
```

```
Clone = 0x00000040,
CrossAppDomain = 0x00000080,
All = 0x000000FF
}
```

Hierarchy	System.Object → System.ValueType → System.Enum(System.IComparable, System.IFormattable, System.IConvertible) → StreamingContextStates
Returned By	StreamingContext.State
Passed To	StreamingContext.StreamingContext( )

SurrogateSelector

System.Runtime.Serialization (mscorlib.dll)   class

This class is the basic implementation of the ISurrogateSelector interface. A formatter uses this class to find the appropriate surrogate object to serialize or deserialize an object of a specific type, assembly, or context.

```
public class SurrogateSelector : ISurrogateSelector {
// Public Constructors
  public SurrogateSelector( );
// Public Instance Methods
  public virtual void AddSurrogate(Type type, StreamingContext context, ISerializationSurrogate surrogate);
  public virtual void ChainSelector(ISurrogateSelector selector);                    // implements ISurrogateSelector
  public virtual ISurrogateSelector GetNextSelector( );                              // implements ISurrogateSelector
  public virtual ISerializationSurrogate GetSurrogate(Type type, StreamingContext context, out ISurrogateSelector selector);
                                                                                     // implements ISurrogateSelector
  public virtual void RemoveSurrogate(Type type, StreamingContext context);
}
```

39

System.Runtime.Serialization.
Formatters

This chapter covers the System.Runtime.Serialization.Formatters namespace, which contains a number of types that are used by serialization formatters. Figure 39-1 shows the types in this namespace. This chapter also features BinaryFormatter and SoapFormatter, two formatters that live in their own namespace and rely on the types in the System. Runtime.Serialization.Formatters namespace.

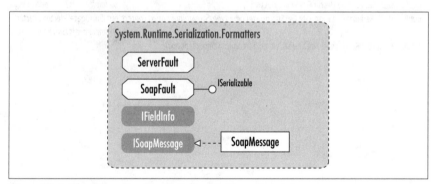

Figure 39-1. The System.Runtime.Serialization.Formatters namespace

BinaryFormatter

System.Runtime.Serialization.Formatters.Binary (mscorlib.dll)   sealed class

This formatter uses a binary format to serialize or deserialize a single object or an object graph.

```
public sealed class BinaryFormatter : System.Runtime.Remoting.Messaging.IRemotingFormatter,
    System.Runtime.Serialization.IFormatter {
// Public Constructors
  public BinaryFormatter( );
```

```
public BinaryFormatter(System.Runtime.Serialization.ISurrogateSelector selector,
    System.Runtime.Serialization.StreamingContext context);
// Public Instance Properties
public FormatterAssemblyStyle AssemblyFormat{set; get; }
public SerializationBinder Binder{set; get; }                    // implements System.Runtime.Serialization.IFormatter
public StreamingContext Context{set; get; }                      // implements System.Runtime.Serialization.IFormatter
public TypeFilterLevel FilterLevel{set; get; }
public ISurrogateSelector SurrogateSelector{set; get; }          // implements System.Runtime.Serialization.IFormatter
public FormatterTypeStyle TypeFormat{set; get; }
// Public Instance Methods
public object Deserialize(System.IO.Stream serializationStream);  // implements System.Runtime.Serialization.IFormatter
public object Deserialize(System.IO.Stream serializationStream,
    System.Runtime.Remoting.Messaging.HeaderHandler handler);
                              // implements System.Runtime.Remoting.Messaging.IRemotingFormatter
public object DeserializeMethodResponse(System.IO.Stream serializationStream,
    System.Runtime.Remoting.Messaging.HeaderHandler handler,
    System.Runtime.Remoting.Messaging.IMethodCallMessage methodCallMessage);
public void Serialize(System.IO.Stream serializationStream, object graph);
                              // implements System.Runtime.Serialization.IFormatter
public void Serialize(System.IO.Stream serializationStream, object graph,
    System.Runtime.Remoting.Messaging.Header[ ] headers);
                              // implements System.Runtime.Remoting.Messaging.IRemotingFormatter
public object UnsafeDeserialize(System.IO.Stream serializationStream,
    System.Runtime.Remoting.Messaging.HeaderHandler handler);
public object UnsafeDeserializeMethodResponse(System.IO.Stream serializationStream,
    System.Runtime.Remoting.Messaging.HeaderHandler handler,
    System.Runtime.Remoting.Messaging.IMethodCallMessage methodCallMessage);
}
```

FormatterAssemblyStyle   serializable

System.Runtime.Serialization.Formatters (mscorlib.dll)   enum

This enumeration controls how assembly names are serialized. Simple serializes assemblies using only the assembly name. The default, Full, includes the assembly name, its culture, public key token, and version.

```
public enum FormatterAssemblyStyle {
  Simple = 0,
  Full = 1
}
```

Hierarchy	System.Object → System.ValueType → System.Enum(System.IComparable, System.IFormattable, System.IConvertible) → FormatterAssemblyStyle
Returned By	System.Runtime.Serialization.Formatters.Binary.BinaryFormatter.AssemblyFormat, System.Runtime.Serialization.Formatters.Soap.SoapFormatter.AssemblyFormat
Passed To	System.Runtime.Serialization.Formatters.Binary.BinaryFormatter.AssemblyFormat, System.Runtime.Serialization.Formatters.Soap.SoapFormatter.AssemblyFormat

FormatterTypeStyle

serializable

System.Runtime.Serialization.Formatters (mscorlib.dll)   enum

This enumeration controls how type information is specified for members. TypesAlways specifies that type information be placed in the serialization stream for all object members. The default, TypesWhenNeeded, places type information in the stream for the following: object arrays, members of type System.Object, and nonprimitive value types (such as structs and enums) that implement the ISerializable interface. XsdString can be bitwise-ORed with another option to specify that strings are represented with the XSD format instead of the SOAP format.

```
public enum FormatterTypeStyle {
  TypesWhenNeeded = 0,
  TypesAlways = 1,
  XsdString = 2
}
```

Hierarchy   System.Object → System.ValueType → System.Enum(System.IComparable,
                   System.IFormattable, System.IConvertible) → FormatterTypeStyle

Returned By   System.Runtime.Serialization.Formatters.Binary.BinaryFormatter.TypeFormat,
                   System.Runtime.Serialization.Formatters.Soap.SoapFormatter.TypeFormat

Passed To   System.Runtime.Serialization.Formatters.Binary.BinaryFormatter.TypeFormat,
                   System.Runtime.Serialization.Formatters.Soap.SoapFormatter.TypeFormat

IFieldInfo

System.Runtime.Serialization.Formatters (mscorlib.dll)   interface

This interface can expose the field names and types of serialized objects. It is used to supply parameter type information to the SoapFormatter when deserializing in SOAP RPC format.

```
public interface IFieldInfo {
// Public Instance Properties
  public string[ ] FieldNames{set; get; }
  public Type[ ] FieldTypes{set; get; }
}
```

ISoapMessage

System.Runtime.Serialization.Formatters (mscorlib.dll)   interface

This type defines the interface used by SoapMessage. This interface is used to serialize and deserialize SOAP in RPC format.

```
public interface ISoapMessage {
// Public Instance Properties
  public Header[ ] Headers{set; get; }
  public string MethodName{set; get; }
  public string[ ] ParamNames{set; get; }
  public Type[ ] ParamTypes{set; get; }
```

```
public object[ ] ParamValues{set; get; }
public string XmlNameSpace{set; get; }
}
```

Implemented By   SoapMessage

Returned By   System.Runtime.Serialization.Formatters.Soap.SoapFormatter.TopObject

Passed To   System.Runtime.Serialization.Formatters.Soap.SoapFormatter.TopObject

ServerFault   serializable

System.Runtime.Serialization.Formatters (mscorlib.dll)   sealed class

This class represents an error that was thrown from a remote server to the client. It is
placed in the Detail section of a SoapFault object.

```
public sealed class ServerFault {
// Public Constructors
  public ServerFault(string exceptionType, string message, string stackTrace);
// Public Instance Properties
  public string ExceptionMessage{set; get; }
  public string ExceptionType{set; get; }
  public string StackTrace{set; get; }
}
```

Passed To   SoapFault.SoapFault( )

SoapFault   serializable

System.Runtime.Serialization.Formatters (mscorlib.dll)   sealed class

This class represents a SOAP fault.

```
public sealed class SoapFault : System.Runtime.Serialization.ISerializable {
// Public Constructors
  public SoapFault( );
  public SoapFault(string faultCode, string faultString, string faultActor, ServerFault serverFault);
// Public Instance Properties
  public object Detail{set; get; }
  public string FaultActor{set; get; }
  public string FaultCode{set; get; }
  public string FaultString{set; get; }
// Public Instance Methods
  public void GetObjectData(System.Runtime.Serialization.SerializationInfo info,
    System.Runtime.Serialization.StreamingContext context);              // implements ISerializable
}
```

SoapFormatter

System.Runtime.Serialization.Formatters.Soap (system.runtime.serialization.formatters.soap.dll)   sealed class

This formatter performs SOAP serialization or deserialization on a single object or an
object graph.

```
public sealed class SoapFormatter : System.Runtime.Remoting.Messaging.IRemotingFormatter,
    System.Runtime.Serialization.IFormatter {
// Public Constructors
  public SoapFormatter( );
  public SoapFormatter(System.Runtime.Serialization.ISurrogateSelector selector,
    System.Runtime.Serialization.StreamingContext context);
// Public Instance Properties
  public FormatterAssemblyStyle AssemblyFormat{set; get; }
  public SerializationBinder Binder{set; get; }                 // implements System.Runtime.Serialization.IFormatter
  public StreamingContext Context{set; get; }                   // implements System.Runtime.Serialization.IFormatter
  public TypeFilterLevel FilterLevel{set; get; }
  public ISurrogateSelector SurrogateSelector{set; get; }       // implements System.Runtime.Serialization.IFormatter
  public ISoapMessage TopObject{set; get; }
  public FormatterTypeStyle TypeFormat{set; get; }
// Public Instance Methods
  public object Deserialize(System.IO.Stream serializationStream);    // implements System.Runtime.Serialization.IFormatter
  public object Deserialize(System.IO.Stream serializationStream,
    System.Runtime.Remoting.Messaging.HeaderHandler handler);
                              // implements System.Runtime.Remoting.Messaging.IRemotingFormatter
  public void Serialize(System.IO.Stream serializationStream,
    object graph);                                              // implements System.Runtime.Serialization.IFormatter

  public void Serialize(System.IO.Stream serializationStream, object graph,
    System.Runtime.Remoting.Messaging.Header[ ] headers);
                              // implements System.Runtime.Remoting.Messaging.IRemotingFormatter
}
```

SoapMessage   serializable

System.Runtime.Serialization.Formatters (mscorlib.dll)   class

This type encapsulates a message sent as part of a SOAP RPC (Remote Procedure
Call).

```
public class SoapMessage : ISoapMessage {
// Public Constructors
  public SoapMessage( );
// Public Instance Properties
  public Header[ ] Headers{set; get; }                          // implements ISoapMessage
  public string MethodName{set; get; }                          // implements ISoapMessage
  public string[ ] ParamNames{set; get; }                       // implements ISoapMessage
  public Type[ ] ParamTypes{set; get; }                         // implements ISoapMessage
  public object[ ] ParamValues{set; get; }                      // implements ISoapMessage
  public string XmlNameSpace{set; get; }                        // implements ISoapMessage
}
```

TypeFilterLevel   .NET 1.1, serializable

System.Runtime.Serialization.Formatters (mscorlib.dll)   enum

This enumeration lists the possible values for the levels of automatic deserialization.
Low provides some security by only suporting basic remoting types.

```
public enum TypeFilterLevel {
  Low = 2,
  Full = 3
}
```

Hierarchy	System.Object → System.ValueType → System.Enum(System.IComparable, System.IFormattable, System.IConvertible) → TypeFilterLevel
Returned By	System.Runtime.Serialization.Formatters.Binary.BinaryFormatter.FilterLevel, System.Runtime.Serialization.Formatters.Soap.SoapFormatter.FilterLevel
Passed To	System.Runtime.Serialization.Formatters.Binary.BinaryFormatter.FilterLevel, System.Runtime.Serialization.Formatters.Soap.SoapFormatter.FilterLevel, System.Runtime. Serialization.FormatterServices.CheckTypeSecurity( )

40

System.Text

The System.Text namespace provides encoding and decoding capabilities for arrays of bytes and characters. These classes allow you to convert characters easily from different subsets of Unicode encodings, such as ASCII, UTF-8, and UTF-16. Additionally, a string-building class allows you to modify strings without creating intermediate string objects. Figure 40-1 shows the types in this namespace.

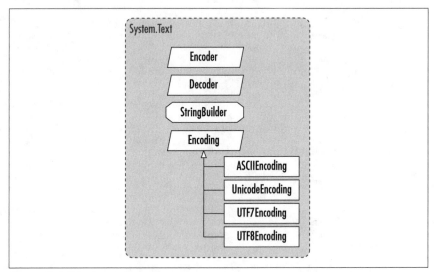

Figure 40-1. The System.Text namespace

ASCIIEncoding

System.Text (mscorlib.dll)   class

This class is a character encoding that encodes Unicode characters as 7-bit ASCII characters. ASCII uses the first 128 chayracters of a Unicode encoding.

```
public class ASCIIEncoding : Encoding {
// Public Constructors
  public ASCIIEncoding( );
// Public Instance Methods
  public override int GetByteCount(char[ ] chars, int index, int count);                  // overrides Encoding
  public override int GetByteCount(string chars);                                         // overrides Encoding
  public override int GetBytes(char[ ] chars, int charIndex, int charCount, byte[ ] bytes, int byteIndex);  // overrides Encoding
  public override int GetBytes(string chars, int charIndex, int charCount, byte[ ] bytes, int byteIndex);   // overrides Encoding
  public override int GetCharCount(byte[ ] bytes, int index, int count);                  // overrides Encoding
  public override int GetChars(byte[ ] bytes, int byteIndex, int byteCount, char[ ] chars, int charIndex);  // overrides Encoding
  public override int GetMaxByteCount(int charCount);                                     // overrides Encoding
  public override int GetMaxCharCount(int byteCount);                                     // overrides Encoding
  public override string GetString(byte[ ] bytes);                                        // overrides Encoding
  public override string GetString(byte[ ] bytes,                                         // overrides Encoding
    int byteIndex, int byteCount);
}
```

Hierarchy   System.Object → Encoding → ASCIIEncoding

Decoder

System.Text (mscorlib.dll)   abstract class

This class converts byte arrays to character arrays using the encoding class from which it was constructed (a decoder is returned by the GetDecoder( ) method of an Encoding subclass). Decoder saves its state between calls to GetChars( ), so leftover bytes from previous input byte arrays are remembered and used in subsequent calls.

```
public abstract class Decoder {
// Protected Constructors
  protected Decoder( );
// Public Instance Methods
  public abstract int GetCharCount(byte[ ] bytes, int index, int count);
  public abstract int GetChars(byte[ ] bytes, int byteIndex, int byteCount, char[ ] chars, int charIndex);
}
```

Returned By   Encoding.GetDecoder( )

Encoder

System.Text (mscorlib.dll)   abstract class

Encoding.GetEncoder( ) returns an instance of this type, which converts character arrays to byte arrays using the encoding subclass from which it was constructed. This class exposes the GetBytes( ) method, which converts a sequence of character blocks into a sequence of byte blocks. Since Encoder maintains state between calls to GetBytes( ), it can deal with partial sequences that occur at block boundaries.

The last argument to GetBytes( ) is a boolean that specifies whether the internal buffer is flushed after the method is called. If true, state information on the object is lost between blocks. If false (the default), the buffer is maintained. A call with flushing set to true is needed on the final call to Encoding.GetBytes( ) to close the byte array properly.

```
public abstract class Encoder {
// Protected Constructors
  protected Encoder( );
// Public Instance Methods
  public abstract int GetByteCount(char[ ] chars, int index, int count, bool flush);
  public abstract int GetBytes(char[ ] chars, int charIndex, int charCount, byte[ ] bytes, int byteIndex, bool flush);
}
```

Returned By   Encoding.GetEncoder( )

Encoding   CF 1.0, ECMA 1.0, serializable

System.Text (mscorlib.dll)   abstract class

This class converts strings of Unicode characters to and from byte arrays. Derived classes implement specific encoding types. The GetBytes( ) method takes an array of characters and returns the corresponding array of bytes. The GetChars( ) method does the opposite conversion. GetByteCount( ) and GetCharCount( ) allow you to get the exact size of the encoding or decoding to size the output buffer appropriately.

The GetEncoder( ) and GetDecoder( ) methods create Encoder and Decoder instances that allow you to do encoding across sequential blocks in which partial byte codes may remain in the buffer.

```
public abstract class Encoding {
// Protected Constructors
  protected Encoding( );
  protected Encoding(int codePage);
// Public Static Properties
  public static Encoding ASCII{get; }
  public static Encoding BigEndianUnicode{get; }
  public static Encoding Default{get; }
  public static Encoding Unicode{get; }
  public static Encoding UTF7{get; }
  public static Encoding UTF8{get; }
// Public Instance Properties
  public virtual string BodyName{get; }
  public virtual int CodePage{get; }
  public virtual string EncodingName{get; }
  public virtual string HeaderName{get; }
  public virtual bool IsBrowserDisplay{get; }
  public virtual bool IsBrowserSave{get; }
  public virtual bool IsMailNewsDisplay{get; }
  public virtual bool IsMailNewsSave{get; }
  public virtual string WebName{get; }
  public virtual int WindowsCodePage{get; }
// Public Static Methods
  public static byte[ ] Convert(Encoding srcEncoding, Encoding dstEncoding, byte[ ] bytes);
```

```
public static byte[ ] Convert(Encoding srcEncoding, Encoding dstEncoding, byte[ ] bytes, int index, int count);
public static Encoding GetEncoding(int codepage);
public static Encoding GetEncoding(string name);
// Public Instance Methods
public override bool Equals(object value);                                          // overrides object
public virtual int GetByteCount(char[ ] chars);
public abstract int GetByteCount(char[ ] chars, int index,  int count);
public virtual int GetByteCount(string s);
public virtual byte[ ] GetBytes(char[ ] chars);
public virtual byte[ ] GetBytes(char[ ] chars, int index, int count);
public virtual byte[ ] GetBytes(string s);
public abstract int GetBytes(char[ ] chars, int charIndex, int charCount, byte[ ] bytes, int byteIndex);
public virtual int GetBytes(string s, int charIndex, int charCount, byte[ ] bytes, int byteIndex);
public virtual int GetCharCount(byte[ ] bytes);
public abstract int GetCharCount(byte[ ] bytes, int index, int count);
public virtual char[ ] GetChars(byte[ ] bytes);
public virtual char[ ] GetChars(byte[ ] bytes, int index, int count);
public abstract int GetChars(byte[ ] bytes, int byteIndex, int byteCount, char[ ] chars, int charIndex);
public virtual Decoder GetDecoder( );
public virtual Encoder GetEncoder( );
public override int GetHashCode( );                                                // overrides object
public abstract int GetMaxByteCount(int charCount);
public abstract int GetMaxCharCount(int byteCount);
public virtual byte[ ] GetPreamble( );
public virtual string GetString(byte[ ] bytes);
public virtual string GetString(byte[ ] bytes, int index, int count);
}
```

Subclasses	ASCIIEncoding, UnicodeEncoding, UTF7Encoding, UTF8Encoding
Returned By	System.IO.StreamReader.CurrentEncoding, System.IO.TextWriter.Encoding, System.Xml.XmlParserContext.Encoding, System.Xml.XmlTextReader.Encoding, System.Xml.XmlValidatingReader.Encoding
Passed To	System.IO.BinaryReader.BinaryReader( ), System.IO.BinaryWriter.BinaryWriter( ), System.IO.StreamReader.StreamReader( ), System.IO.StreamWriter.StreamWriter( ), System.String.String( ), System.Xml.XmlParserContext.{Encoding, XmlParserContext( )}, System.Xml.XmlTextWriter.XmlTextWriter( )

StringBuilder   CF 1.0, ECMA 1.0, serializable

System.Text (mscorlib.dll)   sealed class

This String helper class enables in-place modification of a string without having to create new string instances. Since strings are immutable, their values cannot change once set. (Attempts to assign a new value to an existing string succeed, but at the expense of destroying and re-creating the original string.) The StringBuilder constructor allows you to set the size of the StringBuilder and specify the initial string it contains. The Insert( ) methods put new data (of varying types) into the StringBuilder at a specified position. Append( ) adds data to the end of a StringBuilder. The ToString( ) method converts the StringBuilder into a real string.

```
public sealed class StringBuilder {
// Public Constructors
  public StringBuilder( );
  public StringBuilder(int capacity);
  public StringBuilder(int capacity, int maxCapacity);
  public StringBuilder(string value);
  public StringBuilder(string value, int capacity);
  public StringBuilder(string value, int startIndex, int length, int capacity);
// Public Instance Properties
  public int Capacity{set; get; }
  public int Length{set; get; }
  public int MaxCapacity{get; }
  public char this[int index]{set; get; }
// Public Instance Methods
  public StringBuilder Append(bool value);
  public StringBuilder Append(byte value);
  public StringBuilder Append(char value);
  public StringBuilder Append(char[ ] value);
  public StringBuilder Append(char[ ] value, int startIndex, int charCount);
  public StringBuilder Append(char value, int repeatCount);
  public StringBuilder Append(decimal value);
  public StringBuilder Append(double value);
  public StringBuilder Append(short value);
  public StringBuilder Append(int value);
  public StringBuilder Append(long value);
  public StringBuilder Append(object value);
  public StringBuilder Append(sbyte value);
  public StringBuilder Append(float value);
  public StringBuilder Append(string value);
  public StringBuilder Append(string value, int startIndex, int count);
  public StringBuilder Append(ushort value);
  public StringBuilder Append(uint value);
  public StringBuilder Append(ulong value);
  public StringBuilder AppendFormat(IFormatProvider provider, string format, params object[ ] args);
  public StringBuilder AppendFormat(string format, object arg0);
  public StringBuilder AppendFormat(string format, params object[ ] args);
  public StringBuilder AppendFormat(string format, object arg0, object arg1);
  public StringBuilder AppendFormat(string format, object arg0, object arg1, object arg2);
  public int EnsureCapacity(int capacity);
  public bool Equals(StringBuilder sb);
  public StringBuilder Insert(int index, bool value);
  public StringBuilder Insert(int index, byte value);
  public StringBuilder Insert(int index, char value);
  public StringBuilder Insert(int index, char[ ] value);
  public StringBuilder Insert(int index, char[ ] value, int startIndex, int charCount);
  public StringBuilder Insert(int index, decimal value);
  public StringBuilder Insert(int index, double value);
  public StringBuilder Insert(int index, short value);
  public StringBuilder Insert(int index, int value);
  public StringBuilder Insert(int index, long value);
  public StringBuilder Insert(int index, object value);
```

```
public StringBuilder Insert(int index, sbyte value);
public StringBuilder Insert(int index, float value);
public StringBuilder Insert(int index, string value);
public StringBuilder Insert(int index, string value, int count);
public StringBuilder Insert(int index, ushort value);
public StringBuilder Insert(int index, uint value);
public StringBuilder Insert(int index, ulong value);
public StringBuilder Remove(int startIndex, int length);
public StringBuilder Replace(char oldChar, char newChar);
public StringBuilder Replace(char oldChar, char newChar, int startIndex, int count);
public StringBuilder Replace(string oldValue, string newValue);
public StringBuilder Replace(string oldValue, string newValue, int startIndex, int count);
public override string ToString();                                        // overrides object
public string ToString(int startIndex, int length);
}
```

Returned By   System.IO.StringWriter.GetStringBuilder( )

Passed To   System.IO.StringWriter.StringWriter( )

UnicodeEncoding   CF 1.0, ECMA 1.0, serializable

System.Text (mscorlib.dll)   class

This class encodes Unicode characters as UTF-16, two-byte characters. This class
supports little-endian and big-endian encodings. With zero arguments, the overloaded
constructor for this class uses little-endian byte order by default. The two-argument
constructor can use a boolean true as the first argument to specify big-endian byte
order. If set to true, the second boolean argument specifies the inclusion of the Unicode
byte-order mark in the resulting string. A UnicodeEncoding can also be obtained from two
Encoding properties. A little-endian encoding is returned by Encoding.Unicode. A big-endian
encoding is returned by Encoding.BigEndianUnicode.

```
public class UnicodeEncoding : Encoding {
// Public Constructors
  public UnicodeEncoding( );
  public UnicodeEncoding(bool bigEndian, bool byteOrderMark);
// Public Static Fields
  public const int CharSize;                                              // =2
// Public Instance Methods
  public override bool Equals(object value);                              // overrides Encoding
  public override int GetByteCount(char[ ] chars, int index, int count);  // overrides Encoding
  public override int GetByteCount(string s);                             // overrides Encoding
  public override byte[ ] GetBytes(string s);                            // overrides Encoding
  public override int GetBytes(char[ ] chars, int charIndex, int charCount, byte[ ] bytes, int byteIndex);  // overrides Encoding
  public override int GetBytes(string s, int charIndex, int charCount, byte[ ] bytes, int byteIndex);  // overrides Encoding
  public override int GetCharCount(byte[ ] bytes, int index, int count);  // overrides Encoding
  public override int GetChars(byte[ ] bytes, int byteIndex, int byteCount, char[ ] chars, int charIndex);  // overrides Encoding
  public override Decoder GetDecoder( );                                  // overrides Encoding
  public override int GetHashCode( );                                     // overrides Encoding
  public override int GetMaxByteCount(int charCount);                     // overrides Encoding
  public override int GetMaxCharCount(int byteCount);                     // overrides Encoding
```

```
    public override byte[ ] GetPreamble( );                                                      // overrides Encoding
}
```

Hierarchy   System.Object → Encoding → UnicodeEncoding

UTF7Encoding   CF 1.0, serializable

System.Text (mscorlib.dll)   class

This class encodes Unicode characters as UTF-7, 7-bit characters. UTF-7 is a Unicode
Transformation of the US-ASCII character set, designed for safe use over common
Internet mail and news gateways. RFC 2152, which defines UTF-7, specifies an
optional set of characters in the character set, which may or may not be encoded,
because they may interfere with mail-transfer header fields. The overloaded
constructor has two forms that take this into account. With no arguments, the
encoding object disallows the use of optional characters (such as exclamation points
and dollar signs). With a single boolean argument set to true, these optional characters
are allowed in the encoding.

```
public class UTF7Encoding : Encoding {
// Public Constructors
  public UTF7Encoding( );
  public UTF7Encoding(bool allowOptionals);
// Public Instance Methods
  public override int GetByteCount(char[ ] chars, int index, int count);                          // overrides Encoding
  public override int GetBytes(char[ ] chars, int charIndex, int charCount, byte[ ] bytes, int byteIndex);   // overrides Encoding
  public override int GetCharCount(byte[ ] bytes, int index, int count);                          // overrides Encoding
  public override int GetChars(byte[ ] bytes, int byteIndex, int byteCount, char[ ] chars, int charIndex);   // overrides Encoding
  public override Decoder GetDecoder( );                                                          // overrides Encoding
  public override Encoder GetEncoder( );                                                          // overrides Encoding
  public override int GetMaxByteCount(int charCount);                                             // overrides Encoding
  public override int GetMaxCharCount(int byteCount);                                             // overrides Encoding
}
```

Hierarchy   System.Object → Encoding → UTF7Encoding

UTF8Encoding   CF 1.0, ECMA 1.0, serializable

System.Text (mscorlib.dll)   class

This class encodes Unicode characters as UTF-8, 8-bit characters. The overloaded
constructor allows zero, one, or two boolean parameters. The first argument indicates
whether the encoder should both emit the UTF-8 byte order mark code and recognize
it. The second boolean argument specifies whether to throw an exception when invalid
bytes are encountered.

```
public class UTF8Encoding : Encoding {
// Public Constructors
  public UTF8Encoding( );
  public UTF8Encoding(bool encoderShouldEmitUTF8Identifier);
  public UTF8Encoding(bool encoderShouldEmitUTF8Identifier, bool throwOnInvalidBytes);
// Public Instance Methods
  public override bool Equals(object value);                                                      // overrides Encoding
```

```
public override int GetByteCount(char[ ] chars, int index, int count);          // overrides Encoding
public override int GetByteCount(string chars);                                  // overrides Encoding
public override byte[ ] GetBytes(string s);                                       // overrides Encoding
public override int GetBytes(char[ ] chars, int charIndex, int charCount, byte[ ] bytes, int byteIndex);   // overrides Encoding
public override int GetBytes(string s, int charIndex, int charCount, byte[ ] bytes, int byteIndex);        // overrides Encoding
public override int GetCharCount(byte[ ] bytes, int index,  int count);          // overrides Encoding
public override int GetChars(byte[ ] bytes, int byteIndex, int byteCount, char[ ] chars, int charIndex);   // overrides Encoding
public override Decoder GetDecoder( );                                            // overrides Encoding
public override Encoder GetEncoder( );                                            // overrides Encoding
public override int GetHashCode( );                                              // overrides Encoding
public override int GetMaxByteCount(int charCount);                              // overrides Encoding
public override int GetMaxCharCount(int byteCount);                              // overrides Encoding
public override byte[ ] GetPreamble( );                                           // overrides Encoding
}
```

Hierarchy   System.Object → Encoding → UTF8Encoding

41

System.Text. RegularExpressions

System.Text.RegularExpressions implements an object-oriented system for encapsulating regular expressions. The classes allow you to compile expressions and store matches that can be used with any .NET implementation regardless of the programming language. This namespace supports a regular expression syntax similar to Perl 5. Matches to the regular expression from an input string can be retrieved in fine granularity, allowing you to discern substring captures, groups, and multiple matches. Figure 41-1 shows the classes in this namespace.

Capture
CF 1.0, serializable

System.Text.RegularExpressions (system.dll)   class

This class represents a single result from a capturing group, which is a segment of a regular expression that is delineated, usually by parentheses. The parentheses signal .NET's regular expression engine to save that segment's result for later use. Capture objects compose the collection returned by Group.Captures. The Value property gets the captured substring. The Index property contains the starting position of the capture in the input string, while Length contains the length of the captured string.

```
public class Capture {
// Public Instance Properties
  public int Index{get; }
  public int Length{get; }
  public string Value{get; }
// Public Instance Methods
  public override string ToString( );                                  // overrides object
}
```

Subclasses   Group

Returned By   CaptureCollection.this

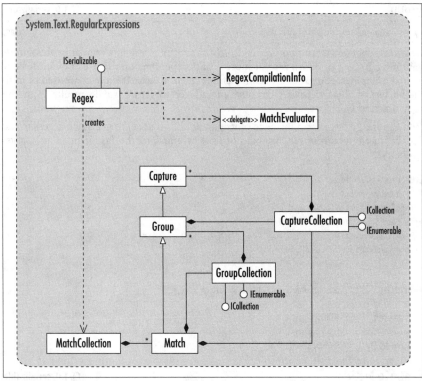

Figure 41-1. *The System.Text.RegularExpressions namespace*

CaptureCollection

CF 1.0, serializable

System.Text.RegularExpressions (system.dll)   class

This class contains a set of captures acquired by a single capturing group. A **CaptureCollec-tion** is returned by **Group.Captures**. An integer indexer returns a single **Capture** object from this collection. The **Count** property gets the number of captures in the collection.

```
public class CaptureCollection : ICollection, IEnumerable {
// Public Instance Properties
  public int Count{get; }                                                    // implements ICollection
  public bool IsReadOnly{get; }
  public bool IsSynchronized{get; }                                          // implements ICollection
  public object SyncRoot{get; }                                              // implements ICollection
  public Capture this[int i]{get; }
// Public Instance Methods
  public void CopyTo(Array array, int arrayIndex);                           // implements ICollection
  public IEnumerator GetEnumerator( );                                       // implements IEnumerable
}
```

Returned By   Group.Captures

Sys.Text.RegEx

Group

CF 1.0, serializable

System.Text.RegularExpressions (system.dll)   class

This class contains a group of results from a capturing group in a regular expression. A capturing group can return zero or more results depending on the use of quantifiers or nested groupings of a subexpression. **Captures** returns a **CaptureCollection** composed of individual **Capture** objects. **Captures** can use an indexer to return single results from the **CaptureCollection**.

You can treat a **Group** as an instance of its parent class (**Capture**) to get quick access to the last captured substring (an instance of **Group** is equal to the last item in its **Captures** property).

```
public class Group : Capture {
// Public Instance Properties
   public CaptureCollection Captures{get; }
   public bool Success{get; }
// Public Static Methods
   public static Group Synchronized(Group inner);
}
```

Hierarchy   System.Object → Capture → Group

Subclasses   Match

Returned By   GroupCollection.this

GroupCollection

CF 1.0, serializable

System.Text.RegularExpressions (system.dll)   class

This class is a collection of the captured groups in a regular expression. A **GroupCollection** is indexed by either a string with the name of the capture group, or with an integer number of the capture group as determined in the regular expression (give a name to a capture group by putting ?<name> immediately after the opening parenthesis). So, **Match.Groups["name"]** would retrieve a capture from the subexpression (?<name>expr), and **Match.Groups[1]** would be the result from the first explicitly grouped subexpression. The entire regular expression is the zero-indexed group (an expression without any groupings is treated as a single group). A **GroupCollection** is returned by **Match.Groups**.

```
public class GroupCollection : ICollection, IEnumerable {
// Public Instance Properties
   public int Count{get; }                                    // implements ICollection
   public bool IsReadOnly{get; }
   public bool IsSynchronized{get; }                          // implements ICollection
   public object SyncRoot{get; }                              // implements ICollection
   public Group this[string groupname]{get; }
   public Group this[int groupnum]{get; }
// Public Instance Methods
   public void CopyTo(Array array, int arrayindex);           // implements ICollection
   public IEnumerator GetEnumerator( );                       // implements IEnumerable
}
```

Returned By   Match.Groups

System.Text.RegularExpressions (system.dll)   class

This class is a single match result of a regular expression. As with **Capture** and **Group**, **Match** has no public constructor. It is returned by **Regex.Match( )** or as a member of a **MatchCollection** returned by **Regex.Matches( )**. A **Match** instance contains the groups that have been captured in a **GroupCollection** returned by **Groups**. A **Match** inherits from **Group** and is equivalent to the zero-indexed group in its **GroupCollection** (the same as **Groups[0]**).

The **NextMatch( )** method finds the next match result in the search string, starting at the end of the previous match. This method disregards any zero-width assertions on the tail of an expression and begins explicitly after the position of the last character of the previous result (even an empty result).

The **Result( )** method takes a replacement pattern and returns the resulting string based on the current match. A replacement pattern is an expression that uses the group replacement syntax, such as **$1** or **${name}**. **Result( )** expands the replacement variables corresponding to the captured groups, within its current result, and returns the string.

```
public class Match : Group {
// Public Static Properties
  public static Match Empty{get; }
// Public Instance Properties
  public virtual GroupCollection Groups{get; }
// Public Static Methods
  public static Match Synchronized(Match inner);
// Public Instance Methods
  public Match NextMatch( );
  public virtual string Result(string replacement);
}
```

Hierarchy   System.Object → Capture → Group → Match

Returned By   MatchCollection.this, Regex.Match( )

Passed To   MatchEvaluator.{BeginInvoke( ), Invoke( )}

System.Text.RegularExpressions (system.dll)   class

This class is a collection of **Match** objects returned by **Regex.Matches( )**. This collection contains each match that an expression finds in the search string. The **Count** property returns the number of matches found in the string.

```
public class MatchCollection : ICollection, IEnumerable {
// Public Instance Properties
  public int Count{get; }                                              // implements ICollection
  public bool IsReadOnly{get; }
  public bool IsSynchronized{get; }                                    // implements ICollection
  public object SyncRoot{get; }                                        // implements ICollection
  public virtual Match this[int i]{get; }
```

```
// Public Instance Methods
    public void CopyTo(Array array, int arrayIndex);                          // implements ICollection
    public IEnumerator GetEnumerator( );                                      // implements IEnumerable
}
```

Returned By   Regex.Matches( )

MatchEvaluator   CF 1.0, serializable

System.Text.RegularExpressions (system.dll)   delegate

This delegate can be called when a match is found during a replace operation. Several
versions of the overloaded Regex.Replace( ) method take a MatchEvaluator as a parameter.
Regex.Replace( ) walks through a search string looking for matches to a given expression
and replaces each match using a specified replacement string. The MatchEvaluator delegate can be called on each match, getting passed the match result as a Match object.

```
public delegate string MatchEvaluator(Match match);
```

Passed To   Regex.Replace( )

Regex   CF 1.0, serializable

System.Text.RegularExpressions (system.dll)   class

This class represents a regular expression. Use it to search for patterns in string data. It
provides static methods that search for a pattern without explicitly creating Regex
instances as well as instance methods that allow you to interact with a Regex object.

The various static methods employed by Regex take the input string to search for as the
first argument and the regular expression pattern string as the second. This is equivalent to constructing a Regex instance with a pattern string, using it, and destroying it
immediately. Most methods are overloaded as instance methods as well. These do not
require a pattern argument, as this is provided with the constructor.

The Match( ) and Matches( ) methods search an input string for a single match or all
matches. Their overloads are the same. The first argument is the input string. You can
specify which position in the string the search should start at using a second integer
parameter. Match( ) also lets you specify the length of substring to search after that position. IsMatch( ) works the same way as Match( ), except that it returns a boolean indicating
whether the string contains a match.

The Split( ) method acts like the System.String.Split( ) method. It uses the Regex pattern as a
delimiter to split the input string into an array of substrings. (The delimiter is not
included in the substrings.) You can provide a maximum number of substrings to
return, in which case the last substring returned is the remainder of the input string.
You can also specify the position to start in the input string and a RegexOptions
parameter.

The Replace( ) method uses a replacement string to replace each pattern match in an
input string. The replacement string can include regular characters and backreference
variable constructs (e.g., $1 or ${name}). Replace( ) can iterate through every match found
in the input string, or it can specify a maximum number of replacements to perform.
Replace( ) can also take an argument specifying a MatchEvaluator delegate, which is called
every time a match is found.

Two additional static methods can transform strings used with regular expressions. Escape() converts a string containing regular expression metacharacters by replacing them with escaped equivalents (for example, ? would be changed to \?). The set of metacharacters converted is \, *, +, ?, |, {, [, (,), ^, $, ., #, and any whitespace. The Unescape() method replaces escaped characters within a string with their unescaped equivalents. Use Escape() and Unescape() when you need to use one of these metacharacters as a literal in a regular expression.

A set of instance methods for Regex provides information on the capturing groups contained in the expression. GetGroupNames() and GetGroupNumbers() each return an array containing the names of all the capture groups or numbers of all capture groups, respectively. The GroupNameFromNumber() and GroupNumberFromName() methods return the corresponding name or number from the argument given to them.

CompileToAssembly() allows you to create your own type for a regular expression object and save it to disk as an assembly. This is a static method that takes a RegexCompilationInfo object and assembly information to build the type. The RegexCompilationInfo object contains the regular expression pattern and additional information needed for the compilation.

```
public class Regex : System.Runtime.Serialization.ISerializable {
// Public Constructors
  public Regex(string pattern);
  public Regex(string pattern, RegexOptions options);
// Protected Constructors
  protected Regex( );
// Public Instance Properties
  public RegexOptions Options{get; }
  public bool RightToLeft{get; }
// Public Static Methods
  public static void CompileToAssembly(RegexCompilationInfo[ ] regexinfos,
    System.Reflection.AssemblyName assemblyname);
  public static void CompileToAssembly(RegexCompilationInfo[ ] regexinfos,
    System.Reflection.AssemblyName assemblyname, System.Reflection.Emit.CustomAttributeBuilder[ ] attributes);
  public static void CompileToAssembly(RegexCompilationInfo[ ] regexinfos,
    System.Reflection.AssemblyName assemblyname,
    System.Reflection.Emit.CustomAttributeBuilder[ ] attributes, string resourceFile);
  public static string Escape(string str);
  public static bool IsMatch(string input, string pattern);
  public static bool IsMatch(string input, string pattern, RegexOptions options);
  public static Match Match(string input, string pattern);
  public static Match Match(string input, string pattern, RegexOptions options);
  public static MatchCollection Matches(string input, string pattern);
  public static MatchCollection Matches(string input, string pattern, RegexOptions options);
  public static string Replace(string input, string pattern, MatchEvaluator evaluator);
  public static string Replace(string input, string pattern, MatchEvaluator evaluator, RegexOptions options);
  public static string Replace(string input, string pattern, string replacement);
  public static string Replace(string input, string pattern, string replacement, RegexOptions options);
  public static string[ ] Split(string input, string pattern);
  public static string[ ] Split(string input, string pattern, RegexOptions options);
  public static string Unescape(string str);
// Public Instance Methods
  public string[ ] GetGroupNames( );
```

```
public int[ ] GetGroupNumbers( );
public string GroupNameFromNumber(int i);
public int GroupNumberFromName(string name);
public bool IsMatch(string input);
public bool IsMatch(string input, int startat);
public Match Match(string input);
public Match Match(string input, int startat);
public Match Match(string input, int beginning, int length);
public MatchCollection Matches(string input);
public MatchCollection Matches(string input, int startat);
public string Replace(string input, MatchEvaluator evaluator);
public string Replace(string input, MatchEvaluator evaluator, int count);
public string Replace(string input, MatchEvaluator evaluator, int count, int startat);
public string Replace(string input, string replacement);
public string Replace(string input, string replacement, int count);
public string Replace(string input, string replacement, int count, int startat);
public string[ ] Split(string input);
public string[ ] Split(string input, int count);
public string[ ] Split(string input, int count, int startat);
public override string ToString( );                                                 // overrides object
// Protected Instance Methods
  protected override void Finalize( );                                              // overrides object
  protected void InitializeReferences( );
  protected bool UseOptionC( );
  protected bool UseOptionR( );
}
```

Passed To   System.Net.WebPermission.{AddPermission( ), WebPermission( )}

RegexCompilationInfo   serializable

System.Text.RegularExpressions (system.dll)   class

This class holds the information that is needed to compile a regular expression to an
assembly with Regex.CompileToAssembly( ). The constructor takes five arguments, which
correspond to its available properties: the pattern string, the RegexOptions option set, the
name of the compiled type, the namespace for the type, and a boolean indicating if the
type is public (true) or private (false).

```
public class RegexCompilationInfo {
// Public Constructors
  public RegexCompilationInfo(string pattern, RegexOptions options, string name, string fullnamespace, bool ispublic);
// Public Instance Properties
  public bool IsPublic{set; get; }
  public string Name{set; get; }
  public string Namespace{set; get; }
  public RegexOptions Options{set; get; }
  public string Pattern{set; get; }
}
```

Passed To   Regex.CompileToAssembly( )

RegexOptions

System.Text.RegularExpressions (system.dll)   enum

This enumeration contains various options that affect the behavior of pattern matching in various methods from the System.Text.RegularExpressions namespace. The values of this enumeration are passed to these methods as a bitwise-OR combination of the specified options.

```
public enum RegexOptions {
  None = 0x00000000,
  IgnoreCase = 0x00000001,
  Multiline = 0x00000002,
  ExplicitCapture = 0x00000004,
  Compiled = 0x00000008,
  Singleline = 0x00000010,
  IgnorePatternWhitespace = 0x00000020,
  RightToLeft = 0x00000040,
  ECMAScript = 0x00000100,
  CultureInvariant = 0x00000200
}
```

Hierarchy   System.Object → System.ValueType → System.Enum(System.IComparable,
                     System.IFormattable, System.IConvertible) → RegexOptions

Returned By   Regex.Options, RegexCompilationInfo.Options

Passed To   Regex.{IsMatch( ), Match( ), Matches( ), Regex( ), Replace( ), Split( )},
                     RegexCompilationInfo.{Options, RegexCompilationInfo( )}

42

System.Threading

A "thread" is an abstraction of the platform, providing the impression that the CPU is performing multiple tasks simultaneously; in essence, it offers to the programmer the ability to walk and chew gum at the same time. The .NET framework makes heavy use of threads throughout the system, both visibly and invisibly. The System.Threading namespace contains most of the baseline threading concepts, usable either directly or to help build higher-level constructs (as the .NET Framework Class Library frequently does).

The "thread" itself is sometimes referred to as a "lightweight process" (particularly within the Unix communities). This is because the thread, like the concept of a process, is simply an operating system (or, in the case of .NET, a CLR) abstraction. In the case of Win32 threads, the operating system is responsible for "switching" the necessary execution constructs (the registers and thread stack) on the CPU in order to execute the code on the thread, just as the OS does for multiple programs running simultaneously on the machine. The key difference between a process and a thread, however, is that each process gets its own inviolable memory space—its "process space"—that other processes cannot touch. All threads belong to a single process and share the same process space; therefore, threads can operate cooperatively on a single object. However, this is both an advantage and a disadvantage—if multiple threads can all access a single object, there arises the possibility that the threads will be acting concurrently against the object, leading to some interesting (and unrepeatable) results.

For example, one common problem in VB and MFC code was the inability to process user input while carrying out some other function; this was because the one (and only) thread used to process user input events (button clicks, menu selections, and so on) was also used to carry out the requests to the database, the calculation of results, the generation of pi to the millionth decimal place, and so on. Users could not negate actions ("Oh, shoot, I didn't mean to click that...."), because the user's UI actions—clicking a "Cancel" button, for example—

wouldn't be processed until the non-UI action finished first. This would lead the user to believe that the program has "hung."

The first reaction might be to simply fire off every "action" from a UI event in its own thread; this would be a naive reaction at best, as a huge source of bugs and data corruption is more likely. Consider, for a moment, a simple UI that runs off to the database and performs a query when the user clicks a button. It would be tempting to simply spin the database query off in its own thread and update the UI if and when the database query completes.

The problems come up when the query returns—when do we put the results up? If the user has the ability to update the information (before the query results are returned), then does the new data overwrite the user's input? Or should the user's input overwrite the query results? What happens if the user clicks the button again? Should we fire off another query? Worse yet, what happens if the user has moved to a different part of the application? Should the UI "suddenly" flip back to the place from which the query was originated and update the values there? This would make it appear to the user that "some weird bug just took over" the program. But if the query silently updates the data, the user may wonder whether that query ever actually finished.

As is common with such capabilities, however, with power comes responsibility. Callous use of threads within an application can not only create these sorts of conundrums regarding UI design, but also lead to mysterious and inexplicable data corruption. Consider the simple expression $x = x + 5$. If x is a single object living in the heap, and two threads both simultaneously execute this code, one of several things can occur.

In the first case, the two threads are slightly ahead of or behind one another; the first thread obtains the value of x, adds 5, and stores that value back to x. The second thread, right behind it, does the same. x is incremented by 10. Consider the case, however, when both threads are in exactly the same place in the code. The first thread obtains the value of x (call it 10). The second thread gets switched in and loads the value of x (again, still 10). The first thread switches back in and increments its local value for x (which is 10, now 15). The second thread switches in and increments its local value for x (which is 10, now 15). The first thread stores its new local value for x back into x (15). The second thread switches in and stores its new local value for x (15). Both threads executed, yet the value of x grows by only 5, not 10, as should have happened.

For this reason, threads must often be held up in certain areas of code, in order to wait until another thread is finished. This is called "thread synchronization," sometimes colloquially referred to as "locks." It is the programmer's responsibility to ensure that any thread-sensitive code (such as the previous $x = x + 5$ example) is properly thread-synchronized. Within C++ and VB 6, this could only be done by making use of Win32 synchronization objects such as events and critical sections; however, a simpler mechanism is available in the CLR.

Each object can have a corresponding "monitor" associated with it. This monitor serves as thread-synchronization primitive, since only one thread within the CLR can "own" the monitor. Synchronization is then achieved by forcing threads to wait to acquire the monitor on the object before being allowed to continue; this is very similar to the Win32 critical section. (This monitor is an instance of the Monitor type; see that type for more details.)

Anytime locks are introduced into a system, however, two dangers occur: safety and liveness. *Safety* refers to the presence of the kind of data corruption discussed earlier—the lack of enough thread synchronization. *Liveness* is the actual time the threads spend executing, and often represents the opposite danger as safety (the presence of too much thread synchronization, particularly the danger of *deadlock*: two threads frozen forever, each waiting for a lock the other one already holds). An excellent discussion of these two concepts can be found in Doug Lea's book *Concurrent Programming in Java: Design Principles and Pattern, Second Edition* (Addison Wesley). (Despite Java code samples, 99% of his discussion pertains to threading in .NET as well.)

Frequently programmers wish to perform some sort of asynchronous operation. One approach is to simply create a Thread object and start it off. Unfortunately, this is also somewhat wasteful, since the cost of creating a thread and destroying it (when the thread has finished executing) is quite high. For this reason, it is often more performant to "borrow" an existing and unused thread—this is the purpose of the ThreadPool type, and one such pool already exists for use by the CLR runtime for processes such as the asynchronous execution of delegates (see System.Delegate for more details).

Figure 42-1 shows many of the classes in this namespace. Figure 42-2 shows the delegates, exceptions, and event arguments. Figure 42-3 shows a state diagram for threads.

ApartmentState serializable

System.Threading (mscorlib.dll) enum

This type is entirely unnecessary for "normal" .NET code; it is needed only for COM interoperability capability.

Apartments are a COM-threading construct. There are two threading apartments: *single-threaded* (STA) and *multithreaded* (MTA). Once a thread joins an apartment, it cannot join another one. If you want to create or access a COM object from a thread, that thread must belong to an apartment. Further, a given COM component may only be compatible with a certain apartment state.

What if an STA thread needs to call a method on a COM object that is only compatible with MTA threads? In that case, a different thread that is already in the MTA state must service the request. The COM Service Control Manager either creates a new thread or uses one allocated for servicing remote procedure calls to accomplish this

Threads in an MTA apartment cannot directly access STA threads either. Instead, the STA thread contains a message sink, and the method is invoked when the thread in that apartment is free. .NET objects do away with this requirement; however, if some of the threads call COM objects, they must first join an apartment. The Thread class usually handles this automatically, but you can join an apartment directly by assigning a parameter from this enumeration to the Thread.ApartmentState property. Unknown indicates that the thread has not joined an apartment.

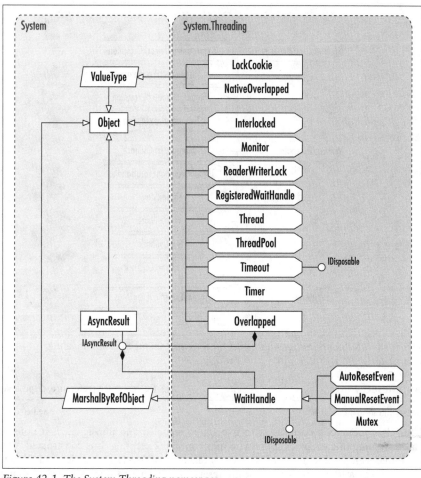

Figure 42-1. The System.Threading namespace

```
public enum ApartmentState {
  STA = 0,
  MTA = 1,
  Unknown = 2
}
```

Hierarchy   System.Object → System.ValueType → System.Enum(System.IComparable,
                System.IFormattable, System.IConvertible) → ApartmentState

Returned By Thread.ApartmentState

Passed To   Thread.ApartmentState

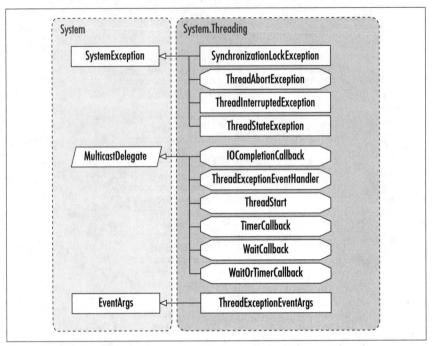

Figure 42-2. Delegates, exceptions, and event arguments in the System.Threading namespace

AutoResetEvent
CF 1.0, marshal by reference, disposable

System.Threading (mscorlib.dll)   sealed class

This class presents a WaitHandle with two states: signaled and nonsignaled. If nonsignaled, waiting threads block; otherwise they continue executing. It is constructed with an initial signal value and can be Set() to signaled or Reset() to nonsignaled. When signaled, the AutoResetEvent automatically resets to nonsignaled once a single blocking thread has been released. Calling Set() with no blocking threads causes it to remain signaled until another thread waits on it.

```
public sealed class AutoResetEvent : WaitHandle {
// Public Constructors
  public AutoResetEvent(bool initialState);
// Public Instance Methods
  public bool Reset( );
  public bool Set( );
}
```

Hierarchy   System.Object → System.MarshalByRefObject → WaitHandle(System.IDisposable) →
                     AutoResetEvent

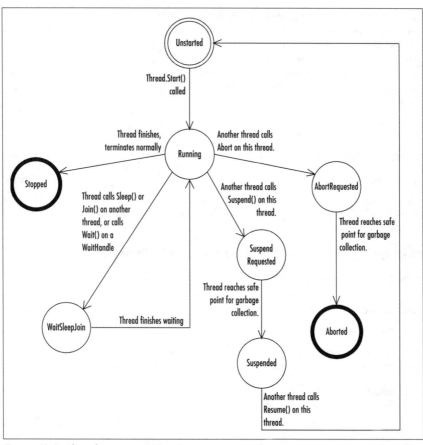

Figure 42-3. Thread state transitions

Interlocked

CF 1.0, ECMA 1.0

System.Threading (mscorlib.dll)   sealed class

The static members of this class provide thread safety for common built-in arithmetic operations, such as increasing and decreasing a variable by one, and exchanging variables.

If two threads increment the same variable, one thread could be interrupted after both have retrieved the initial value of the variable. If this happens, then both operations store the same value, meaning that the variable has been incremented once instead of twice. The Interlocked methods protect against this kind of error. Increment() and Decrement() increase and decrease a variable by one, respectively, and Exchange() switches two variables. CompareExchange() compares the first two variables and, if true, assigns the third value to the first variable.

```
public sealed class Interlocked {
// Public Static Methods
  public static int CompareExchange(ref int location1, int value, int comparand);
  public static object CompareExchange(ref object location1, object value, object comparand);
```

```
public static float CompareExchange(ref float location1, float value, float comparand);
public static int Decrement(ref int location);
public static long Decrement(ref long location);
public static int Exchange(ref int location1, int value);
public static object Exchange(ref object location1, object value);
public static float Exchange(ref float location1, float value);
public static int Increment(ref int location);
public static long Increment(ref long location);
}
```

IOCompletionCallback   serializable

System.Threading (mscorlib.dll)   delegate

This delegate is used to communicate with thread pools that are created using the
Win32 API. This is a delegate to a method that will be called by an unmanaged
process.

```
public delegate void IOCompletionCallback(uint errorCode, uint numBytes, NativeOverlapped *pOVERLAP);
```

Passed To   Overlapped.{Pack( ), UnsafePack( )}

LockCookie   serializable

System.Threading (mscorlib.dll)   struct

This structure returns a LockCookie representing the type of lock (read or write) released.
The same type of lock can be restored by calling ReaderWriterLock.RestoreLock( ).

```
public struct LockCookie {
// No public or protected members
}
```

Hierarchy   System.Object → System.ValueType → LockCookie

Returned By   ReaderWriterLock.{ReleaseLock( ), UpgradeToWriterLock( )}

Passed To   ReaderWriterLock.{DowngradeFromWriterLock( ), RestoreLock( )}

ManualResetEvent   CF 1.0, marshal by reference, disposable

System.Threading (mscorlib.dll)   sealed class

This class is a WaitHandle with two states: signaled and nonsignaled. If nonsignaled,
waiting threads block. If signaled, they continue executing. It is constructed with an
initial signal value and can be Set( ) to signaled or Reset( ) to nonsignaled. Once signaled,
you must manually (hence the name of this type) call Reset( ) to revert it to nonsignaled.

```
public sealed class ManualResetEvent : WaitHandle {
// Public Constructors
public ManualResetEvent(bool initialState);
// Public Instance Methods
public bool Reset( );
```

```
   public bool Set( );
}
```

Hierarchy　　　System.Object → System.MarshalByRefObject → WaitHandle(System.IDisposable) →
ManualResetEvent

Monitor
CF 1.0, ECMA 1.0

System.Threading (mscorlib.dll)
sealed class

This class contains static methods for thread communication and synchronization. The Enter() and Exit() methods allow you to obtain and release a lock on an object, respectively. If an object lock has already been obtained by another thread, Enter() blocks and resumes executing when the lock is released.

Various languages have the ability to silently emit calls on this type as language built-in primitives. C#'s lock{} syntax translates into these two methods: the beginning of the lock block is transformed into a call to Enter(), and the close of the block calls Exit(). (In the presence of exceptions and return calls, the C# compiler must ensure the release of the monitor regardless of how the code exits the lock block.)

TryEnter() attempts to obtain an object lock, but it continues executing and returns false if unsuccessful. Wait() releases an object lock and causes the current thread to wait until another thread calls Pulse() or PulseAll() on the same object. Wait() must be executed from a synchronized block of code.

```
public sealed class Monitor {
// Public Static Methods
  public static void Enter(object obj);
  public static void Exit(object obj);
  public static void Pulse(object obj);
  public static void PulseAll(object obj);
  public static bool TryEnter(object obj);
  public static bool TryEnter(object obj, int millisecondsTimeout);
  public static bool TryEnter(object obj, TimeSpan timeout);
  public static bool Wait(object obj);
  public static bool Wait(object obj, int millisecondsTimeout);
  public static bool Wait(object obj, int millisecondsTimeout, bool exitContext);
  public static bool Wait(object obj, TimeSpan timeout);
  public static bool Wait(object obj, TimeSpan timeout, bool exitContext);
}
```

Mutex
CF 1.0, marshal by reference, disposable

System.Threading (mscorlib.dll)
sealed class

A Mutex is an implementation of a WaitHandle. ReleaseMutex() releases a lock on a WaitHandle. A thread that owns a Mutex lock can call any of the Wait() methods (defined in the parent class, WaitHandle) without blocking, but must then release the Mutex the same number of times as the Mutex was obtained.

```
public sealed class Mutex : WaitHandle {
// Public Constructors
  public Mutex( );
  public Mutex(bool initiallyOwned);
```

**System.
Threading**

```
  public Mutex(bool initiallyOwned, string name);
  public Mutex(bool initiallyOwned, string name, out bool createdNew);
// Public Instance Methods
  public void ReleaseMutex( );
}
```

Hierarchy   System.Object → System.MarshalByRefObject → WaitHandle(System.IDisposable) →
                  Mutex

NativeOverlapped

System.Threading (mscorlib.dll)   struct

This structure has the same layout as the Win32 OVERLAPPED structure, with extra
reserved data at the end, which is provided for backward compatibility. Create a Native-
Overlapped instance by calling Overlapped.Pack( ). Each time an instance is created, it must be
freed by calling the static method Overlapped.Free( ) to avoid a memory leak.

```
public struct NativeOverlapped {
// Public Instance Fields
  public int EventHandle;
  public int InternalHigh;
  public int InternalLow;
  public int OffsetHigh;
  public int OffsetLow;
}
```

Hierarchy   System.Object → System.ValueType → NativeOverlapped

Returned By   Overlapped.{Pack( ), UnsafePack( )}

Passed To   IOCompletionCallback.{BeginInvoke( ), Invoke( )}, Overlapped.{Free( ), Unpack( )}

Overlapped

System.Threading (mscorlib.dll)   class

This class encapsulates the Win32 API OVERLAPPED structure. NativeOverlapped is needed to
mimic the structure the API expects, but this class encapsulates the overlapped structure into a .NET class. You can create NativeOverlapped structures by calling Pack( ), and
create Overlapped objects with the static Unpack( ) method. To avoid a memory leak, each
NativeOverlapped that you create must also be freed by calling the staticFree( ) method.
Unpack( ) does *not* free the memory.

```
public class Overlapped {
// Public Constructors
  public Overlapped( );
  public Overlapped(int offsetLo, int offsetHi, int hEvent, IAsyncResult ar);
// Public Instance Properties
  public IAsyncResult AsyncResult{set; get; }
  public int EventHandle{set; get; }
  public int OffsetHigh{set; get; }
  public int OffsetLow{set; get; }
```

```
// Public Static Methods
  public static void Free(NativeOverlapped *nativeOverlappedPtr);
  public static Overlapped Unpack(NativeOverlapped *nativeOverlappedPtr);
// Public Instance Methods
  public NativeOverlapped* Pack(IOCompletionCallback iocb);
  public NativeOverlapped* UnsafePack(IOCompletionCallback iocb);
}
```

ReaderWriterLock

System.Threading (mscorlib.dll)   sealed class

This class defines a lock that allows multiple readers, but only one writer. A thread can acquire a lock by calling AcquireReaderLock() or AcquireWriterLock(). ReleaseReaderLock() and ReleaseWriterLock() release the specific locks. Calling ReleaseReaderLock() on a writer lock releases both the writer lock and the reader lock. However, calling ReleaseWriterLock() on a reader lock throws a System.ApplicationException.

ReleaseLock() causes any lock to be released, but it returns a LockCookie, which represents the type of lock that RestoreLock can use to obtain the same lock. UpgradeToWriterLock() upgrades a reader lock to a writer lock, and returns a LockCookie representing the original reader lock. Pass that cookie to DowngradeDromWriterLock() to restore the original reader lock.

```
public sealed class ReaderWriterLock {
// Public Constructors
  public ReaderWriterLock( );
// Public Instance Properties
  public bool IsReaderLockHeld{get; }
  public bool IsWriterLockHeld{get; }
  public int WriterSeqNum{get; }
// Public Instance Methods
  public void AcquireReaderLock(int millisecondsTimeout);
  public void AcquireReaderLock(TimeSpan timeout);
  public void AcquireWriterLock(int millisecondsTimeout);
  public void AcquireWriterLock(TimeSpan timeout);
  public bool AnyWritersSince(int seqNum);
  public void DowngradeFromWriterLock(ref LockCookie lockCookie);
  public LockCookie ReleaseLock( );
  public void ReleaseReaderLock( );
  public void ReleaseWriterLock( );
  public void RestoreLock(ref LockCookie lockCookie);
  public LockCookie UpgradeToWriterLock(int millisecondsTimeout);
  public LockCookie UpgradeToWriterLock(TimeSpan timeout);
}
```

RegisteredWaitHandle   marshal by reference

System.Threading (mscorlib.dll)   sealed class

ThreadPool.RegisterWaitForSingleObject( ) returns a RegisteredWaitHandle. To cancel a registered wait (either a new one or one that continuously executes), use Unregister( ).

```
public sealed class RegisteredWaitHandle : MarshalByRefObject {
// Public Instance Methods
  public bool Unregister(WaitHandle waitObject);
// Protected Instance Methods
  protected override void Finalize( );                                          // overrides object
}
```

Hierarchy   System.Object → System.MarshalByRefObject → RegisteredWaitHandle

Returned By   ThreadPool.{RegisterWaitForSingleObject( ), UnsafeRegisterWaitForSingleObject( )}

SynchronizationLockException   ECMA 1.0, serializable

System.Threading (mscorlib.dll)   class

This exception is thrown when Monitor.Exit( ), Monitor.Pulse( ), Monitor.PulseAll( ), or Monitor.Wait( ) is called from unsynchronized code.

```
public class SynchronizationLockException : SystemException {
// Public Constructors
  public SynchronizationLockException( );
  public SynchronizationLockException(string message);
  public SynchronizationLockException(string message, Exception innerException);
// Protected Constructors
  protected SynchronizationLockException(System.Runtime.Serialization.SerializationInfo info,
    System.Runtime.Serialization.StreamingContext context);
}
```

Hierarchy   System.Object → System.Exception(System.Runtime.Serialization.ISerializable) →
                       System.SystemException → SynchronizationLockException

Thread   CF 1.0, ECMA 1.0

System.Threading (mscorlib.dll)   sealed class

Most interaction with the System.Threading namespace occurs via the Thread type. This type encapsulates most of the logic needed to control the way threads behave.

The most commonly used static methods, usually referred to as *thread relative statics*, are methods and properties that refer to the currently executing thread. Sleep( ) causes the calling thread to sleep for a specified amount of time. If for some reason the thread gets woken up, a ThreadInterruptedException is thrown. Because this method can only be called by the current thread and not on a reference to a thread that may also be executing, the thread sleeps immediately and does not need to wait for a safe point for garbage collection as the Suspend( ) method does (see later in this entry).

GetData( ) retrieves data from a specified slot in *thread local storage*. To use this method, slots need to be initialized already (see later in this section). SetData( ) stores data in *thread local storage* to be retrieved using GetData( ). AllocateDataSlot( ) and AllocateNamedDataSlot( ) allocate a data slot for use with the previous two methods.

The Thread class also provides the static property CurrentThread, which returns a reference to the Thread object for the currently running thread. The current thread can then access any of the following instance methods or properties on itself: Abort( ) causes a thread to abort, throwing a ThreadAbortException and executing any finally blocks. You may catch the

ThreadAbortException, but it is automatically rethrown unless you invoke ResetAbort( ), which countermands the Abort() and lets the thread continue to live. Interrupt( ) interrupts a thread that is in the ThreadState.WaitSleepJoin state. If a thread is not in the ThreadState.Wait-SleepJoin state, it is interrupted when it next attempts to enter that state (Join() causes the calling thread to enter that state). The calling thread only starts again once the referenced thread finishes executing and enters the ThreadState.Stopped state. Suspend( ) suspends a thread. The thread is suspended once it has reached a safe point for garbage collection. The current thread can then access any of the following instance methods or properties on itself. Resume( ) resumes a thread that is in the suspended state. Threads in the suspended state are resumed regardless of how many times Suspend( ) was called. Start( ) tells a thread to start executing.

Starting with .NET 1.1, the Thread class provides three new methods (with appropriate overloads) that allow for direct access without respect to any per-processor or per-thread inherent caching mechanism; the VolatileRead( ) and VolatileWrite( ) methods will fetch and set "the value of a field... the latest written by any processor in a computer, regardless of the number of processors or the state of the processor cache" (from the MSDN documentation). This bears some explanation to make sense. Each CPU within the CLR, in the interests of efficiency, is allowed to cache values of objects and data within a thread-local cache, so that requests to access those fields doesn't require a full trip out to the garbage-collected heap. Unfortunately, doing so tends to lead to situations where multiple threads accessing the same fields on the same object (since these values are cached on a per-CPU basis) lead to different values across threads executing on those different CPUs, which is obviously a bad idea. Normally, by using the lock block within C#, a memory barrier is set up, meaning the thread is now required to synchronize its processor cache with the global heap settings, thus forcing the processor-cached field values to match what's in the global heap. These methods (VolatileRead( ) and VolatileWrite( )) force a trip out to the heap, rather than relying on processor cache, useful in situations where an explicit lock is not desired, yet accurate reflection of the object's state is necessary. In addition, the MemoryBarrier( ) method provides the same flushing of cache data to the central heap, but again, this same behavior is seen when using the lock syntax or the Monitor class, both of which provide the same semantics but are clearer and easier to use. For the most part, programmers are encouraged to use lock and/or Monitor where accessing shared data across threads.

```
public sealed class Thread {
// Public Constructors
  public Thread(ThreadStart start);
// Public Static Properties
  public static Context CurrentContext{get; }
  public static IPrincipal CurrentPrincipal{set; get; }
  public static Thread CurrentThread{get; }
// Public Instance Properties
  public ApartmentState ApartmentState{set; get; }
  public CultureInfo CurrentCulture{set; get; }
  public CultureInfo CurrentUICulture{set; get; }
  public bool IsAlive{get; }
  public bool IsBackground{set; get; }
  public bool IsThreadPoolThread{get; }
  public string Name{set; get; }
  public ThreadPriority Priority{set; get; }
  public ThreadState ThreadState{get; }
// Public Static Methods
```

```
public static LocalDataStoreSlot AllocateDataSlot( );
public static LocalDataStoreSlot AllocateNamedDataSlot(string name);
public static void FreeNamedDataSlot(string name);
public static object GetData(LocalDataStoreSlot slot);
public static AppDomain GetDomain( );
public static int GetDomainID( );
public static LocalDataStoreSlot GetNamedDataSlot(string name);
public static void MemoryBarrier( );
public static void ResetAbort( );
public static void SetData(LocalDataStoreSlot slot, object data);
public static void Sleep(int millisecondsTimeout);
public static void Sleep(TimeSpan timeout);
public static void SpinWait(int iterations);
public static byte VolatileRead(ref byte address);
public static double VolatileRead(ref double address);
public static short VolatileRead(ref short address);
public static int VolatileRead(ref int address);
public static long VolatileRead(ref long address);
public static IntPtr VolatileRead(ref IntPtr address);
public static object VolatileRead(ref object address);
public static sbyte VolatileRead(ref sbyte address);
public static float VolatileRead(ref float address);
public static ushort VolatileRead(ref ushort address);
public static uint VolatileRead(ref uint address);
public static ulong VolatileRead(ref ulong address);
public static UIntPtr VolatileRead(ref UIntPtr address);
public static void VolatileWrite(ref byte address, byte value);
public static void VolatileWrite(ref double address, double value);
public static void VolatileWrite(ref short address, short value);
public static void VolatileWrite(ref int address, int value);
public static void VolatileWrite(ref long address, long value);
public static void VolatileWrite(ref IntPtr address, IntPtr value);
public static void VolatileWrite(ref object address, object value);
public static void VolatileWrite(ref sbyte address, sbyte value);
public static void VolatileWrite(ref float address, float value);
public static void VolatileWrite(ref ushort address, ushort value);
public static void VolatileWrite(ref uint address, uint value);
public static void VolatileWrite(ref ulong address, ulong value);
public static void VolatileWrite(ref UIntPtr address, UIntPtr value);
// Public Instance Methods
public void Abort( );
public void Abort(object stateInfo);
public void Interrupt( );
public bool Join(int millisecondsTimeout);
public bool Join(TimeSpan timeout);
public void Join( );
public void Resume( );
public void Start( );
public void Suspend( );
// Protected Instance Methods
```

```
    protected override void Finalize( );                                        // overrides object
}
```

Returned By   System.Runtime.InteropServices.Marshal.GetThreadFromFiberCookie( )

Passed To   System.Diagnostics.StackTrace.StackTrace( )

ThreadAbortException

System.Threading (mscorlib.dll)   sealed class

This exception is thrown on a running thread when Thread.Abort( ) is called. This exception is catchable, but it is automatically rethrown (see Thread for more details).

```
public sealed class ThreadAbortException : SystemException {
// Public Instance Properties
  public object ExceptionState{get; }
}
```

Hierarchy   System.Object → System.Exception(System.Runtime.Serialization.ISerializable) →
                   System.SystemException → ThreadAbortException

ThreadExceptionEventArgs

System.Threading (system.dll)   class

This class represents the event arguments passed to a ThreadExceptionEventHandler. Exception contains the exception raised.

```
public class ThreadExceptionEventArgs : EventArgs {
// Public Constructors
  public ThreadExceptionEventArgs(Exception t);
// Public Instance Properties
  public Exception Exception{get; }
}
```

Hierarchy   System.Object → System.EventArgs → ThreadExceptionEventArgs

Passed To   ThreadExceptionEventHandler.{BeginInvoke( ), Invoke( )}

ThreadExceptionEventHandler
serializable

System.Threading (system.dll)   delegate

This event handler allows an event to be raised whenever a thread exception occurs. The System.Windows.Forms.Application.ThreadException property allows you to set one of these handlers, which takes the sender and ThreadExceptionEventArgs as arguments. The ThreadExceptionEventArgs object contains the exception raised.

```
public delegate void ThreadExceptionEventHandler(object sender, ThreadExceptionEventArgs e);
```

ThreadInterruptedException

serializable

System.Threading (mscorlib.dll)

class

This exception is thrown on a thread in the ThreadState.WaitSleepJoin state when Thread.Interrupt( ) is called.

```
public class ThreadInterruptedException : SystemException {
// Public Constructors
  public ThreadInterruptedException( );
  public ThreadInterruptedException(string message);
  public ThreadInterruptedException(string message, Exception innerException);
// Protected Constructors
  protected ThreadInterruptedException(System.Runtime.Serialization.SerializationInfo info,
    System.Runtime.Serialization.StreamingContext context);
}
```

Hierarchy   System.Object → System.Exception(System.Runtime.Serialization.ISerializable) →
System.SystemException → ThreadInterruptedException

ThreadPool

CF 1.0

System.Threading (mscorlib.dll)

sealed class

Creating or destroying a thread takes a fair amount of work. Therefore, if you pool threads, your program executes more efficiently since you get rid of the overhead associated with creating and destroying threads. There is one thread pool per process. To queue work to execute by this pool of *worker threads*, call any of the ThreadPool static methods. QueueUserWorkItem( ) queues a delegate to execute when one of the pool's threads becomes free. RegisterWaitForSingleObject( ) takes a WaitHandle and executes the specified method either when the WaitHandle is in the signaled state or when a time-out occurs. BindHandle( ) and UnsafeQueueUserWorkItem( ) are provided for compatibility with the Win32 API.

```
public sealed class ThreadPool {
// Public Static Methods
  public static bool BindHandle(IntPtr osHandle);
  public static void GetAvailableThreads(out int workerThreads, out int completionPortThreads);
  public static void GetMaxThreads(out int workerThreads, out int completionPortThreads);
  public static void GetMinThreads(out int workerThreads, out int completionPortThreads);
  public static bool QueueUserWorkItem(WaitCallback callBack);
  public static bool QueueUserWorkItem(WaitCallback callBack, object state);
  public static RegisteredWaitHandle RegisterWaitForSingleObject(WaitHandle waitObject,
    WaitOrTimerCallback callBack, object state, int millisecondsTimeOutInterval, bool executeOnlyOnce);
  public static RegisteredWaitHandle RegisterWaitForSingleObject(WaitHandle waitObject,
    WaitOrTimerCallback callBack, object state, long millisecondsTimeOutInterval, bool executeOnlyOnce);
  public static RegisteredWaitHandle RegisterWaitForSingleObject(WaitHandle waitObject,
    WaitOrTimerCallback callBack, object state, TimeSpan timeout, bool executeOnlyOnce);
  public static RegisteredWaitHandle RegisterWaitForSingleObject(WaitHandle waitObject,
    WaitOrTimerCallback callBack, object state, uint millisecondsTimeOutInterval, bool executeOnlyOnce);
  public static bool SetMinThreads(int workerThreads, int completionPortThreads);
  public static bool UnsafeQueueUserWorkItem(WaitCallback callBack, object state);
```

```
public static RegisteredWaitHandle UnsafeRegisterWaitForSingleObject(WaitHandle waitObject,
   WaitOrTimerCallback callBack, object state, int millisecondsTimeOutInterval, bool executeOnlyOnce);
public static RegisteredWaitHandle UnsafeRegisterWaitForSingleObject(WaitHandle waitObject,
   WaitOrTimerCallback callBack, object state, long millisecondsTimeOutInterval, bool executeOnlyOnce);
public static RegisteredWaitHandle UnsafeRegisterWaitForSingleObject(WaitHandle waitObject,
   WaitOrTimerCallback callBack, object state, TimeSpan timeout, bool executeOnlyOnce);
public static RegisteredWaitHandle UnsafeRegisterWaitForSingleObject(WaitHandle waitObject,
   WaitOrTimerCallback callBack, object state, uint millisecondsTimeOutInterval, bool executeOnlyOnce);
}
```

ThreadPriority   CF 1.0, ECMA 1.0, serializable

System.Threading (mscorlib.dll)   enum

This enumeration encapsulates the various thread priorities. Threads are scheduled to
be executed based on their priority; they default to Normal priority. The runtime can
also update thread priorities if a program window is moved between the foreground
and background. This is done automatically when you create windowed applications.

```
public enum ThreadPriority {
   Lowest = 0,
   BelowNormal = 1,
   Normal = 2,
   AboveNormal = 3,
   Highest = 4
}
```

Hierarchy	System.Object → System.ValueType → System.Enum(System.IComparable, System.IFormattable, System.IConvertible) → ThreadPriority
Returned By	Thread.Priority
Passed To	Thread.Priority

ThreadStart   CF 1.0, ECMA 1.0, serializable

System.Threading (mscorlib.dll)   delegate

This delegate specifies a method for a thread to start executing.

```
public delegate void ThreadStart( );
```

Passed To	Thread.Thread( )

ThreadState   ECMA 1.0, serializable, flag

System.Threading (mscorlib.dll)   enum

This enumeration encapsulates the various states a thread may be in. A thread starts in
the Unstarted state. Once the Thread.Start() method is called, a thread enters the Running
state. If another thread calls Thread.Abort() at any time, the thread shifts into the AbortRequested state, and then into Aborted once the thread reaches a safe point for garbage
collection.

If the running thread calls either the static method Thread.Sleep( ), any of the Wait( ) methods on a WaitHandle, or Thread.Join( ) on another thread, the executing thread enters the WaitSleepJoin state.

If another thread calls Thread.Interrupt( ) on a thread in the WaitSleepJoin state, the thread again enters the Running state. When another thread calls Thread.Suspend( ) on a thread, it enters the SuspendRequested state. Once a thread in the SuspendRequested state reaches a safe point for garbage collection, it enters the Suspended state. A thread then leaves the Suspended state and enters the running state when another thread calls Thread.Resume( ) on it. When a thread has finished running, it enters the Stopped state.

Once a thread has started, it cannot return to the Unstarted state. Similarly, once a thread has aborted or stopped, it cannot return to the Running state. This enumeration is marked with a [Flags( )] attribute, which allows a thread to be in more than one state at a time. For example, if a thread is in the WaitSleepJoin and another thread calls Thread.Abort( ) on it, it will be in both the WaitSleepJoin and AbortRequested states at the same time.

```
public enum ThreadState {
  Running = 0x00000000,
  StopRequested = 0x00000001,
  SuspendRequested = 0x00000002,
  Background = 0x00000004,
  Unstarted = 0x00000008,
  Stopped = 0x00000010,
  WaitSleepJoin = 0x00000020,
  Suspended = 0x00000040,
  AbortRequested = 0x00000080,
  Aborted = 0x00000100
}
```

Hierarchy   System.Object → System.ValueType → System.Enum(System.IComparable, System.IFormattable, System.IConvertible) → ThreadState

Returned By   Thread.ThreadState

ThreadStateException   CF 1.0, ECMA 1.0, serializable

System.Threading (mscorlib.dll)   class

This exception is thrown when an invalid method is called on a thread. For example, once a thread has started, it cannot reenter the ThreadState.Unstarted state. Therefore, an attempt to call Thread.Start( ) on that thread throws this exception.

```
public class ThreadStateException : SystemException {
// Public Constructors
  public ThreadStateException( );
  public ThreadStateException(string message);
  public ThreadStateException(string message, Exception innerException);
// Protected Constructors
  protected ThreadStateException(System.Runtime.Serialization.SerializationInfo info,
    System.Runtime.Serialization.StreamingContext context);
}
```

Timeout   CF 1.0, ECMA 1.0

System.Threading (mscorlib.dll)   sealed class

This class provides a static Infinite property, which is defined as −1 for use with methods that stop a thread's execution for a specific time period.

```
public sealed class Timeout {
// Public Static Fields
  public const int Infinite;                                              // =-1
}
```

Timer   CF 1.0, ECMA 1.0, marshal by reference, disposable

System.Threading (mscorlib.dll)   sealed class

This class can execute actions on a periodic basis. Actions can be performed once or multiple times. The constructor takes a TimerCallback delegate, a state object, a due time, and a period. Both due time and period are measured in milliseconds. Use the state argument to hold state information between delegate calls, or pass in null if you don't have any state to maintain. After the timer is created, it begins counting down until due time has expired, and then it invokes the delegate. The period is the amount of time to wait between delegate invocations before resuming the countdown again.

If the period is zero, the timer executes only once. If either due time or period are negative (and not equal to Timeout.Infinite), the constructor fails, throwing an System.ArgumentOutOfRangeException. Change() changes the due time and period after the timer is created. Specify a due time of Timeout.Infinite to halt the timer. An Infinite period prevents the timer from being raised repeatedly.

```
public sealed class Timer : MarshalByRefObject, IDisposable {
// Public Constructors
  public Timer(TimerCallback callback, object state, int dueTime, int period);
  public Timer(TimerCallback callback, object state, long dueTime, long period);
  public Timer(TimerCallback callback, object state, TimeSpan dueTime, TimeSpan period);
  public Timer(TimerCallback callback, object state, uint dueTime, uint period);
// Public Instance Methods
  public bool Change(int dueTime, int period);
  public bool Change(long dueTime, long period);
  public bool Change(TimeSpan dueTime, TimeSpan period);
  public bool Change(uint dueTime, uint period);
  public bool Dispose(WaitHandle notifyObject);
  public void Dispose( );                                        // implements IDisposable
// Protected Instance Methods
  protected override void Finalize( );                              // overrides object
}
```

Hierarchy   System.Object → System.MarshalByRefObject → Timer(System.IDisposable)

TimerCallback

System.Threading (mscorlib.dll)   delegate

Use this delegate with Timer.

```
public delegate void TimerCallback(object state);
```

Passed To   Timer.Timer( )

WaitCallback

CF 1.0, serializable

System.Threading (mscorlib.dll)   delegate

This delegate is for a ThreadPool work item.

```
public delegate void WaitCallback(object state);
```

Passed To   ThreadPool.{QueueUserWorkItem( ), UnsafeQueueUserWorkItem( )}

WaitHandle

CF 1.0, ECMA 1.0, marshal by reference, disposable

System.Threading (mscorlib.dll)   abstract class

This class encapsulates much of the logic for dealing with synchronization handles, which allow much more fine-grained synchronization control than simple thread locking. Once you have references to one or more WaitHandle subclasses, use the static WaitOne( ) or WaitAny( ) methods to obtain a lock on any single handle or all of the handles, respectively. The WaitOne( ) instance method acquires the lock for a specific WaitHandle. If a thread blocks and cannot obtain the necessary locks, it enters the Thread-State.WaitSleepJoin state until the locks can be obtained.

```
public abstract class WaitHandle : MarshalByRefObject, IDisposable {
// Public Constructors
  public WaitHandle( );
// Public Static Fields
  public const int WaitTimeout;                                               // =258
// Protected Static Fields
  protected static readonly IntPtr InvalidHandle;                             // =-1
// Public Instance Properties
  public virtual IntPtr Handle{set; get; }
// Public Static Methods
  public static bool WaitAll(WaitHandle[ ] waitHandles);
  public static bool WaitAll(WaitHandle[ ] waitHandles, int millisecondsTimeout, bool exitContext);
  public static bool WaitAll(WaitHandle[ ] waitHandles, TimeSpan timeout, bool exitContext);
  public static int WaitAny(WaitHandle[ ] waitHandles);
  public static int WaitAny(WaitHandle[ ] waitHandles, int millisecondsTimeout, bool exitContext);
  public static int WaitAny(WaitHandle[ ] waitHandles, TimeSpan timeout, bool exitContext);
// Public Instance Methods
  public virtual void Close( );
  public virtual bool WaitOne( );
  public virtual bool WaitOne(int millisecondsTimeout, bool exitContext);
  public virtual bool WaitOne(TimeSpan timeout, bool exitContext);
// Protected Instance Methods
```

```
protected virtual void Dispose(bool explicitDisposing);
protected override void Finalize( );                                          // overrides object
}
```

Hierarchy   System.Object → System.MarshalByRefObject → WaitHandle(System.IDisposable)

Subclasses   AutoResetEvent, ManualResetEvent, Mutex

Returned By   System.IAsyncResult.AsyncWaitHandle, System.IO.Stream.CreateWaitHandle( )

Passed To   RegisteredWaitHandle.Unregister( ), ThreadPool.{RegisterWaitForSingleObject( ),
                   UnsafeRegisterWaitForSingleObject( )}, Timer.Dispose( )

WaitOrTimerCallback   serializable

System.Threading (mscorlib.dll)   delegate

This delegate is passed to a ThreadPool. If the wasSignaled parameter is true, then the delegate is invoked in response to a signal; otherwise, it is invoked because the handle timed out.

```
public delegate void WaitOrTimerCallback(object state, bool timedOut);
```

Passed To   ThreadPool.{RegisterWaitForSingleObject( ), UnsafeRegisterWaitForSingleObject( )}

43

System.Timers

The **System.Timers** namespace provides the **Timer** class, which periodically raises an **Elapsed** event. It is a server-based component designed to be used in a multi-threaded environment and is thus more accurate than many other Windows-based timers. Unlike **System.Windows.Forms.Timer**, a server-based timer is not dependent on a user interface message pump. Figure 43-1 shows the class diagram for this namespace.

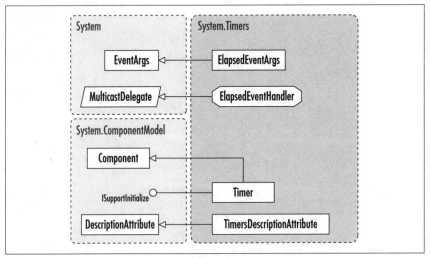

Figure 43-1. The System.Timers namespace

ElapsedEventArgs

System.Timers (system.dll)   class

This class offers the arguments for an **ElapsedEventHandler**.

```
public class ElapsedEventArgs : EventArgs {
// Public Instance Properties
  public DateTime SignalTime{get; }
}
```

Hierarchy   System.Object → System.EventArgs → ElapsedEventArgs

Passed To   ElapsedEventHandler.{BeginInvoke( ), Invoke( )}

ElapsedEventHandler   serializable

System.Timers (system.dll)   delegate

This delegate is used for the Timer.Elapsed event.

```
public delegate void ElapsedEventHandler(object sender, ElapsedEventArgs e);
```

Associated Events Timer.Elapsed( )

Timer   marshal by reference, disposable

System.Timers (system.dll)   class

This class raises an event at regular intervals. It is a server-based timer, which provides much more accuracy than normal Windows timers and ensures that the event is raised at the proper time. To use a Timer, set the Elapsed event, the Interval property, and Enabled to true. Start( ) and Stop( ) provide shortcuts, which respectively assign true and false to Enabled. AutoReset allows you to specify whether the event should be raised only once or periodically. The default is true, which makes the Timer periodic.

```
public class Timer : System.ComponentModel.Component, System.ComponentModel.ISupportInitialize {
// Public Constructors
  public Timer( );
  public Timer(double interval);
// Public Instance Properties
  public bool AutoReset{set; get; }
  public bool Enabled{set; get; }
  public double Interval{set; get; }
  public override ISite Site{set; get; }                          // overrides System.ComponentModel.Component
  public ISynchronizeInvoke SynchronizingObject{set; get; }
// Public Instance Methods
  public void BeginInit( );                                       // implements System.ComponentModel.ISupportInitialize
  public void Close( );
  public void EndInit( );                                         // implements System.ComponentModel.ISupportInitialize
  public void Start( );
  public void Stop( );
// Protected Instance Methods
  protected override void Dispose(bool disposing);                // overrides System.ComponentModel.Component
// Events
  public event ElapsedEventHandler Elapsed;
}
```

Hierarchy	System.Object → System.MarshalByRefObject → System.ComponentModel.Compo-nent(System.ComponentModel.IComponent, System.IDisposable) → Timer(System.ComponentModel.ISupportInitialize)

TimersDescriptionAttribute

System.Timers (system.dll)   class

This class provides a System.ComponentModel.DescriptionAttribute description for a given timer. It can be used by visual tools to display a helpful description of the component.

```
public class TimersDescriptionAttribute : System.ComponentModel.DescriptionAttribute {
// Public Constructors
  public TimersDescriptionAttribute(string description);
// Public Instance Properties
  public override string Description{get; }              // overrides System.ComponentModel.DescriptionAttribute
}
```

Hierarchy	System.Object → System.Attribute → System.ComponentModel.DescriptionAttribute → TimersDescriptionAttribute

Valid On	All

44

System.Xml

The System.Xml namespace provides support for managing XML documents according to a set of standards defined by the World Wide Web Consortium (W3C). The classes implement objects that comply with the XML 1.0 specification and the Document Object Model (DOM) Core Level 1 and Core Level 2. Additional support is provided for XML Schemas (the System.Xml.Schema namespace), XSLT (System.Xml.Xsl), and XPath (System.Xml.XPath).

Figures 44-1 and 44-2 show the types in this namespace. For more information on these technologies and their use, please consult *XML in a Nutshell*, by Elliote Rusty Harold and W. Scott Means (O'Reilly), or *Essential XML: Beyond Markup*, by Don Box (Addison Wesley).

EntityHandling

CF 1.0, serializable

System.Xml (system.xml.dll)

enum

This enumeration defines how entities are expanded. ExpandCharEntities expands only character entities, returning the entity text, while general entities are returned as nodes. ExpandEntities expands all entities; this is the default.

```
public enum EntityHandling {
  ExpandEntities = 1,
  ExpandCharEntities = 2
}
```

Hierarchy	System.Object → System.ValueType → System.Enum(System.IComparable, System.IFormattable, System.IConvertible) → EntityHandling
Returned By	XmlValidatingReader.EntityHandling
Passed To	XmlValidatingReader.EntityHandling

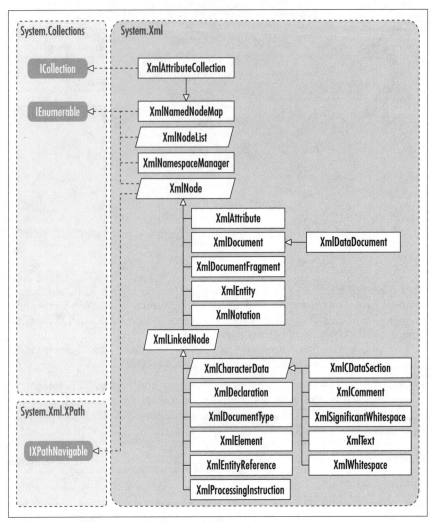

Figure 44-1. XmlNode and related types

Formatting

CF 1.0, ECMA 1.0, serializable

System.Xml (system.xml.dll)

enum

This enumeration specifies whether element content that is output from XmlTextWriter is indented. This is only of interest to human consumers of XML; if the destination of the XML document is another machine or software process, the additional whitespace adds only to the file size.

```
public enum Formatting {
  None = 0,
  Indented = 1
}
```

Hierarchy   System.Object → System.ValueType → System.Enum(System.IComparable, System.IFormattable, System.IConvertible) → Formatting

Returned By   XmlTextWriter.Formatting

Passed To   XmlTextWriter.Formatting

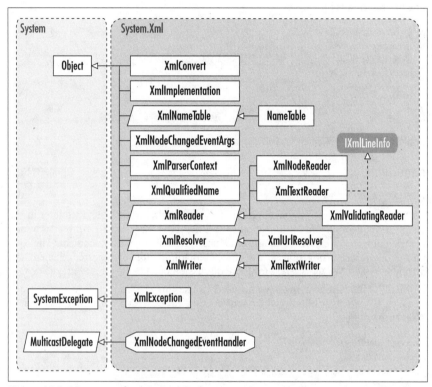

Figure 44-2. More types from System.Xml

IHasXmlNode

System.Xml (system.xml.dll)   interface

This interface is used to get the current or context node from an implementing class, such as XmlDocument or System.Xml.XPath.XPathNavigator. The GetNode( ) method returns the XmlNode that the navigator is currently positioned on.

```
public interface IHasXmlNode {
// Public Instance Methods
  public XmlNode GetNode( );
}
```

System.XML

IXmlLineInfo

CF 1.0

System.Xml (system.xml.dll)   interface

This interface allows XML reader classes (XmlTextReader and XmlValidatingReader) to return
line and position information currently being read. If the class is reading data from a
stream or other form of input, the HasLineInfo() method returns a boolean indicating if
line information is provided.

```
public interface IXmlLineInfo {
// Public Instance Properties
  public int LineNumber{get; }
  public int LinePosition{get; }
// Public Instance Methods
  public bool HasLineInfo( );
}
```

Implemented By XmlTextReader, XmlValidatingReader

NameTable

CF 1.0, ECMA 1.0

System.Xml (system.xml.dll)   class

This class is a concrete implementation of the XmlNameTable type (described later in this
chapter). It is entirely an optimization within the .NET XML stack; it provides a table
of string objects for element and attribute names used in an XML document. The XML
parser uses these string objects for efficient manipulation of repeated element and
attribute names. See XmlNameTable for more discussion of its behavior and usage.

Normally .NET applications have no need to use this class directly. At most, a new
instance is passed in blindly when constructing various XML-related types, such as
XmlNamespaceManager.

```
public class NameTable : XmlNameTable {
// Public Constructors
  public NameTable( );
// Public Instance Methods
  public override string Add(char[ ] key, int start, int len);    // overrides XmlNameTable
  public override string Add(string key);                         // overrides XmlNameTable
  public override string Get(char[ ] key, int start, int len);    // overrides XmlNameTable
  public override string Get(string value);                       // overrides XmlNameTable
}
```

Hierarchy   System.Object → XmlNameTable → NameTable

Passed To   System.Xml.Xsl.XsltContext.XsltContext( )

ReadState

CF 1.0, ECMA 1.0, serializable

System.Xml (system.xml.dll)   enum

This enumeration identifies the current state of an XmlReader instance: closed (Closed); not
yet started (Initial); an error is preventing further reading within the document (Error);
the read is in process (Interactive); or the end of file (or stream, or wherever the XML is
coming from) has been reached (EndOfFile).

```
public enum ReadState {
  Initial = 0,
  Interactive = 1,
  Error = 2,
  EndOfFile = 3,
  Closed = 4
}
```

Hierarchy   System.Object → System.ValueType → System.Enum(System.IComparable,
                System.IFormattable, System.IConvertible) → ReadState

Returned By   XmlReader.ReadState

ValidationType   serializable

System.Xml (system.xml.dll)   enum

This enumeration is used by XmlValidatingReader to determine the type of validation requested: DTD, schema, XDR, or no validation. If the type is set to Auto, the validation type is determined from the document; if there is a reference to a DTD, then DTD-style validation is performed. This is also true if the document contains references to XML Schema types, and so on. (See XmlValidatingReader for details.)

```
public enum ValidationType {
  None = 0,
  Auto = 1,
  DTD = 2,
  XDR = 3,
  Schema = 4
}
```

Hierarchy   System.Object → System.ValueType → System.Enum(System.IComparable,
                System.IFormattable, System.IConvertible) → ValidationType

Returned By   XmlValidatingReader.ValidationType

Passed To   XmlValidatingReader.ValidationType

WhitespaceHandling   CF 1.0, ECMA 1.0, serializable

System.Xml (system.xml.dll)   enum

This enumeration contains settings that determine if whitespace is preserved in text sections of XML documents. This is important if the XML document contains whitespace-sensitive text nodes; for example, HTML is a whitespace-insensitive language.

```
public enum WhitespaceHandling {
  All = 0,
  Significant = 1,
  None = 2
}
```

Hierarchy	System.Object → System.ValueType → System.Enum(System.IComparable, System.IFormattable, System.IConvertible) → WhitespaceHandling
Returned By	XmlTextReader.WhitespaceHandling
Passed To	XmlTextReader.WhitespaceHandling

WriteState   CF 1.0, ECMA 1.0, serializable

System.Xml (system.xml.dll)   enum

As its name implies, this enumeration specifies the state of an XmlWriter instance: closed (Closed), not yet started (Start), or in the process of writing some portion of the XML document (Attribute, Content, Element, or Prolog).

```
public enum WriteState {
  Start = 0,
  Prolog = 1,
  Element = 2,
  Attribute = 3,
  Content = 4,
  Closed = 5
}
```

Hierarchy	System.Object → System.ValueType → System.Enum(System.IComparable, System.IFormattable, System.IConvertible) → WriteState
Returned By	XmlWriter.WriteState

XmlAttribute   CF 1.0

System.Xml (system.xml.dll)   class

This class represents a single attribute of an element. The OwnerElement property returns the element node that contains this attribute. The Specified property indicates if the value was explicitly set or if a default value was used.

```
public class XmlAttribute : XmlNode {
// Protected Constructors
  protected internal XmlAttribute(string prefix, string localName, string namespaceURI, XmlDocument doc);
// Public Instance Properties
  public override string BaseURI{get; }                                          // overrides XmlNode
  public override string InnerText{set; get; }                                   // overrides XmlNode
  public override string InnerXml{set; get; }                                    // overrides XmlNode
  public override string LocalName{get; }                                        // overrides XmlNode
  public override string Name{get; }                                             // overrides XmlNode
  public override string NamespaceURI{get; }                                     // overrides XmlNode
  public override XmlNodeType NodeType{get; }                                    // overrides XmlNode
  public override XmlDocument OwnerDocument{get; }                               // overrides XmlNode
  public virtual XmlElement OwnerElement{get; }
  public override XmlNode ParentNode{get; }                                      // overrides XmlNode
  public override string Prefix{set; get; }                                      // overrides XmlNode
  public virtual bool Specified{get; }
```

```
    public override string Value{set; get; }                                              // overrides XmlNode
// Public Instance Methods
    public override XmlNode CloneNode(bool deep);                                          // overrides XmlNode
    public override void WriteContentTo(XmlWriter w);                                      // overrides XmlNode
    public override void WriteTo(XmlWriter w);                                             // overrides XmlNode
}
```

Hierarchy   System.Object → XmlNode(System.ICloneable, System.Collections.IEnumerable,
                       System.Xml.XPath.IXPathNavigable) → XmlAttribute

Returned By   XmlAttributeCollection.{Append( ), InsertAfter( ), InsertBefore( ), Prepend( ), Remove( ),
                       RemoveAt( ), this}, XmlDocument.CreateAttribute( ), XmlElement.{GetAttributeNode( ),
                       RemoveAttributeNode( ), SetAttributeNode( )}

Passed To   XmlAttributeCollection.{Append( ), CopyTo( ), InsertAfter( ), InsertBefore( ), Prepend( ),
                       Remove( )}, XmlElement.{RemoveAttributeNode( ), SetAttributeNode( )}

XmlAttributeCollection   CF 1.0

System.Xml (system.xml.dll)   class

This class defines a collection of attributes for an XmlElement node. An XmlAttributeCollection
is returned by the XmlElement.Attributes property. The collection contains XmlAttribute objects
that can be specified by either an object name or a zero-based index. Attribute nodes
can be added and removed from the collection with methods, such as InsertBefore( ),
InsertAfter( ), Prepend( ), and RemoveAt( ).

```
public class XmlAttributeCollection, XmlNamedNodeMap : ICollection {
// Public Instance Properties
    public virtual XmlAttribute this[string localName, string namespaceURI]{get; }
    public virtual XmlAttribute this[string name]{get; }
    public virtual XmlAttribute this[int i]{get; }
// Public Instance Methods
    public virtual XmlAttribute Append(XmlAttribute node);
    public void CopyTo(XmlAttribute[ ] array, int index);
    public virtual XmlAttribute InsertAfter(XmlAttribute newNode, XmlAttribute refNode);
    public virtual XmlAttribute InsertBefore(XmlAttribute newNode, XmlAttribute refNode);
    public virtual XmlAttribute Prepend(XmlAttribute node);
    public virtual XmlAttribute Remove(XmlAttribute node);
    public virtual void RemoveAll( );
    public virtual XmlAttribute RemoveAt(int i);
    public override XmlNode SetNamedItem(XmlNode node);                                    // overrides XmlNamedNodeMap
}
```

Hierarchy   System.Object → XmlNamedNodeMap(System.Collections.IEnumerable) →
                       XmlAttributeCollection(System.Collections.ICollection)

Returned By   XmlNode.Attributes

XmlCDataSection

System.Xml (system.xml.dll)   class

This class represents a CDATA (character data) section node of a document. A CDATA section is element content that is unparsed, i.e., entities and markup are ignored.

```
public class XmlCDataSection : XmlCharacterData {
// Protected Constructors
   protected internal XmlCDataSection(string data, XmlDocument doc);
// Public Instance Properties
   public override string LocalName{get; }                               // overrides XmlNode
   public override string Name{get; }                                    // overrides XmlNode
   public override XmlNodeType NodeType{get; }                           // overrides XmlNode
// Public Instance Methods
   public override XmlNode CloneNode(bool deep);                         // overrides XmlNode
   public override void WriteContentTo(XmlWriter w);                     // overrides XmlNode
   public override void WriteTo(XmlWriter w);                            // overrides XmlNode
}
```

Hierarchy   System.Object → XmlNode(System.ICloneable, System.Collections.IEnumerable, System. Xml.XPath.IXPathNavigable) → XmlLinkedNode → XmlCharacterData → XmlCDataSection

Returned By   XmlDocument.CreateCDataSection( )

XmlCharacterData

System.Xml (system.xml.dll)   abstract class

This class is an abstract parent class for the character data node types: XmlCDataSection, XmlComment, XmlSignificantWhitespace, XmlText, and XmlWhitespace. It defines methods for manipulating the text-based data of these nodes.

```
public abstract class XmlCharacterData : XmlLinkedNode {
// Protected Constructors
   protected internal XmlCharacterData(string data, XmlDocument doc);
// Public Instance Properties
   public virtual string Data{set; get; }
   public override string InnerText{set; get; }                          // overrides XmlNode
   public virtual int Length{get; }
   public override string Value{set; get; }                              // overrides XmlNode
// Public Instance Methods
   public virtual void AppendData(string strData);
   public virtual void DeleteData(int offset, int count);
   public virtual void InsertData(int offset, string strData);
   public virtual void ReplaceData(int offset, int count, string strData);
   public virtual string Substring(int offset, int count);
}
```

Hierarchy   System.Object → XmlNode(System.ICloneable, System.Collections.IEnumerable, System. Xml.XPath.IXPathNavigable) → XmlLinkedNode → XmlCharacterData

Subclasses   XmlCDataSection, XmlComment, XmlSignificantWhitespace, XmlText, XmlWhitespace

XmlComment

System.Xml (system.xml.dll)　　　　　　　　　　　　　　　　　　　　　　　　　　　　class

This class represents an XmlComment node. An XML comment is contained within <!--
and --> markup symbols and is not represented in the resulting XML Infoset tree.

```
public class XmlComment : XmlCharacterData {
// Protected Constructors
    protected internal XmlComment(string comment, XmlDocument doc);
// Public Instance Properties
    public override string LocalName{get; }                          // overrides XmlNode
    public override string Name{get; }                               // overrides XmlNode
    public override XmlNodeType NodeType{get; }                      // overrides XmlNode
// Public Instance Methods
    public override XmlNode CloneNode(bool deep);                    // overrides XmlNode
    public override void WriteContentTo(XmlWriter w);               // overrides XmlNode
    public override void WriteTo(XmlWriter w);                      // overrides XmlNode
}
```

Hierarchy　　　　System.Object → XmlNode(System.ICloneable, System.Collections.IEnumerable, System.
　　　　　　　　　　　　Xml.XPath.IXPathNavigable) → XmlLinkedNode → XmlCharacterData → XmlComment

Returned By　　　XmlDocument.CreateComment( )

XmlConvert

System.Xml (system.xml.dll)　　　　　　　　　　　　　　　　　　　　　　　　　　　　class

This type is used to convert XML elements into other, non-XML types, such as CLR
objects. In particular, it is used to convert XSD types into CLR types, for easy transformation of schema-valid XML documents into .NET objects and back again. It is also
used within a variety of other areas, including ADO.NET (for automatic conversion of
XML documents into relational tables and rows).

For the most part, .NET programmers use this type indirectly as part of the .NET Web
Services stack or else directly in order to convert between XML documents and CLR
objects (as part of a home-grown XML-to-RDBMS system, for example).

Note that although a constructor is provided, all methods of any interest are declared
static and therefore require no instance to use. In essence, this type is a collection of C-
style functions.

```
public class XmlConvert {
// Public Constructors
    public XmlConvert( );
// Public Static Methods
    public static string DecodeName(string name);
    public static string EncodeLocalName(string name);
    public static string EncodeName(string name);
    public static string EncodeNmToken(string name);
    public static bool ToBoolean(string s);
    public static byte ToByte(string s);
    public static char ToChar(string s);
    public static DateTime ToDateTime(string s);
```

```
public static DateTime ToDateTime(string s, string format);
public static DateTime ToDateTime(string s, string[ ] formats);
public static decimal ToDecimal(string s);
public static double ToDouble(string s);
public static Guid ToGuid(string s);
public static short ToInt16(string s);
public static int ToInt32(string s);
public static long ToInt64(string s);
public static sbyte ToSByte(string s);
public static float ToSingle(string s);
public static string ToString(bool value);
public static string ToString(byte value);
public static string ToString(char value);
public static string ToString(DateTime value);
public static string ToString(DateTime value, string format);
public static string ToString(decimal value);
public static string ToString(double value);
public static string ToString(Guid value);
public static string ToString(short value);
public static string ToString(int value);
public static string ToString(long value);
public static string ToString(sbyte value);
public static string ToString(float value);
public static string ToString(TimeSpan value);
public static string ToString(ushort value);
public static string ToString(uint value);
public static string ToString(ulong value);
public static TimeSpan ToTimeSpan(string s);
public static ushort ToUInt16(string s);
public static uint ToUInt32(string s);
public static ulong ToUInt64(string s);
public static string VerifyName(string name);
public static string VerifyNCName(string name);
}
```

XmlDataDocument

System.Xml (system.data.dll)   class

The XmlDataDocument is a marriage of XML and RDBMS technology; it is an XmlDocument-inheriting class that particularly understands ADO.NET DataSet objects. This offers a variety of opportunities to the .NET programmer—for example, a DataSet can be loaded into the XmlDataDocument, and then navigated using traditional DOM-style navigation using the XmlNode API. In fact, because XmlDataDocument also inherits the System.Xml.XPath. IXPathNavigable interface, XPath queries can be issued against the DataSet data, as well.

In order to build this relationship, construct the XmlDataDocument with the DataSet holding the data as its constructor parameter. Alternatively, use the Load() method to read in the data via an XmlReader. The resulting XML can also then be written out to another medium with the WriteTo() method.

```
public class XmlDataDocument : XmlDocument {
// Public Constructors
  public XmlDataDocument( );
  public XmlDataDocument(System.Data.DataSet dataset);
// Public Instance Properties
  public DataSet DataSet{get; }
// Public Instance Methods
  public override XmlNode CloneNode(bool deep);                                              // overrides XmlDocument
  public override XmlElement CreateElement(string prefix, string localName, string namespaceURI);
                                                                                              // overrides XmlDocument
  public override XmlEntityReference CreateEntityReference(string name);    // overrides XmlDocument
  public override XmlElement GetElementById(string elemId);                 // overrides XmlDocument
  public XmlElement GetElementFromRow(System.Data.DataRow r);
  public DataRow GetRowFromElement(XmlElement e);
  public override void Load(System.IO.Stream inStream);                     // overrides XmlDocument
  public override void Load(string filename);                               // overrides XmlDocument
  public override void Load(System.IO.TextReader txtReader);                // overrides XmlDocument
  public override void Load(XmlReader reader);                              // overrides XmlDocument
// Protected Instance Methods
  protected override XPathNavigator CreateNavigator(XmlNode node);          // overrides XmlDocument
}
```

Hierarchy   System.Object → XmlNode(System.ICloneable, System.Collections.IEnumerable,
                 System.Xml.XPath.IXPathNavigable) → XmlDocument → XmlDataDocument

XmlDeclaration   CF 1.0

System.Xml (system.xml.dll)   class

This class contains the XML declaration of a document, which is the first element of
an XML document containing the XML version number, encoding, and other optional
information about the file.

```
public class XmlDeclaration : XmlLinkedNode {
// Protected Constructors
  protected internal XmlDeclaration(string version, string encoding, string standalone  XmlDocument doc);
// Public Instance Properties
  public string Encoding{set; get; }
  public override string InnerText{set; get; }                              // overrides XmlNode
  public override string LocalName{get; }                                   // overrides XmlNode
  public override string Name{get; }                                        // overrides XmlNode
  public override XmlNodeType NodeType{get; }                               // overrides XmlNode
  public string Standalone{set; get; }
  public override string Value{set; get; }                                  // overrides XmlNode
  public string Version{get; }
// Public Instance Methods
  public override XmlNode CloneNode(bool deep);                             // overrides XmlNode
  public override void WriteContentTo(XmlWriter w);                        // overrides XmlNode
  public override void WriteTo(XmlWriter w);                               // overrides XmlNode
}
```

System.Object → XmlNode(System.ICloneable, System.Collections.IEnumerable, System.Xml.XPath.IXPathNavigable) → XmlLinkedNode → XmlDeclaration

Returned By   XmlDocument.CreateXmlDeclaration( )

XmlDocument

CF 1.0

System.Xml (system.xml.dll)   class

This class represents an XML document according to the W3C DOM (Document Object Model) specification. The document is represented as a node tree, in which elements and attributes (and their values) are stored as nodes that contain relational information (e.g., parent, child, siblings). XmlDocument derives from the generic XmlNode class and therefore has a node-type of Document.

The set of Create* methods create new objects of any type of node. These objects are created within the context of the XmlDocument; they share the document properties and name table of the parent document. However, they are not inserted into the document. To do this, you need to use the methods for node insertion from XmlNode. A new XmlNode is created from the root node of the XmlDocument; then methods for walking the node tree and appending or inserting nodes can be used to alter the source document.

Events are noted when any nodes (even created node objects that have not been inserted into the document) from this object change. Register an instance of the XmlNodeChangedEventHandler delegate with any of the following event types on XmlDocument to receive the corresponding notification: NodeChanged or NodeChanging for notification when a node has or is in the middle of changing (the element name is being modified, an attribute is being modified, added, or removed, and so on); NodeInserted or NodeInserting for notifications of new nodes having been or in the process of being added to the document; and NodeRemoved or NodeRemoving for nodes removed or in the process of being removed. The XmlNodeChangedEventHandler takes two arguments: the object sending the notification (this object), and an XmlNodeChangedEventArgs instance containing information about the change.

```
public class XmlDocument : XmlNode {
// Public Constructors
   public XmlDocument( );
   public XmlDocument(XmlNameTable nt);
// Protected Constructors
   protected internal XmlDocument(XmlImplementation imp);
// Public Instance Properties
   public override string BaseURI{get; }                              // overrides XmlNode
   public XmlElement DocumentElement{get; }
   public virtual XmlDocumentType DocumentType{get; }
   public XmlImplementation Implementation{get; }
   public override string InnerXml{set; get; }                        // overrides XmlNode
   public override bool IsReadOnly{get; }                             // overrides XmlNode
   public override string LocalName{get; }                            // overrides XmlNode
   public override string Name{get; }                                 // overrides XmlNode
   public XmlNameTable NameTable{get; }
   public override XmlNodeType NodeType{get; }                        // overrides XmlNode
   public override XmlDocument OwnerDocument{get; }                   // overrides XmlNode
   public bool PreserveWhitespace{set; get; }
```

```
     public virtual XmlResolver XmlResolver{set; }
// Public Instance Methods
     public override XmlNode CloneNode(bool deep);                                          // overrides XmlNode
     public XmlAttribute CreateAttribute(string name);
     public XmlAttribute CreateAttribute(string qualifiedName, string namespaceURI);
     public virtual XmlAttribute CreateAttribute(string prefix, string localName, string namespaceURI);
     public virtual XmlCDataSection CreateCDataSection(string data);
     public virtual XmlComment CreateComment(string data);
     public virtual XmlDocumentFragment CreateDocumentFragment( );  internalSubset);
     public virtual XmlDocumentType CreateDocumentType(string name, string publicId, string systemId,  string
     public XmlElement CreateElement(string name);
     public XmlElement CreateElement(string qualifiedName, string namespaceURI);
     public virtual XmlElement CreateElement(string prefix, string localName, string namespaceURI);
     public virtual XmlEntityReference CreateEntityReference(string name);
     public virtual XmlNode CreateNode(string nodeTypeString, string name, string namespaceURI);
     public virtual XmlNode CreateNode(XmlNodeType type, string name, string namespaceURI);
     public virtual XmlNode CreateNode(XmlNodeType type, string prefix, string name, string namespaceURI);
     public virtual XmlProcessingInstruction CreateProcessingInstruction(string target, string data);
     public virtual XmlSignificantWhitespace CreateSignificantWhitespace(string text);
     public virtual XmlText CreateTextNode(string text);
     public virtual XmlWhitespace CreateWhitespace(string text);
     public virtual XmlDeclaration CreateXmlDeclaration(string version, string encoding, string standalone);
     public virtual XmlElement GetElementById(string elementId);
     public virtual XmlNodeList GetElementsByTagName(string name);
     public virtual XmlNodeList GetElementsByTagName(string localName, string namespaceURI);
     public virtual XmlNode ImportNode(XmlNode node, bool deep);
     public virtual void Load(System.IO.Stream inStream);
     public virtual void Load(string filename);
     public virtual void Load(System.IO.TextReader txtReader);
     public virtual void Load(XmlReader reader);
     public virtual void LoadXml(string xml);
     public virtual XmlNode ReadNode(XmlReader reader);
     public virtual void Save(System.IO.Stream outStream);
     public virtual void Save(string filename);
     public virtual void Save(System.IO.TextWriter writer);
     public virtual void Save(XmlWriter w);
     public override void WriteContentTo(XmlWriter xw);                                     // overrides XmlNode
     public override void WriteTo(XmlWriter w);                                             // overrides XmlNode
// Protected Instance Methods
     protected internal virtual XmlAttribute CreateDefaultAttribute(string prefix, string localName, string namespaceURI);
     protected internal virtual XPathNavigator CreateNavigator(XmlNode node);
// Events
     public event XmlNodeChangedEventHandler NodeChanged;
     public event XmlNodeChangedEventHandler NodeChanging;
     public event XmlNodeChangedEventHandler NodeInserted;
     public event XmlNodeChangedEventHandler NodeInserting;
     public event XmlNodeChangedEventHandler NodeRemoved;
     public event XmlNodeChangedEventHandler NodeRemoving;
}
```

Hierarchy	System.Object → XmlNode(System.ICloneable, System.Collections.IEnumerable, System.Xml.XPath.IXPathNavigable) → XmlDocument
Subclasses	XmlDataDocument
Returned By	XmlImplementation.CreateDocument( ), XmlNode.OwnerDocument

XmlDocumentFragment

CF 1.0

System.Xml (system.xml.dll)

class

This class represents a lightweight piece or tree section of an XML document. A document fragment has a null parent node. This object is useful for tree insert operations that use the ImportNode( ) method of the XmlDocument class. To create an XmlDocumentFragment, use the XmlDocument.CreateDocumentFragment( ) method of an XmlDocument instance.

```
public class XmlDocumentFragment : XmlNode {
// Protected Constructors
  protected internal XmlDocumentFragment(XmlDocument ownerDocument);
// Public Instance Properties
  public override string InnerXml{set; get; }                          // overrides XmlNode
  public override string LocalName{get; }                              // overrides XmlNode
  public override string Name{get; }                                   // overrides XmlNode
  public override XmlNodeType NodeType{get; }                          // overrides XmlNode
  public override XmlDocument OwnerDocument{get; }                     // overrides XmlNode
  public override XmlNode ParentNode{get; }                            // overrides XmlNode
// Public Instance Methods
  public override XmlNode CloneNode(bool deep);                        // overrides XmlNode
  public override void WriteContentTo(XmlWriter w);                    // overrides XmlNode
  public override void WriteTo(XmlWriter w);                           // overrides XmlNode
}
```

Hierarchy	System.Object → XmlNode(System.ICloneable, System.Collections.IEnumerable, System.Xml.XPath.IXPathNavigable) → XmlDocumentFragment
Returned By	XmlDocument.CreateDocumentFragment( )

XmlDocumentType

System.Xml (system.xml.dll)

class

This class represents the DOCTYPE element of an XML document and its contents.

```
public class XmlDocumentType : XmlLinkedNode {
// Protected Constructors
  protected internal XmlDocumentType(string name, string publicId, string systemId,
    string internalSubset, XmlDocument doc);
// Public Instance Properties
  public XmlNamedNodeMap Entities{get; }
  public string InternalSubset{get; }
  public override bool IsReadOnly{get; }                               // overrides XmlNode
  public override string LocalName{get; }                              // overrides XmlNode
  public override string Name{get; }                                   // overrides XmlNode
```

```
public override XmlNodeType NodeType{get; }                                              // overrides XmlNode
public XmlNamedNodeMap Notations{get; }
public string PublicId{get; }
public string SystemId{get; }
// Public Instance Methods
public override XmlNode CloneNode(bool deep);                                             // overrides XmlNode
public override void WriteContentTo(XmlWriter w);                                         // overrides XmlNode
public override void WriteTo(XmlWriter w);                                                // overrides XmlNode
}
```

Hierarchy	System.Object → XmlNode(System.ICloneable, System.Collections.IEnumerable, System.Xml.XPath.IXPathNavigable) → XmlLinkedNode → XmlDocumentType

Returned By	XmlDocument.{CreateDocumentType( ), DocumentType}

XmlElement

CF 1.0

System.Xml (system.xml.dll)

class

This class represents an element in an XML document.

```
public class XmlElement : XmlLinkedNode {
// Protected Constructors
  protected internal XmlElement(string prefix, string localName, string namespaceURI, XmlDocument doc);
// Public Instance Properties
  public override XmlAttributeCollection Attributes{get; }                                // overrides XmlNode
  public virtual bool HasAttributes{get; }
  public override string InnerText{set; get; }                                            // overrides XmlNode
  public override string InnerXml{set; get; }                                             // overrides XmlNode
  public bool IsEmpty{set; get; }
  public override string LocalName{get; }                                                 // overrides XmlNode
  public override string Name{get; }                                                      // overrides XmlNode
  public override string NamespaceURI{get; }                                              // overrides XmlNode
  public override XmlNode NextSibling{get; }                                         // overrides XmlLinkedNode
  public override XmlNodeType NodeType{get; }                                             // overrides XmlNode
  public override XmlDocument OwnerDocument{get; }                                        // overrides XmlNode
  public override string Prefix{set; get; }                                               // overrides XmlNode
// Public Instance Methods
  public override XmlNode CloneNode(bool deep);                                           // overrides XmlNode
  public virtual string GetAttribute(string name);
  public virtual string GetAttribute(string localName, string namespaceURI);
  public virtual XmlAttribute GetAttributeNode(string name);
  public virtual XmlAttribute GetAttributeNode(string localName, string namespaceURI);
  public virtual XmlNodeList GetElementsByTagName(string name);
  public virtual XmlNodeList GetElementsByTagName(string localName, string namespaceURI);
  public virtual bool HasAttribute(string name);
  public virtual bool HasAttribute(string localName, string namespaceURI);
  public override void RemoveAll( );                                                      // overrides XmlNode
  public virtual void RemoveAllAttributes( );
  public virtual void RemoveAttribute(string name);
  public virtual void RemoveAttribute(string localName, string namespaceURI);
  public virtual XmlNode RemoveAttributeAt(int i);
  public virtual XmlAttribute RemoveAttributeNode(string localName, string namespaceURI);
```

```
public virtual XmlAttribute RemoveAttributeNode(XmlAttribute oldAttr);
public virtual string SetAttribute(string localName, string namespaceURI, string value);
public virtual void SetAttribute(string name, string value);
public virtual XmlAttribute SetAttributeNode(string localName, string namespaceURI);
public virtual XmlAttribute SetAttributeNode(XmlAttribute newAttr);
public override void WriteContentTo(XmlWriter w);                           // overrides XmlNode
public override void WriteTo(XmlWriter w);                                  // overrides XmlNode
}
```

Hierarchy	System.Object → XmlNode(System.ICloneable, System.Collections.IEnumerable, System.Xml.XPath.IXPathNavigable) → XmlLinkedNode → XmlElement
Returned By	XmlAttribute.OwnerElement, XmlDataDocument.GetElementFromRow( ), XmlDocument.{CreateElement( ), DocumentElement, GetElementById( )}, XmlNode.this
Passed To	XmlDataDocument.GetRowFromElement( )

XmlEntity

System.Xml (system.xml.dll)   class

This class represents an entity in an XML document.

```
public class XmlEntity : XmlNode {
// Public Instance Properties
  public override string BaseURI{get; }                                    // overrides XmlNode
  public override string InnerText{set; get; }                             // overrides XmlNode
  public override string InnerXml{set; get; }                              // overrides XmlNode
  public override bool IsReadOnly{get; }                                   // overrides XmlNode
  public override string LocalName{get; }                                  // overrides XmlNode
  public override string Name{get; }                                       // overrides XmlNode
  public override XmlNodeType NodeType{get; }                              // overrides XmlNode
  public string NotationName{get; }
  public override string OuterXml{get; }                                   // overrides XmlNode
  public string PublicId{get; }
  public string SystemId{get; }
// Public Instance Methods
  public override XmlNode CloneNode(bool deep);                            // overrides XmlNode
  public override void WriteContentTo(XmlWriter w);                        // overrides XmlNode
  public override void WriteTo(XmlWriter w);                              // overrides XmlNode
}
```

Hierarchy	System.Object → XmlNode(System.ICloneable, System.Collections.IEnumerable, System.Xml.XPath.IXPathNavigable) → XmlEntity

XmlEntityReference   CF 1.0

System.Xml (system.xml.dll)   class

This class represents an entity reference in an XML document.

```
public class XmlEntityReference : XmlLinkedNode {
// Protected Constructors
  protected internal XmlEntityReference(string name, XmlDocument doc);
```

```
// Public Instance Properties
  public override string BaseURI{get; }                                              // overrides XmlNode
  public override bool IsReadOnly{get; }                                             // overrides XmlNode
  public override string LocalName{get; }                                            // overrides XmlNode
  public override string Name{get; }                                                 // overrides XmlNode
  public override XmlNodeType NodeType{get; }                                        // overrides XmlNode
  public override string Value{set; get; }                                           // overrides XmlNode
// Public Instance Methods
  public override XmlNode CloneNode(bool deep);                                      // overrides XmlNode
  public override void WriteContentTo(XmlWriter w);                                  // overrides XmlNode
  public override void WriteTo(XmlWriter w);                                         // overrides XmlNode
}
```

Hierarchy System.Object → XmlNode(System.ICloneable, System.Collections.IEnumerable, System.Xml.XPath.IXPathNavigable) → XmlLinkedNode → XmlEntityReference

Returned By XmlDocument.CreateEntityReference( )

XmlException   CF 1.0, ECMA 1.0, serializable

System.Xml (system.xml.dll)   class

This class contains the error thrown by XML-parsing operations. The LineNumber and LinePosition properties store the location of the error in the source document, and Message describes the reason for the error.

```
public class XmlException : SystemException {
// Public Constructors
  public XmlException( );
  public XmlException(string message);
  public XmlException(string message, Exception innerException);
  public XmlException(string message, Exception innerException, int lineNumber, int linePosition);
// Protected Constructors
  protected XmlException(System.Runtime.Serialization.SerializationInfo info,
    System.Runtime.Serialization.StreamingContext context);
// Public Instance Properties
  public int LineNumber{get; }
  public int LinePosition{get; }
  public override string Message{get; }                                              // overrides Exception
// Public Instance Methods
  public override void GetObjectData(System.Runtime.Serialization.SerializationInfo info,
    System.Runtime.Serialization.StreamingContext context);                         // overrides Exception
}
```

Hierarchy System.Object → System.Exception(System.Runtime.Serialization.ISerializable) → System.SystemException → XmlException

XmlImplementation   CF 1.0

System.Xml (system.xml.dll)   class

This class instantiates a new XmlDocument object using the same XmlNameTable of an existing XmlDocument.

```
public class XmlImplementation {
// Public Constructors
  public XmlImplementation( );
// Public Instance Methods
  public virtual XmlDocument CreateDocument( );
  public bool HasFeature(string strFeature, string strVersion);
}
```

Returned By   XmlDocument.Implementation

XmlLinkedNode   CF 1.0

System.Xml (system.xml.dll)   abstract class

This type of node class is the base class for node types that are not top-level (i.e., nodes that require a parent). For example, XmlCharacterData and XmlElement are derived from XmlLinkedNode.

```
public abstract class XmlLinkedNode : XmlNode {
// Public Instance Properties
  public override XmlNode NextSibling{get; }                    // overrides XmlNode
  public override XmlNode PreviousSibling{get; }                // overrides XmlNode
}
```

Hierarchy   System.Object → XmlNode(System.ICloneable, System.Collections.IEnumerable,
                       System.Xml.XPath.IXPathNavigable) → XmlLinkedNode

Subclasses   XmlCharacterData, XmlDeclaration, XmlDocumentType, XmlElement, XmlEntityReference,
                       XmlProcessingInstruction

XmlNamedNodeMap   CF 1.0

System.Xml (system.xml.dll)   class

This class represents a collection of nodes accessed by index or name. This is the abstract parent class of XmlAttributeCollection.

```
public class XmlNamedNodeMap : IEnumerable {
// Public Instance Properties
  public virtual int Count{get; }
// Public Instance Methods
  public virtual IEnumerator GetEnumerator( );                 // implements IEnumerable
  public virtual XmlNode GetNamedItem(string name);
  public virtual XmlNode GetNamedItem(string localName, string namespaceURI);
  public virtual XmlNode Item(int index);
  public virtual XmlNode RemoveNamedItem(string name);
  public virtual XmlNode RemoveNamedItem(string localName, string namespaceURI);
  public virtual XmlNode SetNamedItem(XmlNode node);
}
```

Subclasses   XmlAttributeCollection

Returned By

XmlDocumentType.{Entities, Notations}

XmlNamespaceManager

CF 1.0, ECMA 1.0

System.Xml (system.xml.dll) class

This class represents a collection of namespace prefixes and namespace URIs that are used to manage and resolve namespace information. The namespace manager is constructed using an XmlNameTable. XmlNamespaceManager is used internally by XmlReader to resolve namespace prefixes and track the current scope. XmlNamespaceManager maintains scope in a stack, which can be manipulated with PopScope() and PushScope(). Namespaces must be added explicitly to the namespace manager with AddNamespace(), even if you use an existing XmlNameTable.

```
public class XmlNamespaceManager : IEnumerable {
// Public Constructors
  public XmlNamespaceManager(XmlNameTable nameTable);
// Public Instance Properties
  public virtual string DefaultNamespace{get; }
  public XmlNameTable NameTable{get; }
// Public Instance Methods
  public virtual void AddNamespace(string prefix, string uri);
  public virtual IEnumerator GetEnumerator( );                              // implements IEnumerable
  public virtual bool HasNamespace(string prefix);
  public virtual string LookupNamespace(string prefix);
  public virtual string LookupPrefix(string uri);
  public virtual bool PopScope( );
  public virtual void PushScope( );
  public virtual void RemoveNamespace(string prefix, string uri);
}
```

Subclasses   System.Xml.Xsl.XsltContext

Returned By   XmlParserContext.NamespaceManager

Passed To   XmlNode.{SelectNodes( ), SelectSingleNode( )}, XmlParserContext.{NamespaceManager, XmlParserContext( )}, System.Xml.XPath.XPathExpression.SetContext( )

XmlNameTable

CF 1.0, ECMA 1.0

System.Xml (system.xml.dll) abstract class

This class presents a table of string objects (for element and attribute names) used in an XML document. The XML parser uses these string objects for efficient manipulation of repeated element and attribute names. An XmlNameTable exists for every XmlDocument you create. The XmlImplementation class instantiates a new XmlDocument with the XmlNameTable of another existing XmlDocument.

```
public abstract class XmlNameTable {
// Protected Constructors
  protected XmlNameTable( );
// Public Instance Methods
  public abstract string Add(char[ ] array, int offset, int length);
  public abstract string Add(string array);
```

```
public abstract string Get(char[ ] array, int offset, int length);
public abstract string Get(string array);
}
```

Subclasses   NameTable

Returned By   XmlDocument.NameTable, XmlNamespaceManager.NameTable, XmlParserContext.
                      NameTable, XmlReader.NameTable, System.Xml.XPath.XPathNavigator.NameTable

Passed To   XmlDocument.XmlDocument( ), XmlNamespaceManager.XmlNamespaceManager( ),
                      XmlParserContext.{NameTable, XmlParserContext( )}, XmlTextReader.XmlTextReader( )

XmlNode   CF 1.0

System.Xml (system.xml.dll)   abstract class

This abstract class represents a node in a document. A node is the basic object
described by the Document Object Model for XML. A node can be an element, an
element's attributes, the DOCTYPE declaration, a comment, or the entire document itself.
Nodes are ordered in a hierarchical tree in which child, parent, and sibling relationships are "known" by each node.

The XmlNode class is the parent object of the specific node type classes. The properties of
this class expose the intrinsic values of the node: NamespaceURI, NodeType, parent, child,
sibling nodes, etc. The methods allow a node to add to or removed from a node tree
(in the context of an XmlDocument or XmlDocumentFragment), with respect to a reference
node.

```
public abstract class XmlNode : ICloneable, IEnumerable, System.Xml.XPath.IXPathNavigable {
// Public Instance Properties
  public virtual XmlAttributeCollection Attributes{get; }
  public virtual string BaseURI{get; }
  public virtual XmlNodeList ChildNodes{get; }
  public virtual XmlNode FirstChild{get; }
  public virtual bool HasChildNodes{get; }
  public virtual string InnerText{set; get; }
  public virtual string InnerXml{set; get; }
  public virtual bool IsReadOnly{get; }
  public virtual XmlNode LastChild{get; }
  public abstract string LocalName{get; }
  public abstract string Name{get; }
  public virtual string NamespaceURI{get; }
  public virtual XmlNode NextSibling{get; }
  public abstract XmlNodeType NodeType{get; }
  public virtual string OuterXml{get; }
  public virtual XmlDocument OwnerDocument{get; }
  public virtual XmlNode ParentNode{get; }
  public virtual string Prefix{set; get; }
  public virtual XmlNode PreviousSibling{get; }
  public virtual XmlElement this[string name]{get; }
  public virtual XmlElement this[string localname, string ns]{get; }
  public virtual string Value{set; get; }
```

// Public Instance Methods

```
// Public Instance Methods
  public virtual XmlNode AppendChild(XmlNode newChild);
  public virtual XmlNode Clone( );
  public abstract XmlNode CloneNode(bool deep);
  public XPathNavigator CreateNavigator( );              // implements System.Xml.XPath.IXPathNavigable
  public IEnumerator GetEnumerator( );                                        // implements IEnumerable
  public virtual string GetNamespaceOfPrefix(string prefix);
  public virtual string GetPrefixOfNamespace(string namespaceURI);
  public virtual XmlNode InsertAfter(XmlNode newChild, XmlNode refChild);
  public virtual XmlNode InsertBefore(XmlNode newChild, XmlNode refChild);
  public virtual void Normalize( );
  public virtual XmlNode PrependChild(XmlNode newChild);
  public virtual void RemoveAll( );
  public virtual XmlNode RemoveChild(XmlNode oldChild);
  public virtual XmlNode ReplaceChild(XmlNode newChild, XmlNode oldChild);
  public XmlNodeList SelectNodes(string xpath);
  public XmlNodeList SelectNodes(string xpath, XmlNamespaceManager nsmgr);
  public XmlNode SelectSingleNode(string xpath);
  public XmlNode SelectSingleNode(string xpath, XmlNamespaceManager nsmgr);
  public virtual bool Supports(string feature, string version);
  public abstract void WriteContentTo(XmlWriter w);
  public abstract void WriteTo(XmlWriter w);
}
```

Subclasses	XmlAttribute, XmlDocument, XmlDocumentFragment, XmlEntity, XmlLinkedNode, XmlNotation
Returned By	Multiple types
Passed To	XmlDataDocument.CreateNavigator( ), XmlDocument.ImportNode( ), XmlNamedNodeMap.SetNamedItem( ), XmlNodeReader.XmlNodeReader( )

XmlNodeChangedAction

CF 1.0, serializable

System.Xml (system.xml.dll)   enum

This simple enumeration that describes the change that has occurred within an XmlDocument instance can be one of the following: Change, which indicates that a node within the document has changed in some way; Insert, which indicates that a node has been inserted into the document; or Remove, which indicates that a node has been removed. This is one of the properties specified in the XmlNodeChangedEventArgs parameter to the XmlNodeChangedEventHandler delegate instance registered with the XmlDocument.

```
public enum XmlNodeChangedAction {
  Insert = 0,
  Remove = 1,
  Change = 2
}
```

Hierarchy	System.Object → System.ValueType → System.Enum(System.IComparable, System.IFormattable, System.IConvertible) → XmlNodeChangedAction
Returned By	XmlNodeChangedEventArgs.Action

XmlNodeChangedEventArgs

System.Xml (system.xml.dll)   class

This type contains information about the changes to a node that are passed when an XmlDocument calls through an XmlNodeChangedEventHandler delegate instance. It contains the changed or changing node, the old and new parents to that node, and an enumeration describing the change (modification, insertion, or removal).

```
public class XmlNodeChangedEventArgs {
// Public Instance Properties
  public XmlNodeChangedAction Action{get; }
  public XmlNode NewParent{get; }
  public XmlNode Node{get; }
  public XmlNode OldParent{get; }
}
```

Passed To   XmlNodeChangedEventHandler.{BeginInvoke( ), Invoke( )}

XmlNodeChangedEventHandler   CF 1.0, serializable

System.Xml (system.xml.dll)   delegate

This declared delegate type must be used to receive event notifications from the XmlDocument instance if code wishes to be notified of changes to the document as they occur.

```
public delegate void XmlNodeChangedEventHandler(object sender, XmlNodeChangedEventArgs e);
```

Associated Events XmlDataDocument.{NodeChanged( ), NodeChanging( ), NodeInserted( ), NodeInserting( ),
                       NodeRemoved( ), NodeRemoving( )}, XmlDocument.{NodeChanged( ), NodeChanging( ),
                       NodeInserted( ), NodeInserting( ), NodeRemoved( ), NodeRemoving( )}

XmlNodeList   CF 1.0

System.Xml (system.xml.dll)   abstract class

This class is an enumerated collection of nodes returned by XmlDocument. GetElementsByTagName( ). Nodes contained in the list can be retrieved by index or iterated through via the IEnumerator returned by GetEnumerator( ). Changes to the nodes in the list are immediately reflected in the XmlNodeList's properties and methods. For example, if you add a sibling to a node in the list, it appears in the list.

```
public abstract class XmlNodeList : IEnumerable {
// Protected Constructors
  protected XmlNodeList( );
// Public Instance Properties
  public abstract int Count{get; }
  public virtual XmlNode this[int i]{get; }
// Public Instance Methods
  public abstract IEnumerator GetEnumerator( );                                        // implements IEnumerable
  public abstract XmlNode Item(int index);
}
```

Returned By   XmlDocument.GetElementsByTagName( ), XmlElement.GetElementsByTagName( ),
                       XmlNode.{ChildNodes, SelectNodes( )}

XmlNodeOrder

serializable

System.Xml (system.xml.dll)

enum

These values describe the position of one node relative to another, with respect to document order.

```
public enum XmlNodeOrder {
  Before = 0,
  After = 1,
  Same = 2,
  Unknown = 3
}
```

Hierarchy   System.Object → System.ValueType → System.Enum(System.IComparable,
System.IFormattable, System.IConvertible) → XmlNodeOrder

Returned By   System.Xml.XPath.XPathNavigator.ComparePosition( )

XmlNodeReader

CF 1.0

System.Xml (system.xml.dll)

class

This class is a non-cached, forward-only reader that accesses the contents of an XmlNode. This class can read a DOM subtree, but doesn't provide full-document support such as validation.

```
public class XmlNodeReader : XmlReader {
// Public Constructors
  public XmlNodeReader(XmlNode node);
// Public Instance Properties
```

public override int **AttributeCount**{get; }	// overrides XmlReader
public override string **BaseURI**{get; }	// overrides XmlReader
public override bool **CanResolveEntity**{get; }	// overrides XmlReader
public override int **Depth**{get; }	// overrides XmlReader
public override bool **EOF**{get; }	// overrides XmlReader
public override bool **HasAttributes**{get; }	// overrides XmlReader
public override bool **HasValue**{get; }	// overrides XmlReader
public override bool **IsDefault**{get; }	// overrides XmlReader
public override bool **IsEmptyElement**{get; }	// overrides XmlReader
public override string **LocalName**{get; }	// overrides XmlReader
public override string **Name**{get; }	// overrides XmlReader
public override string **NamespaceURI**{get; }	// overrides XmlReader
public override XmlNameTable **NameTable**{get; }	// overrides XmlReader
public override XmlNodeType **NodeType**{get; }	// overrides XmlReader
public override string **Prefix**{get; }	// overrides XmlReader
public override char **QuoteChar**{get; }	// overrides XmlReader
public override ReadState **ReadState**{get; }	// overrides XmlReader
public override string **this**[string name, string namespaceURI]{get; }	// overrides XmlReader
public override string **this**[int i]{get; }	// overrides XmlReader
public override string **this**[string name]{get; }	// overrides XmlReader
public override string **Value**{get; }	// overrides XmlReader
public override string **XmlLang**{get; }	// overrides XmlReader
public override XmlSpace **XmlSpace**{get; }	// overrides XmlReader

System.XML

```
// Public Instance Methods
  public override void Close( );                                              // overrides XmlReader
  public override string GetAttribute(int attributeIndex);                    // overrides XmlReader
  public override string GetAttribute(string name);                           // overrides XmlReader
  public override string GetAttribute(string name, string namespaceURI);      // overrides XmlReader
  public override string LookupNamespace(string prefix);                      // overrides XmlReader
  public override bool MoveToAttribute(string name);                          // overrides XmlReader
  public override bool MoveToAttribute(string name, string namespaceURI);     // overrides XmlReader
  public override void MoveToAttribute(int attributeIndex);                   // overrides XmlReader
  public override bool MoveToElement( );                                      // overrides XmlReader
  public override bool MoveToFirstAttribute( );                               // overrides XmlReader
  public override bool MoveToNextAttribute( );                                // overrides XmlReader
  public override bool Read( );                                               // overrides XmlReader
  public override bool ReadAttributeValue( );                                 // overrides XmlReader
  public override string ReadString( );                                       // overrides XmlReader
  public override void ResolveEntity( );                                      // overrides XmlReader
  public override void Skip( );                                               // overrides XmlReader
}
```

Hierarchy   System.Object → XmlReader → XmlNodeReader

XmlNodeType   CF 1.0, ECMA 1.0, serializable

System.Xml (system.xml.dll)   enum

This enumeration contains identifiers for node types. All DOM Core Level 2 types are included.

```
public enum XmlNodeType {
  None = 0,
  Element = 1,
  Attribute = 2,
  Text = 3,
  CDATA = 4,
  EntityReference = 5,
  Entity = 6,
  ProcessingInstruction = 7,
  Comment = 8,
  Document = 9,
  DocumentType = 10,
  DocumentFragment = 11,
  Notation = 12,
  Whitespace = 13,
  SignificantWhitespace = 14,
  EndElement = 15,
  EndEntity = 16,
  XmlDeclaration = 17
}
```

Hierarchy   System.Object → System.ValueType → System.Enum(System.IComparable,
                     System.IFormattable, System.IConvertible) → XmlNodeType

Returned By   XmlNode.NodeType, XmlReader.{MoveToContent( ), NodeType}

Passed To   XmlDocument.CreateNode( ), XmlTextReader.XmlTextReader( ),
                  XmlValidatingReader.XmlValidatingReader( )

XmlNotation

System.Xml (system.xml.dll)   class

This class represents a notation declaration (<!NOTATION ...>) in an XML document.

```
public class XmlNotation : XmlNode {
// Public Instance Properties
    public override string InnerXml{set; get; }                    // overrides XmlNode
    public override bool IsReadOnly{get; }                         // overrides XmlNode
    public override string LocalName{get; }                        // overrides XmlNode
    public override string Name{get; }                             // overrides XmlNode
    public override XmlNodeType NodeType{get; }                    // overrides XmlNode
    public override string OuterXml{get; }                         // overrides XmlNode
    public string PublicId{get; }
    public string SystemId{get; }
// Public Instance Methods
    public override XmlNode CloneNode(bool deep);                  // overrides XmlNode
    public override void WriteContentTo(XmlWriter w);             // overrides XmlNode
    public override void WriteTo(XmlWriter w);                     // overrides XmlNode
}
```

Hierarchy   System.Object → XmlNode(System.ICloneable, System.Collections.IEnumerable,
                  System.Xml.XPath.IXPathNavigable) → XmlNotation

XmlParserContext   CF 1.0, ECMA 1.0

System.Xml (system.xml.dll)   class

This class contains document context information normally provided by both the
XML declaration and DOCTYPE elements for parsing XML fragments. XmlTextReader and
XmlValidatingReader use the XmlParserContext for the base URI, internal subset, public and
system identifiers, etc.

```
public class XmlParserContext {
// Public Constructors
    public XmlParserContext(XmlNameTable nt, XmlNamespaceManager nsMgr, string docTypeName, string publd,
        string sysId, string internalSubset, string baseURI, string xmlLang, XmlSpace xmlSpace);
    public XmlParserContext(XmlNameTable nt, XmlNamespaceManager nsMgr, string docTypeName, string publd,
        string sysId, string internalSubset, string baseURI, string xmlLang, XmlSpace xmlSpace, System.Text.Encoding enc);
    public XmlParserContext(XmlNameTable nt, XmlNamespaceManager nsMgr, string xmlLang, XmlSpace xmlSpace);
    public XmlParserContext(XmlNameTable nt, XmlNamespaceManager nsMgr, string xmlLang, XmlSpace xmlSpace,
        System.Text.Encoding enc);
// Public Instance Properties
    public string BaseURI{set; get; }
    public string DocTypeName{set; get; }
    public Encoding Encoding{set; get; }
    public string InternalSubset{set; get; }
```

```
public XmlNamespaceManager NamespaceManager{set; get; }
public XmlNameTable NameTable{set; get; }
public string PublicId{set; get; }
public string SystemId{set; get; }
public string XmlLang{set; get; }
public XmlSpace XmlSpace{set; get; }
}
```

Passed To XmlTextReader.XmlTextReader( ), XmlValidatingReader.XmlValidatingReader( )

XmlProcessingInstruction

CF 1.0

System.Xml (system.xml.dll)   class

This class represents a processing instruction in an XML document.

```
public class XmlProcessingInstruction : XmlLinkedNode {
// Protected Constructors
  protected internal XmlProcessingInstruction(string target, string data, XmlDocument doc);
// Public Instance Properties
  public string Data{set; get; }
  public override string InnerText{set; get; }                                    // overrides XmlNode
  public override string LocalName{get; }                                          // overrides XmlNode
  public override string Name{get; }                                               // overrides XmlNode
  public override XmlNodeType NodeType{get; }                                       // overrides XmlNode
  public string Target{get; }
  public override string Value{set; get; }                                         // overrides XmlNode
// Public Instance Methods
  public override XmlNode CloneNode(bool deep);                                     // overrides XmlNode
  public override void WriteContentTo(XmlWriter w);                                 // overrides XmlNode
  public override void WriteTo(XmlWriter w);                                        // overrides XmlNode
}
```

Hierarchy System.Object → XmlNode(System.ICloneable, System.Collections.IEnumerable, System.Xml.XPath.IXPathNavigable) → XmlLinkedNode → XmlProcessingInstruction

Returned By XmlDocument.CreateProcessingInstruction( )

XmlQualifiedName

CF 1.0

System.Xml (system.xml.dll)   class

This class represents a namespace-qualified local name. This looks like namespace:name within a document. An XmlQualifiedName object is constructed with the element's name and its namespace as string arguments. The namespace field may be empty, in which case the default namespace of the document is assumed.

```
public class XmlQualifiedName {
// Public Constructors
  public XmlQualifiedName( );
  public XmlQualifiedName(string name);
  public XmlQualifiedName(string name, string ns);
```

```
// Public Static Fields
  public static readonly XmlQualifiedName Empty;
// Public Instance Properties
  public bool IsEmpty{get; }
  public string Name{get; }
  public string Namespace{get; }
// Public Static Methods
  public static string ToString(string name, string ns);
  public static bool operator !=(XmlQualifiedName a, XmlQualifiedName b);
  public static bool operator = =(XmlQualifiedName a, XmlQualifiedName b);
// Public Instance Methods
  public override bool Equals(object other);                              // overrides object
  public override int GetHashCode( );                                    // overrides object
  public override string ToString( );                                    // overrides object
}
```

XmlReader

CF 1.0, ECMA 1.0

System.Xml (system.xml.dll)

abstract class

This class is a simple reader for XML documents. XmlReader provides a non-cached, forward-only navigation through an XML data stream. It does not provide validation, nor does it expand general entities. Two derived classes provide these features: XmlTextReader and XmlValidatingReader.

The XmlReader class parses XML in a streaming-based approach (exemplified by the SAX specification). This means the XML parser presents "interesting pieces" (elements, attributes, namespace declarations, and so forth) in a linear order. Within XmlReader, this ordering of nodes is done using successive calls to the Read( ) method. An XmlReader is not positioned on a node at first—an initial call to Read( ) is required to move to the root node of a document. Subsequent calls to Read( ) move the reader sequentially through the nodes. The NodeType property tells you which type of node the reader is currently positioned on, returning values from the XmlNodeType enumeration. A special node-type value for XmlReader is EndElement. As Read( ) moves through the stream, it can be positioned on an element's end tag after it has stepped through the element's children. This is not a real node, in the DOM sense, but is required for XmlReader to parse XML data properly. The Skip( ) method steps through data node by node. A call to Skip( ) moves the reader to the next real node, disregarding the current node's children.

XML documents can also be parsed in a tree-based approach, using the XmlDocument type.

```
public abstract class XmlReader {
// Protected Constructors
  protected XmlReader( );
// Public Instance Properties
  public abstract int AttributeCount{get; }
  public abstract string BaseURI{get; }
  public virtual bool CanResolveEntity{get; }
  public abstract int Depth{get; }
  public abstract bool EOF{get; }
  public virtual bool HasAttributes{get; }
  public abstract bool HasValue{get; }
```

```
    public abstract bool IsDefault{get; }
    public abstract bool IsEmptyElement{get; }
    public abstract string LocalName{get; }
    public abstract string Name{get; }
    public abstract string NamespaceURI{get; }
    public abstract XmlNameTable NameTable{get; }
    public abstract XmlNodeType NodeType{get; }
    public abstract string Prefix{get; }
    public abstract char QuoteChar{get; }
    public abstract ReadState ReadState{get; }
    public abstract string this[string name, string namespaceURI]{get; }
    public abstract string this[int i]{get; }
    public abstract string this[string name]{get; }
    public abstract string Value{get; }
    public abstract string XmlLang{get; }
    public abstract XmlSpace XmlSpace{get; }
// Public Static Methods
    public static bool IsName(string str);
    public static bool IsNameToken(string str);
// Public Instance Methods
    public abstract void Close( );
    public abstract string GetAttribute(int i);
    public abstract string GetAttribute(string name);
    public abstract string GetAttribute(string name, string namespaceURI);
    public virtual bool IsStartElement( );
    public virtual bool IsStartElement(string name);
    public virtual bool IsStartElement(string localname, string ns);
    public abstract string LookupNamespace(string prefix);
    public abstract bool MoveToAttribute(string name);
    public abstract bool MoveToAttribute(string name, string ns);
    public abstract void MoveToAttribute(int i);
    public virtual XmlNodeType MoveToContent( );
    public abstract bool MoveToElement( );
    public abstract bool MoveToFirstAttribute( );
    public abstract bool MoveToNextAttribute( );
    public abstract bool Read( );
    public abstract bool ReadAttributeValue( );
    public virtual string ReadElementString( );
    public virtual string ReadElementString(string name);
    public virtual string ReadElementString(string localname, string ns);
    public virtual void ReadEndElement( );
    public virtual string ReadInnerXml( );
    public virtual string ReadOuterXml( );
    public virtual void ReadStartElement( );
    public virtual void ReadStartElement(string name);
    public virtual void ReadStartElement(string localname, string ns);
    public virtual string ReadString( );
    public abstract void ResolveEntity( );
    public virtual void Skip( );
}
```

Subclasses	XmlNodeReader, XmlTextReader, XmlValidatingReader
Returned By	XmlValidatingReader.Reader, System.Xml.Xsl.XslTransform.Transform( )
Passed To	XmlDocument.{Load( ), ReadNode( )}, XmlValidatingReader.XmlValidatingReader( ), XmlWriter.{WriteAttributes( ), WriteNode( )}, System.Xml.XPath.XPathDocument. XPathDocument( ), System.Xml.Xsl.XslTransform.Load( )

XmlResolver
CF 1.0, ECMA 1.0

System.Xml (system.xml.dll)   abstract class

This class resolves external resources according to their URIs. This class is used to retrieve an external DTD or Schema in XML documents and also obtains resources from imported stylesheets (<xsl:import>) and included files (<xml:include>). This abstract class is implemented by XmlUrlResolver.

```
public abstract class XmlResolver {
// Protected Constructors
   protected XmlResolver( );
// Public Instance Properties
   public abstract ICredentials Credentials{set; }
// Public Instance Methods
   public abstract object GetEntity(Uri absoluteUri, string role, Type ofObjectToReturn);
   public virtual Uri ResolveUri(Uri baseUri, string relativeUri);
}
```

Subclasses	XmlSecureResolver, XmlUrlResolver
Passed To	XmlDocument.XmlResolver, XmlSecureResolver.XmlSecureResolver( ), XmlTextReader.XmlResolver, XmlValidatingReader.XmlResolver, System.Xml.Xsl. XslTransform.{Load(Transform( ), XmlResolver}

XmlSecureResolver

System.Xml (system.xml.dll)   class

This class decorates an XmlResolver instance to provide security restrictions on the normal behavior of an XmlResolver. For example, it can prevent resolving URI references that reference other domains embedded within an XML document. See XmlUrlResolver for the concrete implementation this class will usually wrap around.

```
public class XmlSecureResolver : XmlResolver {
// Public Constructors
   public XmlSecureResolver(XmlResolver resolver, System.Security.Policy.Evidence evidence);
   public XmlSecureResolver(XmlResolver resolver, System.Security.PermissionSet permissionSet);
   public XmlSecureResolver(XmlResolver resolver, string securityUrl);
// Public Instance Properties
   public override ICredentials Credentials{set; }                      // overrides XmlResolver
// Public Static Methods
   public static Evidence CreateEvidenceForUrl(string securityUrl);
// Public Instance Methods
```

```
public override object GetEntity(Uri absoluteUri, string role, Type ofObjectToReturn);    // overrides XmlResolver
public override Uri ResolveUri(Uri baseUri, string relativeUri);                           // overrides XmlResolver
}
```

Hierarchy   System.Object → XmlResolver → XmlSecureResolver

XmlSignificantWhitespace   CF 1.0

System.Xml (system.xml.dll)   class

This class represents a whitespace node in mixed content data, if whitespace is
preserved in the XML document (XmlDocument.PreserveWhitespace is True).

```
public class XmlSignificantWhitespace : XmlCharacterData {
// Protected Constructors
  protected internal XmlSignificantWhitespace(string strData, XmlDocument doc);
// Public Instance Properties
  public override string LocalName{get; }                                     // overrides XmlNode
  public override string Name{get; }                                          // overrides XmlNode
  public override XmlNodeType NodeType{get; }                                 // overrides XmlNode
  public override string Value{set; get; }                              // overrides XmlCharacterData
// Public Instance Methods
  public override XmlNode CloneNode(bool deep);                               // overrides XmlNode
  public override void WriteContentTo(XmlWriter w);                          // overrides XmlNode
  public override void WriteTo(XmlWriter w);                                 // overrides XmlNode
}
```

Hierarchy   System.Object → XmlNode(System.ICloneable, System.Collections.IEnumerable,
                     System.Xml.XPath.IXPathNavigable) → XmlLinkedNode → XmlCharacterData →
                     XmlSignificantWhitespace

Returned By   XmlDocument.CreateSignificantWhitespace( )

XmlSpace   CF 1.0, ECMA 1.0, serializable

System.Xml (system.xml.dll)   enum

This enumeration provides values for the xml:space scope. Used by XmlParserContext.XmlSpace.

```
public enum XmlSpace {
  None = 0,
  Default = 1,
  Preserve = 2
}
```

Hierarchy   System.Object → System.ValueType → System.Enum(System.IComparable,
                     System.IFormattable, System.IConvertible) → XmlSpace

Returned By   XmlParserContext.XmlSpace, XmlReader.XmlSpace, XmlWriter.XmlSpace

Passed To   XmlParserContext.{XmlParserContext( ), XmlSpace},
                     System.Xml.XPath.XPathDocument.XPathDocument( )

XmlText

System.Xml (system.xml.dll)   class

This class represents a text node in an XML document. XmlTest is derived from the XmlCharacterData class and contains the text content of an element.

```
public class XmlText : XmlCharacterData {
// Protected Constructors
   protected internal XmlText(string strData, XmlDocument doc);
// Public Instance Properties
   public override string LocalName{get; }                                  // overrides XmlNode
   public override string Name{get; }                                       // overrides XmlNode
   public override XmlNodeType NodeType{get; }                              // overrides XmlNode
   public override string Value{set; get; }                         // overrides XmlCharacterData
// Public Instance Methods
   public override XmlNode CloneNode(bool deep);                            // overrides XmlNode
   public virtual XmlText SplitText(int offset);
   public override void WriteContentTo(XmlWriter w);                       // overrides XmlNode
   public override void WriteTo(XmlWriter w);                              // overrides XmlNode
}
```

Hierarchy   System.Object → XmlNode(System.ICloneable, System.Collections.IEnumerable,
                       System.Xml.XPath.IXPathNavigable) → XmlLinkedNode → XmlCharacterData → XmlText

Returned By   XmlDocument.CreateTextNode( )

XmlTextReader

System.Xml (system.xml.dll)   class

This class is a text-based reader for XML documents derived from XmlReader. XmlTextReader checks for well-formedness and expands entities, but does not validate data according to a DTD or schema.

```
public class XmlTextReader : XmlReader : IXmlLineInfo {
// Public Constructors
   public XmlTextReader(System.IO.Stream input);
   public XmlTextReader(System.IO.Stream input, XmlNameTable nt);
   public XmlTextReader(System.IO.Stream xmlFragment, XmlNodeType fragType, XmlParserContext context);
   public XmlTextReader(string url);
   public XmlTextReader(string url, System.IO.Stream input);
   public XmlTextReader(string url, System.IO.Stream input, XmlNameTable nt);
   public XmlTextReader(string url, System.IO.TextReader input);
   public XmlTextReader(string url, System.IO.TextReader input, XmlNameTable nt);
   public XmlTextReader(string url, XmlNameTable nt);
   public XmlTextReader(string xmlFragment, XmlNodeType fragType, XmlParserContext context);
   public XmlTextReader(System.IO.TextReader input);
   public XmlTextReader(System.IO.TextReader input, XmlNameTable nt);
// Protected Constructors
   protected XmlTextReader( );
   protected XmlTextReader(XmlNameTable nt);
```

```
// Public Instance Properties
    public override int AttributeCount{get; }                                              // overrides XmlReader
    public override string BaseURI{get; }                                                  // overrides XmlReader
    public override int Depth{get; }                                                       // overrides XmlReader
    public Encoding Encoding{get; }
    public override bool EOF{get; }                                                        // overrides XmlReader
    public override bool HasValue{get; }                                                   // overrides XmlReader
    public override bool IsDefault{get; }                                                  // overrides XmlReader
    public override bool IsEmptyElement{get; }                                             // overrides XmlReader
    public int LineNumber{get; }                                                           // implements IXmlLineInfo
    public int LinePosition{get; }                                                         // implements IXmlLineInfo
    public override string LocalName{get; }                                                // overrides XmlReader
    public override string Name{get; }                                                     // overrides XmlReader
    public bool Namespaces{set; get; }
    public override string NamespaceURI{get; }                                             // overrides XmlReader
    public override XmlNameTable NameTable{get; }                                          // overrides XmlReader
    public override XmlNodeType NodeType{get; }                                            // overrides XmlReader
    public bool Normalization{set; get; }
    public override string Prefix{get; }                                                   // overrides XmlReader
    public override char QuoteChar{get; }                                                  // overrides XmlReader
    public override ReadState ReadState{get; }                                             // overrides XmlReader
    public override string this[int i]{get; }                                              // overrides XmlReader
    public override string this[string name]{get; }                                        // overrides XmlReader
    public override string this[string name, string namespaceURI]{get; }                   // overrides XmlReader
    public override string Value{get; }                                                    // overrides XmlReader
    public WhitespaceHandling WhitespaceHandling{set; get; }
    public override string XmlLang{get; }                                                  // overrides XmlReader
    public XmlResolver XmlResolver{set; }
    public override XmlSpace XmlSpace{get; }                                               // overrides XmlReader
// Public Instance Methods
    public override void Close( );                                                         // overrides XmlReader
    public override string GetAttribute(int i);                                            // overrides XmlReader
    public override string GetAttribute(string name);                                      // overrides XmlReader
    public override string GetAttribute(string localName, string namespaceURI);            // overrides XmlReader
    public TextReader GetRemainder( );
    public override string LookupNamespace(string prefix);                                 // overrides XmlReader
    public override bool MoveToAttribute(string name);                                     // overrides XmlReader
    public override bool MoveToAttribute(string localName, string namespaceURI);           // overrides XmlReader
    public override void MoveToAttribute(int i);                                           // overrides XmlReader
    public override bool MoveToElement( );                                                 // overrides XmlReader
    public override bool MoveToFirstAttribute( );                                          // overrides XmlReader
    public override bool MoveToNextAttribute( );                                           // overrides XmlReader
    public override bool Read( );                                                          // overrides XmlReader
    public override bool ReadAttributeValue( );                                            // overrides XmlReader
    public int ReadBase64(byte[ ] array, int offset, int len);
    public int ReadBinHex(byte[ ] array, int offset, int len);
    public int ReadChars(char[ ] buffer, int index, int count);
    public void ResetState( );
    public override void ResolveEntity( );                                                // overrides XmlReader
}
```

Hierarchy   System.Object → XmlReader → XmlTextReader(IXmlLineInfo)

System.Xml (system.xml.dll)   class

This class adds basic formatting to the text output and is derived from XmlWriter. The Formatting property uses its values to indicate if the output is to be Indented (None is the default). If Formatting is set to Formatting.Indented, the value of the Indentation property is the number of characters to indent each successive level (or child element) in the output. IndentChar sets the character to use for indentation, which must be a valid whitespace character (the default is space). QuoteChar is the character to use to quote attributes and is either a single or double quote.

```
public class XmlTextWriter : XmlWriter {
// Public Constructors
  public XmlTextWriter(System.IO.Stream w, System.Text.Encoding encoding);
  public XmlTextWriter(string filename, System.Text.Encoding encoding);
  public XmlTextWriter(System.IO.TextWriter w);
// Public Instance Properties
  public Stream BaseStream{get; }
  public Formatting Formatting{set; get; }
  public int Indentation{set; get; }
  public char IndentChar{set; get; }
  public bool Namespaces{set; get; }
  public char QuoteChar{set; get; }
  public override WriteState WriteState{get; }                                    // overrides XmlWriter
  public override string XmlLang{get; }                                           // overrides XmlWriter
  public override XmlSpace XmlSpace{get; }                                        // overrides XmlWriter
// Public Instance Methods
  public override void Close( );                                                  // overrides XmlWriter
  public override void Flush( );                                                  // overrides XmlWriter
  public override string LookupPrefix(string ns);                                 // overrides XmlWriter
  public override void WriteBase64(byte[ ] buffer, int index, int count);          // overrides XmlWriter
  public override void WriteBinHex(byte[ ] buffer, int index, int count);          // overrides XmlWriter
  public override void WriteCData(string text);                                   // overrides XmlWriter
  public override void WriteCharEntity(char ch);                                  // overrides XmlWriter
  public override void WriteChars(char[ ] buffer, int index, int count);           // overrides XmlWriter
  public override void WriteComment(string text);                                 // overrides XmlWriter
  public override void WriteDocType(string name, string pubid, string sysid, string subset);  // overrides XmlWriter
  public override void WriteEndAttribute( );                                      // overrides XmlWriter
  public override void WriteEndDocument( );                                       // overrides XmlWriter
  public override void WriteEndElement( );                                        // overrides XmlWriter
  public override void WriteEntityRef(string name);                               // overrides XmlWriter
  public override void WriteFullEndElement( );                                    // overrides XmlWriter
  public override void WriteName(string name);                                    // overrides XmlWriter
  public override void WriteNmToken(string name);                                 // overrides XmlWriter
  public override void WriteProcessingInstruction(string name, string text);       // overrides XmlWriter
  public override void WriteQualifiedName(string localName, string ns);            // overrides XmlWriter
  public override void WriteRaw(char[ ] buffer, int index, int count);             // overrides XmlWriter
  public override void WriteRaw(string data);                                     // overrides XmlWriter
  public override void WriteStartAttribute(string prefix, string localName, string ns);  // overrides XmlWriter
  public override void WriteStartDocument( );                                     // overrides XmlWriter
  public override void WriteStartDocument(bool standalone);                        // overrides XmlWriter
```

System.XML

public override void **WriteStartElement**(string *prefix*, string *localName*, string *ns*);	*// overrides XmlWriter*
public override void **WriteString**(string *text*);	*// overrides XmlWriter*
public override void **WriteSurrogateCharEntity**(char *lowChar*, char *highChar*);	*// overrides XmlWriter*
public override void **WriteWhitespace**(string *ws*);	*// overrides XmlWriter*
}	

Hierarchy   System.Object → XmlWriter → XmlTextWriter

XmlTokenizedType   serializable

System.Xml (system.xml.dll)   enum

This is an enumeration of XML string types based on the XML 1.0 specification.

```
public enum XmlTokenizedType {
  CDATA = 0,
  ID = 1,
  IDREF = 2,
  IDREFS = 3,
  ENTITY = 4,
  ENTITIES = 5,
  NMTOKEN = 6,
  NMTOKENS = 7,
  NOTATION = 8,
  ENUMERATION = 9,
  QName = 10,
  NCName = 11,
  None = 12
}
```

Hierarchy   System.Object → System.ValueType → System.Enum(System.IComparable,
                 System.IFormattable, System.IConvertible) → XmlTokenizedType

XmlUrlResolver   CF 1.0, ECMA 1.0

System.Xml (system.xml.dll)   class

This class resolves URLs of external resources and retrieves them for parsing. XmlUrlResolver implements XmlResolver and provides methods for retrieving external DTDs,
schemas, and imported stylesheets via a URL. To retrieve resources on a network, the
Credentials property can be set to provide usernames and passwords, as well as define
authentication schemes. You can set this property by supplying a System.Net.ICredentials
object. By default, this property is set for anonymous access to a URI resource.

```
public class XmlUrlResolver : XmlResolver {
// Public Constructors
  public XmlUrlResolver( );
// Public Instance Properties
  public override ICredentials Credentials{set; }                              // overrides XmlResolver
// Public Instance Methods
  public override object GetEntity(Uri absoluteUri, string role, Type ofObjectToReturn);   // overrides XmlResolver
}
```

Hierarchy   System.Object → XmlResolver → XmlUrlResolver

XmlValidatingReader

System.Xml (system.xml.dll)   class

This class is an XML reader that supports DTD and schema validation. The type of validation to perform is contained in the ValidationType property, which can be DTD, Schema, XDR, or Auto. Auto is the default and determines which type of validation is required, if any, based on the document. If the DOCTYPE element contains DTD information, that is used. If a schema attribute exists or there is an inline <schema>, that schema is used.

This class implements an event handler that you can set to warn of validation errors during Read() operations. Specifically, a delegate instance of type System.Xml.Schema.ValidationEventHandler can be set for the ValidationEventHandler event in this class. This delegate instance is invoked whenever the XmlValidatingReader finds an schema-invalid construct in the XML document it is reading, giving the delegate a chance to perform whatever error-handling is appropriate. If no event handler is registered, an XmlException is thrown instead on the first error.

```
public class XmlValidatingReader: XmlReader, IXmlLineInfo {
// Public Constructors
   public XmlValidatingReader(System.IO.Stream xmlFragment, XmlNodeType fragType, XmlParserContext context);
   public XmlValidatingReader(string xmlFragment, XmlNodeType fragType, XmlParserContext context);
   public XmlValidatingReader(XmlReader reader);
// Public Instance Properties
   public override int AttributeCount{get; }                                    // overrides XmlReader
   public override string BaseURI{get; }                                        // overrides XmlReader
   public override bool CanResolveEntity{get; }                                 // overrides XmlReader
   public override int Depth{get; }                                             // overrides XmlReader
   public Encoding Encoding{get; }
   public EntityHandling EntityHandling{set; get; }
   public override bool EOF{get; }                                              // overrides XmlReader
   public override bool HasValue{get; }                                         // overrides XmlReader
   public override bool IsDefault{get; }                                        // overrides XmlReader
   public override bool IsEmptyElement{get; }                                   // overrides XmlReader
   public override string LocalName{get; }                                      // overrides XmlReader
   public override string Name{get; }                                           // overrides XmlReader
   public bool Namespaces{set; get; }
   public override string NamespaceURI{get; }                                   // overrides XmlReader
   public override XmlNameTable NameTable{get; }                                // overrides XmlReader
   public override XmlNodeType NodeType{get; }                                  // overrides XmlReader
   public override string Prefix{get; }                                         // overrides XmlReader
   public override char QuoteChar{get; }                                        // overrides XmlReader
   public XmlReader Reader{get; }
   public override ReadState ReadState{get; }                                   // overrides XmlReader
   public XmlSchemaCollection Schemas{get; }
   public object SchemaType{get; }
   public override string this[int i]{get; }                                    // overrides XmlReader
   public override string this[string name]{get; }                             // overrides XmlReader
   public override string this[string name, string namespaceURI]{get; }        // overrides XmlReader
   public ValidationType ValidationType{set; get; }
   public override string Value{get; }                                          // overrides XmlReader
   public override string XmlLang{get; }                                        // overrides XmlReader
```

```
  public XmlResolver XmlResolver{set; }
  public override XmlSpace XmlSpace{get; }                                                  // overrides XmlReader
// Public Instance Methods
  public override void Close( );                                                            // overrides XmlReader
  public override string GetAttribute(int i);                                               // overrides XmlReader
  public override string GetAttribute(string name);                                         // overrides XmlReader
  public override string GetAttribute(string localName, string namespaceURI);               // overrides XmlReader
  public override string LookupNamespace(string prefix);                                    // overrides XmlReader
  public override bool MoveToAttribute(string name);                                        // overrides XmlReader
  public override bool MoveToAttribute(string localName, string namespaceURI);              // overrides XmlReader
  public override void MoveToAttribute(int i);                                              // overrides XmlReader
  public override bool MoveToElement( );                                                    // overrides XmlReader
  public override bool MoveToFirstAttribute( );                                             // overrides XmlReader
  public override bool MoveToNextAttribute( );                                              // overrides XmlReader
  public override bool Read( );                                                             // overrides XmlReader
  public override bool ReadAttributeValue( );                                               // overrides XmlReader
  public override string ReadString( );                                                     // overrides XmlReader
  public object ReadTypedValue( );
  public override void ResolveEntity( );                                                    // overrides XmlReader
// Events
  public event ValidationEventHandler ValidationEventHandler;
}
```

Hierarchy System.Object → XmlReader → XmlValidatingReader(IXmlLineInfo)

XmlWhitespace   CF 1.0

System.Xml (system.xml.dll)   class

This class represents whitespace in element content. Whitespace is ignored if XmlDocument.PreserveWhitespace is not set to true.

```
public class XmlWhitespace : XmlCharacterData {
// Protected Constructors
  protected internal XmlWhitespace(string strData, XmlDocument doc);
// Public Instance Properties
  public override string LocalName{get; }                                                   // overrides XmlNode
  public override string Name{get; }                                                        // overrides XmlNode
  public override XmlNodeType NodeType{get; }                                                // overrides XmlNode
  public override string Value{set; get; }                                                  // overrides XmlCharacterData
// Public Instance Methods
  public override XmlNode CloneNode(bool deep);                                              // overrides XmlNode
  public override void WriteContentTo(XmlWriter w);                                          // overrides XmlNode
  public override void WriteTo(XmlWriter w);                                                 // overrides XmlNode
}
```

Hierarchy   System.Object → XmlNode(System.ICloneable, System.Collections.IEnumerable, System.
                 Xml.XPath.IXPathNavigable) → XmlLinkedNode → XmlCharacterData → XmlWhitespace

Returned By XmlDocument.CreateWhitespace( )

This class is a fast writer used to output XML data to a stream or file. Two methods work with input from an XmlReader object to produce output from the currently positioned node. WriteAttributes( ) outputs all the node's attributes. WriteNode( ) dumps the entire current node to the output stream and moves the XmlReader to the next node.

The remaining Write* methods of this class take string arguments that are output as properly formed XML markup. For example, WriteComment( ) takes a string and outputs it within <!-- ... --> markup. WriteStartAttribute( ) and WriteStartElement( ) provide some flexibility when writing elements and attributes. These two methods provide the opening contents of each type, given the name, prefix, and namespace. The next call can then provide the value of the element or attribute by other means. For example, you can use WriteString( ) for a simple string value, or another WriteStartElement( ) to begin a child element. WriteEndAttribute( ) and WriteEndElement( ) close the writing.

The derived XmlTextWriter class provides formatting functionality to the output data.

```csharp
public abstract class XmlWriter {
// Protected Constructors
  protected XmlWriter( );
// Public Instance Properties
  public abstract WriteState WriteState{get; }
  public abstract string XmlLang{get; }
  public abstract XmlSpace XmlSpace{get; }
// Public Instance Methods
  public abstract void Close( );
  public abstract void Flush( );
  public abstract string LookupPrefix(string ns);
  public virtual void WriteAttributes(XmlReader reader, bool defattr);
  public void WriteAttributeString(string localName, string value);
  public void WriteAttributeString(string localName, string ns, string value);
  public void WriteAttributeString(string prefix, string localName, string ns, string value);
  public abstract void WriteBase64(byte[ ] buffer, int index, int count);
  public abstract void WriteBinHex(byte[ ] buffer, int index, int count);
  public abstract void WriteCData(string text);
  public abstract void WriteCharEntity(char ch);
  public abstract void WriteChars(char[ ] buffer, int index, int count);
  public abstract void WriteComment(string text);
  public abstract void WriteDocType(string name, string pubid, string sysid, string subset);
  public void WriteElementString(string localName, string value);
  public void WriteElementString(string localName, string ns, string value);
  public abstract void WriteEndAttribute( );
  public abstract void WriteEndDocument( );
  public abstract void WriteEndElement( );
  public abstract void WriteEntityRef(string name);
  public abstract void WriteFullEndElement( );
  public abstract void WriteName(string name);
  public abstract void WriteNmToken(string name);
  public virtual void WriteNode(XmlReader reader, bool defattr);
  public abstract void WriteProcessingInstruction(string name, string text);
  public abstract void WriteQualifiedName(string localName, string ns);
```

```
public abstract void WriteRaw(char[ ] buffer, int index, int count);
public abstract void WriteRaw(string data);
public void WriteStartAttribute(string localName, string ns);
public abstract void WriteStartAttribute(string prefix, string localName, string ns);
public abstract void WriteStartDocument( );
public abstract void WriteStartDocument(bool standalone);
public void WriteStartElement(string localName);
public void WriteStartElement(string localName, string ns);
public abstract void WriteStartElement(string prefix, string localName, string ns);
public abstract void WriteString(string text);
public abstract void WriteSurrogateCharEntity(char lowChar, char highChar);
public abstract void WriteWhitespace(string ws);
}
```

Subclasses   XmlTextWriter

Passed To   XmlDocument.Save( ), XmlNode.{WriteContentTo( ), WriteTo( )},
System.Xml.Xsl.XslTransform.Transform( )

45

System.Xml.XPath

XPath is a W3C specification for locating nodes in an XML document. It provides an expression syntax that can determine a node based on its type, location, and relation to other nodes in a document. XPath is generally not useful alone, but works in conjunction with other tools, especially XSLT. Figure 45-1 shows the types in this namespace.

System.Xml.XPath provides types that evaluate expressions and match nodes in XML documents. XPathDocument is a document object designed to provide fast document navigation through XPath and is used by the System.Xml.Xsl classes for XSLT transformations. XPathNavigator is the core entry point for doing XPath expressions; it is abstract, allowing for more than just XML documents to be XPath-navigated. For example, an ADO.NET provider could, if it desired, implement the IXPathNavigable interface and return an XPathNavigator that translated XPath queries into a SQL SELECT statement. (See Aaron Skonnard's MSDN Magazine article "Writing XML Providers for Microsoft .NET" for more details about using XML-based technologies over data sources other than XML documents.)

IXPathNavigable

System.Xml.XPath (system.xml.dll)   interface

This is an interface to XPathNavigator implemented by XPathDocument, System.Xml.XmlNode, and derived classes. It implements one method, CreateNavigator( ), which creates an XPathNavigator instance for the document object.

```
public interface IXPathNavigable {
// Public Instance Methods
  public XPathNavigator CreateNavigator( );
}
```

Implemented By   XPathDocument, System.Xml.XmlNode

Passed To   System.Xml.Xsl.XslTransform.{Load( ), Transform( )}

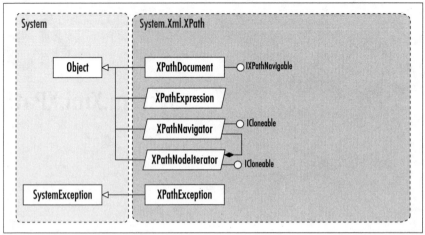

Figure 45-1. The System.Xml.XPath namespace

XmlCaseOrder
serializable

System.Xml.XPath (system.xml.dll)
enum

This enumeration specifies how nodes are sorted with respect to case. A value of None indicates that case is to be ignored when ordering nodes.

```
public enum XmlCaseOrder {
  None = 0,
  UpperFirst = 1,
  LowerFirst = 2
}
```

Hierarchy   System.Object → System.ValueType → System.Enum(System.IComparable, System.IFormattable, System.IConvertible) → XmlCaseOrder

Passed To   XPathExpression.AddSort( )

XmlDataType
serializable

System.Xml.XPath (system.xml.dll)
enum

This enumeration specifies whether to sort node values by type as numeric value (Number) or alphabetically (Text).

```
public enum XmlDataType {
  Text = 1,
  Number = 2
}
```

Hierarchy   System.Object › System.ValueType › System.Enum(System.IComparable, System.IFormattable, System.IConvertible) › XmlDataType

Passed To   XPathExpression.AddSort( )

XmlSortOrder

System.Xml.XPath (system.xml.dll)   enum

This enumeration specifies how nodes are sorted by numerical value, either ascending or descending.

```
public enum XmlSortOrder {
  Ascending = 1,
  Descending = 2
}
```

Hierarchy   System.Object › System.ValueType › System.Enum(System.IComparable, System.IFormattable, System.IConvertible) › XmlSortOrder

Passed To   XPathExpression.AddSort( )

XPathDocument

System.Xml.XPath (system.xml.dll)   class

This class is a concrete implementation of IXPathNavigable for creating an XPathNavigator that knows how to scan through an XML document. There are overloaded forms of the constructor designed to pull an XML document from various sources—a System.IO. Stream, a string, a System.IO.TextReader (which presumably is pulling from some other valid data source), or a System.Xml.XmlReader. Note that if the XmlReader is currently positioned on top of a particular node within a document, the constructed XPathDocument instance is only valid for that element and its children. This allows partial XPath scans of a given document.

This class serves no other purpose than as a factory for producing XPathNavigator instances.

```
public class XPathDocument : IXPathNavigable {
// Public Constructors
  public XPathDocument(System.IO.Stream stream);
  public XPathDocument(string uri);
  public XPathDocument(string uri, System.Xml.XmlSpace space);
  public XPathDocument(System.IO.TextReader reader);
  public XPathDocument(System.Xml.XmlReader reader);
  public XPathDocument(System.Xml.XmlReader reader, System.Xml.XmlSpace space);
// Public Instance Methods
  public XPathNavigator CreateNavigator( );                    // implements IXPathNavigable
}
```

XPathException

System.Xml.XPath (system.xml.dll)   class

This exception indicates a problem with an XPathExpression, such as an invalid prefix.

```
public class XPathException : SystemException {
// Public Constructors
  public XPathException(string message, Exception innerException);
```

```
// Protected Constructors
  protected XPathException(System.Runtime.Serialization.SerializationInfo info,
    System.Runtime.Serialization.StreamingContext context);
// Public Instance Properties
  public override string Message{get; }                                          // overrides Exception
// Public Instance Methods
  public override void GetObjectData(System.Runtime.Serialization.SerializationInfo info,
    System.Runtime.Serialization.StreamingContext context);                      // overrides Exception
}
```

Hierarchy   System.Object → System.Exception(System.Runtime.Serialization.ISerializable) →
                 System.SystemException → XPathException

XPathExpression

System.Xml.XPath (system.xml.dll)   **abstract class**

This class represents a compiled XPath expression. An **XPathExpression** is returned by the
Compile( ) method of **XPathNavigator** from an XPath expression string. The **AddSort( )** method
allows you to specify the order of returned nodes from the expression. **SetContext( )** sets
the namespace to use in the evaluation of the expression.

```
public abstract class XPathExpression {
// Public Instance Properties
  public abstract string Expression{get; }
  public abstract XPathResultType ReturnType{get; }
// Public Instance Methods
  public abstract void AddSort(object expr, System.Collections.IComparer comparer);
  public abstract void AddSort(object expr, XmlSortOrder order, XmlCaseOrder caseOrder, string lang,
    XmlDataType dataType);
  public abstract XPathExpression Clone( );
  public abstract void SetContext(System.Xml.XmlNamespaceManager nsManager);
}
```

Returned By   XPathNavigator.Compile( )

Passed To   XPathNavigator.{Evaluate( ), Matches( ), Select( )}

XPathNamespaceScope   **serializable**

System.Xml.XPath (system.xml.dll)   **enum**

This enumeration defines the namespace scope for certain **XPathNavigator** operations. **All**
includes all namespaces within the scope of the current node (including the xmlns:xml
namespace, whether defined explicitly or not). **ExcludeXml** includes all namespaces
within the scope of the current node, *except* the xmlns:xml namespace. **Local** includes all
locally defined namespaces within the scope of the current node.

```
public enum XPathNamespaceScope {
  All = 0,
  ExcludeXml = 1,
  Local = 2
}
```

Hierarchy	System.Object → System.ValueType → System.Enum(System.IComparable, System.IFormattable, System.IConvertible) → XPathNamespaceScope
Passed To	XPathNavigator.{MoveToFirstNamespace( ), MoveToNextNamespace( )}

XPathNavigator

System.Xml.XPath (system.xml.dll)   abstract class

This class is a read-only representation of an XPathDocument based on the IXPathNavigable interface. It provides an easy-to-use data object for quick XPath-based navigation, particularly for XSLT transformations.

An XPathNavigator instance maintains its state with the current node position to provide the proper context for any XPath expression evaluation. Initially, the current node is the root node. The current node is changed by using the Select( ) method or the various MoveTo* methods. If the XPath expression evaluates to a set of nodes, the first node of the set is the current node for the XPathNavigator. All the Select* methods return an XPathNodeIterator object containing the set of nodes returned by the function. Except for plain old Select( ), the Select* functions do not change the current node of the XPathNavigator they are used on. Any actions on the XPathNodeIterator objects that they return also do not affect the originating object.

The Compile( ) method takes an XPath expression string and encapsulates it into a compiled XPathExpression object. XPathExpression objects are used by Select( ), Evaluate( ), and Matches( ) as input to search a node list.

```
public abstract class XPathNavigator : ICloneable {
// Protected Constructors
  protected XPathNavigator( );
// Public Instance Properties
  public abstract string BaseURI{get; }
  public abstract bool HasAttributes{get; }
  public abstract bool HasChildren{get; }
  public abstract bool IsEmptyElement{get; }
  public abstract string LocalName{get; }
  public abstract string Name{get; }
  public abstract string NamespaceURI{get; }
  public abstract XmlNameTable NameTable{get; }
  public abstract XPathNodeType NodeType{get; }
  public abstract string Prefix{get; }
  public abstract string Value{get; }
  public abstract string XmlLang{get; }
// Public Instance Methods
  public abstract XPathNavigator Clone( );
  public virtual XmlNodeOrder ComparePosition(XPathNavigator nav);
  public virtual XPathExpression Compile(string xpath);
  public virtual object Evaluate(string xpath);
  public virtual object Evaluate(XPathExpression expr);
  public virtual object Evaluate(XPathExpression expr, XPathNodeIterator context);
  public abstract string GetAttribute(string localName, string namespaceURI);
  public abstract string GetNamespace(string name);
  public virtual bool IsDescendant(XPathNavigator nav);
```

```
public abstract bool IsSamePosition(XPathNavigator other);
public virtual bool Matches(string xpath);
public virtual bool Matches(XPathExpression expr);
public abstract bool MoveTo(XPathNavigator other);
public abstract bool MoveToAttribute(string localName, string namespaceURI);
public abstract bool MoveToFirst( );
public abstract bool MoveToFirstAttribute( );
public abstract bool MoveToFirstChild( );
public bool MoveToFirstNamespace( );
public abstract bool MoveToFirstNamespace(XPathNamespaceScope namespaceScope);
public abstract bool MoveToId(string id);
public abstract bool MoveToNamespace(string name);
public abstract bool MoveToNext( );
public abstract bool MoveToNextAttribute( );
public bool MoveToNextNamespace( );
public abstract bool MoveToNextNamespace(XPathNamespaceScope namespaceScope);
public abstract bool MoveToParent( );
public abstract bool MoveToPrevious( );
public abstract void MoveToRoot( );
public virtual XPathNodeIterator Select(string xpath);
public virtual XPathNodeIterator Select(XPathExpression expr);
public virtual XPathNodeIterator SelectAncestors(string name, string namespaceURI, bool matchSelf);
public virtual XPathNodeIterator SelectAncestors(XPathNodeType type, bool matchSelf);
public virtual XPathNodeIterator SelectChildren(string name, string namespaceURI);
public virtual XPathNodeIterator SelectChildren(XPathNodeType type);
public virtual XPathNodeIterator SelectDescendants(string name, string namespaceURI, bool matchSelf);
public virtual XPathNodeIterator SelectDescendants(XPathNodeType type, bool matchSelf);
public override string ToString( );                                        // overrides object
}
```

Returned By   System.Xml.XmlDataDocument.CreateNavigator( ), System.Xml.XmlNode.CreateNavigator( ),
                  IXPathNavigable.CreateNavigator( ), XPathDocument.CreateNavigator( ),
                  XPathNodeIterator.Current

Passed To   System.Xml.Xsl.IXsltContextFunction.Invoke( ), System.Xml.Xsl.XsltContext.
                  PreserveWhitespace( ), System.Xml.Xsl.XslTransform.{Load( ), Transform( )}

XPathNodeIterator

System.Xml.XPath (system.xml.dll)   abstract class

This class is a node-set constructed from a compiled XPath expression. This type is
returned by the Select* methods of XPathNavigator. The MoveNext( ) method moves to the
next node of the node set in document order and does not affect the XPathNavigator on
which the Select( ) was called.

```
public abstract class XPathNodeIterator : ICloneable {
// Protected Constructors
  protected XPathNodeIterator( );
// Public Instance Properties
  public virtual int Count{get; }
  public abstract XPathNavigator Current{get; }
```

```
  public abstract int CurrentPosition{get;}
// Public Instance Methods
  public abstract XPathNodeIterator Clone( );
  public abstract bool MoveNext( );
}
```

Returned By XPathNavigator.{Select( ), SelectAncestors( ), SelectChildren( ), SelectDescendants( )}

Passed To XPathNavigator.Evaluate( )

XPathNodeType
serializable

System.Xml.XPath (system.xml.dll) enum

This enumeration contains the types of nodes that can be listed with the XPathNavigator. NodeType property.

```
public enum XPathNodeType {
  Root = 0,
  Element = 1,
  Attribute = 2,
  Namespace = 3,
  Text = 4,
  SignificantWhitespace = 5,
  Whitespace = 6,
  ProcessingInstruction = 7,
  Comment = 8,
  All = 9
}
```

Hierarchy System.Object → System.ValueType → System.Enum(System.IComparable, System.IFormattable, System.IConvertible) → XPathNodeType

Returned By XPathNavigator.NodeType

Passed To XPathNavigator.{SelectAncestors( ), SelectChildren( ), SelectDescendants( )}

XPathResultType
serializable

System.Xml.XPath (system.xml.dll) enum

This enumeration contains the result types used by the XPathExpression.ReturnType property.

```
public enum XPathResultType {
  Number = 0,
  String = 1,
  Navigator = 1,
  Boolean = 2,
  NodeSet = 3,
  Any = 5,
  Error = 6
}
```

Hierarchy	System.Object → System.ValueType → System.Enum(System.IComparable, System.IFormattable, System.IConvertible) → XPathResultType
Returned By	XPathExpression.ReturnType, System.Xml.Xsl.IXsltContextFunction.{ArgTypes, ReturnType}, System.Xml.Xsl.IXsltContextVariable.VariableType
Passed To	System.Xml.Xsl.XsltContext.ResolveFunction( )

46

System.Xml.Xsl

The System.Xml.Xsl namespace provides support to Extensible Stylesheet Language Transformations (XSLT). XSLT is a W3C specification that describes how to transform one XML document into another with the use of stylesheet templates. For example, a common use of XSLT is to transform an XML document into standard HTML by transforming the specific elements of the input XML document into comparable HTML elements. XSLT templates use XPath expression syntax to specify which nodes of the input XML are transformed.

The XslTransform class constructs the transform object. It loads a stylesheet and applies its templates to an XML document to output the transformed data. The XsltArgumentList class creates objects for XSLT parameters that can be loaded into the stylesheet at runtime. XsltContext provides the XSLT processor with the current context node information used for XPath expression resolution. Figure 46-1 shows the types in this namespace.

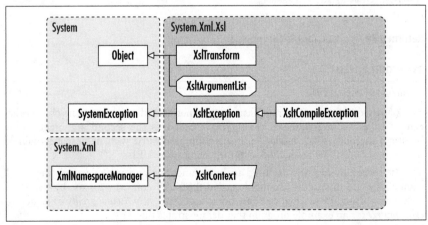

Figure 46-1. The System.Xml.Xsl namespace

IXsltContextFunction

System.Xml.Xsl (system.xml.dll)   interface

The Microsoft .NET XSLT engine, like many other XSLT engines, allows custom functions inside of an XSLT stylesheet document. By providing an "extension object" to an XsltArgumentList instance, an XSLT stylesheet can "call out" to methods in the CLR. See the XsltArgumentList description for an example.

```
public interface IXsltContextFunction {
// Public Instance Properties
   public XPathResultType[ ] ArgTypes{get; }
   public int Maxargs{get; }
   public int Minargs{get; }
   public XPathResultType ReturnType{get; }
// Public Instance Methods
   public object Invoke(XsltContext xsltContext, object[ ] args, System.Xml.XPath.XPathNavigator docContext);
}
```

Returned By   XsltContext.ResolveFunction( )

IXsltContextVariable

System.Xml.Xsl (system.xml.dll)   interface

As with IXsltContextFunction, this interface is used to help the XSLT engine resolve data objects bound into the XSLT engine's executing context while processing an XML document. See the XsltArgumentList method description for an example of how context functions and variables are used with an XSLT instance.

```
public interface IXsltContextVariable {
// Public Instance Properties
   public bool IsLocal{get; }
   public bool IsParam{get; }
   public XPathResultType VariableType{get; }
// Public Instance Methods
   public object Evaluate(XsltContext xsltContext);
}
```

Returned By   XsltContext.ResolveVariable( )

XsltArgumentList

System.Xml.Xsl (system.xml.dll)   sealed class

The XsltArgumentList class constructs lists of parameters and node fragment objects that can be called from stylesheets. This type is called as the second argument to the Transform( ) method of XslTransform. Parameters are associated with namespace-qualified names, and objects are associated with their namespace URIs.

The XsltArgumentList can also be used to bind functions and variables into the XSLT engine's execution space—commonly called the XSLT context—for use by the XSLT stylesheet during processing. See this book's website, *http://www.oreilly.com/catalog/csharpnut2/* for an example program that demonstrates this.

```
public sealed class XsltArgumentList {
// Public Constructors
  public XsltArgumentList();
// Public Instance Methods
  public void AddExtensionObject(string namespaceUri, object extension);
  public void AddParam(string name, string namespaceUri, object parameter);
  public void Clear();
  public object GetExtensionObject(string namespaceUri);
  public object GetParam(string name, string namespaceUri);
  public object RemoveExtensionObject(string namespaceUri);
  public object RemoveParam(string name, string namespaceUri);
}
```

Passed To   XslTransform.Transform()

XsltCompileException   serializable

System.Xml.Xsl (system.xml.dll)   class

The XslTransform.Load() method throws this exception when it encounters an error in an XSLT document.

```
public class XsltCompileException : XsltException {
// Public Constructors
  public XsltCompileException(Exception inner, string sourceUri, int lineNumber, int linePosition);
// Protected Constructors
  protected XsltCompileException(System.Runtime.Serialization.SerializationInfo info,
    System.Runtime.Serialization.StreamingContext context);
// Public Instance Properties
  public override string Message{get; }                                  // overrides XsltException
// Public Instance Methods
  public override void GetObjectData( System.Runtime.Serialization.SerializationInfo info,
    System.Runtime.Serialization.StreamingContext context);              // overrides XsltException
}
```

Hierarchy   System.Object → System.Exception(System.Runtime.Serialization.ISerializable) →
                   System.SystemException → XsltException → XsltCompileException

XsltContext

System.Xml.Xsl (system.xml.dll)   abstract class

This class provides a way to resolve namespaces and determine the current context for XPath variables and expressions. It inherits System.Xml.XmlNamespaceManager and its namespace functions. Additional methods defined for this class resolve variables (ResolveVariable()) as well as references to XPath functions invoked during execution (ResolveFunction()).

```
public abstract class XsltContext : System.Xml.XmlNamespaceManager {
// Public Constructors
  public XsltContext();
  public XsltContext(System.Xml.NameTable table);
```

```
// Public Instance Properties
  public abstract bool Whitespace{get; }
// Public Instance Methods
  public abstract int CompareDocument(string baseUri, string nextbaseUri);
  public abstract bool PreserveWhitespace(System.Xml.XPath.XPathNavigator node);
  public abstract IXsltContextFunction ResolveFunction(string prefix, string name,
    System.Xml.XPath.XPathResultType[ ] ArgTypes);
  public abstract IXsltContextVariable ResolveVariable(string prefix, string name);
}
```

Hierarchy	System.Object → System.Xml.XmlNamespaceManager(System.Collections.IEnumerable) → XsltContext
Passed To	IXsltContextFunction.Invoke( ), IXsltContextVariable.Evaluate( )

XsltException   serializable

System.Xml.Xsl (system.xml.dll)   class

This class returns XSLT exception errors thrown by XslTransform.Transform( ).

```
public class XsltException : SystemException {
// Public Constructors
  public XsltException(string message, Exception innerException);
// Protected Constructors
  protected XsltException(System.Runtime.Serialization.SerializationInfo info,
    System.Runtime.Serialization.StreamingContext context);
// Public Instance Properties
  public int LineNumber{get; }
  public int LinePosition{get; }
  public override string Message{get; }                                        // overrides Exception
  public string SourceUri{get; }
// Public Instance Methods
  public override void GetObjectData(System.Runtime.Serialization.SerializationInfo info,
    System.Runtime.Serialization.StreamingContext context);                    // overrides Exception
}
```

Hierarchy	System.Object → System.Exception(System.Runtime.Serialization.ISerializable) → System.SystemException → XsltException
Subclasses	XsltCompileException

XslTransform

System.Xml.Xsl (system.xml.dll)   sealed class

This object uses the Load( )method to input a stylesheet from either a URL, an XPathNavi-gator object, an object implementing IXPathNavigable, or an XmlReader object (remember, an XSL stylesheet is an XML document itself). The Transform( ) method takes a URL, an XPathNavigator object, or an object implementing IXPathNavigable as its first argument, which contains the XML document to transform. The second argument is an XsltArgumentList object; see XsltArgumentList for an example of using bound functions and/or variables.

The transformed result is output to an XmlReader object by default, or you can specify either a System.IO.Stream, XmlWriter, or XmlTextWriter object in the third argument for the output.

Note that in the .NET 1.1 release, any method or constructor of this class which does not take an XmlResolver instance has been marked obsolete, in favor of overloads that take an XmlResolver instance to resolve external entities (DTD references, entity references, and so on). Change any legacy (pre-1.1) code using those methods to take an XmlResolver instance in the method or constructor call, as these obsolete methods could disappear in a future version of the framework.

```
public sealed class XslTransform {
// Public Constructors
  public XslTransform( );
// Public Instance Properties
  public XmlResolver XmlResolver{set; }                                                    // obsolete
// Public Instance Methods
  public void Load(System.Xml.XPath.IXPathNavigable stylesheet);                           // obsolete
  public void Load(                                                                        // obsolete
    System.Xml.XPath.IXPathNavigable stylesheet, System.Xml.XmlResolver resolver);
  public void Load(System.Xml.XPath.IXPathNavigable stylesheet, System.Xml.XmlResolver resolver,
    System.Security.Policy.Evidence evidence);
  public void Load(string url);
  public void Load(string url, System.Xml.XmlResolver resolver);
  public void Load(System.Xml.XmlReader stylesheet);                                       // obsolete
  public void Load(System.Xml.XmlReader stylesheet, System.Xml.XmlResolver resolver);      // obsolete
  public void Load(System.Xml.XmlReader stylesheet, System.Xml.XmlResolver resolver,
    System.Security.Policy.Evidence evidence);
  public void Load(System.Xml.XPath.XPathNavigator stylesheet);                            // obsolete
  public void Load(System.Xml.XPath.XPathNavigator stylesheet, System.Xml.XmlResolver resolver);  // obsolete
  public void Load(System.Xml.XPath.XPathNavigator stylesheet, System.Xml.XmlResolver resolver,
    System.Security.Policy.Evidence evidence);
  public void Transform(System.Xml.XPath.IXPathNavigable input, XsltArgumentList args,
    System.IO.Stream output);                                                              // obsolete
  public void Transform(System.Xml.XPath.IXPathNavigable input, XsltArgumentList args,
    System.IO.Stream output, System.Xml.XmlResolver resolver);
  public void Transform( System.Xml.XPath.IXPathNavigable input, XsltArgumentList args,
    System.IO.TextWriter output);                                                          // obsolete
  public void Transform(System.Xml.XPath.IXPathNavigable input, XsltArgumentList args,
    System.IO.TextWriter output, System.Xml.XmlResolver resolver);
  public void Transform(System.Xml.XPath.IXPathNavigable input, XsltArgumentList args,
    System.Xml.XmlWriter output);                                                          // obsolete
  public void Transform(System.Xml.XPath.IXPathNavigable input, XsltArgumentList args,
    System.Xml.XmlWriter output, System.Xml.XmlResolver resolver);
  public void Transform(string inputfile, string outputfile);                              // obsolete
  public void Transform(string inputfile, string outputfile, System.Xml.XmlResolver resolver);
  public void Transform(System.Xml.XPath.XPathNavigator input, XsltArgumentList args,
    System.IO.Stream output);                                                              // obsolete
  public void Transform(System.Xml.XPath.XPathNavigator input, XsltArgumentList args,
    System.IO.Stream output, System.Xml.XmlResolver resolver);
  public void Transform(System.Xml.XPath.XPathNavigator input, XsltArgumentList args,
    System.IO.TextWriter output);                                                          // obsolete
```

```
public void Transform(System.Xml.XPath.XPathNavigator input, XsltArgumentList args,
    System.IO.TextWriter output, System.Xml.XmlResolver resolver);
public void Transform(System.Xml.XPath.XPathNavigator input, XsltArgumentList args,
    System.Xml.XmlWriter output);                                                            // obsolete
public void Transform(System.Xml.XPath.XPathNavigator input, XsltArgumentList args,
    System.Xml.XmlWriter output, System.Xml.XmlResolver resolver);
public XmlReader Transform(                                                                  // obsolete
    System.Xml.XPath.IXPathNavigable input, XsltArgumentList args);
public XmlReader Transform(System.Xml.XPath.IXPathNavigable input, XsltArgumentList args,
    System.Xml.XmlResolver resolver);
public XmlReader Transform(System.Xml.XPath.XPathNavigator input, XsltArgumentList args);    // obsolete
public XmlReader Transform(System.Xml.XPath.XPathNavigator input, XsltArgumentList args,
    System.Xml.XmlResolver resolver);
}
```

V

Appendixes

Part V, *Appendixes*, includes reference tables for regular expression syntax (*Regular Expressions*); format specifiers (*Format Specifiers*); C#-to-COM default data mapping (*Data Marshaling*); a glossary of C# keywords (*C# Keywords*); and an alphabetical list of .NET namespaces and the DLLs that expose them (*Namespaces and Assemblies*). You can also look up a method or field and find what type it is defined in the *Type, Method, Property, Event, and Field Index* .

A

Regular Expressions

The following tables summarize the regular-expression grammar and syntax supported by the regular-expression classes in System.Text.RegularExpression. Each of the modifiers and qualifiers in the tables can substantially change the behavior of the matching and searching patterns. For further information on regular expressions, we recommend the definitive *Mastering Regular Expressions* by Jeffrey E. F. Friedl (O'Reilly & Associates, 1997).

All the syntax described in the tables should match the Perl5 syntax, with specific exceptions noted.

Table A-1. Character escapes

Escape code sequence	Meaning	Hexadecimal equivalent
\a	Bell	\u0007
\b	Backspace	\u0008
\t	Tab	\u0009
\r	Carriage return	\u000A
\v	Vertical tab	\u000B
\f	Form feed	\u000C
\n	Newline	\u000D
\e	Escape	\u001B
\040	ASCII character as octal	
\x20	ASCII character as hex	
\cC	ASCII control character	
\u0020	Unicode character as hex	
\non-escape	A nonescape character	

Special case: within a regular expression, \b means word boundary, except in a [ ] set, in which \b means the backspace character.

Table A-2. Substitutions

Expression	Meaning
`$group-number`	Substitutes last substring matched by group-number
`${group-name}`	Substitutes last substring matched by `(?<group-name>)`

Substitutions are specified only within a replacement pattern.

Table A-3. Character sets

Expression	Meaning
`.`	Matches any character except \n
`[characterlist]`	Matches a single character in the list
`[^characterlist]`	Matches a single character not in the list
`[char0-char1]`	Matches a single character in a range
`\w`	Matches a word character; same as `[a-zA-Z_0-9]`
`\W`	Matches a nonword character
`\s`	Matches a space character; same as `[\n\r\t\f]`
`\S`	Matches a nonspace character
`\d`	Matches a decimal digit; same as `[0-9]`
`\D`	Matches a nondigit

Table A-4. Positioning assertions

Expression	Meaning
`^`	Beginning of line
`$`	End of line
`\A`	Beginning of string
`\Z`	End of line or string
`\z`	Exactly the end of string
`\G`	Where search started
`\b`	On a word boundary
`\B`	Not on a word boundary

Table A-5. Quantifiers

Quantifier	Meaning
`*`	0 or more matches
`+`	1 or more matches
`?`	0 or 1 matches
`{n}`	Exactly *n* matches
`{n,}`	At least *n* matches

Table A-5. Quantifiers (continued)

Quantifier	Meaning
{*n,m*}	At least *n*, but no more than *m* matches
*?	Lazy *, finds first match that has minimum repeats
+?	Lazy +, minimum repeats, but at least 1
??	Lazy ?, zero or minimum repeats
{*n*}?	Lazy {*n*}, exactly *n* matches
{*n*,}?	Lazy {*n*}, minimum repeats, but at least *n*
{*n,m*}?	Lazy {*n,m*}, minimum repeats, but at least *n*, and no more than *m*

Table A-6. Grouping constructs

Syntax	Meaning
( )	Capture matched substring
(?<*name*>)	Capture matched substring into group *name*[*]
(?<*number*>)	Capture matched substring into group *number*[*]
(?<*name1-name2*>)	Undefine *name2*, and store interval and current group into *name1*; if *name2* is undefined, matching backtracks; *name1* is *optional*[*]
(?:)	Noncapturing group
(?imnsx-imnsx:)	Apply or disable matching options
(?=)	Continue matching only if subexpression matches on right
(?!)	Continue matching only if subexpression doesn't match on right
(?<=)	Continue matching only if subexpression matches on left
(?<!)	Continue matching only if subexpression doesn't match on left
(?>)	Subexpression is matched once, but isn't backtracked

[*] Single quotes may be used instead of angle brackets—for example (?'name').

The named capturing group syntax follows a suggestion made by Friedl in *Mastering Regular Expressions*. All other grouping constructs use the Perl5 syntax.

Table A-7. Back references

Parameter syntax	Meaning
\count	Back reference count occurrences
\k<*name*>	Named back reference

Table A-8. Alternation

Expression syntax	Meaning
|	Logical OR
(?(*expression*)yes|no)	Matches yes if expression matches, else no; the no is optional
(?(*name*)yes|no)	Matches yes if named string has a match, else no; the no is optional

Table A-9. Miscellaneous Constructs

Expression syntax	Meaning
(?imnsx-imnsx)	Set or disable options in midpattern
(?#)	Inline comment
# [to end of line]	X-mode comment

Table A-10. Regular expression options

Option	Meaning
i	Case-insensitive match
m	Multiline mode; changes ^ and $ so they match beginning and ending of any line
n	Capture explicitly named or numbered groups
c	Compile to MSIL
s	Single-line mode; changes meaning of "." so it matches every character
x	Eliminates unescaped whitespace from the pattern
r	Search from right to left; can't be specified in midstream

B

Format Specifiers

Table B-1 lists the numeric format specifiers supported by the Format method on the predefined numeric types.

Table B-1. Numeric Format Specifiers

Specifier	String result	Datatype
C[*n*]	$XX,XX.XX ($XX,XXX.XX)	Currency
D[*n*]	[-]XXXXXXX	Decimal
E[*n*] or e[*n*]	[-]X.XXXXXXE+xxx [-]X.XXXXXXe+xxx [-]X.XXXXXXE-xxx [-]X.XXXXXXe-xxx	Exponent
F[*n*]	[-]XXXXXXX.XX	Fixed point
G[*n*]	General or scientific	General
N[*n*]	[-]XX,XXX.XX	Number
X[*n*] or x[*n*]	Hex representation	Hex

This example uses numeric format specifiers without precision specifiers:

```
using System;
class TestDefaultFormats {
  static void Main( ) {
    int i = 654321;
    Console.WriteLine("{0:C}", i); // $654,321.00
    Console.WriteLine("{0:D}", i); // 654321
    Console.WriteLine("{0:E}", i); // 6.543210E+005
    Console.WriteLine("{0:F}", i); // 654321.00
    Console.WriteLine("{0:G}", i); // 654321
    Console.WriteLine("{0:N}", i); // 654,321.00
```

```
      Console.WriteLine("{0:X}", i); // 9FBF1
      Console.WriteLine("{0:x}", i); // 9fbf1
  }
}
```

This example uses numeric format specifiers with precision specifiers on a variety of int values:

```
using System;
class TestIntegerFormats {
  static void Main( ) {
    int i = 123;
    Console.WriteLine("{0:C6}", i); // $123.000000
    Console.WriteLine("{0:D6}", i); // 000123
    Console.WriteLine("{0:E6}", i); // 1.230000E+002
    Console.WriteLine("{0:G6}", i); // 123
    Console.WriteLine("{0:N6}", i); // 123.000000
    Console.WriteLine("{0:X6}", i); // 00007B
    i = -123;
    Console.WriteLine("{0:C6}", i); // ($123.000000)
    Console.WriteLine("{0:D6}", i); // -000123
    Console.WriteLine("{0:E6}", i); // -1.230000E+002
    Console.WriteLine("{0:G6}", i); // -123
    Console.WriteLine("{0:N6}", i); // -123.000000
    Console.WriteLine("{0:X6}", i); // FFFF85
    i = 0;
    Console.WriteLine("{0:C6}", i); // $0.000000
    Console.WriteLine("{0:D6}", i); // 000000
    Console.WriteLine("{0:E6}", i); // 0.000000E+000
    Console.WriteLine("{0:G6}", i); // 0
    Console.WriteLine("{0:N6}", i); // 0.000000
    Console.WriteLine("{0:X6}", i); // 000000
  }
}
```

This example uses numeric format specifiers with precision specifiers on a variety of double values:

```
using System;
class TestDoubleFormats {
  static void Main( ) {
    double d = 1.23;
    Console.WriteLine("{0:C6}", d); // $1.230000
    Console.WriteLine("{0:E6}", d); // 1.230000E+000
    Console.WriteLine("{0:G6}", d); // 1.23
    Console.WriteLine("{0:N6}", d); // 1.230000
    d = -1.23;
    Console.WriteLine("{0:C6}", d); // ($1.230000)
    Console.WriteLine("{0:E6}", d); // -1.230000E+000
    Console.WriteLine("{0:G6}", d); // -1.23
    Console.WriteLine("{0:N6}", d); // -1.230000
    d = 0;
    Console.WriteLine("{0:C6}", d); // $0.000000
    Console.WriteLine("{0:E6}", d); // 0.000000E+000
    Console.WriteLine("{0:G6}", d); // 0
```

```
        Console.WriteLine("{0:N6}", d); // 0.000000
    }
}
```

Picture Format Specifiers

Table B-2 lists the valid picture format specifiers supported by the Format method on the predefined numeric types (see the documentation for System.IFormattable in the .NET SDK).

Table B-2. Picture Format Specifiers

Specifier	String result
0	Zero placeholder
#	Digit placeholder
.	Decimal point
,	Group separator or multiplier
%	Percent notation
E+0, E-0 e+0, e-0	Exponent notation
\	Literal character quote
'xx' "xx"	Literal string quote
;	Section separator

This example uses picture-format specifiers on some int values:

```
using System;
class TestIntegerCustomFormats {
    static void Main( ) {
        int i = 123;
        Console.WriteLine("{0:#0}", i);                 // 123
        Console.WriteLine("{0:#0;(#0)}", i);            // 123
        Console.WriteLine("{0:#0;(#0);<zero>}", i);     // 123
        Console.WriteLine("{0:#%}", i);                 // 12300%
        i = -123;
        Console.WriteLine("{0:#0}", i);                 // -123
        Console.WriteLine("{0:#0;(#0)}", i);            // (123)
        Console.WriteLine("{0:#0;(#0);<zero>}", i);     // (123)
        Console.WriteLine("{0:#%}", i);                 // -12300%
        i = 0;
        Console.WriteLine("{0:#0}", i);                 // 0
        Console.WriteLine("{0:#0;(#0)}", i);            // 0
        Console.WriteLine("{0:#0;(#0);<zero>}", i);     // <zero>
        Console.WriteLine("{0:#%}", i);                 // %
    }
}
```

The following example uses these picture format specifiers on a variety of double values:

```
using System;
class TestDoubleCustomFormats {
```

```
static void Main( ) {
  double d = 1.23;
  Console.WriteLine("{0:#.000E+00}", d);      // 1.230E+00
  Console.WriteLine(
    "{0:#.000E+00;(#.000E+00)}", d);          // 1.230E+00
  Console.WriteLine(
    "{0:#.000E+00;(#.000E+00);<zero>}", d);   // 1.230E+00
  Console.WriteLine("{0:#%}", d);             // 123%
  d = -1.23;
  Console.WriteLine("{0:#.000E+00}", d);      // -1.230E+00
  Console.WriteLine(
    "{0:#.000E+00;(#.000E+00)}", d);          // (1.230E+00)
  Console.WriteLine(
    "{0:#.000E+00;(#.000E+00);<zero>}", d);   // (1.230E+00)
  Console.WriteLine("{0:#%}", d);             // -123%
  d = 0;
  Console.WriteLine("{0:#.000E+00}", d);      // 0.000E-01
  Console.WriteLine(
    "{0:#.000E+00;(#.000E+00)}", d);          // 0.000E-01
  Console.WriteLine(
    "{0:#.000E+00;(#.000E+00);<zero>}", d);   // <zero>
  Console.WriteLine("{0:#%}", d);             // %
  }
}
```

DateTime Format Specifiers

Table B-3 lists the valid format specifiers supported by the Format method on the
DateTime type (see System.IFormattable).

Table B-3. DateTime Format Specifiers

Specifier	String result
d	MM/dd/yyyy
D	dddd, MMMM dd, yyyy
f	dddd, MMMM dd, yyyy HH:mm
F	dddd, MMMM dd, yyyy HH:mm:ss
g	MM/dd/yyyy HH:mm
G	MM/dd/yyyy HH:mm:ss
m, M	MMMM dd
r, R	Ddd, dd MMM yyyy HH':'mm':'ss 'GMT'
s	yyyy-MM-dd HH:mm:ss
S	yyyy-MM-dd HH:mm:ss GMT
t	HH:mm
T	HH:mm:ss
u	yyyy-MM-dd HH:mm:ss
U	dddd, MMMM dd, yyyy HH:mm:ss
y, Y	MMMM, yyyy

Here's an example that uses these custom format specifiers on a DateTime value:

```
using System;
class TestDateTimeFormats {
  static void Main() {
    DateTime dt = new DateTime(2000, 10, 11, 15, 32, 14);
    // Prints "2000-10-11T15:32:14"
    Console.WriteLine(dt.ToString());
    // Prints "Wednesday, October 11, 2000"
    Console.WriteLine("{0}", dt);
    // Prints "10/11/2000"
    Console.WriteLine("{0:d}", dt);
    // Prints "Wednesday, October 11, 2000"
    Console.WriteLine("{0:D}", dt);
    // Prints "Wednesday, October 11, 2000 3:32 PM"
    Console.WriteLine("{0:f}", dt);
    // Prints "Wednesday, October 11, 2000 3:32:14 PM"
    Console.WriteLine("{0:F}", dt);
    // Prints "10/11/2000 3:32 PM"
    Console.WriteLine("{0:g}", dt);
    // Prints "10/11/2000 3:32:14 PM"
    Console.WriteLine("{0:G}", dt);
    // Prints "October 11"
    Console.WriteLine("{0:m}", dt);
    // Prints "October 11"
    Console.WriteLine("{0:M}", dt);
    // Prints "Wed, 11 Oct 2000 22:32:14 GMT"
    Console.WriteLine("{0:r}", dt);
    // Prints "Wed, 11 Oct 2000 22:32:14 GMT"
    Console.WriteLine("{0:R}", dt);
    // Prints "3:32 PM"
    Console.WriteLine("{0:t}", dt);
    // Prints "3:32:14 PM"
    Console.WriteLine("{0:T}", dt);
    // Prints "2000-10-11 22:32:14Z"
    Console.WriteLine("{0:u}", dt);
    // Prints "Wednesday, October 11, 2000 10:32:14 PM"
    Console.WriteLine("{0:U}", dt);
    // Prints "October, 2000"
    Console.WriteLine("{0:y}", dt);
    // Prints "October, 2000"
    Console.WriteLine("{0:Y}", dt);
    // Prints "Wednesday the 11 day of October in the year 2000"
    Console.WriteLine(
      "{0:dddd 'the' d 'day of' MMMM 'in the year' yyyy}", dt);
  }
}
```

C

Data Marshaling

When calling between the runtime environment and existing COM interfaces, the CLR performs automatic data marshaling for CLR types into compatible COM types. Table C-1 describes the C# to COM default data type mapping.

Table C-1. C# type to COM type mapping

C# type	COM type
bool	VARIANT_BOOL
char	unsigned short
sbyte	Char
byte	Unsigned char
short	Short
ushort	Unsigned short
int	Int
uint	Unsigned int
long	Hyper
ulong	Unsigned hyper
float	Single
double	Double
decimal	DECIMAL
object	VARIANT
string	BSTR
System.DateTime	DATE[a]
System.Guid	GUID
System.Currency	CURRENCY
1-dimensional arrays	SAFEARRAY
Value types	Equivalently named struct
enum	Equivalently named enum

Table C-1. C# type to COM type mapping (continued)

C# type	COM type
interface	Equivalently named interface
class	Equivalently named CoClass

a COM dates are less precise, causing comparison problems.

Table C-2 shows the mapping of the C# modifiers to their equivalent COM interface attributes.

Table C-2. C# modifier/COM attribute mapping

C# modifier	COM attribute
<no modifier>	[in]
out	[out]
ref	[in, out]
<return value>	[out, retval]

D

C# Keywords

abstract
: A class modifier that specifies that the class must be derived from to be instantiated.

operator
: A binary operator type that casts the left operand to the type specified by the right operand and that returns null rather than throwing an exception if the cast fails.

base
: A variable with the same meaning as this, except that it accesses a base-class implementation of a member.

bool
: A logical datatype that can be true or false.

break
: A jump statement that exits a loop or switch statement block.

byte
: A one-byte, unsigned integral data type.

case
: A selection statement that defines a particular choice in a switch statement.

catch
: The part of a try statement that catches exceptions of a specific type defined in the catch clause.

char
: A two-byte, Unicode character data type.

checked
: A statement or operator that enforces arithmetic bounds checking on an expression or statement block.

class
> An extendable reference type that combines data and functionality into one unit.

const
> A modifier for a local variable or field declaration that indicates that the value is a constant. A const is evaluated at compile time and can be only a predefined type.

continue
> A jump statement that skips the remaining statements in a statement block and continues to the next iteration in a loop.

decimal
> A 16-byte precise decimal datatype.

default
> A marker in a switch statement specifying the action to take when no case statements match the switch expression.

delegate
> A type for defining a method signature so delegate instances can hold and invoke a method or list of methods that match its signature.

do
> A loop statement to iterate a statement block until an expression at the end of the loop evaluates to false.

double
> An 8-byte, floating-point data type.

else
> A conditional statement that defines the action to take when a preceding if expression evaluates to false.

enum
> A value type that defines a group of named numeric constants.

event
> A member modifier for a delegate field or property that indicates that only the += and -= methods of the delegate can be accessed.

explicit
> An operator that defines an explicit conversion.

extern
> A method modifier that indicates that the method is implemented with unmanaged code.

false
> A Boolean literal.

finally
> The part of a try statement to execute whenever control leaves the scope of the try block.

fixed
> A statement to pin down a reference type so the garbage collector won't move it during pointer arithmetic operations.

float
> A four-byte floating-point data type.

for
> A loop statement that combines an initialization statement, continuation condition, and iterative statement into one statement.

foreach
> A loop statement that iterates over collections that implement IEnumerable.

get
> The name of the accessor that returns the value of a property.

goto
> A jump statement that jumps to a label within the same method and same scope as the jump point.

if
> A conditional statement that executes its statement block if its expression evaluates to true.

implicit
> An operator that defines an implicit conversion.

in
> The operator between a type and an IEnumerable in a foreach statement.

int
> A four-byte, signed integral data type.

interface
> A contract that specifies the members that a class or struct may implement to receive generic services for that type.

internal
> An access modifier that indicates that a type or type member is accessible only to other types in the same assembly.

is
> A relational operator that evaluates to true if the left operand's type matches, is derived from, or implements the type specified by the right operand.

lock
> A statement that acquires a lock on a reference-type object to help multiple threads cooperate.

long
> An eight-byte, signed integral data type.

namespace
> A keyword that maps a set of types to a common name.

new
> An operator that calls a constructor on a type, allocating a new object on the heap if the type is a reference type, or initializing the object if the type is a value type. The keyword is overloaded to hide an inherited member.

null
> A reference-type literal that indicates that no object is referenced.

object
> The type all other types derive from.

operator
> A method modifier that overloads operators.

out
> A parameter modifier that specifies that the parameter is passed by reference and must be assigned by the method being called.

override
> A method modifier that indicates that a method of a class overrides a virtual method of a class or interface.

params
> A parameter modifier that specifies that the last parameter of a method may accept multiple parameters of the same type.

private
> An access modifier that indicates that only the containing type can access the member.

protected
> An access modifier that indicates that only the containing type or derived types can access the member.

public
> An access modifier that indicates that a type or type member is accessible to all other types.

readonly
> A field modifier specifying that a field can be assigned only once, either in its declaration or in its containing type's constructor.

ref
> A parameter modifier that specifies that the parameter is passed by reference and is assigned before being passed to the method.

return
> A jump statement that exits a method, specifying a return value when the method is nonvoid.

sbyte
> A one-byte, signed integral data type.

sealed
> A class modifier that indicates a class cannot be derived from.

set
> The name of the accessor that sets the value of a property.

short
> A two-byte, signed integral data type.

sizeof
> An operator that returns the size in bytes of a struct.

stackalloc
> An operator that returns a pointer to a specified number of value types allocated on the stack.

static
> A type member modifier that indicates that the member applies to the type rather than to an instance of the type.

string
> A predefined reference type that represents an immutable sequence of Unicode characters.

struct
> A value type that combines data and functionality in one unit.

switch
> A selection statement that allows a selection of choices to be made based on the value of a predefined type.

this
> A variable that references the current instance of a class or struct.

throw
> A jump statement that throws an exception when an abnormal condition has occurred.

true
> A boolean literal.

try
> A statement that provides a way to handle an exception or a premature exit in a statement block.

typeof
> An operator that returns the type of an object as a System.Type object.

uint
> A four-byte, unsigned integral data type.

ulong
> An eight-byte, unsigned integral data type.

unchecked
> A statement or operator that prevents arithmetic bounds checking on an expression.

unsafe
> A method modifier or statement that permits pointer arithmetic to be performed within a particular block.

ushort
> A two-byte, unsigned integral data type.

using
> A directive that specifies that types in a particular namespace can be referred to without requiring their fully qualified type names. The keyword is overloaded as a statement that allows an object that implements IDisposable to be disposed of at the end of the statement's scope.

value
> The name of the implicit variable set by the set accessor of a property.

virtual

A class method modifier that indicates that a method can be overridden by a derived class.

void

A keyword used in place of a type for methods that don't have a return value.

volatile

A field modifier indicating that a field's value may be modified in a multi-threaded scenario; neither the compiler nor runtime should perform optimizations with that field.

while

A loop statement to iterate a statement block while an expression at the start of each iteration evaluates to false.

E

Namespaces and Assemblies

This appendix allows you to look up a namespace and determine which assemblies export that namespace. This information is helpful when constructing the appropriate /reference:<file list> command-line option for the C# compiler. However, commonly used assemblies are referenced by default.

For a complete list of default assemblies, see the global C# response file, *csc.rsp*, in *%SystemRoot%\Microsoft.NET\Framework\VERSION*, where *VERSION* is the version number of the framework (the first release of .NET is v1.0.3705, and 1.1 is v1.1.4322). You can modify *csc.rsp* to affect all compilations run on your machine, or you can create a local *csc.rsp* in your current directory. The local response file is processed after the global one. You can use the /noconfig switch with *csc.exe* to disable the local and global *csc.rsp* files entirely.

Namespace	DLLs
Accessibility	*Accessibility.dll*
EnvDTE	*envdte.dll*
IEHost.Execute	*IEExecRemote.dll*
Microsoft.CLRAdmin	*mscorcfg.dll*
Microsoft.CSharp	*cscompmgd.dll*
	System.dll
Microsoft.IE	*IEHost.dll*
	IIEHost.dll
Microsoft.JScript	*Microsoft.JScript.dll*
Microsoft.JScript.Vsa	*Microsoft.JScript.dll*
Microsoft.Office.Core	*office.dll*
Microsoft.VisualBasic	*Microsoft.VisualBasic.dll*
	System.dll
Microsoft.VisualBasic.Compatibility.VB6	*Microsoft.VisualBasic.Compatibility.Data.dll*
	Microsoft.VisualBasic.Compatibility.dll

Namespace	DLLs
Microsoft.VisualBasic.CompilerServices	Microsoft.VisualBasic.dll
Microsoft.VisualBasic.Vsa	Microsoft.VisualBasic.Vsa.dll
Microsoft.VisualC	Microsoft.VisualC.Dll
Microsoft.Vsa	Microsoft.JScript.dll
	Microsoft.Vsa.dll
Microsoft.Vsa.Vb.CodeDOM	Microsoft.Vsa.Vb.CodeDOMProcessor.dll
Microsoft.Win32	mscorlib.dll
	System.dll
Microsoft_VsaVb	Microsoft_VsaVb.dll
RegCode	RegCode.dll
System	mscorlib.dll
	System.dll
System.CodeDom	System.dll
System.CodeDom.Compiler	System.dll
System.Collections	mscorlib.dll
System.Collections.Specialized	System.dll
System.ComponentModel	System.dll
System.ComponentModel.Design	System.Design.dll
	System.dll
System.ComponentModel.Design.Serialization	System.Design.dll
	System.dll
System.Configuration	System.dll
System.Configuration.Assemblies	mscorlib.dll
System.Configuration.Install	System.Configuration.Install.dll
System.Data	System.Data.dll
System.Data.Common	System.Data.dll
System.Data.Odbc	System.Data.dll
System.Data.OleDb	System.Data.dll
System.Data.OracleClient	System.Data.OracleClient.dll
System.Data.SqlClient	System.Data.dll
System.Data.SqlTypes	System.Data.dll
System.Diagnostics	mscorlib.dll
	System.Configuration.Install.dll
System.Diagnostics.Design	System.Design.dll
System.Diagnostics.SymbolStore	ISymWrapper.dll
	mscorlib.dll
System.DirectoryServices	System.DirectoryServices.dll
System.Drawing	System.Drawing.dll
System.Drawing.Design	System.Drawing.Design.dll
	System.Drawing.dll
System.Drawing.Drawing2D	System.Drawing.dll
System.Drawing.Imaging	System.Drawing.dll
System.Drawing.Printing	System.Drawing.dll

Namespace	DLLs
System.Drawing.Text	*System.Drawing.dll*
System.EnterpriseServices	*System.EnterpriseServices.dll*
System.EnterpriseServices.CompensatingResourceManager	*System.EnterpriseServices.dll*
System.EnterpriseServices.Internal	*System.EnterpriseServices.dll*
System.Globalization	*mscorlib.dll*
System.IO	*mscorlib.dll* *System.dll*
System.IO.IsolatedStorage	*mscorlib.dll*
System.Management	*System.Management.dll*
System.Management.Instrumentation	*System.Management.dll*
System.Messaging	*System.Messaging.dll*
System.Messaging.Design	*System.Design.dll* *System.Messaging.dll*
System.Net	*System.dll*
System.Net.Sockets	*System.dll*
System.Reflection	*mscorlib.dll*
System.Reflection.Emit	*mscorlib.dll*
System.Resources	*mscorlib.dll* *System.Windows.Forms.dll*
System.Runtime.CompilerServices	*mscorlib.dll*
System.Runtime.InteropServices	*mscorlib.dll*
System.Runtime.InteropServices.CustomMarshalers	*CustomMarshalers.dll*
System.Runtime.InteropServices.Expando	*mscorlib.dll*
System.Runtime.Remoting	*mscorlib.dll*
System.Runtime.Remoting.Activation	*mscorlib.dll*
System.Runtime.Remoting.Channels	*mscorlib.dll* *System.Runtime.Remoting.dll*
System.Runtime.Remoting.Channels.Http	*System.Runtime.Remoting.dll*
System.Runtime.Remoting.Channels.Tcp	*System.Runtime.Remoting.dll*
System.Runtime.Remoting.Contexts	*mscorlib.dll*
System.Runtime.Remoting.Lifetime	*mscorlib.dll*
System.Runtime.Remoting.Messaging	*mscorlib.dll*
System.Runtime.Remoting.Metadata	*mscorlib.dll*
System.Runtime.Remoting.Metadata.W3cXsd2001	*mscorlib.dll*
System.Runtime.Remoting.MetadataServices	*System.Runtime.Remoting.dll*
System.Runtime.Remoting.Proxies	*mscorlib.dll*
System.Runtime.Remoting.Services	*mscorlib.dll* *System.Runtime.Remoting.dll*
System.Runtime.Serialization	*mscorlib.dll*
System.Runtime.Serialization.Formatters	*mscorlib.dll*

Namespace	DLLs
System.Runtime.Serialization. Formatters. Binary	*mscorlib.dll*
System.Runtime.Serialization. Formatters. Soap	*System.Runtime.Serialization.Formatters.Soap.dll*
System.Security	*mscorlib.dll*
System.Security.Cryptography	*mscorlib.dll*
System.Security.Cryptography. X509Certificates	*mscorlib.dll* *System.dll*
System.Security.Cryptography.Xml	*System.Security.dll*
System.Security.Permissions	*mscorlib.dll* *System.dll*
System.Security.Policy	*mscorlib.dll*
System.Security.Principal	*mscorlib.dll*
System.ServiceProcess	*System.ServiceProcess.dll*
System.ServiceProcess.Design	*System.Design.dll* *System.ServiceProcess.dll*
System.Text	*mscorlib.dll*
System.Text.RegularExpressions	*System.dll*
System.Threading	*mscorlib.dll* *System.dll*
System.Timers	*System.dll*
System.Web	*System.Web.dll*
System.Web.Caching	*System.Web.dll*
System.Web.Configuration	*System.Web.dll*
System.Web.Handlers	*System.Web.dll*
System.Web.Hosting	*System.Web.dll*
System.Web.Mobile	*System.Web.Mobile.dll*
System.Web.Mail	*System.Web.dll*
System.Web.RegularExpressions	*System.Web.RegularExpressions.dll*
System.Web.Security	*System.Web.dll*
System.Web.Services	*System.Web.Services.dll*
System.Web.Services.Configuration	*System.Web.Services.dll*
System.Web.Services.Description	*System.Web.Services.dll*
System.Web.Services.Discovery	*System.Web.Services.dll*
System.Web.Services.Protocols	*System.Web.Services.dll*
System.Web.SessionState	*System.Web.dll*
System.Web.UI	*System.Web.dll*
System.Web.UI.Design	*System.Design.dll*
System.Web.UI.Design.MobileControls	*System.Web.Mobile.dll*
System.Web.UI.Design.WebControls	*System.Design.dll*
System.Web.UI.HtmlControls	*System.Web.dll*
System.Web.UI.MobileControls	*System.Web.Mobile.dll*
System.Web.UI.WebControls	*System.Web.dll*

Namespace	DLLs
System.Web.Util	*System.Web.dll*
System.Windows.Forms	*System.Windows.Forms.dll*
System.Windows.Forms.ComponentModel. Com2Interop	*System.Windows.Forms.dll*
System.Windows.Forms.Design	*System.Design.dll* *System.Windows.Forms.dll*
System.Windows.Forms. PropertyGridInternal	*System.Windows.Forms.dll*
System.Xml	*System.Data.dll* *System.XML.dll*
System.Xml.Schema	*System.XML.dll*
System.Xml.Serialization	*System.XML.dll*
System.Xml.XPath	*System.XML.dll*
System.Xml.Xsl	*System.XML.dll*

Type, Method, Property, Event, and Field Index

Use this index to look up a type or member and see where it is defined. For a type (a class or interface), you can find the enclosing namespace. If you know the name of a member (a method, property, event, or field), you can find all the types that define it.

A

AbbreviatedDayNames: DateTimeFormatInfo

AbbreviatedMonthNames: DateTimeFormat-Info

Abort( ): HttpWebRequest, Thread, WebRequest

Aborted: ThreadState

AbortRequested: ThreadState

AboveNormal: ProcessPriorityClass, ThreadPriority, ThreadPriorityLevel

Abs( ): Math

AbsolutePath: Uri

AbsoluteUri: Uri

Abstract: MethodAttributes, TypeAttributes

Accept: HttpWebRequest, NetworkAccess, WebPermissionAttribute

Accept( ): Socket

AcceptConnection: SocketOptionName

Accepted: HttpStatusCode

AcceptList: SocketPermission, WebPermission

AcceptPattern: WebPermissionAttribute

AcceptSocket( ): TcpListener

AcceptTcpClient( ): TcpListener

Access: SocketPermissionAttribute

Accessibility: UserPreferenceCategoryf

Acos( ): Math

AcquireReaderLock( ): ReaderWriterLock

AcquireWriterLock( ): ReaderWriterLock

Action: XmlNodeChangedEventArgs

Activator: System

ActualValue: ArgumentOutOfRangeException

Adapter( ): ArrayList

Add: OpCodes

Add( ): ArrayList, CookieCollection, CookieContainer, CounterCreationDataCollection, CredentialCache, DateTime, Decimal, EventLogPermissionEntryCollection, Hashtable, HybridDictionary, IDictionary, IList, ListDictionary, NameTable, NameValueCollection, PerformanceCounterPermissionEntryCollection, ProcessThreadCollection, SortedList, StringCollection, StringDictionary, TimeSpan, TraceListenerCollection, WebHeaderCollection, XmlNameTable

Add_Ovf: OpCodes

Add_Ovf_Un: OpCodes

AddArgument( ): SignatureHelper

AddDays( ): Calendar, DateTime

AddDeclarativeSecurity( ): ConstructorBuilder, MethodBuilder, TypeBuilder

AddEventHandler( ): EventInfo

AddExtensionObject( ): XsltArgumentList

AddHours( ): Calendar, DateTime

AddInterfaceImplementation( ): TypeBuilder

AddMembership: SocketOptionName

AddMilliseconds( ): Calendar, DateTime

AddMinutes( ): Calendar, DateTime

AddMonths( ): Calendar, DateTime, Gregorian-Calendar, HebrewCalendar, HijriCalendar, JapaneseCalendar, JulianCalendar, KoreanCal-endar, TaiwanCalendar, ThaiBuddhistCalendar

AddNamespace( ): XmlNamespaceManager

AddOtherMethod( ): EventBuilder, Property-Builder

AddParam( ): XsltArgumentList

AddPermission( ): SocketPermission, WebPer-mission

AddRange( ): ArrayList, CounterCreationDataC-ollection, EventLogPermissionEntryCollection, HttpWebRequest, PerformanceCounterPer-missionEntryCollection, StringCollection, TraceListenerCollection

AddRef( ): Marshal

AddResourceFile( ): AssemblyBuilder

Address: HttpWebRequest, IPAddress, IPEnd-Point, ServicePoint, WebProxy

AddressFamily: EndPoint, IPAddress, IPEnd-Point, Socket, System.Net.Sockets

AddressList: IPHostEntry

AddrOfPinnedObject( ): GCHandle

AddSeconds( ): Calendar, DateTime

AddSentinel( ): SignatureHelper

AddSort( ): XPathExpression

AddSourceMembership: SocketOptionName

AddSurrogate( ): SurrogateSelector

AddTicks( ): DateTime

AddValue( ): SerializationInfo

AddWeeks( ): Calendar, GregorianCalendar

AddWithoutValidate( ): WebHeaderCollection

AddYears( ): Calendar, DateTime, GregorianCal-endar, HebrewCalendar, HijriCalendar, Japa-neseCalendar, JulianCalendar, KoreanCal-endar, TaiwanCalendar, ThaiBuddhistCalendar

ADEra: GregorianCalendar

AdjustToUniversal: DateTimeStyles

Administer: PerformanceCounterPermissionAc-cess

After: XmlNodeOrder

AlgorithmId: AssemblyAlgorithmIdAttribute

Aliases: IPHostEntry

All: AttributeTargets, MemberTypes, Streaming-ContextStates, TransportType, Watcher-ChangeTypes, WhitespaceHandling, XPath-NamespaceScope, XPathNodeType

AllCultures: CultureTypes

AllKeys: NameValueCollection

Alloc( ): GCHandle

AllocateDataSlot( ): Thread

AllocateNamedDataSlot( ): Thread

AllocCoTaskMem( ): Marshal

AllocHGlobal( ): Marshal

AllowAutoRedirect: HttpWebRequest

AllowCurrencySymbol: NumberStyles

AllowDecimalPoint: NumberStyles

AllowExponent: NumberStyles

AllowHexSpecifier: NumberStyles

AllowInnerWhite: DateTimeStyles

AllowLeadingSign: NumberStyles

AllowLeadingWhite: DateTimeStyles, Number-Styles

AllowMultiple: AttributeUsageAttribute

AllowParentheses: NumberStyles

AllowThousands: NumberStyles

AllowTrailingSign: NumberStyles

AllowTrailingWhite: DateTimeStyles, Number-Styles

AllowWhiteSpaces: DateTimeStyles

AllowWriteStreamBuffering: HttpWebRequest

AllPorts: SocketPermission

AltDirectorySeparatorChar: Path

Ambiguous: HttpStatusCode

AmbiguousMatchException: System.Reflection

AMDesignator: DateTimeFormatInfo

And: OpCodes

And( ): BitArray

AssemblyTitleAttribute: System.Reflection

AssemblyTrademarkAttribute: System.Reflection

AssemblyVersionAttribute: System.Reflection

Assert( ): Debug, Trace

AssertUiEnabled: DefaultTraceListener

AsyncCallback: System

AsyncResult: Overlapped

AsyncState: IAsyncResult

AsyncWaitHandle: IAsyncResult

Atan( ): Math

Atan2( ): Math

Atm: AddressFamily, ProtocolFamily

Attribute: System, WriteState, XmlNodeType, XPathNodeType

AttributeCount: XmlNodeReader, XmlReader, XmlTextReader, XmlValidatingReader

Attributes: ConstructorBuilder, EventInfo, FieldBuilder, FieldInfo, FileSystemInfo, MethodBase, MethodBuilder, NotifyFilters, ParameterBuilder, ParameterInfo, PropertyBuilder, PropertyInfo, Type, XmlElement, XmlNode

AttributeTargets: System

AttributeUsageAttribute: System

AttrsImpl: ParameterInfo

Audit: EventLogPermissionAccess

Authenticate( ): AuthenticationManager, IAuthenticationModule

AuthenticationManager: System.Net

AuthenticationType: IAuthenticationModule

Authority: Uri, UriPartial

Authorization: System.Net

Auto: CharSet, LayoutKind, ValidationType

AutoClass: TypeAttributes

AutoDispatch: ClassInterfaceType

AutoDual: ClassInterfaceType

AutoFlush: Debug, StreamWriter, Trace

AutoLayout: TypeAttributes

AutoReset: Timer

AutoResetEvent: System.Threading

Available: Socket

AverageBase: PerformanceCounterType

AverageCount64: PerformanceCounterType

AverageTimer32: PerformanceCounterType

B

Background: ThreadState

BadGateway: HttpStatusCode

BadImageFormatException: System

BadRequest: HttpStatusCode

Banyan: AddressFamily, ProtocolFamily

BaseAdd( ): NameObjectCollectionBase

BaseAddress: ProcessModule, WebClient

BaseClear( ): NameObjectCollectionBase

BaseDirectory: AppDomain

BaseGet( ): NameObjectCollectionBase

BaseGetAllKeys( ): NameObjectCollectionBase

BaseGetAllValues( ): NameObjectCollectionBase

BaseGetKey( ): NameObjectCollectionBase

BaseHasKeys( ): NameObjectCollectionBase

BasePriority: Process, ProcessThread

BaseRemove( ): NameObjectCollectionBase

BaseRemoveAt( ): NameObjectCollectionBase

BaseSet( ): NameObjectCollectionBase

BaseStream: BinaryReader, BinaryWriter, StreamReader, StreamWriter, XmlTextWriter

BaseType: EnumBuilder, Type, TypeBuilder, TypeDelegator, UnmanagedMarshal

BaseURI: XmlAttribute, XmlDocument, XmlEntity, XmlEntityReference, XmlNode, XmlNodeReader, XmlParserContext, XmlReader, XmlTextReader, XmlValidatingReader, XPathNavigator

BaseValue: CounterSample

Basic: UriHostNameType

Before: XmlNodeOrder

BeforeFieldInit: TypeAttributes

Begin: SeekOrigin

BeginAccept( ): Socket

BeginCatchBlock( ): ILGenerator

BeginConnect( ): Socket

BeginExceptFilterBlock( ): ILGenerator

BeginExceptionBlock( ): ILGenerator

BeginFaultBlock( ): ILGenerator

BeginFinallyBlock( ): ILGenerator

BeginGetHostByName( ): Dns

BeginGetRequestStream( ): FileWebRequest, HttpWebRequest, WebRequest

BeginGetResponse( ): FileWebRequest, Http-
WebRequest, WebRequest

BeginInit( ): EventLog, FileSystemWatcher,
PerformanceCounter, Timer

BeginInvoke( ): AssemblyLoadEventHandler,
AsyncCallback, CrossAppDomainDelegate,
ElapsedEventHandler, EntryWritten-
EventHandler, ErrorEventHandler,
EventHandler, FileSystemEventHandler, Http-
ContinueDelegate, IOCompletionCallback,
MatchEvaluator, MemberFilter, ModuleRe-
solveEventHandler, ObjectCreationDelegate,
PowerModeChangedEventHandler, Renamed-
EventHandler, ResolveEventHandler, Session-
EndedEventHandler, SessionEndingEv-
entHandler, ThreadExceptionEventHandler,
ThreadStart, TimerCallback, TimerElapsedE-
ventHandler, TypeFilter, UnhandledException-
EventHandler, UserPreferenceChangedE-
ventHandler,
UserPreferenceChangingEventHandler, Wait-
Callback, WaitOrTimerCallback, XmlNo-
deChangedEventHandler

BeginRead( ): FileStream, IsolatedStorage-
FileStream, NetworkStream, Stream

BeginReceive( ): Socket

BeginReceiveFrom( ): Socket

BeginResolve( ): Dns

BeginScope( ): ILGenerator

BeginSend( ): Socket

BeginSendTo( ): Socket

BeginWrite( ): FileStream, IsolatedStorage-
FileStream, NetworkStream, Stream

BelowNormal: ProcessPriorityClass, ThreadPriority, ThreadPriorityLevel

Beq: OpCodes

Beq_S: OpCodes

BestFitMapping: BestFitMappingAttribute,
DllImportAttribute

BestFitMappingAttribute: System.Runtime.
InteropServices

Bge: OpCodes

Bge_S: OpCodes

Bge_Un: OpCodes

Bge_Un_S: OpCodes

Bgt: OpCodes

Bgt_S: OpCodes

Bgt_Un: OpCodes

Bgt_Un_S: OpCodes

BigEndianUnicode: Encoding

BigMul( ): Math

BinaryReader: System.IO

BinarySearch( ): Array, ArrayList

BinaryWriter: System.IO

Bind( ): Socket

Binder: Formatter, IFormatter, System.Reflec-
tion

BindHandle( ): ThreadPool

BindingFlags: System.Reflection

BindToField( ): Binder

BindToMethod( ): Binder

BindToMoniker( ): Marshal

BindToType( ): SerializationBinder

BitArray: System.Collections

BitConverter: System

BitVector32: System.Collections.Specialized

Ble: OpCodes

Ble_S: OpCodes

Ble_Un: OpCodes

Ble_Un_S: OpCodes

BlockCopy( ): Buffer

Blocking: Socket

BlockSource: SocketOptionName

Blt: OpCodes

Blt_S: OpCodes

Blt_Un: OpCodes

Blt_Un_S: OpCodes

Bne_Un: OpCodes

Bne_Un_S: OpCodes

BodyName: Encoding

Bool: UnmanagedType

Boolean: System, TypeCode, XPathResultType

BooleanSwitch: System.Diagnostics

Both: SocketShutdown

Box: OpCodes

Box( ): Pointer

Br: OpCodes

Br_S: OpCodes

Branch: FlowControl

Break: FlowControl, OpCodes

Break( ): Debugger

Brfalse: OpCodes

Brfalse_S: OpCodes

Broadcast: IPAddress, SocketOptionName

Browse: EventLogPermissionAccess, PerformanceCounterPermissionAccess

Brtrue: OpCodes

Brtrue_S: OpCodes

BsdUrgent: SocketOptionName

BStr: UnmanagedType

Buffer: System

BufferedStream: System.IO

Build: Version

BuildNumber: ComCompatibleVersionAttribute

BypassArrayList: WebProxy

BypassList: WebProxy

BypassProxyOnLocal: WebProxy

Byte: System, TypeCode

ByteLength( ): Buffer

ByValArray: UnmanagedType

ByValTStr: UnmanagedType

C

CachePath: AppDomainSetup

Calculate( ): CounterSample

Calendar: CultureInfo, DateTimeFormatInfo, System.Globalization

CalendarType: GregorianCalendar

CalendarWeekRule: DateTimeFormatInfo, System.Globalization

Call: FlowControl, OpCodes

Calli: OpCodes

CallingConvention: DllImportAttribute, MethodBase, MethodBuilder, System.Runtime.InteropServices

CallingConventions: System.Reflection

Callvirt: OpCodes

Cancel: SessionEndingEventArgs

CannotUnloadAppDomainException: System

Canonicalize( ): Uri

CanPreAuthenticate: IAuthenticationModule

CanRead: BufferedStream, FileStream, IsolatedStorageFileStream, MemoryStream, NetworkStream, PropertyBuilder, PropertyInfo, Stream

CanResolveEntity: XmlNodeReader, XmlReader, XmlValidatingReader

CanResume( ): SEHException

CanSeek: BufferedStream, FileStream, IsolatedStorageFileStream, MemoryStream, NetworkStream, Stream

CanWrite: BufferedStream, FileStream, IsolatedStorageFileStream, MemoryStream, NetworkStream, PropertyBuilder, PropertyInfo, Stream

Capacity: ArrayList, CookieContainer, MemoryStream, SortedList, StringBuilder

Capture: System.Text.RegularExpressions

CaptureCollection: System.Text.RegularExpressions

Captures: Group

CaseInsensitiveComparer: System.Collections

CaseInsensitiveHashCodeProvider: System.Collections

Castclass: OpCodes

Category: EventLogEntry, UserPreferenceChangedEventArgs, UserPreferenceChangingEventArgs

CategoryHelp: PerformanceCounterCategory, PerformanceCounterInstaller

CategoryName: PerformanceCounter, PerformanceCounterCategory, PerformanceCounterInstaller, PerformanceCounterPermissionAttribute, PerformanceCounterPermissionEntry

CategoryNumber: EventLogEntry

Ccitt: AddressFamily, ProtocolFamily

CDATA: XmlNodeType, XmlTokenizedType

Cdecl: CallingConvention

Ceiling( ): Math

Ceq: OpCodes

Certificate: ServicePoint

CertificatePolicy: ServicePointManager

Cgt: OpCodes

Cgt_Un: OpCodes

ChainSelector( ): ISurrogateSelector, SurrogateSelector

Change: XmlNodeChangedAction

Change( ): Timer

Changed: FileSystemWatcher, WatcherChange-Types

ChangeExtension( ): Path

ChangeType: FileSystemEventArgs, Wait-ForChangedResult

ChangeType( ): Binder, Convert

ChangeWrapperHandleStrength( ): Marshal

Chaos: AddressFamily, ProtocolFamily

Char: System, TypeCode

CharacterSet: HttpWebResponse

CharEnumerator: System

Chars: String, StringBuilder

CharSet: DllImportAttribute, StructLayoutAttribute, System.Runtime.InteropServices

CharSize: UnicodeEncoding

CheckAccessOnOverride: MethodAttributes

CheckCertificateRevocationList: ServicePoint-Manager

CheckHostName( ): Uri

CheckSchemeName( ): Uri

CheckSecurity( ): Uri

ChecksumCoverage: SocketOptionName

CheckTypeSecurity( ): FormatterServices

CheckValidationResult( ): ICertificatePolicy

ChildNodes: XmlNode

Ckfinite: OpCodes

Class: AttributeTargets, TypeAttributes

ClassesRoot: Registry, RegistryHive

ClassImpl: ParameterInfo

ClassInterfaceAttribute: System.Runtime.InteropServices

ClassInterfaceType: System.Runtime.InteropServices

ClassName: MissingMemberException

ClassSemanticsMask: TypeAttributes

Clear( ): Array, ArrayList, CollectionBase, DictionaryBase, EventLog, Hashtable, HybridDictionary, IDictionary, IList, ListDictionary, NameValueCollection, Queue, SortedList, Stack, StringCollection, StringDictionary, TraceListenerCollection, XsltArgumentList

ClearCache: GC

ClearCachedData( ): CultureInfo

ClearPrivatePath( ): AppDomain

ClearShadowCopyPath( ): AppDomain

ClientCertificate: ServicePoint

ClientCertificates: HttpWebRequest

Clone: StreamingContextStates

Clone( ): Array, ArrayList, AssemblyName, BitArray, CharEnumerator, CultureInfo, DateTimeFormatInfo, Delegate, Hashtable, ICloneable, NumberFormatInfo, OperatingSystem, Queue, SortedList, Stack, String, Version, XmlNode, XPathExpression, XPathNavigator, XPathNodeIterator

CloneNode( ): XmlAttribute, XmlCDataSection, XmlComment, XmlDataDocument, XmlDeclaration, XmlDocument, XmlDocumentFragment, XmlDocumentType, XmlElement, XmlEntity, XmlEntityReference, XmlNode, XmlNotation, XmlProcessingInstruction, XmlSignificantWhitespace, XmlText, XmlWhitespace

Close( ): BinaryReader, BinaryWriter, BufferedStream, Debug, EventLog, EventLogTraceListener, FileStream, FileWebResponse, HttpWebResponse, IsolatedStorageFile, IsolatedStorageFileStream, MemoryStream, NetworkStream, PerformanceCounter, Process, RegistryKey, Socket, Stream, StreamReader, StreamWriter, StringReader, StringWriter, TcpClient, TextReader, TextWriter, TextWriterTraceListener, Timer, Trace, TraceListener, UdpClient, WaitHandle, WebResponse, XmlNodeReader, XmlReader, XmlTextReader, XmlTextWriter, XmlValidatingReader, XmlWriter

Closed: ReadState, WriteState

CloseMainWindow( ): Process

ClosePunctuation: UnicodeCategory

CloseSharedResources( ): PerformanceCounter

CLSCompliantAttribute: System

Clt: OpCodes

Clt_Un: OpCodes

Cluster: AddressFamily, ProtocolFamily

CoClass: CoClassAttribute

CoClassAttribute: System.Runtime.InteropServices

CodeBase: Assembly, AssemblyBuilder, AssemblyName

CodePage: Encoding

CodeTypeMask: MethodImplAttributes

Collect( ): GC

CollectionBase: System.Collections

CollectionsUtil: System.Collections.Specialized

Color: UserPreferenceCategory

ComAliasNameAttribute: System.Runtime.
InteropServices

Combine( ): Delegate, Path

CombineImpl( ): Delegate, MulticastDelegate

ComCompatibleVersionAttribute: System.
Runtime.InteropServices

ComConversionLossAttribute: System.
Runtime.InteropServices

COMException: System.Runtime.InteropServices

ComImportAttribute: System.Runtime.
InteropServices

ComInterfaceType: System.Runtime.InteropS-
ervices

CommandLine: Environment

ComMemberType: System.Runtime.InteropSer-
vices

Comment: Cookie, XmlNodeType, XPathNode-
Type

Comments: FileVersionInfo

CommentUri: Cookie

CommonApplicationData: SpecialFolder

CommonProgramFiles: SpecialFolder

Company: AssemblyCompanyAttribute

CompanyName: FileVersionInfo

Compare( ): CaseInsensitiveComparer, Compare-
Info, Comparer, DateTime, Decimal, IComparer, SortKey, String, TimeSpan

CompareDocument( ): XsltContext

CompareExchange( ): Interlocked

CompareInfo: CultureInfo, System.Globalization

CompareOptions: System.Globalization

CompareOrdinal( ): String

ComparePosition( ): XPathNavigator

Comparer: System.Collections

CompareTo( ): Boolean, Byte, Char, DateTime,
Decimal, Double, Enum, Guid, IComparable,
Int16, Int32, Int64, SByte, Single, String,
TimeSpan, UInt16, UInt32, UInt64, Version

CompatibleImpl: IDispatchImplType

Compile( ): XPathNavigator

Compiled: RegexOptions

CompileToAssembly( ): Regex

Complete: Authorization

CompletedSynchronously: IAsyncResult

Compressed: FileAttributes

CompressedStack: System.Threading

ComputeCounterValue( ): CounterSampleCalculator

ComRegisterFunctionAttribute: System.
Runtime.InteropServices

ComSourceInterfacesAttribute: System.
Runtime.InteropServices

ComUnregisterFunctionAttribute: System.
Runtime.InteropServices

ComVisibleAttribute: System.Runtime.
InteropServices

Concat( ): String

Cond_Branch: FlowControl

ConditionalAttribute: System.Diagnostics

ConditionString: ConditionalAttribute

Configuration: AssemblyConfigurationAttribute

ConfigurationFile: AppDomainSetup

Conflict: HttpStatusCode

Connect: NetworkAccess, WebPermissionAttribute

Connect( ): Socket, TcpClient, UdpClient

Connected: Socket

ConnectFailure: WebExceptionStatus

Connection: HttpWebRequest

ConnectionClosed: WebExceptionStatus

ConnectionGroupId: Authorization

ConnectionGroupName: FileWebRequest, Http-
WebRequest, WebRequest

Connectionless: TransportType

ConnectionLimit: ServicePoint

ConnectionName: ServicePoint

ConnectionOriented: TransportType

ConnectList: SocketPermission, WebPermission

ConnectorPunctuation: UnicodeCategory

ConnectPattern: WebPermissionAttribute

Console: System

ConsoleApplication: PEFileKinds

Constructor: AttributeTargets, MemberTypes

ConstructorBuilder: System.Reflection.Emit

ConstructorInfo: System.Reflection

StringCollection, StringDictionary, TraceListenerCollection, XmlAttributeCollection

CoreNewLine: TextWriter

Cos( ): Math

Cosh( ): Math

Count: ArrayList, BitArray, CaptureCollection, CollectionBase, CookieCollection, CookieContainer, DictionaryBase, EventLogEntryCollection, GroupCollection, Hashtable, HybridDictionary, ICollection, KeysCollection, ListDictionary, MatchCollection, NameObjectCollectionBase, Queue, ReadOnlyCollectionBase, SortedList, Stack, StringCollection, StringDictionary, TraceListenerCollection, XmlNamedNodeMap, XmlNodeList, XPathNodeIterator

CounterCreationData: System.Diagnostics

CounterCreationDataCollection: System.Diagnostics

CounterDelta32: PerformanceCounterType

CounterDelta64: PerformanceCounterType

CounterExists( ): PerformanceCounterCategory

CounterFrequency: CounterSample

CounterHelp: CounterCreationData, PerformanceCounter

CounterMultiBase: PerformanceCounterType

CounterMultiTimer: PerformanceCounterType

CounterMultiTimer100Ns: PerformanceCounterType

CounterMultiTimer100NsInverse: PerformanceCounterType

CounterMultiTimerInverse: PerformanceCounterType

CounterName: CounterCreationData, InstanceDataCollection, PerformanceCounter

Counters: PerformanceCounterInstaller

CounterSample: System.Diagnostics

CounterSampleCalculator: System.Diagnostics

CounterTimer: PerformanceCounterType

CounterTimerInverse: PerformanceCounterType

CounterTimeStamp: CounterSample

CounterType: CounterCreationData, CounterSample, PerformanceCounter

CountPerTimeInterval32: PerformanceCounterType

CountPerTimeInterval64: PerformanceCounterType

Cpblk: OpCodes

Cpobj: OpCodes

Create: FileMode

Create( ): DirectoryInfo, EndPoint, File, FileInfo, IPEndPoint, IWebRequestCreate, PerformanceCounterCategory, WebRequest

CreateAttribute( ): XmlDocument

CreateCaseInsensitiveHashtable( ): CollectionsUtil

CreateCaseInsensitiveSortedList( ): CollectionsUtil

CreateCDataSection( ): XmlDocument

CreateComInstanceFrom( ): Activator, AppDomain

CreateComment( ): XmlDocument

Created: FileSystemWatcher, HttpStatusCode, WatcherChangeTypes

CreateDefault( ): WebRequest

CreateDelegate( ): Delegate

CreateDirectory( ): Directory, IsolatedStorageFile

CreateDocument( ): XmlImplementation

CreateDocumentFragment( ): XmlDocument

CreateDocumentType( ): XmlDocument

CreateDomain( ): AppDomain

CreateElement( ): XmlDataDocument, XmlDocument

CreateEntityReference( ): XmlDataDocument, XmlDocument

CreateEventSource( ): EventLog

CreateEvidenceForUrl( ): XmlSecureResolver

CreateGlobalFunctions( ): ModuleBuilder

CreateInstance: BindingFlags

CreateInstance( ): Activator, AppDomain, Array, Assembly

CreateInstanceAndUnwrap( ): AppDomain

CreateInstanceFrom( ): Activator, AppDomain

CreateInstanceFromAndUnwrap( ): AppDomain

CreateMask( ): BitVector32

CreateMethodBody( ): MethodBuilder

CreateNavigator( ): IXPathNavigable, XmlDataDocument, XmlNode, XPathDocument

CreateNew: FileMode

CreateNode( ): XmlDocument

CreateNoWindow: ProcessStartInfo

CreateObjRef( ): MarshalByRefObject

CreatePermission( ): DnsPermissionAttribute, EventLogPermissionAttribute, PerformanceCounterPermissionAttribute, SocketPermissionAttribute, WebPermissionAttribute

CreateProcessingInstruction( ): XmlDocument

CreateQualifiedName( ): Assembly

CreateSection( ): BitVector32

CreateSignificantWhitespace( ): XmlDocument

CreateSpecificCulture( ): CultureInfo

CreateSubdirectory( ): DirectoryInfo

CreateSubKey( ): RegistryKey

CreateText( ): File, FileInfo

CreateTextNode( ): XmlDocument

CreateTimer( ): SystemEvents

CreateType( ): EnumBuilder, TypeBuilder

CreateWaitHandle( ): Stream

CreateWhitespace( ): XmlDocument

CreateWrapperOfType( ): Marshal

CreateXmlDeclaration( ): XmlDocument

CreationTime: FileSystemInfo, NotifyFilters

CreationTimeUtc: FileSystemInfo

CredentialCache: System.Net

Credentials: FileWebRequest, HttpWebRequest, IWebProxy, WebClient, WebProxy, WebRequest, XmlResolver, XmlSecureResolver, XmlUrlResolver

CrossAppDomain: StreamingContextStates

CrossAppDomainDelegate: System

CrossMachine: StreamingContextStates

CrossProcess: StreamingContextStates

Culture: AssemblyCultureAttribute

CultureInfo: AssemblyName, System.Globalization

CultureInvariant: RegexOptions

CultureTypes: System.Globalization

Currency: NumberStyles, UnmanagedType

CurrencyDecimalDigits: NumberFormatInfo

CurrencyDecimalSeparator: NumberFormatInfo

CurrencyGroupSeparator: NumberFormatInfo

CurrencyGroupSizes: NumberFormatInfo

CurrencyNegativePattern: NumberFormatInfo

CurrencyPositivePattern: NumberFormatInfo

CurrencySymbol: NumberFormatInfo, RegionInfo, UnicodeCategory

CurrencyWrapper: System.Runtime.InteropServices

Current: CharEnumerator, IEnumerator, SeekOrigin, SerializationInfoEnumerator, StringEnumerator, TextElementEnumerator, XPathNodeIterator

CurrentConfig: Registry, RegistryHive

CurrentConnections: ServicePoint

CurrentContext: Thread

CurrentCulture: CultureInfo, Thread

CurrentDirectory: Environment

CurrentDomain: AppDomain

CurrentEncoding: StreamReader

CurrentEra: Calendar

CurrentInfo: DateTimeFormatInfo, NumberFormatInfo

CurrentPosition: XPathNodeIterator

CurrentPrincipal: Thread

CurrentPriority: ProcessThread

CurrentRegion: RegionInfo

CurrentSize: IsolatedStorage, IsolatedStorageFile

CurrentThread: Thread

CurrentTimeZone: TimeZone

CurrentUICulture: CultureInfo, Thread

CurrentUser: Registry, RegistryHive

Custom: MemberTypes

CustomAttributeBuilder: System.Reflection.Emit

CustomAttributeFormatException: System.Reflection

CustomMarshaler: UnmanagedType

D

DashPunctuation: UnicodeCategory

Data: BitVector32, EventLogEntry, XmlCharacterData, XmlProcessingInstruction

DataAvailable: NetworkStream

DataKit: AddressFamily, ProtocolFamily

DataLink: AddressFamily, ProtocolFamily

DataSet: XmlDataDocument

Date: DateTime
DateSeparator: DateTimeFormatInfo
DateTime: System, TypeCode
DateTimeFormat: CultureInfo
DateTimeFormatInfo: System.Globalization
DateTimeStyles: System.Globalization
Day: DateTime
DaylightName: TimeZone
DaylightTime: System.Globalization
DayNames: DateTimeFormatInfo
DayOfWeek: DateTime, System
DayOfYear: DateTime
Days: TimeSpan
DaysInMonth( ): DateTime
DBNull: Convert, System, TypeCode
Debug: SocketOptionName, System.Diagnostics
DebuggableAttribute: System.Diagnostics
Debugger: System.Diagnostics
DebuggerHiddenAttribute: System.Diagnostics
DebuggerStepThroughAttribute: System.Diagnostics
Decimal: System, TypeCode
DecimalDigitNumber: UnicodeCategory
DeclaredOnly: BindingFlags
DeclareLocal( ): ILGenerator
DeclaringType: ConstructorBuilder, EnumBuilder, FieldBuilder, MemberInfo, MethodBuilder, PropertyBuilder, Type, TypeBuilder
DecNet: AddressFamily, ProtocolFamily
DecodeName( ): XmlConvert
Decoder: System.Text
Decrement( ): Interlocked, PerformanceCounter
Default: BindingFlags, CaseInsensitiveComparer, CaseInsensitiveHashCodeProvider, Comparer, Encoding, XmlSpace
DefaultAlias: AssemblyDefaultAliasAttribute
DefaultBinder: Type
DefaultCategory: Debugger
DefaultConnectionLimit: ServicePointManager
DefaultCookieLengthLimit: CookieContainer
DefaultCookieLimit: CookieContainer
DefaultCredentials: CredentialCache
DefaultFileMappingSize: PerformanceCounter

DefaultInvariant: CaseInsensitiveComparer, CaseInsensitiveHashCodeProvider, Comparer
DefaultMaximumResponseHeadersLength: HttpWebRequest
DefaultMemberAttribute: System.Reflection
DefaultNamespace: XmlNamespaceManager
DefaultNonPersistentConnectionLimit: ServicePointManager
DefaultPerDomainCookieLimit: CookieContainer
DefaultPersistentConnectionLimit: ServicePointManager
DefaultTraceListener: System.Diagnostics
DefaultValue: ParameterInfo
DefaultValueImpl: ParameterInfo
DefineByValArray( ): UnmanagedMarshal
DefineByValTStr( ): UnmanagedMarshal
DefineConstructor( ): TypeBuilder
DefineDefaultConstructor( ): TypeBuilder
DefineDocument( ): ModuleBuilder
DefineDynamicAssembly( ): AppDomain
DefineDynamicModule( ): AssemblyBuilder
DefineEnum( ): ModuleBuilder
DefineEvent( ): TypeBuilder
DefineField( ): TypeBuilder
DefineGlobalMethod( ): ModuleBuilder
DefineInitializedData( ): ModuleBuilder, TypeBuilder
DefineLabel( ): ILGenerator
DefineLiteral( ): EnumBuilder
DefineLPArray( ): UnmanagedMarshal
DefineMethod( ): TypeBuilder
DefineMethodOverride( ): TypeBuilder
DefineNestedType( ): TypeBuilder
DefineParameter( ): ConstructorBuilder, MethodBuilder
DefinePInvokeMethod( ): ModuleBuilder, TypeBuilder
DefineProperty( ): TypeBuilder
DefineResource( ): AssemblyBuilder, ModuleBuilder
DefineSafeArray( ): UnmanagedMarshal
DefineType( ): ModuleBuilder
DefineTypeInitializer( ): TypeBuilder

DefineUninitializedData( ): ModuleBuilder, TypeBuilder

DefineUnmanagedMarshal( ): Unmanaged-Marshal

DefineUnmanagedResource( ): Assembly-Builder, ModuleBuilder

DefineVersionInfoResource( ): AssemblyBuilder

DelaySign: AssemblyDelaySignAttribute

Delegate: AttributeTargets, System

Delete( ): Directory, DirectoryInfo, EventLog, File, FileInfo, FileSystemInfo, Performance-CounterCategory

Deleted: FileSystemWatcher, WatcherChange-Types

DeleteData( ): XmlCharacterData

DeleteDirectory( ): IsolatedStorageFile

DeleteEventSource( ): EventLog

DeleteFile( ): IsolatedStorageFile

DeleteSubKey( ): RegistryKey

DeleteSubKeyTree( ): RegistryKey

DeleteValue( ): RegistryKey

Delimiter: Type

Delta: DaylightTime

Depth: XmlNodeReader, XmlReader, XmlTex-tReader, XmlValidatingReader

Dequeue( ): Queue

Descending: XmlSortOrder

Description: AssemblyDescriptionAttribute, IODescriptionAttribute, MonitoringDescrip-tionAttribute, Switch, TimersDescriptionAt-tribute

Deserialize( ): Formatter, IFormatter

Desktop: SpecialFolder, UserPreferenceCategory

DesktopDirectory: SpecialFolder

DestroyStructure( ): Marshal

Detail: SoapFault

Device: FileAttributes

Dgram: SocketType

DictionaryBase: System.Collections

DictionaryEntry: System.Collections

Directory: FileAttributes, FileInfo, System.IO

DirectoryInfo: System.IO

DirectoryName: FileInfo, NotifyFilters

DirectoryNotFoundException: System.IO

DirectorySeparatorChar: Path

DisallowBindingRedirects: AppDomainSetup

DisallowBindings: LoaderOptimization

DisallowCodeDownload: AppDomainSetup

DisallowPublisherPolicy: AppDomainSetup

Discard: Cookie

DiscardBufferedData( ): StreamReader

DispatchWrapper: System.Runtime.InteropSer-vices

DispIdAttribute: System.Runtime.InteropSer-vices

DisplayName: CultureInfo, RegionInfo, Switch

DisplaySettingsChanged: SystemEvents

Dispose( ): BinaryReader, BinaryWriter, EventLog, EventLogTraceListener, FileStream, FileSystemWatcher, FileWebResponse, Http-WebResponse, IDisposable, IsolatedStorage-File, IsolatedStorageFileStream, Network-Stream, PerformanceCounter, Process, Socket, StreamReader, StreamWriter, StringReader, StringWriter, TcpClient, TextReader, Text-Writer, TextWriterTraceListener, Timer, TraceListener, WaitHandle

Div: OpCodes

Div_Un: OpCodes

Divide( ): Decimal

DivideByZeroException: System

DivRem( ): Math

Dll: PEFileKinds

DllImportAttribute: System.Runtime.InteropS-ervices

DllNotFoundException: System

Dns: System.Net, UriHostNameType

DnsPermission: System.Net

DnsPermissionAttribute: System.Net

DoCallBack( ): AppDomain

DocTypeName: XmlParserContext

Document: XmlNodeType

DocumentElement: XmlDocument

DocumentFragment: XmlNodeType

DocumentType: XmlDocument, XmlNodeType

DoFixups( ): ObjectManager

Domain: Cookie, IsolatedStorageScope, NetworkCredential

DomainIdentity: IsolatedStorage

DomainMask: LoaderOptimization

DomainUnload: AppDomain

DontFragment: SocketOptionName

DontLinger: SocketOptionName

DontRoute: SocketFlags, SocketOptionName

Double: System, TypeCode

DoubleToInt64Bits( ): BitConverter

DowngradeFromWriterLock( ): ReaderWriter-Lock

DownloadData( ): WebClient

DownloadFile( ): WebClient

DropMembership: SocketOptionName

DropMulticastGroup( ): UdpClient

DropSourceMembership: SocketOptionName

DTD: ValidationType

Dup: OpCodes

DuplicateWaitObjectException: System

Duration( ): TimeSpan

DynamicBase: AppDomainSetup

DynamicDirectory: AppDomain

DynamicInvoke( ): Delegate

DynamicInvokeImpl( ): Delegate, MulticastDel-egate

DynData: Registry, RegistryHive

E

E: Math

EBCDICCodePage: TextInfo

Ecma: AddressFamily, ProtocolFamily

ECMAScript: RegexOptions

Elapsed: Timer

ElapsedEventArgs: System.Timers

ElapsedEventHandler: System.Timers

ElapsedTime: PerformanceCounterType

Element: WriteState, XmlNodeType, XPathNode-Type

ElementCount: UnmanagedMarshal

ElementIndex: TextElementEnumerator

Embedded: ResourceLocation

Emit( ): ILGenerator

EmitCall( ): ILGenerator

EmitCalli( ): ILGenerator

EmitWriteLine( ): ILGenerator

Empty: CounterSample, EventArgs, EventToken, FieldToken, Guid, Match, MethodToken, ParameterToken, PropertyToken, Signature-Token, String, TypeCode, TypeToken, XmlQualifiedName

EmptyTypes: Type

Enabled: BooleanSwitch, LingerOption, Timer

EnableRaisingEvents: EventLog, FileSystem-Watcher, Process

EnclosingMark: UnicodeCategory

EncodeLocalName( ): XmlConvert

EncodeName( ): XmlConvert

EncodeNmToken( ): XmlConvert

Encoder: System.Text

Encoding: StreamWriter, StringWriter, System.Text, TextWriter, XmlDeclaration, XmlParser-Context, XmlTextReader, XmlValidatingReader

EncodingName: Encoding

Encrypted: FileAttributes

End: DaylightTime, SeekOrigin

End( ): ArgIterator

EndAccept( ): Socket

EndConnect( ): Socket

EndElement: XmlNodeType

EndEntity: XmlNodeType

EndExceptionBlock( ): ILGenerator

Endfilter: OpCodes

Endfinally: OpCodes

EndGetHostByName( ): Dns

EndGetRequestStream( ): FileWebRequest, HttpWebRequest, WebRequest

EndGetResponse( ): FileWebRequest, HttpWe-bRequest, WebRequest

EndInit( ): EventLog, FileSystemWatcher, Perfor-manceCounter, Timer

EndInvoke( ): AssemblyLoadEventHandler, AsyncCallback, CrossAppDomainDelegate, ElapsedEventHandler, EntryWritten-EventHandler, ErrorEventHandler, EventHandler, FileSystemEventHandler, Http-ContinueDelegate, IOCompletionCallback, MatchEvaluator, MemberFilter, ModuleRe-solveEventHandler, ObjectCreationDelegate, PowerModeChangedEventHandler, Renamed-EventHandler, ResolveEventHandler, Session-EndedEventHandler, SessionEndingEv-entHandler, ThreadExceptionEventHandler, ThreadStart, TimerCallback, TimerElapsedE-

ventHandler, TypeFilter, UnhandledException-
EventHandler, UserPreferenceChangedE-
ventHandler,
UserPreferenceChangingEventHandler, Wait-
Callback, WaitOrTimerCallback, XmlNo-
deChangedEventHandler

EndOfFile: ReadState

EndOfStreamException: System.IO

EndPoint: System.Net

EndpointPermission: System.Net

EndRead( ): FileStream, IsolatedStorage-
FileStream, NetworkStream, Stream

EndReceive( ): Socket

EndReceiveFrom( ): Socket

EndResolve( ): Dns

EndScope( ): ILGenerator

EndSend( ): Socket

EndSendTo( ): Socket

EndsWith( ): String

EndWrite( ): FileStream, IsolatedStorage-
FileStream, NetworkStream, Stream

EnglishName: CultureInfo, RegionInfo

Enqueue( ): Queue

EnsureCapacity( ): StringBuilder

Enter( ): Monitor

EnterDebugMode( ): Process

Entities: XmlDocumentType

ENTITIES: XmlTokenizedType

Entity: XmlNodeType

ENTITY: XmlTokenizedType

EntityHandling: System.Xml, XmlValidatingReader

EntityReference: XmlNodeType

Entries: EventLog

Entry: EntryWrittenEventArgs, IDictionaryEnumerator

EntryPoint: Assembly, AssemblyBuilder, DllImportAttribute

EntryPointAddress: ProcessModule

EntryPointNotFoundException: System

EntryType: EventLogEntry

EntryWritten: EventLog

EntryWrittenEventArgs: System.Diagnostics

EntryWrittenEventHandler: System.Diagnostics

Enum: AttributeTargets, System

EnumBuilder: System.Reflection.Emit

ENUMERATION: XmlTokenizedType

Environment: System

EnvironmentVariables: ProcessStartInfo

EOF: XmlNodeReader, XmlReader, XmlTextReader, XmlValidatingReader

Epsilon: Double, Single

Equals( ): ArgIterator, ArrayWithOffset,
Attribute, BitVector32, Boolean, Byte, Char,
CompareInfo, Cookie, CultureInfo, DateTime,
Decimal, Delegate, Double, Encoding,
EndpointPermission, Enum, EventLogEntry,
EventToken, FieldToken, Guid, Int16, Int32,
Int64, IntPtr, IPAddress, IPEndPoint, Label,
MethodBuilder, MethodToken, MulticastDele-
gate, Object, OpCode, ParameterToken, Prop-
ertyToken, RegionInfo, SByte, Section, Signa-
tureHelper, SignatureToken, Single,
SocketAddress, SortKey, StreamingContext,
String, StringBuilder, StringToken, TextInfo,
TimeSpan, Type, TypeToken, UInt16, UInt32,
UInt64, UIntPtr, UnicodeEncoding, Uri,
UriBuilder, UTF8Encoding, ValueType, Version,
XmlQualifiedName

Eras: Calendar, GregorianCalendar, HebrewCalendar, HijriCalendar, JapaneseCalendar,
JulianCalendar, KoreanCalendar, TaiwanCalendar, ThaiBuddhistCalendar

Error: Console, EventLogEntryType, FileSystem-
Watcher, ReadState, SocketOptionName,
TraceLevel, UnmanagedType, XPathResult-
Type

ErrorCode: ErrorWrapper, ExternalException,
SocketException

ErrorDialog: ProcessStartInfo

ErrorDialogParentHandle: ProcessStartInfo

ErrorEventArgs: System.IO

ErrorEventHandler: System.IO

ErrorWrapper: System.Runtime.InteropServices

Escape( ): Regex, Uri

EscapedCodeBase: Assembly, AssemblyName

EscapeString( ): Uri

Evaluate( ): IXsltContextVariable, XPathNavigator

Event: AttributeTargets, MemberTypes

EventArgs: System

EventAttributes: System.Reflection

Formatting: System.Xml, XmlTextWriter

ForwardRef: MethodImplAttributes

Found: HttpStatusCode

Fragment: Uri, UriBuilder

FrameCount: StackTrace

Free( ): GCHandle, Overlapped

FreeBSTR( ): Marshal

FreeCoTaskMem( ): Marshal

FreeHGlobal( ): Marshal

FreeNamedDataSlot( ): Thread

FreePage: ThreadWaitReason

Friday: DayOfWeek

FriendlyName: AppDomain

FromBase64CharArray( ): Convert

FromBase64String( ): Convert

FromDays( ): TimeSpan

FromFileTime( ): DateTime

FromFileTimeUtc( ): DateTime

FromGlobalAccessCache( ): RuntimeEnvironment

FromHex( ): Uri

FromHours( ): TimeSpan

FromMilliseconds( ): TimeSpan

FromMinutes( ): TimeSpan

FromOACurrency( ): Decimal

FromOADate( ): DateTime

FromSeconds( ): TimeSpan

FromTicks( ): TimeSpan

FromXml( ): DnsPermission, SocketPermission, WebPermission

Full: FormatterAssemblyStyle, TypeFilterLevel

FullDateTimePattern: DateTimeFormatInfo

FullName: Assembly, AssemblyName, EnumBuilder, FileSystemInfo, Type, TypeBuilder, TypeDelegator

FullPath: FileSystemEventArgs, FileSystemInfo

FullTypeName: SerializationInfo

FullyQualifiedName: Module, ModuleBuilder

FunctionPtr: UnmanagedType

FusionLog: BadImageFormatException, FileLoadException, FileNotFoundException

G

GatewayTimeout: HttpStatusCode

GC: System

GCHandle: System.Runtime.InteropServices

GCHandleType: System.Runtime.InteropServices

General: UserPreferenceCategory

GenerateGuidForType( ): Marshal

GenerateProgIdForType( ): Marshal

Get( ): BitArray, KeysCollection, NameTable, NameValueCollection, XmlNameTable

GetAbbreviatedDayName( ): DateTimeFormatInfo

GetAbbreviatedEraName( ): DateTimeFormatInfo

GetAbbreviatedMonthName( ): DateTimeFormatInfo

GetAccessors( ): PropertyBuilder, PropertyInfo

GetActiveObject( ): Marshal

GetAddMethod( ): EventInfo

GetAddressBytes( ): IPAddress

GetAllDateTimePatterns( ): DateTimeFormatInfo

GetArray( ): ArrayWithOffset

GetArrayMethod( ): ModuleBuilder

GetArrayMethodToken( ): ModuleBuilder

GetArrayRank( ): Type

GetAssemblies( ): AppDomain

GetAssembly( ): Assembly

GetAssemblyName( ): AssemblyName, AssemblyNameProxy

GetAttribute( ): XmlElement, XmlNodeReader, XmlReader, XmlTextReader, XmlValidatingReader, XPathNavigator

GetAttributeFlagsImpl( ): EnumBuilder, Type, TypeBuilder, TypeDelegator

GetAttributeNode( ): XmlElement

GetAttributes( ): File

GetAvailableThreads( ): ThreadPool

GetBaseDefinition( ): MethodBuilder, MethodInfo

GetBaseException( ): Exception

GetBits( ): Decimal

GetBoolean( ): SerializationInfo

GetBuffer( ): MemoryStream

GetByIndex( ): SortedList

GetByte( ): Buffer, SerializationInfo

GetByteCount( ): ASCIIEncoding, Encoder, Encoding, UnicodeEncoding, UTF7Encoding, UTF8Encoding

GetBytes( ): ASCIIEncoding, BitConverter, Encoder, Encoding, UnicodeEncoding, UTF7Encoding, UTF8Encoding

GetCallingAssembly( ): Assembly

GetCategories( ): PerformanceCounterCategory

GetChar( ): SerializationInfo

GetCharCount( ): ASCIIEncoding, Decoder, Encoding, UnicodeEncoding, UTF7Encoding, UTF8Encoding

GetChars( ): ASCIIEncoding, Decoder, Encoding, UnicodeEncoding, UTF7Encoding, UTF8Encoding

GetComInterfaceForObject( ): Marshal

GetCommandLineArgs( ): Environment

GetComObjectData( ): Marshal

GetCompareInfo( ): CompareInfo

GetComSlotForMethodInfo( ): Marshal

GetConstructor( ): Type

GetConstructorImpl( ): EnumBuilder, Type, TypeBuilder, TypeDelegator

GetConstructors( ): EnumBuilder, Type, TypeBuilder, TypeDelegator

GetConstructorToken( ): ModuleBuilder

GetCookieHeader( ): CookieContainer

GetCookies( ): CookieContainer

GetCounters( ): PerformanceCounterCategory

GetCreationTime( ): Directory, File

GetCreationTimeUtc( ): Directory, File

GetCredential( ): CredentialCache, ICredentials, NetworkCredential

GetCultures( ): CultureInfo

GetCurrentDirectory( ): Directory

GetCurrentMethod( ): MethodBase

GetCurrentProcess( ): Process

GetCurrentThreadId( ): AppDomain

GetCustomAttribute( ): Attribute

GetCustomAttributes( ): Assembly, Attribute, ConstructorBuilder, EnumBuilder, FieldBuilder, ICustomAttributeProvider, MemberInfo, MethodBuilder, Module, ParameterInfo, PropertyBuilder, TypeBuilder, TypeDelegator

GetData( ): AppDomain, Thread

GetDateTime( ): SerializationInfo

GetDateTimeFormats( ): DateTime

GetDaylightChanges( ): TimeZone

GetDayName( ): DateTimeFormatInfo

GetDayOfMonth( ): Calendar, GregorianCalendar, HebrewCalendar, HijriCalendar, JapaneseCalendar, JulianCalendar, KoreanCalendar, TaiwanCalendar, ThaiBuddhistCalendar

GetDayOfWeek( ): Calendar, GregorianCalendar, HebrewCalendar, HijriCalendar, JapaneseCalendar, JulianCalendar, KoreanCalendar, TaiwanCalendar, ThaiBuddhistCalendar

GetDayOfYear( ): Calendar, GregorianCalendar, HebrewCalendar, HijriCalendar, JapaneseCalendar, JulianCalendar, KoreanCalendar, TaiwanCalendar, ThaiBuddhistCalendar

GetDaysInMonth( ): Calendar, GregorianCalendar, HebrewCalendar, HijriCalendar, JapaneseCalendar, JulianCalendar, KoreanCalendar, TaiwanCalendar, ThaiBuddhistCalendar

GetDaysInYear( ): Calendar, GregorianCalendar, HebrewCalendar, HijriCalendar, JapaneseCalendar, JulianCalendar, KoreanCalendar, TaiwanCalendar, ThaiBuddhistCalendar

GetDecimal( ): SerializationInfo

GetDecoder( ): Encoding, UnicodeEncoding, UTF7Encoding, UTF8Encoding

GetDefaultMembers( ): Type

GetDefaultProxy( ): WebProxy

GetDirectories( ): Directory, DirectoryInfo

GetDirectoryName( ): Path

GetDirectoryNames( ): IsolatedStorageFile

GetDirectoryRoot( ): Directory

GetDomain( ): Thread

GetDomainID( ): Thread

GetDouble( ): SerializationInfo

GetDynamicModule( ): AssemblyBuilder

GetElementById( ): XmlDataDocument, XmlDocument

GetElementFromRow( ): XmlDataDocument

GetElementsByTagName( ): XmlDocument, XmlElement

GetElementType( ): EnumBuilder, Type, TypeBuilder, TypeDelegator

GetEmptyWebProxy( ): GlobalProxySelection

GetEncoder( ): Encoding, UTF7Encoding, UTF8Encoding

GetEncoding( ): Encoding

GetEndComSlot( ): Marshal

GetEntity( ): XmlResolver, XmlSecureResolver, XmlUrlResolver

GetEntryAssembly( ): Assembly

GetEnumerator( ): Array, ArrayList, BitArray, CaptureCollection, CollectionBase, CookieCollection, CredentialCache, DictionaryBase, EventLogEntryCollection, GroupCollection, Hashtable, HybridDictionary, IDictionary, IEnumerable, IsolatedStorageFile, KeysCollection, ListDictionary, MatchCollection, NameObjectCollectionBase, Queue, ReadOnlyCollectionBase, SerializationInfo, SortedList, Stack, String, StringCollection, StringDictionary, TraceListenerCollection, XmlNamedNodeMap, XmlNamespaceManager, XmlNode, XmlNodeList

GetEnvironmentVariable( ): Environment

GetEnvironmentVariables( ): Environment

GetEra( ): Calendar, DateTimeFormatInfo, GregorianCalendar, HebrewCalendar, HijriCalendar, JapaneseCalendar, JulianCalendar, KoreanCalendar, TaiwanCalendar, ThaiBuddhistCalendar

GetEraName( ): DateTimeFormatInfo

GetEvent( ): EnumBuilder, Type, TypeBuilder, TypeDelegator

GetEventLogs( ): EventLog

GetEvents( ): EnumBuilder, Type, TypeBuilder, TypeDelegator

GetEventToken( ): EventBuilder

GetException( ): ErrorEventArgs

GetExceptionCode( ): Marshal

GetExceptionPointers( ): Marshal

GetExecutingAssembly( ): Assembly

GetExportedTypes( ): Assembly, AssemblyBuilder

GetExtension( ): Path

GetExtensionObject( ): XsltArgumentList

GetField: BindingFlags

GetField( ): EnumBuilder, IReflect, Module, Type, TypeBuilder, TypeDelegator

GetFieldFromHandle( ): FieldInfo

GetFields( ): EnumBuilder, IReflect, Module, Type, TypeBuilder, TypeDelegator

GetFieldSigHelper( ): SignatureHelper

GetFieldToken( ): ModuleBuilder

GetFile( ): Assembly, AssemblyBuilder

GetFileColumnNumber( ): StackFrame

GetFileLineNumber( ): StackFrame

GetFileName( ): Path, StackFrame

GetFileNames( ): IsolatedStorageFile

GetFileNameWithoutExtension( ): Path

GetFiles( ): Assembly, AssemblyBuilder, Directory, DirectoryInfo

GetFileSystemEntries( ): Directory

GetFileSystemInfos( ): DirectoryInfo

GetFolderPath( ): Environment

GetFormat( ): CultureInfo, DateTimeFormatInfo, IFormatProvider, NumberFormatInfo

GetFrame( ): StackTrace

GetFullPath( ): Path

GetGeneration( ): GC

GetGetMethod( ): PropertyBuilder, PropertyInfo

GetGroupNames( ): Regex

GetGroupNumbers( ): Regex

GetHash( ): Hashtable

GetHashCode( ): ArgIterator, ArrayWithOffset, Attribute, BitVector32, Boolean, Byte, CaseInsensitiveHashCodeProvider, Char, CompareInfo, Cookie, CultureInfo, DateTime, Decimal, Delegate, Double, Encoding, EndpointPermission, Enum, EventToken, FieldToken, Guid, HttpWebRequest, HttpWebResponse, IHashCodeProvider, Int16, Int32, Int64, IntPtr, IPAddress, IPEndPoint, Label, MethodBuilder, MethodToken, MulticastDelegate, Object, OpCode, ParameterToken, PropertyToken, RegionInfo, SByte, Section, ServicePoint, SignatureHelper, SignatureToken, Single, Socket, SocketAddress, SortKey, StreamingContext, String, StringToken, TextInfo, TimeSpan, Type, TypeToken, UInt16, UInt32, UInt64, UIntPtr, UnicodeEncoding, Uri, UriBuilder, UTF8Encoding, ValueType, Version, XmlQualifiedName

GetHINSTANCE( ): Marshal

GetHostByAddress( ): Dns

GetHostByName( ): Dns

neseCalendar, JulianCalendar, KoreanCalendar, TaiwanCalendar, ThaiBuddhistCalendar

GetName( ): Assembly, Enum

GetNamedDataSlot( ): Thread

GetNamedItem( ): XmlNamedNodeMap

GetNames( ): Enum

GetNamespace( ): XPathNavigator

GetNamespaceOfPrefix( ): XmlNode

GetNativeOffset( ): StackFrame

GetNativeVariantForObject( ): Marshal

GetNestedType( ): EnumBuilder, Type, TypeBuilder, TypeDelegator

GetNestedTypes( ): EnumBuilder, Type, TypeBuilder, TypeDelegator

GetNext( ): Formatter

GetNextArg( ): ArgIterator

GetNextArgType( ): ArgIterator

GetNextSelector( ): ISurrogateSelector, SurrogateSelector

GetNextTextElement( ): StringInfo

GetNode( ): IHasXmlNode

GetNumericValue( ): Char

GetObject( ): Activator, ObjectManager

GetObjectData( ): ArgumentException, ArgumentOutOfRangeException, Assembly, AssemblyName, BadImageFormatException, DBNull, Delegate, Exception, FileLoadException, FileNotFoundException, FileSystemInfo, FormatterServices, Hashtable, ISerializable, ISerializationSurrogate, MissingMemberException, Module, MulticastDelegate, NameObjectCollectionBase, NotFiniteNumberException, ObjectDisposedException, ReflectionTypeLoadException, RuntimeTypeHandle, SoapFault, TypeInitializationException, TypeLoadException, WeakReference, XmlException, XPathException, XsltCompileException, XsltException

GetObjectForIUnknown( ): Marshal

GetObjectForNativeVariant( ): Marshal

GetObjectsForNativeVariants( ): Marshal

GetOffset( ): ArrayWithOffset

GetParam( ): XsltArgumentList

GetParameters( ): ConstructorBuilder, MethodBase, MethodBuilder

GetParent( ): Directory

GetPathRoot( ): Path

GetPermission( ): IsolatedStorage, IsolatedStorageFile

GetPreamble( ): Encoding, UnicodeEncoding, UTF8Encoding

GetPrefixOfNamespace( ): XmlNode

GetProcessById( ): Process

GetProcesses( ): Process

GetProcessesByName( ): Process

GetProgIdForType( ): IRegistrationServices, RegistrationServices

GetProperties( ): EnumBuilder, IReflect, Type, TypeBuilder, TypeDelegator

GetProperty: BindingFlags

GetProperty( ): IReflect, Type

GetPropertyImpl( ): EnumBuilder, Type, TypeBuilder, TypeDelegator

GetPropertySigHelper( ): SignatureHelper

GetProxy( ): IWebProxy, WebProxy

GetPublicKey( ): AssemblyName

GetPublicKeyToken( ): AssemblyName

GetRaiseMethod( ): EventInfo

GetRange( ): ArrayList

GetRealObject( ): IObjectReference

GetReferencedAssemblies( ): Assembly

GetRegistrableTypesInAssembly( ): IRegistrationServices, RegistrationServices

GetRemainder( ): XmlTextReader

GetRemainingCount( ): ArgIterator

GetRemoveMethod( ): EventInfo

GetRequestStream( ): FileWebRequest, HttpWebRequest, WebRequest

GetResponse( ): FileWebRequest, HttpWebRequest, WebRequest

GetResponseHeader( ): HttpWebResponse

GetResponseStream( ): FileWebResponse, HttpWebResponse, WebResponse

GetRowFromElement( ): XmlDataDocument

GetRuntimeDirectory( ): RuntimeEnvironment

GetSafeUninitializedObject( ): FormatterServices

GetSatelliteAssembly( ): Assembly

GetSByte( ): SerializationInfo

GetSecond( ): Calendar

GetSerializableMembers( ): FormatterServices

GetService( ): IServiceProvider

GetSetMethod( ): PropertyBuilder, PropertyInfo

GetSignature( ): SignatureHelper

GetSignatureToken( ): ModuleBuilder

GetSignerCertificate( ): Module

GetSingle( ): SerializationInfo

GetSocketOption( ): Socket

GetSortKey( ): CompareInfo

GetStartComSlot( ): Marshal

GetStore( ): IsolatedStorageFile

GetStream( ): TcpClient

GetString( ): ASCIIEncoding, Encoding, Serialization-Info

GetStringBuilder( ): StringWriter

GetStringConstant( ): ModuleBuilder

GetSubKeyNames( ): RegistryKey

GetSurrogate( ): ISurrogateSelector, Surrogate-Selector

GetSymWriter( ): ModuleBuilder

GetSystemVersion( ): RuntimeEnvironment

GetTempFileName( ): Path

GetTempPath( ): Path

GetTextElement( ): TextElementEnumerator

GetTextElementEnumerator( ): StringInfo

GetThreadFromFiberCookie( ): Marshal

GetToken( ): ConstructorBuilder, FieldBuilder, MethodBuilder, ParameterBuilder

GetTotalMemory( ): GC

GetType( ): AppDomain, Assembly, Module, ModuleBuilder, Object, Type

GetTypeArray( ): Type

GetTypeCode( ): Boolean, Byte, Char, Convert, DateTime, DBNull, Decimal, Double, Enum, IConvertible, Int16, Int32, Int64, SByte, Single, String, Type, UInt16, UInt32, UInt64

GetTypedObjectForIUnknown( ): Marshal

GetTypeForITypeInfo( ): Marshal

GetTypeFromAssembly( ): FormatterServices

GetTypeFromCLSID( ): Type

GetTypeFromHandle( ): Type

GetTypeFromProgID( ): Type

GetTypeHandle( ): Type

GetTypeInfoName( ): Marshal

GetTypeLibGuid( ): Marshal

GetTypeLibGuidForAssembly( ): Marshal

GetTypeLibLcid( ): Marshal

GetTypeLibName( ): Marshal

GetTypes( ): Assembly, Module, ModuleBuilder

GetTypeToken( ): ModuleBuilder

GetUInt16( ): SerializationInfo

GetUInt32( ): SerializationInfo

GetUInt64( ): SerializationInfo

GetUnderlyingType( ): Enum

GetUnicodeCategory( ): Char

GetUninitializedObject( ): FormatterServices

GetUnmanagedThunkForManagedMethodPtr( ): Marshal

GetUnmanagedType: UnmanagedMarshal

GetUpperBound( ): Array

GetUserStoreForAssembly( ): IsolatedStorage-File

GetUserStoreForDomain( ): IsolatedStorageFile

GetUtcOffset( ): TimeZone

GetValue( ): Array, FieldBuilder, FieldInfo, PropertyBuilder, PropertyInfo, RegistryKey, SerializationInfo

GetValueDirect( ): FieldInfo

GetValueList( ): SortedList

GetValueNames( ): RegistryKey

GetValues( ): Enum, NameValueCollection, WebHeaderCollection

GetVersionInfo( ): FileVersionInfo

GetWeekOfYear( ): Calendar

GetYear( ): Calendar, GregorianCalendar, HebrewCalendar, HijriCalendar, JapaneseCalendar, JulianCalendar, KoreanCalendar, TaiwanCalendar, ThaiBuddhistCalendar

Ggp: ProtocolType

GlobalAssemblyCache: Assembly

GlobalProxySelection: System.Net

Gone: HttpStatusCode

GregorianCalendar: System.Globalization

GregorianCalendarTypes: System.Globalization

Group: IPv6MulticastOption, MulticastOption, System.Text.RegularExpressions

GroupCollection: System.Text.RegularExpressions

GroupNameFromNumber( ): Regex

GroupNumberFromName( ): Regex

Groups: Match

Guid: System

GUID: EnumBuilder, Type, TypeBuilder, TypeDelegator

GuidAttribute: System.Runtime.InteropServices

H

Handle: FileStream, HandleRef, IsolatedStorageFileStream, Process, Socket, WaitHandle

HandleCount: Process

HandleRef: System.Runtime.InteropServices

HasAttribute( ): XmlElement

HasAttributes: XmlElement, XmlNodeReader, XmlReader, XPathNavigator

HasChildNodes: XmlNode

HasChildren: XPathNavigator

HasDefault: FieldAttributes, ParameterAttributes, PropertyAttributes

HasElementType: Type

HasElementTypeImpl( ): EnumBuilder, Type, TypeBuilder, TypeDelegator

HasExited: Process

HasExtension( ): Path

HasFeature( ): XmlImplementation

HasFieldMarshal: FieldAttributes, ParameterAttributes

HasFieldRVA: FieldAttributes

HashAlgorithm: AssemblyName

Hashtable: System.Collections

HasId( ): ObjectIDGenerator

HasKeys( ): NameValueCollection

HasLineInfo( ): IXmlLineInfo

HasNamespace( ): XmlNamespaceManager

HasSecurity: MethodAttributes, TypeAttributes

HasShutdownStarted: Environment

HasThis: CallingConventions

HasValue: XmlNodeReader, XmlReader, XmlTextReader, XmlValidatingReader

HaveResponse: HttpWebRequest

HeaderIncluded: SocketOptionName

HeaderName: Encoding

Headers: FileWebRequest, FileWebResponse, HttpWebRequest, HttpWebResponse, ISoapMessage, SoapMessage, WebClient, WebRequest, WebResponse

HebrewCalendar: System.Globalization

HebrewEra: HebrewCalendar

HelpLink: Exception

HexEscape( ): Uri

HexNumber: NumberStyles

HexUnescape( ): Uri

Hidden: FileAttributes, ProcessWindowStyle

HideBySig: MethodAttributes

High: ProcessPriorityClass

Highest: ThreadPriority, ThreadPriorityLevel

HijriAdjustment: HijriCalendar

HijriCalendar: System.Globalization

HijriEra: HijriCalendar

History: SpecialFolder

Host: SocketPermissionAttribute, Uri, UriBuilder

Hostname: EndpointPermission

HostName: IPHostEntry

HostNameType: Uri

HostToNetworkOrder( ): IPAddress

Hour: DateTime

Hours: TimeSpan

HttpContinueDelegate: System.Net

HttpStatusCode: System.Net

HttpVersion: System.Net

HttpVersionNotSupported: HttpStatusCode

HttpWebRequest: System.Net

HttpWebResponse: System.Net

HybridDictionary: System.Collections.Specialized

HyperChannel: AddressFamily, ProtocolFamily

I

I1: UnmanagedType

I2: UnmanagedType

I4: UnmanagedType

I8: UnmanagedType

IAsyncResult: System

IAuthenticationModule: System.Net

ICertificatePolicy: System.Net

ICloneable: System

Icmp: ProtocolType

ICollection: System.Collections

IComparable: System

IComparer: System.Collections

Icon: UserPreferenceCategory

IConvertible: System

ICredentials: System.Net

ICustomAttributeProvider: System.Reflection

ICustomFormatter: System

Id: Process, ProcessThread

ID: XmlTokenizedType

IdealProcessor: ProcessThread

IDeserializationCallback: System.Runtime.Serialization

IDictionary: System.Collections

IDictionaryEnumerator: System.Collections

IDispatch: UnmanagedType

IDispatchImplAttribute: System.Runtime.InteropServices

IDispatchImplType: System.Runtime.InteropServices

IDisposable: System

Idle: ProcessPriorityClass, ThreadPriorityLevel

IdleSince: ServicePoint

Idp: ProtocolType

IDREF: XmlTokenizedType

IDREFS: XmlTokenizedType

Ieee12844: AddressFamily, ProtocolFamily

IEEERemainder( ): Math

IEnumerable: System.Collections

IEnumerator: System.Collections

IFieldInfo: System.Runtime.Serialization.Formatters

IfModifiedSince: HttpWebRequest

IFormatProvider: System

IFormattable: System

IFormatter: System.Runtime.Serialization

IFormatterConverter: System.Runtime.Serialization

Igmp: ProtocolType

IgnoreCase: BindingFlags, CompareOptions, RegexOptions

IgnoreKanaType: CompareOptions

IgnoreNonSpace: CompareOptions

IgnorePatternWhitespace: RegexOptions

IgnoreReturn: BindingFlags

IgnoreSymbols: CompareOptions

IgnoreWidth: CompareOptions

IHashCodeProvider: System.Collections

IHasXmlNode: System.Xml

IIDGuid: UnmanagedMarshal

IL: MethodImplAttributes

ILGenerator: System.Reflection.Emit

IList: System.Collections

ImageRuntimeVersion: Assembly, AssemblyBuilder

Implementation: XmlDocument

ImpLink: AddressFamily, ProtocolFamily

Import: TypeAttributes

ImportNode( ): XmlDocument

In: Console, ParameterAttributes

InAttribute: System.Runtime.InteropServices

IncludeSubdirectories: FileSystemWatcher

Increment( ): Interlocked, PerformanceCounter

IncrementBy( ): PerformanceCounter

Indent( ): Debug, Trace

Indentation: XmlTextWriter

IndentChar: XmlTextWriter

Indented: Formatting

IndentLevel: Debug, Trace, TraceListener

IndentSize: Debug, Trace, TraceListener

Index: Capture, EventLogEntry

IndexOf( ): Array, ArrayList, CompareInfo, CounterCreationDataCollection, EventLogPermissionEntryCollection, IList, PerformanceCounterPermissionEntryCollection, ProcessModuleCollection, ProcessThreadCollection, String, StringCollection, TraceListenerCollection

IndexOfAny( ): String

IndexOfKey( ): SortedList

IndexOfValue( ): SortedList

IndexOutOfRangeException: System

Infinite: Timeout

Info: TraceLevel

Information: EventLogEntryType

InformationalVersion: AssemblyInformationalVersionAttribute

Inheritable: FileShare

Inherited: AttributeUsageAttribute

Initblk: OpCodes

Initial: ReadState

Initialize( ): Array

Initialized: ThreadState

InitializeLifetimeService( ): AppDomain, MarshalByRefObject

InitializeReferences( ): Regex

InitialQuotePunctuation: UnicodeCategory

InitLocals: ConstructorBuilder, MethodBuilder

Initobj: OpCodes

InitOnly: FieldAttributes

InitStore( ): IsolatedStorage

InlineBrTarget: OperandType

InlineField: OperandType

InlineI: OperandType

InlineI8: OperandType

InlineMethod: OperandType

InlineNone: OperandType

InlinePhi: OperandType

InlineR: OperandType

InlineSig: OperandType

InlineString: OperandType

InlineSwitch: OperandType

InlineTok: OperandType

InlineType: OperandType

InlineVar: OperandType

InnerException: Exception

InnerText: XmlAttribute, XmlCharacterData, XmlDeclaration, XmlElement, XmlEntity, XmlNode, XmlProcessingInstruction

InnerXml: XmlAttribute, XmlDocument, XmlDocumentFragment, XmlElement, XmlEntity, XmlNode, XmlNotation

INormalizeForIsolatedStorage: System.IO. IsolatedStorage

Insert: XmlNodeChangedAction

Insert( ): ArrayList, CounterCreationDataCollection, EventLogPermissionEntryCollection, IList, PerformanceCounterPermissionEntryCollection, ProcessThreadCollection, String, StringBuilder, StringCollection, TraceListenerCollection

InsertAfter( ): XmlAttributeCollection, XmlNode

InsertBefore( ): XmlAttributeCollection, XmlNode

InsertData( ): XmlCharacterData

InsertRange( ): ArrayList

Install( ): EventLogInstaller, PerformanceCounterInstaller

InstalledFontsChanged: SystemEvents

InstalledUICulture: CultureInfo

InstalledWin32Cultures: CultureTypes

Instance: BindingFlags

InstanceData: System.Diagnostics

InstanceDataCollection: System.Diagnostics

InstanceDataCollectionCollection: System. Diagnostics

InstanceExists( ): PerformanceCounterCategory

InstanceName: InstanceData, PerformanceCounter

Instrument: EventLogPermissionAccess, PerformanceCounterPermissionAccess

Int16: System, TypeCode

Int32: System, TypeCode

Int64: System, TypeCode

Int64BitsToDouble( ): BitConverter

Integer: NumberStyles

Interactive: ReadState

Interface: AttributeTargets, TypeAttributes, UnmanagedType

InterfaceIndex: IPv6MulticastOption

InterfaceIsDual: ComInterfaceType

InterfaceIsIDispatch: ComInterfaceType

InterfaceIsIUnknown: ComInterfaceType

InterfaceMapping: System.Reflection

InterfaceMethods: InterfaceMapping

InterfaceType: InterfaceMapping

InterfaceTypeAttribute: System.Runtime. InteropServices

Interlocked: System.Threading

Intern( ): String

InternalBufferOverflowException: System.IO

InternalBufferSize: FileSystemWatcher

InternalCall: MethodImplAttributes

InternalHigh: NativeOverlapped

InternalImpl: IDispatchImplType

InternalLow: NativeOverlapped

InternalName: FileVersionInfo

InternalServerError: HttpStatusCode

InternalSubset: XmlDocumentType, XmlParser-Context

InternalValidationEventHandler: XmlValidatingReader

InternetCache: SpecialFolder

InterNetwork: AddressFamily, ProtocolFamily

InterNetworkV6: AddressFamily, ProtocolFamily

Interrupt( ): Thread

Intersect( ): DnsPermission, SocketPermission, WebPermission

Interval: Timer

IntPtr: System

InvalidateCachedArrays( ): NameValueCollection

InvalidCastException: System

InvalidComObjectException: System.Runtime.InteropServices

InvalidFilterCriteriaException: System.Reflection

InvalidHandle: WaitHandle

InvalidOleVariantTypeException: System.Runtime.InteropServices

InvalidOperationException: System

InvalidPathChars: Path

InvalidProgramException: System

InvariantCulture: CultureInfo

InvariantInfo: DateTimeFormatInfo, NumberFormatInfo

Invoke( ): AssemblyLoadEventHandler, AsyncCallback, ConstructorBuilder, ConstructorInfo, CrossAppDomainDelegate, ElapsedEventHandler, EntryWrittenEventHandler, ErrorEventHandler, EventHandler, FileSystemEventHandler, HttpContinueDelegate, IOCompletionCallback, IXsltContextFunction, MatchEvaluator, MemberFilter, MethodBase, MethodBuilder, ModuleResolveEventHandler, ObjectCreationDelegate, PowerModeChangedEventHandler, RenamedEventHandler, ResolveEventHandler, SessionEndedEventHandler, SessionEndingEventHandler, ThreadExceptionEventHandler, ThreadStart, TimerCallback, TimerElapsedEventHandler, TypeFilter, UnhandledExceptionEventHandler, UserPreferenceChangedEventHandler, UserPreferenceChangingEventHandler, WaitCallback, WaitOrTimerCallback, XmlNodeChangedEventHandler

InvokeMember( ): EnumBuilder, IReflect, Type, TypeBuilder, TypeDelegator

InvokeMethod: BindingFlags

InvokeOnEventsThread( ): SystemEvents

IObjectReference: System.Runtime.Serialization

IOCompletionCallback: System.Threading

IOControl( ): Socket

IODescriptionAttribute: System.IO

IOException: System.IO

IP: ProtocolType, SocketOptionLevel

IPAddress: System.Net

IPEndPoint: System.Net

IPHostEntry: System.Net

IPOptions: SocketOptionName

IpTimeToLive: SocketOptionName

IPv4: UriHostNameType

IPv6: ProtocolType, SocketOptionLevel, UriHostNameType

IPv6Any: IPAddress

IPv6Loopback: IPAddress

IPv6MulticastOption: System.Net.Sockets

IPv6None: IPAddress

Ipx: AddressFamily, ProtocolFamily, ProtocolType

Irda: AddressFamily, ProtocolFamily

IReflect: System.Reflection

IRegistrationServices: System.Runtime.InteropServices

IsAbstract: MethodBase, Type

IsAlive: Thread, WeakReference

IsAllocated: GCHandle

IsAnsiClass: Type

IsArray: Type

IsArrayImpl( ): EnumBuilder, Type, TypeBuilder, TypeDelegator

IsAssembly: FieldInfo, MethodBase

IsAssignableFrom( ): Type, TypeBuilder

IsAsync: FileStream, IsolatedStorageFileStream

IsAttached: Debugger

IsAutoClass: Type

IsAutoLayout: Type

IsBackground: Thread

IsBadFileSystemCharacter( ): Uri

IsBrowserDisplay: Encoding

IsBrowserSave: Encoding

IsBypassed( ): IWebProxy, WebProxy

IsByRef: Type

IsByRefImpl( ): EnumBuilder, Type, Type-
Builder, TypeDelegator

IsClass: Type

IsCOMObject: Type

IsComObject( ): Marshal

IsCOMObjectImpl( ): EnumBuilder, Type, Type-
Builder, TypeDelegator

IsCompleted: IAsyncResult

IsCompliant: CLSCompliantAttribute

IsConstructor: MethodBase

IsContextful: Type

IsContextfulImpl( ): Type

IsControl( ): Char

IsDaylightSavingTime( ): TimeZone

IsDBNull( ): Convert

IsDebug: FileVersionInfo

IsDefault: XmlNodeReader, XmlReader, XmlTextReader, XmlValidatingReader

IsDefaultAttribute( ): Attribute

IsDefaultPort: Uri

IsDefined( ): Assembly, Attribute, Constructor-
Builder, Enum, EnumBuilder, FieldBuilder,
ICustomAttributeProvider, MemberInfo,
MethodBuilder, Module, ParameterInfo, Prop-
ertyBuilder, TypeBuilder, TypeDelegator

IsDescendant( ): XPathNavigator

IsDigit( ): Char

IsEmpty: XmlElement, XmlQualifiedName

IsEmptyElement: XmlNodeReader, XmlReader,
XmlTextReader, XmlValidatingReader, XPath-
Navigator

IsEnum: Type

IsEquivalentInstaller( ): EventLogInstaller

ISerializable: System.Runtime.Serialization

ISerializationSurrogate: System.Runtime.Seri-
alization

IsError: ObsoleteAttribute

IServiceProvider: System

IsExcludedCharacter( ): Uri

IsExplicitLayout: Type

IsFamily: FieldInfo, MethodBase

IsFamilyAndAssembly: FieldInfo, MethodBase

IsFamilyOrAssembly: FieldInfo, MethodBase

IsFile: Uri

IsFinal: MethodBase

IsFinalizingForUnload( ): AppDomain

IsFixedSize: Array, ArrayList, Hashtable, Hybrid-
Dictionary, IDictionary, IList, ListDictionary,
SortedList

IsHexDigit( ): Uri

IsHexEncoding( ): Uri

IsHideBySig: MethodBase

IsImport: Type

IsIn: ParameterBuilder, ParameterInfo

IsInfinity( ): Double, Single

IsInitOnly: FieldInfo

Isinst: OpCodes

IsInstanceOfType( ): Type

IsInterface: Type

IsInterned( ): String

IsJITOptimizerDisabled: DebuggableAttribute

IsJITTrackingEnabled: DebuggableAttribute

IsLayoutSequential: Type

IsLcid: ParameterInfo

IsLeapDay( ): Calendar, GregorianCalendar,
HebrewCalendar, HijriCalendar, JapaneseCal-
endar, JulianCalendar, KoreanCalendar,
TaiwanCalendar, ThaiBuddhistCalendar

IsLeapMonth( ): Calendar, GregorianCalendar,
HebrewCalendar, HijriCalendar, JapaneseCal-
endar, JulianCalendar, KoreanCalendar,
TaiwanCalendar, ThaiBuddhistCalendar

IsLeapYear( ): Calendar, DateTime, Gregorian-
Calendar, HebrewCalendar, HijriCalendar,
JapaneseCalendar, JulianCalendar, KoreanCal-
endar, TaiwanCalendar, ThaiBuddhistCalendar

IsLetter( ): Char

IsLetterOrDigit( ): Char

IsLiteral: FieldInfo

IsLittleEndian: BitConverter

IsLocal: IXsltContextVariable

IsLogging( ): Debugger

IsLoopback: Uri

IsLoopback( ): IPAddress

IsLower( ): Char

IsMailNewsDisplay: Encoding

IsMailNewsSave: Encoding

IsMarshalByRef: Type

IsMarshalByRefImpl( ): Type

IsMatch( ): Regex

IsMetric: RegionInfo

IsMulticast: EventInfo

IsName( ): XmlReader

IsNameToken( ): XmlReader

IsNaN( ): Double, Single

IsNegativeInfinity( ): Double, Single

IsNestedAssembly: Type

IsNestedFamANDAssem: Type

IsNestedFamily: Type

IsNestedFamORAssem: Type

IsNestedPrivate: Type

IsNestedPublic: Type

IsNeutralCulture: CultureInfo

IsNotPublic: Type

IsNotSerialized: FieldInfo

IsNumber( ): Char

Iso: AddressFamily, ProtocolFamily

ISoapMessage: System.Runtime.Serialization. Formatters

ISOCurrencySymbol: RegionInfo

IsolatedStorage: System.IO.IsolatedStorage

IsolatedStorageException: System.IO.Isolat- edStorage

IsolatedStorageFile: System.IO.IsolatedStorage

IsolatedStorageFileStream: System.IO.Isolat- edStorage

IsolatedStorageScope: System.IO.Isolat- edStorage

IsOptional: ParameterBuilder, ParameterInfo

IsOut: ParameterBuilder, ParameterInfo

IsParam: IXsltContextVariable

IsPatched: FileVersionInfo

IsPathRooted( ): Path

IsPinvokeImpl: FieldInfo

IsPointer: Type

IsPointerImpl( ): EnumBuilder, Type, Type- Builder, TypeDelegator

IsPositiveInfinity( ): Double, Single

IsPrefix( ): CompareInfo

IsPreRelease: FileVersionInfo

IsPrimitive: Type

IsPrimitiveImpl( ): EnumBuilder, Type, Type- Builder, TypeDelegator

IsPrivate: FieldInfo, MethodBase

IsPrivateBuild: FileVersionInfo

IsPublic: FieldInfo, MethodBase, RegexCompila- tionInfo, Type

IsPunctuation( ): Char

IsReaderLockHeld: ReaderWriterLock

IsReadOnly: Array, ArrayList, BitArray, CaptureC- ollection, CookieCollection, CultureInfo, DateTimeFormatInfo, GroupCollection, Hash- table, HybridDictionary, IDictionary, IList, List- Dictionary, MatchCollection, NumberFormat- Info, SortedList, StringCollection, XmlDocument, XmlDocumentType, XmlEn- tity, XmlEntityReference, XmlNode, XmlNota- tion

IsReservedCharacter( ): Uri

IsResource( ): Module

IsRestricted( ): WebHeaderCollection

IsRetval: ParameterInfo

IsSamePosition( ): XPathNavigator

IsSealed: Type

IsSeparator( ): Char

IsSerializable: Type

IsSpecialBuild: FileVersionInfo

IsSpecialName: EventInfo, FieldInfo, Method- Base, PropertyInfo, Type

IsStartElement( ): XmlReader

IsStatic: FieldInfo, MethodBase

IsSubclassOf( ): Type, TypeBuilder

IsSubsetOf( ): DnsPermission, SocketPermis- sion, WebPermission

IsSuffix( ): CompareInfo

IsSurrogate( ): Char

IsSymbol( ): Char

IsSynchronized: Array, ArrayList, BitArray, CaptureCollection, CookieCollection, GroupC- ollection, Hashtable, HybridDictionary, ICollec- tion, ListDictionary, MatchCollection, Queue, SortedList, Stack, StringCollection, StringDic- tionary

IsTerminating: UnhandledExceptionEventArgs

IsThreadPoolThread: Thread

IsTransient( ): ModuleBuilder
IsTypeVisibleFromCom( ): Marshal
IsUnc: Uri
IsUnicodeClass: Type
IsUnrestricted( ): DnsPermission, SocketPermission, WebPermission
IsUpper( ): Char
ISurrogateSelector: System.Runtime.Serialization
IsValueType: Type
IsValueTypeImpl( ): EnumBuilder, Type, TypeDelegator
IsVirtual: MethodBase
IsWhiteSpace( ): Char
IsWriterLockHeld: ReaderWriterLock
Item: ArrayList, BitArray, BitVector32, CaptureCollection, CookieCollection, CounterCreationDataCollection, EventLogEntryCollection, EventLogPermissionEntryCollection, GroupCollection, Hashtable, HybridDictionary, IDictionary, IList, InstanceDataCollection, InstanceDataCollectionCollection, KeysCollection, ListDictionary, MatchCollection, NameValueCollection, ParameterModifier, PerformanceCounterPermissionEntryCollection, ProcessModuleCollection, ProcessThreadCollection, SocketAddress, SortedList, StringCollection, StringDictionary, TraceListenerCollection, XmlNode, XmlNodeReader, XmlReader, XmlTextReader, XmlValidatingReader
Item( ): XmlNamedNodeMap, XmlNodeList
ItemOf: XmlAttributeCollection, XmlNodeList
IUnknown: UnmanagedType
IWebProxy: System.Net
IWebRequestCreate: System.Net
IXmlLineInfo: System.Xml
IXPathNavigable: System.Xml.XPath
IXsltContextFunction: System.Xml.Xsl
IXsltContextVariable: System.Xml.Xsl

J

JapaneseCalendar: System.Globalization
JitImmediate: MethodRental
JitOnDemand: MethodRental
Jmp: OpCodes

Join( ): String, Thread
JoinMulticastGroup( ): UdpClient
JulianCalendar: System.Globalization
JulianEra: JulianCalendar

K

KeepAlive: HttpWebRequest, SocketOptionName
KeepAlive( ): GC
KeepAliveFailure: WebExceptionStatus
Key: DictionaryEntry, IDictionaryEnumerator
Keyboard: UserPreferenceCategory
KeyData: SortKey
KeyEquals( ): Hashtable
KeyFile: AssemblyKeyFileAttribute
KeyName: AssemblyKeyNameAttribute
KeyPair: AssemblyName
Keys: Hashtable, HybridDictionary, IDictionary, InstanceDataCollection, InstanceDataCollectionCollection, ListDictionary, NameObjectCollectionBase, SortedList, StringDictionary
KeysCollection: System.Collections.Specialized
Kill( ): Process
KillTimer( ): SystemEvents
KoreanCalendar: System.Globalization
KoreanEra: KoreanCalendar

L

Label: System.Reflection.Emit
Language: FileVersionInfo
LastAccess: NotifyFilters
LastAccessTime: FileSystemInfo
LastAccessTimeUtc: FileSystemInfo
LastChild: XmlNode
LastIndexOf( ): Array, ArrayList, CompareInfo, String
LastIndexOfAny( ): String
LastModified: HttpWebResponse
LastWrite: NotifyFilters
LastWriteTime: FileSystemInfo
LastWriteTimeUtc: FileSystemInfo
Lat: AddressFamily, ProtocolFamily
Launch( ): Debugger
LayoutKind: System.Runtime.InteropServices

LayoutMask: TypeAttributes

Lcid: ParameterAttributes

LCID: CompareInfo, CultureInfo

LCIDConversionAttribute: System.Runtime.
InteropServices

Ldarg: OpCodes

Ldarg_0: OpCodes

Ldarg_1: OpCodes

Ldarg_2: OpCodes

Ldarg_3: OpCodes

Ldarg_S: OpCodes

Ldarga: OpCodes

Ldarga_S: OpCodes

Ldc_I4: OpCodes

Ldc_I4_0: OpCodes

Ldc_I4_1: OpCodes

Ldc_I4_2: OpCodes

Ldc_I4_3: OpCodes

Ldc_I4_4: OpCodes

Ldc_I4_5: OpCodes

Ldc_I4_6: OpCodes

Ldc_I4_7: OpCodes

Ldc_I4_8: OpCodes

Ldc_I4_M1: OpCodes

Ldc_I4_S: OpCodes

Ldc_I8: OpCodes

Ldc_R4: OpCodes

Ldc_R8: OpCodes

Ldelem_I: OpCodes

Ldelem_I1: OpCodes

Ldelem_I2: OpCodes

Ldelem_I4: OpCodes

Ldelem_I8: OpCodes

Ldelem_R4: OpCodes

Ldelem_R8: OpCodes

Ldelem_Ref: OpCodes

Ldelem_U1: OpCodes

Ldelem_U2: OpCodes

Ldelem_U4: OpCodes

Ldelema: OpCodes

Ldfld: OpCodes

Ldflda: OpCodes

Ldftn: OpCodes

Ldind_I: OpCodes

Ldind_I1: OpCodes

Ldind_I2: OpCodes

Ldind_I4: OpCodes

Ldind_I8: OpCodes

Ldind_R4: OpCodes

Ldind_R8: OpCodes

Ldind_Ref: OpCodes

Ldind_U1: OpCodes

Ldind_U2: OpCodes

Ldind_U4: OpCodes

Ldlen: OpCodes

Ldloc: OpCodes

Ldloc_0: OpCodes

Ldloc_1: OpCodes

Ldloc_2: OpCodes

Ldloc_3: OpCodes

Ldloc_S: OpCodes

Ldloca: OpCodes

Ldloca_S: OpCodes

Ldnull: OpCodes

Ldobj: OpCodes

Ldsfld: OpCodes

Ldsflda: OpCodes

Ldstr: OpCodes

Ldtoken: OpCodes

Ldvirtftn: OpCodes

Leave: OpCodes

Leave_S: OpCodes

LeaveDebugMode( ): Process

LegalCopyright: FileVersionInfo

LegalTrademarks: FileVersionInfo

Length: Array, BitArray, BufferedStream,
Capture, FileInfo, FileStream, IsolatedStorage-
FileStream, MemoryStream, NetworkStream,
Stream, String, StringBuilder, XmlCharacter-
Data

LengthRequired: HttpStatusCode

LetterNumber: UnicodeCategory

Level: TraceSwitch

LicenseFile: AppDomainSetup

LineNumber: IXmlLineInfo, XmlException,
XmlTextReader, XsltException

LinePosition: IXmlLineInfo, XmlException, XmlTextReader, XsltException

LineSeparator: UnicodeCategory

Linger: SocketOptionName

LingerOption: System.Net.Sockets

LingerState: TcpClient

LingerTime: LingerOption

ListDictionary: System.Collections.Specialized

Listen( ): Socket

Listeners: Debug, Trace

ListSeparator: TextInfo

Literal: FieldAttributes

Load( ): AppDomain, Assembly, XmlDataDocument, XmlDocument, XslTransform

LoadedAssembly: AssemblyLoadEventArgs

LoaderExceptions: ReflectionTypeLoadException

LoaderOptimization: AppDomainSetup, System

LoaderOptimizationAttribute: System

LoadFile( ): Assembly

LoadFrom( ): Assembly

LoadModule( ): Assembly

LoadWithPartialName( ): Assembly

LoadXml( ): XmlDocument

Local: XPathNamespaceScope

LocalAddress: MulticastOption

LocalApplicationData: SpecialFolder

LocalBuilder: System.Reflection.Emit

LocalDataStoreSlot: System

Locale: UserPreferenceCategory

LocalEndpoint: TcpListener

LocalEndPoint: Socket

Localized: GregorianCalendarTypes

Localloc: OpCodes

LocalMachine: Registry, RegistryHive

LocalName: XmlAttribute, XmlCDataSection, XmlComment, XmlDeclaration, XmlDocument, XmlDocumentFragment, XmlDocumentType, XmlElement, XmlEntity, XmlEntityReference, XmlNode, XmlNodeReader, XmlNotation, XmlProcessingInstruction, XmlReader, XmlSignificantWhitespace, XmlText, XmlTextReader, XmlValidatingReader, XmlWhitespace, XPathNavigator

LocalPath: Uri

LocalType: LocalBuilder

Location: Assembly, AssemblyBuilder

Lock( ): FileStream

LockCookie: System.Threading

Log: EventLog, EventLogInstaller

Log( ): Debugger, Math

Log10( ): Math

LogDisplayName: EventLog

LogFileName: DefaultTraceListener

LogNameFromSourceName( ): EventLog

Logoff: SessionEndReasons

LongDatePattern: DateTimeFormatInfo

LongLength: Array

LongTimePattern: DateTimeFormatInfo

LookupNamespace( ): XmlNamespaceManager, XmlNodeReader, XmlReader, XmlTextReader, XmlValidatingReader

LookupPrefix( ): XmlNamespaceManager, XmlTextWriter, XmlWriter

Loopback: IPAddress

Low: TypeFilterLevel

LowercaseLetter: UnicodeCategory

LowerFirst: XmlCaseOrder

Lowest: ThreadPriority, ThreadPriorityLevel

LowMemory: SystemEvents

LPArray: UnmanagedType

LpcReceive: ThreadWaitReason

LpcReply: ThreadWaitReason

LPStr: UnmanagedType

LPStruct: UnmanagedType

LPTStr: UnmanagedType

LPWStr: UnmanagedType

m

m_idGenerator: Formatter

m_objectQueue: Formatter

MacCodePage: TextInfo

MachineName: Environment, EventLog, EventLogEntry, EventLogPermissionAttribute, EventLogPermissionEntry, PerformanceCounter, PerformanceCounterCategory, PerformanceCounterPermissionAttribute, PerformanceCounterPermissionEntry, Process

Macro: OpCodeType

MainModule: Process

MainWindowHandle: Process

MainWindowTitle: Process

Major: Version

MajorVersion: ComCompatibleVersionAttribute, TypeLibVersionAttribute

MakeRelative( ): Uri

Managed: MethodImplAttributes

ManagedMask: MethodImplAttributes

ManifestResourceInfo: System.Reflection

ManualResetEvent: System.Threading

MarkLabel( ): ILGenerator

MarkSequencePoint( ): ILGenerator

Marshal: System.Runtime.InteropServices

MarshalAsAttribute: System.Runtime.InteropServices

MarshalByRefObject: System

MarshalCookie: MarshalAsAttribute

MarshalDirectiveException: System.Runtime.InteropServices

MarshalType: MarshalAsAttribute

MarshalTypeRef: MarshalAsAttribute

Mask: Section

Match: System.Text.RegularExpressions

Match( ): Attribute, Regex

MatchCollection: System.Text.RegularExpressions

Matches( ): Regex, XPathNavigator

MatchEvaluator: System.Text.RegularExpressions

Math: System

MathSymbol: UnicodeCategory

Max: AddressFamily, ProtocolFamily

Max( ): Math

Maxargs: IXsltContextFunction

MaxCapacity: StringBuilder

MaxConnections: SocketOptionName

MaxCookieSize: CookieContainer

MaxGeneration: GC

MaxIdleTime: ServicePoint

Maximized: ProcessWindowStyle

MaximumAutomaticRedirections: HttpWebRequest

MaximumResponseHeadersLength: HttpWebRequest

MaximumSize: IsolatedStorage, IsolatedStorageFile

MaxIOVectorLength: SocketFlags

MaxMethodImplVal: MethodImplAttributes

MaxPort: IPEndPoint

MaxServicePointIdleTime: ServicePointManager

MaxServicePoints: ServicePointManager

MaxValue: Byte, Char, DateTime, Decimal, Double, Int16, Int32, Int64, SByte, Single, TimeSpan, UInt16, UInt32, UInt64

MaxWorkingSet: Process

MediaType: HttpWebRequest

Member: ParameterInfo

MemberAccessException: System

MemberAccessMask: MethodAttributes

MemberCount: SerializationInfo

MemberFilter: System.Reflection

MemberImpl: ParameterInfo

MemberInfo: System.Reflection

MemberName: DefaultMemberAttribute, MissingMemberException

MemberType: ConstructorInfo, EventInfo, FieldInfo, MemberInfo, MethodInfo, PropertyInfo, Type

MemberTypes: System.Reflection

MemberwiseClone( ): Object

MemoryBarrier( ): Thread

MemoryStream: System.IO

Menu: UserPreferenceCategory

Message: ArgumentException, ArgumentOutOfRangeException, Authorization, BadImageFormatException, EventLogEntry, Exception, FileLoadException, FileNotFoundException, MissingFieldException, MissingMemberException, MissingMethodException, ObjectDisposedException, ObsoleteAttribute, TypeLoadException, XmlException, XPathException, XsltCompileException, XsltException

MessageLengthLimitExceeded: WebExceptionStatus

Meta: FlowControl

Method: AttributeTargets, ComMemberType, Delegate, FileWebRequest, HttpWebRequest,

HttpWebResponse, MemberTypes, WebRequest

MethodAccessException: System

MethodAttributes: System.Reflection

MethodBase: System.Reflection

MethodBuilder: System.Reflection.Emit

MethodHandle: ConstructorBuilder, MethodBase, MethodBuilder

MethodImplAttributes: System.Reflection

MethodInfo: System.Reflection

MethodName: ISoapMessage, SoapMessage

MethodNotAllowed: HttpStatusCode

MethodRental: System.Reflection.Emit

METHODS_TO_SKIP: StackTrace

MethodToken: System.Reflection.Emit

MiddleEastFrench: GregorianCalendarTypes

Millisecond: DateTime

Milliseconds: TimeSpan

Min( ): Math

Minargs: IXsltContextFunction

Minimized: ProcessWindowStyle

Minor: Version

MinorVersion: ComCompatibleVersionAttribute, TypeLibVersionAttribute

MinPort: IPEndPoint

MinusOne: Decimal

Minute: DateTime

Minutes: TimeSpan

MinValue: Byte, Char, DateTime, Decimal, Double, Int16, Int32, Int64, SByte, Single, TimeSpan, UInt16, UInt32, UInt64

MinWorkingSet: Process

Missing: System.Reflection, Type

MissingFieldException: System

MissingMemberException: System

MissingMethodException: System

Mkrefany: OpCodes

Mode: PowerModeChangedEventArgs

ModifierLetter: UnicodeCategory

ModifierSymbol: UnicodeCategory

Module: AttributeTargets, EnumBuilder, System.Reflection, Type, TypeBuilder, TypeDelegator

ModuleBuilder: System.Reflection.Emit

ModuleMemorySize: ProcessModule

ModuleName: ProcessModule

ModuleResolve: Assembly

ModuleResolveEventHandler: System.Reflection

Modules: Process

Monday: DayOfWeek

Monitor: System.Threading

MonitoringDescriptionAttribute: System.Diagnostics

Month: DateTime

MonthDayPattern: DateTimeFormatInfo

MonthNames: DateTimeFormatInfo

Mouse: UserPreferenceCategory

Move( ): Directory, File

Moved: HttpStatusCode

MovedPermanently: HttpStatusCode

MoveNext( ): CharEnumerator, IEnumerator, SerializationInfoEnumerator, StringEnumerator, TextElementEnumerator, XPathNodeIterator

MoveTo( ): DirectoryInfo, FileInfo, XPathNavigator

MoveToAttribute( ): XmlNodeReader, XmlReader, XmlTextReader, XmlValidatingReader, XPathNavigator

MoveToContent( ): XmlReader

MoveToElement( ): XmlNodeReader, XmlReader, XmlTextReader, XmlValidatingReader

MoveToFirst( ): XPathNavigator

MoveToFirstAttribute( ): XmlNodeReader, XmlReader, XmlTextReader, XmlValidatingReader, XPathNavigator

MoveToFirstChild( ): XPathNavigator

MoveToFirstNamespace( ): XPathNavigator

MoveToId( ): XPathNavigator

MoveToNamespace( ): XPathNavigator

MoveToNext( ): XPathNavigator

MoveToNextAttribute( ): XmlNodeReader, XmlReader, XmlTextReader, XmlValidatingReader, XPathNavigator

MoveToNextNamespace( ): XPathNavigator

MoveToParent( ): XPathNavigator

MoveToPrevious( ): XPathNavigator

MoveToRoot( ): XPathNavigator

MTA: ApartmentState

MTAThreadAttribute: System

Mul: OpCodes

Mul_Ovf: OpCodes

Mul_Ovf_Un: OpCodes

MulticastDelegate: System

MulticastInterface: SocketOptionName

MulticastLoopback: SocketOptionName

MulticastNotSupportedException: System

MulticastOption: System.Net.Sockets

MulticastTimeToLive: SocketOptionName

MultiDomain: LoaderOptimization

MultiDomainHost: LoaderOptimization

Multiline: RegexOptions

MultipleChoices: HttpStatusCode

Multiply( ): Decimal

Mutex: System.Threading

MyComputer: SpecialFolder

MyMusic: SpecialFolder

MyPictures: SpecialFolder

N

Name: AssemblyName, ConstructorBuilder, Cookie, CultureInfo, DirectoryInfo, Enum-Builder, EventLogTraceListener, FieldBuilder, FileInfo, FileStream, FileSystemEventArgs, FileSystemInfo, MemberInfo, MethodBuilder, Module, OpCode, ParameterBuilder, Parame-terInfo, PropertyBuilder, RegexCompilation-Info, RegionInfo, RegistryKey, ResolveEven-tArgs, SerializationEntry, SerializationInfoEnumerator, Thread, TraceLis-tener, TypeBuilder, TypeDelegator, Wait-ForChangedResult, XmlAttribute, XmlCData-Section, XmlComment, XmlDeclaration, XmlDocument, XmlDocumentFragment, XmlDocumentType, XmlElement, XmlEntity, XmlEntityReference, XmlNode, XmlNo-deReader, XmlNotation, XmlProcessingIn-struction, XmlQualifiedName, XmlReader, XmlSignificantWhitespace, XmlText, XmlTex-tReader, XmlValidatingReader, XmlWhitespace, XPathNavigator

NameImpl: ParameterInfo

NameObjectCollectionBase: System.Collec-tions.Specialized

NameResolutionFailure: WebExceptionStatus

Namespace: EnumBuilder, RegexCompilation-Info, Type, TypeBuilder, TypeDelegator, XmlQualifiedName, XPathNodeType

NamespaceManager: XmlParserContext

Namespaces: XmlTextReader, XmlTextWriter, XmlValidatingReader

NamespaceURI: XmlAttribute, XmlElement, XmlNode, XmlNodeReader, XmlReader, XmlTextReader, XmlValidatingReader, XPath-Navigator

NameTable: System.Xml, XmlDocument, XmlNamespaceManager, XmlNodeReader, XmlParserContext, XmlReader, XmlTex-tReader, XmlValidatingReader, XPathNavi-gator

NameValueCollection: System.Collections. Specialized

NaN: Double, Single

NaNSymbol: NumberFormatInfo

Native: MethodImplAttributes

NativeName: CultureInfo

NativeOverlapped: System.Threading

Navigator: XPathResultType

NCName: XmlTokenizedType

ND: ProtocolType

Neg: OpCodes

Negate( ): Decimal, TimeSpan

NegativeInfinity: Double, Single

NegativeInfinitySymbol: NumberFormatInfo

NegativeSign: NumberFormatInfo

NestedAssembly: TypeAttributes

NestedFamANDAssem: TypeAttributes

NestedFamily: TypeAttributes

NestedFamORAssem: TypeAttributes

NestedPrivate: TypeAttributes

NestedPublic: TypeAttributes

NestedType: MemberTypes

NetBios: AddressFamily, ProtocolFamily

NetworkAccess: System.Net

NetworkCredential: System.Net

NetworkDesigners: AddressFamily, Protocol-Family

NetworkStream: System.Net.Sockets

NetworkToHostOrder( ): IPAddress

OpenStandardError( ): Console

OpenStandardInput( ): Console

OpenStandardOutput( ): Console

OpenSubKey( ): RegistryKey

OpenText( ): File, FileInfo

OpenWrite( ): File, FileInfo, WebClient

OperandType: OpCode, System.Reflection.Emit

OperatingSystem: System

OPTIL: MethodImplAttributes

Optional: ParameterAttributes

OptionalAttribute: System.Runtime.InteropServices

OptionalCalendars: CultureInfo

OptionalParamBinding: BindingFlags

Options: Regex, RegexCompilationInfo

Or: OpCodes

Or( ): BitArray

Ordinal: CompareOptions

OriginalFilename: FileVersionInfo

OriginalPath: FileSystemInfo

OriginalString: SortKey

Osi: AddressFamily, ProtocolFamily

OSVersion: Environment

Other: StreamingContextStates

OtherLetter: UnicodeCategory

OtherNotAssigned: UnicodeCategory

OtherNumber: UnicodeCategory

OtherPunctuation: UnicodeCategory

OtherSymbol: UnicodeCategory

Out: Console, ParameterAttributes

OutAttribute: System.Runtime.InteropServices

OuterXml: XmlEntity, XmlNode, XmlNotation

OutOfBand: SocketFlags

OutOfBandInline: SocketOptionName

OutOfMemoryException: System

OutStream: BinaryWriter

OverflowException: System

Overlapped: System.Threading

OwnerDocument: XmlAttribute, XmlDocument, XmlDocumentFragment, XmlElement, XmlNode

OwnerElement: XmlAttribute

P

Pack: StructLayoutAttribute

Pack( ): Overlapped

PacketInformation: SocketOptionName

PackingSize: System.Reflection.Emit, TypeBuilder

PadLeft( ): String

PadRight( ): String

PagedMemorySize: Process

PagedSystemMemorySize: Process

PageIn: ThreadWaitReason

PageOut: ThreadWaitReason

PaletteChanged: SystemEvents

ParagraphSeparator: UnicodeCategory

ParamArrayAttribute: System

Parameter: AttributeTargets

ParameterAttributes: System.Reflection

ParameterBuilder: System.Reflection.Emit

ParameterInfo: System.Reflection

ParameterModifier: System.Reflection

ParameterToken: System.Reflection.Emit

ParameterType: ParameterInfo

ParamName: ArgumentException

ParamNames: ISoapMessage, SoapMessage

ParamTypes: ISoapMessage, SoapMessage

ParamValues: ISoapMessage, SoapMessage

Parent: CultureInfo, DirectoryInfo

ParentNode: XmlAttribute, XmlDocumentFragment, XmlNode

Parse( ): Boolean, Byte, Char, DateTime, Decimal, Double, Enum, Int16, Int32, Int64, IPAddress, SByte, Single, TimeSpan, UInt16, UInt32, UInt64, Uri

ParseCombiningCharacters( ): StringInfo

ParseExact( ): DateTime

Partial: SocketFlags

PartialContent: HttpStatusCode

Password: NetworkCredential, UriBuilder

Path: Cookie, FileSystemWatcher, System.IO, UriBuilder, UriPartial

PathAndQuery: Uri

PathSeparator: Path

PathTooLongException: System.IO

Pattern: RegexCompilationInfo

PaymentRequired: HttpStatusCode

PeakPagedMemorySize: Process

PeakVirtualMemorySize: Process

PeakWorkingSet: Process

Peek: SocketFlags

Peek( ): Queue, Stack, StreamReader, StringReader, TextReader

PeekChar( ): BinaryReader

PEFileKinds: System.Reflection.Emit

Pending: WebExceptionStatus

Pending( ): TcpListener

PercentDecimalDigits: NumberFormatInfo

PercentDecimalSeparator: NumberFormatInfo

PercentGroupSeparator: NumberFormatInfo

PercentGroupSizes: NumberFormatInfo

PercentNegativePattern: NumberFormatInfo

PercentPositivePattern: NumberFormatInfo

PercentSymbol: NumberFormatInfo

PerDomainCapacity: CookieContainer

PerformanceCounter: System.Diagnostics

PerformanceCounterCategory: System.Diagnostics

PerformanceCounterInstaller: System.Diagnostics

PerformanceCounterPermission: System.Diagnostics

PerformanceCounterPermissionAccess: System.Diagnostics

PerformanceCounterPermissionAttribute: System.Diagnostics

PerformanceCounterPermissionEntry: System.Diagnostics

PerformanceCounterPermissionEntryCollection: System.Diagnostics

PerformanceCounterType: System.Diagnostics

PerformanceData: Registry, RegistryHive

PerMilleSymbol: NumberFormatInfo

PermissionAccess: EventLogPermissionAttribute, EventLogPermissionEntry, PerformanceCounterPermissionAttribute, PerformanceCounterPermissionEntry

PermissionEntries: EventLogPermission, PerformanceCounterPermission

Persistence: StreamingContextStates

Personal: SpecialFolder

Phi: FlowControl

PI: Math

Pinned: GCHandleType

PinvokeImpl: FieldAttributes, MethodAttributes

Pipelined: HttpWebRequest

PipelineFailure: WebExceptionStatus

Platform: OperatingSystem

PlatformID: System

PlatformNotSupportedException: System

PMDesignator: DateTimeFormatInfo

Pointer: System.Reflection

Policy: UserPreferenceCategory

Poll( ): Socket

Pop: OpCodes

Pop( ): Stack

Pop0: StackBehaviour

Pop1: StackBehaviour

Pop1_pop1: StackBehaviour

Popi: StackBehaviour

Popi_pop1: StackBehaviour

Popi_popi: StackBehaviour

Popi_popi_popi: StackBehaviour

Popi_popi8: StackBehaviour

Popi_popr4: StackBehaviour

Popi_popr8: StackBehaviour

Popref: StackBehaviour

Popref_pop1: StackBehaviour

Popref_popi: StackBehaviour

Popref_popi_popi: StackBehaviour

Popref_popi_popi8: StackBehaviour

Popref_popi_popr4: StackBehaviour

Popref_popi_popr8: StackBehaviour

Popref_popi_popref: StackBehaviour

PopScope( ): XmlNamespaceManager

PopulateObjectMembers( ): FormatterServices

Port: Cookie, EndpointPermission, IPEndPoint, SocketPermissionAttribute, Uri, UriBuilder

Position: BufferedStream, FileStream, IsolatedStorageFileStream, MemoryStream, NetworkStream, ParameterBuilder, ParameterInfo, Stream

PositionImpl: ParameterInfo

PositiveInfinity: Double, Single

PositiveInfinitySymbol: NumberFormatInfo

PositiveSign: NumberFormatInfo

Pow( ): Math

Power: UserPreferenceCategory

PowerModeChanged: SystemEvents

PowerModeChangedEventArgs: Microsoft.
Win32

PowerModeChangedEventHandler: Microsoft.
Win32

PowerModes: Microsoft.Win32

PreAuthenticate: FileWebRequest, HttpWebRequest, WebRequest

PreAuthenticate( ): AuthenticationManager,
IAuthenticationModule

PreconditionFailed: HttpStatusCode

Prefix: OpCodeType, XmlAttribute, XmlElement,
XmlNode, XmlNodeReader, XmlReader,
XmlTextReader, XmlValidatingReader, XPath-
Navigator

Prefix1: OpCodes

Prefix2: OpCodes

Prefix3: OpCodes

Prefix4: OpCodes

Prefix5: OpCodes

Prefix6: OpCodes

Prefix7: OpCodes

Prefixref: OpCodes

Prelink( ): Marshal

PrelinkAll( ): Marshal

Prepend( ): XmlAttributeCollection

PrependChild( ): XmlNode

Preserve: XmlSpace

PreserveSig: DllImportAttribute, MethodImplAttributes

PreserveSigAttribute: System.Runtime.
InteropServices

PreserveWhitespace: XmlDocument

PreserveWhitespace( ): XsltContext

PreviousSibling: XmlLinkedNode, XmlNode

Primitive: OpCodeType

Priority: Thread

PriorityBoostEnabled: Process, ProcessThread

PriorityClass: Process

PriorityLevel: ProcessThread

Private: FieldAttributes, MethodAttributes,
ResourceAttributes

PrivateBinPath: AppDomainSetup

PrivateBinPathProbe: AppDomainSetup

PrivateBuild: FileVersionInfo

PrivateMemorySize: Process

PrivateScope: FieldAttributes, MethodAttributes

PrivateUse: UnicodeCategory

PrivilegedProcessorTime: Process,
ProcessThread

Process: System.Diagnostics

ProcessExit: AppDomain

ProcessingInstruction: XmlNodeType, XPathNodeType

ProcessModule: System.Diagnostics

ProcessModuleCollection: System.Diagnostics

ProcessName: Process

ProcessorAffinity: Process, ProcessThread

ProcessPriorityClass: System.Diagnostics

ProcessStartInfo: System.Diagnostics

ProcessThread: System.Diagnostics

ProcessThreadCollection: System.Diagnostics

ProcessWindowStyle: System.Diagnostics

Product: AssemblyProductAttribute

ProductBuildPart: FileVersionInfo

ProductMajorPart: FileVersionInfo

ProductMinorPart: FileVersionInfo

ProductName: FileVersionInfo

ProductPrivatePart: FileVersionInfo

ProductVersion: FileVersionInfo

ProgIdAttribute: System.Runtime.InteropSer-
vices

ProgramFiles: SpecialFolder

Programs: SpecialFolder

Prolog: WriteState

Property: AttributeTargets, MemberTypes

PropertyAttributes: System.Reflection

PropertyBuilder: System.Reflection.Emit

PropertyInfo: System.Reflection

PropertyToken: PropertyBuilder, System.Reflec-
tion.Emit

PropertyType: PropertyBuilder, PropertyInfo

PropGet: ComMemberType

PropSet: ComMemberType

ProtectionRealm: Authorization

ProtocolError: WebExceptionStatus

ProtocolFamily: System.Net.Sockets

ProtocolType: Socket, System.Net.Sockets

ProtocolVersion: HttpWebRequest, HttpWebResponse, ServicePoint

ProtocolViolationException: System.Net

Proxy: FileWebRequest, HttpWebRequest, WebRequest

ProxyAuthenticationRequired: HttpStatusCode

ProxyNameResolutionFailure: WebExceptionStatus

PtrToStringAnsi( ): Marshal

PtrToStringAuto( ): Marshal

PtrToStringBSTR( ): Marshal

PtrToStringUni( ): Marshal

PtrToStructure( ): Marshal

Public: BindingFlags, FieldAttributes, MethodAttributes, ResourceAttributes, TypeAttributes

PublicId: XmlDocumentType, XmlEntity, XmlNotation, XmlParserContext

PublicKey: AssemblyNameFlags, StrongNameKeyPair

Pulse( ): Monitor

PulseAll( ): Monitor

Pup: AddressFamily, ProtocolFamily, ProtocolType

Push( ): Stack

Push0: StackBehaviour

Push1: StackBehaviour

Push1_push1: StackBehaviour

Pushi: StackBehaviour

Pushi8: StackBehaviour

Pushr4: StackBehaviour

Pushr8: StackBehaviour

Pushref: StackBehaviour

PushScope( ): XmlNamespaceManager

PutDispProperty: BindingFlags

PutRefDispProperty: BindingFlags

Q

QName: XmlTokenizedType

Query: Uri, UriBuilder

QueryInterface( ): Marshal

QueryString: WebClient

Queue: System.Collections

QueueUserWorkItem( ): ThreadPool

QuoteChar: XmlNodeReader, XmlReader, XmlTextReader, XmlTextWriter, XmlValidatingReader

R

R4: UnmanagedType

R8: UnmanagedType

RaiseDeserializationEvent( ): ObjectManager

Random: System

Rank: Array

RankException: System

RateOfCountsPerSecond32: PerformanceCounterType

RateOfCountsPerSecond64: PerformanceCounterType

Raw: ProtocolType, SocketType

RawBase: PerformanceCounterType

RawFraction: PerformanceCounterType

RawValue: CounterSample, InstanceData, PerformanceCounter

Rdm: SocketType

Read: FileAccess, FileShare

Read( ): BinaryReader, BufferedStream, Console, FileStream, IsolatedStorageFileStream, MemoryStream, NetworkStream, Stream, StreamReader, StringReader, TextReader, XmlNodeReader, XmlReader, XmlTextReader, XmlValidatingReader

Read7BitEncodedInt( ): BinaryReader

ReadAttributeValue( ): XmlNodeReader, XmlReader, XmlTextReader, XmlValidatingReader

ReadBase64( ): XmlTextReader

ReadBinHex( ): XmlTextReader

ReadBlock( ): TextReader

ReadBoolean( ): BinaryReader

ReadByte( ): BinaryReader, BufferedStream, FileStream, IsolatedStorageFileStream, Marshal, MemoryStream, Stream

ReadBytes( ): BinaryReader

ReadCategory( ): PerformanceCounterCategory

ReadChar( ): BinaryReader

ReadChars( ): BinaryReader, XmlTextReader

ReadDecimal( ): BinaryReader

ReadDouble( ): BinaryReader

ReadElementString( ): XmlReader

ReadEndElement( ): XmlReader

Reader: XmlValidatingReader

ReaderWriterLock: System.Threading

ReadInnerXml( ): XmlReader

ReadInt16( ): BinaryReader, Marshal

ReadInt32( ): BinaryReader, Marshal

ReadInt64( ): BinaryReader, Marshal

ReadIntPtr( ): Marshal

ReadLine( ): Console, StreamReader, StringReader, TextReader

ReadNode( ): XmlDocument

ReadOnly: FileAttributes, PerformanceCounter

ReadOnly( ): ArrayList, CultureInfo, DateTimeFormatInfo, NumberFormatInfo

ReadOnlyCollectionBase: System.Collections

ReadOuterXml( ): XmlReader

ReadSByte( ): BinaryReader

ReadSingle( ): BinaryReader

ReadStartElement( ): XmlReader

ReadState: System.Xml, XmlNodeReader, XmlReader, XmlTextReader, XmlValidatingReader

ReadString( ): BinaryReader, XmlNodeReader, XmlReader, XmlValidatingReader

ReadToEnd( ): StreamReader, StringReader, TextReader

ReadTypedValue( ): XmlValidatingReader

ReadUInt16( ): BinaryReader

ReadUInt32( ): BinaryReader

ReadUInt64( ): BinaryReader

ReadWrite: FileAccess, FileShare

ReadWriteTimeout: HttpWebRequest

Ready: ThreadState

ReAllocCoTaskMem( ): Marshal

ReAllocHGlobal( ): Marshal

RealTime: ProcessPriorityClass

Reason: SessionEndedEventArgs, SessionEndingEventArgs

Receive: SocketShutdown

Receive( ): Socket, UdpClient

ReceiveBuffer: SocketOptionName

ReceiveBufferSize: TcpClient

ReceiveFailure: WebExceptionStatus

ReceiveFrom( ): Socket

ReceiveLowWater: SocketOptionName

ReceiveTimeout: SocketOptionName, TcpClient

Recent: SpecialFolder

RecordArrayElementFixup( ): ObjectManager

RecordDelayedFixup( ): ObjectManager

RecordFixup( ): ObjectManager

Redirect: HttpStatusCode

RedirectKeepVerb: HttpStatusCode

RedirectMethod: HttpStatusCode

RedirectStandardError: ProcessStartInfo

RedirectStandardInput: ProcessStartInfo

RedirectStandardOutput: ProcessStartInfo

Refanytype: OpCodes

Refanyval: OpCodes

ReferencedAssembly: ManifestResourceInfo

ReferenceEquals( ): Object

Referer: HttpWebRequest

ReflectedType: ConstructorBuilder, EnumBuilder, FieldBuilder, MemberInfo, MethodBuilder, PropertyBuilder, Type, TypeBuilder

ReflectionTypeLoadException: System.Reflection

Refresh( ): FileSystemInfo, Process

Regex: System.Text.RegularExpressions

RegexCompilationInfo: System.Text.RegularExpressions

RegexOptions: System.Text.RegularExpressions

RegionInfo: System.Globalization

Register( ): AuthenticationManager

RegisterAssembly( ): IRegistrationServices, RegistrationServices

RegisteredModules: AuthenticationManager

RegisteredWaitHandle: System.Threading

RegisterObject( ): ObjectManager

RegisterObjectCreationCallback( ): ExtensibleClassFactory

RegisterPrefix( ): WebRequest

RegisterTypeForComClients( ): IRegistrationServices, RegistrationServices

RegisterWaitForSingleObject( ): ThreadPool

RegistrationServices: System.Runtime.InteropServices

Registry: Microsoft.Win32
RegistryHive: Microsoft.Win32
RegistryKey: Microsoft.Win32
RelativeSearchPath: AppDomain
Release( ): Marshal
ReleaseComObject( ): Marshal
ReleaseLock( ): ReaderWriterLock
ReleaseMutex( ): Mutex
ReleaseReaderLock( ): ReaderWriterLock
ReleaseThreadCache( ): Marshal
ReleaseWriterLock( ): ReaderWriterLock
Rem: OpCodes
Rem_Un: OpCodes
Remainder( ): Decimal
RemoteEndPoint: Socket
Remoting: StreamingContextStates
Remove: XmlNodeChangedAction
Remove( ): ArrayList, CounterCreationDataCollection, CredentialCache, Delegate, EventLogPermissionEntryCollection, Hashtable, HybridDictionary, IDictionary, IList, IsolatedStorage, IsolatedStorageFile, ListDictionary, NameValueCollection, PerformanceCounterPermissionEntryCollection, ProcessThreadCollection, SortedList, String, StringBuilder, StringCollection, StringDictionary, TraceListenerCollection, WebHeaderCollection, XmlAttributeCollection
RemoveAll( ): Delegate, XmlAttributeCollection, XmlElement, XmlNode
RemoveAllAttributes( ): XmlElement
RemoveAt( ): ArrayList, CollectionBase, IList, SortedList, StringCollection, TraceListenerCollection, XmlAttributeCollection
RemoveAttribute( ): XmlElement
RemoveAttributeAt( ): XmlElement
RemoveAttributeNode( ): XmlElement
RemoveChild( ): XmlNode
RemoveEventHandler( ): EventInfo
RemoveExtensionObject( ): XsltArgumentList
RemoveImpl( ): Delegate, MulticastDelegate
RemoveInstance( ): PerformanceCounter
RemoveNamedItem( ): XmlNamedNodeMap
RemoveNamespace( ): XmlNamespaceManager
RemoveParam( ): XsltArgumentList

RemoveRange( ): ArrayList
RemoveSurrogate( ): SurrogateSelector
Renamed: FileSystemWatcher, WatcherChangeTypes
RenamedEventArgs: System.IO
RenamedEventHandler: System.IO
ReorderArgumentArray( ): Binder
ReparsePoint: FileAttributes
Repeat( ): ArrayList
Replace( ): Regex, String, StringBuilder
ReplaceChild( ): XmlNode
ReplaceData( ): XmlCharacterData
ReplacementStrings: EventLogEntry
RequestCanceled: WebExceptionStatus
RequestedRangeNotSatisfiable: HttpStatusCode
RequestEntityTooLarge: HttpStatusCode
RequestTimeout: HttpStatusCode
RequestUri: FileWebRequest, HttpWebRequest, WebRequest
RequestUriTooLong: HttpStatusCode
RequireSecObject: MethodAttributes
ReRegisterForFinalize( ): GC
Reserved2: PropertyAttributes
Reserved3: ParameterAttributes, PropertyAttributes
Reserved4: ParameterAttributes, PropertyAttributes
ReservedMask: EventAttributes, FieldAttributes, MethodAttributes, ParameterAttributes, PropertyAttributes, TypeAttributes
Reset( ): AutoResetEvent, CharEnumerator, IEnumerator, ManualResetEvent, SerializationInfoEnumerator, StringEnumerator, TextElementEnumerator
ResetAbort( ): Thread
ResetContent: HttpStatusCode
ResetIdealProcessor( ): ProcessThread
ResetState( ): XmlTextReader
Resolve( ): Dns
ResolveEntity( ): XmlNodeReader, XmlReader, XmlTextReader, XmlValidatingReader
ResolveEventArgs: System
ResolveEventHandler: System
ResolveFunction( ): XsltContext

ResolveUri( ): XmlResolver, XmlSecureResolver

ResolveVariable( ): XsltContext

ResourceAttributes: System.Reflection

ResourceLocation: ManifestResourceInfo, System.Reflection

ResourceResolve: AppDomain

Responding: Process

Response: WebException

ResponseHeaders: WebClient

ResponseUri: FileWebResponse, HttpWebResponse, WebResponse

RestoreLock( ): ReaderWriterLock

Result( ): Match

Resume: PowerModes

Resume( ): Thread

Ret: OpCodes

Retargetable: AssemblyNameFlags

Rethrow: OpCodes

Return: FlowControl

ReturnType: ConstructorBuilder, IXsltContextFunction, MethodBuilder, MethodInfo, XPathExpression

ReturnTypeCustomAttributes: MethodBuilder, MethodInfo

ReturnValue: AttributeTargets

Retval: ParameterAttributes

ReuseAddress: SocketOptionName

ReuseSlot: MethodAttributes

Reverse( ): Array, ArrayList

Revision: Version

RevisionNumber: ComCompatibleVersionAttribute

RFC1123Pattern: DateTimeFormatInfo

RightToLeft: Regex, RegexOptions

Roaming: IsolatedStorageScope

Rollback( ): EventLogInstaller, PerformanceCounterInstaller

Root: DirectoryInfo, XPathNodeType

Round( ): Decimal, Math

RTSpecialName: EventAttributes, FieldAttributes, MethodAttributes, PropertyAttributes, TypeAttributes

Run: AssemblyBuilderAccess

RunAndSave: AssemblyBuilderAccess

Running: ThreadState

Runtime: MethodImplAttributes

RuntimeEnvironment: System.Runtime.InteropServices

RuntimeTypeHandle: System

S

SafeArray: UnmanagedType

SafeArrayRankMismatchException: System.Runtime.InteropServices

SafeArraySubType: MarshalAsAttribute

SafeArrayTypeMismatchException: System.Runtime.InteropServices

SafeArrayUserDefinedSubType: MarshalAsAttribute

Same: XmlNodeOrder

Sample: InstanceData

Sample( ): Random

SampleBase: PerformanceCounterType

SampleCounter: PerformanceCounterType

SampleFraction: PerformanceCounterType

Saturday: DayOfWeek

Save: AssemblyBuilderAccess

Save( ): AssemblyBuilder, XmlDocument

SByte: System, TypeCode

Schedule( ): Formatter

Schema: ValidationType

Schemas: XmlValidatingReader

SchemaType: XmlValidatingReader

Scheme: Uri, UriBuilder, UriPartial

SchemeDelimiter: Uri

Scope: IsolatedStorage

ScopeId: IPAddress

ScopeName: Module

Screensaver: UserPreferenceCategory

Sealed: TypeAttributes

Second: DateTime

Seconds: TimeSpan

Section: System.Collections.Specialized

Secure: Cookie

SecureChannelFailure: WebExceptionStatus

Security: NotifyFilters

SecurityProtocol: ServicePointManager

SecurityProtocolType: System.Net

SetEntryPoint( ): AssemblyBuilder

SetError( ): Console

SetField: BindingFlags

SetGetMethod( ): PropertyBuilder

SetImplementationFlags( ): Constructor-
Builder, MethodBuilder

SetIn( ): Console

SetLastAccessTime( ): Directory, File

SetLastAccessTimeUtc( ): Directory, File

SetLastError: DllImportAttribute

SetLastWriteTime( ): Directory, File

SetLastWriteTimeUtc( ): Directory, File

SetLength( ): BufferedStream, FileStream,
IsolatedStorageFileStream, MemoryStream,
NetworkStream, Stream

SetLocalSymInfo( ): LocalBuilder

SetMarshal( ): FieldBuilder, MethodBuilder,
ParameterBuilder

SetMinThreads( ): ThreadPool

SetNamedItem( ): XmlAttributeCollection,
XmlNamedNodeMap

SetObjectData( ): ISerializationSurrogate

SetOffset( ): FieldBuilder

SetOut( ): Console

SetParent( ): TypeBuilder

SetPrincipalPolicy( ): AppDomain

SetProperty: BindingFlags

SetPublicKey( ): AssemblyName

SetPublicKeyToken( ): AssemblyName

SetRaiseMethod( ): EventBuilder

SetRange( ): ArrayList

SetRemoveOnMethod( ): EventBuilder

SetSetMethod( ): PropertyBuilder

SetShadowCopyFiles( ): AppDomain

SetShadowCopyPath( ): AppDomain

SetSocketOption( ): Socket

SetSymCustomAttribute( ): ConstructorBuilder,
MethodBuilder, ModuleBuilder

SetThreadPrincipal( ): AppDomain

SetType( ): SerializationInfo

SetupInformation: AppDomain

SetUserEntryPoint( ): ModuleBuilder

SetValue( ): Array, FieldBuilder, FieldInfo, PropertyBuilder, PropertyInfo, RegistryKey

SetValueDirect( ): FieldInfo

ShadowCopyDirectories: AppDomainSetup

ShadowCopyFiles: AppDomain, AppDomain-
Setup

Shl: OpCodes

ShortDatePattern: DateTimeFormatInfo

ShortInlineBrTarget: OperandType

ShortInlineI: OperandType

ShortInlineR: OperandType

ShortInlineVar: OperandType

ShortTimePattern: DateTimeFormatInfo

Shr: OpCodes

Shr_Un: OpCodes

Shutdown( ): Socket

Sign( ): Math

SignalTime: ElapsedEventArgs

Signature: ConstructorBuilder, MethodBuilder,
MissingMemberException

SignatureHelper: System.Reflection.Emit

SignatureToken: System.Reflection.Emit

Significant: WhitespaceHandling

SignificantWhitespace: XmlNodeType, XPath-
NodeType

Simple: FormatterAssemblyStyle

Sin( ): Math

Single: System, TypeCode

SingleDomain: LoaderOptimization

Singleline: RegexOptions

Sinh( ): Math

Site: FileSystemWatcher, Timer

Size: IntPtr, NotifyFilters, OpCode, SocketAddress, StructLayoutAttribute, TypeBuilder,
UIntPtr

Size1: PackingSize

Size16: PackingSize

Size2: PackingSize

Size4: PackingSize

Size8: PackingSize

SizeConst: MarshalAsAttribute

Sizeof: OpCodes

SizeOf( ): Marshal

SizeParamIndex: MarshalAsAttribute

Skip( ): XmlNodeReader, XmlReader

Sleep( ): Thread

Stind_I2: OpCodes

Stind_I4: OpCodes

Stind_I8: OpCodes

Stind_R4: OpCodes

Stind_R8: OpCodes

Stind_Ref: OpCodes

Stloc: OpCodes

Stloc_0: OpCodes

Stloc_1: OpCodes

Stloc_2: OpCodes

Stloc_3: OpCodes

Stloc_S: OpCodes

Stobj: OpCodes

Stop( ): TcpListener, Timer

Stopped: ThreadState

StopRequested: ThreadState

Stream: SocketType, System.IO

StreamingContext: System.Runtime.Serialization

StreamingContextStates: System.Runtime. Serialization

StreamReader: System.IO

StreamWriter: System.IO

String: System, TypeCode, XPathResultType

StringBuilder: System.Text

StringCollection: System.Collections.Specialized

StringDictionary: System.Collections.Specialized

StringEnumerator: System.Collections.Specialized

StringFormatMask: TypeAttributes

StringInfo: System.Globalization

StringReader: System.IO

StringSort: CompareOptions

StringToBSTR( ): Marshal

StringToCoTaskMemAnsi( ): Marshal

StringToCoTaskMemAuto( ): Marshal

StringToCoTaskMemUni( ): Marshal

StringToHGlobalAnsi( ): Marshal

StringToHGlobalAuto( ): Marshal

StringToHGlobalUni( ): Marshal

StringToken: System.Reflection.Emit

StringWriter: System.IO

StrongNameKeyPair: System.Reflection

Struct: AttributeTargets, UnmanagedType

StructLayoutAttribute: System.Runtime. InteropServices

StructureToPtr( ): Marshal

Stsfld: OpCodes

Sub: OpCodes

Sub_Ovf: OpCodes

Sub_Ovf_Un: OpCodes

SubKeyCount: RegistryKey

Substring( ): String, XmlCharacterData

Subtract( ): DateTime, Decimal, TimeSpan

Success: Group, WebExceptionStatus

SuccessAudit: EventLogEntryType

Sunday: DayOfWeek

Supports( ): XmlNode

SupportsIPv4: Socket

SupportsIPv6: Socket

SupportsPipelining: ServicePoint

SuppressChangeType: BindingFlags

SuppressFinalize( ): GC

Surrogate: UnicodeCategory

SurrogateSelector: Formatter, IFormatter, System.Runtime.Serialization

Suspend: PowerModes

Suspend( ): Thread

Suspended: ThreadState, ThreadWaitReason

SuspendRequested: ThreadState

SwapMethodBody( ): MethodRental

Switch: OpCodes, System.Diagnostics

SwitchingProtocols: HttpStatusCode

SynchronizationLockException: System. Threading

Synchronized: MethodImplAttributes

Synchronized( ): ArrayList, Group, Hashtable, Match, Queue, SortedList, Stack, TextReader, TextWriter

SynchronizingObject: EventLog, FileSystem-Watcher, Process, Timer

SyncRoot: Array, ArrayList, BitArray, CaptureCollection, CookieCollection, GroupCollection, Hashtable, HybridDictionary, ICollection, List-Dictionary, MatchCollection, Queue, SortedList, Stack, StringCollection, StringDictionary

SysInt: UnmanagedType

TimeOfDay: DateTime

Timeout: FileWebRequest, HttpWebRequest, System.Threading, WebExceptionStatus, WebRequest

Timer: System.Threading, System.Timers

Timer100Ns: PerformanceCounterType

Timer100NsInverse: PerformanceCounterType

TimerCallback: System.Threading

TimerElapsed: SystemEvents

TimerElapsedEventArgs: Microsoft.Win32

TimerElapsedEventHandler: Microsoft.Win32

TimerId: TimerElapsedEventArgs

TimersDescriptionAttribute: System.Timers

TimeSeparator: DateTimeFormatInfo

TimeSpan: System

TimeStamp: Cookie, CounterSample

TimeStamp100nSec: CounterSample

TimeWritten: EventLogEntry

TimeZone: System

Title: AssemblyTitleAttribute

TitlecaseLetter: UnicodeCategory

Tls: SecurityProtocolType

ToArray( ): ArrayList, MemoryStream, Queue, Stack

ToBase64CharArray( ): Convert

ToBase64String( ): Convert

ToBoolean( ): BitConverter, Convert, Formatter-Converter, IConvertible, IFormatterConverter, XmlConvert

ToByte( ): Convert, Decimal, FormatterCon-verter, IConvertible, IFormatterConverter, XmlConvert

ToByteArray( ): Guid, WebHeaderCollection

ToChar( ): BitConverter, Convert, FormatterCon-verter, IConvertible, IFormatterConverter, XmlConvert

ToCharArray( ): String

ToDateTime( ): Calendar, Convert, Formatter-Converter, GregorianCalendar, HebrewCal-endar, HijriCalendar, IConvertible, IFormatter-Converter, JapaneseCalendar, JulianCalendar, KoreanCalendar, TaiwanCalendar, ThaiBud-dhistCalendar, XmlConvert

Today: DateTime

ToDecimal( ): Convert, FormatterConverter, IConvertible, IFormatterConverter, XmlConvert

ToDouble( ): BitConverter, Convert, Decimal, FormatterConverter, IConvertible, IFormatter-Converter, XmlConvert

ToFileTime( ): DateTime

ToFileTimeUtc( ): DateTime

ToFourDigitYear( ): Calendar, GregorianCal-endar, HebrewCalendar, HijriCalendar, Japa-neseCalendar, JulianCalendar, KoreanCal-endar, TaiwanCalendar, ThaiBuddhistCalendar

ToGuid( ): XmlConvert

ToInt16( ): BitConverter, Convert, Decimal, FormatterConverter, IConvertible, IFormatter-Converter, XmlConvert

ToInt32( ): BitConverter, Convert, Decimal, FormatterConverter, IConvertible, IFormatter-Converter, IntPtr, XmlConvert

ToInt64( ): BitConverter, Convert, Decimal, FormatterConverter, IConvertible, IFormatter-Converter, IntPtr, XmlConvert

Token: EventToken, FieldToken, MethodToken, ParameterToken, PropertyToken, Signature-Token, StringToken, TypeToken

ToLocalTime( ): DateTime, TimeZone

ToLongDateString( ): DateTime

ToLongTimeString( ): DateTime

ToLower( ): Char, String, TextInfo

ToOACurrency( ): Decimal

ToOADate( ): DateTime

ToObject( ): Enum

ToPointer( ): IntPtr, UIntPtr

ToSByte( ): Convert, Decimal, FormatterCon-verter, IConvertible, IFormatterConverter, XmlConvert

ToShortDateString( ): DateTime

ToShortTimeString( ): DateTime

ToSingle( ): BitConverter, Convert, Decimal, FormatterConverter, IConvertible, IFormatter-Converter, XmlConvert

ToString( ): AppDomain, Assembly, Assem-blyName, BadImageFormatException, BitCon-verter, BitVector32, Boolean, Byte, Capture, Char, COMException, CompareInfo, Construc-torBuilder, Convert, Cookie, CultureInfo, DateTime, DBNull, Decimal, DirectoryInfo, Double, EndpointPermission, Enum, Excep-

cess, FileAttributes, FileMode, FileShare, Flow-
Control, FormatterAssemblyStyle,
FormatterTypeStyle, Formatting, GCHandle-
Type, GregorianCalendarTypes, HttpStatus-
Code, IDispatchImplType, IsolatedStorage-
Scope, LayoutKind, LoaderOptimization,
MemberTypes, MethodAttributes, MethodIm-
plAttributes, NetworkAccess, NotifyFilters,
NumberStyles, OpCodeType, OperandType,
PackingSize, ParameterAttributes, PEFile-
Kinds, PerformanceCounterPermissionAccess,
PerformanceCounterType, PlatformID, Power-
Modes, ProcessPriorityClass, ProcessWindow-
Style, PropertyAttributes, ProtocolFamily,
ProtocolType, ReadState, RegexOptions,
RegistryHive, ResourceAttributes, ResourceLo-
cation, SecurityProtocolType, SeekOrigin,
SelectMode, SessionEndReasons, SocketFlags,
SocketOptionLevel, SocketOptionName, Sock-
etShutdown, SocketType, SpecialFolder,
StackBehaviour, StreamingContextStates,
ThreadPriority, ThreadPriorityLevel, Thread-
State, ThreadWaitReason, TraceLevel, Trans-
portType, TypeAttributes, TypeCode, TypeFil-
terLevel, UnicodeCategory, UnmanagedType,
UriHostNameType, UriPartial, UserPreference-
Category, ValidationType, VarEnum, Watcher-
ChangeTypes, WebExceptionStatus,
WhitespaceHandling, WriteState, XmlCase-
Order, XmlDataType, XmlNodeChangedAc-
tion, XmlNodeOrder, XmlNodeType, XmlSor-
tOrder, XmlSpace, XmlTokenizedType,
XPathNamespaceScope, XPathNodeType,
XPathResultType

ValueCount: RegistryKey

Values: Hashtable, HybridDictionary, IDictionary, InstanceDataCollection, InstanceData-
CollectionCollection, ListDictionary, SortedList, StringDictionary

ValueType: System

VarArgs: CallingConventions

VarEnum: System.Runtime.InteropServices

VariableType: IXsltContextVariable

VariantBool: UnmanagedType

Varpop: StackBehaviour

Varpush: StackBehaviour

VBByRefStr: UnmanagedType

Verb: ProcessStartInfo

Verbose: TraceLevel

Verbs: ProcessStartInfo

VerifyName( ): XmlConvert

VerifyNCName( ): XmlConvert

Version: AssemblyFileVersionAttribute, Assem-
blyName, AssemblyVersionAttribute, Cookie,
Environment, OperatingSystem, System,
XmlDeclaration

Version10: HttpVersion

Version11: HttpVersion

VersionCompatibility: AssemblyName

Virtual: MethodAttributes

VirtualMemory: ThreadWaitReason

VirtualMemorySize: Process

VisibilityMask: TypeAttributes

VoiceView: AddressFamily, ProtocolFamily

Void: System

Volatile: OpCodes

VolatileRead( ): Thread

VolatileWrite( ): Thread

VolumeSeparatorChar: Path

VT_ARRAY: VarEnum

VT_BLOB: VarEnum

VT_BLOB_OBJECT: VarEnum

VT_BOOL: VarEnum

VT_BSTR: VarEnum

VT_BYREF: VarEnum

VT_CARRAY: VarEnum

VT_CF: VarEnum

VT_CLSID: VarEnum

VT_CY: VarEnum

VT_DATE: VarEnum

VT_DECIMAL: VarEnum

VT_DISPATCH: VarEnum

VT_EMPTY: VarEnum

VT_ERROR: VarEnum

VT_FILETIME: VarEnum

VT_HRESULT: VarEnum

VT_I1: VarEnum

VT_I2: VarEnum

VT_I4: VarEnum

VT_I8: VarEnum

VT_INT: VarEnum

VT_LPSTR: VarEnum

VT_LPWSTR: VarEnum

VT_NULL: VarEnum

VT_PTR: VarEnum

VT_R4: VarEnum

VT_R8: VarEnum

VT_RECORD: VarEnum

VT_SAFEARRAY: VarEnum

VT_STORAGE: VarEnum

VT_STORED_OBJECT: VarEnum

VT_STREAM: VarEnum

VT_STREAMED_OBJECT: VarEnum

VT_UI1: VarEnum

VT_UI2: VarEnum

VT_UI4: VarEnum

VT_UI8: VarEnum

VT_UINT: VarEnum

VT_UNKNOWN: VarEnum

VT_USERDEFINED: VarEnum

VT_VARIANT: VarEnum

VT_VECTOR: VarEnum

VT_VOID: VarEnum

VtableLayoutMask: MethodAttributes

W

Wait: ThreadState

Wait( ): Monitor

WaitAll( ): WaitHandle

WaitAny( ): WaitHandle

WaitCallback: System.Threading

WaitForChanged( ): FileSystemWatcher

WaitForChangedResult: System.IO

WaitForExit( ): Process

WaitForInputIdle( ): Process

WaitForPendingFinalizers( ): GC

WaitHandle: System.Threading

WaitOne( ): WaitHandle

WaitOrTimerCallback: System.Threading

WaitReason: ProcessThread

WaitSleepJoin: ThreadState

WaitTimeout: WaitHandle

Warning: EventLogEntryType, TraceLevel

WatcherChangeTypes: System.IO

Weak: GCHandleType

WeakReference: System

WeakTrackResurrection: GCHandleType

WebClient: System.Net

WebException: System.Net

WebExceptionStatus: System.Net

WebHeaderCollection: System.Net

WebName: Encoding

WebPermission: System.Net

WebPermissionAttribute: System.Net

WebProxy: System.Net

WebRequest: System.Net

WebResponse: System.Net

Wednesday: DayOfWeek

Whitespace: XmlNodeType, XPathNodeType, XsltContext

WhitespaceHandling: System.Xml, XmlTextReader

Win32NT: PlatformID

Win32S: PlatformID

Win32Windows: PlatformID

Winapi: CallingConvention

WinCE: PlatformID

Window: UserPreferenceCategory

WindowApplication: PEFileKinds

WindowsCodePage: Encoding

WindowStyle: ProcessStartInfo

WorkingDirectory: ProcessStartInfo

WorkingSet: Environment, Process

WrappedObject: CurrencyWrapper, DispatchWrapper, UnknownWrapper

Wrapper: HandleRef

Write: FileAccess, FileShare

Write( ): BinaryWriter, BufferedStream, Console, Debug, DefaultTraceListener, EventLogTraceListener, FileStream, IsolatedStorageFileStream, MemoryStream, NetworkStream, Stream, StreamWriter, StringWriter, TextWriter, TextWriterTraceListener, Trace, TraceListener

Write7BitEncodedInt( ): BinaryWriter

WriteArray( ): Formatter

WriteAttributes( ): XmlWriter

WriteAttributeString( ): XmlWriter

WriteBase64( ): XmlTextWriter, XmlWriter

WriteBinHex( ): XmlTextWriter, XmlWriter

WriteBoolean( ): Formatter

WriteByte( ): BufferedStream, FileStream, Formatter, IsolatedStorageFileStream, Marshal, MemoryStream, Stream

WriteCData( ): XmlTextWriter, XmlWriter

WriteChar( ): Formatter

WriteCharEntity( ): XmlTextWriter, XmlWriter

WriteChars( ): XmlTextWriter, XmlWriter

WriteComment( ): XmlTextWriter, XmlWriter

WriteContentTo( ): XmlAttribute, XmlCDataSection, XmlComment, XmlDeclaration, XmlDocument, XmlDocumentFragment, XmlDocumentType, XmlElement, XmlEntity, XmlEntityReference, XmlNode, XmlNotation, XmlProcessingInstruction, XmlSignificantWhitespace, XmlText, XmlWhitespace

WriteDateTime( ): Formatter

WriteDecimal( ): Formatter

WriteDocType( ): XmlTextWriter, XmlWriter

WriteDouble( ): Formatter

WriteElementString( ): XmlWriter

WriteEndAttribute( ): XmlTextWriter, XmlWriter

WriteEndDocument( ): XmlTextWriter, XmlWriter

WriteEndElement( ): XmlTextWriter, XmlWriter

WriteEntityRef( ): XmlTextWriter, XmlWriter

WriteEntry( ): EventLog

WriteFullEndElement( ): XmlTextWriter, XmlWriter

WriteIf( ): Debug, Trace

WriteIndent( ): TraceListener

WriteInt16( ): Formatter, Marshal

WriteInt32( ): Formatter, Marshal

WriteInt64( ): Formatter, Marshal

WriteIntPtr( ): Marshal

WriteLine( ): Console, Debug, DefaultTraceListener, EventLogTraceListener, TextWriter, TextWriterTraceListener, Trace, TraceListener

WriteLineIf( ): Debug, Trace

WriteMember( ): Formatter

WriteName( ): XmlTextWriter, XmlWriter

WriteNmToken( ): XmlTextWriter, XmlWriter

WriteNode( ): XmlWriter

WriteObjectRef( ): Formatter

WriteProcessingInstruction( ): XmlTextWriter, XmlWriter

WriteQualifiedName( ): XmlTextWriter, XmlWriter

Writer: TextWriterTraceListener

WriteRaw( ): XmlTextWriter, XmlWriter

WriterSeqNum: ReaderWriterLock

WriteSByte( ): Formatter

WriteSingle( ): Formatter

WriteStartAttribute( ): XmlTextWriter, XmlWriter

WriteStartDocument( ): XmlTextWriter, XmlWriter

WriteStartElement( ): XmlTextWriter, XmlWriter

WriteState: System.Xml, XmlTextWriter, XmlWriter

WriteString( ): XmlTextWriter, XmlWriter

WriteSurrogateCharEntity( ): XmlTextWriter, XmlWriter

WriteTimeSpan( ): Formatter

WriteTo( ): MemoryStream, XmlAttribute, XmlCDataSection, XmlComment, XmlDeclaration, XmlDocument, XmlDocumentFragment, XmlDocumentType, XmlElement, XmlEntity, XmlEntityReference, XmlNode, XmlNotation, XmlProcessingInstruction, XmlSignificantWhitespace, XmlText, XmlWhitespace

WriteUInt16( ): Formatter

WriteUInt32( ): Formatter

WriteUInt64( ): Formatter

WriteValueType( ): Formatter

WriteWhitespace( ): XmlTextWriter, XmlWriter

X

XDR: ValidationType

XmlAttribute: System.Xml

XmlAttributeCollection: System.Xml

XmlCaseOrder: System.Xml.XPath

XmlCDataSection: System.Xml

XmlCharacterData: System.Xml

XmlComment: System.Xml

XmlConvert: System.Xml

XmlDataDocument: System.Xml

XmlDataType: System.Xml.XPath

XmlDeclaration: System.Xml, XmlNodeType

XmlDocument: System.Xml

XmlDocumentFragment: System.Xml

XmlDocumentType: System.Xml

XmlElement: System.Xml

XmlEntity: System.Xml

XmlEntityReference: System.Xml

XmlException: System.Xml

XmlImplementation: System.Xml

XmlLang: XmlNodeReader, XmlParserContext, XmlReader, XmlTextReader, XmlTextWriter, XmlValidatingReader, XmlWriter, XPathNavigator

XmlLinkedNode: System.Xml

XmlNamedNodeMap: System.Xml

XmlNameSpace: ISoapMessage, SoapMessage

XmlNamespaceManager: System.Xml

XmlNameTable: System.Xml

XmlNode: System.Xml

XmlNodeChangedAction: System.Xml

XmlNodeChangedEventArgs: System.Xml

XmlNodeChangedEventHandler: System.Xml

XmlNodeList: System.Xml

XmlNodeOrder: System.Xml

XmlNodeReader: System.Xml

XmlNodeType: System.Xml

XmlNotation: System.Xml

XmlParserContext: System.Xml

XmlProcessingInstruction: System.Xml

XmlQualifiedName: System.Xml

XmlReader: System.Xml

XmlResolver: System.Xml, XmlDocument, XmlTextReader, XmlValidatingReader, XslTransform

XmlSecureResolver: System.Xml

XmlSignificantWhitespace: System.Xml

XmlSortOrder: System.Xml.XPath

XmlSpace: System.Xml, XmlNodeReader, XmlParserContext, XmlReader, XmlTextReader, XmlTextWriter, XmlValidatingReader, XmlWriter

XmlText: System.Xml

XmlTextReader: System.Xml

XmlTextWriter: System.Xml

XmlTokenizedType: System.Xml

XmlUrlResolver: System.Xml

XmlValidatingReader: System.Xml

XmlWhitespace: System.Xml

XmlWriter: System.Xml

Xor: OpCodes

Xor( ): BitArray

XPathDocument: System.Xml.XPath

XPathException: System.Xml.XPath

XPathExpression: System.Xml.XPath

XPathNamespaceScope: System.Xml.XPath

XPathNavigator: System.Xml.XPath

XPathNodeIterator: System.Xml.XPath

XPathNodeType: System.Xml.XPath

XPathResultType: System.Xml.XPath

XsdString: FormatterTypeStyle

XsltArgumentList: System.Xml.Xsl

XsltCompileException: System.Xml.Xsl

XsltContext: System.Xml.Xsl

XsltException: System.Xml.Xsl

XslTransform: System.Xml.Xsl

Y

Year: DateTime

YearMonthPattern: DateTimeFormatInfo

Z

Zero: Decimal, IntPtr, TimeSpan, UIntPtr

Index

About the Authors

Peter Drayton is a program manager in the Common Language Runtime team at Microsoft, where his mission is to ensure that Rotor and the CLR are great places for exotic programming languages and virtual machine research and development. Peter was previously an independent consultant, conference speaker, and instructor for DevelopMentor. Originally from Cape Town, South Africa, Peter now lives in Redmond, Washington with his wife, Julie. Peter can be reached at *pdrayton@microsoft.com*.

Ben Albahari is cofounder of Genamics, a provider of components for C# programmers, as well as software for DNA and protein sequence analysis. He is the author of "A Comparative Overview of C#," an early and widely cited comparison of C# with C/C++ and Java. Ben currently works as a program manager in the .NET Compact Framework team at Microsoft.

Ted Neward is an independent software development architect and mentor in the Sacramento, California area. He is also an instructor with DevelopMentor, where he teaches and authors both the Java and .NET curriculum. He speaks frequently for technology user groups, and writes technical papers for *www.javageeks.com* and *www.clrgeeks.com*. He just finished laboring on behalf of the University of California, Davis, architecting a rebuild of the Davis accounting and financial information services software system. His past clients include Pacific Bell/SBC Communications, EdFund, TALX, Transcore, Synergex, and Intuit.

Colophon

Our look is the result of reader comments, our own experimentation, and feedback from distribution channels. Distinctive covers complement our distinctive approach to technical topics, breathing personality and life into potentially dry subjects.

The animal on the cover of *C# in a Nutshell*, Second Edition is a numidian crane. The numidian crane (*Antropoides virgo*) is also called the demoiselle crane because of its grace and symmetry. This species of crane is native to Europe and Asia and migrates to India, Pakistan, and northeast Africa in the winter.

Though numidian cranes are the smallest cranes, they defend their territories as aggressively as other crane species, using their loud voices to warn others of trespassing. If necessary, they will fight. Numidian cranes nest in uplands rather than wetlands and will even live in the desert if there is water within 200 to 500 meters. They sometimes make nests out of pebbles in which to lay their eggs, though more often they will lay eggs directly on the ground, protected only by spotty vegetation.

Numidian cranes are considered a symbol of good luck in some countries and are sometimes even protected by law.

Philip Dangler was the production editor, and Leanne Soylemez was the proofreader for *C# in a Nutshell*, Second Edition. Emily Quill and Claire Cloutier provided quality control. Interior composition was done by Mary Agner and Jamie Peppard. Johnna and Tom Dinse wrote the index.

Emma Colby designed the cover of this book, based on a series design by Edie Freedman. The cover image is an original engraving from the 19th century. Emma Colby produced the cover layout with QuarkXPress 4.1 using Adobe's ITC Garamond font.

David Futato designed the interior layout. He also designed the CD label with QuarkXPress 4.1 using Adobe's ITC Garamond font. This book was converted by Joe Wizda to FrameMaker 5.5.6 with a format conversion tool created by Erik Ray, Jason McIn- tosh, Neil Walls, and Mike Sierra that uses Perl and XML technologies. The text font is Linotype Birka; the heading font is Adobe Myriad Condensed; and the code font is LucasFont's TheSans Mono Condensed. The illustrations that appear in the book were produced by Robert Romano and Jessamyn Read using Macromedia FreeHand 9 and Adobe Photoshop 6. This colophon was written by Linley Dolby.

Other Titles Available from O'Reilly

How to stay in touch with O'Reilly

1. Visit our award-winning web site

http://www.oreilly.com/

★ "Top 100 Sites on the Web"—PC Magazine
★ CIO Magazine's Web Business 50 Awards

Our web site contains a library of comprehensive product information (including book excerpts and tables of contents), downloadable software, background articles, interviews with technology leaders, links to relevant sites, book cover art, and more. File us in your bookmarks or favorites!

2. Join our email mailing lists

Sign up to get email announcements of new books and conferences, special offers, and O'Reilly Network technology newsletters at:

http://elists.oreilly.com

It's easy to customize your free elists subscription so you'll get exactly the O'Reilly news you want.

3. Get examples from our books

To find example files for a book, go to:

http://www.oreilly.com/catalog

select the book, and follow the "Examples" link.

4. Work with us

Check out our web site for current employment opportunites:

http://jobs.oreilly.com/

5. Register your book

Register your book at:
http://register.oreilly.com

6. Contact us

O'Reilly & Associates, Inc.
1005 Gravenstein Hwy North
Sebastopol, CA 95472 USA
TEL: 707-827-7000 or 800-998-9938
         (6am to 5pm PST)
FAX: 707-829-0104

order@oreilly.com
For answers to problems regarding your order or our products. To place a book order online visit:

http://www.oreilly.com/order_new/

catalog@oreilly.com
To request a copy of our latest catalog.

booktech@oreilly.com
For book content technical questions or corrections.

corporate@oreilly.com
For educational, library, government, and corporate sales.

proposals@oreilly.com
To submit new book proposals to our editors and product managers.

international@oreilly.com
For information about our international distributors or translation queries. For a list of our distributors outside of North America check out:

http://international.oreilly.com/distributors.html

adoption@oreilly.com
For information about academic use of O'Reilly books, visit:

http://academic.oreilly.com

O'REILLY®